Law, Mental Health, and Mental Disorder

Related Titles

Psychology and Law, Second Edition
Bartol and Bartol

Psychology and Law for the Helping Professions
Swenson

Psychology and the Legal System, Third Edition
Wrightsman, Neitzel, and Fortune

Law, Mental Health, and Mental Disorder

Edited by

Bruce D. Sales
University of Arizona

Daniel W. Shuman
Southern Methodist University

Brooks/Cole Publishing Company
I(T)P®An International Thomson Publishing Company

Pacific Grove • Albany • Bonn • Boston • Cincinnati • Detroit • London • Madrid • Melbourne
Mexico City • New York • Paris • San Francisco • Singapore • Tokyo • Toronto • Washington

Sponsoring Editor: *Marianne Taflinger*
Marketing Team: *Carolyn Crockett and Margaret Parks*
Editorial Assistant: *Laura Donahue*
Production Editor: *Laurel Jackson*
Manuscript Editors: *Elizabeth Judd and Barbara Kimmel*
Permissions Editor: *Cathleen S. Collins*

Interior and Cover Design: *Roy R. Neuhaus*
Indexer: *James Minkin*
Typesetting: *Kachina Typesetting*
Cover Printing: *Phoenix Color Corporation, Inc.*
Printing and Binding: *Quebecor Printing, Fairfield*

For more information, contact:
BROOKS/COLE PUBLISHING COMPANY
511 Forest Lodge Road
Pacific Grove, CA 93950
USA

International Thomson Publishing Europe
Berkshire House 168-173
High Holborn
London WC1V 7AA
England

Thomas Nelson Australia
102 Dodds Street
South Melbourne, 3205
Victoria, Australia

Nelson Canada
1120 Birchmount Road
Scarborough, Ontario
Canada M1K 5G4

International Thomson Editores
Campos Eliseos 385, Piso 7
Col. Polanco
11560 México D. F. México

International Thomson Publishing GmbH
Königswinterer Strasse 418
53227 Bonn
Germany

International Thomson Publishing Asia
221 Henderson Road
#05-10 Henderson Building
Singapore 0315

International Thomson Publishing Japan
Hirakawacho Kyowa Building, 3F
2-2-1 Hirakawacho
Chiyoda-ku, Tokyo 102
Japan

Printed in the United States of America

10 9 8 7 6 5 4 3 2 1

Library of Congress Cataloging-in-Publication Data
Law, mental health, and mental disorder / edited by Bruce D. Sales,
    Daniel W. Shuman.
        p.   cm.
    Includes bibliographical references and index.
    ISBN 0-534-34090-3
    1. Mental health laws—United States. 2. Insanity—Jurisprudence—
United States. 3. Forensic psychiatry—United States. I. Sales,
Bruce Dennis. II. Shuman, Daniel W.
KF3828.L38 1996
344.73'044—dc20
[347.30444]   95-46616
                                                           CIP

Contents

Part 2
Mental Health Professionals
and the Law   61

Preface

This book evolved from discussions we had a few years ago, in which we explored our mutual frustration with mental health law. We were—and still are—concerned that the field has lost direction and lacks a vision for the future and that the term *mental health* in *mental health law* is without referent or meaning. We are also concerned that, although numerous topics in the law involve mental status issues that require or allow for the expert testimony of mental health professionals, the law relating to mental disorder in criminal contexts receives disproportionate attention. Further, mental health professionals and behavioral and social scientists are disenfranchised from any significant interaction in the law's development. Finally, lawyers seem blithely to assume that their work benefits their clients although no data exists to assess that claim and there is little apparent interest in stimulating behavioral and social scientists to gather that information. These concerns led to numerous meetings in Tucson and to frequent calls, e-mailings, and mailings that culminated in this book.

As we worked on this book, we kept the following in mind:

1. We wanted a book that would reflect the traditional areas of mental health law while presenting legal issues that should be considered part of this law but that have not been included in the past. Our goal, however, was not to cover these issues exhaustively in this first edition, but, rather, to present the range of critical issues that represent our conception of mental health law as we approach the next century. Our introductory chapter presents the criteria for including topics in the newly emerging mental health law.

2. We wanted legal scholars to write all the chapters in this book because legal scholars are in the best position to understand the law.

3. We provided the chapter authors with the following guidelines: briefly review the history of the law you have been asked to write about, describe its current status, identify its therapeutic and antitherapeutic implications, and discuss whether the law needs revision to make it more therapeutic or to remove its antitherapeutic consequences. For some topics, the issue was not whether the law was therapeutic or antitherapeutic, but, rather, whether the psychological consequences it promoted were positive or negative. If the law could not be changed, but some kind of change was needed, the authors were to consider whether changes in other areas (for example, in the mental health community, in mental health practices, or in the political priorities of the state and federal governments) would be appropriate.

4. Although our authors were mostly without formal social science training, we also asked them to consider the implications of the behavioral and social science literature when they addressed the positive and negative consequences of the law. For this book, we wanted the evaluation of the law to reach beyond the narrow confines of traditional legal analysis.

5. We asked authors to write for both the legal and the mental health audiences so that the book would be read by both and would be used to stimulate more—and more significant—interactions in the future.

6. Finally, our primary goals were to rekindle the excitement for mental health law, to invigorate its efforts, and to encourage mental health and legal scholars to work together in this legal area to improve our society.

Part 5

Impact of the Law on the Mental Health of Children and Families 439

The book is organized by categories that should make it easy for the novice in mental health law to learn the lessons that each chapter and each group of chapters offer. This organization will also allow scholars familiar with mental health law to find quickly the topics that will be of most interest to them.

Part 1 of this book contains three chapters that focus on the foundations for the law's interactions with mental health and mental disorder. In the introductory chapter, we explain the newly emerging mental health law. Chapters 2 and 3 cover legal advocacy for people with mental disabilities and the use of mental health expertise in the courtroom.

Because mental health professionals are involved in many different ways in the administration of mental health law, Part 2 centers on foundational issues in the relationship between mental health professionals and the law. The first two chapters of Part 2 focus on confidentiality in the psychotherapeutic relationship and malpractice liability of mental health professionals and institutions, both topics of which all mental health professionals are aware. Then, in Chapters 6 and 7, we turn to two topics with which most legal and mental health scholars and students are less familiar—the roles of antitrust law and state mandates in regulating the marketplace for competition among mental health providers, and legal influences on the financing of mental health care. Although less familiar, both topics are critical to shaping the availability of mental health services.

In Part 3, the focus shifts from mental health professionals to mental health clients and the law. We start Part 3 with a fundamental topic of concern to people who need mental health services—the delivery of those services in the community. Given the emerging importance of the Americans with Disabilities Act and related federal and state law in providing protection for persons with mental disabilities in the community, Chapter 9 is focused on this law. Chapter 10 centers on the judicial imposition of a guardianship over persons who are deemed incompetent

and on whether this law provides a "protection" for incompetent persons. Although a guardian can secure "voluntary" services for the incompetent person, without the legal fiction created by guardianship law, the services are involuntary to the recipient. Our discussion, therefore, turns in Chapter 11 to persons who, under the law, explicitly require the delivery of involuntary mental health services. Only relatively recently have legal scholars begun to focus on the special problems that women and ethnic minorities face regarding the delivery of services; these issues are considered in Chapter 12. Similarly, treatment and refusal rights in mental health, the focus of Chapter 13, also pose special obligations and dilemmas for mental health services. Part 2 ends with a radically different topic—how the law affects compensation for mental and emotional distress caused by the intentional or negligent acts of another.

The focus of Part 4 is on offenders with mental disorders and the law. This part of the book begins with a consideration of classic topics in this field: incompetency to proceed in the criminal process, the insanity defense, dangerousness as a criterion in the criminal process, and the incapacitation by civil commitment of pathologically violent sex offenders. It then concludes with chapters on two more current topics in this area: legal concern about the needs of offenders with mental disorders in the criminal justice–correctional process and the mental health implications of crime victims' rights.

The last section, Part 5, brings the book to a close by presenting a series of topics that traditionally have not been included within the purview of mental health law but that should be. We have placed this section last both for this reason and because these chapters raise issues that integrate concerns of civil, criminal, and juvenile justice. Each chapter focuses on the law's impact on the mental health of children and families. Topics in Part 5 include the legal processing of domestic violence cases, the law's response to child abuse and neglect, the voluntary admission and involuntary hospitalization of minors, mental health issues in juvenile justice, and child-custody decision making.

Although we have just completed this book, we are already thinking about the second edition. Toward this end, we invite you to join in our discussions. In the next edition, we plan to have chapters updated and to add substantial notes and queries at the end of each chapter. We will also consider adding topics that relate to the new mental health law. If you would like to share any of your comments and recommendations with us, you can reach us at the following addresses:

Bruce D. Sales
Department of Psychology
University of Arizona
Tucson, AZ 85721

e-mail address: bsales@ccit.arizona.edu

Daniel W. Shuman
Southern Methodist University
School of Law
Dallas, TX 75214

e-mail address: dshuman@mail.smu.edu

Acknowledgments

We wish to thank the following reviewers of this book for their valuable comments and suggestions: Jose Ashford, Arizona State University; Richard Gonzalez, University of Washington; John S. Kelly, San Jose State University; John Petrila, University of South Florida; Alan J. Tomkins, University of Nebraska, Lincoln; and Curtis E. Wills, Lamar University.

Bruce D. Sales
Daniel W. Shuman

Part 1

Foundations for Law, Mental Health, and Mental Disorder Interactions

1 ■ The Newly Emerging Mental Health Law

Bruce D. Sales
University of Arizona

Daniel W. Shuman
Southern Methodist University

We might begin an examination of mental health law by asking why the topic exists. For instance, why should there be law relating to and affecting the work of mental health professionals (MHPs)? Many MHPs wonder whether they and the mental health system would be better off without the imposition of law, as long as they and mental health administrators act ethically. For example, consider how adherence to four leading moral principles or shared values of the mental health community would affect the interests of patients and society. *Respect* for the client should ensure that clients are fully accorded their right to consent to or avoid services. *Beneficience and nonmalfeasance* should assure clients that therapists will do good—or at a minimum, no harm. *Justice* should ensure that both procedural justice (that is, fairness in procedures applied to persons) and distributive justice (fairness in the distribution of sevices) would be built into services. And *fidelity* should ensure that services are appropriately provided.

Unfortunately, however, adherence to the ethical principles of the mental health disciplines does not ensure that patient or societal interests are protected, because the ethical codes are limited in several ways. First, although ethical guidelines can provide some professional direc-

tion, they speak in generalities; therefore, significant room exists for professional divergence in their implementation. Consider an ethical guideline requiring informed consent to ensure patient autonomy. Without further specific behavioral standards or rules for implementation, decisions about the amount and type of information to provide to the patient will remain idiosyncratic. Must the therapist provide information on alternatives to the suggested treatment (and if so, which alternatives), or can the therapist present only the benefits and risks of the targeted treatment? If risks must be presented, how significant must risk factors be to require disclosure? Does the ethical guideline demand that the information presented during the consent process be understood by the recipient or only that the needed facts be included in the information presented? Because guidelines derived from ethical principles and ethical codes lack detailed behavioral standards or rules with which to interpret them, there is substantial room for disagreement about how therapists should relate to clients of mental health services. This room for disagreement limits the efficacy of professional ethics in protecting the rights of recipients of mental health services.

Second, because ethical guidelines are necessarily generic, often they do not specifically address some of the concerns or needs of clients. For example, what guidelines would guarantee that services will be available for all persons in need? What of those persons in rural areas who have to travel hundreds of miles to gain access to services and are therefore effectively precluded from services? Ethical guidelines do not address these and many other issues that are important to persons with mental disabilities and others in need of services.

Third, a related limitation of ethical principles and codes is that they are created by private

Some portions of this chapter were adapted from "Mental Health Law and Mental Health Care," by B. Sales and D. Shuman, 1994, *American Journal of Orthopsychiatry, 64*(2), 172–179, American Orthopsychiatric Association, Inc.

professional organizations; however, many issues important to persons with mental disabilities should be responded to in public forums. Decisions about whether these persons should be free from discrimination in public services and employment should be entrusted to legislators and other elected officials (see Chapter 9), not to the mental health professions. Similarly, although MHPs should and do provide services to crime victims, it would be inappropriate for them to dictate social policy on victims' rights—even though, for example, the handling of a case by the criminal justice system may affect the mental health of the victims and cause secondary victimization (see Chapter 20). Granting victims' wishes would mean a degree of involvement in criminal law and procedure that is not feasible for MHPs.

Fourth, because the mental health disciplines create their own ethical guidelines, they are likely to be limited by professional self-interest. In drafting guidelines, professionals will probably not create standards for behavior that they cannot easily meet. Rather, they are more likely to incorporate into the guidelines that which is easy to do and likely to be done than that which should be done. In addition, if these guidelines are violated, and there are no legal avenues for redress, what sanctions will the profession impose? Professional ethics committees are much more likely to be concerned with educating practitioners than with punishing them or with compensating harmed clients. Moreover, mental health professionals can avoid ethical sanctions of private, voluntary professional associations simply by resigning from them.

Although professional ethical principles and standards are important, they are insufficient fully to meet the needs of persons with mental disabilities, clients of mental health services, and society. Thus, it should not be surprising that legislators and courts have developed a body of law relevant to the mental health professions and the clients of their services.

For better or worse, MHPs are, and will continue to be, both directly and indirectly affected by that law. Their practice is directly controlled by laws that regulate such matters as licensure and certification, third-party reimbursement, and professional incorporation (for example, Sales & Miller, 1995). The quality of their services is subject to review by courts in malpractice actions (see Chapter 5), while their collective actions are subject to antitrust scrutiny (Chapter 6). Even when not directly affected, MHPs are indirectly affected by the law because their clients are increasingly involved in legal entanglements in which mental status issues are pivotal, such as child custody disputes (Chapter 25), litigation over mental or emotional injury (Chapter 14), and involuntary civil commitment (Chapter 11).

Given the expansiveness of this law and its potential to affect mental health professionals, the clients of their services, and mental health care more generally, this chapter has many purposes: First we will consider the rationale for the initial development of mental health law. Then we will discuss the importance of empirical research for studying the consequences of mental health law and consider a new perspective for studying and improving this area of the law—therapeutic jurisprudence. We will assess the benefits and limits of this approach and discuss its implications for redefining the appropriate terrain of mental health law. Next, we will examine the other grounds for defining the newly emerging mental health law. We then consider factors that threaten the success of mental health law in attaining its goals. Finally, we conclude with a discussion of the relationship that must emerge between the legal and mental health disciplines to make mental health law therapeutic by advancing positive psychological consequences for those it affects.

Early Rationale for Mental Health Law

Mental health law, which grew out of the civil rights and consumer movements of the 1960s and the 1970s, was initially dominated by a deontological perspective that conceives of the law as advancing important values that reflect what *ought* to be done, often ensconced within normative constitutional principles that reflect what customarily *is* done. This orientation resulted in mental health lawyers seeking to achieve a litany of rights for persons who suffered from, or were alleged to suffer from, mental disorders. Indeed, during the 1960s and 1970s, society witnessed the conferral of rights as an end in itself. The vernacular of this rights-based analysis, such as the right to treatment and the right to refuse treatment (Chapter 13), as well as the right to counsel and a hearing (Chapter 2), shaped the discussion of mental health law during that era and defined its original boundaries.

To apply this mode of analysis to interactions between mental health professionals and patients, mental health law borrowed from other areas of law where "rights" were equally important and commonly accepted. For example, involuntary civil commitment of persons with mental disabilities (Chapter 11), one of the early focuses of mental health law, was sufficiently similar to criminal proceedings to justify arguing that the same due process rights should apply (such as the rights to counsel, confrontation and cross-examination of adverse witnesses, and the privilege against self-incrimination) (Chapter 2).

Not all topics considered part of mental health law, however, originated during this period. The contemporary formulation of the insanity defense, for example, was born during the 1800s (Chapter 16). Yet the insanity defense and related topics, such as competency to stand trial (Chapter 15), were comfortably included in books and courses on mental health law because they advanced a concern for the rights of persons with mental disabilities.

The civil rights and consumer movement bases for mental health law lost their strength in the late 1980s and early 1990s for a variety of reasons. First, these driving forces succeeded in accomplishing many of their goals. Many, if not most, of the rights that mental health legal advocates targeted were secured, at least on paper. For example, commitment hearings now require many of the same procedural protections as criminal proceedings, and the conditions under which persons with mental disabilities are involuntarily confined are subject to judicial scrutiny.

Second, because a new conservative national ideology was less receptive to the original goals of the mental health law movement, the U.S. Supreme Court, particularly its newer members, became far less receptive to expanding the rights of persons with mental disabilities, whether those sought-after rights related to institutionalization (Chapters 11 and 23) or to community-based services (Chapter 8). In addition, state legislatures and Congress often shared this conservatism. Thus, the battle for expansion of these rights has dramatically slowed (Chapter 8).

Third, the movement lost vitality because of a growing sense that attaining its goals did not achieve the ends it sought (Shuman, 1992). For example, an increasing number of legal and mental health scholars and practitioners came to doubt that recognizing rights for their own sake was satisfying or beneficial. Despite the legal victories, it was unclear whether the lives of people with mental disabilities had substantially improved. Further, where improvement had occurred, scholars and advocates began to question whether this was because of the legal changes— or in spite of them. For instance, judges and lawyers who played a role in securing rights for persons in civil commitment proceedings did not, for the most part, see beyond these initial goals. In the rush to guarantee a right to counsel, the courts did not ask how counsel would affect the accuracy of commitment decisions, whether the subjects of commitment petitions could cope with an adversarial process, or how those committed to inpatient facilities would respond to the treatment provided in these settings.

Empirical Questioning of Mental Health Law

The deontological perspective of law contrasts with the utilitarian view, which holds that legal rules are important to achieving some end. For example, while the deontological perspective maintains that recognition of a right to a judicial hearing preceding civil commitment should turn on whether commitment is a deprivation of liberty from the standpoint of the Fourteenth Amendment of the U.S. Constitution, the utilitarian perspective maintains that the right to a hearing should turn on the desirability of its consequences, such as improving the accuracy of commitment decisions (Tyler, 1993).

Although much of the previous generation of mental health law scholarship and decision making was deontologically oriented, a significant body of literature developed at the same time that was shaped by this utilitarian perspective, tracing its roots to the early 20th-century Legal Realist movement (Monahan & Walker, 1994). This literature was concerned with empirically testing whether laws were achieving their explicit and implicit goals. This approach to law and behavioral and social science interactions asserts that almost all laws are based on behavioral, social, and economic assumptions whose validity can be empirically determined (Sales, 1983; Sales & Hafemeister, 1985; Shuman, 1984). Thus, when a federal court ordered that persons with mental disabilities residing in state hospitals be accorded their right to privacy, utilitarian-oriented research was able to demonstrate that the subsequent changes in the institutions did not achieve the goals of this court ruling (O'Reilly & Sales, 1986, 1987).

Moreover, empirical questioning will challenge not only the fundamental basis for a law but also the accepted practice of MHPs that the law regulates. Consider, for example, reporting laws, which constitute one exception to confidentiality law. All states require MHPs to report child abuse, including child sexual abuse (Chapter 22); some states also require the reporting of abuse of adults, such as those who are incapacitated, who are particularly vulnerable. Laws such as these opt for protection of the victim over rehabilitation of the perpetrator and have created significant controversy within the mental health community. This controversy is apparent in the debate about

and practice of reporting father-daughter incest perpetrators. Some MHPs argue that to divulge such otherwise confidential information, which was learned in the therapeutic relationship with a client, will decrease the likelihood that offenders will seek therapy and overcome their problems. The utilitarian perspective leads us to ask the following question: To what extent are perpetrators voluntarily seeking therapy and benefiting from it in the absence of reporting? If reporting occurred and resulted in the conviction of the offender, is therapy mandated as part of the court's disposition? If the answer is yes, is this therapy more or less successful than that provided voluntarily?

Therapeutic Jurisprudence Lens on Mental Health Law

Building on this empirical heritage, *therapeutic jurisprudence,* a new school of thought in mental health law, evolved (Wexler & Winick, 1991; Wexler, 1990). Rather than exclusively relying on deontologically driven legal rules, advocates of this new movement analyze the consequences of these legal rules and attempt to incorporate this information in legal decision making. The overarching goal of therapeutic jurisprudence is to ensure that mental health law realizes its potential to advance therapeutic outcomes, at least when it is possible to do so without violating other important principles (such as constitutional principles). Those who subscribe to this school of thought believe not that therapeutic considerations should take precedence over all others but that legal decisions should acknowledge their therapeutic and antitherapeutic consequences.

For example, consider the law's role in the delivery of mental health services in the community. In Chapter 8, Perlin explores the proposition that judicial involvement over the last two decades has had an antitherapeutic impact on the availability of these services. His analysis reveals how myths and stereotypes about persons with mental disabilities, myths to which judges are not immune, limit the therapeutic achievements of the courts.

It can be argued that therapeutic jurisprudence is old wine in a new bottle—that is, the substance of its message is what law and behavioral and social science specialists have been promoting for years—using empirical data and behavioral and social science theory to evaluate the desirability of different legal alternatives. Whether therapeutic jurisprudence is simply a new label for an ongoing major school of thought, however, is not nearly as important as other considerations. Therapeutic jurisprudence can create a climate in which mental health and legal scholars and professionals can agree that mental health law should not be made or carried out without considering its therapeutic consequences, determined empirically, to the extent possible at the time of the legal decision.

Redefining the Boundaries of Mental Health Law

The therapeutic jurisprudence perspective thus suggests the need for one fundamental reorientation of mental health law. Mental health law needs to be examined to determine how its application affects the interests of its intended beneficiaries, and whether therapeutic, or psychologically constructive, outcomes have been or will be advanced. Such work should utilize feedback from MHPs and clients, the work of mental health scholars, and empirical research.

A second fundamental shift needs to occur as well. For mental health law to be therapeutic, it must incorporate a broader vision of what an effective, truly therapeutic, system for the delivery of mental health services would entail. Without this richer view, it is understandable why MHPs have been frustrated with the law's incur-

sions into their domain. In essence, the law has been playing at the fringe of an enormous tapestry that defines mental health care, pulling at individual threads, seemingly oblivious to the larger patterns. The next generation of mental health law and scholarship should have the law participate with MHPs in making appropriate mental health services available to consumers who seek them.

Without abandoning normative constitutional values, such efforts should include a vision of mental health services that incorporates (1) identification of those in need of services and those not being served, and the reasons for this discrepancy; (2) development of a comprehensive plan of integrated services; (3) provision of services with clear outcome goals; (4) systematic collection of accurate information on the delivery of services and the operation of systems providing those services, and the reporting of those data in a meaningful fashion; (5) use of the data to aid in decision making on mental health care; (6) provision of appropriate services to ethnic minorities; (7) provision of sufficient funding to support legally mandated entitlements (for example, National Institute of Mental Health, 1991). This shift in focus should help to reorient mental health law to the core concerns of consumers who need and want mental health services, and of MHPs who provide those services. In addition, these seven requirements support a rational planning and implementation process by legal and public policymakers/administrators responsible for interpreting and implementing legal guidelines. And they facilitate effectiveness and efficiency in the delivery of mental health services. These goals are timely and appropriate because nationally we are plagued by a mental health system that is disjointed and uncoordinated, with no clear communication links between subsystems. The system also suffers from inadequate planning and funding (Chapter 7).

A third fundamental reorientation for mental health law is also necessary. Early mental health law focused on the rights of persons with mental disabilities, primarily in criminal situations—for instance, those involving insanity defense (Chapter 16), competency to stand trial (Chapter 15), and commitment of sex offenders with mental disorders (Chapter 18)—and quasicriminal situations, including situations where the law imposes restrictions on liberty, such as in involuntary civil commitment (Chapter 11) and guardianship (Chapter 10). But early mental health law did not elaborate the other important ways in which the law relates to the mental health professions and its clients: the functions of MHPs, the responsibilities of MHPs, and the operation of systems involved with the delivery of mental health services.

Functions of MHPs

The law affects the functions of MHPs. For example, many legal situations mandate an evaluation of a person by a MHP and specify the legal standard for which the MHP must test (Chapter 17, this volume; Sales & Miller, 1995; Melton, Petrila, Poythress, & Slobogin, 1987). In competency-to-stand-trial determinations, for instance, the court is not directly interested initially in whether the defendant has a mental illness. Rather, the court is concerned with whether the person has the ability to understand the nature of the charges and the legal proceedings, and to aid in the defense. Not all findings of incompetency to stand trial result from a mental illness, and even severe mental illness (that is, psychosis) does not automatically make the person incompetent to stand trial (Chapter 15). Thus, the functions of the mental health professional are articulated in the law and logically should be part of mental health law. Not to incorporate this law as part of mental health law increases the chances that MHPs will not provide appropriate services, and thereby increases the potential of harm to the subjects of legal evaluations. This component of the reorientation requires mental health law to incorporate all topics where MHPs may or are required to testify as to a mental status issue as part of litigation. It also encompasses situations where the clinical work of MHPs will be dictated

by the standard within the law or where their clinical opinion will be asked for in regard to a legal issue in the case (for example, workers' compensation, competency to contract or sign a will, guardianship, dangerousness of alleged or adjudicated offenders).

Responsibilities of MHPs

The law also imposes responsibilities on MHPs in numerous ways. Some laws focus on the requirement that MHPs become licensed or certified to perform certain functions, in addition to requiring them to adhere to certain standards in performing their duties (Simon, Sales, & Sechrest, 1992). Other laws require mental health facilities to be licensed prior to operation. A third type of law constrains the types of practice in the mental health professions, whether it be, for example, in a health maintenance organization (HMO), a preferred provider organization, or a multidisciplinary corporation (one that provides services to different professional disciplines). Although these types of law also cross over into another category (see the section titled "Operation of the System"), they can have a substantial impact on the responsibilities of MHPs and the quality of care that they deliver to their clients. Consider, for example, the explosive growth of HMOs. To the extent that the law allows the HMO to limit the number of patient visits (for instance, to ten sessions), what are the consequences to a client who continues to need care, what are the responsibilities of the therapist who has to terminate the therapy, and will this approach increase malpractice claims by patients who allege inappropriate early termination?

Some laws focus on the responsibilities of MHPs much more directly. The law relating to informed consent requires MHPs to provide certain information to prospective clients and to secure their consent to services prior to initiating treatment. Other laws focus on requiring confidential treatment of information obtained from clients during a professional relationship (Chapter 4). Or they focus on the responsibility of the

MHP to release this information in very explicit circumstances (for instance, pursuant to a valid search by law enforcement authorities, or pursuant to a valid subpoena by a court). Moreover, given the impact of these laws on MHPs and their clients, and the ways services are delivered, it makes little sense to exclude them from the domain of mental health law.

Operation of the System

Finally, the law affects the operation of the mental health system, and other public or private systems, in their provision of services to persons who suffer from some type of mental disorder. There is more than one mental health system. Mental health services are required in a variety of contexts. School systems today must evaluate students for serious emotional disturbance and are obligated to provide appropriate services to students with special needs (Chapter 9). The juvenile justice system often bases dispositions on the treatment needs of the juveniles who come before the court (Chapter 24). A recurring dilemma for the criminal justice system is how to deal with incarcerated persons in jails and prisons who suffer from mental disorder (Cohen, 1995) and how to respond to battered partners (Chapter 21). Mental health law must incorporate these concerns so as to represent the full panoply of laws addressing, and issues facing, persons with mental health service needs. This is important because if law is to be therapeutic, it should be effective across the spectrum of situations where it might apply. For example, if the law allows deprivation of liberty for civil commitment of adults (Chapter 11), juveniles (Chapter 23), and delinquent juveniles (Chapter 24) with mental illness, under what deontological and utilitarian rationales should the commitment be allowed when it is shown that treatment in the prescribed facilities is not effective?

A fourth rationale for fundamentally reorienting our old conception of mental health law is based on the irony that the field is labeled *mental health* law, when it focuses on mental disorder.

Where is the *health*? Indeed, there is a substantial body of law that focuses on people's mental status, where mental illness either is not present or may not be present. By focusing on mental status rather than mental illness, mental health law should be concerned with the continuum of mental status issues that perplex legal decision making. This focus allows mental health law scholars to rephrase critical questions from "Does the institutionalized person with a mental illness have the capacity to consent to services?" to "How should the law best conceptualize and interpret the legal mandate for consent to services for all persons along the continuum from 'the highly intelligent' to 'the severely retarded,' and from 'the normal' to 'the severely mentally disordered'?" Legal standards should be revisited to determine their appropriateness for the spectrum of relevant fact situations faced by the full range of people to whom the law might apply. This reconsideration will probably eventually lead to more thoughtfully defined legal constructs.

In addition, when we focus on mental status, it becomes apparent that mental health law also should be concerned with therapeutic consequences, using the word *therapy* the way mental health professionals use it—to mean positive psychological consequences. What we should be interested in are the psychological consequences of different laws that affect a person's mental health. This broadened conception of mental health law perhaps widens the therapeutic jurisprudence lens, but it is consistent with its basic tenets. By utilizing this broader perspective, topics such as child custody determinations will be incorporated into mental health law scholarship. For example, if the custody decision is based on the child's best interests (Rohman, Sales, & Lou, 1990), mental health law should ask what we know about the mental health consequences to children of various divorce arrangements (Rohman, Sales, & Lou, 1990). Mental health law can also legitimately probe the psychological impact of the legal process on divorcing parents. To be concerned with the therapeutic or antitherapeutic effects of institutionalization, but not be concerned with the potentially devastating psychological effects of other laws such as divorce, foster care, and adoption, diminishes the mental health component of mental health law.

The fifth and final basis for reinventing mental health law is being fueled by the feminist jurisprudence literature (Chapter 12). Feminist scholars point out what we all might have guessed, namely, that our laws reflect a male standard that often ignores the needs of the sizable percentage of women and ethnic minorities that comprise the institutionalized or those in need of services today. David Wexler (1971) and a number of his students reported the outrageous case of a 19-year-old Mexican American woman who was committed to the Territorial Asylum for the Insane in Phoenix in 1912 for "mental problems as being supposedly caused by bathing in cold water at menstrual period and as probably being only temporary in nature" (as quoted from court papers). The woman was still there in 1971, then 78 years of age. The law has redressed some of the problems she faced—in particular, indefinite commitment. But feminist writings are driving mental health and legal scholars to realize that unrecognized prejudice and indifference toward the special needs of women and ethnic minorities still permeate mental health law and practice (Chapter 12, this volume).

Factors Threatening the Success of the New Mental Health Law

Some factors may undermine the success of the effort to reinvent mental health law and put mental health back into it. For example, despite the apparent benefits of the therapeutic jurisprudence orientation on the part of lawyers and legal scholars, MHPs and scholars will not invariably find this approach a panacea. As already noted, therapeutic jurisprudence seeks to advance therapeutic outcomes by encouraging legal decision makers to consider therapeutic consequences; it does not dictate the selection of legal rules that advance a therapeutic outcome. Therapeutic jurisprudence clarifies the stakes involved in the decision but does not purport to resolve them; balancing values cannot be done through a simplistic formulaic analysis. For example, if empirical research reveals that recognition of a right to refuse treatment is antitherapeutic, a court or legislature may either refuse to recognize that right based on that research, or notwithstanding that research, may recognize that right based on a deontological valuation of the importance of autonomy (Schopp, 1993).

When legal decision makers choose to recognize a rule that is therapeutic or refuse to recognize a rule that is antitherapeutic, the judgments of the legal system and the mental health system are congruent. Note, however, that the congruence in the judgments of the two disciplines can either be because legal decision makers utilize a utilitarian approach that accepts the empirical outcomes as dispositive, or because legal decision makers utilize a deontological approach that coincidentally concurs with the empirical research. The absence of congruence occurs when, for deontological reasons, legal decision makers choose laws that are antitherapeutic or reject laws that are therapeutic. This absence of congruence has understandably troubled MHPs whose language and professional values do not share the legal system's deontological concerns. Indeed, MHPs should not expect from therapeutic jurisprudence and the new mental health law a change in legal values or orientation that subordinates normative constitutional values to therapeutic values.

This approach could not only lead to the rejection of therapeutic concerns in favor of normative constitutional values. Emphasizing therapeutic considerations could also lead those who see these considerations as paramount to neglect important normatively derived constitutional values. These normative constitutional values are crucial to the structure and fabric of our society and have enabled our system of government to endure for over 200 years. They have demarcated the protection of the individual from the state in a way that has transcended changes in technology and culture. Thus, they should not be dismissed as mere technicalities; they define us as Americans.

Other factors that may inhibit the ultimate success of this new conception of mental health law derive from the fundamental differences between the legal and mental health systems and between legal and mental health professionals. These differences can lead to conceptual, definitional, and pragmatic schisms and can reduce the ability of the disciplines and systems to work effectively together.

For example, the legal and mental health systems possess different vocabularies with encoded signals that affirm their worldviews but that often lead to miscommunication between the fields. The description of the common law system as an adversary system, for example, which is intended by lawyers to exalt the values of process and participation, is often taken by MHPs to exalt hostility and noncooperation. The illusion that results when lawyers and MHPs believe that they are communicating in a shared language all too often leads to problems like MHPs providing assessment services that do not address the relevant legal issue.

Even where the two groups attempt to communicate effectively, tensions can result because various normative and policy questions are inaccurately and inappropriately identified as involving scientific or technical issues. In an attempt to avoid addressing these normative and policy issues head on, legal decision makers often erroneously recast them as technical questions to be answered by "experts." Even when issues require scientific rather than normative judgments, legal reliance on mental health expertise is problematic because MHPs often do not have relevant empirically grounded knowledge and are willing to render opinions beyond their areas of expertise (Chapters 3 and 25).

Fundamental differences between the fields are also reflected in tensions and conflicts in their respective goals. For example, in dealing with forensic patients, the criminal justice and correctional systems value incapacitation and social control goals, while the mental health system values therapeutic objectives. This conflict continues to occur despite the fact that both systems are charged with the responsibility of treating dangerous persons who have a mental illness as well as protecting society.

Conflicts in goals also occur intraprofessionally, making their resolution all the more complex. Prosecutors may want maximum sentences imposed to protect society, while defense attorneys might argue for the imposition of diversion programs incorporating outpatient services. Similarly, MHPs have strong but divergent views. In considering services, some MHPs value large state hospitals in a mental health service system, while others question the rationale for their existence. It will be difficult for the legal and mental health disciplines to agree on therapeutic, and psychologically constructive, outcomes when this intraprofessional dissension undermines their discussions.

Finally, conflicts can exist between the values, interests, and needs of key participants in law and mental health interactions (that is, policymakers, institutions and organizations providing services, program administrators, providers, clients, family members, and researchers). What if a state institution wishes to deinstitutionalize a minor, but the parents do not wish to have the minor returned to the home (Frohboese & Sales, 1980)? And what if the MHP objects to being used by prison administrators for social control purposes when providing services, such as where the prison asks the MHP to do evaluations to determine dangerousness for security purposes?

But perhaps the most important factors that may limit the therapeutic success of the new mental health law will come from outside the legal or mental health fields. As Rubin notes in Chapter 7, financing drives service systems. The lack of sufficient state or federal appropriations can cripple the best-intentioned public service programs for persons with mental illness and make a sham of government entitlement programs for persons in need of mental health services. The reason is obvious. Without funding, MHPs will not be hired to work, or providers of lesser training and sometimes lesser skills will be substituted. Where funding is provided for the MHP, its level may be so meager that it allows for only a brief or minimal intervention, rather than for the care required for a successful intervention with a client. Moreover, without needed state appropriations to support mental health services, they simply will not exist, either on an inpatient or an outpatient basis. As one person with a mental illness asked in a public forum in a large metropolitan area, "why does the system provide me with drugs to allow me to function but refuse to support psychosocial therapies so that I can function decently?" With limited funding, psychosocial therapies and rehabilitation are out of favor. Indeed, one public employee in that same state reported that a public agency was using a high school graduate to provide mental health services because it could not afford to pay for trained staff. As Perlin observes in Chapter 8, this is an issue of politics, and in the political arena, the need for mental health care has traditionally received only lip service.

A New Relationship for the Legal and Mental Health Disciplines

If the newly emerging mental health law is to be successful, it must create a bridge to overcome the factors that threaten its ability to foster psychologically constructive outcomes. For instance, viewing mental health law from the patient's rights perspective inevitably placed mental health professionals in a defensive posture. A patient right, such as the right to informed consent, concomitantly creates a mental health

professional duty at the same time: the duty to determine the competency of the patient to consent to services, the duty to provide all relevant information about the risks and benefits of services, and so on. So viewed, the law is negative to the MHP, and the less involvement with it the better. Changing that construct to focus on and understand the therapeutic and antitherapeutic consequences of informed consent allows the mental health disciplines to participate in the law in constructive ways that are familiar to them. Equally important, it offers MHPs a legitimate and substantial basis for working with the legal community to change the law when therapeutic outcomes are not achieved or antitherapeutic consequences are generated by it.

The time is ripe for this transition. Although the deontologically driven mental health law substantially succeeded in establishing many rights for persons with mental disabilities, as already noted, our national temperament is unlikely to support dramatic growth in this area in the immediate future (Chapter 8). That may be appropriate. More rights may not be needed to achieve appropriate services for persons with mental disabilities.

A renewed, invigorated interaction between legal and mental health professions should increase the chance of achieving this goal. While MHPs are well versed in the clinical needs of their clients, they are often ill-prepared to design a system to deliver mental health services that would be legally appropriate. Lawyers, on the other hand, are typically trained in setting up complex organizations for their clients, and thus bring a rich set of skills to the table to complement those of MHPs. Together, these professionals can exert significant influence on the shape of politically driven legislative acts and appropriations. The interaction of lawyers and MHPs is particularly needed, since mental health services are provided through a complex array of government and private entities that can easily result in systemic neglect of problems and certain unserved populations falling through the cracks. Whether lawyers will seize this opportunity and

MHPs will view legal participation at this systemic level as intrusive or helpful may depend, in part, on how effective the newly emerging mental health law is in convincing the professions of the need for joint efforts.

In fact, this newly emerging mental health law and the therapeutic jurisprudence lens that can be applied to it should stimulate, for a variety of reasons, renewed discussion and debate about the therapeutic effects of laws and the psychological consequences of different legal arrangements. First, both MHPs and lawyers will find the therapeutic jurisprudence perspective beneficial because it sheds light on the tensions between law and mental health, even if it will not always resolve them. As already noted, therapeutic jurisprudence provides a lens that reminds lawyers and MHPs to examine empirically the therapeutic consequences of legal decision making and that helps make the rationale for these decisions more explicit. As MHPs know, talking openly about conflict has therapeutic value.

Second, in areas of the law where conflicts now exist between the goals of mental health law and mental health care, therapeutic jurisprudence may advance shared therapeutic goals previously frustrated by ill-conceived legal rules (for example, Wexler, 1993). Consider the matter of plea bargaining for sex offenders, in which the defendant is often allowed to avoid a trial by pleading no contest. By doing so, the defendant does not have to acknowledge that he committed the specific acts of abuse. If research reveals that not acknowledging one's guilt promotes the abuser's cognitive distortions and makes treatment less likely to succeed, changing the legal rule to require acknowledgment of the abusive acts in the plea bargain may advance the therapeutic goals of reducing abuse (Klotz, Wexler, Sales, & Becker, 1992).

Third, therapeutic jurisprudence reveals that legal rules often have explicit or implicit therapeutic agendas that sometimes get lost in the tumult of their day-to-day application. Consider guardianship laws. They were implemented to aid incapacitated persons in a variety of ways, such as by creating opportunities for these individuals to continue to live in the community and by having guardians arrange for habilitative and rehabilitative services. Unfortunately, empirical research suggests that guardians are neither trained nor prepared for their responsibilities and that courts fail to monitor guardians' performance despite the statutory obligation to do so. Under the new mental health law, mental health personnel would be encouraged to work with lawmakers and the courts to identify these types of problems and work toward needed solutions. Malpractice laws provide another good example. They are intended to improve the quality of care delivered by MHPs and aid in making whole those injured by substandard care. By understanding the impact of these laws on providers, consumers of mental health services, and mental health care, legal decision makers can better fashion rules that accomplish these goals (Shuman, 1993; Chapter 5, this volume).

Fourth, the new mental health law should invite mental health scholars and professionals to examine the psychological consequences of a broad array of rules that were previously unexamined. By encouraging such an analysis, the mental health disciplines are likely to find a paucity of empirical support for either pro-therapeutic or antitherapeutic claims. This result raises a fascinating opportunity for more research and ongoing interactions between the legal and mental health communities. For example, in Chapter 11, La Fond points to data suggesting that the expansion of the legal standard for involuntary hospitalization, enacted within the last decade for the therapeutic purpose of enhancing mental health care for an expanded group of persons with mental illness, has had significant antitherapeutic effects. How should this law develop in light of this finding?

Conclusion

Although the focus of this discussion has been on legal change, we are not suggesting that lawyers will necessarily have a diminished *traditional* role in the new mental health law. The mental health disciplines will continue to require legal guidance about their obligations and rights in the creation of practices and the delivery of services. In addition, persons with mental disabilities will continue to need legal representation. Despite the best intentions of the mental health professions, the interests of service providers are not always congruent with those of their clients. Whatever other goals they may share, MHPs earn money for their services. If their appointment calendars or hospital beds are not full, they suffer potentially severe financial consequences. These consequences may lead MHPs to recommend overutilization of their services. Concerns over malpractice litigation may also generate recommendations for excessive services to avoid future claims of failure to diagnose. And mental health professionals may recommend overutilization of services because they genuinely believe in the power of their services to do good without considering the empirical data to support that assumption. Finally, rather than keeping people out of the involuntary service system, mental health lawyers will also be involved in securing services for their clients. Lawyers can petition for state and federal entitlements and benefits for clients and help people navigate barriers that may challenge even individuals without disabilities (Chapters 2 and 9).

Similarly, MHPs will continue to have a traditional role in aiding in the administration of the law. They will continue to provide forensic evaluations, testimony, and treatment, as well as empirical research for services planning.

Yet we hope that the new mental health law will stimulate a far broader and richer interaction between the legal and mental health disciplines than has existed previously. The legal and mental health disciplines should see themselves as allied professions, both for the purposes of administering and implementing mental health law and for attempting to achieve therapeutic outcomes and positive psychological consequences.

References

Frohboese, R. F., & Sales, B. D. (1980). Parental opposition to deinstitutionalization: A challenge in need of attention and resolution. *Law and Human Behavior, 4,* 1–88.

Klotz, J. A., Wexler, D. B., Sales, B. D., & Becker, J. V. (1992). Cognitive restructuring through law: A therapeutic jurisprudence approach to sex offenders and the plea process. *University of Puget Sound Law Review, 15,* 579–595.

Melton, G. B., Petrila, J., Poythress, N., & Slobogin, C. (1987). *Psychological evaluations for the courts: A handbook for mental health professionals and lawyers.* New York: Guilford Press.

Monahan, J., & Walker, L. (1994). *Social science in law: Cases and materials* (3rd ed.). Westbury, NY: Foundation Press.

National Institute of Mental Health. (1991). *Caring for people with severe mental disorders: A national plan of research to improve services* (DHHS Publication No. ADM 91-1762). Washington, DC: U.S. Government Printing Office.

O'Reilly, J., & Sales, B. (1986). Setting physical standards for mental hospitals: To whom should the courts listen? *International Journal of Law and Psychiatry, 8,* 301–310.

O'Reilly, J., & Sales, B. (1987). Privacy for the institutionalized mentally ill: Are court-ordered standards effective? *Law and Human Behavior, 11,* 41–53.

Rohman, L., Sales, B., & Lou, M. (1990). The best interests standard in child custody decisions. In D. Weisstub (Ed.), *Law and mental health: International perspectives: Vol. V* (pp. 40–90). Elmsford, NY: Pergamon Press.

Sales, B. D. (1983). The legal regulation of psychology: Professional and scientific interactions. In C. J. Scheirer & B. L. Hammonds (Eds.), *The master lecture series: Vol. 2. Psychology and the law* (pp. 5–36). Washington, DC: American Psychological Association.

Sales, B. D., & Hafemeister, T. (1985). Law and

psychology. In E. Altmaier & M. Meyer (Eds.), *Applied specialties in psychology* (pp. 331–373), New York: Random House.

Sales, B. D., & Miller, M. O. (1995). *Law and mental health professionals.* Washington, DC: American Psychological Association. (A 52-volume book series that covers the law affecting mental health professionals in each of the 50 states, the District of Columbia, and the federal jurisdictions)

Sales, B., & Shuman, D. (1994). Mental health law and mental health care. *American Journal of Orthopsychiatry, 64,* 172–179.

Schopp, R. F. (1993). Therapeutic jurisprudence and conflicts among values in mental health law. *Behavioral Sciences and the Law, 11,* 31–45.

Shuman, D. W. (1984). Decisionmaking under conditions of uncertainty. *Judicature, 67,* 326–335.

Shuman, D. W. (1992). Therapeutic jurisprudence and tort law: A limited subjective standard of care. *Southern Methodist University Law Review, 46,* 323–327.

Shuman, D. W. (1993). Making the world a better place through tort law? Through the therapeutic looking glass. *New York Law School Journal of Human Rights, X,* 739–758.

Simon, Sales, B., & Sechrest. (1992). Licensure of functions. In D. K. Kageiro & W. S. Lawfer (Eds.), *Handbook of psychology and law* (pp. 542–564). New York: Springer-Verlag.

Tyler, T. R. (1993). The psychological consequences of judicial procedures: Implications for civil commitment hearings. *Southern Methodist University Law Review, 46,* 433–445.

Wexler, D. B. (1971). Special project: The administration of psychiatric justice. *Arizona Law Review, 13,* 1–259.

Wexler, D. B. (Ed.). (1990). *Therapeutic Jurisprudence:* The law as a therapeutic agent. Durham, NC: Carolina Academic Press.

Wexler, D. B. (1993). Justice, mental health, and therapeutic jurisprudence. *Cleveland State Law Review, 40,* 517–526.

Wexler, D. B., & Winick, B. J. (Eds.). (1990). *Essays in therapeutic jurisprudence.* Durham, NC: Carolina Academic Press.

2   "Why Would I Need a Lawyer?" Legal Counsel and Advocacy for People with Mental Disabilities

Jan C. Costello
Loyola Law School

Scene 1: The hospital worker assigned to Admissions added one more sheet to the pile of paper in front of the prospective psychiatric patient. "And this is your Waiver of Right to Legal Counsel," she explained. "Sign this before you sign the other forms."

"Why would I need to see a lawyer?" the man asked anxiously.

"No reason I can think of," the staff member replied.

The advocate[1] on duty in Admissions, overhearing this exchange, felt frustrated. Only last week she had conducted a training for hospital staff members on legal issues. She had stressed the importance of making sure that prospective patients understood the *legal* consequences of their hospitalization—both while in the hospital and after discharge. Forms in the stack of papers the patient was about to sign could affect his rights to leave the hospital, to give or withhold informed consent to any proposed treatment, and to control his money and other personal property while in the hospital. If he had been brought to the hospital against his will, the patient could be waiving his right to an administrative review of the need for his hospitalization, or to a more formal judicial hearing. Depending on the circumstances, his hospitalization could have later implications for other legal rights such as to vote, to marry, to make a will, and to qualify for professions or licenses. The admissions worker had listened to the training; how could she possibly say now that there was no reason to consult a legal expert?

The admissions worker saw things differently. The patient (as she thought of him even before he was formally admitted to the hospital) needed reassurance that being hospitalized was in his best interest. The formal admissions process, with the pile of paperwork and questions about previous hospitalizations and insurance coverage, was already daunting to someone experiencing psychological distress. Whether the pa-

My thanks to Michael L. Perlin, Deborah L. Rhode, and Richard A. Rothschild for comments on an earlier version of this chapter.

Both the scenes in this chapter, as well as quotations attributed to clients with mental disabilities, are drawn from my own practice as a lawyer/advocate.

[1]"Legal counsel" or "legal advocacy" may be done by either a lawyer or a lay advocate, depending on the situation. Legal representation in court normally requires a lawyer; however, advocacy in administrative hearings and hospital contexts may be done by either a lawyer or a lay advocate. For the purposes of this chapter, I will use the term *lawyer/advocate* to refer to both kinds of advocates. Where right to counsel refers solely to representation by a lawyer, I will indicate this in the text.

15

tient had been brought to the hospital against his will by police or family members, or whether he had come voluntarily, he should now be encouraged to view the hospital as a safe place in which he would get the help he needed. Warning the patient about some legal rights he might lose would just upset and confuse him—and could undermine his trust in the hospital staff.

Scene 2: "How do you know that my client is dangerous, doctor?" asked the lawyer.

The psychiatrist testifying for the hospital in the commitment hearing replied, "The patient is delusional; she lacks insight into her illness and refuses to cooperate with treatment."

"Objection! Move to strike," the lawyer said. "Nonresponsive."

The psychiatrist, irritated, said, "I am trying to explain why she needs treatment."

The judge intervened. "Just tell the court what you know about the patient's *dangerousness*—that's the legal criterion for involuntary commitment."

The psychiatrist tried again. "Well, she has poor impulse control; she's assaultive."

The patient's lawyer bored in. "Doctor, has she attacked you physically?"

"No."

"Have you personally observed her attacking anyone else?"

"Well, no. I'm not her treating physician—I'm just testifying for the hospital in all the commitment hearings today. But it says in the hospital records that she is violent."

"Where exactly in the hospital record does it say that?"

"Uh . . . wait a minute . . . here in the admissions interview. The patient was brought to the hospital by the police, who said that the patient's neighbor said that the patient had thrown a rock at her."

"Did you interview the neighbor to confirm that statement?"

"Of course not."

"Is the neighbor here in the courtroom to testify to the alleged assault?"

"No."

"Other than that one entry in the hospital records, is there any documented evidence of a violent act by my client, either before or during her hospitalization?"

"I guess not. But whether or not she actually threw the rock isn't the point. She is delusional and she needs treatment. She . . ."

The lawyer cut him off again. "No further questions."

A few minutes later, the lawyer argued, "Your Honor, the statement of the neighbor, reported by the police and simply repeated in the admissions record, is hearsay [a statement made out of court presented as true] and should be found inadmissible. Moreover, its accuracy has not been confirmed; hence even if it is admitted into evidence, it should be given no weight. Since there is no other evidence of violent behavior in the hospital, and since the doctor here admitted that he has no personal knowledge that my client is dangerous, I ask that the court find that the grounds for involuntary hospitalization have not been met."

As he left the courthouse, the psychiatrist was angry and confused. Why hadn't he been allowed to describe his understanding of the patient's illness in his own way? Why must he just answer the questions the lawyers asked? The lawyers, even the one representing the hospital, and the judge didn't have any medical training; they seemed to speak a different language from his. He had been trained to base his opinion on an overall clinical picture, to reach a diagnosis to a reasonable medical certainty. But that wasn't good enough for the lawyers! They seemed to give no deference to his professional judgment, to his years of experience. They wanted observable, provable facts, and not just any facts, only the ones tied to the narrow criteria of the commitment law. He supposed that there had to be some legal review of involuntary hospitalization to avoid rare abuses, but why should it be so adversarial? Why couldn't the judge simply review the paperwork and ask a few questions of the doctor? Why did the lawyers have to be there at all?

The patient's lawyer, by contrast, felt pleased with her day's work—at least to a point. She had won her client's release from the hospital, which in itself was unusual. Today's client, like virtually all of them, couldn't afford to pay for an independent psychiatrist to evaluate and testify on her behalf, so the only expert testimony in the hearing came from the hospital. In the lawyer's experience, most judges deferred far too much to the hospital psychiatrist; if the diagnosis sounded scary enough and the client had "acted out" in the hospital at all, commitment was virtually guaranteed. But today's judge was new and had correctly focused on the commitment criteria and the factual evidence. She had been able to show that the hospital expert's professional opinion on dangerousness was based on unreliable evidence—that double hearsay about throwing the rock. That kind of sloppiness about facts was what really annoyed her about mental health professionals; they just accepted the word of the police, the neighbors, the client's relatives—of everybody but the client, it sometimes seemed. And it was frightening how easy it was to get a damaging label like "assaultive" or "combative" in your record—something that would follow you through life. Well, maybe in the future the hospital doctor would be more careful, would check his facts before jumping to a conclusion. Of course, if he did, he'd be a harder witness to cross-examine! In the meantime, her client was going home.

These scenes, drawn from personal experience, are intended to illustrate two important points: that legal advocacy for people identified as having mental disabilities[2] is not confined to

courtrooms, and that legal advocates and mental health professionals often have very different points of view.

Clash of Two Cultures: Law and Mental Health

Legal advocacy for people with mental disabilities brings into contact—and often into conflict—two very different professional "cultures." Lawyers and mental health professionals (MHPs) are seldom very familiar with the training, methodology, and ethical standards of the "other culture." Each may suspect the other of encroaching on sacred professional turf, performing functions for which he or she is not trained, and pursuing goals out of a desire for personal power or satisfaction, rather than to help the client (Brieland & Lemmon, 1985).

When Clinical Issues Become Legal Issues

Reading about the "legal issues" in the case examples, a MHP is likely to ask, "But aren't these all clinical issues?" Mental health professionals annoyed by a lawyer/advocate arguing for a patient's right to refuse treatment or to be released from the hospital have been known to ask sarcastically, "And what medical school did you attend, counsel?" Whether a patient should be treated in a hospital or as an outpatient and whether a patient should be prescribed antipsychotic medication are surely matters requiring psychiatric evaluation. In that sense they are clinical issues.

But this is so only when the MHP is simply conveying the "answer" to a patient who has complete freedom to reject the professional's advice. The clinical question becomes a legal one when the MHP invokes the power of the law—for example, when the psychiatrist is prepared to

---

[2]Referring to legal advocacy for "mentally disabled people" assumes that all people represented by legal advocates in the mental health system are in fact mentally disabled. Many of the people who are involuntarily hospitalized or proposed for commitment do not believe that they are mentally disabled and would object to being so described. Therefore, for the purposes of this chapter, I will use interchangeably "people identified as mentally disabled" and "people with mental disabilities" or occasionally "mentally disabled people."

initiate involuntary hospitalization proceedings if the patient does not accept the psychiatrist's advice that hospital treatment is appropriate. The psychiatrist may be acting from the highest of motives, from a sincere conviction as to what is in the patient's best clinical interests. But using the power of the law to restrict an individual's liberty changes a clinical matter to a legal one.

A clinical question also becomes a legal issue when following the MHP's advice will have legal consequences for the patient. For instance, a history of inpatient treatment for a psychiatric disorder may later disqualify an individual for certain professions, raise questions about competency to make a will or to enter into a contract, or hinder the ability to assert parental custody rights (Hayman, 1990; Sackett, 1991).

Some MHPs who practiced before the recognition of mental patients' constitutional rights, including right to counsel, may be nostalgic for the good old days when "we could just practice medicine without interference from the law." Indeed, into the late 1960s, in many states a psychiatrist's signature on a paper was sufficient to authorize prolonged involuntary confinement of an individual, as well as to restrict all aspects of a patient's life within an institution. But why did those psychiatrists have so much power? Because the state *law* permitted it. The lack of formal judicial hearings and the deference to MHPs' decisions did not mean that "the law" was not involved in mental health care. Rather, it meant that law was available to support MHPs' authority over patients—but not so available to the patients to resist that authority.

Proof and Certainty in Law and Mental Health

As the psychiatrist's musings in the second case example illustrate, the training of lawyers and MHPs is different in important respects. A MHP evaluating a patient is trying for a "working diagnosis," which will guide the initial course of treatment and which can and should be changed based on subsequent information, including the patient's response or lack of it to treatment. The MHP's subjective impressions of the patient—his or her "hunches" based on previous experience—can legitimately be used in reaching this working diagnosis. To proceed with a treatment plan, a MHP need only be convinced "to a reasonable medical certainty." How certain that is depends on the kind of medical issue at stake: certain physical illnesses can be diagnosed with a much higher degree of certainty than can nonorganic mental disorders. Studies of the validity of psychiatric diagnoses actually assess not "accuracy" but the extent to which several different evaluators arrive at the same diagnosis. That reliability may be 50 percent or less, even given the more precise diagnostic criteria provided in the third revised edition of the Diagnostic and Statistical Manual of Mental Disorders (DSM-IV)[3] (American Psychiatric Association, 1994; Reisner & Slobogin, 1990, pp. 396–397). By contrast, the law favors an approach that is highly dependent on provable facts and on conclusions that may reasonably be deduced from such facts. Subjective impressions are regarded with suspicion, as are conclusory statements giving an overall impression (for example, "the patient has poor impulse control"). Law and mental health have their own vocabularies, which do not have a direct one-to-one correspondence. A psychiatric diagnosis does not correspond directly with a legal concept such as competency to give or withhold consent to medical care. The DSM-III-R text itself cautioned that the courts should not rely on psychiatric diagnosis as determining legal concepts (American Psychiatric Association, 1987, p. xxix), and this admonition has been carried forward in DSM-IV; nevertheless, they often do rely on this diagnosis. Civil commitment laws use criteria such as "mentally disordered" or "gravely disabled" that have no clinical counterparts; a clinical diagnosis may be

---

[3]As of this writing, a comprehensive body of published studies does not yet exist to show whether the fourth edition of the *Diagnostic and Statistical Manual of Mental Disorders (DSM-IV)* will produce greater accuracy in diagnosis.

evidence that the statutory criterion has been met but does not "mean the same thing."

Generally speaking, the law is less interested in the diagnosis (or indeed the origin) of an individual's mental disability than in how it affects the individual's ability to function in a given context. Thus in a civil proceeding to commit an individual as mentally ill and dangerous, the court is concerned with how the individual's mental illness has in the past or could in the future lead to violent behavior. In a hearing to determine *competency* to give or withhold consent to treatment, evidence of dangerousness would be irrelevant; the issue is whether the individual's mental illness impaired or negated her ability to understand the proposed treatment and to weigh the risks and benefits of it and reach a conclusion (Saks, 1991; Winick, 1991). A MHP who does not understand these distinctions may be frustrated, as was the psychiatrist in the second case example, because he simply repeats the diagnosis or makes conclusory statements about the patient that are not relevant to the legal issue.

Existing Law: Right to Legal Counsel

Given the importance of law to people with mental disabilities, where do lawyer/advocates come from, and what are they supposed to do?

Legal assistance for individuals with mental disabilities, whether in the context of a commitment hearing or inside an institution, was the exception rather than the rule until the mid-1970s. Before that time, in many states an individual could be involuntarily hospitalized under civil law without a court hearing. Even where a hearing was required, state law did not necessarily mandate a right to counsel (Perlin, 1992a). Where legal assistance was provided, it was usually "superficial and totally inadequate" (Kittrie, 1973, p. 92). Legal assistance inside institutions was virtually nonexistent.

A right to counsel, both in and out of institutions, developed in the mid-1970s as part of the broader movement to establish constitutional rights of persons with mental disabilities. Courts found a right to counsel based on the constitutional right to due process of law. (See the section titled "Constitutional Law Sources.") In response to such decisions, state legislatures provided for legal assistance from lawyers or nonlawyer legal advocates within institutions. (See the section on "State Statutory Sources.") Finally, the U.S. Congress passed legislation requiring states receiving certain kinds of federal funds to provide legal assistance to individuals with mental disabilities. (See the section titled "Federal Statutory Programs.") By the late 1980s, therefore, every state provided for a legal right to counsel in commitment proceedings, and most states had some type of advocacy program to assist persons with mental disabilities in institutions.

Constitutional Law Sources

The right to counsel in noncriminal proceedings is grounded in the individual's constitutional right to due process. Under the Fourteenth Amendment to the U.S. Constitution, a state cannot deprive any person of life, liberty, or property without "due process of law." When the state legislature enacts a law authorizing involuntary confinement in a mental hospital, and then by its agents (police, hospital employees) confines an individual, the Fourteenth Amendment is triggered. The U.S. Supreme Court has repeatedly recognized that involuntary hospitalization constitutes a "massive curtailment of liberty" (*Addington v. Texas,* 1979, p. 425; *Humphrey v. Cady,* 1972, p. 509). A person confined in a mental hospital loses several important rights falling under the heading of liberty. First and most obvious is the loss of the freedom to move: to leave the hospital and to exercise within the hospital the same liberty as nonpatients. Second is the loss of reputation. The stigma of being identified as mentally ill—indeed, so much so as to require involuntary hospitalization—will likely negatively affect the individual's social, educational, and employment opportunities, and thus will contribute to a future loss of liberty. Finally, the individual may lose the right to give or withhold consent to treatment—whether that is defined as behavioral modification, milieu therapy, or medication (*Vitek v. Jones*, 1980).

An individual facing such a serious loss of liberty is entitled, as a matter of constitutional right, to "due process of law." Due process is a broad and flexible concept; what procedural protections an individual is entitled to vary according to such factors as the seriousness of the deprivation involved, the risk of an erroneous decision to deprive the person of liberty, and the burden on the state of providing additional procedures to protect the person's due process rights (*Mathews v. Eldridge*, 1976). At a minimum, however, due process requires notice of the state's proposed action and a meaningful opportunity for the individual to be heard by a neutral decision maker. In cases establishing the due process rights of defendants in a criminal case, the Supreme Court reasoned that "the right to be heard would be, in many cases, of little avail if it did not comprehend the right to be heard by counsel" (*Powell v. Alabama*, 1932, pp. 68–69—the "Scottsboro Boys" case). The right to counsel developed in the criminal law context; until the mid-1960s, it was unclear whether such a right applied in civil law proceedings such as juvenile delinquency cases and mental disability commitments. In 1967, the Supreme Court ruled that minors facing confinement in juvenile institutions were entitled to due process protections, including the right to counsel (*In re Gault*, 1967, p. 41). The Court rejected the argument that a civil "label" or benevolent state purposes justified a lack of procedural rights; the potential deprivation of liberty was what mattered.

Following this reasoning, lower federal courts quickly recognized a constitutional right to counsel in mental disability commitment proceedings (Perlin, 1989). As in the criminal context, the right to counsel extended to "all significant stages"[4] of the proceeding (*Lynch v. Baxley*, 1974,

p. 389). Counsel must be appointed "as soon after proceedings are begun as is realistically feasible" (*Lessard v. Schmidt*, 1972, pp. 1097–1098), and with enough time prior to the hearing to prepare a defense, including "advancement of an argument for alternative modes of treatment" (*In re Fisher*, 1974, p. 82). The right to counsel usually does not apply to the psychiatric interview in *civil* cases, because the presence of counsel might unduly interfere with the objective evaluation of the patient's mental condition (*Lynch v. Baxley*, *Lessard v. Schmidt*). However, in *criminal* cases there may be a right to have counsel present; at a minimum, defendant and counsel must be notified of the state's intention to obtain a psychiatric interview in order to consult prior to the interview (*Estelle v. Smith*, 1981).

The cases establishing a right to counsel involved mental disability commitment proceedings, presided over by a judge and decided by a judge or jury, which could result in loss of liberty for substantial periods of time. Another group of cases addressed the due process rights of individuals facing lesser deprivations of liberty, made by administrative decisions—for example, the transfer of a convicted incarcerated prisoner from prison to a mental hospital (*Vitek v. Jones*, 1980) or short-term detention for evaluation under a civil statute (*Doe v. Gallinot*, 1981). In such cases, representation by a competent, independent lay advocate has been found to satisfy the federal Constitution.

State Statutory Sources

By the mid-1980s, every state recognized a right to counsel for a person facing involuntary civil commitment (Perlin, 1989). However, states vary widely in how they implement this right. Over a

---

[4] The court in *Lynch* defined a "significant" stage as "all judicial proceedings and any other official proceedings at which a decision is, or can be, made which may result in a detrimental change in the conditions of the subject's liberty" (p. 389 n. 5). A familiar example in the criminal and juvenile justice context is the interrogation of an individual in police custody.

dozen states by statute created a statewide organized "mental health advocacy" program to represent persons identified as mentally disabled. Depending on the law of the state, such programs may be responsible for representing persons with mental illnesses, persons with developmental disabilities, persons proposed for civil commitment, all institutionalized persons, or all persons receiving treatment or services from state programs for those with mental illness or developmental disabilities. Some of the programs are primarily concerned with providing legal services for individuals facing involuntary commitment; others are authorized to assist patients already hospitalized or receiving services.

Some states use multiple mechanisms to provide legal counsel—for example, by allocating funds for counties to contract with individual lawyers or law firms (both for-profit and non-profit). Other states distinguish between counsel in commitment proceedings and nonlawyer advocates to assist individuals within institutions. For instance, California authorizes the public defender to represent individuals seeking to challenge their involuntary hospitalization through habeas corpus hearings and in conservatorship hearings.[5] However, advocacy at administrative hearings to confine the patient for up to 14 days of evaluation and intensive treatment,[6] and at hearings to determine competency to consent to or refuse treatment,[7] is provided by the Office of Patients Rights Advocates (lay as well as lawyer advocates). In addition to statewide advocacy programs, a number of other projects provide legal services to persons with mental disabilities, such as pilot projects funded by the federal Legal Services Corporation, projects of the American Bar Association and/or state or county bar associations, and clinics run by law schools. Some of these programs are local in their focus; others are national projects that concentrate on precedent-setting impact litigation and law reform efforts.

Federal Statutory Programs

Congress has established "Protection and Advocacy" programs to provide legal representation to persons with developmental disabilities (42 U.S.C. sec. 6042(a)(1) *et seq.*). States receiving certain federal funds must establish a Protection and Advocacy (P&A) system. The P&A must have the authority to pursue legal, administrative, and other approaches to ensure the rights of their clients; investigate incidents of abuse and neglect; and establish a grievance procedure to

[5]In California, long-term involuntary confinement of a person with a mental disability in a psychiatric facility may only be accomplished in the civil system through a conservatorship under the Lanterman-Petris-Short Act, Cal. Welf. & Inst. Code sections 5350–5371. If a court finds that the person, by reason of mental disability, is "gravely disabled" (unable to provide for basic needs for food, clothing, and shelter), it may appoint a conservator. The conservator may be authorized by the court to give or refuse consent to treatment related to the "grave disability" (section 5357) and to place the person in a facility for the treatment of the "grave disability" (section 5358).

A conservatee (individual under conservatorship) who wishes to challenge the necessity either for the conservatorship, or for confinement in a treatment facility, may do so in either of two ways. First, under the conservatorship statute itself, the conservatorship must be renewed on a yearly basis (section 5362), and the conservatee has the right to oppose renewal at a hearing (section 5364). Second, whenever the state confines an individual and he or she claims the confine-

ment is unlawful, the individual has a constitutional (and, in California, also a statutory— section 5358.3) right to petition for a writ of habeas corpus. A habeas writ requires the state to produce evidence justifying the continued confinement of the person.

[6]Cal. Welf. & Inst. Code section 5150 permits involuntary detention and evaluation, in a designated psychiatric facility, for up to 72 hours of a person believed by reason of mental disability to be "gravely disabled" or dangerous to self or others. After 72 hours, the individual can be "certified" for up to 14 additional days of intensive treatment if still "gravely disabled" or dangerous to self or others (Cal. Welf. & Inst. Code section 5250). Such an individual is entitled to an administrative "certification review hearing."

[7]Under Cal. Welf. & Inst. Code section 5332, when an individual confined short-term (72 hours or 14 days) refuses medication, a hearing must be held to determine her or his "capacity" for informed consent. Such a "capacity" hearing is presided over by a judge or court-appointed hearing officer.

ensure that clients have full access to services of the state system. The P&A must be independent of any agency that provides treatment, services, or habilitation to persons with developmental disabilities. Congress has established a similar advocacy network, the Client Assistance Program (CAP) for individuals receiving services under the Vocational Rehabilitation Services Act of 1973 (29 U.S.C. sec. 732). Since CAPs perform functions similar to the P&A, states may combine the two in one agency. Finally, under the Protection and Advocacy for Mentally Ill Individuals Act (42 U.S.C. sec. 10801 *et seq.*), Congress made federal funds available to states establishing independent systems that have the authority to investigate incidents of neglect and abuse of persons with mental illness, and to pursue administrative, legal, and other appropriate remedies on behalf of those persons. This act did *not* authorize P&As to represent individuals regularly at civil commitment hearings; that is considered a state function that was not supplanted by the federal program (42 U.S.C. sec. 10821(1)).

State P&As vary considerably in the number of cases they handle, the issues they identify as priorities, and the extent of their funding. Ironically, P&As have been most active in states where there was already at least one other strong advocacy organization and a history of effective representation of people with mental disabilities (Perlin, 1993).

The Role and Ethical Obligations of Counsel

The two scenes with which this chapter began illustrate the range of tasks for legal counsel and advocates. In the first scene, the individual being admitted to the hospital waived his right to consult legal counsel—the patient's rights advocate. Had he not done so, what would the lawyer/advocate's function have been?

Lawyers and nonlawyer advocates generally perform two functions: advocacy and counseling. *Advocacy* means speaking for the client. *Counseling* means informing and advising the client.

Ethical Obligations of Counsel

Legal counsel who are lawyers licensed to practice law are bound by the rules of professional responsibility. Each jurisdiction has its own such rules, but generally these are consistent in principle with the *Model Code of Professional Responsibility* (American Bar Association, 1981) or the *Model Rules of Professional Conduct* (American Bar Association, 1983). Canon 7 of the *Model Code* states: "A lawyer should represent a client zealously within the bounds of the law." In general, the lawyer's responsibility is to pursue the client's interests—as the client defines them—as long as the client does not ask the lawyer to break the law or violate the canons of ethics.[8] The lawyer can consult with the client about both the client's goals and the means by which they are pursued (Model Rule 1.2(a)) and "limit the objectives of the representation if the client consents after consultation" (Model Rule 1.2(c)). But both the *Model Code* and the *Model Rules* recognize the traditional principles of client competency and control over the fundamental decisions in the case.

The *Ethical Considerations* (EC) accompanying the Canons explain that a lawyer can only make decisions as to matters "not affecting the merits of the cause or substantially prejudicing the rights of a client" (EC 7-7). Otherwise, the client has *exclusive* authority to make decisions, and the decisions are binding on the lawyer. For

---

[8]However, many commentators suggest, and ethical codes reflect, the lawyer's right not to participate in what he or she would find morally repugnant (Rhode, 1985; Rhode & Luban, 1992). The *Model Code* (DR 2-110(C)(1)(e)) and *Model Rules* (Rule 1.16) permit a lawyer to withdraw from representation in a matter not pending in court, when the client insists that the lawyer engage in conduct which, although not contrary to the rules of ethics, is contrary to the lawyer's judgment or advice. DR-2-110(C)(1)(d) also permits withdrawal when the client by "other conduct renders it unreasonably difficult for the lawyer to carry out his employment effectively."

example, in a civil matter, the client alone can decide whether to file a lawsuit or to accept a settlement offer. In a criminal matter, the client alone can determine what plea to enter to the charges, whether to testify in her or his own defense, and whether to pursue an appeal. The *Model Rules,* while adhering to the principle that the client chooses the fundamental objectives of the case, acknowledge that "[a] clear distinction between objectives and means sometimes cannot be drawn, and in many cases the client-lawyer relationship partakes of a joint undertaking" (Comment to Rule l.2).

Certainly a client may be influenced by the lawyer's advice in making decisions. It is quite consistent with the concept of "client-centered" decision making (Binder, Bergman, & Price, 1991) for a lawyer to make a recommendation which the client is free to accept or reject. Legal commentators have recognized the dangers of lawyer "paternalism" (Luban, 1981; Tremblay, 1987) and the risk that a lawyer, while appearing to support autonomy, in fact intimidates and manipulates the client (Ellman, 1987).

A lawyer as adviser has a duty to inform the client of relevant information and to assist the client in reaching her or his decision. The *Model Rules* and *Model Code* both assume a principle of competency—that the client, when properly advised and assisted, is capable of making decisions about important matters (Ellman, 1987; Strauss, 1987). The counseling function can include more than simply informing the client of available legal options; the lawyer

may emphasize the possibility of harsh consequences that might result from assertion of legally permissible positions. In the final analysis, however, the lawyer should always remember that the decision whether to forego legally available objectives or methods because of non legal factors is ultimately for the client and not for himself. (EC 7-8)

For example, a lawyer in a divorce case can try to persuade a client to accept a joint custody arrangement, because this will avoid the emotional as well as financial costs of a prolonged custody battle for both the client and the child. But once the client decides to reject the proposal and seek sole custody, the lawyer must follow the client's instructions. Throughout the course of the custody case, the lawyer may continue to recommend that the client rethink her or his goal. However, in representing the client to the outside world, the lawyer must speak for the client as if the lawyer had no doubt as to the merits of the client's position.

Advising and Advocating for the Client

The prospective patient in scene 1 is faced with at least two decisions: whether to request admission to the hospital as a voluntary patient, and whether to exercise or waive his right to a hearing reviewing his involuntary patient status. In assisting an individual with either of these decisions, the lawyer/advocate first must provide the information necessary for an informed decision. Such information includes the legal consequences of becoming a hospitalized patient. It also includes a patient's rights to benefits and services in the hospital, as well as to participate in formulating a treatment plan.

After providing this information, the lawyer/advocate's next task is to assist the client in reaching a decision. This means helping the client identify goals and weigh the pros and cons of the proposed course of action, answering any questions the client has, and expressing a professional opinion as to the practical effect of the client's decision (EC 7-5). The lawyer's role is to facilitate the client's decision, not to make it for the client.

Once the client has determined what he or she wants to do, the lawyer/advocate's task may be over. However, depending on the nature of the decision, the client may want the lawyer/advocate's help in carrying it out. For example, suppose a patient in the hospital wishes to stop taking prescribed antipsychotic medication. The patient consults an advocate who advises her of her legal right to give or withhold consent to treatment, including medication. The patient decides that she wishes to stop taking the medication because she experiences debilitating side-effects. The patient next asks the advocate to assist her in enforcing that right to refuse the medication. Such assistance may involve simply arranging a meeting between the patient and the treating psychiatrist, at which the advocate helps to clarify the patient's concerns for the psychiatrist; the result is a change in medication acceptable to the patient.

However, if the treating psychiatrist believes that the patient is incompetent to make a decision concerning medication and wants to medicate her against her will, the hospital will probably seek a hearing at which a judge or administrative officer will determine the patient's competency. Assisting the patient in carrying out her decision to refuse medication may involve representing her at this competency hearing (Appelbaum, 1988). The lawyer/advocate presents the patient's argument to the judge or hearing officer. This means introducing witnesses in support of the patient's competence, cross-examining witnesses called by the hospital, and possibly even obtaining an evaluation of the patient by an independent psychiatrist, psychologist, or psychopharmacologist.

Suppose the prospective patient in scene 1 had been brought to the hospital against his will and must decide whether to exercise or to waive his right to an administrative review of the need for his hospitalization, or to a more formal judicial hearing. Again the lawyer/advocate's task would be to inform the client of his right to a hearing and to assist the client in reaching a decision. The client's probable chances of winning such a hearing may be a significant factor in the decision; typically, the lawyer/advocate would express an opinion, based on the lawyer/advocate's knowledge of the facts of the client's case and of past decisions of the hearing officer or judge in similar cases. However, if the client decides to pursue a hearing even against the lawyer/advocate's advice, the lawyer/advo-

cate's next task is still to carry out the client's wishes.

If a client in a matter not pending before a court insists on a course of action that the lawyer disapproves of, the lawyer may withdraw from employment (EC 7-8; Model Rule 1.2). Before doing this, however, a lawyer should consider whether the client can readily obtain other legal representation. Where the client is poor, a prisoner, or confined in a mental institution, access to alternative counsel is apt to be nonexistent. Thus withdrawing from representation likely means abandoning the client. In such a case the lawyer should make every effort to reach an understanding with the client that permits continued representation—for example, by limiting, with the client's consent, the goals of the representation.[9] If this is really impossible, the lawyer should assume responsibility for finding another lawyer for the client—for example, by recruiting a "pro bono" volunteer through a local bar association and providing the new lawyer with assistance to develop expertise in mental disability law.

Lawyer's Traditional Role: Adversary System

The role of the lawyer is traditionally described as "adversarial." Contrary to most lawyer jokes, "adversarial" does not mean that the lawyer must be hostile or rude; it means that the lawyer should represent the client consistently with the principles underlying an "adversary system of justice" (EC 7-19). That system assumes that the most accurate decision making will come from each party presenting her or his point of view and challenging that of the other party before a neutral decision maker. The adversary system assumes that parties acting in their own self-defined interest will be motivated to present the strongest case in support of their position.

---

[9]See note 8 for rules permitting such restriction.

The lawyer for either side is not the decision maker; it is not the lawyer's role to decide which party is correct, either in its version of facts or in its legal argument. In a civil commitment proceeding, for example, there might be both disputes about facts (did the hospitalized person throw a rock at a neighbor?) and about the legal significance of those facts (does that act, plus additional information about the person's behavior in the hospital, prove that he or she is dangerous to others?). The lawyer's client expresses her desire not to be involuntarily hospitalized as dangerous. Following that instruction, the lawyer's role is to challenge the accuracy of the facts the hospital presents in support of the petition, as well as to argue that, even if the court finds those facts to be accurate, they do not support a legal conclusion that the client is dangerous and meets the grounds for commitment. Similarly, if a state commitment law uses a term such as "severely disabling mental disorder," the lawyer for the client may attempt to dispute the accuracy of the hospital's diagnosis of the client (for example, by introducing expert testimony in support of a "milder" diagnosis). Or the client's lawyer could argue that the hospital's diagnosis, if accurate, does not satisfy the legal standard (for instance, because it is not usually considered severely disabling, or because in the client's case it has not been shown to have such severe impact).

In both examples, the lawyer is not deciding what diagnosis is "correct" or whether the client is "severely disabled" or "dangerous"; rather, the lawyer is presenting to the decision maker (judge or hearing officer) evidence and arguments that support the client's position. The lawyer is ethically forbidden to fabricate evidence or knowingly to present false testimony (Canon 22; EC 7-26). The lawyer cannot testify as a witness either for or against the client; it is inappropriate for the opposing party or decision maker to ask the lawyer, "Don't you think your client needs to be in the hospital?" or "Why are you so sure your client isn't dangerous?"

Special Problems in Representing Clients with Mental Disabilities

The *Model Code* and *Ethical Considerations* assume that in most cases the client is competent to assess the information and advice provided by the lawyer, to make decisions, and finally, to communicate those decision to the lawyer. If a client is unable to perform these functions because of physical or mental disability, how does this affect the lawyer's responsibilities and role? If a client has a legal guardian or other court-appointed representative such as a conservator, the lawyer informs and advises that representative and takes directions from the representative. But

[i]f a client under disability has no legal representative, his lawyer may be compelled in court proceedings to make decisions on behalf of the client. If the client is capable of understanding the matter in question or of contributing to the advancement of his interests, regardless of whether he is legally disqualified from performing certain acts, the lawyer should obtain from him all possible aid. If the disability of a client and the lack of a legal representative compel the lawyer to make decisions for his client, the lawyer should consider all circumstances then prevailing and act with care to safeguard and advance the interests of his client. But obviously a lawyer cannot perform any act or make any decision which the law requires his client to perform or make, either acting for himself if competent, or by a duly constituted representative if legally incompetent. (EC 7-12)

This part of the lawyer's ethical responsibilities appears to contain a contradiction. On the one hand, the client's mental disability alone does not relieve the lawyer of the responsibility to attempt to inform and advise the client, and to obtain from the client "all possible aid" in determining the client's wishes. Yet by saying that the lawyer may be compelled *in court proceedings* to make decisions on the client's behalf, the *Model Code* seems to indicate that, at least when representing a client in court, the lawyer can make some of the kinds of decisions which the client ordinarily must do (Herr, 1989; Tremblay, 1987). The lawyer in so doing is required to "safeguard and advance the interests of the client." What would this mean in a proceeding to hospitalize the client involuntarily, or to determine whether the client should be placed under conservatorship?

Although the lawyer cannot testify "on the merits" of the issue of dangerousness or need for treatment, can she or he ethically request the court to appoint a *guardian ad litem* for the client? To do so in this situation arguably violates the admonition to "act with care to safeguard and advance the interests of his client" (EC 7-12). Telling the court that one's client is incompetent and asking for a *guardian ad litem* to be appointed essentially concedes the merits of the conservatorship petition.[10] The Commentary to the *Model Rules* acknowleges that such a disclosure by counsel "can adversely affect the client's interest" and ultimately result in involuntary commitment (Herr, 1989). It suggests that a lawyer caught in this difficult situation consult "an appropriate diagnostician for guidance"—presumably on the issue of whether the client is so disabled as to need a guardian.

Model Rule 1.14(b) cautions that "a lawyer shall secure the appointment of a guardian or other legal representative . . . only when the lawyer reasonably believes that the client cannot adequately communicate or exercise judgment in the lawyer-client relationship." This rule would certainly apply to a situation where the lawyer was totally unable to establish a relationship with the client—for example, because the client just stares into space and does not respond to or acknowledge the lawyer's presence. In such a case it would be ethical for the lawyer to petition for appointment of a *guardian ad litem* to instruct her or him on behalf of the client.

But this situation of the client with a severe impairment must be distinguished from a case where the client is resisting the appointment of a conservatorship and communicates this clearly to the counsel. Just because the client shows evidence of delusional thinking or behaves in ways that indicate the presence of a mental disability does *not* mean the lawyer is justified in seeking the appointment of a *guardian ad litem*. Rule 1.14(a) requires that "the lawyer shall, as far as reasonably possible, maintain a normal client-lawyer relationship with the [mentally disabled] client." The Comment to the Rule states that the fact of disability "does not diminish the lawyer's obligation to treat the client with attention and respect." A client with a mental disability may still have "the ability to understand, deliberate upon and reach conclusions about matters affecting the client's own well-being."

Even if a client already has a guardian or other legal representative, the lawyer still has an obligation to maintain communication with the client. Although the lawyer should look to the guardian for decisions ordinarily expected of the client, if the lawyer becomes aware that the guardian "is acting adversely to the [mentally disabled client's] interest," he or she may have a duty to prevent or rectify the guardian's misconduct. This could mean asking a court to review the appropriateness of the guardian's actions, or to appoint a different guardian, or even to reconsider the need for a guardianship at all.

Proposed Alternative Roles

Some early commentators raised the issue of whether a lawyer in the civil commitment context

---

[10]A *guardian ad litem* (GAL) is appointed to represent the interests of an incompetent individual only for the duration of and in the context of a specific legal case. For example, a GAL may be appointed to bring or defend a lawsuit in the name of a minor (who is incompetent "as a matter of law," which means that he or she cannot proceed without a guardian, regardless of the minor's actual capacity to understand or assert his or her interest). A GAL would only be appointed for an *adult* who is incompetent "as a matter of fact," which means the court has considered evidence of the adult's actual capacity and has made a factual determination of incompetency. Although it is theoretically possible that an adult so incompetent as to need a GAL in a conservatorship proceeding could be capable of providing for basic survival needs (and thus *not* meet the definition of "gravely disabled" justifying a conservatorship), a judge is unlikely to appoint a GAL and then deny the petition for conservatorship. Thus, if a lawyer representing an individual proposed for conservatorship asks for a GAL to be appointed for the client, the judge will likely view this as conceding that the client needs a conservator.

should act more like a *guardian ad litem*—that is, should decide what is in the client's best interests and pursue that goal, rather than advocating the client's expressed desires (Andalman & Chambers, 1974; Cohen, 1966). However, such an approach is fundamentally at odds with the principles underlying the *Model Code* and *Model Rules* and was explicitly rejected by both judges and legislatures before the *Model Rules* were drafted (Herr, 1989; Perlin, 1989). Even if a client's abilities are impaired by mental disability, a lawyer is not justified in making decisions for the client based on what the lawyer thinks is in the client's best interests or what the lawyer would have done in the client's place. A client who is so mentally disabled that she or he cannot make the decisions that the law requires the client to make should have a *guardian ad litem* appointed. The *guardian ad litem* then can instruct the lawyer. But the lawyer who simply takes on the role of *guardian ad litem* without being appointed by a court violates the client's legal right to make decisions unless and until declared legally incompetent.

Perhaps the strongest argument against the lawyer–as–*guardian ad litem* approach is that the established role of the lawyer as the advocate of the client's decisions should not suddenly be changed without warning to the client. Persons with mental disabilities, just like other clients, are entitled to expect that their lawyer will "act like a lawyer" and will not suddenly become a *guardian ad litem*—or more than that, the judge of the merits of the client's case. A lawyer who changes role in this way arguably violates an ethical duty of loyalty to the client.

Another role sometimes recommended is as an *amicus curiae*, a friend of the court playing an "investigative" role (Cohen, 1966; Litwak, 1974). Under this proposal, the counsel would simply be responsible for ensuring that the court had before it all relevant information about the client's situation, including available treatment alternatives. This role would normally include cross-examination of the hospital's witnesses or challenging of the accuracy of the hospital's

records, only to clarify or to bring out additional information. The proposed investigative function is indeed valuable, and in some jurisdictions this function is assigned to an employee of the court. For example, in California whenever a conservatorship is proposed, a court representative must investigate alternatives and report on whether the conservatorship is necessary.[11] But the *amicus curiae* role serves the interests of the court, which may differ from the client's interests. The client's interests may call for exclusion of certain information, or for a challenge to the competency of the hospital's expert witness on cross-examination. There is a genuine problem of conflict of roles. Courts have explicitly found that a lawyer who acts as *amicus curiae* does not satisfy the right to counsel (*Anders v. California*, 1967, p. 744).

In practice, lawyers representing clients with mental disabilities in commitment proceedings try to use their counseling function to resolve the dilemma of an impaired client. Where going to a formal hearing would most likely result in involuntary commitment, lawyers often advise their clients to agree to short-term hospitalization as a voluntary patient (Holstein, 1993; Warren, 1982). A lawyer/advocate who believes it is in a client's best interest to remain in the hospital or to take prescribed medication is free to express these convictions to the client and indeed to attempt to persuade the client to follow the lawyer's advice. But to those outside the lawyer/advocate-client relationship, the lawyer/advocate must present the client's point of view only (*McCartney v. United States*, 1965, p. 471).

Ultimately, unless the client is seeking something against the law, the lawyer/advocate has an ethical obligation to represent the client's wishes effectively. Thus, even if the lawyer/advocate tried to persuade the prospective patient to stay in the hospital and to give the treatment a chance, once the client has decided to exercise a right to seek release through a hearing, the lawyer/

---

[11]Cal. Welf. & Inst. Code section 5354.

advocate's responsibility is to pursue that goal for the client.[12] It would be a violation of the lawyer/advocate's ethics to tell the judge or hearing officer (or the psychiatrist) that it would be best for the client to stay in the hospital, or to deliberately provide a weak defense or representation to make it more likely that the client will lose the hearing.

Expansion of Rights of Persons with Mental Disabilities

Thus far the advocates in these examples have simply been advising their clients of their rights under existing law and advocating their client's position in judicial or administrative hearings. However, a major function of many lawyer/advocates is in helping their clients obtain access to services and programs. The fact that a person qualifies for benefits under a state or federal program does not mean that he or she will actually get that benefit without assistance. An advocate can make the difference between a right on paper and a right in reality (Peters & Costello, 1992).

For example, an individual may be eligible for disability benefits but may be either unaware of that fact or unable to go through the complex application process alone. An advocate can first advise the client of her or his eligibility, help the client fill out an application, and obtain supporting documentation. Next the advocate can help the client communicate with the agency worker reviewing the application, making sure that the worker has all the information needed. If the application is denied, an advocate can advise the client about the chances for an appeal and rep-

resent the client through the administrative appeal process.

If the client is denied benefits because of a policy or procedure that the lawyer/advocate concludes is unlawful, the next step may be systemwide advocacy. This could involve trying to change the policy or procedure through strategies ranging from informal approaches to the agency, to legislative lobbying, to the filing of a lawsuit on behalf of the individual client alone or along with others similarly situated (a "class action").[13] Similarly, counsel appointed in commitment hearings may discover that the clients, when they leave the hospital, are not receiving the "individualized discharge plan" provided for under state law. Rather, they are being released with only a telephone number for a community clinic where they can pick up their medication—if that much. Counsel may try to enforce the right for an individual client first, by negotiating with the hospital. If the hospital refuses, the next step may be asking the court to order a discharge plan and follow-up for an individual client—or for many clients.

Suppose the hospital staff responds to counsel by saying the lack of discharge plans is not their fault: community-based services are all but nonexistent. Counsel may try to establish a right to community-based services, again using a range

---

[12]The lawyer may withdraw from representing the client, but only with the permission of the court. The court will appoint alternative counsel to represent the client in the commitment proceeding.

[13]A class action lawsuit is brought on behalf of a class of persons who have common legal interests, or are "similarly situated" with respect to the legal claims at issue in the lawsuit. For example, a class action challenging conditions of confinement in a psychiatric facility as unlawful would name one or more individual patients ("named plaintiffs") in the complaint and ask the court to accept them as representative of the interests of all persons similarly situated, such as all other patients confined in the facility. If the court "certifies" the proposed class, the lawsuit will resolve the claims as to all members of the class. Notice is usually given to all members of the class or their legal representatives (conservators), informing them that they have the right to opt out of the class, and thus not be bound by the outcome of the litigation. A class member who wishes to pursue an individual claim against the facility for, for instance, psychiatric malpractice as well as civil rights violations, and who believes she or he could obtain a more favorable judgment, might choose to opt out.

Class action representation involves special and complex ethical issues (Rhode, 1982).

of advocacy techniques including legislative lobbying and, if necessary, litigation.

Advocates' use of litigation has been sharply criticized as "florid legal schizophrenia," reflecting "aimless hyperactivity and aggressiveness, under which human problems are needlessly turned into legal battle[s], fought without regard to internal system costs, the larger societal interests, or even the best interests of the client" (Brakel, 1988, p. 4). However, most commentators concede that patients rights' litigation has been praised for "significantly improv[ing] the quality of life" for institutionalized individuals, bringing an end to "[t]he filth, squalor, and unsafe conditions" of state institutions (*Ricci v. Callahan*, 1986, p. 379). Sometimes the mere threat of litigation is enough to bring about improvement. One director of a state facility volunteered in a personal conversation that fear of litigation had prompted the legislature to increase funding, enabling him finally to improve conditions to the point of obtaining JCAH accreditation.

Class action lawsuits often precede and form the basis for legislative reform. Early cases such as *Wyatt v. Stickney* had a "massive influence" on the development of state statutes establishing patient's rights to "appropriate treatment and services," to individualized treatment and periodic review of treatment, to a humane treatment environment, and to privacy and safety, as well as to an aftercare plan on discharge (Perlin, 1994, pp. 191–192). The Individuals with Disabilities in Education Act (20 U.S.C. sec. 1400 *et seq.*) drew on the constitutional right to equal protection in education and the factual records established in special education cases (*Mills v. Board of Education*, 1972; *Pennsylvania Association for Retarded Children v. Pennsylvania*, 1972). "Similarly, the institutional reform cases, such as *Wyatt* and Willowbrook [*New York State Ass'n for Retarded Citizens, Inc. v. Rockefeller*, 1973], paved the way for Medicaid standards and the Developmental Disabilities Assistance and Bill of Rights Act" (Herr, 1989, p. 635).

Advocates also have been criticized for protecting clients' liberty at the expense of their treatment needs (Appelbaum & Gutheil, 1979;

Isaac & Brakel, 1992; Treffert, 1973). However, much litigation, from the beginning of the patients' rights movement, attempted to establish a right to treatment and to improve the quality of services both in institutions and in the community (Perlin, 1994; Schwartz, 1989; Wald & Friedman, 1978). More recently, advocates have sought to establish a right to community-based treatment (*Arnold v. Department of Health Services*, 1989; Costello & Preis, 1987). Advocates, while upholding their clients' right to refuse treatment, have also asserted their right to get the new antipsychotic drug known as clozapine (Blackburn, 1990; Perlin, 1993). Advocates are exploring the possibilities of the Americans with Disabilities Act (42 U.S.C. sec. 12102(2) (1990)) to guarantee the rights of individuals with mental disabilities in areas such as employment, housing, and family law, as well as within the mental health care system (Parry, 1993).

Counsel are essential to enforcing rights:

Legal rights are not necessarily self-executing. The declaration by a court of a right "to" a service or a right to be free "from" an intrusion does not *in se* provide that service or guarantee freedom from intrusion. A right is only a paper declaration without an accompanying remedy, and, without counsel (so as to best guarantee enforcement), there is little chance that the rights "victories" that have been won in test case and law reform litigation in this area will have any impact on the mentally disabled population. (Perlin, 1993, p. 175)

Federal statutes creating the protection and advocacy programs recognized that such advocacy was needed "to secure the rights denied at the Willowbrook, Partlow and Pennhurst institutions, and to prevent further human and legal rights abuses" (Herr, 1989, p. 635).

Criticisms of Existing Law

The reality—as opposed to the right on paper—of access to competent, effective counsel varies from state to state and from institution to institution. Two major problems are common: "rolelessness" and fragmentation. The lawyer's role confusion contributes to the problem of perception by MHPs—how can lawyer/advocates educate MHPs about their role if they are unsure themselves?

Fragmentation refers to the lack of a unified, statewide system of advocacy that will provide legal assistance to people with mental disabilities, both in institutions and in the community. Under the current system, a lay advocate employed in a hospital may be able to represent clients in internal hearings to determine matters such as client "privileges"—but not to help the client after discharge to enforce her or his rights to services in the community. Alternatively, a public defender who represents an individual at a commitment proceeding may be prevented by law from assisting the client, once in the hospital, with matters such as consent to medication. Neither may be able to undertake complex litigation necessary to clarify or expand existing rights.

Rolelessness/Counsel in Hearings

Rolelessness refers to the confusion experienced by many lawyer/advocates, who are unsure how to carry out the professional duties discussed above. Lawyers or advocates who are uncertain of their role cannot be effective. Studies consistently show inadequate representation by lawyers appointed in commitment proceedings (Morris, 1978; Perlin, 1992a). Lawyers often defer to the hospital psychiatrist testifying, doing minimal or no cross-examination. Lawyers frequently do not interview their client, much less perform even rudimentary investigation into the facts leading to the client's hospitalization. They often do not explore alternatives to hospitalization or assist their client in obtaining public benefits and services, disdaining this as "social work." Some lawyers think their function is just to look through the paperwork to make sure it is in order, and thus give the false impression that the client has had the benefit of legal representation (Hiday, 1982; Perlin & Sadoff, 1982). These kinds of inadequate representation explain why one study

showed an individual with a lawyer has a worse chance to be released at a commitment hearing than one without (Andalman & Chambers, 1974).

This failure to provide effective representation is not surprising. Few lawyer/advocates start out with the educational background and special training needed to serve clients with mental disabilities effectively. Lawyers are likely to share the general public's unease with people with mental disabilities.[14] A client who cannot readily perform the analytical and decision-making functions that are presumed to be part of the lawyer-client relationship can frustrate the lawyer. A client who has a hard time concentrating on the lawyer's questions because she is hearing voices or is deeply depressed may be frightening.

A client's behavior, demeanor, and decisions may vary from day to day as a result of mental disability, or because of the effects of medication (Costello, 1983). Clients with mental disabilities can be unpredictable in court; their testimony on the stand or behavior at a hearing can be completely unrelated to what they said or did in an interview with the lawyer earlier the same day. All this may be especially unsettling to a lawyer, since one of the attractions of the legal profession is its aura of rationality and control.

A lawyer may respond to such fear and frustration by "paternalism"—deciding what is in the client's best interest. If the lawyer views the client as "sick" and "in need of help," paternalism probably means "rolling over" in the commitment hearing: deferring to the hospital expert or even stipulating to the hospital's allegations and waiving the client's right to testify.

This approach will usually make the lawyer

---

[14] I asked law students in my Mental Disability Law course which they would rather be trapped in an elevator with: a convicted felon or a person who had been diagnosed as schizophrenic. I deliberately did not give the students any more information—for example, whether the felon was a "white-collar" criminal or whether the schizophrenic person had ever been violent—because I wanted to explore their preconceptions. The overwhelming majority chose the felon.

popular with the hospital psychiatrist and lawyer, as well as with the court staff, because the patient's lawyer is "not wasting time." Courts that routinely hear commitment proceedings develop a special subculture within which lawyers are only accepted if they learn the informal procedures and unwritten rules (Holstein, 1993; Warren, 1982).

Some lawyers struggle with wanting to appear credible in the eyes of the judge and court personnel. If the client is behaving in a way that indicates severe mental illness, a lawyer advocating for the client's release may feel foolish. There is a temptation to dissociate himself or herself from the client's "craziness," by adopting a compassionate but condescending manner toward the client, or by stating the client's position but in a tone that conveys a different message to the court. Lawyers may justify this in individual cases by saying they made a pragmatic assessment that the client could not win, and by "rolling over" in this case they are gaining credibility for a future client with a stronger case (Litwack, 1974; Morris, 1978).

Another reaction (although a rarer one) is to take the traditional adversarial model to the extreme as a matter of principle—for example, requesting a jury trial in every case, refusing to stipulate to the qualifications of even well-known "regular" hospital experts, or cross-examining the testifying psychiatrist on philosophical issues ("How can we ever really know who is insane?"). This approach alienates the judge and court personnel, since it goes against the generally shared conviction that the client is of course "sick"—the purpose of the hearing is to see that whatever aid is provided to the person with a mental disability is done with due consideration for his or her rights. It is therefore ineffective in representing the client's interests (Warren, 1982).

Almost any lawyer will resent being portrayed as a "bad guy" who is trying to prevent the poor client from getting needed treatment (Galie, 1978). Yet that is often how legal advocates are viewed. Relatives frequently perceive the lawyer as blocking their attempts to help their mentally disabled family member; especially if the family member is angry or suspicious of the relatives' motives, the relatives see a lawyer advocating the client's view as a personal attack. Hospital workers may encourage this view, for example by explaining to the relatives that they cannot hospitalize or involuntarily medicate the mentally disabled person "because of the lawyer." Often, the client also fails to appreciate the lawyer's efforts; just as the hospital staff and relatives see the lawyer as the enemy, the client decides the lawyer is part of the plot against him or her and in collusion with the hospital or relatives.

Whatever the lawyer/advocate's perspective, the dangers of paternalism in this setting are great. A client with a mental disability may be especially vulnerable to the lawyer's subtle or not-so-subtle efforts to influence a decision (Herr, 1989; Tremblay, 1987). Advocates have been criticized for "disabling" their clients by discouraging them from testifying in court proceedings, or by presenting their case in accordance with the narrow conventions of legal process (Alfieri, 1992). It is difficult to strike a balance between encouraging expression of the client's "own voice" and protecting the client from the likely consequences when the court and MHPs perceive that voice as more evidence of mental disability (Dinerstein, 1992).

Advocates within Institutions

Patients' rights advocacy organizations often employ both lawyers and nonlawyers to represent individuals with mental disabilities within institutions. This representation may be very informal—for example, a meeting between the advocate and a MHP involved in treatment to discuss the client's request—or more formal, such as appearing for the client in an administrative hearing to determine competency to give informed consent. A lawyer/advocate appearing for a client in an institutional setting has the same duty to advance the cause of the client within the bounds of the law (EC 7-15) as would be the case in a more traditional judicial forum.

Nonlawyer advocates face many of the same problems of rolelessness as do lawyers. However, the danger of "paternalism" may be even stronger for nonlawyer advocates than for lawyers because of the lack of a strong tradition of the adversary role. Many nonlawyer advocates were originally trained in health care or social work. This background makes them familiar with the clinical terminology and the perspective of the hospital staff. However, it also may make it easier for them to yield to institutional pressure to "be a team player" or to "go along with what's obviously best for the patient." A mental hospital, as a "total institution," also has its own culture and unwritten rules (Goffman, 1961). An "internal" advocate can be very effective if she or he understands the culture and is perceived by hospital staff as "one of us." However, an "internal" advocate who is an employee of the hospital is especially vulnerable. Such "internal" advocates may correctly perceive that their job security depends on not identifying serious violations of patients' rights, or encouraging patients to compromise their claims (Hospital and Community Psychiatry Service, 1987).

"External" advocates may find it easier to adopt and maintain a traditional advocacy role, because they are not part of the hospital culture. However, they may have trouble getting inside the hospital, literally as well as figuratively; both state and federal laws give lawyer/advocates the right of access to their clients and to clients' records, but again the reality is sometimes different (*Robbins v. Budke*, 1990).

Studies of advocacy programs representing patients in the hospital document the difficulties of developing an appropriate and effective role for lawyer/advocates working in an institution. Lawyer/advocates have been criticized for using the traditional legal approaches in institutional settings and administrative hearings. Especially in the institutional context, where effectiveness of advocacy depends on earning and maintaining the goodwill of the hospital staff, some commentators again recommend an alternative, cooperative "best interest" approach. Brakel (1981) notes that "the patient-hospital relationship is not a simple adversarial one. It is not approached as such by the institution. To approach it that way from the patient's side would, if nothing else, be incongruous" (p. 81).

A number of experienced advocates agree that a cooperative, more informal style may be appropriate within an institution but strongly reject the "best interest" approach:

Consideration for the client militates in favor of representing their subjective wishes. The primary deficit in their lives—the one that renders their legal needs greater than those of others—is the lack of self and community valuation. In a world where they are confined, treated, disenfranchised, unemployed, and zoned out of neighborhoods, persons with mental disabilities suffer as much from such indignities as they do from their disabilities. If advocates do not listen to their clients, respect their views and assist them to achieve some measure of self-determination, it is not clear who will. (Schwartz et al., 1983, pp. 570–571)

If lawyer/advocates in hospitals do *not* perform a function different from that of the caseworker or of other members of the hospital staff, why have them at all? If all that is needed is to inform patients of their legal rights, surely other members of the hospital staff could do that. But what if a patient, on learning of a right to a review of his or her commitment, wishes to exercise that right? A hospital staff person concerned with the patient's need for treatment will refuse to help him or her do that; a lawyer/advocate would, except in rare circumstances, have an ethical duty to pursue the client's goal. A hospital caseworker could advise a patient not to seek release from the hospital "because you need treatment"; a lawyer/advocate might also advise the client not to seek release, but based on the lawyer/advocate's assessment of the client's chances of obtaining release. That is a different role from the caseworker's, and the two should not be confused.

Fragmentation

The best way to illustrate the problem of fragmentation is to return to scene 2.

The lawyer thought: In the meantime, her client was going home—but for how long? The client had mentioned that she was late with her rent. Her disability checks had stopped coming a few months ago and she was not sure why. For a while she had been taking antipsychotic medication and visiting a caseworker at a community mental health center—but the center had closed down, and she had not been referred anywhere else. The hospital, as was routine when a patient won a commitment hearing, had given her a prescription for medication, but no other referral to community-based services. To be fair, there was not much out there; statewide budget cuts had eliminated most of the few community mental health programs left. It was a matter of time before this client's landlord evicted her, or the neighbor called the police again—or she ended up homeless.

The lawyer's office handled only commitment hearings; that was the limit of its authority under state law.[15] So she would do what she could—refer the client to a Legal Aid office that handled landlord-tenant cases and call a social services agency and see if someone could look into the missing disability checks. But Legal Aid had more landlord-tenant cases than it could handle, and its staff had no special training in working

with mentally disabled clients. As for the disability checks, this client might be capable of standing in line for hours, filling out the complex application forms, and organizing the supporting medical documentation—but the lawyer doubted it. She would probably just get so stressed she would walk out of the social services office and keep on wondering what had happened to her checks. When the state announced that the community mental centers were going to close, a group of lawyers filed a class action lawsuit to try to stop it. They had lost a preliminary hearing, but the whole case should go to trial in a year or so—maybe they would win. But where would the client get outpatient care in the meantime? It was crazy trying to lock people up in hospitals when what they really needed was somebody to help them get along outside—to make sure they got their checks, paid their rent, got in to see their counselor. That was a social worker's job, not a lawyer's. Why didn't somebody from the hospital do it?

The lawyer had a feeling she would be seeing the client again.

Therapeutic Impact of Legal Counsel

How has providing lawyer/advocacy affected clients with mental disabilities?

There have been strong criticisms that legal advocates, especially those who use the traditional "adversary" role, are not therapeutic but on the contrary are harmful to therapist-patient and family-patient relationships (Isaac & Brakel, 1992). Legal advocates, it is argued, undermine patient trust in the mental health profession, encourage patients to reject medication, and make court proceedings unnecessarily stressful. Legal representation is claimed to encourage aggression and manipulation; patients file legal petitions just to get attention, to express hostility toward staff or family members, or to avoid facing problems (Warren, 1982).[16]

However, what little research has been done

---

[15]As discussed earlier, a variety of state and federally funded advocacy programs are available for people with mental disabilities. Such programs are frequently circumscribed in the kinds of clients and cases they are eligible to accept. For example, a state public defender's office authorized to represent an indigent person in a conservatorship proceeding would typically *not* be authorized to represent the same person in unrelated civil matters such as a divorce or a contract dispute. A state or federally funded legal services office might be authorized to represent the individual in an administrative hearing concerning eligibility for disability benefits—but not in a suit seeking coverage for an abortion under a state health care plan. Constraints such as these may be imposed by the state or federal law that established the advocacy program, or by "strings attached" to their public funding sources.

In addition, because the demand for services far outstrips available resources, most legal services offices set priorities for the kinds of cases they will accept. In such a situation, an advocacy office which has made obtaining disability benefits a priority may have to refuse to represent a client in a landlord-tenant dispute.

on the therapeutic impact of civil commitment proceedings and access to counsel does not support those conclusions (Ensminger & Liguori, 1978; Perlin, 1989; Tyler, 1992). Procedural protections (at least meaningful ones) and effective counsel could counteract patients' perception of being coerced. Patients' subjective perception of being coerced may affect their treatment compliance and treatment efficacy (Wexler & Winick, 1991). Patients' psychological attitudes toward treatment may affect the outcome even of treatment with organic therapies like psychotropic drugs (Durham & La Fond, 1988).

Legal representation can encourage MHPs not to be paternalistic with their patients, but rather to negotiate with them and explain to them the rationale for recommending a particular course of treatment. This is important because the paternalistic treatment of patients by doctors is well documented (Burt, 1979; Katz, 1984). The advocate's presence may also act as a buffer between the patient and family members, or take some of the pressure off family members to advocate for their relative's wishes. The advocate may help develop an informal "contract" or agreement between the patient and family members that may govern, for example, a proposed visit home. If a court encourages a patient to enter into a behavioral contract and to make a public commitment to comply, the likelihood of compliance is enhanced (Wexler & Winick, 1991).

One of the functions of judicial proceedings when reviewing petitions for commitment or patients' requests for release is "visibly demonstrating a coherence between the decision-

making process and the mandates of the law so that justice 'is seen to be done' " (Warren, 1982, p. 154; Holstein, 1993). Thus the patient is more likely to feel fairly treated, when given the opportunity to hear in a formal setting the reasons why, for example, the hospital psychiatrist believes the patient should be committed. Clients have told their counsel happily, after losing a hearing, "That's OK. I was just glad you made that doctor answer my questions. I've been trying to get him to talk to me all week."

In other cases the opportunity to take the stand and tell the judge his story may reinforce the patient's sense of dignity (Tyler, 1992). This is sometimes criticized as countertherapeutic because it "encourages" the patient's "delusions." True, an advocate speaking for a patient may give the patient's statement or argument more legitimacy. Yet this only compensates in part for the assumption commonly made by MHPs and judges that a speaker with a mental illness is not credible. Some of a patient's beliefs may be delusional, others accurate, but

when they are called upon to testify . . . all their accounts and explanations are suspect . . . . The assumption of mental illness makes it possible to resolve conflicting testimony by framing it as a choice between the claims of a "sane" person (who is frequently a psychiatric professional) or those of a "madman" or "crazy person." (Holstein, 1993, pp. 36–37)

Another well-documented phenomenon is that everything a person with a mental illness does becomes a "symptom." If after consulting a legal advocate/counsel, the patient asks to be released from the hospital or wants to complain to the doctor about side effects of the medication, these acts are proof that the patient "lacks insight into his condition" or that the advocate is "encouraging her denial."

In a system of law, the idea of rights, and the recognition that an individual has a right to something, is all but synonymous with a recognition that the person is worthy of respect: "Rights promote well-being in the broadest

---

[16]Since people without mental disabilities certainly use law for all these things, why should a person identified as mentally disabled suddenly *not* be entitled to use the law, and lawyers, in the same way? Is this part of the infantilization of mental patients? Is this "sanism"? (Perlin, 1992b).

"Sanist" attitudes toward persons with mental disabilities include the beliefs that such individuals are presumptively incompetent, at best childlike and innocent, at worst morally weak and dangerous; that their resistance to confinement in a hospital or to taking medication is proof that they are dangerous and need to be confined.

sense. They secure the dignity and the integrity of human beings. . . . Rights give people control over their lives and are essential to self-respect" (Ziegler, 1987, pp. 678–779). The assistance of a lawyer/advocate affirms both the importance of the right and of the person. Ironically, precisely because persons with mental disabilities, like others in our society, likely view lawyers as "mouthpieces" and "hired guns," they are apt to feel more powerful since they have a lawyer. In the words of a client, "It means they can't push me around."

Is advocacy that fosters a patient's sense of dignity and autonomy by definition counter-therapeutic? Only if *therapeutic* means "cooperating with the treatment plan." How can advocacy be countertherapeutic when it makes those involved in treating a patient actually listen to what the patient has to say?

The question whether legal advocacy is "therapeutic" itself calls for closer scrutiny. Is legal advocacy only "therapeutic" when patients end up doing what MHPs want them to do—for example, signing into the hospital as voluntary patients or taking prescribed medication—but feel better about it because they believe they have made a conscious choice to cooperate? "Enhancing respect for authorities, the willingness to voluntarily accept the decisions of authorities, and the willingness to follow social rules are core objectives to any therapeutic program" (Tyler, 1992, p. 443).

It is questionable whether the "therapeutic" value of advocacy can ever be accurately assessed. Advocacy in our legal system in general is not designed to be "therapeutic," but rather to "assist [. . .] members of the public to secure and protect available legal rights and benefits" (EC 7-1). Whether the act of securing those rights and benefits is "therapeutic" may depend on the client's desires and character. Clients who tell their divorce lawyer to make the other spouse "pay" (economically and emotionally) for wrongs committed during the marriage do not want "therapeutic" advocacy—they want re-

venge. By contrast, clients who instruct their lawyer to "work out a fair custody agreement, something that won't be too hard on the kids" may want, and get, legal representation that will be therapeutic for them as well as for the other family members involved.

But what appears "therapeutic" may not always be so. A "nice" client's conciliatory approach may reflect low self-esteem or a guilty desire to punish herself or himself for failing as a spouse or as a parent. Similarly, seeking "revenge" through an advocate powerful enough to deal with the ex-spouse may be a positive step for a client whose needs were denigrated or denied during the marriage.

It is certainly appropriate for a lawyer/advocate, in advising the client, to raise "therapeutic" concerns. For example, the lawyer/advocate could ask a client to consider the possible impact of a proposed strategy or argument on the client's future relationship with family members. Although some lawyers by temperament are aggressive "bombers," most will use a more cooperative approach if it makes the client happy. But how pleasant and cooperative a lawyer/advocate is depends a great deal on how pleasant and cooperative the other party is. If the other spouse—or the treating psychiatrist—takes the position that "your client is crazy/weak/foolish, and I refuse to discuss the whole matter," an ethical lawyer will concentrate on getting what the client wants, even if not in a "therapeutic" way!

It might be more therapeutic—or at least less stressful—for clients, if MHPs better understood the role of the lawyer/advocate, and vice versa. If there were less temptation to couch the legal issue in terms of win/lose (and the clinical issue in terms of sick/well), clients might be able to see themselves as valued individuals who have the assistance of two different kinds of professionals. An important part of the lawyer/advocate's role should be to serve as an interpreter for clients between the two "cultures" of law and mental health.

Conclusion

The problem of rolelessness can be addressed in a number of ways. First, state and federal laws establishing a right to counsel or advocacy should mandate the basic functions to be performed. The statutes would establish a minimum standard for effective legal representation which would be at once a guide for new lawyers and advocates and a protection for clients.[17]

Second, specialized, standardized training should be developed for lawyer/advocates. Such training must include a basic introduction to the MHP perspective—its terminology and theories of treatment as well as common institutional protocols and procedures. Advocates should be taught how to read and interpret mental health records, and how to examine and cross-examine expert witnesses. They should be familiarized with the most commonly prescribed medications, as well as with any side effects. They should be trained in interviewing techniques appropriate for clients with mental disabilities, with a goal of determining the clients' interests. Finally, they should be trained to recognize and respond to special ethical issues involved in representing these clients.

Similarly, MHPs should be educated about the ethical obligations and role of lawyer/advocates.

The problem of fragmentation must be addressed by coordination of advocacy efforts. The goal should be to develop a consistent approach, ensuring that an individual has effective legal representation both in institutions and in the community. Such an approach would do much to promote the long-term interests of clients. Ideally, each state would have a statewide system of trained lawyers and advocates who would represent clients in all civil proceedings. To make the best use of the experience of established advocacy programs, the statewide system can and should subcontract with existing programs. Lawyers in this system should not be limited to, for example, only commitment hearings, but should be empowered to undertake a full range of advocacy efforts, including legislative lobbying and class action litigation. As to commitment proceedings, an alternative model has been proposed. A state statutory agency able "to bring specialized academic training and practical experience to bear on all facets of commitment representation, including such matters as investigation, diagnosis, referral and placement, within the general framework of an advocacy role" was the specific model endorsed by the President's Commission on Mental Health's Task Panel on Legal and Ethical Issues (Perlin, 1989, p. 765). Finally, representation within institutions should be by "external" advocates who have guaranteed access to the institution. Although these advocates may be physically located and have offices within the institution, they should be employed by and monitored by a "outside" body—the same statewide program.

According to Morris (1978),

[T]he *real* ethical issue is not: Should I adopt the best interest model or should I adopt the adversarial model? It is rather: Am I willing to adequately prepare in order to understand and safeguard the interests of my client? (p. 236)

Schwartz et al. (1983) add that "the real ethical difficulty for legal advocates lies not in whether to represent their client's subjective view but in how to determine those preferences." Advocates must therefore strive to develop an empathic

---

[17]An example of such a statute is the New York law establishing the Mental Hygiene Legal Services (MHLS), which mandates that MHLS (1) study and review the admission and retention of all patients or residents; (2) inform patients or residents of their legal rights; (3) provide legal services to patients or residents and their families related to admission, retention, and care and treatment; (4) be granted access to any hospital, school, or alcoholism facility and to all records; and (5) initiate and take any legal action deemed necessary to safeguard the right of any patient or resident to protection from abuse or mistreatment, which may include investigation into any such allegations of abuse or mistreatment. N.Y. Mental Hygiene Law section 47.03 (McKinney 1986).

For the more detailed Model Statute for Establishing a Developmental Disabilities Advocacy Agency, see Perlin (1989).

understanding of the situation of a person with a mental disability (p. 571).

Effective advocacy thus requires three things: adequate understanding of the lawyer/advocate's role, specialized training to carry it out, and a coordinated system that follows the individual with a mental disability and ensures his or her access to legal services.

References

Addington v. Texas, 441 U.S. 418 (1979).

Alfieri, A. (1992). Disabled clients, disabling lawyers. *Hastings Law Journal, 43,* 769–851.

American Bar Association. (1981). *Model code of professional responsibility (as amended).* Chicago: Author.

American Bar Association. (1983). *Model rules of professional conduct.* Chicago: Author.

American Psychiatric Association. (1987). *Diagnostic and statistical manual of mental disorders* (3rd ed., revised). Washington, DC: Author.

American Psychiatric Association. (1994). *Diagnostic and statistical manual of mental disorders* (4th ed.). Washington, DC: Author.

Andalman, E., & Chambers, D. (1974). Effective counsel for persons facing civil commitment: A survey, a polemic, and a proposal. *Mississippi Law Journal, 45,* 43–91.

Anders v. California, 386 U.S. 738 (1967).

Appelbaum, P. (1988). The right to refuse treatment with antipsychotic medications: Retrospect and prospect. *American Journal of Psychiatry, 145,* 413–414.

Appelbaum, P., & Gutheil, T. (1979). Rotting with their rights on: Constitutional theory and clinical reality in drug refusal by psychiatric patients. *Bulletin of the American Academy of Psychiatry and Law, 7,* 306–311.

Arnold v. Department of Health Services, 160 Az. 593, 775 P.2d 521 (1989).

Binder, D., Bergman, P., & Price, S. (1991). *Lawyers as counselors: a client-centered approach.* St. Paul, MN: West.

Blackburn, C. (1990). New directions in mental health advocacy? Clozapine and the right of medical self-determination. *Mental and Physical Disability Law Reporter, 14,* 453–461.

Brakel, S. (1981). Legal aid in mental hospitals. *American Bar Foundation Research Journal, 21,* 21–93.

Brakel, S. (1988). Legal schizophrenia and the mental health lawyer: Recent trends in civil commitment litigations. *Behavioral Science and the Law, 6,* 3–4.

Brieland, D., & Lemmon, J. (1985). *Social work and the law.* St. Paul, MN: West.

Burt, R. (1979). *Taking care of strangers: The rule of law in doctor-patient relations.* New York: Free Press.

Cohen, F. (1966). The function of the attorney and the commitment of the mentally ill. *Texas Law Review, 44,* 424–469.

Costello, J. (1983). Representing the medicated client. *Mental Disability Law Reporter, 7,* 55–62.

Costello, J., & Preis, J. (1987). Beyond least restrictive alternative doctrine: A constitutional right to treatment for mentally disabled persons in the community. *Loyola Los Angeles of Law Review, 20,* 1527–1557.

Dinerstein, R. (1992). A meditation on the theoretics of practice. *Hastings Law Journal, 43,* 971–989.

Doe v. Gallinot, 657 F.2d 1017 (9th Cir. 1981).

Durham, M., & La Fond, J. (1988). A search for the missing premise of involuntary therapeutic commitment: Effective treatment of the mentally ill. *Rutgers Law Review, 40,* 303–368.

Ellman, S. (1987). Lawyers and clients. *University of California at Los Angeles Law Review, 34,* 717–779.

Ensminger, J., & Liguori, T. (1978). The therapeutic significance of the civil commitment hearing: An unexplored potential. *Journal of Psychiatry and Law, 6,* 5–44.

Estelle v. Smith, 451 U.S. 454 (1981).

In re Fisher, 38 Ohio St. 2d 71, 313 N.E. 1d 851 (1974).

Galie, L. (1978). An essay on the civil commitment lawyer: Or how I learned to hate the adversary system. *Journal of Psychiatry and Law, 6,* 71–87.

In re Gault, 387 U.S. 1 (1967).

Goffman, E. (1961). *Asylums.* New York: Doubleday Anchor.

Hayman, R. (1990). Perceptions of justice: Law, politics, and the mentally retarded parent. *Harvard Law Review, 103,* 1201–1271.

Herr, S. (1989). Representation of clients with disabilities: Issues of ethics and control. *New York University Review of Law and Social Change, 17,* 609–650.

Hiday, V. (1982). The attorney's role in involuntary civil commitment. *North Carolina Law Review, 60,* 1027–1056.

Holstein, J. (1993). *Court-ordered insanity: Interpretive practice and involuntary commitment.* New York: Aldine de Gruyter Press.

Hospital and Community Psychiatry Service. (1987). Protecting patients' rights: A comparison of models. *Rights of the mentally disabled: Statements and standards.* Washington, DC: American Psychiatric Association.

Humphrey v. Cady, 405 U.S. 504 (1972).

Isaac, R., & Brakel, S. (1992). Subverting good intentions: A brief history of mental health law 'reform.' *Cornell Journal of Law and Public Policy, 2,* 89–119.

Katz, J., (1984). *The silent world of doctor and patient.* New York: Free Press.

Kittrie, N. (1973). *The right to be different: Deviance and enforced therapy.* Baltimore, MD: Johns Hopkins University Press.

Lessard v. Schmidt, 349 F. Supp. 1078 (E.D. Wisc. 1972).

Litwack, T. (1974). The role of counsel in civil commitment proceedings: Emerging problems. *California Law Review, 62,* 816–839.

Luban, D. (1981). Paternalism and the legal profession. *Wisconsin Law Review, 81,* 454–493.

Lynch v. Baxley, 386 F. Supp. 378 (N.D. Ala. 1974).

Mathews v. Eldridge, 424 U.S. 319 (1976).

McCartney v. United States, 343 F.2d 471 (9th Cir. 1965).

Mills v. Board of Education, 348 F. Supp. 866 (D.D.C. 1972).

Morris, G. (1978). Conservatorship for the "gravely disabled": California's declaration of nonindependence. *San Diego Law Review, 15,* 201–237.

New York State Ass'n for Retarded Citizens, Inc. v. Rockefeller, 357 F. Supp. 752 (E.D.N.Y. 1973), *consent judgment approved sub nom.* New York State Ass'n for Retarded Children v. Carey, 393 F. Supp. 715 (E.D.N.Y. 1975) (*Willowbrook* or NYSARC).

Parry, J. (1993). Mental disabilities under the ADA: A difficult path to follow. *Mental and Physical Disability Law Reporter, 17,* 100–112.

Pennsylvania Association for Retarded Children v. Pennsylvania, 343 F. Supp. 279 (E.D. Pa. 1972).

Perlin, M. (1989). *Mental disability law: Civil and criminal* (Vol. 2). Charlottesville, VA: Michie.

Perlin, M. (1992a). Fatal assumption: A critical evaluation of the role of counsel in mental disability cases. *Journal of Law and Human Behavior, 16,* 37–59.

Perlin, M. (1992b). On "sanism." *Southern Methodist University Law Review, 46,* 373–408.

Perlin, M. (1993). *Mental disability law: Civil and criminal: Vol. 2. 1993 cumulative supplement.* Charlottesville, VA: Michie.

Perlin, M. (1994). *Law and mental disability.* Charlottesville, VA: Michie.

Perlin, M., & Sadoff, M. (1982). Ethical issues in the representation of individuals in the commitment process. *Law and Contemporary Problems, 45,* 161–192.

Peters, R., & Costello, J. (1992). *Financial empowerment of people with mental disabilities through federally funded government benefits programs.* Los Angeles: Mental Health Advocacy Services.

Powell v. Alabama, 287 U.S. 45 (1932).

Reisner, R., & Slobogin, C. (1990). *Law and the mental health system: Civil and criminal aspects* (2nd ed.). St. Paul, MN: West.

Rhode, D. (1982). Class conflicts in class actions. *Stanford Law Review, 34,* 1183–1262.

Rhode, D. (1985). Ethical perspectives on legal practice. *Stanford Law Review, 37,* 589–652.

Rhode, D., & Luban, D. (1992). *Legal ethics.* New York: Foundation Press.

Ricci v. Callahan, 646 F. Supp. 378 (D.Mass. 1986).

Robbins v. Budke, 739 F. Supp. 1479 (D.M.M. 1990).

Sackett, R. S. (1991). Terminating parental rights of the handicapped. *Family Law Quarterly, 25,* 253–298.

Saks, E. (1991). Competency to refuse treatment. *North Carolina Law Review, 69,* 945–999.

Schwartz, S. (1989). Damage actions as a strategy for enhancing the quality of care of persons with mental disabilities. *New York University Review of Law and Social Change, 17,* 651–687.

Schwartz, S., Fleischner, R., Schmidt, M., Gates, H., Costanzo, C., & Winkelman, N. (1983). Protecting the rights and enhancing the dignity of people with mental disabilities: Standards for effective legal advocacy. *Rutgers Law Journal, 14,* 541, 567–593.

Strauss, M. (1987). Toward a revised model of attorney-client relationship: The argument for autonomy. *North Carolina Law Review, 65,* 315–349.

Treffert, D. (1973). Dying with their rights on. *American Journal of Psychiatry, 130,* 1041–1043.

Tremblay, P. (1987). On persuasion and paternalism: Lawyer decision-making and the questionably competent client. *Utah Law Review, 51,* 515–584.

Tyler, T. (1992). The psychological consequences of judicial procedures: Implications for civil commitment hearings. *Southern Methodist University Law Review, 46,* 433–448.

Vitek v. Jones, 445 U.S. 480 (1980).

Wald, P., & Friedman, P. (1978). The politics of mental health advocacy in the United States. *International Journal of Law and Psychiatry, 1,* 137–152.

Warren, C. (1982). *The court of last resort.* Chicago: University of Chicago Press.

Wexler, D., & Winick, B. (1991). Therapeutic jurisprudence as a new approach to mental health law policy analysis and research. *University of Miami Law Review, 45,* 979–1004.

Winick, B. (1991). Competency to consent to treatment: The distinction between assent and objection. *Houston Law Review, 28,* 15–61.

Wyatt v. Stickney, 325 F. Supp. 781 (M.D. Ala. 1971).

Ziegler, D. (1987). Rights require remedies: A new approach to the enforcement of rights in the federal courts. *Hastings Law Journal, 38,* 665–728.

3 ◼ Mental Health Professional Expertise in the Courtroom

Maureen O'Connor
Bruce D. Sales
University of Arizona

Daniel W. Shuman
Southern Methodist University

Jurors in our legal system are not expected to be experts on the topic of the case before them. Rather, they are expected to decide a case based only on information offered by the parties, screened by the rules of evidence, and provided to them during trial. Ideally, that information consists of the facts of the case presented by lay or fact witnesses who came by that information firsthand ("I saw Mr. Jones drive through the intersection when the light was red"), rather than opinions drawing inferences from those facts ("Mr. Jones was driving recklessly when he went through the red light") (see, for example, Allen & Miller, 1993; Hand, 1901; McCormick, 1954). The ideal trial in our legal system, then, would put the jurors "into the heads of all the witnesses." They would experience the sensory input *and* have access to the "background and experience of each witness" so that the jury could then construct a composite picture of the best evidence free from bias (Allen & Miller, 1993, p. 1).

This goal is of limited value, however, when the case embraces complex scientific and behavioral questions not readily answerable by perception or common experience. In such instances,

the courts recognize the need for "expert" witnesses whose testimony may go beyond the facts to draw inferences in the form of expert judgments or opinions. Experts can assist the jury in understanding information that would otherwise be difficult or impossible for them to evaluate (see Hand, 1901; Imwinkelreid, 1994). For example, an accident reconstruction expert could testify that "in my opinion, Mr. Jones had to have been driving in excess of 50 miles per hour to create skid marks matching those in the intersection."

Courts have struggled with how to structure expert testimony so that it is helpful to the jury but does not overwhelm or confuse it (see Faigman, Porter, & Saks, 1994, nn. 2–3; Sales, Shuman, & O'Connor, 1994). Can procedural and evidentiary rules ensure that jurors will decide a case aided by expert education but not be hindered either by undue deference to experts (Allen & Miller, 1993) or by the "battle of the experts" presented by opposing parties (McCloskey & Egeth, 1983; Resnick, 1986; but see Champagne, Shuman, & Whitaker, 1991, p. 381)?

Nowhere have these issues been more pronounced than when the court is confronted by mental health professional expertise. Psychiatrists, psychologists, and other mental health professionals are often called on to provide "expertise" in the courtroom on fundamental questions of human behavior, motivation, intention, and its consequences. And the criticism that has resulted has been harsh. Perhaps the harshest criticism against psychiatrists (and other mental health professionals) is that they "excuse sin" through cloaking moral judgments in scientific clothing (Resnick, 1986). Not only are some of these questions on which life, death, and liberty turn, but they are also questions that rigorous scientific testing alone cannot answer. In other cases, mental health professionals are criticized for offering testimony that is not grounded in, or flies in the face of, scientific research, when such research exists. Moreover, this testimony differs from some kinds of scientific information, such as the etiology of disease or the proper specifications for building construction, in that most jurors will assume some familiarity with the human conditions in question. What can a psychologist add to a layperson's determination about what is in a child's best interest? Finally, mental health expertise is often complicated by the dual and potentially conflicting role that many mental health professionals play—therapist and expert.

In this chapter, we will examine mental health professional expertise in the courtroom and discuss the issues raised by the content and quality of that expertise from both the legal and mental health professional standpoint.[1] Who is qualified to provide mental health testimony? What is the scope of mental health expertise? What rules govern the admissibility of mental health expertise? To what extent do these rules filter out reliable from unreliable expertise? When discussing admissibility, should courts treat all forms of mental health expertise uniformly? Are there effective safeguards on mental health testimony?

---

[1]Mental health expertise is also relevant to legislative and administrative decision making. Currently, little is known about the scope of mental health professionals' participation in legal decision making outside the courtroom setting (see Smith, 1989; Wursten & Sales, 1988). What we do know suggests that the mental health contribution tends to be based more on clinical expertise than on empirical research (see Boyer & O'Connor, 1994; Wursten & Sales, 1988; Wursten & Sales, 1992).

Mental Health Professional Expertise

Although most cases are settled before going to trial, those that do reach trial are resolved on the basis of the evidence presented by the parties. This evidence consists of documents or other tangible evidence, lay or fact witness testimony, and expert witness testimony. Although the standards for determining the admissibility of all expert testimony have troubled courts, mental health expert testimony has been particularly problematic.

Who May Provide Mental Health Expertise to the Courts?

Historically, few courts ever questioned the appropriateness of asking trained *medical* professionals to comment on a party's relevant mental state. In cases described as representative of the use of experts in the 17th and 18th centuries, Judge Learned Hand (1901) recounted the Witches' case in 1665, in which a physician was called to give his opinion on whether the accused persons were witches, and an insanity case in 1760, in which a surgeon gave an opinion on whether a particular defendant was insane. Such expert medical opinion testimony about a particular defendant's mental state has routinely been provided, before and since (see also Kargon, 1986). But until the middle of this century, courts heard mental health testimony exclusively from medical doctors (psychiatrists, surgeons, and general practitioners).

In the 1940s and 1950s, some courts began to permit a properly qualified psychologist to testify as an expert, albeit within fairly specific boundaries (that is, substantially limited to information provided in psychological tests conducted on the defendant) [see, for example, *People v. Hawthorne*, 1940 (dictum); *State v. Padilla*, 1959 (dictum)]. As late as the 1970s, courts disagreed about whether Ph.D. psychologists were qualified to testify regarding the mental state of a defendant (or witness) (*People v. Lewis*, 1979). But as one well-respected court noted in 1962,

The determination of a psychologist's competence to render an expert opinion based on his findings as to the presence or absence of mental disease or defect must depend upon the nature and extent of his knowledge. It does not depend upon his claim to the title 'psychologist.' (*Jenkins v. U.S.*, 1962, p. at [FN 18])[2]

Some state statutes, such as those dealing with competency to stand trial, still restrict court appointment to examiners within specific disciplines. The trend at least with respect to competency, however, may be to use multidisciplinary teams that include social workers and other paraprofessionals in mental health practice (Winick, 1985).

This more functional approach to admitting expert testimony asks whether the particular expert's actual experience and training will be of "probable probative value" given the precise question being addressed (*Jenkins v. U.S.*, 1962, p. at [FN 24]). As one court explained, "The opinion of a psychologist as to the interpretation and administration of standardized tests would have more weight than that of a psychiatrist. Conversely, a psychiatrist's opinion as to psychotropic medication would carry more weight than that of a psychologist" (*In the matter of Eli*, 1993, p. 538).

Rule 702 of the Federal Rules of Evidence, which applies in federal courts and serves as the model for most state evidence codes, requires that an expert be qualified by knowledge, skill, experience, training, or education, not merely the latter. Under this standard, courts have accepted testimony about mental health issues from non-Ph.D.'s or non-M.D.'s, such as social workers and nurses (*People v. Gans*, 1983; see generally Wilk, 1984; Winick, 1985). Nonetheless, some courts continue to be uncomfortable with experts who do not possess either a Ph.D. or an M.D., particularly with respect to a party's mental state (see, for instance, *Commonwealth v. Dunkle*, 1992; *In the matter of Eli*, 1993; *State v. J. Q.*, 1991).

Alternatively, educational credentials alone will not satisfy the requirement that the expert's training must "fit" with the subject matter of the expertise being offered. In cases involving battered women charged with injuring or murdering their batterers, for example, courts have permitted the testimony of clinical psychologists (*Ibn-Tamas v. United States*, 1979), Ph.D. sociologists (*State v. Borrelli*, 1993), and even noncredentialed experts on domestic violence (*State v. Baker*, 1980; see also Thar, 1982). Conversely, physicians whose primary practice is in the field of internal medicine may not be qualified as experts on battered wife syndrome, even though they may have treated some battered women in their practice (see, for example, *People v. White*, 1980). There is logic to this distinction. Courts should look beyond titles to the actual expertise required to aid the jury, and not all physicians, psychiatrists, psychologists, and social workers are qualified in highly specialized fields. For instance, Myers et al. (1989) list the following factors as critical to establishing expert qualifications for child sex abuse testimony: (1) extensive firsthand experience with sexually abused and non–sexually abused children, (2) thorough and current knowledge of the professional literature on child sexual abuse, and (3) objectivity and neutrality. With increasing specialization among professionals, this attempt to identify particular skills and experience that an expert should possess makes sense and should be welcomed by the courts.

Beyond the minimum level of expertise that the courts are willing to accept, we know surprisingly little about the characteristics of mental health professionals who serve as expert wit-

---

[2]While the courts were divided on the topic, so were the mental health professions. In the *Jenkins* case, the American Psychological Association filed an amicus brief with the court arguing that psychologists should be permitted to testify as expert witnesses, but the American Psychiatric Association urged against expansion of psychologists' role in court. (For a summary of the respective briefs, see Bartol, 1983, pp. 110–111.)

nesses (Gross, 1991). This is particularly troubling because of anecdotal evidence that not all courts look for a match between the mental health professional and the precise question the court is addressing. For instance, are mental health expert witnesses primarily clinicians who provide testimony specific to a particular client or party? Do mental health researchers participate in significant numbers? If not, are the courts receiving state-of-the-art knowledge about the mind and behavior? What percentage of experts are "professional experts" in the sense that they devote more of their time to expert testimony than to either clinical practice or scholarly endeavors? If the percentage is high, we should perhaps be concerned that the courts are basing judgments on outdated or "intuitive" psychology rather than on well-scrutinized and current information. How often can an attorney hire an expert who will say anything to support the attorney's case, as some critics have argued ("Expert Medical Testimony in Jury Trials," 1892; Huber, 1985; Slovenko, 1987)?

What limited empirical information exists can be summarized as follows. Kalven and Zeisel (1966) estimated that psychiatrists appeared in less than 2% of all cases. A Federal Judicial Center study found that clinical psychologists and psychiatrists each testified in approximately 8% of a sample of federal civil trials (M. T. Johnson, personal communication, December 19, 1994). Other more general studies of civil cases have suggested that nearly half of the experts used in civil trials are medical experts. According to Gross (1991), 50% of experts had M.D.'s, while another 9% of trials include clinical psychologists as well as other medical professionals. Champagne, Shuman, and Whitaker (1991) found that 48% of experts possessed M.D.'s. Shuman, Whitaker, and Champagne (1994) determined that 56% were in the medical area and a smaller number from psychology. None of these latter studies distinguished between the medical versus mental health content of the medical experts' testimony. By most accounts, however, use of mental health expertise is on the rise (see Smith, 1989). Two prominent commentators estimate that mental health professionals participate in up to a million legal cases each year (Faust & Ziskin, 1988).

Although experts appear in a large number of trials, a study conducted by Shuman and his colleagues (1994) tends to debunk the myth of "professional experts" spending most of their time testifying in court. In their data, based on surveys from all types of experts in civil trials in three jurisdictions, Shuman and his colleagues found that 73% of the experts made less than 5% of their yearly income from testifying; only 8% derived more than 36% of their income from expert fees. Moreover, the fees paid to experts seemed reasonable given their experience and the demands of testifying (average fee = \$185 per hour). Sixty percent of experts responding to the Shuman et al. (1994) survey claimed that lawyers found out about their services through personal contacts rather than through advertising. Despite this finding, it appears that some smaller percentage of experts is doing a substantial amount of the testifying. Gross (1991) examined actual case records in 529 civil trials and found that nearly 60% of the appearances by expert witnesses in the trials were by witnesses who had testified at least twice over a six-year period. The average number of appearances over the six-year period was 9.4 (median 2.2). Neither of these studies, however, provided any particular information about mental health experts.

What Is the Scope of Mental Health Expert Testimony?

We have little solid information about the actual distribution of the precise content of mental health expertise. We do, however, have a sense of the range of topics informed by mental health expertise. As stated above, mental health experts have traditionally been called on to provide expertise on the connection between mental impairment and criminal behavior (see, for example, *United States v. Hinckley*, 1981); now their expertise is sought on a vast array of other topics, some of which are represented in the chapters in this book. The topics range from routine to emerging issues, including child sexual abuse allegations (for instance, *State v. Michaels*, 1994); children's mental health treatment and placement issues (*Parham v. J. R.*, 1979); likelihood of future dangerousness (*Barefoot v. Estelle*, 1983); defendant and witness competencies to participate in legal proceedings (*Medina v. California*, 1992); competencies to enter a contract or draft a will (*Lucero v. Lucero*, 1994); presence or absence of emotional, physical, or sexual abuse and its consequences (*Frenzel v. State*, 1993); the appropriateness of a particular treatment or disposition (*Foucha v. Louisiana*, 1992); the necessity for involuntary civil commitment (*Addington v. Texas*, 1979); the connection between fundamental rights such as the right to privacy and the regulation of behavior (abortion, sexual conduct) (*Bowers v. Hardwick*, 1986); the likely effect of prior abuse on current behavior (*Hammer v. Hammer*, 1987); the extent of mental suffering caused by fear of developing cancer (*People Against Nuclear Energy v. U.S. Nuclear Regulatory Commission*, 1982); and the postdiction of the cause of suicide, whether death from ambiguous causes was a suicide (*Jackson v. State*, 1989), to name a few.

The content of the expertise offered in these cases varies along a continuum from pure clinical opinion, to clinical expertise based on some empirical support, to scientific opinion based on empirical research (Shuman & Sales, 1995). Pure clinical opinion might come from a clinical social worker who has evaluated a child and observed the child's interactions with both parents and who offers a recommendation about optimal child custody arrangements for the child that is not grounded in any empirical research. In the middle of the continuum, we might observe clinical expertise drawn from scientific research in a case where a neuropsychologist conducts a series of tests as well as brain scans on a person charged with a crime, but then must interpret those tests based on clinical judgment to determine whether the person has a character trait of impulsivity, for example. A researcher

refuting an opposing expert's clinical judgment by relying on disconfirming research evidence, as in the case of citing the empirical research on the suggestibility of children's memories resulting from specific interview techniques ("Brief," 1995), exemplifies the other end of the continuum.

To demonstrate the complexity of the issues as they vary along the continuum, consider a recent case in which a social worker from a psychiatric hospital testified that, in her clinical opinion, a child had been exposed to satanic ritual abuse and was evidencing multiple personality disorder as a result of that abuse (*In re Chrystal and Tasha*, 1994). Researchers have not been able to demonstrate an empirical link between severe childhood sexual abuse and multiple personality disorder (Beitchman, Zucker, Hood, daCosta, & Cassavia, 1992; Lindsay & Read, 1994). Perhaps such a link exists, but it has not been proven empirically; perhaps such a link does not exist, and the witness is basing the opinion on an invalid clinical judgment. Assuming a court wants to admit the best available (that is, reliable and relevant) evidence and keep out highly fallible (invalid and confusing) evidence, how should it respond to admitting expert testimony into evidence?

The admissibility of expert testimony is governed by a set of rules designed to maximize high-quality evidence while minimizing "false or distorted" evidence (Faigman et al., 1994). The trial judge makes the preliminary determination about whether evidence should be admitted under those rules. Once expert testimony is admitted into evidence, the jury has to evaluate the credibility of the witness and decide what weight to give that evidence in relation to all other evidence. Determining whether a given expert's testimony is of sufficient quality to be allowed in the courtroom may require a significantly different analysis than the analysis a jury uses to decide how much weight to give that expert testimony. Whether the law as currently formulated adequately accounts for that difference, particularly with respect to mental health expertise, is a critical law and social policy question that we will examine in the rest of this chapter.

Admissibility of Mental Health Expertise

The American judicial system places a high premium on the ability of juries to decide cases fairly and impartially. At the same time, judges concede that juries can benefit from expert assistance in many cases, from the relatively simple to the highly complex. This conflict between the law's mistrust of juries on the one hand and its faith in juries' abilities on the other creates a "fundamental irony" that colors the courts' approach to the admissibility of expert testimony (Sales, Shuman, & O'Connor, 1994, p. 401). In response, the courts vacillate between a strict admissibility standard (keeping from the jury all but essential and uncontroversial expert evidence) and a lower-threshold admissibility standard (giving the jury any and all potentially helpful expert assistance). We will describe these differing approaches and discuss the implications each raises for mental health professional testimony.

Protecting the Jury

The courts have resorted to various strategies to protect the jury.

Common Law Approach

The pre–20th century approach of American and English courts to expert testimony can be characterized as protective of the jury. To be admissible, the subject of expert testimony had to be "beyond the ken" of the average juror (Cleary, 1984, §13, p. 33; Strong, 1992); that is, the judge had to be convinced that the jury would essentially be unable to make an informed decision in the case without it. In addition, these courts decided whether to admit expert testimony based exclusively on the credentials of the expert, rather than on the quality of the science offered (Osborn, 1935; Shuman & Sales, 1995). Given the limited availability of scientific research, this approach made sense. As the fields of science and their research base expanded, it became possible to evaluate the information offered separately from the expert conveying it (see Faigman et al., 1994).

To evaluate the information conveyed by the expert, one court developed the well-known "general acceptance within the relevant scientific community" test by which to judge the underlying scientific content of the expert testimony separately from its purveyor (*Frye v. United States*, 1923). In *Frye*, the defendant in a murder trial sought to introduce the exculpatory (exonerating) results from an early form of polygraph test that measured systolic blood pressure in order to prove his innocence. The court was faced with novel and unfamiliar science coming from an otherwise qualified expert (see Faigman et al., 1994, n. 20). In essence, the court was no longer comfortable relying on the expert's qualifications. Although the expert's qualifications still mattered, they were no longer the only thing that mattered. Now the expert's testimony was inextricably linked to the scientific quality of the instrument on which his testimony depended. Rather than defer to the one expert, then, the court sought a more measurable demonstration of the scientific merit of the information offered before trusting the jury with it. Given the times, and the long-standing focus on the scientists rather than on the science, it made sense that the court would settle for "consensus within the relevant scientific community" as an acceptable measure of the quality of the underlying science.

The "general acceptance" approach insulates judges from having to undertake their own analysis of the quality of the science (see Giannelli, 1980; Imwinkelreid, 1990). Once the court determines that the person on the stand is qualified to be an expert, the court steps back and allows scientists themselves to determine the quality of the science that will be allowed in the courtroom (Allen & Miller, 1993). "General acceptance" might be demonstrated in the following ways: by an expert on the stand claiming it is so (see, for example, *United States v. Shorter,* 1985), by substantial scholarly writing or even speeches and addresses on the topic (see Giannelli, 1980, p. 1217), or by prior judicial opinions in which a court concluded the same science was generally accepted [see, for instance, *Flanagan v. State,* 1991 (Ervin, J., concurring in part and dissenting in part); *State v. Kelly,* 1984; *United States v. Maivia,* 1990 (science that has received "general judicial recognition" no longer subject to *Frye*)].

None of these approaches guarantees that the scientists or courts proclaiming "general acceptance" of a particular science have carefully examined the validity or reliability of the underlying science. While the sheer volume of writings or professional presentations on a particular topic, and the presence of an expert willing to attest to its "general acceptance," may give some indication of the scientific merit of the testimony, that is not typically how scientists would judge the worthiness of the underlying science in the course of their regular work. Why should the courts settle for less than a scientifically derived evaluation of the expertise? The consequences of such deference to the scientific community are severe, because once a court deems a particular type of expert testimony "generally accepted," it facilitates the introduction of that type of evidence in other courts and may create a "cottage industry" of experts who can be called into service (in a case involving voiceprint techniques, the court cautioned that once testimony has been admitted, precedent may control subsequent trials; see *People v. Kelly,* 1976). Without the assurance that information conveyed by the expert in court cases is scientifically reliable and valid, lawyers are left fighting an uphill battle to overturn the prior determination of "general acceptance."

Application to Mental Health Testimony

Regardless of *Frye*'s merits, historically, courts did not appear to find it relevant at all to medical or mental health testimony based on clinical opinion. As one commentator explains, "The *Frye* debate has almost completely bypassed disputes about the admissibility of medical testimony" (Black, 1988, p. 647). It may be that courts did not see the parallel between a scientific device or process and clinical opinion testimony (see Boyce, 1963; *Campbell v. People,* 1981; McCord, 1987), that courts limited *Frye* to "novel" scientific evidence, or that courts always trusted the jury with opinion testimony, whether from lay or expert witnesses. In any event, a fundamental irony developed. The law imposed what some critics decried as an overly conservative approach to the admissibility of "scientific" expert testimony, waiting for it to become "generally accepted" before admitting it (see, for instance, Boyce, 1963; Imwinkelreid, 1992), while being suspiciously lenient when the expertise was clinically rather than empirically derived (Faigman et al., 1994; Sales, Shuman, & O'Connor, 1994).

To further complicate the issue, it has been noncontroversial, since the middle of the 17th century at least, to allow expert mental health testimony where a party's mental status is at issue (*Ake v. Oklahoma,* 1985; McCord, 1987; Yuille, 1989). That is especially true where the defendant raises an insanity defense, because the presence of a mental disease or defect is the necessary "threshold for tests of criminal responsibility"—that is, the law itself is rooted in a medical model (Bonnie, 1984, p. 19; but see Morse, 1978).[3] Courts have not questioned the scientific basis for the offered testimony on that issue or on others, such as a person's competency to stand trial or to consent to treatment. Moreover, some courts that adhere to *Frye* have drawn an

---

[3]One issue that has engendered substantial debate within the mental health and legal communities (but that is beyond the scope of this chapter) is whether a mental health professional witness should be permitted to testify to the so-called "ultimate issue" in the case—for instance, was the person "insane" at the time of the crime or is the person "competent" (American Psychiatric Association, 1982; Federal Rules of Evidence, 1974, Rule 704(b); Fulero & Finkel, 1991; Melton, Weithorn, & Slobogin, 1985; Morse, 1978; Slobogin, 1989)?

explicit distinction between the clinical expert and experts whose testimony rests on a scientific test or principle underlying the testimony. As one court explained it, a mental health expert's opinion that a defendant is incompetent is "pure opinion testimony" and does not have to meet *Frye* (*Flanagan v. State*, 1991, p. 828).

At the same time, some courts have recognized the gray areas that mental health professional testimony raises. Some judges do invoke the protections of the *Frye* rule for some types of mental health testimony. See, for example, *People v. Bledsoe*, 1984 (applying the *Frye* test to "rape trauma syndrome" when it is used to explain inconsistencies in a rape victim's behavior); *People v. Shirley*, 1982 (subjecting the use of hypnosis to the *Frye* analysis); *Flanagan v. State*, 1991 (applying the *Frye* test to profile testimony); *United States v. Shorter*, 1985 (applying *Frye* to the pathological gambling disorder); *State v. Kelly*, 1984 (applying *Frye* to battered women's syndrome) (see generally, McCord, 1987). In practice, however, it is difficult to discern any coherent pattern in the courts' application of *Frye* to this type of testimony (McCord, 1987).

Trusting the Jury

In large measure, the standard for admission of expert testimony turns on the court's trust of the jury's abilities.

Relevancy Approach

Some courts and commentators were never comfortable with the common law's deference to the scientific community or with such distrust of the jury (see generally Faigman et al., 1994; *State v. Brown*, 1984). An alternative view developed under which all relevant expert and nonexpert evidence would go to the jury for its evaluation. The only limit placed on this approach was that the information would not be admitted into evidence if it would unfairly prejudice or mislead the jury or waste the court's time (see most notably Berger, 1986; McCormick, 1954; McCormick,

1982; see also Cleary, 1984, §203, p. 608). Under such an approach, concerns about the quality or reliability of the science would go to the weight to accord the evidence during jury decision making, rather than to the preliminary question of its admissibility. Just as jurors must decide whether to believe a certain eyewitness or government informant, jurors should be able to evaluate the credibility of clinical opinion testimony or science, and weigh this testimony or information appropriately in their deliberations.

Application to Mental Health Testimony

This broad relevancy approach as applied to mental health testimony is epitomized by the U.S. Supreme Court's decision in *Barefoot v. Estelle* (1983). In *Barefoot*, two psychiatrists testified at sentencing that, in their opinion, Barefoot would likely commit dangerous crimes in the future. Based in part on this prediction, Barefoot was sentenced to death. He appealed the sentence, arguing that the psychiatric experts should not have been allowed to testify given the unreliability of their dangerousness predictions.

The Supreme Court upheld Barefoot's sentence. In doing so, the Court acknowledged the fallibility of future dangerousness predictions, confirming that the best clinical research then suggested that "no more than one out of three predictions of violent behavior" were accurate (*Barefoot*, 1983, p. 901, citing Monahan, 1981, pp. 47–49). Yet, despite the acknowledged unreliability of these clinical predictions, the Court upheld the lower court's decision to allow expert testimony on the prediction of Barefoot's future dangerousness.

Underlying the Court's judgment were two fundamental beliefs about the jury in an adversary system: (1) that the jury should have before it "all possible relevant information about the individual defendant whose fate it must determine" (*Barefoot*, 1983, p. 897, citing *Jurek v. Texas*, 1976, pp. 274–276), and (2) that the jury is perfectly capable of sifting the reliable from the unreliable when it evaluates expert testimony. In the *Barefoot* Court's view,

The differences [among experts] go to the weight of the evidence and not the admissibility of such testimony. . . . Such disputes are within the province of the jury to resolve. Indeed, it is a fundamental premise of our entire system of criminal jurisprudence that the purpose of the jury is to sort out the true testimony from the false, the important matters from the unimportant matters, and when called upon to do so, to give greater credence to one party's expert witnesses than another's. (p. 902, quoting the District Court's opinion)

And, according to the Court, if it is legally permissible for a state to include dangerousness predictions as a factor in death penalty sentencing (*Jurek v. Texas*, 1976), why should a court keep a trained psychiatrist from testifying on that question (*Barefoot*, 1983, p. 896)?

This relevancy approach, as distinct from the *Frye* or general acceptance approach, does not separate experts from the instrumentality of their expertise. Even in the face of scientific data virtually nullifying the basis for the expert's opinion, the Court in *Barefoot* is comfortable permitting that person to give an opinion *as an expert*. The Court does not shy away from cloaking the psychiatrists' testimony as expertise beyond that of a lay witness, while essentially conceding that laypersons could predict as well as psychiatrists.

Recall that under the more restrictive *Frye* approach, some courts recognize a need to assess separately the validity of the underlying scientific principle or test on which mental health expertise relied. Under a pure relevancy approach, however, even where the mental health expert explicitly relies on a testable scientific hypothesis, courts are reluctant to screen out the expertise based on scrutiny of the underlying principles. In *Kruse v. State* (1986), for example, the court permitted an expert in adolescent psychiatry to testify that a child victim, who exhibited no physical symptoms, had suffered a sexual trauma. She based her opinion on her diagnosis of "post-traumatic stress disorder" and on the presumed validity of the history given to her by the victim

and her parents. The court rejected the restrictive *Frye* test in favor of a broad relevancy approach to admissibility of expert testimony. Under this rubric, the court had no difficulty admitting the testimony despite the novelty of this type of testimony and the relative uncertainty of the scientific principles at issue (see *Toro v. State*, 1994, discussing possible problems with such an approach). Obviously, without great faith in the jury's ability to sift the valid from the invalid, this approach would make little sense.

Federal Rules of Evidence

The Federal Rules of Evidence, although applicable in trials in federal court, have also been a model for state evidence codes. Thus, a study of their approach to expert testimony has been regarded as significant.

Rule 702

When Congress enacted the federal rules in 1975, it included broad, inclusive language that all relevant evidence is admissible in the federal courts, unless otherwise provided for in these rules (Federal Rules of Evidence, 1974, Rules 401 & 402).[4] Since 1975, a majority of states have adopted in whole or in part evidence rules patterned on the federal rules (Weinstein & Berger, 1992). This broadening of admissibility rules was intended to expand the admissibility of expert testimony (see *Beech Aircraft Corporation v. Rainey*, 1988; Giannelli, 1991; Strong, 1992).

Unlike the broad relevancy approach discussed above, however, the federal rules dealt explicitly with expert testimony. Rule 702 of the Federal Rules of Evidence reads as follows:

If scientific, technical, or other specialized knowledge will assist the trier of fact to understand the evidence or to determine a fact in issue, a witness qualified as an expert by knowledge, skill, experience, training, or

---

[4]Thus, for example, evidence that is highly prejudicial (Federal Rules of Evidence, 1974, Rule 403) or hearsay (Federal Rules of Evidence, 1974, Rule 803) could still be excluded despite its relevancy to the question in the case.

education, may testify thereto in the form of an opinion or otherwise.

Rule 702 substitutes the "will assist the trier of fact" test for the "beyond the ken" language of the common law and makes no reference to the *Frye* standard or the broad relevancy rules. As a result, courts and commentators have, for two decades, tried to give meaning to Rule 702. Some courts continued to rely on the *Frye* test, using it in conjunction with Rule 702 (see, for instance, *United States v. Tranowski,* 1981). Others viewed the federal rules as initiating a new approach to evaluating expert testimony, one that would turn on the reliability of the science underlying the expert's testimony (see *United States v. Downing,* 1985).

Until 1993, the U.S. Supreme Court did not attempt to resolve the debate. Then, in *Daubert v. Merrell Dow Pharmaceutical, Inc.* (1993), the Court provided some answers to the meaning of Rule 702. It noted that the Federal Rules of Evidence were enacted without mention of the old *Frye* standard. Moreover, in the Court's estimation, the *Frye* standard took a fairly restrictive approach to admissibility of science while the federal rules clearly embody a spirit of broad admissibility. Therefore, the Court concluded, the federal rules superseded the *Frye* test.

Although the Court couched its statutory construction argument in those terms (elimination of "restrictive" *Frye* test and recognition of "broad" admissibility under the federal rules), the remainder of the Court's opinion belies such simplistic reasoning. Having eliminated the test based on general acceptance of the science, the Supreme Court staked out a middle ground, short of unfettered admissibility: "That the *Frye* test was displaced by the Rules of Evidence does not mean, however, that the Rules themselves place no limits on the admissibility of purportedly scientific evidence" (*Daubert v. Merrell Dow Pharmaceutical, Inc.,* 1993, p. 480). Thus while *Frye* might have restrictively kept out "new" research that *Daubert* might let in, *Daubert* should keep out generally accepted, yet low-

quality science that *Frye* would have let in (see Faigman et al., 1994). To assist in this transition, the Court provided a number of pragmatic considerations that should inform judges about the limits of the proffered scientific testimony and guide trial judges in their admissibility determinations. First, the evidence must be sufficiently tied to the facts of the case so as to "assist the trier of fact"—that is, it must be relevant. Second, the subject of an expert's testimony must be "scientific . . . knowledge"—that is, "more than subjective belief" and "ground[ed] in the methods and procedures of science" (*Daubert v. Merrell Dow Pharmaceutical, Inc.,* 1993, p. 2795). The Court looked to "Newtonian experimental science" as the template for those procedures (Imwinkelreid, 1994, p. 2277). In essence, the Court has equated assistance to the jury with evidentiary reliability, which in the case of scientific evidence is measured at least in part by scientific validity.

While emphasizing the flexibility with which validity determinations should be made, the Court suggests some factors to consider. First, is the theory or technique testable, and has it been tested? Second, has the theory or technique been subjected to peer review and publication? Third, in the case of scientific techniques, what is the known or potential error rate, and are there standards controlling the technique's operation? And, finally, is the theory or technique "generally accepted" within its particular field? By including the "general acceptance" language in its suggested guidelines, the Court may not have actually moved evidentiary practice as far as the overruling of *Frye* might suggest (see, for example, Allen, 1994, predicting that lower courts will continue to apply the *Frye* principle while not acknowledging it as the rule).

Application to Mental Health Testimony

Daubert gave no indication of whether courts should apply different standards to different types of scientific expert testimony. The opinion stated explicitly that Rule 702 applies to "novel" techniques as well as to more conventional evidence, for example. Nonetheless, a question remains whether the Supreme Court intended its 702 analysis to apply to mental health professional expertise. The question of *Daubert's* scope is particularly important, given the continuum of types of mental health testimony discussed above—from purely clinical opinion to purely research-based expertise—and the different implications the *Daubert* standard might have for these types of expertise.

Preliminarily, an argument could be made that the Court did not intend the *Daubert* analysis to apply to mental health expert testimony at all. Two features of the opinion might support that view. First, Rule 702 refers to "scientific, technical, or other specialized knowledge" that will assist the trier of fact. *Daubert* explicitly limited its discussion "to the scientific context" because that was the nature of the expertise offered in the case (*Daubert v. Merrell Dow Pharmaceutical, Inc.*, 1993, n. 8). It could be argued, then, that a different set of considerations would come into play when technical or specialized knowledge are at issue. Is mental health expertise, such as clinical opinions on incompetency or insanity, specialized rather than scientific knowledge? Just as the "special knowledge" of police officers make their judgments about the crime situation helpful (see, for instance, *Brown v. Farmers Mutual Insurance Company*, 1991), it could be argued that the "special knowledge" based on years of forensic assessments and evaluations make mental health professionals' insights about a defendant's mental state helpful. Or is mental health expertise technical information, based on a mastery of clinical assessment and evaluation techniques? In some cases, "There is no clear demarcation between scientific, technical, and specialized knowledge" (Graham, 1994, p. 162), as with expert testimony on battered women's syndrome and child sexual abuse syndrome. There, the scientific evidence on people facing those conditions is growing, but the existence of a verifiable "syndrome" is still largely based on clinical, observational experience with victims.

Should those syndromes, nonetheless, be subjected to the exacting scientific standard envisioned by *Daubert?*

Second, the *Daubert* Court did not refer to *Barefoot v. Estelle* (1983), the only other Supreme Court case to deal with the admissibility of expert testimony since the enactment of the federal rules. As noted earlier, *Barefoot* held that expert testimony on the defendant's future dangerousness was admissible despite evidence in the record that psychiatrists were wrong in those predictions two out of three times. Does the Court's failure to address *Barefoot* mean that it did not envision *Daubert* applying to the type of expertise at issue in *Barefoot?* Or did the Supreme Court intend to wipe out decades of routine reliance on clinical opinion testimony that has been admitted without regard to its underlying scientific validity, and assume that all clinical expertise would be subsumed under its *Daubert* analysis?

The better reading of *Daubert*, in our view, is that the Court did not explicitly consider *Daubert's* implications for mental health expertise, so we now turn to this task. First, it is relatively easy to conclude that *Daubert* should apply to mental health expertise based exclusively on experimental science. Such testimony (for example, a psychologist reporting on laboratory research on children's memory fallibilities), fits squarely within the *Daubert* framework—scientific knowledge, testable, determinable error rate, survived peer review. The potentially tougher call relates to whether courts should apply the strictures of *Daubert* to primarily clinically derived opinion testimony or to testimony based on clinical inferences drawn from empirical research, as in the case of much of the syndrome or profile evidence. We now turn to these latter questions.

Application to Clinical Opinion Testimony

Clinical opinion testimony has routinely been admitted if it was relevant to the legal issue in the litigation. *Daubert* did not explicitly or auto-

matically change that. As one post-*Daubert* federal court opinion asserted, medical opinion on the origin of a disease or the consequences of exposure to certain conditions based on "confirmatory data" gained through "clinical experience" is not prohibited by the Federal Rules of Evidence or by *Daubert* (*Cantrell v. GAF Corporation*, 1993, p. 1018).

But why should a court admit such testimony with little scrutiny, including mental health professional clinical opinion testimony, when scientific information must pass a rigorous *Daubert* evaluation to be admitted? Three possible reasons exist. First, despite clinical opinion evidence's lack of scientific foundation, it is inherently reliable because it is based on years of accumulated wisdom and experience. Second, and conversely, jurors will recognize opinion testimony as inherently less credible and be able to assess it accordingly. Third, adversary procedures, such as cross-examination, will ferret out the problems in the reliability of clinical opinion testimony.

The first line of argument is based on the assumption that clinical opinion testimony is sufficiently reliable to be freely admitted without greater scrutiny. One of the most consistent findings in social science research, however, is that the actuarial method of judgment and decision making outperforms the clinical method (Dawes, Faust, & Meehl, 1989). Yet, at least within clinical psychology, few diagnoses or predictions are based on actuarial methods (Dawes et al., 1989). Experienced clinicians differ in their judgments of diagnosis, even with respect to separating persons with actual brain damage from those with simulated brain damage (Faust & Ziskin, 1988, p. 31). One study found that mental health professionals were wrong 47% of the time when they predicted that a mental patient would commit an act of violence within six months (Lidz, Mulvey, & Gardiner, 1993), duplicating earlier research findings on clinical prediction of dangerousness (see, for example, Cocozza & Steadman, 1976; Steadman, 1977; but see Grisso & Appelbaum, 1992).

The growing literature on human judgment and decision making helps explain why clinical determinations fall far short of being inherently reliable. This literature suggests that judgments of experienced clinicians are as susceptible to error as lay judgments, and that expert clinicians, like untrained, lay decision makers, use strategies (or heuristics) in arriving at decisions that contribute to the error rate (Bersoff (1992; see generally Tversky & Kahneman, 1974). After conducting an extensive review of the newer and less extensive research on decision making in forensic settings, Bersoff (1992) concluded that "forensic decisionmaking is just as flawed as typical clinical judgment" (p. 351). This was true for several key mental health expertise content areas, including insanity evaluations, competency-to-stand-trial assessments, predictions of future violence, and the detection of malingering (or faking) of mental disorder. Therefore, courts cannot assume away reliability concerns about the clinical opinions of mental health experts and should not unquestioningly accept mental health expertise without some heightened level of scrutiny or safeguards to guard against erroneous judgments influencing courtroom decisions.

Another rationale for broad admissibility of mental health expertise in the courtroom is that jurors are at their best when determining the credibility of witnesses, and that they are sufficiently skeptical of "mere" opinion testimony so as not to be overly impressed with such testimony even from a designated "expert" witness. This view is well drawn in a post-*Daubert* case from Florida. In *Flanagan v. State* (1993), the Florida Supreme Court (declining to follow *Daubert* and instead adhering to *Frye*) explained that "pure opinion testimony, such as a [mental health] expert's opinion that a defendant is incompetent," did not have to meet the *Frye* or general acceptance standard to be admissible. The *Flanagan* court reasoned that the jury can analyze it as it does any other personal opinion or factual testimony by a witness, despite it being "cloaked with the credibility of an expert." In contrast, the court, relying on *Frye*, refused to admit sexual offender profile testimony. Profile testimony, the

court explained, relies "by its nature" on some scientific principle or test, "which implies an infallibility not found in pure opinion testimony." In the latter case, the court asserted, "[t]he jury will naturally assume that the scientific principles underlying the expert's conclusion are valid," and presumably, then, the court must screen it first for its suitability (*Flanagan v. State*, 1991, p. 828).

This second argument for broad admissibility, then, assumes the fallibility of clinical testimony but argues that jurors recognize this fallibility and can accurately assess the credibility of the expert and the expertise offered. Unfortunately, research does not confirm either point. Jurors are subject to the decision-making errors discussed above. Thus, scientific jargon, scientific principles, and scientific-sounding principles and conclusions in a mental health professional's testimony may be salient bits of information to which jurors would be overly attuned. And, given the decision-making literature discussed above, we are not optimistic that jurors could make accurate credibility determinations. Beyond that, it is well documented in the social psychology literature that an audience will be more influenced by a speaker with higher status or credentials (Bank & Poythress, 1983). A witness who is cloaked in the "white coat" of expertise, then, might be unduly influential merely because of the label.

Moreover, factors that appear from research to be most related to the persuasive impact of testimony may have little or nothing to do with the scientific merit of expert testimony. For example, jurors (as receivers of information) may be most influenced by the perceived trustworthiness of a speaker (Bank & Poythress, 1983; Birnbaum & Stegner, 1979), rather than the content of the testimony. While certainly a showing of actual bias of an expert should legitimately sway a juror, juror attitudes might as easily be affected by incorrectly perceived bias, such as equating hiring by one side with untrustworthiness (see, for example, Petrella &

Poythress, 1984). Vidmar & Schuller (1989) found that jurors "spontaneously indicated to interviewers that experts are chosen to testify because their opinions favor the party that calls them" (p. 171). Even privately retained experts who strictly adhere to the scientist or educator model of expert testimony (see Hans, 1989; Saks, 1990), and can provide reliable testimony, are not immune to this perceived bias. Jurors may dismiss their testimony as untrustworthy, no matter how sound the underlying science, once they hear how much money an expert was paid for rendering an opinion for one side or the other. In addition, social psychological studies have shown repeatedly that presentational and language style (see, for instance, Conley, O'Barr, & Lind, 1978; Erickson, Lind, Johnson, & O'Barr, 1978; Naftulin, Ware, & Donnelly, 1973) and appearance (Chaiken, 1979) affect source credibility ratings (see generally Bank & Poythress, 1983). Moreover, the way experts are questioned may affect ratings of competence, such that experts allowed to present narratives may be more believable than those testifying in a piecemeal fashion (Bank & Poythress, 1983). The available research, then, does not support the assumption that jurors are appropriately skeptical of "mere" opinion testimony. Thus, courts may want to rethink their assumption that jurors should be able to properly weigh the credibility of a mental health professional expert witness.

The third argument in support of admitting clinical opinion testimony rests on the efficacy of adversarial techniques. Research has consistently shown that adversarial procedures are more effective than nonadversarial techniques in several key ways (Lind & Tyler, 1988; Thibaut & Walker, 1975). The adversary system appears to better counteract the decision makers' biases and encourage a diligent search for evidence (Thibaut, Walker, & Lind, 1973). Additionally, it is perceived as more fair, thereby providing greater satisfaction with the legal system (Lind & Tyler, 1988). Justice Blackmun proclaimed the virtues of the adversarial system in *Daubert* (vigorous

cross-examination, presentation of contrary evidence, and careful instruction on the burden of proof), calling them "the traditional and appropriate means of attacking shaky but admissible evidence" (*Daubert*, 1993, p. 2798). Even in the face of its own repeated acknowledgment that psychiatric and psychological judgments are highly fallible (see, for example, *Addington v. Texas*, 1979; *O'Connor v. Donaldson*, 1975), the Supreme Court has explicitly trusted the adversary process to "sort out the reliable from the unreliable evidence and opinion" in mental health expert testimony (*Barefoot v. Estelle*, 1983, p. 901).

Yet this trust in the adversary system may be misplaced when the system is dealing with expert testimony (see Black, Ayala, & Saffran-Brinks, 1994; Brekke, Enko, Clavet, & Seelau, 1991). The adversary nature of the process may circumvent the value in seeking out expert assistance. Many reputable experts simply refuse to be drawn into the adversary process, possibly depriving the courts of the best expertise (Saks & Van Duizend, 1983; Sales & Simon, 1993). Even experts who view themselves as impartial educators may have difficulty maintaining that role when hired and paid by partisan attorneys, pressured to overstate conclusions, or thrust into adversarial battles (see, for instance, Diamond, 1973; McCloskey, Egeth, & McKenna, 1986; Sales & Simon, 1993). Moreover, the limited empirical work on this topic suggests that the way a clinician approaches a particular forensic evaluation can be influenced by which side retains the expert (see Otto, 1989; Rogers, 1987; Shuman, 1994).

The deficiencies of the adversarial system may be particularly devastating in the case of mental health clinical expertise (see, for example, Levine, 1984). Effective cross-examination (a hallmark of the adversary safeguards) is premised on access to the underlying bases of an expert's testimony. Yet, under the Federal Rules of Evidence (Rule 703), experts may rely on any information as long as it is of the type "reasonably relied upon" by experts in the field. If mental health professionals report relying on "years of clinical experience," it is difficult if not impossible to challenge their judgment. Countering vivid, case study–type information with dry scientific or statistical data may not be an effective strategy, given the salience of the more concrete information (Bersoff, 1992). Yet courts seem reluctant to require clinicians to go beyond "years of clinical experience" in providing the basis for their testimony. As Poythress (1977) points out, an attorney's interpretation of the duty to represent a client zealously may include trying to discredit and embarrass an opposing expert. As such, an expert may "hide behind" years of clinical expertise as a defensive gesture. Judge David L. Bazelon (1974), one of the most prominent mental health commentators and jurists, stated his frustration this way:

> One might hope that psychiatrists would open up their reservoirs of knowledge in the courtroom. Unfortunately in my experience they try to limit their testimony to conclusory statements couched in psychiatric terminology. Thereafter they take shelter in a defensive resistance to questions about the facts that are or ought to be in their possession. They thus refuse to submit their opinions to the scrutiny that the adversary process demands. (p. 18)

Other courts have similarly been concerned about the efficacy of cross-examination to neutralize unreliable components of an expert's testimony. One court, faced with expert testimony that a particular child had been a victim of child sexual abuse, observed that "[i]n such a case, the expert's conclusions are as impenetrable as they are unverifiable (*State v. Cressey*, 1993, p. 701; see also *State v. Michaels*, stating that no amount of cross-examination could have undone the harm caused by the expert's testimony). Lawyers may be able to "ferret out" some of the weaknesses in veracity, memory, motivation, prejudices, and biases through cross-examination (see Black et al., 1994, p. 789), but they are not adept at dealing with problems of scientific validity and reliability inherent in mental health clinical opinion testimony.

Conclusion

As this chapter has illuminated, under current evidence law in most jurisdictions, mental health expert witnesses who rely explicitly on empirical evidence to support their testimony will have that "scientific" basis scrutinized for its "quality." In jurisdictions that continue to follow *Frye*, the test will be whether the science is "generally accepted" within the relevant scientific community. In jurisdictions that follow *Daubert*, the test will be whether the science meets reliability standards enunciated by the U.S. Supreme Court. A mental health expert who relies in part on research studies and in part on clinical judgment may or may not undergo such scrutiny, depending on a particular court's attention to reliability concerns. Yet a mental health expert who provides only clinical opinion testimony will ordinarily have that testimony freely admitted with no scrutiny beyond whether the person is qualified in his or her field.

Do these distinctions make sense for mental health expertise? Several approaches are possible. The courts could become more cognizant of the continuum of mental health expertise, from pure clinical opinion to pure science, and adjust its level of scrutiny accordingly (see Shuman & Sales, 1995). Where there is underlying science, the courts should scrutinize its quality. Where the testimony is a mixture of science and clinical opinion, the courts should examine the scientific basis as much as possible.

If it is pure clinical testimony with no scientific basis, the courts could continue to admit it, as they have done for generations, based on the unverified assumption that it is still better than providing no assistance at all to jurors on difficult psychological and behavioral questions. Given the concerns we have identified with the reliability of clinical opinion, with the jury's ability to evaluate it, and with the potential inadequacies of the adversary process, however, it is not unreasonable to argue that courts should simply refuse to admit pure clinical opinion *as expert testimony* until it can pass scientific muster (see Faust & Ziskin, 1988). There is an alternative approach to these two polar opposites that evolves out of a broad reading of *Daubert*. It would extend the Supreme Court's concerns about reliability to all expert testimony (see Imwinkelreid, 1994). While *Daubert* does not itself automatically apply to nonscientific, clinical expertise, it could be read as calling into serious question the uncritical, *Barefoot v. Estelle* type of acceptance of clinical testimony. Clearly, clinical opinion cannot easily be subjected to the rigid scientific analysis associated with Karl Popper, entailing testing and retesting of hypotheses, an approach espoused by Justice Blackmun in *Daubert*. Yet why should we settle for no scrutiny? Good clinical experience and judgment should be distinguishable from totally inadequate opinion. If a mental health expert cannot "point to any experiences supporting the proffered opinion, the opinion is nothing more than conclusory conjecture," lacking experiential validation (Imwinkelreid, 1994, p. 2290). If a psychiatrist claims that a prediction is "100 percent accurate," it would be necessary to show, at a minimum, that his or her prior predictions in actual cases have been 100 percent accurate (see, for example, *Barefoot v. Estelle*, 1983). While it would take substantial work to develop standards for the courts that would permit greater scrutiny of clinical opinion, it would, in our view, be a worthwhile undertaking, and would allow us to derive the best possible reading of the U.S. Supreme Court's statement on Rule 702.

References

Addington v. Texas, 441 U.S. 418 (1979).

Ake v. Oklahoma, 105 S.Ct. 1087 (1985).

Allen R. J. (1994). Expertise and the *Daubert* decision. *Journal of Criminal Law and Criminology, 84*, 1157–1175.

Allen, R. J., & Miller, J. S. (1993). The common law theory of experts: Deference or education? *Northwestern University Law Review, 87,* 1131–1147.

American Psychiatric Association. (1982). *Statement on the Insanity Defense.* Washington, DC: Author.

Bank, S. C., & Poythress, N. G., Jr. (1983). The elements of persuasion in expert testimony. *Journal of Psychiatry and Law, 10,* 173–204.

Barefoot v. Estelle, 463 U.S. 80 (1983).

Bartol, C. (1983). *Psychology and American law.* Belmont, CA: Wadsworth.

Bazelon, D. L. (1974, June). Psychiatrists and the adversary process. *Scientific American, 230*(6), 18–23.

Beech Aircraft Corporation v. Rainey, 488 U.S. 153 (1988).

Beitchman, J. H., Zucker, K. J., Hood, J. E., daCosta, G. A., & Cassavia, E. (1992). A review of the long-term effects of child sexual abuse. *Child Abuse and Neglect, 16,* 101–118.

Berger, M. A. (1986). A relevancy approach to novel scientific evidence. *Federal Rules Decision, 115,* 89–91.

Bersoff, D. N. (1992). Judicial deference to nonlegal decisionmakers: Imposing simplistic solutions on problems of cognitive complexity in mental disability law. *Southern Methodist University Law Review, 46,* 329–372.

Birnbaum, M., & Stegner, S. (1979). Source credibility in social judgment: Bias, expertise, and the judge's point of view. *Journal of Personality and Social Psychology, 37,* 48–74.

Black, B. (1988). A unified theory of scientific evidence. *Fordham Law Review, 56,* 595–695.

Black, B., Ayala, F. J., & Saffran-Brinks, C. (1994). Science and the law in the wake of *Daubert:* A new search for scientific knowledge. *Texas Law Review, 72,* 715–802.

Bonnie, R. J. (1984). Morality, equality, and expertise: Renegotiating the relationship between psychiatry and the criminal law. *Bulletin of the American Academy of Psychiatry and Law, 12,* 5–20.

Bowers v. Hardwick, 478 U.S. 186 (1986).

Boyce, R. N. (1963). Judicial recognition of scientific evidence in criminal cases. *Utah Law Review, 8,* 313–327.

Boyer, C. A., & O'Connor, M. (1994, March). The role of mental health professionals and social science research in Arizona's insanity defense reform: A case study. Paper presented at the meeting of the American Psychology/Law Society, Santa Fe, NM.

Brekke, N. J., Enko, P. J., Clavet, G., & Seelau, E. (1991). Of juries and court-appointed experts: The impact of nonadversarial versus adversarial expert testimony. *Law and Human Behavior, 15,* 451–475.

Brief on behalf of amicus developmental, social, and psychological researchers, social scientists, and scholars in *State v. Michaels. Psychology, Public Policy, and Law.*

Brown v. Farmers Mutual Insurance Company, 468 N.W.3d 105, 114 (Neb. 1991).

Campbell v. People, 814 P.2d 1 (Colo. 1981).

Cantrell v. GAF Corporation, 999 F.2d 1007 (6th Cir. 1993).

Chaiken, S. (1979). Communicator physical attractiveness and persuasion. *Journal of Personality and Social Psychology, 37,* 1387–1397.

Champagne, A., Shuman, D., & Whitaker, E. (1991). An empirical examination of the use of expert witnesses in American courts. *Jurimetrics Journal, 31,* 375–392.

In re Chrystal and Tasha, 1994 WL 174499 (Conn. Super.).

Cleary, E. W. (Ed.). (1984). *McCormick on evidence* (3rd ed.). St. Paul, MN: West.

Cocozza, J. J., & Steadman, H. (1976). The failure of psychiatric predictions of dangerousness: Clear and convincing evidence. *Rutgers Law Review, 29,* 1084–1101.

Commonwealth v. Dunkle, 602 A.2d 830 (Pa. 1992).

Conley, J., O'Barr, W., & Lind, E. (1978). The power of language: Presentational style in the courtroom. *Duke Law Journal, 6*, 1375–1399.

Daubert v. Merrell Dow Pharmaceutical, Inc., 509 U.S., 113 S.Ct. 2786 (1993).

Dawes, R. M., Faust, D., & Meehl, P. E. (1989). Clinical versus actuarial judgment. *Science, 243*, 1668–1674.

Diamond, B. (1973). The psychiatrist as an advocate. *The Journal of Psychiatry and Law, 1*, 5–21.

In the matter of Eli, 607 N.Y.S.2d 535 (1993).

Erickson, B., Lind, A. E., Johnson, B. C., & O'Barr, W. M. (1978). Speech style and impression formation in a court setting: The effects of 'powerful' and 'powerless' speech. *Journal of Experimental Social Psychology, 14*, 266–279.

Expert medical testimony in jury trials. (1892). *Journal of the American Medical Association, 18*, 304 (cited in *JAMA, 267*, 1164).

Faigman, D. L., Porter, E., & Saks, M. J. (1994). Check your crystal ball at the courthouse door, please: Exploring the past, understanding the present, and worrying about the future of scientific evidence. *Cardozo Law Review, 15*, 1101–1136.

Faust, D., & Ziskin, J. (1988). The expert witness in psychology and psychiatry. *Science, 241*, 31–35.

Federal Rules of Evidence. (1974). Westbury, NY: Foundation Press.

Flanagan v. State, 586 So.2d 1085 (Fla. 1st DCA 1991), approv'd by 625 So.2d 827 (Fla. 1991).

Foucha v. Louisiana, 112 S.Ct. 1780 (1992).

Frenzel v. State, 849 P.2d 741 (Wyo. 1993).

Frye v. United States, 293 F. 1013 (D.C. Cir. 1923).

Fulero, S., & Finkel, N. (1991). Barring ultimate issue testimony: An "insane" rule? *Law and Human Behavior, 15*, 495–507.

Giannelli, P. C. (1980). The admissibility of novel scientific evidence: *Frye v. United States*, a half-century later. *Columbia Law Review, 80*, 1197–1250.

Giannelli, P. C. (1991). Criminal discovery, scientific evidence, and DNA. *Vanderbilt Law Review, 44*, 791–825.

Graham, M. H. (1994). *Daubert v. Merrell Dow Pharmaceuticals, Inc.:* No *Frye*, now what? *Criminal Law Bulletin, 30*, 153–171.

Grisso, T., & Appelbaum, P. S. (1992). Is it unethical to offer predictions of future violence? *Law and Human Behavior, 16*, 621–633.

Gross, S. R. (1991). Expert evidence. *Wisconsin Law Review, 1991*, 1113–1232.

Hammer v. Hammer, 418 N.W.2d 23 (Wisc. App. 1987).

Hand, L. (1901). Historical and practical considerations regarding expert testimony. *Harvard Law Review, 15*, 40–58.

Hans, V. (1989). Expert witnessing: Review of Chesler, M. A., Sanders, J., & Kalmuss, D. S. (1989). *Social science in court: Mobilizing experts in the school desegregation cases. Science, 245*, 312–313.

Huber, P. (1985). Safety and the second best: The hazards of public risk management in the courts. *Columbia Law Review, 85*, 277–337.

Ibn-Tamas v. United States, 407 A.2d 626, 637 (D.C. App. 1979).

Imwinkelreid, E. J. (1990). The evolution of the American test for the admissibility of scientific evidence. *Medicine, Science, and the Law, 30*, 60–64.

Imwinkelreid, E. J. (1992). Attempts to limit the scope of the *Frye* standard for the admission of scientific evidence: Confronting the real cost of the general acceptance test. *Behavioral Sciences and the Law, 10*, 441–454.

Imwinkelreid, E. J. (1994). The next step after *Daubert:* Developing a similarly epistemological approach to ensuring the reliability of nonscientific expert testimony. *Cardozo Law Review, 15*, 2271–2294.

Jackson v. State, 553 So.2d 719 (Fl.App. 4 Dist. 1989).

Jenkins v. U.S., 307 F.2d 637 (D.C. Cir. 1962) (en banc).

Jurek v. Texas, 428 U.S. 262 (1976).

Kalven, H. & Zeisel, H. (1966). *The American jury.* Boston: Little, Brown.

Kargon, R. (1986). Expert testimony in historical perspective. *Law and Human Behavior, 10,* 15–27.

Kruse v. State, 483 So.2d 1381 (Fla. 4th DCA 1986).

Levine, M. (1984). The adversary process and social science in the courts: Barefoot v. Estelle. *Journal of Psychiatry and Law, 12*(2), 147–181.

Lidz, C. W., Mulvey, E. P., & Gardiner, W. (1993). The accuracy of predictions of violence to others. *Journal of the American Medical Association, 269,* 1007–1011.

Lind, E. A., & Tyler, T. R. (1988). *The social psychology of procedural justice.* New York: Plenum.

Lindsay, D. S., & Read, J. D. (1994). Incest resolution psychotherapy and memories of childhood sexual abuse: A cognitive perspective. *Applied Cognitive Psychology, 8,* 281–338.

Lucero v. Lucero, 1994 WL 630870 (N.M. App.).

McCloskey, M., & Egeth, H. (1983). Eyewitness identification: What can a psychologist tell a jury? *American Psychologist, 38,* 550–564.

McCloskey, M., Egeth, H., & McKenna, J. (1986). The ethics of expert testimony [Special Issue]. *Law and Human Behavior, 10,* 1–2.

McCord, D. (1987). Syndromes, profiles, and other mental exotica: A new approach to the admissibility of nontraditional psychological evidence in criminal cases. *Oregon Law Review, 66,* 19–108.

McCormick, C. T. (1954). *Handbook of the law of evidence.* St. Paul, MN: West.

McCormick, C. T. (1982). Scientific evidence: Defining a new approach to admissibility. *Iowa Law Review, 67,* 879–916.

Medina v. California, 112 S.Ct. 2572 (1992).

Melton, G., Weithorn, L., & Slobogin, C. (1985). *Community mental health centers and the courts: An evaluation of community-based services.* Lincoln: University of Nebraska.

Monahan, J. (1981). *The clinical prediction of violent behavior.* Crime and delinquency issues: A National Institute for Mental Health monograph series. Washington, DC: American Psychological Association.

Morse, S. J. (1978). Crazy behavior, morals, and science: An analysis of mental health law. *Southern California Law Review, 51,* 527–654.

Myers, J. E. B., Bays, J., Becker, J., Berliner, L., Corwin, D. L., & Saywitz, K. J. (1989). Expert testimony in child sexual abuse litigation. *Nebraska Law Review, 68,* 1–145.

Naftulin, D., Ware, J., & Donnelly, F. (1973). The Doctor Fox lecture: A paradigm of educational seduction. *Journal of Medical Education, 48,* 630–635.

O'Connor v. Donaldson, 422 U.S. 563 (1975).

Osborn, A. S. (1935). Reasons and reasoning in expert testimony. *Law and Contemporary Problems, 2,* 488–494.

Otto, R. K. (1989). Bias and expert testimony of mental health professionals in adversarial proceedings: A preliminary investigation. *Behavioral Sciences and the Law, 7,* 267–273.

Parham v. J. R., 442 U.S. 584 (1979).

People v. Bledsoe, 681 P.2d 291 (Calif. 1984).

People v. Gans, 465 N.Y.S.2d 147 (N.Y. Sup. Ct. 1983).

People v. Hawthorne, 291 N.W. 205 (Mich. 1940).

People v. Kelly, 549 P.2d 1240 (Calif. 1976).

People v. Lewis, 393 N.E.2d 1380 (Ill. 1979).

People v. Shirley, 723 P.2d 1354 (Calif. 1982).

People v. White, 414 N.E.2d 196, 200 (Ill. 1980).

People Against Nuclear Energy v. U.S. Nuclear Regulatory Commission, 678 F.2d 222 (D.C.Cir. 1982).

Petrella, R. C., & Poythress, N. G. (1984). The quality of forensic evaluations: An interdisciplinary study. *Journal of Consulting and Clinical Psychology, 51*(91), 76–85.

Poythress, N. G. (1977). Mental health expert testimony: Current problems. *Journal of Psychiatry and Law, 5,* 201–227.

Resnick, P. J. (1986). Perceptions of psychiatric testimony: A historical perspective on the hysterical invective. *Bulletin of the American Academy of Psychiatry and Law, 14,* 205–219.

Rogers, R. (1987). Ethical dilemmas in forensic evaluations. *Behavioral Sciences and the Law, 5,* 149–160.

Saks, M. J. (1990). Expert witnesses, nonexpert witnesses, and nonwitness experts. *Law and Human Behavior, 14,* 291–313.

Saks, M. J., & Van Duizend, R. (1983). *The use of scientific evidence in litigation.* Williamsburg, VA: National Center for State Courts.

Sales, B. D., Shuman, D. W., & O'Connor, M. (1994). In a dim light: Admissibility of child sexual abuse memories. *Applied Cognitive Psychology, 8,* 399–406.

Sales, B. D., & Simon, L. (1993). Institutional constraints on the ethics of expert testimony. *Ethics and Behavior, 3,* 231–249.

Shuman, D. (1994). The psychology of compensation in tort law. *Kansas Law Review, 43,* 39–77.

Shuman, D., & Sales, B. (1995). *Reconstructing the admissibility of scientific evidence: The difference in clinical and research-based evidence.* Unpublished manuscript, Southern Methodist University, Dallas, TX.

Shuman, D., Whitaker, E., & Champagne, A. (1994). An empirical examination of the use of expert witnesses in the courts. Part II: A three city study. *Jurimetrics Journal, 34,* 193–208.

Slobogin, C. (1989). The "ultimate issue" issue. *Behavioral Sciences and the Law, 7,* 259–266.

Slovenko, R. (1987). The lawyer and the forensic expert: Boundaries of ethical practice. *Behavioral Sciences and the Law, 5,* 119–147.

Smith, S. R. (1989). Mental health expert witnesses: Of science and crystal balls. *Behavioral Sciences and the Law, 7,* 145–180.

State v. Baker, 424 A.2d 171, 172 (N.H. 1980).

State v. Borrelli, 629 A.2d 1105 (Conn. 1993).

State v. Brown, 687 P.2d 751 (Or. 1984).

State v. Cressey, 628 A.2d 696 (N.H. 1993).

State v. J.Q., 599 A.2d 172 (N.J. 1991).

State v. Kelly, 478 A.2d 364 (N.J. 1984).

State v. Michaels, 642 A.2d 1372 (N.J. 1994).

State v. Padilla, 347 P.2d 312 (N.M. 1959).

Steadman, H. J. (1977). A new look at recidivism among Patuxent inmates. *Bulletin of the American Academy of Psychiatry and Law, 5,* 200–209.

Strong, J. W. (1992). Language and logic in expert testimony: Limiting expert testimony by restrictions of function, reliability, and form. *Oregon Law Review, 71,* 349–379.

Thar, A. E. (1982). Comment: The admissibility of expert testimony of battered wife syndrome. An evidentiary analysis. *Northwestern University Law Review, 77,* 348–373.

Thibaut, J., Walker, L. (1975). *Procedural justice: A psychological analysis.* Hillsdale, NJ: Erlbaum.

Thibaut, J., Walker, L., & Lind, E. A. (1973). Adversary presentation and bias in legal decision making. *Harvard Law Review, 26,* 1271–1289.

Toro v. State, 1994 WL 474939 (Fla.App. 5 Dist.).

Tversky, A., & Kahneman, D. (1974). Judgment under uncertainty: Heuristics and biases. *Science, 185,* 1124–1131.

United States v. Downing, 753 F.2d 1224 (3d Cir. 1985).

United States v. Hinckley, 525 F. Supp. 1342 (D.C.D.C. 1981).

United States v. Maivia, 728 F. Supp. 1471 (D. Hawaii 1990).

United States v. Shorter, 618 F. Supp. 255 (D.C.D.C. 1985).

United States v. Tranowski, 659 F.2d 750 (7th Cir. 1981).

Vidmar, N. J., & Schuller, R. A. (1989). Juries and expert evidence: Social framework testimony. *Law and Contemporary Problems, 52,* 133–159.

Weinstein, J. D., & Berger, M. A. (1992). *Weinstein's evidence* (Vol. 3). New York: Matthew Bender.

Wilk, P. A. (1984). Expert testimony on rape trauma syndrome: Admissibility and effective use in criminal rape prosecution. *American University Law Review, 33,* 417–462.

Winick, B. J. (1985). Restructuring competency to stand trial. *UCLA Law Review, 32,* 921–985.

Wursten, A., & Sales, B. (1988). The community psychologist in state legislative decision making. *American Journal of Community Psychology, 16,* 487–502.

Wursten, A., & Sales, B. (1992). Use of psychologists and psychological research in legislative decision making on public interest matters. In D. K. Kagehiro & W. S. Laufer (Eds.), *Handbook of psychology and law* (pp. 119–138). New York: Springer-Verlag.

Yuille, J. C. (1989). Expert evidence by psychologists: Sometimes problematic and often premature. *Behavioral Sciences and the Law, 7,* 181–196.

Part 2
Mental Health Professionals and the Law

4 ▮ Confidentiality in the Psychotherapeutic Relationship

Michele Smith-Bell
William J. Winslade
University of Texas, Medical Branch at Galveston

Clients who seek the assistance of a mental health professional (MHP) reveal private information about their thoughts, feelings, fantasies, and conduct. This disclosure of sensitive, sometimes embarrassing or shameful, personal information makes clients vulnerable to being harmed if unauthorized third parties gain access to such information. Clients assume or seek assurances that sensitive information will be a confidential communication to their MHP, and unless they can trust their therapist and rely on confidentiality, they are unlikely to cooperate fully in their therapy.

Thus, MHPs frequently find themselves caught between clients' desires for privacy and confidentiality and third parties' demands for access to confidential information. The values of privacy and confidentiality, and of privileged communication (that is, confidential information protected from required disclosure in judicial or quasijudicial settings) are codified in law, articulated in ethics codes, and emphasized in professional education. Ordinarily, third parties do not have access to confidential information unless the client consents to it, but law and ethics codes acknowledge exceptions and restrictions to confidentiality; professional education also identifies conflicts arising in clinical settings. Professional practice is replete with difficult decisions about whether or how much otherwise confidential information must be disclosed to third parties such as family members, employers, insurance companies, courts, or government officials. To maximize the effectiveness of and avoid damage to the therapeutic relationship, both MHPs and clients need to understand the scope and limits of privacy, confidentiality, and privilege in mental health care. This chapter clarifies legal and ethical aspects of privacy, confidentiality, and privilege in the context of mental health practice.

After a general review of the concepts of privacy, confidentiality, and privilege, specific problems connected with child abuse reporting laws are discussed in greater detail. Other problem areas—medical records (Winslade, 1982), genetic information (Macklin, 1992), dangerous patients (Felthous, 1989), AIDS (Rennert, 1991), and many others—also warrant close attention but have frequently been discussed in scholarly literature and are not considered here. Child abuse reporting laws have been chosen as a focus for several reasons. Every state requires some form of child abuse reporting that to some degree overrides privacy, confidentiality, and privilege. At the outset of therapy, MHPs must deal with the problem of what, if anything, to tell clients about such laws. In the course of therapy, disclosures made by a client may give rise to a duty to report suspected child abuse. This creates ten-

Adapted from "Privacy, Confidentiality and Privilege in Psychotherapeutic Relationships," by M. Smith-Bell and W. J. Winslade, 1994, *American Journal of Orthopsychiatry, 64*(2). Copyright © 1994 American Orthopsychiatric Association, Inc. Used with permission.

sion within the therapeutic relationship and may inhibit or rupture it. Even if therapy continues, clients may distrust their therapist and withhold important information. Even after child abuse has been reported, such third parties as government officials may seek further access to confidential information, thereby straining the therapeutic relationship even more. Since the scope of laws concerning child abuse reporting differs from state to state, it is possible to assess the variable impact of law on therapeutic practice; here the therapeutic consequences of broad child abuse reporting statutes that lead to overreporting and narrow reporting laws that lead to underreporting are examined.

In this chapter, it is argued that patients have important but limited rights to privacy and confidentiality. Therapists are obligated to protect patient privacy and confidentiality to the extent permitted by law and required by ethical standards. But third parties may have a legitimate interest in access to confidential patient information in particular situations. Therapists should inform patients as much as possible at the beginning of treatment of the rights to, and the limits of, privacy, confidentiality, and privilege. This practice not only respects the autonomy of patients, but also preserves the integrity of the therapeutic relationship (Winslade & Ross, 1985).

Privacy

Concept of Privacy

The concept of privacy embraces the idea of limiting the access of others in certain respects (Gavison, 1980), such as limiting the access of others to one's body or mind, including information about the self contained in dreams, fantasies, thoughts, and beliefs. Privacy in the law is sometimes linked to freedom from intrusion by the state or third persons; it also designates a domain of personal associations, abortion, and bodily integrity. Privacy is important because it preserves and protects individuals as they exercise their freedom to develop their personal identity, choose their values, and shape the course of their lives.

Some legal commentators argue for a constitutional right to privacy, seeing personal information as an integral part of an individual's identity and as crucial to most theories of personhood. This personal interest can be protected from unwarranted governmental intrusions by recognizing a constitutional right to informational privacy based on personhood (Note, 1991). It has been argued that personal interest in mental and emotional health is as basic and fundamental to ordered liberty as are constitutional rights related to family life and childbearing; significant interference with such fundamental interests, in the absence of a compelling state interest, violates the right to privacy (Smith, 1980). Although there is a recognized constitutional right to privacy, the scope of that right is quite narrow. Moreover, the Supreme Court has specifically held that there is no federal constitutional right to informational privacy for medical records, casting further doubt on the idea that there might be a constitutional right to privacy applicable to psychotherapeutic communications (*Whalen v. Roe*, 1976).

Constitutional Right to Privacy

The Supreme Court first recognized a constitutional right to privacy in the case of *Griswold v. Connecticut* (1965), which struck down a Connecticut statute prohibiting use of contraceptives by married couples. The right to privacy was expanded in the case of *Eisenstadt v. Baird* (1972), in which the Supreme Court reversed the defendant's conviction for distributing contraceptives to unmarried persons. In *Roe v. Wade* (1973), the Court held that criminal abortion laws, which proscribed abortion except for the purpose of saving the life of the mother, are unconstitutional. However, the *Roe* Court limited the right to privacy by stating that "only personal rights that can be deemed 'fundamental' or 'implicit in the concept of ordered liberty' . . . are included in this guarantee of personal privacy."

The constitutional right to privacy was restricted in the subsequent case of *Whalen v. Roe* (1976), in which the Court ruled that a patient does not have a constitutional right to informational privacy of communications or records generated in the course of medical treatment when the records are adequately protected from unauthorized disclosure. A more recent Supreme Court case further limits the constitutional right to privacy. In *Bowers v. Hardwick* (1985), the Court upheld a Georgia state antisodomy statute, and rejected the assertion that the right to privacy includes the fundamental right of homosexuals to engage in sodomy. Few federal appellate courts or state courts have recognized a constitutional right to privacy for the psychotherapeutic relationship; only California, Pennsylvania, and the United States Court of Appeals for the Ninth Circuit (covering Alaska, Arizona, California, Guam, Hawaii, Idaho, Montana, Nevada, the North Mariana Islands, Oregon, and Washington) have recognized a constitutionally based psychotherapist-patient privilege for psychotherapeutic communications (Smith, 1980, citing *Bremer v. State*, 1973), and those decisions are 15 to 20 years old.

In the California case (*In re Lifschutz*, 1970), a psychotherapist claimed that he had a privacy interest in psychotherapeutic communications with his patients; the court held that only the patient has a constitutionally protected privacy interest in preventing the release of psychotherapeutic communications. In another case (*Caesar v. Mountanos*, 1976), a psychotherapist refused to answer questions about one of his patients even after the patient specifically waived the psychotherapeutic privilege. The court held that the nature of communications between a patient and a therapist brings the relationship within the constitutional right of privacy through the psychotherapist-patient privilege. But on appeal, the court held that the right to privacy may be limited when necessary to advance a compelling

state interest, such as ascertaining truth in court proceedings; moreover, it was held to be the patient's right to waive or assert the privilege.

The case of *Hawaii Psychiatric Society v. Ariyoshi* (1979) supported a constitutional right to privacy. A federal district court enjoined the State of Hawaii from enforcing a statute that permitted the issuance of administrative inspection warrants to review the mental health records of Medicaid patients. The court held that an individual's decision to seek the aid of a psychiatrist, or to communicate certain personal information to that psychiatrist, fell squarely within the constitutional right to privacy. The court balanced the patient's privacy interest against the state's interest in protecting the Medicaid program from fraud; it found that the state failed to show that the issuance of warrants to inspect the confidential medical records of a psychiatrist was necessary to advance a compelling state interest (Smith, 1980).

The constitutional law of privacy is currently a dormant issue and does not seem likely to awaken much interest in the near future, especially with regard to psychotherapy. Thus, whether other federal and state courts will agree that there is a constitutional right to privacy, and what the boundaries of that right are, are unresolved issues.

Confidentiality

Distinction from Privacy

Privacy and confidentiality are essential features of the psychotherapeutic relationship, despite the limited recognition of the right to privacy in constitutional law. Both are linked to the general notion of limited access and the exclusion of others; sometimes these concepts are used loosely and interchangeably. For example, privacy and confidentiality both stand as polar opposites to what is public and open to everyone. Nevertheless, it is useful to distinguish these concepts in the context of the psychotherapeutic relationship.

When a person enters into a therapeutic relationship, the client relinquishes his or her personal privacy of thoughts, feelings, beliefs, and so on, in exchange for the prospect of therapeutic understanding and assistance. In this respect privacy is an aspect of *individuals*. Once private information has been disclosed to a therapist with an expectation that such information will not ordinarily be disclosed to third parties, it becomes confidential, and one refers to the confidentiality of information in the relationship. Thus, giving a therapist access to private information is necessary by definition for establishing a confidential relationship, and confidentiality is essential, as indicated earlier, to the therapeutic process (Winslade & Ross, 1985).

In some instances, no third parties have access to private information disclosed in confidence to the therapist or even know that the relationship exists at all. Some clients, for example, choose to pay cash for therapy rather than to file an insurance claim (Domb, 1990–1991, citing Sosfin, 1985). Some therapists organize their offices to protect client privacy by the use of separate entrances and exits and of answering machines rather than answering services. The classic image of the exclusive dyadic relationship of the therapist-client, though increasingly rare, is not extinct.

Obstacles to Preservation

Individual and, increasingly, group therapeutic practice often occurs in a larger context of therapist, client, and an array of third parties including family members, employers, insurers, courts, and government agencies. Therapists' general obligation to protect clients' confidential information is overridden by specific obligations to disclose information at the client's request, when the law requires it, or when ethics demands it. For example, a client in a commitment, competency, sanity, or custody proceeding might desire that a therapist testify about disclosures made in ther-

apy. The law might also require disclosures in such contexts even if the client does not consent to them. Legally mandated reporting requirements, such as those concerning child or elder abuse, override confidentiality. Ethics may dictate disclosures in the absence of specific legal authority. Conflicts arise, for example, concerning therapists' obligation to protect third parties threatened by dangerous patients.

The therapeutic consequences of external pressures on the preservation of confidentiality are that therapists may become wary of seeking sensitive information and clients of disclosing it. Even if therapists do not explicitly notify clients of the limits of confidentiality, the style of conducting therapeutic inquiry is influenced by the encroaching shadow of third-party access to information. If therapists inform clients of the limits of confidentiality, clients may then be inhibited in their communication and thereby hamper therapeutic effectiveness. The challenge to policymakers is to balance the need for confidentiality essential to the therapeutic process with the need for access to otherwise confidential information when necessary to protect legitimate public interests.

Patient Expectations

Most therapists should be familiar, even if not happy, with the numerous restrictions placed on the right to confidentiality, but studies indicate that patients have greater expectations of privacy and confidentiality (Weiss, 1982). In a 1986 study, a majority of student psychotherapy patients and nonpatients believed that all communications to psychotherapists are confidential; almost all patients wanted to be informed of exceptions to confidentiality; and most reported that they would react negatively to unauthorized breaches of confidentiality that would undermine their right to privacy (VandeCreek, Miars, & Herzog, 1987). Another study (Weiss, 1982) questioning patients, house staff, and medical students about their expectations concerning patient privacy demonstrated that only a small number of patients expected that their cases would be shared with physicians' spouses (17%) or at parties (18%). House staff and medical students indicated that such discussions occur commonly (57% and 70%, respectively).

Therapists should, of course, protect confidentiality to the extent permitted by law and required by ethical standards. But in view of clients' sometimes unrealistic expectations about the scope of confidentiality, it is important to clarify its limits at the outset of therapy or at least early on. Therapeutic relationships are often tentative and fragile until a client trusts a therapist. Trust is threatened, if not undermined, if a client feels misled by the therapist, and such a client may withhold information or not cooperate in the therapy in overt or subtle ways—by canceling sessions, coming late, failing to pay, and so on. Misunderstandings about confidentiality may even irrevocably rupture a therapeutic relationship. Thus, it is important for therapists to know and disclose what clients can reasonably expect concerning confidentiality. Its precise boundaries may be difficult to mark out in advance, but at least the general issues should be addressed.

When therapists are confronted with a specific conflict between a client's interest in confidentiality and a third party's claim to access, it is almost always appropriate to explore the conflict with the client first. This advances the therapeutic process because it demonstrates respect for both the client and the integrity of the therapeutic relationship. Clients may choose to authorize disclosure even if not legally required to do so. When a client does not want to permit disclosure, therapists have a duty to seek protection of confidentiality to the extent that law and ethics allow. In specific situations, therapists may find it helpful to consult ethics committees of their professional organizations, ethics consultants or attorneys, or experienced colleagues who are familiar with confidentiality rules and practices. Demands to disclose confidential information are sometimes excessive; it may be possible for the client or the therapist to negotiate a limited disclosure that satisfies both the client and the

third party. In other situations a client may have waived or forfeited the right to confidentiality by, for instance, signing a waiver or revealing private information to a third party; the therapist may then have no choice but to disclose otherwise confidential information. The damage to the therapeutic relationship can be minimized, however, if the client has been adequately informed and educated by the therapist early in the relationship.

Privilege

Concept of Privilege

The concept of privilege should be distinguished from that of confidentiality. Privilege is an exception to the general rule that the public has a right to relevant evidence in a court proceeding; confidentiality refers more broadly to legal rules and ethical standards that protect an individual from the unauthorized disclosure of information. Confidentiality alone is not enough to support a privilege; without a privilege statute or a common law rule, a therapist may be charged with contempt of court for refusing a court order to testify about a patient's psychotherapeutic communications. Thus, confidentiality is a professional duty to refrain from speaking about certain matters, while privilege is a relief from the duty to speak in a court proceeding about certain matters (Domb, 1990–1991, citing *In re Lifschutz*, 1970). While the impact of privilege laws, or of their lack, on the utilization of psychotherapeutic services in general is beyond the scope of this chapter, the impact on the use of such services by child abusers is discussed later in this chapter.

Patient Rights

The patient's right to privacy and confidentiality is partially protected by the doctrine of privileged communications. Confidential information that would otherwise be admissible in a judicial proceeding may be withheld if it is classified as a privileged communication. Privilege thus seeks to protect patients' privacy and confidentiality and, in doing so, renders them more disposed to seek mental health services. Privilege generally belongs to the patient, who decides whether it will be exercised or waived. Although the holder of the privilege is the patient, in appropriate circumstances the therapist may invoke the privilege on behalf of the patient, unless that privilege has been waived or the communication in question falls within a statutory exception to the privilege (Brakel, Parry, & Weiner, 1985, citing *In re Lifschutz*, 1970).

To be considered privileged, communications from a patient to a therapist must meet a number of requirements. First, the communications must be to a licensed or certified therapist as described in the state's privilege statute, or to an assistant of the therapist, depending on state law. Second, a professional relationship must exist between the patient and the therapist. Third, the communications must be related to the provision of professional services. Fourth, the communications must be confidential; they may not be released by the client to a third party (Smith, 1986–1987).

Privilege Statutes

While patients tend to expect confidentiality for their communications within the context of psychotherapy, they rarely consider the matter of privilege. Therapists, however, view privilege laws as an important restraint on litigant and governmental intrusion on the therapeutic process. Support for privilege laws also comes from the deontological school of thought, which views privilege as a way to protect significant human interests of the holders of the privileges without regard to its consequences in therapy. It focuses on the societal values preserved by a privilege and considers the disclosure of confidences revealed in certain relationships in and of itself wrong (Shuman, 1985). The fact that privilege laws sometimes result in the exclusion of relevant

and probative evidence, that which tends to prove a material issue, from a trial is then secondary and incidental.

Accordingly, privilege statutes are enacted to encourage full disclosure by patients to their therapist; these statutes usually provide that such communications cannot be revealed without the patient's consent. The term *privileged communication* refers solely to information at issue in litigation. There are generally three forms of privilege statutes applicable to MHPs: a general physician-patient and psychiatrist-patient privilege, a psychologist-patient privilege, and a psychotherapist-patient privilege (Brakel, Parry, & Weiner, 1985). Most states and the District of Columbia have adopted statutes that guarantee the physician-patient and psychologist-patient privilege in judicial settings. A smaller number of states have adopted the psychotherapist-patient testimonial privilege.

Criticism of Privilege

There is no consensus about the importance of a privilege to effective psychotherapy. It has been argued that most people are unaware of the existence of privilege, and it therefore does not affect their seeking therapy or their conduct within therapy (Brakel, Parry, & Weiner, 1985, citing Shuman & Weiner, 1982). Others have concluded that the concept of privilege should be abandoned as a means of determining whether psychotherapeutic communications should be disclosed, noting that standard guidelines in evidentiary matters, materiality and relevancy, adequately protect against unwarranted intervention in the therapeutic relationship (Brakel, Parry, & Weiner, 1985, citing Slovenko, 1974). Still others see privilege laws as insulating therapists from public scrutiny, rather than protecting patients' interests.

Privilege laws and the general obligation of confidentiality have become increasingly subject to exceptions and limitations, effectively reduced by inconsistent federal and state rules, and threatened by changes in health-care financing (Smith,

1986–1987). In addition, privilege statutes afford only limited protection to confidentiality because of the narrowness of their application; in the litigation setting, they are often only applicable to psychiatrists and psychologists, thereby decreasing their scope and effectiveness (Brakel, Parry, & Weiner, 1985). The scope of psychotherapeutic privilege is also reduced when it is waived, sometimes unwisely, by patients.

Waiver

Patients waive the privilege for psychotherapeutic communications when they file a tort or workers' compensation claim for a psychiatric injury, or when litigants otherwise put their mental states at issue. Unlike exception, in which normally privileged information is not privileged in certain situations prescribed by law (as when a defendant to a criminal charge raises his mental state as a defense), waiver requires action or acquiescence from the patient.

At least one court has held that the physician-patient, and hence the psychiatrist-patient, privilege is waived if the patient does not raise it when information concerning psychotherapeutic communications is first sought. There are situations in which a patient's psychotherapeutic communications are at issue, but the patient is not a party to the immediate matter before the court. In those situations, some courts have asserted the privilege on behalf of the patient, to protect the patient's right to confidentiality (Brakel, Parry, & Weiner, 1985).

Mandatory Reporting of Child Abuse

Statutes

The rights to privacy, confidentiality, and privilege in psychotherapy are deeply affected by statutes that make reporting of child abuse mandatory. This is an area in which therapeutic and legal claims may seem divergent, but the exercise of therapeutic jurisprudence may help to bring out areas of congruence.

Child abuse reporting statutes have several purposes: to protect potential victims from future abuse, to facilitate treatment for those already abused, and to deter, punish, and rehabilitate abusers; their general purpose is to protect children (Miller & Weinstock, 1987). All 50 states have mandatory child abuse reporting statutes, and many state evidence codes explicitly recognize that testimony given under a mandatory child abuse reporting law is an exception to the patient's privilege.

For mandatory reporting purposes, a child is defined in most states as someone under 18 years of age, and in a few states as someone under 16 years of age; reporting requirements are extended in many states to age 21 for those who have mental or physical disabilities. Under most statutes, the therapist does not need proof of the maltreatment to report abuse, but must only suspect maltreatment.

Most child abuse reporting statutes place a special burden on members of the helping professions, requiring them to report abuse or neglect to a central register maintained by a state agency (Agatstein, 1989; Slovenko & Grossman, 1991). In a case of suspected child abuse, the legal obligation to report relevant information takes precedence over confidentiality. Statutes differ, but most do not require that the psychotherapist disclose all information about the patient or every instance of abuse (Committee on Confidentiality, 1987). Some go so far as to argue that the state's interest in preventing child abuse is sufficiently strong as to abrogate all privacy interests of patient-perpetrators; therefore, therapists have not only an affirmative duty to report observed or suspected abuse, but also a duty to give evidence in subsequent administrative or court proceedings (Miller & Weinstock, 1987). All states grant immunity from liability to the therapist who, in good faith, reports suspected child abuse or neglect.

Adult Victims of Childhood Abuse

In many instances, the fact that a person was a victim of child abuse is not disclosed until that person is an adult patient in therapy. State laws usually do not address such situations and the psychotherapist is not usually required to report. Any decision to report past child abuse and to initiate an investigation thus belongs to the adult patient, especially if there is no evidence that the abuser is currently engaged in pedophilic activity (Joseph & Onek, 1991).

Child-Abusing Patients

Many psychotherapists assert that a child abuser cannot be treated successfully or the family be restored to reasonably normal functioning unless the abuser admits the violence and apologizes to the child-victim, especially in cases of sexual assault. Thus, an admission of guilt serves to restore family relationships, relieve child abuse victims of guilt and feelings of responsibility for the abuse, and aid in the cognitive restructuring of the abuser (Levine & Doherty, 1991). Forced admissions, however, create problems of self-incrimination for the patient.

The Fifth Amendment privilege against self-incrimination allows an individual to decline to answer questions posed by government officials in any proceeding, civil or criminal, formal or informal, in which answers might incriminate the individual in future criminal proceedings (Levine & Doherty, 1991). The Fifth Amendment generally applies to situations in which an individual is accused of child abuse.

In the private therapy context, if the psychotherapist forces the patient to admit to an act of child abuse, since the abuser cannot count on the therapist to maintain confidentiality because of mandatory reporting requirements, the admission may lead to a demand that the person "testify" against him or herself, in violation of the Fifth Amendment. Furthermore, the abuser may find therapeutically forced admissions used against him or her in a criminal, matrimonial,

or child abuse action (Levine & Doherty, 1991). No Fifth Amendment issue arises when a client makes an admission in the context of voluntary treatment. However, a Fifth Amendment issue does arise when patients' treatment is involuntary, as in court-ordered treatment of a parent on pain of losing parental rights. In such a case, the abuser is forced into treatment that requires a self-incriminating admission (Levine & Doherty, 1991).

Some courts have held that parents can be ordered to undergo treatment for child abuse as long as the order or treatment does not require an admission of abuse and as long as there is no explicit threat to use legal sanctions for not admitting abuse. Accordingly, a court can order treatment and can use the failure of treatment, even if predicated on a refusal to admit abuse, as a factor in terminating parental rights; but the fact that parents refuse to admit abuse presumably cannot be used against them to terminate parental rights (Levine & Doherty, 1991).

Failure to Report Child Abuse

An admission of child abuse by a patient is not always reported by the therapist. Many therapists regard reporting as a breach of the confidential relationship between the therapist and the patient, and in jurisdictions where penalties are not drastic, they may refuse to report. Others may fail to report child abuse because they believe that reporting will not benefit the child (Slovenko & Grossman, 1991).

Almost one-fourth of the professionals who participated in a national survey (Finkelhor & Zellman, 1991) failed to report child abuse because the family had already accepted treatment. One in five of the therapists surveyed was concerned that a report of child abuse would disrupt treatment, one in six cited the poor quality of Child Protective Services (CPS), and even more believed that they themselves could help the child better than could CPS (Finkelhor & Zellman, 1991). Thus, it appears that many therapists do not report suspected or actual cases of child abuse, despite the penalties they face for not reporting.

Problems of Mandatory Reporting

Availability of Treatment

One reason for confidentiality in psychotherapy relates to the availability of treatment, which may be frustrated by a scheme of mandatory reporting. Citing the New York State Assembly Subcommittee on Child Abuse, Finkelhor and Zellman (1991) pointed out that abusive patients may withhold medical treatment from a battered child because they are ashamed or because they fear the legal consequences of disclosure. Moreover, such patients may not only withhold treatment from the child, but may themselves avoid obtaining the treatment they need.

At Johns Hopkins University in Baltimore, a unique study (Berlin, Malin, & Dean, 1991), which assumed that psychotherapy is effective in treating child abusers, illustrated the effects of broad reporting statutes on the rate of self-referrals of child abusers for treatment.

In 1964, Maryland had passed a reporting statute requiring that child abuse be reported when suspicions of abuse emerged during a clinical examination of a child; the law did not mandate reporting disclosures made by adult patients in psychotherapy.

In 1987, Maryland enacted a new statute requiring that child sexual abuse be reported when disclosed by an adult patient either seeking or in treatment unless (1) the suspected abuse occurred before the adult patient sought treatment, (2) knowledge about it was derived solely from the patient's disclosures, and (3) the patient was seeking professional assistance from a program specializing in the treatment of pedophilia.

On July 1, 1989, Maryland's reporting law changed again, this time requiring that all disclosures suggesting sexual abuse of children by adult patients either seeking or already in treatment be reported. The law provided an exception

only if such reporting violated aspects of the attorney-client privilege.

The Johns Hopkins Sexual Disorders Clinic has specialized in the evaluation and treatment of paraphiliac disorders since 1979. Until July 1988, the number of patients varied from 180 to 220 at any one time, and diagnoses of pedophilia averaged 55%. The rate of disclosure of child abuse was a little less than two per month, or about 21 per year. After July 1, 1988, when the law required that patient disclosures be reported, the number of self-referrals dropped to zero and has remained there since. Because patients have made no disclosures of relapse during treatment after the law changed, no children at risk have been identified.

Prior to July 1988, when a patient made a disclosure a variety of clinical actions were quickly initiated; these included immediate hospitalization or voluntary initiation of pharmacotherapy to suppress sexual appetite. In no instances were patients knowingly permitted to continue improper sexual activity. Thus, the availability of clinical information allowed early intervention. Now, in the absence of such disclosures, this is no longer possible. These findings suggest that a broad mandatory child abuse reporting statute reduces the number of child abusers who voluntarily seek treatment. This presumably has the effect of increasing the rate of child abuse, and is thus counterproductive if the goal of the statute is to rehabilitate child abusers.

Effective Diagnosis

The information necessary to make a proper psychotherapeutic diagnosis must almost always come from the patient since it requires full disclosure of the patient's innermost feelings, fantasies, terrors, and shame in a safe environment. A patient who does not expect confidentiality from the therapist may not make the necessary disclosures, making the diagnosis inaccurate. If the diagnosis is inaccurate, the patient may be treated incorrectly. If the untreated illness is related to child abuse, the lack of the confidentiality that promotes disclosures and thus aids in diagnosis may defeat the very purpose of reporting laws.

Another problem with reporting is that the patient, having learned of the therapist's act of reporting, may discontinue treatment entirely or merely withhold, deliberately or subconsciously, the frank disclosure necessary for effective psychotherapy. Moreover, when the patient is the suspected child abuser and is subject to criminal prosecution, reporting may contravene the therapist's duty to promote healing (Finkelhor & Zellman, 1991). Proponents of reporting laws, however, argue that prosecution of the child abuser is therapeutic for the abuser's victim and spouse because it empowers them, and for the abuser because it establishes and subjects the abuser to normative rules and consequences.

Commentators differ on how to address confidentiality problems that are presented by mandatory child abuse reporting statutes. Some argue that a therapist should not disclose a patient's confidences, even with the patient's consent, if the use of the information will have adverse legal consequences for the patient. One commentator noted that "[i]f the psychiatrist speaks out in court in the patient's behalf, he becomes an ally against an outside adversary; if he speaks against his patient, he becomes an enemy. In either case, he abrogates his therapeutic role and takes another, and potentially incompatible role" (Finkelhor & Zellman, 1991, p. 132).

Alternatively, a therapist may choose to warn patients prior to treatment that any information they volunteer regarding past sexual abuse of a child for which they have not already been charged will trigger a report to the authorities, as required by ethical principles, as well as by the Supreme Court's decision in *Estelle v. Smith* (1981) in the case of court-ordered examinations. Similarly, a therapist may choose to warn a patient, either when the therapist believes that disclosure is imminent or in the form of a blanket warning at the beginning of therapy, about mandatory reporting laws. The patient may heed the warning and withdraw from therapy, or fail to

participate effectively. It should be noted that although required child abuse reports are immune from civil liability, ill-advised warnings are not (Agatstein, 1989). Legal risks to therapists from informing their patients about what the law requires, however, are minimal.

Problems with Reporting Statutes

There are many criticisms of current reporting laws. Some statutes are poorly written and very broad, which may interfere with therapy and, in some cases, even be counterproductive (Slovenko & Grossman, 1991). Also, although there is a general consensus among legal scholars and some clinicians that required reporting is essential to deal with the problem of child abuse, other clinicians have argued that child abuse reporting statutes lead to both under- and overreporting (Miller & Weinstock, 1987). Additionally, while mandatory child abuse reporting is demonstrably beneficial to some abused children, it may actually cause problems for other children by premature removal from the home and by interfering with the ability of abusing parents to deal with their problems and reintegrate their families (Miller & Weinstock, 1987).

Child abuse reporting statutes in general may not be effective in preventing or decreasing the incidence of child abuse, for several reasons. First, many child abusers are not prosecuted, chiefly because of the reluctance of child victims to testify due to their lack of credibility. Except in cases in which the abuse falls under sexual assault statutes, criminal sanctions for child abuse are light, and most prosecutors feel that criminal sanctions do not have any deterrent or rehabilitative effects on abusers (Miller & Weinstock, 1987).

Second, successful prosecutions of child abusers are very rare. If suspected child abuse is reported and a prima facie case is made, successful prosecution, particularly in criminal cases, is far from assured. Moreover, the investigation of a child abuse report may do more harm than good. Such an investigation can result in an intrusion by government agents (that is, CPS caseworkers) into intimate family matters that disrupts family unity, breaches family privacy, and is unsettling to the child, the suspected adult, and other family members (Agatstein, 1989).

Third, if there is a successful prosecution, the incarceration of the abuser who is an abusive parent puts a further strain on family stability because it removes a family member who, to some extent, may support the family emotionally or financially. Removal of the child to a foster home, another possible result of criminal or protective proceedings, is also highly inimical to family cohesiveness. The judgment in a successful child protection proceeding also frequently requires mandatory therapy for the abuser. This result may be achieved earlier, more effectively, and at less cost to the state through skillful intervention by the family's own therapist, assuming the family has one (Agatstein, 1989, citing Brandon, 1980; Brakel, Parry, & Weiner, 1985; Joseph & Onek, 1991). Furthermore, government intervention may breed resentment, hostility, and retaliation by the alleged abuser, and thus the incidence of child abuse or family violence may actually increase (Agatstein, 1989, citing Miller & Weinstock, 1987). Of course, some situations are beyond repair, and serious risk of harm to a child takes precedence over family cohesiveness.

Mandatory child abuse reporting laws may have adverse effects on therapists as well as on affected families. Mandatory reporting can violate the therapist's contractual obligation and ethical duty to use his or her best professional judgment on behalf of the patient. Mandatory reporting also involves the therapist in a personal conflict of interest and presents the therapist with the prospect of serious economic harm: in most instances, mandatory and voluntary child abuse reporters are immune from tort liability; however, many statutes expressly create a civil cause of action against therapists who fail to report when required to do so. Thus, the pressure to report all instances of suspected child abuse, as well as the desire to avoid personal liability, may skew professional judgment, forcing the therapist to weigh his or her own legal interests against the therapeutic needs of the patient (Agatstein, 1989, citing Miller & Weinstock, 1987).

Child abuse agencies and the police sometimes wish to involve the therapist in violating the patient's confidentiality solely for the purpose of prosecution, rather than to fulfill the original intent of protecting the child. These trends are often unchallenged or viewed with minimal concern by therapists. It can eventually result in using therapists as de facto "undercover" agents for the police (Weinstock & Weinstock, 1989). Some argue, however, that punishment of the abuser protects the child.

Other serious concerns are raised by mandatory reporting statutes: they are irreconcilable with patients' legitimate interest in privacy, they are irreducibly opposed to the principle of patient care, and they frustrate the exercise of the therapist's independence and professional judgment. Furthermore, attempts by therapists to explain the mandatory reporting requirement to patients may create additional problems, since patients may not be aware of these requirements when they first seek out psychiatric examination and treatment (Agatstein, 1989). Therapists may thus prefer to exercise discretion concerning when to advise their patients about them.

Reporting Statute Reform Proposal

Many proposals for correcting the shortcomings of mandatory child abuse reporting statutes have been advanced. One of these is that statutes should define exactly what behavior constitutes abuse or neglect and what type of evidence is necessary to trigger a report (Miller & Weinstock, 1987).

Flexible Reporting

Another popular proposal is for more flexibility in reporting statutes (Finkelhor & Zellman, 1991). In one version, state CPS agencies would establish a process to grant "registered reporter" status to qualified professionals. Registration would be open only to professionals with documented formal child abuse prevention training and experience who could establish that they had made reports to the CPS agencies in the past. The agencies would establish specific reporting options for those registered reporters, to be implemented under designated circumstances. One such option might be that of deferring a particular report; another option might be to make a confidential report, deferring an investigation; deferral could be indefinite if no child was in immediate jeopardy and if reporting would disrupt an ongoing therapeutic relationship in which the abuse is being addressed.

Such a flexible reporting scheme would include notification requirements; for example, registered reporters would have to notify CPS of the case, with an explanation for the deferral or a description of the treatment plan, but without identifying the child or the family; identification would be required, however, if the situation became more serious or if the child or family left the supervision of the registered reporter without a successful resolution of the problem. CPS would periodically review the records submitted by registered reporters to monitor compliance with the system. Under certain specific circumstances, deferred or confidential reporting would not be permitted—for example, when serious harm was imminent or had already occurred, or when a criminal investigation might otherwise be warranted.

The benefits of such a flexible reporting system would be many. The overloaded child abuse reporting system could be spared from immediate investigation of certain cases already under the supervision of a skilled child abuse professional. The system would formalize and regulate practices that are already widespread but covert and unmonitored. By bringing law and practice into better alignment, professionals would more wholeheartedly support the reporting law.

Flexible reporting might also result in better protective practices. The system would encourage community professionals and agencies to take more responsibility for the investigation, monitoring, and treatment of abusive families, who might not otherwise get attention from CPS agencies, leaving more CPS resources for children who are wholly dependent on them. Such a system would also deprive certain chronically noncomplying professionals of a number of their rationalizations for not reporting and possibly push them into compliance. Finally, the system might result in improved data collection and statistics on child abuse.

A flexible reporting system would also have drawbacks. It would offer greater protection to middle-class families, who seek the care of registered reporters, than to working-class families, who would be reported and investigated by CPS agencies. However, the existing system is already badly skewed by social class, with indications that professionals serving the middle class are the ones least likely to report. If some of these professionals could be drawn into the reporting system because of its greater flexibility, the monitoring of middle-class child abuse might actually increase. It has also been suggested that registered reporter status is unlikely to attract MHPs opposed to reporting, since participation in the system would require effort, both to qualify and to apply for registered reporter status, and would require filing of information when deferred or confidential reports are made (Finkelhor & Zellman, 1991).

Conclusion

Ultimately, in the area of mandatory child abuse reporting statutes society must decide whether it wants to emphasize a criminal justice approach by prosecuting offenders or a public health approach by placing a priority on the identification and treatment of abused children and child abusers (Berlin, Malin, & Dean, 1991). Perhaps legal policies that are sensitive to the impact on therapy but have not lost sight of the need to protect children can include but move beyond these two alternatives. Additional empirical research may help to determine whether such a synthesis is possible.

At the moment it seems that the best available approach is to respect abuser-patients' or victim-patients' autonomy, which means informing them of their right to privacy and confidentiality and of the fact that some of their communications to the therapist are privileged and others are not. The patient should make the ultimate decision regarding which information is kept confidential and which, if any, may be divulged, except when the therapist has a statutory duty requiring restriction of the patient's confidentiality, or when the demands of respect for autonomy have to yield to other moral demands, such as the rights of others. Moreover, the patient should be made as aware as possible at the beginning of treatment of the limitations placed on confidentiality.

In the specific case of child abuse reporting, it is the present authors' contention that confidentiality should be breached only to prevent current or potential danger to a child. In all other situations, confidentiality should be maintained (Weinstock & Weinstock, 1989). Therapists who report suspected child abuse by their patients should also not be required to testify against them in any subsequent criminal proceedings related to the past abuse (Miller & Weinstock, 1987). In this way, the therapist can shield other confidential information of the patient, and this, in turn, will best protect and further the psychotherapeutic relationship.

References

Agatstein, D. J. (1989). Child abuse reporting in New York state: The dilemma of the mental health professional. *New York Law School Law Review, 34,* 115–168.

Berlin, F. S., Malin, H. M., & Dean S. (1991).

Effects of statutes requiring psychiatrists to report suspected sexual abuse of children. *American Journal of Psychiatry, 148,* 449–453.

Bowers v. Hardwick, 478 U.S. 186 (1985).

Brakel, S. J., Parry, J., & Weiner, B. A. (1985). *The mentally disabled and the law* (3rd ed.). Chicago: American Bar Foundation.

Brandon. (1980). The psychiatrist in child abuse: Ethical and role conflicts. In C. Kempe, A. W. Franklin, & C. Cooper (Eds.), *The abused child in the family and in the community: Selected papers from the Second International Congress on Child Abuse and Neglect.* Elmsford, NY: Pergamon Press.

Bremer v. State, 18 Md. App. 291, 307A.2d 503 (1973).

Caesar v. Mountanos, 542 F.2d 1064 (9th Cir. 1976), cert. denied, 430 U.S. 954 (1977).

Committee on Confidentiality. (1987). Official actions, Guidelines on Confidentiality. *American Journal of Psychiatry, 144,* 1522–1526.

Domb, B. (1990–1991). I shot the sheriff, but only my analyst knows: Shrinking the psychotherapist-patient privilege. *Journal of Law and Health, 5,* 209–236.

Eisenstadt v. Baird, 405 U.S. 438 (1972).

Estelle v. Smith, 101 S. Ct. 1886 (1981).

Felthous, A. (1989). *Psychotherapist's duty to warn or protect.* Springfield, IL: Charles C Thomas.

Finkelhor, D., & Zellman, G. (1991). Flexible reporting options for skilled child abuse professionals. *Child Abuse and Neglect, 15,* 335–341.

Gavison, R. (1980). Privacy and the limits of the law. *Yale Law Journal, 89,* 421–472.

Griswold v. Connecticut, 381 U.S. 479 (1965).

Hawaii Psychiatric Society v. Ariyoshi, 481 F. Supp. 1028 (D. Hawaii, 1979).

Joseph, D., & Onek, J. (1991). Confidentiality in psychiatry. In S. Bloch & P. Chodoff (Eds.), *Psychiatric Ethics* (pp. 313–340). Oxford, England: Oxford University Press.

Levine, M., & Doherty, E. (1991). Professional issues, the Fifth Amendment, and therapeutic requirements to admit abuse. *Criminal Justice and Behavior, 18,* 98–112.

In re Lifschutz, 2 Cal. 3d 415, 467 P.2d 557, 85 Cal. Rptr. 829 (1970).

Macklin, R. (1992). Privacy and control of genetic information. In G. J. Annas & S. Elias (Eds.), *Gene mapping: Using law and ethics as guides* (pp. 157–172). New York: Oxford University Press.

Miller, R. D., & Weinstock, R. (1987). Conflict of interest between therapist-patient confidentiality and the duty to report sexual abuse of children. *Behavioral Science and the Law, 5,* 161–174.

Note. (1991). The constitutional protection of informational privacy. *Boston University Law Review, 71,* 133–160.

Rennert, S. (1991). *AIDS/HIV and confidentiality: 333 model policy and procedures.* Washington, DC: American Bar Association.

Roe v. Wade, 410 U.S. 113 (1973).

Shuman, D. W. (1985). The origins of the physician-patient privilege and professional secret. *Southwestern Law Journal, 39,* 661–687.

Shuman, D. W., & Weiner, B. A. (1982). The privilege study: An empirical examination of the psychotherapist-patient privilege. *North Carolina Law Review, 60,* 893–942.

Slovenko, R. (1974). Psychotherapist-patient testimonial privilege: A picture of misguided hope. *Catholic University Law Review, 23,* 649–673.

Slovenko, R., & Grossman, E. (1991). Confidentiality and testimonial privilege. In R. Michels (Ed.), *Psychiatry* (Vol. 3, Ch. 31, pp. 1–18). Philadelphia: Lippincott.

Smith, S. R. (1980). Constitutional privacy in psychotherapy. *George Washington Law Review, 49,* 1–60.

Smith S. R. (1986–1987). Medical and psychotherapy privileges and confidentiality: On giving with one hand and removing with the other. *Kentucky Law Journal, 45,* 473–557.

Sosfin, E. S. (1985). The case for a federal psychotherapist-patient privilege that protects patient identity. *Duke Law Journal,* 1217–1244.

VandeCreek, L., Miars, R. D., & Herzog, C. E. (1987). Client anticipations and preferences for confidentiality of records. *Journal of Counseling Psychology, 34,* 62–67.

Weinstock, R., & Weinstock, D. (1989). Clinical flexibility and confidentiality: Effects of reporting laws. *Psychiatric Quarterly, 60,* 195.

Weiss, B. D. (1982). Confidentiality expectations of patients, physicians, and medical students. *Journal of the American Medical Association, 247,* 2695–2697.

Whalen v. Roe, 429 U.S. 589 (1976).

Winslade, W. J. (1982). Confidentiality of medical records. *Journal of Legal Medicine, 3,* 497–533.

Winslade, W. J., & Ross, J. W. (1985). Privacy, confidentiality, and autonomy in psychiatry. *Nebraska Law Review, 64,* 578–635.

5 ▮ Malpractice Liability of Mental Health Professionals and Institutions

Steven R. Smith
Cleveland State University

The risk of malpractice liability has become an increasingly important concern of mental health professionals (MHPs) and the institutions in which they work (Perlin, 1989; Smith & Meyer, 1987). Part of this concern relates to the economics of practice. Malpractice insurance rates have been increasing, sometimes doubling in less than a decade (Nye, Gifford, Webb, & Dewer, 1988; *Personal Injury Verdict Reviews,* 1986). A wide range of mental health professions are experiencing this increased malpractice liability (Andrade & Andrade, 1979; Gerhart & Brooks, 1985; Watkins & Watkins, 1989). Another reason for concern among MHPs is the growing sense that someone (the legal system) is overseeing the practice of the professions, with a corresponding loss of some professional independence (Smith, 1991).

Despite this heightened concern about malpractice, in reality it does not now represent a significant threat to most MHPs or institutions. The number of claims against MHPs, for example, is lower than for most other medical specialties (Robertson, 1988; Taragin, Wilczek, Karns, Trout,

The author is grateful to Barbara Mills for her assistance in preparing this chapter.

Some portions of this chapter were adapted from "Liability and Mental Health Services," by S. R. Smith, 1994, *American Journal of Orthopsychiatry, 64*(2). Copyright ©1994 American Orthopsychiatric Association, Inc. Used with permission.

& Carson, 1992). Furthermore, only a small percentage of negligent events result in any claim being filed, and only a small proportion of those claims result in any recovery (Danzon, 1985; Harvard Medical Practice Study, 1990). It is also important to note that MHPs are not helpless in the face of malpractice liability—the way they practice has a great impact on the probability that they will face a successful malpractice claim.

In this chapter, I review the malpractice liability principles that apply to MHPs and mental health institutions, discuss the areas of practice in which malpractice claims are most likely to occur, review steps professionals and institutions can take to reduce malpractice claims, consider problems with the current system of liability, and suggest reforms that will address some of these problems. Because the liability problems of mental health institutions (including such small institutions as some professionals' offices) raise special liability issues, I will also consider the concerns of institutions.

The current focus on national health care reform makes it particularly important to consider what changes should be made in the system of malpractice liability. Many of the health reform proposals contain provisions to modify the malpractice system. Even if none of these proposals is adopted immediately, the discussion of professional liability issues is likely to continue for some time. I will, therefore, focus attention on ways mental health malpractice claims might better be resolved. These reforms are described near the end of this chapter.

Malpractice Principles and Process

Injuries arise out of almost any human activity, and one function of a legal system is to decide who will bear the burden of these losses. With some exceptions, our society has generally let the burden of losses fall on those unfortunate enough to have been injured, except where someone has carelessly or intentionally caused harm to another. Where someone's fault has caused harm, we generally shift the loss from the injured party to the one causing the harm. While I take the fault system as a "given" and discuss it throughout this chapter as the primary basis for liability, it is not divinely ordained, and society could decide to take another approach to dealing with injuries resulting from mental health care.

Most mental health malpractice cases are based on the tort of negligence (Simon & Sadoff, 1992). Broadly stated, the principle of negligence is that someone who carelessly causes harm to another should pay for that harm. The primary goals of the negligence system are to compensate those wrongly injured and to deter careless conduct by requiring that the careless party pay for the resulting damage. To prove a negligence claim, the injured plaintiff must demonstrate that the defendant (1) had a *duty* to the plaintiff, (2) *breached* that duty, and (3) thereby *caused* (4) *injury* to the plaintiff. As a general proposition, there is a duty to act with reasonable care to avoid injuring others. In the context of health care, professionals generally have a duty to act reasonably under the circumstances to avoid harming their patients. In a few instances, professionals also owe duties to non-patient "third parties." The question in each case is whether the practitioner acted reasonably under the circumstances.

As a practical matter the "standard of care" by which a professional's duty is judged is commonly established by determining whether the care was "customary in that profession," although custom is not technically dispositive of the question of whether there was negligence. The plaintiff must also prove that the breach of duty caused the injury to the plaintiff. Not every bad event or negative outcome in mental health practice subjects a practitioner to malpractice liability. Only those bad events that result from the professional's negligence appropriately give rise to malpractice claims.

Professional liability in mental health infrequently is based on such other theories of liability as battery, intentional infliction of emotional distress, false imprisonment, breach of contract, or federal civil rights liability (Smith, 1991). Furthermore, new forms of liability continue to arise from mental health practice. For example, in two instances formal action was taken against MHPs for insider trading securities violations. The professionals in these cases received information from patients whose families were business "insiders" and traded in securities based on that confidential information (Nash, 1986; *United States v. Willis*, 1990).

Institutional Liability

Mental health institutions face some special liability issues. Institutions incur liability for the torts of their employees and agents in two major ways: through negligence for failure to provide reasonable care in the selection and supervision of their employees and others in the institution, and through vicarious liability (discussed below) (Berry, 1988; Kanute, 1989; Lisko, 1978; Southwick, 1983). Depending on the nature of the institution, it (or its employees) may also have liability under federal civil rights laws or a variety of other specific state or federal statutes. Because direct liability and vicarious liability have somewhat different implications for mental health institutions, these two forms of liability will be considered separately.

Negligence

Health care institutions have an obligation to exercise care in selecting and supervising their employees and professional staff and in granting practice privileges to nonemployee professionals (Copeland & Brown, 1990). The duty to select staff carefully includes the obligation to establish appropriate employment criteria (educational background and experience), and to check the qualifications and credentials of applicants before they are hired or granted staff privileges. The required level of investigation varies with the sensitivity of the position and the potential harm that an incompetent in that position could cause. Thus, much more careful checking of a staff physician would be required than of a laundry attendant. In the case of professionals, routine checks should include inquiries of established registries and state licensing authorities as to whether discipline and liability claims have been brought against the professional. Given the level of credential fraud that occurs, it is also appropriate to request formal documentation of credentials, including licenses and transcripts, from professionals in the institution.

During the last few decades, health institutions have become responsible for providing increasingly high levels of supervision of the work of professionals (*Darling v. Charleston Community Memorial Hosp.*, 1965). This supervision should include periodic reviews to assess the quality of practice and mechanisms to ensure that professionals are not practicing beyond the scope of their authority or expertise. The failure to exercise adequate supervision may result in liability.

Professional organizations have recognized the importance of such supervision in their accreditation requirements and professional standards (Joint Commission on the Accreditation of Healthcare Organizations, 1993; Roberts, Coale, & Redman, 1987). As mental institutions become more complex and include a greater range of professionals, supervision has become increasingly important. All institutions should have for-

mal, periodic staff reviews to ensure that MHPs and other professionals are competent, that they have the necessary training for practice, that they are adequately supervised, and that they are limiting their practice to those areas in which they have demonstrated competence. Special supervision is required for those in training and for those conducting human experimentation (these issues are considered below). Institutions must also ensure that they have the equipment that is appropriate for the procedures conducted in the institution, that the equipment is properly maintained, and that there is sufficient security to avoid unnecessary accidents.

The obligation to use care in selection and supervision applies not only to employees and agents but also to those with staff privileges and others who are technically not employees of the institution. The failure of an institution to act with reasonable care in the selection and supervision of staff in establishing and enforcing operating policies designed to protect patients from unnecessary injuries, or in acquiring and properly maintaining proper equipment, is negligence for which the institution is subject to liability (Keeton, Dobbs, Keeton, & Owen, 1984).

Vicarious Liability

Vicarious liability or agency liability—an alternative theory of liability—is a legal rule that makes an employer or principal liable for the torts of its employees or agents (Southwick, 1983). Vicarious liability is intended to encourage great care in the selection and supervision of employees and agents and to include the cost of employee carelessness in the price of goods and services. Because the law imposes vicarious liability on mental health institutions whether or not the institution has exercised all possible care, the rules of agency may have a significant impact on the level of institutional liability.

Traditionally, institutions were vicariously liable for the torts of their agents but not for "independent contractors." Vicarious liability did not arise from the actions of such other potential tortfeasors (those who commit torts) as nonemployee physicians with staff privileges, because there was no employment relationship and the physician was merely an independent contractor (Klages, 1988–1989; Southwick, 1983). That doctrine has been significantly eroded in recent years. Courts increasingly find mental health institutions vicariously liable for the torts of independent professionals under the doctrine of "ostensible" or "apparent" agency. This doctrine applies if the institution or professional gives the incorrect impression that the professional is an agent or employee of the institution (Brown, 1988; Combs, 1987; Firman, 1988). Advertising, group practice, professional listings, and the like may all give the appearance of an agency relationship and set up ostensible agency vicarious liability (Thompson, 1990).

Liability Arising in Practice

Negligence liability can arise from virtually any area of mental health practice (Pope, 1989; Robertson, 1988; Smith, 1991). The type of claim that is most common varies from one mental health profession to another. This section briefly identifies a number of areas of practice in which liability may arise. Where institutions have employees or agents (or others who appear to be agents) who are negligent in these areas, they may also be liable through vicarious liability or negligent selection or supervision, as noted above.

Sexual Misconduct

Sexual relationships between patients and therapists are probably the most common source of malpractice claims against MHPs (Perry & Kurue, 1993). Courts have recognized that the nature of the therapist-patient relationship and the patient's great dependence on the therapist

make it easy for the therapist to take advantage of the patient (*Mazza v. Huffaker*, 1983; *Nicholson v. Han*, 1968; *Roy v. Hartogs*, 1976). The therapist who does so is acting unethically and is subject to civil liability (*Doe v. Samaritan Counseling Center*, 1993; Epstein, 1989; Stone, 1976). The recent public attention focused on the harm from therapist-patient sexual relations suggests that liability from this form of misconduct may increase (Robertson, 1992). An increasing number of states also make it a crime for a therapist to engage in sexual relations with a patient (Appelbaum, 1990; Baker, 1993; *Colo. Rev. Stat.* (1989); *Minn. Stat. Ann.* (1989); *N.D. Cent. Code* (1988); Strasburger, Jorgensen, & Randles, 1991; *Wis. Stat. Ann.* (1989)).

Consent is not a defense against these claims. A patient cannot freely consent to engage in therapist-patient sexual relations because of the nature of the relationship between patient and therapist—especially because of the patient's emotional dependence on the therapist.

Many malpractice insurance carriers have sought to reduce their liability exposure from therapists' sexual relations with patients by excluding or limiting policy coverage for such claims. As a result, to seek recovery from liability insurance policies, plaintiffs have come to base their sexual misconduct claims on other bases, notably claiming that injury from the sexual contact was a result of negligence in handling the transference phenomenon—failing to take adequate steps to address the patient's feelings about another person to the MHP (Cummings & Sobel, 1985; Jorgenson, Bisbing, & Sutherland, 1992; Morin, 1989).

Institutions have sometimes successfully claimed that they should not be liable for the sexual misconduct of their employees because, among other things, that misconduct is not part of the professional duties of the employees and is a "personal frolic." Using such legal theories as "negligence in managing transference," plaintiffs have still been able to involve institutions for the liability resulting from the sexual conduct between patients and professional staff.

The Duty to Protect (or Warn)

The landmark decision in *Tarasoff v. Regents of the Univ. of California* (1976) began to establish the principle that therapists have a duty to take reasonable steps to protect identifiable victims of their dangerous patients. Although some commentators and courts emphasize the "duty to warn" the intended victims of the danger so that they can take steps to protect themselves, that does not accurately describe the duty. It is more accurately seen as a duty to take reasonable steps to protect potential victims from dangerous patients. In some circumstances that may not be warning the victim, but rather taking such other action as hospitalizing the patient or removing the patient from a potentially dangerous situation.

Although the exact contours of the duty to protect or warn vary from state to state and are currently unclear in many states, several generalizations are possible. Most states impose some form of *Tarasoff*-type duty on MHPs. That duty requires that a therapist take reasonable steps (especially warning the intended victim or police) where there is a significant risk of physical injury to an identifiable victim of the therapist (Crocker, 1985). Several states have passed "*Tarasoff* statutes." Some professional organizations have sought these laws to limit therapists' responsibility to divulge otherwise confidential information about patients. These laws, however, are often badly written and frequently do not significantly reduce the *Tarasoff* duty (Smith, 1991).

Tarasoff cases have received substantial attention from professionals and commentators despite the fact that relatively few of these cases have been litigated. In part, this reflects the potential for substantial damages in these cases. Of greater importance, however, is the conceptual change that *Tarasoff* brought. The *Tarasoff* duty may require that a therapist breach confidentiality for the good of society at the expense of patient privacy. Moreover, *Tarasoff* expands the limited "duty" of MHPs beyond its traditional limits in that liability is not to the MHPs' patients but to unrelated third parties (Carstensen, 1994).

Other Obligations to Third Parties

If the *Tarasoff* case was notable because it imposed legal duties on therapists to protect third parties, a recent case suggests that such third-party liability may, indeed, be expanding. Because the case involves a trial court jury decision without a formal appellate court decision as this chapter was written, press reports provide the accounts of the case (Ayres, 1994). Defendants Isabella and Rose treated Holly Ramona as a patient. During the course of this treatment, which included a session with sodium amytal used as a "truth serum," Ms. Ramona "remembered" sexual abuse early in her life at the hands of her father. The treatment thus included elements not generally regarded as scientifically sound in recovering previously repressed memories. Ms. Ramona confronted her father, and following the accusations her father lost his job and was divorced. The father (who was a third party because he had not been a patient of the therapists) sued the two therapists and the hospital in which they practiced. The jury returned a verdict in favor of the father for $500,000 (Ayres, 1994).

This case has not been reviewed by appellate courts. Nonetheless, it represents an example of the expansion of third-party duties that may be occurring. The reporting obligations imposed by statutes discussed later in this section are still another example of third-party duties.

Providing Treatment without Consent

MHPs theoretically must obtain informed consent before any treatment is begun, and informed consent issues appear repeatedly in discussions of malpractice claims. In reality, however, failure of informed consent is not a significant source of liability for MHPs unless there is also a physical injury or some form of misconduct or negligence in providing the treatment (Faden, Beauchamp, & King, 1986). For example, where a patient suffered a compression fracture of the spine as a result of electroconvulsive therapy (ECT) but had not been informed prior to treatment of the risk of that injury, the court granted recovery based on a failure of informed consent (*Mitchell v. Robinson*, 1960; *Woods v. Brumlop*, 1962). Other forms of treatment, such as administration of aversive therapies and prescription drugs that involve substantial physical contact, ordinarily require informed consent (*Knecht v. Gillman*, 1973; *Mackey v. Procunier*, 1973). For instance, a patient receiving prescription drugs should be informed about such potential serious side effects as tardive dyskinesia (a neurological disorder, associated with antipsychotic medications, that causes involuntary muscle movements), changes in mood, and addiction (Appleton, 1968; Merrill, 1973; Wettstein, 1983). Therefore, psychiatrists who prescribe drugs should make reasonable efforts to inform patients of how to use the drugs and the consequences of using them, as well as making them aware of alternative treatments that may be available.

Inadequate Diagnosis

Mental health malpractice may result from a therapist's failure to test or diagnose patients adequately when that failure leads to some injury (Slawson & Guggenheim, 1984; Wright, 1981). For instance, liability may be predicated on a negligently conducted examination leading to the prescription of unnecessary medication that injures the patient. Additionally, negligent diagnosis may result from failure to perform an adequate examination; failure to understand the nature, limitations, and proper uses of psychological tests; failure to draw conclusions reasonably arising from the examination; or failure to administer tests properly (Bach, 1989; Busch & Cavanaugh, 1985; *Naccarato v. Grob*, 1970; *Szimonisz v. United States*, 1982).

Failure to Prevent Suicide and Negligent Release

Therapists must act reasonably to diagnose and supervise patients who are at risk for suicide

(*Abille v. United States*, 1980; *Meier v. Ross Gen. Hosp.*, 1968; *Pisel v. Stamford Hosp.*, 1980). Negligence may arise, for example, from suicide that is a result of the failure to examine the patient adequately; recognize common indications of potential suicide; or appropriately supervise, restrain, or treat the patient. The cases are sometimes called "negligent release" cases when patients injure themselves or others following inappropriate release from an institution (Poythress & Brodsky, 1992).

Professionals are not required to prevent all suicides; they need only take reasonable steps to do so (Berman & Cohen-Sandler, 1983; Bongar, 1991). Courts recognize that the threat of suicide must be balanced against other risks and values, including freedom from restraint or the risks of some medications. As one court noted, "Calculated risks of necessity must be taken if the modern and enlightened treatment of the mentally ill is to be pursued intelligently and rationally. Neither the hospital nor the doctor are insurers of the patient's health and safety" (*Baker v. United States*, 1965, p. 135). The risks must be reasonable, however. The problem MHPs encounter is that in hindsight the risk of suicide often appears more obvious than it did before the event (Arkes, Faust, & Guilmette, 1988; Wexler & Schopp, 1989).

Referral to Other Practitioners

Some clients present problems that a particular professional cannot adequately address. For example, the patient may require sophisticated psychological testing that a psychiatrist is not competent to conduct, or a patient being seen by a psychologist may need medical intervention. In such circumstances, the professional must refer the patient to another professional. If injury results from a therapist who negligently fails to refer the patient, the therapist will be subject to liability (*Cestone v. Harkavy*, 1935; Morreim, 1989).

When referral is necessary because of personal feelings or other conflicts with a patient, the professional must make arrangements for the patient to be transferred to another therapist. The therapist must not "dump" or suddenly stop seeing a patient. After treatment has begun, the professional's failure to attend to the patient or to make reasonable provision for the patient to see another competent professional may constitute abandonment (Schutz, 1982; Shapiro, 1986; Weddington & Cavenar, 1979).

Electroconvulsive Therapy

In the past, ECT raised so many malpractice concerns that some insurance companies applied surcharges to cover it. The current claims arising from ECT do not justify this fear (Perr, 1980; Taub, 1987; Winslade, Liston, Ross, & Weber, 1984). Several theories of negligence provide the basis for ECT claims, including failure to obtain proper informed consent, prescribing unnecessary ECT, or negligently administering it (Abrams, 1989).

Prescribing Drugs

The misuse of psychoactive prescription drugs is a potential source of malpractice litigation because of the risk of harm to patients (Farrell, 1992; Slawson & Guggenheim, 1984). By definition, prescription drugs involve risks, and improperly prescribing them or failing to give adequate instructions poses an unnecessary risk to patients. The bases of liability include failure of informed consent, failure to prescribe the proper medication, inappropriate or unnecessary prescription, and negligent administration of drugs (*Clites v. State*, 1982; Kramer, 1988; Mills & Eth, 1987; *Ohligschlager v. Proctor Community Hosp.*, 1973; Tancredi, 1988).

Breach of Confidentiality

Therapists have ethical and legal obligations to maintain the secrets of their patients (Smith, 1987). Failure to do so may result in liability for invasion of privacy, negligence, or breach of contract. The duty to protect confidentiality exists whether or not a psychotherapist-patient testimonial privilege covers the communication (Shuman & Weiner, 1987). (The "privilege" prevents the disclosure in courts and other formal legal proceedings of information from therapy and is, therefore, distinguishable from "confidentiality," which is the broader professional obligation not to reveal patient secrets but which does not apply in legal proceedings.)

The duty of confidentiality is not absolute (Smith, 1987). When competent, patients may waive confidentiality and approve the release of information. A limited waiver by a patient, however, does not permit an unlimited disclosure of such information by the therapist. For instance, permission to inform an insurance company of therapy does not include the right of the professional to write a book describing the patient and the therapy (*Doe v. Roe*, 1977). Therapists are sometimes obligated to breach confidentiality. For example, when therapists receive information concerning child abuse or a valid court order requiring the release of information, they are required to release such information and may do so without incurring liability (Smith & Meyer, 1984).

Involuntary Civil Commitment and Detention

Participation in the civil commitment process infrequently subjects MHPs to liability. Most states provide immunity so long as the professional acts in good faith. If the professional is not acting in good faith, efforts to detain or commit a patient involuntarily may result in liability for false imprisonment or other intentional torts (deliberate, unprivileged harmful or offensive contact with another person) (Knapp & VandeCreek, 1987; *Lanier v. Sallas*, 1985). In addition, the mistreatment of patients (such as through beatings or unreasonable restraint) or the unreasonable withholding of available treatment also may subject the professional to common law or civil rights liability (Perlin, 1989).

In a related area, improper "voluntary" commitment may result in liability. The U.S. Supreme Court has held that civil rights liability may arise when a clearly incompetent patient is held in a mental hospital under his own "consent" (*Zinermon v. Burch*, 1990). In that situation, the consent is legally ineffective and the decision to hold the patient without a judicial proceeding (for example, through civil commitment or guardianship) may deprive the patient of liberty without due process of law in violation of the Fourteenth Amendment to the Constitution.

Reporting Obligations

All states have child abuse reporting statutes (see Chapter 4) (Besharov, 1983; Fraser, 1978; Newberger, 1985), and an increasing number have laws that require persons to report other forms of abuse, such as spouse or elder abuse (Smith, 1987). By requiring reporting, the state can intervene to prevent further injury and decide whether to prosecute the abuser.

State abuse reporting laws generally require the reporting of known or suspected physical, sexual, or emotional abuse, or neglect. Abuse and neglect are generally very broadly defined in these statutes. Although the law varies from state to state, in some states the obligation to report arises regardless of the source of the information (Miller & Weinstock, 1987; Smith & Meyer, 1984; Weinstock & Weinstock, 1988). In most states, MHPs who learn of abuse from patients who have experienced abuse must report that abuse to the state. The failure to file the required reports may result in civil liability, and virtually all states make it a crime to knowingly fail to report abuse (Smith & Meyer, 1987).

Supervision of Other Professionals and Students

All mental health students and many professionals work under the supervision of others. This raises legal issues regarding how carefully the supervisor reviews the supervisee's practice, ensuring acceptable levels of care and the adequacy of informed consent (Kapp, 1984; Wagner, Pollard, & Wagner, 1993). There are few reported legal cases involving injuries suffered because of inadequate treatment by those in training (Kapp, 1983; *McBride v. United States*, 1972; *Rush v. Akron Gen. Hosp.*, 1957). Professionals must nevertheless ensure that those under their supervision maintain the quality of treatment and do not extend themselves beyond their level of training or expertise. This obligation goes beyond merely signing treatment or assessment reports and informing students when they make mistakes. Supervision should be sufficiently intense to protect patients from receiving inferior levels of care.

Test Construction and Validation

MHPs have become increasingly involved in the development and validation of many forms of tests, particularly employment and education tests (Bersoff, 1981; Smith & Meyer, 1987). Defective test design or defective validation may result in a test that does not do what it purports to do or that is illegally discriminatory. This may harm those relying on the test (such as an employer) as well as the test takers (for example, a prospective employee). Traditionally, such defects did not result in significant liability partly because the doctrine of "limited duty"—that the test's developers have a duty only toward the person to whom the test was sold, not toward the person to whom it was administered—made it difficult for test takers to recover (Keeton et al., 1984). MHPs cannot assume that this tradition will continue. In a case involving a psychologist who developed a city employment test that had disparate impact on women (*Zamlen v. Cleveland*, 1988), a claim against the test developer was settled for a substantial amount. The Title VII settlement went to those who had been disadvantaged by the test, not to the city organization that had paid to have the test developed. This again demonstrates the expansion of liability to "third parties."

Nontraditional Therapy

In recent years, a number of nontraditional and "pop" therapies have been developed, some of which attract people with serious emotional problems. The training available to or taken by the practitioners of these forms of therapy varies widely. As a general matter, state licenses are not required to "practice" many nontraditional therapies (Smith & Meyer, 1987).

Unsettled questions remain regarding the extent to which practitioners of unconventional therapies should be held liable when the counseling results in injury (for instance, suicide), and whether practitioners of nontraditional therapies should be held to the standard care of psychotherapists generally (Perlin, 1989). On the one hand, the argument is that to protect patients from ineffective therapy and charlatans, practitioners of nontraditional therapies should be held to the same standard of care as traditional psychotherapists ("Standard of Care," 1974). The application of a lesser standard would encourage the development of potentially harmful "pop" therapies. On the other hand, it is argued that applying the standard of care of ordinary psychotherapy to nontraditional forms is unfair and will discourage the development of new, potentially effective therapies (Hogan, 1974).

There is a strong argument that those practicing nontraditional forms of therapy should have a duty to recognize and refer to appropriate professionals those clients who are suicidal and those with serious emotional problems who may be harmed by the nontraditional therapy (Orr, 1989–1990). By claiming to be counselors or therapists, the nontraditional practitioners hold themselves out as having sufficient training and skills to identify serious emotional problems, and so they should be held to exercising a commensurate standard of care.

Realities of the Malpractice System

While the current system of mental health malpractice liability is an extension of the general tort liability principles of American law, in many ways those principles do not work well when applied to injuries from mental health services. The malpractice system is generally a complex, time-consuming, and difficult process. Plaintiffs often find it hard to meet the requirement to prove a breach of duty, causation, and damages. Furthermore, the process of settlement and negotiation and the role of malpractice insurance frequently complicate matters.

Proving Negligence

Proving the elements of negligence is difficult in many mental health malpractice cases. Negligence requires a standard of professional care against which the actions of the defendant-professional can be measured. Liability exists only if the professional has failed to provide a level of care that would be provided by a reasonably prudent professional (Federici & Doering, 1989). Given professional disagreements about the treatment and causes of mental illness, the standard of practice for MHPs is not as clearly defined as it is in many areas of medicine (Hampton, 1984; Hogan, 1977; Knapp & VandeCreek, 1981). For instance, the standard of practice for the treatment of acute appendicitis is fairly uniform and clear; the standard of practice for the treatment of schizophrenia is not (Modlin, 1990). The absence of a clear "correct" treatment makes it difficult to assess and prove the reasonableness of a therapist's treatment decisions (Federici & Doering, 1989; Leesfield, 1987).

Proving causation may be equally difficult. The causes of emotional and psychological injuries are often difficult to identify with certainty. Therefore, a patient claiming therapy-related injury may not be able to demonstrate that the faulty therapy caused the harm. Additionally, because patients generally suffer from mental problems before seeking therapy, any psychological injury may appear to be part of the preexisting mental illness rather than the result of malpractice (Nieland, 1979).

Damages also may be hard to prove (Paquin, 1988). Emotional injuries are very real and painful, but to a jury they may not be as obvious or gruesome as physical injuries. Furthermore, the law traditionally has been reluctant to recognize emotional or mental injuries, except when they relate to physical harm. Thus, the large verdict awards in mental health cases may occur when clear physical injuries exist—for example, in suicide, prescription drug, and dangerous patient cases.

For these reasons, the negligence system is often unwieldy in mental health cases. Expert witnesses may disagree about whether treatment was reasonable, whether the treatment caused the injury, or even whether there was an injury. Lay juries and judges are left to sort out these issues and to determine disputed scientific questions.

Settlement and Negotiation

Only a very small percentage of civil cases actually go to trial. The vast majority are settled through negotiation. Often the process of negotiation does not begin in earnest until after pretrial discovery of evidence, including depositions, has been completed. At that point, both parties have a reasonably complete understanding of what will be presented at trial. The attorneys know that although they must prepare for trial, it is likely that they will negotiate a settlement. As a result, part of the pretrial process is to gain maximum negotiating advantage over the opponent. A party may try to increase the cost or pain of litigation for the other party to "soften up" the party to encourage settlement on advantageous terms. For example, one party may inundate another party with motions and with requests for extensive and expensive discovery and document review or may seek potentially embarrassing information. The

use of delays, emotional pressure, substantial costs, and the threat of publicity can all be weapons in the extended sparring between parties.

The negotiated settlement of cases has the advantage of limiting the public release of information because a public trial is avoided, and the parties may agree to limit the information that can be released about the settlement. Because discovery has generally occurred before settlement, however, considerable private information may already have been revealed and released. Protective orders can in some instances be obtained to limit the disclosure of information revealed in depositions and other discovery processes, but this is often of limited value in assuring patients that the privacy of intensely personal information can be protected fully.

In mental health malpractice cases where the plaintiff is the former patient, the defense has an incentive to seek to obtain a wide range of embarrassing information from therapy that occurred both before and after the alleged malpractice. For example, during depositions the defense may ask the former patient to discuss in detail the therapy sessions or to repeat very private information revealed in the confidence of therapy. The defendant-therapist may already have some of this information from therapy, but through the discovery process the defense may force the patient to recount this information and obtain additional personal information—for example, from treatment that occurred with another therapist. Thus, the discovery process may be used by the defendant to obtain private information and to inflict pain by requiring that patients retell very difficult therapy experiences. This discourages patients from bringing legitimate malpractice cases, puts emotional pressure on patient-plaintiffs in the negotiating process, and increases the emotional trauma plaintiffs are likely to experience.

Malpractice Insurance

Another feature of the current system is that virtually all malpractice claims involve an insurance company that will have the primary role in selecting an attorney for the defendant and in directing the defense. While malpractice policies commonly provide that the case cannot be settled without the consent of the defendant-professional, the interests of the insurance company and the defendant can diverge in deciding whether to settle the case and in deciding how aggressively to defend. Even if the therapist-defendant is reluctant to force a patient to reveal private information in discovery or in court, the insurance carrier may not share that reluctance in situations where it may obtain an advantage by forcing the plaintiff to reveal very private information.

Delays

Another significant reality is the length of time the process can take. A study of medical malpractice cases indicated that the average time between the filing of a claim and a final disposition was 21 months, with a range that extended to 11 years (U.S. General Accounting Office, 1987). There is generally an extended period during which both defendant and plaintiff endure substantial uncertainty and emotional distress associated with litigation. This may be particularly difficult where a plaintiff or defendant is reliving an extraordinarily painful emotional experience over and over as the case progresses. For the plaintiff it also means a prolonged period of time during which there is no compensation available for the injuries suffered.

Consequences of the Current System

The current malpractice system thus creates serious problems for many patient-plaintiffs, defendant-MHPs, and defendant-institutions. This section reviews the most significant of those problems; the next section discusses alternatives to reduce the problems.

The Effects of the System on Mental Health Professionals

The current system of processing mental health malpractice claims is generally unsatisfactory from the perspective of the defendant-professional. The fact that a malpractice suit is filed may harm the reputation of a professional even if the verdict is ultimately in the defendant's favor. Furthermore, the emotional stress of the case may be as great for a defendant exonerated of negligence as it is for those found liable (Charles & Kennedy, 1985; Hubbard, 1989; Shapiro, 1986; Weiler, 1991).

A malpractice case may also harm the relationship among mental health care providers. In many malpractice cases there are multiple defendants—that is, more than one professional or a professional plus an institution. In some cases plaintiffs use the differences in interest to drive a wedge between defendants by playing one off against the other. This may have the consequence of significantly straining the relationship among defendants who must continue to work closely after the malpractice litigation is concluded.

The Effects of the System on Patients

The current system also creates difficulties for patient-plaintiffs. Although these problems have largely gone unexplored, they are significant and go to the very heart of the values of the mental health professions (Edwards, 1989). The current system is notably inconsistent with maintaining patient confidentiality, for instance.

Confidentiality and the obligation to maintain patient secrets have been hallmarks of the mental health professions. This is logical, because psychotherapy requires that patients reveal the most sensitive information about themselves and their families and patients often disclose information that they would not tell anyone else.

Therapy deals not only with factual information that can be embarrassing, but also with the most intimate fantasies, fears, and anxieties (Smith, 1987). The professions have stressed that confidentiality is essential to successful therapy and to patient well-being (Group for the Advancement of Psychiatry, 1960; Shuman & Weiner, 1982). Publicly revealing patient secrets when patients pursue malpractice cases is, therefore, inconsistent with the basic confidentiality values of the mental health professions.

Any psychotherapist-patient relationship has presumably broken down before any malpractice litigation begins, and breach of confidentiality will therefore not harm that relationship. Concern for patient confidentiality should nevertheless remain for three reasons: (1) because of the traditional interest of the professions in protecting individual patient privacy, (2) because of the broad professional belief that threats to confidentiality generally harm the trust that patients will place in therapists, and (3) because the therapist's disclosure of patient information during litigation may harm the patient.

The public nature of malpractice cases means that the patient's extremely personal information will be revealed not just to a judge in the judge's chambers but will also be available to others. Not only will the information elicited at trial be disclosed, but considerably more information will be revealed during the discovery process described below. Plaintiffs who bring mental health malpractice claims are often forced to relive repeatedly and publicly their most troubling experiences. Like the rape victim who must confront the attacker, publicly describe the rape, and (in days past) disclose prior sexual history, injured mental health malpractice plaintiffs must agree to have the most private aspects of their lives examined, explained, attacked, and viewed in public. The patient will probably be required to publicly confront the therapist, in whom great trust and confidence were developed during therapy. The patient will have to reveal the details of that relationship. The patient may also be required to detail prior and subsequent mental

health history. Plaintiffs who undertake this emotionally difficult process, of course, are often people whose emotional difficulties and fragility probably caused them to seek psychotherapy in the first place, so the risk of emotional harm from the process may be especially high.

The difficulties facing injured patients are particularly well illustrated by patients who have been harmed by therapists' actionable breaches of confidentiality. To pursue such legal claims, plaintiffs must undertake lawsuits that will inevitably require that they publicly reveal considerably more about their emotional conditions than their therapists improperly revealed. Ironically, the patients' lawsuits probably will exacerbate the very harm for which they seek compensation.

Psychotherapist-patient privileges will not protect the patient's sensitive information during a malpractice case. There is a patient-litigant exception that destroys the privilege when the plaintiff brings his or her own mental condition into question by filing the suit (Smith, 1980). The logic for the exception is that patients should not be able to prevent the opposing parties from having information necessary to respond to the legal claims patients themselves have raised. Thus, a potential malpractice plaintiff faces the unhappy choice of giving up a potentially legitimate claim for damages or agreeing to reveal large amounts of very sensitive personal information.[1]

The privacy risk to the patient-plaintiff arises in part because the breadth of discovery in civil cases often permits inspection of the entire mental health history of the patient. Discovery is not limited to information held by the MHP against whom the malpractice case is filed. The plaintiff's mental condition before seeing the professional may be relevant to determine whether

---

[1]Third-party injury claims, where the plaintiff is not the MHP's patient (for example, *Tarasoff*-type suits), do not eliminate the privilege. Because the patient did not raise his or her own mental condition as an issue, the patient-litigant exception does not apply. Other exceptions to the privilege, however, may exist that will require release of the information (Smith, 1987).

malpractice caused the injury. Therefore, much of the information from prior psychotherapy is probably relevant and discoverable. Furthermore, the mental health and treatment of the patient subsequent to any malpractice are usually relevant to the question of damages, so information from that subsequent treatment probably will be discoverable. Thus, virtually the entire mental health history of the plaintiff may be revealed during a mental health malpractice case (Slovenko, 1974; Smith, 1987).

Reform Proposals

The problems that tort litigation presents for plaintiffs and defendants alike in mental health malpractice cases suggest the need for alternative means of handling these cases. The law does not require that all claims of malpractice be resolved through the tort system. Most disputes are settled without resorting to the courts. The formal court system is available where the parties to a dispute cannot agree on a mutually acceptable mechanism for resolving it or when an alternative mechanism was unsuccessful. Once parties are involved in a serious dispute, however, it often becomes difficult for them to agree on mechanisms for resolving the dispute and they are left with the "default" process—the tort system. Establishing a formal process by which parties to disputes can select alternative mechanisms has the advantage of providing a set framework that they need not negotiate themselves (Schor, 1988).

Clearly defined options to the civil trial system should be available to patients injured as a result of faulty mental health care. The options proposed in this chapter are compensation panels and binding arbitration. Neither is an original concept (Dulen, 1992; Paglia, 1991; Saikles, 1992; U.S. General Accounting Office, 1987), but the argument for using them in mental health malpractice cases is particularly compelling because of the extraordinary need to protect patient privacy in those cases and because proving the

elements of negligence is often so complex. Of particular importance to this proposal is that the patient-plaintiff is permitted to choose arbitration, a compensation panel, or a civil trial.

Compensation Panels

One option for handling potential malpractice claims is through compensation funds established by the professions to which those injured by the serious misconduct of a member of the profession could apply for assistance. The American Medical Association (AMA) and the American Psychiatric Association (APA) have endorsed a plan to move malpractice claims to an administrative agency that has some similarities to the panel proposed here (Johnson, Phillips, Orentlicher, & Hatlie, 1989). A critical difference is that in the plan suggested in this chapter it is the patient's option to choose the panel instead of the court, while the AMA/APA plan would preclude a patient from taking a claim to court. In this way, the proposal here is similar to client security funds established by bar associations in some states that supplement, but do not eliminate, judicial remedies (American Bar Association, 1985, 1990).

The compensation panel is an interdisciplinary team appointed to investigate cases and then determine what compensation or restitution is appropriate. Each panel would have at least one MHP to help interpret the scientific data and an attorney to help ensure that the panel understands and follows the law. A cadre of MHPs and others who would have the confidence of patients and who could interpret fairly the scientific and professional evidence presented would be central to the plan. Patients and professionals should be allowed to strike unacceptable professionals from the panel. A third member of the team could be a layperson or patient advocate to remove concern that the panel would have a no-liability, low-damages bias, and to bring to the panel community perspectives and values.

Patients should not be required to have attorneys represent them before the panels. The procedures should be sufficiently simple that patients themselves could request that a panel undertake the investigation and payment of a legitimate claim. Such claims and the information discovered in the investigations would remain confidential. Professional compensation panels could operate as voluntary professional associations, or alternatively, as a required part of the licensing process, as is common with attorney-client security funds (American Bar Association, 1990).

The funding for such programs could be established in several ways. It could be funded as a licensure or membership fee in a professional organization, or as part of the malpractice insurance system. In either event, the patient who opted to accept an award from the fund would do so in lieu of any other malpractice recovery for the injury. The method of investigating and proving negligence, causation, and damages would differ considerably from the current system. By stressing informal investigation and resolution of claims, the system would protect patient confidentiality and, at the same time, work more quickly and efficiently. The membership of the panel should allow it to apply the best available science in resolving cases. One additional advantage of a voluntary compensation system is that the program could establish its own standards for permitting recovery; it would not necessarily be bound by current tort standards. Thus, a profession could offer patients a modified fault standard, or even a range of standards from a fault-based system to one with a schedule of compensation similar to workers' compensation.

Voluntary Binding Arbitration

The mental health professions should also offer injured patients the option of binding arbitration as an alternative to a malpractice lawsuit. The arbitration panel would follow the process of the American Arbitration Association, using three arbitrators if the parties could not agree on a single arbitrator (O'Brien, 1986; Schor, 1988). The substantive tort law described previously would generally apply, although, as described for compensation panels, the professions could offer

other liability standards. All parties would be required to maintain the confidentiality of the proceedings. Arbitration is essentially an adversarial system, although generally less formal than the court system. Most patients would need attorneys to represent them. Furthermore, some form of discovery (a formal process to ask questions of an opposing party, obtain relevant documents, and obtain examinations) would be required, but it should be very limited so that it is as nonintrusive as possible.

Patients would not be required to agree to arbitration before treatment—an approach that has been tried in some malpractice reforms (Dulen, 1992). Rather, MHPs participating in the plan would agree that they would make arbitration available to patients as an alternative to civil trials. Once a patient accepted the arbitration option, it would be binding on both patient and mental health care provider and the patient would relinquish the right to pursue a civil liability case against participating MHPs. Because the arbitration is optional with the patient and the choice of forum is made after injury, it should avoid the constitutional difficulties that some states have found with mandatory arbitration (Saikles, 1992).

The compensation panels and arbitration would remove some cases of mental health malpractice from public view. Yet there is some public interest in knowing when malpractice liability is imposed. To respond to this need, a narrow confidentiality exception would legitimately be made to allow reporting to formal registries of health care professionals and of licensing and credentialing authorities; this would help to remove incompetent and unethical therapists from practice.

Plaintiffs who wish to have the satisfaction of public vindication or a public adjudication of rights would utilize the usual civil jury system, but those plaintiffs who do not want their "day in court" because it is too public should not be required to have it. They should have a less public option. The option may also benefit MHPs who would prefer that any malpractice claims against them be handled as quietly and quickly as possible (Hay, 1992).

Participant Satisfaction

The principles of procedural justice suggest that the compensation panels or arbitration, if structured carefully, could increase the satisfaction of plaintiff-patients and defendant-professionals. Two important elements in increasing procedural justice satisfaction are "process control" (control of, or influence over, the procedures used) and "voice" (the opportunity to tell one's story fairly and clearly) (Lind & Tyler, 1988).

For plaintiffs, the option of selecting a compensation panel, arbitration, or a civil trial would likely increase the sense of process control because they could choose from a fairly wide range of procedural formality and adversarial intensity. Further, the optional processes should increase plaintiffs' sense of control over their personal information. Arbitration, which is adversarial, may provide some of the satisfaction associated with adversarial processes (Sheppard, 1985) while maintaining some information privacy.

The process-control satisfaction for defendant-professionals is somewhat more difficult to consider and would be an interesting area for future research. On the one hand, the MHP would have participated indirectly in adopting the optional compensation and arbitration processes through professional associations, and the formal malpractice reform proposals from the health professions seem to indicate a preference for such options over civil trials (Johnson et al., 1989). On the other hand, it is the plaintiff's choice among the three options and it is possible that the exercise of such a choice by an adverse party may reduce the process-control satisfaction of the professional. Currently, of course, neither the plaintiff nor the defendant has any significant influence on the process used to try a malpractice case.

The "voice" component of procedural justice satisfaction (Lind & Tyler, 1988) is in reality often not well served by the civil process. Because few malpractice claims go to trial, the parties in these cases often do not have a chance to tell their stories to decision makers. Rather, attorneys negotiate a settlement in a way that essentially excludes the parties. Depositions hardly give "voice" to the parties, since they are not taken before a decision maker, and they are essentially controlled by the opposing party. Both the compensation panel and arbitration options should be structured to permit plaintiff and defendant to describe their positions fully before the decision maker.

To promote satisfaction by those involved in cases, the compensation and arbitration panels should permit the parties some flexibility in modifying the procedures and standards to be used. The process should also give both sides a full opportunity to be heard, to express views, and to press arguments before the decision maker. In addition, the decision makers should be (and appear to the parties to be) qualified, well trained, and experienced. They should be instructed to show concern for the parties' rights and to treat them with respect (Lind & Tyler, 1988).

The conventional wisdom suggests that panels and arbitrators are less sympathetic to plaintiffs, or at least give lower awards, than juries (Terry, 1986). Plaintiffs as a group, however, have not done that well in jury trials in mental health cases (Robertson, 1988), and there is some reason to believe that arbitrators are no less sympathetic to injured plaintiffs than are juries, except, perhaps in cases involving very high damages (Zuckerman, Koller, & Bovbjerg, 1986). Plaintiffs who fear arbitrators could choose the usual civil jury trial, and cases presenting outrageous misconduct or the chance of very large awards might well go to trial. Plaintiffs could rationally choose a nonjury option even assuming it meant the possibility of a lower award. The benefits of maintaining the privacy of their mental health information and the ability to conclude the claim quickly in a less threatening environment may well outweigh the chance of a higher economic award. Furthermore, from the plaintiff's perspective, the efficiencies of the options may reduce the total costs of pursuing a claim and offset some of the possible economic disadvantages of the informal mechanism. Attorneys in these cases should remember that the satisfaction with a judicial process is not determined solely by the outcome of a case, but also by the way the parties are treated in the process (Lind & Tyler, 1988).

Other potential advantages of the compensation panels and arbitration include more sophisticated use of expert witnesses (including experts not appointed by either party). These scientifically knowledgeable decision makers should be less likely than lay juries to be misled by scientifically questionable expert testimony or confused by conflicting expert evidence. Further, the informality of the process would allow cases to be concluded without the delays and inefficiencies currently common in civil cases.

In all likelihood, these optional processes would not affect significantly the deterrence goals of the tort system. To the extent that there is a deterrent effect arising from mental health malpractice cases, it probably would not be changed greatly with arbitration or compensation panels (Brown & Rayne, 1989; Wadlington, 1991; Weiler, 1991). Being found liable by a compensation or arbitration panel would be an unpleasant event for a MHP, thereby providing some deterrent effect. Furthermore, because the panel had the participation of the profession, its findings of liability might carry special censure. In fact, the quality of mental health care is less likely to be influenced by malpractice procedures than by research to determine what kinds of therapy are effective for what conditions, and which practitioners are adequately trained and qualified to provide the services they render (Brook, Brutoco, & Williams, 1975; Pierce, 1980; Rush, 1993).

Individual Professionals

The proposals for compensation panels and arbitration assume that MHP associations (or the state) would establish plans that would be generally available to all members of the profession (or holders of licenses). In the absence of such a professionwide plan, individual professionals could offer similar plans on their own by establishing the details of the plan and announcing that it is available to patients. For example, individuals could agree to submit claims to arbitration. Such an approach would present logistical problems, however. Because there is the potential for conflicts with liability insurance carriers, and because any awards probably would not be covered by insurance, an individual practitioner would face significant difficulties in implementing a plan without the cooperation of his or her insurance carrier. Insurance carriers themselves could, of course, establish compensation panels or arbitration options for injured patients.

Avoiding Malpractice Liability

Finally, even more than finding better ways of resolving malpractice claims, it would be better to reduce the number of negligent injuries and malpractice claims. The following suggestions are ways institutions and individual professionals can reduce the possibility that they will face malpractice claims and can reduce even further the possibility of losing a malpractice case if one is filed against them. For the most part, these suggestions are various ways of saying "engage in good, solid, careful professional practice and adopt policies to ensure that others who practice with you or in your institution do the same."

1. Do not engage in any sexual contact with patients or their families. This advice, if followed universally, would significantly reduce the level of mental health malpractice claims. Institutions should adopt and enforce strong policies that prohibit such contact by all employees. This policy may not deter all such contact, but it will help remind the staff of the inappropriateness of such contact.

2. Promote an atmosphere of concern for patients and respect for their legal rights. Problems arise when respect for patients diminishes, or where patients are treated as "income producers."

3. It should be clear how threats to third parties will be handled. In particular, give consideration to steps to protect third parties from the violence of patients. Such steps might include

starting civil commitment proceedings or warning the intended victims. Institutions should have clear policies for dealing with such threats.

4. Clearly identify potentially suicidal patients and inform *all* staff of the proper ways of dealing with suicidal patients. Again, institutions should have clear policies for dealing with such threats.

5. Establish clear procedures for reporting child abuse and other forms of abuse that are subject to state reporting statutes. Institutions should designate someone as responsible for seeing to it that these policies are known throughout the institution, that reporting requirements are enforced, and that members of the staff are advised of their reporting obligations.

6. Be particularly cautious about pressing for the release or dismissal of potentially dangerous patients because of managed care or other third-party reimbursement pressures. Economic pressure is not a justification for negligence or bad practice.

7. Maintain patient records that are complete and up to date. Under no circumstances should alteration of records be tolerated. This is particularly true once litigation involving the records is anticipated.

8. Carefully guard the confidentiality of patient records. Professionals should not release information except with the consent of the patient, for compelling reasons, or subject to clear legal authority. Professionals should be certain that they understand the confidentiality requirements in their jurisdiction.

9. The equipment necessary for procedures done within an office or institution should be readily available and in good working order. The proper maintenance of equipment should be a priority.

10. Establish clear procedures for assessing the competency of voluntary patients when they are admitted to an inpatient facility. If patients are clearly incompetent, there should be a procedure for obtaining a legitimate form of substituted judgment or judicial authority to justify the confinement. If patients object to staying at a facility or are coerced to do so, institutions should consider the possibility of a formal involuntary commitment.

11. Professionals treating children should have clear protocols for dealing with them. These policies should include methods for admitting children to institutions and should deal explicitly with confidentiality. For example, the circumstances under which information will be released to the parents should be set out, and there should be an understanding with the minor and with his or her parents concerning what levels of confidentiality will be respected.

12. Exercise care in the appointment of staff. Institutions should not employ those who are not fully qualified and should check the credentials of all professionals. They should also maintain policies that provide for the removal of staff privileges for misconduct or incompetence.

13. Supervise the activities of staff appropriately. This supervision should ensure that staff are not acting beyond their areas of competence or certification. Evaluations of staff must occur periodically, at regularly scheduled intervals.

14. Carefully follow all accreditation or certification standards for offices or institutions. Use periodic recertification visits as an opportunity to test the adequacy of policies against state and national standards.

15. Implement quality review procedures within the institution faithfully and carefully. This process should help identify problems as early as possible.

16. Carefully supervise students and others in training. The level of supervision must be monitored to ensure that it operates in fact as well as in theory.

17. Do not undertake or become involved with human experimentation unless expressly approved by an institutional review board or similar body.

18. Appoint a patients' rights advocate, if such an advocate does not presently exist, to help identify potential problems and to deal with them at an early stage.

19. Avoid advertising campaigns or other promotions that represent you as having any form of expertise or ability that you do not in fact have.

Such promotions invite unrealistic expectations and may, therefore, increase potential liability when the expectations are not met.

20. Undertake a thorough risk assessment of all areas of practice. Institutions should give particular attention to the pharmacy, equipment, records, and procedures for dealing with dangerous patients. It is generally advisable to have well-qualified consultants assist with this risk assessment. Where unnecessarily risky areas are identified, remedial action must be taken.

21. Undertake periodic reviews of all policies and procedures to account for new legal developments. It is generally useful for institutions to have a continuing relationship with a lawyer and others knowledgeable in mental health law who can help the institution keep abreast of rapid changes in the law.

22. Develop a carefully considered plan to be implemented when potential liability problems arise. Not only should this involve notifying the insurance carrier of the problem, but it also should involve immediate consultation regarding the issue of whether the patient should be charged for services, how relatives should be handled, and the like. There are disagreements about the degree to which patients should be informed when there has been an error. It should be clear who will make those decisions, because time is often of the essence when a potential liability crisis occurs.

Conclusion

The recent insights of therapeutic jurisprudence suggest that the law can profitably be guided by the principles of psychotherapy (Wexler & Winick, 1991). In mental health malpractice cases, the current tort system appears to harm plaintiffs and defendants alike. It is inconsistent with such fundamental psychotherapy principles as the protection of confidentiality. The law should provide injured patients with the option of less public and less intrusive ways of seeking redress for harm suffered during mental health treatment. Until those reforms are made, the mental health professions themselves could do much to offer nonlitigation redress to patients injured in therapy by offering compensation panels or voluntary binding arbitration as alternatives to the tort system. Although neither is a perfect or painless way of resolving malpractice claims, each offers a more private and efficient mechanism for injured patients in a manner more consistent with the values of the mental health professions.

References

Abille v. United States, 482 F. Supp. 703 (N.D. Cal. 1980).

Abrams, R. (1989, December). Malpractice litigation and ECT. *Convulsive Therapy, 5,* 365–367.

American Bar Association. (1985). *Directory of lawyer disciplinary agencies and clients' security funds.* Chicago: Author.

American Bar Association. (1990). *Client protection fund survey.* Chicago: Author.

Andrade, P. D., & Andrade, M. S. (1979). Professional liability of the psychiatric nurse. *Journal of Psychiatry and Law, 7,* 141–186.

Appelbaum, P. S. (1990). Statutes regulating patient-therapist sex. *Hospital and Community Psychiatry, 41,* 15–16.

Appleton, W. S. (1968). Legal problems in psychiatric drug prescription. *American Journal of Psychiatry, 124,* 877–882.

Arkes, H. R., Faust, D., & Guilmette, T. J. (1988). Eliminating the hindsight bias. *Journal of Applied Psychology, 73,* 305–307.

Ayres, B. D., Jr. (1994, May 13). Father who fought "memory therapy" wins damage suit. *New York Times,* §1, p. 1.

Bach, J. P. (1989). Requiring due care in the process of patient deinstitutionalization: Toward a common law approach to mental health care reform [Note]. *Yale Law Journal, 98,* 1153–1172.

Baker, J. R. (1993). Comment—Professional-client sex: is criminal liability an appropriate means of enforcing professional responsibility? *UCLA Law Review, 40,* 1275–1340.

Baker v. United States, 226 F. Supp. 129 (S.D. Iowa 1964) *aff'd,* 343 F.2d 222 (8th Cir. 1965).

Berman, A. L., & Cohen-Sandler, R. (1983). Suicide and malpractice: Expert testimony and the standard of care. *Professional Psychology Research and Practice, 14,* 6–19.

Berry, M. C. (1988). Kirk v. Michael Reese Hospital: A hospital's liability as a health care provider [Note]. *Loyola University of Chicago Law Journal, 19,* 1261–1283.

Bersoff, D. N. (1981). Testing and the law. *American Psychologist, 36,* 1047–1056.

Besharov, D. J. (1983). Child protection: Past progress, present problems, and future directions. *Family Law Quarterly, 17,* 151–172.

Bongar, B. M. (1991). *The suicidal patient: Clinical and legal standards of care.* Washington, DC: American Psychological Association.

Brook, R. H., Brutoco, R. L., & Williams, K. N. (1975). The relationship between medical malpractice and quality of care. *Duke Law Journal, 1975,* 1197–1231.

Brown, H. M. (1988). Hospital liability law: Cost containment, marketing, and consumer expectation. *Defense Counsel Journal, 55,* 159–167.

Brown, J., & Rayne, J. T. (1989). Some ethical considerations in defensive psychiatry: A case study. *American Journal of Orthopsychiatry, 59,* 534–541.

Busch, K. A., & Cavanaugh, J. L., Jr. (1985). Physical examination of psychiatric outpatients: Medical and legal issues. *Hospital and Community Psychiatry, 36,* 958–961.

Carstensen, P. C. (1994). The evolving duty of mental health professionals to third parties: A doctrinal and institutional examination. *International Journal of Law and Psychiatry, 17,* 1–42.

Cestone v. Harkavy, 277 N.Y.S. 438 (1935).

Charles, S., & Kennedy, E. (1985). *Defendant: A psychiatrist on trial for medical malpractice.* New York: Free Press.

Christy v. Saliterman, 179 N.W.2d 288 (Minn. 1970).

Clites v. State, 322 N.W.2d 917 (Iowa Ct. App. 1982).

Colo. Rev. Stat. § 18-3-405.5 (1989).

Combs, C. G. (1987). Hospital vicarious liability for the negligence of independent contractors and staff physicians: Criticisms of the ostensible agency doctrine in Ohio [Note]. *University of Cincinnati Law Review, 56,* 711–738.

Copeland, W. M., & Brown, P. E. (1990). Hospital medical staff privilege issues: "Brother's keeper" revisited. *Northern Kentucky Law Review, 17,* 513–525.

Crocker, E. M. (1985). Judicial expansion of the *Tarasoff* doctrine: Doctors' dilemma. *Journal of Psychiatry and Law, 13,* 83–99.

Cummings, N. A., & Sobel, S. B. (1985). Malpractice insurance: Update on sex claims. *Psychotherapy, 22,* 186–188.

Danzon, P. M. (1985). *Medical malpractice: Theory, evidence, and public policy.* Cambridge, MA: Harvard University Press.

Darling v. Charleston Community Memorial Hosp., 211 N.E.2d 253, 256 (Ill. 1965).

Doe v. Roe, 400 N.Y.S.2d 668, 671 (1977).

Doe v. Samaritan Counseling Center, 791 P.2d 344 (Alaska 1993).

Dulen, M. (1992). Twenty years later . . . Contractual arbitration as medical malpractice tort reform [Comment]. *Journal of Dispute Resolution, 1992,* 325–340.

Edwards, F. (1989). Psychiatric malpractice. In F. Edwards (Ed.), *Medical malpractice: Slowing the crisis* (pp. 73–86). New York: Holt.

Epstein, J. M. (1989, July). The exploitative psychotherapist as a defendant. *Trial, 25*(7), 52–57.

Faden, R. R., Beauchamp, T. L., & King, N. M. P. (1986). *A history and theory of informed consent.* New York: Oxford University Press.

Farrell, M. J. (1992). Medication malpractice: Claims, culprits and defenses. *American Journal of Trial Advocacy, 16*, 65–107.

Federici, W. R., & Doering, S. F., Jr. (1989). Psychiatrists' standard of care. *American Journal of Forensic Psychiatry, 10*(3), 5–12.

Firman, G. J. (1988). Ostensible agency: Another malpractice hazard. *American Journal of Psychiatry, 145*, 510–512.

Fraser, B. G. (1978). A glance at the past, a gaze at the present, a glimpse at the future: A critical analysis of the development of child abuse reporting statutes. *Chicago-Kent Law Review, 54*, 641–686.

Gerhart, U. C., & Brooks, A. D. (1985). Social workers and malpractice: Law, attitudes, and knowledge. *Social Casework: Journal of Contemporary Social Work, 66*, 411–416.

Group for the Advancement of Psychiatry. (1960). *Confidentiality and privileged communication in the practice of psychiatry.* New York: Author.

Hampton, L. P. (1984). Malpractice in psychotherapy: Is there a relevant standard of care? [Note]. *Case Western Reserve Law Review, 35*, 251–281.

Harvard Medical Practice Study. (1990). *Patients, doctors, and lawyers: Medical injury, malpractice litigation, and patient compensation in New York.* Cambridge, MA: Author.

Hay, I. (1992). Courting plaintiffs: Private reform of tort law rights. In I. Hay (Ed.), *Money, medicine, and malpractice in American society* (pp. 183–206). New York: Praeger.

Hogan, D. B. (1974). Encounter groups and human relations training: The case against applying traditional forms of statutory regulation. *Harvard Journal of Legislation, 11*, 659–701.

Hogan, D. B. (1977). *The regulation of psychotherapists: A review of malpractice suits in the United States* (Vol. 3). Cambridge, MA: Ballinger.

Hubbard, F. P. (1989). The physicians' point of view concerning medical malpractice: A sociological perspective on the symbolic importance of "tort reform." *Georgia Law Review, 23*, 295–358.

Johnson, K. B., Phillips, C. G., Orentlicher, D., & Hatlie, M. S. (1989). A fault-based administrative alternative for resolving medical malpractice claims. *Vanderbilt Law Review, 42*, 1365–1406.

Joint Commission on the Accreditation of Healthcare Organizations. (1993). *Accreditation manual for hospitals.* Chicago: Author.

Jorgenson, L., Bisbing, S. B., & Sutherland, P. K. (1992). Therapist-patient sexual exploitation and insurance liability. *Tort and Insurance Law Journal, 27*, 595–614.

Kanute, M. (1989). Evolving theories of malpractice liability for HMOs [Comment]. *Loyola University of Chicago Law Journal, 20*, 841–873.

Kapp, M. B. (1983). Legal implications of clinical supervision of medical students and residents. *Journal of Medical Education, 58*, 293–299.

Kapp, M. B. (1984). Supervising professional trainees: Legal implications for mental health institutions and practitioners. *Hospital and Community Psychiatry, 35*, 143–147.

Keeton, W., Dobbs, D., Keeton, R., & Owen, D. (1984). *Prosser and Keeton on torts* (5th ed.). St. Paul, MN: West.

Klages, G. W. (1988–1989). Medical malpractice liability from a hospital's perspective. *Illinois Bar Journal, 77*, 34–41.

Knapp, S., & VandeCreek, L. (1981). Malpractice as a regulator of psychotherapy. *Psychotherapy: Theory, Research, and Practice, 18*, 354–358.

Knapp, S., & VandeCreek, L. (1987). A review of tort liability in involuntary civil commitment. *Hospital and Community Psychiatry, 38*, 648–651.

Knecht v. Gillman, 488 F.2d 1136 (8th Cir. 1973).

Kramer, D. (1988). Psychiatry, psychology, and the law. *Personal Injury Review, 1988*, 150–177.

Lanier v. Sallas, 777 F.2d 321 (5th Cir. 1985).

Leesfield, I. H. (1987). Negligence of mental

health professionals: What conduct breaches standards of care. *Trial, 23*(3), 57–61.

Lind, E. A., & Tyler, T. R. (1988). *The social psychology of procedural justice.* New York: Plenum.

Lisko, R. K. (1978–1979). Hospital liability under theories of *respondeat superior* and corporate negligence. *University of Missouri–Kansas City Law Review, 47,* 171–184.

Mackey v. Procunier, 477 F.2d 877 (9th Cir. 1973).

Mazza v. Huffaker, 300 S.E.2d 833 (N.C. App. 1983).

McBride v. United States, 462 F.2d 72 (9th Cir. 1972).

Meier v. Ross Gen. Hosp., 445 P.2d 519 (Cal. 1968).

Merrill, R. A. (1973). Compensation for prescription drug injuries. *Virginia Law Review, 59,* 1–120.

Miller, R. D., & Weinstock, R. (1987). Conflict of interest between therapist-patient confidentiality and the duty to report sexual abuse of children. *Behavioral Sciences and the Law, 5,* 161–174.

Mills, M. J., & Eth, S. (1987). Legal liability with psychotropic drug use: Extrapyramidal syndromes and tardive dyskinesia. *Journal of Clinical Psychiatry, 48*(Suppl.), 28–33.

Minn. Stat. Ann. § 609.344 (West 1989).

Mitchell v. Robinson, 334 S.W.2d 11 (Mo. 1960).

Modlin, H. C. (1990). Forensic psychiatry and malpractice. *American Academy of Psychiatry and Law Bulletin, 18,* 153–162.

Morin, L. A. (1989). Civil remedies for therapist-patient sexual exploitation. *Golden Gate University Law Review, 19,* 401–434.

Morreim, E. H. (1989). Conflicts of interest: Profits and problems in physician referrals. *Journal of the American Medical Association, 272,* 390–394.

Naccarato v. Grob, 180 N.W.2d 788 (Mich. 1970).

Newberger, E. H. (1985). The helping hand strikes again: Unintended consequences of child abuse reporting. In E. H. Newberger & R. Bourne (Eds.), *Unhappy families: Clinical and research perspectives on family violence* (pp. 171–178). Littleton, MA: PSG.

Nicholson v. Han, 162 N.W.2d 313 (Mich. App. 1968).

Nieland, R. (1979). Malpractice liability of psychiatric professionals. *American Journal of Forensic Psychiatry, 1*(Pt. 2), 22–36.

N.D. Cent. Code § 12.1–20.06.1 (1988).

Nye, D. G., Gifford, D. G., Webb, B. L., & Dewer, M. A. (1988). The causes of the medical malpractice crisis: An analysis of claims data and insurance company finances. *Georgetown Law Journal, 76,* 1495–1561.

O'Brien, K. R. (1986). Arbitration: An antidote to New York's medical malpractice crisis [Note]. *Vermont Law Review, 11,* 577–601.

Ohligschlager v. Proctor Community Hosp., 303 N.E.2d 392 (Ill. 1973).

Orr, A. W. (1989–1990). Nontherapist counselors: No duty to refer suicidal patients to licensed psychotherapists. *Law and Psychology Review, 13,* 91–102.

Paglia, A. D. (1991). Taking the tort out of court—Administrative adjudication of medical liability claims: Is it the next step? [Note]. *Southwestern University Law Review, 20,* 41–76.

Paquin, G. W. (1988). The malpractice of family therapy: An analysis of two schools. *Law and Psychology Review, 12,* 21–48.

Perlin, M. L. (1989). *Mental disability law: Civil and criminal* (Vol. 3). Charlottesville, VA: Michie.

Perr, I. N. (1980). Liability and electroshock therapy. *Journal of Forensic Sciences, 25,* 508–513.

Perry, C., & Kurue, J. W. (1993). Psychotherapists' sexual relationships with their patients. *Annals of Health Law, 2,* 35–54.

Personal Injury Verdict Reviews. (1986, January 13). P. 1.

Pierce, R. J., Jr. (1980). Encouraging safety: The limits of tort law and government regulation. *Vanderbilt Law Review, 33,* 1281–1331.

Pisel v. Stamford Hosp., 430 A.2d 1 (Conn. 1980).

Pope, K. S. (1989). Malpractice suits, licensing

disciplinary actions, and ethics cases: Frequency, courses, and costs. *Independent Practitioner, 9,* 22–26.

Poythress, N. G., Jr., & Brodsky, S. L. (1992). In the wake of a negligent release lawsuit: An investigation of professional consequences and institutional impact on a state psychiatric hospital. *Law and Human Behavior, 16,* 155–173.

Roberts, J. S., Coale, J. G., & Redman, R. R. (1987). A history of the Joint Commission on Accreditation of Hospitals. *Journal of the American Medical Association, 258,* 936–940.

Robertson, J. D. (1988). *Psychiatric malpractice: Liability of mental health professionals.* New York: Wiley.

Robertson, J. D. (1992). *The psychiatrist in the courtroom: The trial of a sexual misconduct case.* Washington, DC: American Psychiatric Press.

Roy v. Hartogs, 381 N.Y.S.2d 587 (1976).

Rush, A. J. (1993). Clinical practice guidelines: Good news, bad news, or no news? *Archives of General Psychiatry, 50,* 483–490.

Rush v. Akron Gen. Hosp., 171 N.E.2d 378 (Ohio App. 1957).

Saikles, J. L. (1992). *Medical malpractice: Alternatives to litigation* (Publication No. GAO/HRD-92-98). Washington, DC: U.S. General Accounting Office.

Schor, N. D. (1988). Health care providers and alternative dispute resolution: Needed medicine to combat medical malpractice claims [Note]. *Ohio State Journal on Dispute Resolution, 4,* 65–80.

Schutz, B. M. (1982). *Legal liability in psychotherapy.* San Francisco: Jossey-Bass.

Shapiro, E. D. (1986). Defendant: A psychiatrist on trial for medical malpractice [Book review]. *New York Law School Law Review, 31,* 867–871.

Sheppard, B. H. (1985). Justice is no simple matter: Case for elaborating our model of procedural fairness. *Journal of Personality and Social Psychology, 49,* 953–962.

Shuman, D. W., & Weiner, M. F. (1982). The privilege study: An empirical examination of psychotherapist-patient privilege. *North Carolina Law Review, 60,* 893–942.

Shuman, D. W., & Weiner, M. F. (1987). *The psychotherapist-patient privilege: A critical examination.* Springfield, IL: Charles C Thomas.

Simon, R. I., & Sadoff, R. L. (1992). *Psychiatric malpractice: Cases and comments for clinicians* (2nd ed.). Washington, DC: American Psychiatric Press.

Slawson, P. F., & Guggenheim, F. G. (1984). Psychiatric malpractice: A review of the national loss experience. *American Journal of Psychiatry, 141,* 979–981.

Slovenko, R. (1974). Psychotherapist-patient testimonial privilege: A picture of misguided hope. *Catholic University Law Review, 23,* 649–673.

Smith, S. R. (1980). Constitutional privacy in psychotherapy. *George Washington Law Review, 49,* 1–60.

Smith, S. R. (1987). Medical and psychotherapy privileges and confidentiality: On giving with one hand and removing with the other. *Kentucky Law Journal, 75,* 473–557.

Smith, S. R. (1991). Mental health malpractice in the 1990s. *Houston Law Review, 28,* 209–283.

Smith, S. R., & Meyer, R. G. (1984). Child abuse reporting laws and psychotherapy: A time for reconsideration. *International Journal of Law and Psychiatry, 7,* 351–366.

Smith, S. R., & Meyer, R. G. (1987). *Law, behavior, and mental health: Policy and practice.* New York: New York University Press.

Southwick, A. F. (1983). Hospital liability: Two theories have been merged. *Journal of Legal Medicine, 4,* 1–50.

Standard of care in administering non-traditional psychotherapy [Note]. (1974). *U.C. Davis Law Review, 7,* 56–83.

Stone, A. A. (1976). The legal implications of sexual activity between psychiatrist and patient. *American Journal of Psychiatry, 133,* 1138–1141.

Strasburger, L. H., Jorgensen, L., & Randles, R. (1991). Criminalization of psychotherapist-patient sex. *American Journal of Psychiatry, 148,* 859–863.

Szimonisz v. United States, 537 F. Supp. 147, 148 (D. Or. 1982).

Tancredi, L. R. (1988). Malpractice and tardive dyskinesia: A conceptual dilemma. *Journal of Clinical Psychopharmacology, 8*(Suppl.), 71–76.

Taragin, M. I., Wilczek, A. P., Karns, M. E., Trout, R., & Carson, J. L. (1992). Physician demographics and the risk of medical malpractice. *American Journal of Medicine, 93,* 537–542.

Tarasoff v. Regents of the Univ. of California, 551 P.2d 334 (Cal. 1976).

Taub, S. (1987). Electroconvulsive therapy, malpractice, and informed consent. *Journal of Psychiatry and Law, 15,* 7–54.

Terry, N. P. (1986). The technical and conceptual flaws of medical malpractice arbitration. *St. Louis University Law Journal, 30,* 571–631.

Thompson, A. (1990). *Guide to ethical practice in psychotherapy* (pp. 26–30, 218–219). New York: Wiley.

United States v. Willis, 737 F. Supp. 269 (S.D.N.Y. 1990).

U.S. General Accounting Office. (1987, May). *Medical malpractice: A framework for action* (Publication No. GAO/HRD-87-73). Washington, DC: Author.

Wadlington, W. J. (1991). Legal responses to patient injury: A future agenda for research and reform. *Law and Contemporary Problems, 54,* 199–223.

Wagner, K. D., Pollard, R., & Wagner, R. F. (1993). Malpractice litigation against child and adolescent psychiatry residency programs. *Journal of the American Academy of Child and Adolescent Psychiatry, 32,* 462–465.

Watkins, S. A., & Watkins, J. C. (1989). Negligent endangerment: Malpractice in the clinical context. *Journal of Independent Social Work, 3,* 35–50.

Weddington, W. W., & Cavenar, J. O. (1979). Termination initiated by the therapist: A countertransference storm. *American Journal of Psychiatry, 136,* 1302–1305.

Weiler, P. C. (1991). *Medical malpractice on trial.* Cambridge, MA: Harvard University Press.

Weinstock, R., & Weinstock, D. (1988). Child abuse reporting trends: An unprecedented threat to confidentiality. *Journal of Forensic Science, 33,* 418–433.

Wettstein, R. M. (1983). Informed consent and tardive dyskinesia. *Journal of Clinical Psychopharmacology, 8*(Suppl.), 65–70.

Wexler, D. B., & Schopp, R. F. (1989). How and when to correct for juror hindsight bias in mental health malpractice litigation: Some preliminary observations. *Behavioral Sciences and the Law, 7,* 485–504.

Wexler, D. B., & Winick, B. J. (1991). *Essays in therapeutic jurisprudence.* Durham, NC: Carolina Academic Press.

Winslade, W. J., Liston, E. H., Ross, J. W., & Weber, K. D. (1984). Medical, judicial, and statutory regulation of ECT in the United States. *American Journal of Psychiatry, 141,* 1349–1355.

Wis. Stat. Ann. § 940.22 (West 1989).

Woods v. Brumlop, 377 P.2d 520 (N.M. 1962).

Wright, R. H. (1981). Psychologists and professional liability insurance: A retrospective review. *American Psychologist, 36,* 1485–1493.

Zamlen v. Cleveland, 686 F. Supp. 631 (N.D. Ohio 1988). *aff'd,* 906 F.2d 209 (6th Cir. 1990), *cert. denied,* 499 U.S. 936 (1991).

Zinermon v. Burch, 494 U.S. 113 (1990).

Zuckerman, S., Koller, C. F., & Bovbjerg, R. R. (1986). Information on malpractice: A review of empirical research on major policy issues. *Law and Contemporary Problems, 49,* 85–111.

6 ❚ Regulating the Marketplace for Competition among Mental Health Providers: The Roles of Antitrust Law and State Mandates

Thomas L. Greaney
Saint Louis University

Managed competition, the watchword for competitive reform in the 1990s, signifies regularized government intervention to control market conditions, and, more specifically, to mitigate market imperfections. The concept of managing competition is not new, however. Competition among health care providers has been controlled and circumscribed by a variety of regulations, statutes, and common law principles for many years. Perhaps more important, a powerful regime of private regulation has also influenced the behavior of health care professionals.

As consensus builds to impose a system of market-improving mechanisms in health care, it is instructive to consider how judicial and legislative decision makers have determined what conditions and activities improve competitive outcomes and how those potential improvements should be weighed against other considerations. In this chapter, I examine two contrasting kinds of market interventions that regulate competition among professionals: antitrust law, which is judge-made law, and state mandates, which are statutory enactments. I also summarize the scope and purposes of these bodies of law and their impact on health care delivery and insurance. More specifically, I consider how these legal regimes deal with the highly imperfect conditions that characterize markets for mental health services.

Antitrust Law and Mental Health Care Providers

Antitrust Law: History and Rationale

Statutory Framework

The Sherman Act, enacted into federal law in 1890, sets boundaries for cooperative and other relationships among providers. Section 1 of the act prohibits "every contract, combination . . . or conspiracy, in restraint of trade or commerce among the several States, or with foreign nations" (Sherman Act, 1890). By its terms, then, section 1 prohibits an agreement amounting to concerted action, as contrasted with purely unilateral conduct. The Supreme Court has interpreted this provision to require a "meeting of the minds" or a "conscious commitment to a common scheme" (*Interstate Circuit v. United States*, 1939; *Monsanto Co. v. Spray-Rite Serv. Corp.*, 1984). Although its purposes were multifaceted and are the subject of continuing academic debate, the Sherman Act was designed to preserve competitive opportunities and to prevent restraints of trade and monopolies from interfering with the functioning of the marketplace.

The broad sweep of the Sherman Act's prohibition of agreements in restraint of trade reaches both "horizontal" agreements (that is, conspiracies among competing persons or firms) and "vertical" agreements (in which entities at succeeding points in the production process act in concert; examples would include agreements between manufacturers and distributors or insurers and providers). A few such restraints are treated as "per se" illegal, meaning that courts will attach a presumption of illegality to the activity and not require specific proof of anticompetitive effect or purpose. Although the strength and prerequisites for this presumption vary according to the restraint involved, the following categories of activities are generally governed by the per se rule: vertical and horizontal price fixing, market allocations among competitors, certain concerted refusals to deal, and tying arrangements (arrangements in which the sale of a product is conditioned on the buyer's obligation to purchase a different product from the seller). Other agreements are adjudged under the broader "rule of reason" inquiry, which requires an assessment of the activities' pro- and anticompetitive effects, which in turn usually entails examinations of the parties' market power.

By contrast, section 2 of the Sherman Act prohibits unilateral conduct that amounts to monopolization, an attempt to monopolize, or a conspiracy to monopolize. Courts have interpreted this section to require proof that the defendant possesses monopoly power in a relevant market and "the willful acquisition or maintenance of

that power as distinguished from growth or development as a consequence of a superior product, business acumen, or historic accident" (*United States v. Grinnell Corp.*, 1966). For efficiency and juridicial reasons, the law does not punish monopoly or the mere possession of monopoly power; it forbids only those actions that transgress the shadowy line between conduct that constitutes "competition on the merits" and conduct that excludes competitors or limits competition by improper means or without business justifications.

The Sherman Act was supplemented in 1914 with the passage of two other federal statutes, the Clayton Act and the Federal Trade Commission Act, which sought to strengthen antitrust enforcement. These laws deal with specific practices that may have anticompetitive effects and bar mergers and acquisitions that "may substantially lessen competition." The Federal Trade Commission Act also established a federal regulatory agency, the Federal Trade Commission (FTC), to deal with anticompetitive practices. The FTC does this principally through administrative adjudication—that is, resolving claims under the law through evidentiary hearings in which the contesting parties proceed in trial-like proceedings. The FTC also possesses rule-making powers, allowing it to establish rules and regulations governing industrywide behavior through quasi-legislative proceedings. Specifically, the law vests in the FTC the power to prohibit "unfair methods of competition" and "unfair or deceptive acts or practices" (Federal Trade Commission Act, §5). This act has been construed to embody the substance of the Sherman Act and govern other practices as well.

The FTC lacks jurisdiction over any entity not "organized to carry on business for its own profit or that of its members" (Federal Trade Commission Act, §4). Hence, the FTC may not bring actions against not-for-profit entities except to the extent that they operate substantially for the pecuniary benefit of their members. However, the U.S. Department of Justice is not similarly disabled and has on a number of occasions prosecuted not-for-profit entities. Finally, there is abundant incentive for private lawsuits, because persons injured by reason of the Sherman Act may receive treble damages and recover attorneys' fees. Moreover, all but two states have enacted their own antitrust laws, usually modeled on the federal laws.

Antitrust law's place in the context of a free market economy and democratic republic is reflected in the Supreme Court's characterization of the Sherman Act as "a comprehensive charter of economic liberty . . . providing an environment conducive to the preservation of our democratic political and social institutions" (*Northern Pacific Railway v. United States,* 1958). Both economic and normative grounds undergird the nation's reliance on the competitive process as the means for organizing economic relationships. Preservation of business freedom is regarded as reinforcing political freedoms, while economic efficiency produces more societal output and allocates resources according to popular preferences. Accordingly, courts today presume that the antitrust laws will govern the conduct of all participants in the economy, absent an express exemption or a regulatory scheme clearly contemplating displacement of competition with government controls.

To be sure, controversy over the purposes of the antitrust laws has existed over the years. Scholars and jurists identified with the "Chicago School" have urged exclusive reliance on price theory and efficiency analysis (Kovacic, 1990; Kwoka & White, 1989; Posner, 1976). Under this particular economic paradigm, consumer welfare, narrowly defined to include only efficiency concerns associated with allocations of society's resources and not with transfers of wealth between consumers and producers, supplies the exclusive landmark for analysis. Other analysts emphasize that certain noneconomic values such as individual and business freedom and fairness should be taken into account as well (Pitofsky, 1979). More recently, a "Post-Chicago" economic jurisprudence has developed that counsels caution relying on simplified microeconomic models

and stresses the importance of strategic behavior models and appreciation of market imperfections (Krattenmaker & Salop, 1986). Under this approach, antitrust tribunals should take into account, for example, the inadequacy of information, differentiation among services, the peculiarities of insurance markets, and other factors that distinguish health care markets from conventional product markets.

Despite these disagreements, a strong consensus has developed around a number of central principles. Among these are that the primary focus of antitrust inquiries must be on the effect of a practice on competitive conditions, not the welfare of rivals—a policy captured by the Supreme Court's often-repeated maxim that antitrust law is designed to "protect competition, not competitors" (*Brown Shoe Co. v. United States,* 1962, p. 320). In addition, courts have increasingly recognized the importance of assessing the net efficiency consequences of putative restraints of trade while at the same time stressing the practical utility of retaining per se rules for conduct unlikely to yield competitive benefits, contrasting the potential benefits and practicability of enforcement. Finally, as discussed in the following section, antitrust law is to be applied without attempting to factor in various other social policies and societal norms; such considerations are left to the state legislatures and the Congress, which may choose to exempt specific practices or sectors of the economy.

Principles of Special Importance to Health Professionals

Antitrust Law and the "Learned Professions"

Antitrust law's treatment of physicians and other learned professionals has been the subject of considerable debate over the last 20 years. Those advocating leniency for professional activities that restrain trade typically cite the imperfections and market failures affecting most transactions in the health industry and the need to have close cooperation among health professionals concerning standards of care to protect the consumer. Many observers respond that antitrust doctrine is sufficiently flexible to accommodate the peculiar conditions that may be present in the dealings of health professionals, but they conclude that no wholesale exemption is needed to protect those interests. As discussed later in this chapter, the courts have rejected appeals for broad exemptions from antitrust law but at the same time have recognized that collaboration among professionals may improve competitive conditions and in such circumstances do not violate the law's substantive provisions.

In a landmark decision that opened the door for a large number of successful antitrust challenges to practices involving the medical profession, the Supreme Court rejected the notion that "learned professions" were not engaged in "trade or commerce" and hence should be exempt from the antitrust laws (*Goldfarb v. Virginia State Bar*, 1975). The *Goldfarb* opinion, however, did not, on its face, preclude special treatment of the professions under antitrust law in all instances. A suggestive footnote intimated that "it would be unrealistic to view the practice of professions as interchangeable with other business activities" and stated that "the public service aspect, and other features of the professions, may require that a particular practice, which could properly be viewed as a violation of the Sherman Act in another context, be treated differently" (p. 788, n. 17). Despite this language, however, in a series of cases involving medical and other professions, the Supreme Court has repeatedly refused to allow "professional" concerns or public service, safety, or quality-of-care factors to outweigh anticompetitive harms (*Arizona v. Maricopa County Med. Soc'y*, 1982; *FTC v. Indiana Fed. of Dentists*, 1986; *Jefferson Parish Hosp. Dist. No. 2 v. Hyde*, 1984; *National Soc'y of Prof. Eng's v. United States*, 1978; see generally, Greaney, 1989).

The implications of this decision for health professionals were far-reaching: courts and the FTC promptly dissolved a wide assortment of health professionals' ethical codes, trade association rules, and private agreements restricting competition. Perhaps the most important fallout, however, was the erosion of the widely shared assumption that professional decision making was preferable to reliance on decentralized, market forces in health care (Havighurst, 1986).

Cases involving mental health professionals have followed this pattern and have declined to find special circumstances warranting departure from orthodox antitrust rules. For example, in remanding a case (from the appellate court back to the trial court) involving an agreement between two Blue Shield plans and a neuropsychiatric society requiring that psychologists must bill through physicians to obtain reimbursement, the Fourth Circuit left little room for the assertion of professional concerns:

[I]t is not the function of a group of professionals to decide that competition is not beneficial in their line of work. . . . [The court is] not inclined to condone anticompetitive conduct upon an incantation of "good medical practice." (*Virginia Academy of Clinical Psychologists v. Blue Shield of Virginia*, 1980, p. 485)[1]

Promoting Quality of Care and Other Justifications

The Supreme Court has flatly rejected the notion that certain restraints of trade should be excused because they promote safety, improve the quality of care, or advance other worthy causes. In *National Soc'y of Prof. Eng's v. United States* (1978), a trade association defended its ban on competitive bidding by arguing that the ethical code in question prevented shoddy practices and ultimately prevented harm to the public. Stressing that in antitrust "the inquiry is confined to a consideration of impact on competitive conditions," the Court noted that any other approach would invite a standardless and intractable in-

---

[1]See the discussion of this case in section II(c)(3). See also *Welch v. American Psychoanalytic Ass'n* (1986) (refusing to dismiss challenge to an agreement prohibiting psychologists from receiving clinical training in psychoanalysis, because there was "more than a hint of commercial motive behind the defendants' practice").

quiry into social costs and benefits and stated that such appeals were more properly addressed to Congress. In subsequent cases, the Court has applied the "competition only" standard to reject claims by an association of dentists that their collective refusal to supply x-rays to insurers was justified because it allegedly protected patients from unsafe and unwarranted interference with their care (*FTC v. Indiana Fed. of Dentists*, 1986); has treated as irrelevant a hospital's claim that its exclusive contract with anesthesiologists improved patient care (*Jefferson Parrish Hosp. Dist. No. 2 v. Hyde*, 1984); and has refused to countenance price fixing by physicians who claimed their "foundation for medical care" made it easier for consumers to purchase insurance (*Arizona v. Maricopa County Med. Soc'y*, 1982).

While not explicitly weighed when competitive effects are balanced, quality-of-care issues are not totally ignored in antitrust cases. For example, a physician's professional concerns about another provider's competence might support the claim that certain conduct was a unilateral decision by the physician (for example, refusing to make referrals to lay providers) rather than the product of a conspiracy with others (as noted earlier, this is an important distinction because under section 1 of the Sherman Act only the latter is actionable). In addition, concern over quality of care may augment evidence that an activity actually improved competitive conditions by mitigating a market imperfection (Greaney, 1989). Thus mental health professionals might share information about the efficacy of a certain course of treatment or even make recommendations to third-party payers about whether the treatment meets professional standards governing safe and useful therapy. Moreover, Congress has explicitly incorporated a quality-of-care standard in fashioning a defense to antitrust challenges to staff privileges and other peer review actions by physicians and hospitals (Scott, 1991).

As a general matter, courts and the FTC have rarely acknowledged that market imperfections in health care are relevant to antitrust assessments of competitive conditions. Nevertheless, in a variety of circumstances, the problems of inadequate information (for example, the consumers' inability to grasp treatment alternatives) and insurance market imperfections (such as moral hazard, in which individuals are less careful to prevent losses because they have insurance, and adverse selection, in which individuals with a greater than average risk disproportionately seek coverage) should have important ramifications for economic analysis (Furrow, Greaney, Johnson, Jost, & Schwartz, 1994). That is, courts may have to augment traditional analytical tools with a closer understanding of how health care markets work. For example, it may be appropriate to allow mental health professionals greater latitude in acting collectively to regulate advertising or to prevent solicitation of patients given circumstances that disable patients and impede their ability to evaluate provider-supplied information critically.

In a decision of potentially enormous significance to antitrust analyses involving health care, *Eastman Kodak v. Image Technical Services, Inc.* (1992), the Supreme Court has recently given express consideration to imperfect information and related market failures. In that case, the Court expressly found that market power may be present where consumers cannot adequately assess costs and switching costs (costs of changing suppliers after the initial sale) and other factors impaired normal market interactions (*Eastman Kodak v. Image Technical Services, Inc.*, 1992). Although the *Kodak* decision is too recent to have had much impact on the case law, some regard it as signaling an increased willingness to accept "post-Chicago" economic analyses of strategic market behavior and the implications of market imperfections.

Applying Antitrust Law to Specific Professional Practices

Antitrust law has touched virtually every corner of the health care industry (Furrow et al., 1994). While litigation involving mental health professionals and institutions has only surfaced in a few areas, important decisions pertaining to other health care providers offer a generally reliable guide to the principles applicable to them. As discussed below, the primary impact of antitrust law in mental health care has been to reduce the disparate treatment of allied mental health professionals by hospitals and other health care facilities, payers, and educational institutions. In addition, antitrust litigation has served to curtail private agreements often undertaken through professional societies or trade associations—agreements designed to limit competition in the delivery of mental health services.

Although the market for mental health services has much in common with that of other kinds of health services, important differences may affect antitrust analysis. First, the magnitude of market imperfections in some segments of the mental health care market may be more pronounced than in markets for other health services. For example, problems of imperfect information are considerable where the patient has a mental disability or the decision to initiate treatment is the product of coercion. Moreover, in psychotherapy markets the benefits of treatment are uncertain, and there is some evidence that individuals undervalue the utility of those services (McGuire, 1981). Second, mental health insurance markets appear to be characterized by problems of adverse selection. This phenomenon involves the tendency of good insurance risks to congregate in certain insurance plans (prompted by insurers' marketing practices), while unfavorable risks are often driven disproportionately to other insurers. This may cause insurers to set prices at high levels, resulting in too few people buying this form of insurance. On the other hand, the literature is less clear as to the extent of moral hazard —the tendency of insureds to consume more services than they otherwise would because of the presence of insurance—arising out of mental health insurance. (There is strong evidence demonstrating the effect of moral hazard in other forms of health insurance.) Studies do indicate, however, that mental health services can be

provided at lower costs through prepayment plans or health maintenance organizations (HMOs) than could be realized through conventional insurance (McGuire, 1981).

Trade Restraints Involving Professional Associations

The antitrust sword has been used to strike down numerous formal and informal agreements as well as ethical rules and norms promulgated by trade associations and other groups of medical professionals. Such provisions, which are often found in professional codes or other agreements, may reflect laudable, patient-oriented goals. However, to the extent that they also have a purpose or effect of lessening competition, they may violate the antitrust laws. For the most part, these restraints have been treated much like any other horizontal cartel activity (competitors acting in combination) under the antitrust laws. Those challenged have involved price fixing, market divisions (for example, agreements through hospitals not to offer competing services), and boycotts (such as refusals to refer to nurse midwives, psychologists, or other nonphysicians), or other undertakings that have generally enabled professionals to raise prices above marginal cost and reduce output. Courts and commentators regard these activities and their effects on consumers as particularly pernicious because demand for health care is generally inelastic—that is, not very sensitive to changes in price. Moreover, as a result of barriers to entry into the professions, information gaps that limit the ability of consumers to discern quality, and the imperfect agency relationship (involving conflicting interests) between providers and patients, consumers of health services are generally more vulnerable to victimization by professional cartels (Furrow et al., 1994; Lopatka, 1991).

The first important series of cases in this area involved challenges to "ethical" restrictions imposed by professional associations on the price-setting and contracting practices of their members.[2] The government has also successfully challenged other professional norms that directly interfered with the pricing mechanism. Examples include rules prohibiting physicians from accepting "inadequate" compensation or from "underbidding" other physicians (*American Med. Ass'n,* 1979); collective negotiations—which essentially amount to agreed-on pricing—or threats of boycott by providers against payers or hospitals (*Michigan State Med. Soc'y,* 1983); and threats by medical staffs of hospitals designed to coerce hospital administrators into abandoning plans to open HMOs or recruit new physicians on financial terms objectionable to the staff (*Medical Staff of Prince Georges County,* 1988; *Sherman A. Hope, M.D.,* 1981).

A second category of cases involves professional association agreements limiting members' advertising or solicitation of business. Unlike the price restraints previously discussed, these restrictions carry at least arguable claims of improving market performance, and their anticompetitive effects are not always readily apparent. However, most restrictions have been struck down as restraints of trade and unfair methods of competition under the antitrust laws. Or in certain circumstances they have been declared unlawful restraints on speech and in violation of the First Amendment to the Constitution (*Peel v. Attorney Registration and Disciplinary Comm'n of Illinois,* 1990; *Virginia State Bd. of Pharmacy v. Virginia Citizens Consumer Council Inc.,* 1976). For example, the FTC has enjoined a number of private health care associations from adopting or enforcing ethical codes barring advertising or solicitation (*Michigan Optometric Ass'n,* 1985). In the leading antitrust case in this area, the FTC challenged the American

Medical Association's restrictions on dissemination of price information and its ban on advertising. The FTC concluded that suppression of truthful advertising by doctors was an illegal restraint of trade; however, it approved narrowly tailored ethical restrictions that prohibit advertisements that are false and deceptive (*American Med. Ass'n,* 1979). In addition to flat bans on advertising, ethical prohibitions against advertisements mentioning price or discounts, giving information about the practitioner's qualifications, or containing matter deemed undignified or unprofessional have been held unlawful (*Connecticut Chiropractor Ass'n,* 1991).

Groups representing mental health professionals have been involved in several proceedings before administrative agencies where the propriety of private associations' regulation of advertising and other competitively sensitive matters was examined. For example, the American Psychological Association (APA) agreed to an FTC consent order ending the group's restraints on testimonial and comparative advertising and on certain types of patient referral services (*In re American Psychological Association,* 1992).[3] Notably, however, the FTC tailored its relief in this case to accommodate the market peculiarities involved in the provision of mental health care services. While forbidding association actions that in any way discouraged members from engaging in truthful, nondeceptive advertising or participating in patient referral arrangements, the order expressly countenanced the APA's taking actions against both patient solicitation and the use of testimonials from former psychology patients. This unusual leniency, which implicitly acknowledged the special circumstances of the psychotherapist-patient relationship, is noteworthy because it recognizes that antitrust analysis of competitive effects should

---

[2] In several important cases, the federal courts struck down the American Medical Association's rules condemning physicians for associating with HMOs, denouncing collective activity denying staff privileges, and imposing other sanctions on members who in any way assisted innovative financing and delivery plans. See, for example, *American Med. Ass'n v. United States* (1943); *Group Health Coop of Puget Sound v. King County Med. Soc'y* (1951).

[3] See also *State ex rel. Corbin v. Arizona State Psychological Ass'n* (1988) (a consent order to enjoin the association from enforcing a rule on advertising, solicitation, and payment of referral fees).

take into account market imperfections. That is, the FTC's decision appears to rest on the special characteristics of mental health patients such as their inability to function as traditional consumers because of impaired capacity or the nature of their relationships to their providers. Thus, the APA's self-regulatory scheme may be justified by its tendency to prevent abusive practices that take advantage of information gaps and distort competition in the market at large by tainting the value of all advertising.

In another case, the FTC challenged the ethical code of the National Association of Social Workers (NASW), the professional association of clinical social workers, who provide therapeutic and counseling services in the treatment and prevention of psychosocial disorders (*In re Nat'l Ass'n of Social Workers*, 1992). The FTC staff contended that the NASW's Code of Ethics barred its members from soliciting the clients of colleagues. The principal vice of the arrangement lay in the fact that the association did not limit its prohibition to the uninvited, personal solicitation of patients who might be vulnerable to undue influence. The code also prohibited members from paying a fee for referrals, thereby deterring the use of certain commercial patient referral services. In addition, the complaint charged that the NASW's 1984 Standards of Practice for Clinical Social Work restricted the use of testimonials in advertising, as well as other types of truthful advertising. These restrictions, according to the FTC's complaint, deprived consumers of truthful information about social work services and of the benefits of competition among social workers.

The NASW accepted a consent order, agreeing not to impose such restrictions in the future and to undertake certain curative steps (for example, removing all offending statements from guidelines and publications) and prophylactic measures (for instance, adopting antitrust compliance programs) to erase the effects of the violations. Again, however, the FTC's order implicitly acknowledged special features of the market for mental health services that justify departure from conventional antitrust rules governing cooperative behavior. It permitted the NASW to adopt reasonable rules that (1) restrict false or deceptive advertising, (2) regulate solicitation of business or use of testimonials from persons vulnerable to undue influence in advertising, (3) ban all attempts to obtain solicitation of testimonials from current psychotherapy patients, and (4) require disclosure of fees that social workers pay to patient referral services.

Professional Society Membership and Practice Restrictions

A large part of the raison d'être of professional societies is the exchange of scientific information and opinion, both among members and between the society and buyers and others who lack expertise. In addition, professional society membership often carries with it prestige and may signal that members supply services of high quality or have superior training or experience. Finally, norms and standards of practice promulgated by professional societies may serve the market-improving function of offsetting informational deficiencies in the provider-patient relationship.

These potentially salutary effects on competitive conditions find recognition in antitrust law's rule of reason, which mandates that judges and jurors assess and balance the pro-competitive and market-improving effects of horizontal agreements. Weighing on the other side of the ledger is the potential for cartelization (establishing anticompetitive practices) that grows out of standardized professional conduct and exclusionary agreements. For example, membership in a professional society may imply conformity with certain restrictions on the way members compete and with whom they will interact; hence, such membership may raise issues of anticompetitive boycotts, price fixing, or standardization. Profession-imposed standards may also harm competition by ossifying clinical practice methods and by reducing innovation. In economic terms, such standards may enable powerful interests to "raise rivals' costs" by denying certain providers acceptance by mainstream institutions or by forcing them to undertake costly measures to circumvent barriers (Krattenmaker & Salop, 1986; Lopatka, 1991).

A handful of cases have challenged exclusions from membership in professional societies as boycotts covered by the Sherman Act. Courts have rejected these claims where there is no evidence that the exclusion carried with it collateral agreements to standardize medical practice or otherwise limit members' competitive behavior. As one court aptly put it, "It is axiomatic that trade standards must exclude some things as substandard and it is unsurprising that standard-setting bodies sometimes err. A single such error does not amount to a conspiracy" (*Consolidated Metals Products v. American Petroleum Inst.,* 1988, p. 294). As a general matter, courts have been unwilling to impute anticompetitive effects to the mere denial to a single practitioner of membership in an organization, even where doubts exist as to the professional grounds for the exclusion (*Marrese v. American Academy of Orthopedic Surgeons,* 1992).

Where professional society membership has carried with it ancillary agreements concerning practice methods that lack any pro-competitive justification, however, courts and the FTC have overturned such arrangements. For example, trade association rules restricting operation of franchises and branch offices by optometrists, prohibitions against selling products relating to medical services, and bans on affiliations with other providers have been struck down (*American Academy of Ophthalmologists,* 1986; *Iowa Chapter of the American Physical Therapy Ass'n,* 1988; *Michigan Optometric Ass'n,* 1985). On the other hand, where practice restrictions promulgated by a professional society have been supported by plausible justifications based on quality of care, courts have sometimes been willing to take a closer look (although typically concluding ultimately that the conduct restrained trade). A good

example is *Wilk v. American Med. Ass'n* (1990), in which the trial and appellate courts grappled with the American Medical Association's prohibitions on all forms of cooperation by medical doctors with chiropractors. The Seventh Circuit closely examined the pro-competitive justifications, as distinguished from quality-of-care and "public service" justifications, and found them wanting. In particular, it relied on evidence that physicians had a specific intent to destroy chiropractic care and that there were no pro-competitive benefits attributable to the conduct alleged (*Wilk v. American Med. Ass'n,* 1990).

Standard setting in the form of practice guidelines has, for the most part, escaped sanction, especially where plausible market-improving benefits can be demonstrated or where the professional society did no more than dispense a collective opinion. For example, a rule promulgated by a society of surgeons mandating that postoperative care be performed only by surgeons found approval under a rule-of-reason inquiry into its competitive effects (*Koefoot v. American College of Surgery,* 1986). The practice may be likened to establishing a seal of approval for surgeons who agree to abide by norms setting a high level of quality (here, assessing that postoperative care was performed by a provider most capable of delivering the best care). In a case of significance to the legality of profession-promulgated practice standards, *Schachar v. American Academy of Ophthalmology* (1989) upheld the actions of a medical specialty society, addressing the circumstances in which "experimental" procedures should be performed in the face of challenges that the action constituted concerted activity to standardize a service and limit interprofessional competition. The case law suggests that the boundary will be drawn to protect the promulgation of "practice guidelines" that only enhance information in the market, while collective action compelling conformity with a professional society's edicts will transgress the line (*Schachar v. American Academy of Ophthalmology,* 1989).

Credentialing, Peer Review, and Staff Privileges

The lion's share of antitrust litigation involving health care providers has involved conflicts that, in one way or another, concern professional credentials. These disputes highlight tensions between the professions' legitimate concerns and the need to prohibit conduct inhospitable to competition. As discussed below, several courts have held that psychologists, psychiatrists, and other providers are direct competitors. Consequently, action by one such group that arguably excludes or disadvantages another is regarded as a horizontal restraint of trade and may be subject to the strict analysis of the per se rule.

Challenges to denials or curtailment of staff privileges at hospitals have long been a staple of antitrust litigation (Furrow et al., 1994). In most cases, these disputes have arisen in the context of peer review actions by physician staff members concerning the qualifications, competence, or performance of other providers and their suitability for practice in a hospital. In addition, a number of cases have involved challenges to exclusive contracts with staff-based physicians, such as radiologists, pathologists, and anesthesiologists. In both, the claim is usually that members of the medical staff either conspired among themselves or conspired with the hospital to exclude a provider or group of providers from membership. In antitrust terms, the activity is generally characterized as a group boycott, or, in the case of exclusive contracting, an exclusive dealing or tying arrangement.[4]

Despite the enormous number of staff privilege disputes that have been litigated, only a handful of plaintiffs have been successful (*Boczar v. Manatee Hosps. & Health Sys., Inc.*, 1993; see generally, Furrow et al., 1994). Courts have held

that hospitals have no obligation to admit all licensed practitioners who apply for privileges and have recognized that legitimate, pro-competitive impulses often underlie adverse decisions of hospitals on privileges. This is so because of the highly interdependent relationship between hospitals and staff arising from a common interest in promoting cost-effectiveness and high quality (*Kaczanowski v. Medical Center Hospital*, 1985). The cases frequently observe that the credentialing process necessarily requires the active participation and cooperation of the hospital medical staff. In this connection, a number of courts have held that it is impossible, as a matter of law, for a hospital to conspire with its medical staff, reasoning that the two bodies are not separate entities for purposes of antitrust analysis (*Oksanen v. Page Memorial Hosp.*, 1991; *Weiss v. York Hosp.*, 1984). Several courts, however, have concluded that the independent economic interests of physicians provide sufficient reason to view them as separate economic actors for purposes of conspiracy analysis and have permitted allegations involving conspiracies between a hospital and its staff to go forward (*Bolt v. Halifax Hosp. Med. Cntr.*, 1990). Courts may require specific proof that the hospital and staff do not have a complete unity of interests. In a case involving a staff privilege determination made by a psychiatric hospital, the court refused to find a conspiracy between the hospital and its staff in the absence of proof of some divergence of interests between them (*Okusami v. Psychiatric Institute of Washington, Inc.*, 1992).

A conspiracy among the members of the staff is more readily established. Most courts have concluded that the members of medical staffs possess the requisite diversity of interests so that physicians acting on the staff privileges of an applicant can constitute a conspiracy. However, where the hospital retains the ultimate power of final decision over the application, the requisite causal connection between the staff's action and the challenged activity has been found lacking (*Oksanen v. Page Memorial Hosp.*, 1991).

As to the question of whether a denial of

---

[4]*Exclusive dealing* refers to contractual arrangements pursuant to which firms at one level obligate themselves to deal with only a firm operating at another level. A tie-in is a "forced" sale in which the seller compels buyers to purchase a second product in order to be able to buy the primary product.

staff privileges actually restrains trade within the meaning of section 1 of the Sherman Act, courts have generally been unwilling to find that such actions violate the antitrust laws in the absence of evidence of an actual anticompetitive effect. Thus, where the hospital denying privileges lacks market power (defined as the ability to raise price or reduce output), the cases typically conclude that the plaintiff had other alternatives in the market, or rely on other proof of an absence of anticompetitive effect or purpose; in these circumstances, the exclusion has generally been deemed to be "reasonable" (*Bhan v. NME Hosps.*, 1991; *Goss v. Memorial Hosp. Systems*, 1986).

However, where the collective refusal to grant privileges constituted part of a coercive effort against either a class of providers (such as osteopaths, psychologists, or nurse midwives) or attempted coercion to force others into denying staff privileges in order to accomplish an anticompetitive objective, courts have been less reluctant to label the agreement "unreasonable" (*Oltz v. St. Peter's Comm. Hosp.*, 1989). For example, the removal of barriers to psychologists obtaining staff privileges in hospitals was attributable to a challenge by the State of Ohio to Joint Commission on Accreditation of Hospitals rules that had inhibited hospital staff privileges for psychologists (*State of Ohio v. JCAH*, 1979; *Weiss v. York Hosp.*, 1984). The case law and commentary supports closer scrutiny of "class-based" exclusions for several reasons (Kissam, 1982; Note, 1986). First, traditional justifications for privilege denials (that is, the individual practitioner's incompetence or inadequate training, or the hospital's heightened risk of malpractice) would not justify excluding an entire group unless there was evidence tainting the competence of that entire category of practitioners. Indeed, widespread adoption by hospitals and their staffs of policies denying staff privileges to nonphysicians may thwart the competition-enhancing objectives of state licensure laws. Second, the commentary has questioned whether physicians are equipped to judge the skill and training of allied practitioners, especially where the privileges in question limit the scope of the latters' practice within the institution (Note, 1986). On the other hand, exclusion from access to hospitals may not have a serious effect on nonphysician providers who do not need privileges to compete. Moreover, while class-based exclusions may be regarded as suspect, they may be justified by other factors such as a hospital's desire to position itself as a prestigious facility, its commitment to research, or other objectives.

Cases challenging exclusive contracts between a hospital and a group of physicians providing services at the hospital have likewise been unsuccessful in most instances (Furrow et al., 1994). In a leading case, the Supreme Court upheld, in principle, the theory that hospitals' joint provision of anesthesiology services and hospital services could be seen as a "tie-in" sale of separate services. It concluded on the facts before it, however, that the hospital in question lacked market power and hence could not have the power to restrain trade (*Collins v. Associated Pathologists, Ltd.*, 1988; *Jefferson Parish Hosp. Dist. No. 2 v. Hyde*, 1984). Lower courts have followed suit (Furrow et al., 1994). Moreover, they have refused to strike down these arrangements as illegal exclusive-dealing contracts, often noting the availability of alternatives in the relevant market and observing the pro-competitive efficiencies associated with exclusive arrangements between hospitals and a select group of physicians (*Burnham Hosp.*, 1983; *Collins v. Associated Pathologists, Ltd.*, 1988; *Drs. Steuer & Latham v. National Med. Enterprises Inc.*, 1988).

Provider-Payer Conflicts

Conflict arising out of the provider-payer relationship is likely to become a major source of antitrust litigation in a managed competition environment because access to managed care plans is likely to be of critical financial importance to most providers. Among the myriad issues generated by these relationships, three important ones stand out: (1) the permissible bounds of provider cooperation in forming or affiliating with payment systems; (2) the legality of health plans controlled by providers; and (3) the rights of providers excluded from participation in payment plans.

Collusion and Cooperation among Providers

The most clear-cut antitrust abuses in this area involve horizontal price fixing or its functional equivalent. Private agreements among physicians that directly affect price or other terms in dealing with third-party payers have been the subject of numerous civil actions by the government enforcement agencies as well as of criminal prosecutions. For example, collective negotiations undertaken by informal groups of physicians have been repeatedly challenged as illegal price-fixing agreements (*Minnesota v. Mid-West Minnesota Associated Physicians*, 1991; *New York v. Empire Pharmaceutical Society, Inc.*, 1978; *United States v. Alston*, 1992; *United States v. Montana Nursing Home Ass'n, Inc.*, 1982). Likewise, thinly disguised efforts to reduce price competition, such as collective denials to third-party payers of cooperation necessary for cost control, are also clearly illegal (*FTC v. Indiana Fed. of Dentists*, 1986).

Moreover, the fact that physicians enter into a network, such as a preferred provider organization or independent practice association, does not necessarily shield their activities from charges of price fixing. That is, where the arrangement is seen to be a "sham" designed to cover collective bargaining by independent, unaffiliated physicians, the actions have been struck down (*Southbank IPA, Inc.*, 1990). Cases have also found that interprovider cooperation undertaken through a third-party payer can amount to a horizontal conspiracy. The key issue is whether the insurer or its reimbursement mechanism is controlled by providers. For example, where a psychiatric hospital challenged a Blue Cross/ Blue Shield plan, the Sixth Circuit Court of Appeals held that if the plaintiff could establish that hospitals had effective control over the plan's formula for reimbursing hospitals, an illegal conspiracy would be made out (Furrow et al., 1994; *Glen Eden Hospital, Inc. v. Blue Cross and Blue Shield of Michigan*, 1984).

The fault line for determining whether a provider-controlled system will avoid characterization as price fixing is the degree to which it creates a new product. In *Arizona v. Maricopa County Med. Soc'y* (1982), the Supreme Court struck down fee agreements among competing physicians who joined a medical "foundation" that set maximum prices that participating physicians would accept as their terms of reimbursement from insurers. Distinguishing foundations from HMOs, the Court emphasized the absence of any meaningful integration, noting particularly that competing physicians in the foundation did not share risk. In the absence of some risk sharing or other integration so as to create a new product, such cooperative arrangements will be treated as price fixing and not as a joint venture or ancillary restraint. It has yet to be determined whether physician-hospital organizations and management service organizations will merit similar treatment.

Not all forms of provider cooperation face close antitrust scrutiny. The law's treatment of actions that limit competition to some degree, but nevertheless carry plausible justifications, has been considerably more tolerant. For example, physicians sharing information, surveying prices, or establishing advisory benchmarks (such as relative value scales) have come under scrutiny, with courts and agencies generally finding the cooperation pro-competitive under the rule of reason (Furrow et al., 1994). Information-sharing agreements have been approved where providers have established adequate safeguards to avoid spillovers and collusion. For instance, where no present or future price data are disclosed, the arrangements lack any enforcement mechanisms or coercion to pressure individual participants, and the information is exchanged in summary form and made available to nonmembers of the group, government advisory opinions approving the conduct have been routinely granted (*U.S. Department of Justice/ FTC*, 1994; *United States v. Container Corp. of America*, 1969). On the other hand, cooperative activity among physicians involving an exchange of sensitive information about managed care contracting, followed by prompt increases in prices, has led the government to conclude that the agreement to share information "spilled over" into a price-fixing arrangement (*United States v. Burgstiner*, 1991).

In the more problematic area of peer review of fees, the courts have suggested that providers' use of a panel of physicians to review pricing practices of other physicians was legal provided the arrangement was undertaken at the behest of and controlled by the third-party payer. Where, however, the peer review arrangement is controlled by competing providers, only plans that include strict limitations on the nature of the review, the dissemination of the information, and the role of the providers will escape antitrust scrutiny (*Bartholomew v. Virginia Chiropractors Ass'n, Inc.*, 1979; *Iowa Dental Ass'n*, 1982; *Zinser v. Rose*, 1989). The FTC has indicated that it would permit the American Medical Association and local medical societies to engage in mandatory peer review of fees where that review was confined to controlling abusive practices such as fraud or "fee gouging" (*Letter to Kirk B. Johnson and John M. Peterson from Donald S. Clark*, 1994). Organizations that engage in disciplinary actions based on fee levels alone or that are designed to promote uniform prices face antitrust problems.

Provider-Controlled Health Plans A particularly vexing issue for antitrust analysis has been the extent to which providers may control health care networks, including preferred provider organizations (PPOs) and independent practice associations (IPAs) (Furrow et al., 1994). These entities typically contract to provide services to subscribers of insurance plans and commonly join with other entities to bid for the business of employers and other large collective purchasers. They may pose some risk to competitive bargaining, depending on the proportion of the total number of physicians (or hospitals) involved in the PPO or IPA and the extent to which the group has meaningfully integrated, as contrasted with its functioning simply as a price-setting arrangement for its members. The federal enforcement agencies

have issued policy statements indicating that arrangements that share "substantial financial risk" will avoid characterization as price-fixing agreements (Greaney, 1994; *U.S. Department of Justice/ FTC*, 1994). "Substantial financial risk" is defined to mean that either services are provided on a capitation payment basis or a substantial amount of compensation is withheld by the plan as a financial incentive to achieve cost containment.

Where such networks comprise fewer than 20% of the providers in the relevant market, they will fall within a "safety zone" and will not be subject to challenge (*U.S. Department of Justice/ FTC*, 1994). Under the Department of Justice/ FTC analysis, each area of specialization will normally be considered a market. However, physicians from different specialties and nonphysician providers will be placed in the market where insurance plans and their subscribers consider them to be good substitutes for physicians in the network. Hence, it is likely that psychologists, and perhaps others such as certified social workers, would be considered competitors in the same market as psychiatrists when market share figures are calculated.

A particularly difficult judgment in this area has been fixing the level of concentration among providers that unacceptably threatens dominant-firm pricing or oligopolistic coordination among plans or forecloses entry by others—that is, the level of concentration that raises a threat of anticompetitive coordination among firms. In addition, the agencies have tried to balance the competing risks and benefits of exclusive arrangements among providers participating in such plans. While no judicial resolution of this issue has been obtained, the answer is likely to play an important role in shaping the nature and characteristics of large health provider groups forming in anticipation of health care reform in the United States.

Exclusion of Providers Another claim frequently advanced is that the denial of participation in a payment plan such as a PPO or HMO constitutes an actionable antitrust offense by members or by the operator of the plan. Antitrust analysis in these cases turns in large part on who controls the plan and its market power. Where the payment plan is controlled by a third party (that is, an entity that is not a competitor of the excluded provider), courts have likened the situation to vertical distribution arrangements between manufacturers and retailers, emphasizing the right of buyers and sellers to choose the parties with whom they will do business. Consequently, these contracts have been upheld (*Barry v. Blue Cross of California,* 1986) except in the rare instance in which the payer's refusal to deal was shown to be part of a conspiracy to restrain competition in the market for health insurance (*Reazin v. Blue Cross and Blue Shield of Kansas, Inc.,* 1990).

In cases involving provider-controlled plans, exclusion may be scrutinized more closely. Where an entire class of providers has been excluded and no plausible justification advanced, an illegal restraint of trade has been found (*Hahn v. Oregon Physicians Serv.,* 1989). At least in theory, a payer with enough market power to constitute an "essential facility" (that is, one for which there are few, if any, alternatives) may be required to accept all qualified providers willing to accept the plan's terms. As a general matter, however, essential facility claims are rarely successful because the excluded provider must establish that the plan had a monopoly position in the market and meet the doctrine's other stringent requirements (Furrow et al., 1994).

State laws mandating that certain categories of providers should or should not be included in plans may affect the analysis. For instance, where a state law specifically prohibited a Blue Shield plan from offering health services supplied by providers not specifically enumerated in the statute, a court has upheld the exclusion of psychotherapists by the plan under the state action doctrine, which is discussed in the following section (*Alonzo v. Blue Cross of Greater Philadelphia,* 1984).

"Naked" agreements among competitors to exclude providers that lack justifications have been successfully challenged as boycotts. In a well-known case—*Virginia Academy of Clinical Psychologists v. Blue Shield of Virginia* (1980)— an agreement involving two Blue Shield Plans controlled by physicians requiring that psychologists "bill through" a physician was found to constitute an illegal boycott. Although the opinion is less than clear as to the nature of the boycott in question, the court suggested that the agreement effectively rendered psychologists ineffective as competitors and lacked any procompetitive justification. It is important to note that the case involved an agreement between two Blue Shield plans, as well as an agreement among the professionals who controlled each plan. Hence, *Virginia Academy* does not stand for the proposition that all "structural" conspiracies (that is, those arising out of provider control) should result in injunctive relief, specifically ordering the conspirators to cease their anticompetitive activities, thereby affording access to excluded providers. Indeed, such relief seems anomalous because the composition of the plan might be attacked directly and because automatic access is inconsistent with the goals of competition (Havighurst & King, 1983).

Two other aspects of the *Virginia Academy* case are worthy of note. The Court specifically affirmed the lower court's judgment in favor of another defendant, the Neuropsychiatric Society of Virginia (NSV), which had "cooperated closely" with the plans and urged them to adopt the policies in question. The Court noted that there was no proof of a conspiracy between NSV and the plans in the sense of either an agreement to abide by its recommendation or coercion. It went on to emphasize the importance of allowing consumers to solicit proposals freely for health care insurance and to permit sellers to make recommendations aimed at persuading the buyer to purchase their services. Second, in a related case—*Blue Shield v. McCreedy* (1982)—the Supreme Court held that subscribers had standing to sue the plans under the Sherman Act even though the conspiracy's most direct impact was on the excluded psychologists.

In general, however, claims involving provider-controlled plans should not raise significant antitrust issues because the competitive benefits of such plans lie precisely in their ability to be selective. That is, to secure provider participation, PPOs and similar plans must promise a greater number of patients; and to attract the business of insurers and employers, they must offer a panel of providers meeting their customers' quality, geographic coverage, and other needs. Thus, exclusion of certain providers is a necessary (and indeed desirable) aspect of PPOs. Courts have generally acknowledged these considerations by holding that exclusion of a particular provider from a plan, differential reimbursement to participating and nonparticipating providers, and other forms of alleged "discrimination" are not illegal (*Hahn v. Oregon Physicians Servs.*, 1989). If a provider-controlled plan lacks market power, the exclusion of nonparticipating providers has been treated as a justifiable ancillary restraint, reasonably necessary to achieve the benefits of the joint venture (*Capitol Imaging Assocs. v. Mohawk Valley Med. Associates*, 1993; *Hassan v. Independent Practice Assocs.*, 1988; *U.S. Department of Justice/FTC*, 1994).

Defenses and Immunities

Several common law and statutory defenses limit the application of the antitrust laws. For example, the McCarran-Ferguson Act exemption provides that the antitrust laws are only "applicable to the business of insurance to the extent that such business is not regulated by state law." Thus, as long as an activity that would otherwise violate the antitrust laws (such as price fixing) is part of the business of insurance and authorized and regulated by the state, it is immune from attack. However, the Supreme Court has interpreted the business of insurance requirements strictly, holding that insurers' contracts with providers that do not involve spreading and underwriting of a policyholder's risks are not exempt (*Group Life & Health Ins. Co. v. Royal Drug Co.*, 1979).

Because antitrust law is aimed exclusively

at private conduct and not at regulatory decisions of the state or local governments, restraints authorized or compelled by government action are immune under the so-called "state action doctrine." However, states may not confer immunity merely by authorizing antitrust violations. The Supreme Court has enunciated a two-pronged test requiring that (1) the conduct be undertaken pursuant to a "clearly articulated and affirmatively expressed state policy" and (2) the "activity . . . be actively supervised" by the state (*California Retail Liquor Dealers Ass'n. v. MidCal Aluminum, Inc.*, 1980).[5]

While there are both statutory and nonstatutory exemptions for activities involving organized labor, courts and the FTC have rejected the notion that a physician "union" can claim protection under such agreements for their collective bargaining undertaken in negotiating with third-party payers. These cases have emphasized that independent physicians are independent contractors, not employees, and that negotiations concerning reimbursement terms are not the equivalent of labor negotiations over terms of employment (*Colorado v. Colorado Union of Physicians & Surgeons*, 1990; *Indiana Fed. of Dentists*, 1983).

Finally, competitors do not violate the antitrust laws when they act solely to elicit legislative, judicial, or administrative agency action. The Supreme Court has held that the Sherman Act does not reach actions connected with petitioning the government even where those seeking the action do so with the intent of suppressing competition (*Eastern RR. Presidents Conf. v. Noerr Motor Freight, Inc.*, 1961). The doctrine does not protect "sham" petitioning or actions in which the restraint is imposed directly by a boycott or price fixing, albeit with a legislative objective in mind (*Allied Tube & Conduit Co. v. Indianhead, Inc.*, 1988).

---

[5]For a case applying the doctrine to bar a challenge to a Blue Cross/Blue Shield plan's refusal to reimburse for the services of psychotherapists, see *Alonzo v. Blue Cross of Greater Philadelphia* (1984).

Health Care Reform and Antitrust

Recently, a number of states have sought to exempt antitrust activities for joint cooperation and mergers involving health care providers. Several have expressly exempted certain activities where a certificate of public convenience was obtained from the state and explicit approval was received from various state officials. While these acts will probably confer immunity from state antitrust laws, an open question remains as to whether they will satisfy the requirements of the state action doctrine to protect collaboration among providers from challenge under federal antitrust statutes. Recent Supreme Court cases have suggested that only a searching regulatory review that engages in meaningful preapproval and postapproval supervision of a venture's competitive impact will suffice to avoid federal antitrust challenges (*FTC v. Ticor Title Ins. Co.*, 1992; Vance, 1994).

Mental Health Mandates

State law "mandates" governing the provision of health benefits are a pervasive and controversial source of regulation of health care. Health care mandates can be divided into three categories of statutes: (1) *treatment mandates,* which require coverage for particular diseases or conditions, such as alcoholism and mental or nervous disorders; (2) *provider mandates,* which require coverage for the services of particular providers, such as chiropractors, psychologists, or optometrists; and (3) *special-population mandates,* which require coverage for particular groups of people, such as newborns, those with mental or physical disabilities, or adopted children who might otherwise have difficulty finding coverage (Krohm & Grossman, 1990). Treatment mandates come in two forms. The most common are "mandatory-inclusion" laws, which require that all health in-

surance policies contain certain provisions or minimum coverages. As of 1991, 18 states required mandatory inclusion of mental health care benefits (Jensen, 1993). The second form, the "available-for-sale" mandate, requires that insurers offer certain types of supplementary coverage for sale, leaving it up to the buyer whether to purchase that coverage. As of 1991, 10 states required that insurers offer for-sale coverage for mental health care (Jensen, 1993).

By one count, the total number of these laws nationally has risen from 37 in 1970 to 854 in 1990 (Jensen, 1993). Although the pace at which mandates are growing appears to have slowed and some states have begun to examine whether mandates increase costs, some provider groups have advanced legislative initiatives to establish new forms of mandates. Concerned about the potential exclusion of some providers under managed care contracting, many states are considering adopting so-called any willing provider legislation. These laws essentially force health plans to accept as a participating provider any licensed applicant willing to accept the plan's terms and conditions.

At first glance, the effect of mandates may appear beneficial because they serve to broaden insurance coverage and expand the availability of services by requiring more comprehensive coverage or access to a wider array of providers. As discussed below, however, many are now questioning the wisdom of these laws because of their effects on health care costs and the possibility that they dilute the benefits of a competitive marketplace.

The Economics of Mandates

The Economic Rationale for Mandates

The principal economic justification for mandates is that they correct imperfections in the market for group insurance. For example, as discussed in the preceding section, one information-based market failure is that insurance purchasers may

not consider the true value of mental health insurance and may underestimate their risk of ever having to seek mental health treatment (McGuire, 1981). Treatment mandates may cause the population's demand for mental health care coverage to increase to the "appropriate" level—that is, that which would occur if the value of the coverage was understood by well-informed purchasers.

Adverse selection may also distort markets for mental health care (McGuire, 1981). Adverse selection occurs when insurers are unable to price coverage according to buyers' risks. Under adverse selection, groups with a higher incidence of the covered service tend to elect coverage for those services and tend to cluster in plans with the most comprehensive coverage, while low-risk groups choose less extensive coverage or do without insurance altogether. A mandate could in theory strike a balance in premiums and coverage that would be beneficial to both high-risk and low-risk purchasers. Those skeptical of this justification have pointed out, however, that evidence indicating that adverse selection occurs is weak, that governments have no adequate means of determining whether the optimal level of care has been mandated, and that mandates chosen inappropriately may be harmful to consumers (Jensen, 1993).

Another important justification for mental health mandates, discussed below, is that they can encourage individuals to obtain treatment and reduce the need for other health services. Since many individuals receive government-supplied mental health care through public health programs and social welfare agencies, insurance mandates may be a means of shifting costs from public sources to employers and individuals. In addition, mandates may produce "externalities" in that mental health treatment that would not otherwise have been received may benefit not only the insured, but the insured's family, employer, or the community at large. Finally, there may also be noneconomic justifications for mandates. Mandatory-provider

statutes tend to preserve opportunities for alternative forms of health care delivery (that is, nonphysician providers).

The Economic Impact of Mandates

The economic impact of mandates has been controversial. Many contend that mandates increase the total cost of insurance, make it impossible for small employers to offer insurance, and eliminate the possibility of tailoring insurance packages to meet individual needs. One study estimates that as many as 25% of the uninsured lack health care coverage because state mandates make it too expensive (Minnesota Commission on Health Plan Regulatory Reform, 1989).

However, it has proven difficult to pin down the specific effects of mental health mandates. Various studies observe that a significant proportion of health care insurance claims are attributable to mental health care, that mental health mandates increase demand, and that mental health costs increase the costs of premiums (Jensen, 1993; Jensen & Morrissey, 1988; Krohm & Grossman, 1990). For purposes of evaluating mandates, however, these analyses may be misleading. Some mental health costs undoubtedly would be borne by employers even without mandates, and there is substantial evidence that some "offset effect" exists (that is, the availability of mental health services reduces the total cost of other health services). More broadly, the critical question from a policy perspective should be the following: What is the net social cost of mandates? Put another way, it is necessary to evaluate the offset effects that mental health mandates may have on costs outside health care and insurance markets. For instance, how do mandates affect productivity and use of non–health care social services? Although several studies attempt to provide some estimate of the total social cost of certain mental health mandates (Frisman, McGuire, & Rosenbach, 1985; McGuire & Montgomery, 1982), there are considerable difficulties in obtaining reliable evidence.

Perhaps the most important economic criticism of mandates is the adverse effect they may have on competitive contracting under managed competition. Provider mandates, particularly "any willing provider" laws, tend to reduce incentives for discounting and hard bargaining. Providers need not bargain as aggressively because they are assured access to all plans. Moreover, managed care entities cannot promise participating providers access to a greater number of patients because the mandate reduces their ability to limit the number of providers. Mandated access also detracts from the competitive benefits of selectivity in that plans cannot tailor their provider panels to suit competitive goals such as establishing a reputation for excellence.

The Political Economics of Mandates

A considerable literature has developed concerning whether legislatures enact mandates to serve the public interest or advance the legislators' own political interests. On the one hand, mandates may be seen as promoting the public interest to the extent that they correct market imperfections and improve market performance. Ideally, mandates might be justifiable if they offset information and adverse-risk-selection problems without distorting other conditions necessary to a well-functioning market. On the other hand, however, political "capture" theory teaches that well-organized, well-financed special interest groups often interact with legislators in a manner that allows the former to capture economic rents and the latter to reap political dividends. Mandates may thus act as a form of legislative favoritism that serves the financial interests of a few at the expense of the public. Alternatively, legislators may enact mandates because expanded private coverage may reduce the state's expenditures and thus mandates may provide a means to provide more services without raising taxes (Jensen, 1993).

Various interest groups favor different forms of mental health mandates. For example, health care providers such as psychologists and certified social workers—who are at a significant economic disadvantage if they do not qualify for insurance reimbursement—would favor provider mandates. The former groups, together with psychiatrists, mental health institutions, and patients who have a high demand for mental health services but lack insurance coverage, would tend to support treatment mandates. Large self-insured employers that are exempt from mandates under the federal Employee Retirement Income Security Act of 1974 (ERISA) (discussed below) and stand to gain an advantage over competitors might support treatment and provider mandates in order to burden their rivals with costly mandates (Jensen, 1993).

Several studies have examined whether the passage of mandates depended on various political criteria (for example, the strength of the special interest groups favoring and opposing the mandates, the political environment in the state, and the demographics of legislators' constituents). While the results of these analyses are not uniform, they lend support to the political interest or "capture" theory (Jensen, 1993). For instance, studies of mental health and psychologist mandates tend to be consistent with the political interest theory; however, no empirical support has been found regarding substance abuse mandates (Jensen, 1993; Lambert & McGuire, 1990).

States have recently become concerned about the possible negative impact of mandates on insurance and labor markets. Among the new generation of laws are statutes requiring financial and social impact evaluations; "ERISA equalization" laws, which limit the states' ability to mandate benefits unless the mandates also apply to self-insured plans; and waivers of mandated benefits for small firms (Jensen, 1993). Also, several states now allow firms employing fewer than a specified minimum number of workers to offer some "bare-bones" coverage exempt from mandates (Jensen, 1993).

Avoiding the Impact of Mandates: ERISA Preemption

ERISA, which extensively regulates employee pension and welfare plans, contains a broad preemption clause that provides that the act shall "supersede any and all State laws insofar as they may now or hereafter relate to any employee benefit plan" (ERISA, 1974, p. 29 USC §144(a)). However, this broad preemption of state law is limited by a "saving clause" that excepts from preemption any state law regulating insurance, banking, or securities. Yet another provision (the "deemer clause") provides that state laws purporting to regulate insurance cannot simply deem an employee benefit plan to be an insurance company.

Although the purpose of ERISA's preemptive provisions was to give large national employers assurances that they would face uniform regulation of their benefit plans, its consequences have been more far-reaching. It has induced many employers to self-insure their health benefits because it exempts them from state premium taxes and shields them from a variety of costly state regulations, including state insurance mandates. With ERISA substituting very little federal regulation for state regulation, self-insurance rapidly became an attractive option for the vast majority of the nation's larger employers.

The courts have considered a large number of cases challenging state mandates on the basis that ERISA preempts such laws. The Supreme Court has found that a Massachusetts law mandating minimum coverage for mental health services and other state-mandated benefit laws was not preempted by ERISA (*Metropolitan Life Insurance Co. v. Massachusetts*, 1985; *Michigan United Food and Commercial Workers Unions v. Baerwaldt*, 1985). Justice Blackmun, relying in part on the McCarran-Ferguson Act cases interpreting the meaning of the term *business of insurance*, wrote, "In short, the plain language of the saving clause, its relationship to the other ERISA preemption provisions, and the traditional understanding of insurance regulation, all lead us to the conclusion that mandated-benefit laws such as [the Massachusetts mandate] are saved from preemption by the operation of the saving clause" (*Metropolitan Life Insurance Co. v. Massachusetts*, 1985, p. 730).[6] The issue of whether ERISA preempts mandatory *provider* statutes, however, has not been resolved. The courts are split, with some cases and commentary suggesting that contracts between providers and insurers are not within the "business of insurance," following the interpretation of that phrase in cases coming under the McCarran-Ferguson Act.[7]

Conclusion

Both state law mandates and antitrust law attempt to improve market performance. The effects of these interventions in mental health care markets are especially complex because of the nature and extent of market failures and the leeway sometimes afforded to professionals. Antitrust courts have declined, for the most part, to consider noneconomic factors in their evaluations of trade restraints, leaving such concerns to the legisla-

---

[6]Acknowledging the effects of its decision, the Court stated, "We are aware that our decision results in a distinction between insured and uninsured plans, leaving the former open to indirect regulation while the latter are not . . . a distinction created by Congress in [29 U.S.C. 1144 (b)(2)(B)], a distinction Congress is aware of and one it has chosen not to alter." See *Metropolitan Life Insurance Co. v. Massachusetts* (1985).

[7]Compare *Blue Cross Hospital Service, Inc. of Missouri v. Frappier* (1985) (holding no preemption of Missouri's mandatory-provider statutes for chiropractors and psychologists) and *Blue Cross and Blue Shield of Kansas City v. Bell* (1986) (holding no preemption of a Kansas mandatory-provider statute) with *Metropolitan Life Insurance Co. v. Insurance Commissioner* 441 A.2d 1098 (1983), rev'd, 296 Md. 334, 463 A.2d 793 (1983) and ERISA Preemption of State Mandated-Provider Laws (1985) (criticizing *Frappier* for not properly distinguishing between mandatory-provider and mandatory-benefits statutes and noting congressional intent to preempt mandatory-provider statutes for legal services).

ture. However, antitrust evaluations are increasingly likely to take into account market imperfections in health care, a factor that may be of considerable relevance in cases involving mental health care services. Mandates explicitly attempt to address market imperfections by directly increasing the demand for mental health services or guaranteeing providers access to insurance plans. The effects of these laws on market performance are problematic, however, because legislatures do not have reliable means of ensuring that they have chosen the "correct" amount of adjustment and because these interventions may hamper selective contracting and severely dilute the incentives of a competitive marketplace.

References

Allied Tube & Conduit Co. v. Indianhead, Inc., 486 U.S. 492 (1988).

Alonzo v. Blue Cross of Greater Philadelphia, 611 F. Supp. 310 (E.D. Pa. 1984).

American Academy of Ophthalmologists, 108 F.T.C. 25 (1986).

American Med. Ass'n, 94 F.T.C. 701 (1979) (consent order).

American Med. Ass'n v. United States, 317 U.S. 519 (1943).

In re American Psychological Association, FTC File No. 861-0082 (Sept. 9, 1992).

Arizona v. Maricopa County Med. Soc'y, 457 U.S. 332 (1982).

Barry v. Blue Cross of California, 805 F.2d 866 (9th Cir. 1986).

Bartholomew v. Virginia Chiropractors Ass'n, Inc., 612 F.2d 812 (4th Cir. 1979), *cert. denied*, 446 U.S. 938 (1980).

Bhan v. NME Hosps., Inc., 929 F.2d 1404 (9th Cir.), *cert. denied*, 112 S.Ct. 617 (1991).

Blue Cross and Blue Shield of Kansas City v. Bell, 798 F.2d 1331, 1334–35 (10th Cir. 1986).

Blue Cross Hospital Service, Inc. of Missouri v. Frappier, 698 S.W.2d 326 (Mo. 1985).

Blue Shield v. McCreedy, 457 U.S. 465 (1982).

Boczar v. Manatee Hosps. & Health Sys., Inc., 993 F.2d 1514 (11th Cir. 1993).

Bolt v. Halifax Hosp. Med. Cntr., 891 F.2d 810 (11th Cir.), *cert. denied*, 495 U.S. 924 (1990).

Brown Shoe Co. v. United States, 370 U.S. 294, 320 (1962).

Burnham Hosp., 101 F.T.C. 991 (1983) (advisory opinion).

California Retail Liquor Dealers Ass'n. v. MidCal Aluminum, Inc., 445 U.S. 97 (1980).

Capitol Imaging Assocs. v. Mohawk Valley Med. Associates, 996 F.2d 537 (2d Cir. 1993), *cert. denied*, 114 S.Ct. 388 (1993).

Collins v. Associated Pathologists, Ltd., 844 F.2d 473 (7th Cir.), *cert. denied*, 488 U.S. 852 (1988).

Colorado v. Colorado Union of Physicians & Surgeons, Civ. A. No. 90-F-407, 1990 WL 56,176 (D. Colo. 1990).

Connecticut Chiropractor Ass'n, 56 Fed.Reg. 23586 (1991) (consent order).

Consolidated Metals Products v. American Petroleum Inst., 846 F.2d 284 (5th Cir. 1988).

Drs. Steuer & Latham v. National Med. Enterprises Inc., 846 F.2d 70 (4th Cir. 1988).

Eastern RR. Presidents Conf. v. Noerr Motor Freight, Inc., 365 U.S. 127 (1961).

Eastman Kodak Co. v. Image Technical Services, Inc., 112 S.Ct. 2072 (1992).

Employee Retirement Income Security Act of 1974, 29 U.S.C. § 1001 *et seq.* (1974).

ERISA Preemption of State Mandated-Provider Laws (1985), Duke L. J. 1194.

Federal Trade Commission Act, §§ 4, 5 (15 U.S.C. §§ 44, 45).

Frisman, L. K., McGuire, T. G., & Rosenbach, M. L. (1985). Costs of mandates for outpatient mental health care in private health insurance. *Archives of General Psychiatry, 42,* 558–561.

FTC v. Indiana Fed. of Dentists, 476 U.S. 447 (1986).

FTC v. Ticor Title Ins. Co., 112 S.Ct. 2169 (1992).

Furrow, B., Greaney, T. L., Johnson, S. H., Jost, T. S., & Schwartz, R. L. (1994). *Health Law.* St. Paul, MN: West.

Glen Eden Hospital, Inc. v. Blue Cross and Blue Shield of Michigan, 740 F.2d 423 (6th Cir. 1984).

Goldfarb v. Virginia State Bar, 421 U.S. 773 (1975).

Goss v. Memorial Hosp. Systems, 789 F.2d 353 (5th Cir. 1986).

Greaney, T. L. (1989). Quality of care and market failure defenses in antitrust health care litigation. *Connecticut Law Review, 21,* 605–665.

Greaney, T. L. (1994). The Department of Justice/FTC health care policy statements: A critique. *Antitrust, 8,* 20.

Group Health Coop of Puget Sound v. King County Med. Soc'y, 39 WN2d 586, 237 P.2d 737 (1951).

Group Life & Health Ins. Co. v. Royal Drug Co., 440 U.S. 205 (1979).

Hahn v. Oregon Physicians Serv., 868 F.2d 1022 (9th Cir.), *cert. denied,* 493 U.S. 846 (1989).

Hassan v. Independent Practice Assocs., 698 F. Supp. 679 (E.D. Mich. 1988).

Havighurst, C. C. (1986). The changing locus of decision making in the health care sector. *Journal of Health Politics, Policy, and Law, 11,* 697–735.

Havighurst, C. C., & King, N. M. P. (1983). Private credentialing of health care personnel: An antitrust perspective. *American Journal of Law and Medicine, 9*(2), 131–201.

Indiana Fed. of Dentists, 101 F.T.C. 57 (1983), vac'd 745 F.2d 1124 (7th Cir.), rev'd 476 U.S. 447 (1986).

Interstate Circuit v. United States, 306 U.S. 208 (1939).

Iowa Chapter of the American Physical Therapy Ass'n, No. C-3242 (1988) (consent order).

Iowa Dental Ass'n, 99 F.T.C. 648 (1982).

Jefferson Parish Hosp. Dist. No. 2 v. Hyde, 466 U.S. 2 (1984).

Jensen, G. A. (1993). Regulating the content of health plans. In R. B. Helms (Ed.), *American health policy: Critical issues for reform* (pp. 167–193). Washington, DC: American Enterprise Institute Press.

Jensen, G. A., & Morrissey, M. (1988). Employer-sponsored insurance for alcohol and drug abuse treatment. *Inquiry, 28,* 393–402.

Kaczanowski v. Medical Center Hospital, 612 F. Supp. 688 (D.Vt. 1985).

Koefoot v. American College of Surgeons, 1987–1 Trade Cas. CCH para. 67,510 (N.C. Ill. 1986).

Kovacic, W. E. (1990). The antitrust paradox revisited: Robert Bork and the transformation of modern antitrust policy. *Wayne Law Review, 36,* 1413–1471.

Krattenmaker, T. G., & Salop, S. C. (1986). Anticompetitive exclusion: Raising rivals; costs to achieve power over price. *Yale Law Journal, 96,* 209–293.

Krohm, G., & Grossman, M. H. (1990). Mandated benefits in health insurance policies. *Benefits Quarterly,* 51–60.

Kwoka, J., & White, L. (Eds.). (1989). *The antitrust revolution.*

Lambert, D. A., & McGuire, T. G. (1990). Political and economic determinants of insurance regulation in mental health. *Journal of Health, Politics, Policy, and Law, 15,* 169–189.

Letter to Kirk B. Johnson and John M. Peterson from Donald S. Clark, Secretary, Federal Trade Commission, February 14, 1994 (advisory opinion).

Lopatka, J. E. (1991). Antitrust and professional roles: A framework for analysis. *San Diego Law Review, 28,* 301–386.

Marrese v. American Academy of Orthopedic Surgeons, 977 F.2d 585 (7th Cir. 1992).

McGuire, T. G. (1981). *Financing psychotherapy: Costs, effects, and public policy* (pp. 61–72). Cambridge, MA: Ballinger.

McGuire, T. G., & Montgomery, J. T. (1982). Mandated mental health benefits in private health insurance policies. *Journal of Health, Politics, Policy, and Law, 7,* 380–406.

Medical Staff of Prince Georges County, 110 F.T.C. 476 (1988) (consent order).

Metropolitan Life Insurance Co. v. Insurance Commissioner, 51 Md. App. 122, 441 A.2d 1098 (1982), rev'd, 296 Md. 334, 463 A.2d 793 (1983).

Metropolitan Life Insurance Co. v. Massachusetts, 41 U.S. 724 (1985).

Michigan Optometric Ass'n, 106 F.T.C. 342 (1985) (consent order).

Michigan State Med. Soc'y, 101 F.T.C. 191 (1983).

Michigan United Food and Commercial Workers Unions v. Baerwaldt, 767 F.2d 308 (6th Cir. 1985).

Minnesota Commission on Health Plan Regulatory Reform (1989) [citing Freedom of Choice in Health Insurance, National Center for Policy Analysis (1988)].

Minnesota v. Mid-West Minnesota Associated Physicians, 1991–2 Tr. Cas. (CCH ¶ 69,531) (D. Minn. 1991) (consent decree).

Monsanto Co. v. Spray-Rite Serv. Corp., 465 U.S. 752 (1984).

In re Nat'l Ass'n of Social Workers, FTC, File No. 861 0126 (Dec. 15, 1992).

National Soc'y of Prof. Eng's v. United States, 435 U.S. 679 (1978).

New York v. Empire Pharmaceutical Society, Inc., 1978-2 Tr. Cas. (¶ 62,383 (N.Y. Sup. Ct. 1978) (consent decree).

Northern Pacific Railway v. United States, 356 U.S. 1 (1958).

Note (1986). Denying hospital privileges to non-physicians: Does quality of care justify a potential restraint of trade? *Indiana Law Review, 19,* 1219–1251.

Oksanen v. Page Memorial Hosp., 945 F.2d 696, 703 (4th Cir. 1991), *cert. denied,* 112 S.Ct. 973 (1992).

Okusami v. Psychiatric Institute of Washington, Inc., 959 F.2d 1062 (D.C. Cir. 1992).

Oltz v. St. Peter's Comm. Hosp., 861 F.2d 1440 (9th Cir. 1989).

Peel v. Attorney Registration and Disciplinary Comm'n of Illinois, 496 U.S. 91 (1990).

Pitofsky, R. (1979). The political content of antitrust. *University of Pennsylvania Law Review, 127,* 1051–1075.

Posner, R. A. (1976). *Antitrust law: An economic perspective.* Chicago: University of Chicago Press.

Reazin v. Blue Cross and Blue Shield of Kansas, Inc., 899 F.2d 951 (10th Cir. 1990).

Schachar v. American Academy of Ophthalmology, 870 F.2d 397 (7th Cir. 1989).

Scott, C. L. (1991). Medical peer review, antitrust, and the effect of statutory reform. *Maryland Law Review, 50,* 316–407.

Sherman Act, 15 USC §§ 1 *et seq.* §§ 1, 2, 1011.

Sherman A. Hope, M.D., 98 F.T.C. 58 (1981).

Southbank IPA, Inc., 57 Fed. Reg. 2913 (1990) (consent decree).

State ex rel. Corbin v. Arizona State Psychological Ass'n, 1988–1 Trade Cas. (CCH) ¶ 67,928 (Ariz. Super. Ct. 1988).

State of Ohio v. JCAH, Civ. No. C-2-79-1158 (S.D. Ohio, filed Dec. 14, 1979) (later dismissed as moot).

United States v. Alston, 974 F.2d 1206 (9th Cir. 1992).

United States v. Burgstiner, 1991–1 Tr. Cas. (CCH ¶ 69,422) (S.D. Ga. 1991) (consent decree).

United States v. Container Corp. of America, 393 U.S. 333 (1969).

United States v. Grinnell Corp., 384 U.S. 563 (1966).

United States v. Montana Nursing Home Ass'n, Inc., 1982–2 Tr. Cas. (CCH ¶ 64,852) (D. Mont. 1982).

U.S. Department of Justice/Federal Trade Commission. *Statements of enforcement policy and analytical principles relating to health care and antitrust* (Sept. 30, 1994). Reprinted in 4 Trade Reg. Rep. (CCH) ¶ 13,152 at 20,769.

Vance, S. S. (1994). Immunity for state-sanctioned provider collaboration after *Ticor*, 62, Antitrust L. J. 409–431.

Virginia Academy of Clinical Psychologists v. Blue Shield of Virginia, 624 F.2d 476 (4th Cir. 1980).

Virginia State Bd. of Pharmacy v. Virginia Citizens Consumer Council Inc., 425 U.S. 748 (1976).

Weiss v. York Hosp., 745 F.2d 786 (3d Cir. 1984), *cert. denied*, 470 U.S. 1060 (1985).

Welch v. American Psychoanalytic Ass'n, No. 85 Civ 1651 (JFK), S.D. N.Y. 1986 (slip opinion April 14, 1986).

Wilk v. American Med. Ass'n, 895 F.2d 352 (7th Cir.), *cert. denied*, 496 U.S. 927 (1990).

Zinser v. Rose, 868 F.2d 938 (7th Cir. 1989).

7 Legal Influences on the Financing of Mental Health Care

Jeffrey Rubin

Rutgers, The State University of New Jersey

The debate engendered by the introduction of the Health Security Act has focused new attention on the way health care is financed in the United States (Congressional Budget Office, 1994a, 1994b). Efforts to legislate new forms of insurance arrangements and promote alternative service delivery systems are likely to continue for some time. Restructuring key elements in such a large sector of the economy affects so many people in so many ways that achieving a consensus may remain an elusive goal for a very long time.

In connection with the larger question of how to reform the American system for providing health insurance and for delivering health care services, questions continue to arise as to how best to finance and organize mental health services (Arons, Frank, Goldman, McGuire, & Stephens, 1994). Even without the struggle to achieve broad health care reform, the mental health sector has experienced turmoil in recent years. The confluence of numerous developments has prompted legislators, insurers, mental health professionals, advocates for persons with a mental illness, and others to promote alternative views on a wide spectrum of issues.

In both the public and private sectors, the principal players have offered ideas for reform and change (Sharfstein & Stoline, 1992). For example, the private sector has seen extraordinary growth in the use of managed mental health care (Tischler, 1990). Typically, this involves the administrative review of provider decisions regarding the type, location, and extent of mental health treatment. Also, in the face of rising costs for health care and for mental health care, private insurers and firms have collaborated to design benefit packages that reduce the potential financial risks of covering mental health costs (Frank, Salkever, & Sharfstein, 1991). Limits on benefits and financial barriers to care are common and are easily implemented. In the public sector, mental health agencies—often under pressure from state legislators and family advocates—are testing strategies to improve the delivery of mental health care and to contain the costs of such care. For instance, a series of large cities participated in an effort to reorganize their mental health system under an umbrella organization designed to improve the coordination among the many agencies involved in delivering services to persons with a serious mental illness (Morrissey et al., 1994). Other experiments addressed the need for better coordination of services through the creation of case management services (Franklin, Solovitz, Mason, Clemons, & Miller, 1987; Jerrell & Hu, 1989). Still other measures are aimed at combining financial incentives with new organizational structures to improve services and constrain growth in spending.

All these changes are occurring in an environment in which courts and legislators set the parameters. What can be done, how it can be done, by whom, and for whom must fit within the legal rules established through legislation and judicial decisions. In this chapter, the goal is to examine some of the ways courts and legislators affect the financing and delivery of mental health care services. I begin by outlining the fiscal features of the current mental health system. This is followed by a review and analysis of several types of court decisions that affect privately financed mental health care. I also consider some issues associated with legislation to modify private insurance and private delivery systems. In the next section, I report on legal actions intended to force states to increase spending for mental health services. This is followed by a review of recent state legislation, and some related litigation, designed to restructure the system for financing public mental health care. The chapter concludes with some comments about the role of legal advocacy, including its potential limitations, in helping to create a more efficient and more equitable system for delivering quality care to persons with serious and chronic mental health problems.

The Financing and Organization of Mental Health Care

Describing the "mental health system" is difficult. There are two broad perspectives to consider when approaching this task. On the one hand, we can look at the providers of mental health care and use their activities to determine the size and scope of the mental health care system. On the other hand, we can examine the care and services received by persons who meet standardized criteria and are classified as having either a mental illness or a mental health problem. Each approach has advantages and disadvantages.

By looking at providers of mental health care, we acquire a sense of how mental health care is paid for and who delivers such care. This approach does not give a complete picture because many persons with a mental illness may receive other forms of assistance from nonspecialty providers and organizations.

Reviewing spending from the perspective of services received by persons with a mental illness provides useful information on access to care and may also offer insights into financial barriers to care. The problems with this approach stem largely from the need to define which people to include and the difficulty of collecting data on use and costs. In particular, we may wish to focus on only those persons with a serious and chronic mental illness. The system for financing mental health care for persons with short-term problems that cause little functional impairment and require minimal expense is less controversial and less subject to dispute. Furthermore, a clear picture of the functioning and well-being of persons with a chronic mental illness may require collecting information beyond the payments made for mental health services, such as the behavioral consequences of care, that can be difficult to define and measure.

Finally, it is important to emphasize how constrained any analysis is by the way the data are collected and the kinds of data that are collected. Private insurance firms can report on total spending for persons with a particular diagnosis or on payments to certain types of providers. Their data can also be used to develop a description of the services—involving both physical and mental health care—that a particular type of individual receives over the course of some specified time period. The data typically will not include services paid for by other persons or organizations.

Public systems for financing care often have difficulty providing a complete picture of the care an individual has received. Data on amounts spent for certain types of services or payments on behalf of an individual through a public insurance program can be collected. But linking data across programs and individuals is time-consuming, costly, and sometimes not even feasible. The best information on services received by an individual and the costs of these services usually comes from experiments by alternative delivery systems that establish a data system designed to track all services to develop estimates of cost per individual (Weisbrod, 1981).

Epidemiology of Mental Disorders

Spending for mental health care depends on the extent of mental illness in the population, the proportion of the mentally ill population that seeks treatment, and the type and quantity of treatments and services that persons with mental illness receive. Excellent data on prevalence and use rates can be derived from the Epidemiological Catchment Area (ECA) study (Regier et al., 1993). The ECA was a survey, conducted in five metropolitan areas, of over 20,000 persons. Data collection began in 1980, included a 12-month follow-up, and was completed by 1985. Respondents were asked a series of questions that enabled researchers to make diagnostic judgments. In addition, data were collected on the use of medical and mental health services.

Researchers working with the data generated by the ECA concluded that the annual adult prevalence rate for mental or addictive disorders was 28.1%, or about 44.7 million persons.[1] Deleting those with substance abuse disorders reduces the prevalence rate to 22.1%, or just over 35 million individuals in 1980.[2]

Regier et al. (1993) also provide data on the use of the mental health service delivery system. They limit their focus to people who "sought treatment or counseling for what they defined as significant mental or addictive symptoms or emotional distress" (Regier et al., 1993, p. 89). Using this definition will probably result in an undercount of both the number of people receiving services and the quantity of services received by persons who have a mental illness or addictive disorder. Only about 28.5% of those diagnosed as having a mental or addictive disorder received treatment during the course of the year. An even smaller percentage (12.7%) of the 44.7 million adults with a mental or addictive disorder diagnosis received care from the specialty mental health or addictive service sector. The others who received services for a mental or addictive disorder were seen in the general medical sector, the human service sector, or the voluntary support network (for example, 12-step programs, family, and so on).

Narrow, Regier, Rae, Manderscheid, and Locke (1993) present some additional data on patterns of service utilization for mental health or substance abuse reasons. They report that, during 1980, an estimated "22.8 million persons made 326 million outpatient visits to professional or volunteer sources for mental health or substance abuse reasons" (p. 97). These figures indicate that over 10 million people who report being treated for a mental health or substance abuse problem did not meet the diagnostic criteria necessary to be classified as having a mental illness or substance abuse disorder.[3]

Just over 38% (8.8 million) of all those treated were seen by someone in the specialty mental health sector, and about half of these were treated by a mental health specialist in private practice. Of particular interest is the finding that more people (9.4 million) were treated for a psychiatric or substance abuse problem by general medical physicians than were treated by all

---

[1] This rate is the proportion of the adult population in the United States that had a mental or addictive disorder at some time during a one-year period. This rate is the result of summing two different estimates. First, the number of people with a mental disorder at the time of the first interview (a prevalence rate) was determined. Second, the number of people who had no disorder at the time of the first interview but who had a disorder at some time during the one-year follow-up period (an incidence rate) was determined. Combining these two figures yields the 28.1% one-year prevalence rate.

[2] Detailed information on prevalence and one-year incidence rates by diagnostic category are summarized in Regier et al. (1993).

[3] The ECA was designed only to identify people who had a disorder during the one-year survey period. Many who used services but did not have a disorder (based on this survey methodology) either had a history of a mental or substance abuse disorder or had significant, but subthreshold, symptoms of a disorder.

the different providers in the specialty mental health sector. The specialty sector did provide about three and a half times as many visits (122.3 million) as general medical physicians (36.1 million).[4]

Data on use of inpatient care show that 1.4 million people were admitted to an inpatient facility during the year for treatment of a mental health problem. About 21% of these persons did not have a mental illness or substance abuse diagnosis during the course of the year, but most did have a history of a disorder or psychiatric symptoms. Most received inpatient care in either a general hospital (43.3%) or a state and county mental hospital (35.2%). These numbers support two contrasting conclusions. First, substantial resources are available, via either public or private insurance, to pay for inpatient care in general hospitals. Second, the numbers also indicate that for many people a lack of resources and insurance combined with the severity of their illness often necessitates confinement in a state facility.

The ECA data offer a clear picture of who uses which types of providers for treatment of a mental health or substance abuse reason. But the data do not shed any light on how this care is financed, nor do they offer any help in understanding how financial arrangements influence the observed treatment patterns. These figures suggest that careful attention must be given to how financing arrangements influence the decision to use care, the type of care selected, and the quantity of care. Although many factors can hamper utilization, access to public and private insurance policies, the structure of benefits for mental health care in those policies, and the availability of funds to finance public sector services are central to the theme of this chapter. Thus, I turn to the level and scope of funding available for mental health services.

Expenditures and Revenues for Mental Health Care

In this section, I review aggregate spending patterns and briefly summarize data on sources of financing for mental health care. It is important to emphasize that the financing arrangements affecting expenditure and use patterns are the result of many factors, including various legislative enactments and judicial decisions. Consequently, after describing the financing system, I address some significant ways legal factors shape the financing system.

The National Institute of Mental Health collects data on spending and revenue sources for mental health organizations. As the ECA findings indicate, these data are likely to miss a substantial amount of spending that occurs outside the traditional mental health sector, especially among general medical care providers. Nonetheless, the data on spending levels and sources of funds do help clarify where mental health resources are going and the sources of these funds. Of special interest will be the changing distribution of expenditures over time, showing how policy, legal, and other changes result in shifts of funds within the mental health care sector.

In 1988, expenditures in mental health organizations totaled just over $23 billion (Redick et al., 1992).[5] Expenditures in state and county hospitals represent 30% of the total. The three other major sectors are "other organizations" (20%), private psychiatric hospitals (19.9%), and nonfederal general hospitals (15.7%).

The most important trend from the mid-1970s through the late 1980s is the shift of resources away from state and county hospitals.

---

[4]Detailed data on outpatient and inpatient treatments received by sector, as well as information on the quantity of care, are available by diagnostic category. (See Narrow et al., 1993, Tables 1 through 4.)

[5]Mental health organizations include state and county mental hospitals, private psychiatric hospitals, general hospitals with psychiatric services, Veterans Administration (VA) medical centers, federally funded community mental health centers, residential treatment centers for emotionally disturbed children, freestanding psychiatric outpatient clinics, and a variety of other organizations. Many of the federally funded community mental health centers were reclassified into this last category in the early 1980s.

Though critics harp on the inability to shift funds out of the state institutions even as the use of these facilities declined in importance, the data show that there has been a gradual but steady reallocation of funds away from state and county hospitals. In 1975, these facilities spent 48.5% of all dollars expended in mental health organizations. By 1988, the share of spending had fallen to 30.3%. Actual spending in these facilities more than doubled during this period. When the effects of inflation are taken into account, real spending actually declined by about 25%.

Though the share of expenditures in state and county hospitals fell, spending in other inpatient facilities rose. Thus, the proportion of total expenditures made in private psychiatric hospitals rose from 7.1% in 1975 to 19.9% in 1988. The corresponding figures for general hospitals were 9.5% in 1975 and 15.7% in 1988. Combined real spending for these two types of inpatient organizations rose by 150% and, in 1988, exceeded spending in state and county hospitals. Pressure from both private and public insurers during the last six years has probably slowed, if not reversed, the growth in use and expenditures in these facilities.[6]

The shifting expenditure patterns undoubtedly reflect changes in who is paying for care. It is uncertain whether changes in available revenue sources result in new use and expenditure patterns or whether changes in use, perhaps triggered by new treatment methods, result in greater reliance on particular revenue sources. Although causation will remain difficult to determine, it is possible to describe how revenue sources have changed over time.

Just under 35% of the $23.3 billion received by mental health organizations was supplied by state mental health agencies. Another 21% of revenues came from client fees, much of which

is paid for through insurers. Medicaid and Medicare supplied 20% of the funding for mental health organizations, of which about 44% was for care in separate psychiatric units in general hospitals.[7] The sources for the remaining funds included other federal programs (mostly the VA), local governments, and a variety of other sources. The only substantial shift during the mid-1980s was toward relatively more revenues from client fees. This reflected the growing use of private psychiatric hospitals and general hospitals where private insurance typically covers expenses. If recent efforts to introduce restrictions on use of these services are effective, it is reasonable to expect to find a decline in the share of revenues attributable to client fees in the 1990s.

The aggregate revenue and expenditure data necessarily hide extensive variations in the level and distribution of mental health resources across the 50 states (Redick et al., 1993, Table 1.13). Between 1983 and 1988, per capita spending in all mental health organizations rose nearly 50%, from $62.12 to $94.33. The states in which more resources are devoted to mental health care spend about 90% more per capita than the national average (Massachusetts—$174.44; New York—$173.20). At the other extreme, several states spend about half of the national per capita average (Idaho—$45.49; Arkansas—$53.47).

The states also vary in the distribution of spending across different types of mental health organizations. For example, about one-third of mental health spending in Vermont occurs in private psychiatric hospitals. Many Midwestern states exceed the national average in the proportion of spending on general hospital psychiatric services. For example, in Iowa, about 35% of mental health spending occurs in these facilities. At the other end, only about 6% of mental health expenditures in Rhode Island occur in general

---

[6]Controversy over questionable practices in some private psychiatric hospitals contributed to the changes. One major operator of psychiatric hospitals recently settled fraud charges with the federal government and 28 states (Harris, 1994).

[7]See Taube, Goldman, and Salkever (1990) and Lave and Goldman (1990) for discussions regarding the structure of Medicaid and Medicare and their link to financing care for persons with a serious mental illness.

hospitals. These figures are partly related to historical patterns of support for public facilities, the availability of private psychiatric facilities, levels of insurance coverage for inpatient treatment, state decisions about the structure of their Medicaid program, and differences across the population in the demand for care.

The changes in the distribution of spending across mental health organizations and revenue sources over time as well as the differences in spending patterns across the states are partly attributable to differential legal developments. In some instances, states have restructured their mental health systems, sometimes to take advantage of the availability of resources. In other cases, states have passed legislation leading to expanded coverage for mental health care in private insurance policies.[8]

Fiscal problems brought on by the recession in 1990 and 1991 forced states to make difficult choices about tax policy and spending allocations, which in turn affected funding for mental health care. Besides being influenced by budgetary and legislative actions, the organization and structure of mental health care are affected by the results of litigation. In the following section, I discuss some of the legal rulings shaping private health insurance markets.

individual, individuals often take their case to the courts. Major class action lawsuits have been a popular tool that advocates use to force state governments or state agencies to increase funding for mental health care or to force states to change the way they spend available funds (Rubin, 1978; Weiner & Wettstein, 1993). Personal injury litigation and individual challenges to interpretation of insurance contracts have also changed aspects of the financing and delivery of mental health care (Rubin, 1994).

Private health insurance is a major source of funding for mental health care. Generally, most policies provided to employees cover inpatient and outpatient mental health care.[9] Though there are often restrictions on benefits, such as a lifetime or annual cap on insurance payments or higher copayments and deductibles, these policies provide some financial protection against acute psychiatric illness.[10] When these benefits expire because a condition is chronic, individuals either must meet additional expenses from personal funds or, if eligible, may qualify for cash benefits under the Social Security Disability Insurance (SSDI) program.[11] After being eligible for SSDI benefits for two years, these individuals qualify for Medicare coverage. Furthermore, if their income and assets are sufficiently low, they may also qualify for Medicaid coverage.

Case Law and Private Health Insurance

In an effort to affect public policy decisions as well as to achieve a fairly narrow goal for a specific

---

[8]One case involving the interpretation of a state mandate statute is discussed later. A more detailed discussion of mandates can be found in Frank and McGuire (1990). Legal issues surrounding the use of mandates are addressed in Rubin (1991). He also discusses related legal developments affecting health insurance coverage for dependents with mental illness and workers' compensation claims by persons suffering from a mental health problem.

[9]Many of the issues facing employers and insurers with respect to mental health benefits, particularly the problems in projecting costs of different plan provisions, are discussed in McGuire (1994). Some data on the costs of covering mental health care in private insurance plans are summarized in Frank, Salkever, and Sharfstein (1991). Data on mental health benefits in private insurance plans are presented in Blostin (1987) and U.S. Bureau of Labor Statistics (1990).

[10]Some evidence of the impact of various forms of limitations on mental health benefits are discussed in Tsai, Reedy, Bernacki, and Lee (1988) and Custer (1991). Tsai et al. describe how one company's introduction of tighter limits on inpatient care altered utilization patterns and lowered costs. Custer, using a more aggregate approach, also found that restrictions on mental health benefits lowered inpatient use, increased outpatient use, and resulted in lower overall spending for mental health care. Neither paper offers much insight into the impacts of these reductions in use on patient outcomes.

Insurance Contracts

The clauses in private health insurance contracts designed to limit insurer liability for costs of treating mental illness are sometimes the subject of dispute, with many cases winding up in court.[12] From the financing perspective, these contract disputes are significant not because of the way a particular case is resolved but because of the implications of the judicial decision for future contract specifications. In effect, the rulings in cases where the interpretation of terms such as *mental illness* or *mental health care* is at issue establish new boundaries for parties entering into negotiations to draw up a health insurance contract.

The details of several cases and the issues raised by these challenges to insurer efforts to restrict coverage for treatment of mental illness are discussed at length in Rubin (1994). Generally, the major point of contention is how to apply contract language limiting coverage for "mental illness" when there is testimony that a particular condition may have a physical origin but manifests itself in the form of mental problems. In one case, *Saah v. Contel Corporation* (1991), the question was whether the specific condition or the nature of the treatment determined if a limitation applied.[13] In *Saah,* the court, relying on the nature of the treatment to resolve the ambiguity that results when the term *mental illness* is used, ruled that the restriction did apply. After reviewing the contract language, the nature of the proposed treatment, and the origin of the problems requiring treatment, another court decided against an insurer (*Phillips v. Lincoln National Life Insurance Company,* 1992). In another case, the plaintiff first won a partial victory in his effort to obtain additional coverage, only to have that decision overturned on appeal (*Brewer v. Lincoln National Life Insurance Company,* 1990). Basing its decision on the standard that contract terms should be accorded their common meaning, the Court of Appeals decided that the limitations were meant to apply to the plaintiff's situation.

Courts sometimes conduct a detailed examination of the treatment someone is receiving before deciding whether or not a restriction in an insurance contract should apply. In one case, plaintiffs challenged an insurer's determination that the care their daughter was receiving was custodial (*Adelson v. GTE Corporation,* 1992). On the basis of this conclusion, the insurer applied a clause in the contract excluding coverage for custodial services and declined to pay for the care. After an extended review of the treatment program, the court ordered the defendant to pay for the care.

Besides the issues that arise when someone

---

[11]The number of persons receiving SSDI benefits because of a mental illness has grown considerably in the past decade. Over 25% (about 164,100 people) of all SSDI awards to disabled workers in 1992 were for a mental impairment (U.S. General Accounting Office, 1994). Some of the growth has been due to aggressive use of the appeals process and subsequent litigation. For some examples of the issues that are raised in SSDI litigation, see *Case v. Sullivan* (1992) and *Walker v. Secretary of Health and Human Services* (1992). Though relatively few cases reach the courts, Social Security Administration (SSA) officials report "that court decisions may have had a significant impact in increasing awards by causing SSA to liberalize policies and rulings in favor of applicants" (U.S. GAO, 1994, p. 24).

[12]This strategy is not unique to mental health care. For example, numerous cases have raised the question of whether the cost of bone marrow transplants to treat advanced breast cancer is covered in private policies. (As an example, see *Nesseim v. Mail Handlers Benefit Plan,* 1993.) Sometimes, retaining an attorney to pursue the issue is often sufficient to secure an agreement to pay for the care. The increase in litigation has motivated insurers to revise policies to exclude coverage for specific treatments. Another related development is the offer by one insurer to sell supplemental coverage that, for a modest fee, would provide protection against the costs of treatments not covered in the standard policy (Anders, 1994). A potential problem with this approach is that only those persons who anticipate needing the care choose to purchase the insurance (adverse selection). If this occurs, the cost of the coverage might continually rise, and the market may eventually break down.

[13]This case was later affirmed by the Court of Appeals (978 F.2d 1256) without a written opinion.

with a serious psychiatric illness is living in a supported environment without the restrictions typically imposed on a hospital inpatient, the court also brought up an intriguing economic issue. In evaluating the decision by the insurance plan administrator, the court had to determine whether there was an abuse of discretion. In so doing, the court considered whether there was conflict of interest that might color the judgment of the administrator. The court noted that only employees of the corporation are on the committee that makes benefit decisions. The court also emphasized that the employer was self-insured and thus would directly bear the costs of any insurance payments. Under these conditions, the court concluded that "a more direct conflict of interest could scarcely be imagined" (p. 1270).[14]

The continued effort to challenge and broaden the interpretation of health insurance contracts is likely to motivate insurers to refine contract language. Pricing a policy depends on projected use and payments. The uncertainty generated by legal disputes over the applicability of restrictive clauses compounds the problems of making pricing decisions. At the same time, efforts to develop more precise language offer buyers the opportunity to consider the issue of coverage for mental health care. The choices employers and employees make will ultimately determine the scope and extent of financial protection. If legal developments promote reasoned choice based on a balancing of risks and costs, then the case law developments deserve some of the credit for the outcome.

Supporters of more insurance for the costs of mental health care are left with a nagging concern. It is possible that negotiators, in an effort to control the costs of insurance and allow for relatively higher wage gains, will opt to tighten rather than liberalize coverage. If past history is any guide, the relatively small number of persons facing substantial costs, combined with the unpredictability and stigma of mental illness, could weaken efforts to secure more financial protection. In part, past efforts to use legislative approaches, such as mandating certain levels of coverage, are a response to the failure of private negotiations to yield satisfactory coverage. Alternatively, a judgment could be made to let private parties reach their own agreements and then establish a mix of public insurance and mental health service programs to serve as a safety net when private insurance coverage and personal resources become inadequate. Legal actions to ensure that the safety net is there and is sufficiently strong may be essential.

Managed Mental Health Care

Contract disputes over the applicability of coverage restrictions are not the only area of case law likely to influence treatment patterns. Other cases are beginning to come to light on another matter related to health insurance contracts. As pressures mount to control the rapid rise in health insurance premiums, insurers and employers are contracting with firms to manage high-cost cases.[15] Moreover, because of the unique issues arising in mental health care, firms specializing in the management of mental health care are becoming increasingly common. Applying requirements for preadmission review, these firms are demanding that physicians certify that patients meet certain criteria before approving pay-

---

[14]It is useful to recognize that most of the cases just reviewed raise questions about coverage for a dependent with a mental illness. A related question regarding continuation of health insurance coverage for a dependent with a mental illness was litigated in *G.B. v. State Health Benefits Commission* (1988). A discussion of the case and the question of discrimination against persons with mental illness is found in Rubin (1987a).

[15]Some of the problems and issues surrounding the use of different types of managed care arrangements are discussed in Dorwart (1990) and Dickey and Azeni (1992). Of particular note is the finding by Dickey and Azeni that in the two companies they examined, the introduction of managed care was of limited effectiveness, at best.

ment for admission. In addition, the firms may manage the entire process of care by requiring periodic reviews before allowing payment for continued hospitalization or outpatient care. The respective roles and responsibilities of physicians, insurers, and managed care firms are still being clarified, sometimes in the courtroom.

Hoge (1990) briefly traces the use of managed care in psychiatry. The first effort to impose some type of external management controls on use of psychiatric services was developed in response to evidence of excessive use of services in the CHAMPUS program for dependents of military personnel. Hoge goes on to explain that the early program, done in conjunction with the American Psychiatric Association, was very successful and encouraged other insurers to consider some form of managed care.

It is also important to emphasize the provider viewpoint on questions of utilization. In the aggregate, mental health professionals have much to lose if insurers reduce coverage because of high utilization and costs. But at the individual level, fee-for-service medicine and the financial interests of hospitals create incentives to encourage excessive use. The conflict between what is best for all professionals as a group and what is best for an individual professional is at the heart of many disputes over the involvement of reviewers in the provider-patient relationship.

Though there are disagreements between providers and reviewers every day, it is the conflicts that cannot be resolved through negotiations that end up in court. Moreover, the relatively few disputes that do end up in court are important to the entire field. Over time, judicial opinions establish the ground rules under which managed psychiatric care will occur. The precise nature of these rules will determine what conditions providers must meet and how the managed care arrangements and procedures should be structured and implemented to satisfy constitutional and statutory requirements. Because of the

potential importance of managed care for access to mental health services, I present a detailed discussion of several major cases.

One of the first cases to address the responsibilities of physicians, insurers, and managed care firms—*Wickline v. State of California* (1986)—did not involve a person with a mental health problem. The plaintiff claimed she was prematurely discharged from the hospital following a leg amputation. Though a jury awarded damages to Wickline, the Court of Appeals reversed the judgment. The court wrote, "While we recognize, realistically, that cost consciousness has become a permanent feature of the health care system, it is essential that cost limitation programs not be permitted to corrupt medical judgment. We have concluded, from the facts in issue here, that in this case it did not" (p. 820). An important aspect of *Wickline* is the role of Medi-Cal; the case did not involve a private insurance contract but instead related to public health insurance. Consequently, the applicability of *Wickline* to similar questions arising out of activities of managed care firms and private health insurers is limited.

One case involving a patient seeking hospital care for a psychiatric illness did begin to identify the responsibilities of insurers, physicians, and review firms (*Hughes v. Blue Cross of Northern California*, 1989).[16] In *Hughes*, the plaintiff's son was denied coverage for part of a hospital stay to treat a psychiatric problem. The first step in the proceeding was an arbitration hearing in which the insurer was ordered to pay for the hospital stay. The plaintiff then brought additional action "to recover damages for Blue Cross's alleged breach of its implied covenant of good faith and fair dealing" (*Hughes v. Blue Cross of Northern California*, p. 852). The plaintiff received a jury verdict of $150,000 in compensatory damages and $700,000 in punitive dam-

---

[16]Later efforts to get the case reheard were unsuccessful. See *Hughes v. Blue Cross of Northern California* (1989).

ages, which the insurer appealed and the Court of Appeals affirmed.[17]

In its written opinion, the court traced the serious psychiatric problems suffered by Mrs. Hughes's son. It described several hospitalizations, including five stays at Belmont Hills Psychiatric Center. Blue Cross, relying on a review by its psychiatric consultant, would not pay a portion of the charges for the first stay and all charges for the last of those stays at Belmont Hills, totaling about $17,000. Blue Cross asserted that portions of the hospitalizations were essentially custodial care. But after a review of the process employed by Blue Cross and its external reviewer, the court concluded that there was "ample evidence to support a finding that the insurer acted unreasonably in denying benefits" (p. 857). The court was particularly critical of the quality of the review conducted by the Blue Cross consultant prior to reaching an opinion regarding the necessity of a portion of Hughes's hospital care.

The discrepancy between the treating physicians and the reviewing physician in *Hughes* lies at the heart of the controversy over managed care. Though the reviewer of the file on Mr. Hughes did not conduct a review that satisfied the court, rejection of claims based on a thorough review remains feasible. Moreover, it is important to understand that the threat of denial of coverage may alter physician practices and discharge decisions at hospitals. Knowing that an insurer may not pay for care and that a patient lacks the personal resources to cover unreimbursed expenses, it is hoped that a hospital will choose to be careful, while still meeting its legal obligations to provide necessary treatment, to avoid unnecessary hospital care and liability.

Establishing preadmission reviews can help alleviate the uncertainty that arises when insur-

ers review cases after admission or even after discharge. Another option is to conduct periodic reviews while a person is in the hospital. These programs place pressure on physicians to justify each element of the treatment plan. It is reasonable to anticipate that, after a period of trial and error, physicians working with the same review organization will develop a fairly good sense of the conditions under which hospital care will be allowed. Thus, while denials may decline in number, this may reflect effective screening by physicians rather than by the review organization.

The remaining question is how covered individuals will react to restrictions on access to care. These restrictions are intended to limit use and control spending, which in turn will help to constrain premium increases. Tighter limits on admissions and hospital stays, in effect, reduce the value of coverage. In some instances, employees might accept trade-offs between wage increases and insurance policies with varying amounts of managed care. Although the trend has been toward more managed care, it is not unreasonable to expect that in the future some firms may seek to attract skilled workers in short supply by offering a package of wages and benefits that includes fewer restrictions on health care decisions. In the meantime, cases such as *Hughes* have helped establish the guidelines needed to determine what constitutes adequate review prior to denying a claim. One would expect insurers and reviewers to train employees regarding the standards they must meet to avoid the kind of jury verdict secured by the plaintiffs in *Hughes*. Other cases will undoubtedly refine the rules, and their interpretation will vary with the circumstances.

As was the case with disputes over insurance contracts, lawsuits seeking damages for decisions that are the proximate (legally sufficient) cause of harm to someone also can affect access to care and the financing of services. Two of the more common types of cases are those establishing a psychiatrist's duty to protect third parties (Rubin,

---

[17] It is worth noting that the hospital stays in question occurred in 1981 and 1982. The Court of Appeals issued its second ruling upholding the jury decision on November 14, 1989.

1987b)[18] and those claiming professional negligence in releasing (or not confining) a patient who, after discharge, harms another person or persons (Weiner & Wettstein, 1993).[19] A case that began in 1983 and ended with a Court of Appeals decision in 1990 addressed the issues of early release, harm to the patient, and the responsibility of an insurer to conduct a review that meets existing standards of medical practice (*Wilson v. Blue Cross of Southern California*, 1990).

The facts in *Wilson* center around the denial of insurance coverage for an extended hospital stay to treat Howard Wilson, Jr., for major depression, drug dependency, and anorexia. Wilson spent 11 days in a hospital but was released after the insurer determined it would no longer pay for inpatient care. Three weeks after his release, Wilson committed suicide.

Initially, the lower court dismissed the case before trial. The Court of Appeals then reversed and remanded the case to the trial court, which opened the door for a jury trial. The review organization reached a settlement with the plaintiffs, but the case against Blue Cross went forward (Azevedo, 1993). The outcome of the jury trial was somewhat complicated. The jury determined there was no negligence but did conclude that the insurer "had wrongfully withheld insurance benefits and failed to deal in good faith, and that those acts harmed Wilson" (Azevedo, 1993, p. 42). Although no damages were awarded because the jury did not find that the insurer acted with malice, the parties subsequently settled the case rather than proceed with an appeal.

Obviously, because the judicial opinion only governed the question of whether there was a basis for a claim, the opinion does not necessarily establish specific requirements for insurers. Yet certain aspects of the decision are important in providing insight into the developing case law on managed psychiatric care. For example, the Court of Appeals determined that *Wickline* was of limited relevance in this matter because it involved Medi-Cal, while *Wilson* raised questions regarding a private health insurance plan. The case also raised additional questions regarding the responsibility of the treating physician and the review organization. In reversing the trial court's summary dismissal, the Court of Appeals made it clear that this firm could be held liable if it were shown that the firm's "conduct was a substantial factor in causing decedent's death" (*Wilson v. Blue Cross of Southern California*, 1990, p. 883).

One final quirk in *Wilson* is that the role of the physician in challenging or appealing denials remains unclear. Given the facts of this case, the treating physician could only be found liable if one of the defendants (the reviewer organization or the insurer) was judged negligent on the question of wrongful death (Azevedo, 1993). It appears that physicians will have to be careful to apply the same basic standard to all cases. Thus, insurance decisions should not affect treatment decisions. Physicians who alter treatment decisions only because a reviewer denied coverage may not have a particularly strong case should some harm occur and their actions be questioned in court.

Another case sheds some light into how professionals react to the increasing oversight of their treatment decisions. In *Adnan Varol, M.D. v. Blue Cross & Blue Shield* (1989), a group of psychiatrists challenged the use of preauthorization and other managed care requirements. Although the court did grant the defendants' motion to dismiss, the case highlights the conflict between insurers and providers when there is external review of treatment decisions.

In this instance, a managed care pilot pro-

---

[18]See Bowers, Givelber, and Blitch (1984) for a discussion of changes in practice patterns following judicial recognition of a therapist's duty to warn.

[19]An intriguing variation on this issue was recently raised in a New Jersey case (*Perona v. Township of Mullica*, 1994). The plaintiffs were a woman, her husband, and their daughter. They brought a legal action against a township and its police department and some officers, claiming the officers erred in *not* hospitalizing the woman. Believing she was suicidal, the woman's husband summoned the police. The police decided not to commit the woman, and she subsequently was injured in an unsuccessful suicide attempt. The court ruled that the officers were immune from liability.

gram was designed for employees of General Motors who chose the traditional insurance plan. According to one of the briefs filed in this case, the cost of mental health benefits for GM employees rose from $70 million in 1984 to $83 million in 1987, an 18.5% increase. Consistent with its other efforts to control health care spending, GM and the union began negotiations on ways to limit mental health costs. After evaluating cost increases and evidence that mental health benefits were being improperly and inefficiently used, a joint committee consisting of union and management representatives decided to establish a managed psychiatric care program.

The providers in several counties were invited to participate in the pilot program. The agreement with the providers clearly specified the features of the proposed managed care program. A concern in this type of situation is that a large "buyer" of care effectively dominates the market to such an extent that providers must either join the program or lose a large number of their patients. Physicians and other health care providers must decide whether to participate in networks of providers. Providers who delay joining a network sometimes find they subsequently lose market share. Faced with a loss of patients, these providers might then try to join a network only to find that they are unable to get into successful networks.

The court described at length the plaintiffs' claim that the incentives under the pilot program would force them to alter their treatment practices. The court rebutted their contention by noting that nothing in the program prevents providers from delivering services not previously approved. Moreover, the insurer will still pay 80% of the fee. The provider remains free to bill the patient for the other 20%. In general, the court was not persuaded by the plaintiffs' claims that economic incentives will make them do something contrary to their medical judgment.

The last type of case I review concerns what can happen when a state attempts to make health insurers expand coverage for mental health care. One approach is to pass legislation requiring an insurer to offer mental health coverage to each buyer of health insurance. Generally, the buyer is an employer purchasing coverage for an entire group of employees and covered dependents. But a ruling in a recent case (*R.A.K. v. Board of Trustees,* 1993) suggests that a mandate statute can be subject to alternative interpretations. This court found that legislation in Louisiana requires that mental health benefits be offered as an option to individual employees. Unless the legislation or the interpretation is changed, this ruling could cause serious adverse selection problems for insurers: individuals who expect to use large amounts of mental health care will be more likely than others to select coverage. This would impair the ability of insurers to establish a reasonable premium and cover anticipated expenses.

Limitations of Private Litigation

Each type of case discussed in this section contributes to a growing body of mental health law. These opinions help establish standards, which can change over time, that physicians and other types of providers must meet. As with other kinds of cases, the importance of any ruling can go far beyond the immediate impact on the plaintiff and defendant in a single case. The cases are likely to influence practice patterns among insurers and health care providers. The same is essentially true in other liability cases. Many persons and companies engaged in various activities learn what behaviors and practices satisfy the legal standard needed to avoid liability and respond accordingly. Changing practices and policies, redesigning products, attaching warning labels, and other reactions to legal rules all involve costs that are balanced against the benefits of reduced exposure to liability. Consequently, mental health providers, insurers, and others involved in the care of persons with serious mental illness are likely to develop new protocols, policies, and procedures in response to the developing case law.

No one can guarantee that these reactions

enhance the well-being of persons with mental illness or the therapeutic impact of treatment. What might help achieve the goal of an individual plaintiff need not lead to changes preferred by the majority of the seriously mentally ill population. Private litigation simply does not allow one to target precise outcomes. The reactions of all involved are difficult to predict. Rather than view any court decision as a victory, it is necessary to take a larger and more long-run view of how mental health policy develops.

The problems posed by serious mental illness will not go away; no one would suggest that a "cure" or some type of preventive vaccination are on the horizon. Thus, the law must be considered as just one tool among many. No one person or group can consciously develop the best mix of legal actions, political lobbying, public education, program redesign, and other policies. The goal should be to integrate the legal rules and the reactions of those affected into the decision-making process. How to fit the pieces of the puzzle together to create an optimal policy picture remains a daunting task.

Legal Actions against States

In the 1960s and 1970s, public mental health programs came under scrutiny and attack by legal advocates for persons with mental illness. Among the most significant victories were rulings establishing the rights of hospitalized patients and civil commitment standards (Brakel, Parry, & Weiner, 1985; Rubin, 1978). The expansion of patients' rights accomplished two things: it became more expensive for states to provide legally adequate institutional care, and it became more difficult for states to hospitalize people against their will. Whether these two facts alone explain the decline in use of state institutions or whether other factors contributed to the changing pattern of utilization

witnessed in the last three decades may never be satisfactorily answered.[20]

It seems evident that legal victories that forced states to improve staffing ratios could only be satisfied with some combination of more funding and fewer patients. Although class action constitutional challenges to state mental health policies are a less commonly used tactic now, some cases continue to be litigated. Rather than rehash the older decisions, I focus on a recent case that raises some important concerns.

The case (*Casey v. Lewis*, 1993) highlights the growing need to deliver mental health care to persons incarcerated in the criminal justice system. In fact, there could well be a link between the earlier cases (and the related legislation these rulings spawned) and the current levels of need for mental health care in the prison system. With less opportunity to institutionalize people in mental hospitals, many who in the past might have been institutionalized are finding their way into the criminal justice system.[21]

When this lawsuit was tried in early 1992, Arizona had nine prison facilities and over 15,000 inmates. The plaintiffs alleged that the state failed to provide adequate mental health care.[22] Furthermore, there were charges that the quality of mental health care for females was substantially below that available to males. The court provided a lengthy description of each of the prisons in the system and their respective treatment practices. Even with a system in place

---

[20]Competing views suggest that availability of federal funding for Medicaid—which helped pay for nursing home care, inpatient hospital care in specialized psychiatric units, and other health care services—and the development of psychotropic drugs also contributed to the declining long-stay inpatient population in state institutions (Goldman, Adams, & Taube, 1983; Mechanic & Rochefort, 1992; Rochefort, 1993).

[21]This development has spurred increasing support for changes in commitment laws to broaden the capacity of states to involuntarily institutionalize someone (Foderaro, 1994).

[22]There were a number of other allegations regarding the adequacy of medical and dental care. I will not discuss these aspects of the opinion.

that the plaintiffs claimed was inadequate, the extent of mental health services delivered to the prison population is striking.

In 1991, there were just over 19,000 psychiatrist-patient encounters, almost 110,000 mental health encounters, and over 70,000 psychotropic medications dispensed. Notwithstanding the evidence of extensive treatment, the court still found that "seriously mentally ill prisoners go undetected in the prisons, and do not receive treatment" (*Casey v. Lewis*, 1993, p. 1513).

The connections between financing and the adequacy of care are evident in several parts of the court's opinion. For example, in discussing staffing patterns at the prisons, the court noted that the legislature denied requests for funds to add staff and that staffing freezes and limitations on salaries made filling vacancies difficult. The court also cited testimony asserting that facilities placed patients in isolation cells because of "economic conditions."

The court concluded that several facilities do meet the mental health needs of inmates. But "the overwhelming evidence establishes that the defendants are deliberately indifferent to the serious mental health care needs of the inmates in other institutions throughout the state" (p. 1549). The court used strong language in declaring that the system in Arizona violates the Eighth Amendment to the U.S. Constitution. Moreover, the court rejected the claim that a lack of funding could serve as a defense for a violation of constitutional rights. Instead, the court noted that serious harm will likely occur if action is not taken.[23]

Even in the face of these violations of rights and the evident link between the violations and funding problems, the court was reluctant to intervene extensively in the prison mental health system in Arizona. The court rejected the use of a special master and urged the parties to solve the problems identified during the course of the litigation. The court asked the parties to produce a plan to remedy the deficiencies but stopped short of ordering the legislature to appropriate funds. It is unclear what will happen if the legislature fails to provide the resources needed to improve staffing, facilities, and programming for the mental health needs of prisoners.

This case suggests that the problem of finding funds to pay for mental health services has, in part, been shifted from state hospitals to state prisons. Changing the system of providing mental health care for persons with serious illnesses does nothing to alleviate the underlying need for such services. The continued need for services, in turn, suggests the continued need for resources. Regardless of whether these persons are in state hospitals, prisons, or in the community, ultimately their well-being and capacity to function depend on having sufficient funds to staff and maintain adequate systems of care.

One solution to a lack of adequate public funds is to find a way to shift costs to the private sector, perhaps through mandated insurance coverage. But it is unlikely that the private sector can ever come up with sufficient funds to meet the mental health and related service needs of persons with severe and chronic illness. Another option for states is to look to the federal government to assist in funding care for this population. Efforts to shift the burden to the federal government often center on strategies to obtain Medicaid funding for needed services. In the end, it appears that only a greater fiscal commitment from the individual states will be sufficient. Whether state legislators can structure programs and make adequate funds available without the type and scale of judicial intervention witnessed in the 1970s remains uncertain.

[23]One interesting feature of the court's opinion is its speculation of a type of "offset" effect from increased spending for mental health care for inmates. They write that "if these inmates are provided proper mental health care, security staff should be relieved of the time-consuming problems caused when inmates become violent or assaultive due to mental illness. In addition, security staff should be relieved of the duty of performing health and welfare checks, which disrupt security duties and require that personnel perform medical duties which they are not qualified to perform" (p. 1552).

Reform Legislation and State Financing of Mental Health Care

Partly spurred on by the continuing threat of legal challenges and partly motivated by the persistence of problems in meeting the needs of persons with serious mental illness, states have tried numerous strategies to reform their mental health systems. Some of these efforts involve reforms in the way mental health care is financed; others address organizational issues.

Though the focus in this section is on state legislative reforms, it is important to recognize the links between state actions and private sector activities. Generally, people rely on private health insurance to finance their health care needs. Other segments of the population rely on public insurance programs such as Medicare, Medicaid, and the Veterans Administration. But many fall through the cracks, often after exhausting whatever private or public benefits they might have, and into the public mental health system.

State and local governments either use available resources to employ staff and operate buildings and programs or contract with private firms to supply services (Fisher, Dorwart, Schlesinger, & Davidson, 1991). The legislative appropriations for these efforts represent the kind of global budgets being so hotly debated in the context of national health care reform. Mental health agencies have a set budget at the beginning of the year out of which they must fund services to all who qualify for their programs. In some cases, the programs are constrained by the courts to meet certain standards. State mental health agencies do have some opportunities to obtain other funds to increase their budget. For example, they may be able to structure programs to meet requirements for Medicaid funding. They might also work with state housing and welfare departments to determine whether clients are eligible for funds from these programs. Thus, while there is a global budget cap on paper, a sophisticated and experienced manager might be able to push the fiscal boundary further out.

Concern over how widely these fixed budgets are allocated has prompted states to develop financing and organizational systems intended to promote more efficient use of alternatives to expensive inpatient facilities. An increasingly common strategy is to shift the allocation problem from the state to county governments. Along with giving counties a fixed budget to meet local mental health needs, states are also using innovative pricing policies to encourage reduced reliance on state hospitals. We begin by examining how this concept is being applied in Ohio.

Ohio

Ohio constructed a new financing arrangement to change the incentives facing local governments responsible for mentally ill residents in their communities.[24] The design of the new system in Ohio was intended to address the problems associated with what was perceived as excessive use of the state's mental hospitals. As Frank and Gaynor (1994) point out, local governments could avoid the responsibility of delivering community care for difficult patients by sending those patients to the state hospital. This kind of "cost shifting" from one level of government to another was a logical strategy for local communities because the use of the hospital was "free."

Local officials act with several objectives in mind. First, they prefer imposing lower rather than higher taxes on their constituents. Second, they seek to protect their constituents from the kind of behaviors often exhibited by some persons with a serious mental illness. Third, they desire to provide adequate care to constituents who have a mental illness. The ordering of these objectives in terms of their relative importance is difficult for local officials to establish.

---

[24] This discussion relies largely on information presented in Frank and Gaynor (1994) and Hogan (1992).

One goal of the reform effort in Ohio was to reduce the "demand" for state hospital facilities by imposing some cost sharing on local governments. The strategy is essentially the same approach commonly used in private insurance policies to lower use of services and control spending. The difference in this instance is that a government agency bears the copayments for selecting a particular type of care. It is an effort to change the "price of care."

In Ohio, a local mental health board (which might typically coincide with county boundaries) is responsible for administering mental health care. These boards obtain some of their funding by levying a property tax. Under the new financing system, the boards will eventually receive a block grant from the state based on past average annual use of state hospitals by persons from their area. The boards, in turn, will be responsible for paying for the use of state mental hospitals. Thus, compared to the previous arrangement, the board has an incentive to reduce the use of state hospitals.[25]

A second goal of the Ohio reforms was to encourage local boards to identify and enroll persons with more severe mental disabilities in community treatment programs. Under the new policy, the boards receive a "bonus" payment from the state for each enrolled person who meets the definition of severe mental disability. Though the payment does create an incentive to enroll more persons, Frank and Gaynor note that this program does not provide a strong incentive to deliver more services.

Frank and Gaynor assessed how local boards reacted to these new fiscal incentives. If it can be shown that local boards respond to economic incentives in predictable ways, the door is open to formulate other strategies that would increase the quantity and type of care available to persons with mental illness while decreasing the use of less cost-effective services. Success of these kinds of policies depends on two assumptions: first, that local boards respond in predictable ways, and second, that state officials know which responses produce a better system of mental health care. Frank and Gaynor address the first issue but not the second. Evaluations of community care programs offer some insights into the kinds of programs that work for persons with a serious mental illness (Jerrell & Hu, 1989; Weisbrod, 1981). Nonetheless, it is unclear whether the financing reforms adopted in Ohio will cause local boards to implement the kinds of community programs that are effective.

In their assessment of reactions to the new financing arrangements, Frank and Gaynor found that the local mental health boards substantially reduced the use of state hospitals after being faced with "charges" for hospital use. Furthermore, the incentives to increase enrollment of persons with a serious mental illness in programs operated by the local boards were also effective. But the data also show that many of those enrolled received relatively little treatment. Planners considering changes in the incentive system to encourage localities to deliver more community-based services for persons with mental illness must appreciate an inherent conflict in these arrangements. Any policy that requires the boards to deliver more services will increase the cost per enrolled person, which would, in turn, weaken the enrollment incentive.

Past failures of administrative rules and regulations to induce appropriate changes encouraged states to turn to programs built on financial incentives such as those adopted in Ohio. In some respects, these strategies work well, but some serious problems and unanswered questions remain. In particular, states must continue to explore the full scope of responses to these incentives and determine if improvements in client outcomes coincide with the fiscal and structural reorganizations induced by any change in the system of financing public mental health care.

---

[25] The legislation in Ohio also attempts to ease the burden on state hospital employees. Some employees will have an opportunity to work in community mental health programs (Dickey & Cohen, 1993).

Wisconsin

In changing the way local authorities use and finance state hospital care, Ohio was building on a model adopted by Wisconsin some years ago.[26] In the early 1970s, Wisconsin instituted and subsequently fine-tuned a system of financing designed to decentralize care, putting more responsibility on county governments. The counties are responsible for meeting local mental health needs using funds raised through local taxes, as well as state funds paid to counties in the form of a block grant.[27] As in Ohio, counties are required to pay for any inpatient services their clients might use in state mental hospitals. Given the charges for hospital care, counties face a strong incentive to develop alternative community programs that would reduce the "demand" for inpatient days in state hospitals. A potential pitfall of this approach is that counties may choose to deliver inadequate community care while declining to purchase hospital care.

Stein (1989) describes the method Wisconsin developed to overcome the difficulty of establishing new community programs while still providing acceptable hospital care. The state provides counties with the opportunity to seek funds to originate community programs designed to reduce hospital use. If effective, these programs would allow counties to further reallocate funds as the need to pay for inpatient care declined. The program in Wisconsin has succeeded in shifting spending patterns for mental health care services. Proportionally, Wisconsin spends much less than other states for inpatient care, though there are large differences across counties in Wisconsin. While some counties successfully switched to a largely community-based system, others have not changed nearly as much (Dickey & Cohen, 1993).

California

California offers an example of yet another state that has changed the way counties pay for the use of state hospitals. In 1991, California introduced a new system for financing state and county mental health services:[28] "Under such 'realignment legislation' counties received funds from the state and could decide to use that money to fund local programs or to pay the Department for state hospital beds" (*County of San Diego v. Brown*, 1993, p. 825). Under this legislation, counties pay the full price for state hospital beds. Another feature of realignment was the creation of a new source of tax revenue to correct inequities.

Before these changes were implemented, California mental health programs had been operating under a financing structure that was first developed and adopted during the late 1950s and 1960s. It was later refined as changing economic conditions forced the state to adjust its funding for mental health care. This prerealignment system of financing care was the source of many disputes. For example, litigation (*County of San Diego v. Brown*, 1993) raised questions as to the constitutionality of the rules used to allocate resources to counties. Another case (*Board of Supervisors of the County of Los Angeles v. Superior Court (Comer)*, 1989) showed the problems persons with mental illness face in times of tight budgets and their limited opportunity to petition the government to provide adequate funding. These cases document how state efforts to allocate resources to counties, in conjunction with requirements for counties to provide some of their own funding, can be controversial. County officials would prefer more state funding in hopes of reducing the need to tax local residents. This is especially likely to be the case for a service (mental health care) that most residents do not use.

In *Board of Supervisors*, the question at issue was whether to continue to enforce an injunction

---

[26] This section of the chapter draws heavily on the discussion of the Wisconsin system presented in Stein (1989).

[27] The state requires counties to provide funding that is at least 9% of the monies received from the state (Stein, 1989).

[28] The original realignment legislation was amended in 1993.

granted by the Superior Court barring the Board of Supervisors from reducing funding for mental health services. The injunction had been granted at the request of a group of indigent residents of Los Angeles County. The original argument was that the combined state and county allocations for mental health services were inadequate and resulted in a substantial amount of unmet need. These inadequate levels of funding were to be cut further in the 1988–1989 budget. One consequence of the proposed cuts was expected to be the closing of some clinics and reduced services at other clinics. The original plaintiffs contended that this would force them to rely on emergency hospital services. The claims against the county and the state were premised on violations of various state statutes and the state constitution.

The Court of Appeals examined two state statutes: one county general assistance statute that established a county responsibility to care for indigent patients and another that concerned the county requirements under the Short-Doyle Act to provide funds for mental health services. Under Short-Doyle, the state assumed the vast majority of the cost of paying for mental health care while requiring counties to match a portion of state funds. Rather than apply the provisions governing general assistance to require more funding for mental health services, the court held that the specific language in the mental health funding legislation establishing a minimum level of county matching of state funds was relevant. Thus, the county did not have to spend more than what was required under Short-Doyle, though it could if it chose to do so.

In applying the terms of Short-Doyle to establish a minimum county contribution to mental health care, the Court of Appeals acknowledged the need for mental health services while also pointing out that limited resources require public officials to set funding priorities. In addition, the court alluded to limits on the county's ability to raise funds. It concluded by noting that "the legislative arena, rather than the courts, is the appropriate forum in which to raise these concerns" (*Board of Supervisors of the County of Los Angeles v. Superior Court (Comer)*, 1989, p. 913).

Other questions were raised in a lawsuit, originally filed in 1986, challenging the method of allocating state mental health funds (*County of San Diego v. Brown*, 1993, p. 819). Initially, several counties were partially successful in their efforts to force the state to change the method of allocating resources for mental health care across counties. In this case, the Court of Appeals overruled the lower court and "held that [the] state's allocation of mental health funding and state hospital beds to counties did not violate equal protection or due process" (p. 819).

The origin of the complaints was in the system of financing, which began in the 1950s and gave the counties the option of spending more money for community programs as a way to secure more state matching funds. The initial program was voluntary. Some counties developed substantial programs and consequently obtained more state funding than others. The passage of Proposition 13 in 1978 caused state funds for county mental health programs to shrink and led to increasing concerns over the equity of intercounty differences in funding. After much discussion, new legislation was passed with the goal of preserving funding for existing counties while using new funds to promote movement toward a more equitable distribution of funds across counties, based on a measure of need. For several reasons, the new program did not resolve the inequities in funding. A related aspect of the case was a state policy of allocating to counties a certain number of bed days at state hospitals and charging counties for overuse of hospital beds.

The Court of Appeals concurred with the Superior Court's finding that the allocation of mental health dollars under the prerealignment legislation met the necessary constitutional requirements. Among the factors influencing the court's decision was the historical path counties took to end up in their current position. The court expressed concern that reallocating funds to the plaintiff counties would cause "lost economic efficiency and value" and contribute to instability of patient care and maintenance of program infrastructure.

The Court of Appeals differed from the Superior Court on the question of the constitutionality of the hospital bed allocation. Essentially, the Court of Appeals concluded that the bed allocation was part of a county's allocation of mental health resources and thus was protected as part of the county's base allocation. The part of the statute that protected counties from actual decreases in mental health resources in an effort to reduce inequities applied to the bed allocation. Furthermore, the Court of Appeals rejected claims that the bed allocation violated the constitution. It wrote that "the record compels a conclusion [that] the stability of patient care and program infrastructure was a legitimate governmental concern and the method used to allocate state hospital beds including maintaining base allocations was rationally related to providing such stability" (*County of San Diego v. Brown*, 1993, p. 838).[29]

This case highlights the issues that arise when states select a method of allocating dollars to counties to help pay for mental health care. Many strategies exist for making such allocations, including measures of need, measures of the capacity of the county to finance care from its own internally generated revenues, and a simple per capita basis. Matching formulas used in programs like Medicaid are essentially ways to redistribute funds from one set of governments to the other through the use of a larger government entity. In structuring these programs and establishing the formulas and rules for making allocations, the government may have several objectives beside a pure redistribution of resources. In mental health care a key factor in constructing an intergovernmental allocation system is to find a way to induce the counties to alter their mental health care delivery system. Through financing arrangements, California is trying to induce counties to spend more for community care and less for institutional care.[30] The legal record suggests that, in designing programs, states must be careful to meet the statutory standards and also satisfy the constitutional requirements that will be applied if a county challenges the formula or some other aspect of the funding system.

New York

New York State has introduced a number of policies aimed at improving the performance of the public and private mental health care system (Mechanic & Surles, 1992). Unlike the three states discussed previously, New York has not implemented a systemwide reform based on establishing financial incentives for local governments. Rather, New York has adopted programmatic reforms and some financial incentives designed to alter provider behavior.[31] I limit my attention to several of the financial incentives the state recently tried.

Instead of attempting to manipulate local government actions, New York constructed a financing reform strategy focused on providing financial incentives to hospitals and outpatient clinics.[32] Another difference between New York and the other states is that this reform did not directly address issues relating to inpatient care in state hospitals.

---

[29] Realignment legislation did away with the allocation of beds by the state to the counties.

[30] Dickey and Cohen (1993) report that critics questioned how well community programs in California met the needs of those who would otherwise be hospitalized.

[31] Detailed reviews of these efforts and other activities in New York are found in Wilcox-Gök et al. (1994) and Sundram, Stack, and Benjamin (1993).

[32] Using payment methods to control hospital utilization has always proved problematic for psychiatric patients. Variations in the cost of care over the course of a treatment and the need to recognize the distinction between acute care and chronic care are two features of inpatient care that must be addressed in designing payment systems. Fries, Durance, Nerenz, and Ashcraft (1993) discuss the problems with developing a prospective system to pay for inpatient psychiatric care and propose a solution.

Programs focusing only on lowering state hospital use run the risk of successfully reducing use of hospital services without spurring a corresponding increase in community services. New York's reimbursement strategy was premised on the view that a better mix of care in acute care general hospitals and community mental health services was needed.

To accomplish its goals, New York established an alternative payment system for inpatient care for hospitals that volunteered and were selected to participate. Central to the inpatient payment system were incentive payments for hospitals that cared for more seriously ill persons and financial penalties for long stays. Hospitals also received an additional payment if a patient was linked (seen within 10 days of discharge) with an outpatient provider. In addition, New York established a system of bonuses for community care providers for delivering services over an extended period to persons eligible for Medicaid.

Researchers found that, contrary to the objectives of the reimbursement reforms, patients in hospitals participating in the first phase of the experiment had somewhat longer stays than otherwise predicted, all else equal (Wilcox-Gök et al., 1994). There was a somewhat lower readmission rate in participating hospitals. Bonus payments did not significantly increase overall rates of linkage with outpatient providers.

The reimbursement system in New York is being revised to reflect the apparent inability of the incentives in the experiment to achieve the desired outcomes. Stronger financial incentives, more directly focused on those who make treatment decisions, may be essential. Expanding the availability of community providers will also help hospitals speed up the discharge of patients who no longer need intensive inpatient care. Finally, it may be necessary to consider developing a parallel system of incentives to motivate patients and their families to change their behaviors in the desired fashion. For example, offering a voucher of some type to patients who keep outpatient appointments may be a cost-effective way to prevent future hospital care and reduce demands on other public services (such as the criminal justice system).

Other States

Reform at the state level has taken many shapes and sizes. The examples discussed here represent only a few of the reforms being implemented. One approach being tried in some states is the creation of capitation systems for different populations, some of which contain large proportions of persons with a serious mental illness (Moscovice et al., 1993). The basic idea in these models is to give providers a per capita allocation of funds. In return, providers agree to deliver a specified package of benefits for those who enroll. This approach creates an incentive for providers to ensure the efficient delivery of care. These arrangements share the same problem states have when offering counties incentives to reduce hospitalization: the less providers do, the lower the costs and the greater the financial rewards.

Minnesota, Utah, Rhode Island, California, and Arizona are among the states experimenting with some type of capitation program.[33] Colorado is in the midst of implementing a widespread system of capitation as a basis for funding and delivering mental health services (Bloom, Toerber, Hausman, Cuffel, & Barrett, 1994). The decision to go to a capitation system is linked to several legal issues. In Colorado, the legislature adopted a law to establish the pilot program. Moreover, the ability to operate a capitation experiment usually relies on Medicaid legislation allowing states to apply for various waivers from existing Medicaid rules.

Generally, evidence on performance of capitation in health care does not offer much insight into how a similar financial arrangement will work for persons with severe mental illness in a state system. The main problem with these traditional capitation systems is that they limit cover-

---

[33]Other efforts at capitation have been tested in Rochester, New York (Babigian, Mitchell, Marshall, & Reed, 1992) and in Philadelphia (Hadley & Glover, 1989).

age for those with severe mental illness. The long-term chronic illness that may ultimately result in Medicaid eligibility is not the primary focus of standard capitation systems. Thus, one must reconsider how best to apply a reasonable financing mechanism that promotes efficiency to a population not previously covered under such arrangements.

Bloom et al. (1994) describe the features of a typical capitation program and identify the pluses and potential minuses in establishing capitation programs for persons with severe mental illness. One of the most common issues is how much risk to place on an organization that accepts the capitation payments and the requirements that come with it. Because payment per person is predetermined, the organization faces the risk that the actual average costs will exceed the average capitation payment. Much effort has gone into developing measures that correlate with expected costs and trying to find ways to adjust payments by patient characteristics and thus reduce the risk for provider organizations.

A real strength of the capitation approach is that it gives organizations a strong incentive to find less expensive ways of delivering mental health care. This incentive may cause a reallocation of resources away from inpatient care and toward more outpatient services. Depending on the structure of the arrangement, organizations may provide services themselves or contract with others to provide services. In either case, there is a strong incentive to find efficient ways to produce whatever type of care is being delivered.

At this time, the jury is still out on capitation for persons with serious mental illness (and for others with chronic illnesses). Additional data from a variety of states are needed before we can reach any firm opinions on capitation. Moreover, because each trial is somewhat different, it may be hard to tell which factors are responsible for observed outcomes. For example, Colorado is beginning an intensive case management program and is also expanding residential programs at the same time the capitation experiment is being implemented. Identifying which changes lead to which outcomes will be a difficult challenge.

Some Final Comments on State Legislation

State mental health policy is a bit like the seesaw in a playground: tipping from one side to the other as greater amounts of pressure are applied on one side or the other. The federal government is one source of pressure. It applies pressure by passing legislation and regulations governing health insurance programs such as Medicare and Medicaid. Medicare can be considered an external factor because it is unaffected by state actions. Rules regarding Medicaid, however, have a much more direct effect on state mental health policy choices. The share of state matching, the conditions governing eligibility, and the specific services that can be covered all influence state policy choices. In addition, the opportunity to request a waiver from Medicaid rules gives states some flexibility to use Medicaid dollars in different ways.

Judicial actions also represent one type of pressure acting on state mental health policy. The interpretation of state laws and constitutions establishes boundaries within which states may act. A case in Pennsylvania raised some questions regarding the fiscal strategies used in that state and also about which individuals or agencies would be responsible for the consequences of choices influenced by the financial incentive (*Lee v. Gateway Institute & Clinic, Inc., et al.*, 1989). The case highlights both the difficult problems associated with using fiscal rules to encourage less expensive and intensive treatment methods and the sad consequences that sometimes surround serious mental illness.

The plaintiffs were relatives of a man who was killed by a patient who was a resident at the Gateway Institute & Clinic, a supervised residence for persons with mental illness. The patient was also under the care of professionals at the local mental health center. Before the murder, the patient had been treated as an inpatient at DuBois Regional Medical Center. The patient created many problems as an inpatient but was nevertheless released to Gateway. The plaintiffs contend that financial factors motivated the hospital and the treating physicians to release the patient and get him into Gateway and the community mental health center.

The plaintiffs argued that because counties in Pennsylvania have to "bear the cost of reimbursing patient costs for both private entities and the more intensive state facilities . . . there is an incentive to downgrade a patient's treatment regardless of what sound medical judgment dictates" (p. 574). Although the Court granted the defendants' motion to dismiss, the case raises some important questions about the consequences of state policies designed to encourage certain treatment choices. If the incentives are too strong, those who stand to benefit from available funds may make errors in judgment. Safeguards must be built into any legislation affecting the mental health system that enable injured parties to hold professionals accountable for their actions. Although financial incentives can alter provider decisions, it is important that patients' interests and the public's safety be factored into the equation.

Private health insurance is yet another force applying pressure to state mental health policy. The proportion of the population with coverage for treatment of serious mental illness affects the need for state resources. One other factor is the current knowledge among mental health professionals regarding the effectiveness of alternative treatments and organizational approaches to serving persons with serious and chronic mental illnesses.

A change in any of these forces can tip the seesaw toward a different outcome. Differences in the extent of these pressures across the states may help to explain why some states have followed one path while others use an alternative strategy. In each instance, it is reasonable to expect that the goal remains the establishment of an equitable and efficient system of care. Whether more money, better organizational structures, or more talented administrative and service delivery personnel will produce the system that advocates desire remains to be seen. Though model programs continue to offer evidence of success, achieving comparable success with large-scale, state-level, systemwide reform remains an elusive goal. The dollars remain limited, and the problems posed by serious and chronic mental illness remain difficult to resolve. Incremental improvements and setbacks that come when the seesaw tips back and forth appear certain to remain the norm for years to come.

Conclusion

Within the bounds of established rules and regulations, the decisions of politicians and bureaucrats control vast sums of public dollars intended to assist persons with a serious mental health problem. Employers and employees also make decisions that affect the amount and distribution of funds available to persons with a serious mental illness. The competing demands from others for the limited public and private funds constrain the capacity of the system to devote sufficient resources to enable society to cope with all the consequences of mental illness. Moreover, current knowledge and skills also limit the effectiveness of programs for persons with a serious mental illness.

In the midst of these dilemmas, there exists a legal system composed of statutes, constitutional rules, administrative regulations, and judicial interpretations. This legal system, as evidenced by the review in this chapter, has an enormous impact on an extraordinarily wide range of parties. Each action, each rule, and each statute motivates all those affected to respond with a series of reactions and responses. Whether "the law" has a positive net therapeutic effect is impossible to determine.

It is certainly clear that many individuals enjoy the benefits of statutes that create programs offering services and money to those who qualify. Still others obtain valuable services as a result of judicial rulings requiring public and private officials to finance or deliver needed care. But not all programs are effective. Not all of those in need are served. And not all judicial rulings support efforts to expand access to resources for those who have a serious mental illness.

It is useful to consider for a moment the origin of legal actions that affect persons with a serious mental illness. One set of activities are initiated by private individuals dissatisfied with a public decision (for example, an SSDI determination) or a private decision (for instance, rejection of a health insurance claim). Legal representation may be provided by a private attorney—either on a fee-for-service or contingency basis—or a legal advocacy organization. The result of these cases is first noticed by the individual plaintiffs and defendants and could, depending on the decision, have implications for a wider group of people. Except for instances in which a mental health advocacy organization is involved, these cases cannot reasonably be considered a part of any concerted effort to manipulate the size or the form of the system to finance mental health care.

A second set of legal developments are those that begin with lobbying efforts directed to convincing legislators to correct a failing in the mental health financing system. The subsequent legislation that is prepared can be fairly narrow (such as rewriting a misinterpreted portion of a mandate law) or exceptionally broad (for example, passing legislation that restructures the process by which the state allocates dollars to local governments). Though intended to accomplish a specific objective, even these actions could produce unexpected and undesirable results. For example, changes in a mandate law that increase the financial burden of providing insurance for employees could cause at least two reactions. One option is for some employers to self-insure, thereby avoiding the mandate's requirements. The self-insurance policy may contain weaker-than-desired protection for the costs of chronic psychiatric care. Reducing employment is yet another possible employer reaction.

There is also the possibility that legal developments totally unrelated to mental health care might subsequently affect the mental health system. For example, broadening the scope of rules that require manufacturers to warn users of their products of potential dangers could also ultimately influence judicial views on the responsibilities of therapists to warn potential victims of possible harm from a person under treatment. Another possibility is that legislatively enacted tax cuts could lead to reductions in state revenues, which could have consequences for the level of funding available to pay for public mental health programs.

Though the impact of new statutes or new judicial interpretations of existing constitutional, statutory, and common law opinion is difficult to predict, this approach to improving the financing of mental health services cannot be overlooked or ignored. Legal action will function best when it is part of a larger effort to improve the well-being of persons with a serious mental illness. For instance, appeals to taxpayers to provide better support for mental health programs and efforts to convince persons without mental illness to purchase more insurance protection against the costs of mental illness are avenues that should also be pursued. Nonetheless, it remains an unfortunate feature of our legal system that the efforts of individuals or groups to pursue their own interests need not always result in outcomes that promote the common good. Consequently, we face a situation where one legal action begets another. Though this may be an optimal world for attorneys, it cannot ensure that the resulting system of financing care for persons with a serious mental illness is either cost-effective or equitable.

References

Adelson v. GTE Corporation, 790 F. Supp. 1265 (1992).

Adnan Varol, M.D. v. Blue Cross & Blue Shield, 708 F. Supp. 826 (1989).

Anders, G. (1994, February 15). More insurers pay for care that's in trials. *Wall Street Journal*, pp. B1, B6.

Arons, B. S., Frank, R. G., Goldman, H. H., McGuire, T. G., & Stephens, S. (1994). Mental health and substance abuse coverage under health reform. *Health Affairs, 13*(1), 192–205.

Azevedo, D. (1993, January 25). Courts let UR firms off the hook—and leave doctors on. *Medical Economics*, pp. 30–44.

Babigian, H. M., Mitchell, O. S., Marshall, P. E., & Reed, S. K. (1992). A mental health capitation experiment: Evaluating the Monroe-Livingston experience. In R. G. Frank & W. G. Manning, Jr. (Eds.), *Economics and mental health* (pp. 307–331). Baltimore, MD: Johns Hopkins University Press.

Bloom, J. R., Toerber, G., Hausman, J. W., Cuffel, B., & Barrett, T. J. (1994). *Colorado's capitation plan: An analysis of capitation for mental health services.* Berkeley, CA: Institute for Mental Health Services Research.

Blostin, A. (1987, July). Mental health benefits financed by employers. *Monthly Labor Review, 110,* 23–27.

Board of Supervisors of the County of Los Angeles v. Superior Court (Comer), 254 Cal.Rptr. 905 (1989).

Bowers, W., Givelber, D., & Blitch, C. (1986). How did *Tarasoff* affect clinical practice? *Annals of the American Academy of Political and Social Science, 484,* 70–86.

Brakel, S. J., Parry, J., & Weiner, B. A. (1985). *The mentally disabled and the law* (3rd ed.). Chicago: American Bar Foundation.

Brewer v. Lincoln National Life Insurance Company, 730 F. Supp. 292 (1989), 921 F.2d 150 (1990), *cert. denied,* 111 S.Ct. 2872 (1991).

Case v. Sullivan, 810 F. Supp. 52 (1992).

Casey v. Lewis, 834 F. Supp. 1477 (1993).

Congressional Budget Office (1994a). *An analysis of the administration's health proposal.* Washington, DC: U.S. Government Printing Office.

Congressional Budget Office. (1994b). *An analysis of the Managed Competition Act.* Washington, DC: U.S. Government Printing Office.

County of San Diego v. Brown, 23 Cal.Rptr 2d 819 (1993).

Custer, W. S. (1991). Employer health care plan design and its effect on plan costs. *Inquiry, 28,* 81–86.

Dickey, B., & Azeni, H. (1992). Impact of managed care on mental health services. *Health Affairs, 11*(3), 197–204.

Dickey, B., & Cohen, M. D. (1993). Changing the financing of state mental health programs: Using carrots, not sticks, to improve care. *Administration and Policy in Mental Health, 20,* 343–355.

Dorwart, R. A. (1990). Managed mental health care: Myths and realities in the 1990s. *Hospital and Community Psychiatry, 41,* 1087–1091.

Fisher, W. H., Dorwart, R. A., Schlesinger, M., & Davidson, H. (1991). Contracting between public agencies and private psychiatric inpatient facilities. *Medical Care, 29,* 766–774.

Foderaro, L. W. (1994, June 17). New York considers easing rules for committing the mentally ill. *New York Times,* pp. A1, B4.

Frank, R., & Gaynor, M. (1994). Organizational failure and transfers in the public sector. *Journal of Human Resources, 29,* 108–125.

Frank, R., & McGuire, T. G. (1990). Mandating employer coverage of mental health care. *Health Affairs, 9*(1), 31–42.

Frank, R. G., Salkever, D. S., & Sharfstein, S. S. (1991). A new look at rising mental health insurance costs. *Health Affairs, 10*(2), 116–123.

Franklin, J. L., Solovitz, B., Mason, M., Clemons, J. R., & Miller, G. E. (1987). An evaluation of case management. *American Journal of Public Health, 77,* 674–678.

Fries, B. E., Durance, P. W., Nerenz, D. R., & Ashcraft, M. L. F. (1993). A comprehensive payment model for short- and long-stay psychiatric patients. *Health Care Financing Review, 15*(2), 31–50.

G. B. v. State Health Benefits Commission, 222 N.J. Super. 83 (1988).

Goldman, H. H., Adams, N. H., & Taube, C. A. (1983). Deinstitutionalization: The data demythologized. *Hospital and Community Psychiatry, 34,* 129–134.

Hadley, T. R., & Glover, R. (1989). Philadelphia: Using Medicaid as a basis for capitation. In D. Mechanic & L. H. Aiken (Eds.), *Paying for services: Promises and pitfalls of capitation* (pp. 65–76). San Francisco: Jossey-Bass.

Harris, R. J., Jr. (1994). National Medical agrees to settlement of fraud charges totaling $380 million. *Wall Street Journal,* p. A4.

Hogan, M. F. (1992). New futures for mental health care: The case of Ohio. *Health Affairs, 11*(3), 69–83.

Hoge, S. K. (1990). Utilization review: A house divided. *Hospital and Community Psychiatry, 41,* 367–368.

Hughes v. Blue Cross of Northern California, 263 Cal. Rptr. 850 (1989), *cert. denied,* 495 U.S. 944 (1990).

Jerrell, J. M., & Hu, T. (1989). Cost-effectiveness of intensive clinical case management compared with an extended system of care. *Inquiry, 26,* 224–234.

Lave, J. R., & Goldman, H. H. (1990). Medicare financing for mental health care. *Health Affairs, 9*(1), 19–30.

Lee v. Gateway Institute & Clinic, Inc., et al., 732 F. Supp. 572 (1989).

McGuire, T. (1994). Predicting the cost of mental health benefits. *Milbank Quarterly, 72,* 3–23.

Mechanic D., & Rochefort, D. A. (1992). A policy of inclusion for the mentally ill. *Health Affairs, 11*(1), 128–150.

Mechanic, D., & Surles, R. C. (1992). Challenges in state mental health administration. *Health Affairs, 11*(3), 34–50.

Morrissey, J. P., Calloway, M., Bartko, W. T., Ridgely, M. S., Goldman, H. H., & Paulson, R. I. (1994). Local mental health authorities and service system change: Evidence from the Robert Wood Johnson program on chronic mental illness. *Milbank Quarterly, 72,* 49–80.

Moscovice, I., Lurie, N., Christianson, J., Finch, M., Popkin, M., & Akhtar, M. R. (1993). Access and use of health services by chronically mentally ill Medicaid beneficiaries. *Health Care Financing Review, 14,* 75–87.

Narrow, W. E., Regier, D. A., Rae, D. S., Manderscheid, R. W., & Locke, B. (1993). Use of services by persons with mental and addictive disorders. *Archives of General Psychiatry, 50,* 95–107.

Nesseim v. Mail Handlers Benefit Plan, 995 F.2d 804 (1993).

Perona v. Township of Mullica, 270 N.J. Super. 19 (1994).

Phillips v. Lincoln National Life Insurance Company, 978 F.2d 302 (1992).

R.A.K. v. Board of Trustees, 619 So.2d. 126 (1993).

Redick, R. W., Witkin, M. J., Atay, J. E., & Manderscheid, R. W. (1992). Specialty mental health system characteristics. In R. W. Manderscheid & M. A. Sonnenschein (Eds.), *Mental health, United States, 1992* (pp. 1–141). Washington, DC: U.S. Government Printing Office.

Regier, D. A., Narrow, W. E., Rae, D. S., Manderscheid, R. W., Locke, B. Z., & Goodwin, F. K. (1993). The de facto US mental and addictive disorders service system. *Archives of General Psychiatry, 50,* 85–94.

Rochefort, D. A. (1993). *From poorhouses to homelessness: Policy analysis and mental health care.* Westport, CT: Auburn House.

Rubin, J. (1978). *Economics, mental health, and the law.* Lexington, MA: Heath.

Rubin, J. (1987a). Discrimination and insurance coverage of the mentally ill. In T. McGuire & R. Scheffler (Eds.), *Advances in health economics and health services research* (Vol. 8, pp. 195–209). Greenwich, CT: JAI Press.

Rubin, J. (1987b). Mental health professionals and the duty to warn. *International Journal of Law and Psychiatry, 10,* 311–337.

Rubin, J. (1991). Paying for care: Legal developments in the financing of mental health services. *Houston Law Review, 28,* 143–173.

Rubin, J. (in press). Issues in the financing and organization of mental health services. In B. Sales & S. Shah (Eds.), *Mental health and the law: Research, policy, and practice.* Durham, NC: Carolina Academic Press.

Saah v. Contel Corporation, 780 F. Supp. 311 (1991).

Sharfstein, S. S., & Stoline, A. M. (1992). Reform issues for insuring mental health care. *Health Affairs, 11*(3), 84–97.

Stein, L. I. (1989). Wisconsin's system of mental health financing. In D. Mechanic & L. H. Aiken (Eds.), *Paying for services: Promises and pitfalls of capitation* (pp. 29–41). San Francisco: Jossey-Bass.

Sundram, C. J., Stack, E. W., & Benjamin, W. P. (1993). *Discharge planning practices of general hospitals: Did incentive payments improve performance?* Albany: New York State Commission on Quality of Care for the Mentally Disabled.

Taube, C. A., Goldman, H. H., & Salkever, D. (1990). Medicaid coverage for mental illness. *Health Affairs, 9*(1), 5–18.

Tischler, G. L. (1990). Utilization management of mental health services by private third parties. *American Journal of Psychiatry, 147,* 967–973.

Tsai, S. P., Reedy, S. M., Bernacki, E. J., & Lee, E. S. (1988). Effect of curtailed insurance benefits on use of mental health care. *Medical Care, 26,* 430–440.

U.S. Bureau of Labor Statistics. (1990). *Employee benefits in medium and large firms* (Bulletin No. 2363). Washington, DC: U.S. Government Printing Office.

U.S. General Accounting Office. (1994). *Social security disability rolls keep growing, while explanations remain elusive* (Publication No. GAO/HEHS-94-34). Washington, DC: Author.

Walker v. Secretary of Health and Human Services, 980 F.2d 1066 (1992).

Weiner, B. A., & Wettstein, R. M. (1993). *Legal issues in mental health care.* New York: Plenum Press.

Weisbrod, B. A. (1981). Benefit-cost analysis of a controlled experiment: Treating the mentally ill. *Journal of Human Resources, 16,* 523–548.

Wickline v. State of California, 192 Cal. App. 3d 1630, 239 Cal. Rptr. 810 (1986).

Wilcox-Gök, V., Boyer, C. A., Rubin, J., Shern, D., Evans, M., & Mechanic, D. (1994). *General hospital responses to changing economic incentives in New York State's mental health system.* Unpublished manuscript, Institute for Health, Health Care Policy, and Aging Research, New Brunswick, NJ.

Wilson v. Blue Cross of Southern California, 271 Cal. Rptr. 876 (1990).

Part 3

Mental Health Clients and the Law

8 ■ The Voluntary Delivery of Mental Health Services in the Community

Michael L. Perlin
The New York Law School

The past two decades have seen a tremendous proliferation of case law, statutes, and scholarly commentary about virtually every phase of mental disability law. Many of these developments have been cyclical. Early judicial opinions and legislative enactments dramatically expanded the civil, political, social, and economic rights of individuals subjected to institutionalization because of mental disability (*Lessard v. Schmidt,* 1972; *O'Connor v. Donaldson,* 1975; Perlin, 1987, 1989; *Wyatt v. Stickney,* 1971, 1972, 1974). Public concern or dissatisfaction then led frequently to the "swing of the pendulum" (Durham & La Fond, 1985; Shuman, 1985) that often resulted in more restrictive court decisions and statutes that, in some cases, cut back severely on the earlier rights expansion (La Fond & Durham, 1992; *Parham v. J. R.,* 1979; *Wash. Rev. Co. Ann.,* 1984; *Youngberg v. Romeo,* 1982). This trend has not been entirely consistent, however. More recently, other cases have expanded rights in areas that had previously lacked public attention (*Foucha v. Louisiana,* 1992; *Riggins v. Nevada,* 1992; *Zinermon v. Burch,* 1990), and new statutes have, for the first time, expanded federal civil rights laws to include persons with mental disabilities (see Americans with Disabilities Act, 1992; Federal Fair Housing Act Amendments, 1988).

Yet, in spite of all this turmoil, little attention has been paid in the last decade to what is potentially one of the most important areas of patients' rights: the right to voluntary mental health services in the community. Only a trickle of cases has been litigated, and only a handful of statutes have been enacted (see, generally, Perlin, 1989, pp. 566–737). The legal literature is largely bereft of any doctrinal analysis or theoretical inquiries in this area (for an important recent exception, see Seicshnaydre, 1992). By and large, for the last decade, this has appeared to be a "nonarea."

And yet it was not always this way. During the late 1970s and early 1980s, the question of the right of people with mental disabilities to community services (especially people who had formerly been institutionalized) was a topic of great interest. An early line of cases had asserted a "right to deinstitutionalization" or a "right to services in the community" (*Dixon v. Weinberger,* 1975; *Halderman v. Pennhurst State School & Hospital,* 1978). Several states amended their mental health statutes to provide for such rights (*Ariz. Rev. Stat.,* 1993). Commentators urged expanded and creative readings of due process–Fourteenth Amendment decisions as providing support for such rights (Perlin, 1980). It appeared that this expansion was the next logical step in the progress of litigation and that, for mental health advocates and patients' rights litigators,

I wish to thank Lori Kranczer for her invaluable research assistance.

the right to community services would be "the next frontier" (Perlin, 1980).

Why did this area of the law seem to shrivel up and die? Why did litigators abandon strategies to assert rights in this area? Why did legislators turn their back on this question? Why did scholars give up on these issues?

Any answer must consider the surrounding social context. A sharp reduction in government funds for all social service programs during the Reagan and Bush years resulted in drastically fewer discretionary dollars being made available to fund such programs (Dinerstein, 1984; Hendon, 1990; Sardell, 1990; Smith, 1990). In addition, any public consensus that had supported expanded civil rights and discretionary programs for persons with mental disabilities was sharply eroded during the same period—an erosion best exemplified by the public debate over the relationship between deinstitutionalization and homelessness (Perlin, 1991a).

These changes in administrative and social attitudes were also clearly reflected in a series of Supreme Court decisions. These cases define as well as any the social agenda of the Supreme Courts headed by Chief Justice Warren Burger and his successor, Chief Justice William Rehnquist. This agenda was "aggressively majoritarian" and responded directly to "mainline America's" fears and concerns through means "insensitive or at least unempathetic to those most in need of its protection" (Stone, 1984, pp. 19, 22). It also underscored the Court's overt hostility toward plaintiffs seeking to expand civil rights in this substantive area (*De Shaney v. Winnebago County Department of Social Services*, 1989; *Pennhurst State School v. Halderman*, 1981, 1984; Perlin, 1987, pp. 1258–1259; *Youngberg v. Romeo*, 1982). Along with the political changes that came with the "Reagan revolution" and increasingly negative attitudes toward persons with mental disabilities, they explain the atrophied state of the law in this area.

These changes have also influenced the way scholars think and talk about mental disability law issues. The seeming end of the civil rights revolution—the revolution that directly spurred the exponential growth of mental health law in the 1970s (Wexler, 1992)—has caused scholars to consider new approaches to the study of mental disability law jurisprudence, and to reevaluate developments in that field. Perhaps the most important of these new approaches has been the development of the school of therapeutic jurisprudence (Wexler, 1990; Wexler & Winick, 1991) and the use of therapeutic jurisprudence as a tool for critical analysis.[1]

The application of therapeutic jurisprudence to this area of the law yields provocative results. As I will subsequently demonstrate, the Supreme Court decisions that led directly to the shriveling up of the law in this area are profoundly antitherapeutic. What is especially striking is the fact that, in each case, the antitherapeutic end was the inevitable result of a litigation victory by a government agency: in three decisions, the Attorney General of Pennsylvania (counsel for the state hospital system in *Youngberg v. Romeo* and in *Pennhurst State School and Hospital v. Halderman*).[2]

The irony here should be obvious. For the past several years, a standard critique of the patients' rights movement has been that vigorous advocacy on the part of patients is antitherapeutic—that patients now "die with their rights on" (Hiday & Markell, 1980, pp. 418–419; Treffert, 1973) or that the right to refuse treatment is "one right too many" (Rachlin, 1975). Prominent psychiatrists such as E. Fuller Torrey and H. Richard Lamb have flayed the mental health advocacy movement for contributing to homelessness, and criticized judges hearing civil commitment cases for interpreting commitment statutes too literally (Lamb, 1984; Perlin, 1991a, 1991b, 1993c; Torrey, 1988). "Ordinary common sense"

---

[1]See section titled "New Developments."

[2]For an early analysis of the way advocacy on the part of state agencies may result in antitherapeutic outcomes, see Wexler (1982).

(Perlin, 1990b; Sherwin, 1988) would suggest that lawyers representing mental patients are somehow antitherapeutic (Ensminger & Liguori, 1978). And yet the most profoundly antitherapeutic decisions in the cases above flowed directly and inexorably from arguments made by lawyers representing public hospital systems.

I will consider these issues in the following manner. In the next section, I will trace the early development of right-to-services case law and will review early cases seeking to vindicate the civil rights of persons with mental disabilities in community and aftercare settings, and cases that sought to bring an end to exclusionary zoning laws. Then I will explain the significance of the four Supreme Court decisions that define this area of the law. In the following section, I will consider the impact of homelessness on developments in this area of the law. I will then discuss the few cases that have expressed a different vision of the law. I will apply therapeutic jurisprudence principles to these questions in the next section. In the final section, I will consider briefly the potential impact on this area of recent federal legislation such as the Americans with Disabilities Act, will consider all developments through the filter of "sanism" (Perlin, 1992a; Perlin & Dorfman, 1993), and will offer some concluding thoughts.

The Right to Services in the Community

The Basic Constitutional Rights: In the Beginning

The theoretical underpinnings of a right to services in the community are found in the early cases that established both a right to treatment and a right to the least restrictive alternative in commitment decision making (Rhoden, 1982).[3] These cases (for example, *Lessard v. Schmidt,* 1972; *O'Connor v. Donaldson,* 1975; *Wyatt v.* *Stickney,* 1971, 1972, 1974) established the basic principles that served as the groundwork for the attempt to structure a right to deinstitutionalization and to community services (Perlin, 1980). Scholars suggested that predischarge planning and development of aftercare services were specific enforceable aspects of the constitutional right to treatment (Saphire, 1976), and cases proceeded on several parallel fronts: as outgrowths of right-to-treatment cases and challenges to involuntary-civil-commitment statutes (Rhoden, 1982, pp. 421–422), as outgrowths of cases seeking to extend the least-restrictive-alternative doctrine beyond intrahospital decision making (Rhoden, 1982, pp. 422–424; see generally Chapter 11, this volume), and as discrete cases seeking the promulgation of a discrete constitutional or statutory right to community care (*Dixon v. Weinberger,* 1975; Ferleger, 1983; Ferleger & Boyd, 1978).

Early cases found that, as part of the constitutional right to treatment, the state was obligated to provide "adequate transitional treatment and care for all patients released after a period of confinement" (*Wyatt v. Stickney,* 1972, p. 386); the provision of these services was explicitly seen as a major "disincentive to unnecessary institutionalization" (Wald & Friedman, 1978, p. 146). Another early institutional rights case found that a settlement that had provided residents with the "least restrictive and most normal living conditions possible" required state officials to fund "natural home placements" for such residents where it was needed to meet the settlement's deinstitutionalization criteria (*New York State Ass'n for Retarded Children, Inc. v. Carey,* 1980).

Similarly, an early case that had struck down a state civil commitment statute as overbroad required the state or committing agency to bear the burden of exploring alternatives to institutionalization, listing a spectrum of alternatives that

---

[3]The material in this section is largely adapted from Perlin (1989, pp. 567–608).

included "voluntary or court-ordered out-patient treatment, day treatment in a hospital, night treatment in a hospital, placement in the custody of a friend or relative, placement in a nursing home, referral to a community mental health clinic, and home health aide services" (*Lessard v. Schmidt*, 1972, p. 1096). Other courts found that the right to treatment included the right to such treatment in the least restrictive alternative (*Romeo v. Youngberg*, 1980).[4]

The first case that focused explicitly on a right to community treatment found a statutory right to aftercare under local law and specifically concluded that the District of Columbia had an affirmative obligation to place those patients suitable for placement in "less restrictive alternatives" in community settings (*Dixon v. Weinberger*, 1975, p. 979). Although, operationally, compliance with this court decree was sporadic (see "Accord Reached," 1989; "Landmark Agreement," 1989; Perlin, 1989, pp. 578–583), the legal principle was never seriously challenged, and subsequent cases in other jurisdictions settled on terms that were close to those ordered in the *Dixon* decree (*Brewster v. Dukakis*, 1987; *Wuori v. Zitnay*, 1978).

A somewhat different approach was put forth in New Jersey, where the state Supreme Court ruled that individuals who no longer met involuntary civil commitment criteria, but for whom there was no adequate or suitable placement, would be entitled to special placement hearings. The court would make inquiry as to "the needs of the individual for custodial and supportive care, the desires of the individual regarding placement, the type of facility that would provide the needed level of care in the least restrictive manner, the availability of such placement, [and] the efforts of the State to locate such placement" (*In re S.L.*, 1983, p. 1258; Perlin, 1985).

Deinstitutionalization and Community Services

Subsequently, other litigation sought the declaration of a constitutional right to deinstitutionalization and community services. Merging arguments in support of constitutional rights to treatment and the least restrictive alternative (Ferleger & Boyd, 1978, p. 739), this theory argued that, where further inpatient confinement is "predictably anti-therapeutic, further confinement must be deemed to effect a continuing violation of due process" in violation of the Fourteenth Amendment (Saphire, 1976, p. 286). When this theory was advanced in the case of *Halderman v. Pennhurst State School & Hospital* (1978), it was at first remarkably successful. The district court found that the Pennhurst facility was "inappropriate and inadequate for the habilitation of the retarded," violated residents' rights to minimally adequate habilitation,[5] their right to freedom from harm, and their right to "non-discriminatory habilitation," as well as state and federal statutory rights to minimally adequate habilitation. The court ordered the facility closed, finding that every resident removed from the facility had to be "accommodated in a community facility which will provide minimally adequate habilitation."[6]

On appeal, the Court of Appeals substantially affirmed, but on a nearly totally different legal basis, finding that the federal Developmentally Disabled Assistance and Bill of Rights Act (1976) (DD Act) provided an enforceable statu-

---

[4]The plaintiff in *Youngberg v. Romeo*, Nicholas Romeo, was institutionalized in a facility in the Pennhurst State School and Hospital. He was seeking a less restrictive option for services.

[5]Although there are great differences between facilities established to care for persons with mental retardation and those established for persons with mental illness, the case law has rarely focused on these differences. Most important cases have been cited interchangeably in subsequent decisions without regard to the particular condition of the institutionalized persons in question. But see *Heller v. Doe* (1993) (holding the statutory scheme providing for lesser standard of proof in case of involuntary civil commitment based on mental retardation than in case based on mental illness not unconstitutional).

[6]The court found support for its decision in the Fourteenth Amendment, § 504 of the Rehabilitation Act of 1973 (29 U.S.C. § 504), and state statutes (*Halderman v. Pennhurst State School & Hospital*, 1978; Pa. Stat. Ann., 1969).

tory right to treatment in the least-restrictive-alternative setting (*Halderman v. Pennhurst State School & Hospital,* 1979, pp. 95–107). However, it disagreed with the trial court's conclusion that the facility needed to be closed, concluding that, for some patients, such a transfer to community settings "might be too unsettling a move." Thus, it ordered a remand to the trial court for individual determinations as to the appropriateness of "an improved Pennhurst for each such patient."

Other Civil Rights of Individuals with Mental Disabilities in Community and Aftercare Settings

Beyond the provision of services, a panoply of other legal determinations affects the lives of people in the community with mental disabilities.[7]

In the Community

There has also been a significant amount of idiosyncratic litigation over the way that a person's status as an ex-patient could affect his or her civil rights in the community. These lawsuits were not initially intended to reform the law, but rather had the simpler goal of "vindicat[ing] the civil rights and basic rights of citizenship of individual mentally handicapped persons" (Perlin, 1980, p. 38; see generally Dennison, 1988). In these cases, courts have outlawed status discrimination against former patients and community mental health center residents in such areas as drivers' license suspensions, firearms purchases, employment, welfare, and Supplemental Security Income (SSI) benefits. They have also considered the impact of mental disability on such questions as parental rights, marriage dissolution, and sexual autonomy and have outlawed similar discrimination against *current* patients in matters involving voting rights (Perlin, 1989, pp. 652–654).

In Aftercare Settings

Several important cases have now been brought on behalf of formerly institutionalized patients currently receiving services in community mental health centers or other aftercare facilities (*Alessi v. Pa. Dep't of Pub. Welfare,* 1990; *Hanson v. Clarke Cty.,* 1989; *Martone v. Lensink,* 1988). Most have concentrated on common law and statutory issues involving the records of patients' stays at facilities: the degree of confidentiality required and the applicability of expungement statutes to such records (*N.J. Stat. Ann.,* 1981, §§ 30:4-80.8 to 30:4-80.11). In one consent decree, a federal district court in Pennsylvania ruled that city outpatient clinics must adopt stringent rules "with respect to maintaining the confidentiality of the medical records of all persons who have undergone or are presently undergoing treatment" at such centers (*Doe v. Beal,* 1977, reported in Perlin, 1980, p. 42); in a Pennsylvania state case, it was ordered that a former patient was entitled to copies of "all medical records" amassed during his hospitalization at a private psychiatric clinic (*Bala v. Auer,* 1978, reported in Perlin, 1980, p. 42).

Freedom from Discrimination in Exclusionary Zoning Cases

The most common focus of litigation brought on behalf of persons with mental disabilities in community settings has involved the right to be free from housing discrimination.[8] Most of these cases (but see *New York v. 11 Cornwall Co.,* 1983) have been based on state law and most frequently have turned on whether residents of group homes or other congregate living facilities should be considered as "families" for zoning law purposes. This categorization would allow courts to rebuff attempts to exclude such residences from a community (*Incorporated Village of Freeport v. Ass'n*

---

[7]This section is largely adapted from Perlin (1989, pp. 654–657) and Perlin (1994a, pp. 375–379).

[8]This section is largely adapted from Perlin (1989, pp. 657–671) and Perlin (1994b, pp. 368–375).

for the Help of Retarded Children, 1977; *Little Neck Community Ass'n v. Working Org. for Retarded Children,* 1976). Others have pursued a parallel strategy of seeking to bring such facilities within an "educational use" exemption to zoning codes (Tuoni, 1981) or to apply a state preemption doctrine as a basis on which discriminatory local laws could be struck down, on the theory that the municipal exclusion seeks to allow what the state has legislatively forbidden (*City of Torrance v. Transitional Living Centers, Inc.,* 1982). While most such attacks have been successful, some have not. In the latter cases, courts have generally refused to apply either a family or educational use exemption and have sustained local ordinances barring congregate facilities (for example, *Zoning Bd. of Hammond v. Tongipahoa Ass'n for Retarded Citizens,* 1987).

The sharpest judicial focus on this question came as a result of the U.S. Supreme Court's consideration in *City of Cleburne v. Cleburne Living Center* (1985) of the Fourteenth Amendment's equal protection implications of local zoning ordinances that exclude the disabled from congregate living. The facts in *Cleburne* were virtually uncontested. A private individual purchased a building in the city with the intention of leasing it to Cleburne Living Center (CLC) so that this nonprofit corporation could operate a group home for 13 mentally retarded (the term used in the case) individuals, who would be under the "constant supervision" of CLC staff members. He was told by city officials that, under a city ordinance, a special use permit was required to operate the group home. Subsequently, CLC submitted an application for such a permit.

After both the city's Planning and Zoning Commission and the city council held hearings and voted to deny the special use permit, CLC filed suit in federal court, alleging that the ordinance was facially invalid because it discriminated against persons with mental retardation in violation of the equal protection clause. The district court upheld the constitutionality of the operative ordinance on the theory that it was "rationally related to the City's legitimate inter-

ests in 'the legal responsibility of CLC and its residents . . . , the safety and fears of residents in the adjoining neighborhood,' and the number of people to be housed in the home" (*City of Cleburne v. Cleburne Living Center,* 1985, p. 437).

The Court of Appeals reversed, holding that mental retardation was a quasisuspect classification, demanding heightened scrutiny. The constitutional consequence of that conclusion was that more would be required of the municipality than to show that the ordinance was reasonable, but that it was not necessary to satisfy a more rigorous standard requiring a demonstration of a "compelling state interest" to uphold it. The Court of Appeals ruled that the ordinance's validity should therefore be assessed under the intermediate standard of scrutiny. It thus held the ordinance facially invalid and invalid as applied (*Cleburne Living Center v. City of Cleburne,* 1984). The Supreme Court then granted the city's petition for *certiorari* and agreed to review the case.

The Supreme Court concluded that the Court of Appeals had erred in its characterization of mental retardation as a quasisuspect classification that called for "a more exacting standard of judicial review than is normally accorded economic and social legislation" (*City of Cleburne v. Cleburne Living Center,* 1985, p. 442). On the other hand, the Court stressed, this refusal to adopt quasisuspect classification "does not leave [persons with mental retardation] entirely unprotected from invidious discrimination" (*City of Cleburne v. Cleburne Living Center,* 1985, p. 446). Use of the rational relationship standard "affords governments the latitude necessary, both to pursue policies designed to assist the retarded in reaching their full potential, and to freely and efficiently engage in activities that burden the retarded in what is essentially an incidental manner" (*City of Cleburne v. Cleburne Living Center,* 1985, p. 446).

The Court characterized the difference between the proposed home and other facilities that would be permitted in the same zone without a special use permit as "largely irrelevant." The record reflected no rational basis for suggesting that CLC's home would "pose any special threat to the city's legitimate interests." The Supreme Court thus affirmed the Court of Appeal's judgment "insofar as it holds the ordinance invalid as applied" (*City of Cleburne v. Cleburne Living Center*, 1985, p. 448).

The Court then scrutinized—and rejected— the factors on which the city based its insistence on a special use permit. First, although the city was concerned with "negative attitudes" of adjacent property owners and fears of nearby elderly neighborhood residents, such "unsubstantiated" negative attitudes or fear were not permissible bases for discriminatory treatment: "Private biases may be outside the reach of the law, but the law cannot, directly or indirectly, give them effect" (*Cleburne Living Center v. City of Cleburne*, 1985, pp. 432–434).

Second, the Court dismissed objections to the facility being located both across the street from a junior high school (whose students might "harass" CLC residents) and on a "five hundred year flood plain." Because 30 students with mental retardation attended the nearby school, the Court found the city's fears concerning the school to be "vague [and] undifferentiated" (Cleburne, 1985, p. 449). The Court also found that concern as to a possible bimillennial flood could not justify a meaningful distinction in treatment between a group home and, for instance, a permitted nursing home.

Third, while the city expressed concern about the house's size and the number of people who would occupy it, "its use would be permitted under the zoning ordinance" if all other factors were the same but the potential residents did not have mental retardation (*City of Cleburne v. Cleburne Living Center*, 1985, p. 449). Finally, the Court rejected the city's argument that its ordinance was aimed at "avoiding concentration of population and at lessening congestion of the streets." Such concerns "obviously fail to explain why apartment houses, fraternity and sorority houses, hospitals and the like, may freely operate without a permit" (*City of Cleburne v. Cleburne Living Center*, 1985, p. 450).

Justice Stevens concurred, arguing that unlike cases involving race, gender, or age, cases involving categorizations based on conditions such as mental retardation "do not fit well into sharply defined classifications," from which he reasoned that a properly defined "rational basis" test would better result in a single standard that could be applied in a "reasonably consistent fashion" (*City of Cleburne v. Cleburne Living Center*, 1985, pp. 451–452). While not all laws that place persons with mental retardation in a special class are "presumptively irrational," given the history of "unfair and often grotesque mistreatment" to which persons with mental retardation have been subjected, Justice Stevens was "convince[d]" that the city required a permit "because of the irrational fears of neighboring property owners, rather than for the protection of the mentally retarded persons who will reside in [CLC's] home" (*City of Cleburne v. Cleburne Living Center*, 1985, pp. 454–455).

Justice Marshall concurred in part and dissented in part (on his own behalf, and for Justices Brennan and Blackmun), taking sharp issue with both the way the Court reached its result and with the "narrow, as-applied remedy it provide[d]" (*City of Cleburne v. Cleburne Living Center*, 1985, p. 456). First, he characterized the interest of persons with retardation in the establishment of such homes as "substantial." Second, he saw persons with mental retardation as having been subject to a "'lengthy and tragic' history of segregation and discrimination that can only be called grotesque" (*City of Cleburne v. Cleburne Living Center*, 1985, p. 461). Because of the importance of the interest at stake and the history of discrimination that "the retarded" have suffered, according to Justice Marshall, the equal protection clause "requires us to do more than review the [ordinance's] distinctions . . . as if they appeared in a taxing statute or in economic or commercial legislation" (*City of Cleburne v. Cleburne Living Center*, 1985, p. 464). The "searching scrutiny" the dissenters would employ leads to the conclusion that the city's "vague generalizations . . . are not substantial or important enough to overcome the suspicion that the ordinance rests on impermissible assumptions or outmoded and perhaps invidious stereotypes" (*City of Cleburne v. Cleburne Living Center,* 1985, p. 465).

The most important recent jurisprudential perspective on *Cleburne* has come from legal scholar Martha Minow. Drawing especially on Justice Marshall's opinion identifying a "chief root of prejudice" as "separation among groups [that] exaggerates indifference," Minow has read *Cleburne* from a "social relations" perspective:

[T]he premise is that relationships between people are what matter, and attributions of difference that build obstacles to such relationships are suspect. Isolation itself may contribute to false views of difference that impede or obstruct relationships, and isolation of a powerless minority group by a powerful majority should raise special suspicions for a court that focuses on relationships and power. (Minow, 1987, pp. 135–136)

Summary

By the early 1980s, it appeared as if the concept of a right to community services had won widespread support. Courts appeared willing to premise this right on both constitutional and statutory bases, and appeared comfortable with seeing it as the logical next step in right to treatment and right to least-restrictive-alternative litigation. The decisions by the Supreme Court in *Youngberg* and in *Pennhurst,* however, made it clear that this vision was not shared by that Court.

The Supreme Court Speaks

The Supreme Court first heard the state's appeal from the *Pennhurst* case—the first major constitutional challenge seeking to mandate community services—in 1981. In an opinion written by Justice Rehnquist, it rejected out of hand the Third Circuit's legal reasoning and ruled that the DD Act did not create enforceable rights. The Court interpreted the statute as merely a voluntary federal-state grant program through which the federal government could provide financial assistance to states to aid in the creation of programs to treat persons with developmental disabilities. It further found that nothing in the legislative history of the act suggested that Congress intended to require the states to provide "appropriate treatment" in the "least restrictive environment" to citizens with mental retardation. It reached this conclusion despite the fact that, in the DD Act, Congress had made specific findings that "persons with developmental disabilities have a right to appropriate treatment, services, and habilitation" (Developmentally Disabled Assistance and Bill of Rights Act, 1976, § 6010(1)) and that treatment should be provided "in the setting that is least restrictive of the person's personal liberty" (§ 6010(2)). The Court then remanded the case to the Court of Appeals to consider other arguments that had been made by the plaintiffs but that had not yet been decided.

On remand, the Court of Appeals reinstated in its entirety its initial ruling, but on an entirely different basis. Premising its holding solely on Pennsylvania law, it found that state residents were entitled to treatment in the least-restrictive-alternative setting and that that formulation meant that "mentally retarded persons and [their] family shall have the right to live a life as close as possible to that which is typical of the general population" (*Halderman v. Pennhurst State School & Hospital,* 1982). Again, state officials appealed this decision to the Supreme Court.

Before the Supreme Court reached that appeal, however, it granted the state's application for review in *Youngberg,* the case that had sought a constitutional declaration of a right to treatment or habilitation for institutionalized persons with mental disabilities. Although the Supreme Court did articulate a right to "minimally adequate [institutional] training," including specific substantive rights to food, shelter, medical care, and clothing—a right conceded by the state—it reaffirmed its earlier holdings in other social welfare areas that there was no general right to services in community settings. The Court stressed the "established principle that a state is under no constitutional duty to provide substantive services for those within its borders." While conceding that the state owed a duty "to provide services and care" to an "institutionalized [person who is] wholly dependent on the state," it added that the state had "considerable discretion in determining the scope and nature of its responsibilities." In the course of its decision, the Court also established a stringent "substantial professional judgment" standard for assessing the behavior of state officials in institutional decision making. Constitutional norms would be violated only where a professional's decision "is such a substantial departure from accepted professional judgment, practice or standards as to demonstrate that the person responsible actually did not base the decision on such a judgment" (Perlin, 1990b; Stefan, 1992).

Then, in 1984, the Supreme Court once more reversed the Court of Appeals' decision in *Pennhurst*. This time it based its decision on a set of constitutional principles that on the surface seemed to have nothing to do with mental disability law: the scope of the Eleventh Amendment,[9] and whether that amendment precludes federal courts from hearing under its "pendent jurisdiction"[10] state law claims against state officials. In what was "clearly the Court's most bitterly split

institutional decision of the century" (Perlin, 1989, p. 627; Rudenstine, 1984, pp. 71–72), the Court ruled that such actions were entirely barred by the Eleventh Amendment, and that for a federal court to instruct state officials on how to conform their conduct to comply with state law was an "intrusion on state sovereignty" that conflicted squarely with "principles of federalism."

One other important non–mental disability Supreme Court case must also be considered: *De Shaney v. Winnebago County Department of Social Services* (1989). There, the mother of a small child complained to the county social services department that her son's father, who had been granted custody in their divorce, was physically abusing him. After these complaints and a series of abortive efforts by the county, the father continued to abuse the child, eventually causing him permanent brain damage. The mother sued, claiming that the county owed her son an affirmative duty to protect him in a reasonably competent manner. The Supreme Court disagreed, holding that the due process clause of the Fourteenth Amendment did not obligate the state to protect its citizens from one another; the state's affirmative act of restraining an individual's freedom to act on his or her own behalf—through institutionalization or other similar restraint on personal liberty—was a prerequisite to any state obligation to provide care.[11]

Together, these four cases—the two *Pennhurst* decisions, *Youngberg,* and *De Shaney*—reflect a Supreme Court vision of the state's obligation to provide services for persons with disabilities that is drastically at odds with the one offered by advocates for such persons. Although the persons with mental disabilities who were at risk in *Pennhurst* and *Youngberg* may not have

---

[9] The relevant part of the Eleventh Amendment reads as follows: "The judicial power of the United States shall not be construed to extend to any suit in law or equity, commenced or prosecuted against any one of the United States by citizens of another state." Decisions construing this amendment have been characterized by the Third Circuit as "a wonderland of judicially created and perpetuated fiction and paradox" (*Spicer v. Hilton*, 1980, p. 235; see generally Schwartz, 1984, pp. 151–152).

[10] Under this constitutional and jurisdictional doctrine, there are significant limits to the ability of federal courts to hear claims brought against state officials on state law bases (Perlin, 1989, pp. 627–636).

[11] At least one court has held that those aspects of *Youngberg* imposing affirmative duties on the state (for minimal institutional services) have survived the Supreme Court's decision in *De Shaney* (*Shaw by Strain v. Strackhouse*, 1990, pp. 1146–1147 n. 4; see also *Matter of McKnight*, 1990, p. 863 n. 11, noting that *De Shaney* distinguished the circumstances (specific facts) present in *Youngberg*).

been the Court's specific targets in its decisions, the cases are clearly linked to the Court's desire "to ban 'public law' litigation in general, and 'institutional' litigation in particular, from federal courts" (Brown, 1985, p. 344), as well as to the Court's ongoing transformation of its role "from guardian of individual rights to the guardian of majority rule" (Sherry, 1986, p. 662). Within months of the second *Pennhurst* decision, commentators had thus gloomily concluded that the Court's opinion had "distressing tactical implications for proponents of a right to community treatment for mental patients" ("Establishing a Right," 1984) and predicted that the case would "foreclose" further federal involvement in institutional reform and deinstitutionalization litigation ("The Reinstitutionalization," 1986).

Homelessness and Deinstitutionalization

In recent years, the problems of urban homeless persons have drawn significant attention from lawyers, the media, government officials, and the general public.[12] Though it is clear that homelessness is *not* a new phenomenon and that its causes are "many and complex" (Arce & Vergare, 1984; Hatfield et al., 1984, pp. 283–289), it is equally apparent that, in the public's eye, the increase in homelessness and the urban trouble spawned by this increase have been "caused" by the policy of deinstitutionalization (Lamb, 1984; Rhoden, 1982). It is thus necessary to consider briefly the range of social and economic factors that have contributed to deinstitutionalization and to homelessness in an effort to determine their relationship, if any, with the questions confronted elsewhere in this chapter.

---

[12] This section is largely adapted from Perlin (1989, pp. 671–686; Perlin, 1991a; Perlin, 1994b, pp. 379–391).

The Development of Deinstitutionalization

At least five separate forces have provided the impetus for the development of deinstitutionalization as a social policy since the early 1960s (Langdon & Kass, 1985; Mills & Cummins, 1982). First, as the extent of serious deficiencies in state hospitals became apparent to social reformers, psychiatrists, lawyers, and political leaders, it became relatively apparent that alternatives to large, impersonal institutions needed to be developed (Deutsch, 1949; Ferleger, 1983; Solomon, 1958).

Second, mental health professionals and others began to turn their attention to the different mechanisms through which community care could be provided (Bassuk & Gerson, 1978).

Third, new and amended federal grant and entitlement programs provided a mechanism through which community programs could be reimbursed for the care of persons with mental disabilities (Ewing, 1979; Talbott, 1978).

Fourth, the development of antipsychotic drugs created a modality of treatment that could, in many instances, be administered in the community in much the same manner as in institutions (Baldessarini, 1977; Brill & Patton, 1957; but see Scull, 1984, questioning this view).

Fifth, as courts more readily applied the due process clause of the Constitution to cases involving the rights of institutionalized persons with mental disabilities, they began to strike down vaguely drafted involuntary civil commitment statutes, to impose durational limitations on commitments, and to extend the least-restrictive-alternative doctrine to institutional decision making (Perlin, 1989, pp. 1–28). In addition, legislatures passed more restrictive commitment laws and adopted periodic review mechanisms that limited the universe of those who would be initially institutionalized and who would subsequently remain institutionalized (Perlin, 1989, pp. 29–454).

Notwithstanding these roots, there is no question that deinstitutionalization subsequently became a scapegoat for what has been perceived as a massive social failure that, in some instances, "worsened conditions of care, created community resistance, and undermined patient reintegration" (Mills & Cummins, 1982, p. 274). On the other hand, there is an ample body of evidence indicating that a well-conceived deinstitutionalization program with a variety of rehabilitative services offered intensively has a positive and significant effect on the length of the ex-patients' tenure in the community (Durham & LaFond, 1988).

Homeless Persons with Mental Illness

Blaming homelessness on deinstitutionalization is a serious error. Beyond the obvious fact that this blame laying ignores the tens (if not hundreds) of thousands of homeless persons who have never been institutionalized or who do not have a mental illness (Langdon & Kass, 1985), even the sharpest critics of deinstitutionalization policies have recognized that (1) even in the broadest reading, deinstitutionalization cannot be seen as the *sole* cause of the increase in homelessness (Lamb, 1984), and (2) it is not the *concept* of deinstitutionalization—characterized as "clinically sound and economically feasible" (Talbott & Lamb, 1984)—but its misexecution that has helped exacerbate the problems in question (Lamb, 1984).

Factors Contributing to Homelessness

At least five separate factors have had a significant impact on the problems of the homeless: (1) the baby boom, (2) the shrinking housing market, (3) deinstitutionalization policies, (4) reduction in government benefits, and (5) high unemployment rates (Fischer & Breakey, 1986; Marmor & Gill, 1989). It is necessary to consider each factor separately to understand the full scope of the problems the homeless face and the extent of the connection—if any—between these problems and the right of persons with mental disabilities to community services:

1. *The baby boom.* While the numbers of the homeless are growing steadily, their average age is also dropping precipitously. As successive cohorts of post–World War II, baby-boom babies reach maturity, "the absolute number of young persons at risk for developing schizophrenia and other chronic mental disorders has increased dramatically." Because younger people, including the "episodic or permanently homeless," are generally more mobile—traveling more extensively and relocating more frequently—there have developed "magnet" communities "that attract the more mobile of the homeless mentally ill," and there is evidence of "migration streams within which the chronically mentally ill move" (Bachrach, 1984, pp. 14–15). Younger people also show a greater "recreational use of addictive substances" (both drugs and alcohol) that often "exacerbate [and alter] the symptoms of illness" and make homelessness more likely (Bachrach, 1984, pp. 14–15).

2. *The shrinking housing market.* The elimination of available housing stock has had a tremendous impact on the growth of the homeless, especially in the biggest cities. A study by the New York State Department of Social Services concluded that "homelessness is by its nature a crisis of housing" (Carmody, 1984). This merely echoes the findings of a state study issued two years before: "The single most critical factor which prevents effective service coordination and implementation of rational discharge planning is the lack of provision for adequate specialized housing for the chronically disabled" (Baxter & Hopper, 1984, p. 113). This problem is exacerbated further by states and communities that—fearing they will become a "magnet" for the homeless—systematically "compete to have the least attractive provisions in an effort to minimize their populations of homeless people" ("Homelessness," 1985a, pp. 555–556).

3. *Deinstitutionalization policies.* A variety of reasons have been suggested regarding why deinstitutionalization policies have not "worked" as they were intended to. What is no longer in serious dispute is that a significant percentage of

the homeless exhibit certain key characteristics of mental illness, that this percentage is probably growing, and that shelters have become "permanent institutions" for some persons with mental disabilities who are no longer under the supervision of state departments of mental health (Appleby & Desai, 1985; Bassuk, Rubin, & Lauriat, 1984).

Though it is "abundantly clear" that deinstitutionalization has "failed to live up to its initial promise" (Rhoden, 1982, pp. 393–394), countless community programs and facilities are known to exist that are able to facilitate the reintegration of chronic patients into the community by providing supportive social structures (Mosher & Keith, 1980). Further, when patients are deinstitution-alized into alternative outpatient treatment programs, the latter are invariably more effective than inpatient treatment (Kiesler, 1982).

4. *The reduction in government benefits.* The procedures initiated by the Reagan Administration to seek review of all SSI recipients resulted in over 350,000 people losing their benefits since the fall of 1981 (*Stieberger v. Heckler*, 1985). Mental disability was found to be overrepresented in this group by a factor of three in cases where benefits were discontinued, and about a third of all persons whose benefits have been discontinued have mental impairments (Baxter & Hopper, 1984).

Although these cutbacks have diminished in the face of public outrage and congressional response (*Bowen v. City of New York*, 1986; 42 U.S.C. § 423, 1995), there is no question that the reduction of disability benefits was a significant factor in the increase in the number of homeless persons (Bassuk & Lauriat, 1984). There is also no reason to suggest that the more recent amelioration in entitlement policy has aided those whose benefits were reduced or cut off in the early 1980s ("Building a House of Legal Rights," 1985b).

5. *High unemployment rates.* Most of the "new homeless" are unskilled and were chronically unemployed even *before* they became homeless. Although they are mobile and physically and mentally capable, they have had little opportunity for advancement because of poverty and skill levels. To a significant extent, this group has helped reshape the demographic picture of the homeless: more and more, members of the racial and ethnic minority groups who have been disproportionately hurt by the increase in unemployment rates in unskilled and semiskilled jobs are joining the ranks of the homeless (Langdon & Kass, 1985).

A Different Vision?

Other Legal Strategies

In spite of the clear signals by the Supreme Court in the two *Pennhurst* cases, *Youngberg,* and *De Shaney,* and in spite of the public's linkage of deinstitutionalization with homelessness, litigators representing persons with mental disabilities have continued to pursue other theories that would compel states to provide community rights to services. One circuit expanded *Youngberg*'s right to training to apply to an individual not institutionalized *at the time of suit* but who, by the time he was 19 years old, had been "shuffled" through 40 foster homes and institutions, on the theory that he was in constant peril of being reinstitutionalized (*Thomas S. v. Morrow*, 1984, p. 1057). Another found that community care was required when professional judgment was unanimous that further institutionalization was improper (*Clark v. Cohen*, 1986). In the latter case, the court relied on *Youngberg* to find that a plaintiff had a right *not* to be institutionalized if it were possible to create a community living arrangement for her (*Clark v. Cohen*, 1986, p. 702). Yet most courts took the lead of the Supreme Court and rejected plaintiffs' arguments seeking noninstitutional services (*Clift v. Fincannon*, 1987; *Department of Mental Health v. Doe*, 1987; *Gieseking v. Schafer*, 1987; *P. C. v. McLaughlin*, 1990) or a right to community placement (*Phillips v. Thompson*, 1983; *Society for Good Will to Retarded Children v. Cuomo*, 1984).

In perhaps the most important of these unsuccessful cases, a federal trial court invalidated a city budgetary plan that had denied certain support services and benefits for individuals with mental disabilities who lived at home; the court ordered the state to pay for such services (*Philadelphia Police & Fire Ass'n v. City of Philadelphia*, 1988). It had found that failure to maintain the basic skills of such persons in the community violated their right to "personal autonomy," protected by the due process clause. On appeal, however, the Court of Appeals reversed the decision, finding that the Supreme Court's *De Shaney* decision handed down after the trial but before the appeal "eliminate[d] all support" for the trial court's due process finding, "constrain[ing]" it to hold that the service reductions did not violate plaintiffs' rights (*Philadelphia Police & Fire Ass'n v. City of Philadelphia*, 1989). This decision was a major "setback in the battle for the rights of citizens [with mental disabilities]" (*"Philadelphia Police and Fire Association,"* 1990).

Decisions such as these led some other litigators to forgo the federal forum and bring suits instead in state court, a tactical move that reflected the reality that state high courts often interpreted state constitutions and statutes more liberally than the federal courts when construing the counterpart federal documents (Perlin, 1987; *Rivers v. Katz*, 1986). In the broadest state court decision, the Arizona Supreme Court ruled that both the state and county were statutorily compelled to provide mental health care to community patients with chronic mental disabilities (*Arnold v. Department of Health Services*, 1989; Santiago, 1990). Such suits have not been universally successful, however; the Rhode Island Supreme Court, for example, has ruled that a community mental health center had the statutory right to refuse admission to an outpatient: "[N]o [center] should be ordered to accept a patient suffering from mental disability unless its officials are willing to do so" (*Rhode Island Dep't of Mental Health v. R.B.*, 1988).

Commentators have continued to proffer arguments to support constitutionally based rights to mental health services in the community (Seicshnaydre, 1992), and to demonstrate the constitutional and moral inadequacies of the *Youngberg* "substantial professional judgment" standard (Stefan, 1992). It is by no means clear, though, that the federal courts—as currently constituted—will be a receptive audience for these arguments.

The Legal Rights of Homeless Persons with Mental Disabilities

To the public, increases in homelessness and the urban troubles spawned by this increase were caused primarily by deinstitutionalization (Lamb, 1984, pp. 56–60), a position embraced by policymakers, elected officials, and the media in spite of both empirical data and theoretical arguments that effectively rebut this position (Perlin, 1991a).[13] It is clear, however, that many homeless individuals do have mental disabilities (Perlin, 1985, pp. 657–686), and it is thus necessary to consider carefully legal strategies that have been forwarded on behalf of this population.

The Right to Shelter

The first litigated case—*Callahan v. Carey* (1979)—resulted in an initial ruling that, under the New York State Constitution and state regulatory scheme, both the city and state were obligated to provide shelter to homeless males. When city defendants refused to extend the terms of the decree to homeless women, a subsequent suit was filed on behalf of the latter group (*Eldredge v. Koch*, 1983). A trial court ruled that the *Callahan* decree must be made equally applicable to women and found that several of the women's shelters violated *Callahan*'s substantive standards (*Eldredge v. Koch*, 1983, p. 961). Although the appellate division ruled that more

---

[13] This section is largely adapted from Perlin (1989, pp. 391–396) and Perlin (1993a, § 2.53).

evidence was needed on the question of specific violations, it affirmed the aspect of the trial court's opinion that found *Callahan* applicable to women.

In what has been characterized as "perhaps the most far-reaching" right-to-shelter case (Stille, 1986, p. 25), a New Jersey trial court judge has used state law as the basis for an order compelling Atlantic City to develop a comprehensive plan to deal with its homeless problems (*Maticka v. City of Atlantic City*, 1986, 1987). The city submitted such a plan to the court, through which it presented 10 specific recommendations to implement a "comprehensive and coordinated system to address the needs of Atlantic City's homeless population on a long-term basis" (*Maticka v. City of Atlantic City*, 1986).

The Right to Psychiatric Services

In the first case concerning the right to psychiatric services, the highest state court in New York ordered a trial in a suit brought on behalf of, among others, homeless ex-patients seeking adequate aftercare facilities, ruling that "failure to provide suitable and adequate treatment cannot be justified by lack of staff or facilities," especially where the plaintiffs claim a constitutional violation (*Klostermann v. Cuomo*, 1984a, p. 253). On remand, the trial court held that ex-patients had no federal constitutional right to mental health treatment at public expense. It did, however, hold that their claim that they were refused residential care, placement, and supervision that had been provided to others with less severe disabilities stated a claim on which relief could be granted under both the equal protection clause and section 504 of the Rehabilitation Act of 1973 (*Klostermann v. Cuomo*, 1984b, pp. 583–584). On a related question, that state's Appellate Division ruled in favor of homeless patients with mental illness who had argued that they were entitled to a sample of discharge service plans during the discovery phase of a suit they had brought seeking to require state defendants to prepare such plans for all patients prior to discharge (*Heard v.*

Cuomo, 1988). In subsequent developments in the same case, the trial court ruled, based on state law (McKinney's Mental Hygiene Law §§ 7.07(c), 29.15) that the city owes patients discharged from city psychiatric facilities appropriate housing conditions (*Heard v. Cuomo*, 1991).

Notwithstanding this handful of modest victories in the past decade in litigation seeking to establish a right to community services, most innovative litigation has slowed to a trickle. This, of course, stands in stark contrast to such other areas of constitutionally based mental disability law as the right to refuse treatment, where case law developments continue to increase exponentially (Perlin, 1991c, 1993b, 1994).

The Impact of Therapeutic Jurisprudence

The most important and exciting new jurisprudential insights into mental disability law of the last two decades have come from the development of the construct of therapeutic jurisprudence.[14] *Therapeutic jurisprudence* presents a new model to assess the ultimate impact of case law and legislation that affects individuals with mental disabilities. It studies the role of the law as a therapeutic agent, recognizing that substantive rules, legal procedures, and lawyers' roles may have either therapeutic or antitherapeutic consequences. It also questions whether such rules, procedures, and roles can or should be reshaped to enhance their therapeutic potential, while not subordinating normatively derived legal principles (Perlin, 1989, pp. 5–9; Wexler, 1990, 1992; Wexler & Winick, 1991). An inquiry into therapeutic outcomes does not mean that therapeutic concerns "trump" civil rights and civil liberties. The law's use of "mental health information to

---

[14] This section is largely adapted from Perlin (1993d, pp. 2–4).

improve therapeutic functioning [cannot] impinge upon justice concerns" (Wexler, 1993, p. 17). *Therapeutic jurisprudence* does not, cannot, and must not mean, in Nicholas Kittrie's (1971) famous phrase, "a return to the therapeutic state." This approach to jurisprudence calls for an examination of the therapeutic consequences of legal rules and decisions; it does not provide an excuse to return to the 1950s, when courts were comfortable with a "hands-off" policy toward mental hospitals and their residents (Perlin, 1987; Perlin, 1989, pp. 5–15).

Therapeutic jurisprudence looks, then, at a variety of mental disability law issues in an effort both to shed new light on past developments and to offer new insights for future developments (articles cited in Perlin, 1989, pp. 6–7 nn. 156.6–156.17; Perlin, 1991c, 1992b, 1993b, 1993d; Perlin & Dorfman, 1993; Wexler, 1990, 1992, 1993; Wexler & Winick, 1991). No attention has been paid, however, to the area of the law under consideration here: the right to community services. The application of such a mode of analysis reveals some startling findings.

Therapeutic Jurisprudence and the Right to Community Services

Some of the original deinstitutionalization litigation was explicitly anti-institutional. The aim of plaintiffs' counsel was to "spell the end of more than a century of incarceration of the retarded in the United States" (Ferleger, 1978). Yet, at the same time, it was not nihilistic. Virtually every early case explicitly sought an expansive provision of community services: aftercare, transitional services, and suitable community living arrangements (*Dixon v. Weinberger*, 1975; *Halderman v. Pennhurst State School & Hospital*, 1978) in which persons with mental disabilities would be more likely "to develop maximum potential in self-help, language, personal, social, educational, vocational and recreational skills" (*Halderman v. Pennhurst State School & Hospital*, 1979). The vast majority of literature written by mental health professionals and behaviorists has endorsed such community-based care as generally preferable to institutional care (see, for example, Ellis & Luckasson, 1985; Menolascino, 1977; Rubin, 1991; Scheerenberger, 1976; Weithorn, 1988).

The success that these arguments met with in the lower federal courts before 1982, however, was matched by their failure in the U.S. Supreme Court. As previously noted, the current court is, in most instances, overtly hostile to public law litigation in general, and to institutional litigation in particular. Its specific hostility to litigation on behalf of persons with mental disabilities may also stem from judges' "sanist" attitudes (that is, the use of stereotypical thinking and deindividualization about persons with mental disabilities) (Perlin, 1992a; Perlin & Dorfman, 1993).[15] There is yet another factor present in these cases, however, that requires some further analysis: the position taken in institutional reform litigation by counsel for state hospital departments (Wexler, 1983).

A review of the briefs filed by the state in the U.S. Supreme Court in the two *Pennhurst* cases and in *Youngberg* reveals positions almost identical to those ultimately endorsed by the Supreme Court. In the first *Pennhurst* appeal, for instance, the hospital's lawyers argued that the "DD Act does not compel the States either to fund treatment or to provide the least restrictive environment" and that the Bill of Rights in that act was "nothing more than a statement of federal policy, to be encouraged through federal funding" (*Pennhurst*, Brief for Petitioners, 1980 Term, Summary of Argument). In *Youngberg*, counsel argued that "by assuming responsibility for satisfying [the plaintiff's] basic needs, the [State] did not assume a constitutional duty to provide him with additional services such as treatment," and that the Third Circuit "plainly erred in holding that . . . the institutionalized mentally retarded

---

[15] See "Summary."

have a right . . . to receive treatment, which is both acceptable in light of present medical or other scientific knowledge and the least intrusive available under the circumstances" (*Youngberg,* Brief for Petitioners, 1980 Term, Summary of Argument). The Court also stressed that "states are under no affirmative constitutional obligation to provide its residents with governmental services" (*Youngberg,* Brief for Petitioners, 1980 Term, Text of Argument). Finally, in the second *Pennhurst* case, the state's lawyers focused explicitly on the Eleventh Amendment arguments ultimately adopted by the Supreme Court:

The decision below, ordering costly and extensive relief solely under state law, does considerable violence to established principles under the Eleventh Amendment and to notions of comity [according respect to the decisions of the state by other governments]. Unless it is reversed, the decision will give federal courts a free hand in the management of state programs despite the absence of [any] federal interest. (*Pennhurst,* Brief for Petitioners, 1982 Term, Summary of Argument)

These arguments must be read in the factual context of the records developed in these cases. In the initial *Pennhurst* trial, the district court judge made the following findings: Pennhurst was "inappropriate and inadequate for the habilitation of the retarded"; the physical environment was "so poor that it contributed to [residents'] losing skills already learned"; many of the residents "have suffered physical deterioration and intellectual and behavioral regression during their residency" (*Halderman v. Pennhurst State School & Hospital,* 1978, pp. 1304–1309). The defendants never offered any "serious" factual objections to these findings in any subsequent aspect of the litigation, or to other findings of sexual abuse, excrement-laden floors, infectious diseases, lack of toilet paper, and general unsanitary conditions (*Halderman v. Pennhurst State School & Hospital,* 1979, pp. 92–93). In short, the defendants conceded the antitherapeutic conditions of the facility and focused their legal assault entirely on the court's

ability to order community care and services for the plaintiff classes. Indeed, following the second Supreme Court decision in *Pennhurst,* the parties settled the case under an order that provided "virtually all" of the relief initially sought when the suit was filed (*Halderman v. Pennhurst State School & Hospital,* 1985; Perlin, 1989).

The Court's decisions are profoundly antitherapeutic. Their failure to find a generic constitutional right to community services curbed litigation seeking to establish such a right. The initial *Pennhurst* decision, for all practical purposes, eviscerated the DD Act as a potential litigational tool for institutionalized persons with mental disabilities; the reaffirmation of the no-general-right-to-community-services in *Youngberg* ended most advocacy efforts to have such a right established. The second *Pennhurst* opinion effectively put an end to deinstitutionalization/ aftercare litigation as a strategy of patients' rights advocates.

What is especially ironic here is the topsy-turvy spin on the rhetoric that places the blame for inappropriate deinstitutionalization and homelessness squarely on the shoulders of patients' rights advocates. The American Psychiatric Association Task Force on the Homeless Mentally Ill has argued that legal advocacy on behalf of institutionalized mental patients "neglected [the patients'] right to high-quality comprehensive outpatient care" (Talbott & Lamb, 1984, p. 7). Its chair, H. Richard Lamb (1984), has asserted that "some mental health lawyers and patients' rights advocates . . . have contributed heavily to the problems of homelessness" (p. 62). E. Fuller Torrey has characterized inappropriate deinstitutionalization as the "primary" cause of homelessness and accused "civil liberties lawyers" of "compound[ing] the disaster" by filing such suits as *Lessard v. Schmidt, Wyatt v. Stickney,* and *Dixon v. Weinberger* (Perlin, 1991a).

The truth is just the opposite. First, each of the cases identified by Torrey sought the constitutionally mandated provision of appropriate and accessible aftercare and community services (Perlin, 1989, p. 576, discussing this aspect of *Lessard;* p. 574, discussing this aspect of *Wyatt;* pp. 578–582, discussing this aspect of *Dixon*). Early proponents of deinstitutionalization envisioned that a broad array of community services would emerge as institutional care declined (Rubenstein, 1986, pp. 384–385; Seicshnaydre, 1992, p. 1974, n. 10). Beyond this, patients' rights litigators have been praised by federal judges for "significantly improv[ing] the quality of life" for institutionalized persons, helping to bring an end to the "filth, squalor, and unsafe conditions" that had characterized state institutional life (*Ricci v. Callahan*, 1986, p. 379). While some prominent lawyers sought the abolition of involuntary civil commitment, others focused on the need to fund mental health care and services adequately (Wald & Friedman, 1978; Rhoden, 1982). Finally, most of the cases criticized by Torrey resulted in consent orders, in which state defendants agreed with plaintiffs as to the ultimate disposition of the case (Perlin, 1989, p. 34, discussing stipulation to standards in *Wyatt v. Stickney,* 1972; Perlin, 1989, p. 581, discussing compromise implementation plan agreed on in *Dixon v. Harris*, 1980; Perlin, 1989, p. 575, discussing consent judgment in *New York State Ass'n for Retarded Children, Inc. v. Carey*, 1980).

New Developments

This does not end the necessary inquiry. The enactment of the Americans with Disabilities Act (ADA) and the passage of the Fair Housing Amendments Act of 1988 represent Congress's most innovative attempts to address pervasive problems of discrimination against persons with physical and mental disabilities. The ADA, especially, has the potential to restructure relationships between such persons and employers, government agencies, and places of public accommodations.

The Fair Housing Amendments Act of 1988

Advocates for persons with mental disabilities have begun to formulate litigation strategies to ensure the availability of adequate housing in community settings (*Edge v. Pierce*, 1982; *Knutzen v. Nelson*, 1985; *Quaker Hill Place v. Saville*, 1987).[16] Some of this early litigation led the Department of Housing and Urban Development to publish regulations prohibiting a landlord or property manager from limiting disabled tenants "in the enjoyment of any right, privilege, advantage, or other opportunity enjoyed by other qualified individuals receiving the housing aid, benefit, or service" (53 Fed. Reg. 20233, 1988). The most important tool in such advocates' arsenal, however, will likely prove to be the federal Fair Housing Amendments Act of 1988 (FHAA).

In 1968, Congress enacted Title VIII of the Civil Rights Act to end racial segregation in housing (42 U.S.C. §§ 3601–3617, 1968). The purpose of the Fair Housing Act (FHA) was to promote open, integrated residential housing patterns and to prevent the increase of segregation in ghettos on the part of racial groups whose lack of opportunities the FHA was designed to combat (*Williamsburg Fair Hous. Comm. v. NYC Housing Auth.*, 1978). Through the FHAA, the promise of the FHA was extended, for the first time, to reach the mentally and physically disabled (41 U.S.C. §§ 3602, 3604). The FHAA widened the FHA's coverage by seeking to achieve two goals: to secure to people with disabilities the right to establish a home free of discrimination in any community they choose, and to integrate people with handicaps into the mainstream of American life (Kotkin, 1989–1990; Simring, 1991). Under the FHAA, a person is "handicapped" if he or she

(1) [has] a physical or mental impairment which substantially limits one or more of such person's major life activities,

---

[16]This section is largely adapted from Perlin (1989 (1993 pocket part), §6.44B) and Perlin (1994a, pp. 321–329).

(2) [has] a record of having such an impairment, or

(3) is regarded as having such an impairment. (42 U.S.C. § 3602(b), 1968)

The Act makes the following practices unlawful:

(1) To discriminate in the sale or rental, or to otherwise make unavailable or deny, a dwelling to any buyer or renter because of a handicap of:

  (A) that buyer or renter;

  (B) a person residing in or intending to reside in that dwelling after it is so sold, rented, or made available; or

  (C) any person associated with that buyer or renter.

(2) To discriminate against any person in the terms, conditions, or privileges of sale or rental of a dwelling, or in the provision of services or facilities in connection with such dwelling, because of a handicap of:

  (A) that person; or

  (B) a person residing in or intending to reside in that dwelling after it is so sold, rented, or made available; or

  (C) any person associated with that person. (42 U.S.C. §§ 3604 (f), 1968)

Under the FHAA, landlords and owners may not ask a prospective tenant or buyer blanket questions about the individual's disabilities (24 C.F.R. § 100.202(c)). The only exception applies to applicants for government housing programs for persons with disabilities, allowing inquiries to ensure eligibility (24 C.F.R. § 100.202(c)). Landlords must make reasonable accommodations in rules, policies, and practices, with an exception provided for tenants whose tenancy would constitute a direct threat to the health or safety of other individuals or whose tenancy would result in substantial damage to the property of others (42 U.S.C. § 3604(f)(3)(B), 1988). Discrimination includes "a refusal to make reasonable accommodations in rules, policies, practices, or services, when such accommodations may be necessary to afford such person equal opportunity to use and enjoy a dwelling" (42 U.S.C. § 3604(f) (3)(B), 1988); reasonable accommodation means that a person's disability must be taken into account in making a modification that will allow that person to have an equal chance to benefit from the housing (Simring, 1991).

In the first relevant federal court decision, a health care provider attempted to open a home for homeless persons terminally ill with AIDS. The city denied him a special use permit because of the arguments of community opponents that people with AIDS posed a direct threat to the community at large, including students attending two nearby schools. The court rejected this argument and found that "persons who are HIV-positive pose no risk of its transmission to the community at large" (*Baxter v. City of Belleville*, 1989, p. 726). The case is significant because it supports the view that it will be difficult to prove that a person with a disability poses a direct threat to the health or safety of others; also, it stands for the proposition that the burden to show that a danger exists is on the party attempting to deny housing, not on the individual with a disability (Simring, 1991).

In a second case, the United States alleged that the defendant township discriminated on the basis of handicap in violation of the FHAA when it amended its zoning ordinance in 1989 to permit only persons who are considered a "family" to reside in single-family residential districts unless they are granted a special exception by the Zoning Hearing Board. In so doing, the township effectively blocked the creation of a Community Living Arrangement (CLA) for five males with mental retardation. The court held that the 1989 zoning ordinance amendment discriminated on the basis of handicap in violation of the FHAA and that it had a disparate impact and discriminatory effect on persons with mental disabilities (*United States v. Schuylkill Twp.*, 1990).

At least one zoning ordinance, has, however, been found to pass muster under the FHAA. In *Familystyle of St. Paul, Inc. v. City of St. Paul* (1990), plaintiffs challenged a state and local zoning ordinance regulating the licensing of facilities that required that no new community facility be built within 1320 feet of an existing residential facility. Plaintiffs claimed that the zoning ordinance violated section 3615 of the

FHAA[17] and was thus invalid as requiring or permitting a discriminatory housing practice. The district court upheld the zoning ordinance because it did not directly bar individuals with disabilities from residing at a residence of their choice. However, it advised that future generations would look on these laws "as archaic trappings of an unenlightened society" (*Familystyle of St. Paul, Inc. v. City of St. Paul*, 1990, p. 1405).

On appeal, the Court of Appeals affirmed the decision, reasoning that the dispersal requirements in the ordinance addressed the need of providing residential services in mainstream community settings while avoiding neighborhoods made up entirely of group homes that re-create institutional environments. The dispersal requirements, the court found, will ensure that individuals with mental disabilities who are in need of residential treatment will not be forced into enclaves of treatment facilities that would "replicate and thus perpetuate" institutionlike isolation (*Familystyle of St. Paul, Inc. v. St. Paul, Minn.*, 1991, p. 95).

The Americans with Disabilities Act

The purpose of the ADA is nothing less than "a national mandate to end discrimination against individuals with disabilities and to bring those individuals into the economic and social mainstreams of American life" (House Committee on Energy and Commerce, 1990). Through the ADA, Congress chose to provide clear, strong, enforceable standards and to ensure that the federal government plays a central role in the enforcement of such standards.

---

[17]That section reads as follows:

Nothing in this subchapter shall be construed to invalidate or limit any law of a State or political subdivision of a State, or of any other jurisdiction in which this subchapter shall be effective, that grants, guarantees, or protects the same rights as are granted by this subchapter; but any law of a State, a political subdivision, or other such jurisdiction that purports to require or permit any action that would be a discriminatory housing practice under this subchapter shall to that extent be invalid.

Initially, the ADA makes important fact findings that underscore this congressional commitment. The act makes clear that one of its purposes is the elimination of discrimination against individuals with disabilities in a variety of areas: "employment, housing, public accommodations, education, transportation, communication, recreation, institutionalization, health services, voting and access to public services" (42 U.S.C. § 12101(a)(3), 1993). The inclusion here of institutionalization underscores that the ADA is a law whose impact will be felt both in the community and in state facilities.

Second, Congress found specifically that individuals with disabilities are a "discrete and insular minority . . . subjected to a history of purposeful unequal treatment, and relegated to a position of political powerlessness" (42 U.S.C., § 12101(a)(7), 1993). This section paraphrases the famous *Carolene Products* case (*United States v. Carolene Products*, 1938, p. 152 n. 4), the Supreme Court case decision that has served as the springboard for almost all challenges to state and municipal laws that operate in discriminatory ways against minorities (Perlin, 1992a, pp. 380–381 n. 51). Under this analysis, a discriminatory law will not be upheld unless justified by a "compelling state interest," a difficult standard to meet (Perlin, 1993a, pp. 2–3).

Third, Congress explicitly states its purpose to "invoke the sweep of congressional authority, including the power to enforce the Fourteenth Amendment" (42 U.S.C. § 12101(4)). Any violation of the ADA must be read in the same light as a violation of the equal protection clause of the Constitution. Congress rarely invokes this power; in doing so here, it underscores the depth of its commitment through the ADA. Congress's conscious decision to incorporate the equal protection clause within the ADA itself is a strong signal that Congress expects the "compelling state interest" standard to be used to interpret ADA cases.

The three substantive titles of the ADA deal with employment, public entities, and public accommodations. It specifically bans any "public entity" from discriminating against any person with a disability or excluding any such person "from participation in" or denying such person "the benefits of the services, programs or activities of a public entity" (42 U.S.C. § 12132). The final operational title legislatively overrules those cases that suggest that states have an out—under the Eleventh Amendment—to exempt them from complying with the act (42 U.S.C. § 12202; *Halderman v. Pennhurst State School & Hospital*, 1984).

What will this act's meaning be for those with mental disabilities? It seems clear that, in matters involving employment and public accommodations, the ADA will be an important enforcement tool. No longer will employers be able to ask questions about prior mental health treatment on job application forms; no longer will towns be able to exclude the formerly institutionalized from access to local services. Because it is clear that having a residence and a job are frequently the two key variables that allow ex-patients to remain and function in the community, the ADA may ultimately have a significant impact on the future of all deinstitutionalization programs (Perlin, 1993a).

The ultimate impact of the antidiscrimination language of the public entity title, however, is still not clear. In the only major piece of analysis yet done, the late Timothy Cook—formerly head of the National Disability Action Center and one of the architects of the entire ADA—was explicit. He saw this title as ending what he termed the segregation of institutions for persons with mental disabilities (Cook, 1991). He read congressional intent through the legislative history to abolish, in Senator Weicker's words, "the monoliths of isolated care in institutions and segregated educational settings. . . . Separate is not equal. It was not for blacks; it is not for the disabled." The House Judiciary Report here was equally explicit: "Integration is fundamental to the purposes of the ADA. Provisions of segregated accommodations and services relegate persons with disabilities to second-class citizen status" (1990 USC CAN 449). Cook further read

the act to bar intentional and unintentional discrimination, and quoted researchers who concluded that "institutions and other segregated settings are simply unacceptable" (p. 413).

If these arguments are accepted, what impact would they have on rights to services in the community? Cook's thesis suggests that the plaintiffs' original arguments in the first phase of the *Pennhurst* case must prevail—that institutional treatment is unacceptable at least for persons with mental retardation. Can the same arguments be made about people with mental illness? Are there clear differences? Do police power considerations inherent in the involuntary civil commitment process make a difference? (Perlin, 1989, pp. 29–188).

Cook argued further that the ADA—by invoking the Fourteenth Amendment's equal protection language—effectively overrules the "substantial professional judgment" standard of *Youngberg*. This is the boldest argument that has been made on behalf of the ADA; if it is to be accepted, then the state of the right to community services may be drastically altered (Perlin, 1993a).

If the ADA is taken at face value, it would appear to be a powerful weapon for litigators to advance the cause of individuals with mental disabilities in community settings. It would also appear to be a significantly therapeutic law. On the other hand, any predictions as to its ultimate impact may be nothing more than speculation. The history of all civil rights law enforcement is rocky; the passage of civil rights laws meant to empower African Americans and women have not entirely eradicated discrimination against such persons (Rebell, 1986), and it would be folly to expect a significantly different outcome as to people with disabilities. Nevertheless, Stephan Haimowitz (1991) has stressed the incalculable symbolic significance of the ADA in this context:

While the [ADA] is no more likely to completely eliminate the myths, fears, and discrimination faced by persons with disabilities than earlier civil rights law eliminated discrimination based on race, the new legislation will nonetheless contribute to the enormous educational effort needed to combat widespread misinformation and stereotypes about disabilities. (p. 23)

On "Sanism"

This leads to the final wild card, the impact of "sanism." "Sanism" is an irrational prejudice of the same quality and character of other irrational prejudices that cause (and are reflected in) prevailing social attitudes of racism, sexism, homophobia, and ethnic bigotry (Allport, 1955). It infects both our jurisprudence and our lawyering practices (Birnbaum, 1974; Perlin, 1991a, 1992a; Perlin & Dorfman, 1993).

Sanism is largely invisible and largely socially acceptable. It is based predominantly on stereotype, myth, superstition, and deindividualization, and is sustained and perpetuated by our use of alleged "ordinary common sense" and heuristic reasoning in an unconscious response to events both in everyday life and in the legal process. Judges are not immune to sanism. "[E]mbedded in the cultural presuppositions that engulf us all" (D'Amato, 1991, p. 614), they express discomfort with social science or any other system that may appear to challenge law's hegemony over society and skepticism about new thinking; this discomfort and skepticism allows them to take deeper refuge in heuristic thinking and flawed, nonreflective ordinary common sense, both of which perpetuate the myths and stereotypes of sanism. As a result, the discomfort that judges often feel in having to decide mental disability law cases is often palpable (Perlin, 1990b).

Sanism and the Court Process in Mental Disability Law Cases

Judges reflect and project the conventional morality of the community, and judicial decisions in all areas of civil and criminal mental disability law continue to reflect and perpetuate sanist stereotypes (Perlin, 1992a; Perlin & Dorfman, 1993). Their language demonstrates bias against individuals with mental disabilities and often shows contempt for the mental health professions (Perlin, 1992a). Courts frequently appear impatient with litigants having mental disabilities, ascribing their problems in the legal process to weak character or poor resolve. Thus, a popular sanist myth is that "[m]entally disabled individuals simply don't try hard enough. They give in too easily to their basest instincts, and do not exercise appropriate self-restraint" (Perlin, 1992a, p. 396; see also Balkin, 1990, p. 238).

Sanist thinking allows judges to avoid difficult choices in mental disability law cases; their reliance on nonreflective, self-referential, alleged "ordinary common sense" helps explain the case law that has developed in all areas of mental disability law jurisprudence. Until and unless the existence and extent of this sort of judicial behavior is confronted, it is doubtful that the lofty promises of any law—even the ADA—will ever become a reality.

Conclusion

This chapter examining the impact of law on the voluntary delivery of mental health services in the community describes mixed results. Once seen as "the next frontier" (Perlin, 1980), the right of persons with mental disabilities to services in community settings has atrophied over recent years, the victim of a series of Supreme Court decisions that effectively foreclosed patients' lawyers from pressing such claims in federal courts. These decisions are antitherapeutic and ironically (perhaps tragically) stemmed from litigation strategies on the part of state mental health departments.

There is nonetheless cause for optimism. The ADA offers the promise of a "national mandate to end discrimination against individuals with disabilities" (House Committee on Energy and Commerce, 1990, p. 25). Whether this promise will be fulfilled is far from clear. However, it stands as the most significant congressional commitment to persons with mental disabilities, both in institutional and in community settings. In therapeutic jurisprudence terms, it has potentially profound therapeutic potential: it may truly be an "Emancipation Proclamation for persons with disabilities" (Ackourey, 1991, p. 1183 n. 2; Dorfman, 1993). However, if it is truly to restructure the way that society deals with individuals with mental disabilities, it must also provide a way of challenging sanist attitudes (Perlin, 1993a). If it can do this, it will fulfill its therapeutic promise, and the damage done by *Youngberg* and the *Pennhurst* cases to the idea of community services rights may yet be undone.

References

42 U.S.C. § 423 (1995).

53 Fed. Reg. 20233 (June 2, 1988).

Accord reached on community services plan for D.C. patients. (1989). *Hospital and Community Psychiatry, 40,* 973.

Ackourey, K. (1991). Insuring Americans with disabilities: How far can Congress go to protect traditional practices? *Emory Law Journal, 40,* 1183–1225.

Alessi v. Pa. Dep't of Pub. Welfare, 893 F.2d 1444 (3d Cir. 1990), *rev'g,* 710 F. Supp. 127 (E.D. Pa. 1989).

Allport, G. (1955). *The nature of prejudice.* Cambridge, MA: Addison-Wesley.

Americans with Disabilities Act, 42 U.S.C. §§ 12101 *et seq.* (1993).

Appleby, L., & Desai, P. N. (1985). Documenting the relationship between homelessness and psychiatric hospitalization. *Hospital and Community Psychiatry, 36,* 732–737.

Arce, A. A., & Vergare, M. J. (1984). Identifying and characterizing the mentally ill among the homeless. In H. R. Lamb (Ed.), *The homeless mentally ill* (pp. 75–89). Washington, DC: American Psychiatric Association Press.

Arnold v. Department of Health Services, 160 Ariz. 593, 775 P.2d 521 (1989).

Bachrach, L. (1984). The homeless mentally ill and mental health services: An analytical review of the literature. In H. R. Lamb (Ed.), *The homeless mentally ill* (pp. 55–74). Washington, DC: American Psychiatric Association Press.

Bala v. Auer, No. 6075 (Pa. Ct. C.P. 1978).

Baldessarini, R. (1977). Schizophrenia. *New England Journal of Medicine, 297,* 988–993.

Balkin, J. M. (1990). The rhetoric of responsibility. *Virginia Law Review, 76,* 197–263.

Bassuk, E. L., Rubin, L., & Lauriat, A. (1984). Is homelessness a mental health problem? *American Journal of Psychiatry, 141,* 1546–1550.

Bassuk, E. L., & Gerson, S. (1978). Deinstitutionalization and mental health services. *Scientific American, 238,* 46–53.

Bassuk, E. L., & Lauriat, A. (1984). The politics of homelessness. In H. R. Lamb (Ed.), *The homeless mentally ill* (pp. 301–313). Washington, DC: American Psychiatric Association Press.

Baxter v. City of Belleville, 720 F. Supp. 720 (S.D. Ill. 1989).

Baxter, E., & Hopper, K. (1984). Shelter and housing for the mentally ill. In H. R. Lamb (Ed.), *The homeless mentally ill* (pp. 109–139). Washington, DC: American Psychiatric Association Press.

Birnbaum, M. (1974). The right to treatment: Some comments on its development. In F. J. Ayd (Ed.), *Medical, Moral, and Legal Issues in Mental Health Care* (pp. 97–107). Baltimore, MD: Williams & Williams.

Bowen v. City of New York, 476 U.S. 467 (1986), *aff'g,* City of New York v. Heckler, 578 F. Supp. 1109 (E.D.N.Y.), *aff'd,* 742 F.2d 729 (2d Cir. 1984).

Brewster v. Dukakis, No. 76-4423-F (D. Mass., Mar. 12, 1987).

Brill, H., & Patton, R. (1957). Analysis of 1955–1956 population fall in New York State mental hospitals in first year of large scale use of tranquilizing drugs. *American Journal of Psychiatry, 114,* 509–517.

Brown, G. D. (1985). Beyond Pennhurst—protective jurisdiction, the eleventh amendment, and the power of Congress to enlarge federal jurisdiction in response to the Burger Court. *Virginia Law Review, 71,* 343–402.

Building a house of legal rights: A plea for the homeless [Note]. (1985). *St. John's Law Review, 59,* 530–557.

Callahan v. Carey, No. 79-42582 (N.Y. Super. Ct., N.Y. Cty. 1981), *reported in* N.Y.L.J. (Dec. 11, 1979).

Carmody, D. (1984, Nov. 2). Study blames poverty for most homelessness. *New York Times,* p. B2.

City of Cleburne v. Cleburne Living Center, 473 U.S. 432 (1985).

City of Torrance v. Transitional Living Centers, Inc., 30 Cal. 3d 5165, 638 P.2d 1304, 179 Cal. Rptr. 907 (1982).

Clark v. Cohen, 794 F.2d 79 (3d Cir. 1986), *cert. denied,* 479 U.S. 962 (1986).

Cleburne Living Center v. City of Cleburne, 726 F.2d 191 (5th Cir. 1984), *mod.,* 473 U.S. 432 (1985).

Clift v. Fincannon, 657 F. Supp. 1535 (E.D. Tex. 1987).

Cook, T. (1991). The Americans with Disabilities Act: The move to integration. *Temple Law Review, 64,* 393–469.

D'Amato, A. (1991). Harmful speech and the culture of indeterminacy. *William and Mary Law Review, 32,* 329–351.

Dennison, M. (1988). Ex-mental patients have rights too. *New York Law School Journal of Human Rights, 6,* 135–155.

Department of Mental Health v. Doe, 533 A.2d 536 (R.I. 1987).

De Shaney v. Winnebago County Department of Social Services, 489 U.S. 189 (1989).

Deutsch, A. (1949). *The mentally ill in America: A history of their care and treatment from colonial times.* New York: Doubleday, Doran & Co.

Developmentally Disabled Assistance and Bill of Rights Act, 42 U.S.C. §§ 6001 *et seq.* (1976).

Dinerstein, R. (1984). The absence of justice. *Nebraska Law Review, 63,* 680–708.

Dixon v. Harris, Civ. No. 74-285 (D.D.C. 1980), reported in *Clearinghouse Review, 14,* 784 (1980).

Dixon v. Weinberger, 405 F. Supp. 974 (D.D.C. 1975).

Doe v. Beal, Civ. No. 76-1396 (E.D. Pa. 1977).

Dorfman, D. A. (1993). Effectively implementing Title I of the Americans with Disabilities Act for mentally disabled persons: A therapeutic jurisprudence analysis. *Journal of Law and Health, 8,* 105–121.

Durham, M., & La Fond, J. Q. (1985). The empirical consequences and policy implications of broadening the statutory criteria for civil commitment. *Yale Law and Policy Review, 3,* 395–446.

Durham, M., & La Fond, J. Q. (1988). A search for the missing premise of involuntary therapeutic commitment: Effective treatment of the mentally ill. *Rutgers Law Review, 40,* 303–368.

Edge v. Pierce, 540 F. Supp. 1300 (D.N.J. 1982).

Eldredge v. Koch, 118 Misc. 2d 163, 459 N.Y.S. 2d 960 (Sup. Ct.), *rev'd in part on other grounds,* 98 A.D. 2d 675, 469 N.Y.S. 2d 744 (1983).

Ellis, J. W., & Luckasson, R. A. (1985). Mentally retarded criminal defendants. *George Washington Law Review, 53,* 414–493.

Ensminger, J. J., & Liguori, T. (1978). The therapeutic significance of the civil commitment hearing: An unexplored potential. *Journal of Psychiatry and Law, 6,* 5–44.

Establishing a right to shelter for the homeless [Note]. (1984). *Brooklyn Law Review, 50,* 939–994.

Ewing, M. (1979). Health planning and deinstitutionalization: Advocacy within the administrative process. *Stanford Law Review, 31,* 679–715.

Fair Housing Act, 42 U.S.C. §§ 3601–3617 (1968).

Fair Housing Amendments Act of 1988, 42 U.S.C. §§ 3601 *et seq.* (1988).

Familystyle of St. Paul, Inc. v. City of St. Paul, 728 F. Supp. 1396 (D. Minn. 1990).

Familystyle of St. Paul, Inc. v. St. Paul, Minn., 923 F.2d 91 (8th Cir.), *reh'g denied* (1991).

Ferleger, D. (1983). Anti-institutionalization and the Supreme Court. *Rutgers Law Journal, 14,* 595–636.

Ferleger, D., & Boyd, P. (1978). Anti-institutionalization: The promise of the *Pennhurst* case. *Stanford Law Review, 31,* 717–765.

Fischer, P. J., & Breakey, W. R. (1986). Homelessness and mental health: An overview. *International Journal of Mental Health, 6,* 14–21.

Foucha v. Louisiana, 112 S. Ct. 1780 (1992).

Gieseking v. Schafer, 672 F. Supp. 1249 (W.D. Mo. 1987).

Haimowitz, S. (1991). Americans with Disabilities Act of 1990: Its significance for persons with mental illness. *Hospital and Community Psychiatry, 42,* 23–24.

Halderman v. Pennhurst State School & Hospital, 446 F. Supp. 1295 (E.D. Pa. 1978), *modified,* 612 F.2d 84 (3d Cir. 1979), *rev'd,* 451 U.S. 1 (1981), *reinstated,* 673 F.2d 647 (3d Cir. 1982), *rev'd,* 465 U.S. 89 (1984).

Halderman v. Pennhurst State School & Hospital, 610 F. Supp. 1221 (E.D. Pa. 1985).

Hanson v. Clarke City, 867 F.2d 1115 (8th Cir. 1989).

Hatfield A. B., et al. (1984). The family's perspective on the homeless. In H. R. Lamb (Ed.), *The homeless mentally ill* (pp. 279–300). Washington, DC: American Psychiatric Association Press.

Heard v. Cuomo, 142 A.D. 2d 537, 531 N.Y.S. 2d 253 (1988), *appeal after remand,* 160 A.D. 2d 590, 554 N.Y.S. 2d 234 (1990).

Heard v. Cuomo, 150 Misc. 2d 257, 567 N.Y.S. 2d 594 (Sup. Ct. 1991).

Heller v. Doe, 113 S. Ct. 2637 (1993).

Hendon, S. M. (1990). The possibility of tax incentives for lending to charitable organizations. *Yale Law and Policy Review, 8,* 414–435.

Hiday, V. A., & Markell, S. J. (1980). Components of dangerousness: Legal standards in civil commitment. *International Journal of Law and Psychiatry, 3,* 405–419.

Homelessness: Halting the race to the bottom [Note]. (1985). *Yale Law and Policy Review, 3,* 551–570.

House Committee on Energy and Commerce. (1990). H.R. Rep. No. 485 (1990, 101st Cong., 2d Sess., pt. 4). Washington, DC: U.S. Government Printing Office.

Incorporated Village of Freeport v. Ass'n for the Help of Retarded Children, 94 Misc. 2d 1048, 406 N.Y.S. 2d 221 (Sup. Ct.), *aff'd,* 60 A.D. 2d 644, 400 N.Y.S. 2d 727 (1977).

Kiesler, C. (1982). Mental Hospitals and alternative care: Noninstitutionalization as potential public policy for mental patients. *American Psychologist, 37,* 349–360.

Kittrie, N. (1971). *The right to be different: Deviance and enforced therapy.* Baltimore, MD: Johns Hopkins University Press.

Klostermann v. Cuomo, 61 N.Y. 2d 525, 463 N.E. 2d 588, 475 N.Y.S. 2d 247 (1984a).

Klostermann v. Cuomo, 126 Misc. 2d 247, 481 N.Y.S. 2d 580 (Sup. Ct. 1984b).

Knutzen v. Nelson, 617 F. Supp. 977 (D. Colo. 1985).

Kotkin, M. (1989–1990). The Fair Housing Amendments Act of 1988: New strategies for new procedures. *N.Y.U. Review of Law and Social Change, 17,* 755–786.

La Fond, J. Q., & Durham, M. (1992). *Back to the asylum: The future of mental health law and policy in the United States.* New York: Oxford University Press.

Lamb, H. R. (1984). Deinstitutionalization and the homeless mentally ill. In H. R. Lamb (Ed.), *The homeless mentally ill* (pp. 55–74). Washington, DC: American Psychiatric Association Press.

Landmark agreement to create community mental

health system. (1989). *Mental and Physical Disability Law Reporter, 13*, 229.

Langdon, J. K., & Kass, M. A. (1985). Homelessness in America: Looking for the right to shelter. *Columbia Journal of Law and Social Problems, 19*, 305–392.

Lessard v. Schmidt, 349 F. Supp. 1078 (E.D. Wis. 1972).

Little Neck Community Ass'n v. Working Org. for Retarded Children, 52 A.D. 2d 90, 383 N.Y.S. 2d 364 (1976), *leave to appeal denied*, 40 N.Y. 2d 803, 356 N.E.2d 482, 387 N.Y.S. 2d 1030 (1977).

Marmor, T. R., & Gill, K. C. (1989). The political and economic context of mental health care in the United States. *Journal of Health Politics, Policy and Law, 14*, 459–475.

Martone v. Lensink, 207 Conn. 296, 541 A.2d 488 (1988).

Maticka v. City of Atlantic City, No. L8306-84E (N.J. Super. Ct., Law Div. 1986), *supplemented*, 216 N.J. Super. 434, 524 A. 2d 416 (App. Div. 1987).

Matter of McKnight, 406 Mass. 787, 550 N.E.2d 856 (1990).

Menolascino, F. (1977). *Challenges in mental retardation: Progressive ideology and services.*

Mills, M. J., & Cummins, B. D. (1982). Deinstitutionalization reconsidered. *International Journal of Law and Psychiatry, 5*, 271–284.

Minow, M. (1987). When difference has its home: Group homes for the mentally retarded, equal protection, and legal treatment of difference. *Harvard Civil Rights–Civil Liberties Law Review, 22*, 111–189.

Mosher, L. R., & Keith, S. J. (1980). Psychosocial treatment: Individual, group, family, and community support approaches. *Schizophrenia Bulletin, 6*, 10–41.

New York v. 11 Cornwall Co., 508 F. Supp. 273 (E.D.N.Y. 1981), *aff'd*, 695 F.2d 34 (2d Cir. 1982), *modified on other grounds*, 718 F.2d 22 (2d Cir. 1983).

New York State Ass'n for Retarded Children, Inc.

v. Carey, 492 F. Supp. 1099 (E.D.N.Y. 1980) (NYSARC).

N.J. Stat. Ann. §§ 30:4-80.8 to 30:4-80.11 (1981).

O'Connor v. Donaldson, 422 U.S. 563 (1975).

Palmore v. Sidoti, 466 U.S. 429 (1984).

Pa. Stat. Ann., tit. 50, §§ 4104–4704 (1969).

Parham v. J. R., 442 U.S. 584 (1979).

P. C. v. McLaughlin, 913 F.2d 1033 (2d Cir. 1990).

Pennhurst State School v. Halderman, 454 U.S. 808 (1981).

Perlin, M. L. (1980). Rights of ex-patients in the community: The next frontier? *Bulletin of the American Academy of Psychiatry and Law, 8*, 33–43.

Perlin, M. L. (1985). "Discharged pending placement": The due process rights of the nondangerous institutionalized mentally handicapped with "nowhere to go." *Directions in Psychiatry, 5*, Lesson 21.

Perlin, M. L. (1987). State constitutions and statutes as sources of rights for the mentally disabled: The last frontier? *Loyola of Los Angeles Law Review, 20*, 1249–1327.

Perlin, M. L. (1989) (1993 pocket part). *Mental disability law: Civil and criminal.* Charlottesville, VA: Michie.

Perlin, M. L. (1990a). Are courts competent to decide questions of competency? Stripping the facade from *United States v. Charters. University of Kansas Law Review, 38*, 957–1001.

Perlin, M. L. (1990b). Psychodynamics and the insanity defense: "Ordinary common sense" and heuristic reasoning. *Nebraska Law Review, 69*, 3–70.

Perlin, M. L. (1991a). Competency, deinstitutionalization, and homelessness: A story of marginalization. *Houston Law Review, 28*, 63–142.

Perlin, M. L. (1991b). Morality and pretextuality, psychiatry, and law: Of "ordinary common sense," heuristic reasoning, and cognitive dissonance. *Bulletin of the American Academy of Psychiatry and Law, 19*, 131–150.

Perlin, M. L. (1991c). Reading the Supreme Court's tea leaves: Predicting judicial behavior in civil and criminal right to refuse treatment cases. *American Journal of Forensic Psychiatry, 12,* 37–67.

Perlin, M. L. (1992a). On "sanism." *Southern Methodist University Law Review, 46,* 373–407.

Perlin, M. L. (1992b). *Tarasoff* and the dilemma of the dangerous patient: New directions for the 1990's. *Law and Psychology Review, 16,* 29–63.

Perlin, M. L. (1993a). The ADA and mentally disabled persons: Can sanist attitudes be undone? *Journal of Law and Health, 8,* 15–45.

Perlin, M. L. (1993b). Decoding the right to refuse treatment law. *International Journal of Law and Psychiatry, 16,* 151–177.

Perlin, M. L. (1993c). Pretexts and mental disability law: The case of competency. *University of Miami Law Review, 47,* 625–688.

Perlin, M. L. (1993d). What is therapeutic jurisprudence? *New York Law School Journal of Human Rights, 11,* 623–636.

Perlin, M. L. (1994a). *The law and mentally disabled persons.* Charlottesville, VA: Michie.

Perlin, M. L., & Dorfman, D. A. (1993). Sanism, social science, and the development of mental disability law jurisprudence. *Behavioral Sciences and the Law, 11,* 47–66.

Petrila, J. P. (1992). Redefining mental health law: Thoughts on a new agenda. *Law and Human Behavior, 16,* 89–106.

Philadelphia Police & Fire Ass'n v. City of Philadelphia, 699 F. Supp. 1106 (E.D. Pa. 1988), *reversed,* 874 F.2d 156 (3d Cir. 1989).

Philadelphia Police and Fire Association for Handicapped Children, Inc. v. City of Philadelphia: Citizens with mental retardation and the courts—new barriers for equal protection and due process? [Note]. (1990). *Arkansas Law Review, 43,* 423–452.

Phillips v. Thompson, 715 F.2d 365 (7th Cir. 1983).

Quaker Hill Place v. Saville, 523 A.2d 947 (Del. Super. Ct.), *aff'd,* 531 A.2d 201 (Del. 1987).

Rachlin, S. (1975). One right too many. *Bulletin of the American Academy of Psychiatry and Law, 3,* 99–102.

Rebell, M. (1986). Structural discrimination and the rights of the disabled. *Georgetown Law Journal, 74,* 1435–1501.

The reinstitutionalization of the mentally retarded [Comment]. (1986). *Wayne Law Review, 32,* 1105–1136.

Rhode Island Dep't of Mental Health v. R. B., 549 A.2d 1028 (R.I. 1988).

Rhoden, N. (1982). The limits of liberty: Deinstitutionalization, homelessness, and libertarian theory. *Emory Law Journal, 31,* 375–440.

Ricci v. Callahan, 646 F. Supp. 378 (D. Mass. 1986).

Riggins v. Nevada, 112 S. Ct. 1810 (1992).

Rivers v. Katz, 67 N.Y. 2d 485, 495 N.E. 2d 337, 504 N.Y.S. 2d 74 (1986).

Romeo v. Youngberg, 644 F.2d 147 (3d Cir. 1980), *vacated,* 457 U.S. 307 (1982).

Rubenstein, L. S. (1986). Access to treatment and rehabilitation for severely mentally ill poor people. *Clearinghouse Review, 20,* 382–391.

Rubin, J. (1991). Paying for care: Legal developments in the financing of mental health services. *Houston Law Review, 28,* 143–173.

Rudenstine, D. (1984). *Pennhurst* and the scope of federal judicial powers to reform institutions. *Cardozo Law Review, 6,* 71–110.

In re S. L., 94 N.J. 128, 462 A.2d 1252 (1983).

Santiago, J. M. (1990). The evolution of systems of mental health care: The Arizona experience. *American Journal of Psychiatry, 147,* 148–155.

Saphire, R. (1976). The civilly-committed public mental patient and the right to aftercare. *Florida State University Law Review, 4,* 232–289.

Sardell, A. (1990). Child health policy in the U.S.: The paradox of consensus. *Journal of Health Politics, Policy, and Law, 15,* 271–304.

Scheerenberger, R. (1976). *Deinstitutionalization*

and community adjustment of mentally re-tarded people.

In re Schmidt, 496 Pa. 86, 429 A.2d 631 (1981).

Schwartz, M. (1984). The eleventh amendment and state law claims. *Clearinghouse Review, 18,* 151–154.

Scull, A. T. (1984). *Decarceration: Community treatment and the deviant: A radical view.* New Brunswick, NJ: Rutgers University Press.

Seicshnaydre, S. E. (1992). Community mental health treatment for the mentally ill—when does less restrictive treatment become a right? *Tulane Law Review, 66,* 1971–2001.

Shaw by Strain v. Strackhouse, 920 F. 2d 1135 (3d Cir. 1990).

Sherry, S. (1986). Issue manipulation by the Burger Court: Saving the community from itself. *Minnesota Law Review, 70,* 611–663.

Sherwin, R. (1988). Dialects and dominance: A study of rhetorical fields in confessions. *University of Pennsylvania Law Review, 136,* 729–849.

Shuman, D. W. (1985). Innovative statutory approaches to civil commitment: An overview and critique. *Law, Medicine, and Health Care, 13,* 284–289.

Simring, R. (1991). The impact of federal anti-discrimination laws on housing for people with mental disabilities. *George Washington Law Review, 59,* 413–450.

Smith, C. E. (1990). The Supreme Court's emerging majority: Restraining the high court or transforming its role? *Akron Law Review, 24,* 393–421.

Society for Good Will to Retarded Children v. Cuomo, 737 F. 2d 1239 (2d Cir. 1984) (SGW).

Solomon, H. (1958). The American Psychiatric Association in relation to American psychiatry. *American Journal of Psychiatry, 115,* 1–10.

Spicer v. Hilton, 618 F.2d 232 (3d Cir. 1980).

Stefan, S. (1992). Leaving civil rights to the "experts": From deference to abdication under the professional judgment standard. *Yale Law Journal, 102,* 639–717.

Stieberger v. Heckler, 615 F. Supp. 1315 (S.D.N.Y. 1985).

Stille, A. (1986, February 10). Seeking shelter in the law. *National Law Journal,* 1.

Stone, G. R. (1984). O. T. 1983 and the era of aggressive majoritarianism: A court in transition. *Georgia Law Review, 19,* 15–30.

Talbott, J. A. (1978). *The death of the asylum: A critical study of state hospital management, services, and care.* New York: Grune & Stratton.

Talbott, J. A., & Lamb, H. R. (1984). Summary and recommendations. In H. R. Lamb (Ed.), *The homeless mentally ill* (pp. 1–10). Washington, DC: American Psychiatric Association Press.

Thomas S. v. Morrow, 601 F. Supp. 1055 (W.D.N.C. 1984), *aff'd & modified,* 781 F.2d 367 (4th Cir. 1986), *cert. den. sub. nom.,* Kirk v. Thomas S., 476 U.S. 1124 (1986).

Torrey, E. F. (1988). *Nowhere to go: The tragic odyssey of the homeless mentally ill.* New York: Harper & Row.

Treffert, D. (1973). Dying with their rights on. *American Journal of Psychiatry, 140,* 1041.

Tuoni, G. (1981). Deinstitutionalization and community resistance by zoning restrictions. *Massachusetts Law Review, 66,* 125–139.

United States v. Carolene Products Co., 304 U.S. 144 (1938).

United States v. Schuylkill Twp., 1990 WL 180980 (E.D. Pa. 1990).

Wald, P., & Friedman, P. (1978). The politics of mental health advocacy in the United States. *International Journal of Law and Psychiatry, 1,* 137–152.

Wash. Rev. Co. Ann. § 71.05.020(1) (1984).

Weithorn, L. A. (1988). Mental hospitalization of troublesome youth: An analysis of skyrocketing admission rates. *Stanford Law Review, 40,* 773–838.

Wexler, D. (1982). Inappropriate patient confinement and appropriate state advocacy. *Law and Contemporary Problems, 45,* 193–209.

Wexler, D. (1990). *Therapeutic jurisprudence: The*

law as a therapeutic agent. Durham, NC: Carolina Academic Press.

Wexler, D. (1992). Putting mental health in mental health law: Therapeutic jurisprudence. *Law and Human Behavior, 16,* 27–38.

Wexler, D. (1993). Therapeutic jurisprudence and changing concepts of legal scholarship. *Behavioral Sciences and the Law, 11,* 17–29.

Wexler, D., & Winick, B. (1991). *Essays in therapeutic jurisprudence.* Durham, NC: Carolina Academic Press.

Williamsburg Fair Hous. Comm. v. NYC Housing Auth., 450 F. Supp. 602 (S.D.N.Y. 1978).

Wuori v. Zitnay, Civ. No. 75-80-P (D. Me., July 14, 1978).

Wyatt v. King, 803 F. Supp. 377 (M.D. Ala. 1992).

Wyatt v. King, 811 F. Supp. 1533 (M.D. Ala. 1993a).

Wyatt v. King, 1993 WL 7101 (M.D. Ala. 1993b).

Wyatt v. Stickney, 325 F. Supp. 781 (M.D. Ala. 1971), 344 F. Supp. 373 (M.D. Ala. 1972), 344 F. Supp. 387 (M.D. Ala. 1972), *aff'd sub. nom.,* Wyatt v. Aderholt, 503 F.2d 1305 (5th Cir. 1974).

Youngberg v. Romeo, 457 U.S. 307 (1982).

Zinermon v. Burch, 494 U.S. 113 (1990).

Zoning Bd. of Hammond v. Tangipahoa Ass'n for Retarded Citizens, 510 So.2d 751 (La. App.), reh'g denied (1987).

9 ▌Protections for Persons with Mental Disabilities: Americans with Disabilities Act and Related Federal and State Law

Laura F. Rothstein
University of Houston

It is only since the mid-1970s that federal policy has recognized the right to nondiscrimination on the basis of disability (including mental disability) in elementary and secondary education, higher education, places of public accommodation, public services, housing, and the workplace. The major relevant laws include the Rehabilitation Act of 1973 (prohibiting discrimination on the basis of disability by federal agencies, federal contractors, and recipients of federal financial assistance) and the Education for All Handicapped Children Act of 1975 (amended in 1990 and title changed to the Individuals with Disabilities Education Act (IDEA), requiring a free appropriate public education in the least restrictive environment and procedural safeguards and individualization). Other important laws include the 1988 amendments to the Fair Housing Act (prohibiting housing discrimination on the basis of handicap) and the Americans with Disabilities Act (ADA) of 1990 (prohibiting discrimination on

the basis of disability by most employers, by state and local government agencies, and by private providers considered to be public accommodations).

All four laws incorporate common principles of nondiscrimination, reasonable accommodation, and mainstreaming. The IDEA goes even further and is considered to be a hybrid statute because it provides for benefits in the form of educational services as well as for the right to be treated nondiscriminatorily.

The IDEA is based on principles of due process and equal protection, and it incorporates more than a simple requirement that public schools not discriminate in providing education to children with disabilities (including mental disabilities). The IDEA includes a mandate to provide appropriate special education programming and related services to all children of public school age who have disabilities—at no cost to the parents—and to do so in the least restrictive environment. It incorporates procedural safeguards designed to ensure that the mandates of the statute are carried out.

All four laws protect individuals with mental disabilities. However, it is not enough to have a mental disability to claim protection under the three federal nondiscrimination laws. The Rehabilitation Act, the Fair Housing Act Amend-

I thank Lisa Wilson and Kristi Schrode, students at the University of Houston Law Center, for their research assistance.

ments, and the ADA all require that the individual be qualified to carry out the essential requirements of the program (for example, job, higher education program, housing) in spite of the disability. What that means in various contexts has been the subject of an increasing amount of litigation and judicial interpretation. For instance, if someone is dangerous to others in the workplace, that individual is likely to be unqualified, even though the person has the technical ability to carry out the job functions. Under the IDEA, the presumption is that *all* age-eligible children are entitled to special education and related services if they meet the statutory definition of a student with a disability.

The following sections explore each of these laws as they apply to people with mental disabilities in education, higher education, employment, public services, public accommodations, and housing. This chapter will explore whether these laws accomplish the underlying policy goal of the full participation of individuals with disabilities in all aspects of life in a mainstream setting to the extent that can reasonably be achieved. It further considers whether there is a need for statutory amendment and whether new policies or practices are needed to achieve this result.

Unfortunately, little data analyzing the impact of current federal law on individuals with mental illness are available. Most of the studies focus on the laws' impact on people with all disabilities and do not present information by type of disability. For example, a study of the impact of the Rehabilitation Act on integration of individuals with disabilities in public services indicates that although there have been a few successes in the area of removing architectural barriers and providing more interpreter service, segregation continues due to factors such as "continued fear, ignorance, hostility, and . . . inertia" (Cook, 1991, p. 397). Indeed, the legislative history of the ADA mentioned that persons with disabilities were still largely excluded from the economic mainstream of America even after the Rehabilitation Act (U.S. Congress, Senate

Committee on Labor and Human Resources, 1989, p. 195).

Education

Statutory Coverage

Education of elementary and secondary school age children with disabilities is provided primarily through the Individuals with Disabilities Education Act. The Rehabilitation Act and the Americans with Disabilities Act also apply, particularly with respect to students with mental and emotional disabilities.

The Individuals with Disabilities Education Act (IDEA), enacted in 1975, was originally called the Education for All Handicapped Children Act. It provides for a free appropriate public education to all children with disabilities who require special education and related services. This education must be individualized for each child and must be provided in the least restrictive appropriate environment. Its most important improvement over previous legislation is that it incorporates procedural safeguards allowing individuals protected by these statutes to pursue remedies through administrative and judicial proceedings. These procedural safeguards include notice and a right to hearing at virtually all stages of the educational process (Rothstein, 1995).

Children covered by the IDEA are those who are "mentally retarded, hard of hearing, deaf, speech impaired, visually handicapped, *seriously emotionally disturbed*, orthopedically impaired, or other health impaired children, or children with specific learning disabilities, who by reason thereof require special education and related services" (emphasis added). In 1990, autism and traumatic brain injury were added to the list of conditions. Children fitting this definition are entitled to the benefit of special education, which goes far beyond what is mandated by a nondiscrimination statute. It is significant to note that during the 1990 hearings surrounding the amendment of the IDEA, Congress found children with serious emotional disturbance to be the most underserved group of students with disabilities (*Individuals with Disabilities Education Act of 1990*, 1990, p. 39).

One condition on which much discussion has focused is attention deficit disorder. As part of the 1990 IDEA amendments, the Department of Education was required to evaluate this condition and to determine whether children with the condition receive adequate services under other disability categories. After making this evaluation, the Department has determined that they are already covered either in the category of learning disabilities or, where the condition is a result of a chemical imbalance or other biological condition, as other health impaired or as seriously emotionally disturbed (Davila, Williams, & McDonald, 1991).

Although the two major nondiscrimination statutes do not go as far as the IDEA, both require reasonable accommodation. Section 504 of the Rehabilitation Act and the Americans with Disabilities Act apply to schools. The Rehabilitation Act applies only to schools receiving federal financial assistance, thus excluding some private schools; the ADA, however, applies to both public and private schools. The statutory requirements relevant to public and private schools are substantially the same, and both statutes prohibit discrimination on the basis of disability. The definition of disability covers individuals with a physical or mental impairment that creates a *substantial* limitation of one or more major life activities (which include learning), individuals with a record of such an impairment, and those who are regarded as having such an impairment.

As mentioned previously, although section 504 and the ADA are not as comprehensive either in terms of the procedural safeguards available to the student or the substantive education to be provided by the school, both statutes contemplate reasonable accommodations and programming in the least restrictive appropriate environment.

Case Law Interpretations

The courts have directed attention to several issues concerning students with emotional and psychological disabilities. Issues include the definition of what individuals are protected under these statutes, the services that must be provided to these individuals under these statutes, and the disciplinary removal of dangerous and disruptive students. Most of these cases have been brought under the IDEA and therefore provide little guidance as to the impact of section 504 or the ADA. The major reason that the IDEA is the only statutory lens through which the courts examine these issues is a U.S. Supreme Court decision holding that when the IDEA resolves an issue of special education, the IDEA is the only statute that may be applied (*Smith v. Robinson*, 1984). Only when the IDEA does not provide a resolution may parents pursue remedies under section 504 (and by implication the ADA). Nevertheless, situations could still exist in which the two nondiscrimination statutes apply to students with emotional disabilities. These statutes would apply when the student has a substantial impairment of a major life activity and does not require special education or related services as a result of that disability, but does require reasonable accommodation. The courts have not addressed the application of these statutes to such situations in the educational context to any great extent, however, because few cases have been brought since the *Smith* decision claiming violations of IDEA and section 504 or the ADA.

Individuals Covered

Courts have decided several education cases involving mental impairments. One court held that a student with a conduct disorder who disrupted classes and attempted suicide was not "seriously emotionally disturbed" and thus not entitled to coverage under the IDEA (*A. E. v. Independent School District*, 1991). Another court found that having a weak attention span is not a disability covered under the IDEA (*Hiller v. Board of Education*, 1990). Nor was there IDEA protection for a child who was socially maladjusted but not seriously emotionally disturbed (*Evans v. District No. 17*, 1988). In none of these cases did the court address the possible application of section 504 or the ADA. Had they done so, there might have been guidance on whether the school should have made accommodations to the conditions. In sum, the courts have reached disparate conclusions on various conditions and whether they are covered under the IDEA. It is an issue that would benefit from policy development or at least guidance from the Department of Education.

Services Provided

An enormous amount of judicial attention has been given to cases involving the types of psychological counseling and residential treatment that should be provided under the IDEA (Rothstein, 1992). The courts have not reached any consensus on the proper standard for determining when these services must be provided. Again, the courts seem to concentrate on whether such programming fits the IDEA definition of special education and related services, but they do not focus on whether the student might be entitled to at least some of this programming as a reasonable accommodation under section 504 or the ADA.

Disciplinary Removal

The courts also have decided a significant number of cases involving disciplinary removal, including one Supreme Court case that set some universal standards but left many issues unresolved (*Honig v. Doe*, 1988). A child who is covered by the IDEA may not be excluded from special education. IDEA permits temporary removal for a short period (no more than 10 days in any school year) in emergency situations, but in no case may a child protected by IDEA be totally excluded from educational programming. This provision might require homebound instruction, but the school cannot cease to provide educational services. What this leaves unresolved is whether services may be terminated for students who are not covered by the IDEA but

who may be protected by section 504 or the ADA. Many children do not exhibit emotional problems until adolescence and thus may not be identified as being eligible for special education under the IDEA. As the cases involving psychological counseling demonstrate, it is not always obvious—even for students fitting the IDEA definition—whether certain types of programming and services are required under the IDEA, because this programming does not clearly meet the definition of special education and related services within the statute. In addition, the courts have not applied section 504 and the ADA to cases involving students with emotional disabilities who do not require special education and related services. Therefore, it is difficult to predict whether these services might be available if the courts were to address requests for such services under the nondiscrimination statutes instead of the IDEA.

Policy Gaps

The area of education combines more programming and services with nondiscrimination mandates than is found in other areas such as employment, housing, and public accommodations. Yet even in the area of education there are some significant gaps in accomplishing the goal of full participation of children with mental illness in the educational program.

One excellent analysis of the barriers to participation by students with emotional disabilities is based on an interpretation of the IDEA as a statute and the judicial interpretations of the IDEA in the context of children with emotional disabilities. The analysis also draws on statistical studies of children with emotional disabilities and the placement of such children as well as on research by social scientists and educators. The analysis concludes that the major barrier is how "educators understand and respond to actions of these children" (Glennon, 1993, p. 295). This analysis finds that educators respond primarily to the disruptive or disturbing behavior by implementing either punitive measures or medical measures. Glennon's study indicates that children are both underidentified as seriously emotionally disturbed and inconsistently identified. This results from the varying causes of emotional disabilities as well as the different methods of identifying these children. In addition, students with serious emotional disabilities are more likely to drop out of school.

Glennon's evaluation of current literature and her own conclusions indicate that in spite of the legislative preference for mainstream education, students with serious emotional problems are generally educated in highly restrictive settings. This is particularly true for students in their teen years. Not only do the schools place these students in restrictive settings, but these students often end up in restrictive settings throughout the mental health, juvenile justice, or child welfare systems (Glennon, 1993, pp. 308–309). Those who are not identified as subject to the IDEA protections often suffer from severe disciplinary measures that would not be legally permitted if they had been identified.

The lack of a coordinated service delivery system among various agencies and the failure to prioritize mental health services have meant that children with emotional disabilities are often underserved (pp. 310–313). The response of educators to this population is a socially constructed determination that these children are either bad or sick, which justifies a failure to serve them appropriately (pp. 313–319). As a result of this construct, the educational response is to take either punitive or medical measures (pp. 319–350), rather than implementing a learning model. Individual efforts to challenge this way of thinking seem ineffective because of the systemic failure to respond appropriately to children with emotional disabilities that has resulted from the deeply held attitudes of the majority of educators toward these children (Glennon, 1993, pp. 350–354).

Fortunately, Glennon's study proposes concrete policy changes that would improve societal response to these children (pp. 354–363). These responses include broadening key statutory definitions as to who is covered to be more inclusive (by not requiring that the emotional disability be "severe" before there is coverage). The definition of who is covered should also be revised to clarify that a child should be covered when the emotional condition adversely affects educational performance in a broad sense, including social skills development—not simply when it affects academic performance. Children would thus be identified as entitled to services *before* their emotional state reaches a crisis level. Presently, students who are emotionally disturbed are not entitled to services unless this condition adversely affects *academic* performance. The definition of special education should be revised to include instruction in behavior, social, and emotional skills. Finally, Congress should reemphasize the "least restrictive" element of special education to avoid segregating these students as much as possible.

Additional policy changes that would support improvement in this area include mandating that the Department of Education provide more constructive guidance to states, local school districts, parents, and advocates about educating children with emotional disabilities (Glennon, 1993, pp. 357–359). Congressional and Department of Education attention to the issue of discipline is also necessary. Information dissemination is essential to the difficult task of changing attitudes. Glennon proposes a coordinated system of services encouraged by congressional incentives. She suggests that financial incentives for changes such as better teacher preparation could ultimately result in changed attitudes (pp. 359–360).

Advocates and parents are provided their own set of activities to achieve policy change. These include "lobbying, raising public awareness, and litigation" (pp. 360–363). It is through these combined efforts that attitudes will change and children with emotional disabilities will find supportive learning environments in the public schools rather than exclusion and medical treatment.

It is difficult to add much to Glennon's

excellent analysis of the current status and the needed policy changes. It should be noted, however, that the major barrier identified in this study is attitude. That same barrier is a major obstacle in virtually all other areas discussed in this chapter. Although steps have been taken to change conduct, without changes in attitude, current policy can only go so far to achieve the goal.

One major issue not touched on in depth in the Glennon analysis is the relationship of drugs and alcohol to emotional disability. Although a high correlation exists, Congress has specified limited protection for students whose status is related to drug and alcohol use and abuse. Until there is greater understanding of and attention to the issue of teen substance abuse, there will be a significant gap in our policy response to educating these students.

In sum, elementary and secondary education requires policy responses to negative attitudes, funding for additional educational services, and systemic change. Case-by-case challenges under current law are unlikely to produce the desired results.

Higher Education

Statutory Coverage

Students in higher education and applicants to colleges and universities are protected from discrimination on the basis of disability under both section 504 of the Rehabilitation Act and by Titles II and III of the Americans with Disabilities Act (ADA). Section 504 applies to virtually all colleges and universities because most receive federal financial assistance. Title II of the ADA applies to higher education programs operated by state or local government agencies. Title III of the ADA applies to institutions operated by private entities.

Another statute of importance to the college student with mental illness is the Family Educational Rights and Privacy Act (FERPA), commonly known as the Buckley Amendment. FERPA applies to student records and requires that institutions receiving federal financial assistance follow certain policies with respect to access to student records and the accuracy of those records. Because mental illness carries such a stigma, this is an important area of protection for the student. But, as noted in the section on judicial interpretation, FERPA does not necessarily provide as much protection as might be desired in all instances.

Case Law Interpretations

As the following discussion illustrates, the courts have addressed a number of higher education cases involving students with mental illness. The general themes that emerge from these decisions include taking an individualized approach to each factual setting and giving substantial deference to the educational institutions with respect to academic standards and other criteria for participation. Although the courts give deference to the institution, they also require that the institution provide justification for its standards.

For an applicant or student to be protected by the Rehabilitation Act or the ADA, he or she must meet the definition of an individual with a disability and must also be otherwise qualified. This means that the individual must have a substantial physical or mental impairment to one or more major life activities, have a record of such an impairment, or be regarded as having such an impairment. In addition, the individual must be able to meet the essential requirements of the educational program (either with or without reasonable accommodations) *in spite of* the impairment (*Southeastern Community College v. Davis*, 1979). Higher education institutions are not required to make fundamental alterations to the program, nor are they required to lower standards or provide accommodations that would be unduly burdensome either administratively or financially.

Most of the case law has been decided under section 504 alone, but the ADA is intended to be interpreted consistently with section 504. The results in most cases would probably be the same if either law were applied. Courts have evaluated a number of mental conditions in the context of higher education (Rothstein, 1992). They have been particularly deferential to colleges and universities in determining what the essential elements of the program are, including academic standards and other qualifications. This is particularly true for medical programs because of the judicial concern for patient safety.

Cases in which courts have not ruled in favor of students with mental conditions include a case where a student claimed test phobia and neurotic dependency on professors. The court found that the student was not otherwise qualified because she had failed oral exams; thus, her academic dismissal was upheld (*Schuler v. University of Minnesota*, 1986). A law student suffering from alcoholism was not protected because he had not met the academic standards. Interestingly, in that case, the law school had given him more opportunities for rehabilitation than it may have been legally required to provide (*Anderson v. University of Wisconsin*, 1988). Failure to meet the academic standards was also the basis for upholding the denial of admission to a doctoral program where the claimant sought the accommodation of conditional admission. This was requested to alleviate the stress of performing to meet admission standards. Her claim of posttraumatic stress disorder was not found to excuse the regular performance requirements (*Crancer v. Board of Regents*, 1986). A 1992 decision found that a college had not violated section 504 when a student with schizophrenia was found not to be academically qualified (*Wood v. President & Trustees of Spring Hill College*, 1992).

Perhaps the best-known case on this issue involved a student who was initially admitted to medical school. The school learned of her mental illness in a postadmission medical exam and she was ultimately denied participation in the program. The court found substantial evidence of previous violent, self-destructive conduct, which indicated an appreciable risk that these behaviors would recur (*Doe v. New York University*, 1981). This case involved a student who met the academic criteria but was found not to be qualified because of her behavior. Similarly, a 1981 decision permitted dismissal of a student suffering from chronic paranoia because the college catalog reserved the right to dismiss students in these cases (*Aronson v. North Park College*, 1981). It is questionable, however, whether this decision would be reached today in light of more recent case precedents.

There have been only a few cases in which the courts have found unlawful discrimination against individuals with mental impairments. In one decision, the court recognized that a medical program had improperly rejected a medical student with multiple sclerosis who was applying to a psychiatric residency program. On the basis of short interviews with the applicant, four faculty members concluded that the individual lacked the necessary emotional stability to be a psychiatrist, believing that he would have difficulty dealing with probable patient reactions to his condition. This deduction was made in spite of the applicant's psychological record to the contrary, and the court recognized that this was an unfounded determination (*Pushkin v. Regents of University of Colorado*, 1981). This case illustrates that the major barrier to participation by individuals with mental disabilities is often the negative attitudes of educators and educational administrators, which result from fear and unfounded misunderstandings about individuals with mental impairments.

Thus far, the courts have not addressed whether colleges and universities should be permitted to ask about treatment for mental illness or history of mental illness in the application process. It seems likely that unless such questions are narrowly tailored to ask about past conduct or disciplinary action or are based on a clear relationship of the condition to the qualifications for the program, they are likely to be found to violate section 504 and ADA prohibitions against preadmissions inquiries about disabilities. In spite of this, many colleges and universities still have questionable practices in this regard. Some judicial guidance will probably result from current challenges to similar questions asked by credentialing and professional licensing agencies. All such programs are likely to be required to justify the relevance of asking questions such as, "Have you ever been treated for mental illness?" Although higher education programs and licensing agencies will probably be given substantial deference in establishing relevant academic criteria and performance standards, they will have to establish the relationship of asking such questions to these standards. The courts will need to evaluate whether programs are safer asking questions related to relevant behavior and conduct, such as, "Have you ever been disciplined by an educational agency or government authority for violent and dangerous behavior?" rather than, "Have you ever been treated for psychological problems?" Appropriate questions related to conduct seem more likely to be upheld than broad-based questions related to status. The latter types of questions not only are probably impermissible under nondiscrimination statutes, but they have the additional problem of being a disincentive to individuals to seek treatment, for fear that they would have to report such treatment.

A catch-22 problem arises in the context of these broad-based questions about past mental treatment. A problem can occur if students falsely answer the question (because they are justifiably concerned about stigma) and then are later rejected from admission to the program, not because of the mental health status but because they lied. It will be important for courts to address this dilemma if students with mental illness are to be fairly treated in the admissions process. This is relevant in both admission to the higher education program and admission in a professional certification context.

There has been little judicial interpretation of the Family Educational Rights and Privacy Act of relevance to this issue, primarily because individuals are not permitted to go to court to seek personal remedies under the act. Basically, the student's remedy is to complain to the Department of Education, which may investigate but probably would not grant the student an individual remedy in most instances. Department of Education findings would not be reflected in reports of judicial decisions.

FERPA allows students 18 or older to have access to their own educational records; the opportunity to challenge inaccurate, misleading, or other privacy-violating information; and a right to deny disclosure to third parties without consent. Although the educational agency is required to list the names and positions of personnel who may have access to those records, this requirement is somewhat vague and is rarely subject to any challenge. In addition, there are a variety of contexts in which an educational agency is arguably privileged to release such records. For example, if a student seeks to transfer to another institution, the transferring college would probably be permitted to send all educational records (including any information reflecting mental illness that might be contained in such records) to the transferee college.

Similarly, students seeking certification from a licensing board or admission to the legal or medical profession must grant the college a waiver to send such student records information. Because there is no private right of action under FERPA, it is difficult to challenge practices related to the handling of student records. In addition, these practices are likely to be upheld in any case as justifiable and privileged. One case involved a law student who challenged the law school's reporting of his disruptive and difficult behavior to the board of bar examiners. He claimed that his behavior was a result of his epilepsy and that the law school had violated the Rehabilitation Act and the ADA by reporting this conduct to bar admission authorities (*Rothman v. Emory University*, 1993). This case is currently still in litigation. In one of the few other cases related to the issue of privileged disclosure, a student who was HIV-positive was unsuccessful in obtaining damages under the Rehabilitation Act when the school to which he was transferring was informed of his status (*Doe v. Southeastern University,* 1990).

Part of the problem with student records may be that, unlike health records in the employment context that are required to be kept separate from the individual's employment records, student educational records may include health-related information. Indeed, it may be necessary to have such information in the student educational record as the basis for documenting why a particular reasonable accommodation has been provided. For example, a student suffering from stress disorder may request to take an exam in a separate room. In granting the request, the administrator may require a physician's documentation to be included in the student's record. The problem arises later when that same administrator is required to certify character and fitness (not just completion of academic requirements at a satisfactory level). The administrator faces the dilemma of whether in a particular context it might be necessary to report this concern. Arguably, the administrator should report only relevant behavior or discipline problems.

For example, a student with a mental illness who has problems meeting deadlines may still have met the academic requirements for graduation. However, when the student seeks to enter a profession, such as the legal profession, where timeliness is an essential criterion, the information may be relevant to professional qualifications. Perhaps the appropriate response is that administrators who provide information to certifying agencies or to transferee institutions should have to advise the student *before* the negative information is sent. The student then could have an opportunity to object, although courts may be likely to hold that academic institutions are privileged to provide this information to certifying agencies, particularly in situations where the student has by virtue of the certification process granted permission for disclosure of information in student records. Administrators, however, may think that a requirement to notify students before

sending negative information is unduly burdensome, particularly in light of the fact that students have a right—and an obligation—to inspect and review their individual files. The advantage in advance notification is that potential litigation may be avoided through this process.

Policy Gaps

The gaps in ensuring appropriate access to higher education for individuals with mental illness are somewhat complex. Although the ADA and the Rehabilitation Act prohibit discrimination on the basis of disability, including mental disability, individuals with mental illness seem not to be very successful in court. Perhaps this is because most individuals with mental illness seeking entry into higher education institutions meet the academic requirements and are not in court seeking redress in the first place. Statistical information on the percentages and numbers of college students with mental illness is difficult to obtain.

Many individuals with mental illness are screened out even before they are admitted as a result of preadmissions inquiries that are probably impermissible. It is extremely difficult to prove that rejection was based on mental illness in a higher education context. In many admissions processes, factors other than grades and standardized test scores are used. Although subjective factors such as leadership, maturity, service, and work experience are certainly important, the inclusion of these subjective factors may also permit higher education programs to hide behind them in rejecting an applicant who has noted a history of mental illness in response to a question (which is probably illegal) about the applicant's mental health history.

Although the Department of Education has a policy guideline permitting applicants to have access to comments of evaluators made in the admissions process, this is likely to be of little benefit in proving impermissible discrimination. The reasons are, first, that admissions evaluators are (as a result of this policy guideline) now less likely to write comments that could be used as the basis for a discrimination charge, and second, that admissions offices are allowed to destroy these comments after the admissions process is complete.

The policy gap of proving discrimination may be resolved once the courts begin to resolve the issue of permissible preadmissions inquiry. This resolution is already in progress in the area of professional certification questions, as discussed in the section on employment. These cases will be instructive. In addition, the Department of Education has also issued a number of opinion letters finding certain preadmissions questions about disabilities to be impermissible (Jaschik, 1993). Although these decisions and opinion letters point out that certain questions are impermissible, they do not provide guidance as to exactly what type of preadmissions inquiry language would be permissible in a particular application context. This may be an area where the Department of Education could serve both higher education institutions and applicants by providing guidance.

The fact that a student has no individual remedy under FERPA may be problematic in terms of ensuring that unfairly stigmatizing information is not included in student records. It may be, however, that additional challenges under tort theories (such as libel, slander, defamation, invasion of privacy, and infliction of emotional distress) and discrimination theories may result in new protections in this area. Again, however, it would be more efficient and constructive for the Department of Education to examine this issue and to provide regulations or clearer guidelines as to what information related to disabilities (including mental disabilities) can be asked and placed in student records.

This guidance needs to provide clearer instruction as to what information can and must be included, what may be provided in credentialing, transfer, and other contexts, and who may have access, such as faculty members and other administrators who have reason to need access to some aspects of student records.

Significant attention is also required as to how student records are kept and the degree to which it is appropriate to incorporate academic records, health records, and disciplinary records into one student record.

As the previous comments suggest, student affairs administrators face growing concerns about their obligations and liabilities in regard to the handling of student records. In addition, student affairs administrators, whose role may have been to discuss concerns with students, increasingly find themselves in the role of a personal counselor without counseling training. Student affairs professionals today need more awareness and sensitivity, not only about legal requirements but also about the resources available to provide help to students with mental illness. Student affairs administrators cannot be expected to provide mental health counseling, but they may need an adequate understanding of when and where to refer students who need such help.

Related to the gap in preparation by student service providers is the gap in the availability of mental health services on most campuses. Although most college campuses have an administrative office that provides counseling and testing, the level of service varies from campus to campus. And in an era of fiscal constraints in higher education, such services are often the first to be cut. Campus counseling programs are rarely equipped to provide long-term counseling or other mental health treatment. Similarly, student health insurance rarely provides coverage for long-term treatment or other coverage for serious mental health problems. This gap demonstrates the need for a national health insurance policy that will provide adequate access to health care, including mental health services.

Finally, of course, the common theme of lack of understanding should be mentioned. Because of the misunderstandings and myths surrounding mental illness, members of the academic community, including fellow students, administrators, faculty, staff, and campus law enforcement personnel, often respond inappropriately to some situations involving students with mental illness. While it is reasonable to want to be safe and to be concerned about a student whose behavior is threatening or dangerous, the level of knowledge and understanding needs to be improved dramatically in order for individuals in the community to respond appropriately to students whose mental illnesses may make them behave strangely.

Employment Discrimination

Statutory Coverage

Studies show that discrimination against people with mental disabilities is greater than against those with physical disabilities (U.S. Congress, Senate Committee on Labor and Human Resources, 1990, p. 199). In considering what policy changes might be necessary to ensure that individuals with mental illness are adequately protected in terms of access to employment, it is essential to examine the current status of the law as it applies to this issue.

The major coverage is under federal law—the Rehabilitation Act, the ADA, and to some extent the Family Medical Leave Act (FMLA). While state law prohibiting employment discrimination is relevant, for the most part it is subsumed by federal coverage as a result of the ADA.

Until 1990, there was virtually no federal protection against employment discrimination on the basis of disability for most of the private sector. The Rehabilitation Act of 1973 only prohibits employment discrimination on the basis of disability by federal government employers, federal contractors with $10,000 or more in annual federal contracts, and programs receiving federal financial assistance.

In 1990, Congress passed the ADA, which prohibits discrimination on the basis of disability by virtually all private employers as well as by state and local government employers. The only employers not covered by the ADA are small

employers (some of whom are nonetheless covered by state law) and federal employers (who are covered by sections 501 and 504 of the Rehabilitation Act). One of the reasons the ADA was needed was that state laws provided inadequate and inconsistent coverage (that is, in terms of who was protected and which programs were covered), enforcement, and remedies.

The Rehabilitation Act and the ADA have common basic principles. The definition of who is protected is virtually identical in the two cases. Individuals who have substantial impairments to major life activities, those with records of such impairments, or those who are regarded as having such impairments are covered under both statutes. Both the Rehabilitation Act and the ADA require that the individual be qualified (able to carry out the essential requirements of the job in spite of the disability) with or without reasonable accommodations (*Southeastern Community College v. Davis,* 1979).

Both the ADA and the Rehabilitation Act specifically exclude several conditions, many of which are related to mental health. Excluded conditions are homosexuality, bisexuality, transsexualism, transvestism, pedophilia, exhibitionism, voyeurism, gender identity disorders not resulting from physical impairments, other sexual behavior disorders, compulsive gambling, kleptomania, pyromania, and psychoactive substance use disorders resulting from current use of drugs. Coverage of individuals with alcohol and drug problems is now consistent under the ADA and the Rehabilitation Act. In both statutes, individuals who are alcoholics or addicted to drugs are protected so long as they can perform the duties of the job, where there is no direct threat to the property or safety of others and they are not currently using illegal drugs or illegally using legal drugs.

Employers are required to make reasonable accommodations for employees not only to determine whether they are otherwise qualified to be hired or remain in the job, but after the employee has been hired. Reasonable accommodation does not require waiver of fundamental or essential aspects of the job. In defining what is reasonable, the employer is not required to make accommodations that would be unduly burdensome, either financially or administratively. Barrier removal (for example, installing a ramp or an elevator) and accommodations to existing policies, practices, and procedures (such as providing for flexible work hours) are among the types of reasonable accommodations contemplated.

Both major federal statutes incorporate the principle of *mainstreaming*. In the context of employment, this means that employers are not allowed to segregate employees with disabilities or to assign them only to specific kinds of jobs. This principle applies to all aspects of employment. For example, an inaccessible lunchroom would probably violate this principle.

One employment practice prohibited by the ADA is preemployment medical exams. Such tests can only be required after a conditional offer has been made and only if all employees in the same job category are subject to the examination. Tests of current employees must be job-related. Drug tests are not considered medical exams, so an employer can give a drug test to job applicants before making an employment offer or to current employees. Information related to disability that is obtained through such a drug test cannot be used in a manner that would discriminate against someone with a disability. It is difficult, however, to prove that impermissible uses of drug tests have occurred. Preemployment questions that might tend to screen out individuals with disabilities (for instance, questions about whether an individual has a driver's license where driving is not part of the job being sought) can also be problematic. Both the ADA and the Rehabilitation Act prohibit these practices.

Case Law Interpretations

Who Is Protected?

A number of judicial decisions have addressed issues related to the employment of individuals with mental health problems. One issue that the courts have addressed is whether a specific condition is covered under state or federal law. State courts applying state statutes have reached a variety of conclusions. Courts in various states have held that the following types of disabilities fit the state definition: being perceived to have a mental impairment (*Ashker v. IBM*, 1990), short-term memory problems resulting from a head injury (*LaMott v. Apple Valley Health Care Center*, 1991), phobic reaction to carbon monoxide (*Barnes v. Barbosa*, 1986), manic depression (*Balzac v. Columbia University Press*, 1985), and depression (*Henkel Corp. v. Iowa Civil Rights Commission*, 1991). Conditions that have not met the state definition for protection in various judicial decisions include gender dysphoria and transsexualism (*Doe v. Boeing Co.*, 1993), chronic lateness (*School District v. Friedman*, 1984), occasional episodes of stress, depression, and mental exhaustion (*Pressman v. University of North Carolina*, 1985), and claustrophobia and depression (*Bowers v. Estep*, 1992).

Addiction to drugs and alcohol is treated differently by the various states (Rothstein, 1992), and although epilepsy is considered a disability by most judicial opinions, many courts do not find that it is protected under the state statute because the individual with epilepsy is not qualified to perform the job. Another condition that some states have found to relate to mental health problems is obesity. Courts and policymakers are currently evaluating whether obesity is a physiological condition, is self-induced, or is simply a condition meriting no special treatment as a disability.

The differing state law treatment of mental disabilities and related conditions is one of the major reasons why it was important for the sake of consistency that the ADA be passed. Both the ADA and the Rehabilitation Act provide basically the same definitional coverage as to who is protected. They both protect individuals with impairments that substantially affect one or more major life activities, those who are regarded as having such impairments, and those who have records of such impairments. Major life activities include caring for one's self, performing manual tasks, walking, seeing, hearing, speaking, breathing, learning, and *working.*

Several judicial opinions have addressed federal laws as they apply to employment cases involving individuals with mental health problems. These cases have resulted in findings that the following conditions are disabilities at least in the jurisdiction where the case was decided: depressive illness and medication regime (*Guice-Mills v. Derwinski*, 1991), epilepsy (*Duran v. City of Tampa*, 1977), and mental illness (*Overton v. Reilly*, 1992). Other courts have found that the following conditions do *not* meet the statutory definition: stress symptoms and panic disorder (*Margeson v. Springfield Terminal Railway Co.*, 1993), bipolar modal disorder (*Mackey v. Runyon*, 1992), ambiguous existence of learning disability (*Pandazides v. Virginia Board of Education*, 1992), fear of heights (*Forrisi v. Bowen*, 1986), sexual obsession (*Winston v. Maine Technical College System*, 1993), and mild cerebral palsy (*Pridemore v. Legal Aid Society*, 1985).

Unlike people with some other types of disabilities, "individuals with mental disabilities may move in and out of protected status" (Mickey & Pardo, 1993, p. 532), which can make it difficult to determine who is protected. Litigation for individuals with mental health problems in employment has focused not on whether a person is protected, though, but on whether the individual is qualified and on what type of reasonable accommodation is required.

Qualification for Protection

To be entitled to protection under the ADA or the Rehabilitation Act, it is not enough to meet the definition of being disabled. One must also be qualified. This means that the individual must be able to carry out the essential requirements of the job or program "in spite of the handicap" or disability (*Southeastern Community College v. Davis*, 1979). In addressing this issue, the courts must take into account whether reasonable accommodations could be provided so that the

individual would then be qualified. Accommodations that are fundamental alterations of the program are not required, nor are those that are unduly burdensome either financially or administratively.

A number of judicial decisions under the Rehabilitation Act have addressed this issue. Judicial decisions favorable to the employee have addressed a variety of situations. Some of these decisions have found that the employee was otherwise qualified and was not hired or was discharged because of a disability that did not affect the employee's ability to meet the job requirements. In other cases, the court has found that the individual would be otherwise qualified if reasonable accommodations were provided.

For example, one court held that a person with apraxia (loss of coordination) should be provided with the reasonable accommodation of a distraction-free environment by being provided a private work space (*Arneson v. Sullivan*, 1991). Another court held that an employee was otherwise qualified and had been improperly denied eligibility by requiring medical proof of recovery from mental illness (*United States v. Cook*, 1984). One employer's failure to provide appropriate supervision of a laundry worker who had mental retardation and emotional disabilities was found to be constructive discharge (when an employer creates such unpleasant working conditions that an employee is compelled to resign) when the employee was taunted and inappropriately disciplined by coworkers (*Kent v. Derwinski*, 1991). Another court found that it was unlawful to discharge an otherwise qualified employee with cerebellar ataxia (a neurological impairment) (*Carter v. Casa Centenary*, 1988).

Several courts have reached decisions unfavorable to the employee. In cases addressing whether the employee was otherwise qualified, the courts have found that an employee with work-anxiety depressive disorders was not otherwise qualified because the job required him to be able to get along with coworkers (*Pesterfield v. Tennessee Valley Authority*, 1991); that a nurse with depressive illness interfering with the ability to arrive at work on time was not qualified to be head nurse (*Guice-Mills v. Derwinski,* 1991); that extending the probationary period was not required for a word processor with depression (*Baxter v. Wisconsin Department of Natural Resources,* 1991); and that an employee who sought a job as a splice service technician was not qualified because he was unable to climb telephone poles and had not been discriminated against because of his brain injury (*Cox v. New England Telephone & Telegraph,* 1993). The courts have also found that a psychiatric worker was not otherwise qualified because her suicidal tendencies would adversely affect her work (*Doe v. Region 13 Mental Health–Mental Retardation Commission,* 1983); that an individual with paranoid schizophrenia was not otherwise qualified (*Franklin v. United States Postal Service,* 1988); that a person with manic depression was not otherwise qualified (*Matzo v. Postmaster General,* 1987); and that it was permissible to revoke a security clearance of a psychiatrically impaired employee when the decision was based on his conviction of felony child abuse (*Swann v. Walters,* 1984).

Other courts have addressed issues involving reasonable accommodations in reaching results adverse to the employee. In one case it was held that the Postal Service was not required to accommodate an employee with anxiety disorder by assigning him to a post closer to home because it would violate the collective bargaining agreement (*Shea v. Tisch,* 1989); that a teacher with psychiatric disorder could not be reasonably accommodated to perform the essential functions of an English teacher (*Marlow v. Department of Education,* 1987); and that an individual with borderline personality need not be transferred or reassigned where it would usurp the rights of other employees (*Fields v. Lyng,* 1988).

Although the ADA may be interpreted to require that employers consider reasonable accommodations related to stress reduction, keeping on schedule, and complying with supervision, courts recognize that it is not always possible to provide accommodations to individuals with mental illness without fundamentally altering the essential nature of the job or creating an undue hardship (Mickey & Pardo, 1993, pp. 539–541).

No reported judicial opinions have been decided under the ADA so far that have directly involved employment and mental illness, but the ADA is intended to incorporate for the most part the judicial interpretation of the Rehabilitation Act. It is likely that there will be ADA decisions in the near future. Of the 14,334 ADA Title I charges received by the Equal Employment Opportunity Commission between July 26, 1992 (the initial date of application of Title I of the ADA) and August 31, 1993, 9.7% were by individuals with mental illness. The only other disability category in which more complaints were made was back problems.

Statistics as of June 30, 1993, provide a more detailed breakdown of this data (Mickey & Pardo, 1993, p. 531 n. 2). Of the charges claiming failure to make reasonable accommodations, 8.5% were from individuals claiming mental illness. Of the hiring complaints, 7.4% were from individuals with mental illness, and 11.1% of the complaints related to discharge were from individuals claiming mental illness. This breakdown might indicate that it is more difficult for individuals with mental illness to ascertain that there was discrimination in the hiring process than it is once they are on the job.

Licensing Boards

Professional certification cases under the ADA do not directly involve Title I but nonetheless involve employment. A common practice of professional certification boards has been to ask questions about mental health history of individuals seeking to be admitted to practice law or medicine, or to obtain a license to be a dentist, an accountant, or a barber. Before 1990, most of these licensing agencies were not subject to the Rehabilitation Act because they were either state government agencies or private entities not receiving federal financial assistance or federal contracts. The ADA, however, applies to state and local agencies and to private entities considered to be public accommodations. Thus, most licensing agencies are now subject to the ADA prohibition against discrimination on the basis of disability. Prohibited practices would probably include asking questions that would tend to screen out individuals with disabilities (including mental disabilities) that are unrelated to legitimate requirements for licensure.

The practice of asking questions such as "Have you ever been treated for mental illness?" are being challenged in the courts, and for the most part, the challenges are likely to be successful in striking down such questions. In one case, it was found that reliance on questions about past drug abuse or psychological problems by a board of medical examiners violates the ADA by placing extra burdens on qualified individuals with disabilities (*Medical Society of New Jersey v. Jacobs*, 1993).

Licensing boards will be required to tailor questions more carefully to legitimate information related to occupational functions. They will need to focus their questions on misconduct and behavior related to the character and fitness in the particular profession. Asking about treatment or past illness is not appropriate to address these concerns.

Although current judicial opinions indicate that such questions are likely to be struck down, an additional concern—as noted—is that individuals who might have falsely answered these questions in the past because they were concerned about discriminatory treatment are now being excluded, not because they have a history of mental health treatment, but because they lied on the questionnaire. Until the courts address this catch-22 problem, these individuals may face unfair treatment in seeking their employment goals. An amendment to the ADA and the Rehabilitation Act might also resolve this problem, by holding that programs subject to these statutes that asked impermissible questions may not penalize individuals because they falsely answered impermissible questions.

Policy Gaps

Testimony in hearings on the ADA indicates that discrimination against people with mental disabilities is greater than against people with physical disabilities (U.S. Congress, House Committee on Small Business, 1990, pp. 120, 129). This testimony cites a study authorized by the Rehabilitation Act that asked employers to rank various groups in terms of which ones they believed employers would be most likely to hire. The data indicated that physical disability groups were clustered together and ranked lower than all minority groups and the elderly, but higher than all mental disability groups. The study found that employers would be more likely to hire student radicals or prison parolees than people with physical or mental disabilities (Colbert, Kalish, & Chang, 1973, p. 194). Although individuals with mental impairments are included in the broad statutory coverage of the ADA and the Rehabilitation Act, the courts may not be appropriately addressing whether certain individuals fit the definition. As mentioned previously, a current policy debate concerns the coverage of individuals who are obese and some mental disorders.

The relationship of alcohol and drug use and addiction in exacerbating mental illnesses has not been fully explored. This is an area where more research is necessary to evaluate whether individuals with certain conditions are being given adequate protection under current discrimination statutes. This research is needed in order to develop an appropriate policy response to definitional coverage of certain mental impairments.

The courts have been inconsistent in determining whether individuals with mental disabilities could be reasonably accommodated in the workplace. Although in one case, as we have seen, a court ordered an accommodation of providing a distraction-free environment via a private work space for an individual with apraxia, courts in general are not inclined to permit employees to disrupt or present a danger in the workplace.

While it is understandable that the courts have reached these judicial results, employers might benefit from a greater awareness of issues related to mental illness and more technical assistance about providing accommodations. A 1993 publication of the American Bar Association and the National Mental Health Association provides this technical assistance. This publication, titled *The ADA and People with Mental Illness: A Resource Manual for Employers*, includes a section discussing appropriate accommodations and another section with case studies in developing reasonable accommodations. The *ADA Resource Manual* suggests accommodations such as education in the workplace, changing the physical environment, flexible scheduling, job restructuring, job training, improved communication and support, feedback (both critical and positive), and on-the-job support (such as allowing the employee to call friends or counselors).

The awareness of the availability of information about mental illness is key for both employers and the courts. A technical assistance resource that has been in existence since the mid-1980s is the Job Accommodation Network (JAN). This federally funded program is a service of the President's Committee on Employment of People with Disabilities. JAN is available to employers and others as a clearinghouse of ideas and information for accommodating individuals with disabilities in the workplace. Since its beginning in 1985, it has received only 209 inquiries related to mental illness. There has been a significant increase in the number of employer-initiated inquiries since the passage of the ADA. The inquiries since the ADA have most often involved retention, while before the ADA they usually involved job seeking. The types of solutions for mental illness offered by JAN have included promoting coworker understanding, rearranging work schedules to avoid rush-hour traffic, educating supervisors about the impact of stress from deadlines and criticism, reassignment into less stressful positions, and rearranging office locations to be near a window. Most of the solutions involved training and education. JAN is clear that absenteeism need not be excused to any greater degree than it would be for other employees with other serious health problems. One of the barriers to educating others in the workplace is the limitations on disclosure of the disability. The employee in many cases would have to permit the disclosure in order for the education of the employer and coworkers to occur.

As just noted, the vast majority of reported decisions involving employment and individuals with mental illness address the issue of nondiscrimination against an employee who is already in the workplace. Few have addressed the issue of whether someone has been unfairly precluded from obtaining a job in the first place. Although the courts have not yet decided these cases, we can expect that some of those currently in the pipeline will soon reach judicial determination. As noted previously, however, proving discrimination in the hiring process can be extremely difficult. The employer is not required to indicate any reason for a refusal to hire. One possible policy change might require employers to provide, on request, justifications for not hiring, similar to disclosures that are required on request when someone is denied credit by a lender. The counterargument to this policy change would be that this might be unduly burdensome on employers, given the large number of applicants in many situations.

One area in which a policy change is necessary involves medical screening practices, particularly drug testing by employers (Rothstein, 1989). Preemployment drug tests are not prohibited by the ADA, although it is technically illegal to use the results of such tests for discriminatory purposes. Realistically, however, it is difficult to prove that employers are making impermissible use of such information. It is quite possible that employers are using drug tests of both applicants and current employees to ascertain whether they are currently taking drugs for mental illness. It would be difficult, however, to prove that they are doing so. Some employers may be using this information in refusing to hire and in terminating employees, though it is probably illegal to use the information this way.

Drug testing is one way of screening out individuals with mental illness. Inquiring about past mental health is another. The legislative history of the ADA indicates that employers were troubled by the inability to screen job applicants by inquiring about mental illness (U.S. Congress, 1989, p. 66). As genetic information becomes more readily available, attention to practices of screening out individuals with genetic indications of mental illness will also become essential.

Employers are interested in screening out employees with mental illness for three main reasons. First, they are concerned about the health insurance costs that these employees would incur, as well as about lost productivity due to absenteeism for treatment permitted by the Family Medical Leave Act or as a reasonable accommodation under the ADA or other laws. Second, employers are concerned about the employee not being able to do the job because of the mental condition. This attitude is based on general perceptions and attitudes toward mental illness rather than individualized determinations of the abilities of each applicant or employee. Third, employers are concerned about disruption or even danger in the workplace. An employee whose behavior is bizarre or unusual may distract fellow employees or even customers. Employees whose mental illness may result in violent behavior would be undesirable. The screening out for this reason is also usually based on generalized attitudes and prejudices about mental illness without a complete understanding of the probable manifestations for the particular individual involved. Testimony from the mental health advocates related to the ADA bears out the problem with employers' negative attitudes (U.S. Congress, House Committee on Education and Labor, 1988, pp. 37, 131, 173, 200, 221, 229). Although the courts have been fairly consistent in requiring individualized determinations in the cases that reach court, the problem is that the vast number of instances of discrimination never reach the courts. Increased funding of education about mental illness is essential to combat this prejudice and the resulting discrimination.

Another area where policy correction is needed involves confidentiality of mental health information about employees in the possession of the employer. Employers gain access to mental health information related to employees in three main ways. First, because under the ADA, post-offer exams (exams following a conditional job offer) need not be job related, employers can require access to the medical records of conditional offerees (those offered jobs conditional on their exams), even though it is unlawful to discriminate against individuals for non–job-related reasons. Second, employers, especially those who are self-insured and pay medical bills directly rather than through an insurance company, receive the bills for mental health as well as other health treatment with diagnostic information included. Third, many companies have employee assistance plans (EAPs) that encourage employees to seek help for drug abuse, mental health, and related problems. When these programs are run in-house, although the employees are usually promised confidentiality, conflicts of interest often arise and confidentiality may be breached. Attention to these problems should result in appropriate policy changes (Ravid, 1992; Rothstein, 1989).

Many of these issues have not received attention from the courts. One reason there may not be more judicial attention to the issue of employment discrimination is the lack of access to legal representation. Although successful litigants under the Rehabilitation Act and the ADA can obtain attorneys' fees and court costs, many private attorneys seem reluctant to take such cases in the first place. This may be because they are concerned about the likelihood of success. It may also be because of personal fear and lack of understanding of individuals with mental illness. Until the 1986 passage of the Protection and Advocacy for Mentally Ill Individuals Act, little specialized subsidy was available in terms of public Legal Aid–type services for individuals with mental illness. Because that statute applies primarily to legal representation involving individuals who are in residential facilities, rather than mentally ill individuals generally who might wish to pursue discrimination claims, people with mental disabilities still have little access to affordable legal services.

In addition to the problems with medical screening and lack of judicial guidance, there may be a practical problem with the employment statutes in terms of ensuring employment for individuals who have a mental illness. The problem is simply that in some cases, even with appropriate reasonable accommodations, the individuals may not be otherwise qualified. Individuals with a severe mental illness, even when they are in appropriate therapy programs, cannot always consistently carry out the requirements of a particular job. Although certain low-skill jobs require little training and allow for erratic work attendance, most employment situations do not. And some individuals who could maintain constant fitness if they accepted treatment, including drug therapy or counseling, also have the right to refuse such treatment. Such refusal may result in a change in behavior and conduct such that the individual is not fit for employment on certain days. The availability of more technical assistance in terms of education for employers in dealing with employees with various mental illnesses would probably enhance the employment opportunities of individuals with mental illness.

There is, however, a limit to what current therapies can do to make some individuals fit for some employment situations. The various laws that apply to individuals with mental illness do not coordinate well. Laws prohibiting employment discrimination do not require coordination of appropriate housing arrangements and supervisory services to ensure that the individual with mental illness has the necessary support system to ensure appropriate employment behavior (Haimowitz, 1991).

Even if the problems of discrimination and stigma were eliminated, the problem of access to

mental health treatment services remains. If these services were readily available, many individuals whose work is impeded by symptoms of mental illness could function satisfactorily. The policy change that is necessary is the expansion of access to mental health treatment. Insurance programs currently provide both inadequate medication and insufficient psychological counseling or other therapy. For many types of mental illness, both interventions are essential. Current policy interpretation from the Equal Employment Opportunity Commission indicates that employers may limit coverage for mental illness without violating discrimination laws (Equal Employment Opportunity Commission, 1993, p. 6).

The Family Medical Leave Act provides some assistance in terms of permitting the employee a right to some time off to obtain treatment, assuming the employee has the financial means to obtain such treatment. The lack of access to such treatment is the problem. It is essential that national health care policy not only provide services for mental illness, but that these services include both medication and counseling. A 1994 survey indicates public support for providing substantially more benefits in the area of mental health (Bazelon Center for Mental Health Law, 1994).

In addition to the lack of available support services due to inadequate funding, there is the lack of such services due to lack of personnel. Even if more funding were available, a serious shortage of personnel exists in the psychiatry, psychology, and social work fields to provide services to this population (Hollingsworth & Hollingsworth, 1994, pp. 154–155).

Related to the issue of employment is the issue of housing, which is addressed in a later section. It should be noted at this point, however, that unless individuals with mental illness have appropriate housing in the community that is reasonably close to employment opportunities, it will be difficult to ensure that individuals with mental illness have an appropriate level of access to the workplace. This raises the entire policy problem with the social service delivery system for people with mental illness in the United States. The system is decentralized and provided on a state or local level; for the most part, services are not coordinated. What is necessary is centralized responsibility for working with a client with mental illness who has needs in the area of employment, housing, crisis intervention, social services, counseling, and daily living (Hollingsworth & Hollingsworth, 1994, pp. 157–161). Without better coordination of comprehensive services, only so much can be accomplished through nondiscrimination statutes. The individual seeking employment must be qualified to be protected by nondiscrimination law. If that individual's behavior is out of control, or if the individual's housing is not located close enough to work, the ADA will be of little value in ensuring employment.

Public Accommodations and Public Services

Statutory Coverage

Until the passage of the ADA, little comprehensive protection existed for people with mental disabilities in public accommodations and public services. Public accommodations in this context refer to privately operated facilities provided to the public. Under Title III of the ADA, there are 12 categories. These are lodging, eating establishments, entertainment facilities, public gathering places, stores and sales establishments, service establishments (including law offices and health care provider facilities), transportation stations, public display facilities, places of recreation, places of education, social service centers, and exercise facilities.

Public services under Title II of the ADA refer to public service programs operated by state or local government entities. This would include such programs as public colleges, courthouses and jail facilities, and social service agencies. Public services operated by the federal govern-

ment are not covered by the ADA but would be subject to the mandates of sections 501 and 504 of the Rehabilitation Act.

In this area, both the ADA and the Rehabilitation Act prohibit discrimination against individuals with disabilities who are qualified to carry out the essential aspects of the program. They also require that reasonable accommodations be made.

The protections involving public accommodations and public services have a much greater impact on individuals with physical disabilities (including sensory, mobility, and health impairments) than on individuals with mental disabilities. In many instances, the nondiscrimination and reasonable accommodation mandates involve removing physical barriers or altering how a particular program can be provided. These requirements also apply to individuals with mental impairments. For example, a physician may not refuse to treat a patient simply because the patient has a mental illness. Nor may a store refuse to wait on a customer because of the customer's mental illness.

Case Law Interpretations

There is little, if any, reported case law interpretation of these requirements as they have been applied to individuals who have a mental illness. This is probably because many of the requirements are too new to have reached the level of reported judicial interpretation. It may also be that individuals with mental illness who have encountered discrimination in these areas may not be aware of their rights or may not be able to retain legal counsel to represent them.

Policy Gaps

We can only speculate on the policy gaps in this area. There is clearly a need for greater availability of public services to be provided to individuals with mental illness, but in the area of nondiscrimination, the degree to which such discrimination on the basis of mental illness occurs and why it occurs is unclear. In some cases, a lack of understanding of mental illness is the problem, especially when this lack of understanding takes the form of irrational fears. This occurs when all mental illnesses are lumped together in the perception of the public accommodation or public service provider.

Housing

Statutory Coverage

Housing is one of the major areas of life not covered in any comprehensive way by either the ADA or the Rehabilitation Act. The Rehabilitation Act prohibits discrimination in some government housing, but the major statutory coverage against discrimination on the basis of disability is found in the 1988 amendments to the Fair Housing Act (FHA) of 1968. The FHA prohibits discrimination in the sale or rental of housing when it is based on a handicapping condition, including a mental impairment. The definition of who is protected is substantially similar to the definitions provided by the Rehabilitation Act and the ADA. Individuals currently using illegal drugs or addicted to controlled substances are not protected. As with the Rehabilitation Act and the ADA, individuals are required to be qualified to perform the essential requirements of the program, with or without reasonable accommodation, in spite of the handicap. Reasonable accommodations include modifying rules, policies, practices, and services.

In addition, some states prohibit housing discrimination on the basis of handicap or disability. Many of these protect individuals with mental impairments.

Case Law Interpretations

A number of housing cases have involved individuals who have a mental illness. These cases are of two major types. The first type involves individuals who have claimed discrimination. The second type includes attempts to restrict group homes for individuals with mental impairments. The courts have generally tried to protect individuals with mental illness in both types of cases.

In one case decided under state law, a New Hampshire court held that a landlord could not evict a low-income tenant with a psychiatric disability because she was in violation of the no-pets clause. The court found that she was emotionally dependent on her cat and that she should be allowed to keep the cat as a reasonable accommodation (*Whittier Terrace Associates v. Hampshire*, 1989). A similar result was reached in a case in New York (*Crossroads Apartments Association v. LeBoo*, 1991). In another case, it was decided that the Rehabilitation Act required the landlord to allow a tenant to continue living in a government-subsidized housing project even though there had been some minor damage to the walls when the tenant hit the walls with a broom. The tenant's conduct was a result of a mental impairment (*City Wide Associates*, 1991). The court considered the damage so minor that it was a reasonable accommodation not to evict the tenant because of the damage, although she may be required to pay for it. Similarly, in a 1993 case under the FHA, a court required a federally subsidized apartment complex to explore whether reasonable efforts could be made to accommodate a tenant with mental illness before evicting him. The tenant had threatened an elderly tenant with obscene and offensive language (*Roe v. Sugar River Mills Associates*, 1993). Unfortunately, the court provided no guidance on the type of accommodations that should be considered. In a simple discrimination case, not involving reasonable accommodations, a court in 1987 found a Rehabilitation Act violation when a landlord refused to rent to an individual with cerebral palsy and another individual who suffered from schizophrenia (*Bolthouse v. Continental Wingate Co.*, 1987).

Restrictions on group-home housing have been successfully challenged on several occasions. These challenges have involved both government regulation and private deed restrictions. Not all cases have involved group homes for individuals with mental illness, but they have established principles that are likely to be applied to such cases. Successful challenges have included invalidation of spacing requirements (that is, requiring group homes to be a certain distance from each other) and restrictive definitions of family that would effectively prohibit group homes from single-family neighborhoods (Rothstein, 1992, § 11.11).

Policy Gaps

In the area of housing, the gap is not primarily in the nondiscrimination mandates. Substantive protection exists, and the courts have responded sensitively to the reasonable-accommodation requirement as well as to the attempts by neighbors and government bodies to exclude group homes. It should be noted that the courts in general require reasonable accommodation but do not tolerate violent or unreasonably disruptive behavior. In many cases, if access to mental health treatment is inadequate, the individual's behavior may become intolerable. The individual would thus no longer be otherwise qualified and could be out on the streets. Some data indicate that individuals with mental problems are disproportionately represented in the homeless population (Robertson, Zlotnick, & Westerfelt, 1993). This illustrates the important relationship of nondiscrimination mandates to other services.

Many instances of unlawful discrimination probably never reach the courts, either because the individuals involved are unaware of their legal rights or because they lack access to legal representation.

The other major gap is funding. Without sufficient funding to provide the housing and the supervisory staffing in the community near employment and a mainstream environment, the goal of full participation cannot be achieved. Although more needs to be done in changing attitudes of landlords and neighbors so that they will not resist the presence of individuals with mental disabilities in the community, the major problem is that insufficient housing is available in the community because of a lack of funding. Until this is addressed, probably by both Con-

gress and state legislatures, housing for individuals with mental impairments will remain a significant problem. Without some form of subsidized or staff-supported housing, many of these individuals would not have the financial means to obtain the necessary housing.

Conclusion

The major barrier that has been identified in the previous sections is attitudinal. Although it may be difficult to legislate attitudes, the important first step of prohibiting discrimination is a start. Policymakers must now take the steps outlined earlier to educate the various service providers about mental illness and the myths and realities surrounding mental disabilities. They must also make greater efforts to ensure that the various social service providers coordinate the delivery of services. Access to mental health care is essential. Health care policy must ensure that mental health services, including both medication and counseling, are available to individuals who need them. And finally, funding for services is essential. More support for housing as well as mental health treatment, teacher training for children in schools, employment training, and legal representation are required. Perhaps if the educational efforts included information about the societal costs of *not* doing these things, policymakers and their constituents would be more inclined to make these significant improvements.

References

A. E. v. Independent School District, 936 F.2d 472 (10th Cir. 1991).

American Bar Association and National Mental Health Association. (1993). *The ADA and people with mental illness: A resource manual for employers.* Washington, DC: ABA Commission on the Mentally Disabled.

Americans with Disabilities Act, 42 U.S.C. §§ 12101 *et seq.*

Anderson v. University of Wisconsin, 841 F.2d 737 (7th Cir. 1988).

Arneson v. Sullivan, 946 F.2d 90 (8th Cir. 1991).

Aronson v. North Park College, 94 Ill. App. 3d 211, 418 N.E.2d 776 (1981).

Ashker v. IBM, 168 A.D.2d 724, 563 N.Y.S.2d 572 (1990).

Balzac v. Columbia University Press, 114 A.D.2d 792, 495 N.Y.S.2d 45 (1985).

Barnes v. Barbosa, 144 Ill. App. 3d 860, 494 N.E.2d 619 (1986).

Baxter v. Wisconsin Department of Natural Resources, 477 N.W.2d 648 (Wis. Ct. App. 1991).

Bazelon Center for Mental Health Law. (1994, February 22–24). *Survey of voters' views on coverage of mental health care and substance abuse treatment under health care reform.* Author.

Bolthouse v. Continental Wingate Co., 656 F. Supp. 620 (W.D. Mich. 1987).

Bowers v. Estep, 204 Ga. App. 615, 420 S.E.2d 336 (1992).

Carter v. Casa Centenary, 849 F.2d 1048 (7th Cir. 1988).

Colbert, J. N., Kalish, R. A., & Chang, P. (1973). Two psychological portals of entry for disadvantaged groups. *Rehabilitation Literature, 34,* 194.

Cook, T. (1991). The Americans with Disabilities Act: The move to integration. *Temple Law Review, 64,* 393.

Cox v. New England Telephone & Telegraph, 414 Mass. 375, 607 N.E.2d 1035 (1993).

Crancer v. Board of Regents, 156 Mich. App. 790, 402 N.W.2d 90 (1986).

Crossroads Apartments Association v. LeBoo, 478 N.Y.S.2d 1004 (City Ct. 1991).

Davila, R. R., Williams, M. L., & McDonald, J. T. (1991, September 16). *Department of Education, clarification of policy to address the needs of children with attention deficit disorders within general and/or special education* (memorandum to chief state school officers).

Doe v. Boeing Co., 121 Wash. 2d 8, 846 P.2d 531 (1993).

Doe v. Region 13 Mental Health–Mental Retardation Comm'n, 704 F.2d 1402 (5th Cir. 1983).

Doe v. New York University, 666 F.2d 761 (2d Cir. 1981).

Doe v. Southeastern University, 732 F. Supp. 7 (D.D.C. 1990).

Duran v. City of Tampa, 430 F. Supp. 75 (M.D. Fla. 1977).

Equal Employment Opportunity Commission. (1993, June 8). *Interim enforcement guidance on the applications of the Americans with Disabilities Act of 1990 to disability-based distinctions in employer-provided health insurance* (Publication No. N-915.002). Washington, DC: Author.

Evans v. District No. 17, 841 F.2d 824 (8th Cir. 1988).

Fair Housing Act, 42 U.S.C. §§ 3601 *et seq.* (1968).

Family Educational Rights and Privacy Act, 20 U.S.C. § 1232g (1994).

Family Medical Leave Act, 29 U.S.C. §§ 2601–2654 (1993).

Fields v. Lyng, 705 F. Supp. 1134 (D. Md. 1988).

Forrisi v. Bowen, 794 F.2d 931 (4th Cir. 1986).

Franklin v. United States Postal Service, 687 F. Supp. 1214 (S.D. Ohio 1988).

Glennon, T. (1993). Disabling Ambiguities: Confronting barriers to the education of students with emotional disabilities. *Tennessee Law Review, 60,* 295.

Guice-Mills v. Derwinski, 772 F. Supp. 188 (S.D.N.Y. 1991).

Haimowitz, S. (1991). Americans with Disabilities Act of 1990: Its significance for persons with mental illness. *Hospital and Community Psychiatry, 42,* 23.

Henkel Corp. v. Iowa Civil Rights Commission, 471 N.W.2d 806 (Iowa 1991).

Hiller v. Board of Education, 743 F. Supp. 958 (N.D.N.Y. 1990).

Hollingsworth, J. R., & Hollingsworth, E. J. (1994). *Care of the chronically and severely ill: Comparative social policies.* New York: Aldine De Gruyter.

Honig v. Doe, 484 U.S. 305 (1988).

Individuals with Disabilities Education Act, 20 U.S.C. §§ 1400–1461 (1990).

Individuals with Disabilities Education Act of 1990, H.R. Rep. No. 544, 101st Cong., 2d sess. 39 (1990).

Jaschik, S. (1993, April 21). 46 colleges found to have violated rights of disabled, U.S. documents show. *Chronicle of Higher Education, 39*(33), A-18–A-19.

Job Accommodation Network. (1993, December 1). Mental illness cases handled by the job accommodation network. Morgantown, WV: Author. (The Job Accommodation Network is a service of the President's Committee on Employment of People with Disabilities.)

Kent v. Derwinski, 790 F. Supp. 1032 (E.D. Wash. 1991).

LaMott v. Apple Valley Health Care Center, 465 N.W.2d 585 (Minn. Ct. App. 1991).

Mackey v. Runyon, 804 F. Supp. 1508 (M.D. Fla. 1992).

Margeson v. Springfield Terminal Railway Co., F. Supp. (D. Mass. 1993).

Marlow v. Department of Education, 820 F.2d 581 (2d Cir. 1987).

Matzo v. Postmaster General, 685 F. Supp. 260 (D.D.C. 1987).

Medical Society of New Jersey v. Jacobs, 1993 U.S. Dist. Lexis 14294 (D.N.J. 1993).

Mickey, P., & Pardo, M. (1993). Dealing with mental disabilities under the ADA. *Labor Lawyer, 9,* 531.

Overton v. Reilly, 977 F.2d 1190 (7th Cir. 1992).

Pandazides v. Virginia Board of Education, 804 F. Supp. 794 (E.D. Va. 1992).

Pesterfield v. Tennessee Valley Authority, 941 F.2d 437 (6th Cir. 1991).

Pressman v. University of North Carolina, 78 N.C. App. 296, 337 S.E.2d 644 (1985).

Pridemore v. Legal Aid Society, 625 F. Supp. 1171 (S.D. Ohio 1985).

Protection and Advocacy for Mentally Ill Individuals Act, 42 U.S.C. §§ 12801–12827, Pub. L. No. 102, 321, § 199, 106 Stat. at 352, 42 U.S.C. § 290ff-1(d)(2) (1986).

Pushkin v. Regents of University of Colorado, 658 F.2d 1372 (10th Cir. 1981).

Ravid, R. (1992). Disclosure of mental illness to employers: Legal resources and ramifications. *Journal of Psychiatry and Law, 20,* 85.

Rehabilitation Act of 1973, 29 U.S.C. §§ 791, 793, 794 (1993).

Roe v. Sugar River Mills Associates, 820 F. Supp. 636 (D.N.H. 1993).

Robertson, M. J., Zlotnick, C., & Westerfelt, A. (1993). Homeless adults: A special population in public alcohol treatment programs. *Contemporary Drug Problems, 20,* 499.

Rothman v. Emory University, 828 F. Supp. 537 (N.D. Ill. 1993).

Rothstein, L. F. (1992). *Disabilities and the law.* Colorado Springs, CO: Shepard's/McGraw-Hill.

Rothstein, L. F. (1995). *Special education law.* White Plains, NY: Longman.

Rothstein, M. A. (1989). *Medical screening and the employee health care cost crisis.* Washington, DC: BNA Books.

School District v. Friedman, 96 Pa. Commw. 267, 507 A.2d 882 (1984).

Schuler v. University of Minnesota, 788 F.2d 510 (8th Cir. 1986).

Shea v. Tisch, 870 F.2d 786 (1st Cir. 1989).

Smith v. Robinson, 468 U.S. 992 (1984).

Southeastern Community College v. Davis, 442 U.S. 397 (1979).

Swann v. Walters, 620 F. Supp. 741 (D.D.C. 1984).

United States v. Cook, 628 F. Supp. 38 (D. Colo. 1984).

U.S. Congress. (1989, September 7). *Proceedings and debates of the 101st Cong., 1st Sess., 135,* 112. Washington, DC: Government Printing Office.

Chapter 9 / Protections for Persons with Mental Disabilities **201**

U.S. Congress, House Committee on Education and Labor. *Oversight hearings on H.R. 4498, Americans with Disabilities Act of 1988, Hearing before the Subcommittee on Select Education.* 100th Cong., 2d sess.

U.S. Congress, House Committee on Small Business. (1990). *Americans with Disabilities Act: Hearing before the Committee on Small Business.* 101st Cong., 2d sess.

U.S. Congress, Senate Committee on Labor and Human Resources. (1989). *Americans with Disabilities Act: Hearing before the Subcommittee on the Handicapped.* 101st Cong., 1st sess. (statement of former Attorney General Dick Thornburgh).

Whittier Terrace Associates v. Hampshire, 26 Mass. App. 1020, 532 N.E.2d 712 (1989).

Winston v. Maine Technical College System, Maine Sup. Jud. Ct. 6638 (1993).

Wood v. President & Trustees of Spring Hill College, 978 F.2d 1214 (11th Cir. 1992).

10 ■ Guardianship for Incapacitated Persons

Phillip B. Tor
Bruce D. Sales
University of Arizona

A state may impose a guardianship on a person who lacks the ability to care for himself or herself or to manage personal property and assets. In such cases, a guardian is appointed to make personal or financial decisions for the person, who becomes legally known as the *ward*. The legal justification for placing persons with disabilities into such a restrictive arrangement is rooted in the feudal English doctrine of *parens patriae*, where the English crown assumed the role of parent. In the United States, the power of *parens patriae* is invoked by state sovereignties to protect individuals unable to protect themselves. Custody of children, the mentally incompetent, and the physically incapacitated through guardianship proceedings falls within the doctrinal ambit of *parens patriae*.

The ramifications of imposing a guardianship can be far-reaching. It can result in the loss of liberty and many legal and civil rights; rights once taken for granted may no longer exist for the ward (Sales, Powell, Van Duizend, & Associates, 1982). Through the court's action, for example, a guardian may have the final word on whether and whom the ward can marry or whether the ward may validly enter into a contract.

Because guardianship can have such a profound impact on an individual's life, many legal and mental health professionals have been concerned about the absence of legal safeguards in the guardianship system (for example, Axilbund, 1979; Mitchell, 1979; Parry & Hurme, 1991; Pecora, 1990; Radcliffe, 1982; Rein, 1992; Sales et al., 1982; Schmidt, Miller, Peters, & Loewenstein, 1988). In addition, critics have argued that the state's power to protect the interests of incompetents under the doctrine of *parens patriae* drifts into an exercise of the state's *police power*, which is intended to control persons, because the imposition of a guardianship can result in the ward's liberty being severely restricted (Mitchell, 1979; Sales et al., 1982). Unless state guardianship statutes have built-in safeguards to protect the rights of proposed wards, these individuals may become the victims of a system that does less to help than to control them. For example, because there are gradations of incapacity, and a ward's incompetency may be limited to specific areas of functioning, a plenary (total) guardianship can constitute an unreasonable deprivation of the wards's autonomy. It would prevent a ward from functioning where he or she is capable, and would "foster . . . further degeneration of existing competent behaviors and obstruct . . . the development of new ones" (Massad & Sales, 1981, p. 759). Thus, courts should consider limiting the scope of a guardian's power.

Over the past decade, research has revealed a number of weaknesses in the guardianship laws and practices of many states, including vague and overbroad standards for determining incompetency, inadequate due process protection, infrequent use of less restrictive alternatives to plenary guardianship, inadequate monitoring of guardianships, and the lack of training programs

This chapter is adapted with permission from "A Social Science Perspective on the Law of Guardianship: Directions for Improving the Process and Practice," by P. B. Tor and B. D. Sales, 1994, *Law and Psychology Review, 18,* 1–41. Copyright © 1994 University of Alabama School of Law.

for guardians (*Guardians of the Elderly*, 1987). These shortcomings have fostered antitherapeutic consequences (for example, guardianships being imposed too often and, as already noted, a loss of existing skills on the part of wards) (Massad & Sales, 1981).

This chapter will consider the laws regarding guardianship practices in the United States and their therapeutic and antitherapeutic consequences. It also will make specific recommendations for improving the guardianship process, to help more effectively persons subjected to a guardianship petition and placed under a guardian's control. The chapter is organized into five sections, each focusing on a different critical part of the guardianship process: guardianship standards, due process in guardianship proceedings, alternatives to full guardianship, monitoring and enforcement of guardianships, and the selection of guardians.

To simplify the discussion, *guardian* and *guardianship* will be used throughout this chapter as generic terms. Some states distinguish between guardianship and guardians, and conservatorship and conservators, but the distinction is not always based on the same criteria among the 51 jurisdictions (the 50 states and the District of Columbia). For example, in California a conservator is appointed by the court to care for a person found to be mentally disabled, and a guardian is appointed to care for a minor (*California Probate Code*, 1991). In other jurisdictions, the conservator looks after the ward's estate, while the guardian looks after the welfare of the person (see generally Sales et al., 1982).

Guardianship Standards

The chief purpose of the guardianship hearing is to make a legal determination about a person's competency. Since determination of incompetency is a legal conclusion, each state spells out in its guardianship statute the legal requirements

for making such a finding. The statutory standards can be categorized into three groups: the causal link approach, the Uniform Probate Code (UPC) approach, and the functional approach (Nolan, 1984).

Causal Link Approach

The causal link approach refers to the traditional standards of incompetency where mental or physical conditions are linked to a generalized incapacity for self-care. Under these statutes, the court could declare a person incompetent on the basis of a diagnostic label, such as "aged" or "mentally retarded," if there is testimony that the subject is inadequately caring for himself or herself or for personal property (Nolan, 1984). For example, a discontinued version of the Minnesota guardianship statute included the categories of "old age," "imperfection or deterioration of mentality," and "incompetent to manage his person" (*Minn. Stat.*, 1975). This type of statute is based on classifications, with incompetence and inability to care for one's self or manage one's responsibilities being viewed as inevitable consequences of that classification. If the petitioner (the party who initiates the guardianship action) can convince the court that the proposed ward has a disabling condition and is not taking proper care of himself or herself or of personal assets, the court could approve the guardianship and severely limit the ward's civil rights.

Where the statute calls for more than the diagnosis of a condition before a person can be placed in the care of a guardian, judges rely on the diagnostic opinion of physicians rather than on behavioral evidence (for example, Pleak & Appelbaum, 1985). In a Florida guardianship study, for instance, incompetency was established by the psychiatric evaluations of physicians on examining committees (Peters, Schmidt, & Miller, 1985). About 90% of these reports lacked evidence about specific behaviors.

Because causal link statutes offer only vague standards for incompetency, they give the judge wide discretion in deciding what evidence is admissible. In turn, broad judicial discretion gives rise to the likelihood of different outcomes of incompetency determinations for persons with similar disabilities who are adjudicated in the same jurisdiction. It also increases the likelihood of discrepant decisions by the same judge when hearing cases for persons with similar conditions. Moreover, individuals who fit into a statutory category but are capable of some degree of self-maintenance may still be forced into a plenary guardianship (see section titled "Alternatives to Full Guardianship"), rather than one limited to their specific disabilities.

Uniform Probate Code Approach

In an effort to escape the stigmatic labels of the traditional causal link statutes, the UPC approach uses the term *incapacity* and defines it as an impairment of cognitive and communicative abilities resulting from one of a number of mental or physical conditions. The operative wording for incapacity in UPC statutes is a person's lack of "sufficient understanding or capacity to make or communicate responsible decisions concerning his person" (*Uniform Probate Code*, 1993). Most state legislatures have made changes to their guardianship statutes by incorporating this language. For example, the Alabama guardianship statute states:

Incapacitated person. Any person who is impaired by reason of mental illness, mental deficiency, physical illness or disability, physical or mental infirmities accompanying advanced age, chronic use of drugs, chronic intoxication, or other cause (except minority) to the extent of lacking sufficient understanding or capacity to make or communicate responsible decisions. (*Ala. Code*, 1991)

This legislative desire to measure incapacity by the impairment of cognitive processes does not alleviate many of the problems with the causal link approach. UPC statutes perpetuate the use of causal categories and give the court too much discretion because the key cognitive processes

on which they focus (that is, understanding or capacity to make or communicate responsible decisions) remain vague. In addition, although the UPC emphasizes the person's ability to make decisions, it allows the court to discount that ability if the decisions are not deemed responsible (*In re Boyer*, 1981). The UPC standard fails to distinguish the capacity to make a decision, albeit a foolish one from some people's perspective, from the capacity to make a socially or morally responsible decision. Thus, the court's finding of incapacity continues to turn on its own values, rather than on functional deficiencies. Finally, courts in UPC jurisdictions may seldom have sufficient information about the proposed ward's conduct to make an objective determination about the proposed ward's decision-making abilities. Unless the judge asks specific questions about the proposed ward's conduct, objective information about the person's ability to make decisions may not be considered (Pleak & Appelbaum, 1985). For these reasons, judicial inconsistencies may continue to plague guardianship proceedings. The UPC modification may thus have gained little ground over the causal link approach to ensure that determinations of incapacity have a sound, objective basis.

Functional Approach

The functional approach represents the most recent innovation in guardianship standards (Nolan, 1984). It requires that the court look at objective behavioral evidence of functional limitations in the person's daily activities when determining an individual's need for assistance. These statutes list specific activities, such as securing food, clothing, and health care for oneself. Courts will thereby have useful guidelines for determining when and how much assistance is needed to protect the individual from that person's incapacity, without imposing unnecessary restrictions on the individual's autonomy.

The functional approach is familiar and useful to mental health professionals because it focuses on behavioral objectives in the care and treatment of people with mental and physical disabilities (Nolan, 1984). Nolan has argued that the functional approach can aid judicial decision making by referring to the same objective criteria used by geriatric nurses, social workers, psychologists, physicians, and related health workers to evaluate patients with mental, physical, and social disabilities. This information is expected to help the court in deciding when and to what degree intervention is called for.

A growing number of states have adopted the functional approach. The New Hampshire code, for example, defines *functional limitations* as

behavior or conditions . . . which impair [one's] ability to participate in and perform minimal activities of daily living that secure and maintain proper food, clothing, shelter, health care or safety for himself or herself. . . .

"Incapacity" means legal, not medical, disability and shall be measured by functional limitations. . . . Inability to provide for personal needs or to manage property shall be evidenced by acts or occurrences, or statements which strongly indicate imminent acts or occurrences. (*N.H. Rev. Stat. Ann.*, 1992)

The statute also discusses the minimum frequency and duration of the observed limitations that demonstrate the need for guardianship. Functional statutes use the term *incapacity* instead of *incompetency*, in part to avoid the stigma of the latter term.

It has been argued that legislatures should write statutes that not only require evidence of functional deficits, but that also mandate prehearing standardized functional evaluations (Tor, 1993). These assessments can provide the court with objective information about the nature and extent of the person's deficits before a hearing takes place. Both requirements would serve to screen out petitions that do not present a prima facie case worthy of judicial consideration, bring consistency to the determinations of legal incapacity, and create a more accurate and fair adjudicatory process.

When a guardianship petition presents a prima facie case for incompetency, the court

should order a formal evaluation, which should generally include systematic observations of the prospective ward's behavior, ideally in the ward's normal environment, so that the behavior can be measured against normative levels of competent behaviors. The court can appoint a mental health professional or a "visitor" (that is, a trained layperson) to make and record observations of the proposed ward in the natural milieu. To ensure that no conflict of interest will taint the results of the evaluation, funding for these evaluations should be provided by public sources, rather than by either party.

Because functional statutes provide objective criteria of incapacity, standardized assessment instruments can be developed for routine evaluations of proposed wards. These instruments can aid the court in achieving greater certainty in its legal determination, guarantee equivalent treatment from the court of all proposed wards, and reduce evaluation costs (Grisso, 1986; Schmidt, 1984).

A legitimate concern with mandating functional assessments is the intrusion into the prospective ward's privacy (Nolan, 1984). Considering the legal and civil rights a proposed ward stands to lose if found legally incapacitated, however, the temporary invasion of privacy is not an unreasonable inconvenience to ensure an accurate judicial outcome. The law also reaches this result by ruling that a judge may order a psychological examination of a person when his or her mental condition is at issue (for example, *Fed. R. Civ. P.*, 1992).

Due Process in Guardianship Proceedings

Due process protections also should be used to ensure that the person who is the subject of a guardianship petition is fairly treated during the proceeding. Indeed, due process protections are provided in the law whenever a person faces the loss of liberty or civil rights. For example, most states require proof by clear and convincing evidence of the proposed ward's incompetence or incapacity (Tor, 1993). This is a higher standard of proof than the preponderance-of-the-evidence standard typically used in civil cases, but lower than the beyond-a-reasonable-doubt standard used in criminal cases. Therefore, a person may arguably have greater protection against an incorrect finding of incompetency or incapacity (hereafter incompetency) than he or she would have in most other civil actions.

The importance of due process rights cannot be overemphasized in guardianship proceedings because proposed wards are even more susceptible to abuses or violations of their civil rights than defendants in other kinds of civil actions. Perhaps because courts place so much confidence in a physician's undocumented opinions, most proposed wards, particularly the elderly (*Guardians of the Elderly*, 1987), are perceived to be incompetent even before the guardianship hearing begins (see generally, Sales & Kahle, 1980). This perception leads to a relaxation of important procedural rights, including the right to notice, an indigent's right to appointed legal counsel, and the right to be present at one's hearing to confront the allegations of incompetency. Some critics note a paternalistic attitude among courts toward guardianship subjects (see generally, Griffith, 1991; Mitchell, 1979). Instead of conducting an impartial hearing, courts may tend to look out for what they believe to serve the best interests of the proposed ward. The result may be that some persons are being subjected to unnecessary guardianships. Because of the importance of these issues, we will examine due process failures at each phase of the guardianship process next.

Preadjudication

Guardianship Petitions

Petitions for guardianship are typically motivated by the prospective ward's inability to manage personal affairs. Occasionally, however, an un-

seemly desire to control the prospective ward's estate may constitute the petitioner's true goal (see, for example, *Guardians of the Elderly*, 1987), or a family member or business partner may be interested in preserving property and not in protecting the welfare of the ward (Alexander & Lewin, 1972). The court has the duty to consider petitions based on legitimate concerns for the welfare of the incapacitated. The court should screen allegations of incompetency to determine if the pleading or petition contains a statement of the grounds on which a claim of incapacity is made (such as *Fed. R. Civ. P.* 8(a), 1992). As with any other pleading filed with the court, if the petition fails to make a prima facie case, the action should be subject to dismissal upon a motion for judgment on the pleadings (for example, *Fed. R. Civ. P.* 12(c), 1992). A pleading that simply restates the law's criteria should not be acceptable. For instance, a statement that the subject of the guardianship petition is incompetent to make rational decisions is a legal conclusion and should not be considered sufficient as a cause of action without further supporting facts.

By dismissing a petition that lacks particularity, the court can prevent an invalid claim from clogging up an already crowded docket. This is a particularly important concern. In the Associated Press study (*Guardians of the Elderly*, 1987), 2200 guardianship files from numerous jurisdictions throughout the United States were randomly sampled. Specific medical evidence supporting the allegations was found to be absent in 7 out of every 10 files. Instead, undocumented medical or psychological conclusions often formed the basis for the claim that the person was incompetent.

Unfortunately, without a statutory provision listing objective criteria for proving incapacity, a petition presenting a physician's conclusory opinions may be acceptable to the court. At best, the subject of the guardianship petition can only gainsay the physician's opinion about his or her own competence, and the court is unlikely to give much weight to the respondent's opinion because he or she has been described as incompetent by a "competency expert." Grisso (1986) emphasizes that "the difficulty courts have in making [competency] decisions, the prestige of the expert, and other factors can converge to give the expert's opinion considerable influence on the ultimate legal decision" (p. 10). Unless the proposed ward has a reasonably able attorney who can answer the petition with a pleading that points out that the petition does not state a valid legal claim, or who can present an expert to support the person's claim of competency, the defendant is not likely to have the petition dismissed by the court. A requirement for a statement of particularized behavioral facts in the petition should make it clear to the proposed ward how to mount a challenge to the proposed guardianship.

Research has found that courts seldom dismiss cases that do not provide enough evidentiary explanation to make a prima facie case (Peters et al., 1985). Courts may sometimes grant guardianship petitions because the defense attorneys do not zealously defend their clients in their answers. This result can occur because of ignorance and misperceptions about their client's condition (see the subsection titled "Adjudication" for further discussion in this regard). Judges, like attorneys, also may suffer from ignorance and misperceptions about incompetency and may rely too much on medical opinion. State bars should make available materials to educate judges and lawyers about both the legal meaning of incompetency and about appropriate evidence to prove its existence. A better-informed bar and judiciary may result in fairer and more expedient disposals of specious guardianship petitions.

Notice

Once a petition is filed, due process requires that notice be served on a party in any civil action (see, for example, *Fed. R. Civ. P.*, Rules 4 and 5, 1992). Its purpose is to inform the party that an action involving that party's interest has been taken. Good notice provides the party sufficient information about the action, and his or her rights in regard to that action, to allow the person a reasonable opportunity to prepare and present an adequate defense. If a proposed ward is not apprised of this information and the meaning of the proposed guardianship, the ward may not be motivated to seek legal and other expert assistance.

Studies reveal that notice to a prospective ward may often be deficient (*Guardians of the Elderly*, 1987; Peters et al., 1985). Although most prospective wards are given some form of notice about an impending hearing (*Guardians of the Elderly*, 1987), several problems with notification have become evident. One is that in many jurisdictions the language of the notice is too legalistic, with the result that ordinary citizens have difficulty understanding it. In addition, the notice is often served by mail or by deputies without further explanation to the individual about his or her rights as a potential ward. And the particular basis for or implications of the guardianship hearing may not be set forth in the notice.

At the time that data were collected by the Associated Press study, only 14 states required that notification of an impending guardianship proceeding include information about proposed wards' rights to oppose the petition and the rights they stand to lose (*Guardians of the Elderly*, 1987). Furthermore, the study reported instances where a ward discovered after the fact that a guardian had been appointed to make decisions on his or her behalf. Individuals who became wards were sometimes not even aware that a hearing had taken place.

Another notice problem arises when a prospective ward does not have much time to prepare for a hearing. In 29% of the cases in one study, the proposed ward was notified one week or less before a scheduled hearing (Peters et al., 1985). Considering the seriousness of the rights and liberty interest at stake, it is doubtful that one week is a reasonable amount of time for a person to prepare an adequate defense to challenge an unwanted guardianship.

Some courts have taken measures to ensure that adequate notice is given. For example, one appellate court (*In re Bouchant*, 1974) voided a guardianship for lack of notice to the ward. Since

1987 at least 17 states are reported to have modified their notice requirement (McCue, 1992). Important changes in notice requirements include more advanced notification of the appointment hearing, and the use of simpler language and large type to spell out the purpose and seriousness of the matter and to explain the defendant's rights. How proposed wards respond to these stricter notice requirements, and whether a clear explanation of the potential impact of guardianship on that individual triggers self-protective behaviors and produces fairer hearings, needs to be examined.

Legal Representation

In preparing a defense, legal representation is essential and should be required in order to put the prospective ward on a level playing field with the petitioner and the court. Apart from informing the client about his or her rights and obligations, legal counsel can advise the client about the petition and implement legal strategies to respond to it. When petitions are prepared by nonlawyers, they are less likely to contain relevant evidence or make legally meaningful statements concerning an individual's competence. An attorney for the proposed ward can then move for dismissal of the petition by bringing to the attention of the court the failure of the petition to establish a prima facie case of incompetency.

Despite the indispensable need for the services of counsel, legal representation has been absent during the guardianship hearing in the majority of the cases (*Guardians of the Elderly*, 1987). In a Pennsylvania study where 27 guardianship hearings were observed, legal counsel was absent in all 27 cases (Pleak & Appelbaum, 1985). In many cases, prospective wards do not seek out formal counsel (Bulcroft, Kielkopf, & Tripp, 1991), and even where they do, they may not always get it (Friedman & Savage, 1988). In some states, for example, legal representation is not mandatory, and in others, court-appointed counsel is at the discretion of the judge (*Guardians of the Elderly*, 1987).

At least 35 states, however, have adopted legislation providing for the right to an attorney to represent the person or the right to a guardian ad litem to act as advocate for the individual's best interests (McCue, 1992). Yet, by statute or court practice, the function of court-appointed attorney or guardian ad litem may be to investigate for the court the proposed ward's condition and need for a guardian (Iris, 1988), rather than to carry out or advocate the proposed ward's desires. Whether the person who is supposed to represent the interests of the proposed ward should do so as an advocate or as a court investigator is subject to dispute (see Parry, 1988). In addition, some court functionaries reportedly doubt that attorneys have a useful role in guardianship proceedings (Friedman & Savage, 1988). We will examine the roles of the attorney and the guardian ad litem further in the next subsection.

Adjudication

In addition to preadjudication problems, several factors during the adjudicatory phase of the process work to ensure the petitioner's success. Research has shown that the ward is likely to be absent from the hearing, to have no legal representation, to voice no protest to the appointment of a particular guardian or any guardian, to have a plenary guardian appointed even where a limited guardian (one who has specified and limited power to make decisions on behalf of the ward) might be more appropriate, and to have little relevant information about his or her functional capacities presented at the hearing. We will discuss this research in detail.

Attendance at Hearing

A proposed ward's attendance at the hearing depends on some factors beyond the control of the court. For instance, the individual may be comatose or too disabled to attend. Of the 2200 case reports examined by the Associated Press (*Guardians of the Elderly*, 1987), only 8% indicated that elderly wards attended their hearings.

Other studies confirm a high rate of nonattendance by proposed wards (Friedman & Savage, 1988; Pleak & Appelbaum, 1985; Schmidt, 1981). Not all the absences are due to infirmity, however. As already noted, the individual may not attend because he or she has not received notice or is not encouraged or required to do so by the court. For example, one elderly ward discovered that she was under the protection of a guardian only when she was turned away from a polling booth (*Guardians of the Elderly*, 1987).

One danger in not attending is that the court may conclude that the ward is unable to attend because of an incapacitating condition. This in turn may support an assumption of incompetence merely because the court is deprived of an opportunity to directly observe the proposed ward before passing judgment on that person's competency. McCrary and Walman (1990) describe a typical case where affidavits from physicians concerning a hospitalized patient formed the sole basis of a judge's finding of incompetency. In addition, the proposed ward who fails to show up may be deprived of an opportunity to contest the proceeding or to demonstrate to the court that less than a plenary guardian (the decision-making authority on all facets of the ward's life) would suffice.

Objections

However, even when they do attend their hearings, prospective wards seldom raise objections or contest the hearing (Bulcroft et al., 1991; Friedman & Savage, 1988). One study found that objections to the guardian or guardianship were raised in only 6 of the 63 cases reviewed (Bulcroft et al., 1991). In a California study where 178 guardianship cases were examined, 23 of the proposed wards objected to the guardianship or some aspect of it, but only 2 filed formal objections (Friedman & Savage, 1988). Of all the cases considered in these two studies, only one resulted in a denial of guardianship, and that was because the court lacked jurisdiction to hear the case.

Legal Representation

These findings may not be surprising given the paucity of legal representation for prospective wards. Research findings indicate that only 16% (Friedman & Savage, 1988) to 44% (*Guardians of the Elderly*, 1987) of proposed wards are represented by legal counsel during the guardianship process. This is particularly unfortunate because of the importance of legal representation to an individual facing the prospect of losing his or her autonomy. Without legal representation, proposed wards seldom know or learn how to lodge formal objections that are recognizable by the court (Friedman & Savage, 1988); are unable to raise legally valid objections, such as the court's lack of jurisdiction; are unfamiliar with the many specialized issues of law that arise in controversies; and may be unable to understand the allegations, the impact of a judicial determination, what his or her rights are, and what rights he or she may lose. Ironically, as already noted, not all states provide a guarantee of counsel. How the absence of legal counsel affects the guardianship process needs to be studied.

One important reason for the proposed ward to have legal counsel at a guardianship hearing is to help restrain the court's tendency to grant plenary powers to the guardian. Plenary guardianship is almost always granted (Bulcroft et al., 1991; Peters et al., 1985), even though all states have provisions for less restrictive arrangements. There is reason to believe that even where limited guardianship would fulfill the needs of the proposed ward, too few limited guardianship arrangements are ordered. As Friedman & Savage (1988) found, judges are far more likely to expand the authority of a guardian than to augment the rights of a ward. In only one case these authors studied did the court use its discretion to expand the ward's rights, notwithstanding the ability of about 60% of the wards to make "intelligible" responses to questions. Without clear statutory guidelines to define behavioral criteria for incompetency, without better documentation of the proposed ward's deficiencies and needs, and without mandatory legal representation for the ward, it is not surprising that judges seldom recognize the need for limited guardianship arrangements (see the section on "Alternatives to Full Guardianship" for further discussion of this issue).

Despite the importance of legal representation, ironically, attorneys do not always advocate for their alleged incompetent clients. For example, data indicate that attorneys who represent psychiatric patients at civil commitment hearings do not employ strong advocacy techniques to challenge the credibility of expert witnesses testifying on behalf of the petitioning party (Poythress, 1978). This result occurred even when the defense attorneys were trained in the use of vigorous cross-examination techniques and were provided with substantive materials about the limits of psychiatric expertise that could be useful in their cross-examinations. Though it would be wrong to conclude from this one study that training lawyers to be better advocates at guardianship hearings is futile, it may be safe to say that lawyers do not instinctively advocate for clients who have been branded with a psychiatric or psychological diagnosis before the hearing. The reasons for this lack of client support are not clear. Attorneys may either be ignorant or harbor negative attitudes about incompetency, which in turn may cause them to misperceive their role and impair their ability to advocate for their clients. In addition, attorneys may be ignorant of or insensitive to the desires of their client and may instead act on what they believe is in the best interests of the client and other related parties (such as the family).

Guardian ad Litem

At least 35 jurisdictions have guardianship laws providing for the appointment of a *guardian ad litem* (McCue, 1992), someone to protect the interests of the proposed ward in this hearing. Some states require only that a *guardian ad litem* be appointed to protect the interests of the proposed ward. This is problematic where the

guardian ad litem is related to the ward, is not a lawyer, is not trained to represent the ward's legal interests, or is unprepared for the vigorous advocacy expected of a lawyer (Massad & Sales, 1981). Even their statutory responsibilities may not always be clear, because they can serve as an advocate, surrogate decision maker, or court investigator for the proposed ward. According to a study of guardianship proceedings in Washington State, for example, the courts assumed that the function of an attorney *guardian ad litem* is "to investigate the accuracy of the testimony filed concerning the alleged incompetency," rather than to advocate for a finding of competency (Bulcroft et al., 1991, p. 157). One investigation into the decision-making process of elder guardianship in Illinois, on the other hand, shows that the *guardian ad litem* investigates the proposed ward's need for guardianship and can recommend to the court a plenary guardianship, notwithstanding opposition by the proposed ward (Iris, 1988). Statutory or judicial guidelines are obviously needed to establish the role and duties of the *guardian ad litem*, and these guidelines should be made explicitly clear to the person serving in that role.

Evidence

Guardianship proceedings usually fall within the jurisdiction of a probate court, which sits without a jury. The judge is therefore the trier of fact as well as the interpreter of the law in the case. To the extent that a subject of a guardianship petition is not being properly represented, the judge has the authority to seek further information. Yet one study reports that "[n]either attorneys nor judges challenged the nominal or explicit evidence presented in support of incompetency petitions or the similarly terse medical diagnoses submitted by examining committees in support of incompetency rulings" (Peters et al., 1985, p. 537). This finding points to the need for statutes to specify the kinds of evidence courts should require when incompetency is at issue.

Postadjudication

Guardianship Plan

Although most states have laws that require periodic reviews (typically annually) of the guardianship and the status of the ward, only a few states have guardianship statutes that require the guardian to prepare a prospective plan for the care of the ward or estate or both (Hurme, 1991). A guardianship plan is needed to set a baseline against which to judge the progress of the ward and the performance of the guardian, and to set goals for both to reach (Hurme, 1991). Until courts monitor the design and implementation of individual guardianship plans, wards will not be fully protected against neglectful or abusive practices, nor are they likely to receive the appropriate habilitative or rehabilitative services that they require.

Termination of Guardianship

Most states provide for the termination of a guardianship when competency is restored (Hurme, 1991). Unfortunately, without specific observable indications of incompetency recorded in the ward's file, the reviewing court will have few facts about the ward's initial functional deficits with which to compare the ward's current condition. Other factors that may play a role in a termination hearing include a presumption of incompetence (for example, *In re Guardianship of Walters*, 1951), judicial bias and overbroad discretion (see Mitchell, 1979), and the absence of legal representation. In addition, depending on who must pay for legal counsel to initiate a termination proceeding and to represent the ward at the hearing, indigent wards may have little chance of ever reclaiming their legal rights.

Finally, the fact that the courts monitor so few guardianship arrangements makes restoration of rights difficult for the ward. The Associated Press study (*Guardians of the Elderly*, 1987) indicated that only 16% of the files contained annual reports of the ward's posttrial condition,

with information concerning the ward's physical and financial condition seldom being up to date (Schmidt, 1984). Thus, it is not surprising that in a study of 200 wards with public guardians,[1] competency was restored to only four (Schmidt, 1984); it is possible that these few cases were the only ones with up-to-date status reports in their files (see the section "Monitoring and Enforcement of Guardianships" for more discussion of this issue).

Alternatives to Full Guardianship

As noted at the beginning of this chapter, there are several sound public policy reasons for promoting the least restrictive form of guardianship: limited guardianship. Thus, "there should be statutory specification of decisional standards and dispositional alternatives to assure factually sound decisions and consequences for the respondent, which are no more limiting of personal responsibility and authority than necessary to remediate or compensate for proven disabilities" (Axilbund, 1979, p. 13). These recommendations have been incorporated in a widely cited model statute on guardianship (Sales et al., 1982).

Over the past decade, state legislatures have given the courts greater latitude in limiting the role of the guardian, with the legal distinction between plenary and limited guardianship being well entrenched today (McCue, 1992; Parry & Hurme, 1991). For instance, some states limit the scope of the guardian's decision-making power to no more than is justified by the ward's actual limitations (as an example, see *Cal. Prob. Code*,

---

[1]Public entities serve in the guardian role in situations where there are no private individuals or entities that are qualified, able, and willing to serve (Sales et al., 1982).

1991). A few states achieve the effect of limited guardianship by relying on the least-restrictive-alternative principle—that is, they tailor the duties and powers of the plenary guardian to the needs of the ward in the least-restrictive manner (Parry & Hurme, 1991).

Although, ideally, the level of guardian assistance should be matched to the ward's disability, this may be difficult to achieve. Even in jurisdictions where limited guardianship laws had been on the books for over a decade, a limited guardianship is seldom granted (Axilbund, 1979; Friedman & Savage, 1988; Peters et al., 1985). For example, in a report on the implementation of a limited guardianship law in Washington State, Axilbund (1979) noted that the number of guardianship petitions filed in the most populated county rose by more than a third in the first three years after the law was adopted. However, only about 10% of the guardianship filings in the same county resulted in limited guardianship. Limited guardianship was estimated to be less frequently employed statewide.

The reluctance of courts to recognize or consider limited assistance as an available and appropriate alternative to plenary control may come from numerous sources. First, a thorough diagnostic examination of the guardianship petition subject is needed to determine whether a guardianship is warranted and to pinpoint how limited the guardianship should be. Yet assessments in guardianship cases are typically undocumented and lack standardization (Bulcroft et al., 1991; Peters et al., 1985; Pleak & Appelbaum, 1985). Second, comprehensive reports to the court reviewing the methods, findings, and conclusions of the assessments are needed. Unfortunately, as already noted, these reports often present conclusory diagnoses rather than objective behavioral information (for example, Pleak & Appelbaum, 1985). Without a detailed appraisal of the ward's condition, the judge will not usually have enough information about a ward's functional disabilities to determine that the appointment of a limited rather than a plenary guardian would be in the ward's best interest

(Bulcroft et al., 1991). Third, statutes are not always clear on what constitutes grounds for limited guardianship. Vague standards of incompetence may leave the court mystified about what constitutes partial incompetence and uncertain about when a limited guardianship is appropriate. Fourth, courts may not consider alternatives to plenary guardianship because petitioners or guardianship subjects are not aware of them, because of the extra time it adds to guardianship hearings, or because of the inadequacy of legal representation. Fifth, although almost all jurisdictions have the option of granting a limited guardian to a potential ward, not all states mandate that the judge consider a limited guardianship before ordering a plenary one (Parry & Hurme, 1991). Sixth, there may not be sufficient judicial resources available to allow for full consideration of the case. With the size of our elderly population growing, many courts have undoubtedly experienced a dramatic increase in guardianship filings—but without a concomitant increase in court personnel to handle them (see, for example, Hurme, 1991). For instance, only one judge, one commissioner, one probate counselor, and seven administrative personnel were available to handle the 389 petitions filed in 1988 in Pima County, Arizona. Adding to the strain on the court's attention to these cases, these workers had duties other than those associated with guardianship petitions. Forced by constraints on time and money, guardianship hearings may last no more than three minutes if not contested (Dvorchak, 1987; *Guardians of the Elderly*, 1987), giving the court insufficient time to determine whether a guardianship is warranted and how limited it should be. Seventh, even if a limited guardianship is warranted, an appropriate guardian may not be available (Schmidt & Peters, 1987). And even if one is found, there may be pressures on the guardian to want a plenary guardianship. The policies and practices of some convalescent homes are to reject prospective residents unless they have been declared totally incompetent (Friedman & Savage, 1988). Finally, those responsible for implementing guardianship may hold the attitude that disabled adults are totally incapacitated (Mesibov, Conover, & Saur, 1980).

An underlying assumption of this discussion is that a limited guardian is an attractive alternative for the ward. However, this may not always be the case; "the least restrictive alternative does not direct the court to insist that the intervenor better the ward's situation by taking positive steps to improve the ward's health, restore or enhance her mental powers, make her subjectively happier, or at least prevent further . . . deterioration" (Rein, 1992, pp. 1882–1883). Factors such as the following can make a limited guardianship more onerous to the ward than a plenary guardianship: the availability of and access to needed services that would otherwise be provided under a plenary guardianship, whether the ward's wishes and decisions are more likely to be carried out under limited arrangements, the duration of the imposed limits on autonomy under the two kinds of arrangements, and whether courts maintain interest in both kinds of guardianship to the same degree. In addition, the availability of limited guardianship may lead to the indiscriminate inclusion of prospective wards who would otherwise not have been considered candidates for guardianship. Massad and Sales (1981) give an example of this "net-widening" effect where parents were appointed guardians to "deprogram" their adult children, who were members of the Unification Church (*Katz v. Superior Court*, 1977). The large increase in guardianship filings in Washington State three years after limited guardian provisions were adopted (see Axilbund, 1979) may also be evidence of a net-widening effect.

Monitoring and Enforcement of Guardianships

A monitoring and enforcement scheme is needed to prevent neglect and abuse of wards and to guard against the opportunistic squandering of their property by others. Court investigators can play an active and independent fact-finding role in monitoring guardianships and in uncovering abuses by the guardian. All jurisdictions have monitoring statutes governing the review and enforcement of guardianship orders, although a minority of states leave the decision about whether to require a financial accounting and a personal status report on the ward to the discretion of the court (Parry & Hurme, 1991). Despite the enactment of statutes that require periodic reports, in over a third of the jurisdictions, no court action was taken when guardians failed to file the requisite materials (Parry & Hurme, 1991). In a few jurisdictions, no one noticed when they were filed. Based on the results of their survey, Parry and Hurme (1991) conclude that compliance with and enforcement of the monitoring statutes are seriously lacking in many jurisdictions and are sometimes drastically inconsistent across counties within the same state.

One cause of this problem may be court personnel untrained in guardianship matters. Since compliance with the monitoring statute is generally enforced through the courts, if key court personnel are unaware of the monitoring requirements, of guardian reporting requirements, of court-imposed limits on the guardian's role, or of guardians' practices in the jurisdiction, there will be no enforcement. As evidence of this fact, a survey of persons actively involved in the implementation of guardianship—including judges, court personnel, attorneys, and public and private guardians—revealed that they were not always aware of the monitoring requirements of their jurisdictions (Hurme, 1991). If judges are not aware of or do not enforce state mandates for accountability, then who will?

Court participation in overseeing guardianship arrangements is essential to the delivery of quality services and eradication of abusive practices by guardians. Court personnel and judges may need training to learn what the legal requirements for guardians are and to interpret their status reports. Programs that also educate judges and court personnel on the significance of regular monitoring in spotting abusive practices might encourage the courts to impose sanctions for improper guardian conduct. These programs should include information on disabilities and their impact on wards' behavior, financial planning for wards, and the available services to help both the ward and the guardian.

Alternatively, the monitoring function can be assigned to nonjudicial personnel. For example, courts might employ social workers, paralegals, or community boards to assume the responsibilities of advising and evaluating guardians in helping courts meet their statutory duty of review (Peters et al., 1985). And a majority of the states have visitor programs in which a "visitor" meets periodically with the ward to evaluate the ward's well-being and the continuing need for a guardian (McCue, 1992; Parry & Hurme, 1991). Visitors may be attorneys, government employees, or community volunteers. While a visitor's primary function may be to regularly meet with the ward and evaluate his or her well-being, a visitor may also be used to "investigate complaints, track missing reports, and recommend alternatives to continued guardianship or less restrictive placements" (Parry & Hurme, 1991).

Changing some features of guardianship laws may also enhance enforcement and compliance rates. As already noted, the guardian should be required to submit a plan for the upcoming year describing how the ward will be cared for, and statutes should provide guidelines for the contents of periodic status reports (Hurme, 1991). Periodic reports provide a source of data for answering questions about the ward's behavior and about the guardian's performance. In addition, requiring greater specificity in the guardianship plan and status reports should make the guardian aware of what the court or monitoring agency will be looking for in both the condition of the ward and the performance of the guardian; in the absence of guardian guidelines, the newly appointed guardian may proceed on his or her own instincts, whims, sympathies, and prejudices. Reports should ask for financial, medical, and behavioral information about the ward in a structured or semistructured format. Unstructured reports or reports that are lengthy or complicated may encourage guardians to avoid preparing them.

Guardians can obviously assist the court in its monitoring function, their timely reports providing the needed information to help the court carry out its work more routinely and smoothly. Thus, guardians should be trained in what the law requires of them and in how to prepare a periodic report. Requiring guardians to attend a class to learn about periodic filing requirements and how to fill out status reports will not only increase their awareness of the statutory requirements, but it may also make them more sensitive to the specialized needs of their charges.

It is important to distinguish a guardian's need to provide information to the court from the adequacy of those reports and the guardian's performance more generally. Assigning a public or private guardian the duty of evaluating his or her own performance creates a pernicious conflict of interest. This conflict is amplified for public guardians, who are responsible for many wards and thus have less time to provide comprehensive services to each one. In addition, if the public guardian is related to a service provider, the relationship may influence decisions regarding services for the ward. The solution, of course, is to stop the practice of asking persons who deliver guardianship services to evaluate both their own performance and their wards' progress. Instead, independent evaluators should be employed to assume these responsibilities.

Finally, the use of sanctions for monitoring violations by the guardian should be seriously considered. The law's specification of sanctions for violating the reporting requirements should encourage guardian compliance with the law and improve monitoring effectiveness. Although sanctions also may discourage some persons from service as private guardians, the loss should be compensated for by an increase in the quality of their service.

Moreover, significant improvements in the quality of care for wards should occur if guardianship laws and the courts require guardians to file guardianship plans for, and periodic status reports on, their wards, present clear statements to guardians about the reporting requirements, provide reporting forms, mandate training for guardians, implement procedures for notifying guardians when reports are due, and enforce timely filings. The laws and the courts should also establish review procedures and criteria for court personnel to evaluate the content of the guardians' reports, establish investigation procedures for suspect cases, hold periodic hearings on the need for continuing a guardianship, allocate state and local funding to carry out a meaningful monitoring program, establish practice and ethical guidelines for attorneys involved in guardianship cases, and motivate community involvement in local guardianship programs (see generally, Hurme, 1991).

Selection of Guardians

Perhaps the most important protection for wards is not procedural; rather, it is the selection of appropriate guardians. By making decisions for wards, guardians can directly and indirectly secure services that will ultimately make the guardianship therapeutic or antitherapeutic. Thus, the selection and qualifications of the guardians represent a critical issue.

But who are the guardians? According to the Associated Press study (*Guardians of the Elderly*, 1987), 70% of the guardians are family members of the ward, 25% are not, and 4% are of unknown relationship to the ward. Of the family-member guardians, 35% are children of the wards, 6% are spouses, 8% are siblings, and 20% are other relatives such as grandchildren or nieces or nephews. Attorneys (5%), friends (7%), agencies (7%), public guardians (2%), banks (4%), other (3%), and unknown (3%) comprise the non–

family-member guardians. A study of cases from two different states indicates that when family members are appointed as guardians, they are more likely to be male than female, possibly because of the emphasis on estate management (Bulcroft et al., 1991). Relative to the number of proposed elderly wards with spouses, few spouses file for guardianship. This is due to the fact that many of the spouses are themselves too frail or impaired to perform the caretaking functions of a guardian (Bulcroft et al., 1991).

As might be expected, wards of public guardians are generally poorer than those of private guardians (see Friedman & Savage, 1988; Schmidt, 1990). The correspondence between a ward's assets and the likelihood he or she will have a private guardian has not gone unnoticed:

Dependents institute proceedings to secure their needs. Co-owners of property find incompetency proceedings convenient ways to secure the sale of realty. Heirs institute actions to preserve their dwindling inheritances. Beneficiaries of trusts or estates seek incompetency as an expedient method of removing as trustee one who is managing the trust or estate in a manner adverse to their interests. All of these motives may be honest and without any intent to cheat . . . , but none of the proceedings are commenced to assist the debilitated. (Alexander & Lewin, 1972).

The inherent conflict of interest that can arise from these situations is sometimes avoided by the appointment of a disinterested third party as guardian. Moreover, opportunities for self-aggrandizement could be minimized by barring the petitioner from also being the appointed guardian.

When it comes to the appointment of a guardian, the ward probably rarely makes the choice. Support for this proposition comes from several researchers who have concluded that guardianship adjudications tend to favor the interests of the petitioner over those of the proposed ward (Bulcroft et al., 1991; Peters et al., 1985). In addition, though the ward may object to a particular guardian or to the guardianship itself, the court seldom hears these objections (Bulcroft et al., 1991). If the courts turn a deaf ear to the informally expressed desires of disabled persons, guardians may have little incentive outside of their own sense of ethical duty to listen and give their wards more than basic care. The qualifications, training, and goals of guardians are thus integral to the effectiveness of a humane guardianship program.

Formal training programs for private guardians are scarce, even though they are strongly recommended by professionals (American Bar Association, 1989) and other special interest groups (for example, the National Guardianship Association). The Florida legislature has responded to this need by enacting a statute providing for a mandatory eight hours of instruction covering "the guardian's duties and responsibilities, the ward's rights, local resources to aid the ward and the preparation of habilation plans, annual reports and financial accounts" (Hurme, 1991, p. 28). Other nonprofit sources have developed training handbooks, courses, and videotape materials.

Many wards are too poor and too disconnected from family to afford a private guardian. Public and corporate institutions have been set up to provide state-funded guardian services. The use of these types of guardians varies from state to state. Data taken from guardianship proceedings in Washington and Ohio indicate that 25% of the elderly wards are under public and corporate guardianship (Bulcroft et al., 1991). Nationwide, according to the Associated Press investigation (*Guardians of the Elderly*, 1987), only 2% of the wards have public guardians, although there may be a much greater need for them than is evidenced by this statistic (see, for example, Schmidt & Peters, 1987).

Although public and corporate guardians are needed, there are problems with them. Wards of these guardians receive little personal attention, are rarely granted limited guardianships, and receive only perfunctory review of their guardianship arrangements (Schmidt et al., 1981). Effective public guardianship programs should limit the number of wards assigned to a public guardian. In addition, opportunities for self-aggrandizement should be precluded; guardians should not have the right to provide services and the right to consent to these services on behalf of the ward.

Despite the great potential for conflicts of interest, the public guardian appears to be more beneficial to wards than no guardian at all (see Schmidt et al., 1988). In a climate of deinstitutionalization, public and corporate guardians are necessary to provide services to incapacitated individuals where private guardians are not available. Quality-of-care concerns—such as fostering consumer satisfaction among wards served by a public guardian, finding the maximum number of wards a single guardian can maintain while providing needed comfort and attention to the wards, and determining whether corporate programs can be run more efficiently or produce better consumer satisfaction than government-run programs—remain to be resolved.

Conclusion

Based on the foregoing analysis, we offer the following recommendations. First, statutes pertaining to incompetency should contain specific, narrow, and functional standards with objectively defined terms. Second, evidentiary requirements should be set forth in the statutes that govern guardianships. This should include the kind of evidence required to prove the person's functional incapacity. Such evidence should focus on the individual's ability to communicate, make decisions, accurately perceive ordinary life situations, and reach reasonable conclusions (Appelbaum & Grisso, 1988). Third, the burden of proof and persuasion, which should be on the petitioner, and the quantum of proof, preferably a clear and convincing standard, should also be prescribed by statute. Fourth, due process guarantees such as notice and the right to counsel should be expressly stated in the statute to remind the court and counsel of their duties to the defendant. Fifth, when a statute voids the effect of a person's act, such as a marriage, or prohibits the individual from exercising a specific right because of a prior finding of incompetency, the right should be abrogated only if the prior adjudication specifically addressed it. Courts would then be unable to make inappropriate, overly broad competency determinations. Sixth, and finally but perhaps most important, guardianships should not be viewed as custodial arrangements that operate as institutions without walls. Guardians should see themselves as responsible for helping their ward maintain a quality lifestyle and for gaining or regaining independence to the maximum extent possible. Only then will guardianship ultimately fulfill its therapeutic potential.

References

Ala. Code § 26-2A-20 (1991).

Alexander, G., & Lewin, T. (1972). *The aged and the need for surrogate management.* Syracuse, NY: Syracuse University Press.

American Bar Association (1989). Guardianship: An agenda for reform, recommendations of the National Guardianship Symposium and policy of the American Bar Association. *Mental and Physical Disabilities Law Reporter, 13,* 271–313.

Appelbaum, P. S., & Grisso, T. (1988). Assessing patients' capacities to consent to treatment. *New England Journal of Medicine, 319*(25), 1635–1638.

Axilbund, M. T. (1979). *Exercising judgment for the disabled.* Washington, DC: American Bar Association Commission on the Mentally Disabled.

In re Bouchant, 522 P.2d 1168 (Wash. App. 1974).

In re Boyer, 535 P.2d 1085 (Utah 1981).

Bulcroft, K., Kielkopf, M. R., & Tripp, K. (1991). Elderly wards and their legal guardians: Analysis of county probate records in Ohio and Washington. *Gerontologist, 31*(2), 156–164.

Cal. Prob. Code § 1801 (1991).

Dvorchak, B. (1987, September 25). Pennsylvania's law is ripe for abuse. *Los Angeles Daily Journal,* p. 6.

Fed. R. Civ. P. 35(a) (1992).

Friedman, L., & Savage, M. (1988). Taking care: The law of conservatorship in California. *Southern California Law Review, 61,* 273–290.

Griffith, D. B. (1991). The best interests standard: A comparison of the state's parens patriae authority and judicial oversight in best interests determinations for children and incompetent patients. *Issues in Law and Medicine, 7*(3), 283–338.

Grisso, T. (1986). *Evaluating competencies: Forensic assessments and instruments.* New York: Plenum.

Guardians of the elderly: An ailing system. (1987). (Associated Press Special Report: Many AP reporters investigated guardianship records and cases across the United States in a series of reports published in over 300 newspapers.)

In re Guardianship of Walters, 231 P.2d 473 (Cal. 1951).

Hurme, S. B. (1991). *Steps to enhance guardianship monitoring.* Washington, DC: American Bar Association Commission on the Mentally Disabled and Commission on Legal Problems of the Elderly.

Iris, M. A. (1988). Guardianship and the elderly: A multi-perspective view of the decision-making process. *Gerontologist, 28*(Suppl.), 39–45.

Katz v. Superior Court (1977), Ca. App. 3d 952, 141 Cal. Rptr 234.

Massad, P. M., & Sales, B. D. (1981). Guardianship: An acceptable alternative to institutionalization? *American Behavioral Scientist, 24,* 755–770.

McCrary, S. V., & Walman, A. T. (1990). Procedural paternalism in compentency determinations. *Law, Medicine, and Health Care, 18,* 108–113.

McCue, J. (1992, July). The states are acting to reform their guardianship statutes. *Trusts and Estates,* pp. 32–37.

Mesibov, G. B., Conover, B. S., & Saur, W. G. (1980). Limited guardianship laws and developmentally disabled adults: Needs and obstacles. *Mental Retardation, 18,* 221–226.

Minn. Stat. § 525.24 (1975).

Mitchell, A. M. (1979). Objects of our wisdom and our coercion: Involuntary guardianship for competents. *Southern California Law Review, 52,* 1405–1449.

N.H. Rev. Stat. Ann. § 464-1:2(VII) & (XI) (1992).

Nolan, B. S. (1984). Functional evaluation of the elderly in guardianship proceedings. *Law, Medicine, and Health Care, 12,* 210–218.

Parry, J. W. (1988). Selected recommendations from the National Guardianship Symposium at Wingspread. *Mental and Physical Disability Law Reporter, 12,* 398–406.

Parry, J. W., & Hurme, S. B. (1991). Guardianship monitoring and enforcement nationwide. *Mental and Physical Disability Law Reporter, 15*(3), 304–314.

Pecora, A. K. (1990). The constitutional right to court-appointed adversary counsel for defendants in guardianship proceedings. *Arkansas Law Review, 43,* 345–372.

Peters, R., Schmidt, W. C., Jr., & Miller, K. S. (1985). Guardianship of the elderly in Tallahassee, Florida. *Gerontologist, 25*(5), 532–538.

Pleak, R. R., & Appelbaum, P. S. (1985). The clinician's role in protecting patients' rights in guardianship proceedings. *Hospital and Community Psychiatry, 36*(1), 77–78.

Poythress, N. G. (1978). Psychiatric expertise in civil commitment: Training attorneys to cope with expert testimony. *Law and Human Behavior, 2*(1), 1–23.

Radcliffe, A. (1982). Guardianship of incapacitated adults in Utah. *Utah Law Review, 1982,* 427–443.

Rein, J. E. (1992). Preserving dignity and self-determination of the elderly in the face of competing interests and grim alternatives: A proposal for statutory refocus and reform. *George Washington Law Review, 60,* 1818–1887.

Sales, B. D., & Kahle, L. R. (1980). Law and attitudes toward the mentally ill. *International Journal of Law and Psychiatry, 3,* 391–403.

Sales, B. D., Powell, D. M., Van Duizend, R., & Associates. (1982). *Disabled persons and the law: State legislative issues.* New York: Plenum Press.

Schmidt, W. C., Jr. (1981). Guardianship of the elderly in Florida. *Florida Bar Journal, 55,* 189–195.

Schmidt, W. C., Jr. (1984). The evolution of a public guardianship program. *Journal of Psychiatry and Law, 12,* 349–372.

Schmidt, W. C., Jr. (1990). Quantitative information about the quality of the guardianship system: Toward the next generation of guardianship research. *Probate Law Journal, 10,* 61–80.

Schmidt, W. C., Jr., Miller, K. S., Bell, W., & New, E. (1981). *Public guardianship and the elderly.* Cambridge, MA: Ballinger.

Schmidt, W. C., Jr., Miller, K. S., Peters, R., & Loewenstein, C. (1988). A descriptive analysis of professional and volunteer programs for the delivery of public guardianship services. *Probate Law Journal, 8,* 125–156.

Schmidt, W. C., & Peters, R. (1987). Legal incompetents' need for guardians in Florida. *Bulletin of the American Academy of Psychiatry and Law, 15*(1), 69–83.

Tor, P. (1993). Finding incompetency in guardianship: Standardizing the process. *Arizona Law Review, 35*(3), 739–764.

Tor, P. B., & Sales, B. D. (1994). A social science perspective on the law of guardianship: Directions for improving the process and practice. *Law and Psychology Review, 18,* 1–41.

Uniform Probate Code § 5-103(7) (Supp. 1993).

11 ◼ The Impact of Law on the Delivery of Involuntary Mental Health Services

John Q. La Fond
Seattle University

During the late 19th and early 20th centuries, most states enacted involuntary civil commitment laws to provide care for individuals with mental illness who needed commitment but, because of their mental illness, could not recognize their need (Brakel, Parry, & Weiner, 1985). Progressive reformers had argued persuasively that public institutions could help many individuals with disabilities who previously had been left to fend for themselves. Hospitalization and treatment of people with mental illness, even without the patient's informed consent, were considered necessary to help a person in need (La Fond & Durham, 1992).

Between 1900 and 1940, the hospitalized population in mental health facilities in the United States increased from 150,000 to approximately 445,000 (Grob, 1983). By 1955, there were almost 819,000 inpatients in state and county mental hospitals in the United States (Kiesler & Sibulkin, 1987).

Over the last 30 years, however, the normative vision embodied in the American legal system regulating the delivery of involuntary mental health services has changed dramatically. During this period the law has sometimes emphasized the civil liberties of individuals; at other times it has emphasized community safety (Isaac & Armat, 1990; La Fond & Durham, 1992). Consequently, it is impossible to comprehend fully the impact law has had on these services and on the mental health professionals (MHPs) who provide them unless the discussion is placed in historical context.

The Liberal Era

Beginning in the early 1960s and extending to about 1980, American society experienced a tumultuous time of social change, with special emphasis on expanding civil rights, greater toleration for the disadvantaged, and a proclivity for social innovation and reform. The civil rights movement, buoyed by its earlier epic victory in *Brown v. Board of Education* (1954), which held that segregated school systems violated the Constitution's promise of equal protection, actively campaigned for the dismantling of lawfully ordered racial segregation, first in the South and then throughout America. Civil rights lawyers developed new theories and skills on behalf of other disadvantaged groups, including individuals with mental illness (Wyatt & Stickney, 1971). In the late 1960s, with the antiwar movement becoming more intense as America's involvement in the Vietnam War deepened, popular distrust of government increased. The large, impersonal bureaucracies of the modern state were seen as posing the greatest threat to individual liberties (Fiss, 1982).

Increasingly, courts acknowledged that gov-

219

ernment action intended to help individuals could actually harm them and that, despite good intentions, erroneous decisions were possible (*In re Gault*, 1972). To ensure fairness and to protect against inaccurate fact finding, courts interpreted due process requirements more broadly when government agencies made decisions that affected individual citizens, such as denying welfare benefits or revoking parole (*Goldberg v. Kelly*, 1970; *Morrisey v. Brewer*, 1972). These procedural due process rights often included written notice of proposed government action, the assistance of counsel, the opportunity to present evidence and to confront adverse witnesses, the right to appeal, and the right to periodic review.

A new judicial activism emerged. Judges, especially federal judges, embraced evolving theories of individual constitutional rights that limited governmental authority. Equally important, courts seemed willing to take steps intended to change the behavior of government agencies. The Supreme Court, under the leadership of Chief Justice Earl Warren, imposed new restraints on how the police investigated crimes and arrested criminal suspects. The Court constructed a new paradigm for criminal trials and juvenile delinquency hearings. It expanded the concept of "procedural due process" by conferring on defendants such rights as the assistance of counsel and the right to jury trials, and by placing higher burdens of proof on the government. In short, the contemporary due process paradigm emphasized the adversarial and accusatorial nature of fact finding that must occur before a citizen could be deprived of liberty. Persons with mental illness were among the beneficiaries of this due process explosion.

In the 1950s and 1960s, influential critiques cast doubt on the need for and wisdom of involuntary commitment. Radical psychiatrists like Thomas Szasz attacked the concept that mental illness should be considered a medical disease. Instead, he argued that mental illness was a social construct used by a powerful elite, namely psychiatrists, to impose unwanted and unnecessary control over those who simply had problems in

living (Laing, 1960; Szasz, 1974). Others claimed that confinement in institutions created a dependency on their structured environment, diminishing patients' ability to function in the outside world (Goffman, 1961). Civil rights attorneys used these critiques, along with powerful stories of individual clients abused by the public mental health system, to argue that citizens with mental illness needed special constitutional protection and that the law should regulate this system more aggressively (Ennis, 1972).

The popular culture reinforced a general skepticism about the motives and competence of MHPs, especially those who worked in the public mental health system. Books and films like *One Flew Over the Cuckoo's Nest* (1962) portrayed MHPs as abusive, power-hungry individuals who made a bad system even worse.

Fiscal conservatives joined forces with civil libertarians to reduce the number of individuals confined to large state hospitals. Many of these facilities were quite old and required extensive and costly renovation to meet the new, stricter accreditation standards. Burgeoning state populations would generate increased demand for involuntary commitment under lax commitment laws. To avoid additional state expenditures on expanding and upgrading these massive institutions, policymakers decided to decrease institutional populations by discharging large numbers of patients and enacting restrictive commitment laws to ensure that the new national policy of deinstitutionalization was maintained (Scull, 1984).

Involuntary Civil Commitment Law Reform

Federal courts were sympathetic to criticisms of the public mental health system. Judges became increasingly skeptical as to whether state involuntary commitment systems served constitutionally acceptable government goals and whether citizens facing commitment were provided with sufficient procedural protection. Courts were in the vanguard in this era of legal reform, issuing decisions that limited state authority to commit individuals with mental disorders and requiring generous due process protection for commitment ("Developments in the Law," 1974; La Fond, 1981).

Involuntary commitment came to be seen as state action that resulted in the loss of an individual's constitutionally protected right to liberty. It was no longer viewed as a "medical" decision to be made by a trained professional on behalf of one who, as a result of mental illness, could not make a competent decision based on self-interest. Rather, it was seen as a legal decision to be made by a neutral decision maker.

Grounds for Commitment

Because individual liberty was now characterized as a "fundamental interest"—an individual right accorded special status under the Constitution— civil rights activists persuaded courts that only a compelling state interest could justify the loss of liberty occasioned by commitment. Increasingly, courts ruled that this compelling interest could only be met if the government were seeking to prevent persons with mental illness from doing serious harm to themselves or others (La Fond, 1981). Consequently, many states changed their involuntary commitment laws to require a finding of mental illness and dangerousness to self or to others as the only grounds for commitment (La Fond, 1981). A number of states, either by statute or by court decision, required the government to present evidence of recent overt acts demonstrating that the individual was dangerous (Groethe, 1977). Often, this new generation of commitment laws also permitted hospitalization of individuals found "gravely disabled"—that is, unable as a result of mental illness to provide themselves with the basic necessities of life, including food, shelter, and clothing. Generally, commitment for treatment only was no longer permitted.

Procedural Protection

In addition to narrowing the substantive grounds for involuntary commitment, courts also required more procedural due process protection. Landmark decisions like *Lessard v. Schmidt* (1972) provided patients with mental illness subjected to involuntary civil commitment with most of the procedural rights held by criminal defendants in a criminal trial. Faced with the distinct possibility that court decisions would invalidate their involuntary commitment laws, many state legislatures made fundamental changes, adopting a legal model of civil commitment and providing patients facing involuntary hospitalization with generous due process rights, including the right to remain silent. Under these new statutes, judges or juries—not MHPs—made the commitment decision.

Least Restrictive Alternative

Moreover, a number of courts ruled that, under contemporary constitutional theory, the government must use the least drastic means available to accomplish the purposes of involuntary civil commitment, taking away no more liberty than was necessary. This led to the development of the *least-restrictive-alternative* doctrine, which required the state to avoid confining an individual in a state psychiatric facility if other placement in the community could adequately serve the purpose of commitment (Hoffman & Foust, 1977). Most state commitment laws were amended to specify that patients had a right to placement in the least restrictive alternative.

Restraints and Seclusion

Courts also ruled that involuntary commitment in a psychiatric facility did not extinguish patients' residual interest in liberty and safety (*Youngberg v. Romeo*, 1982). Within reasonable limits, patients still had the right to move around in the ward and to be protected against violence by other patients. Thus, a patient confined to a hospital could not be kept indefinitely in seclusion or in mechanical restraints. The use of these techniques had to be medically indicated; they could not be used simply for the convenience of the staff. Many states enacted statutes (often after lawsuits challenging their improper use) to ensure that restraints and seclusion were used appropriately and only for legitimate medical or security reasons (Brakel, Parry, & Weiner, 1985; *Davis v. Balson*, 1978; *Eckerhart v. Hensley*, 1979; *Rogers v. Okin*, 1979; *Wyatt v. Stickney*, 1972). In general, restraints and seclusion could be used only for a limited time and pursuant to a written order. Patients' conditions had to be charted at regular intervals, and any extension of their use must be authorized by a doctor and sometimes also reviewed by others (Brakel, Parry, & Weiner, 1985). Consequently, staff spent more time creating a written record documenting when and why they used these devices.

Right to Privacy

Committed patients were also accorded a right to privacy. Thus, for example, patients could visit with family or friends or talk to them on the telephone without their conversations being monitored (*Davis v. Watkins*, 1976). This right could be qualified, however. An MHP could impose reasonable restrictions in a written order specifying why the restrictions were necessary. In addition, virtually every state passed legislation generally prohibiting the disclosure of civilly committed patients' records, subject to very limited exceptions. Violation of these laws could result in stiff fines (Brakel, Parry, & Weiner, 1985). Thus, MHPs must not disclose any information relating to their committed patients unless authorized by law.

A basic assumption of this law reform was that privacy is important to everyone, including persons with mental illness. It appears that patients with mental illness who are confined in hospitals do value their privacy. In one study, a majority of patients, when interviewed, said that privacy was important to them (O'Reilly & Sales,

1987). Privacy may also have a therapeutic benefit by helping them to calm down and to develop their individuality. However, courts generally set only constitutionally mandated *minimum* standards of privacy. Consequently, these legal "floors" often become "ceilings" in practice. That is, public hospitals frequently complied with the literal terms of a court order to provide facilities that afford some personal privacy, but they seldom did any more than they were ordered to by the court.

Too often, courts focused almost exclusively on visual privacy, paying little or no attention to other intrusions on privacy, like excessive noise or noxious odors. Some astute commentators have urged state mental health departments to provide the degree of privacy that quality patient care demands rather than simply doing no more than required by law (O'Reilly & Sales, 1987). It is, therefore, not surprising that some evidence suggests that the *Wyatt* standards are insufficient to ensure that most patients in fact perceive themselves as having suitable overall privacy (O'Reilly & Sales, 1987). It is also likely that the physical conditions in many hospitals, though frequently improved as a result of legal intervention, in many instances still do not provide the optimal level of individual privacy and tranquillity that would facilitate the ability of MHPs to provide patients with the optimal level of treatment and care.

Forced Labor and Work Therapy Programs

For the last 30 years, the issue of whether or not patients should be compensated for labor performed while hospitalized, even in a work therapy program, has been in flux. In mental health hospitals, work therapy had traditionally been included in the treatment program because it was viewed as having therapeutic value for patients. Thus, it was not considered as employment that should be compensated (Safier, 1976). The law reflected this attitude. Before 1966, the Fair Labor Standards Act (FLSA) exempted from its coverage service establishments, including hospitals for persons with mental illness, so long as more than 50% of the establishment's sales were made in the state where it was located. In a 1966 amendment, Congress extended the FLSA to institutions engaged primarily in the "care of the sick, the aged, [or] the mentally ill or defective who reside on the premises of such institutions" (Fair Labor Standards Act, Amendments of 1966). The legislative history of these amendments, however, left unresolved whether Congress intended to extend coverage of the FLSA to patients in such institutions.

The 1973 federal court ruling in *Souder v. Brennan* forced a change in the older, traditional view. The court held that patients working in institutions for persons with mental illness and persons with developmental disabilities must be paid in accordance with the minimum wage and other provisions of the FLSA whenever they perform any activity that confers an economic benefit on the institution in which they reside. The court determined that the FLSA applied regardless of whether the activity has therapeutic value for the patient, or whether the work activity was undertaken in the interest of the patient or in the interest of the institution. In other words, a patient must be paid what he or she earns. Although the decision did not prohibit institutions from operating work programs, it did require states to pay patients for their work. Many states simply could not afford to pay. So far-reaching was the impact of the *Souder* decision that, within a year, a majority of states had either reduced or eliminated their patient work programs (Blaine, 1987).

In 1977, the U.S. Supreme Court declared that federal wage and hour laws did not apply to employees of state institutions, thereby limiting the jurisdiction of *Souder v. Brennan* to private hospitals (*National League of Cities v. Usery*, 1976). In doing so, the Court exempted the very type of institution against which the claim in *Souder* had originally been brought and where patient exploitation had been widely acknowledged to exist. However, in 1985, the *Usery*

decision itself was overturned by a 5 to 4 vote of the Supreme Court, with the probable effect of reinstating the *Souder* decision (even though there is continued speculation that the latest reversal may likewise be impermanent) (*Garcia v. San Antonio Metropolitan Transit Authority*, 1986).

What is not a debatable issue is the importance of work programs for institutionalized persons with mental illness (Blaine & Mason, 1986). Most MHPs consider work programs as having therapeutic value for at least some patients, and virtually all believe that such programs cannot be replaced by another type of activity (Blaine, 1987). Other evidence suggests that patients like structured work programs and recognize their benefits.

Because of the continuing uncertainty whether patients must be compensated for their labor, MHPs frequently find themselves unable to use work as an effective therapeutic tool in helping patients establish a greater sense of self-worth and in acquiring the skills they will need to lead self-sufficient lives after discharge. Some MHPs undoubtedly conclude that the law has needlessly (and even foolishly) constrained their ability to provide individuals with mental illness with the type of treatment virtually all MHPs would, in their professional judgment, consider most appropriate. Some might further assert that the law has actually undermined patients' right to treatment.

Civil Rights and Legal Authority

Contemporary laws also provided patients committed to public mental health facilities with extensive rights even while they were hospitalized. Unlike the approach used before the liberal era, involuntary commitment to a hospital was no longer seen as a judicial finding of general incompetence. Patients retained a wide range of civil rights and legal authority. For example, they had the right to communicate with individuals outside the hospital, including families and lawyers. Though these rights could be restricted for important reasons, patients could send and receive mail and read newspapers (Ennis & Siegel, 1973; Ferleger, 1973). Many states have also enacted laws guaranteeing patients the right to have their personal possessions with them (Brakel, Parry, & Weiner, 1985).

Commitment to a mental hospital did not extinguish the right to vote unless the person had been judicially determined to be incompetent. One study conducted in 1977 concluded that the hospitalized patient who has a mental illness is competent to vote and is capable of doing so in an informed and thoughtful manner (Howard & Anthony, 1977). The data indicated that hospitalized patients with mental illness vote much like their fellow citizens. Where the patients were exposed to information about candidates and issues, their vote reflected consideration of this information in casting their ballots. These facts also indicated that the patient vote was an independent one.

Patients were also accorded a constitutional right to practice their religion while institutionalized. Unfortunately, there has been very little research on the availability of religious services for patients or their access to clergy. Nor has there been any research concerning whether being able to practice their religion has had any impact on institutionalized patients with mental illness.

Summary

In sum, most states enacted restrictive civil commitment laws during the 1970s, severely limiting the authority of the state to hospitalize persons with mental illness involuntarily. Often, authority to commit individuals with mental illness was taken away from MHPs and given to judges or juries. Also, at specified intervals, MHPs had to persuade judges that committed individuals should be kept in hospitals. Lawyers representing patients had general access to their clients in the institutions where they were placed. This access, in turn, permitted lawyers to keep abreast of conditions in state mental health facilities, enabling them to seek legal redress. As a

result of such litigation, courts often issued injunctions preserving patients' civil rights and ordering hospitals to use restraints and seclusion only when medically appropriate, to compensate patient labor, to protect patient privacy, and to ensure patients' ability to exercise their other civil and legal rights. There was undoubtedly a wide range of reaction among MHPs to these legal developments. Some probably saw them as hindering their ability to control patients and to provide appropriate care and treatment. Others no doubt saw them as helpful in preserving patient self-esteem and in ensuring that patients retained important legal rights.

Duty to Prevent Harm

Not content with circumscribing the state's commitment authority, courts also began to impose legal accountability on how MHPs exercised their commitment authority. In a landmark case, *Tarasoff v. Regents of the University of California* (1976), the California Supreme Court imposed a legal duty on MHPs to take reasonable steps to prevent a patient whom they knew or should have known was mentally disturbed and dangerous from harming anyone. Though subsequent California case law limited the scope of the therapist's duty to readily identifiable victims (*Mavroudis v. Superior Court*, 1980; *Thompson v. County of Alameda*, 1980), courts in other states have imposed a general duty on MHPs to commit dangerous individuals if necessary to prevent harm to any member of the public, even those who could not be readily identified, because the possibility of harm toward *someone* should have been foreseen (*Petersen v. State*, 1983). Unless protected by statutory immunity, MHPs could be sued if they negligently failed to take reasonable measures to prevent such individuals from harming third persons.

Beginning in the late 1960s, lawyers also brought civil rights lawsuits on behalf of one or more involuntary patients seeking to enforce newly recognized constitutional rights. Many of these lawsuits sought to recover damages personally from MHPs for not providing adequate treatment; some sought personal damages for wrongful commitment to, and confinement in, psychiatric facilities. Many MHPs were unsettled by the prospect of personal financial liability, even though, in most cases, state laws provided immunity from such suits except for the most extreme cases of negligence (Brakel, Parry, & Weiner, 1985).

Impact of Liberal Reform on MHPs

During this era, MHPs found that they often lacked the legal authority to make important medical decisions on behalf of patients they considered mentally incompetent. MHPs could not hospitalize an individual with a serious mental illness whom they felt needed treatment but who refused hospitalization. Instead, judges and juries, who had no training in mental health, would make these decisions.

Moreover, patients had new and powerful advocates: lawyers. In the eyes of many MHPs, lawyers needlessly interfered with their attempts to establish a therapeutic doctor-patient relationship and instead spawned an adversary relationship that would not advance therapeutic goals. Though the evidence is mixed, it appears that lawyers generally discharged their responsibilities aggressively and, from their own professional perspective of furthering their clients' expressed preferences, successfully. Lawyers were generally made available to most patients, hearings lasted longer, and evidence offered in support of commitment was examined more carefully. Lawyers were more likely to challenge the opinions of MHPs and to seek alternative placement for their clients in lieu of hospitalization. Consequently, patients were more likely to be released in the face of recommendations for commitment by MHPs (Hiday, 1981, 1982; Miller & Fiddleman, 1983; Warren, 1977a, 1977b, 1982; Wenger & Fletcher, 1969).

These studies on the impact of revised commitment procedures and lawyer functioning furnish indirect but probative evidence that

MHPs, in turn, spent more time preparing for commitment hearings. It is fair to surmise that they spent more time interviewing patients and reviewing charts and that they also spent more time in court.

Many professionals felt that time spent preparing for and participating in legal proceedings was time lost from treating patients and was therefore wasteful of a scarce resource and not in their patients' best interests. In cross-examining MHPs, lawyers would often disparage their expertise, their professionalism, and even their motivation. Many MHPs, unused to the courtroom setting, felt less valued in this new era.

Processing a patient through the involuntary commitment process can indeed be time-consuming. There is evidence that, to minimize the time spent with individuals brought in for emergency commitment, some MHPs bartered with patients by promising them hospital privileges, like an off-grounds pass, in return for agreeing to voluntary admission. If that did not work, some MHPs apparently used threats to coerce patients into accepting admission on a voluntary basis. If necessary, they sought continuances in the judicial proceedings pursuant to the emergency commitment that would keep these individuals hospitalized until the MHPs felt the patients were ready to be discharged. Patients' lawyers, too, frequently urged their clients to accept voluntary admission (Reed & Lewis, 1990).

Often, lawyers actually negotiated with MHPs over placement of their clients and even over treatment regimes. It was not unusual for lawyers to secure placement in a less restrictive environment as a result of these negotiations or to secure physician agreement on what drugs would be prescribed for their clients. Many MHPs were not pleased with what some of them viewed as officious intrusion into their professional domain.

Even if judges agreed with their recommendations and committed patients with mental illness to hospitals, new court decisions imposed significant constitutional restraints on the authority of MHPs to provide the treatment they deemed medically appropriate. Indeed, these decisions often imposed what many MHPs considered hopelessly confusing, even conflicting, directives (Kapp, 1994). For example, patients had the right to receive treatment (*Rone v. Fireman*, 1979; *Wyatt v. Stickney*, 1971, 1972), yet they also had the right to refuse treatment (*Rennie v. Klein*, 1979; *Rogers v. Okin*, 1979).

This ambiguity imposed impossible demands on MHPs. They were required to take measures that offered patients a reasonable prospect of getting better (*Rouse v. Cameron*, 1966), while at the same time acquiescing in a disturbed patient's refusal to take the medications considered necessary for getting better (*Rogers v. Commissioner of the Department of Mental Health*, 1983). MHPs could also be personally sued if they failed to provide any treatment to patients committed for treatment (*O'Connor v. Donaldson*, 1975).

In addition, an emerging right-to-treatment doctrine generally required MHPs to prepare individual treatment plans for each involuntarily committed patient. To some, this simply meant being diverted from their treatment tasks to process paper rather than provide therapy.

The least restrictive alternative to commitment required MHPs to spend time finding placements for patients in nursing homes or other facilities. In some cases, commentators argued that states were required to create less restrictive placements if they did not already exist (Frug, 1978). Services outside hospitals for persons with mental illness involved MHPs in greater planning and oversight than did services provided in an institution.

Many observers predicted that the restrictive civil commitment laws limiting involuntary hospitalization to individuals with mental illness who were dangerous would leave only the most violent patients in hospitals. However, although the data available are not definitive, a number of researchers found that the behavior of patients committed as dangerous under the restrictive commitment laws did not in fact appear to be violent, assaultive, or threatening (Hiday, 1991; Peters, Miller, Schmidt, & Meeter, 1987; Warren, 1982). Thus,

these laws did not, after all, seem to expose MHPs to an especially dangerous patient population.

An intended consequence of narrow commitment laws was to limit the use of involuntary hospitalization and, after their enactment, admission rates decreased for at least two years. The decline was temporary, however, and admission rates soon reached or exceeded prereform levels (Bagby & Atkinson, 1988).

How, then, did public hospitals reduce their beds, close wards, or limit their patient censuses? Contrary to public opinion, hospitals did not close; the number of state mental hospitals has not varied much over the last three decades, even though there was a dramatic reduction in hospital patient population, mostly between 1965 and 1975. The average length of hospitalization, however, declined so significantly that institutions were able to reduce their average daily census by almost 80%. Thus, the size of the inpatient population served by MHPs in hospitals contracted substantially (Kiesler & Sibulkin, 1987).

Some MHPs felt that these restrictive laws prevented them from providing the long-term institutional treatment many patients with mental illness needed and that early discharge simply created a "revolving door" phenomenon in which patients returned because of inadequate treatment. This conclusion is misleading, however. The evidence indicates that the increase in commitment rates was due both to accelerating rates of first-time admissions and to rising readmission rates (Bagby, 1987; Faulkner, Bloom, & Kudndahl-Stanley, 1982; Lamb, Sorkin, & Zusman, 1981).

In addition, most mental health agencies eventually adopted policies of short-term hospitalization whenever possible in response to court rulings that patients have the "right to the least restrictive alternative to hospitalization." Furthermore, institutions must comply with accreditation agencies that limit the number of patients that may be treated in a given hospital at any one time. Given daily admissions, daily discharges are required to maintain the status quo (Reed & Lewis, 1990). It seems fair to conclude that, under these circumstances, MHPs began focusing primarily on crisis intervention and stabilization rather than on long-term treatment.

Mental Health Services in the Criminal Justice System

If MHPs found the new system unwieldy at times, police officers often found it unworkable. Suddenly, many more people with mental disorders were living in the community than before, but the dispositions available in the mental health system to an officer faced with an offender with a mental illness were restricted both by stringent commitment criteria and by scarce community-based resources. Commentators have argued that, as a consequence, arrest became the preferred strategy of police officers in dealing with individuals with mental illness (Abramson, 1972; Teplin, 1986; Teplin & Voit, 1994).

Studies of police interaction with individuals with mental illness showed that most of these individuals came into contact with officers because they needed assistance, not because they were suspected of committing a crime. However, when the individual's behavior clearly was outside the community's tolerance level but not sufficiently disturbed to warrant hospital evaluation, arrest was often the only available option (Teplin, 1986).

While police observation supports the criminalization hypothesis, it is not necessarily supported by other data. If jails are increasingly being used to contain individuals with mental illness, one would expect research to show that the incidence of mental illness is higher in the jail population than in the population as a whole and that it has increased since deinstitutionalization. Unfortunately, there are few longitudinal data, and the current data are flawed by small sample sizes and inconsistencies in sample selection and diagnostic criteria. Findings range from 16% of jail inmates having had any lifetime mental illness (Bolton, 1976) to approximately two-thirds of those surveyed (Teplin & Voit, 1994). Rates of severe mental illness (such as

schizophrenia or psychosis) in the general jail population varied from 5% to 12% (Teplin & Voit, 1994). And no one knows whether these numbers are higher or lower than they were 20 years ago.

Whether or not these numbers have increased due to deinstitutionalization, they demonstrate that jails play a major role in the mental health system. It is a role assumed reluctantly, to be sure. In 1972, the American Medical Association found that less than 3% of jails performed routine medical examinations at intake. Nearly 50% said they *never* gave a medical examination (Singer, 1982). Then, in 1976, the U.S. Supreme Court found that such deliberate indifference to inmates' medical needs constituted "cruel and unusual punishment" in contravention of the Eighth Amendment (*Estelle v. Gamble*, 1976). In 1980, a federal appellate court extended that principle to include failure to provide jail mental health services (*Inmates of Allegheny County v. Pierce*, 1979). What followed was a "deluge" of standard setting by medical and legal groups. In turn, inmate lawsuits seeking damages for attempted or actual suicide or seeking changes in the delivery of mental health services validated these standards (Singer, 1982; Steadman, McCarty, & Morrissey, 1989).

Increased awareness of mental health needs by correctional system administrators has led to new programs that seek to divert nonviolent offenders with a mental illness from jails to treatment programs, as well as to better serve the needs of persons with mental illness charged with more serious offenses. But here, as in civil commitment, a lack of resources limits the availability of appropriate services.

In 1991, researchers studied the mental health services connected with the King County Correctional Facility located in Seattle, Washington. They found that, even though a wide range of services were available for them, including a crisis intervention program, a central emergency room, a prebooking diversion program, a detox program, a jail mental health unit, and an aftercare case management service, persons with mental illness were, nonetheless, incarcerated for inappropriate periods of time (Policy Research Associates, 1991). The average length of stay in jail for such offenders was 34 days, compared to an average stay for all offenders of 11 days. The researchers found that police officers were often deterred from using the crisis intervention and prebook diversion programs because they were located away from the jail and took too much time and training to use. Thus, the jail was receiving inmates who would have been more appropriately placed in a community mental health program.

Once in jail, inmates had to wait their turn for attention from MHPs whose limited time was spent primarily on required assessment, treatment, and reporting, leaving little time for developing referral and linkage services that could speed the inmates' return to the community. Jail-based MHPs often could not even find out whether an inmate had received or was receiving community-based services prior to arrest. Psychiatric coverage was also found to be inadequate. Less than a quarter of all mental health unit admittees were seen by a psychiatrist. Only about half of those receiving psychotropic medication were seen. Despite its shortcomings, however, the King County program was seen as a model for jail-based mental health services because it was integrated with community-based programs.

If the model for jail mental health programs is to include better linkage between community and jail-based services, community MHPs must be willing to treat individuals referred to them by the correctional system. Jails and community providers will have to work together, rather than carefully delineating and defending their respective "turf." Some commentators have expressed concern that such linkage is made too difficult because the custody orientation of corrections professionals conflicts with the treatment orientation of MHPs. However, there is surprisingly little evidence of day-to-day conflict (Steadman et al., 1989). The MHP's goal of stabilizing inmates so that they are no longer a danger to themselves or others also enhances security for everyone.

The most effective mental health–criminal justice programs are characterized by the presence of at least one individual whose primary responsibility it is to manage the interaction of the staffs, or what Steadman (1992) has artfully termed a *boundary spanner*. One example might be a social worker working for a corrections department whose job is to move minor offenders quickly out of jail by working with the public defender and judges as well as with community-based MHPs. In the future, more MHPs will be needed to act as "boundary spanners" in a cooperative system, working to ensure the most appropriate placement of each individual. Whether or not there has been criminalization of individuals with mental illness, diversion programs, properly implemented, can ensure that many of these individuals remain in or return to the community rather than languishing inappropriately in jail.

If the effect of deinstitutionalization on jails is uncertain, its effect on prisons is even less well documented. Researchers working with jail inmates arrested for felonies have found very high percentages with prior arrests, hospitalizations, and severe, overt psychopathology (Lamb & Grant, 1982, 1983). They surmise that, prior to reform, this population would likely have become lifetime residents of state hospitals. However, between 1968 and 1978, when mental hospital populations fell by two-thirds, the percentage of men entering prisons with prior histories of mental hospitalization only increased from 7.9% to 10.4% (Monahan & Steadman, 1984). In half the states studied, the percentage actually *fell*. Thus, it does not appear that more restrictive commitment laws have had much impact on prison populations or generated greater demand on prison mental health providers.

It is apparent that our corrections system contains a large number of individuals who need treatment for serious mental illness. In a sense, this population suffers from a dual diagnosis; they are both "bad" and "mad." Consequently, they may well have low priority when scarce public funds are allocated. The available research suggests that the needs of this increasing population remain woefully unmet. It seems fair to conclude, therefore, that MHPs who work in the criminal justice system often find themselves overwhelmed by the demands on their time and expertise. Much of their time is spent responding to the bureaucratic needs of the system, like "evaluating" and "reporting," rather than treating. And given the mobility of this population within the criminal justice system, much of any treatment they are able to provide is likely to be acute crisis intervention rather than long-term care. Clearly, public policy must give more attention to providing more resources to serve this somewhat invisible population of individuals with mental illness and to providing continuity of treatment for them.

The Duty to Prevent Harm Revisited

The duty to protect potential victims from the violent acts of MHPs' clients that was introduced by *Tarasoff v. Regents of the University of California* (1976) and its progeny also had an impact on how MHPs practiced. The case law has treated *Tarasoff*-like situations inconsistently, with results varying from jurisdiction to jurisdiction, including states that flatly reject a *Tarasoff* duty altogether. Nonetheless, some prominent MHPs have concluded that the duty to protect is "now a national standard of practice" and that MHPs should practice as if the "duty to protect" were the law (Perlin, 1992).

Though the evidence is not clear, there is some indication that *Tarasoff* has produced some negative clinical effects. MHPs may have developed an excessive fear of litigation that has affected their clinical judgment. Many MHPs believe that they are more likely to be sued for the release of a dangerous patient than for the incarceration of a nondangerous patient. As a result, they may utilize involuntary commitment more readily to avoid possible tort liability for harms caused by a dangerous patient. Thus, patients who have demonstrated violent behavior may be committed in the short term, pending court approval, even though they may not actually

be suffering from a mental illness. This stratagem allows MHPs to escape liability by leaving the decision to commit to the courts (Brown & Rayne, 1989). Furthermore, once committed, "dangerous" patients may be hospitalized for much longer than actually warranted because of the MHPs' fear of liability for negligent release. Because these patients may be kept longer, the staff-to-patient ratio may be negatively affected, resulting in a dilution of services to all patients (Poythress & Brodsky, 1992).

There is evidence that physicians involved in litigation have significantly more psychological and emotional distress than physicians who have not been sued. As a result, they may refrain from treating a certain type of patient or retire early (Perlin, 1992; Simon, 1987). The same negative impact has been observed in MHPs who have been involved in a lawsuit for negligent release of a dangerous psychiatric patient (Poythress & Brodsky, 1992). In addition, some clinicians have reported a reluctance to probe subjects with patients that may uncover violence; others have simply changed how they keep their records (that is, eliminating anything that might suggest violence or adding information that would support a decision not to warn) (Perlin, 1992). Others may have been more willing to discard therapist-patient confidentiality and warn possible victims or resort to involuntary civil commitment more often.

A fundamental premise underlying the duty to protect third parties from patient violence is that MHPs have the ability to predict future dangerousness accurately. It is not surprising that courts and legislatures believe that MHPs have this expertise, because MHPs make decisions about dangerousness daily in emergency rooms, psychiatric hospitals, and outpatient practices.

However, this belief is not supported by corroborating evidence. Although evidence exists that MHPs have some ability to predict imminent dangerousness accurately, there is little to suggest that they are any better at predicting long-term dangerousness than the average layperson. What the MHP really predicts is the probability of dangerousness, not whether a specific individual will commit a future dangerous act (Greenberg, 1989). In the absence of clear legislative guidelines, *Tarasoff* and its progeny often induce MHPs to predict many individuals as dangerous even when there is, in fact, a low probability they will actually do harm. As a result, MHPs generally overpredict dangerousness. In any event, the threat of tort liability imposed by cases like *Tarasoff* has clearly increased the complexity of MHPs' practice and its accompanying psychological and financial pressures.

Because of the increased legal regulation of involuntary mental health services during this era, MHPs who work in this field have had to keep abreast of legal developments through continuing education programs. For example, the University of Southern California offers a one-year program to enhance the skills of practicing psychiatrists by offering subsequent training in psychiatry and law (Pollack, 1985). It has been suggested that psychiatric facilities should retain skilled legal counsel "on call" to advise on legal questions that arise (Weitzel, 1977). Many MHPs have taken training in the law as well as in their own area of expertise.

The Neoconservative Era

At the twilight of the liberal era, America's values were once more changing. The economy began to decline, with a concomitant loss of high-paying jobs. Many felt that the Great Society programs had failed, that instead of providing the means for the poor and disadvantaged to help themselves, the programs had created a large dependent welfare class who lacked any desire to be productive citizens (Bell, 1976; Coser & Howe, 1974; Kristol, 1976; Moynihan, 1973). Despite massive government expenditures designed to solve the "root causes" of crime, crime rates soared during the liberal era; violent crime increased almost 50% between 1971 and 1980

(Federal Bureau of Investigation, 1971, 1980, 1988).

Early in the 1980s, concern for civil liberties and fairness to the disadvantaged gave way to a growing conservatism in American politics. Traditional values, such as family and religion and a belief in individual responsibility and the free market, emerged as driving forces in economic and political discourse. Government was no longer perceived as a threat to individual rights; rather, it was seen as crucial to the preservation of community safety and the conditions necessary for individuals to enjoy their rights (van den Haag, 1975).

Elected politicians responded to this new public ethos. Grassroots political movements, such as victims' rights groups, developed into a national force and pressed for law reform emphasizing community security. Legislatures became more responsive to the will of the majority, abandoning rehabilitation as the primary purpose of criminal incarceration and adopting a just-deserts theory that criminals deserved to be punished for their past crimes. They enacted determinate sentencing laws, reenacted death penalty statutes, and imposed greater responsibility on juveniles (La Fond & Durham, 1992).

Congress revised the federal insanity test to make it more difficult for criminal defendants to escape criminal responsibility by use of the insanity defense. Eight states changed their insanity test to the same end. Idaho, Montana, and Utah abolished the insanity defense entirely (La Fond & Durham, 1992).

Interestingly, the need for these insanity defense reforms was not substantiated by empirical research. The insanity defense is raised in less than 1% of all felony cases. Its success rate, when raised, is only 23% (Steadman et al., 1993). Of the 19,971 admissions to facilities for offenders with mental illness in 1978, only 8.1% had been adjudged not guilty by reason of insanity (NGI) (Steadman & Braff, 1983). Many more of those admittees were found incompetent to stand trial (IST) or were prison inmates transferred because they evidenced severe mental illness.

The NGIs, however, constitute a larger share— 22.3%—of all residents of these facilities because they stay far longer than the more numerous ISTs. Clearly, the insanity defense is used much less and is even less successful than the public thinks. Though its use appears to have increased somewhat over time, it is not a major "loophole" in the penal system (Steadman & Braff, 1983).

The Supreme Court has sent mixed messages with regard to the incarceration of insanity acquittees. On the one hand, it has held that individuals acquitted of even a minor criminal charge by reason of insanity could be held in a psychiatric facility beyond the maximum term for the charged crime until they proved they were not mentally ill or dangerous (*Jones v. United States*, 1983). On the other hand, the Court held that Louisiana could not continue to confine an NGI who was no longer mentally ill solely because he was dangerous. In effect, the Court held that dangerousness alone would not justify indefinite civil commitment (*Foucha v. Louisiana*, 1992).

The results of neoconservative insanity defense reforms are mixed. Reforms that shifted the burden of proof to the defense not only reduced the use of the defense but tended to confine its use to those who had a serious mental illness. Changing the legal standard for insanity, however, appeared to have no effect. Abolition of the plea altogether amounted to a mere "sleight of hand." Those who might have used the insanity defense were, instead, often found incompetent to stand trial. As ISTs, they were treated in the same hospitals that they would have been treated in had they been found NGIs. Only the legal terminology and status changed (Steadman et al., 1993).

No matter how the labels are rearranged, treatment of offenders with a serious mental illness remains both a legal obligation and a commonsense prison management strategy. It is worth noting that many more offenders with mental illness were transferred from prisons than were NGIs. Of all those admitted to such facilities, 54.1% were transferred from prison. Trans-

ferees account for an average of 36.5% of the population of offenders with mental illness (Monahan, Davis, Hartstone, & Steadman, 1983). Consequently, even when denied NGI or IST status, these offenders may simply stop briefly in prison on their way to a psychiatric hospital.

In 1980 the Supreme Court held in *Vitek v. Jones* that prisoners must have a hearing before a neutral decision maker with the assistance of a lawyer before they can be transferred from a prison to a mental hospital. Even with these procedural due process protections, however, it is probably easier for the government to prove that offenders are mentally ill and dangerous in this context than it is for criminal defendants to persuade a jury that they were legally insane at the time of the crime. Thus, abolition of the insanity defense could simply shift the forum for adjudicating the mental status of an offender from the trial court to an administrative hearing officer, often an individual chosen from within the correctional system, or to an MHP advising a judge on a defendant's competency to stand trial. Given these options, NGI reform is not likely to reduce the population of forensic psychiatric facilities or the demands made on MHPs working in the corrections system.

Courts and Public Institutions

Courts, including federal courts—once the mainstay of liberal era reform—retreated from judicial activism. In part, this can be explained by the appointment by Presidents Reagan and Bush of a large number of conservative federal judges who rejected judicial activism (Goldman, 1989). But even liberal judges became more reluctant to interfere with the administration of large state institutions, including mental hospitals. Activist judges came to realize that their ability to change the day-to-day operation of prisons or hospitals was extremely limited and would realistically entail a great deal of time appointing committees, reviewing reports, and holding hearings. Moreover, ordering more resources for such institutions as large state mental hospitals would simply result in less resources for other programs, like community mental health (Weinstein, 1982).

Other Consequences of Deinstitutionalization

Critics of deinstitutionalization and civil libertarian commitment laws, though acknowledging the laudatory goals of these reforms, argued that both society and those with mental illness now faced a "second generation" of problems spawned by these policy changes (Stromberg & Stone, 1983). As noted earlier, some commentators argued that restrictive commitment laws had resulted in persons with mental illness being jailed rather than hospitalized (Abramson, 1972). Others claimed that citizens with mental disorders had found their way into dilapidated housing in the cities, forming "psychiatric ghettos," or were being warehoused in uncaring nursing homes (Aviram & Segal, 1973). More strident critics argued that persons with mental illness were "dying with their rights on" (Treffert, 1975).

The growing and visible number of homeless people in America became one of the most provocative problems of the 1980s. Early estimates placed the number of homeless people at anywhere from 250,000 to 3,000,000 (*Creative Non-Violence v. Pierce*, 1987; Mascari, Note, 1987). The 1990 census reported about 230,000 people homeless, but current, more accurate estimates conservatively put the number between 500,000 and 600,000 (Barringer, 1991; Caton, 1990). At first, research inaccurately indicated that as many as 90% of the homeless were mentally ill. Later, more reliable research showed no more than one-quarter to one-third of homeless people with a diagnosable mental disorder (Cohen & Thompson, 1992; Dennis, 1990; Kiesler, 1991; Rossi, Wright, Fisher, & Willis, 1987).

The mental health professions and families with members who have a mental illness, once at odds with one another, adopted allied policy positions and became politically more active. Increasingly, they argued that state mental health systems had abandoned those with serious mental illness to the streets and doorways of America and had failed to provide them with safe and humane treatment. Families and MHPs proposed that commitment criteria be expanded to encompass those who, though not dangerous, would nonetheless suffer serious psychological or physical harm without hospitalization (Dunham, 1985; Stromberg & Stone, 1983).

Involuntary Civil Commitment Law Reform

In 1979, the Supreme Court made it clear in the *Parham* case that children were not entitled to an adversary hearing in an impartial tribunal before their parents could admit them to a state hospital for treatment (*Parham v. J. R.*, 1979). Though the Court said that children have a constitutional liberty interest and were entitled to procedural due process, it concluded that a medical review of the parents' admission application is all the process due. Consequently, unless state laws require it, MHPs do not have to participate in the kind of adversary judicial hearings required to commit adults in most states.

Beginning in 1979, a number of states—Washington, then Alaska, Hawaii, Arizona, Kansas, North Carolina, Oregon, and Texas—revised their involuntary commitment laws to make it easier to hospitalize persons with mental illness for a therapeutic purpose (La Fond & Durham, 1992). Though framed in different ways, this reform was mainly intended to permit involuntary hospitalization of patients who had started to decompensate. This allowed intervention before the individual became dangerous to self or others. The Washington law has been used to commit homeless individuals with mental illness who wanted to spend evenings in public shelters or to camp out in public forests, even though thousands of homeless Americans do so (*In re La Belle*, 1986). Other states, including New Jersey, California, and Pennsylvania, decided against such laws because of the significant funding increase they would probably require (Durham & La Fond, 1985).

New York City has reinterpreted existing commitment laws to make it easier to place individuals with mental illness in city hospitals. In October, 1986, the city adopted a scheme permitting the police forcibly to transport during cold weather homeless individuals who refused to go voluntarily either to a shelter or to a psychiatric hospital. In October, 1987, New York City implemented Project Help, which enabled teams of psychiatrists, social workers, and nurses to forcibly bring homeless individuals they considered to have a serious mental illness to city hospitals.

Outpatient Commitment

By 1988, almost every state had enacted laws authorizing outpatient commitment of individuals with mental illness. Many permitted outpatient commitment of persons with mental illness who were not dangerous but were expected to deteriorate and become dangerous if they did not receive treatment (Keilitz & Hall, 1985; Miller, 1988). Some of these state statutes authorize outpatient commitment of individuals who could not be committed to hospitals and also provide fewer procedural protections for outpatient commitment than for inpatient commitment (Stefan, 1987). Patients subjected to outpatient commitment can be ordered to take medications and to keep appointments at mental health centers. Failure to comply can result in the initiation of involuntary commitment proceedings as inpatients to psychiatric hospitals.

Courts have recently been far more reluctant to find unconstitutional state laws that expanded the authority of the state to commit patients to hospitals for treatment or to make it easier to commit them as outpatients. Increasingly, courts seem to agree that many individuals with mental illness are unable to seek vital mental health treatment in their own best interest and must instead receive it through the involuntary commitment system.

Ironically, however, in the 1990 *Zinermon v. Burch* case, the Supreme Court indicated that an individual with mental illness had to be competent before consenting to voluntary hospitalization in a state psychiatric hospital and that due process required a meaningful inquiry into competency prior to hospitalization (*Zinermon v. Burch*, 1990). Consequently, it held that state mental health facilities and staff could be sued for violating an individual's civil rights if they did not provide constitutionally adequate procedures to ensure such competency. This decision may require mental health providers to have some documented form of medical evaluation or legal consultation before individuals can voluntarily admit themselves to a state mental health facility (Winick, 1991).

Yet the Supreme Court has also signaled that judges should give greater deference to the judgment of MHPs in deciding how to treat persons with mental illness while they are committed involuntarily. In *Youngberg v. Romeo* (1982), Justice Blackmun stated that

there certainly is no reason to think judges or juries are better qualified than appropriate professionals in making [treatment decisions.] . . . For these reasons, the decision, if made by a professional, is presumptively valid; liability may be imposed only when the decision by the professional is such a substantial departure from accepted professional judgment that the person responsible actually did not base his decision on such a judgment. (pp. 322–323)

The decision also held that

[i]n an action for damages against a professional in his individual capacity, however, the professional will not be liable if he was unable to satisfy his normal professional standards because of budgetary constraints; in such a situation good-faith immunity would bar liability. (p. 323)

The Supreme Court reinforced the view that judges should not try to make medical decisions when it held in *Harper v. Washington* (1990) that prisoners with mental illness do not have a constitutional right to a court hearing to decide whether they should be given psychotropic medication without their consent. The Court held that administrative review provides inmates with constitutionally adequate due process.

Although conditions in state psychiatric facilities caused some controversy, it appears that courts apparently paid less attention to them. During the 1980s, fewer right-to-treatment lawsuits were evidently brought seeking to improve these conditions.

In sum, a modest but discernible trend toward expanding the state's authority to commit individuals with mental illness who are not dangerous but are considered in need of treatment has become apparent over the last decade or so. In addition, states are more willing to use their commitment authority to seek treatment compliance of noninstitutionalized patients through more aggressive outpatient commitment. Both federal and state courts have become more reluctant to strike down these expansive commitment laws or to monitor conditions in state hospitals. Finally, courts have increasingly characterized treatment issues involved in commitment as medical rather than legal. Consequently, the expertise of MHPs receives more deference in legal attacks brought on behalf of patients seeking protection of constitutional rights.

Impact of Reform on MHPs

What happens when a state legislature revises its laws to make it easier to commit individuals for treatment? There is powerful evidence that expanding a state's therapeutic commitment authority leads to a sharp increase in the number of patients hospitalized involuntarily.

When the state of Washington made such revisions in 1979, commitment rates increased so rapidly—beginning nine months *before* the effective date of the new law—that the largest state hospital imposed a "cap" on new admissions at 90% of bed capacity. One government jurisdiction sued the hospital, claiming that under state law the hospital had to accept all patients committed to it. The Washington State Supreme Court agreed and ordered the hospital to accept all involuntary patients even if there were no beds for them. The court concluded that "treatment delayed and inadequate must surely be better than no treatment at all" (*Pierce County v. Western State Hospital,* 1982).

The influx of new admissions caused systemic overcrowding throughout Washington State and made the staff's work next to impossible. Voluntary patients found access to treatment so difficult that they virtually disappeared from the state's public mental health system.

By 1981, three out of every four commitments in Washington were based on the therapeutic commitment ground of "grave disability" rather than on dangerousness (Durham & La Fond, 1985). Yet the increase in the number of patients committed as "gravely disabled" did not change the clinical or demographic profile of patients committed to the state's mental health system, nor did the behavior that brought them to the attention of commitment authorities change (Durham & La Fond, 1985).

The Washington State experience, though not matched by all states that broadened grounds for commitment, demonstrates that the expansion of therapeutic commitment authority can generate significant new demand for institutional care. Without careful management of rate of admissions or bed space, expanding a state's commitment authority may impose overwhelming demands on MHPs who work in the commitment system.

Overcrowding in state psychiatric facilities is now more likely to be ignored; lawyers are more reluctant to bring right-to-treatment lawsuits, and courts are less eager to interfere with the management of state institutions. Also, as the Supreme Court made clear in the *Youngberg v. Romeo* (1982) case, judges give substantial deference to professional judgment and take into account the resources available to MHPs in determining their immunity in cases of failure to exercise professional judgment. The *Youngberg* case, together with state immunity statutes, should also, in all but the most egregious cases, protect MHPs from personal liability when they are sued for depriving committed patients of their constitutional rights.

As a result, MHPs may find they will have greater freedom of action in running mental health facilities for committed patients. Judges are less likely to be looking over their shoulders and second-guessing their treatment decisions. One suspects MHPs will welcome this new freedom.

On the other hand, judges are also less likely to order state mental health institutions to provide more resources for treating committed patients. As a result, many MHPs will no longer have the powerful persuasion of a court order to secure additional funding for these institutions. If this prediction proves correct, then more MHPs may find themselves working in overcrowded and understaffed facilities, providing only minimal treatment. This state of affairs would surely please no one.

Conclusion

Mental health law and policy, particularly as they relate to involuntary civil commitment and insanity defense reform, appear to be driven primarily by prevailing social values and ideology, rather than by sound, empirically derived knowledge. During the present neoconservative era, policymakers have increasingly come to believe that involuntary hospitalization or outpatient commitment will serve the needs of both society and those with mental illness. The rugged individualism and distrust of the government so pervasive during the liberal era have given way both to a growing demand to make our communities safer and, it is to be hoped, to help those in need.

Society must be on guard, however, lest compassion give way too readily to convenience (Rothman, 1980). MHPs in particular may need to remind the public that they are therapists, not jailers. The current trend is clear. Society is giving MHPs more power and responsibility in caring for people with mental disabilities through the involuntary civil commitment system. Unfortunately, this broadened mandate is all too seldom accompanied by the resources required for the task.

The public seems to have renewed confidence in the expertise of MHPs, and they are being asked to solve one of society's most difficult and persistent human problems: how best to care for and control persons with serious and chronic mental illness. MHPs should perhaps be wary of creating expectations that, if not fulfilled, could lead to renewed criticism and recrimination.

Wise, compassionate, and cost-effective social policy toward those with mental illness must be based on sound empirical knowledge. The ideology of the moment must be tempered by a critical comprehension of what is known and what is not known. Equally important, more work is needed to ascertain whether law and social policy in fact produce the outcomes desired (La Fond & Durham, 1992; Wexler, 1990; Wexler & Winick, 1991).

References

Abramson, J. (1972). The criminalization of mentally disordered behavior: Possible side effects of a new mental health law. *Hospital and Community Psychiatry, 23*(4), 101–105.

Aviram, U., & Segal, S. P. (1973). Exclusion of the mentally ill: Reflection of an old problem in a new context. *Archives of General Psychiatry, 29*, 126–131.

Bagby, R. M. (1987). The effects of legislative reform on admission rates to psychiatric units of general hospitals. *International Journal of Law and Psychiatry, 10*, 383–394.

Bagby, R. M., & Atkinson, L. (1988). The effects of legislative reform on civil commitment admission rates: A critical analysis. *Behavioral Science and Law, 6*, 45–61.

Barringer, F. (1991, April 12). Federal count of homeless is far below other figures. *New York Times*, p. A14.

Bell, D. (1976). *The cultural contradictions of capitalism.* New York: Basic Books.

Blaine, J. G. (1987). Patient work programs a decade after *Souter v. Brennan:* A survey of selected state psychiatric hospitals. *Psychiatric Hospital, 18*(2), 71–77.

Blaine, J. G., & Mason, J. (1986). Application of the Fair Labor Standards Act to patient work programs at mental health institutions: A proposal for change. *Boston College Law Review, 27,* 553–577.

Bolton, A. (1976). *A study of the need for and availability of mental health services for mentally disordered jail inmates and juvenile detention facilities.* Boston: Arthur Bolton Associates.

Brakel, S. J., Parry, J., & Weiner, B. (1985). *The mentally disabled and the law.* Chicago: American Bar Foundation.

Brown, J., & Rayne, J. T. (1989). Some ethical considerations in defensive psychiatry: A case study. *American Journal of Orthopsychiatry, 59,* 534–541.

Brown v. Board of Education, 347 U.S. 483 (1954).

Caton, C.L.M. (1990). *Homeless in America.* New York: Oxford University Press.

Cohen, C. I., & Thompson, K. S. (1992). Homeless mentally ill or mentally ill homeless. *American Journal of Psychiatry, 149,* 816–823.

Coser, L. A., & Howe, I. (Eds.) (1974). *The new conservatives: A critique from the left.* New York: Quadrangle.

Creative Non-Violence v. Pierce, 814 F.2d 663 (D.C. Cir. 1987). (Citing a report to the Secretary of Housing & Urban Development on the homeless and emergency shelters)

Davis v. Balson, 461 F. Supp. 842 (N.D. Ohio 1978).

Davis v. Watkins, 384 F. Supp. 1196 (N.D. Ohio 1976).

Dennis, D. (1990). Exploring myths about "street people." *Access, 2*(2), 1–3.

Developments in the law: Civil commitment of the mentally ill. (1974). *Harvard Law Review, 87,* 1190–1406.

Dunham, A. C. (1985). APA's model law: Protecting the patients' ultimate interests. *Hospital and Community Psychiatry, 36,* 973–975.

Durham, M., & La Fond, J. (1985). The empirical consequences and policy implications of broadening the statutory criteria for civil commitment. *Yale Law and Policy Review, 3,* 395–446.

Eckerhart v. Hensley, 475 F. Supp. 908 (W.D. Mo. 1979).

Ennis, B. (1972). *Prisoners of psychiatry—Mental patients, psychiatrists, and the law.* New York: Harcourt, Brace, Jovanovich.

Ennis, B., & Siegel, L. (1973). *The rights of mental patients.* New York: Discus Books.

Estelle v. Gamble, 429 U.S. 97 (1976).

Fair Labor Standards Act of 1938, 29 U.S.C. § 201.

Faulkner, L. R., Bloom, J. D., & Kudndahl-Stanley, K. (1982). Effects of a new involuntary civil commitment law: Expectations and reality. *Bulletin of the American Academy of Psychiatry and Law, 10*(4), 249–259.

Federal Bureau of Investigation. (1971). *Crime in the U.S.: Uniform crime reports for the United States.* Washington, DC: U.S. Department of Justice.

Federal Bureau of Investigation. (1980). *Crime in the U.S.: Uniform crime reports for the United States.* Washington, DC: U.S. Department of Justice.

Federal Bureau of Investigation. (1988). *Crime in the U.S.: Uniform crime reports for the United States.* Washington, DC: U.S. Department of Justice.

Ferleger, D. (1973). Loosing the chains: In-hospital civil liberties of mental patients. *Santa Clara Law Review, 13,* 447–500.

Fiss, O. (1982). The social and political foundations of adjudication. *Law and Human Behavior, 6,* 121–128.

Foucha v. Louisiana, 112 S. Ct. 1780 (1992).

Frug, G. E. (1978). The judicial power of the purse. *University of Pennsylvania Law Review, 126,* 715–794.

Garcia v. San Antonio Metropolitan Transit Authority, 469 U.S. 528 (1986).

In re Gault, 387 U.S. 1 (1972).

Goffman, E. (1961). *Asylums: Essays on the social situation of mental patients and other inmates.* Garden City, NY: Doubleday.

Goldberg v. Kelly, 397 U.S. 254 (1970).

Goldman, S. (1989). Reagan's judicial legacy: Completing the puzzle and summing up. *Judicature, 72,* 318–330.

Greenberg, L. (1989). The psychiatrist's dilemma. *Journal of Psychiatry and Law, 17,* 381–411.

Grob, G. (1983). *Mental illness and American society, 1875–1940.* Princeton, NJ: Princeton University Press.

Groethe, R. (1977). Overt dangerous behavior as a constitutional requirement for involuntary civil commitment of the mentally ill. *University of Chicago Law Review, 44,* 562–593.

Harper v. Washington, 110 U.S. 1028 (1990).

Hiday, V. A. (1981). Court decisions in civil commitment: Independence or deference. *International Journal of Law and Psychiatry, 4,* 159–170.

Hiday, V. A. (1982). The attorney's role in involuntary civil commitment. *North Carolina Law Review, 60,* 1027–1056.

Hiday, V. A. (1991). Arrest and incarceration of civil commitment candidates. *Hospital and Community Psychiatry, 42,* 729–743.

Hoffman, P. B., & Foust, L. L. (1977). Least restrictive treatment of the mentally ill: A doctrine in search of its senses. *San Diego Law Review, 14,* 1100–1154.

Howard, G., & Anthony, R. (1977). The right to vote and voting patterns of hospitalized psychiatric patients. *Psychiatric Quarterly, 49*(2), 124–132.

Inmates of Allegheny County v. Pierce, 612 F.2d 754 (3d Cir. 1979).

Isaac, R. J., & Armat, V. C. (1990). *Madness in the streets.* New York: Free Press.

Jones v. United States, 463 U.S. 354 (1983).

Kapp, M. B. (1994). Treatment and refusal rights in mental health: Therapeutic justice and clinical accommodation. *American Journal of Orthopsychiatry, 64,* 223–234.

Keilitz, I., & Hall, T. (1985). State statutes governing involuntary outpatient civil commitment. *Mental and Physical Disability Law Report, 9,* 378–400.

Kesey, K. (1962). *One flew over the cuckoo's nest.* New York: New American Library.

Kiesler, C. A. (1991). Homelessness and public policy priorities. *American Psychologist, 46,* 1245–1252.

Kiesler, C. A., & Sibulkin, A. E. (1987). *Mental hospitalization: Myths and facts about a national crisis.* Newbury Park, CA: Sage.

Kristol, I. (1976, January 19). "What is a Neoconservative?" *Newsweek,* p. 87.

In re La Belle, 107 Wn.2d 196, 728 P.2d 138 (1986).

La Fond, J. Q. (1981). An examination of the purposes of involuntary civil commitment. *Buffalo Law Review, 30,* 499–535.

La Fond, J. Q., & Durham, M. L. (1992). *Back to the asylum: The future of mental health law in the United States.* New York: Oxford University Press.

Laing, R. D. (1960). *The divided self.* Baltimore: Penguin.

Lamb, H., & Grant, R. (1982). The mentally ill in an urban county jail. *Archives of General Psychiatry, 39,* 17–22.

Lamb, H., & Grant, R. (1983). Mentally ill women in a county jail. *Archives of General Psychiatry, 40,* 363–368.

Lamb, H. R., Sorkin, A. P., & Zusman, J. (1981). Legislating the control of the mentally ill in California. *American Journal of Psychiatry, 138,* 334–339.

Lessard v. Schmidt, 349 F. Supp. 1078 (E.D. Wis. 1972), vacated and remanded, 414 U.S. 473 (1974), order on remand, 379 F. Supp. 1376 (1974), vacated and remanded on other grounds, 421 U.S. 957 (1975), order reinstated on remand, 413 F. Supp. 1318 (1976).

Mascari, D. [Note]. Homeless families: Do they have a right to integrity? (1987). *UCLA Law Review, 35,* 159–204.

Mavroudis v. Superior Court, 102 Cal. App. 3d 594 (1980).

Miller, R. D. (1988). Outpatient civil commitment of the mentally ill: An overview and update. *Behavioral Sciences and Law, 6,* 99–117.

Miller, R. D., & Fiddleman, P. B. (1983). Changes in North Carolina commitment statute: The impact of attorneys. *Bulletin of the American Academy of Psychiatry and Law, 11,* 43–50.

Monahan, J., Davis, S. K., Hartstone, E., & Steadman, H. (1983). Prisoners transferred to mental hospitals. *Mentally disordered offenders* (J. Monahan & H. Steadman, Eds.) (pp. 233–244). New York: Plenum.

Monahan, J., & Steadman, H. (1984). *Crime and mental disorder.* Washington, DC: Department of Justice.

Morrisey v. Brewer, 408 U.S. 471 (1972).

Moynihan, D. P. (1973). *The politics of guaranteed income: The Nixon administration and the family assistance plan.* New York: Random House.

National League of Cities v. Usery, 426 U.S. 833 (1976).

O'Connor v. Donaldson, 422 U.S. 563 (1975).

O'Reilly, J., & Sales, B. (1987). Privacy for the institutionalized mentally ill: Are court-ordered standards effective? *Law and Human Behavior, 11*(1), 41–53.

Parham v. J. R., 442 U.S. 584 (1979).

Perlin, M. (1992). *Tarasoff* and the dilemma of the dangerous patient: New directions for the 1990s. *Law and Psychology Review, 16,* 29–63.

Peters, R., Miller, K. S., Schmidt, W., & Meeter, D. (1987). The effects of statutory change on the civil commitment of the mentally ill. *Law and Human Behavior, 11,* 73–99.

Petersen v. State, 100 Wn.2d 421, 671 P.2d 230 (1983).

Pierce County v. Western State Hospital, 97 Wash.2d 264, 268 P.2d 131, 133–134 (1982).

Policy Research Associates. (1991). *Diversion and treatment services for mentally ill detainees in the KCCF.* Delwar, NY: Author.

Pollack, S. (1985). Observations on the outcome of specialty education and training in forensic psychiatry. *Bulletin of the American Academy of Law and Psychiatry, 13,* 117–119.

Poythress, N., & Brodsky, S. (1992). In the wake of a negligent release lawsuit. *Law and Human Behavior, 16,* 155–173.

Reed, S. C., & Lewis, D. A. (1990). The negotiation of voluntary admission in Chicago's state mental hospitals. *Journal of Law and Psychiatry, 18,* 137–163.

Rennie v. Klein, 462 F. Supp. 1131 (1979).

Rogers v. Commissioner of the Department of Mental Health, 390 Mass. 489, 458 N.E.2d 308 (1983).

Rogers v. Okin, 478 F. Supp. 1342 (D. Mass. 1979).

Rone v. Fireman, 473 F. Supp. 92 (N.D. Ohio 1979).

Rossi, P. H., Wright, J. D., Fisher, G. A., & Willis, G. (1987). The urban homeless: Estimating composition and size. *Science, 235,* 1336–1341.

Rothman, D. J. (1980). *Conscience and convenience: The asylum and its alternatives in progressive America.* Boston: Little, Brown.

Rouse v. Cameron, 373 F.2d 451 (1966).

Safier, M. A. (1976). Patient work under fair labor standards: The issue in perspective. *Hospital and Community Psychiatry, 27*(2), 89–92.

Scull, A. T. (1984). *Decarceration: Community and the deviant—A radical view.* Englewood Cliffs, NJ: Prentice-Hall.

Simon, R. I. (1987). A clinical philosophy for the (unduly) defensive psychiatrist. *Psychiatric Annals, 17*(3), 197–200.

Singer, R. (1982). Providing mental health services to jail inmates: Legal perspectives. In C. Dunn & H. Steadman (Eds.), *Mental health services in local jails* (pp. 69–99). Rockville, MD: National Institute of Mental Health.

Souder v. Brennan, 367 F. Supp. 808 (D.C. 1973).

Steadman, H. (1992). Boundary spanners: A key component for the effective interactions of the justice and mental health systems. *Law and Human Behavior, 16,* 75–87.

Steadman, H., & Braff, J. (1983). Defendants not guilty by reason of insanity. In J. Monahan & H. Steadman (Eds.), *Mentally disordered offenders* (pp. 109–129). New York: Plenum.

Steadman, H., McCarty, D., & Morrissey, J. (1989). *The mentally ill in jail: Planning for essential services.* New York: Guilford Press.

Steadman, J., McGreevy, M., Morrissey, J., Callahan, L., Robbins, P. C., & Cirincione, C. (1993). *Before and after Hinckley: Evaluating insanity defense reform.* New York: Guilford Press.

Stefan, S. (1987). Preventive commitment: The concept and its pitfalls. *Mental and Physical Disability Law Reporter, 11,* 288–302.

Stromberg, C. D., & Stone, A. A. (1983). A model state law on civil commitment of the mentally ill. *Harvard Journal on Legislation, 20,* 275–396.

Szasz, T. (1974). *The myth of mental illness.* New York: Hoeber-Harper.

Tarasoff v. Regents of the University of California, 17 Cal. 3d 358 (1976).

Teplin, L. (1986). *Keeping the peace: The parameters of police discretion in relation to the mentally disordered.* Washington, DC: U.S. Department of Justice.

Teplin, L., & Voit, E. (1994). Criminalizing the seriously mentally ill: Putting the problem in perspective. *Mental health and the law: Research, policy, and services.* Durham, NC: Carolina Academic Press.

Thompson v. County of Alameda, 27 Cal. 3d 741, 614 P.2d 728 (1980).

Treffert, D. (1975). The practical limits of patients' rights. *Psychiatric Annals, 5,* 91–96.

van den Haag, E. (1975). *Punishing criminals: Concerning a very old and painful question.* New York: Basic Books.

Vitek v. Jones, 445 U.S. 480 (1980).

Warren, C.A.B. (1977a). Involuntary civil commitment for mental disorder: The application of California's Lanterman-Petris-Short Act. *Law and Society Review, 11,* 629–649.

Warren, C.A.B. (1977b). *The social construction of dangerousness.* Los Angeles: University of Southern California Press.

Warren, C.A.B. (1982). *Court of last resort: Judicial review of involuntary mental illness and the law.* Chicago: University of Chicago Press.

Weinstein, J. B. (1982). The effect of austerity on institutional litigation. *Law and Human Behavior, 6,* 145–151.

Weitzel, W. D. (1977). Changing law and clinical dilemmas. *American Journal of Psychiatry, 134,* 293–295.

Wenger, D. L., & Fletcher, C. R. (1969). The effect of legal counsel on admissions to a state mental hospital: A confrontation of professions. *Journal of Health and Social Behavior, 10,* 66–72.

Wexler, D. B. (1990). *Therapeutic jurisprudence: The law as a therapeutic agent.* Durham, NC: Carolina Academic Press.

Wexler, D. B., & Winick, B. J. (1991). *Essays in therapeutic jurisprudence.* Durham, NC: Carolina Academic Press.

Winick, B. J. (1991). Competency to consent to voluntary hospitalization: A therapeutic jurisprudence analysis of *Zinermon v. Burch. International Journal of Law and Psychiatry, 14,* 169–214.

Wyatt v. Stickney, 325 F. Supp. 781 (M.D. Ala. 1971).

Wyatt v. Stickney, 344 F. Supp. 373 (M.D. Ala. 1972).

Youngberg v. Romeo, 457 U. S. 307 (1982).

Zinermon v. Burch, 110 S. Ct. 975 (1990).

12 ▌ Issues Relating to Women and Ethnic Minorities in Mental Health Treatment and Law

Susan Stefan
University of Miami

By the year 2000, almost one in three Americans will be members of ethnic minorities (Day, 1993). Presently, more than half our population are women (U.S. Bureau of the Census, 1992). Two-thirds of individuals with chronic mental illness in this country are women (Bachrach, 1986). Yet the unstated assumption that the typical mental health client is a white male permeates mental health law as well as mental health policies and programs. Issues that particularly affect minorities and women in mental health law or policy either are ignored or are labeled "special" concerns and relegated to a special issue of a journal,[1] a special chapter of a textbook,[2] a special portion of a report,[3] or, occasionally, a separate textbook for a separate course (Jones & Gray, 1986).

As a result, presentations in textbooks or diagnostic manuals such as the *Diagnostic and Statistical Manual of Mental Disorders* (DSM-IV) (American Psychiatric Association, 1994) about a particular diagnosis, such as schizophrenia, typically do not mention the well-documented tendency of mental health professionals to misdiagnose minorities. For example, blacks[4] are

I would like to thank Delores Parron, King Davis, Len Rubenstein, and Juan Mezzich for sharing their time and knowledge. I owe much to the research assistance of Shannon Campbell, to the patience of the librarians at the University of Miami School of Law, and to the fine editing of Dan Shuman and Bruce Sales. This chapter was finished with the support of the Center for Public Representation in Northampton, Massachusetts. Finally, I would like to dedicate this effort to my husband, Wes Daniels.

[1]This is not to say that these "special issues" are not an excellent compendium of information, only that such information tends to be relegated to them.

[2]Major psychiatric textbooks, 1000 to 2000 pages long, give these issues a few paragraphs at most. The most recent edition of the leading textbook in psychiatry (Kaplan & Sadock, 1987) devotes a few lines to racism in its chapters on the "related disciplines" of anthropology and sociology. No mental health law textbook or treatise considers issues related to minorities at all. Consideration of women's issues is limited to the discussion of battered women's syndrome as a defense to homicide in the leading treatise in the field. I do not fault the editors of the lawbooks: as will be discussed later in this chapter, there has been very little litigation in these areas.

[3]This is even true when reports deal solely with women's problems. See, for example, McGrath, Keita, Strickland, and Russo's *Women and Depression: Risk Factors and Treatment Issues* (1990). (The third section of their report is on "special female populations," which include African Americans/Blacks, Hispanics/Latinas, Asian Americans, Native Americans, adolescents, substance abusers, women in poverty, professional women, older women, lesbians, and so on.) I confess my own dereliction in this chapter; by dividing "women's" issues and "minority" issues, I have failed women of color, who are subject to the intersecting stresses and stereotypes associated with their race and their gender.

[4]I am using blacks here as an example of distorted diagnoses and treatment given to minorities; a fuller discussion of this issue with respect to other minorities will follow.

often misdiagnosed, usually by overdiagnosing schizophrenia[5] and underdiagnosing affective disorders and depression. This results in inappropriate medication of black patients, which is likewise not mentioned in textbooks or reference works on psychotropic medication. Nor do these books reveal that even when correctly diagnosed, black patients are given disproportionately higher doses of psychotropic medications, and disproportionately less therapy of any other kind. Finally, the leading materials in the field of seclusion and restraint (American Psychiatric Association, 1994; Tardiff, 1984) do not mention the controversy over the disproportionate use of seclusion and restraint on black patients (Flaherty & Meagher, 1980; Lawson, Yesavage, & Werner, 1984; Soloff & Turner, 1982).

The number of gender-related issues in mental health treatment is even greater. Overt gender stereotypes are evident in diagnoses of women as mentally ill because they are angry or aggressive (Ussher, 1991) and in decisions to commit women involuntarily because they are "promiscuous" (Chesler, 1989), pregnant (*Oregon v. Johnson*, 1992; Stefan, 1989), lesbian (Kitzinger & Perkins, 1993), or living in an unsafe place (although men living in the same place would be allowed to stay) (Holstein, 1993).[6] Such decisions reflect gender discrimination by mental health professionals. In addition, the indifference of treatment professionals, policymakers, and lawyers to issues of crucial concern to women patients is illustrated by the failure to consider a history of prior sexual abuse when making decisions to

restrain female patients or forcibly medicate them (Herman, 1992; Stefan, 1994). The absence of housing programs that permit women with psychiatric disabilities to live with their children is another such example (Nicholson, Geller, Fisher, & Dion, 1993; Stefan, 1987).[7]

All of these examples raise issues of both patient abuse and race and gender discrimination in the policies and practices of the mental health system in this country. Yet the civil rights organizations that might be expected to focus on mistreatment of women and minorities in the mental health system, such as the National Association for the Advancement of Colored People (NAACP) or National Organization for Women (NOW), have been silent. After an initial forceful critique of the mental health system during the late 1970s and 1980s, many feminists backed away from challenging the mental health profession's diagnosis and treatment of women.[8] This may be due to heightened sensitivity to women's issues by mental health professionals, who in the 1970s began to develop concepts such as battered women's syndrome and rape trauma syndrome. By the 1980s, lawyers were introducing these concepts into the courtroom setting.

Although these steps have been perceived as victories for women, the use of these diagnoses in legal settings can cause unforeseen damage. For example, the use of rape trauma syndrome against men accused of rape may lead to the reintroduction of recently abolished practices, such as the psychiatric examination of the victim,

---

[5]For a list of studies documenting this, see the section titled "History of the Mental Health Profession's Theory and Practice toward Women and Minorities." At least fairly substantial research has taken place regarding diagnosis and treatment of black patients. Less research has been done in this area on diagnosis and treatment of patients who are members of other minorities, such as Native Americans and Eskimos, Asian Americans, and Hispanics.

[6]Holstein's book presents an illuminating discussion of the subtle way in which gender stereotypes influence commitment decisions, and a brilliant sociological and linguistic analysis of the commitment process generally.

[7]One of the best indications that mental health programs are developed with the implicit assumption that the typical client is male is the general absence of concern for the client's children. Although male clients are typically single with no dependents, many women with psychiatric disabilities have children. If they seek treatment or rehabilitation, they often ultimately lose custody of their children.

[8]There have been signs that the silence of feminists about issues relating to mental health treatment is beginning to change, with the opposition of NOW to new psychiatric diagnoses related to premenstrual stress and "masochistic" personality disorder. However, women's groups generally slight mental health issues, and no organized women's group has challenged the treatment of women in institutional settings.

defendants' access to the woman's medical and psychiatric records, admission of evidence of the victim's past sexual behavior, and even corroboration requirements (Stefan, 1994).[9] Although tort lawyers have begun to grasp the significance of sexual abuse perpetrated by therapists and clinicians on women patients, and the number of malpractice suits arising out of such abuse is proliferating, only rare attempts have been made at feminist analysis or practice in this area (LeBoeuf, 1988).[10] For the most part, however, the feminist legal community and personal injury lawyers have been indifferent to the injuries of women who are institutionalized or have a serious mental illness.

Minority mental health professionals also focused their attention productively on issues of race and mental health, but the legal community has yet to pay attention to and use this material, even innovative material directly aimed at the legal community (Griffith & Griffith, 1986). Attempts to end the mistreatment of minorities in the mental health system through legal means have been even less forthcoming. After early efforts to desegregate mental institutions, the NAACP has retreated from any involvement with blacks in the mental health system.

Mental health lawyers and activists on behalf of people labeled "mentally ill" have done no better for women and minorities in the mental health system. Although Protection and Advocacy systems, funded by the federal government to provide advocacy and legal services to institutionalized people, were given an explicit congressional mandate to be more sensitive to issues of race and culture among their clients,[11] not one of the 54 programs[12] have brought a single action based on race discrimination in the eight years of their existence.[13]

The law's impact on women and minorities in the mental health system is, for the most part, very different. To combine these two groups in a single chapter may initially seem inappropriate. But ultimately, there are some unifying themes common to women and minorities in the mental health system and as subjects of mental health law. The mental health system exists in a political and social culture, and reflects that culture in ways that are damaging to both women and minorities (Mercer, 1984; Stefan, 1992). Yet mental health professionals behave as if they are free from cultural constructs and preconceptions, and the image of the mental health profession as detached and objective (Menzies, 1989; Starr, 1982; Stefan, 1992) allows society to lose sight of the fact that clinicians rely "on a distinctive set of cultural presuppositions that may be different from those of the patient" (Mezzich, Kleinman, et al., 1993, p. 8).

History suggests that the mental health profession has embodied both racism and sexism in its theory and practice, not only accepting pre-

---

[9]Elizabeth Schneider (1986), one of the first lawyers to use battered woman syndrome evidence, was also one of the first to warn about the dangers to women of medicalizing issues of violence against them.

[10]LeBoeuf, though highlighting the genuine damage done to women who have sex with their therapists, nevertheless takes a situation with obvious implications for feminist political and cultural analysis and appears to accept the medical model at face value without question. For example, after detailing a long list of abuses by psychiatrists of their women clients, she states without caveat, "Because of the effect of the victim's pre-existing illness [which was often diagnosed by the same psychiatrist who exploited the woman, but whose judgment as to the woman's condition remains unquestioned] on her ability to consent, women who are victims of psychotherapeutic exploitation can be presumed to be incapable of full consent" (LeBoeuf, 1988, p. 85). Thus, she accepts without challenge the current legal structure, which severely limits women's legal relief unless they present themselves to legal decision makers as diminished or defective (Stefan, 1992).

[11]See U.S. Congress (1988). The full text is reproduced in Rosenthal and Carty (1988).

[12]Protection and Advocacy agencies are also funded for the District of Columbia, Puerto Rico, the Virgin Islands, and Guam.

[13]In part, as we will see later, this is due to the fact that cases involving race discrimination are difficult to structure. These programs have also not made any efforts to bring lawsuits involving gender discrimination. The Wisconsin and Kentucky Protection and Advocacy Agencies have each worked on race discrimination issues through administrative advocacy: the Wisconsin P&A addressed broad-based discrimination issues in one facility, and the Kentucky P&A worked on lowering the number of black patients in highly restrictive wards.

vailing stereotypes of women and minorities, but systematically classifying members of those groups who were angry, who protested, or who simply behaved differently as suffering from illness.[14] Even when acting from the best of motives, mental health professionals tend to focus on treating anger, distress, and depression as personal problems: the political becomes purely and relentlessly personal.

The law, both through judicial deference to professionals and by requirements for the structuring of litigation, strongly reinforces these approaches. Existing legal mechanisms for challenging race and gender discrimination are difficult to adapt to the mental health context. Requirements relating to standing, immunity from suit, intent, causation, class representation, and state action, operate to impede legal remedies for race and gender discrimination in the mental health system. Even if these obstacles are overcome, courts are deferential—perhaps too much so—to presumed expertise and neutrality that may simply be race and gender discrimination cloaked in elaborate terminology (Stefan, 1992).

The extent to which the mental health profession's research and practice are shaped by the assumptions and biases of the dominant culture even today is best illustrated by hindsight. Therefore, this chapter will begin with a brief history of the mental health profession's theory and practice toward women and minorities.[15] Next, I will examine traditional issues in mental health law—civil commitment, right to treatment, right to refuse treatment, and right to be free from

seclusion and unreasonable restraint—and their impact on women and minorities. The final section will be devoted to legal matters of particular concern to women and minorities in the mental health system.

History of the Mental Health Profession's Theory and Practice toward Women and Minorities

History of the Mental Health Profession's Theory and Practice toward Women

Sigmund Freud, the father of modern psychiatry, was one of the most influential theorists of women's psychological development. His ideas helped form both professional and popular images of women. Freud portrayed women as naturally passive and masochistic. After a period of believing the stories of childhood sexual abuse that many of his women clients told him, Freud decided that these stories simply reflected women's fantasies, setting the stage for almost 50 years of clinical disbelief and discrediting of women's stories of sexual abuse (Masson, 1984).

In the unlikely event that women were believed when they told of being raped or abused, the therapist's job was to discover what pathology of theirs led this situation to occur: "[T]herapists concentrated on the reasons that women supposedly chose to be in abusive situations. Until recently, many therapists believed that one of their primary tasks was to discover the underlying

---

[14]See the following two sections of this chapter. Interestingly, this perception is shared in other countries. See Mercer (1984), who notes that "psychiatry [in Britain] has played an active role in attempts to medicalise black resistances and define them not as aspects of a political struggle but as individualised, medico-psychological problems of 'alienation' or 'inter-generational conflict' or 'identity crises' " (p. 22).

[15] Throughout this chapter, emphasis is placed on African Americans, simply because more research is available on this group than for all other members of minority groups combined. When possible, I have included information about Hispanic Americans, Asian Americans, and Native Americans. Although there is much more research relating to African

Americans, that research has come under some criticism. For example, Mary Gauvain (1994) has noted that social science research about blacks has often concentrated on poor blacks rather than working-class or middle-class blacks. In addition, research often assumes that blacks share a common experience and common response.

psychological reasons that women provoked assaults" (Kutchins & Kirk, 1989, p. 91).

This preoccupation was reflected in law as well as social science literature. The eminent Dean Wigmore (1970), who wrote the leading treatise on evidence, advised that many if not most women fabricated rape accusations, and all women who came forward with such accusations should be subjected to psychological examination. An article coauthored by a prominent law professor with substantial mental health training claimed that women sought out rape because they feared it and simply wanted to get it over with (Slovenko & Phillips, 1962, p. 807).[16]

The mental health profession's theories with regard to women in the 1940s and 1950s also used the writings of Freud and his followers to legitimate gender roles. It was not only inappropriate for women to be intellectual and ambitious, it was a sign of maladjustment and mental illness: "Woman's intellectuality is to a large extent paid for by the loss of valuable feminine qualities. . . . All observations point to the fact that the intellectual woman is masculinized; in her, warm, intuitive knowledge has yielded to cold unproductive thinking" (Deutsch, 1944, pp. 289, 291). The woman's proper role was maternal and domestic. Mental health theorists from Freud on did not stop there but emphasized that women craved pain and domination. As Deutsch (1944) wrote, "The attraction of suffering is comparably stronger for women than for men" (p. 273).

Not surprisingly, the women's movement began by identifying the mental health system's theorists and practitioners as partners in the oppression of women. Kate Millett spent a lengthy chapter in *Sexual Politics* (1970, pp. 249–329) dissecting the role of the mental health profession in providing the ideological

support for patriarchy.[17] Nor was she the only prominent feminist author attacking the mental health system (Brownmiller, 1975; Chesler, 1989; Martin, 1981).[18]

At first, psychiatric theory was the most common target of critique by feminists. They worked on debunking the theory of penis envy and the contention that women were "naturally" docile, submissive, and timid (Brownmiller, 1975; Millett, 1970). Later feminists—including men—probed the complicity of the mental health profession in concealing the extent of child abuse, especially incest. Jeffrey Masson (1984) provoked intense controversy with his research finding that Freud had initially believed girls' stories of sexual abuse and had recanted because of concerns for his career and reputation. Even less well-known collections put together by women's consciousness-raising groups repeatedly mentioned abuses at the hands of a mental health profession chiefly concerned with keeping women in their proper places (Connell & Wilson, 1974).

The classic feminist critique of the mental health system remains Phyllis Chesler's *Women and Madness*, originally published in 1972. This was the first book to focus on the connection between the political and psychiatric oppression of women.[19] Chesler pointed out that women were being diagnosed as mentally ill for being promiscuous, for getting raped, for acting rebellious, and for disobeying their husbands. They were then "treated" by men who were patronizing and condescending at best and whose cure for them

---

[16]With no supporting citation, Slovenko and Phillips (1962) state that "fear of rape in females may activate a 'riddance mechanism' whereby they allow themselves to be raped in actuality in order to deal with the ever-present fear that it may actually happen. Quite often in cases of alleged sexual assault, we find the victim herself unconsciously tempting the offender" (p. 867). Slovenko is still well respected and publishing today.

[17]Ironically, Millett would later herself be involuntarily committed by her family. Representation by an ACLU attorney won her quick release. She documents her personal odyssey through the mental health system in *The Loony Bin Trip* (1990).

[18]The very first pages of Susan Brownmiller's *Against Our Will: Men, Women, and Rape* (1975) begin with an indictment of the mental health profession for ignoring the problem of rape. Brownmiller discusses the support the mental health profession provided for the theory that women craved rape on pages 350–362 of her book.

[19]Some psychiatric survivors have criticized Chesler's belief that psychotherapy can be helpful if informed by feminist principles (Chamberlin, 1978).

involved a return to submissiveness and docility. Although much has changed since Chesler wrote her book, the most fundamental aspects of her critique still hold true today (Chesler, 1989).

Nevertheless, the feminist critique of the mental health system virtually disappeared in the late 1970s and 1980s. It may be plausibly argued that this was because the mental health establishment—especially female mental health professionals—responded to feminist criticism by beginning to study subjects of interest to women: rape, battering, child abuse, and other forms of violence against women, and by developing feminist theories of mental health and feminist forms of therapy. Among the theorists who emerged among mental health professionals were Lenore Walker, Mary Ann Dutton, Judith Herman, Elissa Benedek, Nancy Felipe Russo, Mary Koss, Dianna Russell, and Jean Hamilton. These women did groundbreaking work in substantiating the existence of an enormous level of violence against women and the psychological damage it caused. Their work transformed the national consciousness about violence against women and its consequences.

But in the process, the angry, empowered women of the feminist movement who marched, held speakouts, and organized the first rape crisis centers and battered women's shelters were gradually marginalized, as federal grants and funding went to professionals interested in studying and treating victims rather than to organizers who saw violence against women as a political issue. Raped women's reactions were studied, organized, and labeled as syndromes. Every aspect of women's lives that had called forth a political response was turned into a psychiatric condition: battered women's syndrome, rape trauma syndrome, child abuse accommodation syndrome, and therapist-patient sex syndrome. Women began to be believed when they reported sexual assault, but only if they accepted the role of victim. Their reactions were considered genuine traumas, but once again it was women who had to be cured. The American Psychiatric Association began in the 1980s to create a number of new diagnoses. These diagnoses were either gender-specific, such as late luteal

dysphoric disorder,[20] or could be seen as pathologizing and blaming women for problems more properly characterized as social issues, such as the diagnosis of "masochistic personality disorder"—"a diagnosis for people who stay in abusive relationships."[21]

Few mental health professionals suggested that a society that accepted such a staggeringly high rate of violence against women itself needed to be transformed. Yet there was some opposition to the new psychiatric diagnoses, both within and outside the mental health profession. The organized opposition brought a measure of success. Self-defeating personality disorder, which was placed in the appendix to DSM-III-R, was removed entirely in the DSM-IV edition. However, periluteal dysphoric disorder remains in the appendix to DSM-IV.

History of the Mental Health Profession's Theory and Practice toward Members of Minority Groups

Although increasing research is being pursued regarding diagnosis, treatment, and utilization of mental health services by members of minority groups, as a threshold matter, one has to distinguish carefully in making generalizations about

---

[20]*Periluteal dysphoric disorder* or *late luteal dysphoric disorder* is the psychiatric term for a subset of premenstrual stress syndrome, popularly known as PMS, in which mood disturbance is the predominant symptom (Spitzer, Severino, Williams, & Parry, 1989).

[21]This diagnosis was first proposed in 1985 by the Work Group to Revise DSM-III (Kutchins & Kirk, 1989). The nomenclature for this diagnosis was later changed to "self-defeating personality disorder" (Kutchins & Kirk, 1989, p. 92 n. 1). While gender-neutral on its face, the diagnosis raised the specter of pathologizing women who were involved in battering relationships and was opposed by women, both within psychiatry and outside the profession. The head of the committee that proposed this diagnosis, Frederick Kass, stated that he did not have battered women in mind when the diagnosis was developed, but rather "the martyrish mother who always arranges to get the short end of the stick and whose manipulative, resentful, long-suffering manner reflects a profound lack of self-esteem" (Holden, 1986, p. 328).

"minorities."[22] Although many government statistics until very recently were presented as "white" and "all other races," the change to "White," "Black," and "all other races"[23] does not represent much progress. "All other races" does not distinguish among the very different cultural and social situations of Asians, Hispanics, and Native Americans in the United States.[24] For example, many recent Indochinese refugees have experienced extreme trauma and even torture (Mollica et al., 1990).[25] The "all other races" category gives a clear indication of the significance placed by those who collect statistics on these distinctions between different races and cultures.

History

The history of the delivery of mental health services to minorities is replete with overt racism as well as crushing neglect: "Historically, the question of black mental health status has been used politically as a justification for slavery, as a 'scientific' rationale for segregation, and to reinforce the concept of black racial inferiority" (Neighbors, 1984, p. 69). Most mental institutions across the South were legally segregated until recently. The first time that any mental institution was required to be integrated was in 1948, when Harry Truman ordered that Veterans Administration Hospitals be desegregated.[26] Desegregation was vigorously opposed by many of the most respected mental health professionals of the time;[27] they argued on the basis of their professional judgment and expertise that "integration was not in the best interest of the patients, that psychiatric care could be best delivered in a segregated setting" (Prudhomme & Musto, 1973, p. 47).

Most mental institutions in the South remained segregated well past *Brown v. Board of Education* (1954) and into the late 1960s.[28] In 1969, the Legal Defense Fund of the NAACP

---

[22]Issues of ethnic identity raise complex questions. Most existing categories do not account for dual or multiple ethnic identities. For example, "black" is not synonymous with "African American" in that a significant number of black people in the United States are of Caribbean origin and do not identify as African Americans. The group often designated "Hispanic" contains Mexican Americans, Cuban Americans, Puerto Ricans, and immigrants from Nicaragua, El Salvador, and other Latin American countries, who may have very different cultural identities. "Blacks" include African-Americans and people from the Caribbean islands. "Native Americans" include Eskimos from Alaska as well as Navajo from Arizona, and the category "Asian American/Pacific Islanders" includes Japanese, native Hawaiians, Filipinos, Chinese, Vietnamese, Laotian/Hmongs, and Koreans. These people come from very different cultures and have different responses to different forms of treatment.

[23]Compare the data presented in Mental Health (1992), pp. 283–284, 288–290 (presenting errata sheet from Mental Health United States 1990) with that on pp. 265–266.

[24]As noted above, even within those categories, there are numerous cultural differences between, for example, Japanese, Vietnamese, and Koreans, or Puerto Ricans, Cuban Americans, and Mexican Americans, or between the Aleut from Alaska and the Navajo from Arizona.

[25]The article by Mollica et al. (1990) makes clear the importance of distinguishing between cultural groups: Vietnamese, Cambodians, and Laotian/Hmong had experienced different levels of trauma and torture and responded in different ways to treatment provided them.

[26]Harry S. Truman, Executive Order No. 9980, *Regulations Governing Fair Employment Practices Within the Federal Establishment*, July 26, 1948, quoted in Prudhomme and Musto (1973). This chapter of the Prudhomme and Musto book provides a fascinating overview of the development of the mental health profession with regard to racial issues and contains material not found elsewhere.

[27]For example, Dr. Winifred Overholser, the director of St. Elizabeth's Hospital, at the time nationally known as a leading research facility, opposed desegregation as against the interests of the patients (Prudhomme & Musto, 1973).

[28] Tenn. Code Annotated 33-602 ("Colored insane kept in separate buildings") was apparently repealed in 1965; Va. Code Ann. Title 37-5 through 37-7 ("no white person shall be transferred to an institution used exclusively for colored persons or vice versa") was apparently repealed in 1964; Ga. Code Ann. 35-225 ("in no case shall Negroes and white persons be together"). Interestingly, when Georgia revised its code in 1960, this section "was expressly retained" (Editorial note, Ga. Code Ann. 35-225); North Carolina Code Ann. 122-3 (reserving Cherry Hospital "exclusively for colored persons") was repealed in 1963. For a curious and isolated case challenging racial discrimination in mental hospitals, see *Johnson v. Crawfis* (1955). The plaintiffs sought the admission to a mental hospital of an 11-year-old boy, who apparently did not have a mental illness but had severe retardation. They charged that the institution refused to admit the boy because of his race; the defendants claimed that the beds for children were full, and no child of any race would be admitted. Over the course of the opinion, it seems clear that the institution

sued the state of Alabama over its mental institutions—segregated by statute as of 1969—as well as discrimination against black employees in the case of *Marable v. Alabama Mental Health Board* (1969).[29]

Marable illustrates a fairly common picture of mental health treatment in the Southern United States in the late 1960s and early 1970s. The court noted as "undisputed facts" to which all sides agreed that Bryce, the "white" institution, contained 4700 white patients and 400 black patients. One hundred and sixty of the black patients lived in a facility eight miles from Bryce's main complex. The rest lived in segregated units called "Ward X, the Lodge and the Colony" "for purposes of performing work at or around the [white] facilities." The Colony was an "old, dimly lighted building" where "Negroes are housed solely to work in the laundry and certain kitchen areas at Bryce." They slept in one large room with 87 beds. The Lodge was a converted stable.

Searcy, the black institution, housed only black patients in far worse conditions than those experienced by black patients at Bryce. The facility, with cement floors and backless wooden benches, had "a TV set, dominoes and cards if requested, and a weekly visit from the Recreation Department." One white doctor and four Cuban refugee doctors treated the 2500 black patients at Searcy. The court ordered the state to desegregate its institutions and end racial discrimination against black staff members, finding that black patients could sue over discrimination against black employees because it adversely affected patient treatment.

Interestingly, although the decision in *Marable* was written by Judge Frank Johnson—who less than two years later decided the famous right-to-treatment case of *Wyatt v. Stickney* challenging conditions at Bryce—no mention of racial issues was ever made in *Wyatt*. And ironically, *Wyatt* is commonly regarded as the first class action lawsuit involving the rights of persons in mental institutions in this country. Although in fact *Marable* was the first class action involving the rights of patients in a mental institution, no mental health law textbook contains any citation to the *Marable* case.[30]

The *Marable* case marked the beginning and the end of successful race-related mental health litigation in the United States. A few scattered cases charging race discrimination in the delivery of mental health services were filed in the early 1970s and rebuffed by the courts.[31]

This is not because racism ceased in mental health theory and practice. In 1967, the *Journal of the American Medical Association* published a letter from several prominent neurologists speculating that participants in the race riots of the 1960s had neurological brain disfunctions and implying that psychosurgery might be a treatment of choice for these aberrant and violent people.[32]

---

was segregated by ward, a practice defended by the state in its brief, although evidently not codified in statutory form. The issue was argued in court, but the judge held that the boy lacked standing to challenge the segregation because he was never admitted to the hospital.

[29]This litigation actually began after the U.S. Department of Health, Education, and Welfare (HEW) refused to give federal funds to Alabama for mental health care on the grounds that its facilities were segregated. Alabama sued HEW, and attorneys representing the patients intervened in the litigation, as did the United States.

---

[30]Indeed, the first individual case regarded as the beginning of the legal formulation of the right to treatment, *Rouse v. Cameron* (1966), involved a black man. No textbook excerpt of this case makes this fact clear.

[31]In *North Philadelphia Community Board v. Temple University* (1971), the plaintiffs charged that the defendants failed to provide the kind of mental health services available in predominantly white communities and failed to recognize and provide for the specific mental health needs of black clients; the court dismissed the case for failure to exhaust administrative remedies. In *Davis v. Hubbard* (1980), a federal district court rejected the plaintiffs' argument that black patients in an institution were entitled to a representative number of black employees among the staff of the institution.

[32]The letter noted that

[i]t is important to realize that only a small number of the millions of slum dwellers have taken part in the riots, and that only a sub-fraction of these rioters have indulged in arson, sniping, and assault. Yet, if slum conditions alone determined and initiated riots, why are the vast majority of slum dwellers able to resist the temptations of

The ascription of violent behavior in poor, crime-filled neighborhoods plagued with unemployment and police brutality to biological causes, susceptible to cure by biological interventions, did not cease in the 1960s. A recent article titled "Psychology's Role in the Public Health Response to Assaultive Violence among Young African American Males" considered the possibility of biological risk factors for violence, while noting the controversies surrounding this theory (Hammond & Yung, 1993).

In 1992, after the riots in Los Angeles following the acquittal of the police officers accused of beating Rodney King, Frederick Goodwin, then head of the Alcohol, Drug Abuse and Mental Health Administration, made remarks comparing the inner city to the jungle and youths of the inner city to rhesus monkeys who only want to kill each other, have sex, and reproduce.[33] Although Goodwin later apologized for any misunderstanding arising from these remarks, he continued to advocate a federal program on violence that called for establishing biological markers for the early identification of conduct-disordered children. This program would predict future violence by examining and assessing very young children and begin interventions, including the use of drugs for behavior control such as Ritalin, with children as young as five years old ("Study to Quell Violence," 1992).[34]

The mental health system continues to be characterized by an abundance of practices that could be fairly described as racially discriminatory or at the very least racially insensitive. The law enforces and exacerbates the damage of these practices. This process will be described in greater detail in the following section.

Impact of Mental Health Law on Women and Members of Minority Groups

Mental health law can be described in a number of ways. Even by the most narrow definition, it includes a wide range of legal issues within the civil setting. Because of considerations of length, this chapter will be devoted primarily to civil law (Perlin, 1990), ranging from involuntary civil commitment to the rights of institutionalized people, including the right to treatment and the right to refuse treatment. It also includes rights outside institutions, such as the right not to be discriminated against on the basis of disability, first established by the Rehabilitation Act of 1973 and recently expanded by Congress when it passed the Americans with Disabilities Act in 1990.

---

unrestrained violence? Is there something peculiar about the violent slum dweller that differentiates him from his peaceful neighbor? . . . The real lesson of the urban rioting is that, besides the need to study the social fabric that creates the riot atmosphere, we need intensive research and clinical studies of the *individuals* committing the violence. The goal of such studies would be to pinpoint, diagnose, and treat those people with low violence thresholds before they contribute to further tragedies. (Ervin, Mark, & Sweet, 1967, p. 895; emphasis in original)

[33] The exact text of Goodwin's remarks is as follows:

If you look, for example, at male monkeys, especially in the wild, roughly half of them survive to adulthood. The other half die by violence. That is the natural way of it for males, to knock each other off, and, in fact, there are some interesting evolutionary implications of that because the same hyperaggressive monkeys who kill each other are also hypersexual, so they copulate more and reproduce more to offset the fact that half of them are dying.

Now, one could say that if some of the loss of social structure in this society, and particularly within the high impact inner city areas, has removed some of the civilizing evolutionary things that we have built up, and maybe it isn't just the careless use of the word when people call certain cities jungles, that we may have gone back to what might be more natural, without all of the social controls that we have imposed upon ourselves as a civilization over thousands of years in our evolution. (From a transcript of the February 11, 1992, meeting of the National Mental Health Advisory Council, available through the Center for the Study of Psychiatry, 4628 Chesnut Street, Bethesda, Md. 20814)

[34] The proposed conference on genetics and crime was canceled ("U.Md. Cancels Conference," 1992; "New Storm Brews," 1992). The development of this program was halted by the Clinton Administration at the time. After the controversy died down, the conference was reinstituted. Goodwin remains in place as the head of the National Institute of Mental Health.

Another way to describe mental health law is to see it in terms of the legal needs of people who are considered to have a mental illness. Thus, although search and seizure law governed by the U.S. Constitution's Fourth Amendment is not typically thought of as mental health law, when an individual is taken from his or her home to be detained at a mental institution, and the court analyzes this individual's rights in terms of the protection of the Fourth Amendment (*Villanova v. Abrams,* 1992), this may be seen as a mental health law issue. Although family law is not typically considered to be mental health law, if an individual loses custody of a child because of a diagnosis of mental illness or because of refusal to take psychotropic medication (*In re M.M.M.,* 1984), those situations may be seen as involving mental health law issues.

This chapter will look at the law in both categories as it affects women and minorities. First, we will look at the traditional issues of civil commitment, right to treatment, and right to refuse treatment, and then we will turn to specific mental health law issues raised by the special circumstances of women and minorities in this country.

Civil Commitment

The act of involuntarily committing an individual constitutes a deprivation of liberty and freedom of movement. In a society where "liberty is the norm, and detention prior to trial or without trial is the carefully limited exception" (*United States v. Salerno,* 1987, p. 755), the standards that must be met before an individual may be civilly committed and many of the procedures that must be followed have been set forth by the U.S. Supreme Court.

An individual must both have a mental illness and be either dangerous to himself or herself or dangerous to others to justify involuntary civil commitment (*Foucha v. Louisiana,* 1992; *O'Connor v. Donaldson,* 1975).[35] Therefore, to commit an individual, the state must prove by clear and convincing evidence (*Addington v. Texas,* 1979) two things: that the individual has a mental illness, and that, by reason of that mental

illness, the individual is dangerous. Both the requirement of a finding of mental illness and the requirement of a finding of dangerousness take on special meanings in the context of women and members of minority groups in this country.

The Requirement of a Finding of Mental Illness and Its Impact on Minorities and Women

Although a court must make a legal finding that the individual has a mental illness, in civil commitment cases judges defer almost completely to mental health professionals in the determination of mental illness. Thus, if a professional diagnoses an individual as having a mental illness, the court very rarely investigates the basis for this conclusion or the procedures by which the professional reached this conclusion. This is not because courts feel themselves unable to undertake this sort of review. In the criminal justice system, searching inquiries often accompany professional pronouncements that a defendant was insane at the time of the offense, incompetent to stand trial, or competent (or incompetent) to be executed. For instance, in *Ford v. Wainwright* (1986)—a case involving execution of a man alleged to be insane—the Supreme Court noted that

[c]ross-examinaton of the psychiatrists, or perhaps a less formal equivalent, would contribute markedly to the process of seeking truth in insanity disputes by bringing to light the bases for each expert's beliefs, the precise factors underlying those beliefs, any history of error or caprice of the examiner, any personal bias with respect to the issue of capital punishment, the expert's degree of certainty about his or her own conclusions,

---

[35]Whereas *Donaldson,* a civil commitment decision, left open the possibility that an individual could be involuntarily committed if he or she received mental health treatment, *Foucha* eliminated that option, finding that a person could only be involuntarily held in a mental hospital if he or she was mentally ill and a danger to self or others. Indeed, one passage in *Foucha* raises the possibility that a person may only be committed if "the person sought to be committed is mentally ill and . . . requires hospitalization for his own welfare *and* the protection of others" (p. 1783; emphasis added).

and the precise meaning of ambiguous words used in the report. (p. 415)

Although cross-examination is available in civil settings, and some attorneys do cross-examine professionals about their diagnoses, an examination of hundreds of civil commitment cases revealed that none of the factors listed above—or indeed, anything related to the validity or accuracy of the diagnosis of mental illness—was ever mentioned in any case.[36] Yet the accuracy and validity of diagnoses in general and diagnoses of minorities in particular has been repeatedly called into question (Bersoff, 1992; Ennis & Lit- wack, 1974; Lawson, 1986; Lipton & Simon, 1985).

Although diagnoses such as schizophrenia and depression appear race and gender neutral, they are not distributed evenly among the population. Of the five leading diagnoses for admission to outpatient clinics, schizophrenia ranks first for black men (145.2 per 100,000 population), and last for white women (60.9 per 100,000) (Olmedo & Parron, 1981). Depression is by far the most likely diagnosis for women; women are diagnosed with depression significantly more often than men.[37] Anorexia and other eating disorders are also manifested far more frequently in women

than in men, as are multiple personality disorder and histrionic personality disorder (American Psychiatric Association, 1994). Men, on the other hand, are much more often diagnosed as having antisocial personality disorder or substance abuse problems (American Psychiatric Association, 1994; Robins & Regier, 1991).

The research literature consistently shows that the high rate of diagnosis of schizophrenia for blacks is at least in part the product of error in diagnosis (Adebimpe, 1981; Lipton & Simon, 1985; Neighbors & Jackson, 1989). Since schizophrenia is considered one of the most severe mental illnesses, a diagnosis of schizophrenia might be expected to result in a higher likelihood of involuntary civil commitment. Research confirms that blacks are involuntarily committed at a much higher rate than whites. Because an individual must be found to have a mental illness by clear and convincing evidence in order to be involuntarily committed, mistaken diagnoses may have a major impact on the process of civil commitment.

Race, Diagnosis, and Involuntary Commitment   Blacks are consistently diagnosed as schizophrenic far more often than whites—up to twice as often (Adams, Dworkin, & Rosenberg, 1984, p. 971; Neighbors & Jackson, 1989, pp. 303–304; Robins & Regier, 1991, p. 40; Snowden & Cheung, 1990, p. 349), and more in some Southern states.[38] In a study of state hospital admissions in South Carolina, the fewer blacks who lived in

---

[36] The distinction between the frequently thorough evaluation of the evidence of mental illness in criminal cases, when the diagnosis is perceived as a way of "getting the defendant off," and the virtually total deference to diagnosis in civil commitment settings, where the diagnosis will result in the person's institutionalization, is an example of what Michael Perlin (1991, 1993) has described and documented as *pretextuality* in mental health proceedings. Perlin is referring to hearings that purport to be guided by due process but whose outcome is often predetermined by the preexisting and often unconscious stereotypes employed by the decision maker.

[37] The Epidemiological Catchment Area Survey found that "over twice as many women as men have major depression and dysthimia [a chronic] (of at least two years' duration) [disturbance of mood involving either depressed mood or loss of interest or pleasure in most usual activities along with some of the symptoms used to diagnose major depression]" (Robins & Regier, 1991, p. 65; the definition of dysthimia is on p. 55). Table 4-10 in Robins and Regier (1991) shows a lifetime prevalence rate of major depression in men at 2.6% and women at 7.0%. Another recent study indicated that "of the 11 million adults who suffered from major depression in 1990, approximately 7.8 million, or 71 percent, were women" ("Cost of Depression," 1994, p. 85).

---

[38] In South Carolina state hospitals, for example, a third of all black patients were diagnosed with schizophrenia, a figure three times higher than that of white patients (Ramm, 1989, p. 15). In Tennessee in 1990, among involuntarily committed inpatients, African Americans constituted nearly half of those with a diagnosis of schizophrenia (Lawson, Hepler, Holladay, & Cuffel, 1994). The significantly greater rate of diagnoses of schizophrenia among blacks in the South is an ironic inverse of the situation in 1840, when the census revealed that "the South had almost no insane Blacks, but as one moved north the rate of insanity increased." John C. Calhoun of South Carolina interpreted these statistics to mean that the elimination of the "protected condition" of blacks in slavery produced insanity. The census figures were later shown by research to be in error, but the government refused to alter them or admit mistake (Prudhomme & Musto, 1973, pp. 30–31).

the area from which black patients were admitted, the greater the likelihood that they would be diagnosed as having schizophrenia rather than affective disorder (Wright, Scott, Pierre-Paul, & Gore, 1984). On average, 17.2 black persons with the diagnosis of schizophrenia were admitted to the state hospitals for every black admitted with a major affective disorder (the comparable statistic for whites was 3.1 to 1) (Wright et al., 1984). In counties where blacks constituted less than 20% of the population, 44.5 black persons were admitted with a diagnosis of schizophrenia for every black diagnosed as having an affective disorder (Wright et al., 1984).

Studies have confirmed that the disproportionate diagnosis of schizophrenia among blacks reflects misdiagnosis (Adebimpe, 1981; Lawson, 1986; Lipton & Simon, 1985; Neighbors & Jackson, 1989). Interestingly, this finding holds true in other Western countries. Blacks are also misdiagnosed in Britain (Mercer, 1984). When diagnoses are reexamined by trained diagnosticians, the number of blacks diagnosed with schizophrenia plummets, and those diagnosed with depression or affective disorder rises. The Epidemiological Catchment Area Survey, the largest epidemiological survey ever conducted, found that "controlled for age, gender, marital status and, most importantly, SES level [citation omitted] the significant difference between black and white prevalence rates [of schizophrenia] disappears" (Robins & Regier, 1991, p. 41).

But most diagnoses made prior to involuntary commitment hearings are not done so carefully, as the misdiagnosis studies confirm. Because "the diagnosis that is most often associated with violence is schizophrenia" (Carpenter, Hannon, McCleery, & Wanderling, 1988, p. 729), the result of misdiagnoses of schizophrenia may be reflected in predictions of violent or dangerous behavior, the second prong in the standard for involuntary commitment.

Gender, Diagnosis, and the Transformation of Oppression into Illness
While blacks and other minorities face the problem of misapplication of diagnoses that most mental health profes-

sionals agree are valid, women face a different problem: the proliferation of gender-specific diagnoses whose validity professionals dispute. While it is unthinkable that the psychiatric profession would explicitly designate race-specific diagnoses, the last 10 years have seen a number of syndromes and pathologies described that are exclusive or virtually exclusive to women: late luteal dysphoric disorder (a version of premenstrual stress), battered women's syndrome, rape trauma syndrome, and self-defeating personality disorder.

In addition, women's dissatisfaction and anger with their life situations are often diagnosed as either depression or borderline personality disorder. These diagnoses often decontextualize behavior that makes sense considered in relation to the woman's environment and history, and then pathologize the behavior and the woman.

Depression is the woman's diagnosis. Women are diagnosed with depression at rates two to four times greater than men (Kaschak, 1992). This holds true across race and national boundaries. Symptoms of major depression include feelings of worthlessness, fatigue or loss of energy nearly every day, markedly diminished interest or pleasure in all or almost all activities most of the day, nearly every day (American Psychiatric Association, 1994).

The clinical studies of depression decontextualize these symptoms from the facts of women's lives. For example, while acknowledging that women who are on public welfare with difficulties in their marriage or caring for their children are more likely to be depressed, one study interpreted this finding as showing

> the general impairment in social and occupational functioning characteristic of those with affective disorders. [A previous study] demonstrated the social and interpersonal morbidity of depression in women, that is, the difficulty depressed women have in caring for their children and in their marriages and social life. (Robins & Regier, 1991, pp. 76–77)

The source of women's depression is located in themselves, and environmental factors that might be seen as contributing to women's depression are seen instead as the result of their depression.

One excellent study of women, the Stress and Families Project, confirmed that low-income mothers in the study experienced a high rate of depressive symptoms and other mental health problems (Belle, 1982) but found that "many traditional therapeutic approaches are counter-productive for low-income mothers" (p. 198). These women, who in the study and in the larger society are likely to be minority women, were concerned with lack of money and related problems in paying bills, finding a decent place to live, putting food on the table, and getting adequate medical care. When asked by a researcher what she thought caused emotional problems, one of them "succinctly stated, 'No money or food would cause emotional problems'" (Belle, 1982, p. 198). These women often did not seek treatment because of "the fear of being called crazy and locked up, and the danger of having one's children taken away" (p. 202). These fears were not illusory.[39] Of the varied forms of treatment tried by the women in the study, hospital inpatient treatment was viewed most negatively (p. 205).[40]

Thus, although a woman could be correctly diagnosed as depressed, insufficient attention to the environment in which she found herself might lead to the erroneous conclusion that involuntary treatment in an institutional setting would be beneficial. In fact, it could simply exacerbate problems far more deep-rooted and intractable by leading to the loss of children, housing, and benefits, making food harder to come by and employment even more difficult to find. Involuntary commitment might simply deepen the woman's depression rather than resolving it. The act of involuntary commitment and treatment, or loss of custody, can only follow from a judge's order. The judge's order is often based on a mental health professional's diagnosis and recommendation. Thus, interaction with the mental health profession and with the legal system may have separate, harmful effects on women; the combination can be devastating.

Borderline personality disorder—also more prevalent in women than in men (American Psychiatric Association, 1994; Gunderson & Zanarini, 1987)—has been the subject of considerable controversy (Gunderson & Zanarini, 1987; Kramer, 1989). Patients who are diagnosed as having borderline personality disorder are almost universally described as "difficult"[41] or "manipulative" (Gunderson & Zanarini, 1987). Supposedly neutral articles about this disorder bristle with barely concealed manifestations of clinician distaste and anger. "'Borderline' is also used pejoratively in many clinics and wards, and more than one clinician has pointed out a possible sexist underpinning to the concept" (Dawson & MacMillan, 1993, p. 10).

Reading a description of borderline personality disorder makes it easy to understand why it is more prevalent in women. People who are considered to have this disorder are characterized by "[a] marked and persistent identity disturbance . . . manifested by uncertainty about several life issues, such as self-image, sexual orientation, long term goals or career choices, types of friends or lovers to have, or which values to adopt" (Dawson & MacMillan, 1993, p. 346). It is characterized by "impulsiveness in at least two areas that are potentially self-damaging, e.g. spending, sex, substance use, shoplifting, reckless driving, binge eating" (p. 346). Another hallmark of the disorder is "inappropriate intense anger or lack of control of anger, e.g. frequent

---

[39]One example involved a woman advised by a therapist not to begin treatment with him or anyone; "he feared that her acknowledgement of parenting problems and her desire for treatment could result in her being seen as an unfit mother" (Belle, 1982, p. 201). Another woman, who in fact lost her child, said, "If you've had a breakdown, it'll follow you further and faster than a prison record" (p. 201). Also see p. 206.

[40] The contributors to the Belle volume did note that the low level of satisfaction might be related to the severity of the problems that precipitated treatment (p. 206).

[41]The first line of a review of a recent book about borderline personality disorder begins, "The authors are to be applauded for devoting much of their clinical energy to a difficult patient population." The last line is as follows: "I highly recommend the book for practitioners who continue to have the courage and resiliency to treat patients with borderline syndrome" (Weddige, 1994, pp. 81, 82).

displays of temper, constant anger, or recurrent physical fights," as well as "chronic feelings of emptiness and boredom" (p. 346).

Women who are diagnosed as having borderline personality disorder are angry and express it: "Anger expressed directly or in the form of bitterness, demandingness, or sarcasm is clearly the most discriminating feature of borderline personality disorder" (Gunderson & Zanarini, 1987, p. 6).

A substantial number of involuntarily committed women are diagnosed with borderline personality disorder. Very recently, women researchers have begun to trace a connection between a diagnosis of borderline personality disorder and a history of sexual abuse as a child. In a study of patients diagnosed as having borderline personality disorder,

[e]very patient who was positive for the following six symptoms had been sexually abused: compulsive sexual behavior, chemical dependency, sadomasochistic sexual fantasy, sexual identity issues, low energy and chronic fatigue, and loss of interest in or enjoyment of sex. There were sexually abused patients who did not exhibit all six symptoms, but no patients who exhibited all six symptoms had not been sexually abused. (Craine, Henson, Colliver, & Maclean, 1988, pp. 302–303)

Some of these symptoms—low energy and chronic fatigue, and loss of interest in or enjoyment of sex—are also frequently cited as symptoms of depression.

Diagnoses are a way that the mental health profession and the law structure an individual's experience of the world, often in quite different ways than the individual herself (or himself) would describe (Estroff, Lachicotte, Illingworth, & Johnston, 1991). Diagnoses often contradict or at least reframe an individual's story about personal difficulties,[42] inexorably drawing attention away from social and environmental pressures and refocusing them on the individual's inability to cope with these pressures.[43] Often, the patients themselves resist this reconstruction of their versions of reality,[44] resulting in a greater likelihood

that they will be diagnosed as " mental ill," "in denial," and "treatment resistant." Interestingly, African American males diagnosed as "seriously mentally ill" are dramatically less likely to accept and internalize this description of themselves than white males (4.2% versus 43.6%) (Estroff et al., 1991), and also more likely to be involuntarily committed.

Women and minorities' understanding of their own stories includes the pressures of poverty, discrimination, and physical danger. For women, these pressures coexist with the pressures to be physically attractive, to seek validation and self-esteem primarily from satisfying emotional relationships, to take primary responsibility for nurturance in emotional relationships with men and with children, and to live as though threats of violence were not omnipresent. These pressures disappear in the diagnoses of mental

---

[42] These stories—those of people diagnosed as mentally ill about their perceptions of what really happened in their lives—are admittedly scarce, for the very reasons outlined here. People whose credibility has been robbed will have a hard time finding a publisher. Therefore, such stories rarely appear as material for research (but see Estroff et al., 1991) but instead usually appear in anthologies put together by people who have themselves experienced the mental health system, such as *The Madness Network New Reader* (Hirsch et al., 1974) or Michael Susko's *Cry of the Invisible* (1991). Sometimes authors with already established credibility can tell stories of their experience with madness and treatment; see Kate Millett's *The Loony Bin Trip* (1990) or Sylvia Plath's novel *The Bell Jar* (1971). The best books remain the less well known but striking and eloquent *Too Much Anger, Too Many Tears* by Janet and Paul Gotkin (1992), *How to Survive Being Committed to a Mental Hospital* (1979) by Doug Cameron, and *On Our Own* by Judi Chamberlin (1978).

[43] See Helen Gremillion's (1992) discussion of anorexia: "The 'disguise' of scientific psychiatry is the belief that objective methodologies do not actively participate in creating clinical realities . . . [in] psychiatry's intrapsychic presentation of emotional distress . . . sociocultural 'pathology' is never possible; as psychiatric interpretations of anorexia illustrate, pathology is strictly bounded by the ill 'self.' . . . Like the anorectic herself, psychiatry locates the illness as a discreet, internal problem or set of problems in need of 'objective' control and ordering" (p. 59).

[44] As psychiatrist Peter Kramer (1989) put it, "My diagnostic doggedness may make her feel I will dismiss as meaningless her understanding of her individual history" (p. 38).

illness of women and minorities to which courts defer. The reframing of reality experienced by women or minorities in this way is often the most crazy-making part of all.

The Legal Requirement of a Finding of Dangerousness and Its Impact on Minorities and Women

The Supreme Court has made it clear that an individual cannot be committed simply because he or she is found to have a mental illness (*Foucha v. Louisiana*, 1992; *O'Connor v. Donaldson*, 1975;). It is a violation of the constitutional right to due process to confine a harmless person with mental illness against his or her will.

To involuntarily commit a person, a legal finding must be made that the person's mental illness has caused him or her to behave in ways that constitute a danger either to others or to himself or herself. Predictably, both categories—danger to self and danger to others—raise interesting questions with regard to minorities and women. Taken together, they provide a fascinating insight into the construction of violence in this society.

Race and Perceptions of Dangerousness to Others   For a person to be involuntarily committed, that person's behavior must first be identified as dangerous, and then the dangerousness must be attributed to that person's mental illness.

Violent behavior and socially perceived dangerousness are far from identical. One of the most prevalent and unjust stereotypes about mental disability is that people with a diagnosis of mental illness are dangerous. Thus, in one case an individual was found to be dangerous where the court conceded that "the psychiatrist could not give any degree of probability of dangerousness, and although there was no evidence of prior dangerous conduct." The court found the individual dangerous because he believed that people were "after him" and a psychiatrist testified that other patients with the same delusions had injured other people (*People v. Sansone*, 1974).

People also perceive black males as danger-ous, even in the absence of any violent behavior (Bond, DeCandia, & MacKinnon, 1988). Research has shown that "when Whites act in ambiguous ways, their behavior is given an innocent interpretation; when Blacks act identically, they are attributed with aggressive intent" (Bond et al., 1988, p. 7). One study showed that evaluators of different races evaluated the same behavior very differently. Non–African Americans viewing a video of an interaction between an African American mother and daughter rated them as having a much higher level of conflict than African American raters (Gauvain, 1994).

Because aggressiveness or even assertiveness is beyond women's traditional social role, it is often perceived in an exaggerated fashion (Coughlin, 1994). Women who express anger are often viewed as behaving inappropriately, even dangerously (Geller & Munetz, 1986). Violent women are seen as much more dangerous and deviant than violent men.

At the same time, some violent behavior is not perceived as dangerous. Domestic violence against women by men of both races rarely results in the perception that men who inflict domestic violence are dangerous, or that they are mentally ill or have a personality disorder of any sort.

Gender and Perceptions of Dangerousness to Self   The classic way in which a person can be a danger to himself or herself is to attempt suicide. Other forms of danger to self include self-injury and failure to care for one's self adequately.

Research shows that women make far more suicide attempts than men, and women are far more likely to try to injure themselves than are men. In addition, women who have been battered, raped, or sexually abused are far more likely to attempt suicide or to injure themselves than women who have not been raped or sexually abused (Briere, 1988; Herman, 1992).

Self-injury, most often by cutting but sometimes by tearing out clumps of hair or burning the skin, has often been interpreted as attempted suicide, whereas both the accounts of those who do it (Mazelis, 1994) and the observations of those who research it strongly suggest that it is a very different act from attempting suicide (Herman, 1992). In fact, Mazelis suggests that for some people, cutting themselves is a way of avoiding suicide, a means of survival. Certain kinds of self-injury, such as cutting, are so strongly associated with coping and survival mechanisms of women who have been sexually abused that the people who engage in such conduct are overwhelmingly likely to be women. For many women with histories of sexual abuse, one of the keys to recovery is to gain a sense of control over their lives (Herman, 1992). Yet involuntary commitment removes every vestige of control over every aspect of life, from the time one gets up in the morning to the time one goes to bed at night.

The category of dangerousness to self because of an inability to care for one's self is also strongly informed by gendered assumptions. James Holstein's brilliant book, *Court Ordered Insanity* (1993), makes the point that judgments about whether people can adequately care for themselves are informed by gender stereotypes, with women more likely to be committed if they are living in situations perceived as inappropriate or dangerous. For example, men diagnosed as having a mental illness who are homeless appear to be more likely to avoid commitment for being unable to care for themselves, even when they live in states like Oregon or North Dakota (*In re J.A.D.*, 1992; *In re Stanley*, 1992); homeless women with mental illness get committed routinely in far warmer climates as being unable to care for themselves.

Civil Commitment: A Summary of the Impact on Minorities and Women and Suggestions for Analysis and Improvement

The findings of the last two sections suggest the possibility that blacks will be subject to involuntary commitment at a higher rate than whites, and studies bear out this hypothesis as well. It is clear that blacks are overrepresented in state mental hospitals, and underrepresented in private psychiatric hospitals in proportion to their numbers

in the general population (Adebimpe, 1994; Flaskerud & Hu, 1992; Lawson et al., 1994; Lindsey & Gordon, 1989). In 1980, for example, whites were admitted to state and county mental hospitals at a rate of 136.8 per 100,000. Blacks were admitted at a rate of 364.2 per 100,000 (Snowden & Cheung, 1990). Asians, on the other hand, are consistently underrepresented in both state and private mental hospitals (Flaskerud & Hu, 1992; Snowden & Cheung, 1990). Data vary for Hispanics (Snowden and Cheung observed that of 17 evaluations of Mexican Americans in psychiatric hospitals, 12 found evidence of underrepresentation and 5 found proportional representation or overrepresentation). Native Americans are tremendously overrepresented: they are admitted at almost three times the rate of whites, not including treatment at Indian Health Service Hospitals, which would have raised the rate even more.[45] These findings about state mental hospitals are replicated in studies of civilian admissions to Veterans Administration Hospitals (Snowden & Cheung, 1990). The most recent national data about rates of institutionalization suggest that men are hospitalized for psychiatric illness at a higher rate than women; of all persons receiving inpatient services on April 1, 1986, 59.1% were men and 40.9% were women (U.S. Department of Health and Human Services, 1993). The difference between the rates of hospitalization of white men and women is much smaller (55.5% men versus 44.5% women) than the difference between the rates of "all other races" (68.2% men versus 31.8% women).

About one-third of all psychiatric hospitalizations are involuntary (Snowden & Cheung, 1990); the rate is even higher when only state and county institutions are taken into account. Blacks are even more overrepresented among those involuntarily committed to state institutions than they are among general admissions (Lawson et

---

[45]All of this discussion of "overrepresentation" and "underrepresentation" assumes, of course, a norm of commitment represented by white people. This assumption should not go unnoticed.

al., 1994). In the South, blacks are nearly three times more likely to be involuntarily committed to state mental institutions than whites (Ramm, 1989). The overrepresentation of blacks in the public mental health system is also true in out-patient settings. Studies show that blacks are overrepresented as clients of community mental health centers relative to their proportion in the population (O'Sullivan, Peterson, Cox, & Kirkcby, 1989).

Why are blacks overrepresented in state mental facilities and as subjects of involuntary civil commitment? A number of explanations have been offered. One popular explanation is that there is a greater rate of pathology among the lower socioeconomic classes, and the disproportionate rate of black representation in these statistics is explained by their disproportionate representation among the poor. However, this does not turn out to be the case. Even when controlled for socioeconomic differences, the rate of admissions for blacks is higher (Snowden & Cheung, 1990).

The true reason appears to be that diagnoses of mental illness are made by observing behavior. Behavior that is culturally explainable or even appropriate for members of racial minorities tends to be seen as pathological by white professionals. For example:

[N]ormal (for blacks) protective wariness is often mistaken as paranoia, symptomatic of schizophrenia . . . strict control over affective response and a resistance to establishing rapport and communication. These behaviors are often misinterpreted as flat or blunted affect and problems relating to others and may be mistaken as further evidence of schizophrenia. (Jones & Gray, 1986, p. 63)[46]

While the effect of coercion on an individual's behavior is only now beginning to be studied,[47] none of the studies so far have addressed the differences that race or gender could make in reactions to coercion. In fact, none of the studies even differentiate responses to coercion by race or gender.

To be diagnosed as having a mental illness for engaging in conduct that is necessary for survival, and to have that stigmatizing diagnosis accepted without question by a judge and used as the basis for deprivation of liberty, is likely to increase rather than decrease an individual's stress, frustration, and what might be seen as "pathology" or "symptomatology." The role of the law is crucial here. If a black person were misdiagnosed as schizophrenic by a mental health professional, the diagnosis, while unsettling, could simply be rejected as erroneous and unhelpful by the individual. Many blacks, especially males, do just that (Estroff et al., 1991). Misdiagnosis is particularly disastrous in the legal context because it is the court, and not the mental health professional, with the power to deprive the individual of liberty by committing him or her involuntarily. Involuntary commitment wrenches an individual out of context: out of the neighborhood, community, and family. This can cause particular hardship to women and minorities.[48] Women who are involuntarily committed may lose custody of their children during even the briefest period of institutionalization. Blacks and other members of ethnic minorities are torn from their neighborhoods and networks and thrown into an institution whose culture and expectations may be difficult to comprehend. For

---

[46]Nothing illustrates the position of blacks in an institutional setting more vividly than a vignette in the documentary *Hurry Tomorrow*, set on the psychiatric ward of a Los Angeles hospital. In the documentary's opening scenes, a black patient is being interviewed by an all-white treatment team. His responses are monosyllabic and difficult to understand; he avoids making eye contact with the team and appears mute and uncomprehending. After the meeting is over and he returns to the ward, he is shown talking freely and articulately to another black patient; he seems to the viewer to be a completely normal person.

[47]See, for example, "Coercion in Mental Health Care" (1993); Group for the Advancement of Psychiatry (1994).

[48]In one study of coercion in an emergency room, the following exchange is recorded between a patient and an attending physician:

Patient: I'll go to outpatient every day. Please let me go home! Anything! Don't separate me from my children! . . . I need to be with my children. (Lidz, Mulvey, Arnold, Bennett, & Kirsch, 1993, p. 277)

Although the patient's gender is not identified, it is not hard to guess that this patient is a woman.

members of some minority groups, it may be that no one speaks their native language and supportive family are far away.

Yet the law on involuntary commitment assumes that the individual exists in a vacuum. It assumes that an individual either has a mental illness or does not have one, without looking to the effect of the person's environment on his or her behavior, or the effect of race or gender stereotypes on the diagnosis (Stefan, 1993). Likewise, dangerousness associated with mental illness is considered a clinical issue rather than one brought on by interpersonal or contextual factors such as prior physical or sexual attacks on the person alleged to be dangerous (Estroff, Zimmer, Lachiotte, & Benoit, 1994).

The liberty of the individual is seen by the law as a fundamental right of constitutional magnitude to be protected; the violation of the person's connections with others (or freedom of association) has never been addressed as a legal issue in commitment cases. Nor has the right to be free from race or gender discrimination ever been legally contested in commitment cases, although the research suggests ample grounds for suspicion in that area.

One of the reasons for the failure to challenge involuntary commitments as discriminatory on race or gender grounds is that the structure of the law makes it difficult to do so, for a number of reasons.[49] First of all, who would the proper defendant be in such a lawsuit? Officially, the judge has the final power of commitment, and judges are completely immune from suit (*Stump v. Sparkman*, 1978). True, the judges defer to the recommendations of mental health professionals. If a recommendation or diagnosis had its basis in intentional racism, the commitment might be appealed and a damage action brought against the mental health professional. Although this kind of case would itself be difficult to prove, it is probably not the consciously racist actions of

one or two mental health professionals that lead to the racial disparity in involuntary commitments. Rather, it is the stereotypes held and unconsciously applied by many mental health professionals, resulting in misdiagnosis, the greater likelihood that behavior of black men would be interpreted as indicating dangerousness and violence, the exaggeration of the dangerousness of violent women who are acting against social stereotype, or the assumption that a woman might be less able to care for herself than a man.

Most statutory or constitutional protections against race discrimination require that either the defendant be a state actor, or that the defendant act intentionally, or both. Some mental health professionals who testify for the state at commitment hearings are not employed by the state, and contracting with the state may or may not be sufficient to constitute state action. Even for those employed by the state, discrimination may be difficult to prove, both because of the presumption that professionals act neutrally and objectively, and because of the scientific mystique surrounding mental health diagnoses and predictions (Stefan, 1992). In *Addington v. Texas* (1979), for example, the Supreme Court stated that "[w]hether the individual is mentally ill and dangerous to either himself or others and is in need of confined therapy turns on the meaning of the facts which must be interpreted by expert psychiatrists and psychologists. . . . Psychiatric diagnosis . . . is to a large extent based on medical 'impressions' drawn from the subjective analysis and filtered through the experience of the diagnostician" (pp. 429–430).[50] While subjective analysis based on racial or gender stereotypes filtered through experience that may have con-

---

[49]I am indebted to Len Rubenstein, director of the Bazelon Mental Health Law Center (formerly the Mental Health Law Project), who has been thinking about this issue for almost 10 years and suggested the inclusion of this material.

[50]This summary of the process of diagnosis might seem to indicate the need for greater procedural protections rather than fewer, but the Supreme Court endorsed a lower standard of proof in *Addington* precisely because mental health professionals could not meet the higher standard: "This process [diagnosis] often makes it very difficult for the expert physician to offer definite conclusions about any particular patient. . . . Given the lack of certainty and the fallibility of psychiatric diagnosis, there is a serious question as to whether a state could ever prove beyond a reasonable doubt that an individual is both mentally ill and likely to be dangerous" (pp. 430, 429).

firmed or reinforced these stereotypes is acting intentionally for purposes of proving gender or race discrimination, it may be extremely difficult to prove that the mental health professional's decision was based on a race or gender stereotype in any individual case.[51]

In addition, laws prohibiting discrimination generally require a causal relationship between the defendants' actions and the claimed harm. The significant racial disparity in commitments could be brought about by a number of different factors. Some of these factors are a result of racism on the part of other actors in the mental health system, such as the greater tendency of police to also view ambiguous behavior on the part of black males as indicating dangerousness; others may be a reaction to racism, such as the reluctance of black family members to bring their family members in voluntarily for help (K. Davis, personal communication, February 22, 1994). One researcher noted that the statistically significant racial disparity in involuntary commitments in her study could be explained by the fact that involuntary commitments are more likely to arise out of detentions initiated by police rather than family members, and that blacks were significantly more likely to be brought into the mental health system through police actions than through their families (Rosenfeld, 1984).

Thus, the structure of the legal system obstructs a legal solution to race and gender discrimination manifestly evident from the research: the rate of misdiagnosis of blacks; the racial disparity in involuntary commitments, rising as one moves farther southward and into the more rural areas in the South; the tendency to view women as unable to care for themselves or as

having a mental illness for engaging in "inappropriate" behavior.

Nevertheless, there is room for some solutions to the problem of unconscious racism and sexism in involuntary commitment. Some are even relatively simple. The requirement in civil commitment, currently in place in a number of states, that "dangerousness" be manifested by a recent overt act (Massachusetts General Laws, 1994) may help to counteract unconscious racism that would label more ambiguous behavior as dangerous. Likewise, if "dangerous to self" were limited to situations where the state could show that a person's life was in *imminent* danger, some of the harm to women by gender assumptions around inability to care for themselves, or misunderstandings of self-injury as suicidal behavior, would be diminished.

In other words, broad, vague language in commitment statutes, like broad, vague language in criminal statutes, increases the chances that involuntary commitment will have a disparate impact on minorities, or be used mistakenly with women, because it cedes to professional discretion the definition of dangerous, and permits unconscious racism or sexism to have wider play. If objective, conduct-based, observable evidence is required, then the judge or jury is in a better position to evaluate whether those acts have been proven and the statutory criteria have been met.

The passage of the Americans with Disabilities Act (ADA) and the regulations implementing it raise the possibility of transforming and reframing the legal perspective on involuntary commitment from one primarily concerned with individual liberty to a new focus on the harm done by isolating individuals from their community and context. Under the ADA, exclusion and segregation of individuals because of their disability is illegal discrimination (Cook, 1991). Unnecessary institutionalization, when available alternatives would not segregate the individual from her family, her neighborhood, and her community, may now be illegal under the ADA (*Helen S. v. Didario*, 1994). It has been almost 10 years since a federal judge found that institutionalizing

---

[51]Traditionally, problems of proving discrimination individual by individual have been alleviated by the class action mechanism, where a group of people similarly situated sues for relief, and the evidence introduced can be much broader, such as the statistical evidence cited in this chapter. For problems with bringing cases as class actions, see the section titled "Key Legal Issues for Women and Minorities in the Mental Health System."

people with mental retardation constituted segregation in violation of the equal protection clause of the Fourteenth Amendment to the U.S. Constitution. This argument could have particular force and poignancy in the case of black people institutionalized because of misdiagnosis, misperceptions of dangerousness, misunderstandings of culture and behavior, and perhaps outright racism. This legal doctrine presents hope for a new analysis of the involuntary commitment and institutionalization of blacks and minorities in general.

In addition, considering exclusion from the community, separation from family, and inability to associate with others as the harm of involuntary commitment may be truer to the experience of women. The well-known work of Carol Gilligan (1982) suggests that women place a high value on maintaining relationships and on association, work hard to protect relationships, and are particularly damaged when relationships are destroyed. Thus, an ADA analysis of the harm done by exclusion may be needed to complement the traditional loss-of-liberty analysis when measuring the harm done by involuntary commitment to the individual.

But the first step to solving the problem of racism and sexism in the process of diagnosis, evaluation of dangerousness, and involuntary commitment is educating lawyers and mental health professionals to look for it—in the mental health system, in the legal system, and in themselves.

The Right to Treatment

History of the Right to Treatment (Revisited)

The first constitutional right to treatment case was *Wyatt v. Stickney*, filed on October 23, 1970.[52]

---

[52]Although the action was originally brought on behalf of two classes—the patients at the hospital and employees terminated for budgetary reasons—the latter group soon dropped out of the litigation (*Wyatt v. Aderholt*, 1974).

Bryce was the "white" hospital that had been compared so favorably to Searcy, the "black" hospital in the case of *Marable v. Alabama Mental Health Board*. Less than two years previously, Judge Johnson had written that

[i]n contrast to the main complex at Bryce, the physical facilities at Searcy are very old and crowded, have no dayrooms, and have bare cement floors and seating consisting of backless wooden benches. Bryce has many recreational and occupational programs and craft shops; Searcy has a television set, dominoes and cards, if requested, and a weekly visit from the recreation department. (*Marable v. Alabama Mental Health Board*, 1969, p. 294)

Bryce was now portrayed by the same judge who wrote *Marable* as "dehumanizing," "degrading," "humiliating," and "critically substandard" (*Wyatt II*, 1971, p. 1343). The judge ruled on March 12, 1971, that patients at Bryce had a constitutional right to treatment, which was violated by the conditions there (*Wyatt I*, 1971).

It was not until several months after patients at Bryce were granted the constitutional right to treatment that the lawyers in *Wyatt* filed a motion to add the patients at Searcy to the *Wyatt* case (*Wyatt III*, 1972, pp. 374–375). Interestingly, no reference to Searcy, either by Judge Johnson or by the U.S. Court of Appeals for the Fifth Circuit on review, ever identified it as anything but simply "the other mental hospital in Alabama" or "also a State institution designed to treat the mentally ill" (*Wyatt III*, 1972; *Wyatt v. Aderholt*, 1974). The role of a patient's race in determining the adequacy of treatment, and the comparison of conditions at institutions that serve predominantly minority populations with those that serve primarily white populations, was never considered in *Wyatt* and remains untouched in case law to this day.

The issue decided in *Wyatt*—that an institutionalized individual was constitutionally entitled to treatment—was first considered by the U.S. Supreme Court in 1982. In that year, the Court held that once a person is institutionalized,[53] the due process clause of the Fourteenth Amendment to the Constitution requires that the person receive minimally adequate treatment (*Youngberg v. Romeo,* 1982).[54] The constitutional measure of adequacy is that the treatment may not be a substantial departure from professional judgment, practice, or standards.

Women and Minorities Have Distinctive Treatment Needs

Professional judgment, practice, and standards are established through the requirements and guidelines of certification bodies, as well as through the testimony of experts. Both certification bodies and the experts rely on their familiarity with research in the area to develop standards, teach future practitioners, and testify with authority. The research and the standards in turn shape the practice and the professional judgment of the field.

The research literature has confirmed for a number of years that women's treatment needs are different from those of men. This is true even when men and women are diagnosed as having the same mental illness; research documents major differences between the course of major mental illnesses such as schizophrenia in men and women (American Psychiatric Association, 1994; Seeman, 1983). As one leading text noted, "Our findings suggest strongly that sensitivity to . . . gender differences should inform the planning of services and treatment for chronic mental patients" (Bennett, Handel, & Pearsall, 1986,

p. 41). Professional standards have for many years distinguished between the treatment needs of men and women. Yet treatment practices in state institutions do not appear to account for these differences.

The research also shows that mental health needs of minorities are significantly different from those of whites. Persons of African descent, Asian descent, and whites have substantially different reactions to the same dosage of medication: "Hispanics, like blacks and Asians, may show sensitivity to drugs with anticholinergic properties (such as tricyclic antidepressants and neuroleptics) and they have a higher incidence of side effects at the recommended dosages, and therefore require lower doses" (Adams & Dworkin, 1984, p. 971).

Culture may also play a role in the kind of therapy that is most appropriate. One study suggested that group therapy worked better than an individual relationship with a therapist for Hispanics, because "in the latter arrangement, the Hispanic client views the therapist as a powerful authority who has all the answers; the relationship exaggerates the patient's dependency and encourages her regression into the culturally syntonic role of the helpless patient" (Olarte & Masnik, 1985, p. 1094).

Understandably, therapy needs are different for recent immigrants and refugees from Asia than they are for Asian Americans, and very different than those of other minorities. Both men and women in this population have been through privation and culture shock, and some endured torture before coming to this country (Mollica et al., 1990). The needs of women in the population of recent refugees, many of whom are likely to have been raped and assaulted in the voyage to this country, are different from the needs of men in those populations, who may misunderstand and even reject the women as defiled (Mollica & Son, 1989).

Considerable evidence suggests not only that the distinctive treatment needs of women and minorities are ignored in the mental health system, but that mental health professionals discrim-

---

[53] There are legal issues as to when a person is constitutionally entitled to adequate treatment. Some courts have held that voluntary patients are not entitled under the Constitution to minimally adequate treatment, while others have held that labels such as *voluntary* were illusory. Some courts have found that patients in private facilities were not entitled to the same constitutional guarantees as those in state facilities. Reviewing these controversies is beyond the scope of this chapter.

[54] *Youngberg* used the term *training* rather than *treatment* because *Youngberg* involved a man with mental retardation, which cannot be treated. People with mental retardation are entitled to habilitation or training. Courts since *Youngberg* have applied it to the mental health setting and used its standards to guide decisions in cases involving the right to treatment in the mental health system.

inate by providing less of the generic services offered to black patients than to white patients. For example, one study showed that on a treatment unit that served 66 black and 35 white patients, "recreational therapy was ordered for 47% of blacks and 78% of whites; occupational therapy was ordered for 47% of blacks and 75% of whites" (Flaherty & Meagher, 1980, p. 681). The same study showed that all-white treatment teams spent more time discussing white patients than black patients; treatment teams with a majority of black members spent more time discussing black patients. Or insight therapy might be helpful in discussing problems of stress related to economic conditions or racism in society, but black patients who are equivalent in every other respect to white patients are consistently judged as less suitable for "insight" therapy (Umbenhauer & DeWitte, 1978).

Legal Remedies for Race or Gender Discrimination in the Provision of Mental Health Treatment

One possible solution to these problems is increasing the recruitment of minority professionals, and generally greater use of minority staff members to increase majority sensitivity and improve the quality of treatment and discharge planning (Flaherty & Meagher, 1980). However, the only lawsuit to raise this issue, *Davis v. Hubbard* (1980)—which argued that patients in a hospital where the population was 44.8% black were entitled to "a representative number of black employees, as well as a staff varied in sex"—was unsuccessful in persuading the court that these measures were needed for adequate treatment (p. 919).

The plaintiffs in the case apparently simply argued that adequate treatment required a staff roughly in proportion (racially) to the racial composition of the patient population. Much of the research on misdiagnosis of black patients had not been done, and the *Davis* plaintiffs could not have relied on it. Recent research on misdiagnosis may provide stronger support for specific claims that black patients are receiving inade-

quate treatment, since misdiagnosis can lead to tragic mistakes in treatment. For example, lithium carbonate has been shown to be effective in the treatment of affective disorder, but a patient misdiagnosed as schizophrenic may not receive the medication that would alleviate his or her symptoms. This happens on a regular basis (Bell & Metha, 1980).

Statutes exist that might provide the springboard for legal action to ensure that blacks received the treatment they needed, or at least the same level of treatment as white patients. Title VI of the Civil Rights Act of 1964 prohibits discrimination on the basis of race in any program that receives federal financial assistance such as Medicaid, Medicare, or other federal funds (42 U.S.C. 2000(d), 1982). Title VI has never been used to challenge the treatment accorded to minorities or women in the mental health system.

There are many reasons for this. Race discrimination in the provision of treatment is difficult to prove on an individual level. A mental health professional may be able to point to a plausible nondiscriminatory reason for actions adverse to an individual black patient, or to a range of other factors that may have influenced the individual result being challenged. It is only when studies are done of the entire state mental health system, or of a region in the state, or a particular facility, that the cumulative impact of individual decisions shows such strong racial disparity as to forcefully suggest racial discrimination is taking place in the system or facility.

The recognition of the difficulty of showing race discrimination through individual decisions is one of the reasons that many race discrimination cases are brought as class actions. In a class action, statistics such as those discussed here can be introduced into evidence to show that on a systemic level, there is an enormous disparity between the treatment accorded to blacks and whites who are otherwise similarly situated. This evidence might be crucial in mental health cases, where professionals may not act with conscious racism.

Yet a class action on behalf of all black

persons involuntarily committed would face legal problems of its own. To certify a class, a court must find that the situation of class representatives is typical of class members,[55] and some might argue that each person's mental health difficulties are unique, defeating class certification. However, problems with class certification are not the only—or even the greatest—obstacles that an attorney seeking to bring such a case would encounter.

The case of *Lora v. New York Board of Education* (1978, 1980) is instructive in highlighting the difficulty and complexity of bringing systemic race discrimination litigation in a mental health context. However, there are a number of distinctions between such a case and *Lora*, where plaintiffs challenged the practice of "dumping" minority children into "special" schools for the disabled, where they received little assistance and were segregated from other students (*Lora v. New York Board of Education*, 1978, 1980).[56]

The statistics in *Lora* were similar to the statistics presented here: minorities constituted a significant and disproportionate percentage of children in the special, separate schools created by New York. The plaintiffs charged that defendants were achieving segregation by race under cover of providing special assistance to children with disabilities.

Judge Weinstein, in a lengthy decision in favor of the plaintiffs, painstakingly traced through all the various reasons advanced for the statistically significant preponderance of minority children in the special schools. Predictably, a key justification offered by defendants was that children with emotional handicaps and behavioral problems tended to come from poor and deprived

families, and that these families were predominantly made up of minorities. Although the poverty and deprivation that led to the children's emotional problems might well be a result of racism, it was not the result of defendants' racism: indeed, defendants were now taking on the task of remedying the damage done by others.

Judge Weinstein found in favor of the plaintiffs, holding that "isolation of minority students in special education settings with small hope of a truly fruitful education or movement into less restrictive environments constitutes a denial of equal protection" (*Lora v. New York Board of Education*, 1978, p. 1276). The analogy to institutionalization of minorities with little hope for meaningful treatment is clear, as is the analogy between the assessment and diagnosis of minorities as having mental illness and being dangerous and "the referral and assignment of students to these schools [which was] based upon vague and subjective criteria. . . . [T]he combination of processes, practices and policies has a racially discriminatory effect on Black and Hispanic children" (*Lora v. New York Board of Education*, 1978, p. 1216).

The Second Circuit Court of Appeals, however, vacated Judge Weinstein's order in *Lora*, determining that he had not made sufficient findings that defendants acted with the intent to discriminate, even though their actions had discriminatory impact (*Lora v. New York Board of Education*, 1980). Title VI, the Second Circuit held, required findings of discriminatory intent, as does a claim for violation of the equal protection clause, on which Title VI is largely based.

Since the Second Circuit's decision in *Lora*, however, the U.S. Supreme Court has held that although Title VI itself requires a showing of discriminatory intent, plaintiffs can seek declaratory and limited injunctive relief for discriminatory impact under the regulations promulgated pursuant to Title VI, which prohibit discrimination in selection for or eligibility to receive services and in the provision of services (*Alexander v. Choate*, 1985; *Guardians Association v.*

---

[55]This requirement, and other requirements that must be satisfied before a case may proceed as a class action, are found in Rule 23 of the Federal Rules of Civil Procedure.

[56]Underscoring the problem with class certification referred to above, it is noteworthy that the plaintiffs in *Lora* initially failed to win class certification; the judge in their case died, and the new judge, Judge Jack Weinstein, reconsidered their motion and certified the class.

Civil Service Commission, 1983). Therefore, there is still some opportunity to use Title VI—or at least its regulations—as a vehicle for remedying racial discrimination in the mental health system.

Title VI itself and the equal protection clause of the Fourteenth Amendment to the Constitution still require a showing of intent to discriminate before a plaintiff or plaintiff class may prevail. The need to show a specific intent to discriminate is particularly difficult in a systemic context, where many different people make decisions along the way that are responsible for a structure that clearly and consistently disadvantages members of minorities. Thus, race discrimination claims regarding treatment in institutional settings may be seen as conceptually resembling legal claims that the death penalty is discriminatory because it is disparately applied to blacks. Such claims have failed under the federal equal protection clause (*McKleskey v. Kemp,* 1987) but have been received more hospitably under state constitutional guarantees of equal protection (*State v. Marshall,* 1992). Other similar cases include arguments that habitual offender statutes are disparately applied to blacks (*Miller v. Florida,* 1987). Often, actors in the mental health system may not act with conscious desire to harm an individual because he is black or believe in racial inferiority. But as Charles Lawrence (1987) has so persuasively written, an outlook incorporating false stereotypes may be so ingrained as to not be consciously intentional; yet actions based on these stereotypes are equally, if not more, harmful:

[M]ost of us are unaware of our racism. We do not recognize the ways in which our cultural experience has influenced our beliefs about race or the occasions on which those beliefs affect our actions. In other words, a large part of the behavior that produces racial discrimination is influenced by unconscious racial motivation. (p. 322)

The needs relating to both race and gender that must be addressed in the area of the right to treatment are to end outright discriminatory treatment such as provision of less desirable treatment

or no treatment beyond medication to members of minority groups, mistaken use of medications based on misdiagnosis of blacks and women based on stereotypes, or diagnosis of patients who can barely speak English by clinicians who have neither knowledge nor understanding of the patient's background and culture.

Although the difficulties of proving intent may counsel against federal equal protection cases and damage actions under Title VI, there is still room for attorneys to bring actions under the regulations to Title VI[57] under a state constitution's equal protection clause, which may be interpreted by the state supreme court more broadly than the federal equal protection clause. Or a plaintiff may simply plead a substantive due process violation: that errors in medication due to misdiagnosis, or diagnoses based on insufficient familiarity with the patient's language or culture, are departures from the professional standards in the field of mental health treatment. Further, there is a need to equate the right to "minimally adequate treatment" with the professional standards recognizing that women and men often need different forms of treatment, just as members of a given culture may need a different modality of treatment (for example, doing better with group therapy, or not being able to derive any benefit at all from group therapy).

The Right to Refuse Treatment

Some forms of treatment are experienced as frightening or noxious by their recipients, who wish to avoid them. The extent to which psychiatric patients have a right to refuse treatment has been a heavily litigated and controversial subject. The U.S. Supreme Court has considered the dimensions of an individual's constitutional right to refuse both psychiatric and nonpsychiatric treatment in several cases (*Cruzan v. Missouri*

---

[57]One advantage of Title VI litigation is that Congress abrogated state immunity under Title VI, 42 U.S.C. 2000d(7), so that while states can claim Eleventh Amendment immunity from suits under 42 U.S.C. 1983, they are foreclosed from doing so in Title VI litigation.

Department of Health, 1990; *Washington v. Harper,* 1990).

In *Washington v. Harper,* the Supreme Court held that a prisoner's liberty interest in being free from forcible medication could be overcome if the prison could show that he (1) had mental illness, (2) was dangerous to himself or others as a result of that mental illness (pp. 227, 1040),[58] and (3) would benefit from the medication.[59] Although the prisoner, Walter Harper, was a black man in a state that is predominantly white, neither the opinions in his case nor any law review commentary speculated on the role that this may have played in his diagnoses, in the behavior on which the diagnoses were based, or in the conclusion that he was so dangerous that he needed involuntary medication.[60]

_____

[58]This standard is almost identical to the civil commitment standard in the state of Washington, which was adopted by the prison as its standard to justify forced medication. While the prison standard also allowed damage to property to suffice as justification for forced medication, the Supreme Court included only danger to self or others in its own formulation of the appropriate standard.

[59]There is some confusion about the exact nature of the Court's holding, since it both required a finding of medical benefit (p. 227) and explicitly upheld a state policy that did not require such a finding (p. 227). The Court assumed that no mental health professional would medicate an individual unless the medication would benefit the individual, an assumption contradicted by several *amicus* briefs pointing out the widespread use of psychotropic medication in prisons for purposes of behavior control (p. 227, n. 13).

[60]A number of plaintiffs in famous right-to-refuse-treatment cases have been black or female or both, but no case has ever considered either of these to be relevant factors in either the decision to forcibly medicate or the individual's desire to refuse the medication. Rubie Rogers of *Rogers v. Okin* was black (Appelbaum, 1993, p. 116). Joyce Jones of *State ex. rel. Jones v. Gerhardstein* (1987) was a black woman as well; like Harper, she was black in a predominantly white state (T. Zander, attorney in the case, personal communication, September 24, 1994). The plaintiffs in *In re Bryant* (1988) and *In re Rosa M.* (1991) were black women, less surprising given that they were from the District of Columbia and New York, respectively. However, plaintiffs in both federal and state court right-to-refuse-treatment cases in Maryland were black men. The plaintiffs in *Williams v. Wilzack* (1990) and *Johnson v. Silvers* (1984) were black men, as was the plaintiff in a federal suit from North Carolina, *United States v. Charters* (1987, 1988). The diagnosis given to almost all of these people was paranoid schizophrenia.

Most recently, in *Riggins v. Nevada* (1992), the Supreme Court considered the standard for forcibly medicating a pretrial detainee prior to and during his trial for murder. It decided that the state must make a compelling showing that the medication was necessary and that all less restrictive alternatives had been considered.

Both the *Harper* and *Riggins* cases discussed the side effects of psychotropic medications in determining that individuals have a liberty interest in refusing these drugs. The side effects include

acute dystonia, a severe involuntary spasm of the upper body, tongue, throat or eyes. . . . Other side effects include akathesia (motor restlessness, often characterized by an inability to sit still); neuroleptic malignant syndrome (a relatively rare condition which can lead to death from cardiac dysfunction). (*Washington v. Harper,* 1990, pp. 229–230)

The most frequently discussed side effect is tardive dyskinesia, "a neurological disorder, irreversible in some cases, that is characterized by involuntary, uncontrollable movements of various muscles, especially around the face" (pp. 229–230). The Supreme Court implied, and other courts have directly held, that concern over tardive dyskinesia constituted a rational reason for refusing medication.

The literature shows that both women (Seeman, 1983) and nonwhite patients (Glazer, Morgenstern, & Doucette, 1994) face a significantly disproportionate risk of suffering from tardive dyskinesia. In the case of minorities, this may be a result of the fact that they receive psychotropic medication more often than whites (Adams, Dworkin, & Rosenberg, 1984; Glazer, Morgenstern, & Doucette, 1994)[61] and in higher doses (Adams, Dworkin, & Rosenberg, 1984)— both factors associated with tardive dyskinesia.

Other reasons for wanting to refuse drugs are

_____

[61]This in turn may be related to the fact that in this study nonwhites were more frequently diagnosed as schizophrenic than whites. No effort was made to discover the accuracy of those diagnoses.

given less credence by courts. For example, although lithium, widely used to treat depression, can cause abnormalities in fetuses (Office of Technology Assessment, 1992), courts have not been sympathetic to refusals of medication by women for these reasons.[62] In some cases, even clinicians themselves are relatively unsympathetic to the woman's dilemma (Mogul, 1985).

Both the selection of forms of treatment (that is, individual therapy, group therapy, psychotropic medication, electric shock treatments) and the duration or dosage of treatment have been shown to be correlated with gender and ethnicity. Sometimes there may be clinically based explanations for these phenomena. For example, electric shock, because it is believed to be helpful in cases of severe depression, is given far more often to women than to men, because far more women than men are severely depressed and indicate suicidal ideas. Of course, these clinically based explanations beg the question of whether the source of a woman's depression is primarily in her brain or in her environment, and, if the latter, whether electric shock will ultimately provide relief. Women also receive a higher percentage of psychotropic medication prescribed than men. Of psychotropic medication prescribed by general physicians, 70% of prescriptions were given to women. Women receive more prescriptions for the so-called major and minor tranquilizers than men.

Treatment often aims at adaptation; some wish to refuse treatment because they do not want to adapt. Forced treatment may be perceived by the patient as punishment, regardless of the intentions of the treatment professional. Appropriate behavior is thus achieved through fear, and inconvenient expressions of suffering and anger are silenced.

In fact, the ideal patient in institutional settings is very similar to older ideals of perfect womanhood: docile, acquiescent to the will of others, and obedient. In her autobiography, Janet Gotkin realizes after attempting suicide in a private psychiatric hospital that the hospital is considering transferring her to the state hospital, a fate that terrifies all the patients at the private hospital. She resolves to

> become the model patient: cooperative, submissive and cheerful. I would admit my mistakes, bow to their wisdom, demonstrate my good intentions and promise to behave and continue to pursue the path of mental health. . . . It took two months to fully implement my plan, two months of silent hidden suffering, during which a new Janet emerged. Dr. Maynard smacked his lips in satisfaction; he was taking credit for the transformation. And in a way, he was responsible. After my failed suicide attempt, he had said, in effect, "If you continue to act in accordance with your deepest feelings, we will send you away to a state institution. If you stop acting on the truth of your despair, we will give you your freedom." (Gotkin & Gotkin, 1992, p. 120)

Being forced to submit to white male authority figures may have particularly traumatic and troubling resonance for women and for members of minority groups. Forced medication often involves injections in the buttocks, a position of vulnerability for sexually abused women (indeed, any woman). By the same token, retaining control over treatment has been shown to be effective in a number of different programs, especially those for women who have been battered or sexually abused, or with a history of borderline personality disorder (which research is beginning to show may overlap substantially with the first two categories) (Dawson & MacMillan, 1993; Dutton, 1992; Herman, 1992).

Although scores of right-to-refuse-treatment cases have been litigated, many with black or female plaintiffs, no case has ever focused on the interaction between a plaintiff's race or gender

---

[62]Sometimes a case must be read closely to discern the issue of pregnancy and danger to the fetus. In *In re M.M.M.* (1984), a woman lost custody of a child born on December 30, 1979; among other reasons cited for termination of parental rights was her failure to accept psychotropic medication beginning in June 1979, which would have been just after she learned she was pregnant. The court did not make the connection. In other cases, it is clear-cut. In *Lefebvre v. North Broward Hospital District* (1990), a woman went off lithium specifically because she was pregnant; hospital authorities then tried to force her to have an abortion she did not want because of her "uncontrolled" mental illness.

and the right to refuse treatment. Nor have mental health professionals writing about treatment refusal ever carefully examined the role that race or gender plays in treatment refusal or the response to treatment refusal.

The Right to Be Free from Seclusion and Restraint

The U.S. Supreme Court confirmed in *Youngberg v. Romeo* (1982) that institutionalized individuals have a right to be free from unreasonable bodily restraint. The Court held that an individual could only be restrained to ensure safety or to provide treatment. The measure of whether safety or treatment concerns actually require restraint is the professional judgment standard, referred to earlier. According to the Court, an individual's right to be free from unreasonable restraint is sufficiently protected if the decision to restrain the individual followed professional judgment, standards, or practice. (For a critique of this standard, see Stefan, 1992.)

A decision to restrain an individual that is based on gender or racial stereotypes or myths is not a "professional" judgment. Like predictions of violence and decisions to commit an individual involuntarily, to the extent that restraint decisions are made on erroneous perceptions of dangerousness based on race stereotypes, they are unconstitutional. Although some studies come to contradictory conclusions, the literature appears to support the notion that at least some restraint decisions are made because of racial stereotypes. Thus, one study showed that although blacks were restrained at 10 times the rate that whites were restrained at in a psychiatric facility for adolescents when they first arrived at the facility, after a month the restraint rates were roughly equivalent (Bond, DeCandia, & MacKinnon, 1988). The authors suggest that "as the White staff at Altobello became familiar with individuals' expressive styles, perhaps they were less likely to infer aggressive intent [but] it is noteworthy that the effect did not generalize beyond the individuals involved. Despite their experi-

ences with Black individuals, the staff continued to restrain new arrivals" (Bond et al., 1988, p. 456). Another study showed that, when measured in terms of indicators such as assault and verbal abuse, black patients in a Veterans Administration Hospital were less violent than their white counterparts. In this study, blacks spent less time than whites in seclusion and restraint. The authors hypothesized, among other explanations, that blacks with mental illness who were more violent had been diverted to the criminal justice system (Lawson, Yesavage, & Werner, 1984).

The response to patients considered at risk of suicide is almost always to restrain them. Patients who express suicidal ideations, or make suicidal gestures, or try to commit suicide are likely candidates for restraint. Women attempt suicide at a far higher rate than men. Women who have a history of rape or sexual abuse attempt suicide at a rate 10 to 12 times that of women who have no history of sexual abuse (Gise & Paddison, 1988). Attempts at self-injury also result in restraint, and a high percentage of women who engage in self-injurious behavior have been sexually abused. One study found that women with a history of sexual abuse were significantly more likely to be subjected to restraints when they were institutionalized.

Against this background, consider the impact of restraints. A patient who is secluded or restrained is often stripped of all clothing (Lion & Soloff, 1984), often by male attendants, almost always by a number of attendants acting together (American Psychiatric Association, 1994; Tardiff, 1984). She is then taken (dragged, if she resists) to a room empty except for a bed, to which she is tied with either leather or cloth restraints.

Restraints are used despite the fact that every study of patient attitudes toward seclusion and restraint has shown that even long after the episode of seclusion or restraint, many patients are still frightened and angry at the experience (Norris & Kennedy, 1992; Wadeson & Carpenter, 1976). For women, the damage from restraint experiences may be especially severe. Wadeson and Carpenter noted that

[t]he question arises as to whether paranoid tendencies are actually provoked by the seclusion room experience . . . a sexually preoccupied college girl responded to the forceful physical contact [of being taken involuntarily to the seclusion room] with a delusion that she was raped in the seclusion room by a male aide. (Wadeson & Carpenter, 1976, p. 327)

Restraints are used without regard to a patient's prior history. Indeed, they are sometimes used when a patient's known history contraindicates them:

As a child the patient had been repeatedly tied up and forced to perform fellatio on her father. During her last hospitalization, she became severely suicidal and anorexic. The staff members tried to feed her through a naso-gastric tube, but she kept pulling it out. Consequently, they felt compelled to place her in four-way restraints. The patient was now tied to her bed and having a tube forced down her throat, all in the name of saving her life. (Herman, 1992, p. 139)

Professional judgment would clearly call for a patient's prior history to be taken into account before a decision was made to restrain that person. For example, in one case, prison mental health professionals strongly opposed a proposed prison policy of random strip-searching of women prisoners (many of whom also have a history of sexual abuse) by male guards on the grounds that this would be unbearably traumatic to the women (*Jordan v. Gardner,* 1993). The United States Court of Appeals for the Ninth Circuit in *Jordan* found that to do this constituted cruel and unusual punishment under the U.S. Constitution's Eighth Amendment. Surely what is true for women prisoners is no less true for institutionalized women. After all, the Supreme Court found that they are entitled to "more considerate treatment and conditions of confinement than criminals, whose conditions of confinement are designed to punish" (*Youngberg v. Romeo,* 1983, pp. 321–322).

After years of concentrating on ensuring equality, courts are beginning to recognize the relevance of gender differences in deciding the meaning of equality (MacKinnon, 1991). Sexual harassment is measured in several Circuits by the standard of the "reasonable woman" (*Dey v. Colt Construction & Development Company,* 1994; *Steiner v. Showboat Operating Co.,* 1994). Some courts have recognized in self-defense cases that the jury must be instructed to consider whether the reasonable woman would have feared for her life (*State v. Leidholm,* 1983; *State v. Wanrow,* 1977). It is time for courts considering mental health law cases to follow this trend. To do so would be both good jurisprudence and good for the mental health of the women involved.

Key Legal Issues for Women and Minorities in the Mental Health System

The Psychiatric and Legal Consequences of Sexual Abuse of Women

As should be clear from this chapter, one of the most important gender-specific mental health issues for women is the impact of sexual abuse on their entry into and treatment by the mental health system. As noted previously, mental health professionals played an important role in minimizing both the prevalence of rape and incest (by not believing women who reported such occurrences) and in minimizing the damage and pain women felt as a result of being sexually violated: "As recently as 1975, an authoritative textbook of psychiatry was unable to conclude whether incest had deleterious effects" (Jacobson & Herald, 1990, referring to Kaplan & Sadock, 1987). A number of researchers have contributed enormously to uncovering the truth about the prevalence of rape and sexual abuse.[63] Their studies have shown that over 50% of institutionalized women have suffered sexual abuse, usually as children or adolescents (Craine et al., 1988; Stefan, 1994).

It appears that chronic, continual sexual abuse can play a significant role in making women crazy. Women who have been sexually abused are regularly diagnosed as depressed, as suffering from alcohol or drug abuse, or as having borderline personality disorder. Yet institutionalized women are rarely asked whether they have been sexually abused when they are admitted to institutions,[64] and their diagnoses and treatment almost never take abuse and its consequences into consideration.

The reaction of treatment professionals to revelations of sexual abuse helps explain why women are so rarely asked about their abuse histories. One study reported that even listening to accounts of sexual abuse resulted in reactions in staff that "bore a resemblance to post-traumatic stress disorder [citation omitted]. Staff reported nightmares, intrusive and repetitive images, and somatic symptoms such as headaches, nausea and sleeplessness" (Lyon, 1993, p. 410). Even when women do report a history of sexual abuse, professionals often either do not react to it (Starke & Flitcraft, 1988) or explicitly express skepticism: "Although I confronted my doctor with my childhood sexual abuse, we did little work in the area. I'd go in and say I was an abused child. He'd say, Maybe you are, maybe you're not" (Susko, 1991, p. 133).

Yet the treatment reported by some institutionalized women seems to replicate the conditions women who were sexually abused endured in their families. They are denied privacy, disbelieved, punished for any manifestation of anger or rebellion, and their bodies are forcibly in-truded upon "for their own good," to medicate them or place them in restraints (Stefan, 1994). When they are in restraints, they may be raped or molested again (*Alphonso v. Charity Hospital of Louisiana*, 1982; Musick, 1984).

Some treatment professionals sexually abuse their clients. While these constitute a minority of professionals, the amount of litigation generated by this abuse is rising sharply (*College Hospital v. Superior Court*, 1993; *Dillon v. Callaway*, 1993; *Koren v. Weihs*, 1993; *Omer v. Edgren*, 1984; *St. Paul Fire and Marine Insurance Co. v. Love*, 1990; *St. Paul Fire and Marine Insurance Co. Inc. v. Mitchell*, 1982; *Vigilant Insurance Co. v. Employers Ins of Wausau*, 1986; *Zipkin v. Freeman*, 1968), and defendants include both the mental health professionals themselves and the institutions or mental health centers that employ them (*St. Paul Fire and Marine Insurance Co. v. Downs*, 1993). In fact, some states are passing statutes that specifically permit a cause of action against the employer of a therapist who has sexual relations with his patient, if the employer has reason to know the therapist has done so (Illinois, 1991).

The number of cases has been substantial enough for malpractice insurers to include clauses in their policies limiting or excluding coverage for liability arising out of sexual misconduct (*American Home Assurance Co. v. Cohen*, 1993; *Chicago Insurance Co. v. Griffin*, 1993; *Cranford Insurance Co. Inc. v. Allwest Ins. Co. Inc.*, 1986; *Govar v. Chicago Insurance Co.*, 1989; *Rivera v. Nevada Medical Liability Insurance Co.*, 1991; *St. Paul Fire and Marine Insurance Co. v. Downs*, 1993). These provisions have been declared void as against public policy by some courts (*American Home Assurance Co. v. Cohen*, 1993) but upheld by most others (*St. Paul Fire and Marine Insurance Co. v. Downs*, 1993).

Although much of the litigation charging sexual abuse by a professional is initiated by women who were treated as outpatients, there is a considerable amount that relates to sexual molestation of institutionalized women: *State v. Tonzola*, 1993 (a technician was convicted of

---

[63]Among them are Diana Russell, Dean Kilpatrick, and Mary Koss. In addition, Elaine Carmen, Andrea Jacobsen, Steven Rose, Patricia Reiker, James Beck, and Judith Herman have done outstanding work in documenting the connection between institutionalization and a history of sexual abuse.

[64]Women patients themselves report this (see Susko, 1991, pp. 117, 133). These stories are confirmed by studies by professionals as well (Jacobson & Herald, 1990; Craine et al.,

fondling women patients and exposing himself to them); *Astorino v. Lensink,* 1993 (a woman with mild retardation was repeatedly raped at an institution for people with mental retardation); *Andrea N. v. Laurelwood Convalescent Hospital,* 1993 (involving girls who were abused); *L. V. v. Liberto,* 1992 (charging sexual battery by a teacher assigned to a psychiatric hospital to educate children). Other cases have involved boys abused either by staff or by other patients.

The sexual abuse of women or girls with a mental disability raises a number of legal questions for administrators, regardless of the identity of the perpetrator. Institutional administrators are being charged with and found liable for negligent hiring of staff, supervision of staff or of patients, and investigation of allegations of sexual abuse (*Astorino v. Lensink,* 1993; *Rogers v. Alabama Department of Mental Health and Mental Retardation,* 1993). A common theme of these lawsuits is that the supervisory authority had no policy in place to prevent these occurrences, or did not investigate allegations or take steps to prevent the recurrence of harm when the allegations were found to be true (*Shaw by Strain v. Strackhouse,* 1990). Lawsuits are charging administrators of institutions with violations of residents' constitutional rights to safety pursuant to the Fourteenth Amendment to the Constitution, guaranteed by the Supreme Court in *Youngberg v. Romeo* (1982).

Different courts have created different standards to judge the liability of administrators in these cases. Some find that to prevail in such a challenge, the plaintiff must show that the administrator or mental health professional made decisions that constituted a substantial departure from professional judgment (*Astorino v. Lensink,* 1993; *Shaw by Strain v. Strackhouse,* 1990). Others hold administrators liable only if they were deliberately indifferent to the patient's right to safety by failing to train and supervise staff adequately, and if this failure was causally connected to the sexual assault (*Rogers v. Alabama Department of Mental Health and Mental Retardation,* 1993).

Lack of Access to Mental Health Treatment and Criminalization of Mental Illness among Members of Minority Groups

There are many legal issues that are of particular concern to minorities in the mental health system, but one of the most pressing is the lack of meaningful, culturally sensitive mental health services, and the lack of access to those services that do exist. Lack of access to mental health services is caused both by the reluctance of many members of minority groups to seek treatment (K. Davis, personal communication, February 22, 1994) and by the tendency to divert blacks with mental health problems—especially males—into the criminal justice system.

Black women may avoid seeking mental health services, for either themselves or their children, because of fear of losing custody of their children (Belle, 1982). Black families tend to avoid seeking services for their family members because of mistrust of the mental health system, often amply justified, and a belief that families ought to care for their own ill members (K. Davis, personal communication, February 22, 1994; Townsend, 1994).

Some blacks in desperate need of mental health services are in prison or jail. Blacks in 1991 made up 12% of America's population but between 46% and 48% of both prison and jail inmates (Tonry, 1994, quotes a rate of 48%; U.S. Bureau of Justice Statistics, 1991, cites 46%). There is evidence that white adolescents with behavior problems end up in the mental health system, while black adolescents with similar behavior end up in the criminal justice system (Lewis, Shanok, Cohen, & Ritvo, 1980). The skyrocketing rates of mental illness in jails and the generally abysmal absence of treatment there were the subject of a comprehensive report (Torrey et al., 1992). It is striking, in view of the high proportion of blacks in jails, that this otherwise extensive report makes no effort to examine issues of race, but that is unfortunately typical of many of the reports about the need for mental health services in jails and prisons.

The prison system also has a rising number of individuals with serious mental illness and provides generally inadequate mental health care to these people.[65] Although the increasing numbers of people who have a mental illness in prisons and jails is well recognized, as is the disproportionate representation of blacks in prisons and jails, the connection between these two facts—that a high number of the people needing mental health care in the prison system must by definition be members of minority groups—has not been the subject of attention. Mental health treatment resources in the prison system are extremely scarce, and, if drug treatment statistics are any indication,[66] blacks may be excluded from treatment, while whites receive what little is available. Nor has any connection been made between these facts and the prevalent misdiagnosis of mental illness in blacks and resulting errors in treatment common throughout the country.

Conclusion

To describe mental disability as an illness suffered by an individual eliminates the effect of racism and sexism on a person's behavior. To focus solely on the allegedly mentally ill person diverts attention from the impact of racist and sexist assumptions on the perceptions of the mental health professional, who has the power through diagnosis to reinterpret a person's behavior as a set of symptoms, even when the person does not see his or her behavior in those terms. History shows that mental health professionals often share the prejudices and stereotypes typical of their time, of their class, of their race, and of their gender. Some act with conscious racism; many simply act according to constructs and assumptions that may not even be the subject of conscious evaluation.

Nevertheless, courts, with few exceptions, adopt the reinterpretations of a person's behavior framed by mental health professionals in legal proceedings affecting a person's most fundamental rights to liberty, bodily integrity, and freedom of association: involuntary commitment, or involuntary medication with psychotropic drugs, or seclusion and restraint. The history of mental health law, especially its most recent history, reflects a combination of deference to the opinions of mental health professionals and a total absence of reflection on the part that race and gender may play in diagnosis, assessment of dangerousness, need for treatment, adequacy of treatment, and the individual's need to shape his or her treatment.

This is not due to an absence of social science research pointing out the relevance of race and gender in these areas, nor to an absence of historical precedent suggesting that mental health professionals have been mistaken in diagnoses and treatments before in ways that grievously and permanently injured the patients in their power. Beyond the deference to mental health professionals lie structural problems in the law that make it extremely difficult to present these issues in their larger context.

Like the judgments and diagnoses of mental health professionals, some of these legal structures are not accidental: they have been con-

---

[65]In the conservative estimate of the federal government, 54,000 prison inmates—7% of all prison inmates—have serious mental illnesses, while 95,000 inmates—12.5%— have significant psychiatric problems requiring intermittent care (Office of Consumer, Family and Public Information, Center for Mental Health Services, Room 13-103, 5600 Fisher's Lane, Rockville, MD 20857, May 1994). The figure seems low. A study published seven years ago found that 8% of the prison population in New York had severe disabilities from mental illness and another 16% had significant disabilities (Steadman, Fabisiak, Dvoskin, & Holokean, 1987). Since California alone apparently has 28,000 inmates with mental illness in its prison system (*Coleman v. Wilson*, 1994), it seems safe to assume that the number nationwide is higher than the government figures would indicate. For a description of the types of problems these inmates face, see Hans Toch (1992).

[66]While whites account for only 7% of drug offenders incarcerated in the state of New York, they occupy 47% of state-funded drug treatment slots (Edna McConnell Clark Foundation, 1993).

sciously constructed to get courts out of the business of large-scale social reform. Thus, the U.S. Supreme Court has not always held that intentional discrimination must be proven to recover under Title VI; originally it held just the opposite (*Lau v. Nichols*, 1974). The Supreme Court of the 1960s, faced with a case involving a man injured more than 70 times in two years in an admittedly overcrowded, underfunded institution, might not have responded by preferring to ease the administrative burdens of such an institution by minimizing interference by the federal judiciary (*Youngberg v. Romeo*, 1982, pp. 322, 324).

Although women constitute more than half the population, and minorities will soon constitute one-third of the population, neither the practices of mental health professionals nor the legal doctrines adopted by courts reflect their situations and needs. Unfortunately, in many ways law and the mental health profession collaborate in reconstructing these situations and needs, reinterpreting them, and redefining them. In this process, struggle and complexity are erased, as are the coexistence of strength with desperate distress, and failure with resilience. People's real experiences are obliterated by a diagnosis that puts the individual in the category of "mental patient," discredited or at least doubted. There are few more effective ways of silencing individuals than to label them as having a mental illness. These labels and the legal coercion that often accompanies them can transform angry, disenchanted, disenfranchised, and frustrated people into "the mentally ill," to be pitied and provided services at best and ignored, abused, or jailed at worst.

Racism and sexism are clearly only part of the story of mental health treatment and mental health law. But mistaken diagnoses, gender-specific diagnoses, significantly disparate involuntary commitment rates by race, and forced treatment of women and minorities who do not accept that they are sick are also part of the story of racism and sexism in this country—a part of the story that has been ignored for too long by mental health professionals, legal scholars, and historians.

References

42 U.S.C. 2000(d) (1982).

Abramson, R. K., & Wright, H. H. (1981). Diagnosis of black patients. *American Journal of Psychiatry, 138*, 1515.

Adams, G. L., Dworkin, R. J., & Rosenberg, S. (1984). Diagnosis and pharmacotherapy issues in the care of Hispanics in the private sector. *American Journal of Psychiatry, 141*, 970–974.

Addington v. Texas, 441 U.S. 418 (1979).

Adebimpe, V. (1981). Overview: White norms and psychiatric diagnosis of black patients. *American Journal of Psychiatry, 138*, 279–285.

Adebimpe, V. (1994). Race, racism, and epidemiological surveys. *Hospital and Community Psychiatry, 45*, 27–31.

Alexander v. Choate, 469 U.S. 287 (1985).

Alphonso v. Charity Hospital of Louisiana, 413 So.2d 982 (La.Ct.App. 1982).

American Home Assurance Co. v. Cohen, 815 F. Supp. 365, 368 (W.D.Wash. 1993).

American Psychiatric Association. (1994). *Diagnostic and statistical manual of mental disorders* (4th ed.). Washington, DC: Author.

Andrea N. v. Laurelwood Convalescent Hospital, 16 Cal.Rptr. 894 (Cal.App. 1993).

Appelbaum, P. (1993). *Almost a revolution: Mental health law and the limits of change.* Oxford, England: Oxford University Press.

Astorino v. Lensink, U.S.Dist.LEXIS 12748 (D.Conn. 1993).

Bachrach, L. (1986). Chronically mentally ill women: An overview of service delivery issues. In L. Bachrach & C. Nadelson (Eds.), *Treating chronically mentally ill women.* Washington, DC: American Psychiatric Association Press.

Bachrach, L. (1985). Chronic mentally ill women: Emergence and legitimation of program issues. *Hospital and Community Psychiatry, 36,* 1063–1069.

Bell, C. C., & Metha, H. (1980). The misdiagnosis of black patients with manic-depressive illness. *Journal of the National Medical Association, 72,* 141–145.

Belle, D. (Ed.). (1982). *Lives in stress.* Beverly Hills, CA: Sage.

Bennett, M. B., Handel, M., & Pearsall, D. (1986). Behavioral differences between female and male hospitalized chronically mentally ill patients. In L. Bachrach & C. Nadelson (Eds.), *Treating chronically mentally ill women.* Washington, DC: American Psychiatric Association Press.

Bersoff, D. (1992). Judicial deference to nonlegal decisionmakers: Imposing simplistic solutions on problems of cognitive complexity in mental health law. *Southern Methodist Law Review, 46,* 329–372.

Bond, C. F., DeCandia, C. G., & MacKinnon, J. (1988). Responses to race in a psychiatric setting: The role of patient's race. *Personality and Social Psychology Bulletin, 14,* 448–458.

Briere, J. (1988). Long-term clinical correlates of childhood sexual victimization. *Annals of the New York Academy of Sciences, 528,* 327–334.

Brown v. Board of Education, 347 U.S. 184 (1954).

Brownmiller, S. (1975). *Against our will: Men, women and rape.* New York: Simon & Schuster.

In re Bryant, 542 A.2d 1216 (1988).

Cameron, D. (1979). *How to survive being committed to a mental hospital.* New York: Vantage Press.

Carpenter, M., Hannon, V. R., McCleery, G., & Wanderling, J. A. (1988). Ethnic differences in seclusion and restraint. *Journal of Nervous and Mental Disease, 176,* 726–731.

Chamberlin, J. (1978). *On our own.* New York: McGraw-Hill.

Chesler, P. (1989). *Women and madness* (Rev. ed.). New York: Harcourt Brace Jovanovich.

Chicago Insurance Co. v. Griffin, 817 F. Supp. 861, 865 (D. Hawaii 1993).

"Coercion in mental health care." (Summer 1993). [Symposium Issue] *Behavioral Sciences and the Law, 11*(3), 237–345.

Coleman v. Wilson, No. 90-0520 (E.D.Ca. July 7, 1994).

College Hospital v. Superior Court, 16 Cal.Rptr. 833 (Cal. App. 1993).

Connell, N., & Wilson, C. (Eds.). (1974). *Rape: The first sourcebook for women.* New York: New American Library.

Cook, T. (1991). The Americans with Disabilities Act: The move to integration. *Temple Law Review, 64,* 393–469.

"Cost of depression estimated at nearly 44 billion: Time lost from work accounts for largest share." (1994). *Hospital and Community Psychiatry, 45*(1), 85.

Coughlin, A. M. (1994). Excusing women. *California Law Review, 82,* 1–93.

Craine, L. S., Henson, C. E., Colliver, J. A., & Maclean, D. G. (1988). Prevalence of a history of sexual abuse among female patients in a state hospital system. *Hospital and Community Psychiatry, 39,* 300–304.

Cranford Insurance Co. Inc. v. Allwest Ins. Co. Inc., 645 F. Supp. 1440 (N.D. Ca. 1986).

Cruzan v. Missouri Department of Health, 110 S.Ct. 2841 (1990).

Davis v. Hubbard, 506 F. Supp. 915 (N.D. Ohio 1980).

Dawson, D., & MacMillan, H. (1993). *Relationship management of the borderline patient: From understanding to treatment.* New York: Brunner/Mazel.

Day, J. C. (1993, October). *Current population reports: Population projections of the United States by age, sex, race, and Hispanic origin.* (Publication No. P25-1104). Washington,

DC: U.S. Department of Commerce, Economics and Statistics Administration, Bureau of the Census.

Deutsch, H. (1944). *Psychology of women.* New York: Grune & Stratton.

Dey v. Colt Construction & Development Company, 1994 U.S. App. LEXIS 17031 (7th Cir. July 11, 1994).

Dillon v. Callaway, 609 N.E.2d 424 (Ind. App. 1993).

Dutton, M. A. (1992). *Empowering and healing the battered woman: A model for assessment and intervention.* New York: Springer.

Edna McConnell Clark Foundation. (1993). *Americans behind bars.* New York: Author.

Ennis, B., & Litwack, T. (1974). Psychiatry and the presumption of expertise: Flipping coins in the courtroom. *California Law Review, 62,* 693–752.

Ervin, F., Mark, V., & Sweet, W. (1967). Role of brain disease in riots and urban violence. *Journal of the American Medical Association, 201,* 895.

Estroff, S. E., Lachicotte, W. S., Illingworth, L., & Johnston, A. (1991). Everybody's got a little mental illness: Accounts of illness and self among people with severe, persistent mental illness. *Medical Anthropology Quarterly, 5,* 331–369.

Estroff, S. E., Zimmer, C., Lachiotte, W., & Benoit, J. (1994). The influence of social networks and social support on violence by persons with severe mental illness. *Hospital and Community Psychiatry, 45,* 669–678.

Flaherty, J. A., & Meagher, R. (1980). Measuring racial bias in inpatient treatment. *American Journal of Psychiatry, 137,* 679–682.

Flaskerud, J. H., & Hu, L.-t. (1992). Racial/ethnic identity and amount and type of psychiatric treatment. *American Journal of Psychiatry, 149,* 379–384.

Ford v. Wainwright, 477 U.S. 399 (1986).

Foucha v. Louisiana, 112 S.Ct. 1780 (1992).

Gauvain, M. (1994, August). *Slouching toward cultural competence: Lessons from research on African-American adolescents and street youth.* Paper presented at the meeting of the American Psychological Association, Los Angeles.

Geller, J., & Munetz, M. (1986). The iatrogenic creation of psychiatric chronicity in women. In L. L. Bachrach & C. C. Nadelson (Eds.), *Treating chronically mentally ill women.* Washington, DC: American Psychiatric Association Press.

Gilligan, C. (1982). *In a different voice.* Cambridge, MA: Harvard University Press.

Gise, L. H., & Paddison, P. (1988). Rape, sexual abuse, and its victims. *Psychiatric Clinics of North America, 11,* 629–648.

Glazer, W. M., Morgenstern, H., & Doucette, J. (1994). Race and tardive dyskinesia among outpatients at a CMHC [Community Mental Health Center]. *Hospital and Community Psychiatry, 45,* 38–42.

Gotkin, J., & Gotkin, P. (1992). *Too much anger, too many tears* (2nd ed.). New York: HarperCollins.

Govar v. Chicago Insurance Co., 879 F.2d 1581 (8th Cir. 1989).

Gremillion, H. (1992). Psychiatry as social ordering: Anorexia nervosa, a paradigm. *Sociology of the Science of Medicine, 35,* 57–71.

Griffith, E. E. H., & Griffith, E. J. (1986). Racism, psychological injury, and compensatory damages. *Hospital and Community Psychiatry, 37,* 71–75.

Group for the Advancement of Psychiatry. (1994). *Forced into treatment: The role of coercion in clinical practice* (Report No. 137). Washington, DC: American Psychiatric Press.

Guardians Association v. Civil Service Commission, 463 U.S. 582 (1983).

Gunderson, J. G., & Zanarini, M. C. (1987). Current overview of the borderline diagnosis. *Journal of Clinical Psychiatry, 48* (Suppl. 8), 5–11.

Hammond, W. R., & Yung, B. (1993). Psychology's role in the public health response to assaultive violence among young African American males. *American Psychologist, 48,* 142–154.

Helen S. v. Didario, 1994 U.S. Dist. LEXIS 595 (E.D. Pa. 1994).

Herman, J. (1992). *Trauma and recovery.* New York: Basic Books.

Hirsch, S., Adams, J. K., Frank, L. R., Hudson, W., Keene, R., Krawitz-Keene, G., Richman, D., & Roth, R. (Eds.). (1974). *The madness network news reader.* San Francisco: Glide Publications.

Holden, C. (1986). Proposed new psychiatric diagnoses raise charges of gender bias. *Science, 231,* 327–328.

Holstein, J. A. (1993). *Court ordered insanity: Interpretive practice and involuntary commitment.* New York: Aldine de Gruyter.

ILCS Ann. 14/1 & 14/2 70.800 *et seq.* (Michie 1995).

In re J.A.D., 492 N.W.2d 82 (N.D. 1992).

Jacobson, A., & Herald, C. (1990). The relevance of childhood sexual abuse to adult psychiatric inpatient care. *Hospital and Community Psychiatry, 41,* 154–158.

Johnson v. Crawfis, 128 F. Supp. 230 (D.C.E.D. Ark. 1955).

Johnson v. Silvers, 742 F.2d 823 (4th Cir. 1984).

Jones, B., & Gray, B. (1986). Problems in diagnosing schizophrenia and affective disorders among blacks. *Hospital and Community Psychiatry, 37,* 61–65.

Jordan v. Gardner, 986 F.2d 1521 (9th Cir. 1993) (en banc).

Kaplan, H. I., & Sadock, B. J. (1987). Comprehensive textbook of psychiatry. Baltimore, MD: Williams & Wilkins.

Kaschak, E. (1992). *Engendered lives.* New York: Basic Books.

Kitzinger, C., & Perkins, R. (1993). *Changing our minds: Lesbian feminism and psychology.* New York: New York University Press.

Koren v. Weihs, 593 NYS2d 222 (A.D. 1993).

Kramer, P. (1989). *Moments of engagement.* New York: Norton.

Kutchins, H., & Kirk, S. A. (1989). DSM-III-R:

The conflict over the new psychiatric diagnoses. *Health and Social Work, 14,* 91–101.

L. V. v. Liberto, 612 So.2d 812 (La.App. 1992).

Lau v. Nichols, 414 U.S. 563 (1974).

Lawrence, C. (1987). The Id, the Ego, and equal protection: Reckoning with unconscious racism. *Stanford Law Review, 39,* 317–387.

Lawson, W. B. (1986). Chronic mental illness and the black family. *American Journal of Social Psychiatry, 6,* 57–61.

Lawson, W. B., Hepler, N., Holladay, J., & Cuffel, B. (1994). Race as a factor in inpatient and outpatient admissions and diagnosis. *Hospital and Community Psychiatry, 45,* 72–74.

Lawson, W. B., Yesavage, J., & Werner, P. (1984). Race, violence, and psychopathology. *Journal of Clinical Psychiatry, 45,* 294–297.

LeBoeuf, D. (1988). Psychiatric malpractice: Exploitation of women patients. *Harvard Women's Law Journal, 11,* 83–116.

Lefebvre v. North Broward Hospital District, 566 So.2d 568 (Fla.App. 1990).

Lewis, D. O., Shanok, S. S., Cohen, R. J., & Ritvo, E. (1980). Race bias in the diagnosis and disposition of violent adolescents. *American Journal of Psychiatry, 137,* 1211–1216.

Lidz, C., Mulvey, E. B., Arnold, R. P., Bennett, N. S., & Kirsch, B. L. (1993). Coercive interactions in a psychiatric emergency room. *Behavioral Sciences and the Law, 11,* 269–280.

Lindsey, K., & Gordon, P. (1989). Involuntary commitments to public mental hospitals: Issues involving the overrepresentation of blacks and assessment of relevant functioning. *Psychological Bulletin, 106,* 171–183.

Lion, J., & Soloff, P. (1984). Implementation of seclusion and restraint. In K. Tardiff (Ed.), *The psychiatric uses of seclusion and restraint.* Washington, DC: American Psychiatric Press.

Lipton, A. A., & Simon, F. S. (1985). Psychiatric diagnosis in a state hospital: Manhattan State revisited. *Hospital and Community Psychiatry, 36,* 368–373.

Lora v. New York Board of Education, 456 F.

Supp. 1211 (E.D.N.Y. 1978), vacated and remanded, 623 F.2d 248 (2nd Cir. 1980), on remand, 587 F. Supp. 1572 (E.D.N.Y. 1984) (approving settlement decree).

Lyon, E. (1993). Hospital staff reactions to accounts by survivors of childhood abuse. *American Journal of Orthopsychiatry, 63,* 410–416.

In re M.M.M., 485 A.2d 180 (D.C. 1984).

MacKinnon, C. (1991). Reflecting on sex equality under law. *Yale Law Journal, 100,* 1281–1328.

Marable v. Alabama Mental Health Board, 297 F. Supp. 291 (M.D.Ala. 1969) (three-judge court).

Martin, D. (1981). *Battered wives* (Rev. ed.). San Francisco: Volcano Press.

Massachusetts General Laws, C. 123 § 1 (1994).

Masson, J. (1984). *The assault on the truth: Freud's suppression of the seduction theory.* New York: Farrar, Straus & Giroux.

Mazelis, R. (Ed.). (1994). *The cutting edge, 5.* (Newsletter)

McGovern, D., & Cope, R. V. (1987). First psychiatric admission rates of first and second generation Afro Caribbeans. *Social Psychiatry, 22,* 139–149.

McGrath, E., Keita, G., Strickland, B., & Russo, N. F. (1990). *Women and depression: Risk factors and treatment issues.* Washington, DC: American Psychological Association.

McKleskey v. Kemp, 481 U.S. 279 (1987).

Mental Health, United States. (1992). Rockville, MD: National Institute for Mental Health.

Menzies, R. (1989). *Survival of the sanest: Order and disorder in a pretrial psychiatric clinic.* Toronto: University of Toronto Press.

Mercer, K. (1984). Black communities' experience of psychiatric services. *International Journal of Social Psychiatry, 30,* 22–27.

Mezzich, J. E., Kleinman, A., Fabrega, H., Jr., Parron, D., Good, B. J., Johnson-Powell, G., Lin, K.-M., & Manson, S. (1993). Revised cultural proposals for DSM-IV (Taskforce report).

Miller v. Florida, 482 U.S. 423 (1987).

Millett, K. (1970). *Sexual politics.* Garden City, NY: Doubleday.

Millett, K. (1990). *The Loony Bin Trip.* New York: Simon & Schuster.

Mogul, K. M. (1985). Psychological considerations in the use of psychotropic medications with women patients. *Hospital and Community Psychiatry, 36,* 1080–1085.

Mollica, R. F., & Son, L. (1989). Cultural dimensions in the evaluation and treatment of sexual trauma: An overview. *Psychiatric Clinics of North America, 12,* 363–379.

Mollica, R. F., Wyshak, G., Lavelle, J., Truong, T., Tor, S., & Yang, T. (1990). Assessing symptom change in Southeast Asian refugee survivors of mass violence and torture. *American Journal of Psychiatry, 147,* 83–88.

Musick, J. (1984). Patterns of institutional sexual assault. *Response to violence and sexual assault* (No. 7). Washington, DC: Center for Women Policy Studies.

Neighbors, H. W. (1984). The distribution of psychiatric morbidity in black Americans: A review and suggestions for research. *Community Mental Health Journal, 20,* 169–181.

Neighbors, H., & Jackson, J. (1989). The influence of racial factors on psychiatric diagnosis. *Community Mental Health Journal, 25,* 301–311.

"New storm brews over whether crime has roots in genes." (1992, September 15). *New York Times,* p. C1.

Nicholson, J., Geller, J., Fisher, W., & Dion, G. (1993). State policies and programs that address the needs of mentally ill mothers in the public sector. *Hospital and Community Psychiatry, 44,* 484–489.

Norris, M., & Kennedy, C. (1992). The view from within: How patients perceive the seclusion process. *Journal of Psychosocial Nursing, 30,* 7–13.

North Philadelphia Community Board v. Temple University, 330 F. Supp. 1107 (E.D. Pa. 1971).

O'Connor v. Donaldson, 422 U.S. 563 (1975).

Office of Technology Assessment. (1992). *The biology of mental disorders.* Washington, DC: Author.

Olarte, S., & Masnik, R. (1985). Benefits of long-term group therapy for disadvantaged Hispanic outpatients. *Hospital and Community Psychiatry, 36,* 1093–1097.

Olmedo, E., & Parron, D. (1981). Mental health of minority women: Some special issues. *Professional Psychology, 12,* 103–111.

Omer v. Edgren, 685 P.2d 635 (Wash. App. 1984).

Oregon v. Johnson, 843 P.2d 985 (Or. App. 1992).

O'Sullivan, M. J., Peterson, P. D., Cox, G., & Kirkeby, J. (1989). Ethnic populations: Community mental health services ten years later. *American Journal of Community Psychology, 17,* 17–30.

People v. Sansone, 309 N.E.2d 733, 741 (Ill. App. 1974).

Perlin, M. (1990). *Mental disability law.* Charlottesville, Va.: Michie.

Perlin, M. (1991). Morality and pretext, psychiatry and law: Of ordinary common sense, heuristic reasoning, and cognitive dissonance. *Bulletin of the American Academy of Psychiatry and Law, 19,* 131–150.

Perlin, M. (1993). Pretexts and mental disability law: The case of competence. *University of Miami Law Review, 47,* 625–688.

Plath, S. (1971). *The bell jar.* New York: Harper and Row.

Prudhomme, C., & Musto, D. F. (1973). Historical perspectives on mental health and racism in the United States. In C. Willie, B. Kramer, & B. Brown (Eds.), *Racism and mental health.* Pittsburgh, PA: University of Pittsburgh Press.

Ramm, D. (1989). Over committed. *Southern Exposure, 27,* 14–17.

Riggins v. Nevada, 112 S.Ct. 2572 (1992).

Rivera v. Nevada Medical Liability Insurance Co., 814 P.2d 71 (Nev. 1991).

Robins, L. N., & Regier, D. A. (Eds.). (1991). *Psychiatric disorders in America: The Epidemiological Catchment Area Study.* New York: Free Press.

Rogers v. Alabama Department of Mental Health and Mental Retardation, 825 F. Supp. 986 (M.D.Ala. 1993).

Rogers v. Okin, 478 F. Supp. 1342 (D. Mass. 1979).

In re Rosa M., 155 Wisc.2d 103, 597 NYS2d 555 (1991).

Rosenfeld, S. (1984). Race differences in involuntary hospitalization: Psychiatric vs. labeling perspectives. *Journal of Health and Social Behavior, 25,* 14–23.

Rosenthal, E., & Carty, L. (1988). Impediments to services and advocacy for black and Hispanic people with mental illness. Washington, DC: Mental Health Law Project.

Rouse v. Cameron, 373 F.2d 451 (D.C.Cir. 1966).

Sabshin, M., Diesenhaus, H., & Wickerson, R. (1970). Dimensions of institutional racism in psychiatry. *American Journal of Psychiatry, 127,* 787–793.

Schneider, E. (1986). Describing and changing: Women's self defense work and the problem of expert testimony on battering. *Women's Rights Law Reporter,* Vol. 9 (1986), 195–222.

Seeman, M. V. (1983). Schizophrenic men and women require different treatment programs. *Journal of Psychiatric Treatment and Evaluation, 5,* 143–148.

Shaw by Strain v. Strackhouse, 920 F.2d 1135 (3rd Cir. 1990).

Slovenko, R., & Phillips, C. (1962). Psychosexuality and the criminal law. *Vanderbilt Law Review, 15,* 797–828.

Snowden, L. R., & Cheung, F. K. (1990). Use of inpatient mental health services by members of ethnic minority groups. *American Psychologist, 45,* 347–355.

Soloff, P., & Turner, S. M. (1982). Patterns of seclusion: A prospective study. *Journal of Nervous and Mental Disorders, 169,* 37–44.

Spitzer, R., Severino, S. K., Williams, J.B.W., & Parry, B. (1989). Late luteal dysphoric disorder and DSM-III-R. *American Journal of Psychiatry, 146,* 892–897.

In re Stanley, 843 P.2d 1018 (Or. 1992).

Starke, E., & Flitcraft, A. (1988). Personal power and institutional victimization: Treating the dual trauma of woman battering. In F. Ochsberg (Ed.), *Post-traumatic therapy and victims of violence.* New York: Brunner/Mazel.

Starr, P. (1982). *The social transformation of American medicine.* New York: Basic Books.

State *ex. rel.* Jones v. Gerhardstein, 416 N.W.2d 883 (Wis. 1987).

State v. Leidholm, 334 N.W.2d 811 (N.D. 1983).

State v. Marshall, 613 A.2d 1059 (N.J. 1992).

State v. Tonzola, 621 A.2d 243 (Vt. 1993).

State v. Wanrow, 559 P.2d 548 (Wash. 1977).

Steadman, H. S., Fabisiak, S., Dvoskin, J., & Holokean, E. J., Jr. (1987). The prevalence of mental disability among state prison inmates: A statewide survey. Albany: New York State Office of Mental Health.

Stefan, S. (1987). Mothers in the mental health system. In L. C. Insensee & L. Tarr-Whelan (Eds.), *The women's economic justice agenda: Ideas for the states.* Washington, DC: National Center for Policy Alternatives.

Stefan, S. (1989). Whose egg is it anyway? The reproductive rights of incarcerated, institutionalized, and incompetent women. *NOVA Law Review, 13,* 406–456.

Stefan, S. (1992). Leaving civil rights to the 'experts': From deference to abdication under the professional judgment standard. *Yale Law Journal, 102,* 639–717.

Stefan, S. (1993). Silencing the different voice: Competence, feminist theory and law. *University of Miami Law Review, 47,* 763–815.

Stefan, S. (1994). The protection racket: Rape trauma syndrome, psychiatric labelling, and law. *Northwestern University Law Review, 88,* 1271–1345.

Steiner v. Showboat Operating Company, 25 F.3d 1459 (9th Cir. 1994).

St. Paul Fire and Marine Insurance Co. v. Downs, No. 1-91-3880 (Ill.App.Ct. May 26, 1993) 17 Mental and Physical Disability Law Reporter 644 (Nov/Dec 1993).

St. Paul Fire and Marine Insurance Co. v. Love, 459 N.W.2d 698 (Minn. 1990).

St. Paul Fire and Marine Insurance Co. Inc. v. Mitchell, 296 S.E.2d 126 (Ga.App. 1982).

"Study to quell violence is racist, critics charge." (1992, November 2). *Detroit Free Press,* p. 1.

Stump v. Sparkman, 435 U.S. 349 (1978).

Susko, M. (Ed.). (1991). *Cry of the invisible: Writings from the homeless and survivors of psychiatric hospitals.* Baltimore, MD: Conservatory Press.

Tardiff, K. (Ed.). (1984). *The psychiatric uses of seclusion and restraint.* Washington, DC: American Psychiatric Press.

Task Force on the Psychiatric Uses of Seclusion and Restraint. (1985). *The psychiatric uses of seclusion and restraint.* Washington, DC: American Psychological Association Press.

Toch, H. (1992). *Human breakdowns in prison.* Washington, DC: American Psychological Association. (Revised edition of *Men in crisis,* 1975)

Tonry, M. (1994). Racial disproportion in US prisons. *British Journal of Criminology, 34,* 97–115.

Torrey, E. F., Stieber, J., Ezekiel, J., Wolfe, S. M., Sharfstein, J., Noble, J., & Flynn, L. (1992). *Criminalizing the seriously mentally ill: The abuse of jails as mental hospitals.* Washington, DC: National Alliance for the Mentally Ill/Public Citizen's Health Research Group.

Townsend, W. (1994, May). Cultural competence in the mental health treatment of people of color. Paper presented at the National Symposium of Involuntary Interventions, Houston, TX. (Copies of the paper are available from the author at the Ohio Department of Mental Health, Columbus.)

Umbenhauer, S. L., & DeWitte, L. L. (1978). Patient race and social class: Attitudes and decisions among three groups of mental health professionals. *Comprehensive Psychiatry, 19,* 509–515.

"U.Md. cancels conference on genetic link to crime." (1992, September 5). *Washington Post,* p. 1.

United States v. Charters, 829 F.2d 479 (4th Cir. 1987), *rev'd* 863 F.2d 302 (4th Cir. 1988) *(en banc).*

United States v. Salerno, 481 U.S. 739 (1987).

U.S. Bureau of the Census. (1992). *Statistical abstract of the United States: 1992* (112th ed.). Washington, DC: U.S. Government Printing Office.

U.S. Bureau of Justice Statistics. (1991). *Sourcebook of criminal justice statistics.* Washington, DC: U.S. Government Printing Office.

U.S. Congress. (1988, September 9). *H. Rept. 100-903 on H.R. 5155, Protection and Advocacy for Mentally Ill Individuals Amendments Act of 1988,* 100th Cong., 2d sess., sec. 4.

U.S. Department of Health and Human Services, Public Health Division. (1993). *Mental health, United States, 1992.* Rockville, MD: Author.

Ussher, J. M. (1991). *Women's madness: Misogyny or mental illness?* Amherst: University of Massachusetts Press.

Vigilant Insurance Co. v. Employers Ins of Wausau, 626 F. Supp. 262 (S.D.N.Y. 1986).

Villanova v. Abrams, 972 F.2d 792 (7th Cir. 1992).

Wadeson, H., & Carpenter, W. T. (1976). Impact of the seclusion room experience. *Journal of Nervous and Mental Disease, 163,* 318–329.

Washington v. Harper, 494 U.S. 210 (1990).

Weddige, R. D. (1994). [Review of *Relationship management of the borderline patient: From understanding to treatment* by D. Dawson & H. McMillan]. *Hospital and Community Psychiatry,* 81–82.

Wigmore, J. H. (1970). *Evidence* (Vol. 3A, Sec. 924a). (Chadbourne, rev. ed.)

Williams v. Wilzack, 573 A.2d 809 (Md. 1990).

Wright, H., Scott, H. R., Pierre-Paul, R., & Gore, T. (1984). Psychiatric diagnosis and the black patient. *Psychiatric Forum, 12,* 65–71.

Wyatt v. Aderholt, 503 F.2d 1305 (5th Cir. 1974).

Wyatt v. Stickney, 325 F. Supp. 781 (M.D.Ala. 1971) (Wyatt I).

Wyatt v. Stickney, 334 F. Supp. 1341 (M.D.Ala. 1971) (Wyatt II).

Wyatt v. Stickney, 344 F. Supp. 373 (M.D.Ala. 1972) (Wyatt III).

Youngberg v. Romeo, 457 U.S. 307 (1982).

Zipkin v. Freeman, 436 S.W.2d 753 (Mo. 1968).

13 ∎ Treatment and Refusal Rights in Mental Health: Therapeutic Justice and Clinical Accommodation

Marshall B. Kapp
Wright State University

Modern mental health professionals have been able to intervene effectively in the lives of persons with severe mental illness, especially through the prescription of psychoactive medications, for only a relatively short time. Ironically, the interventions of the last quarter century have spawned considerable legal activism, leading to firmly entrenched rights to treatment and to refuse treatment in American jurisprudence.

Judicial and legislative actions setting forth treatment and refusal rights were met immediately by many clinicians, institutional administrators, and observers with great dismay and predictions of dire consequences. This chapter addresses whether the adverse expectations expressed by many in the 1970s and early 1980s in reaction to the announcement of treatment and refusal rights have been borne out.

The chapter first outlines the right to treatment and the right to refuse it, next examines clinicians' stated objections and anxieties, and then looks at the manner in which the legal edicts have been implemented in everyday activity in terms of the impact of these legal constructs on persons with mental illness, their families and clinicians, and society as a whole. This chapter argues that, in practice, the divergent actors in this sphere have reached workable clinical ac-commodations, and the implementation of these rights in practice has not exerted an unduly disruptive or destructive effect on mental health services and their clienteles. Swimming largely against the tide of opinion over a dozen years ago, forensic psychiatrist Loren Roth (1981) suggested:

As in other arenas where there is a legitimate clash of values, the hope is that a reasonable compromise can be fashioned, one that respects both the needs and the rights of the mentally ill. My guess is that such a compromise will ultimately be achieved and that, once the furor abates, that compromise will be one of procedures, not concepts. (p. 233)

This prediction has proven correct for the most part. Thus, the goals of law and mental health care have not proven to be irreconcilable, perhaps because both disciplines are intended to promote human welfare (Melton, 1992).

Although the goals of law and mental health care have not proven to be irreconcilable, they have yet to be fully achieved. Put differently, while recognition of these rights has not had the deleterious impact predicted by critics, neither has it led to the positive therapeutic impact envisioned by some of its proponents (Wexler & Winick, 1991). The law has not appreciably worsened or improved the quality of care available. Legal advocates, clinical caregivers, and their intended beneficiaries will need to contribute jointly to strategies for bringing better mental health services to individuals within a framework of patients' decisional rights (Margulies, 1992).

Origins of Patients' Rights to Treatment and to Refuse Treatment

The Right to Treatment

A right to treatment for patients with mental illness who were involuntarily confined (that is, civilly committed) in state institutions was first enunciated by federal trial courts in the early 1970s (Perlin, 1989), primarily in response to the revolting living conditions prevalent in many facilities (La Fond & Durham, 1992). A strange group of political bedfellows pursuing independent, sometimes hidden, but strategically consistent agendas initiated or supported early challenges to the lack of meaningful treatment (or decent surroundings) in state institutions for patients at that time.

The more radical patient advocates envisioned judicial proclamation of an expansive right to treatment as a way to raise the economic costs of maintaining large numbers of persons with severe mental illness in public hospitals to a high enough level that states would decide to return many patients to the community rather than to incur those costs. Thus, under this agenda, the right to treatment would serve as a backdoor strategy for defeating involuntary hospitalization altogether (Isaac & Armat, 1990). Less radical patient advocates, as well as many mental health professionals, institutional administrators, and labor unions, saw judicial decrees of a right to treatment as a powerful political club that could be wielded over the heads of state legislators reluctant to appropriate sufficient tax dollars to ensure decent, humane conditions for institutionalized patients and reasonable wages for their caregivers. For these advocates, enunciation of a right to treatment was the key to improved institutional conditions.

Early challenges to involuntary commitment without treatment based on the U.S. Constitution's Fourteenth Amendment's equal protection clause and the Eighth Amendment's cruel and unusual punishment clause were largely unsuccessful. The equal protection argument was that the state lacked adequate justification for setting apart persons labeled mentally ill and dangerous to themselves for what amounted to a discriminatory intervention. No other group, it was suggested, was locked up against its will without being convicted of a crime and without treatment. The Eighth Amendment argument was that involuntarily confining a person indefinitely, without criminal conviction or treatment, was an unjustified and inhumane punishment.

The constitutional hook on which judicial decisions were primarily hung, first suggested in a 1960 journal article (Birnbaum, 1960), was the Fourteenth Amendment's guarantee that no person could be deprived by the state of life, liberty, or property without due process of law. Commitment statutes embodied the states' *parens patriae* (that is, parental) authority to protect those who were unable to protect themselves, by involuntarily hospitalizing persons whose mental illness was self-endangering. The Birnbaum idea, as embraced by the federal courts in *Wyatt v. Stickney* (1972) and its progeny, was that indefinite physical protection (such as through isolation) of the vulnerable individual was not enough. Instead, the courts began to hold that to deprive a person of liberty, the state had to provide treatment aimed at maximizing the potential functional ability of the patient and the possibility of return to the community as a minimal constitutional quid pro quo. The Supreme Court endorsed involuntary commitment as a legitimate exchange for the state's treatment or habilitation obligations in *Youngberg v. Romeo* (1982), though (as discussed later in this chapter) the treatment duties were imposed in a conservative fashion.

A second constitutional path for requiring treatment of civil committees arose out of the state's *police power* commitment rationale. The Tenth Amendment to the U.S. Constitution grants states the right, under the police power rationale, to enact laws to secure the safety of its citizens, among other things. The states interpreted this authority as granting them the right to commit involuntarily persons with mental illness who posed a danger to others. In 1975, the Supreme Court in *Donaldson v. O'Connor* prohibited states from involuntarily keeping a *non*dangerous individual in a mental facility without "more"—the "more" presumably connoting some form of treatment. *Donaldson*, however, left open the issue of treatment rights for dangerous mentally ill persons committed under the state's police power (*Rone v. Fireman*, 1979).

But what if the patient has not been involuntarily committed? A significant number of patients in state mental institutions have been admitted voluntarily, at least ostensibly. (This patient category may shrink in light of the Supreme Court's holding in *Zinermon v. Burch*, 1990, that a federal civil rights claim against the state may arise where the state unconstitutionally permits the "voluntary" admission of a decisionally incapacitated patient.) The due process, quid pro quo rationale would not apply to voluntarily admitted persons, and the courts generally have been reluctant to extend a legal right to treatment, with corresponding obligations for the state, to this group. Theoretically, a voluntary patient dissatisfied with the treatment options afforded by the state institution is free to leave, although in reality both the ability to leave and acceptable alternatives may be limited.

While involuntary and voluntary residents of state facilities are an important part of the mental health picture, a much more common contemporary scenario involves the individual who lives in the community and desires outpatient mental health treatment but lacks health insurance or independent financial means to purchase that treatment in the private sector. With few exceptions (*Dixon v. Weinberger*, 1975), the courts have neither embraced a constitutional substantive due process right (Costello & Preis, 1987) nor interpreted federal statutes to create a legislative right (*Halderman v. Pennhurst*, 1981) to community-based mental health services. Some jurisdictions have addressed this need, however, through limited, conditional statutes that the courts, in turn, have sought to enforce through injunctive relief (that is, a court decree forbidding, permitting, or commanding some action) and consent decrees (for example, an agreement between the parties that is sanctioned by the court) (*Lelsz v. Kavanagh*, 1991). To the extent that a right to publicly funded treatment in the community exists today, it is essentially the result of state statutes (Weiner, 1985). Hence it is an issue to be battled out primarily in the political arena, with perhaps the strongest argument being that adequate community treatment can forestall or prevent unnecessary hospitalization (Arrigo, 1992). Injunctions based on constitutional or statutory provisions are not needed for patients who pay for and receive private mental health services; vindication of their right to treatment is a matter of contract or tort law (that is, the law dealing with remedying private, civil wrongs other than breaches of contract) (Klerman, 1990).

The Right to Refuse Treatment

The chief focus for some mental health advocates was the independence, privacy, and freedom of the individual patient against outside interference. For them, securing the right of persons with mental illness to be left alone was a natural enterprise, though others regarded this as the right to be mentally ill (Stone, 1987). This quest involved not only an attack on involuntary hospitalization but also, particularly as psychoactive drugs began to proliferate as a behavioral management instrument, a proclamation of the patient's right to consent to or refuse recommended medical interventions. While the interventions that might be subsumed under a right to refuse treatment include psychotherapy, electroconvulsive therapy, psychosurgery, and programs of behavior modification and aversive therapy, most of the legal and clinical attention of the past decade and a half—especially concerning persons involuntarily committed to state institutions—has surrounded the forcible administration versus patient refusal of psychoactive drugs.

Although at least one commentator seems to want to argue to the contrary (based on the idea that mind-altering drugs are not intrusive) (Slovenko, 1992), several important federal cases originating in the late 1970s broke the initial ground in developing the right of an involuntarily confined mental patient to refuse drugs (*Rennie v. Klein*, 1981; *Rogers v. Okin*, 1982). Judicial recognition of this right was premised on the due process (Fourteenth Amendment protection of liberty) and freedom of thought and free exercise of religion (First Amendment) clauses enumerated or read into the federal constitution intended to promote individual privacy or autonomy (Rhoden, 1980; Tancredi, 1980). In addition, attorneys' arguments and court decisions cited the common law right of bodily integrity that also furthers personal autonomy and reinforces the informed consent doctrine (Hermann, 1989). This doctrine holds that mentally competent adults have a right to control—that is, to consent to or refuse—any external interventions involving their own bodies. It also holds that unconsented-to treatment that violates another's bodily integrity should expose the invader to liability under either battery (intentional wrongdoing) or negligence (unintentional but culpable wrongdoing) theories. Slanted judicial impressions (Bursztajn et al., 1991) about the adverse side effects (for example, tardive dyskinesia and tardive dystonia) of powerful psychoactive substances, and their frequent misuse for staff convenience and the control and punishment of patients (Plotkin, 1978), also influenced a number of landmark decisions. These problems convinced courts to impose significant restrictions on mental health professionals' ability to force drugs on unwilling patients (La Fond & Durham, 1992).

Advocates and courts also drew a sharp distinction between the legal criteria necessary to hospitalize a person involuntarily (for example, mental illness and dangerousness) and the criteria to find a person incompetent to make personal decisions. The former did not automatically imply an inability to understand and manipulate information about risks, benefits, and alternatives or to engage in a rational decision-making process about one's own treatment plan. Thus a shift in orientation occurred from treatment-oriented commitment that presumed incompetence to dangerousness-oriented commitment that presumed competence. With reference to the difference between earlier therapeutic concerns and contemporary public safety concerns, one astute commentator has remarked that "the treatment-oriented commitment system of the 1960s, which had survived through the 1830s, became the dangerousness-oriented system of the 1970s and 1980s" (Appelbaum, 1988, p. 414).

Although thus far the Supreme Court has chosen not to address the right to refuse treatment directly (*Mills v. Rogers*, 1982), a plethora of state and lower federal courts have relied on specific state as well as federal constitutional clauses (Brooks, 1991), plus a number of state statutes, to establish solidly the right to refuse treatment. The Supreme Court did set forth a related ruling in *Washington v. Harper* (1990) that a state prisoner with mental illness may be forcibly medicated with psychoactive drugs as long as the prison's review procedure (in this instance a panel of institution-based clinicians and administrators not directly involved in that prisoner's care) was "reasonably related to legitimate penological interests." The *Harper* decision, however, in no way diminishes the prerogative of state and federal courts to enunciate a broader right for involuntary mental patients to refuse treatment based certainly on state, and possibly on federal, law (Appelbaum, 1990). Additionally, *Harper* in no way infringes on the prerogative of states to restrict their own power to compel treatment; such state-level restrictions could be imposed legislatively or through administrative regulation (Eagle & Kirkman, 1990).

While the involuntary patient's right to refuse treatment is now generally accepted as a given in the state institutional context, it is not absolute. The various states have adopted an array of procedural mechanisms for implementing that right in practice and mediating treatment disputes between caregivers and patients, based on valid state police power and *parens patriae* rationales (Feather, 1985). The police power is the state's inherent authority to promote and protect the general health, safety, and welfare of the community. The *parens patriae* authority is the state's inherent power to intervene to protect persons who cannot protect themselves. This range of mechanisms will be discussed later in this chapter, because a jurisdiction's particular administrative and review procedures have vital implications for the interface of legal theory and clinical practice in this arena.

Most public institutions provide voluntary patients a "take it or leave it" choice (that is, the patient must accept recommended treatment or leave the institution), although a few states statutorily establish a right to refuse treatment. Most private mental facilities impose rules that set out nonnegotiable conditions of treatment. As a general matter, patients receiving outpatient treatment may elect to follow or decline treatment recommendations, although here, too, termination from a treatment program or a specific clinician may result from noncompliance.

The situation becomes more complicated when the patient has been involuntarily committed to receive outpatient treatment. This is an option that courts in many states are grasping as an alternative to inpatient commitment, in an attempt to conserve scarce resources and place individuals who need treatment in the least restrictive setting. Picking up on an idea proposed some time ago (Bleicher, 1967), a number of states today legislatively authorize involuntary treatment of these individuals (Keilitz & Hall, 1985). In this scenario, a report of outpatient noncompliance submitted by the mental health professional may subject the patient to involuntary hospitalization and, after applicable procedures have been exhausted, to forced medication (McCafferty & Dooley, 1990). However, for outpatients who do not meet the criteria for forced medication, the state's options may be limited to (1) initiating involuntary inpatient commitment where that would serve only to warehouse the individual, (2) permitting the person to "walk the streets" without treatment, or (3) waiting for the person to enter the legal system through the criminal justice doorway.

Additionally, it has been suggested that, even where legal authority is present, coerced treatment may be counterproductive to community-based services because of a connection between the patient's attitudes about treatment and treaters, and the effectiveness of such treatment, including antipsychotic drugs (Wisor, 1993). This hypothesis is worthy of empirical investigation. Evidence regarding the effectiveness of compelled outpatient treatment will provide a basis for discussing the philosophical objections to this practice voiced by some critics (Schwartz & Costanzo, 1987).

Objections and Fears

The Right to Treatment

Few have objected to the general sentiment that persons needing and desiring appropriate mental health services ought to have convenient and affordable access to them. Some clinicians and other critics, though, have noted several inherent and applied difficulties with the courts' proclamation of treatment rights.

First, the financial expense entailed in properly fulfilling judicial treatment mandates is thought to have encouraged many states to depopulate their public mental institutions prematurely, indiscriminately "dumping" patients into unprepared and unwelcoming communities, rather than to incur the costs of substantially upgrading their institutions.

Second, an external intrusion into clinical practice, such as the setting and enforcement of treatment standards by the judiciary, is likely to be met with distrust and dislike. Weiner and Wettstein (1993, p. 113) describe how clinical staff may become so distracted by, and upset with, the perceived intrusion of judicial or administrative personnel that their ability to provide good care is jeopardized.

Third, there is a recognition that legally imposed treatment standards can, at best, deal only with the structural elements of care, such as minimal educational and licensure requirements for providers. These structural elements may have little effect on the important aspects of the process and outcome of treatment. Put differently, judicial or legislative announcement of minimal, structural mandates for treatment providers or programs is inherently incapable of ensuring real change—optimal, effective, freely chosen treatment for all needy patients (Appelbaum & Gutheil, 1991).

Fourth, some commentators have complained that a right to treatment, although meritorious on its own, is logically and practically incongruous with judicial enunciation of the negative right to refuse treatment that took place around the same time, and therefore asked mental health professionals to behave inconsistently (Simon, 1992). Finally (or perhaps initially), because treatment is a concept that refers to many varieties and intensities of intervention, delineating a right to treatment entails questions about type, duration, and quality. As Weiner and Wettstein (1993) ask, "Does a right to treatment convey to the patient a right to select a particular treatment modality, a particular therapist, or a particular treatment setting, for a particular time period?" (p. 113).

The Right to Refuse Treatment

The courts' recognition of a right to refuse treatment also has been attacked on several fronts (Brooks, 1980). First, clinicians and others submitted that the care of the mentally ill would be adversely affected. Under this view, courts and other preapproval review bodies would presume that involuntary patients do not want to be treated, a presumption that slights patients' true desires to get better so that they can exercise their autonomy again (Gutheil, 1985). According to these critics, the purported refusal of treatment by patients with serious mental illness is not an accurate reflection of those patients' consistent, authentic values and preferences. Most patients, it was submitted, would thank the clinician afterward for treating them against their objections, thereby proving that the ostensible refusals were based on mental pathology rather than principle or rational analysis. Thus, this issue should be handled clinically instead of legally (Schwartz, Vingiano, & Perez, 1990). Even substituted judgment exercised by proxy decision makers on behalf of decisionally incompetent patients (Hermann, 1989) begs the question of what the patient actually would want if presently competent enough to exercise autonomy.

Second, it has been argued that, paradoxically, patients who refused treatment would end up being involuntarily hospitalized, in a more restrictive setting, for a longer period than if they were treated effectively over their objection. For example, the increased use of seclusion and physical restraints for the unmedicated patient would increase the possibility of accidental injury. Untreated patients would thus be forced to "rot with their rights on." The therapeutic milieu of the institution might be disrupted by widespread treatment refusal, precipitating patient violence to staff or other patients (Weiner & Wettstein, 1993). The fundamental thrust of this position is that psychotropic medicines are safer and more efficacious and mental health professionals have more positive motives than most attorneys and courts believe. Therefore, clinical practice ought to determine legal doctrine instead of the other way around (Appelbaum & Gutheil, 1979). Clinicians complained that their ethical integrity and sense of professional self-esteem were potentially compromised by legal rules that changed their role from healer to jailer (Rodenhauser, 1984, 1986).

Although rarely stated so bluntly, much of the criticism leveled against judicial and legislative recognition of a right to refuse treatment, especially in the institutional context, can be reduced to a frustration and anger on the part of mental health professionals to a perceived threat to their proper sphere of professional autonomy and judgment, and a general opposition to legal interference in clinical matters (Baldessarini & Cohen, 1986; Brown, 1984). Although the underlying sentiments are noble and sincere, in many cases beneficence or concern for patient well-being has been overextended into the sort of parentalistic "doctor knows best" attitude that helped to inspire external oversight in the first place. At its worst, this overextension takes on more the form of a diatribe than a reasoned argument (Isaac & Armat, 1990).

Third, it was lamented that the cost of procedural implementation would be unacceptably high. The treatment approval process was expected to be cumbersome and slow, and endowed with an adversarial tone, resulting in valuable personnel and resources diverted away from treatment of receptive patients toward fulfilling due process procedures for unreceptive patients. Further, there was concern that the adversarial process would exert an antitherapeutic effect on the patient's health and the professional's enthusiasm. This effect would be compounded by guardians acting more as court-appointed watchdogs than as surrogate decision makers.

Implementing the Law in Practice

The experience of the past decade and a half has, for the most part, not substantiated the apprehensions and anxieties of clinicians and other critics. The predicted problems have failed to materialize, have been less severe than anticipated, or cannot be causally traced directly to legal recognition of mental health patients' rights

to treatment and to refuse treatment. Writing in 1982, the attorney representing the state in one of the landmark mental patients' rights cases noted perceptively that

[m]any psychiatrists seem to have a common misperception regarding the law that it deals in absolutes. . . . In fact, the law balances interests far more than it creates absolutes and is structured in such a way as to consider clinical realities when determining legal boundaries. (Schultz, 1982, p. 187)

It should be acknowledged that the observations made here concerning the law's impact on actual practice and patients' lives are drawn much more from the literature—ordinarily reflecting anecdotal, impressionistic, and single-institution experience—and from my personal conversations with mental health and legal professionals and observers than from reference to a comprehensive, large-scale, rigorously collected multisetting empirical database. Indeed, such a database is sorely needed to measure accurately the tangible therapeutic outcomes of the jurisprudential changes of the past several decades. Unfortunately, the construction and maintenance of this database remains a glaring unfulfilled research agenda at this point in time and ought to constitute the next major component of the therapeutic jurisprudence inquiry.

The Right to Treatment

Notwithstanding the foregoing data constraints, it appears that the right to treatment that was greeted with such hope and expectation by patients' advocates 20 years ago has turned out in practice to be so limited in scope as not to be much of a factor in either a positive or negative direction. In the institutional setting, important judicial decisions have tended to defer heavily to the clinical expertise of the patient's mental health professionals to determine the (limited) extent and types of treatments minimally necessary to prevent patients' further deterioration, instead of imposing an external, objective standard of minimum treatment (Bersoff, 1992;

Parham v. J. R., 1979; Stefan, 1993; *Youngberg v. Romeo*, 1982). Recent judicial decisions, based on painful lessons learned in the 1970s and 1980s about the practical limitations of the courts to micromanage large public service delivery systems like mental institutions and prisons (Rosenberg, 1991), have also taken into account (at least implicitly) the fiscal and administrative realities faced by the states responsible for fulfilling even the minimal treatment plans designed by their mental health professionals. This approach is a far cry from the spectre of pervasive, detailed intrusion into the everyday operation of institutional care that many envisioned in the heyday of *Wyatt*. Thus, contrary to predictions, this does not seem to be an arena where legal doctrine has unduly disrupted good clinical care (although some would maintain that administrative rules often are sufficiently burdensome to affect care negatively, at least indirectly).

Similarly, in the outpatient setting, the idea of a legally enforceable right to treatment does not appear to have interfered with proper mental health services. Litigation has been largely unsuccessful in enforcing a right to treatment unless it is based on an existing state statute (*Heard v. Cuomo*, 1993). Virtually all state statutes that provide a right to outpatient mental health treatment do so in a limited and conditional fashion, with many taking into account explicitly the status of the jurisdiction's present financial resources. The same is true for consent decrees imposing government obligations (*Arevalo v. City and County of Denver*, 1993). Again, the constraints imposed by a legal right to treatment on professional autonomy are not a major issue.

But lack of detriment is not enough. Policymakers must take the next step and ask what type of legal rule would be most likely to exert a positive therapeutic effect. For example, should such a rule specify that involuntary commitment be conditioned on a treatment plan with proof of the state's ability and willingness to deliver resources, perhaps enforced through recognition of a person's right to bring a civil rights action for specific dollar damages? A private right of action

against the state or its subdivisions for liquidated damages also could be created by legislation for voluntary inpatients and outpatients if the legislature were convinced of the therapeutic impact of such a remedy. As state officials in some jurisdictions attempt to shift mental health care for those with chronic illness to the private sector in an experiment intended to provide better care at lower cost, it will be important to evaluate whether privatization can achieve that goal without excessive intrusion into patient autonomy (Wisor, 1993).

No matter how well thought through and articulated the legal rules are, the real difficulty with establishing a meaningful right to treatment in the inpatient or outpatient settings are economic and political (Seicshnaydre, 1992). This is so, even though some argue that courts defer to health care professionals in setting standards and should therefore. recognize a right to treatment indicated by health care professionals without regard to economic cost (Posner, 1992). The dilemma of inadequate resources, especially for community-based care, is not limited to the United States. In commenting on a proposed amendment to the Mental Health Act in Great Britain and Wales that would give the government new legal power to supervise patient discharges from institutions and to ensure compliance with community care, a member of the Royal College of Psychiatrists' education committee said, "The proposed supervision order is a legal figleaf to disguise the diminishing substance of psychiatric services" (Dean, 1993; Groves, 1993). Although a thorough analysis of this problem is well beyond the scope of this chapter, suffice it to note that these deficiencies are attributable to political and economic dynamics involving labor unions, budgets, competing social demands, administrative inefficiencies, and the attitudes of taxpayers.

The Right to Refuse Treatment

It has been suggested that if the United States adequately funded and enforced a more extensive right to treatment, where a menu of appropriate services were readily accessible to the consumer in a continuum of congenial environments, the right to refuse treatment would be exercised less frequently (Michels, 1981). While this thesis has not been verified or disproved, there are abundant anecdotal reports of a significant number of mental health patients in both inpatient and outpatient settings today who exercise the right to refuse certain treatment modalities for a number of reasons.

For some, refusal may be a symptom and result of illness. A classic feature of serious mental illness is that the patient has no insight into his or her condition; "[m]adness is reality to the person who is afflicted" (Stone, 1987, p. 296). For others, though, the decision to decline treatment, including psychoactive drugs, may be a rational reflection of a personal risk-benefit analysis about the specific treatment in question. Refusal may also result from inadequate communication taking place with the patient (Johnson, 1990) or other problems in the provider-patient relationship; many patients reverse their treatment refusal decisions when clinicians probe their origins and remedy information or understanding deficiencies on the patient's part. This is an example of an area where the therapeutic jurisprudence concept could play a constructive role by asking what kinds of legal rules would encourage better communication and a more constructive provider-patient relationship: rules that enforce a legalistic/bureaucratic or a medical model, fixed or flexible rules, and so on.

Where treatment refusal by an involuntarily hospitalized individual persists, different states have established, by judicial decision or legislative or administrative creation, a variety of procedural models to utilize in balancing the patient's decisional rights against the legitimate interests of the state in protecting the patient and public. These models vary regarding the extent of due process required before forcible treatment, who has ultimate decision-making authority, the definition of an emergency, and the authority of

guardians to consent to psychiatric interventions (Weiner, 1985).

Psychiatrist Paul Appelbaum has broken down these various models into two main categories (Appelbaum, 1988). *Rights-driven* approaches, exemplified by Massachusetts, take the form of court adjudication programs aimed at determining the patient's mental competence to make health care decisions. In these programs, the adequacy and appropriateness of the proffered medication regimen usually have been a secondary concern. On the other hand, *treatment-driven* approaches such as New Jersey's have relied on clinical review (generally by facility staff), which has been more focused on the propriety of the proposed treatment plan for the patient's clinical problems. This approach devotes relatively little formal attention to the issue of competency, which better belongs in the courts. At least one state (New York) has attempted a hybrid of the two approaches (Zito, Craig, & Wanderling, 1991).

In practical outcome, the specific due process model adopted by a jurisdiction for adjudicating disputes between involuntarily hospitalized patients and their attending clinicians appears to make little difference, at least for disagreements that wind their way through the formal dispute resolution mechanism. In treatment-driven, rights-driven, and hybrid models, the vast majority of adjudicated cases result in the patient's objection being overruled and the treatment eventually permitted (Farnsworth, 1991). This phenomenon is strengthened by the proclivity of clinicians and the courts to employ as the substantive decision-making standard the patient's "best interests" (as seen by the caregivers) rather than a "substituted judgment" of what the patient personally would have wanted under the circumstances (*In re Jeffers*, 1992). In effect, clinical, administrative, and judicial reviewers tend to act, after going through the motions of gathering data and hearing arguments, more on the basis of pragmatic imperatives (for example, evidence of violent incidents) than clinical diagnosis or legal theory (Appelbaum,

1988; Cournos, McKinnon, & Adams, 1988; Veliz & James, 1987; Zito, Craig, & Wanderling, 1991). Courts and legislatures are likely to look to clinicians for proof of the impact that application of the right to refuse treatment would have on patient welfare and that of the community (Perlin, 1989). Although some appellate judges have enunciated sweeping legal principles, lower courts and those who apply those principles have crafted pragmatic strategies that are more managerial than jurisprudential.

A somewhat distinct procedural approach to the right-to-refuse issue is found in a few jurisdictions that make a patient's incapacity to decide about medications one of the mandatory criteria for involuntary commitment in the first place. By moving the determination to the front end, no additional hearing is needed for involuntary treatment after hospitalization has occurred (*A. E. and R. R. v. Mitchell*, 1983; *Estate of Roulet*, 1979). In this schema, the professional discretion of the treating mental health professional goes unchallenged, while patients' decisional rights are not diminished without judicial oversight (Stone, 1981). The ultimate result is the same as in other jurisdictions, however, except that some decisionally incapacitated patients may go untreated because they do not satisfy the dangerousness criteria for involuntary commitment (Hoge, Appelbaum, & Greer, 1989).

Regardless of its impact (or lack of impact) on the substantive result, some argue that the type of process used to make particular decisions has an important therapeutic value in itself (Tyler, 1992; Wolf, 1992). Thus, it is quite likely that the alternative process models discussed above exert differing psychological effects on patients involved and on clinicians' perceptions of outside intrusiveness.

However, when the inquiry is restricted to impact on actual substantive outcomes (that is, whether people with mental illness who could clearly benefit from therapeutic interventions go without those interventions to their mental and physical detriment), there is support for the conclusion that both psychiatrists and legal ad-

vocates had inflated the likely impact of judicial enunciation of a right to refuse treatment (Appelbaum, 1988). Expressed psychiatric objections to this right are muted today by comparison with those of a decade ago, and predominantly center on administrative inconvenience and unnecessary resource dedication under rights-driven due process models rather than on dire consequences to patients from not taking their medications. Support for independent clinical review panels, as a mechanism for quality control, and maintaining professional standards, without enduring the administrative waste of formal judicial intervention or the antitherapeutic experience of an adversarial proceeding, is strong and cuts across ideological boundaries (Appelbaum, 1988; Curran, 1989; DeLand & Borenstein, 1990; Isaac & Armat, 1990; Zito, Craig, & Wanderling, 1991). A therapeutic effect of the internal clinical review panel mechanism, as opposed to judicial review of treatment refusal, on the self-concept of patients with mental illness has been posited (Ciccone, Tokoli, Gift, & Clements, 1993). Advocates of the review panel model refer to this model's encouragement of negotiated settlements and strong clinician-patient relationships, as opposed to the zero-sum judicial process, which essentially precludes interaction other than by legal fiat (Zito, Vitrai, & Craig, 1993).

Especially in jurisdictions using the internal clinical review panel mechanism to effectuate the right to refuse treatment, clinicians have developed practice strategies for communicating and collaborating more effectively with patients about treatment options (Appelbaum & Gutheil, 1991). Many welcome the impetus to create a therapeutic alliance that a qualified right to treatment has inspired (Simon, 1992).

When an institution has contested a patient's right to refuse treatment, an administrative or judicial order authorizing treatment often results. This forced treatment frequently prepares the patient for return to the community, provided that he or she continues taking the prescribed medication. However, the threat of judicial review may encourage some institutional providers to forgo potentially beneficial treatment attempts for patients whose decisional capacity is uncertain, thus depriving those patients of useful treatments they might have received under other review models (Zito, Vitrai, & Craig, 1993).

The problem of enforcing medication compliance by a patient once he or she has been discharged from an institution also is serious, especially in an age of extensive homelessness (Cournos, 1989; Perlin, 1991). It is dwarfed, though, according to most discharge planners and case managers, by the phenomenon of people with mental disabilities living in the community who would like but cannot afford to obtain appropriate services or lack the physical or mental wherewithal to navigate the delivery system (Pepper & Ryglewicz, 1982).

A few mental patient advocates have expressed disappointment that the right to refuse treatment has not turned institutional psychiatry on its head, calling the evolving flexibility in the implementation of this rule a descent into a neoconservative era of mental health law (La Fond & Durham, 1992). This is clearly a minority perspective today. Leading mental health lawyers take the general position that courts and legislatures crafting right to refuse public policies have mainly accommodated competing interests and forged reasonable, workable compromises. The unfolding of the right-to-refuse story over the past decade and a half has caused attorneys and clinicians to talk to each other and to join together to advocate for a better treatment system with better treatment alternatives, as advocates' emphasis has shifted from an unbridled zeal for individual liberty at all costs to a concern about quality and benefits of care (Rubenstein, 1986).

Conclusion

In spite of earlier predictions to the contrary, societal recognition over the past 20 years of a mental health patient's rights to treatment and to refuse treatment have not set up an irreconcilable conflict in practice between the goals of law and mental health care. Therapeutic jurisprudence (Wexler, 1990; Wexler & Winick, 1991, 1992) posits that law should act therapeutically as well as procedurally and that to accomplish this outcome, lawmakers must converse much more closely with mental health professionals. Under this philosophy, legal policymaking should consider not only patient rights but also economic factors, public safety, and the therapeutic ramifications of proposed rules and their alternatives as values reflecting the preferences held by the community influencing the result. This relatively new approach is consistent with the older theory of legal realism, which insists on an evaluation of any part of law in terms of its effects (Llewellyn, 1931).

Much empirical research is still to be done evaluating the impact of judicially and legislatively declared rights to treatment and to refuse on patient, community, and professional well-being. Based on the limited existing research record and a substantial body of anecdotal reports and impressions, this chapter has maintained that recognition of these rights has not exerted the antitherapeutic effect that many had anticipated.

This judgment, however, by no means suggests that the courts or legislatures, simply by declaring these rights, have brought about a satisfactory, let alone ideal, mental health delivery system. While the nightmares of mental health professionals have not materialized, neither have the dreams of patient advocates. We have learned (or at least should have) by now that the best the law can do is to provide agents who desire social progress with support, useful tools, and a congenial environment (Rosenberg, 1991).

Many of the prerequisites to social progress will depend on the collection and interpretation of data, as opposed to speculation and anecdote, about the effect of legal influences on the lives of mental health professionals and their patients. The research areas needing further careful exploration include the extent to which persons with mental illness desiring community-based services actually are impeded in their access to such services, the explanations for those impediments (for example, services do not exist, are user-unfriendly, are hard to reach geographically, and so on), and the effects of those access impediments on their mental, physical, and economic health; the extent to which individuals with mental illness in the community have access to services but refuse them, and with what impact on their mental, physical, and economic health; the extent to which patients with mental illness who refuse treatment either languish unnecessarily in institutions or are released uncontrolled; and the effectiveness or counterproductivity of compelled outpatient treatment on the functioning of patients in society.

This sort of information should exert a powerful influence on the development of future public policy, in terms of both legal parameters and the setting of priorities for the expenditure of limited public funds. For example, if the homelessness phenomenon in the United States were clearly shown to be related to the depopulation of public mental institutions coupled with the unavailability of mental health services or the refusal of those services by people living in the streets, the implications for compelled treatment (and perhaps for involuntary commitment law as well) and the allocation of tax dollars would be obvious. Answering such questions and turning the data into effective social responses is the challenge, and the potential, of the therapeutic jurisprudence movement.

References

A. E. and R. R. v. Mitchell, 724 F.2d 864 (10th Cir. 1983).

Appelbaum, P. S. (1988). The right to refuse treatment with antipsychotic medications: Retrospect and prospect. *American Journal of Psychiatry, 145*, 413–419.

Appelbaum, P. S. (1990). *Washington v. Harper*:

Prisoners' rights to refuse antipsychotic medication. *Hospital and Community Psychiatry, 41*, 731–732.

Appelbaum, P. S., & Gutheil, T. G. (1979). Rotting with their rights on: Constitutional theory and clinical reality in drug refusal by psychiatric patients. *Bulletin of the American Academy of Psychiatry and Law, 7*, 306–315.

Appelbaum, P. S., & Gutheil, T. G. (1991). *Clinical handbook of psychiatry and the law* (2nd ed.). New York: McGraw-Hill.

Arevalo v. City and County of Denver, No. 81-CV-6961 and 81-MH-270 (Colo. Dist. Ct., Denver County, September 9, 1993).

Arrigo, B. A. (1992). The logic of identity and the politics of justice: Establishing a right to community-based treatment for the institutionalized mentally disabled. *New England Journal on Criminal and Civil Confinement, 18*, 1–31.

Baldessarini, R. J., & Cohen, B. M. (1986). Regulation of psychiatric practice. *American Journal of Psychiatry, 143*, 750–751.

Bersoff, D. N. (1992). Judicial deference to non-legal decisionmakers: Imposing simplistic solutions on problems of cognitive complexity in mental disability law. *Southern Methodist University Law Review, 46*, 329–372.

Birnbaum, M. (1960). The right to treatment. *American Bar Association Journal, 46*, 499–503.

Bleicher, B. K. (1967). Compulsory community care for the mentally ill. *Cleveland Marshall Law Review, 16*, 93–115.

Brooks, A. (1980). The constitutional right to refuse antipsychotic medications. *Bulletin of the American Academy of Psychiatry and Law, 8*, 179.

Brooks, W. B. (1991). A comparison of a mentally ill individual's right to refuse medication under the New York and United States Constitution. *Touro Law Review, 8*, 1.

Brown, P. (1984). The right to refuse treatment and the movement for mental health reform. *Journal of Health Politics, Policy and Law, 9*, 291–313.

Bursztajn, H., Chanowitz, B., Kaplan, E., Gutheil, T., Hakim, R. M., & Alexander, V. (1991). Medical and judicial perceptions of the risks associated with use of antipsychotic medication. *Bulletin of the American Academy of Psychiatry and Law, 19*, 271–275.

Ciccone, J. R., Tokoli, J. F., Gift, T. E., & Clements, C. D. (1993). Medication refusal and judicial activism: A reexamination of the effects of the *Rivers* decision. *Hospital and Community Psychiatry, 44*, 555–560.

Costello, J. C., & Preis, J. J. (1987). Beyond least restrictive alternative: A constitutional right to treatment for mentally disabled persons in the community. *Loyola L.A.* Law Review, 20, 1527–1557.

Cournos, F. (1989). Involuntary medication and the case of Joyce Brown. *Hospital and Community Psychiatry, 40*, 736–740.

Cournos, F., McKinnon, K., & Adams, C. (1988). A comparison of clinical and judicial procedures for reviewing requests for involuntary medication in New York. *Hospital and Community Psychiatry, 39*, 851–855.

Curran, W. J. (1989). The management of psychiatric patients: The legal right to refuse treatment (pp. 262–267). In W. J. Curran (Ed.), *Law-medicine notes: Progress in medicolegal relations*. Waltham, MA: New England Journal of Medicine Books.

Dean, M. (1993). Psychiatric patients in the community. *Lancet, 342*, 485.

DeLand, F. H., & Borenstein, N. M. (1990). Medicine court: II. Rivers in practice. *American Journal of Psychiatry, 147*, 38–43.

Dixon v. Weinberger, 405 F. Supp. 974 (D.D.C. 1975).

Donaldson v. O'Connor, 422 U.S. 563 (1975).

Eagle, S. J., and Kirkman, M. (1990). *Ohio mental health law* (2nd ed.). Cleveland, OH: Baldwin-Banks Law Publishing Company.

Estate of Roulet, 590 P.2d 1 (Cal. Sup. Ct. 1979).

Farnsworth, R. (1991). The impact of judicial review of patients' refusal to accept antipsychotic medications at the Minnesota Security Hospital. *Bulletin of the American Academy of Psychiatry and Law, 19*, 33–42.

Feather, R. B. (1985). The institutionalized mental health patient's right to refuse psychotropic medication. *Perspectives in Psychiatric Care, 23*, 45–68.

Groves, T. (1993). Government wants wider legal powers for community care. *British Medical Journal, 307*, 463.

Gutheil, T. G. (1985). *Rogers v. Commissioner*: Denouement of an important right-to-refuse treatment case. *American Journal of Psychiatry, 142*, 213–216.

Halderman v. Pennhurst, 451 U.S. 1 (1981).

Heard v. Cuomo, 80 N.Y.2d 684, 594 N.Y.S.2d 675, 610 N.E.2d 348 (1993).

Hermann, D. H. J. (1989). The basis for the right of committed patients to refuse psychotropic medication. *Journal of Health and Hospital Law, 22*, 176–185.

Hoge, S. K., Appelbaum, P. S., & Greer, A. (1989). An empirical comparison of the Stone and dangerousness criteria for civil commitment. *American Journal of Psychiatry, 146*, 170–175.

Isaac, R. J., & Armat, V. C. (1990). *Madness in the streets: How psychiatry and the law abandoned the mentally ill. New York: Free Press.*

In re Jeffers, 606 N.E.2d 727 (Ill.App.Ct. 1992).

Johnson, A. B. (1990). *Out of bedlam: The truth about deinstitutionalization.* New York: Basic Books.

Keilitz, I., & Hall, T. (1985). State statutes governing involuntary outpatient civil commitment. *Mental and Physical Disability Law Reporter, 9*, 378–397.

Klerman, G. L. (1990). The psychiatric patient's right to effective treatment: Implications of *Osheroff v. Chestnut Lodge. American Journal of Psychiatry, 147*, 409–418.

La Fond, J. Q., & Durham, M. L. (1992). *Back to the asylum: The future of mental health law and policy in the United States.* New York: Oxford University Press.

Lelsz v. Kavanagh, No. 3-85-2462-H (N.D. Tex. December 30, 1991).

Llewellyn, K. N. (1931). Some realism about realism—Responding to Dean Pound. *Harvard Law Review, 44*, 1222.

Margulies, P. (1992). The cognitive politics of professional conflict: Law reform, mental health treatment technology, and citizen self-governance. *Harvard Journal of Law and Technology, 5*, 25–63.

McCafferty, G., & Dooley, J. (1990). Involuntary outpatient commitment: An update. *Mental and Physical Disability Law Reporter, 14*, 277–287.

Melton, G. B. (1992). The law is a good thing (psychology is, too). *Law and Human Behavior, 16*, 381–398.

Michels, R. (1981). The right to refuse treatment: Ethical issues. *Hospital and Community Psychiatry, 32*, 251–255.

Mills v. Rogers, 457 U.S. 291 (1982).

Parham v. J. R., 442 U.S. 584 (1979).

Pepper, B., & Ryglewicz, H. (1982). Testimony for the neglected: The mentally ill in the post-deinstitutionalized age. *American Journal of Orthopsychiatry, 52*, 388–392.

Perlin, M. L. (1989). *Mental disability law: Civil and criminal* (Vol. 2). Charlottesville, VA: Michie.

Perlin, M. L. (1991). Competency, deinstitutionalization, and homelessness: A story of marginalization. *Houston Law Review, 28*, 63–142.

Plotkin, R. (1978). Limiting the therapeutic orgy: Mental patients' right to refuse treatment. *Northwestern University Law Review, 72*, 461–525.

Posner, M. J. (1992). The *Estelle* medical professional judgment standard: The right of those in state custody to receive high-cost medical treatments. *American Journal of Law and Medicine, 18*, 347–368.

Rennie v. Klein, 653 F.2d 836 (3rd Cir. 1981).

Rhoden, N. (1980). The right to refuse psychotropic drugs. *Harvard Civil Rights–Civil Liberties Law Review, 15*, 363–413.

Rodenhauser, P. (1984). Treatment refusal in a forensic hospital: Ill-use of the lasting right.

Bulletin of the American Academy of Psychiatry and Law, 12, 59–63.

Rodenhauser, P. (1986). Lasting rights and last rites: A case report. *Bulletin of the American Academy of Psychiatry and Law, 14*, 281–286,

Rogers v. Okin, 634 F.2d 650 (1st Cir. 1982).

Rone v. Fireman, 473 F.Supp. 92 (N.D. Ohio 1979).

Rosenberg, G. N. (1991). *The hollow hope: Can courts bring about social change?* Chicago: University of Chicago Press.

Roth, L. H. (1981). The right to refuse treatment. *Hospital and Community Psychiatry, 32*, 233.

Rubenstein, L. S. (1986). Treatment of the mentally ill: Legal advocacy enters the second generation. *American Journal of Psychiatry, 143*, 1264–1269.

Schultz, S. (1982). The Boston State Hospital case: A conflict of civil liberties and true liberalism. *American Journal of Psychiatry, 139*, 183–188.

Schwartz, H. I., Vingiano, W., & Perez, C. B. (1990). Autonomy and the right to refuse treatment: Patients' attitudes after involuntary medication (pp. 189–199). In D. B. Wexler (Ed.), *Therapeutic justice: The law as a therapeutic agent.* Durham, NC: Carolina Academic Press.

Schwartz, S. J., & Costanzo, C. E. (1987). Compelling treatment in the community: Distorted doctrines and violated values. *Loyola L.A. Law Review, 20*, 1329–1429.

Seicshnaydre, S. E. (1992). Community mental health treatment for the mentally ill—When does less restrictive treatment become a right? *Tulane Law Review, 66*, 1971–2001.

Simon, R. I. (1992). *Clinical psychiatry and the law* (2nd ed.). Washington, DC: American Psychiatric Press.

Slovenko, R. (1992). The right of the mentally ill to refuse treatment revisited. *Journal of Psychiatry and Law, 20*, 407–434.

Stefan, S. (1993). What constitutes departure

from professional judgment? *Mental and Physical Disability Law Reporter, 17,* 207–213.

Stone, A. A. (1981). The right to refuse treatment: Why psychiatrists should and can make it work. *Archives of General Psychiatry, 38,* 358–362.

Stone, A. A. (1987). Justice Blackmun: A survey of his decisions in psychiatry and law. *American Journal of Law and Medicine, 13,* 291–313.

Tancredi, L. R. (1980). The right to refuse psychiatric treatment: Some legal and ethical considerations. *Journal of Health Politics, Policy, and Law, 5,* 514–522.

Tyler, T. (1992). The psychological consequences of judicial procedures: Implications for civil commitment hearings. *Southern Methodist University Law Review, 46,* 433–445.

Veliz, J., & James, W. S. (1987). Medicine court: *Rogers* in practice. *American Journal of Psychiatry, 144,* 62–67.

Washington v. Harper, 110 S.Ct. 1028 (1990).

Weiner, B. A. (1985). *Treatment rights.* In S. J. Brakel, J. Parry, & B. Weiner (Eds.), *The mentally disabled and the law* (3rd ed., pp. 327–367). Chicago: American Bar Foundation.

Weiner, A., & Wettstein, R. M. (1993). *Legal issues in mental health care.* New York: Plenum.

Wexler, D. B. (1990). *Therapeutic jurisprudence: The law as a therapeutic agent.* Durham, NC: Carolina Academic Press.

Wexler, D. B., & Winick, B. J. (1991). *Essays in therapeutic jurisprudence.* Durham, NC: Carolina Academic Press.

Wexler, D. B., & Winick, B. J. (1992). Therapeutic jurisprudence and criminal justice mental health issues. *Mental and Physical Disability Law Reporter, 16,* 225–231.

Wisor, R. L., Jr. (1993). Community care, competition, and coercion: A legal perspective on privatized mental health care. *American Journal of Law and Medicine, 19,* 145–175.

Wolf, S. M. (1992). Toward a theory of process. *Law, Medicine, and Health Care, 20,* 278–290.

Wyatt v. Stickney, 344 F. Supp. 387 (M.D.Ala. 1972), *aff'd sub. nom.* Wyatt v. Aderholt, 503 F.2d 1305 (5th Cir. 1974).

Youngberg v. Romeo, 457 U.S. 307 (1982).

Zinermon v. Burch, 110 S.Ct. 975, 108 L.Ed.2d 100 (1990).

Zito, J. M., Craig, T. J., & Wanderling, J. (1991). New York under the *Rivers* decision: An epidemiologic study of drug treatment refusal. *American Journal of Psychiatry, 148,* 904–909.

Zito, J. M., Vitrai, J., & Craig, T. J. (1993). Toward a therapeutic jurisprudence analysis of medication refusal in the court review model. *Behavioral Sciences and the Law, 11,* 151–163.

14 ▌ Compensation for Mental and Emotional Distress

Daniel W. Shuman
Cynthia E. Daley
Southern Methodist University

Tort law shares with mental health professionals a common concern for reduction of harm in society and the restoration of those who are harmed. It attempts to discourage harmful activities by all members of society, including mental health professionals; it compensates injuries, including mental and emotional distress, for which mental health professionals provide treatment and assessment; and it involves a process that mental health professionals have the potential to shape therapeutically if they correctly understand its operation. Thus, tort law ought to be of innate interest to mental health professionals.

To assist mental health professionals' understanding of the tort process for compensating mental and emotional distress and making their input therapeutic, this chapter first explores the law that governs compensation for mental and emotional distress caused by the intentional or negligent acts of others. It then examines its goals, operation, and problems and its linkage of deterrence and compensation in a single system. It proceeds to examine tort claiming, including how people decide whether to institute a tort claim, and the role of mental health professionals in tort claims. Next, the chapter examines compensation for mental and emotional distress outside of the tort system through workers' compensation and first-party insurance. Finally, the

chapter examines tort law's impact on claimants' mental health.

Compensation for Mental and Emotional Distress in Tort Law

The Goals, Operation, and Problems of Tort Law

Tort law addresses the harm that results from people's activities by furthering two conjunctive goals—deterrence and compensation (Arlen, 1993; Owen, 1985; Pierce, 1985; Priest, 1987). Deterrence focuses on the potential injurers, to deter their unreasonably unsafe conduct and reduce injuries. Compensation focuses on the injured, to compensate their injuries and assist their recovery (Shuman, 1994). These conjunctive goals are apparent in the requirements for tort recovery; a plaintiff must establish both liability (that is, that the defendant's conduct was intentionally or negligently unreasonable and should be deterred) and damages (that is, that the plaintiff has suffered injury and should be compensated) (Keeton, Dobbs, & Owen, 1984).

Neither the need for deterrence nor the need for compensation alone is sufficient to trigger tort sanctions. Plaintiffs are not compensated merely because they are injured by the defendant's conduct. Plaintiffs also must establish that the defendant's intentional or negligent conduct falls below the standard of reasonable care society expects and that this conduct proximately caused their injury.

To prove an intentional tort, the plaintiff must establish that the defendant intentionally and without consent invaded the plaintiff's person. Because intentional torts require a showing of a violation of the plaintiff's person, intentional torts presume some harm. Engaging in sexual relations without the other party's consent constitutes the intentional tort of battery, for example, and confining another without consent or lawful authority constitutes the intentional tort of false imprisonment. Intentional torts recognize an individual's right to be free from purposeful, nonconsensual intrusions on physical and mental sanctity.

To prove a negligent tort, the plaintiff must establish that the defendant breached a duty to act reasonably owed to the plaintiff that proximately caused harm to the plaintiff. Driving an automobile faster than the speed limit that results in accidentally striking another vehicle and causing harm is an example of negligently inflicted injury. Negligent torts recognize an individual's right to be free from unreasonably caused harm.

However, even where a plaintiff prevails on the issue of liability, all injuries may not be compensated; that is, not all injury suffered as the result of the defendant's tortious conduct is legally compensable. Some loss is regarded as too speculative, remote, or insignificant to require tort damage awards, and mental and emotional distress is one category that has been singled out for special scrutiny. Traditionally, tort law has viewed mental and emotional injuries with suspicion (Magruder, 1936; Perrin & Sales, 1993).

Tort claims for mental and emotional injury present two pragmatic concerns for courts. Because there are no natural limits to these claims, as there are for physical injury, mental and emotional injury presents the potential of limitless damage claims. The value of a car damaged in an accident is finite; the value of the emotional loss to the parents of the child who died in that accident is infinite. In addition, without the objective criteria that courts thought existed for physical injuries, courts feared that fraud, somatization, and malingering would not permit them to adjudicate these claims accurately.

Apart from this skepticism about the practicability of accurately assessing claims for mental and emotional injuries, the causation requirement present in all tort cases poses unique problems for proof of these claims. To prevail, the plaintiff must prove a causal connection between the plaintiff's injury and the defendant's conduct. In traditional tort parlance, the plaintiff must show that "but for" the defendant's action, the injury would not have occurred. In cases of mental and emotional distress, this burden can be difficult to sustain, especially if the plaintiff has any preexisting psychological disorder or treatment. Although defendants are charged with the responsibility to take a plaintiff's preexisting circumstances into account in their actions, defendants are not required to compensate plaintiffs for preexisting injury caused by others.

Notwithstanding the traditional reluctance of courts to award compensation for mental and emotional injury, this reluctance has been less of a problem in the case of intentional torts. Traditionally, courts have allowed claims for mental and emotional injury caused by intentional torts such as assault, battery, and false imprisonment. In part, this willingness is due to the moral judgment about the defendant's conduct implicit in finding an intentional tort and, in part, it is because the essence of the wrong in an intentional tort is an intrusion on the person's integrity.

Although intentional tort claims such as assault and battery have remained largely unchanged through this century, one new intentional tort claim has evolved that has emotional distress as its principle concern—intentional infliction of emotional distress. Assault and battery involve intentional physical intrusion on the person's integrity. Intentional infliction of emotional distress addresses intentional emotional intrusion on the person's integrity; it grew out of threats to emotional rather than physical security. A person is subject to liability under this tort for intentionally or recklessly inflicting emotional distress on another if the actor's conduct is outrageous beyond the bounds of decency, the harm intended (or risked by the actor's recklessness) is severe, and the actual resulting emotional harm is also severe (Dobbs, 1993).

As noted above, courts have been far more reluctant to compensate a plaintiff for mental or emotional harm that is the result of negligent conduct than for harm that results from intentional or reckless behavior. The lack of objective criteria for measuring mental or emotional injury and the difficulty in placing a monetary value on emotional or mental distress is no more problematic for negligently caused harm than intentionally caused harm; however, the potential volume of suits for negligently inflicted mental or emotional harm is greater because there is more negligently caused harm than intentionally caused harm (Levit, 1992). For example, whereas few of us ever attack our neighbors, most of us occasionally drive carelessly. In response to this fear of a flood of suits for negligently inflicted mental or emotional harm, courts have fashioned myriad rules that limit the circumstances under which recovery will be recognized for negligently inflicted emotional harm.

One manifestation of the fear of feigned mental or emotional harm is that courts historically denied recovery for negligently caused emotional injury unless there was a concurrent physical impact (for example, a jolt) or injury (such as a broken arm). This rule provided a limit, albeit artificial, on the potential number of claimants and corresponded to an intuitive sense that emotional suffering may accompany physical injury. Most jurisdictions subsequently expanded this test to include those in the danger zone who might legitimately fear physical impact or injury from the defendant's negligent conduct. The zone-of-danger test allowed recovery for psychic harm without physical injury. This test enabled a plaintiff who was within the range of immediate physical danger to recover for his or her fright or

shock. Again, the rule provided an artificial limit on claimants.

Many jurisdictions have abandoned the zone-of-danger test in favor of a pragmatic approach that permits recovery by those who might reasonably suffer foreseeable emotional harm from the defendant's acts. Although the test of foreseeability is a prospective test to be applied from the perspective of the defendant at the time of the injury-producing event, its trial application is affected by hindsight bias. Thus, because jurors are aware of the consequences of the defendant's acts, jurors are more likely to conclude that the defendant's acts were foreseeable (Fischhoff, 1975). To address this problem of hindsight bias, some suggest bifurcation of trials so that jurors are unaware of the outcome when asked to assess its foreseeability (Wexler & Winick, 1991).

Although damages for mental or emotional distress have always had their share of critics, these criticisms have recently been tied to tort reform proposals that enjoy substantial support. A common theme in tort reform proposals is capping or eliminating damages for intangible injuries such as mental or emotional distress (Komesar, 1990). The wisdom of that decision entails a thoughtful examination of why tort damages are awarded for mental and emotional injury. Tort damages are intended to aid in the plaintiff's restoration by awarding a dollar amount sufficient to permit the plaintiff to purchase services necessary for recovery. This intent is clearest in the case of damages for physical injuries. A defendant whose conduct breaks a plaintiff's arm is assessed damages that include an amount of money that will permit the plaintiff to purchase rehabilitation services necessary to restore the arm to its preaccident condition.

But what of the pain and suffering that this injury has caused the plaintiff? Damages for intangible injuries like pain and suffering present two sets of concerns: one pragmatic, the other theoretical. The pragmatic concern, discussed earlier, is that these intangible losses lack a reliable method of valuation (Ingber, 1985).

The theoretical concern about awarding damages for these intangible injuries reveals a significant problem for tort law. Unlike damages awarded to purchase medical services for the rehabilitation of nonpermanent physical injuries, tort-financed medical services cannot make whole the intangible losses represented by pain and suffering. Because these losses do not fit neatly within tort law's avowed goal of making people whole through compensation, tort law faces the decision whether to award damages for these injuries and, if so, how to justify them.

Tort law justifies an award of damages for these intangible losses on the basis of two different conceptually troubling premises. One premise, a creative conceptualization of compensation, justifies an award of damages for intangible loss such as pain and suffering to permit the plaintiff to purchase offsetting substitute pleasures. The notion is that, although a child's life, for example, is irreplaceable, damages that allow parents to purchase a new sports car or a vacation condo may distract them from thinking about their loss as much. That these damage awards offset suffering lacks empirical validation (Shuman, 1994).

Another justification for awarding damages for intangible loss is based on deterrence, to avoid conferring on the defendant an entitlement to injure. This is simply an attempt to compute the amount that the defendant should pay for the damage award to have the appropriate deterrent effect.

Both suggestions, that we can offset intangible loss by awarding funds to purchase a substitute pleasure and that we should value incalculable injuries to achieve deterrence, are troubling explanations for damage awards for intangible loss. Moreover, if the best plaintiffs can expect from tort compensation is the ability to purchase restorative goods or services or substitute pleasures, there is no particular reason, assuming that damages are calculated in equivalent ways, that plaintiffs should care whether the payment is made by the defendant, an insurance company, or the government. To the contrary, because the financial and emotional costs of obtaining tort compensation are higher than for other compensation systems, if money alone were the goal and damages were calculated in equivalent ways, there is no reason for anyone to choose tort compensation. And, if providing money to injured persons is the sole goal of tort compensation, it hardly seems likely that society could justify maintaining the present tort system with its costs and inefficiencies. Why then maintain a fault-based tort system?

The Impact of Linking Deterrence and Compensation

Tort law awards damages only against people whose conduct it concludes should be deterred. This linkage of deterrence and compensation is based on two assumptions: (1) it is only appropriate to visit moral blameworthiness and financial responsibility for harm where an actor's conduct falls below some societal norm, and (2) tort law is the appropriate vehicle to deter conduct from falling below societal norms. "The general principle of our law is that loss from accident must lie where it falls" (Holmes, 1946, p. 76). The assumption that responsibility for harm should require a showing of fault is based on the belief that fault is the only compelling reason to shift the consequences of loss, absent some prior agreement of the parties.

Even if deterrence of unreasonable behavior is an appropriate goal, tort law may be unnecessary to satisfy that goal. People may act reasonably without regard to tort law because they believe it is the right thing to do, because they think it advances their economic interests, or because they are concerned about their own safety. Indeed, it may be beneficial for people to choose suitable behavior without governmental coercion (Skolnick, 1968). Even if it is necessary and appropriate to coerce reasonable behavior through legal sanctions, the criminal law or administrative regulation (for example, licensing and regulatory agencies) may be preferable to tort law.

There is no body of research that supports the conclusion that tort law, as it is currently structured, accurately or precisely deters injurious behavior (Shuman, 1993). At best, tort law likely either over- or underdeters. To be an effective deterrent, tort law, like criminal law, should create clear behavioral expectations by setting clear parameters for acceptable behavior that actors may use to guide their behavior and to avoid sanctions (Bovbjerg, Sloan, & Blumstein, 1989). Inconsistent determinations of liability and wide-ranging damage assessments from one trial to the next and from one jurisdiction to the next leave actors with unclear parameters for acceptable behavior (Shuman, 1993).

In addition, if tort law is to be an effective deterrent, tort law expectations for reasonable behavior should be communicated to the public. However, no formal mechanism exists to accomplish this goal. Although appellate court rulings on legal questions are published in official legal reporting services, trial court judgments are not. Public recognition of the consequences of tortious conduct usually occurs through the media, and then only in headline grabbing cases involving large monetary awards. This not only skews public knowledge of cases tried but also wrongly implies that cases are typically resolved by trial. Ninety to ninety-five percent of all civil cases are resolved by settlement agreements rather than formal adjudication by judge or jury (Trubek, Sarat, Felstiner, Kritzer, & Grossman, 1983). The terms of these agreements most often are not available to those other than the participating parties (FitzGerald, 1990). Although defendants are often interested in limiting public disclosure of these settlements, nondisclosure limits another important source of information that might otherwise communicate precise behavioral expectations to others so that tort law could be an effective deterrent. Thus, all tort settlements judge and jury determinations should be published to enhance the deterrent capacity of tort law to reduce unnecessary harm.

Despite these questions regarding deterrence's necessity and effectiveness, commentators continue to tout deterrence as an important goal of tort law (Atiyah, 1980). No-fault compensation schemes have not supplanted the traditional domain of tort law. And deterrence—which is concerned with the conduct of defendants, not the effects of that conduct on plaintiffs—remains a prerequisite to their tort compensation.

Questions and concerns also arise about tort law's goal to compensate for injury (that is, to return the injured to their preaccident condition) (Hutchinson, 1985). Tort sanctions take the form of monetary damages designed to compensate loss of earning capacity, property damage, medical expenses, and mental and emotional distress. Yet tort law's capacity to compensate is limited by its fault-based structure (Holmes, 1946). Tort law affords compensation only to people injured as the result of unsafe behavior thought to be in need of deterrence. People seriously injured through behavior not thought to be in need of deterrence (that is, reasonable mistakes and errors of judgment) are not afforded compensation under the fault-based tort system. In addition, people seriously injured through unsafe behavior thought to be in need of deterrence are not likely to institute a tort claim unless the injurer has sufficient assets or insurance to satisfy an award and the potential award is substantial. If compensation for all injured persons is desirable, tort law should be supplanted with a compensation system that focuses only on injury and provides compensation without regard to the injurer's capacity to pay by distributing the cost of compensation across the entire population.

Under the current fault-based system, it is largely coincidental that one seriously injured person institutes a tort claim and ultimately receives compensation and another does not. Some of this inequity is explained by the injurer's behavior, and some of this is explained by the serendipitous nature of the process through which injured persons decide to institute a tort claim.

Tort Claiming

The Decision to Institute a Tort Claim

The goals of tort law are not self-effectuating; they require the injured person, or someone on their behalf, to act. A necessary condition for their fulfillment is the institution of a tort claim by the person injured. Before a person can file a tort claim, however, he or she must make a series of decisions. First, a person must decide that he or she has been injured by the actions of another. For example, is my back bothering me more than it usually does, and, if so, is it from gardening or from an automobile accident in which I was involved? Normative expectations about what life has to offer guide personal assessments of injury. People who grow up in homes where abuse is common, for example, are less likely to perceive abuse or its emotional consequences as abnormal (Wartel, 1991). Changes in these normative expectations over time (and as the result of experiences such as therapy) and a statute of limitations (the time within which a claim must be brought or abandoned)[1] may have an impact on a plaintiff's decision and ability to bring a claim (Glimcher, 1982). Particularly in claims seeking damages for mental or emotional distress, where the date of the defendant's wrongful conduct alleged to have caused the plaintiff's injury and the onset of that injury may be uncertain, the impact of statutes of limitations is significant.

Consider, for example, claims in cases involving repressed memory of child sexual abuse. Ordinarily, the statute of limitations for a tort claim that arose during childhood is between one

and three years after age 18. Thus, without some special rule affecting the running of the statute of limitations, a person instituting a tort claim for childhood sexual abuse must do so at least by age 21. Although this may be fair to both parties where the potential claimant is then aware of the claim, what of individuals who assert that they repressed memory of the childhood abuse until they were older than 21?

Some states apply an exception to the running of the statute of limitations, known as the *discovery rule*, to adult survivors of childhood sexual abuse. The discovery rule developed in surgical malpractice cases in which the harm did not become apparent and could not reasonably have been discovered until a subsequent surgery, conducted after the running of the statute of limitations. In cases applying the discovery rule, the statute of limitations does not begin to run until the date the victim should have reasonably discovered the wrongful act, here, the psychological harm from the sexual abuse. One statutory codification of this approach for childhood sexual abuse, the *Cal Code Civ. Proc.* 340.1a, states:

In any civil action for recovery of damages suffered because of childhood sexual abuse, the time for commencement of the action shall be within eight years of the date the plaintiff attains the age of majority or within three years of the date the plaintiff discovers or should have reasonably discovered that psychological injury or illness occurring after the age of majority was caused by the sexual abuse, whichever occurs later.

The process through which repressed memories of child sexual abuses are retrieved is fraught with controversy. The pattern of memory retrieval, as reflected in the cases, reveals two scenarios. Some adults who claim to be victims of childhood sexual abuse contend that they repressed any memory of the childhood sexual abuse, and then suddenly recalled the abuse while engaged in counseling, or shortly before filing suit (Rogers, 1994; Summit, 1989). Other plaintiffs acknowledge earlier recall of the childhood sexual abuse but assert that they did not

---

[1]Statutes of limitations serve two purposes. First, these statutes restrict potentially unending liability of defendants. Second, statutes of limitations prevent evidentiary problems associated with stale claims, or claims unjustly brought due to the passage of time (Dobbs, 1993). Statutes of limitations typically range from one to three years from the date of injury occasioned by the defendant's intentional or negligent conduct.

causally link it with their current emotional or mental problems until engaged in counseling, or shortly before filing suit. Courts have been more inclined to recognize claims of complete repression of any memory of childhood abuse as fitting the discovery rule than cases in which claimants acknowledge earlier memories of childhood abuse but failed to identify them as the cause of current difficulties (Snelling & Fisher, 1992).

The application of the discovery rule to repressed memories of childhood sexual abuse has met with criticisms by legal and mental health professionals. Some in the legal community have criticized the discovery rule as leaving defendants indefinitely subject to suit. Criticisms from the mental health field question the accuracy of repressed memory of sexual abuse. These critics point out that memory recovery therapists who make suggestions about memory of an event across sessions are likely to make memory fallible, and that there is little empirical support for the proposition that childhood sexual abuse is often totally repressed or forgotten (Lindsay & Read, 1994). Thus, whereas mental health professionals have the potential to alert their client-patients to events that may give rise to a decision to institute a tort claim in a timely manner, mental health professionals also risk creation of a fallible memory that may give rise to an unjustified claim of childhood sexual abuse and subject the therapist to a claim by the person wrongly accused. The law should not reinforce the use of therapeutic techniques that make memory fallible by recognizing claims that arise from these techniques.

After recognizing the existence of an injury by another, a person next must allocate the responsibility for the injury to that other person before filing a tort action. Central to the concept of fault-based tort liability is that the plaintiff may recover only if the defendant, not the plaintiff, is primarily responsible for causing the plaintiff's injury. *Attribution theory* assists in understanding how the injured allocate responsibility for their injury.

Attribution theory attempts to explain people's perceptions of what causes events that happen to them. It posits that attribution begins with a person's perception of an event, leads to a causal judgment about that event, and finally, ends with a behavioral outcome. Thus, according to attribution theory, before instituting a tort claim, a plaintiff must make a causal connection between the injury and the defendant's conduct.

Research regarding attributional processes has centered on external and internal causation of events to explain how people respond to what has happened to them (Heider, 1958). The fundamental attribution error people make is a well-researched phenomenon; people overestimate the internal causes of an event, such as personality traits, and underestimate the external causes, such as the environment (Ross, 1977). An attribution error of this type may result in the failure to consider a viable tort claim.

Mental or emotional harm such as anxiety or depression may be more difficult to identify as an injury occasioned by the acts of another than physical injuries such as broken limbs and bruises. Erroneous attribution may result in failing to make a causal connection between the injury and the tortious conduct. However, even if a person does identify the mental or emotional injury, he or she nevertheless may erroneously fail to attribute the injury to an external source, attribute it internally instead, and fail to connect that injury to the tortious act. Only by moving to a no-fault compensation system in which responsibility for causing harm is irrelevant could the law minimize the consequences of attribution error in compensation of the injured.

A person who identifies a compensable injury and allocates responsibility to another may nonetheless be unwilling to institute a tort claim. Tort litigation is time-consuming and expensive, and there is often economic or environmental pressure to settle. Claimants who seek recovery for mental or emotional harm may face additional difficulties. Tort litigants are subject to rigorous scrutiny by opponents and cannot come to emotional closure until resolution of their legal claims. Claimants may choose to abandon claims rather than prolong emotional distress or disclose personal information publicly. A plaintiff who seeks damages for any personal injury must waive confidentiality of all relevant medical and mental health records. During the discovery phase of any tort litigation, either side may gain access to relevant information through the formal discovery process. Seeking mental health care prior to the tortious conduct at issue is discoverable and admissible, when relevant, and plaintiffs may be reluctant to disclose this information and be labeled as mentally ill. Only by moving to a less public and less adversarial compensation system could the law minimize these negative consequences of tort litigation (Chapter 5, this volume).

The consequence of the decision-making process for tort claiming is that most injured persons do not make decisions that lead them to institute tort claims (Abel, 1987). Fewer than one patient in eight injured by negligent medical care institutes a tort claim (Harvard Medical Practice Study, 1990). Only 10% of injuries from defective products result in claims (U.S. Department of Commerce, 1978). Except for victims of motor vehicle accidents, only a small percentage of injured persons ever institute a tort claim (Hensler, 1991). The legal system may exacerbate this situation because plaintiffs' lawyers, who are typically paid on a contingency fee, are unlikely to take cases unless damages are valued at more than $50,000 (Saks, 1992). Many smaller claims are not compensated by the tort system, and only when unsafe behavior coincides with serious injury caused by a solvent defendant is a tort claim likely to be instituted. If we wish to encourage legal assistance in pursuing valid tort claims, the law should award attorneys fees even in smaller claims to increase the number of injured persons who are compensated. The law, however, is not the only major player affecting injured persons' tort claiming; mental health professionals also play a significant role in the process.

The Role of Mental Health Professionals in Tort Claims

The decision to institute tort litigation and the outcome of that litigation is also affected by the actions of mental health professionals. They provide the forensic and clinical bases for asserting the mental and emotional harm that informs the client-patient and legal actors. The recognition and application of diagnostic criteria is used to validate injury. For example, claims for what is now diagnosed as posttraumatic stress disorder increased dramatically after its recognition in 1980 in the third edition of the *Diagnostic and Statistical Manual of Mental Disorders* (DSM-III) (American Psychiatric Association, 1980), although mental health professionals had discussed this psychological phenomenon for at least a century (Shuman, 1995). Not only do mental health professionals provide evidence of mental and emotional harm, they also may play two different but equally critical roles.

Tort litigation may grow out of the injuries for which mental health professionals provide treatment, and mental health professionals also may play an important role in tort litigation other than as caregivers. As opposed to traditional clinical psychology and psychiatry, forensic psychiatry and psychology involves evaluations in a litigation context. The purposes of traditional and forensic evaluations and the relationships between the parties in these two settings differ in significant ways. Traditional psychiatric or psychological evaluations are performed to aid in the management and treatment of a patient, are written for another member of the psychiatric or psychological community such as a physician or case manager, are confidential and privileged, and are rarely seen by the patient (Hoffman, 1986). In addition, the traditional evaluation is performed in the context of a voluntary relationship that the patient chose to enter and may choose to terminate.

Conversely, a psychiatric or psychological forensic consultant in a tort action performs an evaluation to explain a plaintiff's symptoms to members of the legal and insurance communities and assess the connection between these symptoms and the tortious act. Unlike treatment records, forensic reports are not confidential or privileged. Moreover, forensic evaluations are not made in the context of a voluntary relationship that the examinee may enter into or terminate at will. For example, a person who institutes a tort claim for mental or emotional harm will be required to submit to an evaluation by a mental health professional chosen by the opposing party as a condition of bringing the claim.

In traditional psychiatry and psychology, the external validity of the patient's worldviews are not at issue, thus there is no need for the therapist to verify this information. In forensic psychiatry and psychology, the external validity of the patient's worldviews is at issue, and the weight given forensic assessments turn on the validity of the information on which they are based. Thus, forensic reports in tort cases include information about the history of the accident or incident in question, the postaccident course, past legal history, and familial medical and psychiatric history regarding dysfunction following an accident or other traumatic event (Hoffman, 1986). Because of this context for forensic assessments, mental health professionals must document each piece of data gathered with great care, keeping in mind that the validity of their opinion rests on the accuracy of this information, which will be tested in adversary proceedings. Accordingly, some forensic professionals recommend video recording as much of the evaluation process as possible (Borum, Otto, & Golding, 1993).

The role of mental health professionals in forensic assessment is crucial not only in individual assessments but also in shaping judicial attitudes about mental and emotional injuries. As noted above, courts have viewed the legitimacy of mental and emotional injuries with suspicion and consider these injuries speculative and difficult to assess. Courts often demand objective proof of injuries and their relationship to the defendant's tortious conduct (that is, concurrent physical impact or injury), which are rarely present for psychic injury.

Notwithstanding these attempts to demand objective proof of mental and emotional injuries, it is far from clear how these legal rules affect the conduct of these cases. There has been little empirical assessment of this approach. Perrin and Sales's research suggest that these standards are complied with more often in negligence than in intentional tort claims for mental and emotional injuries where "the claimed injuries were less specifically identified, less severe, and less frequently supported by expert testimony" (Perrin & Sales, 1993, p. 202).

Crucial to assessing psychic injury in a context in which injury may be rewarded is the ability to identify malingering, intentionally produced false or exaggerated physical or psychological symptoms motivated by external incentives such as monetary compensation (American Psychiatric Association, 1994). Mental health professionals have utilized three approaches to detect malingering—psychometric measurements, clinical interviews and observations, and psychophysiological measurements (Drob & Berger, 1987). Psychometric detection entails the use of psychological tests to provide an indirect measurement of malingering. The Minnesota Multiphasic Personality Inventory, or MMPI and MMPI-2 (Hathaway & McKinley, 1983), has been found to be the most helpful psychological test in identifying exaggeration and minimization of symptoms (Pope, Butcher, & Sellen, 1993; Rogers & Mitchell, 1991). It does not identify all malingering, however, and it erroneously identifies malingering in other instances. Projective tests such as the Rorschach Inkblot Test (Exner, 1986) have been found less helpful in identifying malingering (Stermac, 1988). Malingering on the Rorschach presents an even greater problem when secondary gain is at issue (Albert, Fox, & Kahn, 1980; Perry & Kinder, 1990). Clinical observation and interviewing, although often relied on in judicial proceedings, have not proved to be effective in the scientific literature in the detection of malingering with the exception of gross malingering (Rogers & Mitchell, 1991). Psychophysiological measurement of malingering, by use of the polygraph and similar devices, is mired in the controversy surrounding its use in general, and its utility in the detection of malingering is not clear (Szucko & Kleinmuntz, 1981). Understandably, courts have been skeptical of a mental health professional's ability to detect deception or malingering.

Mental health professionals can also aid the legal system by helping to determine whether a causal connection exists between an emotional or mental injury and a tortious act. For example, if a plaintiff is experiencing depression, a mental health professional may help to assess the relationship between the plaintiff's depressive symptoms, such as weight loss and sleeplessness, to a car accident. This assessment may involve separating the plaintiff's current psychological dysfunction from any emotional stressors, such as a divorce or death in the family, that occurred concurrently or before the accident (Weissman, 1990). Although the psychiatric and psychological communities have worked to combine psychological assessment instruments and legal demands to provide valid and reliable evaluations (Elwork, 1992), courts continue to question mental health professionals' capability of assessing mental or emotional difficulties accurately.

The consequences of error matters in different ways for the clinical and forensic activities of mental health professionals. Diagnostic errors in clinical practice, for example, can often be corrected in a subsequent session as new information or the failure of a particular therapy appears. On the other hand, diagnostic errors in forensic practice are not so easily corrected, as trials are not redone in light of information acquired later. Thus, the standards by which the law reviews the judgments of forensic mental health professionals must be rigorous and supported by good data.

Compensation for Mental and Emotional Distress Outside the Tort System

Given the problems in gaining recovery through tort law, it is not surprising that most people who seek compensation for accidental injury do not invoke the tort system and are more likely to seek nonfault-based recovery, such as workers' compensation or their own first-party insurance (Hensler, 1991). It is appropriate therefore to examine those systems and their treatment of claims for mental and emotional distress.

Workers' Compensation

In the 19th century the "three sisters"—contributory negligence (plaintiff barred from recovery if his or her own fault contributed to the injury), assumption of the risk (plaintiff barred from recovery if he or she voluntarily assumed the risk of harm posed by the defendant's conduct), and the fellow servant rule (plaintiff barred from recovery from employer if the injury was caused by a fellow worker)—were tort defenses available in negligence cases. These defenses had a devastating impact on employee claims against employers for work-related injuries and minimized the employee's chances of prevailing in a tort action. For example, under the fellow servant rule, recovery was precluded if an injury was caused by a fellow employee's negligence, which was invariably the case (Dobbs, 1993). And, because in many jobs risks are endemic to the vocation, courts often deemed that employees assumed the risks that resulted in their injuries and precluded their claims.

Workers' compensation statutes are legislative creations that came into existence in most states at the end of the 19th century as a response to the defenses that all but barred employee's tort claims against employers for work-related injury. In contrast to tort liability claims that make fault a prerequisite to compensation, fault is irrelevant in workers' compensation claims. The primary function of workers' compensation is to compensate victims of work-related injuries without regard to fault. In theory, the costs of compensating an injured worker are passed on to price conscious consumers who will choose more safely produced goods and services, thereby encouraging greater employer safety measures.

Mental or emotional injury caused by a physical injury or trauma is compensable in workers' compensation systems in virtually all states. Most workers' compensation schemes authorize awards for work-related stress not caused by physical injury or trauma, particularly when the stress exceeds that experienced in normal working conditions (for example, witnessing the death of a coworker). However, the stressors and injuries that are covered vary widely among the states (Pattison & Varca, 1994). One trade-off for removing the tort barriers to recovery in workers' compensation is a difference in the amount of compensation. Workers' compensation awards are typically less than tort damage awards for equivalent injuries, with workers' compensation schemes consisting of fixed scale payments. In addition, punitive damages are not available in the workers' compensation system.

State law requires compensation for covered employees in the event of injury. In exchange for an assurance of compensation, the employer cannot be liable in tort for work-related injuries. However, courts tend to make judicial exceptions for intentional torts such as sexual assault (Love, 1985).

First-Party Insurance

Although workers' compensation is a legally required program, many people seek compensation for accidental injury from first-party insurance they have purchased for that eventuality. An injury from a fall off of a stepladder resulting in a trip to the emergency room to suture a wound or set a broken bone is likely to result in a claim on the injured person's health insurance policy, not a suit against the manufacturer of the ladder (Hensler, 1991).

The availability of compensation from a health insurance plan for the costs of treating mental or emotional harm is a matter of private agreement between the insured and the insurer, subject to state mandates that may require the provision of certain health benefits (Chapter 6, this volume). The severity of the injury for which benefits will be provided and the extent of the benefits are determined before an occurrence of mental or emotional injury. Unions may choose to press for extensive mental health coverage in their insurance benefits or trade these benefits for wage increases. Employers who do offer mental health care may offer only managed mental health benefits to reduce costs of providing this coverage (Chapter 7, this volume). To some, this bargaining process is the direction to be undertaken for all compensation reform. According to this view, insurance is an accurate vehicle for people to express competing preferences about risk. Insurance is an opportunity for people to express the value they place on certain losses by insuring against them.

Conclusion

Although most injured people do not seek compensation from the tort system, the tort system is an important public forum accessible to private citizens to address personal and social policy concerns. Its symbolic importance may transcend its actual usage. And, notwithstanding the barrage of criticism, the tort system appears likely to continue in some form.

Although both intentional and negligent torts may permit recovery for mental and emotional distress,[2] it may seem strange to use a fault-based tort scheme to redress these injuries. As already noted, fault-based tort recovery presents problems of proving that the defendant's intentional or negligent conduct caused the plaintiff's mental or emotional distress, establishing a dollar value of the harm, and subjecting a plaintiff who suffers these injuries to adversarial scrutiny. Given these problems, an overarching question is whether the tort system has a beneficial or therapeutic effect on plaintiffs sufficient to outweigh its limitations, particularly for plaintiffs who have suffered mental or emotional distress.

The notion that law may have therapeutic or antitherapeutic effects, although not new, is a concern about which we are reminded by a new mode of legal analysis, therapeutic jurisprudence. Therapeutic jurisprudence examines the law's potential as a therapeutic agent; it posits that laws have both therapeutic and antitherapeutic consequences that should be empirically examined, without offending other normative values (Wexler, 1990, 1992; Wexler & Winick, 1991). Therapeutic jurisprudence is a useful lens to examine the impact of tort law because tort law's goals of deterrence (or avoidance of injury) and compensation (or restoration of the injured) are therapeutically driven.

Fault, the defining element of tort law, may be the central issue in examining tort law's restorative powers. Although the requirement of finding the defendant at fault denies tort compensation to some injured persons, for those who are compensated, this finding of fault may be therapeutic in ways that no-fault compensation is not. A finding of fault may play an important psychological role in undoing the harm caused by the defendant's wrongful conduct. Plaintiffs often say that they institute tort litigation because they expect it to produce a beneficial result (Shuman, 1994). Students of human behavior note that punishment of wrongdoers relieves the outraged feelings of those who have been hurt (Shuman,

1994). And, even if fully compensated elsewhere, some plaintiffs would nonetheless pursue tort litigation because of a "need for dignity, respect, empowerment, and an ideology of fairness that a system of justice provides" (Bender, 1990, p. 877).

Yet there is also speculation that fault-based tort litigation reinforces psychopathology by holding out a damage award for remaining unhealthy. Although this view of secondary gain is widely held, the research addressing the effects of being a claimant does not show convincingly that, in general, claiming plays a role in creating or perpetuating illness or injury (Shuman, 1994). Even if claimants improve dramatically after their claims are resolved and not a moment before, that describes only *what* occurs and does not explain *why* it occurs. Improvement following tort compensation is consistent with tort compensation having both a therapeutic and an antitherapeutic impact. If plaintiffs improve dramatically after they have received tort compensation, the improvement may result from the removal of the negative effect of tort litigation or it may result from the receipt of its positive benefits.

Tort litigation may be therapeutic not only because of its result (the fault-based compensation decision) but also because its process empowers and gives voice to the injured in ways that no-fault compensation does not. Tort claimants may tell their stories in an important public forum and invoke the coercive power of the courts to reshape power imbalances in their relationships with their injurer (Shuman, 1994). Thus understood, fault-based tort law offers restorative benefits that no-fault compensation does not. At its restorative best, the tort system offers claimants the opportunity to be heard in a dignified and culturally meaningful proceeding that conveys a message that society cares what happened, determined by a trusted decision maker who will make a judgment of responsibility that may help reshape the balance of power between claimant and injurer (Shuman, 1994).

---

[2] Strict products liability, another vehicle for the imposition of tort liability, is used to impose liability for injuries caused by defective products. This law generally excludes damages for nonphysical harm.

References

Abel, R. L. (1987). The real tort crisis—too few claims. *Ohio State Law Journal, 48*, 443–467.

Albert, S., Fox, H. M., & Kahn, M. W. (1980). Faking psychosis on the Rorschach: Can expert judges detect malingering? *Journal of Personality Assessment, 44*, 115–119.

American Psychiatric Association. (1980). *Diagnostic and statistical manual of mental disorders* (3rd ed.). Washington, DC: Author.

American Psychiatric Association. (1994). *Diagnostic and statistical manual of mental disorders* (4th ed.). Washington, DC: Author.

Arlen, J. H. (1993). Compensation systems and efficient deterrence. *Maryland Law Review, 52*, 1093–1136.

Atiyah, P. S. (1980). *Accidents, compensation and the law* (3rd ed.). London: Weidenfeld and Nicolson.

Bender, L. (1990). Feminist (re)torts: Thoughts on the liability crisis, mass torts, power, and responsibilities. *Duke Law Journal, 1990*, 848–912.

Borum, R., Otto, R., & Golding, S. (1993). Improving clinical judgment and decision making in forensic evaluation. *Journal of Psychiatry and Law, 21*, 35–76.

Bovbjerg, R. R., Sloan, F. A., & Blumstein, J. F. (1989). Valuing life and limb in tort: Scheduling "pain and suffering." *Northwestern University Law Review, 83*, 908–976.

Cal. Code Civ. Proc. 340.1a (Deering 1995).

Dobbs, D. B. (1993). *Torts and compensation: Personal accountability and social responsibility for injury*. St. Paul, MN: West.

Drob, S. L., & Berger, R. H. (1987). The determination of malingering: A comprehensive clinical-forensic approach. *Journal of Psychiatry and Law, 15*, 519–538.

Elwork, A. (1992). Psycholegal treatment and intervention: The next challenge. *Law and Human Behavior, 16*, 175–183.

Exner, J. E. (1986). *The Rorschach: A comprehensive system: Vol. 1. Basic Foundations* (2nd ed.). New York: Wiley.

Fischhoff, B. (1975). Hindsight ≠ foresight: The effect of outcome knowledge on judgment under uncertainty. *Journal of Experimental Psychology: Human Perception and Performance, 1*, 288–299.

FitzGerald, B. T. (1990). Sealed v. sealed: A public court system going secretly private. *Journal of Law and Politics, 6*, 381–413.

Gallagher, B. D. (1993). Damages, duress, and the discovery rule: The statutory right of recovery for victims of childhood sexual abuse. *Seton Hall Legislative Journal, 17*, 505–540.

Glimcher, S. D. (1982). Statutes of limitations and the discovery rule in latent injury claims: An exception or the law? *University of Pittsburgh Law Review, 43*, 501–523.

Harvard Medical Practice Study. (1990). *Patients, doctors, and lawyers: Medical injury, malpractice litigation, and patient compensation in New York*. Report to the State of New York.

Hathaway, S. R., & McKinley, J. C. (1983). *The Minnesota Multiphasic Personality Inventory Manual*. New York: Psychological Corporation.

Heider, F. (1958). *The psychology of interpersonal relations*. New York: Wiley.

Hensler, D. (1991). Compensation for accidental injuries in the United States. Santa Monica: Rand.

Hoffman, B. F. (1986). How to write a psychiatric report for litigation following a personal injury. *American Journal of Psychiatry, 143*, 164–169.

Hoffman, B. F., & Spiegel, H. (1989). Legal principles in the psychiatric assessment of personal injury litigants. *American Journal of Psychiatry, 146*, 304–310.

Holmes, O. W. (1946). *The common law*. Boston: Little, Brown.

Hutchinson, A. C. (1985). Beyond no-fault. *California Law Review, 73*, 755–771.

Ingber, S. (1985). Rethinking intangible injuries:

A focus on remedy. *California Law Review, 73*, 772–856.

Keeton, R. E., Dobbs, D. B., & Owen, D. G. (1984). *Prosser and Keeton on torts* (5th ed.). St. Paul, MN: West.

Komesar, N. K. (1990). Injuries and institutions: Tort reform, tort theory, and beyond. *New York University Law Review, 65*, 23–77.

Levit, N. (1992). Ethereal torts. *George Washington Law Review, 61*, 136–192.

Lindsay, D. S., & Read, J. D. (1994). Incest resolution psychotherapy and memories of childhood sexual abuse: A cognitive perspective. *Applied Cognitive Psychology, 8*, 281–338.

Love, J. C. (1985). Actions for nonphysical harm: The relationship between the tort system and no-fault compensation (with an emphasis on Workers' Compensation). *California Law Review, 73*, 857–897.

Magruder, C. (1936). Mental and emotional disturbance in the law of torts. *Harvard Law Review, 49*, 1033–1067.

Marcus, E. H. (1983). Causation in psychiatry: Realities and speculations. *Medical Trial Technique Quarterly, 29*, 424–433.

Owen, D. G. (1985). Deterrence and desert in tort: A comment. *California Law Review, 73*, 665–676.

Pattison, P., & Varca, P. E. (1994). Workers' compensation for mental stress claims in Wyoming. *Land and Water Law Review, 29*, 145–173.

Perrin, G., & Sales, B. D. (1993). Artificial legal standards in mental/emotional injury litigation. *Behavioral Sciences and the Law, 11*, 193–203.

Perry, G. G., & Kinder, B. N. (1990). The susceptibility of the Rorschach to malingering: A critical review. *Journal of Personality Assessment, 54*, 47–57.

Pierce, R. (1985). Institutional aspects of tort reform. *California Law Review, 73*, 917–940.

Pope, K. S., Butcher, J. N., & Sellen, J. (1993). *The MMPI, MMPI-2 & MMPI-A in court: A practical guide for expert witnesses and attorneys*. Washington, DC: American Psychological Association.

Priest, G. L. (1987). Modern tort law and its reform. *Valparaiso University Law Review, 22*, 1–38.

Rogers, M. L. (1994). Factors to consider in assessing adult litigants' complaints of childhood sexual abuse. *Behavioral Sciences and the Law, 12*, 279–298.

Rogers, R., & Mitchell, C. N. (1991). *Mental health experts and the criminal courts*. Ontario, Canada: Thomson Professional Publishing Canada.

Ross, L. D. (1977). The intuitive psychologist and his shortcomings: Distortions in the attribution process. In L. Berkowitz (Ed.), *Advances in experimental social psychology* (Vol. 10). New York: Academic Press.

Saks, M. J. (1992). Do we really know anything about the behavior of the tort litigation system—and why not? *University of Pennsylvania Law Review, 140*, 1147–1292.

Shuman, D. W. (1993). The psychology of deterrence in tort law. *Kansas Law Review, 42*, 115–168.

Shuman, D. W. (1994). The psychology of compensation in tort law. *Kansas Law Review, 43*, 39–77.

Shuman, D. W. (1995). Persistent reexperiences in psychiatry and the law: Current and future trends in posttraumatic stress disorder litigation. In R. Simon (Ed.), *Posttraumatic stress disorder in litigation: Guidelines for forensic assessment*. Washington, DC: American Psychiatric Press.

Skolnick, J. H. (1968). Coercion to virtue: The enforcement of morals. *Southern California Law Review, 41*, 588–641.

Snelling, T., & Fisher, W. (1992). Adult survivors of childhood sexual abuse: Should Texas courts apply the discovery rule? *South Texas Law Review, 33*, 377–415.

Stermac, L. (1988). Projective testing and dissimulation. In R. Rogers (Ed.), *Clinical Assessment of malingering and deception*. New York: Guilford Press.

Sugarman, S. D. (1985). Doing away with tort law. *California Law Review, 73*, 555–664.

Summit, R. C. (1989). The centrality of victimization: Regaining the focal point of recovery for survivors of child sexual abuse. *Psychiatric Clinics of North America, 12*, 413–430.

Szucko, J. J., & Kleinmuntz, B. (1981). Statistical versus clinical lie detection. *American Psychologist, 36*, 488–496.

Trubek, Sarat, M., Felstiner, W. L. F., Kritzer, H. M., & Grossman, J. B. (1983). The costs of ordinary litigation. *UCLA Law Review, 31*, 72–127.

U.S. Department of Commerce, Interagency Task Force on Product Liability. (1978). Final report. Springfield, VA.

Wartel, S. G. (1991). Clinical considerations for adults abused as children. *Families in Society, 72*, 157–163.

Weissman, H. N. (1990). Distortions and deceptions in self-presentation: Effects of protracted litigation in personal injury cases. *Behavioral Sciences and the Law, 8*, 67–74.

Wexler, D. B. (1990). *Therapeutic jurisprudence: The law as therapeutic agent.* Durham, NC: Carolina Academic Press.

Wexler, D. B. (1992). Putting mental health into mental health law: Therapeutic jurisprudence. *Law and Human Behavior, 16*, 27–38.

Wexler, D. B., & Winick, B. J. (1991). *Essays in therapeutic jurisprudence.* Durham, NC: Carolina Academic Press.

Part 4

Offenders with Mental Disorders and the Law

15 ■ Incompetency to Proceed in the Criminal Process: Past, Present, and Future

Bruce J. Winick
University of Miami

If, at any time in the criminal proceedings, a defendant appears to have a mental illness, the issue of his or her competence to proceed may be raised. This may occur when the defendant seeks to plead guilty or to stand trial. It may occur when the defendant seeks to waive certain constitutional rights, such as the right to counsel or to a jury trial. Even after conviction, the issue may be raised at a sentencing hearing, or when the government attempts to administer punishment, including capital punishment. The issue usually is raised by defense counsel, but also may be raised by the prosecution or the court itself, even over the opposition of the defendant, who may prefer to proceed despite his or her mental illness.

When the competency issue is raised, a court typically will appoint several clinical evaluators to conduct a formal assessment of the defendant's competency. These clinical evaluators examine the defendant and then submit written reports to the court. The court then decides the issue, sometimes following a hearing at which the examiners testify and are subject to cross-examination. If the court finds the defendant incompetent,

the criminal proceedings are suspended and the defendant is ordered into treatment, typically on an inpatient basis. Treatment is designed not to cure the defendant but to restore competence. If such restoration is thought to have been achieved, a new round of evaluations and hearings will occur, and if the court is satisfied concerning the defendant's competence, the criminal proceedings will be resumed.

This chapter examines the competency process, analyzing the legal framework that has evolved for competency determination and the disposition of those found incompetent to proceed. It discusses the origins of the competency process, the purposes the doctrine is designed to accomplish, and the costs and burdens that existing practices impose. It criticizes existing practices as costly, burdensome to defendants, and often inconsistent with the stated justifications for the doctrine. The various rules and procedures used in this area are analyzed from a therapeutic jurisprudence perspective (see generally "Bibliography," 1993; Perlin, 1993a; Wexler, 1993; Wexler & Winick, 1991a, 1991b, 1992a, 1992b). Not only do these rules and procedures often impose heavy burdens on criminal defendants with mental illness whom they are designed to protect, but they also frequently produce antitherapeutic consequences for those found incompetent and divert limited clinical resources from treatment to evaluation.

I would like to acknowledge the research assistance of Katherine Diamandis and Douglas Stransky.

Substantial reforms thus are needed. Ten years ago, I proposed a radical restructuring of the incompetency doctrine (Winick, 1985). In this chapter I review that proposal and offer several refinements growing out of my more recent work in therapeutic jurisprudence. I suggest changes in the way competency should be defined and evaluated and attempt to reshape the existing doctrine in order to eliminate its most objectionable features.

This chapter analyzes problems of incompetency to stand trial resulting from mental illness. Sometimes defendants are found incompetent as a result of mental retardation. The issues raised by mental retardation are considerably different from those raised by mental illness. Unlike mental illness, mental retardation is congenital, untreatable, and unchangeable. Moreover, individuals with mental retardation are always of subaverage intelligence and are often extremely vulnerable to suggestive influences, making waiver issues always problematic. For these and other reasons, the discussion in this chapter is limited to incompetency produced by mental illness, and its suggestions are not intended to apply to those with the distinct problems caused by mental retardation (Ellis, 1992; Ellis & Luckasson, 1985).

Incompetency in the Criminal Process: Past and Present

Historical Origins of the Incompetency Doctrine

The common law origins of the incompetency doctrine have been traced to mid-17th-century England (Group for the Advancement of Psychiatry, 1974; Hale, 1736; Winick, 1983, 1985). Blackstone (1783/1979) wrote that a defendant who becomes "mad" after the commission of an offense should not be arraigned "because he is not able to plead . . . with the advice and caution

that he ought," and should not be tried, for "how can he make his defense?" The ban on trial of an incompetent defendant has been traced to the common law prohibition on trials in absentia (trials held in defendant's absence), and to the difficulties encountered by the English courts when a defendant frustrated the ritual of the common law trial by remaining mute instead of pleading to the charges (Foote, 1960; Gobert, 1973; Group for the Advancement of Psychiatry, 1974; Winick, 1983; see for example, *Frith's Case*, 1790; *Kinloch's Case*, 1746). Without a plea the trial could not go forward. In such cases, English courts were obliged to determine whether the defendant was "mute by visitation of God" or "mute of malice." If "mute of malice" the defendant was subjected to a form of medieval torture, the *peine forte et dure*, in which increasingly heavier weights were placed on the defendant's chest in an effort to compel a plea. If "mute by visitation of God," the defendant was spared this painful ritual. The category "mute by visitation of God" originally encompassed the "deaf and dumb," but its scope gradually expanded to include "lunatics." At the discretion of the Chancellor, a jury could be empaneled to conduct an inquiry into the defendant's competency.

At this early stage of the development of the incompetency doctrine in England, self-representation rather than representation by counsel was the common practice (*Faretta v. California*, 1975; Winick, 1989). Indeed, in serious criminal cases, counsel was prohibited, and the defendant was required to "appear before the court in his own person and conduct his own defense in his own words" (*Faretta v. California*, 1975, p. 823, quoting Pollock & Maitland, 1898/1968). The prohibition against the assistance of counsel continued for centuries in felony and treason cases (Pollock & Maitland, 1898/1968; Stephen, 1883/1964). Thus, during the formative period of the incompetency doctrine, in many cases the defendant stood alone before the court and trial was merely "a long argument between the prisoner and the counsel for the Crown" (*Faretta v. California*, 1975, pp. 823–824, citing Stephen,

1883/1964). During the time when the incompetency doctrine was shaped, it was imperative that the defendant be competent because he or she was required to conduct his or her own defense.

The common law rationale for the incompetency doctrine has now largely become obsolete (Gobert, 1973; "Incompetency to Stand Trial," 1967; Winick, 1983, 1987). Today the assistance of counsel is available as a matter of constitutional right (*Argersinger v. Hamlin*, 1972; *Gideon v. Wainwright*, 1963; U.S. Constitution, amendment 6, 1791; Winick, 1989). As a result, in the modern criminal case, it is counsel who must be competent, and the competence of the defendant, although still required, takes on secondary importance.

Modern Justifications for the Incompetency Doctrine

Although the historical justifications for the doctrine have largely been eclipsed, a number of justifications for the modern doctrine remain. In part, the doctrine is justified based on *parens patriae* (protectionist) considerations—the desire to prevent unfairness to the defendant and to prevent a potentially erroneous conviction that could result from requiring the defendant to stand trial while significantly impaired by mental illness. Even though many of the strategic decisions in the modern criminal trial process are made by counsel, the defendant, if impaired, may be unable or unwilling to communicate facts that might be critical to counsel or the court (Bonnie, 1993; Weihofen, 1954). This concern has led the Supreme Court to deem the bar against trying an incompetent defendant "fundamental to an adversary system of justice" (*Drope v. Missouri*, 1975). Avoiding inaccuracy in criminal adjudication serves not only the individual's interests in avoiding unjust conviction, but also the societal interest in the reliability of the criminal process (Bonnie, 1993; Winick, 1985).

The incompetency doctrine also may be defended as necessary for preserving the moral dignity of the criminal process. This process would be threatened by trying defendants who lack a meaningful understanding of the nature of the criminal proceedings (Bonnie, 1993). This justification relates to the need to ensure public respect and confidence in the criminal process—considerations basic to the legitimacy of the criminal justice system (Winick, 1983, 1985).

The competency doctrine also protects the criminal defendant's interest in autonomous decision making concerning his or her defense (Winick, 1992). Although many issues of strategy and tactics are decided by counsel, certain key decisions must be made by the defendant (Bonnie, 1993). In our system, the defendant must make the decisions whether to plead guilty, to waive jury trial, to be present during trial, and to testify (see generally American Bar Association, 1992b; for example, *Adams v. United States ex rel. McCann*, 1942; *Brookhart v. Janus*, 1966; *Jones v. Barnes*, 1983; O'Neil, 1990; *Rock v. Arkansas*, 1987; *Wainwright v. Sykes*, 1977; Winick, 1985). As a result, the defendant must be competent to make these decisions.

A final justification for the incompetency doctrine is the need to preserve the decorum of the courtroom and the resulting dignity of the trial process, which could be threatened by permitting the trial of a mentally impaired defendant unable to control his or her courtroom conduct ("Incompetency to Stand Trial," 1967; Winick, 1985). However, in light of alternative measures for dealing with this problem, it alone should not justify barring the trial of an otherwise competent defendant (Bonnie, 1993; Winick, 1985).

The Modern Practice

Under the modern practice applicable in all American jurisdictions, a criminal defendant is deemed incompetent to stand trial if, as a result of mental illness, he or she is unable to understand the nature of the proceedings or to assist counsel in making a defense (see generally American Bar Association, 1989; Roesch & Golding, 1980; Steadman, 1979; Winick, 1991d). Virtually all criminal defendants who appear to have mental illness at any time in the criminal trial process are ordered by the court to be evaluated for competency (*Drope v. Missouri,* 1975; Winick, 1985). The competency issue usually is raised by motion of defense counsel requesting a competency evaluation. The prosecution may also raise the issue by motion. In addition, the judge may, on his or her own motion, request a competency evaluation when the evidence presents a bona fide doubt as to the defendant's competency (*Drope v. Missouri,* 1975). Failure of a court to order a competency evaluation when reasonable grounds exist to question the defendant's competency will violate the defendant's right to due process,[1] requiring reversal of any conviction obtained (*Drope v. Missouri,* 1975; *Pate v. Robinson,* 1966). As a result, courts typically order a formal competency evaluation in virtually every case in which doubt about the defendant's competency is raised, necessitating an evaluation by two to three court-appointed clinicians, who then submit written reports to the court (Roesch & Golding, 1980; Winick, 1985). Several studies have concluded that the vast majority of defendants are referred inappropriately for competency evaluations and have suggested that the competency process is often invoked for strategic purposes (Winick, 1985; see, for example, American Bar Association, 1983; Chernoff & Schaffer, 1972; Cooke, Johnston, & Pogany, 1973; Ennis & Emery, 1978; Golding, Roesch, & Schreiber, 1984; Halpern, 1975; McGarry, 1969; Roesch & Golding, 1979, 1980; Shah, 1981; Steadman & Braff, 1978; Steadman & Hartstone, 1983; Stone, 1978; Wexler & Scoville, 1971).[2]

It is estimated that 25,000 defendants are evaluated for competency in America each year, and that the number is increasing (Steadman & Hartstone, 1983). Perhaps because the threshold for requiring a competency hearing is so low, a large percentage of defendants evaluated are found competent—as many as 96% or more in some jurisdictions, and probably no less than 75% in most (Winick, 1993a). Nearly all of those found incompetent are hospitalized for treatment (Roesch & Golding, 1979; Winick, 1985). These defendants are treated, usually with psychotropic drugs (Winick, 1993b), and most will be returned to court within several months as having been restored to competency (Winick, 1985). Some are hospitalized for longer periods, and some are never restored to competency (Winick, 1985).[3]

The Costs and Burdens of the Incompetency Process

The existing competency process imposes serious burdens on defendants and is extremely costly. Virtually all criminal defendants exhibiting symptoms of mental illness are subjected to a formal evaluation for competency; yet a considerable number of defendants may not require formal evaluation (Winick, 1985).

Empirical research on the costs of competency evaluation and treatment is almost nonexistent. However, data from a study I conducted 10 years ago of costs in Dade County, Florida, are useful as a rough basis for projecting costs nationally (Winick, 1985). Evaluation costs for an initial competency assessment averaged $2327, excluding court costs and the expense of additional defense attorney, prosecutor, and judge time. These costs were based on outpatient evaluation. Inpatient evaluation for competency, still used in some jurisdictions, could easily double

---

[1] The 14th Amendment to the U.S. Constitution imposes the requirement that the states not deprive a person of liberty without "due process of law." This requires that the states use fair procedures in the criminal process, including a prohibition on proceeding against an individual who is incompetent to stand trial.

[2] The incompetency process may be invoked by both sides to obtain delay, by prosecutors to avoid bail or an insanity acquittal or to effect hospitalization that might not otherwise be possible under the state's civil commitment statute, or by defense attorneys to obtain mental health recommendations for use in making an insanity defense, in plea bargaining, or in a sentencing.

[3] Those who are permanently incompetent or are unlikely to be restored to competency within a reasonable period must either be civilly committed or released (see *Jackson v. Indiana,* 1972). Their criminal charges, however, may remain unresolved, and they may be prosecuted in the future should they then become competent.

and even quadruple these costs (Winick, 1985). If a defendant is found incompetent at this initial stage, he or she is hospitalized for several months of treatment, at an added average cost of $20,351, excluding several thousand dollars in court costs attributable to attorney time and hearings (Winick, 1985). Total cost for the typical defendant found incompetent in Dade County thus exceeded $22,678, excluding attorney and court costs. Costs for some cases ran considerably higher (Winick, 1985).[4]

Using these Dade County figures, which I assume to be low and which are based on costs prevailing 10 years ago, it can be estimated that in excess of $185 million is spent annually on competency evaluation and treatment in America (Winick, 1985). The actual costs today may be two to three times as high. With attorney and court costs included, the costs of the incompetency process nationally may well exceed $1 billion per year. Moreover, formal competency evaluations occur in many cases in which less formal screening could suffice. Therefore, the competency determination results in a diversion of limited clinical resources to evaluation that otherwise could be used for treatment.

The incompetency process also frequently imposes serious burdens on defendants. Prior to the Supreme Court's 1972 decision in *Jackson v. Indiana*, defendants hospitalized for incompetency to stand trial received what amounted to an indeterminate sentence of confinement in a mental hospital, typically for many years, often exceeding the maximum sentence for the crime charged, and sometimes lasting a lifetime (Winick, 1985). In *Jackson*, the Court recognized a constitutional limit on the duration of incompetency commitment, holding that a defendant committed solely based on trial incompetency "cannot be held more than a reasonable period of time necessary to determine whether there is

a substantial probability that he will attain that capacity in the foreseeable future" (p. 738). Any continued confinement, the Court held, must be based on the probability that the defendant will be returned to competency within the foreseeable future. If the treatment provided does not succeed in advancing the defendant toward that goal, then the state either must institute customary civil commitment proceedings, if it wishes to detain the defendant, or must release him or her (*Jackson v. Indiana*, 1972; Winick, 1985). Although *Jackson* marked an end to the most egregious cases of indefinite incompetency commitment, many states have responded insufficiently to the Court's decision and abuses persist (Melton, Weithorn, & Slobogin, 1985; Winick, 1985).

Lengthy incompetency commitment is particularly burdensome for defendants charged with misdemeanors, perhaps a majority of those found incompetent (Winick, 1985). Many of these defendants would pay a small fine or receive a period of probation were they convicted. Instead, they might spend many months and even years confined as incompetent. Many of the hospitals in which the defendants are confined are maximum security institutions that are poorly funded and staffed (Winick, 1985). Although many states now authorize outpatient treatment for trial incompetency, most defendants found incompetent are still hospitalized (Winick, 1985). Such hospitalization is frequently unnecessarily restrictive of defendant's liberty and unnecessarily stigmatizing (Winick, 1985). In some jurisdictions, a short-term commitment based on incompetency to stand trial is used as an alternative to ordinary civil commitment. In misdemeanor cases, these defendants often will be released after several months with their charges dismissed. However, even this period of hospital confinement may be unnecessary, may not satisfy state commitment criteria, and will be more restrictive and less therapeutic than typical civil hospitalization.

Even for those not ultimately found incompetent, a court-ordered competency evaluation often prevents the setting of bail, ensuring that the defendant is held in custody, separated from

---

[4]Dade County uses a relatively inexpensive system of outpatient evaluations. Expensive inpatient evaluations are used more frequently in some other jurisdictions.

family, friends, and other community ties for a lengthy period (Winick, 1985). Moreover, this period of confinement for evaluation or treatment often is not credited against a sentence later received (Winick, 1985). As a result, defendants who are evaluated are potentially confined for longer than they would have been had they been permitted to waive their incompetency and either plead guilty or stand trial at the outset.

These delays undermine the Sixth Amendment's guarantee to a speedy trial. While an incompetency determination is being made witnesses may die or disappear, memories may fade, and evidence may become lost or unavailable. These difficulties can burden both the defense and the prosecution, and may significantly impede a just and reliable determination of the charges. In addition, lengthy delays may compromise the basic purposes of the criminal law. If the defendant is guilty, delay in the trial process diminishes the possibilities for rehabilitation. Delayed punishment may also weaken the deterrent effect of the criminal sanction and frustrate the interests of victims in seeing that justice is done. Undue delay will be especially prejudicial if the defendant is innocent (Winick, 1993a).

The incompetency determination also imposes a serious stigma on defendants labeled incompetent to stand trial. Even though these defendants already bear the stigma of criminal accusation, the added stigma of being labeled incompetent may be considerably worse than being accused of a crime (American Bar Association, 1983). Moreover, these defendants are further stigmatized by their being associated with the often notorious institutions to which they are committed—high-security mental health correction facilities like Dannamoura, Bridgewater, or Ionia—that evoke in the public mind an image of the dangerously mad (Burt, 1974; Winick, 1977, 1985).

In addition to its impact on how others may perceive the defendant, an incompetency label may also impose serious negative psychological effects on the individual so labeled (see generally Sales & Kahle, 1980; Winick, 1995). The label "incompetent" has an unfortunate general connotation that may make people feel not only that they are unfit to stand trial, but that they are broadly incompetent to do anything. Moreover, the "incompetent" label suggests a permanent deficit, rather than a temporary impairment. Individuals so labeled may, therefore, come to think that their difficulties cannot be helped. This can impede successful treatment. Imposition of an incompetency label can thus be seriously debilitating to the individual. Many criminal defendants already have serious problems that they may feel are outside their control. Labeling them incompetent, particularly against their will, can foster what Martin Seligman (1975) called "learned helplessness," a syndrome characterized by generalized feelings of helplessness, hopelessness, depression, and lack of motivation (Abramson, Garber, & Seligman, 1980; Abramson, Seligman, & Teasdale, 1978; Maier & Seligman, 1976; Seligman & Garber, 1980) that mirrors the symptoms of clinical depression (Peterson & Bossio, 1989).

In practice, the incompetency doctrine thus raises significant problems and imposes serious burdens on defendants and high costs on states. Although designed for their protection, the burdens it places on defendants are so substantial that the American Bar Association (ABA) committee that developed the ABA's *Criminal Justice Mental Health Standards* (1983) suggested that defense counsel may conclude that it is in their clients' best interests not to raise the issue.

Restructuring the Incompetency Process

Distinguishing Assent from Objection

The ABA committee has indicated that if the severe problems associated with the competency doctrine continue, "perhaps we should address more clearly the concept of possible waiver on the part of a defendant" (§ 7.162). Under existing practices, a defendant deemed incompetent may not stand trial or plead guilty even if he or she wishes to do so (American Bar Association, 1983; *Drope v. Missouri*, 1975; see, for example, *Hamm v. Jabe*, 1983; *Medina v. California*, 1992). Indeed, existing practices require the defense attorney to raise the competency question with the court whenever a genuine doubt about competency arises, even if counsel believes that raising the issue will not be in the defendant's best interests (American Bar Association, 1989).

In my previous article (Winick, 1985), I suggested that waiver might be possible in limited circumstances for defendants impaired by mental illness who, with the concurrence of counsel, clearly and voluntarily express the desire to stand trial or plead guilty notwithstanding their mental impairment. I suggested that the incompetency process be restructured to distinguish two different types of cases. The first is when defendants assert their own incompetency as a ground for temporarily halting the criminal proceedings. The second is when the defendant wishes to proceed notwithstanding his or her impairment, but the incompetency status is sought either by motion of the prosecution or by action of the court itself. In the former case, a system of trial continuances should be substituted for the existing formal competency process. In the latter, waiver could be considered, with appropriate safeguards, when the defendant clearly and voluntarily expresses a preference for trial or a guilty plea and counsel concurs. In the alternative, even if the defendant is deemed incompetent to waive the supposed benefits of the incompetency doctrine, counsel should be permitted to do so on behalf of the defendant, on the basis that the defense lawyer, as a fiduciary (a person in a position of trust), should be permitted to substitute his or her judgment for that of an incompetent client.

This proposal for restructuring the incompetency-to-stand-trial doctrine was controversial. It challenged thinking that regarded competency as an essential prerequisite for waiver of rights in the criminal process, and seemed inconsistent with the Supreme Court's jurisprudence in this area. I argued, however, that allowing a defendant of doubtful competence to waive the "benefits" of the incompetency doctrine would not violate the purposes of the doctrine as long as safeguards, including the advice and agreement of counsel, were required (Winick, 1985). I also argued that the Supreme Court's language in *Pate v. Robinson* (1966), suggesting that incompetent defendants could not waive the incompetency status, was dicta (not essential to the decision in that case), and could easily be discarded (Winick, 1985). I discussed legal and clinical practices, both in the criminal area and elsewhere, that accept waiver in many situations in which the individual whose rights are waived never participates in the decision or is of doubtful competence (Winick, 1985). These practices support a distinction between assent and objection. That distinction should justify the application of differential standards of waiver in the incompetency-to-stand-trial context based on whether the defendant seeks to accept trial or a guilty plea or to object to trial on the basis of his or her mental illness. I suggested that our conceptions of competency in the criminal process were artificial and were based on myth and unrealistic models of the criminal process and of the differences between criminal defendants with mental illness and "normal" defendants (Winick, 1985).

In the 10 years since advancing my original proposals for restructuring the incompetency process, I have developed further some of the ideas on which my proposals were based. More specifically, my work in therapeutic jurisprudence explored in greater detail the distinction between assent and objection and its implications for defining competency (Wexler & Winick, 1991a, 1991b). I have analyzed the use of this distinction in two noncriminal areas—competency to consent to treatment (Winick, 1991a) and competency to consent to voluntary hospitalization (Winick, 1991b). Further, I have analyzed the value of autonomy and its role in mental health law (Winick, 1992), and explored the psychological value of allowing individuals to exercise choice (Winick, 1992, 1994a) and the corresponding disadvantages of denying them the opportunity to be self-determining (Winick, 1994b). In addition, I have analyzed the various procedural modes for determining competency (Winick, 1991b), including the role of presumptions and burdens of proof in this process (Winick, 1993a). The further thinking in the last 10 years on restructuring competency to stand trial has led to several refinements in the argument and additional proposals. In what follows in this section, I set forth an expanded proposal for how the incompetency process can be reformed.

Waiver and the Purposes of the Incompetency Doctrine

Can defendants who may be incompetent waive the "benefits" of the incompetency status? The incompetency doctrine is not designed solely to protect the defendant's interests, but also serves societal interests in preserving the moral dignity of the criminal process and in avoiding erroneous convictions, both of which might be compromised by permitting trial of an incompetent defendant (Winick, 1993a). In my original article I acknowledged these and other societal interests that are thought to justify the incompetency doctrine (Winick, 1985), but questioned "whether in practice the competency doctrine actually accomplishes these asserted benefits" (p. 950). We can speculate that some of these benefits of the incompetency doctrine are present for defendants who assert their incompetency as a basis for postponing the trial ("objectors" to trial), and that these benefits outweigh the burdens the doctrine would impose on the defendant (Bonnie, 1993). But for defendants who prefer trial or a guilty plea in accordance with the advice of counsel, or at least with the approval of counsel ("assenters"), these benefits may be more theoretical than real, and may fall far short of outweighing the burdens imposed.

My proposal assumes that the defendant has the ability clearly and voluntarily to articulate a preference either for trial or a guilty plea. It also assumes that defense counsel, after careful consideration, concurs in the judgment that this preference seems reasonable in the circumstances and that the client's assent is not basically irrational. This requirement is consistent with the role of the defense lawyer. After the defense lawyer receives sufficient information from the defendant and investigates the facts and the law, he or she typically will select an appropriate defense strategy (Winick, 1985). When the defendant assents to this strategy, and counsel thinks the defendant has a basic understanding of the choice made, counsel's judgment is entitled to great weight. In most cases it will be counsel's recommendation to go to trial or to enter a guilty plea to which the defendant assents. In some cases, however, the choice will originate with the defendant and counsel will approve or at least acquiesce in that choice. Counsel's agreement with the client's choice provides an assurance by a person who has a professional fiduciary relationship with the defendant that proceeding to trial or entering a guilty plea is in the defendant's best interests. In such cases, deference both to the autonomy of the defendant and to the professional expertise of counsel makes it appropriate to erect a presumption in favor of competency, that is, a rule that assumes that defendants are competent until proven otherwise. Counsel's acquiescence to the client's decision provides reasonable assurance that accuracy in adjudication will not be frustrated. A defense attorney concerned that allowing a guilty plea or proceeding to trial with an impaired defendant might result in an unjust conviction, because either the client lacks a basic understanding of the choice made, or the choice made seems clearly inconsistent with the defendant's interests, should not and presumably would not provide the concurrence that my proposal requires.

Allowing a trial that both the defendant and his or her counsel wish to proceed with is a provisional decision that the trial judge can rescind if, as the case unfolds, concerns for accuracy arise. Moreover, if defense counsel, during trial, realizes that the defendant's impairment is more significant than earlier thought, and that the client's inabilities seem likely to produce an inaccurate result, then counsel can seek a determination of incompetency based on this new information. Because competency is a fluctuating state and a defendant's condition may change during the course of a trial, the trial judge has a continuing duty to reconsider the issue of competency at any time when reasonable doubt about the defendant's competency is raised (*Drope v. Missouri*, 1975; Winick, 1993a). At best, a pretrial competency determination constitutes a prediction about how the defendant will perform at a future trial. If during trial, defense counsel, contrary to an initial assessment, concludes that the defendant's impairment is materially interfering with the ability to communicate or provide essential assistance, the attorney then can bring concrete examples of such incapacities to the court's attention and seek a mistrial. The court possesses broad discretion concerning the grant of a mistrial (Federal Rules of Criminal Procedure, Rule 43(b)–(c), 1986; *Illinois v. Allen*, 1970; *Snyder v. Massachusetts*, 1934; see, for example, *Hamm v. Jabe*, 1983), and can at that point order a clinical evaluation of competency to assist in determining the issue.

The risk of inaccuracy in adjudication also may be minimized through use of the trial court's power to set aside verdicts in the interest of justice (for example, Federal Rules of Criminal Procedure, Rule 33, 1986), or to allow a new trial if additional evidence affecting the verdict later materializes that would have been available but for the defendant's incompetency (Burt & Morris, 1972). Thus, a number of safety valves prevent truly incompetent defendants from subjecting themselves to trials.

Let us consider the concern for accuracy in adjudication in perspective. Waivers are customarily accepted in other criminal contexts, even though allowing such waivers might affect accuracy. First, the Supreme Court has held that a defendant may waive the right to counsel and represent himself or herself (*Faretta v. California*,

1975). Thus, the Court recognizes that respect for individual autonomy may override the societal concern for accuracy in adjudication (Winick, 1985). Second, a defendant may plead guilty (and thereby waive all trial-related constitutional rights) even if unwilling to concede commission of a crime (*North Carolina v. Alford*, 1970; *White Hawk v. Solem*, 1982, 1983; see also American Law Institute, 1972), and even in the absence of a factual basis to believe that he or she has done so (Barkai, 1977; Goldstein, 1981; Halberstam, 1982; see, for example, Federal Rules of Criminal Procedure, Rule 11(f), 1986). Even though acceptance of such a plea may lead to an erroneous conviction, the desire to let the accused resolve the charges together with society's interest in facilitating negotiated settlements outweigh the concern for accuracy. These waiver-of-counsel and guilty-plea cases arose in contexts in which the defendant's competency was not questioned, and therefore may not be as persuasive in contexts in which competency is in issue. However, they demonstrate that deference to autonomy sometimes trumps reliability concerns.

Finally, an incompetent defendant whose "free will" is impaired by mental illness may confess to a crime (*Colorado v. Connelly*, 1986). These confessions are given great weight by juries, and if inaccurate, can produce unjust convictions. If a defendant without counsel may confess to a crime and thereby waive Fifth Amendment and *Miranda* rights, notwithstanding his or her substantial mental impairment, why should a mentally impaired defendant who wishes to accept counsel's recommendation not be able to waive the due process right to avoid trial while incompetent?

In addition to the societal concern for accuracy in adjudication, the incompetency doctrine serves other significant societal interests. For example, the doctrine may be essential to preserving the moral dignity of the criminal process. Does this interest justify barring conviction of defendants who can be said to lack a meaningful moral understanding of wrongdoing and punishment or the nature of criminal prosecution (Bonnie, 1993)? Would concern for the moral dignity of the criminal process be frustrated by permitting a mentally impaired defendant to be tried in accordance with his or her wish to follow defense counsel's recommendation? Would this concern be frustrated if the choice for trial was the defendant's and counsel acquiesced in that choice as reasonable in the circumstances?

Two types of cases seem plainly not to justify a bar on trial. First, a defendant lacking any meaningful understanding of wrongdoing might qualify for the insanity defense, and if so, would be neither convicted nor punished. A defendant who otherwise possesses sufficient abilities to make an insanity defense thus should not be disqualified from doing so by a lack of moral understanding of his or her wrongdoing. Second, it can be conceded that a defendant lacking a meaningful understanding of punishment should not be punished (Winick, 1985). However, such a lack of understanding can be taken into account at sentencing, or at the time of administration of punishment, or such punishment can be deferred (Winick, 1985). This concern therefore should not be used as a justification for putting off a trial desired by the defendant and his or her lawyer.

The concern with avoiding trial for a defendant lacking a meaningful understanding of the nature of criminal prosecution is more serious. But how much understanding should be required before a defendant's trial would threaten the moral dignity of the criminal process? We should be careful not to set this standard too high lest we disqualify not only defendants with mental illness from facing their charges, but also many "normal" defendants. Indeed, many criminal defendants who do not have a mental illness may lack a meaningful understanding of the nature of criminal prosecution (Winick, 1985). Defendants generally are willing to defer to their attorneys, just as most medical patients are willing to defer to their doctors concerning appropriate medical treatment (Winick, 1985). Many defendants do not comprehend the nature of their choices and are willing to delegate decision making to a professional in whom they place their trust.

Moreover, a complete understanding of the nature of criminal prosecution is unnecessary in the overwhelming number of cases in which the charges are resolved through a guilty plea (Winick, 1985). Defendants who plead guilty do not need to possess a high level of understanding concerning the trial process because they will not participate in it. These defendants need to possess sufficient skills to help counsel reconstruct the alleged crime and evaluate possible defenses in order to allow counsel to assess the strength of the prosecution's case. However, we should not ignore the fact that in a substantial number of cases the defendant with mental illness, like defendants generally, probably has committed the crime with which he or she is charged and lacks a credible defense. For these defendants, a guilty plea is almost always the best option. The plea negotiation process is conducted exclusively by counsel, with little need for the client's assistance. Therefore, when the negotiation produces a plea that the defendant finds more desirable than an incompetency adjudication (which will only postpone trial or a guilty plea to a later date), the defendant should be permitted to accept the plea, provided he or she possesses a rudimentary understanding of the consequences (that is, the sentence to be imposed and that he or she forgoes trial and various trial-related rights). A more complete understanding of the nature of a criminal prosecution thus may be only rarely required. Its absence therefore should not disqualify a defendant with mental illness who has a basic understanding of the nature of a guilty plea from being able to accept such a plea.

In *Godinez v. Moran* (1993), the Supreme Court rejected the contention that competency to plead guilty should require a higher standard than competency to stand trial. Therefore, the Court suggested that the general standard for competency to stand trial should apply as well to other competency issues arising in the criminal process. The Court did not consider, however, whether in an appropriate case the test of competency to plead guilty might be a lower standard than for competency to stand trial. In fact, the notion of competency is best understood in the context of the decisions presented (American Bar Association, 1989; Bonnie, 1993; Roesch & Golding, 1979). To the extent that *Godinez* holds that the same standard of competency must be applied across the board, regardless of the particular issue or the nature of the case, it is open to serious criticism.

We should not insist on an abstract notion of competency based on a model of the criminal case as involving a full-blown trial in which the defendant will testify and must have considerable skills in order to participate with counsel in complicated strategic decision making. Rather, we should apply a flexible standard of competency that requires only that the defendant possess the abilities that will be necessary in the particular case. This is particularly true in misdemeanor cases, where an overwhelming majority of defendants plead guilty. In the past 20 years, tightening civil commitment standards and the practice of deinstitutionalization have had the effect of funneling many former civil patients who commit minor nuisances into the criminal process, with the result that a majority of defendants evaluated for competency are charged only with minor misdemeanors (see Bonovitz & Guy, 1979; Dickey, 1980; Geller & Lister, 1978; Shah, 1981; Teplin, 1983; Wexler, 1983; Winick, 1985, 1987). A defendant arrested for a petty offense such as disorderly conduct or shoplifting usually will be able to plead guilty and pay a small fine. If the defendant is imcompetent to stand trial, however, he or she may face many months of incarceration in a jail and in a maximum security mental hospital that resembles one. If the defendant then is restored to competency and returned to court, he or she probably will accept the same plea bargain at that point. When acceptance of a guilty plea imposes such nominal consequences on the defendant, the degree of competency required to accept a plea that is clearly and voluntarily sought by the defendant, with the advice and concurrence of counsel, should be relatively modest. When the consequences are substantial—a felony conviction carrying a lengthy prison sentence, for example—the degree of competency required to plead guilty can be higher. And in cases in which the defendant seeks to plead guilty to a capital offense, thereby being exposed to a possible death sentence, a relatively high degree of competency and understanding should be required (*Beck v. Alabama*, 1980; *Coker v. Georgia*, 1977; *Eddings v. Oklahoma*, 1982; *Enmund v. Florida*, 1982; *Furman v. Georgia*, 1972; *Gardner v. Florida*, 1977; *Gregg v. Georgia*, 1976; *Lockett v. Ohio*, 1978; *Solem v. Helm*, 1983; *Winick*, 1982; *Woodson v. North Carolina*, 1976).

Such a sliding-scale approach to defining competency is reasonable and consistent with the desire to protect the accuracy and moral dignity of the criminal process. Indeed, basic principles of criminal procedure reflect such a sliding-scale approach by requiring less procedural protections in the trial of petty offenses than in more serious cases. For example, the U.S. Supreme Court has recognized a petty-offense exception to the Sixth Amendment right to trial by jury (*Baldwin v. New York*, 1970; *Bloom v. Illinois*, 1968). Under this exception, jury trial is unavailable in cases in which the authorized penalty does not exceed six months imprisonment (see *Duncan v. Louisiana*, 1968; *Singer v. United States*, 1965). Similarly, although the right to counsel is an essential feature of our adversary system (see *Faretta v. California*, 1975; *Powell v. Alabama*, 1932), indigent defendants are not entitled to the appointment of counsel in misdemeanor cases in which the defendant does not receive a sentence of imprisonment (see *Argersinger v. Hamlin*, 1972; *Scott v. Illinois*, 1980), and thus must face a professional prosecutor without assistance. When the stakes are relatively low, as they are in misdemeanor cases in which a prison sentence is either ruled out or will not exceed six months, important procedural safeguards are dispensed with.

A similar distinction between petty offenses and more serious cases could be applied in the incompetency-to-stand-trial context. To the extent that concerns with accuracy and the moral dignity of the criminal process make us reluctant to permit guilty pleas or trials for assenting defendants whose competency is in question, we should have considerably less reluctance when the defendant seeks to plead guilty or stand trial for a petty misdemeanor. Imposing the burdens of an incompetency adjudication on an unwilling defendant who would prefer to plead guilty in accordance with counsel's advice or with counsel's acquiescence seems unjustified unless the defendant is grossly incompetent. When competence is more marginal, the societal concerns for accuracy and the moral dignity of the criminal process should not be deemed to outweigh the defendant's desire to have an expeditious resolution of the charges.

Even if we continue generally to bar guilty pleas by defendants when there is doubt about their competence, a petty-offense (or even a misdemeanor) exception to the incompetency doctrine should be recognized. This exception should apply in cases in which the defendant clearly and voluntarily expresses assent to counsel's recommendation or expresses a desire to plead with which counsel approves. Because such a high percentage of incompetency cases arise in the misdemeanor context, such a rule would eliminate many of the high costs and burdens of the incompetency process. Limitations on civil commitment and the deinstitutionalization process have had the unintended effect of funneling into the criminal process many thousands of individuals who previously would have been committed civilly. The incompetency process has become a sort of "backdoor" commitment route. In effect, these misdemeanor incompetency-to-stand-trial commitments are short-term alternatives to civil commitment, and not truly criminal dispositions. Following a brief period of incompetency hospitalization, these defendants typically are released and their criminal charges are dismissed. Many of these individuals do not belong in the criminal process, and most do not belong in the hospital. They belong in the community but require continued services. Instead of spending millions of dollars in the criminal system on the processing of these mis-

demeanor incompetency cases, this money should be spent on services in the community to meet the continued medical and social needs of these individuals. By adopting the petty-offense misdemeanor exception proposed, we could effectuate such savings and reallocate the funds to the community services that are needed. Such an exception would be easy to adopt legislatively. An amendment to state incompetency-to-stand-trial statutes or court rules could provide that in all misdemeanor cases (or in all misdemeanor cases in which a prison sentence is ruled out), a defendant clearly and voluntarily electing to plead guilty or *nolo contendere* (no contest) with the approval of counsel will be presumed to be competent to do so.

Many defendants, of course, whether charged with a misdemeanor or a felony, will wish to stand trial rather than to plead guilty. Even when the defendant does not elect to plead guilty, but wishes to face the charges and to put the prosecution to its proof, the concerns for accuracy and for preserving the moral dignity of the criminal process will not necessarily be compromised by applying a low standard of competency for defendants assenting to the recommendation of counsel. These concerns assume that in our adversary system the truth determination process will be unfairly skewed in favor of the prosecution whenever the defendant's ability to understand the nature of the proceeding and participate fully in the defense is impaired. Yet there are some cases in which the defense strategy does not require the defendant's participation or understanding, and other cases in which the defendant's participation would not help significantly (see American Bar Association, 1983; Chernoff & Schaffer, 1972; Winick, 1985). Indeed, in cases in which the insanity defense is raised—which it will be in many cases involving defendants whose competency is in question—defense counsel may find it more advantageous to present the defendant to the trier of facts in his or her existing condition, rather than after having been restored to competency and returned to court on what may be a high dose of psychotropic medication that may affect the jury's assessment of the person's credibility (see American Bar Association, 1983; *Commonwealth v. Louraine*, 1983; *In re Pray*, 1975; *Riggins v. Nevada*, 1992; *State v. Jojola*, 1976; *State v. Murphy*, 1960; Winick, 1985). In addition, there are many cases in which defense counsel will raise a legal defense that does not require the defendant's participation, and that may be determined based on a pretrial motion. These include cases involving a motion to dismiss the indictment for lack of a speedy trial or for violation of the ban on double jeopardy. These also include cases involving a motion to suppress critical evidence obtained in violation of the defendant's Fourth, Fifth, or Sixth Amendment rights, or some other legal attack on the indictment or on the admissibility of key evidence. In addition, they include cases in which counsel raises police or prosecutorial misconduct. Deferring consideration of these legal challenges to the prosecution until after the defendant has received what might be a lengthy period of confinement for incompetency treatment seems questionable in cases in which counsel wishes to proceed and the defendant clearly and voluntarily agrees (*Jackson v. Indiana*, 1972). Requiring an incompetency delay in such cases cannot reasonably be justified based on concerns for accuracy or for preserving the dignity of the criminal process.

Instead of a rigid bar on the trial of a defendant of questionable competency, we should adopt a more flexible sliding-scale approach. We should use standards that reflect the highly contextualized nature of competency and that seek to determine it based on the precise degree of ability that a defendant will require in the case in question. Especially when the consequences to the defendant are relatively minor and the defense strategy in the case requires little assistance and participation by the defendant, we should be more willing to defer to the autonomy of a defendant who is clearly able to agree to the trial strategy recommended by counsel, even if his or her autonomy is reduced by mental illness. In many cases, respecting such autonomy, and

permitting the case to proceed, at least provisionally, will produce just, fair, and accurate results that do not compromise the moral dignity of the criminal process.

A Presumption in Favor of Competency

Even if the protections of the incompetency doctrine should be deemed waivable, what procedures should be used to ensure the validity of waiver in individual cases? When fundamental rights like the right to counsel or to a trial are involved, expression of a preference to waive the right alone cannot suffice to create a valid waiver. To waive such rights, "the waiver must 'be knowing and intelligent' and the court must assure, on the record that these criteria have been satisfied" (Bonnie, 1993, p. 944). Absent any understanding of the nature and consequences of the decision, the ability to express a preference cannot itself resolve the competency question.

Although the mere expression of a preference cannot alone meet the requirements for competency to waive at least certain fundamental constitutional rights, my proposal does not suggest that expression of preference alone should be an acceptable definition of competency. Rather, defendants whose competency is in question should be permitted to waive these rights when they clearly and voluntarily express a preference to do so, provided certain other conditions are satisfied, including the concurrence of counsel. I do not equate the ability to express such a preference with competency or suggest that incompetent defendants should be permitted to waive these rights: "[T]he high value attached to the principle of individual autonomy does not mean that incompetent expressions of autonomy are or should be accepted" (Winick, 1985, p. 966).

Determining whether an expression of preference is competent, however, is often difficult, and a large percentage of cases could be decided either way. It is difficult to ascertain an individual's ability to process information and engage in rational decision making. Moreover, evaluators may tend to confuse the quality of the decision-making process with the reasonableness of the result reached. As a result, an approach to determining competency that presumed the competency of an individual able to articulate a preference should be used in cases in which counsel concurred with the choice made (Winick, 1985). Many cases will involve marginal defendants on the borderline of competence. To prevent excessive paternalism we should presume that individuals who are able to express a choice are competent. Moreover, existing practices in both criminal and noncriminal contexts support such a presumption (Winick, 1985).

How would a presumption of this type work? A presumption in favor of competency in cases in which the defendant can clearly and voluntarily express a preference is not the same as adopting the ability to express a preference as a substantive definition of competency. In my original article I recognized that when the defendant's expressed preference is based on "irrelevant reasons ('I will plead guilty because I am an insect'), irrational beliefs ('I will stand trial and thereby become a movie star'), or outright delusions ('I am an extraterrestrial and will return to my planet')," that expression of choice does not represent a sufficient degree of autonomy to be worthy of respect (Winick, 1985, p. 967). However, "[a]n individual able to express a choice is exercising at least some autonomy, and our respect for the principle of autonomy makes it appropriate to utilize a presumption of competency to guide the decision-maker in such a case" (p. 967). The presumption of competency would not shield clearly incompetent expressions of choice. Such a presumption "does not always decide a case; it is a rebuttable presumption" (p. 967; see also Winick, 1992, p. 1776; 1993a, p. 862).

As a result, a presumption in favor of competency is not a substantive test of competency to waive rights, but is a procedural rule concerning how such competency should be ascertained. There are elements of both a substantive and a procedural rule encompassed in my proposal. In my initial article, I suggested that the law "should apply only a relatively low standard of competency and minimal scrutiny when the defendant, with the concurrence of his attorney, expresses the wish to stand trial, and a higher standard and more intense scrutiny when the state asserts that the defendant should be tried over his objection that he is incompetent" (Winick, 1985, p. 968). Clearly expressed choice by the defendant in favor of resolving the charges speedily, either by trial or a guilty plea, is entitled to a degree of respect that permits only limited scrutiny of that choice by the courts. A high degree of scrutiny is appropriate, however, when the state seeks to prevent the defendant from invoking incompetency as a shield to an immediate trial, asserting a desire for treatment designed to improve his or her final functioning. Other than suggesting a low standard of competency for assent and a higher standard for objection, my proposal did not set forth a substantive definition of competency. It did, however, offer a procedural tool to be used in making competency determinations.

For the presumption in favor of competency to apply, I would require both the defendant's voluntary expression of choice and counsel's concurrence. By requiring the concurrence of counsel, my proposal would leave the matter of whether the defendant possesses sufficient competence largely to the judgment of counsel. A lower threshold of competence would be used for decisions that assent to counsel's recommendation than for those that object. When the defendant objects to counsel's recommendation concerning a matter for which the law requires a personal decision by the defendant—such as waiver of jury trial or the decision to testify or to decline to do so—the client's preference should be honored unless he or she is highly incompetent. If counsel believes the client to be competent, counsel must defer to the defendant's expression of preference with regard to at least one of these issues that the law leaves to the defendant, and probably also should do so for many other issues. If, on the other hand, counsel believes the client to be incompetent in this regard, counsel should raise the competency issue and the court would then conduct an inquiry into the matter. When there is assent, however, if the defendant is able clearly and voluntarily to express a decision, counsel's concurrence would constitute an implicit representation that the client is sufficiently competent to make the decision.

Unless the prosecution could produce evidence suggesting a lack of competence to engage in decision making concerning one of these crucial issues, or unless the court's own contact with the defendant produces statements by the defendant suggesting a lack of decisional competence in this regard, no further inquiry should occur. With regard to decisions that are not among the limited number requiring a defendant's personal decision—the myriad tactical and evidentiary decisions arising at the pretrial and trial stages—I would allow counsel to act on behalf of a client even when competence to engage in rational decision making is in doubt.

My proposal thus has the effect of moving much of the competency determination process from the formal judicial arena to the attorney-client relationship. Rather than having extensive clinical evaluation of competence followed by judicial determination, the bulk of the determinations of competence would be subsumed within the professional relationship. Counsel would always remain free to obtain a clinical consultation if needed, as part of the defendant's Sixth Amendment right to effective assistance of counsel (see *Ake v. Oklahoma*, 1985), or could always obtain consultation from another attorney to help in the decision-making process. However, leaving the bulk of competency assessment within the attorney-client relationship should produce fair decisions that do not conflict with the societal purposes underlying the competency doctrine. The ability of the prosecutor to obtain specific evidence of incompetency when it is available, or of the court to conduct its own inquiry of the defendant in court, provides additional assurance that leaving much of the decision making in this area to the attorney-client relationship will not undermine the moral dignity of the criminal process or the concern for accuracy in adjudication.

My original proposal drew heavily on an analogy between the attorney-client relationship and the doctor-patient relationship (Winick, 1985). In the context of competency to make treatment and hospitalization decisions, clinicians typically are trusted to make their own assessments of their patients, at least in cases of patient assent to interventions recommended by the physician (Winick, 1991a, 1991b). Attorneys, like physicians, have a fiduciary relationship with their clients. Both attorneys and physicians are charged with a professional duty to promote and protect the best interests of their clients. Moreover, like physicians, attorneys are best situated to understand the specific aspects of their clients' cases and to assess competence.

Competence to stand trial is fundamentally a legal question. The skills needed to participate in the criminal process are skills that a lawyer is better able to assess than would be a clinical evaluator. Moreover, the lawyer is in the best position to understand the skill that will be needed in the context of the particular case. The special constitutional obligation that the Sixth Amendment places on attorneys to provide effective assistance of counsel to their clients "entails a wide sphere of discretion to define and implement the strategic objectives of the defense" (Bonnie, 1993, p. 565). The Sixth Amendment policies also justify insulating the attorney-client relationship from undue prosecutorial or judicial inquiry (Bonnie, 1993).

In my initial article, as an alternative to allowing a defendant of questionable competency to waive the protections of the incompetency doctrine, I proposed that counsel should be able to "waive" the doctrine on the defendant's behalf as long as the client assents (Winick, 1985). I have now concluded that the concept of "waiver" seems awkward in this context. Counsel may waive a variety of trial-related rights through action or inaction, thereby binding the client whether or not the client has participated in the decision (Winick, 1985). However, there are several critical constitutional rights that, under existing constitutional and ethical theory, require the client's own voluntary and knowing waiver, including the right to plead guilty, the decision whether to have a jury trial, and the decision whether to testify (Bonnie, 1993; Winick, 1985). Because permitting an attorney to waive these rights would conflict with deeply ingrained principles, an across-the-board waiver theory would go too far. However, surrogate decision making by the attorney would be possible with regard at least to certain issues in cases that involve trials (Bonnie, 1993). In the case of at least certain fundamental rights, permitting waiver by counsel would be inconsistent with accepted doctrine. But these instances aside, counsel may waive virtually all the rights and strategic options that a defendant enjoys in our criminal system.

I strongly disagree with the current requirement that attorneys and courts initiate an inquiry into competency whenever they harbor a genuine doubt about the defendant's competence, even when counsel believes that raising the issue is not in the client's best interests (American Bar Association, 1989; Bonnie, 1993; Chernoff & Schaffer, 1972; Uphoff, 1988). In my view, this judgment should be left largely in the hands of defense counsel. The current requirement imposes a responsibility on defense counsel that is basically inconsistent with counsel's obligations to protect and promote the best interests of the client. Such a conflict seriously burdens the professional relationship. It erodes client trust and confidence in counsel and impairs the ability of counsel to function effectively. Placing counsel in such an untenable position undermines the Sixth Amendment right to counsel and should be deemed constitutionally suspect (see American Bar Association, 1980; *Polk County v. Dodson*, 1981).

My original proposal talked about waiver in this context, arguing that counsel should be permitted not to raise the competency question when both counsel and client conclude that reso-

lution of the criminal charges would be more in the defendant's interests than an incompetency adjudication (Winick, 1985). Because the attorney is in the best position to decide whether an inquiry into competency should be undertaken, in the context of most rights and strategic options, waiver or surrogate decision making by counsel should be permitted. In addition, the requirement that counsel initiate a formal competency inquiry whenever doubt is raised about the defendant's competency should be relaxed. With the exception of the waiver of certain fundamental rights, the judgment should be left to the attorney-client relationship.

By leaving such a large measure of discretion in the hands of counsel, my proposal might be subject to three criticisms. First, given the inconsistent quality of the criminal defense bar, can counsel be counted on to perform this role effectively? Second, will adoption of the proposal produce excessive appellate or habeas corpus litigation challenging guilty verdicts or guilty pleas on the ground that the defendant was incompetent? Third, will counsel abuse the authority delegated under the proposal to attempt to gain strategic advantage? Although these concerns are legitimate, none is so serious as to make the presumption proposal unfeasible.

First, placing the bulk of competency decision making in the hands of defense counsel assumes an attorney who is competent and will zealously safeguard the defendant's interests. The Sixth Amendment guarantees the effective assistance of counsel. However, it must be conceded that the quality of the criminal defense bar is varied, and that in some areas, the promise of the Sixth Amendment remains unfulfilled. Many criminal attorneys are talented, energetic advocates who effectively represent their clients' interests. Sadly, however, some are not. Some suffer under caseloads too heavy to devote sufficient time to a particular case. Some are incompetent, and some even are unethical.

Leaving incompetency decision making largely in the hands of counsel thus raises certain risks. These risks increase in cases involving defendants with mental disabilities because such clients are particularly vulnerable to malpractice by counsel. Notwithstanding these risks, in designing legal rules it seems sensible in general to make the assumption that defense attorneys are competent and will vigorously represent their clients' interests. To minimize this risk, a trial court should be particularly sensitive to the possibility of ineffectiveness of counsel, and when appropriate, should question counsel to ensure that the defendant's interests are properly represented. Counsel for an impaired client bears a special degree of professional responsibility (see American Bar Association, 1992a). A court must be especially alert to the potential breakdown in the adversary system when defense counsel is ineffective in representing a defendant with mental illness (Winick, 1993a). Although in general, under the proposal outlined here, the trial court should leave the competency question to counsel, when the court has concerns in this area, it would be appropriate to inquire of counsel whether the defendant's mental condition has been fully considered by counsel, and whether counsel has had the opportunity to consult with a defense clinician concerning the question (Bonnie, 1993). There is "a problem of quality assurance" in this area, but "[if] attention to 'competence' should be enhanced in this context, it should be directed toward the competence of counsel, not the competence of the defendant" (pp. 567, 578). To the extent that some attorneys fail effectively to perform the role my proposal would assign them, the possibility of a collateral attack on any resulting conviction based on ineffective assistance of counsel would be available.

Second, will my proposal produce extensive appellate or habeas corpus litigation by defendants allowed to stand trial or plead guilty? The use of an informal process utilizing a presumption in favor of competency should not have the effect of promoting extensive appellate litigation by defendants who are convicted or collateral attacks on their guilty pleas. In cases in which the presumption of competence is not rebutted, the discussion between the trial judge and the defendant suggested above should create an adequate record that would insulate the case from appeal or collateral attacks questioning competence. Insulation from subsequent attack could be further ensured if the court required counsel to make a statement on the record that the defendant's decision has been made after consultation with counsel, that it seems to the attorney to be reasonable and to be in the client's best interests, and that counsel believes that the defendant possesses sufficient competence to make the decision. Such a statement by counsel would not necessarily preclude counsel from later raising the question of competency if, as the trial unfolded, counsel became convinced that the defendant's condition had changed, or that counsel's original assessment of competency was in error. Should counsel become convinced during trial that, contrary to his or her initial conclusion, the defendant actually was incompetent, counsel's motion, together with a detailed recitation of the circumstances giving rise to this change of view, should create enough doubt to require the trial court to hold a new inquiry (Burt & Morris, 1972; *Drope v. Missouri*, 1975; *Illinois v. Allen*, 1970; *Snyder v. Massachusetts*, 1934; Winick, 1993a).

Third, will adoption of my proposal invite defense counsel to use the presumption process to gain discovery concerning the prosecution's case? Will defense counsel be tempted to abuse the process by opting for a trial to test the strength of the prosecution's evidence, but preserving the ability to bail out if the case appears to be going poorly? This concern underestimates the professional ethics of the defense bar and the ability of trial judges to police counsel appearing in their courts to prevent attorney abuse. When counsel certifies that the client seems competent and that the choice to go forward seems to be in his or her best interests, we should be willing to assume that counsel is acting in good faith, and that any subsequent representation to the court by counsel that counsel now has come to the belief that the client is incompetent also is made in good faith.

Few attorneys will wish to risk even a trial judge's suspicion that they are attempting to perpetuate a fraud on the court.

These three concerns, therefore, do not justify rejection of the proposal. If adopted, the proposal made here would avoid many unnecessary formal judicial determinations of competency. It also would avoid much unnecessary clinical evaluation, thereby allowing a reallocation of scarce clinical resources from evaluation to treatment. Furthermore, it would reduce many of the costs and burdens of existing practices. When a defendant of questionable competency is willing voluntarily to assent to counsel's recommendation concerning a defense strategy that seems more in the defendant's interests than an incompetency adjudication, the defendant's wishes should generally be respected. Both allowing a measure of surrogate decision making or waiver by counsel and substituting a presumption in favor of competency in cases of assent for the present practice of requiring a formal competency determination whenever doubt about competency is raised would do much to reform the law in this area. The proposed restructuring would provide greater deference to the autonomy both of the individual and of the attorney-client relationship consistent with the protective objectives and societal concerns underlying the incompetency doctrine.

But would adoption of the proposal be constitutional? My argument that we should allow defendants of questionable competency to waive the "benefits" of the incompetency doctrine must contend with the dilemma that, under *Pate v. Robinson* (1966), incompetent defendants could not waive their rights. To avoid this dilemma, I propose use of a presumption that would avoid further inquiry into whether a mentally impaired defendant actually was incompetent in cases in which the defendant was able to assent to a recommendation of counsel in favor of trial or a guilty plea. In such cases, a formal competency evaluation and determination would be avoided. Use of a procedural presumption would not violate *Pate v. Robinson*'s holding that a fair proce-

dural determination of the competency issue should occur whenever a reasonable doubt about the question is raised. Although a conclusive or irrebuttable presumption is really a substantive rule, a rebuttable presumption such as the one contemplated is a procedural device that determines how a substantive issue will be decided. A presumption allocates (and sometimes reallocates) a burden of proof. The party challenging a presumption has the burden of demonstrating its falsity. Moreover, a presumption requires the party challenging the presumption to present some evidence tending to negate it. In the absence of such a showing, further inquiry usually is considered unnecessary, the presumption is deemed unrebutted, and the truth of the issue that is the subject of the presumption is treated as having been established.

When reasonable doubt about competency is raised in a criminal case, due process requires a fair determination of the issue. This is actually the holding of *Pate v. Robinson* and *Drope v. Missouri*, two leading Supreme Court competency-to-stand-trial cases that often are construed to place a total bar on trying an incompetent defendant. My proposal suggests the use of a presumption in favor of competency in cases in which the defendant, with the advice and agreement of counsel, clearly and voluntarily expressed a preference in favor of trial or a guilty plea. This presumption would not be destroyed by the existence of reasonable doubt about the defendant's competency (Winick, 1993a). Even when doubt about competency triggers an inquiry under *Pate* and *Drope*, the presumption in favor of competency would continue to inform the adjudication of the issue by placing the burden of proving incompetency on the party challenging the presumption, which in this context would be the prosecution (Winick, 1993a).

If the prosecution fails to produce specific evidence of the defendant's incompetency, the presumption remains unrebutted, and the criminal proceeding then may continue (Winick, 1993a). To rebut the presumption, the prosecution would need to produce some evidence suggesting that the defendant's express choice was the product of his or her mental illness. This production burden could be carried by adducing evidence that suggested, for example, that the defendant's choice was the product of pathological delusions or hallucinations, was based on beliefs that were intrinsically irrational or on reasons that were clearly irrelevant, or was the result of a mood disorder that impaired the defendant's judgment or motivation to act self-interestedly (see Winick, 1985, 1991a; see also Murphy, 1974; Tepper & Elwork, 1984). In addition, the trial judge would always be free to engage in a short exchange with the defendant of the kind that typically occurs in connection with the acceptance of a guilty plea (see, for example, Federal Rules of Criminal Procedure, Rule 11, 1986), and would be required to do so when the defendant seeks to plead guilty or waive certain fundamental rights, like the right to counsel. The judge's questioning would provide additional assurance that the defendant's expressed preference is indeed voluntary, that the defendant has at least a rudimentary understanding of the nature of the right sought to be waived, and that the defendant's responses do not suggest that the decision is the product of cognitive impairment or a mood disorder.

In the absence of such evidence produced by the prosecution or responses by the defendant that themselves raise such questions, the presumption in favor of competency would remain unrebutted, and no further inquiry would occur. As previously mentioned, in the case of a defendant wishing to stand trial, a decision at the outset honoring the defendant's choice can be regarded as provisional, and may be reconsidered as the trial unfolds if the defendant's conduct or demeanor suggests incompetency or if defense counsel decides to raise the issue. If at the initial competency inquiry, the prosecution comes forward with evidence suggesting that the defendant's choice of a trial or a guilty plea is incompetent, or if the defendant's responses to the trial judge's inquiries raise a serious question of competency, the court can always then order a more formal competency

evaluation and hold a further hearing on the issue. In many cases, however, applying a procedural presumption of competency and placing the burden of proof on the party challenging competency can succeed in avoiding the formal clinical evaluation of competency that now typically (and often unnecessarily) occurs.

This procedure should satisfy the due process requirement of conducting an inquiry into competency when reasonable doubt is raised about the issue. *Pate v. Robinson* imposes a constitutional obligation on the trial judge to raise the competency issue and hold a hearing to appraise a defendant's competency whenever sufficient evidence of incompetency comes to his or her attention. *Pate* does not, however, specify the nature of the hearing required. Due process is a flexible notion and does not always require a formal trial-type hearing. Even if the defendant appears to have mental illness or has a history of mental illness, an informal inquiry into competency using the presumption proposed here should meet the requirement of due process. That presumption, it should be emphasized, applies only in cases in which the defendant, with the advice and concurrence of counsel, clearly expresses a preference for trial or a guilty plea. A more elaborate hearing can always be held should the presumption of competency be rebutted, if the court finds this to be necessary.

Although under *Pate*, the existence of mental illness might trigger the need for an inquiry into the competency question, an informal inquiry into the issue using a presumption in favor of competency in cases in which the defendant, with the concurrence of counsel, wishes to go forward should suffice. A more formal inquiry could be held if the presumption is rebutted. Although it may trigger the need for some inquiry under *Pate*, mental illness alone—even one of the major mental illnesses like schizophrenia, major depression, or bipolar disorder—would not be sufficient to rebut the presumption of competency that I argue should exist when a defendant can clearly express a preference that counsel concurs in. Mental illness should not be equated with incompetency. Many individuals suffering from even serious mental illness retain full decision-making capacity, and even when such illness impairs capacity in one area of functioning, it may leave capacity unimpaired in others (American Psychiatric Association, 1993b; Appelbaum & Gutheil, 1991; McKinnon, Cournos, & Stanley, 1989; Morse, 1978; Winick, 1991a, 1991b). More than mental illness alone thus should be required to rebut the presumption of competency; specific evidence suggesting that the defendant's decision is the product of mental illness would be needed.

The Supreme Court's decision in *Medina v. California* (1992) clearly supports the constitutionality of the use of the presumption of competence suggested here (see Winick, 1993a). *Medina* upheld the constitutionality of a statutory presumption in favor of the competency of a criminal defendant and the placement of the burden of proof in an adjudication of the issue on the party challenging competency. The Court's rejection of the challenge to the statutory presumption involved there, raised by a defendant who asserted that it was constitutionally unfair to place the burden on him of establishing his own incompetency, constitutes an endorsement of the constitutionality of the use of presumptions in the competency-to-stand-trial area. The use of a presumption in favor of competency will prevent full inquiry into the matter in some cases, and therefore may produce a risk of error. But *Medina* shows that such a risk of error in the determination of competency will not violate *Pate* (Winick, 1993a). As a result, although the presumption procedure outlined here might result in permitting waiver by at least some defendants presumed competent who actually are incompetent, *Medina* demonstrates that a procedural rule governing the determination of criminal competency is not unconstitutional because it fails to eliminate the possibility of error in the application of the incompetency test.

Medina's endorsement of the constitutionality of presumptions in favor of competency stands in sharp contrast to the Supreme Court's decision two years earlier in *Zinermon v. Burch* (1990; see also Winick, 1991b). In the course of discussing the necessity of a procedural determination of the competency of a mental patient seeking voluntary admission to a psychiatric hospital, the Court in *Zinermon* noted that even if a request for admission to a hospital for medical treatment might justifiably be taken at face value, "a state may not be justified in doing so without further inquiry as to a mentally ill person's request for admission and treatment at a mental hospital" (Winick, 1991b, p. 133 n. 18). This language seems to disapprove of the presumption in favor of the competency of mentally ill persons that has been the trend of modern mental health law, and to call for an "inquiry" into the issue whenever a person with mental illness seeks hospitalization. Construed broadly, the *Zinermon* language could also suggest the need for such an inquiry whenever a person with mental illness seeks to exercise any rights, including the assertion or waiver of rights in the criminal process. This language, however, was dicta, and if taken literally, would seriously undermine the institution of voluntary hospitalization and impose unintended antitherapeutic consequences on patients and serious fiscal costs on the states (Winick, 1991b).

The presumption in favor of the competency of persons with mental illness, which the *Zinermon* dicta seems to question, has been a significant recent development in mental health law (Winick, 1991a). The presumption in favor of competency constitutes a recognition that mental illness does not necessarily produce incompetency, and frequently does not do so (American Psychiatric Association, 1993b; Appelbaum & Gutheil, 1991; Winick, 1991b). Moreover, it reflects a preference in favor of individual autonomy grounded in both political and legal theory and psychological principles (Winick, 1992).

Although the implications of the *Zinermon* dicta are questionable (Winick, 1991b), the holding of the case—that some "inquiry" into competency should have been made when the patient involved in that case sought admission to a mental hospital—seems clearly correct and can be used to illustrate the kind of case in which a presumption in favor of competency should be considered to have been rebutted. The patient in *Zinermon* was able to express a preference for hospitalization but appeared confused and delusional at the time, was unable to state the reasons for his choice, and was hallucinating in ways that related directly to his decision (Winick, 1991b). In fact, he apparently believed that the psychiatric hospital he was entering was "heaven" (*Zinermon v. Burch*, 1990, pp. 118–120; Winick, 1991b). These facts certainly suggest the need for an inquiry into competency and would rebut any presumption in favor of competency that would apply in this and other cases. However, in the absence of facts such as these suggesting that the individual's expressed choice is the product of mental illness, competency should be presumed, and a formal inquiry into the competency question should be unnecessary (American Psychiatric Association, 1993a; Winick, 1994a).

Although the issues presented in *Medina v. California* were quite different from those presented in *Zinermon*, the *Medina* decision seemed to endorse a presumption in favor of competency, whereas the *Zinermon* decision had challenged it (Winick, 1993a). California's statutory presumption in favor of competency examined in *Medina* represents "the enlightened approach of modern mental health law" (Winick, 1993a, p. 863). *Medina* upheld the constitutionality of the California statute, and hence in no way affects the Court's earlier holding in *Zinermon*. But the Court's endorsement of the presumption in favor of competency in *Medina* is a welcome step away from the questionable implications of *Zinermon*'s broad dicta.

Medina paves the way for adoption of the proposal made here—that a presumption of competency should exist when a defendant, with the advice and concurrence of counsel, can clearly and voluntarily express a preference for trial or a guilty plea, and that unless the prosecution can produce specific evidence showing that the defendant's expressed preference is incompetent, or this conclusion is suggested by the defendant's own statements in a discussion with the trial judge, the defendant's waiver should be accepted. By upholding the constitutionality of a statutory presumption in favor of competency and assigning the burden of proof on the issue to the party asserting incompetency, *Medina* suggests that the proposal advanced here also would meet constitutional requirements. Once it is recognized that the use of the procedural presumption of competency suggested here would be constitutionally permissible, the reasons for adopting it become compelling. Such a procedure would further the value deeply ingrained in our American constitutional heritage of protecting and promoting individual autonomy (for example, *Faretta v. California*, 1975; see generally, Winick, 1992). In addition, it would have the effect of reducing some of the unnecessary costs of the existing incompetency process as well as the serious burdens it imposes on defendants. Moreover, as suggested earlier, the use of the procedural presumption proposed here could further these interests without sacrificing the concern for fairness and accuracy in adjudication and without undermining the moral dignity of the criminal process.

Substituting "Treatment Continuances" for the Formal Incompetency Process

In view of the constitutional questions that this waiver proposal raises, further scholarly work may be necessary before legal changes are likely to occur. However, there should be no constitutional impediment to adoption of one aspect of this initial proposal—the suggestion that much of the competency evaluation process should be replaced with a system of trial continuances. Cases in which a defendant seeks to waive the incompetency doctrine and stand trial or plead guilty over an objection by the prosecution that he or she is incompetent probably represent only a very small percentage of total cases. In the overwhelming majority of cases, it is the defendant through his or her counsel who raises the incompetency doctrine as a bar to trial. Under existing practices, the defendant's request triggers a formal competency evaluation. In my initial proposal, I suggested that rather than invoking the formal evaluation process in such cases, a continuance of reasonable duration could be granted to the defendant based on a written certification of counsel that, in counsel's view, the defendant is incompetent (Burt & Morris, 1972; Szasz, 1971; Winick, 1985).

Under this proposal, counsel could be required to certify that the continuance is sought in good faith and on reasonable grounds, and to set forth the specific observations and statements of the defendant that form the basis for the request. Once such a continuance has been granted, a request for a further continuance would need to be supported by a statement from a clinician certifying that the defendant is incompetent, stating that the defendant is receiving appropriate treatment, and predicting a restoration of the defendant's competence within a reasonable period (Winick, 1985). The clinician's statement could also be required to include a specific treatment plan, detailing the kinds of treatment attempted and proposed. The defendant would be permitted substantial choice in electing the type of treatment desired to improve his or her trial functioning. The place of treatment, of course, will depend on the defendant's bail status. If the defendant is in custody, such treatment will occur either in a jail or in a security mental health facility; if released, in the community as an outpatient or voluntary inpatient. The defendant would bear the cost of treatment if not in custody unless he or she is indigent.

In addition to avoiding the cost of unnecessary clinical evaluation and formal judicial determination of the defendant's competency, this proposal could have considerable therapeutic advantages for the defendant. Based on the literature on the psychology of choice (see Winick, 1991a, 1991b, 1992, 1994b), it can be hypothesized that the potential for successful treatment of defendants who are incompetent to stand trial is increased when the defendant accepts treatment voluntarily rather than when the defendant

is forced to enter a forensic facility (Wexler & Winick, 1991a; Winick, 1985; see generally Wexler, 1991; Winick, 1992, 1994a). Placing the burden on the defendant (and his or her counsel) to arrange for treatment with a provider of choice as a condition for receiving the requested continuance can thus be justified not only as efficient, but also as therapeutic. With active treatment, particularly treatment the defendant seeks to obtain, the great majority of mentally impaired defendants can be expected to gain sufficient competency to participate in trial within several weeks or months (Winick, 1985).

Whereas, under existing practice, an incompetency determination suspends the criminal proceedings, the treatment continuance proposed need not do so. During the continuance the defense attorney may be required to file any pretrial motions that can be resolved without the client's assistance (see *Jackson v. Indiana*, 1972). Although the grant of a treatment continuance would suspend the defendant's right to a speedy trial, defense counsel, at any time, would be permitted to file a notice with the court that the defendant has become competent, and proceedings should thereafter resume, with speedy trial periods again running.

Requiring certificates from counsel and from a clinician as conditions for the grant or renewal of a continuance, coupled with judicial supervision, should prevent abuse of the treatment continuance process as a means of obtaining delay. The trial judge maintains wide discretion over whether to grant or deny requested continuances (see *Morris v. Slappy*, 1983; Winick, 1985), and the judge could condition granting of a treatment continuance on receipt of weekly or monthly reports from the defendant's attorney or the treating clinician. The court would always be able to order an independent clinical evaluation and court-supervised treatment if deemed necessary. The process, of course, also would be monitored by the prosecutor, who could always move for a formal competency evaluation if abuse of the continuance process was suspected (Winick, 1985).

The proposal that a defendant voluntarily accept treatment as a condition for the grant of a trial continuance also could be joined with a form of "wagering" or behavioral contracting (Wexler, 1991; Wexler & Winick, 1991a; Winick, 1991c). Under this proposal, to further increase the efficacy of treatment, the defendant and the trial court could enter into a contingency contract under which the defendant would receive the continuance sought in exchange for an agreement to participate in an appropriate treatment program and for making periodic progress toward the goal of restoration to competency. A schedule of target goals and dates could be included, culminating in a restoration to competency within a period specified in the contract. The incentive to perform effectively in treatment could be increased in jurisdictions in which the defendant does not automatically receive credit against any ultimate sentence received for time spent in incompetency commitment (Winick, 1985). In such jurisdictions, a credit against sentence may be used as a reinforcer in the contingency contract to provide an additional inducement for an expeditious restoration to competency (Wexler & Winick, 1991a).

Substituting a system of trial continuances for the existing formal incompetency process also would have the salutary effect of avoiding unnecessary incompetency labeling. As previously indicated, the term *incompetency to stand trial* has an unfortunate connotation, implying a traitlike immutable impairment rather than a temporary difficulty that in most cases can easily be remedied (Sales & Kahle, 1980; Winick, 1995). The negative psychological effects of using an incompetency label in this area can be avoided by granting what can be called a *treatment continuance*, a label that has no similar negative connotations. Even when it is necessary to make a formal incompetency determination—for example, when the defendant seeks to waive a right that he or she is determined to be incompetent to waive—the defendant could be found *temporarily impaired* or *temporarily unable to waive* the right in question (Sales & Kahle, 1980; Winick, 1995).

Such a label suggests hope rather than hopelessness, and encourages the individual to view his or her "temporary" problem as one that can be resolved through appropriate treatment. Such a redesigned label will be less stigmatizing to defendants and will have the effect of limiting the risk that the individual will interpret the impairment as global and relatively stable, an attribution that would increase the likelihood of learned helplessness and other inhibitory patterns that will interfere with competency in the future (Bonnie, 1992; Gould, in press; Winick, 1995).

Defining and Evaluating Competency in the Criminal Process

The Supreme Court's classic formulation of the standard for incompetency in the criminal process was adopted in the 1960 case of *Dusky v. United States* (see Winick, 1985). The Court held that a court was required to determine whether the defendant "has sufficient present ability to consult with his lawyer with a reasonable degree of rational understanding and whether he has a rational as well as factual understanding of the proceedings against him" (*Dusky v. United States*, 1960, p. 402). Although some courts had applied a more demanding standard of competency when a defendant attempted to plead guilty or waive counsel (requiring the ability to make a reasoned choice), in *Godinez v. Moran* (1993) the Supreme Court rejected such a higher standard. Instead, the Court found that the *Dusky* formulation was the appropriate test of competency throughout the criminal process. The *Dusky* standard emphasizes the ability to understand and consult, not necessarily the ability to engage in rational decision making. In *Godinez*, the Court distinguished between competency and the knowledge and voluntariness required for the waiver of certain fundamental rights. A competency inquiry, the Court noted, focuses on the defendant's "mental capacity; the question is whether he has the *ability* to understand the proceedings" (*Godinez v. Moran,* 1993, p. 2687 n. 12). By contrast, the Court noted, the inquiry into "knowing and voluntary . . . is to determine whether the defendant actually *does* understand the significance and consequences of a particular decision and whether the decision is uncoerced" (p. 2687 n. 12).

Although the Court thus clarified that its competency standard was not as broad as some courts had thought, the standard still is broad, open-textured, and vague, permitting clinical evaluators substantial latitude in interpreting and applying the test (Bonnie, 1993; Winick, 1985). The clinical instruments available for competency assessment compound the problem (Grisso, 1986). These instruments typically list the many potentially relevant capacities that a defendant might need without prescribing scoring criteria for how these capacities should be rated (Bonnie, 1993). Moreover, because clinical evaluators rarely consult with counsel to ascertain the particular skills the defendant will need to have to function effectively in the particular case, the assessment instruments encourage clinical evaluators to apply a generalized, abstract standard of competency, rather than following a more appropriate contextualized approach to competency assessment (American Bar Association, 1989; Grisso, 1986; Melton et al., 1985; Roesch & Golding, 1980). By simply relying on clinical judgment based on all the circumstances, these instruments make competency assessment a highly discretionary exercise in clinical judgment (Bonnie, 1993). Many clinical evaluators are paternalistically oriented, and without more concrete guidance tend to classify marginally competent mental patients as incompetent (Winick, 1985). The literature documents the tendency of clinical evaluations in the criminal courts to misunderstand the legal issues involved in incompetency, frequently confusing it with legal insanity or with the clinical definition of psychosis (Winick, 1985). Some clinicians overdiagnose incompetency to bring about what to them seems a more humane disposition of the case or to secure mental health treatment because they assume it will be helpful (Winick, 1985). The discretion

vested in clinical evaluators is both increased and made more troubling by the fact that appellate courts rarely review and almost never reverse trial court competency determinations (Bonnie, 1993), and that trial judges almost always defer to clinical evaluators (Bonnie, 1993; Golding, Roesch, & Schreiber, 1984; Hart & Hare, 1992; Reich & Tookey, 1986).

Decision making in this area thus is effectively delegated to clinical evaluators making low-visibility and essentially unreviewed decisions pursuant to a vague, abstract standard. This situation tends to obscure the distinction between the clinical and legal components of incompetency in the criminal process and allows clinicians to regard a competency assessment as largely an exercise in clinical description. Assessing competency, however, inevitably involves cultural, social, political, and legal judgments that are more normative in nature than clinical (Grisso, 1986; Winick, 1985, 1991a). Recognizing the essentially legal nature of the concept of competency in the criminal process calls for courts and legislatures to define competency with greater precision. Moreover, recognition of the high costs and burdens imposed by the incompetency-to-stand-trial process argues for a narrow definition of competency that results in classifying marginally competent defendants as competent rather than as incompetent (Winick, 1993a). In defining competency to stand trial, the law should not apply to defendants suffering from mental illness artificially high standards for decision-making capacity that many "normal" criminal defendants are unable to satisfy (Perlin, 1991, 1992, 1993a; Perlin & Dorfman, 1993; Winick, 1985). For this reason, Bonnie's efforts to delineate in detail the various components of competency to stand trial is to be applauded (Bonnie, 1993). Moreover, his efforts and those of his co-researchers in the MacArthur Network on Mental Health and the Law to develop more detailed assessment instruments and to conduct empirical research on the decision-making abilities of both "normal" and mentally ill defendants will be most useful.

As previously suggested, the definition of competency should vary depending on whether the defendant assents to a recommendation made by counsel or objects to it. Assent to counsel's recommendation provides an assurance that the choice made by the defendant is reasonable and likely to be in the defendant's best interests. Erring on the side of finding a marginally competent assenting defendant to be competent therefore will not undermine the societal interests in accuracy and the moral dignity of the criminal process. When the defendant objects to counsel's recommendation, this assurance that the defendant's choice is reasonable is not present, and these societal concerns justify a higher degree of scrutiny of the defendant's competency.

Bonnie's analysis of incompetency decision making in the context of decisions whether to raise an insanity defense has demonstrated that existing practice reflects a distinction in the way defendants are dealt with depending on whether they assent or object to the recommendations of counsel (Bonnie, 1992, 1993). Bonnie found that when the defendant pleads insanity in accordance with counsel's recommendation, the courts in practice used a "basic understanding" test of competency in which capacity to understand the nature and consequences of the decision sufficed. When defendants refused a recommended insanity plea, however, and the defense attorney raised doubts about competency, a higher test of competency was applied, requiring an appreciation of the reasons for the decision.

Agreeing with my proposal, Bonnie has recommended a two-level test for decisional competence based on whether the defendant assents or objects to counsel's advice. In general, he suggests that a basic understanding test of competency is all that should be required for decisions, including those waiving constitutional rights, when the defendant assents to counsel's recommendation. Under this low-level test, only the ability to express a choice and to understand its nature and consequences would be required, and deficits or impairments bearing on the defendant's reasons for accepting counsel's recommen-

dation would not be the subject of inquiry. When, however, the defendant insists on acting contrary to counsel's advice in a manner that raises doubts about competency, Bonnie suggests that the test should require ability to make a reasoned choice. This is a more stringent test that requires appreciation and the ability to engage in rational decision making.

While my proposal for a lower standard of competency in cases of assent to counsel's recommendation and a higher standard in cases of objection did not attempt to define those differing standards, Bonnie's approach attempts to do so. The results of his further work with the MacArthur Network on Mental Health and the Law to operationalize these standards in assessment instruments and to test their administration are eagerly awaited. Although the Supreme Court in *Godinez* refused to depart from the unitary standard of competency associated with the *Dusky* formulation, it declined to do so on constitutional grounds. Thus, the states must accept the *Dusky* standard as a constitutional minimum, but they are free to go beyond it and fashion differing tests of competency for different contexts, including recognizing a distinction between assent and objection.

Conclusion

I have recommended a restructured incompetency process that recognizes a distinction between assent and objection, and that presumes competency in cases in which the defendant assents to counsel's recommendation or in which counsel approves the defendant's choice. I have further recommended the use of certifications by counsel, both in cases in which such a presumption is applied and in those in which the defendant seeks to raise his or her mental impairment as a bar to trial and counsel seeks what I would call a *treatment continuance*. These recommendations will have the effect of subsuming the bulk of the competency determination process within the attorney-client relationship. This would be preferable to the present process, in which almost all determinations are made through a formal judicial process that relies heavily on often unnecessary clinical evaluations. Under this proposal, many decisions about competency will be left to counsel, a professional with a duty to act in the defendant's best interests and who is best situated to ascertain the client's deficits and their impact on the skills needed to participate in the criminal case at hand. When necessary, of course, counsel will have access to clinical assistance in making these decisions, but in most cases, the decision will be left to counsel.

Moving competency determinations from clinicians to defense attorneys should increase the accuracy of competency decision making, particularly in light of the tendency of clinical evaluators to misunderstand the incompetency standard and to overdiagnose incompetency (Winick, 1985). Moreover, it would recognize that competency in the criminal process is more a legal than a clinical question, involving legal and normative judgments and not merely clinical ones. In addition, it would avoid a serious conflict of interest for counsel that can undermine the attorney-client relationship and threaten the values underlying the Sixth Amendment right to counsel. Finally, subsuming the bulk of competency determination under the attorney-client relationship would avoid an unnecessary drain on scarce clinical time, allowing a reallocation of clinical resources from evaluation to treatment. This reallocation can increase the quality of the incompetency treatment process and limit existing delays, allowing defendants impaired by mental illness to improve more rapidly and to obtain a more expeditious disposition of their criminal charges.

If implemented, these recommendations thus can transform the existing way we define and evaluate competency in the criminal process, and the way we deal with defendants whose abilities to assume the role of criminal defendants are impaired by mental illness. The most seriously

impaired would still be able to claim the protections of the existing doctrine, although most would receive treatment continuances rather than being labeled incompetent. Those whose impairment is marginal would be able either to obtain treatment, which they themselves arrange and choose as a condition for receiving a brief continuance, or if they prefer, would be permitted to plead guilty or face their charges. Most defendants assenting to counsel's recommendations would be able to have their choices honored. Only those whose assent seems clearly to be a product of mental illness would have their choices interfered with. The result can be a restructured competency doctrine that fulfills its protective purposes in a way that is more sensitive to individual autonomy, and that avoids many unnecessary costs and many of the burdens of delay, stigma, and unnecessary hospitalization that existing practices too often impose.

References

Abramson, L. Y., Garber, J., & Seligman, M. E. P. (1980). Learned helplessness in humans: An attributional analysis. In J. Garber & M. E. P. Seligman (Eds.), *Human helplessness: Theory and applications* (pp. 3–34). New York: Academic Press.

Abramson, L. Y., Seligman, M. E. P., & Teasdale, J. (1978). Learned helplessness in humans: Critique and reformulation. *Journal of Abnormal Psychology, 87,* 49–74.

Adams v. United States *ex rel.* McCann, 317 U.S. 269 (1942).

Ake v. Oklahoma, 470 U.S. 68 (1985).

American Bar Association. (1980). *Standards for criminal justice* (2nd ed.). Boston: Little, Brown.

American Bar Association. (1983). *First tentative draft: Criminal justice mental health standards.* Washington, DC: Author.

American Bar Association. (1989). *Criminal jus-*

tice mental health standards. Washington, DC: Author.

American Bar Association. (1992a). *Model Rules of Professional Conduct.* Chicago: Center for Professional Responsibility.

American Bar Association. (1992b). *Standards for criminal justice: Providing defense service* (3rd ed.). Washington, DC: Author.

American Law Institute. (1972). *Model code of pre-arraignment procedures* (tentative draft No. 5). Philadelphia: Author.

American Psychiatric Association, Task Force on Consent to Voluntary Hospitalization. (1993a). *Consent to voluntary hospitalization* (Task Force Report No. 34). Washington, DC: Author.

American Psychiatric Association, Task Force on DSM-IV. (1993b). *DSM-IV Draft Criteria.* Washington, DC: Author.

Appelbaum, P. S., & Gutheil, T. G. (1991). *Clinical handbook of psychiatry and the law* (2nd ed.). Baltimore, MD: Williams & Wilkins.

Argersinger v. Hamlin, 407 U.S. 25 (1972).

Baldwin v. New York, 399 U.S. 66 (1970).

Barkai, J. L. (1977). Accuracy inquiries for all felony and misdemeanor pleas: Voluntary pleas but innocent defendants. *University of Pennsylvania Law Review, 126,* 88–146.

Beck v. Alabama, 447 U.S. 625 (1980).

Bibliography of therapeutic jurisprudence. (1993). *New York Law School Journal of Human Rights, 10,* 915–926.

Blackstone, W. (1979). *Commentaries on the laws of England.* Chicago: University of Chicago Press. (Original work published 1783)

Bloom v. Illinois, 391 U.S. 194 (1968).

Bonnie, R. J. (1992). The competence of criminal defendants: A theoretical reformulation. *Behavioral Sciences and the Law, 10,* 291–316.

Bonnie, R. J. (1993). The competence of criminal defendants: Beyond *Dusky* and *Drope. University of Miami Law Review, 47,* 539–601.

Bonovitz, J. C., & Guy, E. B. (1979). Impact of restrictive civil commitment procedures on

a prison psychiatric service. *American Journal of Psychiatry, 136,* 1045–1048.

Brookhart v. Janus, 384 U.S. 1 (1966).

Burt, R. A. (1974). Of mad dogs and scientists: The perils of the "criminal-insane." *University of Pennsylvania Law Review, 123,* 258–296.

Burt, R. A., & Morris, N. (1972). A proposal for the abolition of the incompetency plea. *University of Chicago Law Review, 40,* 66–95.

Chernoff, P. A., & Schaffer, W. G. (1972). Defending the mentally ill: Ethical quicksand. *American Criminal Law Review, 10,* 505–531.

Coker v. Georgia, 433 U.S. 584 (1977).

Colorado v. Connelly, 479 U.S. 157 (1986).

Commonwealth v. Louraine, 453 N.E.2d 437 (Mass. 1983).

Cooke, G., Johnston, N., & Pogany, E. (1973). Factors affecting referral to determine competency to stand trial. *American Journal of Psychiatry, 130,* 870–875.

Dickey, W. (1980). Incompetency and the nondangerous mentally ill client. *Criminal Law Bulletin, 16,* 22–40.

Drope v. Missouri, 420 U.S. 162 (1975).

Duncan v. Louisiana, 391 U.S. 145 (1968).

Dusky v. United States, 362 U.S. 402 (1960).

Eddings v. Oklahoma, 455 U.S. 104 (1982).

Ellis, J. W. (1992). Decisions by and for people with mental retardation: Balancing considerations of autonomy and protection. *Villanova Law Review, 37,* 1779–1809.

Ellis, J. W., & Luckasson, R. A. (1985). Mentally retarded criminal defendants. *George Washington Law Review, 53,* 414–493.

Enmund v. Florida, 458 U.S. 782 (1982).

Ennis, B. J., & Emery, R. D. (1978). *The rights of mental patients: The revised edition of the basic ACLU guide to a mental patient's rights.* New York: Avon Books.

Faretta v. California, 422 U.S. 806 (1975).

Federal Rules of Criminal Procedure, 18 U.S.C. (1986).

Foote, C. (1960). A comment on pre-trial commitment of criminal defendants. *University of Pennsylvania Law Review, 108,* 832–846.

Frith's Case, 22 How. St. Tr. 307 (1790).

Furman v. Georgia, 408 U.S. 238 (1972).

Gardner v. Florida, 430 U.S. 349 (1977).

Geller, J. L., & Lister, E. D. (1978). The process of criminal commitment for pretrial psychiatric examination: An evaluation. *American Journal of Psychiatry, 135,* 53–60.

Gideon v. Wainwright, 372 U.S. 335 (1963).

Gobert, J. J. (1973). Competency to stand trial: A pre- and post-*Jackson* analysis. *Tennessee Law Review, 40,* 659–688.

Godinez v. Moran, 113 S. Ct. 2680 (1993).

Golding, S. L., Roesch, R., & Schreiber, J. (1984). Assessment and conceptualization of competency to stand trial: Preliminary data on the interdisciplinary fitness interview. *Law and Human Behavior, 8,* 321–334.

Goldstein, A. S. (1981). *The passive judiciary: Prosecutorial discretion and the guilty plea.* Baton Rouge: Louisiana State University Press.

Gould, K. A. (in press). Therapeutic jurisprudence and the arraignment process: The defense attorney's dilemma: Whether to request a competency evaluation. In S. Verdun-Jones & M. Layton (Eds.), *Mental health law and practice through the life cycle.*

Gregg v. Georgia, 428 U.S. 153 (1976).

Grisso, T. (1986). *Evaluating competencies: Forensic assessment and instruments.* New York: Plenum.

Group for the Advancement of Psychiatry. (1974). *Misuse of psychiatry in the criminal courts: Competency to stand trial.* New York: Author.

Halberstam, M. (1982). Towards neutral principles in the administration of criminal justice: A critique of Supreme Court decisions sanctioning the plea bargaining process. *Journal of Criminal Law and Criminology, 73,* 1–49.

Hale, M. (1736). *The history of the pleas of the crown.* London: E. and R. Nutt and R. Gosling.

Halpern, A. L. (1975). Use and misuse of psychiatry in competency examinations of criminal defendants. *Psychiatric Annals, 5,* 123–150.

Hamm v. Jabe, 706 F.2d 765 (6th Cir. 1983).

Hart, S. D., & Hare, R. D. (1992). Predicting fitness to stand trial: The relative power of demographic, criminal, and clinical variables. *Forensic Reports, 5,* 53–59.

Illinois v. Allen, 397 U.S. 337 (1970).

Incompetency to stand trial. (1967). *Harvard Law Review, 81,* 454–473.

Jackson v. Indiana, 406 U.S. 715 (1972).

Jones v. Barnes, 463 U.S. 745 (1983).

Kinloch's Case, 18 How. St. Tr. 395 (1746).

Lockett v. Ohio, 438 U.S. 586 (1978).

Maier, S. F., & Seligman, M.E.P. (1976). Learned helplessness: Theory and evidence. *Journal of Experimental Psychology: General, 105,* 33–46.

McGarry, L. A. (1969). Demonstration and research in competency for trial and mental illness: Review and preview. *Boston University Law Review, 49,* 46–61.

McKinnon, K., Cournos, F., & Stanley, B. (1989). *Rivers* in practice: Clinicians' assessments of patients' decision making capacity. *Hospital and Community Psychiatry, 40,* 1159–1162.

Medina v. California, 112 S. Ct. 2572 (1992).

Melton, G. B., Weithorn, L. A., & Slobogin, C. (1985). *Community mental health centers and the courts: An evaluation of community-based forensic services.* Lincoln: University of Nebraska Press.

Morris v. Slappy, 461 U.S. 1 (1983).

Morse, S. J. (1978). Crazy behavior, morals, and science: An analysis of mental health law. *Southern California Law Review, 51,* 527–654.

Murphy, J. (1974). Incompetency and paternalism. *Archiv für Rechts- und Sozialphilosophie, 60,* 465–474.

North Carolina v. Alford, 400 U.S. 25 (1970).

O'Neil, T. P. (1990). Vindicating the defendant's constitutional right to testify at a criminal trial: The need for an on-the-record waiver. *University of Pittsburgh Law Review, 51,* 809–839.

Pate v. Robinson, 383 U.S. 375 (1966).

Perlin, M. L. (1991). Competency, deinstitutionalization, and homelessness: A story of marginalization. *Houston Law Review, 28,* 63–142.

Perlin, M. L. (1992). On "sanism." *SMU Law Review, 46,* 373–407.

Perlin, M. L. (1993a). Pretexts and mental disability law: The case of competency. *University of Miami Law Review, 47,* 625–688.

Perlin, M. L. (1993b). What is therapeutic jurisprudence? *New York Law School Journal of Human Rights, 10,* 623–636.

Perlin, M. L., & Dorfman, D. A. (1993). Sanism, social science, and the development of mental disability law jurisprudence. *Behavioral Sciences and the Law, 11,* 47–66.

Peterson, C., & Bossio, L. M. (1989). Learned helplessness. In R. C. Curtis (Ed.), *Self-defeating behaviors: Experimental research, clinical impressions, and practical implications* (pp. 235–236). New York: Plenum.

Polk County v. Dodson, 454 U.S. 312 (1981).

Pollock, F., & Maitland, F. W. (1968). *The history of English law before the time of Edward I* (2nd ed.). London: Cambridge University Press. (Original work published 1898)

Powell v. Alabama, 287 U.S. 45 (1932).

In re Pray, 336 A.2d 174 (Vt. 1975).

Reich, J. H., & Tookey, L. (1986). Disagreements between court and psychiatrist on competency to stand trial. *Journal of Clinical Psychiatry, 47,* 29–30.

Riggins v. Nevada, 112 S. Ct. 1810 (1992).

Rock v. Arkansas, 483 U.S. 44 (1987).

Roesch, R. J., & Golding, S. L. (1979). Treatment and disposition of defendants found incompetent to stand trial: A review and a proposal. *International Journal of Law and Psychiatry, 2,* 349–370.

Roesch, R. J., & Golding, S. L. (1980). *Competency to stand trial.* Urbana: University of Illinois Press.

Sales, B. D., & Kahle, L. R. (1980). Law and attitudes toward the mentally ill. *International Journal of Law and Psychiatry, 3,* 391–403.

Scott v. Illinois, 440 U.S. 367 (1980).

Seligman, M.E.P. (1975). *Helplessness: On depression, development, and death.* San Francisco: Freeman.

Seligman, M.E.P., & Garber, J. (Eds.). (1980). Human helplessness: Theory and applications. New York: Academic Press.

Shah, S. A. (1981). Legal and mental health system interactions: Major developments and research needs. *International Journal of Law and Psychiatry, 4,* 219–270.

Singer v. United States, 380 U.S. 24 (1965).

Snyder v. Massachusetts, 291 U.S. 97 (1934).

Solem v. Helm, 463 U.S. 277 (1983).

State v. Jojola, 553 P.2d 1296 (N.M. Ct. App. 1976).

State v. Murphy, 355 P.2d 323 (Wash. 1960).

Steadman, H. J. (1979). *Beating a rap? Defendants found incompetent to stand trial.* Chicago: University of Chicago Press.

Steadman, H. J., & Braff, J. (1978). Crimes of violence and incompetency diversion. *Journal of Criminal Law and Criminology, 66,* 73–78.

Steadman, H. J., & Hartstone, E. (1983). Defendants incompetent to stand trial. In J. Monahan & H. J. Steadman (Eds.), *Mentally disordered offenders: Perspectives from law and social science.* New York: Plenum.

Stephen, J. F. (1964). *A history of the criminal law of England.* New York: B. Franklin. (Original work published 1883)

Stone, A. A. (1978). Comment. *American Journal of Psychiatry, 135,* 61–63.

Symposium—Therapeutic jurisprudence: Restructuring mental disability law. (1993). *New York Law School Journal of Human Rights, 10,* 623–926.

Szasz, T. S. (1971). *Psychiatric justice.* New York: Collier.

Teplin, L. A. (1983). The criminalization of the mentally ill: Speculation in search of data. *Psychological Bulletin, 94,* 54–67.

Tepper, A. M., & Elwork, A. (1984). Competence to consent to treatment as a psycholegal construct. *Law and Human Behavior, 8,* 205–223.

Uphoff, R. J. (1988). The role of the criminal defense lawyer in representing the mentally impaired defendant: Zealous advocate or officer of the court? *Wisconsin Law Review, 1988,* 65–109.

Wainwright v. Sykes, 433 U.S. 72 (1977).

Weihofen, H. (1954). *Mental disorder as a criminal defense.* Buffalo, NY: Dennis.

Wexler, D. B. (1983). The structure of civil commitment: Patterns, pressures, and interactions in mental health legislation. *Law and Human Behavior, 7,* 1–30.

Wexler, D. B. (1991). Health care compliance principles and the insanity acquitee conditional release process. *Criminal Law Bulletin, 27,* 18–41.

Wexler, D. B. (1992). Justice, mental health, and therapeutic jurisprudence. *Cleveland State Law Review, 40,* 517–526.

Wexler, D. B. (1993). Therapeutic jurisprudence and changing concepts of legal scholarship. *Behavioral Sciences and the Law, 11,* 17–29.

Wexler, D. B., & Scoville, S. E. (1971). Special project—The administration of psychiatric justice: Theory and practice in Arizona. *Arizona Law Review, 13,* 1–259.

Wexler, D. B., & Winick, B. J. (1991a). *Essays in therapeutic jurisprudence.* Durham, NC: Carolina Academic Press.

Wexler, D. B., & Winick, B. J. (1991b). Therapeutic jurisprudence as a new approach to mental health law policy analysis and research. *University of Miami Law Review, 45,* 979–1004.

Wexler, D. B., & Winick, B. J (1992a). The potential of therapeutic jurisprudence: A new approach to psychology and the law. In J.R.P. Ogloff (Ed.), *Law and psychology: The broadening of the discipline* (pp. 211–239). Durham, NC: Carolina Academic Press.

Wexler, D. B., & Winick, B. J. (1992b). Therapeutic jurisprudence and criminal justice mental health issues. *Mental and Physical Disability Law Reporter, 16,* 225–231.

White Hawk v. Solem, 693 F.2d 825 (8th Cir. 1982), *cert. denied,* 460 U.S. 1054 (1983).

Winick, B. J. (1977). Psychotropic medication and competency to stand trial. *American Bar Foundation Research Journal, 81,* 769–816.

Winick, B. J. (1982). Prosecutorial peremptory challenge practices in capital cases: An empirical study and a constitutional analysis. *Michigan Law Review, 81,* 1–98.

Winick, B. J. (1983). Incompetency to stand trial: Developments in the law. In J. Monahan & H. J. Steadman (Eds.), *Mentally disordered offenders: Perspectives from law and social science* (pp. 3–38). New York: Plenum.

Winick, B. J. (1985). Restructuring competency to stand trial. *UCLA* Law Review, 32, 921–985.

Winick, B. J. (1987). Incompetency to stand trial: An assessment of costs and benefits, and a proposal for reform. *Rutgers Law Review, 39,* 243–287.

Winick, B. J. (1989). Forfeiture of attorney's fees under RICO and CCE and the right to counsel of choice: The constitutional dilemma and how to avoid it. *University of Miami Law Review, 43,* 765–869.

Winick, B. J. (1991a). Competency to consent to treatment: The distinction between assent and objection. *Houston Law Review, 28,* 15–61.

Winick, B. J. (1991b). Competency to consent to voluntary hospitalization: A therapeutic jurisprudence analysis of *Zinermon v. Burch. International Journal of Law and Psychiatry, 14,* 169–214.

Winick, B. J. (1991c). Harnessing the power of the bet: Wagering with the government as a mechanism for social and individual change. *University of Miami Law Review, 45,* 737–816.

Winick, B. J. (1991d). The mentally disordered defendant in Florida. In *Florida Criminal Rules and Practice* (Part 2, §§ 7.1–7.95). Tallahassee, FL: Continuing Legal Education.

Winick, B. J. (1992). On autonomy: Legal and psychological perspectives. *Villanova Law Review, 37,* 1705–1777.

Winick, B. J. (1993a). Presumptions and burdens of proof in determining competency to stand trial: An analysis of *Medina v. California* and the Supreme Court's new due process methodology in criminal cases. *University of Miami Law Review, 47,* 817–866.

Winick, B. J. (1993b). Psychotropic medication in the criminal trial process: The constitutional and therapeutic implications of *Riggins v. Nevada. New York Law School Journal of Human Rights, 10,* 637–709.

Winick, B. J. (1994a). How to handle voluntary hospitalization after *Zinermon v. Burch. Administration and Policy in Mental Health, 21,* 395–406.

Winick, B. J. (1994b). The right to refuse mental health treatment: A therapeutic jurisprudence analysis. *International Journal of Law and Psychiatry, 17,* 99–117.

Winick, B. J. (1995). The side effects of incompetency labeling and the implications for mental health law. *Psychology, Public Policy, and Law, 1*(1), 6–42.

Woodson v. North Carolina, 428 U.S. 280 (1976).

Zinermon v. Burch, 494 U.S. 113 (1990).

16 ■ The Insanity Defense: Deconstructing the Myths and Reconstructing the Jurisprudence

Michael L. Perlin
New York Law School

The insanity defense is unique among criminal defenses. If it is successful, it does not result in acquittal and outright release; rather, it results in the entry of a special verdict—not guilty by reason of insanity—generally followed by commitment to a forensic (often maximum security) psychiatric institution. Its purpose is to divert defendants who, as a result of mental disease or disorder, are not responsible for the criminal act with which they have been charged (LaFave & Scott, 1986).

No aspect of the criminal justice system is more controversial than the insanity defense. No other successful defense regularly brings about cries for its abolition; no other aspect of the criminal law inspires position papers from trade

I wish to thank Janet Abisch and Dave Scott for their extraordinary editing assistance, and Lori Kranczer for her excellent research assistance.

This chapter is adapted from Michael L. Perlin, *The Jurisprudence of the Insanity Defense* (1994), © 1994, Carolina Academic Press. A similar version of this article will be published as "Current Status of the Insanity Defense," in *Innovations in Clinical Practice* (forthcoming, Professional Resource Press). Other portions of this chapter draw heavily on Michael L. Perlin, *Mental Disability Law: Civil and Criminal*, Chapter 15 (1989), and Michael L. Perlin, *Law and Mental Disability*, Chapter 4 (1994).

associations spanning the full range of professions and political entities. When the insanity defense is successful in a highly publicized case, especially when it involves a defendant whose commission of the act is clear, the acquittal triggers public outrage and serves vividly as a screen on which each relevant interest group can project its fears and concerns. It symbolizes "the most profound issues [of responsibility, guilt, moral accountability, punishment, good and evil] in social and criminal justice" (Keilitz, 1987, p. 322).

Although, on one hand, the defense is characterized as a reflection of the "fundamental moral principles of our criminal law" (*United States v. Lyons*, 1984), or as a bulwark of the law's "moorings of condemnation for moral failure" (Livermore & Meehl, 1967, p. 797), it remains as a symbol of all that is "wrong" with the criminal justice system and as a source of social and political anger. It is seen as a "loophole" through which the legally, morally, and factually guilty can escape punishment. It was thus attacked by the nation's Attorney General as a major stumbling block in the restoration of the "effectiveness of Federal law enforcement" and as tilting the balance "between the forces of law and the forces of lawlessness" (U.S. Congress, 1982, p. 27).

Our fixation with the insanity defense has evolved into a familiar story. The insanity defense, so common wisdom goes, encourages the factually (and morally) guilty to seek refuge in an excuse premised on pseudoscience, shaky rehabilitation theory, and sleight of hand. The defense, allegedly, is frequently used in abusive ways, is generally successful, and often results in brief slap-on-the-wrist periods of confinement in loosely supervised settings; because it is basically a no-risk maneuver, the story continues, even when it fails, the defendant will suffer no harm. Purportedly, the defense is used disproportionately in death penalty cases, often involving garish multiple homicides, and inevitably results in trials in which high-priced experts do battle in front of confused jurors who are inevitably unable to make sense of contradictory, highly abstract, and speculative testimony. Finally, the defense is seen as being subject to the worst sort of malingering or feigning, and it is assumed that, through this gambit, clever defendants can "con" gullible, "soft" experts into accepting a fraudulent defense.

The largely unseen counterworlds of empirical reality, behavioral advance, scientific discovery, and philosophical inquiry paint a different picture. Empirically, the insanity defense is rarely used, is less frequently successful, and generally results in lengthy stays in restrictive maximum security facilities for far longer periods than the defendants would have been subject to had they been sentenced criminally (Perlin, 1989–1990).

It is also a risky plea; where it fails, prison terms are generally significantly longer than in like cases where the defense was not raised. The defense is most frequently pled in cases *not* involving a victim's death and is often raised in cases involving minor property crimes. The vast majority of cases are so-called "walkthroughs" where both state and defense experts agree as to both the severity of the defendant's mental illness and his or her lack of responsibility. Feigned insanity is rare, successfully feigned insanity even rarer. It is far more likely for a jury to convict in a case in which the defendant meets the relevant substantive insanity criteria than to acquit where the defendant does not (Perlin, 1989–1990).

Nonetheless, the myths continue and we demand legislative reform. This reform leads to a variety of changes in insanity defense statutes—in substantive standards, in burdens of proof, in standards of proof, in the creation of hybrid verdicts such as guilty but mentally ill, even, in a few instances, in supposed abolition of the defense itself. No matter what their final reform, these reforms stem from one primary source: "the public's overwhelming fear of the future acts of [released insanity] acquittees" (Steadman, 1993, p. 69).

Behaviorally, researchers are beginning to develop sophisticated assessment tools that can translate insanity concepts into quantifiable variables that appear to easily meet the traditional legal standard of "reasonable scientific certainty" (Rodriguez, LeWinn, & Perlin, 1983). Scientifically, the development of "hard science" diagnostic tools such as computerized tomography (CAT scanning) or magnetic resonance imaging (MRI) has helped determine the presence and severity of certain neurological illnesses that may be causally related to some forms of criminal behavior (see, for example, Garber, 1988). Finally, moral philosophers are increasingly trying—with some measure of success—to clarify such difficult underlying issues as the contextual meaning of terms like *causation, responsibility,* and *rationality* (Moore, 1984).

Yet these discoveries and developments have had virtually no impact on the basic debate. They are ignored, trivialized, and denied. And the gap between myth and reality is a vast one that widens exponentially with the passage of time. Although virtually every empirical researcher who has studied any of these issues acknowledges the gap (Callahan, Steadman, McGreevy, & Robbins, 1991; Steadman, 1993), it continues to grow. We continue to honor and reify the myths through legislative action and judicial decisions and in public forums. The public continues to endorse a substantive standard for insanity that approximates the "wild beast" test of 1724 (Roberts, Golding, & Fincham, 1987). Moreover, legislators look to the potential abolition of the insanity defense as a remedy for rampant crime problems in spite of statistics showing that the defense is raised in a fraction of 1% of felony prosecutions (and is successful only about one-fourth of the time) (Callahan et al., 1991, p. 334–336). Illustrative is our response to the most celebrated insanity acquittal of the 20th century—that of John W. Hinckley—which is to shrink the insanity defense in federal jurisdictions to a narrower and more restrictive version of an 1843 test that was seen as biologically, scientifically, and morally outdated at the time of its creation (Perlin, 1989, pp. 292–294).

Why is this? What is there about the insanity defense that allows for, and perhaps encourages, such a discontinuity between firmly held belief and statistical reality? Why is our insanity defense jurisprudence so irrational? Why do we continue to be obsessed by questions that are irrelevant to the core jurisprudential inquiry of who should be exculpated because of lack of mental responsibility? Why do we allow ourselves to be immobilized by this debate? Why does our willful blindness lead us to ignore scientific and empirical developments and instead force us to waste time, energy, and passion on a series of fruitless inquiries that will have negligible impact on any of the underlying social problems? Why, most importantly, do we continue to ignore the most fundamental and core question: why do we feel the way we do about "these people," and why, when we engage in our endless debates and incessant retinkering with insanity defense doctrine, do we not seriously consider our answer to this question?

Our thinking about the insanity defense has been shaped by these empirical myths and related broad social myths. The result of a medieval and fundamentalist religious vision of the roots of mental illness and the relationships between mental illness, crime, and punishment, the myths continue to dominate the landscape in spite of, and independent of, the impressive scientific and behavioral evidence to the contrary (Rogers, Seman, & Clark, 1986).

Our efforts to understand the insanity de-

fense and insanity-pleading defendants are doomed to intellectual, political, and moral gridlock unless we are willing to take a fresh look at the underlying doctrine through a series of filters: empirical research, scientific discovery, moral philosophy, cognitive and moral psychology, sociology, communications theory, and political science. Only in this manner can we attempt to articulate a coherent and integrated perspective and reconstruct a meaningful insanity defense jurisprudence.

In this chapter, I will (1) trace the doctrinal development of the insanity defense and show how the public has always demanded a rigid all-or-nothing construct of criminal responsibility; (2) demonstrate the role of the insanity acquittal of John W. Hinckley, Jr., in the reformulation of our contemporary insanity defense laws; (3) examine the role of punishment and demonstrate how our culture of punishment is dominated by the obsessive fear that a responsible defendant will beat the rap; (4) discuss the role of externalities in the formulation of the insanity defense; and (5) offer some modest conclusions as to *why* the current debate over the insanity defense is doomed to result in moral and empirical failure.

The Development of Insanity Defense Doctrine

Pre-*M'Naghten* History

The insanity defense, which has been in existence since at least the 12th century, has always aroused more discussion than any other topic of substantive criminal law, despite the fact that few insanity pleas were entered prior to the mid-18th century (Eigen, 1984). Prior to the famous decision in the *M'Naghten* case (1843), which still shapes the contemporary defense (Insanity Defense Reform Act, 1984), the substantive insanity defense went through three significant stages: the good-and-evil test, the wild beast test, and the right-and-wrong test.

Good and Evil

The good-and-evil test—which apparently first appeared in a 1313 case involving the capacity of an infant under the age of seven—revealed the "moral dogmata reflected in [the medieval] theological literature" (Platt & Diamond, 1966, pp. 1231–1233). The insane, like children, were incapable of "sin[ning] against [their] will" because people's freedom "is restrained in children, in fools, and in the witless who do not have reason whereby they can choose the good from the evil" (Platt & Diamond, 1966, p. 1233). During the 14th through the 16th centuries, this test—the source of which was most likely biblical—remained constant in English law. And by the end of that time, coinciding with the reign of Elizabeth I, insane persons who met this test were treated as "nonpersons" who were not fit subjects for punishment, "since they did not comprehend the moral implications of their harmful acts."

Wild Beast

In *Rex v. Arnold* (1724), a case in which the defendant shot and wounded a British lord in a homicide attempt, Judge Tracy instructed the jury that it should acquit by reason of insanity in the case of

a mad man . . . must be a man that is totally deprived of his understanding and memory, and doth not know what he is doing, no more than *a brute,* or *a wild beast,* such a one is never the object of punishment. (*Rex v. Arnold,* 1724, in Howell, 1812, p. 695)

In short, the emphasis was on lack of *intellectual ability* rather than on the violently wild, ravenous beast image that the phrase calls to mind. The wild beast test continued to be used until at least 1840 (Platt & Diamond, 1966, p. 1236).

Right and Wrong

The following step—the right-and-wrong test, the forerunner of *M'Naghten*—emerged in two 1812 cases. In the second of the two, the jury was

charged that it must decide whether the defendant "had sufficient understanding to distinguish good from evil, right from wrong . . ." (Lewinstein, 1969, p. 279). It was finally expanded on in 1840 in *Regina v. Oxford* (1840), where Lord Denman charged the jury that it must determine whether the defendant, "from the effect of a diseased mind," knew that the act was wrong, and that the question that must thus be answered was whether "he was quite unaware of the nature, character, and consequences of the act he was committing" (*Regina v. Oxford,* 1840, p. 525).

Even with these rigid tests in place, the public's perceptions of abuse of the insanity defense then differed little from its reactions today. The public's representatives demanded an all-or-nothing sort of insanity, a conceptualization "peculiarly foreign" to psychiatry since at least the middle of the 19th century (Diamond, 1961, p. 62).

M'Naghten

In 1843, the "most significant case in the history of the insanity defense in England" arose out of the shooting by Daniel M'Naghten of Edward Drummond, the secretary of the man he mistook for his intended victim, Prime Minister Robert Peel. After *nine* medical witnesses testified that M'Naghten was insane, and after the jury was informed that an insanity acquittal would lead to the defendant's commitment to a psychiatric hospital, M'Naghten was found not guilty by reason of insanity (NGRI) (Hermann & Sor, 1983; *M'Naghten,* 1843; Moran, 1981).

Enraged by the verdict, Queen Victoria questioned why the law was of "no avail," because "everybody is morally convinced that [the] malefactor . . . [was] perfectly conscious and aware of what he did," and demanded that the legislature "lay down the rule" so as to protect the public "from the wrath of madmen who they feared could now kill with impunity" (Eule, 1978, p. 644). In response, the House of Lords asked the Supreme Court of Judicature to answer five questions regarding the insanity law, and the judges' answers to two of these five became the *M'Naghten* test:

[T]he jurors ought to be told in all cases that every man is presumed to be sane, and to possess a sufficient degree of reason to be responsible for his crimes, until the contrary be proved to their satisfaction; and that to establish a defence on the ground of insanity, it must be clearly proved that, at the time of the committing of the act, the party accused was labouring under such a defect of reason, from disease of the mind, as not to know the nature and quality of the act he was doing; or, if he did know it, that he did not know he was doing what was wrong. (*M'Naghten*, 1843, 722)

This rigid responsibility test established under royal pressure and focusing on the defendant's *knowledge* reflected "the prevailing intellectual and scientific ideas of the times." It stemmed from an "immutable philosophical and moral concept which assumes an inherent capacity in man to distinguish right from wrong and to make necessary moral decisions" (Hovenkamp, 1981, p. 551).

The *M'Naghten* rules reflected a theory of responsibility that was outmoded long before its adoption and that bore little resemblance to contemporaneous study and inquiry about the human mind. Nonetheless, with almost no exceptions, American courts eagerly embraced this formulation and codified it as the standard test "with little modification" in virtually all jurisdictions until the middle of the 20th century (Weiner, 1980, p. 1060).

Post-*M'Naghten* Developments

Irresistible Impulse

Although there was some interest in the post-*M'Naghten* years in the so-called irresistible impulse exception—allowing for the acquittal of a defendant if a mental disorder caused him or her to experience an "irresistible and uncontrollable impulse to commit the offense, even if the defendant remained able to understand the nature of the offense and its wrongfulness"—this formulation was not more than a brief detour in

the development of an insanity jurisprudence (Dix, 1986, p. 7). At its highwater mark, it was endorsed in 18 jurisdictions (Goldstein, 1967, pp. 241–242 n. 1), but it is virtually unused today (Perlin, 1989, pp. 294–296).

Durham

The first important theoretical alternative to *M'Naghten* emerged in the District of Columbia in the 1954 case of *Durham v. United States* (1954). Writing for the court, Judge David Bazelon rejected both *M'Naghten* and the irresistible impulse tests on the theory that the human mind was a functional unit and that a far broader test would be appropriate (*Durham v. United States*, 1954, pp. 870–874). *Durham* thus held that an accused would not be criminally responsible if his "unlawful act was the product of mental disease or mental defect" (pp. 874–875). This test provided for a broad range of psychiatric expert testimony, "unbound by narrow or psychologically inapposite legal questions" (Weiner, 1985, p. 710). Further, the court reiterated the jury's function in such a case:

Juries will continue to make moral judgments, still operating under the fundamental precept that "Our collective conscience does not allow punishment where it cannot impose blame." But in making such judgments, they will be guided by wider horizons of knowledge concerning mental life. The question will be simply whether the accused acted because of a mental disorder, and not whether he displayed particular symptoms which medical science has long recognized do not necessarily or even typically, accompany even the most serious disorder. (*Durham v. United States*, 1954, p. 876)

Durham was the first modern, major break from the *M'Naghten* approach and created a "feeling of ferment" as the District of Columbia "became a veritable laboratory for consideration of all aspects of insanity (medical *and* legal), in its fullest substantive and procedural ramifications" (Goldstein, 1967, p. 83). Both the substantive test—how nonresponsibility should be defined—and the procedural aspects—how nonresponsibility should be proven—were vigorously debated anew in the aftermath of *Durham*. Within a few years, however, *Durham* was judicially criticized, modified (Acheson, 1963), and ultimately dismantled by the court that had decided it (*Frigillana v. United States*, 1962; *McDonald v. United States*, 1962). Its burial was completed by the decision in *United States v. Brawner* (1972) to adopt the Model Penal Code/American Law Institute Test.

United States v. Brawner

Brawner discarded *Durham*'s product test but added a *volitional* question to *M'Naghten*'s cognitive inquiry. Under this test,

A defendant would not be responsible for his criminal conduct if, as a result of mental disease or defect, he "lack[ed] substantial capacity either to appreciate the criminality of his conduct or to conform his conduct to the requirements of law." (*United States v. Brawner*, 1972, p. 973; Model Penal Code § 4.01, 1955)

Although the test was rooted in *M'Naghten*, there were several significant differences. First, its use of the word *substantial* was meant to respond to case law developments that had required "a showing of total impairment for exculpation from criminal responsibility." Second, the substitution of the word *appreciate* for the word *know* showed that "a sane offender must be emotionally as well as intellectually aware of the significance of his conduct," and "mere intellectual awareness that conduct is wrongful when divorced from an appreciation or understanding of the moral or legal import of behavior, can have little significance." Third, by using broader language of mental impairment than *M'Naghten* had, the test "capture[d] both the cognitive and affective aspects of impaired mental understanding." Fourth, its substitution in the final proposed official draft of the word *wrongfulness* for *criminality* reflected the position that the insanity defense dealt with "an impaired moral sense rather than an impaired sense of legal wrong" (Goldstein, 1967, p. 87).

Although it was incorrectly assumed that the

spreading adoption of *Brawner* would augur the death of *M'Naghten* (Diamond, 1962, p. 189; Insanity Defense Reform Act, 1988), *Brawner* did serve as the final burial for the *Durham* experiment (Diamond, 1973).

Guilty But Mentally Ill (GBMI)

Perhaps the most important development in substantive insanity defense formulations in the 20 years post-*Brawner* has been the adoption in over a dozen jurisdictions of the hybrid guilty-but-mentally-ill (GBMI) verdict (McGraw, Farthing-Capowich, & Keilitz, 1985). It received its initial recent impetus in 1975 in Michigan as a reflection of legislative dissatisfaction with and public outcry over a state Supreme Court decision prohibiting automatic commitment of insanity acquittees (Mickenberg, 1987; *People v. McQuillan*, 1974).

The rationale for the passage of GBMI legislation was that the implementation of such a verdict would decrease the number of persons acquitted by reason of insanity. The jury would have an alternative verdict that would acknowledge the defendant's mental illness while allowing them to not enter an NGRI verdict, and that would ensure treatment of those who were GBMI within a correctional setting (*People v. Smith*, 1984, p. 106). A GBMI defendant would purportedly be evaluated on entry to the correctional system and be provided appropriate mental health services, either on an inpatient basis as part of a definite prison term or, in specific cases, as a parolee or as an element of probation (Weiner, 1985, p. 715).

Practice under GBMI statutes reveals that the verdict does little or nothing to ensure effective treatment for offenders with mental disabilities. Because most statutes vest discretion in the director of the state correctional or mental health facility to provide a GBMI prisoner with such treatment as he or she "determines necessary," the GBMI prisoner is not ensured treatment "beyond that available to other offenders" (Slobogin, 1985, p. 513). One comprehensive study of the operation of the GBMI verdict in

Georgia revealed that only 3 of the 150 defendants who were found GBMI during the period in question were being treated in hospitals (Steadman, 1993, p. 195).

Hinckley and Its Aftermath

The acquittal of John W. Hinckley of the attempted murder of President Ronald Reagan galvanized the American public in a way that led to the reversal of 150 years of study and understanding of the complexities of psychological behavior and the relationship between mental illness and certain violent acts (Caplan, 1984; Perlin, 1989–1990). The public's outrage over a jurisprudential system that could allow a defendant who shot an American president on national television to plead not guilty for *any* reason became a "river of fury" after the jury's verdict was announced (Perlin, 1985, p. 859). To the public, the defense strategy, the trial, and the subsequent verdict were vivid reifications of many of the most powerful insanity defense myths: an intelligent albeit troubled defendant who plans a fiendish crime—not coincidentally, against one of the nation's most beloved political leaders—hires a top-dollar Washington, D.C., law firm, retains a panel of heavily credentialed forensic mental health witnesses, and bamboozles a lay jury so as to avoid severe punishment (Caplan, 1984).

Congressional Reaction: The Insanity Defense Reform Act

Members of Congress responded quickly to the public's outpouring of outrage by introducing 26 separate pieces of legislation designed to limit, modify, severely shrink, or abolish the insanity defense in federal trials (Mickenberg, 1987; Perlin, 1985, 1989–1990). The Reagan Administration originally had called loudly for the abolition of the insanity defense (Perlin, 1985,

p. 860 n. 9). However, in the face of a nearly unified front presented by most of the relevant professional organizations and trade associations, it eventually quietly dropped its loud public call for abolition and supported the Insanity Defense Reform Act (IDRA) as a "reform compromise" (Perlin, 1989, pp. 398–399 n. 743). The legislation ultimately enacted by Congress—legislation that closely comported with the public's moral feelings—returned the insanity defense to "*status quo ante* 1843: the year of . . . *M'Naghten*" (Perlin, 1985, p. 862).

The IDRA changed the burden of proof in insanity trials from the government to defendants (18 U.S.C. § 17), established strict procedures for the hospitalization and release of defendants found not guilty by reason of insanity (18 U.S.C. § 4243 *et seq.*, 1988), and severely limited the scope of expert testimony in federal insanity cases (Federal Rules of Evidence 704(b)). It also discarded the Model Penal Code test applied in almost all federal judicial districts (Perlin, 1989, pp. 300–303) and adopted a more restrictive version of *M'Naghten*, by specifying that the level of mental disease or defect that must be shown to qualify be "severe" (18 U.S.C. § 17(a), 1988).

Two-thirds of the states quickly followed the federal government's lead by reevaluating their laws, but not, in all cases, with the same ultimate results. Twelve states adopted the GBMI test, seven narrowed the substantive test, sixteen shifted the burden of proof, and twenty-five tightened release provisions in the cases of defendants found to be NGRI. Three states adopted legislation that purported to abolish the defense but actually retained a *mens rea* exception. That is, if defendants were so *severely* impaired that they thought, for instance, that they were squeezing a lemon rather than strangling a person, they would be exculpated (Callahan, Mayer, & Steadman, 1987; Perlin, 1989, pp. 404–406; Steadman, 1993). All this had the ultimate effect of returning the law to "do its punitive worst," so that it had "the rigidity of an army cot and the flexibility of a Procrustean bed," retained the flavor "of the celebrated concepts of Hale and

Coke of the 17th century," and was, simply, "bad psychiatry and bad law" (English, 1988, p. 47; Sadoff, 1986, p. 20).

The Role of Punishment

Social Role

Courts and legislators have often feared that acceptance of psychodynamic principles, allegedly characterized by the psychiatrist's "peculiar tolerant attitude toward criminal behavior" and perceived urge to "replace the negative pattern of fear and repression which has dominated penology," would wrongly undermine the powerful force of punishment in the criminal justice process (Guttmacher, 1958, pp. 633, 642). This fear is mirrored in President Reagan's campaign rhetoric on behalf of conservative Republican Senate candidates, whom he could count on to support his efforts to appoint "tough" federal judges ("We don't need a bunch of sociology majors on the bench") (Krisberg, 1991, p. 141; Rowland, Songer, & Carp, 1988, p. 194). Although we know that these fears are inaccurate—perhaps even irrational—they help explain, as much as any other source, the incoherence of our insanity defense jurisprudence (Perlin, 1989–1990, 1990; Perlin & Dorfman, 1993).

Criminologists and philosophers have identified at least five major aims of corrections: restraint, general deterrence, individual deterrence, rehabilitation, and "desert" (sometimes referred to as retaliation, retribution, or simply punishment) (Andenaes, 1956, 1971; Rychlak, 1990; Rychlak & Rychlak, 1990). The Supreme Court's decision upholding a first offender's sentence of life imprisonment without parole for a cocaine possession conviction specifically invokes punishment as one of the acceptable correctional rationales (*Harmelin v. Michigan*, 1991, p. 2706).

Punishment was originally needed to "re-move the evil spirit thought to cause an individual to transgress against society" ("The Modern Day Scarlet Letter," 1989, p. 1360). It is also a "ritualistic device" conveying "moral condemnation," inflicting humiliation, and dramatizing evil through a public "degradation ceremony" (Boldt, 1986, p. 1004; Hibbert, 1968, p. 32; "The Modern Day Scarlet Letter," 1989, p. 1360). By nurturing emotions of vengeance, the punishment of criminals "furthers social solidarity and protects against the terrifying anxiety that the forces of good might not triumph against the forces of evil after all" (Diamond, 1973, p. 110). It does this through the context of a trial process that is a "moral parable [with] a religious meaning essential as a public exercise in which the prevailing moral ideals are dramatized and reaffirmed" (Roche, 1958, p. 245). The celebration of "punishment as *punishment*" legitimized the institutional "infliction of suffering" in much the same way as disease was seen as having to be "completely suffered" as a way of ensuring that one's soul would find purification (Pillsbury, 1989, p. 773).

More than mere disapproval, punishment expresses "a kind of vindictive resentment" as a "way of getting back at the criminal" (Feinberg, 1970, pp. 98–100). This may be the reason that "the moment . . . rehabilitative impulses emerge into expressions, the legal system is doomed to encounter contradiction, confusion, and frequent public criticism" (Watson, 1958, p. 226). This symbolic function explains "why even those sophisticated persons who abjure resentment of criminals and look with small favor generally on the penal law are likely to demand that certain kinds of conduct be punished when or if the law lets them go by" (Feinberg, 1970, p. 102).

The standards enforced by such punishment transcend the "rock-bottom prohibitions of the criminal law"; they include "the affirmative standards and ideals of the group with which we wish to identify" (Weihofen, 1967, p. 30). Punishment expresses to other members of the community "its self-image as a society" that places great value on the "preservation of designated interests"

(Sendor, 1986, pp. 1428–1429 n. 208). This expression is all the more pointed when the defendant is enough unlike us that we neither empathize nor sympathize (Perlin, 1989–1990).

Our "Culture of Punishment"

The acceptance of psychodynamic principles is seen as an approach that might temper this societal need for punishment, thus threatening our core social values. These principles seem to reflect some cognitive dissonance or psychological reactance: if some individuals with mental illness are deemed to not be criminally culpable, and if we accept the notion that *some* individuals will receive special treatment from the law by reason of their mental disability, such exemptions can exist *only* where those so selected accurately reflect society's moral judgments that such special treatment is warranted (Brehm & Brehm, 1981; Perlin, 1991). Society's concern that exemptions from responsibility can be granted only when they reflect society's judgment that they are warranted may help to explain why there is increasing support for relaxing the legal protections available to the mentally ill, by making them equally subject to the same "draconian penalties" now generally in good currency (Forer, 1987, p. 187).

This may help explain why so much of our insanity defense debate is obsessively dominated by our fear of defendants faking so as to beat the rap, whereas in reality, research shows that offenders often *deny* mental illness and its symptomatology, even where recognition of the existence of such symptoms might literally save their lives (Grossman & Cavanaugh, 1989; Lewis et al., 1988).

Thus, in analyzing the decision of the legislature in Idaho (an isolated, highly religious state) to reduce the insanity defense to solely a consideration of *mens rea* (Perlin, 1989, pp. 404–406), Geis and Meier (1985, p. 73) have found that the state's residents strongly held the view that *all* human beings ought to take personal responsibility for their behavior. As a result, Idaho residents

concluded that criminal defendants with mental disabilities should not be able to avoid punitive consequences of criminal acts by reliance on either a "real *or* faked plea of insanity," an attitude also endorsed by a member of the Louisiana Supreme Court (*State v. Perry*, 1992, p. 781).

This example may help explain why, despite recidivism of 35% to 65% reported by all prison systems, the public is more incensed at the crimes of insanity acquittees than it is by those of ex-convicts (Rappeport, 1983).

The Role of Externalities

One underlying theme throughout the centuries of insanity defense test formulation has been the question of to what extent *externalities*—empirical research, scientific advances, political confrontations, and teachings of moral philosophers—have had and should have a significant impact on the structuring of the substantive legal formula for responsibility. The empiricist, the scientist, and the moral philosopher all base their arguments on the important but unarticulated premise that fact finders are ready, willing, and able to be rational, fair, and bias-free in their assessment of insanity defense cases, and it is only the absence of a missing link—the additional, irrefutable data as to NGRI demographics, the newest discovery in brain biology, the exact calibration of moral agency in the allocation of responsibility—that stands in the way of a coherent and well-functioning system. Yet there is virtually no evidence that the addition of any or all of these extra factors would make any difference.

Empirical Data and Myths

Deconstructing the Myths

In the wake of the Hinckley verdict, commentators began to examine carefully the myths that had developed about the insanity defense, in an effort to determine the extent "to which this issue has been distorted in the public eye" (Rodriguez, LeWinn, & Perlin, 1983, p. 400). The research shows that (1) the insanity defense opens only a "small window of nonculpability," (2) defendants who successfully use the NGRI plea "do not beat the rap," and, perhaps more important, (3) the "tenacity of these [false] beliefs in the face of contrary data is profound" (Jeffrey, Pasewark, & Bieber, 1988, p. 39; Pogrebin, Regoli, & Perry, 1986, p. 240; Rogers, 1987a, p. 840).

Myth 1: The insanity defense is overused

All empirical analyses have been consistent: the public at large and politicians (especially legislators) grossly overestimate both the frequency and the success rate of the insanity plea, an error which is "undoubtedly . . . abetted" by the media's "bizarre depictions," "distortion[s]," and inaccur[acies]" in portraying individuals with mental illness charged with crimes (Rodriguez, LeWinn, & Perlin, 1983, p. 401). The most recent research reveals, for instance, that the insanity defense is used in only about 1% of all felony cases, and is successful just about one-quarter of the time (Callahan et al., 1991; Steadman, 1993). What is as startling as any other fact unearthed by empiri-cists is the realization that, as recently as 1985, directors of forensic services in only 10 of the 50 states could even provide researchers with baseline information regarding the frequency of the insanity plea and its success, and that officials in 20 states could provide no information whatever about the use of the plea (Pasewark & McGinley, 1985).

Myth 2: Use of the insanity defense is limited to murder cases

In one jurisdiction where the data have been closely studied, contrary to expectations, slightly less than one-third of the successful insanity pleas entered over an eight-year period were reached in cases involving a victim's death (Rodriguez, LeWinn, & Perlin, 1983). Further, individuals who plead insanity in murder cases are no more successful in being found NGRI than persons charged with other crimes (Steadman, Keitner, Braff, & Arvanites, 1983).

Myth 3: There is no risk to the defendant who pleads insanity

Defendants who asserted an insanity defense at trial, and who were ultimately found guilty of their charges, served significantly longer sentences than defendants tried on similar charges who did not assert the insanity defense. The same ratio is found when only insanity defense–homicide cases are considered (Rodri-guez, LeWinn, & Perlin, 1983).

Myth 4: NGRI acquittees are quickly released from custody

Of the entire universe of individuals found NGRI over an eight-year period in one jurisdiction, only 15% had been released from all restraints; 35% remained in full custody, and 47% were under partial court restraint following conditional release (Rodriguez, LeWinn, & Perlin, 1983, p. 403). A comprehensive study of California practice showed that only 1% of insanity acquittees were released following their NGRI verdict and that another 4% were placed on conditional release, the remaining 95% being hospitalized (Steadman, 1993). In other recent research, Stephen Golding and his colleagues discovered, in their study of all persons found NGRI in the Canadian province of British Columbia over a nine-year period, that the average time spent in secure hospitalization or supervision was slightly over nine and a half years (Golding, Eaves, & Kowaz, 1989).

Myth 5: NGRI acquittees spend much less time in custody than do defendants convicted of the same offenses

On the contrary, NGRI acquittees spend almost *double* the amount of time that defendants convicted of similar charges spend in prison settings, and they often face a lifetime of postrelease judicial oversight (Rodriguez, LeWinn, & Perlin, 1983). In California, while the length of confinement for individuals acquitted by reason of insanity on murder charges was less than for those convicted, defendants found NGRI for other violent crimes were confined twice as long as those found guilty of such charges, and those found NGRI for nonviolent crimes were confined for periods over *nine* times as long (Steadman, 1993).

Myth 6: *Criminal defendants who plead insanity are usually faking* This is perhaps the oldest of the insanity defense myths and has bedeviled American jurisprudence since the mid-19th century (Ray, 1853). Of the 141 individuals found NGRI in one jurisdiction over an eight-year period, there was no dispute that 115 were schizophrenic (including 38 of the 46 cases involving a victim's death), and in only 3 cases was the diagnostician unwilling or unable to specify the nature of the patient's mental illness (Rodriguez, LeWinn, & Perlin, 1983). Also, most studies show that a large number of NGRI defendants have significant histories of prior hospitalizations (Hawkins & Pasewark, 1983).

Myth 7: *Most insanity defense trials feature "battles of the experts"* The public's false perception of the circuslike "battle of the experts" is one of the most telling reasons for the legal system's distrust of psychological explanations of human behavior. A dramatic case such as the Hinckley trial thus "reinforced the public's perception that the insanity defense is characterized by battles of experts" who "overwhelm[ ]" the jury, engendering judicial and public skepticism as to the ability of psychiatrists to actually come to reasoned and reasonable judgments in cases involving individuals with mental disabilities charged with crime (Anchor, 1982; "The Right to a Partisan Psychiatric Expert," 1986, p. 721).

The empirical reality is quite different. In a Hawaii survey, there was examiner congruence on insanity in 92% of all cases; in Oregon, prosecutors agreed to insanity verdicts in 80% of all cases (Fukunaga, Pasewark, Hawkins, & Gudeman, 1981; Rogers, Bloom, & Manson, 1984). Most important, these are not recent developments: over 25 years ago, a study of the impact of the *Durham* decision in Washington, D.C., found that between two-thirds and three-quarters of all insanity defense acquittals were uncontested (Acheson, 1963). In short, the empirical evidence refuting this myth has been available to judges, legislators, and scholars since almost a decade *prior* to the adoption of the American Law Institute–Model Penal Code test in *Brawner.*

Myth 8: *Criminal defense attorneys—perhaps inappropriately—employ the insanity defense plea solely to "beat the rap"* Attorneys representing defendants with mental disabilities have been routinely criticized for "seeking refuge" in the insanity defense as a means of technically avoiding a deserved conviction (Kavanagh, 1928, p. 90). The reality is quite different. First, the level of representation afforded to defendants with mental disabilities is frequently substandard (Perlin, 1992b). Second, the few studies that have been done paint an entirely different picture; lawyers also enter an insanity plea to obtain immediate mental health treatment of their client, as a plea-bargaining device to ensure that their client ultimately receives mandatory mental health care, and to avoid malpractice litigation (Pasewark & Craig, 1980). Third, the best available research suggests that jury biases exist relatively independent of lawyer functioning and are generally "not induced by attorneys" (they predate jurors' involvement in the legal system) (Tanford & Tanford, 1988, pp. 48–49).

Myth 9: *Mental health professionals cannot accurately assess insanity at the time of the crime* Through the use of such instruments as the Mental State at the Time of the Offense Screening Evaluation (MSO), the Schedule of Affective Disorders and Schizophrenia (SADS), the Research Diagnostic Criteria (RDC), and the Rogers Criminal Responsibility Assessment Scales (R-CRAS), behaviorists have focused on the provision of standardized and empirically based approaches to criminal responsibility (Rogers & Cavanaugh, 1981; Rogers, Cavanaugh, Seman, & Harris, 1984; Rogers, Seman, & Clark, 1986; Slobogin, Melton, & Showalter, 1984; Spitzer, Endicott, & Robins, 1978). These instruments were designed to translate legal insanity concepts into quantifiable variables that meet the standard of reasonable scientific certainty (Golding & Roesch, 1987).

In a series of studies, R-CRAS has been validated for the American Law Institute–Model Penal Code standard, and for the *M'Naghten* rules and GBMI as well (Rogers, 1987b; Rogers & Cavanaugh, 1981; Rogers, Dolmetsch, & Cavanaugh, 1981; Rogers, Seman, & Wasyliw, 1983; Rogers, Wasyliw, & Cavanaugh, 1984). The instrument revealed that malingering was not associated in criminal defendants either with severe psychopathology or with expert opinion regarding sanity (Rogers, Dolmetsch, & Cavanaugh, 1981; Rogers, Gillis, & Bagby, 1990). These tools remain, however, virtually irrelevant both to the policy debate over the future of the insanity defense and to the substantive and procedural contours of the defense itself (English, 1988).

We have known for 150 years of the depths of insanity defense mythology. Over the past 15 years, researchers and other scholars have been patiently rebutting these myths (Steadman, 1993). The recent publication by Henry Steadman and his colleagues of their extended multijurisdiction study of virtually every empirical facet of insanity defense pleading proves—beyond *any* doubt— that the basic tenets are mythic. The extent to which the dissemination of this data alters the terms of the insanity defense debate will reveal whether these myths, in fact, can be reinterpreted by lawmakers and the general public (Perlin, 1993a).

The Significance of Scientific Evidence

It might be assumed that, as our database of the etiology, epidemiology, pathology, and physiology of mental disability increases, our construct of mental responsibility becomes increasingly more sophisticated, especially in light of the attention legal commentators have recently paid to the scientific method and its implications for the law. Of course, no such thing has happened. Development of insanity defense jurisprudence has proceeded with extreme indifference to new scientific discoveries. If anything, the retrenchment of the cognitive-only test as reflected in the *M'Naghten* rules and the even more restrictive IDRA may have reflected a conscious decision on the part of politicians to ignore Freud's revo-

lution and its aftermath. In short, where science does appear to inform us of ways the criminal justice system is operating unfairly, we choose to reject it rather than to confront the underlying issues raised.

The Abolitionist Movement

The Contemporary Revival

Although the movement to abolish the insanity defense dates to the turn of the century (Perlin, 1989, pp. 314–317), its contemporary revival can be traced to the Nixon Administration's unsuccessful attempts to "gut the [insanity] defense" by limiting it to cases where the defendant, by mental disease or defect, "lacked the state of mind required as an element of the offense charged" (Wales, 1976, p. 687). This proposed limitation has been characterized as the "lemon squeezer" exception: the defense would apply only where the defendant thought the strangulation victim's head was a lemon (American Law Institute, 1956, p. 156).

President Nixon had charged that this limitation was necessary so as to end the "unconscionable abuse" to which the defense had been subjected by unscrupulous defendants (Perlin, 1979, p. 1889). Although the source of this charge has never been made clear, there has been informed speculation that it flowed from press accounts of the case of one Garrett Trapnell, who allegedly boasted that he had successfully conned the defense (Gerber, 1984). If so, it is but one additional instance of the way that the fear-of-faking myth and the solitary vivid case have combined to impede a rational insanity discourse (Perlin, 1989–1990).

The intellectual vacuity among politically motivated abolitionists (Halpern, 1991, 1993; Perlin, 1990) is illuminated by the striking lack of interest shown in the empirical data in jurisdictions where abolition has been attempted. The *mens rea* (criminal intent) reduction in Montana, Idaho, and Utah should provide an ideal opportunity for emulating the laboratory conditions envisioned by Justice Brandeis when he dissented in *New State Ice Co. v. Liebmann* (1932, p. 311). (That is, this experiment should provide empirical data by which legislators in other jurisdictions should be able to assess the real-life impact of such abolition.) It is ironic that so little attention has been paid to the experiences in the *mens rea* states, especially since there has been some evidence that, as a result of the new legislation, there may be "more claims of mental disturbance" rather than fewer (Keilitz, 1987, p. 305).

Actual Results of Abolition

On the other hand, some useful data are emerging (Steadman, 1993). This research reveals that, basically, abolition in Montana was a pretext (Perlin, 1993b). First, abolition had no meaningful statistical impact on the number of defendants pleading NGRI. Defendants continued to allege that they lacked the requisite *mens rea* for criminal responsibility (Steadman, 1993). Second, defendants who previously would have been found NGRI are now found incompetent to stand trial. Two-thirds of these were subsequently committed indefinitely to state hospitals, where they were frequently treated on the same units as patients who had been found NGRI prior to abolition reform. In short, "the insanity statutes were reformed, but the detention system was not" (Steadman, 1993, pp. 220–222). Some of the postabolition pleas may have been the result of defense counsel wanting to emphasize to the court that the defendants had a serious mental illness and were in need of psychiatric hospitalization. This is precisely the same strategy often employed by counsel in jurisdictions where the defense has not been abolished.

If the Montana experience is representative, the full measure of the abolition charade is clear. The defense is abolished in name only. Criminal defendants with severe mental illness are treated in the same wards of the same forensic hospitals to which they would have been sent had they been found NGRI. This suggests the deceptiveness of much of the politically based abolition move-

ment: voters are being told that their representatives are doing something about the crime problem, but only the labels describing the patients' forensic status change. In short, the abolition movement is a textbook example of the way that insanity defense mythology and opportunistic politicians have helped corrupt our jurisprudence. Empiricism, science, and philosophy are subverted; old shibboleths are repeated, and little changes.

Conclusion

It is impossible to understand the current state of insanity defense jurisprudence without reflecting on the links between mental illness and sin, criminal law, and theology, and the impact of medievalism on our conscious and unconscious social attitudes. Despite the development of psychology and psychiatry, we have regularly rejected psychodynamic explanations for behavior because such explanations were cognitively dissonant with our need to punish: we choose to reinterpret information and experience that conflicts with our internally accepted beliefs to avoid the unpleasant state that such inconsistency produces (Perlin, 1991). As a result, our jurisprudence has developed out of subjective consciousness.

The development of the insanity defense has tracked the tension between psychodynamics and punishment, and reflects our most profound ambivalence about both. On the one hand, we are especially punitive toward those with mental disabilities, "the most despised and feared group in society" (Scott, Zonana, & Getz, 1989, p. 982). On the other hand, we recognize that in some narrow and carefully circumscribed circumstances, exculpation is—and historically has been—proper and necessary. This ambivalence infects a host of criminal justice policy issues that involve mentally disabled criminal defendants beyond insanity defense decision making: on issues of expert testimony, mental disability as a mitigating or aggravating factor at sentencing and in death penalty cases, and the creation of a compromise GBMI verdict.

The post-Hinckley debate revealed the fragility of our insanity defense policies and demonstrated that there was simply not enough "tensile strength" in the criminal justice system to withstand the public furor (Wexler, 1985, p. 537) that followed the jury verdict. In spite of doctrinal changes and judicial glosses, the public remains wed to the wild beast test of 1724 (Roberts, Golding, & Fincham, 1987). It should thus be no surprise that, when Congress chose to replace the American Law Institute–Model Penal Code insanity test with a stricter version of *M'Naghten,* insanity defense supporters saw that decision as a victory (Milner, 1984).

These dissonances, tensions, and ambivalences—again, rooted in medieval thought—continue to control the public's psyche. They reflect the extent of the gap between academic discourse and social values, and the "deeply rooted moral and religious tension" that surrounds responsibility decision making (Golding, 1990). Ours is a culture of punishment. Only when we acknowledge that psychic and physical reality can we expect to make sense of the underlying jurisprudence.

References

18 U.S.C. § 4243 *et seq.* (1988).

Acheson, D. (1963). *McDonald v. United States:* The *Durham* rule redefined. *Georgetown Law Journal, 51,* 580–591.

American Law Institute. (1956). Comments to *Model Penal Code* § 4.01. Philadelphia: Author.

Anchor, K. (1982). Expert witness testimony in the John Hinckley trial. *American Journal of Trial Advocacy, 6,* 153–162.

Andenaes, J. (1956). Determinism and criminal law. *Journal of Criminal Law, Criminology, and Police Science, 47,* 406–413.

Andenaes, J. (1971). The moral or educative influence of criminal law. *Journal of Social Issues, 27*(2), 17–31.

Boldt, R. (1986). Restitution, criminal law, and the ideology of individuality. *Journal of Criminal Law and Criminology, 77,* 969–1022.

Brehm, S., & Brehm, J. (1981). *Psychological reactance: A theory of freedom and control.* New York: Academic Press.

Callahan, L., Mayer, C., & Steadman, H. (1987). Insanity defense reform in the United States—Post-Hinckley. *Mental and Physical Disability Law Reporter, 11,* 54–59.

Callahan, L., Steadman, H., McGreevy, M., & Robbins, P. (1991). The volume and characteristics of insanity defense pleas: An eight-state study. *Bulletin of the American Academy of Psychiatry and Law, 19,* 331–338.

Caplan, L. (1984). *The insanity defense and trial of John W. Hinckley, Jr.* Boston: Godine.

Diamond, B. (1961). Criminal responsibility of the mentally ill. *Stanford Law Review, 14,* 59–86.

Diamond, B. (1962). From *M'Naghten* to *Currens* and beyond. *California Law Review, 50,* 189–205.

Diamond, B. (1973). From *Durham* to *Brawner:* A futile journey. *Washington University Law Quarterly, 1973,* 109–154.

Dix, G. (1986). Criminal responsibility and mental impairment in American criminal law: Responses to the Hinckley acquittal in historical perspective. In D. Weisstub (Ed.), *Law and mental health: International perspectives* (pp. 1–44). New York: Pergamon Press.

Durham v. United States, 214 F.2d 862 (D.C. Cir. 1954), *overruled in* United States v. Brawner, 471 F.2d 969 (D.C. Cir. 1972).

Eigen, J. P. (1984). Historical developments in psychiatric forensic evidence: The British experience. *International Journal of Law and Psychiatry, 6,* 423–429.

English, J. (1988). The light between twilight and

dusk: Federal criminal law and the volitional insanity defense. *Hastings Law Journal, 40,* 1–52.

Eule, J. (1978). The presumption of sanity: Bursting the bubble. *University of California at Los Angeles Law Review, 25,* 637–699.

Federal Rules of Evidence 704(b).

Feinberg, J. (1970). *Doing and deserving: Essays in the theory of responsibility.* Princeton, NJ: Princeton University Press.

Forer, L. (1987). Law and the unreasonable person. *Emory Law Journal, 36,* 181–201.

Frigillana v. United States, 307 F.2d 665 (D.C. Cir. 1962).

Fukunaga, K. K., Pasewark, R. A., Hawkins, M., & Gudeman, H. (1981). Insanity plea: Interexaminer agreement in concordance of psychiatric opinion and court verdict. *Law and Human Behavior, 5,* 325–328.

Garber, H. J. (1988). Use of magnetic resonance imaging in psychiatry. *American Journal of Psychiatry, 145,* 164–171.

Geis, G., & Meier, R. F. (1985). Abolition of the insanity plea in Idaho: A case study. *Annals, 477,* 72.

Gerber, R. (1984). The insanity defense revisited. *Arizona State Law Journal, 1984,* 83–127.

Golding, S. (1990). Mental health professionals and the courts: The ethics of expertise. *International Journal of Law and Psychiatry, 13,* 281–307.

Golding, S., Eaves, D., & Kowaz, A. (1989). The assessment, treatment, and community outcome of insanity acquittees. *International Journal of Law and Psychiatry, 12,* 149–179.

Goldstein, A. (1967). *The insanity defense.* New Haven, CT: Yale University Press.

Grossman, L., & Cavanaugh, J. (1989). Do sex offenders minimize psychiatric symptoms? *Journal of Forensic Sciences, 34,* 881–886.

Guttmacher, M. (1958). The psychiatric approach to crime and correction. *Law and Contemporary Problems, 23,* 633–649.

Halpern, A. L. (1991). The insanity defense in the 21st century. *International Journal of*

Offender Therapy and Comparative Criminology, 35, 187–189.

Halpern, A. L. (1993). The insanity verdict, the psychopath, and post-acquittal confinement. *Pacific Law Journal, 24,* 1125–1164.

Harmelin v. Michigan, 111 S. Ct. 2680, 2706 (1991) (Kennedy, J., concurring in part & concurring in judgment).

Hawkins, M. R., & Pasewark, R. A. (1983). Characteristics of persons utilizing the insanity plea. *Psychological Reports, 53,* 191–195.

Hermann, D., & Sor, Y. (1983). Convicting or confining? Alternative directions in insanity law reform: Guilty but mentally ill versus new rules for release of insanity acquittees. *Brigham Young University Law Review, 1983,* 499–638.

Hibbert, C. (1968). *The roots of evil: A social history of crime and punishment.* Boston: Little, Brown.

Hovenkamp, H. (1981). Insanity and responsibility in progressive America. *North Dakota Law Review, 57,* 541–575.

Insanity Defense Reform Act, 18 U.S.C. § 17 (1988).

Insanity defense: Should the shock of the *Hayes* verdict compel North Carolina to fix what "ain't broke"? [Comment]. (1990). *Wake Forest Law Review, 25,* 547–589.

Jeffrey, R. W., Pasewark, R. S., & Bieber, S. (1988). Insanity plea: Predicting not guilty by reason of insanity adjudications. *Bulletin of the American Academy of Psychiatry and Law, 16,* 35–39.

Johnson v. State, 439 A.2d 542 (Md. 1982).

Kaplan, L., & Rinella, V. (1988). Jurisprudence and the appropriation of the psychoanalytic: A study in ideology and power. *International Journal of Law and Psychiatry, 11,* 215–248.

Kavanagh, M. (1928). *The criminal and his allies.* Indianapolis, IN: Bobbs-Merrill.

Keilitz, I. (1987). Researching and reforming the insanity defense. *Rutgers Law Review, 39,* 289–322.

Krisberg, B. (1991). Are you now or have you ever been a sociologist? *Journal of Criminal Law and Criminology, 82,* 141–155.

LaFave, W., & Scott, A. (1986). *Substantive criminal law.* St. Paul, MN: West.

Lewinstein, S. (1969). The historical development of insanity as a defense in criminal actions, Part I. *Journal of Forensic Sciences, 14,* 275–293.

Lewis, D., Pincus, J., Bond, B., Richardson, E., Pitcher, L., Feldman, M., & Yeager, C. (1988). Neuropsychiatric, psychoeducational, and family characteristics of 14 juveniles condemned to death in the United States. *American Journal of Psychiatry, 145,* 584–589.

Livermore, J., & Meehl, P. (1967). The virtues of *M'Naghten. Minnesota Law Review, 51,* 789–856.

M'Naghten's Case, 8 Eng. Rep. 718 (1843).

McDonald v. United States, 312 F.2d 847 (D.C. Cir. 1962).

McGraw, B., Farthing-Capowich, D., & Keilitz, I. (1985). The "guilty but mentally ill" plea and verdict: Current state of the knowledge. *Villanova Law Review, 30,* 117–191.

Mickenberg, I. (1987). A pleasant surprise: The guilty but mentally ill verdict has succeeded in its own right and successfully preserved the insanity defense. *University of Cincinnati Law Review, 55,* 943–996.

Milner, N. (1984). What's old and new about the insanity plea. *Judicature, 67,* 499–509.

Model Penal Code (1955 Tent. Draft No. 4), § 4.01.

The modern day scarlet letter: A critical analysis of modern probation conditions [Note]. (1989). *Duke Law Journal, 1989,* 1357–1385.

Moore, M. (1984). *Law and psychiatry: Rethinking the relationship.* New York: Cambridge University Press.

Moran, R. (1981). *Knowing right from wrong: The insanity defense of Daniel McNaughtan.* New York: Free Press.

New State Ice Co. v. Liebmann, 285 U.S. 262 (1932) (Brandeis, J., dissenting).

Pasewark, R., & Craig, P. (1980). Insanity plea: Defense attorneys' view. *Journal of Psychiatry and Law, 8,* 413–441.

Pasewark, R., & McGinley, H. (1985). Insanity plea: National survey of frequency and success. *Journal of Psychiatry and Law, 13,* 101–108.

People v. McQuillan, 221 N.W.2d 569 (Mich. 1974).

People v. Seefeld, 290 N.W.2d 123 (Mich. App. 1980).

People v. Smith, 465 N.E.2d 101 (Ill. App. 1984).

Perlin, M. L. (1979). Overview of rights in the criminal process. In P. Friedman (Ed.), *Legal rights of mentally disabled persons* (Vol. 3, pp. 1879–1897). New York: Practicing Law Institute.

Perlin, M. L. (1985). "The things we do for love": John Hinckley's trial and the future of the insanity defense in the federal courts [Book review]. *New York Law School Law Review, 30,* 857–875.

Perlin, M. L. (1987). The Supreme Court, the mentally disabled criminal defendant, and symbolic values: Random decisions, hidden rationales, or "doctrinal abyss"? *Arizona Law Review, 29,* 1–98.

Perlin, M. L. (1989). *Mental disability law: Civil and criminal.* Charlottesville, VA: Michie.

Perlin, M. L. (1989–1990). Unpacking the myths: The symbolism mythology of insanity defense jurisprudence. *Case Western Reserve Law Review, 40,* 599–731.

Perlin, M. L. (1990). Psychodynamics and the insanity defense: "Ordinary common sense" and heuristic reasoning. *Nebraska Law Review, 69,* 3–70.

Perlin, M. L. (1991). Morality and pretextuality, psychiatry and law: Of "ordinary common sense," heuristic reasoning, and cognitive dissonance. *Bulletin of the American Academy of Psychiatry and Law, 19,* 131–150.

Perlin, M. L. (1992a). Fatal assumption: A critical evaluation of the role of counsel in mental disability cases. *Law and Human Behavior, 16*, 39–59.

Perlin, M. L. (1992b). On "sanism." *Southern Methodist University Law Review, 46*, 373–407.

Perlin, M. L. (1993a). Back to the past: Why mental disability law "reforms" don't reform [Book review]. *Criminal Law Forum, 4*, 403–412.

Perlin, M. L. (1993b). Pretexts and mental disability law: The case of competency. *University of Miami Law Review, 47*, 625–688.

Perlin, M. L., & Dorfman, D. A. (1993). Sanism, social science, and the development of mental disability law jurisprudence. *Behavioral Sciences and the Law, 11*, 47–66.

Pillsbury, S. (1989). Understanding penal reform: The dynamics of change. *Journal of Criminal Law and Criminology, 80*, 726–780.

Platt, A., & Diamond, B. (1966). The origins of the "right and wrong" test of criminal responsibility and its subsequent development in the United States: An historical survey. *California Law Review, 54*, 1227–1260.

Pogrebin, M., Regoli, R., & Perry, K. (1986). Not guilty by reason of insanity: A research note. *International Journal of Law and Psychiatry, 8*, 237–241.

Rappeport, J. R. (1983). The insanity plea scapegoating the mentally ill—much ado about nothing. *South Texas Law Journal, 24*, 686–704.

Ray, I. (1853). *Medical jurisprudence of insanity* (3rd ed.). Boston: Little, Brown.

Regina v. Oxford, 9 Carr. & P. 525 (1840).

Rex v. Arnold, 16 How. St. Tr. 695 (1724), reprinted in *A complete collection of state trials* (T. B. Howell ed. 1812).

The right to a partisan psychiatric expert: Might indigency preclude insanity? [Note]. (1986). *New York University Law Review, 61*, 703–707.

Roberts, C. F., Golding, S. L., & Fincham, F. D. (1987). Implicit theories of criminal responsibility decision making and the insanity defense. *Law and Human Behavior, 11*, 202–232.

Roche, P. (1958). *The criminal mind.* Westport, CT: Greenwood Press.

Rodriguez, J. H., LeWinn, L. M., & Perlin, M. L. (1983). The insanity defense under siege: Legislative assaults and legal rejoinders. *Rutgers Law Journal, 14*, 397–430.

Rogers, J. L., Bloom, J. D., & Manson, S. M. (1984). Insanity defense: Contested or conceded? *American Journal of Psychiatry, 141*, 885–888.

Rogers, R. (1987a). APA's position on the insanity defense: Empiricism versus emotionalism. *American Psychologist, 42*, 840–848.

Rogers, R. (1987b). Assessment of criminal responsibility: Empirical advances and unanswered questions. *Journal of Psychiatry and Law, 15*, 73–82.

Rogers, R., & Cavanaugh, J. (1981). Application of the SADS diagnostic interview to forensic psychiatry. *Journal of Psychiatry and Law, 9*, 329–344.

Rogers, R., Cavanaugh, J., Seman, W., & Harris, M. (1984). Legal outcome and clinical findings: A study of insanity evaluations. *Bulletin of the American Academy of Psychiatry and Law, 12*, 75–83.

Rogers, R., Dolmetsch, R., & Cavanaugh, J. (1981). An empirical approach to insanity evaluations. *Journal of Clinical Psychology, 37*, 683–687.

Rogers, R., Gillis, J. R., & Bagby, R. M. (1990). The SIRS as a measure of malingering: A validation study with a correctional sample. *Behavioral Sciences and the Law, 8*, 85–92.

Rogers, R., Seman, W., & Clark, C. R. (1986). Assessment of criminal responsibility: Initial validation of the R-CRAS with the M'Naghten and GBMI standards. *International Journal of Law and Psychiatry, 9*, 67–75.

Rogers, R., Seman, W., & Wasyliw, O. (1983). The R-CRAS and legal insanity: A cross validation study. *Journal of Clinical Psychology, 39*, 554–559.

Rogers, R., Wasyliw, O., & Cavanaugh, J. (1984). Evaluating insanity: A study of construct validity. *Law and Human Behavior, 8*, 293–303.

Romanucci-Ross, L., & Tancredi, L. (1986). Psychiatry, the law, and cultural determinants of behavior. *International Journal of Law and Psychiatry, 9*, 265–293.

Roth, L. (1986–87). Preserve but limit the insanity defense. *Psychiatric Quarterly, 58*, 91–105.

Rowland, C. K., Songer, D., & Carp, R. A. (1988). Presidential effects on criminal justice policy in the lower federal courts: The Reagan judges. *Law and Society Review, 22*, 191–300.

Rychlak, R. J. (1990). Society's right to punish: A further exploration of the denunciation theory of punishment. *Tulane Law Review, 65*, 299–338.

Rychlak, R. J., & Rychlak, J. F. (1990). The insanity defense and the question of human agency. *New Ideas in Psychology, 8*, 3–4.

Sadoff, R. L. (1986, September). *Insanity: Evolution of a medicolegal concept.* Paper presented at College Night, the College of Physicians of Philadelphia.

Schulhofer, S. (1974). Harm and punishment: A critique of emphasis on the results of conduct in the criminal law. *University of Pennsylvania Law Review, 122*, 1497–1607.

The scientific model in law [Note]. (1987). *Georgetown Law Journal, 75*, 1968–2003.

Scott, D. C., Zonana, H. V., & Getz, M. A. (1989). Monitoring insanity acquittees: Connecticut's Psychiatric Review Board. *Hospital and Community Psychiatry, 41*, 980–984.

Sendor, B. (1986). Crime as communication: An interpretative theory of the insanity defense and the mental elements of crime. *Georgetown Law Journal, 74*, 1371–1434.

Slobogin, C. (1985). The guilty but mentally ill verdict: An idea whose time should not have come. *George Washington Law Review, 53*, 494–527.

Slobogin, C., Melton, G., & Showalter, C. (1984). The feasibility of a brief evaluation of mental state at the time of the offense. *Law and Human Behavior, 8*, 305–320.

Spitzer, R. L., Endicott, J., & Robins, E. (1978). Research diagnostic criteria: Rationale and reliability. *Archives of General Psychiatry, 35*, 773–782.

State v. Perry, 610 So.2d 746 (La. 1992) (Cole, J., dissenting).

Steadman, H. (1993). Reforming the insanity *defense: An evaluation of pre- and post-Hinckley reforms.* New York: Guilford.

Steadman, H., Keitner, L., Braff, J., & Arvanites, T. (1983). Factors associated with a successful insanity plea. *American Journal of Psychiatry, 140*, 401–405.

Tancredi, L., & Volkow, N. (1988). Neural substrates of violent behavior: Implications for law and public policy. *International Journal of Law and Psychiatry, 11*, 13–49.

Tanford, J., & Tanford, S. (1988). Better trials through science: A defense of psychologist-lawyer collaboration. *North Carolina Law Review, 66*, 741–780.

United States v. Brawner, 471 F.2d 969 (D.C. Cir. 1972).

United States v. Lyons, 739 F.2d 994 (5th Cir. 1984) (Rubin, J., dissenting).

U. S. Congress, Senate Committee on the Judiciary. (1982). *Insanity defense hearings.* 97th Cong., 2d sess.

van den Haag, E. (1975). *Punishing criminals.* New York: Basic Books.

Virgin Islands v. Fredericks, 578 F.2d 927, 936–37 (3rd Cir. 1978) (Adams, C. J., dissenting).

Wales, H. (1976). An analysis of the proposal to "abolish" the insanity defense in S.1: Squeezing a lemon. *University of Pennsylvania Law Review, 124*, 687–712.

Watson, A. (1958). A critique of the legal approach to crime and correction. *Law and Contemporary Problems, 23*, 611–632.

Weihofen, H. (1967). Capacity to appreciate "wrongfulness" or "criminality" under the A.L.I.–Model Penal Code test of mental responsibility. *Journal of Criminal Law, Criminology, and Police Science, 58,* 27–31.

Weiner, B. (1980). Not guilty by reason of insanity—A sane approach. *Chicago-Kent Law Review, 56,* 1057–1085.

Weiner, B. (1985). Mental disability and criminal law. In S. Brakel, J. Parry, & B. Weiner (Eds.), *The mentally disabled and the law* (pp. 693–801). Chicago: American Bar Foundation Press.

Wexler, D. (1985). Redefining the insanity problem. *George Washington Law Review, 53,* 528– 561.

17 ■ Dangerousness as a Criterion in the Criminal Process

Christopher Slobogin
University of Florida

As used in the law, *dangerousness* usually refers to a person's propensity to commit antisocial behavior and involves more than a prediction about whether such behavior will occur (see Schopp & Quattrocchi, 1994). So defined, the dangerousness criterion permeates the criminal process. After first detailing this point, I analyze whether and when dangerousness is a legitimate consideration in the criminal context and how it should be conceptualized and predicted. The positions advanced in this chapter are different from those normally found in the literature. Most scholarship appears to accept dangerousness as a valid legal criterion but questions whether we can implement it in practice. The argument explored here, in contrast, is that dangerousness should not be grounds for intervention in many of the contexts it currently is grounds for intervention; and when it is a legitimate legal criterion, deciding who meets it is not as significant a problem as much of the literature would lead us to believe.

When Dangerousness Could Be Relevant

In theory, a prediction that a person will commit an antisocial act could be relevant at virtually any stage of the criminal process. This part of the chapter describes, for each stage, the extent to which the law has recognized its relevance in each stage of the process. Although many of the interventions identified here typically do not involve people with a serious mental disorder, understanding the scope of each intervention is helpful for comparison when exploring the impact of the law of dangerousness on mental health care.

During the earliest stage of the criminal process—the investigative phase—police frequently treat individuals whom they perceive to be dangerous differently from other suspects. Far from penalizing these practices, the courts have facilitated them by relaxing many of the usual constitutional limitations on police investigative conduct. For instance, under the Fifth Amendment to the U.S. Constitution, the courts usually require that *Miranda* warnings be given before any custodial interrogation (*Miranda v. Arizona,* 1966); however, the U.S. Supreme Court created a "public safety" exception to this rule for cases when the warnings might silence a suspect who knows the location of a weapon (*New York v. Quarles,* 1984). Similarly, under the Fourth Amendment, the courts usually require that police obtain a warrant before they enter a person's home (*Payton v. New York,* 1980); but courts have long permitted warrantless entries when police are in hot pursuit of a dangerous suspect (*Warden v. Hayden,* 1967). Finally, dangerousness assessments have led to a relaxation of Fourth Amendment rules regarding the degree of certainty police must have before they search or seize an individual. Until 1968, the U.S. Supreme Court required that the police have probable cause—

that is, a more-likely-than-not belief—that a person they seized or a place they searched was involved in criminal activity. In *Terry v. Ohio* (1968), however, the court decided that police can "stop and frisk" an individual in the absence of probable cause as long as they have "reasonable suspicion" that "criminal activity is afoot" and that the person confronted "may be armed and presently dangerous." The *Terry* Court sanctioned reliance on the more easily met reasonable suspicion standard after balancing society's interest in crime prevention against the relatively limited intrusion represented by a brief stop and a limited patdown. Although *Terry* itself has found widespread acceptance, its balancing test has since been applied to authorize more questionable police actions on less than probable cause (and, in some instances, on less than reasonable suspicion), including searches of a schoolchild's purse and a public employee's desk, seizures of illegal immigrants and drunk drivers at roadblocks, and drug testing of railway workers involved in accidents and safety violations (Slobogin, 1991, pp. 43–46).

Once an arrest has been made, a judge or magistrate decides either to release the individual on personal recognizance or bail or to detain the individual pending trial. Here again dangerousness assessments may have a significant impact; a prediction that the arrestee will engage in criminal conduct if released is more likely to lead to continued confinement or particularly strict bail conditions. For some time, judicial decisions indicated that ensuring appearance for trial was the only constitutionally acceptable criterion for evaluating pretrial release (*Stack v. Boyle*, 1951). But in practice, judges and magistrates often consider the dangerousness of an arrestee when setting bail (Mitchell, 1969). By the 1980s, several jurisdictions had explicitly authorized consideration of dangerousness in making the bail decision (see, for example, Bail Reform Act, 1984). Finally, in *United States v. Salerno* (1987), the U.S. Supreme Court made clear that dangerousness *is* a constitutionally permissible basis for pretrial detention, when it upheld a provision in the federal Bail Reform Act of 1984 permitting pretrial detention of an accused criminal to "reasonably assure . . . the safety of any other person and the community" (p. 741). In rejecting the argument that the act violated the Fifth Amendment's due process clause because it deprived arrestees of liberty prior to conviction, the Court emphasized that the pretrial detention was "regulatory" rather than "punitive" in intent. It also noted that "[t]he government's interest in preventing crime by arrestees is both legitimate and compelling," that the act "operates only on individuals who have been arrested for a specific category of extremely serious offenses," that the prosecutor must show "[i]n a full-blown adversarial hearing . . . by clear and convincing evidence that no conditions of release can reasonably assure the safety of the community or any person," and that the "maximum length of pretrial detention is limited by the stringent time limitations of the Speedy Trial Act" (pp. 749–751).

At or near the time the detention decision is being made, the prosecutor is determining the formal charge against the defendant. Research on charging decisions indicates that dangerousness assessments play a role here as well, although—in contrast to the bail determination—that role remains largely implicit. For instance, when surveyed, federal prosecutors did not list dangerousness or lack of it as a reason for prosecuting or declining to prosecute (Frase, 1980, pp. 261–266). But they did state that the decision to charge is heavily influenced by the nature of the offense and moderately influenced by the prior record of the defendant, both possible proxies for dangerousness (see also Miller, 1969, pp. 287–292). A related prosecutorial decision—the selection of a suspect for inclusion in a pretrial "diversion" program, successful completion of which results in dismissal of charges—seems to be even more clearly affected by a person's perceived risk to the community (Zimring, 1974, pp. 238–239). Although the Supreme Court has yet to address whether dangerousness may be used as a criterion in these types of decisions, it would likely be receptive to the practice, given its general willingness to give the prosecutor's charging determination wide latitude. As it stated in *Bordenkircher v. Hayes* (1978), "so long as the prosecutor has probable cause to believe that the accused committed an offense defined by statute, the decision whether or not to prosecute, and what charge to file or bring before a grand jury, generally rests entirely in his discretion."

Sometime after charging, the formal discovery process begins. Here again dangerousness may be an issue: in particular, the prosecution may want to withhold the identity of witnesses who it fears may be intimidated or harassed by the defendant or the defendant's colleagues. Rather than engage in an individualized assessment of this danger, many jurisdictions simply prohibit witness depositions by the defense (see, for example, Federal Rules of Criminal Procedure 15(a)); disclosure of other prosecution witness identities and statements is not required until the witness has testified at trial (see, for instance, Bail Reform Act of 1984, § 3500). Because in its supervisory capacity over the federal courts the U.S. Supreme Court has been responsible for the promulgation of rules of this type, it is not likely to declare them unconstitutional.

During the adjudication process, a defendant's potential danger to others is not normally a consideration. The issue to be decided by the judge or jury is whether the accused committed a particular crime, not whether he or she might commit a crime in the future.[1] Indeed, the rules of evidence specifically prohibit injecting issues of propensity into the adjudication process unless the defendant decides to present character evidence, and then only as a way of determining whether the defendant committed the *past* act with which he or she is charged (see, for example,

Federal Rules of Evidence 404(a)). This rule is founded on the idea, developed further in the next section of this chapter, that people are deserving of punishment only for what they have done, not for what they might do. It must be noted, though, that there is one way, albeit rare, in which a form of dangerousness assessment can affect the trial process. In *Illinois v. Allen* (1970), the Supreme Court held that a defendant may be removed from the courtroom despite the Sixth Amendment right to confront accusers if, after being warned, the defendant continues to act "in a manner so disorderly, disruptive, and disrespectful of the court that his trial cannot be carried on with him in the courtroom."

It is during the dispositional stage that dangerousness predictions have played the most significant role. Although modern sentencing jurisprudence tends to favor a backward-looking "just-deserts" orientation and thus rejects incapacitation as a sentencing consideration (Melton, Poythress, Petrila, & Slobogin, 1987, pp. 172–177), in many jurisdictions assessments of dangerousness (and the related issue of the offender's rehabilitative potential) continue to influence the degree of punishment meted out. Most dramatically, in approximately eight states, a prediction of dangerousness can spell the difference between life imprisonment and execution for those convicted of capital murder (Bonnie, 1980). An even greater number of states provide for "special track" sentencing, which permits indeterminate confinement of special groups of offenders (for example, those convicted of sex offenses) for as long as they are considered dangerous (American Bar Association, 1989, pp. 459–460). Finally, in connection with regular noncapital sentencing, judges in states that have not adopted the just-deserts model continue to enhance sentences, within the range permitted by the legislature, on the basis of their beliefs about the offender's violence proneness (Diamond, 1983; Morris, 1974, pp. 62–63). Parole boards similarly have routinely considered dangerousness in deciding whether to grant early release to a sentenced offender (Dawson, 1969, pp. 263–278).

---

[1]Of course, some crimes, like conspiracy or attempt, may implicitly be based on dangerousness. Although not developed in this chapter, an argument can be made, derived from the ideas discussed in the next section, that such actions should be criminalized only on retributive grounds. In this view, attempt and conspiracy should be punishable only if what has already happened is culpable, not because of something that may occur in the future.

All these practices appear to be constitutional. The Supreme Court has held that dangerousness predictions may form the basis for the death penalty as long as "the [sentencing] jury ha[s] before it all possible relevant information about the individual defendant whose fate it must determine" (*Jurek v. Texas*, 1976). The Court has also rejected the claim that enhanced sentences beyond the normal term for dangerous sex offenders violate the Fourteenth Amendment's equal protection clause (*Minnesota ex rel. Pearson v. Probate Court*, 1940). Many lower courts have upheld these special track schemes against due process and Eighth Amendment cruel and unusual punishment claims as well, although most temper their holdings by requiring that the offender receive treatment, or at least treatment reviews, during incarceration (*People v. Feagley*, 1975; *State v. Little*, 1978). Presumably, in light of these decisions, the use of dangerousness predictions in regular sentencing proceedings and in connection with parole is also permissible. Moreover, the Court has refused to place any evidentiary limitations, beyond a relevance requirement, on the type of dangerousness testimony that sentencing bodies may consider (*Barefoot v. Estelle*, 1983). The only significant restrictions the Court has imposed in this area have been procedural. Sentencing proceedings traditionally have been very informal, but in the death penalty context, the Court has required procedures akin to a trial (see *Bullington v. Missouri*, 1981). And in *Specht v. Patterson* (1967) the Court held that, because the finding of dangerousness under special track sentencing laws raises a "distinct issue" involving "the making of a new charge leading to criminal punishment," the offender sentenced under such a statute is entitled to counsel as well as to the rights to be heard, to confront witnesses, and to offer evidence.

Two other types of dispositions make use of the dangerousness criterion. The first is the indeterminate commitment of persons who have been acquitted by reason of insanity. In every state, such commitment is predicated on a finding that the person is mentally disordered and dangerous, a practice the Supreme Court has condoned (*Jones v. United States*, 1983). The Court has also held, however, that such commitment may not be based on dangerousness *alone* (*Foucha v. Louisiana*, 1992), a decision that will receive detailed analysis later in this chapter.

A final type of disposition involves transfer of a convicted offender from prison to a mental hospital. Although most states simply provide that such transfer may occur when a prisoner needs "treatment that cannot be provided in the prison" (Favole, 1983), those transferred under such statutes frequently are those who are violent or disruptive due to mental illness (Dell, 1980). Thus, dangerousness is, at the least, an implicit consideration in these transfer determinations. The Supreme Court has (apparently) sanctioned transfers based on dangerousness but has also imposed procedural requirements (that is, notice, a hearing with an independent decision maker, and the opportunity to present evidence and confront accusers), given the heightened stigma and the coerced treatment that accompanies relocation to a hospital (*Vitek v. Jones*, 1980).

The foregoing should have made clear both the criminal system's extensive reliance on the dangerousness criterion and the courts' reluctance to upset this practice. The remainder of this chapter investigates the wisdom of the courts' position.

When Dangerousness Should Be Relevant

Protecting innocent members of society from dangerous individuals should be a prominent goal of any government. Nonetheless, the use of dangerousness as a legal criterion can be attacked on two grounds. First, one can argue that, as a conceptual matter, dangerousness should not be considered a justification for the particular intervention at issue. Second, one can concede that dangerousness is a legitimate consideration in a given context but also contend that it cannot be predicted with sufficient accuracy to allow government intervention. I address the first contention in this section and the second argument in the next section.

Conceptual Arguments against Dangerousness as a Legal Criterion

Assume that we can know, beyond a reasonable doubt, that John will commit a violent act against another person within the next year if he is not confined in a jail or prison. Is there any reason to refrain from confining him? One reason might be that, because we are not *positive* that he will commit the act, we cannot incarcerate John. But this type of argument does not concern the relevance of dangerousness as a legal criterion, only its inevitable uncertainty, an issue addressed in the next section. For present purposes, we are assuming, as indicated above, that John's confinement will last only so long as we are able to show beyond a reasonable doubt that it is necessary to prevent him from harming another person. That level of certainty is all we require to confine someone for commission of past acts (*In re Winship*, 1970). On what ground can we require an even greater showing when the government intervention is based on a prediction rather than a reconstructive judgment?

The only potentially persuasive ground would seem to be this: confinement under such circumstances would undermine the tenet of free will that underlies the criminal justice system (and most of Western civilization). When we deprive John of liberty based not on what he has done but rather on a prediction of what he will do—even if the prediction is likely to be accurate—we are treating him as an automaton or an inanimate object. We are in effect asserting that John does not possess the "willpower," or the capacity to choose, necessary to refrain from acting violently. Institutionalizing this decision would violate our notion of what it means to be human. As Packer (1968) eloquently put it:

It is important, especially for a society that likes to describe itself as "free" and "open," that a government should be empowered to coerce people only for what they do and not for what they are. . . . Now, this self-denying ordinance can be and often is attacked as being inconsistent with the facts of human nature. People may in fact have little if any greater capacity to control their conduct . . . than their emotions or their thoughts. It is therefore unrealistic or hypocritical, so the argument runs, to deal with conduct as willed or to treat it differently from personality and character. This attack is, however, misconceived. . . . The idea of free will in relation to conduct is not, in the legal system, a statement of fact, but rather a value preference having very little to do with the metaphysics of determinism and free will. . . . (pp. 74–75)

But, one might respond, cannot a prediction that John will hurt another simply mean we believe he will *choose*, of his own free will, to act in that way? The distinction between acting as if a person can choose to commit a violent act and predicting that he cannot do otherwise is an important one. However, when the state intervention consists of prolonged confinement, thus depriving John of any opportunity to exercise his will in the right direction, the effect, if not the intent, is to assert that he cannot choose that course; it thus "coerces" him "for what [he is]." By way of comparison, prolonged confinement after a conviction for a past act reaffirms the free will paradigm, because it occurs only after a person has chosen to act (Schoeman, 1979).

This last statement suggests another way of reconciling the dangerousness criterion with the free will paradigm. The argument might be made as follows. Dangerous people like John know—or can be told if they do not know—that unless they remain confined and undergo whatever treatment is available, they pose a substantial risk to others. Assuming so, if they choose instead to walk the streets, they are, in the words of the Model Penal Code's "reckless endangerment" provision, "recklessly engag[ing] in conduct which places or may place another person in danger of death or serious bodily injury" (American Law Institute, 1962, § 211.2). This rationale for the dangerousness criterion, so the argument would go, focuses not on the "status" of the individual but on his or her culpability for failing to do something about it. It would allow continued incarceration even if the punishment for such a crime is minimal, because the state could reconvict as reckless any "dangerous" person who wanted to leave prison.

Although seductive, this analysis is also flawed. Admittedly, many types of "inchoate" crimes can be justified on grounds analogous to reckless endangerment. Consider, for instance, persons involved in an attempt to commit crime, a conspiracy, or speeding. In each of these cases, the individual has chosen to engage in particular conduct that, if he or she knows or should know of its dangerousness, is justifiably punished. In contrast, incarcerating John because he declines to surrender "voluntarily" despite knowledge of his dangerousness undermines the free will paradigm because his refusal is not a choice of any *specific* dangerous behavior. Rather it is merely a decision to exist in a certain place (outside of prison). The effect of confining him for making that type of decision would again be tantamount to punishing him for being himself.[2]

For those who prefer instrumental reasoning, one can identify two distinct harms that might result from locking up people on the basis of predicted status rather than acts they have committed. First, this type of intervention will harm the confined individual in a way that is counterproductive for society. A fundamental assertion of those who endorse "therapeutic jurisprudence," for instance, is that, when possible, people should be treated as capable of choice so

as to facilitate their rehabilitation. As Winick (1994) says, "[a] variety of studies show that allowing individuals to make choices is intrinsically motivational, while denying choice 'undermines motivation, learning, and . . . well-being'" (pp. 108–109). In another article, Winick (in press) relies on the same research in asserting:

People who think they lack the capacity to control their harmful conduct because of an internal deficit that seems unchangeable predictably will develop expectations of failure. As a result, they may not even attempt to exercise self-control, or may do so without any serious commitment to succeed.

On this view, confinement of John for something he has not yet done could convince him that he is "incorrigible" and that further antisocial behavior is inevitable. At the same time, such confinement could easily lessen his respect for the system, an attitude that has been found to correlate positively with recidivism (Zamble & Porporino, 1990, p. 59).

The second harm such confinement could bring is essentially the harm Winick identifies applied to society as a whole. To the extent people believe they can be confined for what they are rather than for what they have done, the moral tone of society is undermined. Although this point can be inferred from Packer's comments, it is even more concretely made by Robinson (1993), who has argued that confinement of "blameless" individuals can directly affect societal allegiance to the law. On the basis of empirical studies (see, for example, Grasmick & Green, 1980; Tyler, 1990), he asserts that "most people obey the law, not because they fear the pain of criminal sanction, but because they want to do what is right." But a society "that imposes criminal liability on persons that the community regards as not sufficiently blameworthy risks destroying this motive to adhere to the laws [and] becoming a society in which the only motive not to commit criminal conduct is to avoid being caught and punished" (pp. 707–708). In a more recent piece, Robinson (1994) states the point even more bluntly: By "shifting to a system of pure social control, which

---

[2]A question to the issue would be raised if John rejects treatment (such as medication) that he knows can curb his dangerous tendencies and has begun exhibiting symptoms known to him to presage violence (for example, threats to family members). Because not he is choosing to engage in threatening behavior that he knows will get worse, punishing such an individual under a reckless endangerment type of statute may not be inconsistent with the freewill paradigm (although the incapacity exception would often apply in such situations in any event) (Wexler, 1990).

sentences according to dangerousness rather than desert, the system loses its ability to claim that offenders deserve the sentence they get [and thus] dilutes its ability to induce personal shame and to instigate social condemnation" (p. 44). Confinement of people like John for something they have not yet done may be perceived as undeserved arbitrary punishment; this in turn could lead potential criminals to conclude that they may as well commit crime (as they will be confined anyway if the state becomes aware of them) and could demoralize other members of the public (because doing "what's right" does not immunize them from government intervention). If so, such confinement could not only undermine John's incentive to be law abiding and to respect the commands of the criminal law but also diminish the incentive of others.[3]

In short, the use of dangerousness as a criterion for long-term state intervention can be challenged on a deontological ground (the belief in free will) and on two instrumental grounds derived from the free will paradigm: the self-fulfilling prophecy and societal disobedience hypotheses. The responses to these arguments are numerous, and the instrumental reasons are admittedly based on speculation. They may lose further force when, as is usually the case, the person confined as dangerous has already committed a violent act sometime in the past: both the individual and society may view confinement as "deserved" even if the act occurred long ago and the present confinement is explicitly based solely on dangerousness. More important, even if the harms identified above are real, most would probably conclude that they do not outweigh the harm caused by a "dangerous" person who is released. In the face of such a conclusion, rigid allegiance to the deontologically based free will premise is also difficult.

The (tentative) claim made here, however, is that the free will premise is worth taking seriously and that the harms Winick and Robinson allude to are plausible phenomena. The accumulated impact of these harms could result in greater danger to others than that posed by release of dangerous individuals if inappropriate reliance on the dangerousness criterion becomes widespread. At the same time, accepting the conclusion that this criterion violates the free will premise does not mean that all state intervention based on it should be prohibited. Indeed, it follows that intervention that does *not* undermine that premise is justifiable. Two broad sets of circumstances might fall into this latter category: (1) when the state intervention does not significantly denigrate a person's ability to choose, and (2) when the person does not possess an ability to choose. Because the first exception is linked to the effect of the state intervention, it can be called the *effect exception*. Because the second exception is associated with the incapacity of the person subjected to the intervention, I will call it the *incapacity exception*.

The Effect Exception

The scope of the effect exception depends on such factors as the nature and the duration of the state intervention. All the state actions described in the first section of this chapter, to the extent that they are based on dangerousness predictions, might undermine the presumption that the affected person is a free agent. But it is also plausible to argue that some state actions do so only to a trivial extent. For instance, consider a stop and frisk of a "suspicious" individual, a decision to withhold witness names from a defendant charged with a serious crime, or a court order barring a disruptive defendant from the courtroom. Because these are relatively unintrusive interventions and of short duration, they do not significantly denigrate the free will paradigm. They do not impose, or even appear to impose, the "moral condemnation" of which Robinson speaks or announce to the affected individuals,

---

[3]Robinson himself is willing to ascribe these consequences only to *conviction* of a blameless person. On the other hand, he does not believe that *commitment* of such a person undermines allegiance to the law. This chapter takes the view that, as far as society is concerned, the difference between the two is too subtle to be noticed.

in the way Winick contemplates, that they are passive victims of forces they can neither understand nor control. In short, they do not signal that the affected individuals lack ability to refrain from antisocial activity.

In contrast, a sentence of imprisonment based in whole or in part on a prediction of dangerousness has all these effects and to a nontrivial degree. Because it occurs after conviction, a sentence is directly associated with moral condemnation and the determination that the person is culpable; thus, to the extent that it is based instead on a dangerousness assessment, it undermines the credibility of the criminal justice system in the manner Robinson indicates. More important, its prolonged duration and confining nature exert significantly greater control over a person's life than do stops, discovery rules, and sequestration orders, thus suggesting much more dramatically that the person has no such control. This message clearly undermines the free will paradigm and may also have the antitherapeutic effects posited by Winick (at least the latter hypothesis is worth testing empirically). For these reasons, capital, special track, and regular sentencing based on dangerousness predictions are suspect manifestations of state power, even assuming the predictions are accurate. So too is the charging decision to the extent that it is based on such predictions, because it initiates the process of moral condemnation implemented by sentencing.

A utilitarian caveat to these conclusions might be registered with respect to regular sentencing and charging, however. As I suggested in the previous section, the Supreme Court's probable rationale for holding that a charging decision may incorporate dangerousness is that any charge for which there is probable cause is justifiable. A similar analysis might permit any sentence within the range determined by just-deserts principles (Monahan, 1982; Morris & Miller, 1985, pp. 35–37). According to this view, use of dangerousness as a criterion in these contexts is "harmless error" because it merely allows exercise of discretion within limits set by other,

legitimate criteria. By itself, this reasoning does not overcome the type of argument made here: if a prosecutor differentiates between two suspects who have committed the same crime on dangerousness grounds, then the free will paradigm has been violated in the same way that a sentence enhancement based on dangerousness undermines that paradigm even though it falls within the legislative range. At the same time, precisely because prosecutors and sentencing judges have so much discretion, society and the defendant may not be *aware* that dangerousness is being considered in determining the charge or sentence. If so, then the instrumental reasons for prohibiting this practice suggested by Winick and Robinson, which depend on such awareness, disappear.

Note, however, that to the extent that this analysis is valid, it affects only the charging decision and regular sentencing. Capital and special track sentencing of the type described in the previous section remain unjustifiable even on instrumental grounds, because they cannot avoid making explicit their reliance on predictions of violence.

The practice of basing pretrial release decisions on dangerousness is more difficult to evaluate. Like a sentence of imprisonment, preventive pretrial confinement is much more global in effect than the types of state interventions discussed at the beginning of this section. Furthermore, as with capital and special track sentencing, the fact that the confinement is based on an assessment of dangerousness will often be evident. On the other hand, if pretrial detention is not perceived as "punishment," as the Supreme Court asserted in *Salerno*, then it avoids Robinson's problem. Because the confinement resulting from a pretrial release decision is of limited and determinate duration and occurs *prior* to conviction, as the Court noted, there is some strength to this conclusion.

The same conclusion cannot be reached with respect to criminal commitment, however. The Supreme Court's decision in *Jones* goes well beyond *Salerno* by upholding *prolonged, indeterminate, posttrial* confinement for persons found not guilty by reason of insanity. Echoing *Salerno*, the Court's principle reason for its ruling was that the purpose of such commitment is not punitive, but rather incapacitative and rehabilitative. Although not an inaccurate statement about the purported reasons for such commitment, this characterization ignores reality. As the lower court opinion in *Jones* concluded, such commitment, although premised on an "acquittal" rather than a conviction, is at least "partially punitive": it occurs not just for medical reasons but "because society is unwilling to allow those who have committed crimes to escape without paying for their crime" (*Jones v. United States*, 1983, p. 381). Others have suggested that, given the involuntary nature of the confinement, both society and the committed individual are likely to view the confinement as condemnatory in nature (Note, 1981b, p. 618; Note, 1982, pp. 287–288). Further indication of the public's mindset comes from efforts to replace the "not guilty" label with a "guilty except for insanity" verdict (see, for example, *Or. Rev. Stat.* § 161.295). In any event, whether or not the punitive label should be affixed to criminal commitment, the fact that the associated confinement exerts a tremendous degree of control over the person's autonomy alone warrants the conclusion that it has significant potential for undermining the free will paradigm.

Thus, whatever its application to pretrial detention, the effect exception does not encompass criminal commitment. Nor should it apply to prison transfers based on a prediction of dangerousness because there, too, prolonged confinement results purely from that prediction. However, both types of state intervention may implicate the second exception to the general rule that dangerousness should not be used as a legal criterion—the incapacity exception.

The Incapacity Exception

The fact that a particular state intervention undermines the free will paradigm should not matter if the intervention affects only those without free will; telling these people they are not in control

of their lives harms neither the individual nor society because it is palpably true. This assumption is the premise of the incapacity exception and is the justification frequently given for both civil and criminal commitment (Morse, 1982, pp. 64–65; Note, 1974, p. 1230). The difficulty, of course, is in first defining when a person is lacking free will and then linking that condition to violence proneness. These are large subjects that are discussed primarily in Chapters 16 (on the insanity defense) and 18 (on civil commitment). However, a few observations about these topics will be made here.

The first observation concerns the relationship between the incapacity exception and the insanity defense (and other excuse doctrines, such as the duress and automatism defenses, which are based on lack of volitional conduct). The insanity defense is meant to identify individuals who, because of the type of people they are, cannot be considered responsible for past criminal actions. The incapacity exception is meant to encompass precisely the same people but in connection with their future actions. Thus, if a person is found insane at the time of the offense and that condition persists or is likely to recur if involuntary confinement is not imposed, then commitment would be permissible under the incapacity exception if it is based on a prediction that the condition causes violent behavior. In contrast, a mere finding that a person is "mentally ill" or "mentally abnormal"—the language usually found in criminal commitment statutes—is insufficient justification for a finding of incapacity. The existence of some type of mental dysfunction is only the beginning of the inquiry under the incapacity exception.

As to the precise type of dysfunction that suggests the absence of free will, only some broad notions can be outlined here. As recognized in the *M'Naghten* test and subsequent formulations of the insanity defense (see generally, Melton et al., 1987, § 6.02), a person who does not understand that he or she is committing criminal acts (as is often the case with those suffering from psychosis) is lacking free will and should qualify for the incapacity exception. Similarly, a person whose actions are truly "involuntary" because there is no link between mind and body (as during seizures) fits the exception (Melton et al., 1987, § 6.03). More difficult to evaluate are the much more prevalent situations in which the individual appears to be cognitively and volitionally intact enough to know what he or she is doing and is able to control it physiologically, in the minimal way described above, but commits apparently random antisocial acts (for example, the "psychopath" who sexually assaults strangers or who kills for exceedingly trivial reasons). Analogous to a duress defense, to the extent that individuals can be said to be compelled to act *against* their will (as might be true with some "sex psychopaths"), free will may be absent. Analogous to the automatism defense, to the extent that the individual's reasons for acting are so insubstantial that they could apply in any situation and thus make the act literally "unthinking" (as might be the case with the casual killer described above), free will may also be absent. Indeed, even less virulent forms of psychopathy could be associated with a lack of free will; as Stephen Morse (1994) has noted, "the psychopath lacks attributes that give people perhaps the best reasons not to harm others . . . [and thus] seems 'morally insane,' unable successfully to reason practically about moral issues, to include moral concerns among his reasons for action" (p. 1636).[4] Again, the goal—which turns out to be very difficult to achieve—is to identify people so lacking in the ability to choose or control their dangerous behavior that we can feel comfortable confining them for what they are (see generally, Slobogin, 1985).

---

[4]In contrast to the terminology used in this chapter, however, Morse (1994) eschews "freewill" terminology. To him, "[t]he will and free will are not legal criteria, and agents in the criminal justice system would do well to dispense with employing them in responsibility analysis and attribution" (p. 1559). Although I do not disagree with the first part of this statement, I continue to use the phrase because it captures the essence of the way laypeople think of control over their lives; as argued earlier, that is one of the instrumental reasons for disfavoring broad use of the dangerousness criterion.

But when the incapacity exception, however defined, is not met, dangerousness-based commitment should not be permitted, regardless of how dangerous an individual may seem. This conclusion not only flows from the premise of this chapter but also may be the holding of the Supreme Court's decision in *Foucha*, briefly mentioned in the first section. In that case, an individual who had been committed after his acquittal by reason of insanity challenged his continued confinement on the ground that, although dangerous, he was no longer "mentally ill" (the hospital staff diagnosed him as a sociopath). Without deciding whether sociopathy is a mental illness (and thus avoiding the difficult issue described above), four members of the Court concluded that Louisiana could not hold an acquittee purely on the basis of a dangerousness prediction. They distinguished this case from *Salerno* by noting that the detention in the latter case "was strictly limited in duration." Permitting the confinement sought by Louisiana, on the other hand, "would . . . be only a step away from substituting confinements for dangerousness for our present system which, with only narrow exceptions and aside from permissible confinements for mental illness, incarcerates only those who are proved beyond reasonable doubt to have violated a criminal law" (*Foucha v. Louisiana*, 1992, p. 83).

However, there is some difficulty with concluding that *Foucha* recognizes only the effect and incapacity exceptions endorsed in this chapter, because the fifth vote for the majority came from Justice O'Connor, who wrote a separate concurring opinion. She agreed that Louisiana's objective in *Foucha* was unconstitutional but stated that because acquittees have usually been found, beyond a reasonable doubt, to have committed an offense "with the required level of criminal intent," it might be permissible to confine a dangerous but sane acquittee "if, unlike the situation in this case, the nature and duration of detention were tailored to reflect pressing public safety concerns related to the acquittee's continuing dangerousness" (p. 87). She then suggested that if there were some "medical justification" for doing so, continued confinement of acquittees, at least those charged with serious crimes, would be constitutional. In short, Justice O'Connor's opinion seemed to condone indeterminate confinement of a sane acquittee if the acquittee is dangerous and the dangerousness is *treatable*. Recall from the previous section of this chapter that similar reasoning has led some lower courts to uphold special track sentencing beyond the normal term for the offense charged.

The insult to the free will paradigm produced by indeterminate confinement of dangerous people who do not meet the incapacity exception does not disappear simply because their dangerousness is treatable. Such confinement is coercion of people—who are, by definition, capable of exercising free will—for what they are and are predicted to be rather than for what they have done; thus from a deontological perspective, such confinement cannot be countenanced. One might argue that, at least from an instrumental perspective, a treatment disposition does not undermine the free will paradigm in the same way a strict dangerousness disposition does, because neither society nor the individual is likely to view it as "punishment." Furthermore, if treatment is directed at making the individual take responsibility for his or her actions (Winick, 1991a, p. 70), Winick's concern about exacerbating fatalism could be curtailed. In reality, however, the involuntary confinement that occurs based on a prediction of treatability is not very different than confinement based on a prediction of dangerousness (see *Allen v. Illinois*, 1986; Burt, 1979; Durham & La Fond, 1988; Note, 1982). Indeed, the former prediction may lead to even greater infringement on a person's autonomy and sense of self-worth (Rothman, 1973, pp. 21–24).

In short, treatment or treatability in the absence of a finding of incapacity is no more a justification for prolonged confinement than is dangerousness.[5] On the other hand, treatment *is* an entitlement of those who are justifiably confined. This conclusion stems from the least-

drastic-means doctrine, first developed in First Amendment cases as a limitation on the exercise of government power (see Chambers, 1972). Under this doctrine, when a dangerous person is legitimately confined under the incapacity (or effect) exception, the state is required to reach its goal in the least drastic manner possible. Meeting this requirement means that treatment must be provided if doing so will render the person less dangerous and thus shorten the confinement (see Spece, 1978, pp. 34–35).

Note also the therapeutic effect of this approach to treatment considerations. Current special track and commitment statutes, to the extent that they are based on reasoning like Justice O'Connor's, tell dangerous people that they will be confined so long as they are "treatable." Some commentators suggest that this message reduces the incentive to appear treatable or even to undergo treatment prior to a commitment or periodic review hearing (see Klotz, Wexler, Sales, & Becker, 1993, p. 594). The approach proposed above, on the other hand, tells dangerous people that they will be confined only if they remain lacking in free will, which increases their incentive to obtain treatment to eliminate the dysfunction before the hearing. Treatment becomes not an end in itself but the means to an end, which is likely to make it more attractive to detainees.[6]

Summary: The Washington Sexual Predator Statute

In this part of the chapter, I have argued that if a person is dangerous due to a lack of free will,

---

[5]However, if the state proves the person lacks capacity to make a treatment decision, intervention for treatment purposes may be permissible under the *parens patriae* authority of the state (that is, the power of the state to stand in the shoes of the parent) (Note, 1974, pp. 216–217).

[6]It might be argued that creating this type of "incentive" to undergo treatment makes it involuntary and thus *less* likely to succeed (Morris, 1974, pp. 12–27). But such an incentive is better seen as "positive reinforcement" rather than as coercion (Winick, 1991b), and is certainly preferable to the disincentive to seek treatment mentioned in the text.

the state may infringe on his or her liberty until the condition disappears (the incapacity exception). If dangerousness is not due to the absence of free will, the permissibility of state intervention based on that ground depends on its intrusiveness and duration, the extent to which it smacks of moral condemnation or punishment, and the extent to which it is explicitly based on a dangerousness prediction (the effect exception).

Using these criteria, we can look at a statute that has occasioned much comment in recent years, the Washington Sexual Predator Statute. This statute is different from most laws discussed to this point in that it permits indeterminate commitment of dangerous persons—in this case, persons convicted of serious sex offenses who have served their sentence—*without* any showing that they have a serious mental disorder or are treatable (*Wash. Rev. Code* § 71.09.010, 1994). Nonetheless, in *In re Young* (1993), the Washington Supreme Court upheld the constitutionality of the statute. *Young* distinguished *Foucha* by noting that, in the latter case, the U.S. Supreme Court assumed for purposes of its decision that Foucha was not mentally ill, whereas the Washington statute requires proof that the dangerousness comes from a "personality disorder" or a "mental abnormality" (the latter defined as a "congenital or acquired condition affecting the emotional or volitional capacity which predisposes the person to the commission of criminal sexual acts"). Although persons confined under the statute are not required to be treatable (thus seemingly undermining an O'Connor-type argument in its favor), the Washington Court further held that as long as confinement occurs under conditions "compatible" with treatment and not identical to conditions in prison, due process is not violated (see *Allen v. Illinois*, 1986).

Under the analysis proposed in this chapter, however, the Washington statute fails. Admittedly, for reasons made clear above, the fact that it permits commitment of untreatable individuals would not invalidate it. As long as either the effect or incapacity exception is met, the state may intervene against a dangerous person; treatment is necessary only to the extent that it can shorten the intervention. On the other hand, neither exception appears to apply to this statute. The potential lifetime commitment under the statute clearly disqualifies it for the effect exception. And since the act merely requires proof of a "predisposition" to commit sexual acts, with no further requirement that the "mental abnormality" disable a person from controlling his or her behavior,[7] it is not valid under the incapacity exception either.

Of course, if one does not accept the analysis proposed in this part of the chapter, the Washington statute is harder to fault, even if it does result in prolonged confinement of those who seem capable of controlling their actions. If one rejects the free will premise, or believes that using dangerousness as a legal criterion does not undermine it, or is convinced that the harm in undermining the premise is outweighed by the harm to society that can be prevented by locking up dangerous individuals, then there is no theoretical ground for invalidating statutes like the sexual predator law. But the Washington statute and other interventions that rely on dangerousness predictions can still be challenged on the practical ground that we lack the ability to predict individual violence. It is to this topic that we now turn.

---

[7]Compare a similar statute in Minnesota, which has been judicially construed to cover only "those persons who, by a habitual course of misconduct in sexual matters, have evidenced an utter lack of power to control their sexual impulses" (*State ex rel. Pearson v. Probate Court*, 1939, p. 273), and which has also recently been upheld against a constitutional challenge in *In re Blodgett* (1994). It is possible that, "as applied," the Washington statute is unobjectionable. According to the Office of the Attorney General of Washington (1992, pp. 871–877), only 9 people, all of whom had extensive records of sexual crime, were committed under the statute in its first 20 months of operation. Prosecutors *may* be singling out sex offenders who experience uncontrollable urges and who thus may come under the incapacity exception.

What Is Dangerousness?

To facilitate analysis of when dangerousness might be a legitimate legal criterion, we have assumed that we can prove beyond a reasonable doubt whether a person will harm someone in the future. Left undiscussed to this point is the possibility that we cannot prove dangerousness with this degree of certainty. If we cannot, should the state be prevented from intervening even when the effect or incapacity exception is met? Answering this question requires consideration of several issues: the state of the prediction art, the substantive definition of dangerousness, and the evidentiary and procedural rules that should be followed in assessing a person's dangerousness.

The State of the Art

Until recently, the "common wisdom" about the accuracy of "expert" dangerousness predictions, accepted even by a traditionalist Supreme Court (*Barefoot v. Estelle*, 1983), was that only one out of every three such predictions are correct. Worse yet, this ratio, which came from Monahan's summary of research conducted in the 1970s (Monahan, 1981), described the accuracy of assessments of populations with high base rates for violence, meaning that the predictions of dangerousness in those studies had a much better chance of turning out right than did predictions involving more ordinary populations. In only one of the state interventions discussed in the first section—special track sentencing—do the relevant state statutes normally explicitly identify a group with a high base rate for violence. The other types of interventions focus on the general population of those convicted, charged, or suspected of crime, for which the base rate for violence may be appreciably lower. The "old generation" of research, then, indicated that the state would have difficulty showing that violent behavior is even probable, much less that it would occur beyond a reasonable doubt.

But the accepted wisdom is being challenged. Although Monahan's summary of the older studies suggested an accuracy rate of no better than 33%, more recent research on prediction by mental health professionals has produced accuracy rates close to or somewhat above 50% (Klassen & O'Connor, 1988; Lidz, Mulvey, & Gardner, 1993; McNiel & Binder, 1991; Otto, 1992; Sepejak, Menzies, Webster, & Jensen, 1983). Most of this new research focuses on short-term predictions of dangerousness rather than on the long-term predictions involved in criminal commitment and sentencing. But this fact, if it makes any difference, is likely to underestimate prediction accuracy compared to studies with a longer follow-up period.

There are two possible reasons for this increase in accuracy rates. The first and least important is the improvement in predictive "science." Behavioral scientists have become more aware of the factors associated with violence. Indeed, there is increasing recognition that "actuarial" prediction, based on factors shown to correlate statistically with violence (for example, number of violent acts, age, gender, diagnosis), can supplement "clinical" prediction based on a more amorphous behavioral analysis (Monahan, 1981, pp. 85–90). However, the advent of this "hybrid" approach probably does not explain most of the increase in accuracy found in the newer research. As Poythress (1992, p. 144) has stated, "to date only the promise, and not the practicality [of this approach], has been delivered" (but see Harris, Rice, & Quinsey, 1993).

The more significant reason for the lower "false positive" rates found in the newer research is simply the better methodology of the new studies. Much of the older research suffered from at least two major flaws: (1) the studied interventions were based on predictions of dangerousness defined broadly (that is, *any* type of harm to others) but were tested using narrow outcome criteria (indications of violent physical harm), thus underestimating accuracy; and (2) the studies often relied on deficient outcome data, such as arrest records, which underreported the amount of violent activity by a significant margin (Brooks, 1993, pp. 740–749; Monahan, 1981). The newer studies have largely avoided these two problems by carefully defining dangerousness and by relying on self-reports and other outcome variables, thus helping to obtain better accuracy rates.

In short, improvements in predictive science and research methodology suggest that predictions of dangerousness can exceed the 33% accuracy rate once thought unsurpassable. At the same time, the available data indicate that such predictions may still be inaccurate as much as 40% or 50% of the time. How should the law respond to this conclusion?

A Contextual Definition of Dangerousness

The most obvious way of addressing the preceding question requires determining the appropriate level or "standard" of proof the state must meet before it may base an intervention on dangerousness. Historically, the law has recognized three primary standards of proof: beyond a reasonable doubt, clear and convincing evidence, and preponderance of the evidence. Although this approach is somewhat arbitrary, one might characterize the reasonable doubt standard as demanding a level of certainty over 95%; whereas the preponderance ("more-likely-than-not") standard can be quantified at the 51% level; and the clear and convincing standard would fall somewhere in between, at a 70% to 80% level of certainty (see Stone, 1975).

Obviously, if the reasonable doubt or clear and convincing rubrics apply to the dangerousness criterion, even the "improved" predictive accuracy reported in recent studies falls short. Although we might occasionally be "certain" that an individual is violence prone, current research suggests that, in the usual case, we cannot be certain enough to meet either of these two standards, and so we are likely to risk an unacceptably large number of false positive decisions. Accordingly, an important first task in assessing the legitimacy of a particular dangerousness-based intervention is determining the appropriate standard of proof for that intervention.

We can begin tackling the standard-of-proof issue with the Supreme Court's observations on the subject. According to the Court's decision in *Addington v. Texas* (1979), the standard of proof "serves to allocate the risk of error between the litigants and to indicate the relative importance attached to the ultimate decision" (p. 423). When litigation involves "a monetary dispute between private parties . . . society has a minimal concern with the outcome," and thus the preponderance standard, in which "[t]he litigants . . . share the risk of error in roughly equal fashion" is appropriate (p. 423). In contrast, "[i]n a criminal case . . . the interests of the defendant are of such magnitude that historically . . . they have been protected by standards of proof designed to exclude as nearly as possible the likelihood of an erroneous judgment" (p. 423). Finally, the clear and convincing standard has been assigned to cases where "[t]he interests at stake . . . are deemed to be more substantial than mere loss of money," but not as substantial as the punishment that accompanies criminal conviction (p. 423).

Addington itself dealt with the standard of proof at civil commitment proceedings, concluding that the state must prove its case—including the element of dangerousness—by clear and convincing evidence. The Court rejected the preponderance standard in this context primarily because the consequence of commitment is loss of liberty, as it is in criminal cases. But the Court rejected the reasonable doubt standard as well, for several reasons: (1) given the layers of professional review in the commitment process, erroneous commitments are more likely to be corrected; (2) given the treatment goals of commitment, the negative consequences of commitment are not as significant as those associated with conviction; and (3) the issues in the civil commitment hearing—mental illness and dangerousness—are more difficult to prove than those in a criminal case.

If *Addington* is correct, one might conclude

that criminal commitment (that is, hospitalization of insanity acquittees) should also require clear and convincing evidence of dangerousness, given the similarity between civil and criminal commitment in the three areas noted above. But in *Jones v. United States* (1983), the Court permitted, for a minimum of 50 days, *automatic* commitment of a person acquitted by reason of insanity, at least when the acquittee's trial establishes insanity by a preponderance of the evidence and the commission of a criminal act beyond a reasonable doubt. The Court reasoned that, because this type of trial proves both that the person was mentally ill and committed a dangerous act, mental illness and dangerousness can be assumed after the trial; therefore *no* further proof is necessary to justify commitment. The Court did not directly address the proper standard of proof at any subsequent review hearing but seemed to have no problem with a District of Columbia statute that adopted the preponderance standard (Ellis, 1986, p. 972).

The Court has addressed the standard of proof in only one of the other situations discussed earlier. As noted before, the Court has permitted stops and frisks and some other types of investigative techniques when there exists a reasonable suspicion of dangerousness (a "standard of proof" that is even lower than the preponderance-of-the-evidence test). The Court has yet to address specifically the proof of dangerousness required to implement the "public safety" exception to *Miranda*; the warrant exception based on dangerousness; pretrial preventive detection schemes; prosecutorial charging decisions; discovery provisions; the "*Allen* rule" allowing removal of disruptive defendants; or sentencing, parole, and prison transfers. Lower courts and legislatures have typically filled in the gaps only in connection with pretrial detention, special track sentencing, and capital sentencing (leaving the standard of dangerousness required for other interventions up to the decision maker). With respect to pretrial detention, the law has usually required clear and convincing evidence of dangerousness (see, for example, *United States v. Townsend,* 1990). In special track sentencing, the Court has adopted

either the reasonable doubt or clear and convincing standard, sometimes depending on whether the initial hearing or a review hearing is at issue (see, for example, *Ill. Stat.* § 105-3.01 *et seq.*). In capital sentencing, it has usually required proof beyond a reasonable doubt (Dix, 1981).

Addington correctly recognized that determining the standard of proof requires balancing individual and state interests. But whether *Addington* appropriately characterized those interests in the civil commitment context is more open to question. As noted above, the decision minimized the committed individual's interest in avoiding erroneous confinements by noting the possibility of subsequent "correction" and the intervention's treatment orientation. But the Court does not give any reason for believing that subsequent "reviews" will be any more accurate than the initial decision. Moreover, it has recognized in *Vitek* (the prison transfer case) that the stigma and coerced treatment that follow hospitalization may render the latter intervention *more* inimical to individual interests than confinement alone. A more discerning assessment of the individual values at stake would have compared the stigma and coerced treatment concerns, together with the indeterminate nature of commitment, with the stigma and generally longer and more onerous terms of confinement associated with conviction. The *Addington* Court also tried to heighten the state interest by noting the difficulty of proving dangerousness. Again, this reasoning is not so much wrong as it is incomplete. The mere fact that something is difficult to prove does not justify lowering the standard of proof. A more finely tuned argument for such a relaxation of the standard is that the state's interest (prevention of harm by individuals with mental illness) is compelling and that it cannot be achieved without relaxing the standard. Only after more accurately loading the individual and state scales in this way should the Court have attempted the difficult task of deciding which side was heavier and to what extent.

Whether or not *Addington's* rejection of the reasonable doubt standard for civil commitment proceedings is correct, *Jones'* implication that insanity acquittees may be confined on less than clear and convincing evidence is clearly wrong. On the individual side of the balance, criminal commitment is even more like imprisonment, in terms of length and conditions, than is civil commitment (see the summary of research in Melton et al., 1987, § 6.02(a)(3)). Moreover, there is nothing on the state side to counteract this additional infringement of individual interests: the harm to be prevented by criminal commitment appears no greater than the harm the state seeks to prevent with its civil counterpart (Note, 1981a, p. 1079). The Court's assertion (which it used to differentiate civil and criminal commitment) that one can infer dangerousness from conviction of one offense is not supported by the literature (see Monahan, 1981, pp. 71–72). This assertion is especially suspect because, at the time of a criminal commitment hearing, the supposed "cause" of that offense (that is, mental illness) has been treated sufficiently to render the person competent to stand trial. If the clear and convincing standard is constitutionally mandated for civil commitment, it should be required for criminal commitment as well.

Space limitations prevent detailed examination of the proof necessary to justify other types of state interventions. But to give some idea of how the analysis might flow, a brief discussion of the standard that might be required for each type of intervention follows (including sentencing and charging, in case the reader remains unconvinced that these interventions should not be based on dangerousness assessments). If the clear and convincing standard is mandated for criminal commitment, it should also apply to regular sentencing and parole decisions, because the individual consequences of these interventions are as significant and the harm the government is trying to prevent is no greater. And the criminal reasonable doubt standard should apply where the consequences to the individual are even more significant, as is the case with special track and capital sentencing, the charging process, and the *Allen* situation (the latter because the individual

might suffer erroneous conviction, as well as punishment, if not present at trial). On the other hand, the much lower reasonable suspicion standard may be justifiable for stops and frisks because, as *Terry* indicated, the intrusion is relatively minimal and the likelihood is great that requiring probable cause for such police actions would significantly undermine the state's interest in preventing crime. The same lower standard might be applicable in the discovery situation as well, given that the "intervention" at most delays the defendant's ability to prepare for trial.

Perhaps falling somewhere in between is the preventive detention authorized by *Salerno.* Although clearly more onerous than an investigative detention or discovery delay, the consequences of such detention do not compare to those associated with commitment or sentencing. Thus, the clear and convincing proof that many preventive detention statutes require may not be necessary. In further support of this conclusion, note that an arrest (which authorizes detention for the entire period prior to trial when the person cannot make bail) has traditionally been permitted on "probable cause"—a level of certainty that is, at most, no higher than the preponderance-of-the-evidence standard. The same standard might also apply to decisions about prisoner transfers. Although the stigma and coerced treatment concerns identified in *Vitek* are important individual interests to consider, the fact remains that transfer usually does not prolong the duration of confinement (but see Churgin, 1983, p. 220).

If these conclusions about the appropriate standards of proof are accepted, and if we assume further that predictive accuracy is unlikely to be much better than 50%, then proving the requisite degree of dangerousness at commitment and sentencing may be particularly difficult. Some commentators (see, for example, Gordon, 1977; Morris & Miller, 1985, pp. 18–26) have suggested a way out of this conundrum. They argue that dangerousness should be redefined to mean a *probability* of violent behavior, rather than violent behavior per se. With dangerousness so defined, proving dangerousness by clear and convincing evidence, or even beyond a reasonable doubt, would not be difficult. Assuming "probability" is equated with nothing greater than a more-likely-than-not standard, proving a probability (.51) of dangerousness beyond a reasonable doubt (.95) requires only a showing somewhat below the 50% level (.51 × .95) (see Monahan & Wexler, 1978). But this move is a mere sleight of hand to the extent that it is thought to avoid the key issue: whether the state's interest in executing, imprisoning, or committing someone who has only a 50% chance of being violent in the future outweighs the individual's interest in avoiding an erroneous decision. The answer, if one accepts the foregoing analysis, remains no.

Evidentiary and Procedural Considerations

Up to this point, the discussion has suggested that, even if conceptually permissible, certain interventions—specifically, commitment and sentencing—must be prohibited on practical grounds to the extent that they are based on dangerousness predictions. But this conclusion does not necessarily follow. It is possible that, using evidentiary and procedural rules, the law can structure the dangerousness inquiry in such a way that the legally required standard of proof can be met in these two contexts, at least for a narrow subset of individuals. Furthermore, recognizing the possibility of erroneous determinations, the law can use procedure to limit the consequences of a dangerousness prediction.

In terms of structuring the inquiry, the principal step the law can take is to require certain types of proof before a finding of dangerousness can be made. Before describing this proof in more detail, further analysis of the research on predictive accuracy is necessary. Recall from earlier discussion that the older studies of prediction suffered from two flaws that the newer studies have corrected. Unfortunately, a third methodological problem with the earlier research continues to bedevil newer studies as well. For obvious legal and ethical reasons, a prediction of danger-

ousness usually leads to confinement or treatment or both, which presumably suppresses violent behavior. This fact means that virtually any research attempting to assess the accuracy of predictions based on subsequent behavior by the subjects will probably underestimate validity. Bolstering this conjecture are recent epidemiological studies comparing people in the community who have mental disabilities to demographically similar people in the same community without mental disabilities (Link, in press; Swanson, Holzer, Ganju, & Jono, 1990). Contrary to studies that focus on people *in or released from* hospitals and jails, which in general found no difference in violent behavior between the mentally ill and others (Monahan, 1981, pp. 77–82), these studies found that people in the community *currently* suffering from psychoses are three to five times more likely to be violent than those who are not so diagnosed (see Monahan, 1992, p. 517). This latter finding suggests that prediction research that uses behavior in confinement or after treatment as its outcome criterion (as does most prediction research) underreports the "true" dangerousness of the people it studies—at least, those with psychoses. This underestimate, in turn, distorts conclusions concerning the accuracy of predictions about what those people would do if not confined or treated.

Building on this insight, Litwack and Schlesinger (1987) have argued that certain types of predictions *can* meet at least the "clear and convincing" level of proof. In particular, they contend, this level of accuracy can be reached when predictions rely on one of three types of information: (1) "a recent history of repeated violence[8] (absent treatment or evidence of significant changes in the circumstances or attitudes

---

[8]Although Litwack and Schlesinger do not say so, the word *repeated*, as used here, might refer to four or more previous violent acts. Research indicates that, for persons under 30, a person arrested four times has an 80% chance of being arrested a fifth time (Wolfgang, 1978). See also Gottfredson & Gottfredson (1994, p. 464), indicating that having three prior incarcerations is a significant predictor for crimes against persons and serious drug offenses.

that led to violence in the past)"; (2) "a more distant history of violence" together with proof that the personality traits and attitudes, physical abilities, and circumstances that led to the past violence still exist; or (3) "unequivocal threats or other like evidence of serious intentions to commit violence, especially when based on delusional thinking" (p. 224). Although Litwack and Schlesinger admit that

research has yet to establish the predictive power of these indices—and because of the practical and ethical problems involved may never do so—neither (to our knowledge) is there any evidence that refutes the legitimacy of relying on these indices to establish 'clear and convincing' evidence of 'dangerousness.' (p. 224)

At the same time, they caution, this level of accuracy may not be possible without these indications. If the law prohibited a finding of dangerousness unless proof of the circumstances identified by Litwack and Schlesinger exists, it might obtain predictions at the clear and convincing or even beyond a reasonable doubt levels (see generally, Monahan & Steadman, 1994).[9]

Adopting this proposal should not, of course, prevent use of additional information that might further improve the accuracy of the prediction (recall the Court's statement in *Jurek* that all relevant information must be given the fact finder). One type of evidence, already alluded to, that could fall in this category is actuarial data. Statistical information may confuse the fact finder or distract the finder from considering individualized criteria like those suggested by Litwack and Schlesinger (see Goodman, 1987, pp. 523–527). But *if* it can help refine the prediction process, it should be made available.

One objection to this position has been that,

to the extent that actuarial data incorporate "immutable" characteristics of the individual (such as race, age, and gender), its use violates the Fourteenth Amendment's equal protection clause (Goodman, 1987). When the immutable characteristic relied on is race, this type of argument is persuasive. The negative consequences to a democratic society of explicitly relying on race as a basis for state intervention far outweigh its usefulness as a predictive tool (Slobogin, 1991, pp. 85–86). On the other hand, use of factors such as age or gender is unlikely to induce the kinds of societal repercussions that use of race would. A different ground for rejecting use of the latter variables is that their immutable quality is inconsistent with the free will premise underlying the criminal justice system (Note, 1982, p. 321). Use of such evidence could also be said to be countertherapeutic: telling someone he is going to be confined as dangerous, in part because he is a young male, is not likely to promote his feeling of autonomy. These arguments might be persuasive to the extent that the analytical scheme described in the second section of the chapter is not followed. But if predictions of dangerousness are used only in the situations identified by the effect and incapacity exceptions—where the free will paradigm is not undermined—they lose much of their force. Furthermore, at least under Litwack and Schlesinger's scheme, the prediction will continue to be based primarily on behavior the individual *can* do something about (for example, antisocial behavior, delusions). In short, outside of race, if demographic characteristics improve the predictive process, they should be used.

A third way evidentiary rules might improve the prediction decision has to do with the use of experts. Much of the information relevant to a dangerousness prediction, such as an individual's history of violence, can be gleaned from lay witnesses and public records. But the description of the personality traits and delusions to which Litwack and Schlesinger refer, as well as explanations of other dynamics of violent behavior, may best come from mental health professionals

---

[9]A major caveat to this conclusion is that most of the research suggesting that predictions may be fairly accurate focuses on populations diagnosed with some type of psychosis. When the population studied is nonpsychotic, accuracy rates might be lower (see Ewing, 1991). Even for the latter populations, prediction accuracy may be high *if* the criteria Litwack and Schlesinger (1987) suggest are followed. See Note 8.

or other experts on human behavior.[10] If so, two rules that are not radical in theory but that are not often practiced should be strictly followed in this context. First, to the extent that the types of "facts" just discussed (for example, the individual's history of violence and interaction with family members) form the basis for the expert opinion, they should be corroborated with lay and documentary evidence rather than, as is often the case, "proved" solely by the expert's testimony (see Note, 1977). The assumption here is not that experts will lie, but that they consciously and unconsciously "shape" facts based on their professional and theoretical background, the context and timing of their interviews, and their conclusions (Ennis & Litwack, 1974). Second, in the absence of good actuarial data demonstrating precise probabilities, the expert should be limited to stating which factors might enhance or decrease the likelihood of an individual's violent acts (Grisso & Appelbaum, 1993; Melton et al., 1987, pp. 203–204). Experts should be prohibited from stating conclusions as to whether a particular person is "dangerous" or even "likely to be" violent, not only because the degree and type of dangerousness required for legal intervention is ultimately a legal determination rather than a scientific one but also because such testimony "overinfluences" the fact finder, thus possibly contributing to inaccurate decisions (Slobogin, 1989). Indeed, one could argue that psychiatric prediction testimony should be *prohibited* unless the defendant decides to rely on it

first, given its otherwise prejudicial impact on the dangerousness decision (Slobogin, 1984).

In addition to adopting the foregoing evidentiary rules, predictive accuracy can be enhanced through procedural mechanisms. First, as the Court itself has required in many situations described in the first section of the chapter, the individual whose dangerousness is at issue should be entitled to counsel, to confront accusers, and to present evidence. More controversially, rather than relying on a judge or jury, this type of decision—whether made in the commitment or the sentencing context—might best be made by an interdisciplinary panel composed of lawyers and mental health professionals or other experts in prediction. Although the ultimate decision on dangerousness is clearly a legal one, the types of information that may be considered, including actuarial as well as diagnostic material, might be difficult for lawyers or laypeople to grasp (see *Parham v. J. R.,* 1979). Furthermore, a consortium of decision makers versed in prediction research are less likely to succumb to easy stereotyping or undue reliance on the experts (see Bonnie & Slobogin, 1980, pp. 512–515).

Even if these precautions are taken, there are bound to be erroneous predictions of dangerousness, just as there are erroneous convictions. Furthermore, the former type of error is more likely to lead to disproportionate consequences because dangerousness is not as concrete an entity as culpability. Whereas a conviction for murder suggests a measurable level of desert that can be translated, however loosely, into a specific sentence, a prediction that one will kill does not carry with it *any* intrinsic limitation. In theory, dangerousness can "disappear" at some later point in time; but once the label is attached it can be exceedingly difficult to shake off (Lord, Ross, & Lepper, 1979, p. 2099; Note, 1982, p. 327). This bootstrapping tendency is exacerbated by the fact that, in contrast to a guilty verdict, we can never really know whether a prediction of dangerousness *was* erroneous. In effect, once found to be dangerous, those who are

---

[10]An issue not addressed in this chapter is whether expert testimony on dangerousness is admissible under the rules of evidence. Even if such testimony generally produces clear and convincing evidence of dangerousness, it should not be admissible if it produces results that are worse than chance (that is, no better than the base rate for violence of the population from which the subject comes) or no better than lay or actuarial data could obtain (Slobogin, 1984, pp. 131–137). This view of admissibility has been bolstered by the Supreme Court's decision in *Daubert v. Dow Chemical* (1993), which seems to require that "scientific" testimony pass a "falsifiability" test of admissibility. Even under this strict test of admissibility, however, it appears that, at this point, "good" clinical prediction is better than chance (Lidz, Mulvey, & Gardner, 1993; Mossman, 1994).

sentenced or committed carry a heavy burden, de facto if not de jure, to show they no longer are (see American Bar Association, 1989, p. 442).

Thus, several procedural mechanisms meant to reduce the consequences of erroneous decisions should be considered. First, there must be periodic review of the dangerousness finding that incorporates all the evidentiary and procedural suggestions made above. Even today, not every jurisdiction provides such review for insanity acquittees (Note, 1981a, p. 1071), and it is far from routine in the sentencing context (see *State v. Little*, 1978). Second, at the review hearing, the state should have the burden of showing that nothing in effect has changed; that is, it should have to show, with the requisite degree of certainty, that without the intervention the individual will cause harm to others. Thus, for instance, as *Foucha* held, if mental illness is the cause of the danger and it has been treated, the individual should be released unless the state can show that the illness will recur on release (see American Bar Association, 1989, Standard 7-7.4(d)).

Finally, given the ease with which an initial prediction of dangerousness can translate into a lifetime label, there should be a specified period of time at the end of which the state must, at the least, conditionally release the committed or sentenced individual (unless new proof of violence proneness arises in the meantime). This period might be completely arbitrary (that is, two years for everyone), or it could be based on the duration of the sentence the person would have received if convicted for the predicted act. The latter proposal is based on the theory that, if the prediction is correct, then without intervention the person would have committed this act and received the appropriate sentence, at the end of which he or she would have been released. Whatever its content, this maximum-limit proposal should not only undercut the effect of erroneous predictions, but should also have a therapeutic effect in giving the confined individual a specific behavioral goal to achieve (that is, no violent activity within the specified period in order to obtain conditional release).

Conclusion

Assuming free will, it would be morally wrong, as well as "countertherapeutic" for both the individual and society, to use dangerousness as the basis for state intervention, unless the intervention has a minimal effect on the free will paradigm (the "effect exception") or is aimed solely at those who lack free will (the "incapacity exception"). For circumstances in which a prediction of dangerousness may be used as a legal criterion, it should lead to intervention only when the state can show, with the required degree of certainty, that the individual will engage in harmful activity in the absence of the intervention. When the requisite standard of proof is above the preponderance level (which should be the case for all commitment and sentencing proceedings), a finding of dangerousness should be permitted only if the following conditions are met. Certain facts concerning past behavior and personality traits must be proved, and certain procedures—including use of an administrative panel, periodic review, and time-limited intervention—must be implemented. These proposals, it is submitted, will achieve the best balance between public safety, individual rights, and therapeutic goals.

References

Addington v. Texas, 441 U.S. 418 (1979).

Allen v. Illinois, 478 U.S. 364 (1986).

American Bar Association. (1989). *Criminal justice mental health standards*. Washington, DC: Author.

American Law Institute. (1962). *Model Penal Code* (proposed official draft). Philadelphia: Author.

Bail Reform Act of 1984. 18 U.S.C.A. §§ 3141–3150 (1984).

Barefoot v. Estelle, 463 U.S. 880 (1983).

In re Blodgett, 510 N.W.2d 910 (Minn. 1994).

Bonnie, R. (1980). Psychiatry and the death penalty: Emerging problems in Virginia. *Virginia Law Review, 66,* 167–198.

Bonnie, R., & Slobogin, C. (1980). The role of mental health professionals in the criminal process: The case for informed speculation. *Virginia Law Review, 66,* 427–522.

Bordenkircher v. Hayes, 434 U.S. 357 (1978).

Bullington v. Missouri, 451 U.S. 430 (1981).

Brooks, A. (1993). The constitutionality and morality of civilly committing violent sexual predators. *University of Puget Sound Law Review, 15,* 709–754.

Burt, R. (1979). *Taking care of strangers: The rule of law in doctor-patient relations.* New York: Free Press.

Chambers, D. (1972). Alternatives to civil commitment of the mentally ill: Practical guides and constitutional imperatives. *Michigan Law Review, 70,* 1107–1200.

Churgin, M. (1983). The transfer of inmates to mental hospitals. In J. Monahan & H. Steadman (Eds.), *Mentally disordered offenders: Perspectives from law and social science.* New York: Plenum.

Daubert v. Dow Chemical, 113 S. Ct. 2680 (1993).

Dawson, R. (1969). *Sentencing: The decision as to type, length, and conditions of sentence.* Boston: Little, Brown.

Dell, S. (1980). Transfer of special patients to the NHS. *British Journal of Psychiatry, 136,* 222–234.

Diamond, S. (1983). Order in the court: Consistency in criminal court decisions. In J. Scheirer & B. Hammonds (Eds.), *Psychology and the law* (American Psychological Association Master Lecture Series, No. 2). Washington, DC: American Psychological Association.

Dix, G. (1981). Expert prediction testimony in capital sentencing: Evidentiary and constitutional considerations. *American Criminal Law Review, 19,* 1–48.

Durham, M., & La Fond, J. (1988). A search for the missing premise of involuntary therapeutic commitment: Effective treatment of the mentally ill. *Rutgers Law Review, 40,* 303–376.

Ellis, J. (1986). The consequences of the insanity defense: Proposals to reform post-acquittal commitment law. *Catholic University Law Review, 35,* 961–1020.

Ennis, B., & Litwack, T. (1974). Psychiatry and the presumption of expertise: Flipping coins in the courtroom. *California Law Review, 62,* 693–757.

Ewing, C. (1991). Preventive detention and execution: The constitutionality of punishing future crimes. *Law and Human Behavior, 15,* 139–153.

Favole, R. (1983). Mental disability in the American criminal process. In J. Monahan & H. Steadman (Eds.), *Mentally disordered offenders: Perspectives from social science and law.* New York: Plenum.

Federal Rules of Criminal Procedure 15(a).

Federal Rules of Evidence 404(a).

Foucha v. Louisiana, 504 U.S. 71 (1992).

Frase, R. (1980). The decision to file federal criminal charges: A quantitative study of prosecutorial discretion. *University of Chicago Law Review, 47,* 246–330.

Goodman, D. (1987). Demographic evidence in capital sentencing. *Stanford Law Review, 39,* 499–543.

Gordon, R. (1977). A critique of the evaluation of Patuxent Institution, with particular attention to the issues of dangerousness and recidivism. *Bulletin of the American Academy of Psychiatry and Law, 5,* 210–255.

Gottfredson, S. D., & Gottfredson, D. M. (1994). Behavioral prediction and the problem of incapacitation. *Criminology, 32,* 441–474.

Grasmick, H., & Green, D. (1980). Legal punishment, social disapproval, and internalization as inhibitors of illegal behavior. *Journal of Criminal Law and Criminology, 71,* 325–345.

Grisso, T., & Appelbaum, P. (1993). Structuring the debate about ethical predictions of future violence. *Law and Human Behavior, 17,* 482–485.

Harris, G., Rice, M., & Quinsey, V. (1993). Violent recidivism of mentally disordered offenders: The development of a statistical prediction instrument. *Criminal Justice and Behavior, 20,* 315–335.

Illinois v. Allen, 397 U.S. 337 (1970).

Jones v. United States, 463 U.S. 354 (1983).

Jurek v. Texas, 428 U.S. 262 (1976).

Klassen, D., & O'Connor, W. (1988). Crime, inpatient admissions, and violence among male mental patients. *International Journal of Law and Psychiatry, 11,* 305–312.

Klotz, J., Wexler, D., Sales, B., & Becker, J. (1993). Cognitive restructuring through law: A therapeutic jurisprudence approach to sex offenders and the plea process. *University of Puget Sound Law Review, 15,* 579–595.

Lidz, C., Mulvey, E., & Gardner, W. (1993). The accuracy of predictions of violence to others. *Journal of the American Medical Association, 269,* 1007–1011.

Link, B., Cullen, F., & Andrews, H. (in press). Violent and illegal behavior of current and former mental patients compared to community controls. *American Sociological Review.*

Litwack, T., & Schlesinger, B. (1987). Assessing and predicting violence: Research, law, and applications. In I. Weiner & A. Hess (Eds.), *Handbook of forensic psychology.* New York: Wiley.

Lord, C., Ross, L., & Lepper, M. (1979). Biased assimilation and attitude polarization: The effects of prior theories on subsequently considered evidence. *Journal of Personality and Social Psychology, 37,* 2098–3019.

McNiel, D., & Binder, R. (1991). Clinical assessment of the risk of violence among psychiatric inpatients. *American Journal of Psychiatry, 148,* 1317–1321.

Melton, G., Poythress, N., Petrila, J., & Slobogin, C. (1987). *Psychological evaluations for the courts: A handbook for mental health professionals and lawyers.* New York: Guilford Press.

Miller, F. (1969). *Prosecution: The decision to charge a suspect with a crime.* Boston: Little, Brown.

Minnesota *ex rel.* Pearson v. Probate Court, 309 U.S. 270 (1940).

Miranda v. Arizona, 384 U.S. 436 (1966).

Mitchell, J. (1969). Bail reform and the constitutionality of preventive detention. *Virginia Law Review, 55,* 1223–1242.

Monahan, J. (1981). *The clinical prediction of violent behavior.* Washington, DC: National Institute of Health.

Monahan, J. (1982). *The* case for prediction in the modified desert model of criminal sentencing. *International Journal of Law and Psychiatry, 5,* 103–113.

Monahan, J. (1992). Mental disorder and violent behavior: perceptions and evidence. *American Psychologist, 47,* 511–521.

Monahan, J., & Steadman, H. (1994). *Violence and mental disorder: Developments in risk assessment.* Chicago: University of Chicago Press.

Monahan, J., & Wexler, D. (1978). A definite maybe: Proof and probability in civil commitment. *Law and Human Behavior, 2,* 37–42.

Morris, N. (1974). *The future of imprisonment.* Chicago: University of Chicago Press.

Morris, N., & Miller, M. (1985). Predictions of dangerousness. In M. Tonry & N. Morris (Eds.), *Crime and justice: An annual review of research* (Vol. 6). Chicago: University of Chicago Press.

Morse, S. (1982). A preference for liberty: The case against involuntary commitment of the mentally disordered. *California Law Review, 70,* 54–106.

Morse, S. (1994). Culpability and control. *University of Pennsylvania Law Review, 142,* 1587–1660.

Mossman, D. (1994). Assessing predictions of violence: Being accurate about accuracy. *Journal of Consulting and Clinical Psychology, 62,* 783–792.

New York v. Quarles, 467 U.S. 649 (1984).

Note (1974). Developments in the law: Civil

commitment of the mentally ill. *Harvard Law Review, 87,* 1190–1406.

Note (1977). Hearsay bases of psychiatric opinion testimony: A critique of Federal Rule of Evidence 703. *Southern California Law Review, 51,* 129–158.

Note (1981a). Commitment and release of persons found not guilty by reason of insanity: A Georgia perspective. *Georgia Law Review, 15,* 1065–1103.

Note (1981b). Commitment following an insanity acquittal. *Harvard Law Review, 94,* 618–645.

Note (1982). Rules for an exceptional class: The commitment and release of persons acquitted of violent offenses by reason of insanity. *New York University Law Review, 57,* 281–329.

Office of the Attorney General of Washington. (1992). Sexually violent predator civil commitment statistics. *University of Puget Sound Law Review, 15,* 871–877.

Or. Rev. Stat. § 161.295 (1994).

Otto, R. (1992). Prediction of dangerous behavior: A review and analysis of "second-generation" research. *Forensic Reports, 5,* 103–133.

Packer, H. (1968). *The limits of the criminal sanction.* Stanford, CA: Stanford University Press.

Parham v. J. R., 442 U.S. 584 (1979).

Payton v. New York, 445 U.S. 573 (1980).

People v. Feagley, 535 P.2d 373 (Cal. 1975).

Poythress, N. (1992). Expert testimony on violence and dangerousness: Roles for mental health professionals. *Forensic Reports, 5,* 135–150.

Robinson, P. (1993). Foreword: The criminal-civil distinction and dangerous blameless offenders. *Journal of Criminal Law and Criminology, 83,* 693–717.

Robinson, P. (1994). A failure of moral conviction? *Public Interest, 117,* 40–48.

Rothman, D. (1973). Decarcerating prisoners and patients. *Civil Liberties Review, 1,* 8–30.

Schoeman, F. D. (1979). On incapacitating the dangerous. *American Philosophical Quarterly, 16,* 27–35.

Schopp, R., & Quattrocchi, M. R. (1994, March). *Predicting the present: Expert testimony and civil commitment.* Paper presented at the annual meeting of the American Association of Psychology and Law, Santa Fe, NM.

Sepejak, D., Menzies, R., Webster, C., & Jensen, R. (1983). Clinical predictions of dangerousness: Two-year follow-up of 408 pre-trial forensic cases. *Bulletin of the American Academy of Psychiatry and Law, 11,* 171–199.

Slobogin, C. (1984). Dangerousness and expertise. *University of Pennsylvania Law Review, 133,* 79–174.

Slobogin, C. (1985). A rational approach to responsibility. *Michigan Law Review, 83,* 820–848.

Slobogin, C. (1989). The "ultimate issue" issue. *Behavioral Sciences and the Law, 7,* 259–266.

Slobogin, C. (1991). The world without a Fourth Amendment. *U.C.L.A. Law Review, 39,* 1–107.

Spece, R. (1978). Preserving the right to treatment: A critical assessment and constructive development of constitutional right to treatment theories. *Arizona Law Review, 20,* 1–47.

Specht v. Patterson, 386 U.S. 605 (1967).

Stack v. Boyle, 342 U.S. 1 (1951).

State ex rel. Pearson v. Probate Court, 287 N.W. 297 (Minn. 1939).

State v. Little, 261 N.W.2d 847 (Neb. 1978).

Stone, A. (1975). *Mental health and the law: A system in transition.* Washington, DC: U.S. Government Printing Office.

Swanson, J. W., Holzer, C., Ganju, V., & Jono, R. (1990). Violence and psychiatric disorder in the community: Evidence from the Epidemiological Catchment Area Surveys. *Hospital and Community Psychiatry, 41,* 761–770.

Terry v. Ohio, 392 U.S. 1 (1968).

Tyler, T. (1990). *Why people obey the law.* New Haven, CT: Yale University Press.

United States v. Salerno, 481 U.S. 739 (1987).

United States v. Townsend, 897 F.2d 989 (9th Cir. 1990).

Vitek v. Jones, 445 U.S. 480 (1980).

Warden v. Hayden, 387 U.S. 294 (1967).

Wash. Rev. Code § 71.09.010 (1994).

Wexler, D. (1990). Inducing therapeutic compliance through the criminal law. *Law and Psychology Review, 14*, 43–64.

Winick, B. (1991a). Competency to consent to treatment: The distinction between assent and objection. In D. Wexler & B. Winick (Eds.), *Essays in therapeutic jurisprudence.* Durham, NC: Carolina Academic Press.

Winick, B. (1991b). Harnessing the power of the bet: Wagering with the government as a mechanism for social and individual change. *Miami Law Review, 45*, 737–816.

Winick, B. (1994). The right to refuse mental health treatment: A therapeutic jurisprudence analysis. *International Journal of Law and Psychiatry, 17*, 99–117.

Winick, B. (in press). Ambiguities in the legal meaning and significance of mental illness: A therapeutic jurisprudence analysis of *Foucha v. Louisiana.*

In re Winship, 397 U.S. 358 (1970).

Wolfgang, M. (1978). *An overview of research into violent behavior.* Testimony before the U.S. House of Representatives Committee on Science and Technology, 95th Cong., 2d Sess., January 10–12.

In re Young, 857 P.2d 989 (Wash. 1993).

Zamble, E., & Porporino, F. (1990). Coping, imprisonment, and rehabilitation. *Criminal Justice and Behavior, 17*, 53–65.

Zimring, F. (1974). Impact of pretrial diversion from the criminal justice system. *University of Chicago Law Review, 41*, 224–241.

18 ■ The Incapacitation by Civil Commitment of Pathologically Violent Sex Offenders

Alexander D. Brooks

Rutgers, The State University of New Jersey

In May, 1987, a long-term sex offender, Earl Shriner, was about to complete a 10-year-term in a Washington State prison. Shriner had been sentenced in 1977 to a 20-year term for kidnapping and assaulting two 16-year-old girls. But the sentencing judge had made a trivial mistake in his sentencing order, as a result of which an appellate court reduced Shriner's 20-year sentence to 10 years. He was now about to be released (Boerner, 1992).

Shriner had a 25-year history of criminal sexual assaults against children and young people, including a sexually motivated murder. Twenty-one years earlier, in 1966, he killed a 15-year-old girl whom he had tied to a tree and strangled. But he was not prosecuted for that crime; instead he was institutionalized as a defective delinquent.

Despite years of counseling and treatment for earlier sex offenses, Shriner continued to fantasize about torturing and killing children. Shortly before he was due to be discharged from prison, corrections officials learned of Shriner's intention to torture children after he was released. While waiting out the final months of his prison sentence, Shriner designed elaborate plans to maim or kill youngsters and made entries in a diary that included lists of apparatus to be used for that purpose. He told a cellmate that he wanted a van customized with cages so that he could pick up children, molest them, then kill them (Kaplan, 1993).

On learning of Shriner's plans, state officials made vigorous efforts to have him civilly committed immediately on his release from prison. But the civil commitment judge before whom the case was presented, despite this evidence, ruled that Shriner did not meet a requirement of the general civil commitment statute that he must be found to have committed a recent "overt act" that would confirm his dangerousness. Of course, since Shriner had been imprisoned for 10 years, he had had no opportunity to commit sexual offenses against children or young people. The judge chose not to characterize Shriner's statements of his intentions, his keeping a diary, and his making lists of torture equipment as required "overt acts."

With great foreboding on the part of prison staff as to what Shriner would do, he was released. He had "maxed out" (served the maximum time under his sentence). Four months later he was arrested for stabbing a 16-year-old boy with a knife. After plea bargaining, Shriner pled guilty only to the misdemeanor of attempted simple assault and was sentenced to the statutory maximum for that lesser nonsexual crime of a mere 90 days in jail. At the time, a psychologist stated in a presentence report that Shriner was at high risk for future violent acts, especially against children. The judge ignored the report. When interviewed later about why he did so, the judge said, "[Y]ou can't give an exceptional sentence based simply on someone's thought that they might be dangerous in the future" (Boerner, 1992, p. 528). The judge was either not informed of, or disregarded, Shriner's long-term criminal record of sexual crimes, including murder. The murder may not have been included in Shriner's presentence report.

A short time later, Shriner served 66 days in a county jail for another second degree assault. Part of his sentence was suspended. In 1988, Shriner was next convicted of the unlawful imprisonment of a 10-year-old boy whom Shriner tied to a fence post and beat. Shriner was charged with attempted statutory rape in the first degree and unlawful imprisonment, crimes for which he could have been sentenced to nearly four years in prison. Again Shriner successfully plea bargained; the charge was reduced to attempted unlawful imprisonment, for which Shriner served only 67 days in jail. The prosecutor actually recommended that 30 days of this lenient sentence be converted to community service. Later, in attempting to justify the plea bargain, the prosecutor insisted that the victim had moved to Florida and could not be induced to return to testify against the defendant. But this explanation was never confirmed. There was no explanation for the prosecutor's recommendation of community service as a substitute for jail.

Shriner's postprison sexual career culminated in a crime that horrified the people of Washington. On May 20, 1989, he kidnapped a 7-year-old boy, raped him orally and anally, stabbed him in the back, strangled him with a cord, and cut off his penis. The boy was found mute and naked, covered with mud and dried blood. The police quickly determined that it was Shriner who was responsible.

The firestorm of public rage and indignation over the repeated failure of the criminal justice system to protect children and women from violent sexual offenders such as Earl Shriner ultimately led to the enactment in Washington of a new omnibus sex offender statute. The statute provides for increased sentences for convicted sex offenders, for their registration, and for the involuntary civil commitment of pathological and particularly dangerous sex offenders who are highly likely to repeat their crimes. The increased sentences and registration features have not yet been challenged in the courts, but the Sexually Violent Predator (SVP) Statute—the topic of this chapter—immediately became the focus of a constitutional attack. This chapter focuses on the SVP Statute, rather than on other sex offender issues, because the statute is on the cutting edge of a new approach in the relationship between the criminal justice and mental health systems: the civil confinement of extremely dangerous offenders. Moreover, this approach is currently being adopted by other states and is therefore the focus of national attention.

A central question that confronted the Washington legislature, and that now confronts other legislatures as well, is whether a state is helpless to protect women and children from the palpable dangers caused by previously convicted dangerous sex offenders who are again at large, who are known to be recidivistic and pathological, and whose persistent and repeated sex crimes over a long period of time establish beyond a reasonable doubt that their future victims are in immense danger.

The Shriner case illustrates the limitations of the criminal justice system in providing sufficient protection from violent sexual predators. For years, sentences for sexual offenses, even violent ones, have been relatively lenient. A 1989 survey conducted by the Department of Justice has concluded that while the median sentence for men convicted of rape was six years, the average time served was only 29 months, a little over two years (U.S. Department of Justice, 1989). A Montana study found that under a new reform statute that provided for sentences up to 40 years, 41% of convicted rapists served less than 2 years, and 24% were not confined at all (Yarnold, 1994). As in the Shriner cases, many convicted violent sex offenders are released from prison or jail after relatively short periods, to offend again. Victims often refuse to testify at a trial, which encourages plea bargaining. Judges are frequently unaware of the offender's actual history of sex crimes because records are seriously inadequate and presentence reports incomplete. Plea bargaining is far more common than trials. Serious sexual crimes are commonly bargained down to minor nonsexual offenses, as a result of which there are not only lenient sentences for the offender, but also a record that does not accurately reflect the defendant's history of sexual crimes. Although little systematic research on the issue of plea bargaining in sex offense cases has been done, it is widely acknowledged that most convictions in rape cases are a result of plea bargaining, ending up with a guilty plea rather than a trial. In Montana, for example, one study showed that 75% of convictions in cases where rape was charged resulted from guilty pleas (Yarnold, 1994). Moreover, many sentencing judges ignore presentence evaluations that predict offenders to be dangerous. Shriner's history and the history of many sex offenders illustrate these widespread problems. Shriner was convicted over and over again of significant sexual offenses but was generally given trivial sentences. Even where longer-term confinement was available, prosecutors recommended community service instead.

Finally, the criminal justice system, for a variety of reasons, does not effectively identify sex offenders who are particularly dangerous, whose offenses stem from a pathology that is demonstrated by the repetitiveness of their offenses, the brutality involved, the irrationality of risks taken by the offender, the obsessive sexual fantasies that drive their behavior, and the enormous harm they inflict on their victims. Deficiencies in the criminal justice system tend, over time, to conceal the real character of these hard-core offenders until it is too late. Then a rape-murder suddenly horrifies the community. A major function of the SVP statute discussed here is that it presents an overall view of the entire career of a dangerous sex offender, providing the basis for appropriate incapacitation.

The mental health system is also inadequately protective of victims of sex crimes. At the time of Shriner's 1987 release, the judge decided that Shriner could not be civilly committed under the then-existing general commitment statute because he had not committed a "recent overt act." But that general civil commitment statute was intended for the most part to provide short-term hospitalization for psychotic persons and was not enacted with violent sex offenders in mind. The legislature later pointed out that while that statute was "intended to be a short-term civil commitment system that is primarily designed to provide short-term treatment to individuals with serious mental disorders and then return them to the community," sexually violent predators "generally have antisocial personality features which are unamenable to existing mental illness treatment modalities" (Sexually Violent Predator Statute, Wash. 71.09.010, Findings, 1990–1991).

The Shriner crime, and others of similar seriousness, convinced Washington State legislators that a new approach had to be developed to deal with extremely dangerous and pathological sex offenders who are not adequately incapacitated by the criminal justice system. The legislature concluded that involuntary civil commitment and treatment for sexually violent offenders, especially following the expiration of their prison terms, should be tried. The major feature of the approach discussed in this chapter is that involuntary civil confinement takes place after the expiration of a criminal sentence rather than as an alternative to prison, a strategy that has already been used in many states and rejected by some ("Repeal of the Wisconsin Sex Crimes Act," 1980). The SVP legislation is intended to apply only to a relatively "small but dangerous group" of pathological sex offenders who are deemed by a judge or jury to be too violent to be set free, even though they have already served prison terms for specific crimes (Sexually Violent Predator Statute, Wash. 71.09.010, 1990–1991).

Although the new statute features treatment, the Washington legislature has made it clear that the protection of women and children is its principal objective (*In re Young*, 1993, p. 992). Moreover, the legislature has acknowledged the difficulty of successfully treating this particular cohort of offenders (Sexually Violent Predator

Statute, Wash. 71.09.010, Findings, 1990–1991). Researchers studying the efficaciousness of treatment for sex offenders have generally concluded that there is no evidence that clinical treatment has been particularly successful in reducing recidivism (Furby & Weinrott, 1980), although treatment for certain selected offenders may have some effect (Marshall & Barbaree, 1988). There is common agreement that the outlook for successful treatment is cloudy, and it is assumed, but without much research as yet, that for violent and pathological sex offenders treatment is particularly questionable. Nevertheless, the Washington legislature has rested the constitutional and moral validity of its SVP statute on the state's readiness to provide, in good faith, whatever state-of-the-art treatment is available. It is important to note that violent sex offenders are not to be confined either with criminal prisoners or with general psychiatric patients. They are housed in a unit that is separate from both prison and mental hospital—a segregation intended to ease administrative and management problems. Violent sex offenders must be treated very differently from patients with other mental disorders. Moreover, those with psychopathic characteristics can be very disruptive of the environment in a general psychiatric hospital.

The statute applies to sexual offenders who have been convicted of at least one crime of sexual violence as defined in the statute and who also suffer from a "mental abnormality" or "personality disorder" that makes the offender likely to engage in future predatory acts of sexual violence (Sexually Violent Predator Statute, Wash. 71.09.020, 1990–1991). An Attorney General's guideline published subsequent to the statute's enactment is intended to ensure that virtually all SVPs will be career offenders. Moreover, the Washington Supreme Court's reference to the requirement that an SVP be an offender with a "proven history" of sexual crimes underscores this requirement (*In re Young*, 1993, p. 1003).

The familiar term *personality disorder* is not defined in the statute but is defined in the

American Psychiatric Association's (1994) *Diagnostic and Statistical Manual of Mental Disorders* (DSM-IV). But *mental abnormality*, not defined as such in DSM-IV, is defined in the statute as a "congenital or acquired condition affecting the emotional or volitional capacity which predisposes the person to the commission of criminal or sexual acts" (Sexually Violent Predator Statute, Wash. 71.09.020(2), 1990–1991). "Predatory" acts are those directed against strangers or against nonstranger victims who have been deliberately groomed by the offender for the purpose of sexual victimization (Sexually Violent Predator Statute, Wash. 71.09.020(3), 1990–1991). Thus, most acts of incest are not covered by the statute, even if violent.

The statute provides that when a convicted offender's sentence for a sexually violent offense has expired or is about to expire, the state may petition for his involuntary civil commitment. If probable cause is found, the offender is evaluated and a hearing is held within 45 days to determine whether he is a SVP.

At the hearing the offender is provided a broad array of procedural rights, including the right to a jury trial, the right to a lawyer, and the right to be examined by an expert of his own choice (Sexually Violent Predator Statute, Wash. 71.09.050 & 71.09.060, 1990–1991). The right to an examination by an independent expert psychiatrist or psychologist is an important protection against the possible bias of state-retained experts. Finally, the state bears the burden of proving that the offender is a SVP beyond a reasonable doubt (Sexually Violent Predator Statute, Wash. 71.090.060(2), 1990–1991). If determined to be a SVP, the offender is committed to the special facility referred to earlier for "control, care, and treatment" until "safe to be at large" (Sexually Violent Predator Statute, Wash. 71.09.090(2), 1990–1991).

Each SVP must be examined by state examiners annually to determine whether he is nondangerous enough to be released. He may also be evaluated by an examiner of his own choice. An institutional determination that he is safe to be discharged is submitted to a court, which then holds a release hearing. In some cases the SVP may petition for a hearing if none is requested by the institution.

Even though it may be difficult for sex offenders to persuade the authorities that they are no longer dangerous, it is likely that a number of them will, in time, be released. That has been the experience in other sex offender treatment programs (Dix, 1975). But, at least theoretically, some offenders may be confined for long periods of time, including life.

Challenges to the SVP Legislation

Objections to the SVP legislation were voiced soon after its enactment ("Predators and Politics," 1992). Shortly after the statute was passed, two confined offenders, Young and Cunningham, brought a lawsuit challenging the statute's constitutionality (*In re Young*, 1993). Both were long-term career sex offenders. Young had been diagnosed as suffering from a severe personality disorder and severe paraphilia. Cunningham was diagnosed as suffering from severe paraphilia. The Young-Cunningham challenge was several-fold. First, they argued that the involuntary civil commitment was in reality a criminal punishment cloaked in civil clothing, but without adequate criminal protection. They claimed that the statute ran afoul of two basic constitutional rights: the prohibition against ex post facto legislation (*Calder v. Bull*, 1798) and the bar against double jeopardy (*U.S. v. Halper*, 1989). As part of this argument, they claimed that treatment for them would be ineffective. The challengers argued that if treatment is useless, confinement is really punishment.

The petitioners' second argument was that the sex offenders described in the SVP statute are not mentally ill in a "medically recognized sense" and that, since they are not mentally ill, they are confined simply because they are dangerous, a basis of confinement that has been prohibited by the U.S. Supreme Court in *Foucha v. Louisiana* (1992). This contention was reinforced by the claim that one of the terms used in the statute, *mentally abnormal*, is not a term recognized by psychiatry and that the other term, *personality disorder*, is unconstitutionally vague and overbroad in its reach.

A third argument was that the prediction of future dangerousness required by the statute, which applies to an offender who is "likely to engage in predatory acts of sexual violence," is impossible to make with an acceptable degree of accuracy (La Fond, 1992, p. 770). This claim rested on empirical findings that purportedly demonstrated that two out of three predictions of dangerousness of persons with mental illness are likely to be wrong, resulting in the confinement of an unacceptably high number of "false positives"—persons predicted to be dangerous who turn out not to be (Monahan, 1981).

A fourth argument was that the SVP statute did not provide a requirement, included in the general civil commitment statute, that a finding of dangerousness should be based on evidence of an offender's "recent overt act."

The Washington Supreme Court Decides

The SVP statute was enacted in January 1990 and became effective on July 1, 1990. Its constitutionality was challenged shortly thereafter, in October and December 1990, by Young and Cunningham. Two trials were held in December 1990 and May 1991, but it was not until August 1993 that the Washington Supreme Court finally delivered its decision on the constitutionality of the SVP statute. In *In re Young* (1993), the Court, by a vote of 6 to 3, upheld the statute's constitutionality.

The Washington Supreme Court acknowledged at the outset of its opinion in the *Young* case that it should evaluate the validity of the SVP statute using the so-called "strict scrutiny" standard of review set forth by the U.S. Supreme Court. This standard is used in cases where fundamental liberty interests are threatened. The federal constitution requires that a person shall not be deprived of life, liberty, or property without due process of law. When a state statute threatens one of these fundamental rights it will be found to be constitutional only if the statute serves "compelling state interests" and is "narrowly drawn" to serve those interests. In other words, the statute must not limit the liberty of persons needlessly.

The Washington Court began its analysis by noting that the statute's objective—the protection of society from sexual predators and the treatment of such offenders to prevent their reoffending—is the type of compelling state interest that has been upheld in earlier U.S. Supreme Court cases. The Court then focused on the question of whether the statute is sufficiently narrowly drawn.

Petitioners argued that the SVP statute violates constitutional guarantees against ex post facto law and double jeopardy. The constitutional bar against ex post facto legislation prohibits a legislature from making a crime greater than it was when committed or from subsequently imposing a different or more severe punishment. The bar against double jeopardy prohibits a jurisdiction from imposing more than one punishment for the same offense.

In effect, the petitioners claimed that after serving a prison term for a sexual crime, they were being "punished" again. This would be double jeopardy if true. They further claimed that the rule against ex post facto punishment was violated because their punishment was changed between the commission of their crime and the hearing on their status as violent sexual predators.

But constitutional law is clear that these two provisions apply (with rare exceptions) only in situations where the additional state action is "punishment." Thus, both the petitioners' arguments necessarily rested on an assumption that the SVP statute is in reality a criminal statute, imposing punishment, even though the legislature had designated it "civil."

The Washington Supreme Court rejected petitioners' argument, ruling that the SVP statute is indeed civil and that ex post facto and double jeopardy limitations therefore did not apply. The Court explained that its conclusion did not depend on the civil label. Even though the Washington legislature had called the statute civil, that label would be disregarded if it were shown by the "clearest proof" that the statute was punitive, either in purpose or effect.

In so ruling the Court invoked the holding of a leading U.S. Supreme Court case, *Allen v. Illinois* (1986), which was an Illinois sex offender case. The Supreme Court had upheld the Illinois statute as civil, in the face of a similar attack, finding several of the statute's aspects to be dispositive of the outcome: the designation as civil by the legislature; the provision of care and treatment intended to bring about recovery; and the prospect of discharge where the detainee is regarded as no longer dangerous, rather than at the end of a fixed term. It is worth noting that in the *Allen* case the U.S. Supreme Court did not require that the state provide "efficacious" treatment, only that the state's treatment be intended to bring about recovery.

The Washington Supreme Court said that

[t]he Washington sexually violent predator statute is not concerned with the criminal culpability of petitioners' past actions. Instead, it is focused on treating petitioners for a current mental abnormality, and protecting society from the sexually violent acts associated with that abnormality. (*In re Young*, 1993, p. 997)

Being civil, not criminal, the statute did not violate constitutional prohibitions against ex post facto legislation or double jeopardy.

Inasmuch as the Washington Supreme Court decided that the SVP program involves civil, and not criminal, commitment, the statute next had to be evaluated in terms of traditional civil commitment standards, which must meet substantive due process requirements. These standards require that to be constitutionally valid, civil commitment should be based on a showing that the candidate for commitment is mentally ill, disordered, or abnormal (*Foucha v. Louisiana,* 1992) and that, in addition, he should be dangerous or incapacitated in such a way as to require confinement. Being "gravely disabled" is one such alternative incapacitation (*O'Connor v. Donaldson,* 1975). For some jurisdictions, dangerousness is the only requirement in addition to mental disorder.

Petitioners thus attacked the SVP statute on both grounds, claiming that the statute's mental illness standard was constitutionally flawed and that the dangerousness of this cohort of sex offenders could not adequately be predicted.

Mental Abnormality and Personality Disorder

On the mental illness issue, the petitioners claimed that the SVP statute does not require the traditional form of mental illness required by well-established civil commitment statutes. The petitioners said that the two terms used in the SVP statute to describe pathology—*mental abnormality* and *personality disorder*—either did not describe a mental disorder or were void for vagueness, because they were insufficiently precise. As to the term *personality disorder,* the petitioners had an arguable point, not because of the *Foucha* case, but because the term may be subject to abuse. But petitioners did not focus on the problems of this term, and the *amicus curiae* brief of the Washington State Psychiatric Association even seemed satisfied with it, because the term is included in the DSM. Instead, petitioners bore down heavily on the term *mental abnormality,* which, they charged, is not listed in the DSM.

The Court ruled that the terms used in the SVP were constitutionally acceptable. Citing Brooks (1992), the Court said that the statutory term *mental abnormality*—though admittedly not in the DSM as such—was intended by the Wash-

ington legislature to cover a large variety of mental disorders and pathologies, including paraphilias. Paraphilias are sexual disorders defined in the DSM as involving recurrent intense and inappropriate sexual urges and sexually arousing fantasies. Each of the two petitioners in the *Young* case, both of whom had committed a number of sexual crimes, had been diagnosed by clinical experts as suffering from a severe "paraphilia not otherwise specified," a condition listed in the DSM and requiring treatment. One of the petitioners (Young) was diagnosed as also suffering from a severe "antisocial personality disorder," a condition included in the DSM.

The petitioners' argument on the mental illness issue was particularly weak. Statutes dealing with mental illness, disease, or disorder frequently contain legal terms not used by psychiatrists in their diagnoses. The term *insanity,* for example, though used in many statutes, is nowhere to be found in the DSM. It is a legal term, as is *mental abnormality.* Moreover, the American Psychiatric Association in the DSM has made it clear that whether or not a term is used in the DSM may not be "wholly relevant to legal judgments" (American Psychiatric Association, 1987, p. xxix).

Said the Court:

In using the concept of "mental abnormality" the legislature has invoked a more generalized terminology that can cover a much larger variety of disorders. Some, such as the paraphilias, are covered in the DSM-III-R; others are not. The fact that pathologically driven rape, for example, is not yet listed in the DSM-III-R does not invalidate such a diagnosis. The DSM is, after all, an evolving and imperfect document. Nor is it sacrosanct. Furthermore, it is in some areas a political document whose diagnoses are based, in some cases, on what American Psychiatric Association ("APA") leaders consider to be practical realities. *What is critical for our purposes is that psychiatric and psychological clinicians who testify in good faith as to mental abnormality are able to identify sexual pathologies that are as real and meaningful as other pathologies already listed in the DSM.* (In re Young, 1993, p. 1001, quoting from Brooks, 1992, p. 733; italics added by the Washington Supreme Court)

Petitioners further argued that the statute did not satisfy the mental disorder requirement because treatment of violent sex offenders is impossible. The Washington State Psychiatric Association filed an *amicus curiae* brief in which it made the remarkable argument that since involuntarily committed violent sex offenders cannot be successfully treated, they do not suffer from a mental disorder such as is required by constitutionally valid civil commitment statutes. Put otherwise, a nontreatable disorder, they said, is not a disorder!

The Washington Court made short shrift of this. First, the Court said, difficulty of treatment does not invalidate a diagnosis. Even if some forms of schizophrenia cannot be treated, the diagnosis of schizophrenia is nevertheless valid. Second, the petitioners had not demonstrated that the specific conditions of confinement provided in the Washington statute were in fact incompatible with efficacious treatment. Thus, the Court said, terms used in the statute to describe mental condition were constitutionally valid.

Dangerousness

The petitioners' second due process argument was that the dangerousness of SVPs cannot be accurately predicted, and that this statute, because it calls for such predictions, is constitutionally invalid. The Washington Court acknowledged that a constitutionally valid commitment of a mentally disordered or abnormal person must rest on a finding that he or she is also dangerous. In *O'Connor v. Donaldson* (1975), the U.S. Supreme Court had ruled that mental illness alone is an insufficient ground on which to commit, and held that dangerousness, coupled with mental illness, is one of several sufficient grounds for civil commitment. (The U.S. Supreme Court also stated that other grounds, such as being gravely disabled or being in need of treatment, might also suffice to support a commitment.) The Washington Supreme Court went a step beyond the U.S. Supreme Court in ruling that dangerousness was the exclusive additional requirement. In an earlier case

the Washington Court had said that "the only basis for involuntary commitment [in addition to mental illness] is dangerousness" (*In re Harris,* 1982). In the *Young* case, the Court ruled that the SVP statute applies only to dangerous offenders who have a "proven history of rape and sexually motivated violence" and whose likelihood of reoffending is "extremely high" (p. 1003).

Petitioners argued that permitting mental health professionals to predict the future dangerousness of violent sex offenders would violate substantive due process because such predictions, according to the research they cited, are highly inaccurate, resulting in two "false positives" (mistakes) out of every three predictions. But the research relied on by the petitioners is methodologically flawed. The petitioners' arguments are therefore highly questionable (Brooks, 1992).

Most of the empirical research on which the petitioners relied is based on outcome studies in which social scientists have attempted to determine whether clinical predictions of dangerousness turned out to be accurate. Early studies concluded that such predictions were highly inaccurate (Monahan, 1981, pp. 47–49). More recently, however, a number of social scientists doing more rigorous studies have concluded that the earlier studies were methodologically flawed, and their conclusions about low predictive accuracy wrong (Litwack, 1994). Earlier studies excluded and ignored significant samples, did not take into account undetected behavior, and confused individuals with the average. Moreover, petitioners used findings drawn from studies of cohorts of psychotic persons to apply to an entirely different cohort, violent sex offenders—a group to which those earlier findings simply do not apply. In fact, the validity of predictions of the future dangerousness of violent sex offenders has not yet been adequately studied. Most of the research cited by the petitioners was not relevant to predictions about violent sex offenders, whose behavior tends to be substantially more predictable than that of psychotic persons (Brooks, 1992). The Washington Supreme Court cited with approval the conclusion of Vernon Quinsey, a distinguished expert on sexual offenders, who has concluded that predictions of future violence by violent sex offenders "can realistically be expected to be in the 80% range [of accuracy]" (*In re Young*, 1993, pp. 1003–1004).

The Court did not, however, engage in a full-scale analysis of the dangerousness issue, being satisfied to rely instead on its own previous case law. In the civil commitment case of *In re Harris* (1982), the Washington Supreme Court had earlier ruled that clinical predictions of future violence, even if inherently uncertain, do not violate substantive due process. The Court pointed out in *Harris* that a ruling to the opposite effect would "eviscerate the entire law of involuntary commitment." In a later case dealing with exceptional sentences for sex offenders based on predictions of future dangerousness (*State v. Pryor*, 1990), the Washington Court came down with a ruling implying that predictions of future dangerousness are "sufficiently accurate and reliable" to meet constitutional standards. The Court said that it saw no reason to reconsider those holdings. Finally, the Court said in *Young*, the state is required to prove the dangerousness of a SVP beyond a reasonable doubt, a very high burden of proof that is used almost exclusively in criminal cases.

The Inapplicability of the *Foucha* Case

The Court also dealt with the petitioners' claim that the U.S. Supreme Court's decision in *Foucha v. Louisiana* (1992) forbade the involuntary civil commitment of sex offenders under the SVP statute, on the ground that they do not suffer from a mental disorder. This argument was a red herring. The *Young* Court pointed out that the Louisiana statute declared unconstitutional in *Foucha* was vitally different from the SVP statute.

In *Foucha* the U.S. Supreme Court struck down a statute that provided for the continued confinement of an insanity acquittee in a psychi-

atric hospital solely on the ground that he was dangerous, without requiring that he be found mentally ill or disordered.

Foucha had been acquitted by reason of insanity of two crimes and had been confined in a psychiatric hospital for four years. Then hospital psychiatrists recommended that Foucha be conditionally discharged and testified at a hearing that Foucha was no longer mentally ill, if he had ever been. They further testified that Foucha suffered from an "antisocial personality," a condition that they did not regard as a "mental illness" that warranted further confinement in a psychiatric hospital where he could not be efficaciously treated. The psychiatrists did, however, consider Foucha to be dangerous. They testified that because of Foucha's violent behavior in the hospital they could not "certify" that he "would not constitute a menace to himself or others if released." On the basis of the testimony that Foucha was dangerous, the court ordered his retention in the psychiatric hospital.

The U.S. Supreme Court reversed that decision and struck down the Louisiana statute on the ground that it permitted the confinement in a psychiatric hospital of a person solely because he or she was dangerous, without regard to whether or not he or she had a mental illness.

The U.S. Supreme Court's reasons for the reversal were threefold. First, they said, the Louisiana statute did not meet the substantive due process requirement set forth in *Jackson v. Indiana* (1972), to the effect that the nature of a commitment must bear a reasonable relationship to the purpose for which the person is committed. It was unconstitutional, said the Supreme Court, to confine in a psychiatric hospital a person whom doctors had testified was not mentally ill.

Second, the Supreme Court said, the Louisiana statute did not provide procedures that were constitutionally acceptable. The Court, equating insanity acquittees with noncriminal mentally ill and dangerous persons, focused its attention primarily on the requirement of the Louisiana statute that an insanity acquittee seeking discharge must prove that he or she is no longer dangerous. In *Addington vs. Texas* (1979), the Court had ruled that in a civil commitment case the state must bear the burden of establishing mental illness and dangerousness by clear and convincing evidence. The Court now invoked the equal protection clause of the Fourteenth Amendment to rule that the *Addington* standard be applied as well to insanity acquittees and, without identifying other deficiencies, ruled the Louisiana statute to be discriminatory against insanity acquittees, thus procedurally objectionable (*Addington v. Texas,* 1979).

Third, the Supreme Court said, while it is true that certain non–mentally ill persons who are dangerous can be confined, such confinement is permissible only under special circumstances approved by the Court in *U.S. v. Salerno* (1987), which had upheld brief jail confinements prior to trial of dangerous criminal defendants. Foucha's confinement, they said, did not fit the *Salerno* limitations.

The ruling of the *Foucha* case is tenuous and its future highly problematic because the bare five-justice majority decision in that case was made up, in part, by the vote of Justice Sandra Day O'Connor, who concurred only in the very narrow and limited holding and not in most of the rationale used by the other four majority justices. Furthermore, two of the majority justices—White and Blackmun, one of whom (White) wrote the majority opinion in *Foucha*—have since retired from the Court. One can only speculate how the two new justices—Ginsburg and Breyer—will vote on a future *Foucha*-type case. Justice O'Connor emphasized that her concurring vote applied only to the specific Louisiana statute before the Court and not to any other statute that might be more narrowly drawn. She insisted that the majority rationale not be applied more broadly. Justice O'Connor said that she could envision the confinement of non–mentally ill dangerous persons as constitutional, but not in a psychiatric hospital, a confinement that she regarded as anomalous.

Petitioners in *Young* claimed that the term *antisocial personality disorder* used in the SVP statute is similar to the condition accepted as "non–mental illness" by the U.S. Supreme Court in *Foucha*. The Washington Supreme Court responded to this argument by pointing out that the condition described in *Foucha* was "antisocial personality," which is not a DSM mental disorder, whereas "antisocial personality disorder" was a disorder listed in DSM-III-R, operative at the time. (DSM-III-R has since been superseded by DSM-IV.) Moreover, said the Washington Court, petitioners overlooked the fact that the U.S. Supreme Court had said that its *Foucha* ruling was based not on the Court's own view of what constitutes mental illness, but rather on the testimony presented by two hospital psychiatrists at a court hearing. In other words, the U.S. Supreme Court in *Foucha* did not purport to define what is or is not a mental illness sufficient to support the constitutionality of a commitment statute. It simply relied on a record in which testimony had been presented by two Louisiana doctors about Foucha's mental condition. As has already been pointed out, the Washington Court concluded that the terms for pathology used in the SVP statute fully comply with the U.S. Supreme Court's requirement that a constitutional involuntary civil commitment be based on some form of mental abnormality or disorder as well as on dangerousness.

Furthermore, the Washington Court said, the procedural guarantees of the SVP statute are much more protective of the offender than were those of the rejected Louisiana statute. Unlike the Louisiana statute, which placed the burden of proof on the offender, the Washington SVP statute places the burden of proving both dangerousness and mental condition beyond a reasonable doubt on the state. SVP detainees are confined only after a full trial with a full panoply of procedural protections. The Washington Court said that this made the SVP statute the kind of "sharply focused scheme" called for by the U.S. Supreme Court in *Foucha*. The SVP commitment is tailored to the nature and duration of the mental offender's condition and the dangerousness resulting from it.

The Court concluded that since the SVP statute requires a bona fide finding of mental pathology and dangerousness, it is, unlike *Foucha*, directly in the tradition of civil commitment programs that have been traditionally upheld by the Supreme Court.

The Recent-Overt-Act Requirement

The petitioners finally claimed that the SVP statute was unconstitutional because it did not contain a requirement that a finding of dangerousness be based in part on evidence of a recent overt act committed by the offender. In *In re Harris* (1982), the Washington Court had read into the general civil commitment statute the requirement that psychiatric testimony that a respondent was dangerous should be supported by other evidence that he or she had committed a recent overt act that had caused harm or reasonable apprehension of harm to self or another. The recent-overt-act requirement was generated during a period of extreme skepticism that has since diminished about the accuracy of clinical predictions.

Inasmuch as most sex offenders presented for commitment under the SVP statute are likely to have been in prison up to the time of their SVP hearings, a requirement of a recent and harmful overt act would, in most cases, be impossible for the state to meet. Accordingly, the Court rejected this argument, except in the case of offenders who had been discharged from prison and who were living in the community prior to their detention and hearing. In such situations, said the Court, the recent-overt-act requirement would apply. One of the two petitioners in the *Young* case, Cunningham, had in fact lived in the community for several months before a petition was filed against him. Because the petition against Cunningham did not include an allegation of a recent overt act, the court reversed his commitment and ordered his release.

Conclusion

The decision of the Washington Supreme Court to uphold the constitutionality of the SVP Statute is likely to encourage other states to experiment with the SVP approach. Indeed, as of this writing, three states—Wisconsin, Minnesota, and New Jersey—have enacted statutes that provide for the civil commitment of violent sexual offenders. Moreover, it now seems likely that the U.S. Supreme Court will ultimately validate the constitutionality of civilly committing violent sexual predators.

It is necessary, however, notwithstanding constitutional validation, that the implementation of these novel statutes be carefully evaluated and that valid criticisms of their operation be taken into consideration in making modifications that may seem necessary both to make the statutes more effective and to safeguard the civil liberties of sex offenders to the fullest extent possible. For example, it should be asked what criteria are being used to determine which, and how many, of the hundreds of sex offenders released from prison each year are to be selected for further commitment. How will the term *personality disorder* be defined in practice? What treatment modalities will be used, and with what success? What criteria will be used for the discharge of committed predators? What rate of recidivism of offenders discharged from the program as safe to be at large will there be?

A significant question is the extent to which the criminal justice system will be modified so as to make postsentence civil commitment somewhat less necessary. Certainly, plea bargaining practices can be improved, with a more careful selection being made, through more responsible prebargain investigations of an offender's record, so that hard-core violent and pathological offenders will not be given inappropriately lenient sentences for serious offenses unless prosecutions are certain to fail. Furthermore, the development of computerized record-keeping is likely to provide more accurate and complete presentence reports for judges, so that sentences will be more realistic than in the past.

From the outset, SVP legislation has been perceived by its supporters as a "fail-safe" measure to provide for the incapacitation of very dangerous sex offenders who have managed, one way or another, to slip through the cracks of the criminal justice system. However improved the criminal justice system may become, and improvements are likely to take a long time in developing, it is highly probable that, given the systemic imperfections of that system, the civil commitment backup may always be necessary to provide sufficient societal protection.

The debate and controversy over the Washington legislation has shed much needed light on the deficiencies in earlier research on such questions as predicting the dangerousness of sex offenders. We are, for instance, now rejecting an earlier view that clinical predictions of dangerousness are necessarily inaccurate. The revealed methodological defects in many of the studies supporting that conclusion have rendered them substantially useless, especially for evaluating sex offenders. The extent to which we can now be more confident of the dangerousness predictions of clinical experts is likely to enhance our readiness to incapacitate truly violent offenders without the fear that we are confining an inappropriate number of false positives.

Furthermore, we know much less about the treatment of sex offenders than we should. Our treatment modalities are relatively primitive, and some modalities, such as antiandrogens, which suppress sexual drive, have not yet been adequately experimented with, although such treatment modalities hold great promise for helping a significant number of offenders cope with their overpowering sexual drive. Although we may not be able to change the sexual orientation of most offenders, we may be able to help many of them resist their unacceptable and criminal behavior. Moreover, we know too little about the outcomes of treatments in current use, although some studies and much anecdotal evidence strongly suggest that many treatments in current use are ineffective. The Washington legislature has candidly admitted that pathologically violent sexual predators are extremely difficult to treat. In fact, treatment may be useless for many of them. The debate over SVP legislation has sharpened our awareness of the need for further rigorous research in this area.

Finally, the rapid growth and widespread interest in the civil confinement of our most serious sex offenders reflects a basic shift in the attitude of our society toward sexual predators. Sexual crimes that have been dealt with tolerantly for many years are now being punished with increasing severity. Even critics of the civil commitment approach discussed here acknowledge that we must be "tougher" on violent sex offenders, although they argue that toughness should be implemented exclusively through the criminal justice system. But a convincing case can be made that the criminal justice system alone does not, and currently cannot, provide sufficient protection. In today's new climate of opinion, the civil SVP statutes are likely to play an increasing role.

Note: While this book was in press, a federal district in *Young v. Weston* (1995) held the Sexually Violent Predator Statute unconstitutional, finding that permitting indefinite confinement of people who are not mentally ill is in violation of the due process clause of the U.S. Constitution. Subsequent appeal of this decision is likely.

References

Addington v. Texas, 441 U.S. 418 (1979).

Allen v. Illinois, 478 U.S. 364 (1986).

American Psychiatric Association. (1994). *Diagnostic and statistical manual of mental disorders* (4th ed.). Washington, DC: Author.

American Psychiatric Association. (1987). Diagnostic and statistical manual of mental disorders (3rd ed. rev.). Washington, DC: Author.

Boerner, D. (1992). Confronting violence: In the act and in the word. *University of Puget Sound Law Review, 15,* 525–535.

Brooks, A. (1992). The constitutionality and morality of civilly committing violent sexual predators. *University of Puget Sound Law Review, 15,* 709–754.

Calder v. Bull, 3 U.S. 386 (1798).

Dix, G. (1975). Determining the continued dangerousness of psychologically abnormal sex offenders. *Journal of Psychiatry of Law, 3,* 327–344.

Foucha v. Louisiana, 112 S.Ct. 1780 (1992).

Furby, L., & Weinrott, M. (1980). Sex offenders' recidivism: A review. *Psychological Bulletin, 105,* 3–30.

In re Harris, 654 P.2d 109 (Wash. 1982).

Jackson v. Indiana, 406 U.S. 715 (1972).

Kaplan, D. (1993, January 18). The incorrigibles. *Newsweek,* pp. 48–49.

La Fond, J. (1992). Washington's Sexually Violent Predator Statute: Law or lottery? A response to Professor Brooks. *University of Puget Sound Law Review, 15,* 755–779.

Litwack, T. (1994). Assessments of dangerousness: Legal, research, and clinical developments. *Administration and Policy in Mental Health, 21,* 361–377.

Marshall, W., & Barbaree, H. (1988). The long-term evaluation of a behavioral treatment program for child molesters. *Behavioral Research Therapy, 26,* 499–511.

McCoy, C. (1993). *Politics and plea bargaining: Victim's rights in California.* Philadelphia: University of Pennsylvania Press.

Monahan, J. (1981). *The clinical prediction of violent behavior.* Washington, DC: National Institute of Mental Health.

O'Connor v. Donaldson, 422 U.S. 563 (1975).

Predators and politics: A symposium on Washington's sexually violent predators statute. (1992). *University of Puget Sound Law Review, 15,* 507–911.

Repeal of the Wisconsin sex crimes act. (1980). *Wisconsin Law Review, 1980,* 941–975.

Robinson, P. (1993). The criminal-civil distinction and dangerous blameless offenders. *Journal of Criminal Law and Criminology, 83,* 693–717.

Sexually Violent Predator Statute, Wash. Rev. Code ch. 71.09 (Supp. 1990–1991).

State v. Pryor, 799 P.2d 244 (Wash. 1990).

U.S. v. Halper, 490 U.S. 435 (1989).

U.S. v. Salerno, 481 U.S. 739 (1987).

U.S. Department of Justice. (1989). Criminal victimization in the United States. Washington, DC: Government Printing Office.

Yarnold, B. M. (1994). A political court's rape sentencing in Montana. *Behavioral Sciences and the Law, 12,* 299–312.

In re Young, P.2d 989 (Wash. 1993).

Young v. Weston, 1995 U.S. Dist. LEXIS (D.W.D.Wa. 1995).

19 Offenders with Mental Disorders in the Criminal Justice–Correctional Process

Fred Cohen

State University of New York at Albany

Mental disorder is an issue that may arise at any point in the criminal process from arrest to trial to sentencing, during incarceration, and even as an aspect of capital punishment (*Ford v. Wainwright*, 1986). Unfortunately, there is no coordinated or integrated approach to mental disorder within the criminal process. Definitions of mental illness or disorder vary from stage to stage and depend on who asks the question and for what purpose; conceptual and semantic confusion is endemic; and the path to needed treatment for the offender with a mental disorder is strewn with obstacles that cast doubt on whether any coherent policy exists or is even possible.

After exploring preconfinement screening mechanisms, this chapter is devoted to correctional mental health issues—the law and practice concerning mental health care for those in penal confinement. The sheer number of persons in penal confinement and continuously headed that way establishes this as an area of enormous concern. With state and federal prison populations hovering at the million mark, with approximately 10 million persons passing through jails annually (U.S. Department of Justice, 1993),[1] and with perhaps about 10% of this number having serious mental illness, the dimensions of the problem begin to take shape (Bland, Newman, Dyck, & Orn, 1990; Fabisiak, Steadman, Dvoskin, & Holohean, 1987; Motiuk & Porporino, 1991; Neighbors et al., 1987; Spitzer, Williams, & Gibbon, 1986).

For a variety of reasons, penal systems are repeatedly, and often successfully, sued in federal court under section 1983 of the Civil Rights Act, claiming that the jail, prison, or prison system denied captives with mental disorders their constitutional right to minimally adequate mental health care (Cohen, 1988). The elimination of needless suffering and deterioration is at the core of these lawsuits. Thus, when plaintiffs prevail there is a sense of urgency involved in the recruitment of mental health staff and the creation of appropriate physical space for treatment purposes. The judgment of the court often requires that a certain number of psychiatrists,

I wish to thank Elizabeth R. Walsh, attorney-at-law and Ph.D. student at the School of Criminal Justice, State University of New York at Albany, for her research and editorial assistance.

[1]Total admissions of adults to local jails in June 1989, June 1990, and June 1991 were 9,720,102; 10,005,138; and 10,206,086, respectively. Releases from local jails for the same time periods were 9,442,773; 9,811,198; and 9,873,048 (U.S. Department of Justice, 1993, p. 592). The average daily population of U.S. jails for those three years was approximately 400,000 (U.S. Department of Justice, 1993, p. 590).

psychologists, social workers, or nurses be hired within a specified time. Salary levels may be specified to make the recruitment competitive.[2]

We turn now to a brief exploration of various preconfinement stages of the criminal justice system where a person's mental disorder might serve as a basis for the various informal and formal processing available. From there, we will move to a more detailed examination of the mentally disordered captive's right to appropriate treatment.

Entry into the System

Persons with mental disorders who enter the criminal justice–correctional system usually encounter the law initially through contact with a law enforcement agency. A police officer considering arrest has considerable discretionary authority and may charge a person with such amorphous, broadly defined crimes as loitering, disorderly conduct, harassment, criminal nuisance, or public lewdness (Cohen, 1991). Although several U.S. Supreme Court decisions narrow this law enforcement discretion, their impact in practice is negligible (*Kolender v. Lawson*, 1983; *Papachristo v. City of Jacksonville*, 1972).

Police officers retain substantial discretion in addressing minor criminal conduct. However, there is no mandate that a police officer arrest someone who, for example, lives on the street, panhandles for money but occasionally throws proffered money back, uses the street as a toilet, and walks recklessly among vehicular traffic (*Matter of Boggs*, 1987). Such a person may be ignored, although politically this may not be possible or may be made the subject of the civil commitment process. The more serious the harm, and thus, the more serious the crime, the more likely it is that a criminal charge will be invoked. Thus, in a situation involving public nuisance–type behavior engaged in by someone who may have a mental disorder, police officers may invoke the criminal process or the civil commitment process, or they may ignore the conduct or attempt to reach some informal resolution (such as listen and give counsel, bring the person home, or take the person to an appropriate helping agency).

Most police agencies have no outreach-type program, no working relationship with a mental health agency, and no special training or guidelines for dealing with offenders with mental disorders (Murphy, 1986). Thus, whether a person with a mental disorder is brought into the criminal justice conveyor belt, and for what type of charge, is often a matter of happenstance. The police response may be explained by the amount of paperwork required for an alternative response or simply by how far it is to the police station or to an alternative solution.

Without any clear policy or consistently applied screening-out criteria and process at the entryway to the criminal system, some persons with mental disorders will be ignored, a few may receive appropriate help, and others will find their way to prison. Unless we view prison as an inherently desirable facility for those with mental disorders, a serious problem exists at the threshold of the system.[3] If we believe that the further the entry into the criminal justice system by persons who have mental disorders, the more negative the consequences, it is obvious that some consistently applied screening-out criteria and process should exist at this entryway to the criminal process.

---

[2]Privatization is growing in significance, with organizations like Correctional Medical Services (CMS) providing mental health care in about 19 jails in 16 states and 30 prisons in some 10 states (Jane Haddad, Vice-President, CMS, personal communication, July 26, 1994).

---

[3]This is not to argue for the filtering out of the criminal justice process—or even prison—of all defendants with mental disorders. It is to suggest that we need clear policy on the subject—policy that may well turn on the seriousness of the offense, considerations of dangerousness, seriousness of the illness, and the like.

For the vast number of minor offenders, the homeless, and those with a chronic mental illness, there is no realistic prospect of a lawyer arguing incompetence or entering a plea of not guilty by reason of insanity. These people will live out their lives on the street, in shelters, in adult homes, and through turnstile jail experiences. Indeed, some may say, "I like jail. It's better than the shelter" (Johnson, 1990, p. 112). The poignancy of this observation aside, it says as much about shelters as about jail, and it raises a systemic concern about prospective patients not fitting program, staffing, or administrative arrangements instead of the obvious need to fit the program to the individual.

Legal Filters for Offenders with Mental Disorders

Fitness to Be Tried

When criminal charges have been brought and neither the police nor the prosecutors have exercised their discretion to divert the defendant with a mental disorder, the initial court-focused hurdle is the competency question. One has a constitutional right under the due process clause of the Fourteenth Amendment to avoid a hearing or a trial during a period of incompetency. In *Pate v. Robinson* (1966), the Supreme Court held that it is unconstitutional to convict a person who is incompetent to stand trial and that the states must have adequate procedures in place to determine competency (or "triability").

In most cases, a recognized mental disorder is the essential base point for a determination of competence, and the disorder must substantially affect the defendant's ability to understand the charges and to assist counsel. This is a relatively undemanding test and does not, for example, require that the defendant be particularly skilled as a client or witness or make wise decisions. It seems to require only a present ability to absorb and process the most rudimentary information (I am charged with killing someone and not with being the Easter Bunny) and, in turn, to transmit the most rudimentary, defense-related information to counsel.

The *Pate* case did not address what should occur during a period of incompetence. Nine years later, in *Jackson v. Indiana* (1975), the Supreme Court decided that an incompetent criminal defendant cannot be held for more than the reasonable period of time necessary to determine that there is a substantial probability that he or she will attain competence in the foreseeable future. Not being triable does not by itself give the state the right to detain a defendant indefinitely while awaiting a return (or restoration) to competence. If competency cannot be restored during this period, the state must begin civil commitment proceedings or release the defendant.

The irony of this ruling is that as civil commitment law and procedure became more restrictive (Chapter 11, this volume), there is some evidence that police and prosecutors increasingly filed criminal charges, typically for disorderly conduct, against persons with mental disorders, using the procedurally more relaxed incompetency commitment. Frequently the criminal charges were dropped at the end of the competency commitment. Thus, the criminal process–competency proceeding was utilized as a mechanism to avoid the strictures of civil commitment but without the intent to complete the criminal process (Dickey, 1980).

There are a substantial number of commitments to restore competency. Data for New York State, for example, reveal that in 1992 there were 430 felony defendants found incompetent to be tried, 405 in 1993, and 187 as of June 1994. For 1992, 373 have been restored, with a mean stay of 143 hospital days; for 1993, 331 were restored, with a mean stay of 112 hospital days; and for 1994 (June), 56 had been restored. Fifty-five persons found incompetent in 1992 and 1993 were still in process—that is, hospitalized awaiting restoration—11 of these from 1992

(R. Miraglia, Asst. Dir., Bureau of Forensic Services, N.Y.S. Division of Mental Health, oral communication, 1994).

Although the numbers are substantial if extrapolated to the 50 states, the District of Columbia, and the federal jurisdictions, competency—or fitness to be tried—does not operate as a significant filter for defendants with mental disorders. New York's prison population in 1991 was approximately 58,000 inmates. If 10% of this population have a serious mental illness, there are some 5800 such inmates in New York's prisons.

Insanity Defense

The next potential filter for offenders with mental disabilities is the insanity defense. Yet if the insanity defense is supposed to divert even defendants with the most serious mental illness from the correctional process, it too fails miserably at this task. Few offenders with mental disorders are affected by this defense; the defense is raised in only about 1% of all felony cases and is successful about 25% of the time (Callahan, Steadman, McGreevy, & Robbins, 1991). In addition, after *Hinckley* (*United States v. John Hinckley, Jr.,* 1982), the federal government, as well as many states, narrowed the defense to cognitive impairments only; emphasized the need for a serious mental disease; engaged in procedural and burden-of-proof shifting designed to narrow the potential for success; moved toward automatic commitment; and made release increasingly difficult (Perlin, 1994).

There are nonetheless countervailing moves to expand the insanity defense, albeit in backdoor fashion, and also to transpose it to the area of self-defense. Examples of this countermovement include pre- and postmenstrual syndrome, sexual addiction (*Winston v. Maine Technical College System,* 1993), compulsive gambling disorder (or the Pete Rose disease), battered wife syndrome, urban survival syndrome, the "black rage" insanity defense, and the "adopted child syndrome" (McQuiston, 1994).

Beyond the various syndromes and compulsions seeking admittance to the world of self-defense or mitigation, we encounter other disorders that seek recognition as an acceptable mental disease to be used as a basis for the insanity defense. There are, in other words, "good" and "bad" mental disorders, and what may be "good" (or acceptable) for one legal purpose (such as insurance benefits) is "bad" (unacceptable) for another.

Alcoholism and drug addiction alone, for example, will not formally qualify as the mental disease required for the insanity defense. Indeed, neither will such addiction alone qualify for the "serious illness" that both the Eighth and Fourteenth Amendments mandate for requiring treatment of the convicted prisoner or detainee. However, the life-threatening consequences that may accompany withdrawal will, of course, mandate appropriate care (Cohen, 1993).

Vaillant (1983), in his classic work on alcoholism, ultimately decides that calling alcoholism a disease rather than a behavior disorder is a useful device for treatment purposes, for admission to the health care system, and for purposes of understanding and study. Thus, on pragmatic grounds he arrives at a verdict of alcoholism-as-disease. Others with a different agenda may argue that substance abuse represents moral failure calling for moral, regenerative measures, or that the disease label may, in fact, be antitherapeutic.

Vaillant (1983) states, "The argument may be legitimately made that there is no more reason to subsume alcohol abuse under the medical model than to include compulsive fingernail biting, gambling, or child molesting in textbooks on medicine" (p. 19).[4] However that may be, if substance abuse and the various compulsions and syndromes noted earlier served as a basis for an insanity-type defense, the consequences would be enormous.

---

[4] The argument for inclusion of alcoholism, and not the others in the text, rests on a variety of individual pathological consequences; the need for medical care, as in detoxification; and frequent abuse of loved ones.

Do we wish to admit alcoholism or drug addiction into the halls of mental disease for the purposes of the required basis for an insanity defense? If so, we presumably would not make it a total free pass—that the alcoholic or addict would have to be under the influence of the substance at the time of the harm-producing conduct.

By some counts, perhaps 40% to 80% of the persons entering our prisons are substance abusers (Powell, 1994). If we allow being addicted and "under the influence" to serve as a type of mental illness that qualifies for the insanity defense, it is clear that society would not simply allow such acquittees to walk out of the courtroom. Rather, any expansion of the disease concept to accommodate an enlarged mission for the insanity defense will simply result in more people being channeled into coercive treatment programs (Kramer, 1970).

It is extremely unlikely that legislatures or courts will soon voluntarily engage in any doctrinal or definitional maneuvering to expand defenses to criminal responsibility or to expand opportunities for rehabilitation or treatment of the criminally committed. Thus, viewing the insanity defense and the current gaggle of compulsion and syndrome defenses as likely diversionary vehicles for defendants with mental disorders is illusory.

Under these circumstances, it is reasonable to assume that meaningful diversion of defendants with mental disorders is unlikely, that prison populations will continue to swell in the foreseeable future, that persons with mental illness will continue to stream into our jails and prisons, and that litigation will be the driving force in achieving whatever affirmative change is accomplished.

Persons with Mental Disorders in Prison

There are now more persons with serious mental illness in prison than ever before. In particular, there are more cases of schizophrenia and clinical depression and there are more violent persons with mental illnesses. These findings are clear whether one relies on anecdotal or empirical information.

In their study of 3684 New York State prisoners, Fabisiak, Steadman, Dvoskin, and Holohean (1987) used standardized surveys to collect data from health workers and correctional counselors on randomly selected inmates throughout the state. They were interested in determining the presence of psychiatric disability and functional disability. They found that 5% of the sample had severe psychiatric disability and 10% had significant psychiatric disability.

Ron Jamelka and his colleagues (1989) did an overview of a number of studies focusing on the prevalence of mental illness in prisons and concluded:

[P]revalence rates for major psychiatric disorders . . . have increased slowly and gradually in the last 20 years and probably will continue to increase. Facility surveys suggest that only six to eight percent of adjudicated felons are currently being designated as seriously mentally ill. Clinical studies, however, suggest that 10 to 15 percent of prison populations have a major DSM-III-R . . . disorder . . . and need the services usually associated with severe or chronic mental illness. (pp. 483–484)

Crowded into the same facilities with these persons with serious mental illness are large numbers of people who are socially and psychologically dysfunctional—often labeled antisocial personalities—for whom adjustment anywhere is difficult. Such offenders will be joined by many other inmates who are substance abusers and whose criminal career often will be linked to obtaining the drug of choice or acting out under its influence.

Once an individual is confined, there is a constitutional obligation to provide treatment for any *serious* medical or mental health condition (*DeShaney v. Winnebago Department of Social Services,* 1989; *Estelle v. Gamble,* 1976). The constitutional mandate is to not be deliberately indifferent to those with serious illnesses (Cohen, 1993). Ironically, because treatment is mandated only for those with serious ailments, another sorting out process begins.

The prison world puts many obstacles in the path of obtaining adequate mental health care. The security staff guards the door to treatment, suspicious of those who are "manipulators." A typically small and embattled mental health staff opens its door only slightly, guarding against those seeking "secondary gain" and those who are merely violent and not also ill. In addition, diagnoses too often are made with one eye on available treatment space and the other on the inmate's tractability.

Gone is the search for responsibility as well as the defining element of criminal law. A captive's access to treatment likely will be governed by the human and physical treatment resources available in a particular correctional system and not primarily by a clinical assessment of need. In the terribly crowded world of jails and prisons, every unit assigned to treatment (or rehabilitation) will be filled. Thus, we encounter intense competition for scarce resources.

The captive must negotiate the worlds of security and mental health professionals to gain access to the scarce resource of care. For example, the wildly acting out and violent captive is both the best candidate for care and the one who creates the most suspicion. Is he or she really "mad" or just "bad"? The quietly decompensating captive usually is not a problem for security; he or she is desperately quiet and manageable and will not likely be sought out by clinicians. Because in prison there is no such thing as homelessness—no dazed individual, lightly clothed in winter, sleeping on exhaust vents, hawking money, buying wine, living in filth, and testing law enforcement discretion—it is easy to ignore or rationalize away the need for mental health services.

Yet when it is afforded, mental health care and placement is a welcome respite for some captives, and they are willing to pay the price. The price may include being labeled a "bug" by fellow inmates and either being shunned or victimized, waiting for medication in stigmatizing "bug" pill lines, having parole denied or delayed, or experiencing the often terrifying side effects of psychotropic medication.

Legal Mandates for Treatment

Under the Eighth Amendment, which prohibits cruel and unusual punishment, persons convicted of crime and sentenced to prison are entitled to at least the minimum conditions of human survival, including a right to protection from staff and fellow inmates (*Rhodes v. Chapman*, 1981; *Wilson v. Seiter*, 1991). Thus, a prison official's duty to preserve life and health can be separated from the duty to identify and treat mental illness.

As mentioned earlier, the crucial components of a captive's constitutional right to mental health care are diagnosis of a *serious* mental disorder and a showing that the lack of care *or* the manner in which care was provided meets the mental element of *deliberate indifference*. Prisoners may be transferred to a mental hospital for treatment; when the inmate resists such a transfer, some interesting procedural issues are involved that will be addressed later in the chapter. Also, an inmate who refuses antipsychotic or psychotropic medication has a limited liberty interest in remaining drug-free and has some procedural rights to contest this form of enforced treatment (this will be addressed after consideration of seriousness and deliberate indifference).

The "Seriousness" Component

Based on the *Estelle v. Gamble* (1976) formulation of when medical and mental health care is mandated, the twin concepts of "serious need or disorder" and "deliberate indifference" form the crucial components for establishing constitutionally required care.[5] Serious medical need or disorder is the threshold requirement for the duty of care, whereas deliberate indifference—an apparent oxymoron—is an awkward and slippery reference to the mental element requirement needed to establish a breach of the constitutional duty to provide care.

Whether the legal challenge (that is, a claim for damages or prospective relief) is to the system or individual failure, all claims must lead first to a finding of "seriousness" and only then to a consideration of the culpable mental state of deliberate indifference (*Langley v. Coughlin*, 1989). One Federal Court of Appeals described "serious medical need" as follows:

A "serious medical need" exists if the failure to treat a prisoner's condition could result in further significant injury or the "unnecessary and wanton infliction of pain." . . . Either result is not the type of "routine discomfort [that] is 'part of the penalty that criminal offenders pay for their offenses against society.'" . . . The existence of an injury that a doctor or patient would find important and worthy of comment or treatment; the presence of a medical condition that significantly affects an individual's daily activities; or the existence of chronic and substantial pain are examples of indications that a prisoner has a "serious" need for medical treatment. (*McGuckin v. Smith*, 1992, pp. 1059–1060)

This description of "serious" by the Ninth Circuit Court of Appeals, although flawed, is more detailed and more useful than the more standard approach taken by federal courts' "obviousness" test. That test provides that a

medical need is serious if it is one that has been diagnosed by a physician as mandating treatment, or one that is so obvious that even a lay person would easily recognize the necessity for a doctor's attention. . . . The "seriousness" of an inmate's needs may also be determined by reference to the effect of the delay of treatment. (*Gaudreault v. Municipality of Salem, Mass.*, 1990, p. 208)

The "obviousness" test is seriously flawed in

several respects. First, doctors frequently diagnose minor ailments as calling for minimal care. Thus, medical involvement by itself does not determine seriousness. Second, in the exercise of professional judgment, clinicians disagree and a correctional decision maker is entitled to select from among such differing opinions. Third, the "obviousness" test does not mention pain and avoidable, gratuitous suffering as a key ingredient of the *Estelle v. Gamble* (1976) Eighth Amendment formulation. Fourth, the obvious-to-a-layperson factor has not become clearer by virtue of its repetition. A broken bone protruding through the skin is one type of obvious-to-a-layperson's call, but serious mental illness is another matter. Are the acts of inmates in a prison disciplinary unit—climbing the bars, disrobing and displaying their genitals, and letting loose a string of profanities—mental illness or rebellion?

In arriving at a judgment of "seriousness" or disease, the possibility of secondary gain in the jail and prison setting appears to color the perceptions and reactions of mental health professionals as well as security staff. Inmates may be seeking any of the following things: hospitalization and a chance to earn more money there, greater freedom, an excuse not to work, a chance to establish mental illness as a basis for an incompetence finding or an insanity defense (obviously more critical in jail), or the experience of being locked down to avoid something bothersome or threatening in the general population.[6] Thus, the appearance of objectivity, of cold clinical judgment in the world of captives, may mask a basic distrust for the captive.

Both tests for seriousness refer to the consequences of a failure to treat as evidence of the seriousness of the condition. The "obviousness" test refers only to the consequences of delay, but improper care, no matter how quickly provided,

---

[5]The material on "seriousness" and much of the material on "deliberate indifference" is drawn from "Captives' Legal Rights to Mental Health Care," by Fred Cohen, 1993, *Law and Psychology Review*, *17*, pp. 17–25. Adapted with permission.

[6]Notwithstanding the *One Flew Over the Cuckoo's Nest* (Kesey, 1962) syndrome, and with vast improvements made in some of the bleakest forensic mental hospitals, I have encountered many inmates who make no effort to disguise their desire and their various techniques for being hospitalized.

must also be a part of the formulation. The Ninth Circuit test refers to further significant injury or "needless" pain, and although the reference to "significant injury" is flawed and actually contradicted by the holding, overall this is a somewhat more desirable approach.

There simply is no *definitional* clarity on what is a serious disorder for the purposes of mandated medical or mental health care. What pose as definitions tend to be descriptions. Whether an illness is serious will likely be the subject of a battle of expert witnesses, and the battle may even be waged over whether the condition is a mental disease at all while the words employed may refer only to seriousness. There are conflicting views on whether certain dysfunctional states qualify as a mental disorder. This is true, for example, for whether a dysthymic disorder, or transsexualism, is a mental disorder (*Farmer v. Carlson,* 1988). If the condition is accepted as a mental disorder, the seriousness question then arises, and the battle is raged over the modalities of treatment.

Although the opinion of experts, now clearly validated by the Court in *Youngberg v. Romeo* (1982), is perhaps the single most important factor in the "serious/disease" decision, a few more generalities may be distilled from the case law:

1. The diagnostic test is one of medical or psychiatric necessity.
2. Minor aches, pains, or distress will not establish such necessity.
3. A desire to achieve rehabilitation from alcohol or drug abuse, to lose weight to simply look or feel better, will not suffice.
4. A diagnosis based on professional judgment and resting on some acceptable diagnostic tool, e.g., DSM-IV, is presumptively valid.
5. By the same token, a decision by a mental health professional that mental illness is not present also is presumptively valid.
6. While "mere depression" or behavioral and emotional problems alone do not qualify as serious mental illness, acute depression, paranoid schizophrenia, "nervous collapse," and suicidal tendencies do qualify. (Cohen, 1988, p. 24)

With regard to the sixth point above, it is actually the clinicians' choice of the diagnostic terminology that will move these cases from no care to discretionary care or to mandated care. Regretfully, as suggested earlier, diagnosis in a custodial setting is likely to say as much about the availability of resources, security concerns, and a judgment about the captive's possible pursuit of secondary gain as about an objective diagnosis based on signs and symptoms. Indeed, even epidemiological data may be significantly influenced by the availability of solutions. The number of captives identified as having serious mental illness may be responsive to the space and personnel available to deal with them, as opposed to clinically sound assessments.

In accepting or rejecting various diagnostic categories, courts are strongly influenced by accounts of the inmate's behavior. For example, in *Torraco v. Maloney* (1991)—a Massachusetts prison suicide case—a Federal Court of Appeals held that "the record contains sufficient evidence that Torraco had a serious mental health need" (p. 236 n. 5). In support of this conclusion, the court referred to an earlier suicide attempt while in confinement, an assault on a prison official later attributed to impaired mental health, and an overdose of THC (an active component of marijuana) pills somewhat later (p. 235 n. 4). Thus, clinical diagnoses supported by incidents supportive of those judgments are likely to be at the core in determining serious disorders.

Deliberate Indifference

Deliberate indifference is the constitutionally mandated mental element for liability in medical or mental health care litigation. *Estelle v. Gamble* (1976) established this culpability requirement, although a search of all Supreme Court decisions back to 1790 reveals no prior reference to deliberate indifference or to any variation of the phrase (Boston, 1992, p. 43). Given the novelty of the phrase, one might have expected some effort at definition. Instead, the *Estelle* decision labored to explain only what deliberate indifference was not:

[A]n inadvertent failure to provide adequate medical care cannot be said to constitute "an unnecessary and wanton infliction of pain" or to be "repugnant to the conscience of mankind." Thus, a complaint that a physician has been negligent in diagnosing or treating a medical condition does not state a valid claim of medical mistreatment under the Eighth Amendment. Medical malpractice does not become a constitutional violation merely because the victim is a prisoner. (*Estelle v. Gamble*, 1976, pp. 104–105)

In *Wilson v. Seiter* (1991) the Court determined that the deliberate indifference standard applied to all prison-condition cases—cases involving crowding, exercise, ventilation, and so on. Although *Seiter* expands the reach of the deliberate indifference formulation, it offers nothing new on its meaning.

Justice Scalia's opinion in *Seiter* did emphasize that the mental element requirement of deliberate indifference is not simply the predilection of the Court but is fundamental to the Eighth Amendment, which focuses on punishment (*Wilson v. Seiter*, 1991). Punishment, in turn, in any of its several definitions, includes some reference to pain or suffering (Cohen, 1980).[7]

Pain, of course, is essentially a subjective matter. Indeed, like the mental state of deliberate indifference, pain is known when it is reported by the sufferer or through inferences drawn from observation of the individual or his or her behav-ior. Ascertaining the presence of pain—whether needless or unavoidable—is not a problem limited to Eighth Amendment jurisprudence. Chronic pain with no discernible physical cause is the most common reason for lost workdays in this country, yet doctors remain uncertain of causation, treatment, or even the validity of the complaint (Rosenthal, 1992).

Recent studies have failed to link chronic pain to physical injury or x-ray findings, but they have found that it correlates with such factors as job satisfaction, depression, and the resolution of lawsuits (Rosenthal, 1992). This, of course, closely resembles the kind of secondary gains (for example, housing changes, hospital admission) attributed to prisoners whose behavior patterns create the disciplinary/need-for-care dichotomy.

A football player in a championship game may redouble his efforts after a bloody gash to the forehead; a factory worker may go home with a minor scratch to a finger. An inmate acts out, and a clinician may eventually have to make the call on the etiology of the behavior and perhaps invoke either a disciplinary process or a mental health process responsive to the pain of mental illness. If the illness and pain are serious, care is mandatory; if not, it is discretionary. The avoidance of needless pain, however, is the link between the trigger of a serious disorder and the mental state of deliberate indifference.

One of the most intellectual-appearing, pre–*Farmer v. Brennan* (1994) discussions of deliberate indifference, which culminates in the most defense-oriented of definitions, is by Judge Richard Posner in *Duckworth v. Franzen* (1985). After marking off negligence, recklessness, and deliberateness as the three traditional mental elements to be consulted to locate the appropriate space for deliberate indifference, Judge Posner states:

If the word "punishment" in cases of prisoner mistreatment is to retain a link with normal usage, the infliction of suffering on prisoners can be found to violate the Eighth Amendment only if that infliction is either deliberate, or reckless in the criminal law sense. Gross negligence is not enough. Unlike criminal recklessness it does not import danger so great that knowledge of

---

[7]In *Bell v. Wolfish* (1979) the Court determined that under the due process clause, pretrial detainees could not be punished. However, while the Court indicated that not every disability imposed during detention was punishment, the closest it came to a definition was a reference to the earlier decision in *Kennedy v. Mendoza-Martinez* (1963).

Punishment in the simple form of restraint, banishment, or public humiliation ceremonies may involve more generalized suffering than actual pain. In medical and mental health cases the claimed deprivation-as-punishment and punishment-as-pain is not as difficult to ascertain as in the above examples.

the danger can be inferred; and we remind that the "indifference" to the prisoner's welfare must be "deliberate" . . . implying such knowledge. (p. 652)

More recent decisions from the Seventh Circuit do not retreat from the *Duckworth* formulation and, indeed, actually may increase the burden for plaintiffs. For example, in *Salazar v. City of Chicago* (1991), the court reiterated the reckless-in-a-criminal-sense formulation, emphasizing the complete indifference to risk—where the actor does not care whether the other person lives or dies despite knowing there is a significant risk of death. Here, there clearly was a serious medical need—a bleeding liver resulting from the trauma of an automobile accident—and plainly a serious consequence—the detainee died in his cell from internal bleeding. However, the decedent's behavior was said to be consistent with intoxication, and the failure to obtain tests or medical care, although perhaps negligent, did not reach the stringent requirements of deliberate indifference (*Salazar v. City of Chicago*, 1991). That instead seems to be actual knowledge of the condition and risk and a failure to act attributable to either a desire that the detainee suffer or an absolute lack of concern about whether the detainee lives or dies.

In June 1994, the Supreme Court rendered its first decision defining deliberate indifference. *Farmer v. Brennan* (1994) dealt with a transsexual, federal prisoner who alleged that he was raped while in confinement and that prison officials violated his Eighth Amendment right to personal security in being deliberately indifferent to the risks associated with this inmate's rather obvious condition. The Court in *Farmer* ultimately adopted the Seventh Circuit's views on deliberate indifference.

Justice Souter, writing for the Court, reaffirmed that prison officials have a clear duty to protect prisoners from violence at the hands of other prisoners and that the challenged act or omission is to be governed by the deliberate indifference standard that first arose in the area of health care obligations (*Farmer v. Brennan*,

1994). Deliberate indifference is described by Justice Souter as a mental state positioned somewhere between negligence at one end and purpose or intent at the other. The mental state between these two extremes is recklessness—that is, a high degree of risk creation followed by conduct that seemingly ignores the risk (*Farmer v. Brennan*, 1994).

Having settled on recklessness as the closest analogue to deliberate indifference, the Court still had to choose between a "mild" and a "hot" version of recklessness. The essential difference between these two extremes is the extent to which a corrections official must actually know and disregard a risk or whether recklessness might be based on a more objective standard, which in turn places a certain duty of inquiry on the official.

In opting for the Seventh Circuit's version of recklessness—criminal recklessness—the Court accepted the subjective or "actually knew" approach. We may now ask if the *Farmer* definition of deliberate indifference will apply to medical and mental health cases, and the answer is clearly yes. Perhaps more important, what difference might this test make for inmate claims to unconstitutional mental health care? Minimally, the rhetoric will change somewhat, and within the federal judicial system the courts should now be at least more linguistically consistent.

While *Farmer* plainly states that corrections officials have no particular duty of inquiry, it also states that knowledge of a risk is to be determined from the facts, including inferences to be drawn from circumstantial evidence. Thus, in a *Farmer* situation, officials know they have in their custody in a male prison, a full-breasted, rouged, off-the-shoulder-dressing inmate. What are the risks that must be inferred here from what is known by even a remotely competent corrections official? The real possibility of sexual attack or exploitation is obvious.

Of course, mental disorder need not be, and often is not, worn as a badge, and thus there need not always or even regularly be actual knowledge that an inmate falls into the general class of having a mental disorder, to say nothing of having a serious disorder. Does general knowledge that perhaps 10% of incoming male inmates may have serious mental disorders, and that incoming females may have double that percentage, place a duty of inquiry on prison officials (Ohio Department of Rehabilitation and Corrections, 1993)? Is there a duty to perform intake screening to determine if there is a mental health history, prior suicide attempts, or a current mental health crisis lurking just below the surface?

The case law on custodial suicide before *Farmer* has been very difficult from the claimants' perspective. Although state laws may often be more relaxed, requiring only a negligence standard for liability, "[w]ithout some actual or potential knowledge of an individual's potential for committing suicide, custodians simply have no [constitutional] liability. . . . The distressing aspect of modern case law is the premium it appears to place on ignorance; a premium which is antitherapeutic and life threatening" (Cohen, 1991, pp. 1, 9).

Intake screening as a means of detecting mental disorder among incoming inmates is viewed generally as one of the most basic aspects of a constitutionally acceptable mental health system (Cohen, 1988). Does *Farmer* allow room for an argument that intake screening is not a constitutional requirement and deliberate indifference exists only when, for example, the acting-out, aggressive type of inmate with a mental disorder presents himself or herself; or when a psychiatric record accompanies the inmate, making it clear that there is a relevant history that cannot now be ignored?

Such an argument can and undoubtedly will be made, but if it prevails, it would be the worst of pyrrhic victories. Calculated ignorance in the face of an opportunity to avoid the violence, deterioration, institutional tension, and use of force often associated with inmates with mental disorders is a self-destructive, inhumane, and ultimately costly policy. It is the worst policy for staff and is antitherapeutic in the most basic sense for inmates. Early detection and intervention is clearly the most therapeutic approach, and

no prison or jail system should view *Farmer* as an invitation to reduce or eliminate intake screening for mental health problems and to simply do classification for security.

Prison systems have been and will remain vulnerable to class action lawsuits claiming systemic deficiencies in the system's mental health services. On June 6, 1994, for example, after some 39 days of trial preceded by months of fruitless negotiation, the magistrate-judge in *Coleman v. Wilson* (1994) handed down his Findings and Recommendations in a suit lodged against the California Department of Corrections. With a prison population of just over 118,000 (as of May 1994), operating at about 175% of rated capacity, the Magistrate-Judge found the California system to be constitutionally deficient in virtually every material respect.[8]

The heart of this, or any similar lawsuit, relates to three major components: (1) *staff*—how many, with what credentials, perform what functions? (2) *space* (physical resources and programs)—how much of what kind of space (often expressed as beds) is available for what type of mental health care and programming? and (3) *access*—how do inmates gain access to staff and appropriate space; how long does it take to gain access to diagnosis, treatment, medication, medication monitoring, and the like?

In *Coleman* the magistrate-judge found that California inmates do not have adequate access to necessary care, primarily because of inadequate screening and referral (*Coleman v. Wilson*, 1994). Medication management was found deficient. Disciplinary measures and the use of force (use of tasers and 37-mm stunguns) were condemned; mental health records—necessary for continuity of care—were disorganized and incomplete; and staffing ratios effectively denied access to appropriate care which, in turn, often

---

[8] These findings may be challenged and even modified before they are accepted by the federal district court judge and an enforceable judgment is issued. However, the facts and the record seem so overwhelmingly in favor of the plaintiff's position that I seriously doubt any major changes will result.

did not exist. The appointment of a special master was recommended with a three-year term, a sure sign that the magistrate-judge had virtually no faith in the ability of California officials to deliver adequate care without constant oversight and the threat of contempt.

How the magistrate-judge arrived at his finding of deliberate indifference illustrates whether the *Farmer* approach might have changed the result. The defendants knew of the serious problems of understaffing at least since 1985, when an in-house study concluded that the workload was excessive. They also were held to know that using even a relatively low percentage of inmates with mental illness—let us say 10%—meant that thousands of inmates with serious illness were unidentified and thus untreated (*Coleman v. Wilson,* 1994). The combination of known historical facts and the inferences to be drawn from epidemiological data and the actual number of inmates receiving any mental health care may be said to meet the *Farmer* standard of actual knowledge.

In another illustrative case, *Casey v. Lewis* (1993), the Arizona Department of Corrections was found to be deliberately indifferent to the minimally adequate care of its inmates with serious mental illness. Millions have been spent—including over $3 million in legal fees—in somewhat fruitless litigation and now in delay-tactic appeals. Arizona was faulted on virtually every aspect of its mental health care system for inmates: failure to identify the mentally ill, excessive delay in accessing care, excessive use of lockdown (that is, isolation) for inmates with mental illness, inadequate medication practices, lack of appropriate staff and physical space for care, and disparity between the care afforded female inmates and that afforded males. These flaws were apparent and remediable prior to the litigation, but little or nothing was done. Now it will cost perhaps $6 million to comply with the ruling. Again, the lawsuit created the crisis, which led, in turn, to remedial measures that could have been taken earlier.

Moreover, in evaluating a claim of systemic failure to provide adequate medical or mental health care, the basic components of such evaluation are the available physical and human resources, including qualifications and training; the modalities of care, especially the reliance on and handling of drugs; access to such care, including diagnostic and screening activities; and record-keeping and maintenance, including tracking captives into and out of care.[9] Consideration may also be given to an assessment of how any given care was provided, whether there was an abrupt termination (*Smith v. Jenkins,* 1990) of a given treatment, whether security staff actually prevented delivery of prescribed care, and the accuracy of a particular diagnosis (*Lynsky v. City of Boston,* 1990).

Resistance to Treatment

Resisting Transfer to a Treatment Facility

Although there is a limited constitutional right to mental health services, can the correctional authority transfer the prisoner to another institution to receive them? In *Vitek v. Jones* (1980) the Supreme Court addressed whether the due process clause of the Fourteenth Amendment entitles a prisoner to certain procedural protections with which to resist a proposed transfer for treatment from a state prison to a state mental hospital.

Four years earlier, the Supreme Court held that a prisoner has no right to procedures by which to resist a prison-to-prison transfer, even to conditions far less favorable. *Meacham v. Fano*

---

[9]I base these criteria primarily on my experience as a legal consultant on prison mental health issues in the states of Michigan, Utah, Pennsylvania, Vermont, and Ohio. That experience has enabled me to visit virtually every prison and every prison-connected mental health service in those states, observe their operations, and interview many inmates and staff. Of course, this experience is filtered through a case law–based legal prism.

(1976) held that as long as any given prison met minimally acceptable conditions of confinement, an inmate did not have sufficient legal autonomy to challenge a state's decision on the place of confinement. In *Meacham* there was no claim of a lost right to mandated care or rehabilitation, nor any claim that invasive procedures awaited the transferee. The inmate claimed a grievous loss in the greater distance from visiting family, loss of work opportunities, even the prospect of danger in adjusting to the turf of a new prison.

Would *Vitek*—involving transfer from prison to mental hospital—then be governed by *Meacham*, or is there something *qualitatively* different about a prison–to–mental hospital transfer? The Court concluded that a prisoner has a reasonable expectation of not being transferred to a mental hospital absent a finding of mental illness and that adequate treatment was not available in the sending facility. In addition, the stigma of being labeled "mentally ill," and the prospect of being subjected to what was termed "mandatory behavior modification" programs, created a liberty interest in the inmate and thus the need for a procedural format to resist.

Vitek, of course, does not require that a transfer hearing be held; and when held, such hearing need only be of the administrative variety. *Vitek* provides an opportunity to resist—an opportunity that few inmates appear to exercise.

Indeed, the problem is exactly the opposite of that confronted in *Vitek*: How may desperately ill inmates gain access to the care they need given the relatively limited bed space available? In many states, delays in hospital transfers can extend for weeks and even months.

Vitek does, of course, extend some autonomy to the prisoner, although, as noted, it hits at the wrong side of the problem. In addition, and perhaps inadvertently, the Court's assertion that the stigma of mental illness creates the basis for a protected liberty interest actually nourishes the stigma. It is one thing to say that a protesting inmate simply has sufficient legal identity or autonomy to resist enforced, and possibly invasive, care or simply to resist a qualitatively different place of confinement. If we are to view mental illness as illness, it is not the Court's finest moment to say to the inmate that "you have a procedural opportunity to avoid being stigmatized on your way to needed care" (Cohen, 1988).

Resisting Treatment

Whereas *Vitek* deals with the physical location of treatment, *Washington v. Harper* (1990) dealt with an inmate's right to resist unwanted antipsychotic drugs. Harper was an inmate in the Washington prison who for six years had consented to the administration of antipsychotic medication. He then said he would rather die than take the medication, but Washington officials were determined to forcibly medicate him.

First, the Court recognized that an inmate has a protected, liberty interest in avoiding the unwanted administration of antipsychotic drugs. However, even if an inmate is competent—that is, understands the nature and consequences of his or her decision—the state is also accorded an interest in pursuing the prisoner's medical interests and in overriding his or her protest with the use of forced medication. Thus, the prisoner does not have an absolute right to resist this form of treatment, and the state does not have an unconditional right to impose it. Dilemmas such as this tend to be resolved legally by procedural and burden-of-proof requirements. And this is what occurred in *Harper*.

To medicate forcibly, the state must establish that a mental disorder exists, that the treatment is in the prisoner's medical interests (and not simply prison security), and that the drug is administered under the direction of a licensed psychiatrist. An administrative hearing—not a judicial proceeding—may suffice to meet due process.

Although the Court abjures the possibility that prison security is, or could be, of paramount concern here, the reality is quite the contrary. The prime candidate for forced medication is the violent, acting-out inmate with a mental disorder. And although the medication may defuse the inmate, it also contributes a great deal to prison security and management.

The majority acknowledged the risks of negative side effects, although not with the vigor of the dissenters. Those risks were not enough to allow a competent inmate to refuse or to require judicial proceedings. If a doctor weighs the risks and monitors the inmate, a majority was satisfied. In *Sullivan v. Flannigan* (1993), an inmate sought to persuade the panel that he could function without medication. The court held that an inmate had no right to a drug-free interlude prior to a *Harper* hearing, a ruling that means a doctor may choose to medicate an inmate for his or her entire term.

Inmates who are noncompliant with their medication—either refusing or simply lapsing—are frequently involved in prison disciplinary proceedings. Often, the refusal or lapse relates to a failure of prison personnel to educate the inmate about the disorder and the consequences of taking or not taking the medication. A drug education program should be in place, inducements to continue on medication should be required before even contemplating force, and medication should be utilized as a last resort and then only in a hospital or residential treatment unit after *Harper* procedures, at a minimum, are employed.

A *Vitek* transfer hearing might actually be used to reach a forcible medication decision, and in some jurisdictions that is the case. When transfer and medication are decided in a single proceeding, the right to administer the drug should be severely time limited—10 days perhaps—until there is a review by the psychiatrist at the receiving facility.

Conclusion

A recent study of federal inmates' access to health care, including mental health care, found serious deficiencies in that system's capacity to provide adequate care. The finding of inadequate staff is framed by a larger picture of a failure to project inmate needs into the near future, inject quality assurance programs, and review cost effective alternatives (General Accounting Office, 1994).

Although a number of similar studies exist about other agencies responsible for inmates' mental health care, those studies rarely lead directly to change. Ironically, when a change agent does appear, typically in the form of a lengthy class action complaint filed in federal court, these very studies—as in the *Coleman* case in California—serve as evidence to support a finding of deliberate indifference.

Federal courts consistently find challenged prisons dangerously overcrowded and populated by inmates with serious mental disorders who are constitutionally entitled to mental health care. While the state loses case after case, there is no self-initiated change in corrections. Corrections systems have every reason to know of the current problems with inmates with mental disorders and to anticipate the future.

Without a crisis—one often created by a lawsuit or, less often, a riot—corrections seems paralyzed. For example, any corrections system that retained some credible experts in advance of a lawsuit and then followed any of their reasonable recommendations on staff, treatment space, and provisions for access would be virtually certain of insulating itself from successful legal challenge. This would be inexpensive insurance, but even the minimal "premium" seems unavailable.

In a crisis-oriented, reactive system, at a time when legislative appropriations for anything other than "bricks and mortar" and security staff seem nearly impossible, we may be doomed to sit on the sidelines and watch the inevitable events play themselves out. A lawsuit is filed, attorneys' fees and expert witness costs begin to mount, and mountains of discovery material are generated until someone gets the point: "We are going to lose; let's hire some people, find some beds, and provide some treatment."

Surely the best law here is preventive. The

legal factors used to assess the constitutionality of prison mental health services are rather clear, making it tragic that the sick inmates will suffer needlessly and scarce resources will go to a legal fight instead of to needed care. The lawsuits involving correctional mental health care will go on, and many of them will be resolved either in court or through settlement, leading to some form of consent decree.

A cautionary note might be sounded here— one that suggests that we ought to have a look at the policy consequences of what appears to be the transmigration of thousands of people with mental illness from our embattled and shrinking mental hospitals[10] to our prisons, with intermediate stops for many on our city streets and local jails. If we continue to confine large numbers of offenders with serious mental illness, we must continue to provide them with treatment—with extensive staff, treatment beds, programs, access—and more. Yet should we as a society want to provide extensive mental health care in prisons, or should we seek to divert such persons into a variety of other settings for care? Research is needed in this area that looks at the costs, outcomes, and alternatives—research that could easily be framed in the language of therapeutic jurisprudence.

References

Andrews v. Glenn, 768 F. Supp. 668 (C.D. Ill. 1991).

Bell v. Wolfish, 441 U.S. 520 (1979).

Bland, R. C., Newman, S. C., Dyck, R. J., & Orn, H. (1990). Prevalence of psychiatric disorders and suicide attempts in a prison population. *Canadian Journal of Psychiatry, 35,* 407–413.

Boston, J. (1992). *Wilson v. Seiter:* A preliminary analysis. In S. Saltzman & B. Wolvuitze (Eds.), *Civil rights litigation and attorney fees annual handbook, 8,* 41–54.

Callahan, L. A., Steadman, H. J., McGreevy, M. A., & Robbins, P. C. (1991). The volume and characteristics of insanity defense pleas. *Bulletin of the American Academy of Psychiatry and Law, 19*(4), 331–338.

Casey v. Lewis, 834 F. Supp. 1477 (D. Arizona 1993).

Cohen, F. (1980). *The law of deprivation of liberty: A study in social control.* Durham, NC: Carolina Academic Press.

Cohen, F. (1988). *Legal issues and the mentally disturbed prisoner.* Washington, DC: National Institute of Corrections.

Cohen, F. (1991). *The law of the deprivation of liberty: Cases and material.* Durham, NC: Carolina Academic Press.

Cohen, F. (1993). Captives' legal rights to mental health care. *Law and Psychology Review, 17,* 1–39.

Coleman v. Wilson, No. Civ. 5-90-0520 (E.D. Ca. June 6, 1994).

DeShaney v. Winnebago Department of Social Services, 489 U.S. 189 (1989).

Dickey, W. (1980). Incompetency and the nondangerous mentally ill client. *Criminal Law Bulletin, 16*(1), 22–40.

Duckworth v. Franzen, 780 F.2d 645 (7th Cir. 1985).

East v. Lemos, 768 F.2d 1000 (8th Cir. 1985).

Estelle v. Gamble, 429 U.S. 97 (1976).

Fabisiak, S., Steadman, H. J., Dvoskin, J., & Holohean, E. J. (1987). A survey of mental disability among state prison inmates. *Hospital and Community Psychiatry, 38,* 1086–1090.

Farmer v. Brennan, 114 U.S. 1970 (1994).

Farmer v. Carlson, 685 F. Supp. 1335 (M.D. Pa. 1988).

Ford v. Wainwright, 106 S. Ct. 2595 (1986).

---

[10]From 1960 to 1989, the number of psychiatric beds in the United States fell from 722,000 to 161,000. In Japan, psychiatric beds increased by 274%, from 95,000 to over 355,000; Germany has doubled its capacity (see Spector, 1994, reporting on data from the United Nations' 1994 *Human Development Report*).

Gaudreault v. Municipality of Salem, Mass., 923 F.2d 203 (1st Cir. 1990).

General Accounting Office Report to Chair, Subcommittee on Intellectual Property and Judicial Administration, Committee on the Judiciary, House of Representatives. (1994). *Bureau of prisons health care: Inmates' access to health care is limited by lack of clinical staff.* Washington, DC: Author.

Grisso, T. (1986). *Evaluating competencies: Forensic assessments and instruments.* New York: Plenum.

Jackson v. Indiana, 406 U.S. 715 (1975).

Jamelka, R., Trupin, E., & Chiles, J. A. (1989). The mentally ill in prisons: A review. *Hospital and Community Psychiatry,* 481–491.

Johnson, A. B. (1990). *Out of bedlam: The truth about deinstitutionalization.* New York: Basic Books.

Kennedy v. Mendoza-Martinez, 372 U.S. 144 (1963).

Kesey, K. (1962). *One flew over the cuckoo's nest.* New York: Viking.

Kolender v. Lawson, 461 U.S. 352 (1983).

Kramer, J. (1970). The state versus the addict: Uncivil commitment. *Boston University Law Review, 50*(1), 1–22.

Langley v. Coughlin, 715 F. Supp. 522 (S.D.N.Y. 1989), aff'd. 888 F.2d 252 (2d Cir. 1989).

Lynsky v. City of Boston, 761 F. Supp. 858 (D.Mass. 1990).

Matter of Boggs, 523 N.Y.S.2d 71 (1st Dept. 1987).

McGuckin v. Smith, 974 F.2d 1050 (9th Cir. 1992).

McQuiston, J. T. (1994, May 11). Form of insanity defense planned for next Rifkin trial. *New York Times,* p. B7.

Meacham v. Fano, 427 U.S. 215 (1976).

Motiuk, L. L., & Porporino, F. J. (1991). *The prevalence, nature and severity of mental health problems among federal male inmates in Canadian penitentiaries.* Ottawa: Correctional Services of Canada.

Murphy, G. R. (1986). *Special care: Improving police response to the mentally disabled.* Washington, DC: Police Executive Research Forum.

Neighbors, H. W., Williams, D. H., Gunnings, T. S., Lipscomb, W. D., Broman, C., & Lepowski, J. (1987). *The prevalence of mental disorder in Michigan prisons.* Final Report submitted to the Michigan Department of Corrections.

Ohio Department of Rehabilitation and Corrections. (1993). *1992 intake study and report: Final report.* Columbus, OH: Author.

Papachristo v. City of Jacksonville, 405 U.S. 156 (1972).

Pate v. Robinson, 383 U.S. 375 (1966).

Perlin, M. (1994). *The jurisprudence of the insanity defense.* Durham, NC: Carolina Academic Press.

Powell, T. (1994). *Prevalence of mental illness among rural prisoners.* Waterbury: Vermont Department of Corrections.

Rhodes v. Chapman, 452 U.S. 337 (1981).

Rosenthal, E. (1992, December 29). Chronic pain fells many but lacks clear cause. *New York Times,* pp. C1, C3.

Salazar v. City of Chicago, 940 F.2d 233 (1991).

Smith v. Jenkins, 919 F.2d 90 (8th Cir. 1990).

Smith-Bey v. Hospital Adm'r, 841 F.2d 751 (7th Cir. 1988).

Spector, P. (1994, September 24). "Failure by the numbers." *New York Times,* p. 23.

Spitzer, R. L., Williams, J. B., & Gibbon, M. (1986). *Structured clinical interview for DSM-III-R (SDID).* New York: New York State Psychiatric Institute.

Sullivan v. Flannigan, 8 F.3d 591 (7th Cir. 1993).

Torraco v. Maloney, 923 F.2d 231 (1st Cir. 1991).

United States v. John Hinckley, Jr., Findings and Order, Criminal Number 81-306, August 10, 1982.

U.S. Department of Justice, Bureau of Justice Statistics. (1993). *Sourcebook of criminal justice statistics 1992* (K. Maguire, A. L. Pastore, & T. J. Flanagan, Eds.). Washington, DC: U.S. Government Printing Office.

Vaillant, G. E. (1983). *The natural history of alcoholism: Causes, patterns, and paths to recovery.* Cambridge, MA: Harvard University Press.

Vitek v. Jones, 455 U.S. 480 (1980).

Washington v. Harper, 110 S.Ct. 1028 (1990).

White v. Farrier, 849 F.2d 322 (8th Cir. 1988).

Wilson v. Seiter, 111 S.Ct. 2321 (1991).

Winston v. Maine Technical College System, 631 A.2d 70 (1993), *cert. denied* 114 S.Ct. 1643 (1994).

Youngberg v. Romeo, 457 U.S. 307 (1982).

20 | The Mental Health Implications of Crime Victims' Rights

Richard P. Wiebe
University of Arizona

U.S. citizens expect their federal, state, and local governments to provide the police, court, and correctional services necessary to enforce the criminal law. This public responsibility evolved over several centuries from a system of dispute resolution that was predominantly private. In England and Europe following the fall of the Roman Empire, around the fifth century A.D., the family of a victim seeking redress could declare a "blood feud" against the person, property, and family of the wrongdoer, seeking both payment and vengeance (Henderson, 1992). English law, from which U.S. jurisprudence evolved, began to limit the extent of the blood feud in the 11th century, permitting it only where the injured party had demanded and been refused reasonable payment for the injury from the offender (Henderson, 1992); soon, the offender became responsible for the payment of a fine to the king as well (Schafer, 1968). At first, some crimes—such as killing by stealth, arson, treason, housebreaking, and open theft—required the death or mutilation of the offender; the offender could not merely pay compensation to the victim or the victim's family (Greenburg, 1984). Eventually, the transition to public enforcement of criminal law was complete. Current U.S. criminal law views crimes as of-

fenses against the state, not against the victims (Elias, 1986).

In the interests of public order, and in the face of centralized criminal justice, rights of criminal defendants were easily ignored. The U.S. Constitution's Bill of Rights, however, contains some protections for specific defendants. Enacted after the original Constitution, the Bill of Rights contains the following provisions governing the rights of persons suspected, accused, or convicted of committing a crime:

AMENDMENT IV: The right of the people to be secure in their persons, houses, papers, and effects, against unreasonable searches and seizures, shall not be violated, and no warrants shall issue but upon probable cause, supported by oath or affirmation, and particularly describing the place to be searched, and the persons or things to be seized.

AMENDMENT V: No person shall be held to answer for a capital, or otherwise infamous crime, unless on a presentment or indictment of a grand jury, except in cases arising in the land or naval forces, or in the militia, when in actual service in time of war or public danger; nor shall any person be subject to the same offense to be twice put in jeopardy of life or limb; nor shall be compelled in any criminal case to be a witness against himself; nor be deprived of life, liberty or property, without due process of law; nor shall private property be taken for public use without just compensation.

AMENDMENT VI: In all criminal prosecutions, the accused shall enjoy the right to a speedy and public trial, by an impartial jury of the State and district wherein the crime shall have been committed, which district shall have previously ascertained by law, and to be informed of the nature and cause of the accusation; to be confronted with the witnesses against him; to have compulsory process for obtaining witnesses in

I thank Wendy A. Gagnon for her assistance with research for this chapter, Daniel A. Krauss and Bruce D. Sales for their editorial comments and help with the structure of the chapter, and Christina Bouwkamp and Daniel W. Shuman for their editing and ideas. Any remaining problems are, of course, my responsibility.

his favor; and to have the assistance of counsel for his defense.

AMENDMENT VIII: Excessive bail shall not be required, or cruel and unusual punishments inflicted.

Initially, these rights applied only to persons accused of federal crimes, but they were applied to state defendants through the post–Civil War Supreme Court's interpretation of the Civil Rights Amendments (*Yick Wo v. Hopkins*, 1886). However, it was not until the 1950s that rights of criminals began to assume paramount importance in the criminal justice system. Defendants received "Miranda warnings" and court-appointed lawyers. The exclusionary rule, allowing only evidence obtained legally to be used against the accused (*Weeks v. United States*, 1913), was applied. Prison conditions were scrutinized; prisoners received counseling, employment training, schooling, medical care, and libraries, because their absence could be construed as "cruel and unusual punishment" under the Eighth Amendment (Karmen, 1984).

During this period of emphasis on defendants' rights, neither the Supreme Court nor state or national legislatures focused on the needs of crime victims. Although the right to protect individuals from the government was constitutionally compelling, the focus on the rights of defendants without talk of the rights of those they injured was not politically persuasive. Thus, in the aftermath of defendants' rights, a picture began to emerge of the "forgotten victim," victimized twice: first by the criminal, then by the system (Karmen, 1984; President's Task Force on Victims of Crime, 1982). In response, legislatures began to enact laws establishing rights for victims, at first focusing on government-funded victim compensation to crime victims. California passed the first such statute in 1965, followed by New York in 1966, Hawaii in 1967, and Massachusetts in 1968 (Roberts, 1990). Other victims' rights began to populate statute books and state constitutions; currently, there may be up to 30,000 different state and federal victims' rights laws (S. S. Howley, personal communication, December 30,

1993). Public interest peaked during the early Reagan years, with the establishment of the President's Task Force on Victims of Crime and the release of its final report in 1982. Many of the recommendations of the Task Force have been enacted (see, for example, U.S. Department of Justice, Office of Justice Programs, 1986), but nowhere have they and other victim-oriented measures been systematically evaluated for their effects on the psychological recovery of victims themselves. An evaluation of this type may help guide the future of victims' rights, so that victims may avoid being victimized a third time.

The goals of this chapter are to survey the scope and purposes of victims' rights provisions; to discuss, from current psychological research, the effects of those provisions on the mental health of victims; to compare these effects with those intended by lawmakers and advocates— that is, whether intended goals have been attained, and whether the laws resulted in unintended consequences; and to suggest possible directions for victims' rights that would better serve victims' mental health. The analysis fits the framework of *therapeutic jurisprudence,* which attempts to determine the extent to which legal processes benefit or harm the people involved (Wexler & Winick, 1991). However, it would be naive to assert that therapeutic jurisprudence alone can, or should, dictate the agenda of victims' rights. Laws are enacted within the context of the existing social structure, and other political and moral considerations may prevail over therapeutic outcomes (Sales & Shuman, 1994).

Before going forward, one caveat is in order. Crimes can be placed, with overlap and exceptions, into three broad categories. The first, so-called victimless crimes, such as vandalism of a public place, drunken driving, prostitution, drug use, insider trading, and desertion from the armed forces, lack specific victims (although they can clearly result in harm). Other crimes, like illegal dumping of toxic waste and espionage, may have specific victims, but their consequences may be delayed and the identity of the victims and extent of harm may not be readily apparent. The third broad category, including "street crimes" such as assault, homicide, robbery, rape, and burglary, together with fraud against individuals, involves specific, readily ascertainable victims; victims' rights provisions tend to focus on these crimes. Thus, the rest of this chapter focuses on this third category.

The Scope and Purposes of Victims' Rights

The word *victim* stems from the Latin *victima*, a person or animal sacrificed during a religious ceremony. The word has since acquired more connotations—for example, there are victims of floods, cancer, accidents, prejudice, and crime (Karmen, 1984). Unlike the sacrificial victim, a crime victim suffers consequences unintended by society and may have certain rights under law that accrue after victimization. Aside from the quest for justice, a topic beyond the scope of this chapter, the proliferation of victims' rights has stemmed from the desire to ease victims' psychological suffering. The next section outlines the details of that suffering.

The Experience of the Victim

Criminal victimization can leave psychological scars that endure as long as or longer than any physical or financial damage (Fischer, 1984; Frank, 1988; Henderson, 1992). Criminal victimization may result in anxiety disorders, depression, drug and alcohol abuse, fear, flashbacks, lowered self-esteem, sexual dysfunction, somatic complaints, suicidal ideation, suspiciousness, and a sense of social isolation (Fischer, 1984; Keane, 1989; Lurigio & Resick, 1990). In some cases victims may suffer from posttraumatic stress disorder (PTSD) (American Psychiatric Association, 1994).[1]

Although much of the research on the impact of crime has focused on rape, victims of other crimes may suffer qualitatively similar consequences (Resick, 1987). Other factors being equal, like level of violence and victim's perception of danger, rape may harm the victim's mental health more than do other violent crimes (Kilpatrick, 1989; Kilpatrick et al., 1985), but this issue is not settled (Resick, 1987; Riggs, Kilpatrick, & Resnick, 1992). Significant psychological injuries have been reported among victims of many other crimes, including assault (Lurigio & Resick, 1990; Riggs et al., 1992; Shepherd, 1990; Steinmetz, 1984; Wirtz & Harrell, 1987), attempted rape (Becker, Skinner, Abel, Howell, & Bruce, 1982), bank fraud (Ganzini, McFarland, & Cutler, 1990), burglary (Brown & Harris, 1989), child abuse (Cavaiola & Schiff, 1988), kidnapping (Terr, 1983), and robbery (Kilpatrick et al., 1985). In addition, families of crime victims in general (Riggs & Kilpatrick, 1990) and of rape (Mio, 1991; Orzek, 1983) and homicide (Amick-McMullen, Kilpatrick, & Resnick, 1991; McCune, 1989) victims in particular often develop psychological symptoms as a result of the crime. Finally, community residents may suffer as a result of public vandalism, a crime with no specific victim (Reiss, 1986).

The consequences of victimization are not necessarily intuitively obvious. Although crime victims indeed experience more mental health problems than do other persons (Ganzini, McFarland, & Cutler, 1990; Kilpatrick et al., 1985; Riggs et al., 1992; Santiago, McCall-Perez, Gorcey, & Beigel, 1985), the severity of the crime does not necessarily predict the severity of the symptoms. For example, Becker et al. (1982) found that victims of attempted rape and rape did not significantly differ in their short- and long-term responses to the assault; Ganzini et al.

---

[1]Victims of other kinds of trauma, such as serious accidents and illnesses, war, and technological and natural disasters, often develop the same mental health problems as crime victims (Frieze, Hymer, & Greenberg, 1987; Keane, 1989).

(1990) found significant levels of depression in victims of the relatively placid crime of bank fraud. Furthermore, though it is clear that support from family members and friends can assist a victim's recovery (Janoff-Bulman & Frieze, 1983), those persons do not always understand the extent of psychological trauma and may think the victim should have recovered earlier than is reasonable to expect (Mio, 1991; Riggs & Kilpatrick, 1990; Sales, Baum, & Shore, 1984). In addition, not all crime victims will react the same way to similar victimizations (Lurigio & Resick, 1990; Shapland, 1986).

Similarly, the duration of symptoms is difficult to predict. Symptoms can begin immediately after the attack and persist over a lifetime (Santiago et al., 1985). Fifty-seven percent of rape victims in a community survey reported having suffered PTSD symptoms at some point in their lives, with 16% reporting current PTSD symptoms, an average of 17 years after the rape (Kilpatrick, Saunders, Vernonen, Best, & Von, 1987).

Cognitive and behavioral psychologists have attempted to explain this persistence of symptoms through several mechanisms. Through classical conditioning, a crime victim may unconsciously associate an aversive event, the crime itself, with a previously neutral stimulus, such as the street on which the crime occurred (Wirtz & Harrell, 1987). The victim would then respond with fear and anxiety to the street itself, even when it appears objectively to be safe. These responses may be extremely resistant to extinction (Kilpatrick et al., 1987; Veronen, Kilpatrick, & Resick, 1979). In addition, depression may result from learned helplessness, where a victim has been traumatized as a result of an experience over which he or she had no control (Peterson & Seligman, 1983). Persistence of symptoms may also be associated with an enduring modification of beliefs. Studies have shown that violent crime can alter victims' beliefs regarding their safety, self-esteem, and trust, whereas property crimes affect victims' beliefs concerning safety; these beliefs, in turn, affect psychological distress

(Janoff-Bulman & Frieze, 1983; Norris & Kaniasty, 1991).

Symptoms may also endure because, left to themselves, crime victims may select inefficacious techniques for recovery. Research focusing on victims' coping strategies outside a therapeutic relationship found that some victims' methods, such as changing phone numbers, staying at home, moving, not going out alone, installing new locks, bolting locks more, owning or carrying a weapon, changing jobs, and generally exercising more caution, failed to facilitate their recovery significantly. In fact, changing phone numbers and staying home more correlated with *higher* psychological distress levels both one and six months after the crime (Wirtz & Harrell, 1987; see also Cohen, 1987). Similarly, remaining at home and withdrawing from others correlates with poor postrape adjustment (Meyer & Taylor, 1986). Without assistance, then, many crime victims will continue to experience significant adverse psychological symptoms.

The Framework of Victims' Rights

Despite their suffering, recognition and establishment of a societal obligation to crime victims has been long delayed. The constitutional framework of American criminal procedure seeks to limit governmental power over individuals. The constitution does not obligate the government to provide services or benefits to individuals. This framework implicitly assumes that crime victims benefit from just prosecution of the perpetrator. Thus, in the absence of affirmative statutory recognition of crime victims' rights, the American criminal justice system grants the victim no special stature within it other than as a complaining witness, and it assumes no obligation to the crime victim as an individual, such as by according the victim a right to compensation or services. In the absence of victims' rights and victim assistance programs, crime victims must provide their own transportation to and from court and must assist the prosecution, over whose conduct they have no control, by identifying witnesses, attending the trial, and subjecting themselves to intrusive cross-examination by the defendant's attorney. They also must pay their own medical and counseling bills (Sales, Rich, & Reich, 1987). Because many crimes go unreported, most reported crimes fail to result in an arrest, and most arrests do not lead to a trial. Thus, whatever benefits crime victims enjoy from criminal prosecution will not be available to most crime victims.

Victims' rights attempt to address these problems of victims through various means. The first broad category of victims' rights contains measures aimed at benefiting victims through increasing penalties for, and decreasing the liberties of, accused and convicted criminals. Thus, the provisions recommended under this rubric of victims' rights address the accused directly and the victim indirectly. "Getting tough" on criminals by, for example, increasing sentences, limiting bail, and abolishing the exclusionary rule, focuses directly on the criminal. The desired result of more convictions, longer sentences, and a safer society benefits crime victims by decreasing their chances of being revictimized (President's Task Force on Victims of Crime, 1982) and may satisfy victims' desire for revenge (Henderson, 1992). This orientation has been dubbed the "crime control" model of victims' rights (see, for example, McShane & Williams, 1992).

A second category of provisions and services, compatible with the crime control perspective, affects victims directly within the criminal justice system. Some, such as victim or witness assistance programs, help victims negotiate the criminal justice system by, for example, providing transportation to and from court, court escorts, and referrals to other community agencies. Others, such as statutes requiring victim impact statements at sentencing, provide a significant role for the victim in the proceedings themselves. These statements include testimony from or on behalf of the victim regarding the effects the crime had on the victim, whether physical, economic, psychological, or social. This category of provisions may also affect offenders: for example,

with support from a victim or witness assistance program, a crime victim may become a better and more cooperative witness, resulting in a greater probability of conviction.

A third category provides alternatives to traditional criminal justice procedures and outcomes. Examples include mediation between offenders and victims, restitution from offenders to victims, and civil rights suits by victims against offenders. These procedures can address individual aspects of victimization more easily than conventional criminal court and are more amenable to victim control.

The final category bestows direct benefits on victims, including victim compensation and mental health services. Provisions in the third and fourth categories can also be encompassed by the crime control model (President's Task Force on Victims of Crime, 1982), but radical victimologists are more concerned with the possibility that, in the implementation of provisions within the first two categories, crime control can be emphasized and victims ignored (Elias, 1993; McShane & Williams, 1992).

Although concern for the victim began to emerge in the 1960s, many of these provisions, both victim- and crime-oriented, have only recently become law. Several protections for victims of federal crimes appeared in the Federal Victim and Witness Assistance Act in 1982 (the Victim/Witness Act). This act protected the privacy of victims of federal crimes and gave them a presumptive right to restitution from offenders. The Victim/Witness Act also mandated that evidence concerning the impact of the crime on the victim, or "victim impact statements," be accepted in federal trials (U.S. Department of Justice, Office of Justice Programs, 1986). The laws of most of the states as well now require these statements (National Victim Center, 1993).

Two years later, Congress passed the Victims of Crime Act (VOCA) (Public Law 98-473), whose most significant provision established the Crime Victims Fund. This fund provides up to $100,000,000 annually to state and local victim compensation and victim/witness assistance programs (Roberts, 1990). Currently, every state, as well as the federal government and the District of Columbia, has a victim compensation program (National Association of Victim Compensation Boards, 1993b) and provides some services to crime victims (National Victim Center, 1993). Furthermore, 17 states have so-called Victims' Bills of Rights; 9 appear in state constitutions (Reske, 1992). Finally, mandatory sentencing guidelines have been enacted on the federal level and in many states (National Victim Center, 1993).

Let us consider these four categories in greater detail.

Crime Control: Increased Sanctions

Where convictions are not obtained or tough sentences not imposed, many crime victims believe the system has failed. Victims often believe that the scales of justice have tilted in favor of criminals and that the current system "has proven itself incapable of dealing with crime" (Harrington, 1982, p. vi). They may therefore feel neglected and vulnerable, exacerbating the consequences of their victimization. In response, much of what has been enacted as victims' rights limit the rights of accused and convicted criminals in the hope of making convictions easier and detention longer (Dittenhoffer & Ericson, 1992). Cross-examination has been curtailed, hearsay permitted at preliminary hearings, preventive detention authorized, mandatory minimum and "true" life sentences imposed, concurrent sentences reduced, and the exclusionary rule limited (Viano, 1987). The constitutionality of such victims' rights initiatives is the subject of current debate, with courts nationwide having disagreed on their constitutionality, but it appears that many will survive judicial scrutiny (Carrington & Nicholson, 1989).

No Right to Safety The most important victims' right would be a right not to be a victim. However, a specific person generally has no right to safety unless the government has accepted some special duty to protect that particular person, such

as when a witness is under police protection (see *American Law Reports,* 1985). A person cannot successfully claim that his or her rights have been violated simply because he or she was victimized, for example, in a town that maintained regular police patrols at or near the crime scene. The criminal justice system represents an attempt to maintain public safety; it does not provide a guarantee.

Crime Control: Crime Victims and the Criminal Trial

Believing that their special status is not acknowledged, crime victims have long complained of being ignored and used by the criminal justice system. Provisions to address these concerns fall into two main types: those guaranteeing the victim a "voice" in criminal proceedings, and those governing out-of-court interactions between the victim and the system.

Granting Victims a "Voice" Although the Bill of Rights applies to all U.S. citizens, the Constitution grants victims of crime no rights comparable to those protecting the accused (Goddu, 1993). This omission has created what many have perceived as a system that favors the accused at the expense of the victim (President's Task Force on Victims of Crime, 1982). For example, whereas criminal defendants have the absolute right to confront the witnesses against them, victims do not have the reciprocal right to confront the accused; in criminal proceedings, the prosecutor, not the victim, decides whether the victim will be a witness.

More broadly, the victim has little or no control over whether, or to what extent, the accused will be prosecuted. Though, in many jurisdictions, a victim may hire an attorney to assist with the prosecution (Sales et al., 1987), this is not practical for many crime victims: violent crimes strike members of poor households more often than persons of higher income (Bastian, 1993).

To increase victim involvement in the system, the President's Task Force proposed adding victims' rights to the Sixth Amendment of the U.S.

Constitution. The Task Force suggested that "the victim in every criminal prosecution shall have the right to be present and to be heard at all critical stages of judicial proceedings" (President's Task Force on Victims of Crime, 1982). This does not specify the extent to which the trier of fact (the jury in a jury trial, the judge in a nonjury trial) shall consider the victim's statements, and does not specify what a "critical" stage might be; it might not give victims the right to participate, for example, in plea bargaining negotiations, but only to attend court when the plea is accepted by the judge. For instance, the Washington State Constitution grants victims the rights to be informed of and attend court proceedings and to make statements at sentencing and any other stage, such as a parole hearing, where the defendant's release is being considered, but does not address plea bargaining (Washington State Constitution, 1989).

Other, narrower statutes permit or require statements regarding the impact of the crime on the victim and the victim's family to be introduced when the case is being tried, when the defendant is being sentenced, or both. Victim impact statements have been challenged by defendants who claim that the character or eloquence of the victim or the victim's family should have no bearing on the defendant's sentence. However, the U.S. Supreme Court recently permitted such evidence to be introduced in capital cases (*Payne v. Tennessee*, 1991, overruling *Booth v. Maryland*, 1989).

Relations with the System   A victims' bill of rights, or similar scheme, seeks to compel the criminal justice system to treat the crime victim with respect. Some of the common statutes grant victims the right:

1. To be informed of the final disposition of the case;
2. To be notified if any court proceeding for which they have received a subpoena will not occur as scheduled;
3. To receive protection from victim intimidation and to be provided with information as to the level of protection available;

4. To be informed of the procedure for receiving witness fees;
5. To be provided, wherever practical, with a secure waiting area away from defendants;
6. To have personal property in the possession of law enforcement agencies returned as expeditiously as possible, where feasible, photographing the property and returning it to the owner within ten days of being taken; and
7. To be provided with appropriate employer intercession so that loss of pay and other benefits resulting from court appearances will be minimized. (Goddu, 1993, p. 251)

None of these provisions has a direct impact on the conduct of the trial itself; rather, each indirectly affects the outcome by facilitating the victim's participation as a witness against the defendant.

In addition, some states require that victims be notified of the offender's status at all stages of the proceedings, through sentence completion. The victim, and, under some statutes, the community, would be told when the defendant has been released for any reason, including parole, work release, furlough, or completion of the full term of the sentence. They would also be informed if the prisoner escapes (National Victim Center, 1993).

Alternatives to Traditional Justice

A criminal who completes a prison sentence is considered to have satisfied his or her debt to society. However, the debt to the victim may not have been addressed at all. For a victim who still suffers from the effects of the crime, alternatives to this traditional paradigm, including restitution, mediation, and civil litigation, can reestablish the connection between the criminal and the victim that was broken when the state took over the prosecution and can compel the criminal to take responsibility for the consequences of the crime.

Restitution   Theoretically, restitution affords the victim a chance to be fully compensated for losses or injuries by the person responsible, the perpetrator. Restitution comprises a judicially ordered payment from offender to victim, either after trial or as part of a plea agreement. It is often made a condition of probation to encourage compliance. Restitution is available in most states and in federal court. Under the Victim/Witness Act (1982), a judge in a federal case must order restitution or expressly state reasons for not so doing. Restitution may also be ordered as part of a mediated agreement between the offender and the victim (Dittenhoffer & Ericson, 1992).

Mediation Victim-offender mediation (VOM), or reconciliation, takes advantage of the "potential for activity, for participation" inherent in conflicts between victims and offenders (Christie, 1977, p. 7). Through VOM, an agreement between the offender and the victim replaces a judicial determination. The agreement can require the offender to make payments or provide services directly to the victim, to perform community service, or to fulfill a combination of these obligations (Umbreit, 1989).

VOM attempts to grant crime victims some control over criminal justice, with the extent of control dependent on the program design. In some designs, the judge refers a case to mediation only after conviction with the instruction that the victim and offender agree on the amount of restitution, often not to exceed a limit set by the judge (Dittenhoffer & Ericson, 1992). Other designs require that both victim and offender opt out of the criminal trial process voluntarily and allow a full range of possible outcomes, as described above (Umbreit, 1989).

Civil Courts and Crime Victims Concurrent with the takeover of criminal justice by the state, separate civil tort systems evolved where victims could sue offenders for money damages in the civil courts. However, this remedy, still theoretically available to all crime victims, can be used successfully in only a minority of cases (Roberts, 1990).

For a tort action to succeed, a *tortfeasor*—an entity responsible for the harm—must be identified and found to have breached a legal duty to the injured party. For the injured party to attain complete relief, the tortfeasor must have assets or insurance to pay the judgment. These requirements limit the feasibility of torts for most crime victims. Even if identified, the offender may be a family member or acquaintance whom the victim does not wish to sue, or the evidence in the case may be weak. Moreover, not all criminals have easily identifiable assets, if they have assets at all. If the offender is a family member, the assets may be identical to those of the victim. In addition, insurance policies generally do not insure persons against the consequences of their own intentional criminal actions. Finally, it is very difficult for an incarcerated offender to earn enough money to pay a civil judgment.

A poor offender may occasion a search for "deep pockets," an entity other than the primary offender that may be held responsible for the victimization. Deep pockets can be found, for example, in landlords who have undertaken the duty of providing security services but whose services are provided negligently (*American Law Reports*, 1975).

Victims may also bring suit seeking money damages from the government for a denial of constitutional rights. For example, in *DeShaney v. Winnebago County Department of Social Services* (1989), the family of a child left brain damaged by his father sued—albeit unsuccessfully—the local social services agency, claiming that the agency had deprived the child of his life, liberty, or property without due process of law under the Fourteenth Amendment to the U.S. Constitution because it failed to take appropriate action to protect the child despite reports of previous abuse. Although the Court held that the Constitution recognized no such claim, it acknowledged the possibility of a state law tort claim in such a case.

Direct Benefits to Victim: Compensation, Services

Other programs exist for crime victims whose needs the various court systems cannot address fully. Victim compensation programs make government payments directly to eligible crime victims, partly in response to the inadequacies of restitution. Most require that the victim apply for an award; awards generally extend to compensation for physical injuries and "necessary" personal property only, such as wheelchairs and eyeglasses (Geis, 1990). Victim compensation can also pay for therapy of the victim's choice, subject, in most states, to time or money limitations (National Association of Victim Compensation Boards, 1993b). These programs exist in all 50 states, the District of Columbia, and the federal government (National Association of Victim Compensation Boards, 1993a).

Victims may also be assisted by victim service agencies, which are often nonprofit and exist at least in part on government grants (Roberts, 1990). These services emerged to overcome limitations placed on victims by the criminal justice system. Although this system provides many avenues for victims to seek recompense and recovery, victims must participate in the system to gain access to these rights. Unfortunately, low reporting rates for many of the most serious crimes hinder the reach of many victim rights' provisions, especially those based solely in the courts. A community survey conducted by Kilpatrick et al. (1987) revealed that almost 25% of the sample of women had been victims of a completed rape during their lifetime, but only 15% of these rapes had ever been reported to the police. In addition, restrictions on victim compensation can further inhibit what victims recover.

Victim service programs grew out of grassroots organizations of the 1970s dedicated to, and often founded by, victims of particular crimes, like sexual assault or drunk driving. Funding under the Victims of Crimes Act and various state initiatives has encouraged the establishment of these programs, with their number currently exceeding 5000 (Davis & Henley, 1990). These agencies generally assist victims of any crime. In a survey of 184 local victim service programs, summarized in Table 20.1, Roberts (1990) found they most commonly provided explanations of the court process and referrals to other agencies, and less commonly provided lock repair and emergency money. In addition, crime victims may take advantage of other public services that are open to all, like county mental health departments and public hospitals.

The Mental Health Consequences of Victims' Rights

The past 15 years have seen victims' rights and services proliferate. What remains to be established, however, is which of these provisions and programs actually benefit victims, where *benefit* is not simply defined within the terms of the theory that generated the right. For example, an advocate of the crime control model may be concerned with convictions and sentence length,

Table 20-1   Services Provided by Programs

Type of Service	Number of Programs	Percentage
Explain court process	131	71
Make referrals	126	69
Provide court escort	120	65
Help with victim compensation applications	118	64
Public education	112	61
Assist with employers	111	60
Provide transportation to court	109	59
Provide crisis intervention	99	54
Provide child care	69	38
Provide emergency money	45	25
Repair locks	22	12

Source: Roberts (1990, p. 47).

whereas a radical victimologist may applaud any victim-oriented measure that does not result in harsher punishment for the criminal.

Evaluation of rights and services may be approached by combining examinations of the actual, not theoretical, effects of crime on victims (for example, Kilpatrick et al., 1985) and the efficacy of various therapies (Frank, 1988; Kilpatrick and Calhoun, 1988). Under this perspective, laws should seek to deliver the proper therapies to the proper victims. This assumes, however, that the only necessary treatment for the consequences of victimization happens in the clinic, and it ignores the role of the rest of the victim's environmental context.

A broader approach is illustrated by two trends in social science research that seek explicitly to determine the effects of laws and legal processes on the people they affect. The first, *procedural justice*, studies user satisfaction with courts and other adjudicative processes (Thibaut & Walker, 1975). This research shows that, regardless of the outcome of their case, persons who believe that they have been heard, taken seriously, and treated with respect are more likely to be satisfied with their court experience than those who believe otherwise (Fischer, 1984). The procedural justice research suggests that citizens are more likely to accept a system if they believe the authorities will listen to their concerns (Tyler, 1987). A procedure is "just" when people affected thereby are satisfied with it.

Unlike procedural justice, the second law and social science perspective, *therapeutic jurisprudence*, does not limit itself to a single dependent variable. Therapeutic jurisprudence seeks to assist the law to achieve its potential to advance therapeutic outcomes (Sales & Shuman, 1994). This norm need not conflict with other views on victims' rights that also aim to help crime victims. From the perspective of therapeutic jurisprudence, then, an analysis of victims' rights should seek to discover the effects of laws and legal processes on the recovery of previctimization psychological functioning of victims. Some research does attempt to make

procedural justice part of therapeutic jurisprudence. However, it appears to assume that its outcome measures, such as satisfaction with the court process, belief in the fairness of the procedure, and trust in the system, benefit the consumers of the system without empirically confirming this benefit (see, for example, Tyler, 1992).

Evaluation of Increased Criminal Sanctions

The crime control model of victims' rights, designed to benefit victims primarily by incarcerating criminals, has been criticized by radical victimologists (Elias, 1983a; Fattah, 1992; Goddu, 1993; Henderson, 1992; Karmen, 1984; McShane & Williams, 1992). These critics do not accept the "common assumptions about crime victims—that they are all 'outraged' and want revenge and tougher law enforcement" (Henderson, 1992, p. 111). Radical victimology argues that this is only incidentally a victim-oriented perspective. Furthermore, some have accused conservative political groups of using the rhetoric of "victims' rights" to advance their "law and order" agenda (Elias, 1986, 1993; McShane & Williams, 1992).

Research has not yet demonstrated a link between conviction or harsh punishment of offenders and victims' recovery (Halleck, 1989; Umbreit, 1989). However, victims may benefit from the satisfaction of their desires for safety or vengeance.

Safety

The interjection of victims' rights initiatives into American jurisdictions has occurred as public fear of crime, specifically street crime, has escalated, while the crime rate generally has leveled out. In fact, according to the U.S. Department of Justice, the total number of criminal victimizations in America actually *declined* slightly between 1972 and 1992, with per capita rates of personal theft, household larceny, and burglary sinking significantly during that period. Assault, robbery, and rape rates have remained about the same, which means (with population growth) that the total number of such violent crimes has risen slightly (Bastian, 1993).

The proposition that incarceration following a serious crime will prevent future crime has been questioned. Because the crime rate declines sharply with age irrespective of incarceration or apprehension rates, serious offenders should be incarcerated *before* they begin to commit serious offenses if we are to prevent crime (Gottfredson & Hirschi, 1990). Problems, of course, arise: predictions are not necessarily accurate, and concerns for the civil liberties of both children and parents mitigate against intrusive programs for at-risk youth.

Thus, it is not clear that victims do, or should, feel safer today as a consequence of these victims' rights initiatives. Ironically, measures aimed at increasing sentences and convictions, which are partially aimed at incapacitation of the criminal and safety of society, could actually increase the tendencies of the victim to withdraw by making the world appear to be an even harsher place than it is (Elias, 1993). Unfortunately, there has been very little research on this subject.

Vengeance

Aside from a desire for safety, a desire for justice or vengeance may motivate victims, and this desire may interfere with recovery if left unresolved. Victimization appears to lead to a loss of the sense of control over one's life. Recovery occurs only after the victim assumes responsibility for dealing with the traumatic experience, instead of attempting to shut it out of consciousness (Henderson, 1992). Past and future victimization can be distinguished: coping strategies may represent the attempt to deal with past victimization by preventing future victimization. Yet, if the existential perspective has some weight, recovery will not occur until the victim makes the past victimization part of his or her life (Henderson, 1992). Indeed, cognitive and behavioral therapies aim to allow the victims to return to normal, previctimization functioning in the world, instead of withdrawing from it (Foa, 1991; Frank, 1988). To achieve previctimization func-

tioning, it may be necessary to abandon vengeance to recover precrime mental health (Halleck, 1989). And if it is important to help restore the victim's belief system (Kennedy, 1983; Norris & Kaniasty, 1991), victims may need to abandon vengeance. Victims who retain their anger or who attempt to avoid situations that resemble the conditions of the earlier victimization, for example by refusing ever to walk outside after dark, can become phobic and never approach any situation, no matter how harmless, that resembles the crime conditions.

Anger may be important in initiating the recovery process; anger has been positively correlated with longer life among cancer patients (Wortman, 1983), though, by itself, it increases the risks of heart disease and hypertension. Perhaps anger connected with a desire for vengeance can benefit crime victims, as long as that anger is resolved; as discussed below, successful recovery has been reported for torture victims who testify publicly about their experiences (Pope & Garcia-Peltoniemi, 1991).

In sum, it is not clear whether provisions that simply increase penalties for offenders have any salutary effects on the psychological recovery of victims. However, measures requiring the active participation of victims, like victim impact statements, could satisfy victims as well as crime control advocates.

Victims in the Justice System: Consequences of Provisions

Provisions designed either to give victims a voice in or to smooth their relations with the criminal justice system can affect victims' mental health either directly or indirectly. If, for example, a victim's postcrime anxiety diminishes as a result of testifying to the impact of the crime on his or her life, the testimony has had a direct effect. If, however, the victim's improvement is due to satisfaction at the long sentence the judge imposed after hearing the victim impact statement, the testimony had an indirect effect.

Three major questions arise concerning the relationships between (1) criminal sanctions and victim psychological functioning, (2) victim participation in the trial and sanctions, and (3) the victim's dealings with the criminal justice system and victim mental health. As discussed above, little research exists to illuminate the first question.

With regard to the second, some evidence suggests that victim impact statements in capital trials increase the likelihood that the jury will impose the death sentence (Burkhead, Luginbuhl, & Wrenn, 1994), but this question is not settled. Indeed, a simple answer to the second question has proved elusive; most research in this area has focused on the decision making of the judge and jury without specifically testing the victims' role as a predictor. The third question has been studied more extensively. However, there has been no consensus on the criteria used to evaluate effects, which may reflect an underlying clash of goals. Although therapeutic jurisprudence measures the benefit to victims of laws and legal processes, procedural justice measures the more specific variable of satisfaction with such processes and assumes that satisfaction, besides being therapeutic, benefits society (Tyler, 1992). If not satisfied with the justice system, crime victims add their voice to the democratic cacophony of competing desires and may lose respect for, and even disobey, the law themselves (see Tyler, 1992). Therefore, satisfaction of consumers becomes a legitimate and sometimes overriding goal of the system, and procedural justice an important perspective.

It is important, however, to retain sight of crime victims' long-term psychological outlook and not focus only on their immediate satisfaction with court procedures. As satisfied customers, victims may assume they have received the limit of the system's assistance and may cease their quest for full recovery. To explore the relationship between procedural justice and recovery, victims' satisfaction with court procedures could be used as an *independent* variable, or predictor, of subsequent mental health functioning. Other variables, such as the outcome of the trial, the seriousness of the harm, and the treatment of the victim outside the justice system, may also be important predictors; this area remains largely unexplored. Although legislatures have enacted a plethora of statutes attempting to ease the victim's experience with the court system, research does not yet support the contention that the quality of this experience significantly aids the victim's eventual psychological recovery (see, for example, Cluss, Boughton, Frank, Stewart, & West, 1983; Lurigio & Resick, 1990).

Maximizing procedural justice, however, most likely does no harm. It is difficult to see how provisions that seek respectful treatment of victims in court could interfere with their recovery, and such provisions may be of significant benefit (Resick, 1987). Furthermore, because a victim's perception of control has been shown to be important to recovery (Kelly, 1990), and persons who believe they have had a voice in court proceedings are generally more satisfied with those proceedings than those who do not so believe, it is possible that the notions of "voice" and "control" represent the same underlying psychological process. If so, victim participation in the court process may be therapeutic, including at plea bargaining and other stages generally closed to the public.

Effects of Granting Victims a "Voice"

As already noted, because a major concern of victims seems to be their alienation from and lack of involvement in criminal proceedings, allowing victims to make a statement at sentencing and other stages of the criminal process could benefit victims psychologically (Fischer, 1984). However, the mere fact that victims have been heard does not guarantee that their wishes will be followed. For example, in a study of sexual assault cases in Ohio, the expressed wishes of victims regarding sentencing options were not followed to any significant degree by the judge (Walsh, 1992). Research is needed to determine the psychological effects on victims of having their wishes ignored, even though Tyler (1987) suggests that being heard may be sufficient.

Testimony and Oral Histories It is possible that testifying in court, and especially informing the court about the personal impact of the crime, benefits the victim (see Sahjpaul & Renner, 1988). Support for the idea that public disclosure can help victims recover is found in the success of testimonial and oral history therapy for victims of torture (C. Bouwkamp, personal communication, July 13, 1994). Such persons can, with the assistance of a therapist, either prepare oral histories to be shared with other victims and their families (Herbst, 1992), prepare a written document from tape-recorded testimony in a therapeutic setting (Cienfuegos & Monelli, 1983), or publicly denounce their tormentors (Pope & Garcia-Peltoniemi, 1991). Consistent with research on victim involvement in sentencing, however, torture victims may suffer negative consequences when their testimony is ignored (Pope & Garcia-Peltoniemi, 1991). The same may be true regarding the overall responsiveness of the criminal justice system. Furthermore, testimony may not be appropriate for everybody, as the popularity of laws protecting the privacy of sexual assault victims attests.

Victims' Rights: Rights without Remedies

Although victims' rights—to privacy, notification of the status of the victim, to have personal property used at trial returned expeditiously, and so forth—may be couched in the rhetoric of "rights" (as in "victims' bills of rights"), they differ significantly from criminals' rights: they generally are not enforceable (Goddu, 1993). Sanctions for a failure to honor the rights of the accused differ starkly from those available to a victim whose rights are violated. The best known of the sanctions for violations of the rights of the accused is the "exclusionary rule."

The Exclusionary Rule   The exclusionary rule excludes evidence gathered in violation of a defendant's Fourth Amendment rights under the U.S. Constitution. The decision to exclude illegally obtained evidence is unrelated to the probative value of the evidence or the consequence of exclusion to a conviction or acquittal (*Weeks v. United States*, 1913). No equivalent rule exists

under current victim rights' schemes: sanctions against the government for failing to observe and protect the rights of victims do not exist (Eikenberry, 1989; Polito, 1990; Roland, 1989), unless, in some cases, the government breached a special duty and the victim was injured as a result of the breach (*American Law Reports*, 1986). Furthermore, it would probably be inappropriate to punish the *accused* for the government's failure to follow the letter of victims' rights. For example, under the Washington State Constitution the victim has the right to attend all court proceedings. If the consequence of a denial of this right were easier conviction of the defendant, this would violate the defendant's well-established right to be judged only on evidence actually presented in the courtroom. However, the fact that many victims' rights are unenforceable may harm victims.

Notification of the Status of the Offender
One victim right deserves special mention because it may operate to harm the victim if enforced. Where a statute requires notification of the status of the convicted and imprisoned offender, victims who are not so notified but who are not harmed by that particular offender will have no recourse (*American Law Reports*, 1985, 1986). On the other hand, notification may not benefit victims. Although no definitive research could be found addressing this issue, it is possible that this could actually harm victims by causing them to lead a fearful, socially restricted lifestyle (C. Bouwkamp, personal communication, July 13, 1994), at least in the absence of other effective supports.

The Effects of Alternative Criminal Justice

The victims' rights discussed above involve the traditional criminal justice system, where the state, not the victim, plays the role of the injured party. Alternatives, including restitution, mediation, and civil torts, still cast the victim as victim, and still within a government context. On the other hand, the amount of control ceded to victims varies among individual programs, ranging from restitution ordered without consulting the victim to face-to-face mediation between the victim and the offender.

Evaluating Restitution

Aside from the obvious monetary benefit to victims, successful restitution can have a salutary effect on the victim's satisfaction with the court process (Rosen & Harland, 1990). It can also increase the offender's chances of rehabilitation by fostering a fruitful relationship between the offender and the probation officer (Galaway, 1988), which may itself benefit the victim. Restitution can be made part of any reasonable model of corrections, either as punishment, equity, recompense, or rehabilitation (Matthews, 1981). When made part of an agreement between the victim and the offender, it can help the victim achieve closure of the criminal experience and enhance recovery (Henderson, 1992; Umbreit, 1989).

Although theoretically restitution could fully compensate victims for their losses, practically it cannot be relied on to do so. Despite the fact that advocacy for its implementation came primarily from the victims' rights movement (Rosen & Harland, 1990), restitution serves primarily the aims of the system, and only tangentially the needs of the victim. For example, an American Bar Association study revealed victim dissatisfaction with attempts made to collect from offenders, as well as with the failure of restitution programs both to consult with victims regarding the amounts of awards and to keep them apprised of the progress of collections (Hillenbrand, 1990). Probation officers often cease attempting to collect from an offender who has not made full payment but is leading a stable family life because the probation officer's main interest is in the offender, not the victim (Zapf & Cole, 1985). Furthermore, restitution orders generally seek to compensate victims only for economic losses, such as lost or destroyed property, medical bills, and lost wages; offenders need not pay victims to compensate for the pain and suffering caused by the crime (Rosen & Harland, 1990).

Inadequacies of restitution for victims is not surprising, as justice to the victim is not the primary goal of restitution orders. The U.S. Supreme Court has made it clear that restitution does not operate strictly to assist victims:

Although restitution does resemble a judgment "for the benefit of" the victim, the context in which it is imposed undermines that conclusion. The victim has no control over the amount of restitution awarded or over the decision to award restitution. Moreover, the decision to impose restitution generally does not turn on the victim's injury, but on the penal goals of the State and the situation of the defendant. . . . Because criminal proceedings focus on the State's interests in rehabilitation and punishment, rather than on the victim's desire for compensation, we conclude that restitution orders . . . operate "for the benefit of" the State. (*Kelly v. Robinson*, 1986, pp. 362–363)

This means that a restitution order that operates unfairly toward the victim will nonetheless be acceptable to the courts if it advances a correctional purpose. The victim's irrelevance is also illustrated by orders that restitution be paid to third parties, such as insurance companies (see, for example, *Hagler v. State*, 1993).

A further difficulty with restitution lies in the uneven distribution of resources among criminals. As in 11th-century England, restitution could allow the successful modern criminal to buy his or her way out of an offense (Geis, 1990). This could actually lead to more crime because money, not prison time, would be the cost of getting caught. Such a system could harm both actual and potential crime victims.

Evaluation of Mediation

The major failure of restitution surfaces when it is imposed by a court and administered without regard to the victim's needs. Mediation, or reconciliation, can integrate the victim into the restitution process as well as offer a return to the "golden age of the victim," when criminal justice "served only [the victim's] private interests. No other aspects of crime could compete with this concept in this privately administered criminal law" (Schafer, 1968, pp. 7, 20). Further, it is consistent with a characterization of criminal justice as essentially a private matter that has been usurped by the state (Christie, 1977) and with the theory that no victim will recover from a crime until he or she finds meaning in the experience, to reassert control over his or her life (Henderson, 1992). Programs seeking to mediate agreements between the victim and offender in face-to-face meetings offer victims hope for control.

Victim-offender mediation, currently limited mainly to family disputes and juvenile property crimes (Menard & Salius, 1990), has not been exhaustively researched. It could, however, afford certain crime victims the chance to reinstitute their precrime equilibrium by, among other things, allowing them to confront both the offender and the crime. A strictly voluntary program has the additional advantage of allowing the victim complete autonomy of choice, hence retention of control.

Reservations exist regarding mediation's potential, however. For example, some believe that domestic violence victims should never meet face to face with the offender, as the underlying dynamics of the relationship will prevent the victim from achieving a satisfactory resolution (Geffner, 1992; Menard & Salius, 1990). In fact, mediation may be inappropriate in all cases of extreme violence (Geffner, 1992).[2] Nevertheless, because of its potential for personal resolution of the victimization experience, mediation offers many crime victims hope of real procedural justice and the possibility that their alienation from the system may be substantially reduced.

Evaluation of Civil Courts and Victims

A final alternative to the criminal trial may be found in the civil courts, where the burden of proof is lower and the reparation from the defendant potentially unlimited. Whomever the defendant may be, a civil trial can provide an opportunity to a crime victim to receive full compensation for any and all financial, psychological, and physical injuries suffered as a result of the crime (minus legal fees, which can be substantial). However, some legislatures limit the damages that may be awarded in such suits (Sales et al., 1987). Because economic security appears to be associated with psychological recovery (Lurigio & Resick, 1990), successful suits can facilitate victims' recovery; however, research is needed to determine the extent to which these suits are used by crime victims, and whether awards actually help victims to recover (Sales et al., 1987).

When the defendant is indigent, suit may be brought against a third party, usually a government entity. However, unless the agency has breached a specific duty resulting in injury, the suit will not succeed. The case of *Martinez v. California* (1980) helps illuminate the boundaries of the responsibility of the criminal justice system. Here, the family of a woman killed by an ex-convict five months after he was released sued the state on the basis of the alleged gross negligence of penal authorities. The Court unanimously held that the act resulting in the death was that of the murderer, not the state, and that the woman had been in no unique danger relative to the general populace. It is not likely that these boundaries of state responsibility will be extended by the courts in the near future. In their analysis of victim-related decisions of the Reagan-era Court, Carrington and Nicholson (1989) concluded that "while the conservative majority of the Court are willing to protect society from the criminals themselves, they are not willing to extend that protection to those endangered by the negligence of the bureaucrats" (p. 11; see also McShane & Williams, 1992).

Finally, it may matter against whom a victim is successful. Suits against third parties, though potentially lucrative, do not allow the victim to deal directly with the offender. For example, in the case of *DeShaney v. Winnebago County Department of Social Services* (1989), brought as a constitutional claim rather than a tort claim, the

---

[2]With regard to its impact on corrections as well, it is possible that mediation may promise more, such as a substantial reduction in imprisonment, than it can deliver. A Canadian study suggested that judges may view mediation not as an alternative to incarceration, but as a supplement to probation or other nonprison sanctions (Dittenhoffer & Ericson, 1992).

11-year-old plaintiff was left brain-damaged after an assault by his father, following months of repeated complaints by third parties to the local child protective agency. The agency had intervened earlier but later returned the child to the father and subsequently chose to take no action in the face of new complaints. The Court held that, because the agency had not then taken custody of the boy, it had assumed no duty to him, though in dissent, Justice Blackmun pointed out that, under the law, the agency had sole jurisdiction over the child's case and provided the only legal alternative to the father's care. Even if the suit had succeeded, however, the boy may have benefited more psychologically from a settlement with, or award from, his father instead of a third party (Shuman, 1994).

Evaluation of Victim Compensation

Victim compensation schemes represent a more clinical perspective than do interactive solutions to victimization. Instead of the result of an interaction between two persons, criminal victimization is considered a disorder to be treated physically, financially, and psychologically. Under this perspective, if fully funded and liberally distributed, victim compensation could represent the best hope for many crime victims' psychological recovery because it could pay for all the therapy a victim needs. However, many victim compensation programs are restrictive in their reach and miserly in their execution. A study of an Ohio state program, for example, revealed that less than $6 million of the $18 million allocated by the state legislature was actually awarded in 1988, and 52% of the applicants for awards in 1987 were denied (Roberts, 1990). Similar results had earlier been obtained in New York and New Jersey (Elias, 1983b). In addition, the programs do not necessarily reach deep into the pool of potential claimants: Elias estimated in 1983 that only 1% to 2% of New York and New Jersey crime victims sought compensation, and a 1989 study revealed that only 8% of eligible New Jersey crime victims filed claims (Roberts, 1990). Instead of making all

crime victims eligible for awards, states limit them in various ways, including setting maximum awards, denying awards to persons victimized by members of their own households, making poverty a prerequisite for an award, granting awards only where there was physical injury, and not compensating for pain and suffering (Roland, 1989).

These limits may be necessary because the total costs of crime are staggering. By using jury awards as a measurement, one investigator has estimated the annual cost of crime, including pain and suffering, at over $90 billion (Cohen, 1988). In contrast, the total amount awarded by state victim compensation programs was approximately $200 million in 1992, or about one-fifth of 1% of the total cost of crime. California alone accounted for $75 million (National Association of Victim Compensation Boards, 1993b). Obviously, without full funding, some limitations on awards will be necessary, and many have been justified on public policy grounds. However, by placing the burden of proof for eligibility on the victim (Sales et al., 1987), compensation programs may harm even successful applicants. One study demonstrated significant dissatisfaction with the criminal justice process among successful and unsuccessful applicants who were required to show financial need to receive compensation (Elias, 1983b).

Many states also place significant limitations on compensation to fund psychological services but do not similarly limit the use of monies for other medical expenses (National Association of Victim Compensation Boards, 1993a). An examination of limitations placed on postvictimization counseling by various state compensation boards reveals that, of 46 states surveyed, 14 do not pay for counseling for family members of homicide victims, 28 do not pay for counseling for the families of rape victims, and 3 others assist parents or caretakers only—not children. Furthermore, though many states place no limits on the extent of counseling or require a treatment plan if the counseling extends past a certain point, other states severely restrict payment:

South Carolina limits coverage to the greater of 15 sessions or 90 days, and Montana places a $500-per-person cap on counseling expenses (National Association of Victim Compensation Boards, 1993b). Such limitations do not appear empirically justified, because symptoms can persist for years and extend to family members (for example, Kilpatrick et al., 1987; Amick-McMullen et al., 1991). In addition, victims of unreported crimes have no access to victim compensation but still represent a major public health concern.

Finally, limitations on awards and severe scrutiny of applications may also cause ineligible victims or unsuccessful applicants to blame themselves for their victimization. Until compensation and services are available to victims of all crimes—including but not limited to crimes within the family, white-collar, and environmental crimes—victims of noncovered crimes may suffer additionally because society has not acknowledged their victimization. Self-blame has been associated with poor recovery (Meyer & Taylor, 1986). But even if acknowledged, because victim compensation comes from a third party, it broadens the gulf between the criminal and the victim. Thus it eliminates the hope inherent in mediation, for example, for reconciliation with and restitution from the offender.

Consequences of Victim Services

It is beyond the scope of this chapter to evaluate individual victim service agencies. The great number of them ensures that they will range in quality. However, an understanding of the experience and needs of the crime victim assists any specific evaluation. Governments, whether by establishing public programs or funding nonprofit agencies, should attempt to provide victims with the right to access to victim services in accordance with current research and should provide for ongoing evaluation of the effectiveness of these programs (Salasin, 1981). Particular attention should be paid to the choice of criteria used in the evaluations. Agency bureaucracies should not be permitted to dictate research and evalua-

tion agendas because their first loyalties will tend to be to the institution (Chelimsky, 1981). Concern for victims' long-term functioning should underlie any evaluation, and evaluations should be conducted such that they are comparable to each other. In this way, public dollars can be directed to achieve maximum benefits to victims.

Because the entire court process can be stressful to crime victims, they should receive some sort of counseling, not only for the effects of the crime but also to prepare them for court itself, especially for the experience of testifying (Resick, 1987). Such counseling, as well as other services provided by victim service agencies, should take into account the following knowledge about victims, their symptoms, and their recovery.

Victim Characteristics: Gender and Age
Responses to criminal victimization vary across victims and crimes. Specific responses to trauma are difficult to predict simply from victim characteristics, even when characteristics of the crime are also considered (Resnick, Kilpatrick, & Lipovsky, 1991). However, trauma seems less severe in younger, male, higher-socioeconomic-status persons whose precrime psychological adjustment was strong and who have been relatively free from previous victimization (Lurigio & Resick, 1990). In addition, research on "resilient" adults, who function well despite severely traumatic childhoods, reveals that they share several characteristics: they are intelligent, creative, economically successful, socially and politically active, and have maintained close ties to others throughout their lives (Higgins, 1994, p. 20). Instead of being inherent, many of these characteristics probably developed after victimization; as such, they would provide goals for therapy.

Although many of these characteristics seem to require little explanation, the fact that men may react less severely to crime is more problematic. It may be that the difference is due to measurement error: men may underreport assault-related trauma because of the cultural dictates of masculinity (Stanko & Hobdell, 1993). If the differences are real, it may be that women's coping strategies fail more often than men's, because women generally take fewer risks than men due to both internal and external domestic social controls. The same controls that reduce their vulnerability to crime also lead to their reluctance to abandon their roles within the family following victimization, and prevent their search for "exits" from family structures that may have become harmful (Hagen, 1990). Finally, distress from sexual assault, because of women's evolved psychology, may be responsible for the difference. If rape is maladaptive from an evolutionary perspective, because it robs women of their ability to be sexually selective in order to control their reproduction, women of reproductive age should suffer more psychological pain following rape than girls or older women because it is more important, genetically, for them to avoid it. Significant psychological pain resulting from rape would be adaptive, because women of reproductive age would be motivated by the threat of such pain to avoid rape more than would other women. In support of this hypothesis, research has found psychological pain following rape to be greatest during the reproductive years (Thornhill & Thornhill, 1990; see also Buss, 1994, p. 165).

Therapy   Researchers have directed much attention to the diagnosis and treatment of mental health problems resulting from crime, with work concentrated on rape victims. Success has been reported for general cognitive behavioral therapy, including systematic desensitization (Frank, 1988; but see Kilpatrick & Calhoun, 1988), the cognitive-behavioral techniques of stress inoculation and prolonged exposure (Foa, 1991), and group therapy (Yassen & Glass, 1984), among other interventions. However, there seems to be no consensus as to the single best treatment to use (Foa, 1991). Furthermore, improvements have not consistently been measured against base rates: victims seem to improve over time even with no formal treatment (Shapland, 1986).

These observations comport with the general findings of clinical psychology that, overall, different psychotherapies generate similar outcomes

(Stiles, Shapiro, & Elliot, 1986). However, most clinical research has not examined treatment by subject interactions. As victims vary in their responses to crime, they may vary in their responses to therapy. Where specific treatments can be matched with particular subjects, the possibility for successful therapy increases (Shoham & Rohrbaugh, 1993).

Social Support   Finally, victim service agencies should take into account the amount, quality, and victim's perception of social support, which can affect recovery (Kaniasty & Norris, 1992). However, families of victims, especially rape victims, go through their own victimization and may not be able to give adequate support (Mio, 1991; Riggs & Kilpatrick, 1990). Therefore, families should be involved in counseling to aid in the recovery of the victim and for themselves (Mio, 1991; Orzek, 1983; Sales et al., 1984). Families do not always have realistic expectations regarding the victim's progress, and their impatience could be detrimental (Riggs & Kilpatrick, 1990). It is interesting to note that the victim's perception of the quality and quantity of social support may be more important than the amount actually received (Kaniasty & Norris, 1992).

The Future of Victims' Rights

It is important to utilize empirical evidence when deciding to implement or retain specific victims' rights. Specific victims' rights provisions should be examined to determine the extent to which they facilitate the victim's psychological functioning and should not be lauded merely because they are called "victims' rights." However, if no psychological benefit to victims is found for a particular right, political realities or cultural norms may still require its retention (Sales & Shuman, 1994).

Under the current structure of American law, it would be a mistake to assume that all the psychological needs of victims can be addressed through the traditional criminal justice system. Pre-Norman England, characterized by private justice, may indeed have been the "golden age of the victim" (Schafer, 1968), or it may have been that the status of the victim, especially one of low social standing, was enhanced only after the king took over the burdens of prosecution (Greenburg, 1984). However, it does not seem to be either the effect or intent for victims' rights to return to the ninth century, when victims had sole responsibility for resolving conflicts with offenders. Modern victims' rights generally have not diminished the power of the state by returning control to the victims. Instead, they involve the victim more extensively in the state's campaign against criminals and create new bureaucracies to serve and assist victims (see, for example, Elias, 1993). Restitution, for instance, in old England belonged to the victim; in modern America, it is another tool of corrections (*Kelly v. Robinson,* 1986). Unless victims gain real control over criminal justice proceedings, society, not the individual victim, will remain the injured party in the eyes of the court, and the government, not the victim, will be the prosecutor's client. Because the criminal justice system will retain its present form for the foreseeable future, and because harm to victims can persist long after a criminal case is completed, meaningful victim participation in the criminal courts—including, in some cases, the opportunity to resolve disputes directly with offenders—should be combined with services geared toward the victim's psychological needs.

The reliance on large government entities such as victim compensation agencies and the courts to address victims' concerns clashes with the perspective that conceptualizes crime as a form of conflict belonging to the parties involved (Christie, 1977). Theoretically, the harm resulting from crimes against specific persons could be handled privately (Greenburg, 1984). However, because crimes are considered offenses against the state or against its citizens as a whole, the prosecution and incarceration of a criminal is generally the sole responsibility of the government entity: a victim cannot privately imprison or execute his or her offender and has only a limited right to assist with the prosecution (Sales et al., 1987). It can be argued that the government that prosecutes takes property—specifically, the debt, monetary or moral, owed by the offender—from the victim (Christie, 1977). The modern victims' rights movement stems from the perception that crime victims have not received enough in return.

On the other hand, where bureaucracies exist, they should respond to the needs of the victim in light of their purposes. For example, a victim who is entitled to compensation should not have to jump through procedural hoops to obtain that award. Rather, eligibility for compensation should routinely be made part of every criminal investigation and a determination mailed to the victim as a matter of course; part of the determination would include the amount of insurance available to the victim, and as part of the award, the compensation board could authorize future medical or psychological services, if insurance were unavailable. The victim would either accept or appeal the determination; if accepted, the award could be in the victim's hands within a month of the crime. Information gathered would also be useful for the determination of restitution at later stages of the proceedings as well as in plea bargaining negotiations. This would require funding of victim compensation beyond current levels.

Control over the process seems to be important to crime victims (Henderson, 1992; Kelly, 1990; Resick, 1987; but see Tyler, 1987), and this should be also factored into victims' rights laws. Plea bargaining, currently the exclusive domain of the prosecution, might provide an avenue for victims to gain some control over the process. The process of plea bargaining, when a prosecutor and a defendant negotiate a plea to an offense, generally occurs without the victim's approval.

Only the defendant, not the victim, has a right to a trial. A necessary concomitant of plea bargaining is the defendant's waiver of this right, but the victim cannot insist the case be brought to trial. Some states, including Washington, have amended their constitutions to guarantee some victim involvement in the trial and sentencing. However, these generally do not cede control of the trial to the victim (see, for example, Eikenberry, 1989).

Even the quest for vengeance could accommodate victims' desires for control. Active vengeance may be gained by confronting a surrogate for the offender; for example, rape victims may benefit from confronting convicted rapists, even if not their own (Warshaw, 1988). More directly, researchers should seek to determine whether vengeance is compatible with victim-involving procedures like mediation, and compare results with the effects of other judicial actions that seem to encompass vengeance, such as mandatory prison sentences and routine denial of bail.

Finally, because many victims fall outside the reach of victims' rights, these laws should be reevaluated. Currently, victims' rights laws cover those who typically fit a societally accepted view of the "ideal victim"; the victim most easily accepted as blameless by society is a physically weak person, engaged in a respectable activity in a place they could not be blamed for being, victimized by a stronger person unknown to him or her (Christie, 1977). An actual victim can vary in several ways from this profile. For example, it is possible to view drug addicts as victims of the crime of drug selling. Drug treatment would then be provided as a right, in a nonjudgmental atmosphere, not, for example, as a condition of probation. Society's attraction to protecting and avenging the "ideal victim" ignores the prevalence of crime within socioeconomic class or within the family, the reality of white-collar, environmental, and corporate crime, the relationship between victim and criminal in date and acquaintance rape, and official negligence or wrongdoing (McShane & Williams, 1992; Warshaw, 1988, see, for example, *DeShaney v. Winnebago County Department of Social Services*, 1989).

Conclusion

Victims need to feel in control and safe, able to live normal lives. If crime control provisions control crime, they may someday be all that are needed. Until then, there will be victims and the need for victims' rights. Victims' rights should be oriented toward the psychological recovery of victims, focusing on the needs of specific victims. This means taking into account the variability and persistence of symptoms and accepting that victims must participate in their own recovery (Higgins, 1994).

References

American Law Reports 3rd, *66*, 202 (1975).

American Law Reports 4th, *38*, 1194 (1985).

American Law Reports 4th, *46*, 948 (1986).

American Psychiatric Association. (1994). *Diagnostic and statistical manual of mental disorders* (4th ed.). Washington, DC: Author.

Amick-McMullen, A., Kilpatrick, D. G., & Resnick, H. S. (1991). Homicide as risk factor for PTSD among surviving family members [Special issue: Environmental risk factors in the development of psychopathology]. *Behavior Modification, 15*(4), 545–559.

Bastian, L. D. (1993). *Criminal victimization 1992: A national crime victimization survey report.* Washington, DC: U.S. Department of Justice, Bureau of Justice Statistics.

Becker, J., Skinner, L. J., Abel, G. G., Howell, J., & Bruce, J. (1982). The effects of sexual assault on rape and attempted rape victims. *Victimology, 7*(1–4), 106–113.

Booth v. Maryland, 482 U.S. 496 (1989).

Brown, B. B., & Harris, P. B. (1989). Residential burglary victimization: Reactions to the invasion of a primary territory. *Journal of Environmental Psychology, 9*(2), 119–132.

Burkhead, M. L., Luginbuhl, J. S., & Wrenn. (1994, March). *Victim impact evidence in capital trials: What are its effects?* Paper presented at the meeting of the American Psychology-Law Society, North Carolina State University, Raleigh.

Buss, D. B. (1994). *The evolution of desire: Strategies of human mating.* New York: Basic Books.

Carrington, F., & Nicholson, G. (1989). Victims' rights: An idea whose time has come—Five years later: The maturing of an idea. *Pepperdine Law Review: Follow-Up Issue on Victims' Rights, 17*(1), 1–18.

Cavaiola, A. A., & Schiff, M. (1988). Behavioral sequelae of physical and/or sexual abuse. *Child Abuse and Neglect, 12*(2), 181–188.

Chelimsky, E. (1981). Serving victims: Agency incentives and individual needs. In S. E. Salasin (Ed.), *Evaluating victim services* (pp. 21–37). Newbury Park, CA: Sage.

Christie, N. (1977). Conflicts as property. *British Journal of Criminology, 17*(1), 1–15.

Cienfuegos, A. J., & Monelli, C. (1983). The testimony of political repression as a therapeutic instrument. *American Journal of Orthopsychiatry, 53*(1), 43–51.

Cluss, P. A., Boughton, J., Frank, E., Stewart, B. D., & West, D. (1983). The rape victim: Psychological correlates of participation in the legal process. *Criminal Justice and Behavior, 10*(3), 342–357.

Cohen, L. J. (1987). The psychological aftermath of rate: Long-term effects and individual differences in recovery. *Journal of Social and Clinical Psychology, 5*(4), 525–534.

Cohen, M. A. (1988). Pain, suffering, and jury awards: A study of the cost of crime to victims. *Law and Society Review, 22*(3), 537–555.

Davis, R. C., & Henley, M. (1990). Victim service programs. In A. J. Lurigio, W. G. Skogan, & R. C. Davis (Eds.), *Victims of crime: Problems, policies, and programs* (Sage Criminal Justice System Annals No. 25, pp. 50–68). Newbury Park, CA: Sage.

DeShaney v. Winnebago County Department of Social Services, 109 S.Ct. 998 (1989).

Dittenhoffer, T., & Ericson, R. V. (1992). The victim/offender reconciliation programme: A message to the correctional reformers. In E. A. Fattah (Ed.), *Towards a critical victimology* (pp. 311–346). New York: St. Martin's Press.

Eikenberry, K. (1989). The elevation of victims' rights in Washington State: Constitutional status. *Pepperdine Law Review: Follow-Up Issue on Victims' Rights, 17*(1), 19–33.

Elias, R. (1983a). The symbolic politics of victim compensation. *Victimology, 8*(1–2), 213–224.

Elias, R. (1983b). *Victims of the system: Crime victims and compensation in American politics and criminal justice.* New Brunswick, NJ: Transaction Books.

Elias, R. (1986). *The politics of victimization: Victims, victimology, and human rights.* New York: Oxford University Press.

Elias, R. (1993). *Victims still: The political manipulation of crime victims.* Newbury Park, CA: Sage.

Fattah, E. A. (1992). The need for a critical victimology. In E. A. Fattah (Ed.), *Towards a critical victimology.* New York: St. Martin's Press.

Fischer, C. T. (1984). Being criminally victimized: An illustrated structure. *American Behavioral Scientist, 27*(6), 723–738.

Foa, E. B. (1991). Treatment of posttraumatic stress disorder in rape victims: A comparison between cognitive-behavioral procedures and counseling. *Journal of Consulting and Clinical Psychology, 59*(5), 715–723.

Frank, E. (1988, August). Immediate and delayed treatment of rape victims. Conference of the New York Academy of Sciences: Human sexual aggression: Current perspectives. *Annals of the New York Academy of Sciences, 528*, 296–309.

Frieze, I. H., Hymer, S., & Greenberg, M. S. (1987). Describing the crime victim: Psychological reactions to victimization. *Profes-*

sional Psychology: Research and Practice, *18*(4), 299–315.

Galaway, B. (1988). Crime victim and offender mediation as a social work strategy. *Social Service Review, 62*(4), 668–683.

Ganzini, L., McFarland, B. H., & Cutler, D. (1990). Prevalence of mental disorders after catastrophic financial loss. *Journal of Nervous and Mental Disease, 178*(11), 680–685.

Geffner, R. (1992). Guidelines for using mediation with abusive couples. *Psychotherapy in Private Practice, 10*(1–2), 77–92.

Geis, G. (1990). Crime victims: Practices and prospects. In A. J. Lurigio, W. G. Skogan, & R. C. Davis (Eds.), *Victims of crime: Problems, policies, and programs* (Sage Criminal Justice System Annals No. 25, pp. 50–68). Newbury Park, CA: Sage.

Goddu, C. R. (1993). Victims' "rights" or a fair trial wronged. *Buffalo Law Review, 41*(1), 244–272.

Gottfredson, M. R., & Hirschi, T. (1990). *A general theory of crime.* Stanford: Stanford University Press.

Greenburg, J. (1984). The victim in historical perspective: Some aspects of the English experience. *Journal of Social Issues, 40*(1), 77–102.

Hagen, J. (1990). The structuration of gender and deviance: A power-control theory of vulnerability to crime and the search for deviant role exits. *Canadian Review of Sociology and Anthropology, 27*(2), 137–156.

Hagler v. State, 625 So.2nd. 1190 (Ala. 1993).

Halleck, S. L. (1989). Vengeance and victimization. *Victimology, 5*(2–4), 99–109.

Harrington, L. H. (1982). Statement of the Chairman. In President's Task Force on Victims of Crime, *Final report.* Washington, DC: Author.

Henderson, L. N. (1992). The wrongs of victims' rights. In E. A. Fattah (Ed.), *Towards a critical victimology* (pp. 100–192). New York: St. Martin's Press.

Herbst, P. R. (1992). From helpless victim to empowered survivor: Oral history as a treatment for survivors of torture [Special issue: Refugee women and their mental health: I. Shattered societies, shattered lives]. *Women and Therapy, 13*(1–2), 141–154.

Higgins, G. O. (1994). *Resiliant adults: Overcoming a cruel past.* San Francisco: Jossey-Bass.

Hillenbrand, S. (1990). Restitution and victim rights in the 1980's. In A. J. Lurigio, W. G. Skogan, & R. C. Davis (Eds.), *Victims of crime: Problems, policies, and programs* (Sage Criminal Justice System Annals No. 25, pp. 188–204). Newbury Park, CA: Sage.

Janoff-Bulman, R., & Frieze, I. H. (1983). A theoretical perspective for understanding reactions to victimization. *Journal of Social Issues, 39*(2), 1–17.

Kaniasty, K., & Norris, F. H. (1992). Social support and victims of crime: Matching event, support, and outcome. *American Journal of Community Psychology, 20*(2), 211–241.

Karmen, A. (1984). *Crime victims: an introduction to victimology.* Pacific Grove, CA: Brooks/Cole.

Keane, T. M. (1989). Post-traumatic stress disorder: Current status and future directions. *Behavior Therapy, 20,* 149–153.

Kelly, D. (1990). Victim participation in the criminal justice system. In A. J. Lurigio, W. G. Skogan, & R. C. Davis (Eds.), *Victims of crime: Problems, policies and programs* (Sage Criminal Justice System Annals No. 25, pp. 172–187). Newbury Park, CA: Sage.

Kelly v. Robinson, 479 U.S. 36 (1986).

Kennedy, D. B. (1983). Implications of the victimization syndrome for clinical intervention with crime victims. *Personnel and Guidance Journal, 62*(4), 219–222.

Kilpatrick, D. G. (1989). Victim and crime factors associated with the development of crime-related post-traumatic stress disorder. *Behavior Therapy, 20*(2), 199–214.

Kilpatrick, D. G., Best, C. L., Veronen, L. J., Amick, A. E., Villeponteaux, L. A., & Ruff, G. A. (1985). Mental health correlates of crime victimization: A community survey.

Journal of Consulting and Clinical Psychology, 53(6), 866–863.

Kilpatrick, D. G., & Calhoun, K. S. (1988). Early behavioral treatment for rape trauma: Efficacy or artifact? *Behavior Therapy, 19*(3), 421–427.

Kilpatrick, D. G., Saunders, B. E., Veronen, L. G., Best, C. L., & Von, J. M. (1987). Criminal victimization: Lifetime prevalence, reporting to police, and psychological impact. *Crime and Delinquency, 33*(4), 479–489.

Lurigio, A. J., & Resick, P. A. (1990). Healing the psychological wounds of criminal victimization: Predicting postcrime distress and recovery. In A. J. Lurigio, W. G. Skogan, & R. C. Davis (Eds.), *Victims of crime: Problems, policies, and programs* (Sage Criminal Justice System Annals No. 25, pp. 50–68). Newbury Park, CA: Sage.

Martinez v. California, 444 U.S. 27 (1980).

Matthews, W. G. (1981). Restitution: The chameleon of corrections. *Journal of Offender Counseling, Services, and Rehabilitation, 5*(3–4), 77–92.

McCune, N. (1989). Children surviving parental murder. *British Journal of Psychiatry, 154,* 889.

McShane, M. D., & Williams, F. P. (1992). Radical victimology: A critique of the concept of victim in traditional victimology. *Crime and Delinquency, 38*(2), 258–271.

Menard, A. E., & Salius, A. J. (1990). Judicial response to family violence: The importance of message. *Mediation Quarterly, 7*(4), 293–302.

Meyer, C. B., & Taylor, S. E. (1986). Adjustment to rape. *Journal of Personality and Social Psychology, 50*(6), 1226–1234.

Mio, J. S. (1991). The effects of rape upon victims and families: Implications for a comprehensive family therapy. *American Journal of Family Therapy, 19*(2), 147–159.

National Association of Victim Compensation Boards. (1993a). *Counseling expense comparison, 1989–1992.* Washington, DC: Author.

National Association of Victim Compensation Boards. (1993b). *State mental health cost control rules.* Washington, DC: Author.

National Victim Center. (1993). *Database on victims' rights.* Alexandria, VA: Author.

Norris, F. H., & Kaniasty, K. (1991). The psychological experience of crime: A test of the mediating role of beliefs in explaining the distress of crime. *Journal of Social and Clinical Psychology, 10*(3), 239–261.

Orzek, A. M. (1983). Sexual assault: The female victim, her male partner, and their relationship. *Personnel and Guidance Journal, 62*(3), 143–146.

Payne v. Tennessee, 111 S.Ct. 2597 (1991).

Peterson, C. S., & Seligman, M.E.P. (1983). Learned helplessness and victimization. *Journal of Social Issues, 39*(2), 103–116.

Polito, K. E. (1990). The rights of crime victims in the criminal justice system: Is justice blind to the victims of crime? *New England Journal on Criminal and Civil Confinement, 16,* 241–269.

Pope, K. S., & Garcia-Peltoniemi, R. E. (1991). Responding to victims of torture: Clinical issues, professional responsibilities, and useful resources. *Professional Psychology: Research and Practice, 22*(4), 269–276.

President's Task Force on Victims of Crime. (1982). *Final report.* Washington, DC: Author.

Reiss, A. J. (1986). Policy implications of crime victim surveys. In E. A. Fattah (Ed.), *From crime policy to victim policy: Reorienting the justice system* (pp. 246–260). London: Macmillan.

Resick, P. A. (1987). Psychological effects of victimization: Implications for the criminal justice system. *Crime and Delinquency, 33*(4), 468–478.

Resick, P. A. (1990). Victims of sexual assault. In A. J. Lurigio, W. G. Skogan, & R. C. Davis (Eds.), *Victims of crime: Problems, policies and programs* (Sage Criminal Justice System Annals No. 25, pp. 69–86). Newbury Park, CA: Sage.

Reske, H. J. (1992). Helping crime's casualties. *American Bar Association Journal, 78*, 34–38.

Resnick, H. S., Kilpatrick, D. G., & Lipovsky, J. A. (1991). Assessment of rape-related posttraumatic stress disorder: Stressor and symptom dimensions [Special section: Issues and methods in assessment of posttraumatic stress disorder]. *Psychological Assessment, 3*(4), 561–572.

Riggs, D. S., & Kilpatrick, D. G. (1990). Families and friends: Indirect victimization by crime. In A. J. Lurigio, W. G. Skogan, & R. C. Davis (Eds.), *Victims of crime: Problems, policies, and programs* (Sage Criminal Justice System Annals No. 25, pp. 120–138). Newbury Park, CA: Sage.

Riggs, D. S., Kilpatrick, D. G., & Resnick, H. S. (1992). Long-term psychological distress associated with marital rape and aggravated assault: A comparison to other crime victims. *Journal of Family Violence, 7*(4), 283–296.

Roberts, A. R. (1990). *Helping crime victims: Research, policy, and practice.* Newbury Park, CA: Sage.

Roland, D. L. (1989). Progress in the Victim Reform Movement: No longer the "forgotten victim." *Pepperdine Law Review: Follow-Up Issue on Victims' Rights, 17*(1), 35–58.

Rosen, C. J., & Harland, A. T. (1990). Restitution to crime victims as a presumptive requirement in criminal case dispositions. In A. R. Roberts (Ed.), *Helping crime victims: Research, policy, and practice* (pp. 233–248). Newbury Park, CA: Sage.

Sahjpaul, S., & Renner, K. E. (1988). The new sexual assault law: The victim's experience in court. *American Journal of Community Psychology, 16*(4), 503–513.

Salasin, S. E. (1981). Services to victims: Needs assessment. In S. E. Salasin (Ed.), *Evaluating victim services* (pp. 21–37). Newbury Park, CA: Sage.

Sales, B., Rich, R. F., & Reich, J. (1987). Victimization policy research. *Professional Psychology: Research and Practice, 18*(4), 326–337.

Sales, B. D., & Shuman, D. W. (1994). Mental health law and mental health care. *American Journal of Orthopsychiatry, 64*, 172–179.

Sales, E., Baum, M., & Shore, B. (1984). Victim readjustment following assault. *Journal of Social Issues, 40*(1), 117–136.

Santiago, J. M., McCall-Perez, F., Gorcey, M., & Beigel, A. (1985). Long-term psychological effects of rape in 35 rape victims. *American Journal of Psychiatry, 142*(11), 1338–1340.

Schafer, S. (1968). *The victim and his criminal: A study in functional responsibility.* New York: Random House.

Shapland, J. (1986). Victim assistance and the criminal justice system: The victim's perspective. In E. A. Fattah (Ed.), *From crime policy to victim policy: Reorienting the justice system* (pp. 218–233). Hong Kong: Macmillan.

Shepherd, J. (1990). Victims of personal violence: The relevance of Symonds' model of psychological response and loss-theory. *British Journal of Social Work, 20*(4), 309–332.

Shoham, V., & Rohrbaugh, M. (1993). Aptitude × treatment interaction (ATI) research: Sharpening the focus, widening the lens. In M. Aveline & D. A. Shapiro (Eds.), *Research foundations for psychotherapy.* New York: Wiley.

Shuman, D. W. (1994). The psychology of compensation in tort law. *Kansas Law Review, 43*, 39–77.

Stanko, E., & Hobdell, K. (1993). Assault on men: Masculinity and male victimization. *British Journal of Criminology, 33*(3), 400–415.

Steinmetz, C. H. (1984). Coping with serious crime: Self-help and outside help. *Victimology, 9*(3–4), 324–343.

Stiles, W. B., Shapiro, D. A., & Elliot, R. (1986). Are all psychotherapies equivalent? *American Psychologist, 41*(2), 165–180.

Terr, L. C. (1983). Chowchilla revisited: The effects of psychic trauma four years after a school-bus kidnapping. *American Journal of Psychiatry, 140*(12), 1543–1550.

Thibaut, J., & Walker, L. (1975). *Procedural justice: A psychological analysis.* Hillsdale, NJ: Erlbaum.

Thornhill, N. W., & Thornhill, R. (1990). An evolutionary analysis of psychological pain following rape: III. Effects of force and violence. *Aggressive Behavior, 16*(5), 297–330.

Tyler, T. R. (1987). Conditions leading to value-expressive effects in judgments of procedural justice: A test of four models. *Journal of Personality and Social Psychology, 52*(2), 333–344.

Tyler, T. R. (1992). The psychological consequences of judicial procedures: Implications for civil commitment hearings. *Southern Methodist University Law Review, 46*, 433–445.

Umbreit, M. S. (1989). Crime victims seeking fairness, not revenge: Toward restorative justice. *Federal Probation, 53*(3), 52–57.

U.S. Department of Justice, Office of Justice Programs. (1986). *Four years later: A report of the President's Task Force on Victims of Crime.* Washington, DC: Government Printing Office.

Veronen, L. G., Kilpatrick, D. G., & Resick, P. A. (1979). Treating fear and anxiety in rape victims: Implications for the criminal justice system. In W. H. Parsonage (Ed.), *Perspectives in victimology.* Newbury Park, CA: Sage.

Viano, E. (1987). Victim's rights and the Constitution: Reflections on a Bicentennial. *Crime and Delinquency, 33*(4), 438–451.

Victims of Crimes Act (1984). Public Law 98-473.

Walsh, A. (1992). Placebo justice: Victim recommendations and offender sentences in sexual assault cases. In E. A. Fattah (Ed.), *Towards a critical victimology* (pp. 294–310). New York: St. Martin's Press.

Warshaw, R. (1988). *I never called it rape.* New York: HarperCollins.

Washington State Constitution 8200, 51st sess. (1989).

Weeks v. United States, 232 U.S. 883 (1913).

Wexler, D. B., & Winick, B. J. (1991). *Essays in therapeutic jurisprudence.* Durham, NC: Carolina Academic Press.

Wirtz, P. W., & Harrell, A. V. (1987). Effects of postassault exposure to attack-similar stimuli on long-term recovery of victims. *Journal of Consulting and Clinical Psychology, 55*(1), 10–16.

Wortman, C. B. (1983). Coping with victimization: Conclusions and implications for future research. *Journal of Social Issues, 39*(2), 195–221.

Yassen, J., & Glass, L. (1984). Sexual assault survivors groups: A feminist practice perspective. *Social Work, 29*(3), 252–257.

Yick Wo v. Hopkins, 118 U.S. 356 (1886).

Zapf, M. K., & Cole, B. (1985). Yukon restitution study. *Canadian Journal of Criminology, 27*(4), 477–490.

Part 5

Impact of the Law on the Mental Health of Children and Families

21 ◼ The Legal Processing of Domestic Violence Cases

Leonore M. J. Simon
Washington State University

Media coverage of the O. J. Simpson murder case has focused public attention on the legal system's chronic failure to respond more effectively to domestic violence cases (Buzawa & Buzawa, 1992; Gordon, 1988; Pleck, 1987; U.S. Commission on Civil Rights, 1982). For example, a study by the Justice Department found that slightly more than half (51.4%) of the defendants in spouse killings had been previously arrested (Dawson & Langan, 1994). As the O. J. Simpson case illustrates, the legal response to domestic violence cases has been so weak that offenders seem to walk away from a legal encounter believing that they can batter their intimate partner or ex-partner with impunity.

The term *domestic violence* carries different meanings across the literature. In this chapter, the term is used to refer to violence between spouses, ex-spouses, intimates, and ex-intimates. Although both males and females are victimized by partners, injuries and lethal injuries from such partner violence fall disproportionately on women (Straus & Gelles, 1986). The focus of this chapter, then, is on violent behavior committed by men against women that would be considered a violent crime if it were committed against a stranger. These violent behaviors include physical assault, sexual assault, and homicide committed, threatened, or attempted by intimate partners.

Although our legal system has become less accepting of the physical assault of wives, especially in severe cases, a husband's assault on his wife continues to carry fewer legal sanctions than a similar assault of a stranger (Ford, 1983; Langan & Innes, 1986). Only in the last two decades have laws and policies about domestic violence undergone major changes, with their implementation varying widely among jurisdictions (Lemon, 1993; Zorza, 1993).

The legal system's failure to respond more consistently and effectively to such cases has alarming implications for battered women and their children. For instance, when a spouse kills a spouse, wives are the victims in nearly two-thirds of the cases (Browne & Williams, 1989; Wilson & Daly, 1992). The escalation of violence against women can, and all too frequently does, result in their deaths (Dawson & Langan, 1994; Saunders & Browne, 1991; Zahn, 1989). Compared with victims of stranger violence, victims of domestic violence are at far greater risk of recurring victimization (Langan & Innes, 1986). Even in cases where the battered woman leaves the relationship, evidence suggests that the greatest risk of domestic violence is faced by separated

Research for this chapter was made possible by a summer research fellowship from Temple University. I especially wish to thank Bradford Beyer, Howard Evans, Jennifer Nooney, and Tammy Schmidt for their research assistance. I am also grateful for the helpful editorial suggestions of Alan Harland, Richard Lamma, Michael Perlin, Bruce Sales, and David Wexler. Lastly, Phil Harris and the Department of Criminal Justice, Temple University, have been very generous with their research support.

Adapted from "A Therapeutic Jurisprudence Approach to the Legal Processing of Domestic Violence Cases," by L. M. J. Simon, 1995, *Psychology, Public Policy, and Law, 1,* 43–79. Copyright 1995 American Psychological Association. Adapted with permission.

and divorced women (Kennedy & Dutton, 1989; Wiersema & Loftin, 1994). In addition, men who abuse their wives are more likely to be abusive toward their children (Browne, 1987; Hart, 1992; Straus, 1983). Some investigators believe that as many as 80% of men who batter women also batter a child (Giles-Sims, 1985; Hofford & Gable, 1989; Jaffe, Wolfe, & Wilson, 1990). The more severely the mother is abused, the worse the child is abused (Bowker, 1988).

In general, criticisms leveled at the legal system have emphasized the comparative lack of serious consequences accorded domestic violence acts; similar criminal behavior against strangers incurs severe sanctions (Dawson & Langan, 1994; Herrell & Hofford, 1990). The hesitancy to invoke legal sanctions in cases of spouse abuse has historically been linked to the view that such incidents are family affairs and not the true business of the legal system (Goolkasian, 1986; U.S. Commission on Civil Rights, 1982; Zimring, 1989). Traditionally, police have not responded to battered woman calls (Buzawa & Buzawa, 1992; Dobash & Dobash, 1979; Parnas, 1967; Walker, 1979), and prosecutors and judges have treated domestic violence as a noncriminal event (Ellis, 1984; Field & Field, 1973; Lerman, 1986; Schafran, 1987; Stanko, 1985; Vera Institute of Justice, 1981). The low sanction severity traditionally associated with domestic violence cases may actually reinforce the underlying causes of marital violence. Batterers tend to deny or minimize their violent behavior (Fagan & Browne, 1994), a perception fueled both by police annoyance with victims (Ferraro, 1989) and by prosecution and judicial indifference (Buzawa & Buzawa, 1992).

This insensitivity to domestic violence victims has not been the domain solely of the criminal justice system (Frieze & Browne, 1989). The civil justice system has presented its own obstacles to these victims (Clark, 1986; Gagnon, 1992; Topliffe, 1992). Historically, civil remedies such as restraining orders have been unavailable to the majority of victims of domestic violence (Chaudhuri & Daly, 1992) and when issued have not been enforced by legal officials (Harrell, Smith, & Newmark, 1993). Consequently, when civil remedies such as restraining orders have been used to avert further violence, they have provided victims with a false sense of security. The ineffectiveness of restraining orders is due to the legal system's failure to sanction violators, and there is increased risk of harm to victims who separate from or divorce abusers. Another thorny issue—the issuance of mutual restraining orders by the courts—has further compromised the safety of victims by sending mixed messages to the perpetrators and to the police about the seriousness of the batterer's actions (Finn & Colson, 1990). The argument against the issuance of mutual restraining orders is that doing so perpetuates the historical fallacy that battered women are responsible for the batterer's behavior. Mutual orders of protection are also believed to perpetuate the violence by exonerating the abuser and giving confusing directions to the police.

Less severe legal sanctions include treatment programs available to domestic violence offenders that are not available to offenders in crimes against strangers. The current trend in the legal processing of domestic violence offenders emphasizes mental health treatment in lieu of punishment (Burns & Meredith, 1993; Harrell, 1991; Pence & Paymar, 1993). This treatment policy toward domestic violence offenders contrasts sharply with the denial of rehabilitation programs to general criminal offenders based on skepticism about the effectiveness of offender treatment (Lab & Whitehead, 1990). Outcome evaluations of hundreds of domestic violence offender treatment programs have yielded mixed and unpromising results (Burns & Meredith, 1993; Hamberger & Hastings, 1990; Harrell, 1991; Saunders & Azar, 1989). In contrast, application of criminal sanctions in domestic violence cases has a consistent small effect on the likelihood of reducing repeat violence under certain circumstances (Edelson & Syers, 1990; Harrell, 1991; Jaffe, Wolfe, Telford, & Austin, 1986; Sherman & Berk, 1984; Tolman & Bennett,

1990). For example, men who batter are best deterred from further violence if they believe that the penalties for recidivism are both certain and severe (Carmody & Williams, 1987; Harrell et al., 1993).

Because of the intersection of therapeutic and justice concerns in domestic violence cases, this chapter utilizes the framework of therapeutic jurisprudence to address ways in which the legal system advances or impedes therapeutic goals (Perlin, 1993). The schema of therapeutic jurisprudence suggests that the law can act as a therapeutic agent (Wexler, 1990, 1993a; Wexler & Winick, 1991a) whereby legal rules, legal procedures, and the roles of legal actors (such as police, lawyers, and judges) can constitute social forces that often produce therapeutic or antitherapeutic results (Wexler, 1991, 1993b). As Wexler (1993a) says, "therapeutic jurisprudence proposes that we be sensitive to such consequences rather than ignore them, and that we ask whether the law's antitherapeutic consequences can be reduced and its therapeutic consequences enhanced without subordinating due process and justice values" (p. 762). Consequently, therapeutic jurisprudence attempts "to identify—and ultimately examine empirically—relationships between legal arrangements and therapeutic outcomes" (Wexler, 1992, p. 32). The therapeutic jurisprudence schema does not advocate that therapeutic concerns supplant other factors, only that legal decision making can and should benefit from the insights of the mental health and related disciplines (Wexler, 1993a; Wexler & Winick, 1991b). Within the limits set by principles of justice, therapeutic jurisprudence suggests that the law should be designed to serve more effectively as a therapeutic agent (Klotz, Wexler, Sales, & Becker, 1992; Shuman, 1994; Winick, 1991). The emphasis incorporating research from varied disciplines facilitates a new perspective on an old problem.

Using the therapeutic jurisprudence perspective, the next section examines the psychology of offenders who commit domestic violence crimes. The section after that explores the psychology of domestic violence victims. Then we turn to the impact of the arrest and prosecution stages of the criminal justice system. The following section explores trials, plea bargains, and sentencing issues. Finally, I examine the use of restraining orders. The discussion of these issues and the therapeutic jurisprudence perspective presented in this chapter can inform law reform efforts, criminal justice policy, and mental health policy.

Psychology of Domestic Violence Offenders

Characteristics of Domestic Violence Offenders

Little is known about the psychological characteristics of batterers or about men who kill current or ex-wives or girlfriends. Most of the knowledge we have is based on interviews with women victims (Fagan & Browne, 1994; Frieze & Browne, 1989). A comprehensive review published by the National Academy of Sciences indicates that "the few studies of violent men have been limited to small samples of repeatedly assaultive participants in treatment programs, voluntary or self-selected samples, or assailants identified by the criminal justice system who also frequently are violent" (see review by Fagan & Browne, 1994, p. 185).

Characteristics of domestic violence offenders that can be gleaned from the various studies indicate that men tend to neutralize (Bandura, 1979; Dutton, 1986; Sykes & Matza, 1957) their violent behavior by rationalization or externalization of blame (Ptacek, 1988). They are likely to underreport their violence (Browning & Dutton, 1986; Edelson & Brygger, 1986; Jouriles & O'Leary, 1985; Szinovacz, 1983), minimize its harm and severity (Fagan & Browne, 1994), and even deny their behavior (O'Leary & Arias, 1988). They tend to attribute more involvement to the victim than is justified by either witness or police reports (Sonkin & Murphy, 1985) or to blame their violent behavior on alcohol (Coleman & Straus, 1983; Collins, 1988; Dawson & Langan, 1994; Sonkin, Martin, & Walker, 1985; Speiker, 1983). While blaming the victim, offenders also tend to perceive themselves as the victim (Hastings & Hamberger, 1988; Holtzworth-Munroe & Hutchinson, 1993). As a result of these characteristics, batterers are not likely to seek treatment voluntarily (Hamberger & Hastings, 1986).

An examination of reported personality characteristics of batterers suggests that they have many psychological problems. These include histories of mental illness (Dawson & Langan, 1994; Hamberger & Hastings, 1988), histories of childhood exposure to violence (Caesar, 1988; Fagan, Stewart, & Hansen, 1983; Neidig, Friedman, & Collins, 1986; Rosenbaum & O'Leary, 1981; Straus, 1983), attachment deficits (Stosny, 1994), extreme fluctuations in mood (Walker, 1979), suicidal ideation (Browne, 1987), alcohol abuse (Dawson & Langan, 1994; Gondolph, 1988; Kantor & Straus, 1987; Miller, Downs, & Gondoli, 1988; Shields, McCall, & Hanneke, 1988; Walker, 1984), low self-esteem (Okun, 1986; Pagelow, 1984; Stosny, 1994), chronic hostility or anger (Gottman et al., in press; Holtzworth-Munroe & Hutchinson, 1993; Maiuro, Cahn, & Vitaliano, 1986; Novaco, 1976), extreme jealousy (Bowker, 1983; Davidson, 1978; Okun, 1986), need for control (Browning & Dutton, 1986; Dutton & Strachan, 1987; Okun, 1986), unassertiveness (Holtzworth-Munroe, 1992; Holtzworth-Munroe & Anglin, 1991), physical abuse toward children (Browne, 1987), cognitive distortions of social cues (Holtzworth-Munroe, 1992; Holtzworth-Munroe & Anglin, 1991), distortions in information processing and social skills deficits (Holtzworth-Munroe, 1992; Holtzworth-Munroe & Anglin, 1991), strong gender-role stereotypes (Gondolph, 1988), and lack of verbal skills (Browne, 1987). Typologies of offenders that have been developed (Dutton, 1988) have been discrepant in their findings, however (Hamberger & Hastings, 1988; Holtzworth-Munroe & Stuart, 1994).

Do Domestic Violence Offenders Specialize?

No discussion of the characteristics of domestic violence offenders is complete without asking whether they victimize only intimate partners or are instead generalists in assaultive behavior and other crime. Most criminological research suggests that general criminal offenders do not specialize in violence (Gottfredson & Hirschi, 1990; Simon, 1994). However, the legal and academic treatment of domestic violence as separate from general criminal violence has implied that it is a specialty (Sherman, 1992). The notion of specialization is so entrenched that current research and practice singles out family violence (O'Leary, 1993) in general and spouse abuse (Frieze & Browne, 1989) in particular as special and distinct types of violence that are not to be viewed as a subset of violent behavior (Yllo, 1993).

Yet, after years of treating domestic violence as a specialty, researchers are beginning to find that a sizable proportion of domestic violence offenders are also violent outside the home (Fagan et al., 1983; Shields et al., 1988; Walker, 1979). There is little evidence that the majority of domestic violence offenders specialize in assaults toward intimates (Hotaling & Straus, 1989). Instead, the evidence is consistent with the research on general criminal offenders indicating that they are generalists who commit a wide variety of offenses. As a result, domestic violence offenders do not need a separate explanation for their violent acts. Singling out domestic violence offenders for special treatment by the legal system not only perpetuates the myth of specialization but also communicates to offenders and victims that offenses are not as serious when committed against an intimate as they are when committed against a stranger.

A Cognitive Therapy Approach

In addressing the legal and therapeutic concerns of domestic violence offenders, the legal system can effect therapeutic changes in offenders by applying some of the principles of cognitive therapy used in psychology. Cognitive interventions have been effective in the psychological treatment of a broad range of disorders (Beck, 1976; Beck, Rush, Shaw, & Emery, 1979; Beck, Freeman, & Associates, 1990; Hollon & Beck, 1994; Lutzer & Van Hasselt, 1992; Masters, Burish, Hollon, & Rimm, 1987; Meichenbaum, 1977) and provide a useful framework for the legal processing of domestic violence offenders. Based on the idea that thinking plays a role in the etiology and maintenance of at least some disorders, these treatments seek to improve mental health by changing maladaptive beliefs and providing new information processing skills (Hollon & Beck, 1994).[1]

Cognitive learning theorists believe that conscious thoughts play a major role in mediating emotional and instrumental behavior in human beings. In particular, Aaron Beck's Cognitive Therapy approach asserts that individuals with emotional problems possess dysfunctional automatic thoughts that are exaggerated, distorted, mistaken, or unrealistic (Craighead, Evans, & Robins, 1992). These dysfunctional, automatic thoughts, called *cognitive distortions*, shape the perception and interpretation of events (McMullin, 1986).

A therapeutic jurisprudence approach to the legal handling of domestic violence offenders can utilize the principles of cognitive therapy to confront batterers' faulty thinking and promote more adaptive cognitive processing. The various techniques of neutralization used by domestic violence offenders can be categorized into four types of cognitive distortions about the offense: (1) cognitive distortions that morally justify or euphemistically label the violence; (2) cognitive

distortions that disavow responsibility; (3) cognitive distortions that minimize the effects of the violence; and (4) cognitive distortions that dehumanize or blame the victim (Fagan & Browne, 1994). By challenging these techniques of neutralization in the articulation and enforcement of its laws and policies, the legal system can achieve therapeutic results for the offender and the victim. For example, the police can confront offender denial by taking domestic violence calls seriously, responding quickly, and making arrests where legally appropriate. Prosecutors can challenge offender neutralization by prosecuting these cases fully and granting diversion only in extraordinary cases. The use of plea bargains by the prosecutor in domestic violence cases may not be advisable, particularly the use of charge bargaining, because the offender is allowed to escape responsibility for the actual crime in question. Prosecutors can also confront offender minimization by recommending sentences commensurate with comparable stranger crimes. Judges can confront offender denial and minimization by taking these cases seriously and by sentencing these offenders in the same way stranger offenders are sentenced. Once judges enter any type of court order in a domestic violence case, they can confront offender minimization of violations by monitoring, identifying, and sanctioning them. Judicial development of a means of monitoring compliance is essential in both civil and criminal orders.

Psychology of Domestic Violence Victims

Characteristics of Domestic Violence Victims

Empirical research on domestic violence consists mostly of research on victims. According to the existing literature, "other than their abuse histories and socioeconomic status, there do not ap-

---

[1]Note that the term *cognitive therapy* encompasses cognitive as well as cognitive-behavioral approaches. Although cognitive and cognitive-behavioral approaches differ in terms of their developmental histories, each approach has borrowed from the other over the years, blurring the distinctions (Hollon & Beck, 1994).

pear to be consistent patterns that differentiate victims from nonvictims" (Fagan & Browne, 1994, p. 198). A thorough reading of the literature on victims indicates that victims are well-adjusted individuals whose maladaptive symptoms "are sequalae of marital violence rather than antecedents or concurrent factors" (Fagan & Browne, 1994, citing Walker, 1984; Margolin, 1988).

The few victim characteristics that have been isolated include witnessing family violence as a child or adolescent, being young in age, and abusing alcohol (Fagan & Browne, 1994). Evidence suggests that victims are more likely to abuse alcohol than are nonvictims, although researchers argue that the causal relationship between alcohol abuse and victimization is not clear. Younger women are at greater risk for victimization than older women. Experiencing abuse as children and witnessing parental violence increases a woman's probability of being abused by her partner (Hotaling & Sugarman, 1986; Kalmus, 1984).

Research evidence indicates that battered women have difficulty leaving battering relationships, with various reasons postulated. Such reasons include learned helplessness (Walker, 1984), "traumatic bonding" (Dutton & Painter, 1981), the intensification of violence and threats after the victim leaves or attempts to separate from the abuser (Browne, 1987), shock reactions of victims to abuse, and practical problems in separating (Browne, 1987).

Although treatment programs for batterers are quite common, there appear to be few treatment programs for women outside the supportive services found in women's shelters (Dutton, 1992). The absence of meaningful treatment for victims seems to be a combination of a hesitancy to assign any responsibility or blame to the woman and an insistence that any symptoms the victim may have are the effects of rather than the precursors to battering (Dutton, 1992). Even accepting the argument that the victim's symptoms result from the battering, it is clinically

accepted that battered women have many of the symptoms of posttraumatic stress disorder (PTSD) (American Psychiatric Association, 1994; Ochberg, 1988) found in other trauma victims and thus desperately need meaningful treatment.[2] The lack of mental health treatment also increases the likelihood that if a woman leaves a battering relationship, she will enter another violent relationship (Kalmus & Seltzer, 1986).

A reading of the relevant literature suggests that the battered woman is likely to indulge in specific dysfunctional thoughts that perpetuate her relationship to the batterer. These include denial or minimization of the abuse and excusing the batterer's behavior. Her cognitive distortions are likely to involve maladaptive beliefs, such as "it is better to have an abusive relationship than no relationship at all" (Dutton, 1992, p. 98), and related beliefs, such as "if I don't remain in this relationship, I'm never going to be in another one," or "any cost is worth paying for a relationship" (Dutton, 1992, p. 98). Additional faulty thinking by battered women leads them to the conclusion that they are helpless in escaping the violence. Many of these dysfunctional thoughts are likely to impair their judgment. For example, it is not uncommon for battered women to ignore or minimize signals of danger, not responding in a manner that would potentially increase their safety (Dutton, 1992).

Cognitive restructuring as a result of cognitive therapy can be employed to challenge many of these dysfunctional thoughts. Much of the therapy involves assisting the client in ferreting out automatic thinking and the underlying dys-

---

[2]Posttraumatic stress disorder (PTSD) is classified as an anxiety disorder in which symptoms are developed "following exposure to an extreme traumatic stressor involving direct personal experience of an event that involves actual or threatened death or serious injury, or other threat to one's physical integrity." DSM-IV describes posttraumatic stress disorder as characterized by symptoms of intrusive thoughts or memories, avoidance of stimuli associated with the trauma or the feelings associated with the trauma, and heightened autonomic arousal (American Psychiatric Association, 1994).

functional assumptions, and then in retraining the individual to think more logically and realistically and to modify fundamental underlying beliefs. The approach relies heavily on the process of empirical disconfirmation; clients are taught to treat their beliefs as hypotheses that can be tested, and to gather information and conduct behavioral experiments to test them. In monitoring and evaluating their dysfunctional thoughts, clients are taught to modify self-defeating thinking by countering their automatic thoughts with adaptive responses, a form of cognitive restructuring. As applied to domestic violence victims, the self-blame commonly seen in battered women can be confronted by reattributing responsibility for the violence to the batterer. The cognitive distortion of helplessness can be confronted by persuading a victim to accept personal responsibility for her safety and her choices.

Much of this cognitive restructuring can be achieved without therapy, however, by altering the response of those representing social institutions that are chief among the external barriers to battered women's seeking safety (Dutton, 1992). Ensuring that the legal system will protect the battered woman from violence and will arrest, prosecute, convict, and sentence the batterer will facilitate the woman's reattribution of blame for the violence (Hart, 1993). This intervention requires that legal actors—including police officers, prosecutors, attorneys in general, judges, and probation officers—be sensitive to the problems and dynamics of domestic violence cases. Criminal justice system actors can be educated about the impact of not prosecuting a domestic violence case. Treating each act of domestic violence as a criminal act against the state rather than as merely a family matter is essential in challenging the fear and ambivalence many victims feel in cooperating with the batterer's prosecution.

This sensitivity should extend beyond the criminal justice system to civil proceedings that involve battering couples. For example, the legal system has considerable power in determining the level of protection available to a victim through restraining orders, divorce, custody, and visitation decisions (Dutton, 1992).

Arrest and Prosecution of Offenders

Having thus far described the psychology of domestic violence offenders and victims, the remainder of the chapter addresses the different stages of the legal system and how they can be restructured to provide therapeutic processes and outcomes for both parties. As was pointed out in the introduction, the legal system has a history of failing to respond appropriately to domestic violence cases. In addition to reinforcing offender and victim cognitive distortions about their respective roles in the violence, these legal policies have been physically dangerous for the victims and their children. A stage-by-stage analysis of these problems and potential remedies follows.

Prior theory and research suggests that non-stranger offenses are treated more leniently at all stages of the legal proceedings (Black, 1976; Gottfredson & Gottfredson, 1988). The closer the relationship between the victim and the offender, the less likely the police are to make an arrest (Black, 1971; Ford, 1983; Parnas, 1971; Worden & Politz, 1984; U.S. Commission on Civil Rights, 1982); the less likely the prosecutor is to bring formal charges (Boland, Brady, Tyson, & Bassler, 1983; Brosi, 1979; Field & Field, 1973; Lerman, 1986; Lundsgaarde, 1977; Rauma, 1984; Williams, 1978); the less likely a conviction or prison sentence will result (Cannavale & Falcon, 1976; Erez & Tontodonato, 1990; Forst, Lucianovic, & Cox, 1977; Gross & Mauro, 1984; LaFree, 1980, 1989; Miethe, 1987; U.S. Commission on Civil Rights, 1982; Vera Institute of Justice, 1981); the shorter prison sentences are likely to be (Erez & Tontodonato, 1990; Parnas, 1970; Rhodes & Conly, 1981); and the less likely a sentence of capital punishment will be handed down (Gross & Mauro, 1984).

These legal system responses are troubling, given that a large number of homicides and aggravated assaults are committed by and against intimate partners (Dawson & Langan, 1994). The legal system offers the last and sometimes the only protection available to domestic violence victims who hope to end the violence in their lives (Herrell & Hofford, 1990). Failure to deal effectively with perpetrators and victims of family violence leads to victimization by the legal system itself and to certain repetition of violent behavior in the next generation (Jaffe et al., 1990).

The arrest and prosecution phase of the criminal justice system may have either therapeutic or antitherapeutic effects on offenders and victims of domestic violence. Laws, policies, and legal decisions can either reinforce cognitive distortions of offenders and victims or promote more adaptive cognitions. Because the police and prosecutors are gatekeepers for the number and type of domestic violence cases that are criminally pursued (Ford, 1983), decisions to arrest and prosecute may have mental health implications for the offender and the victim.

Arrest

The police historically have failed to intervene effectively in domestic violence cases (Beck, 1987; Hathaway, 1986; Pleck, 1987). For instance, one study found that the pattern of police response was directly related to the rates of domestic homicide: police had been repeatedly called to the scenes of most domestic homicides (Wilt & Bannon, 1977). Other evidence suggests that police intentionally delay their response to domestic violence calls, hoping that the conflict will be resolved by the time they arrive (Oppelander, 1982). The literature in general suggests that police have traditionally felt more comfortable responding to stranger crimes, such as robbery, because they hold stereotypes of the participants in domestic violence cases and lack knowledge

of how to respond to those cases effectively (Ford, 1983).

One commentator has characterized police intervention as *iatrogenic,* meaning that police presence exacerbates conflict (Barocas, 1973). This is understandable. Because the police are typically the first legal actors to be apprised of the incident (Ford, 1983), the priority they assign to the case can not only have detrimental effects on the victim and her children but can also continue to legitimize the offender's violence at home (Fleming, 1979). When police respond slowly or not at all to domestic violence cases (Ford, 1983), offenders are encouraged to deny or minimize their behavior, whereas victims continue to feel helpless and blameworthy. Police policies can promote therapeutic effects for both offenders and victims by mandating that domestic violence calls receive priority over less serious personal crimes or property crimes (Herrell & Hofford, 1990).

Once the decision is made to go to the scene of a domestic violence report, police officers are likely to be met by a terrorized and probably injured victim (and her children) and an angry offender who denies his violence and blames the victim. Only a warrantless, probable cause arrest of domestic violence perpetrators commiting an assault or any other crime (Hart, 1992; Lerman, 1986) can challenge the entrenched, destructive, and maladaptive thoughts of the offender while empowering and protecting the victim and her children. By taking the offender into custody, the police are communicating to him and the victim that he has committed a criminal act and that he is responsible for his violent behavior (Sherman & Berk, 1984). By not making an arrest at this time, the police would be facilitating offender denial (Wexler & Winick, 1992) and encouraging the victim to continue to feel helpless, blamed, and worthless (Dutton, 1992).

By taking domestic violence cases seriously and arresting offenders when legally warranted, the police can validate the victim's right to be free from personal violence. Given the likelihood that threats or additional violence will occur unless the offender is arrested, such arrest can provide at least temporary safety from harm for the victim and her children. This is also a timely opportunity for the police to inform the victim of other services available to her (Herrell & Hofford, 1990; Langan & Innes, 1986).

Except for making a formal arrest (or warrant for an arrest if an offender is not found at the scene), the manner in which police deal with domestic violence cases currently has anti-therapeutic effects on the victims. It is not un-common for police to blame the victim or disparage her in some other way (Ferraro, 1989). This type of behavior merely reinforces the victim's low self-esteem and feelings of isolation and helplessness. Police training could make officers more sensitive and helpful to victims. Training could address general aspects of the dynamics of domestic violence, the potential lethality of these cases, services available for battered women and their children, and the legal obligation of the police to provide protection (Buzawa & Buzawa, 1992; Herrell & Hofford, 1990). Receiving training in handling domestic violence cases may enable officers to respond to these calls with more sensitivity and effective-ness.

Not surprisingly, the indifference of police to victims of domestic violence has led to a number of lawsuits (see review by Zalman, 1992). One of the most publicized cases of this kind involved a woman who was brutally assaulted and left para-lyzed by her estranged husband after she had repeatedly sought police protection (*Thurman v. City of Torrington*, 1984). The $2.3 million award granted to Tracey Thurman in that suit and awards in other lawsuits are believed to have prompted police departments to effect policy changes in domestic violence cases (Buzawa & Buzawa, 1992). Another spur to change has been attributed to the results (Sherman & Berk, 1984) and wide publicity (Lempert, 1989) of a pilot study in Minneapolis finding that arrests in mis-demeanor domestic violence assaults had a sig-nificantly greater effect than other responses by police in reducing future acts of violence by

offenders. These factors and others (Binder & Meeker, 1992) are leading to policy changes in the police's role in domestic violence cases.

Prosecution

The prosecution of an offense usually occurs in response to a police report (Ford & Regoli, 1992; Goolkasian, 1986; Lerman, 1986; Schmidt & Steury, 1989). Generally, prosecutors wield a great deal of discretion regarding whom to charge and what charge to file (Gottfredson & Gottfred-son, 1988). Prosecutors use this discretion to screen some suspects out of the criminal justice system altogether, divert others to community programs outside the system, bargain for informa-tion and guilty pleas, and prosecute some defen-dants fully. For example, studies of the screening function indicate that only 25% of cases brought to the attention of 94 U.S. attorneys ended in formal prosecution (Frase, 1980). This type of day-to-day decision making is conducted by pros-ecutors who make their decisions relatively free of control, although they may be influenced by the desires and opinions of the public, by the police, and by other government officials.

Case law accords the prosecutor wide lati-tude in the discretionary exercise of his or her prosecutorial powers so long as the decision is not deliberately based on unjustifiable standards such as race, religion, or other arbitrary classifi-cations (*Bordenkirscher v. Hayes*, 1978; *Oyler v. Boles*, 1962; *Town of Newton v. Rumery*, 1987; *United States v. Cox*, 1965; *United States v. Goodwin*, 1982; *Wayte v. United States*, 1985). Legality of this discretion extends to decisions of whether to charge with a crime or not, to refer the individual elsewhere (that is, diversion), to drop charges, to negotiate guilty pleas, and to try contested cases.

In general criminal cases, we know that the prosecutor considers various factors in deciding whether to bring formal charges against a suspect, including seriousness of the crime (Bernstein, Kelly, & Doyle, 1977; Eisenstein & Jacob, 1977; Forst & Brosi, 1977; Kaplan, 1965), strength of the evidence and adequacy of witnesses (Bernstein et al., 1977; Forst & Brosi, 1977; Kaplan, 1965), the suspect's background and characteristics (Bernstein et al., 1977; Forst & Brosi, 1977; Frase, 1980), the costs and benefits of obtaining a conviction (Frase, 1980; Kaplan, 1965), and attitude of the community toward the offense the suspect is believed to have committed (Miller, 1970). In addition, evidence shows that the decision to prosecute is based on characteristics of the victim (Miller, 1970; Williams, 1978) and the victim-offender relationship (Gottfredson & Gottfredson, 1988; Vera Institute of Justice, 1981; Williams, 1978).

In domestic violence cases, prosecutors may use the same broad range of tools used in general criminal cases. They have the discretion to effect a variety of policies, ranging from dismissing a case through prosecuting to convicting with harsh punishment (Ford, 1986; Ford & Regoli, 1992). They also can recommend sentences not specifically prescribed by statute but allowed as conditions of probation. For example, offenders may be required to participate in rehabilitative treatment programs as a requirement of probation (Ford & Regoli, 1992).

Although a great deal of attention has been paid to investigating the police decision to arrest domestic violence offenders, very little research has examined the prosecutor's decision making in these cases. An early, thought-provoking study concluded that the prosecution of domestic violence cases had the effect of converting a system thought to function under standard rules into a system whose processes are subject to chance (Ford, 1983). For example, the manner in which a victim's complaint was processed depended on who was taking complaints on any particular day. In addition, careless handling and errors in processing complaints resulted in legal inaction in many cases. These and other findings indicated that the victim's efforts to prosecute an offender had little institutional support and often had the effect of wearing the victim down long before the offender was due to stand trial.

Like other actors in the legal system, prosecutors historically have not been very sympathetic to the plight of domestic violence victims (Cahn, 1992; Ford, 1983; Loseke, 1989; Pagelow, 1992). Prosecutorial decisions in these cases are often complicated by the fact that victims commonly change their minds and ask that the charges against the offender be dismissed (Ferraro & Boychuk, 1992; Ford, 1983; Ford & Regoli, 1992). As a result, prosecutorial policy sometimes places the filing decision on the victim, which typically severely reduces the number of charges filed (Cahn, 1992). For example, one study of the reasons prosecutors gave for deciding not to charge domestic violence cases found that, in 45% of the cases, the primary reason for the failure to go forward was the victim's wishes (Schmidt & Steury, 1989). An antitherapeutic effect of following such a policy is that it provides an opportunity for the abuser to intimidate and prevent the victim from pursuing the charges (Cahn, 1992). Other factors also prevent prosecutors from going forward with the case; a common prosecutorial perception is that such crimes are trivial (Cahn, 1992), and some prosecutors blame victims and assume that women provoke the violence against them (Lerman, 1986; Schafran, 1987; U.S. Commission on Civil Rights, 1982).

This lack of enthusiasm for prosecution is unfortunate. By going forward with these cases, prosecutors provide a powerful message that offenders cannot avoid criminal sanctions through their control over the victim (Cahn, 1992). And precluding victims from influencing prosecution forces prosecutors to take these cases seriously and establishes that domestic violence is a crime against society. In addition, a number of jurisdictions have demonstrated that victims are more helpful if the prosecution will go forward with or without their cooperation (Cahn, 1992; Herrell & Hofford, 1990). If victims ultimately decide to take an active part in the prosecution of the offender, they can gain feelings of empowerment that can alter the balance of power in battering relationships and lower rates of future violence (Cahn, 1992; Ford, 1983).

To promote prosecution, some jurisdictions

have found it helpful to implement guidelines on when to file charges in domestic violence cases (Cahn, 1992; Ford, 1983). Such guidelines encourage the filing of domestic violence charges (Cahn, 1992) and make offenders less likely to think they can use violence against their wives. The effect on the victims is likely to be less tolerance of violent behavior.

A current prosecutorial trend is to divert these offenders and refer them to a treatment program (Herrell & Hofford, 1990). Diversion programs are an alternative to traditional criminal prosecution and sentencing through which case processing is suspended while the defendant completes a treatment program (Cahn, 1992; Goolkasian, 1986; Lerman, 1986). The decision as to whether diversion should occur prior to or after pleading guilty is controversial (Cahn & Lerman, 1991). Given the batterer's lack of motivation to seek treatment on his own, it makes sense to condition diversion on an admission of guilt and attendant conditions of probation (Hamberger & Hastings, 1989). Otherwise, offenders may believe that they are "getting off" their criminal charges if they do not receive the message that domestic violence is a crime (Cahn, 1992). Diversion also extends the time that a case is held open so that, if there is a violation, the offender can be prosecuted (Waits, 1985). Having the charges hanging over the offender's head and the threat of prosecution at any misstep will provide the victim with some power over his compliance.

Given the controversy over diversion programs, the National Council of Juvenile and Family Court Judges recommends that diversion be granted only in extraordinary cases, and then only after a guilty plea has been entered (Herrell & Hofford, 1990). The organization notes that diversion is inappropriate when it is used to weed out cases from the court's calendar, when first offenders are chronic abusers, when the required treatment is only of brief duration and is not monitored, and when the use of diversion is perceived as a less-than-serious response to the crime.

In sum, a variety of prosecutorial functions in domestic violence cases can have an antitherapeutic effect on both offenders and victims. Lenient treatment by the prosecutor communicates to the offender and the victim that the violent behavior is considered trivial. This is likely to feed the offenders' perceptions that they have done nothing wrong and encourage them to continue to blame the victim. Reform aimed at more vigorous prosecution of domestic violence cases can help offenders take responsibility for their hurtful behavior (Herrell & Hofford, 1990). Consistent prosecution can also empower victims and help them believe that the violence is not their responsibility. Written guidelines can assist prosecutors with decisions about when and whom to charge in these cases. As with the police, prosecutors can be trained to understand the dynamics of domestic violence and the potential dangerousness of the offenders if not sanctioned. Training can also alter prosecutorial stereotypes of battered women, enabling them to respond more sensitively to domestic violence cases.

When diversion programs are employed, the National Council of Juvenile and Family Court Judges' eligibility guidelines should be followed. The most important element in the use of diversion appears to be that an offender enter a guilty plea. Otherwise, offenders can continue to rationalize their violence or think they have escaped liability for their conduct. In addition, active monitoring of the offender's participation in the treatment program with the threat and use of sanctions for noncompliance are critical to combat batterers' cognitive distortions that they have done nothing wrong or illegal.

Trials, Plea Bargains, and Sentencing Issues

Certain aspects of the adjudication and sentencing of domestic violence offenders can have therapeutic and antitherapeutic consequences for the offender and victim. For instance, the decision to go to trial or not, the types of pleas and plea bargains employed, and the sentencing decisions can extend the cognitive distortions of both parties or promote more adapative and functional thinking and behavior.

Trials and Plea Bargains

The practice of plea bargaining enters into the prosecutor's decision to prosecute and, if so, on what charge (Gottfredson & Gottfredson, 1988). Plea bargaining is widespread, typically requiring that the defendant give up the right to go to trial in exchange for a reduction in the charge or sentence or both (Alschuler, 1968; Casper, 1979; Eisenstein & Jacob, 1977). Although there is considerable variation among jurisdictions in guilty plea rates, about 90% of persons adjudicated guilty are guilty as a result of a guilty plea (U.S. Department of Justice, 1984).

Controversy exists as to whether defendants who plea bargain and plead guilty get lighter sentences than defendants who exercise their right to trial. Some studies report sentencing differentials favoring those who plead guilty (Brereton & Casper, 1981–1982; Nardulli, 1978; Rhodes & Conly, 1981; Tiffany, Avichai, & Peters, 1975; Uhlman & Walker, 1980), whereas others indicate that other factors, such as seriousness of the charge and nature of the offender's prior record, may be more important in determining the sentence (Eisenstein & Jacob, 1977). In fact, several studies have found an association between offense seriousness and mode of disposition, with more serious cases being more likely to go to trial (Eisenstein & Jacob, 1977; Hagan, 1975).

As discussed in the previous section on the prosecution of offenses, many domestic violence cases are diverted prior to or after a plea of guilty. In the latter case, the plea bargaining process is used to encourage offenders to plead guilty in exchange for diversion into a treatment program in lieu of other sanctions. Offenders who do not

qualify for diversion programs may still utilize plea bargains to avoid the maximum punishment. No research is available on the utilization of plea bargains in domestic violence cases, making this a fertile ground of inquiry for future studies.

There is also no research on factors that influence a domestic violence offender to forgo his right to trial and enter into a plea bargain. Given the cognitive distortions most offenders harbor about their violence, one would expect that they are more likely to go to trial because they feel unjustly prosecuted. It is likely, however, that pleading guilty instead of fighting the charges in a full trial may have more therapeutic effects for both the offender and the victim. This would be expected to be more true for offenders who plead guilty as charged and not as true for offenders whose charges are bargained down or who plead no contest (see Klotz et al., 1992). Consequently, any manner of proceeding in court other than a guilty plea to the offense as charged may reinforce the domestic violence offender's denial and minimization of his violent behavior (Wexler & Winick, 1992). When the offender takes responsibility in this way, the victim can desist from self-blame and begin the process of healing. The therapeutic impact of a guilty plea can be reinforced by a judicial sentencing policy that recognizes a guilty plea as a first step in the offender's rehabilitation (Wexler & Winick, 1992).

Clearly, research is needed on the effects of various types of guilty pleas and trial postures on the entrenched dysfunctional thoughts of the domestic violence offender. In particular, does pleading guilty as charged therapeutically alter the cognitive distortions of the offender? Does proceeding to trial further cement the cognitive distortions? When treatment is part of a plea bargain, can the effects of pleading guilty be teased out from the effects of treatment per se? Other research questions involve the role of the prosecuting and defense attorneys in the case (Klotz et al., 1992). For example, how does zealous, adversarial posturing by defendant's attorney affect the defendant's thinking about the offense?

Sentencing

After a guilty plea or a finding of guilt at trial in a domestic violence case, the offender faces two possibilities: probation and/or fine, or imprisonment (Cahn, 1992). Probation generally includes participation in counseling or other diversionary programs. The National Council of Juvenile and Family Court Judges indicates that the primary goals of domestic violence sentencing are to stop the violence, protect the victim and family members, and hold the offender accountable (Herrell & Hofford, 1990). The council suggests that provision be made for formal supervision and monitoring of the offender's behavior if he is granted probation.

Although research suggests that stranger offenders fare worse than nonstranger offenders in sentencing outcome (Erez & Totodonato, 1990), no research examines the sentencing differential between domestic violence offenders and stranger offenders. Clearly, the dearth of research on this matter suggests that future researchers may want to examine sentencing outcome differentials between domestic violence offenders and stranger assault/homicide offenders. We do know, however, that batterers are rarely sentenced to incarceration (Waits, 1985); imprisonment is extremely rare, even for felonious aggravated assaults (Ferraro & Boychuk, 1992).

Prosecutors can request tougher sentences, thereby educating the abuser, the victim, and the court about the seriousness of the crime. Some jurisdictions statutorily mandate that prosecutors make all reasonable efforts to persuade the court to impose the most severe authorized sentence on a person convicted of spouse abuse (Cahn, 1992). Other jurisdictions provide judicial and probation guidelines that set out a presumptive sentence recommendation for misdemeanor offenses, beginning with 30 to 60 days in jail, suspended on conditions that protect the victim and rehabilitate the offender (Goolkasian, 1986). Requiring prosecutors to recommend sentences commensurate with other crimes could have therapeutic effects

on offenders and victims by communicating to them that a serious crime has occurred and that the perpetrator will be punished. In addition, one could even argue that domestic violence offenders should be treated more harshly than, say, stranger offenders committing comparable crimes because of the greater frequency of their offending and the higher likelihood of their offenses becoming fatal to the victim.

Judges can also confront offender denial and minimization by sentencing these cases as they would other crimes, and by recognizing that offenders will violate sentencing orders and conditions with impunity if they believe nothing will happen to them (Herrell & Hofford, 1990). Consistently ordering some sort of additional penalty for those found guilty of past violations of court orders or conditions of sentencing can communicate to offenders that they will be punished for each infraction. As with any form of behavior modification, offenders need to know that they cannot escape liability for single lapses in compliance. To be consistent, courts should develop a means of monitoring compliance with both criminal and civil court orders. The National Council of Juvenile and Family Court Judges suggests that judges may wish to set cases for periodic review, whether or not a violation has been reported (Herrell & Hofford, 1990).

If judges use diversion or conditions of probation, psychological principles can be used to facilitate offender compliance. For example, Wexler (1991) reviews the literature that sets forth ways of achieving patient compliance with treatment regimens and then applies those principles to achieving greater compliance with conditions of probation on the part of probationers. Wexler suggests that probationers might be more likely to comply with conditions of their probation if the court order is individually tailored to fit their needs, and if the judge seeks input and commitment from the defendant. One could apply Wexler's reasoning to fashioning diversion and probation orders for domestic violence offenders. To increase adherence with conditions, hearings can actively involve the offender in arriving at the conditions, ensure that he understands what is expected of him, and solicit his agreement with and commitment to the conditions. Research is needed to assess the effectiveness of such an approach to the achievement of compliance by domestic violence offenders.

Restraining Orders

In addition to the invocation of criminal sanctions against domestic violence offenders, legal reforms over the last 10 years have made it possible for victims to seek help and protection from the civil justice system (McHardy, 1993). Remedies available through civil courts include temporary and permanent restraining orders (Murphy, 1992), divorce and child custody proceedings (Hart, 1992), and suits for compensatory and punitive damages for marital torts (Spector, 1993). This section focuses on restraining orders because they complement the use of criminal remedies in domestic violence cases. Therapeutic and antitherapeutic effects can result from the accessibility, use, and enforcement of these protective orders.

Civil restraining orders can be an effective remedy for obtaining immediate relief for domestic violence victims (Finn & Colson, 1990; Harrell et al., 1993). They may be used in conjunction with criminal sanctions or as an exclusive legal remedy and are now available to battered women in every jurisdiction (Hart, 1992). The order typically offers a domestic violence victim a judicial injunction that directs the offender to cease battering, threatening, or harming the woman and, where appropriate, other family members such as children (Chaudhuri & Daly, 1992). Many state codes authorize the trial court to award the victim a temporary restraining order if imminent danger exists, and a hearing on the permanent order is scheduled within a reasonable period of time (Harrell et al., 1993; Hart, 1992; Herrell & Hofford, 1990).

The forms required to obtain a restraining order, however, may be discouragingly complex for women not represented by an attorney or assisted by someone familiar with the forms and the courts (Harrell et al., 1993). The utility of the restraining orders depends on the specificity of relief ordered, enforcement practices of the police and courts, the severity of violence in the year prior to the order, and the level of resistance by the man during the hearing (Harrell et al., 1993; Hart, 1992). Moreover, research indicates that violations of restraining orders are reported by over half the women who obtain them. And despite provision of criminal sanctions for restraining order violations, men who continued abuse faced low risks of arrest or return to court (Harrell et al., 1993).

The legal system can accomplish therapeutic as well as legal goals by improving the accessibility, issuance, and enforcement of restraining orders in domestic violence cases. For example, judges can facilitate the process of obtaining both temporary and permanent restraining orders by ensuring that women get the legal papers served on the offenders (Harrell et al., 1993). This is important because over 40% of women who obtained a temporary restraining order did not return for a permanent order because they were unable to get the temporary order served on the batterers (Harrell et al., 1993). Judicial facilitation of service may necessitate redefining the role of the judge in these proceedings (Harrell et al., 1993). The judge's role can also be improved by personalizing the orders to fit each victim's needs (Harrell et al., 1993).

Empirical findings indicate that the majority of offenders violate a restraining order within one year of its issuance, and that the severity of preorder abuse and the intensity of the offender's resistance to the order at the hearing are highly predictive of noncompliance (Harrell et al., 1993). Consequently, judges are presented with a challenge to ensure that their orders are carried out. Several suggestions based on the psychological literature can be made to encourage offenders to comply with the court order.

First, offenders are more likely to comply with restraining orders if they believe that judges are neutral, honest authorities who allow them to state their views and who treat them with dignity (Lind & Tyler, 1988; Tyler, 1990). Tyler suggests that people obey the law because they view it as just and moral; they react to their experiences by evaluating justice or unjustice; and in evaluating the justice of their experiences, they consider factors unrelated to outcome, such as whether they have had a chance to state their case and been treated with dignity and respect. Consequently, if offenders feel respectfully listened to, believe they have greater input into fashioning the order, and view the proceedings as fair, they may be more likely to comply with a court order.

Second, the behavioral psychological technique of contingency contracting (Masters, 1987; Meichenbaum & Turk, 1987; Winick, 1991) may increase compliance by offenders with restraining orders. In a therapeutic setting, this involves the therapist and client entering into a formal agreement wherein they jointly choose the behavioral goals to be achieved and the reinforcement or aversive consequences that the client will receive on achievement or nonachievement of those goals (Winick, 1991). Several conditions increase the effectiveness of these contracts in a therapeutic setting (Meichenbaum & Turk, 1987). These include tailoring the agreement to fit individual needs, defining in detail the specific behavior expected of the individual, listing in detail the consequences of compliance or noncompliance, specifying the dates that the contract covers, attaining the individual's commitment to follow the agreement in both oral and written form, and requiring that the individual sign the contract. Such an approach has been suggested for use by judges to increase an insanity acquitee's compliance with conditions of release (Wexler, 1991, 1993a).

Therapeutic jurisprudence principles suggest that judges composing restraining orders might increase compliance by asking offenders to enter into a behavioral contract with the court. The success of this venture would depend on following the guidelines associated with effective agreements. Victims would experience greater feelings of satisfaction with the legal process involved in obtaining the protective order if judges made an effort to tailor each order to fit the needs of the individual victim. In addition to affecting victim satisfaction, specially tailoring the restraining order can protect women from severe future violence (Harrell et al., 1993). Judges also need to use clear and unambiguous language in composing restraining orders. Confusion over what it covered by the order can be eliminated by explaining the conditions to the women and specifically tailoring conditions for the men, using nonlegal jargon. Finally, judges can benefit from training designed to instill an understanding of the dynamics of domestic violence, the effects of civil orders of protection, and the types of conditions courts may impose in these cases (Harrell et al., 1993; Schafran, 1987).

Therapeutic objectives can also be accomplished by the police who are called out on restraining order violations. It is recommended that police training and supervision emphasize the importance of arresting offenders who violate valid restraining orders (Harrell et al., 1993). This training might educate officers about how failure to arrest in these cases can reduce a woman's sense of empowerment and safety that accompanied obtaining the order in the first place, as well as the probable lethal outcomes of their failure. Not arresting and prosecuting such offenders also encourages them to violate the law in the future and makes a mockery of the legal system. If victims view restraining orders as an exercise in futility, they are less likely to turn to the legal system for help in the future.

Conclusion

It is clear from the preceding discussion that ample research exists verifying that the laws, policies, and legal actors involved in domestic violence cases can have iatrogenic or therapeutic effects on both offenders and victims. This chapter explored the ways in which the legal system reinforces maladaptive behavior by offenders and victims and how it can influence changes in such behavior through legal mechanisms. Where empirical research was found to address these issues, it was cited. However, in most cases, empirical research is not available to support many of the recommendations that were made. This is an area where behavioral scientists can empirically demonstrate ways in which the law can improve the legal processing of domestic violence cases.

Because the chapter focused on offenders and victims in domestic violence cases, only minimal attention was paid to the consequences for children in these relationships. Future scholarly writing needs to address these issues more fully. Such investigations might examine the effects of legal decisions on children of violent couples—for example, in child custody and visitation matters. Other future research could investigate the effects on children whose mothers are incarcerated for killing a battering spouse. Also, given that battered women have posttraumatic stress disorder symptoms and are likely to abuse their children, the effect of a battered woman's treatment on the well-being of her children might provide interesting information on the possible prevention of psychopathology and violent behavior among children.

References

Alschuler, A. (1968). The prosecutor's role in plea bargaining. *University of Chicago Law Review, 36,* 50.

American Psychiatric Association. (1994). *Diagnostic and statistical manual of mental disorders* (4th ed.). Washington, DC: Author.

Armstrong, L. (1983). *The home front: Notes from the family war zone.* New York: McGraw-Hill.

Bandura, A. (1979). The social perspective: Mechanisms of aggression. In H. Toch (Ed.), *Psychology of crime and criminal justice.* New York: Holt, Rinehart & Winston.

Barocas, H. A. (1973). Iatrogenic and preventive intervention in police-family crisis situation. *International Journal of Social Psychiatry, 20,* 113–121.

Beck, A. T. (1976). *Cognitive therapy and emotional disorders.* New York: International Universities Press.

Beck, A. T., Freeman, A., & Associates. (1990). *Cognitive therapy of personality disorders.* New York: Guilford Press.

Beck, A. T., Rush, J., Shaw, B., & Emery, G. (1979). *Cognitive therapy of depression.* New York: Guilford Press.

Beck, L. R. (1987). Protecting battered women: A proposal for comprehensive domestic violence legislation in New York. *Fordham Urban Law Journal, 15,* 999.

Bernstein, I., Kelly, W., & Doyle, P. (1977). Societal reaction to deviants: The case of criminal defendants. *American Sociological Review, 42,* 743.

Binder, A., & Meeker, J. (1992). Arrest as a method to control spouse abuse. In E. S. Buzawa & C. G. Buzawa (Eds.), *Domestic violence: The criminal justice response* (pp. 129–140). Westport, CT: Auburn House.

Black, D. (1971). The social organization of arrest. *Stanford Law Review, 23,* 1087.

Black, D. (1976). *The behavior of law.* New York: Academic Press.

Boland, B., Brady, E., Tyson, H., & Bassler, J. (1983). *The prosecution of felony arrests.* Washington, DC: U.S. Department of Justice, Bureau of Justice Statistics.

Bordenkircher v. Hayes, 434 U.S. 357 (1978).

Bowker, L. (1983). *Beating wife-beating.* Lexington, MA: Health.

Bowker, L. (1988). On the relationship between wife beating and child abuse. In K. Yllo & M. Bograd (Eds.), *Feminist perspectives on wife abuse* (pp. 133–157). Newbury Park, CA: Sage.

Brereton, D., & Casper, J. (1981–1982). Does it pay to plead guilty? Differential sentencing and the functioning of criminal courts. *Law and Society Review, 16*(1), 45–70.

Brosi, K. (1979). *A cross-city comparison of felony case processing.* Washington, DC: Institute for Law and Social Research.

Browne, A. (1987). *When battered women kill.* New York: Macmillan/Free Press.

Browne, A., & Williams, K. (1989). Exploring the effects of resource availability and the likelihood of female-perpetrated homicides. *Law and Society Review, 23,* 75–94.

Browning, J. J., & Dutton, D. G. (1986). Assessment of wife assault with the conflict tactics scale: Using couple data to quantify the differential reporting effect. *Journal of Marriage and the Family, 48,* 375–379.

Burns, N., & Meredith, C. (1993). Evaluation of the effectiveness of group treatment for men who batter. In J. Hudson & J. Roberts (Eds.), *Evaluating Justice* (pp. 241–263). Toronto, Ontario: Thompson Education Publishing Company.

Buzawa, E. S., & Buzawa, C. G. (1992). Introduction. In E. S. Buzawa & C. G. Buzawa (Eds.), *Domestic violence: The criminal justice response* (pp. vii–xxii). Westport, CT: Auburn House.

Caesar, P. L. (1988). Exposure to violence in families of origin among wife abusers and maritally nonviolent men. *Violence and Victims, 3,* 49–64.

Cahn, N. (1992). Innovative approaches to the prosecution of dometic violence crimes: An overview. In E. S. Buzawa & C. G. Buzawa (Eds.), *Domestic violence: The criminal justice response* (pp. 161–180). Westport, CT: Auburn House.

Cahn, N., & Lerman, L. (1991). Prosecuting woman abuse. In M. Steinman (Ed.), *Woman battering: Policy responses.* Cincinnati, OH: Anderson Publishing.

Cannavale, F. J., Jr., & Falcon, W. D. (1976). *Witness cooperation.* Institute for Law and Social Research, Lexington, MA: Lexington Books.

Carmody, D. C., & Williams, K. R. (1987). Wife assaults and perceptions of sanctions. *Violence and Victims, 2,* 25–38.

Casper, J. (1979). Reformers vs. abolitionists: Some notes for further research on plea bargaining. *Law and Society Review, 13,* 567.

Chaudhuri, M., & Daly, K. (1992). Do restraining orders help? Battered women's experience with male violence and legal process. In E. S. Buzawa & C. G. Buzawa (Eds.), *Domestic violence: The criminal justice response* (pp. 227–252). Westport, CT: Auburn House.

Clark, N. L. (1986). Marital privacy: New remedies for old wrongs. *Cumberland Law Review, 16,* 229.

Coleman, D. H., & Straus, M. A. (1983). Alcohol abuse and family violence. In E. Gottheil, K. A. Druley, T. E. Skoloda, & H. M. Waxman (Eds.), *Alcohol, drug abuse, and aggression* (pp. 104–124). Springfield, IL: Charles C Thomas.

Collins, J. J., Jr. (1988). Suggested explanatory frameworks to clarify the alcohol use/violence relationship. *Contemporary Drug Problems, 15,* 107–121.

Craighead, W. E., Evans, D. D., & Robins, C. J. (1992). Unipolar depression. In S. M. Turner, K. S. Calhoun, & H. E. Adams (Eds.), *Clinical behavior therapy* (2nd ed., pp. 99–116). New York: Wiley.

Davidson, T. (1978). *Conjugal crime.* New York: Hawthorne Books.

Dawson, J. M., & Langan, P. A. (1994). *Murder in families.* Washington, DC: U.S. Department of Justice.

Dobash, R. E., & Dobash, R. P. (1979). *Violence against wives: A case against patriarchy.* New York: Free Press.

Dutton, D. G. (1986). Wife assaulter's explanations for assault: The neutralization of self-punishment. *Canadian Journal of Behavioural Science, 18,* 381–390.

Dutton, D. G. (1988). Profiling of wife assaulters: Preliminary evidence for a trimodal analysis. *Violence and Victims, 3,* 5–30.

Dutton, D. G., & Painter, S. L. (1981). Traumatic bonding: The development of emotional attachments in battered women and other relationships of intermittent abuse. *Victimology: An International Journal, 6,* 139–155.

Dutton, D. G., & Strachan, C. E. (1987). Motivational needs for power and dominance as differentiating variables of assaultive and non-assaultive male populations. *Violence and Victims, 2,* 145–156.

Dutton, M. A. (1992). *Empowering and healing the battered woman.* New York: Springer.

Edelson, J., & Brygger, M. P. (1986). Gender differences in reporting of battering incidences. *Family Relations, 35,* 377–382.

Edelson, J., & Syers. (1990). *The relative long-term effects of group treatment for men who batter.* Minneapolis, MN: Domestic Abuse Project.

Eisenstein, J., & Jacob, H. (1977). *Felony justice.* Boston: Little, Brown.

Ellis, J. E. (1984). Prosecutorial discretion to charge in cases of spouse assault: A dialogue. *Journal of Criminal Law and Criminology, 75,* 56–102.

Erez, E., & Tontodonato, P. (1990). The effect of victim participation in sentencing outcome. *Criminology, 28,* 451.

Fagan, J. (1989). Cessation of family violence. In L. Ohlin & M. Tonry (Eds.), *Family violence: Vol. 11. Crime and justice: An annual review of the research* (pp. 377–425). Chicago: University of Chicago Press.

Fagan, J., & Browne, A. (1994). Violence between spouses and intimates. In A. J. Reiss & J. A. Roth (Eds.), *Understanding and preventing violence: Vol. 3. Social influences* (pp. 115–292). Washington, DC: National Academy Press.

Fagan, J., Stewart, D., & Hansen, K. (1983). Violent men or violent husbands? Background factors and situational correlates of domestic and extra-domestic violence. In D. Finkelhor, R. Gelles, G. Hotaling, & M. Straus (Eds.), *The dark side of families* (pp. 49–68). Newbury Park, CA: Sage.

Ferraro, K. (1989). Policing woman battering. *Social Problems, 36,* 61–74.

Ferraro, K., & Boychuk, T. (1992). The court's response to interpersonal violence: A comparison of intimate and nonintimate assault. In E. S. Buzawa & C. G. Buzawa (Eds.), *Domestic violence: The criminal justice response* (pp. 209–225). Westport, CT: Auburn House.

Field, M. H., & Field, H. F. (1973). Marital violence and the criminal process: Neither justice nor peace. *Social Service Review, 47,* 221–240.

Finn, P., & Colson, S. (1990). *Civil protection orders: Legislation, current court practice, and enforcement.* Washington, DC: National Institute of Justice, U.S. Department of Justice.

Fleming, J. B. (1979). *Stopping wife abuse.* Garden City, NY: Anchor/Doubleday.

Ford, D. A. (1983). Wife battery and criminal justice: A study of victim decision-making. *Family Relations, 32,* 463–475.

Ford, D. A. (1986). Prosecution as a victim power resource: A note on empowering women in violent conjugal relationships. *Law and Society Review, 25,* 313.

Ford, D. A., & Regoli, M. J. (1992). The preventive impact of policies for prosecuting wife batterers. In E. S. Buzawa & C. G. Buzawa (Eds.), *Domestic violence: The criminal justice response* (pp. 181–208). Westport, CT: Auburn House.

Forst, B., & Brosi, K. (1977). A theoretical and empirical analysis of the prosecutor. *Journal of Legal Studies, 6,* 177.

Forst, B., Lucianovic, J., & Cox, S. (1977). *What happens after arrest?* Washington, DC: Institute for Law and Social Research.

Frase, R. (1980). The decision to file federal criminal charges: A quantitative study of prosecutorial discretion. *University of Chicago Law Review, 47,* 246.

Frieze, I. H., & Browne, A. (1989). Violence in marriage. In L. Ohlin & M. Tonry (Eds.), *Family violence: Vol. 11. Crime and justice: An annual review of the research* (pp. 163–218). Chicago: University of Chicago Press.

Gagnon, A. G. (1992). Ending mandatory divorce mediation for battered women. *Harvard Women's Law Journal, 15,* 272.

Giles-Sims, J. (1985). A longitudinal study of battered children of battered wives. *Family Relations, 34,* 205.

Goldstein, H. (1967). Policy formulation: A proposal for improving police performance. *Michigan Law Review, 65,* 1123.

Gondolf, E. Q. (1988). Who are those guys? Toward a behavioral typology of batterers. *Violence and Victims, 3,* 187–204.

Goolkasian, G. A. (1986). *Confronting domestic violence: The role of the Criminal Court judges.* Washington, DC: U.S. Department of Justice.

Gordon, L. (1988). *Heroes of their own lives: The politics and history of family violence.* New York: Penguin Books.

Gottfredson, M., & Gottfredson, D. (1988). *Decision making in criminal justice: Towards a rational exercise of discretion* (2nd ed.). New York: Plenum.

Gottfredson, M., & Hirschi, T. (1990). *A general theory of crime.* Stanford, CA: Stanford University Press.

Gottman, J. M., Jacobson, N. S., Rushe, R. H., Short, J. W., Babcock, J., & La Taillade, J. J. (in press). The relationship between heart rate reactivity, emotionally aggressive behavior, and general violence in batterers. *Journal of Family Psychology.*

Gross, S., & Mauro, R. (1984). Patterns of death: An analysis of racial disparities in capital sentencing and homicide victimization. *Stanford Law Review, 37,* 27.

Hagan, J. (1974). Extra-legal attributes and criminal sentencing: An assessment of a socio-logical viewpoint. *Law and Society Review, 8,* 357.

Hagan, J. (1975). Parameters of criminal prosecution: An application of path analysis to a problem of criminal justice. *Journal of Criminal Law and Criminology, 65*(4), 536–544.

Hamberger, L. K., & Hastings, J. E. (1986). Characteristics of spouse abusers: Predictors of treatment acceptance. *Journal of Interpersonal Violence, 1,* 363–373.

Hamberger, L. K., & Hastings, J. E. (1988). Characteristics of male spouse abusers consistent with personality disorders. *Hospital and Community Psychiatry, 39,* 763–770.

Hamberger, L. K., & Hastings, J. E. (1989). Counseling male spouse abusers: Characteristics of treatment completers and dropouts. *Violence and Victims, 4,* 275–286.

Hamberger, L. K., & Hastings, J. E. (1990). Recidivism following spouse abuse abatement counselling. *Violence & Victims, 5,* 157.

Harrell, A. (1991). *Evaluation of court-ordered treatment for domestic violence offenders: Final report.* Washington, DC: Urban Institute.

Harrell, A., Smith, B., & Newmark, L. (1993). *Court processing and the effects of restraining orders for domestic violence victims.* Washington, DC: Urban Institute.

Hart, B. J. (1992). State codes on domestic violence: Analysis, commentary, and recommendations. *Juvenile and Family Court Journal, 43,* 1–81.

Hart, B. (1993). Battered women and the criminal justice system. *American Behavioral Scientist, 36,* 624–638.

Hastings, J. E., & Hamberger, L. K. (1988). Personality characteristics of spouse abusers: A controlled comparison. *Violence and Victims, 3,* 31.

Hathaway, C. R. (1986). Case comment: Gender based discrimination in police reluctance to respond to domestic assault complaints. *Georgetown Law Journal, 75,* 667.

Herrell, S. B., & Hofford, M. (1990). *Family*

violence: Improving court practice. Reno, NV: Family Violence Project, National Council on Juvenile and Family Court Judges.

Hofford, M., & Gable, R. (1989). *Significant interventions: Coordinated strategies to deter family violence.* In *Families in court: A national symposium* (pp. 1–36). Washington, DC: National Institute of Justice.

Hollon, S. D., & Beck, A. T. (1994). Cognitive and cognitive-behavioral therapies. In A. E. Bergin & S. L. Garfield (Eds.), *Handbook of psychotherapy and behavior change* (4th ed., pp. 428–466). New York: Wiley.

Holtzworth-Munroe, A. (1992). Social skill deficits in maritally violent men: Interpreting the data using a social information processing model. *Clinical Psychology Review, 12,* 605–617.

Holtzworth-Munroe, A., & Anglin, K. (1991). The competency of responses given by maritally violent versus nonviolent men to problematic marital situations. *Violence and Victims, 6,* 257–269.

Holtzworth-Munroe, A., & Hutchinson, G. (1993). Attributing negative intent to wife behavior: The attributions of maritally violent versus nonviolent men. *Journal of Abnormal Psychology, 102,* 206–211.

Holtzworth-Munroe, A., & Stuart, G. L. (1994). Typologies of male batterers. *Psychological Bulletin, 116,* 474–497.

Hotaling, G. T., & Straus, M. A. (1989). Intrafamily violence and crime and violence outside the family. In L. Ohlin & M. Tonry (Eds.), *Family violence: Vol. 11. Crime and justice: An annual review of the research* (pp. 315–375). Chicago: University of Chicago Press.

Hotaling, G. T., & Sugarman, D. B. (1986). An analysis of risk markers in husband to wife violence: The current state of the knowledge. *Violence and Victims, 1,* 101–124.

Jacobson N. S., Gottman, J. M., Waltz, J., Rushe, R., & Babcock, J. (1994). Affect, verbal content, and psychophysiology in the arguments of couples with a violent husband. *Journal of Consulting and Clinical Psychology, 62,* 982–988.

Jaffe, P. G., Wolfe, D. A., Telford, A., & Austin, G. (1986). The impact of police charges in incidents of wife abuse. *Journal of Family Violence, 1,* 37–49.

Jaffe, P. G., Wolfe, D. A., & Wilson, S. K. (1990). *Children of battered women.* Newbury Park, CA: Sage.

Jouriles, E. N., & O'Leary, K. D. (1985). Interspousal reliability of reports of marital violence. *Journal of Consulting and Clinical Psychology, 53,* 419–421.

Kalmus, D. (1984). The intergenerational transmission of marital aggression. *Journal of Marriage and the Family, 46,* 11–19.

Kalmus, D., & Seltzer, J. (1986). Continuity of marital behavior in remarriage: The case of spouse abuse. *Journal of Marriage and the Family, 48,* 113.

Kantor, G. K., & Straus, M. A. (1987). The "drunken bum" theory of wife beating. *Social Problems, 34,* 213–321.

Kaplan, J. (1965). Prosecutorial discretion—A comment. *Northwestern University Law Review, 60,* 174.

Kennedy, L. W., & Dutton, D. G. (1989). The incidence of wife assault in Alberta. *Canadian Journal of Behavioural Sciences, 21,* 40–54.

Klotz, J. A., Wexler, D. B., Sales, B. D., & Becker, J. V. (1992). Cognitive restructuring through law: A therapeutic jurisprudence approach to sex offenders and the plea process. *University of Puget Sound Law Review, 15,* 579–595.

Lab, S. P., & Whitehead, J. T. (1990). From "nothing works" to "the appropriate" works: The latest stop on the search for the secular grail. *Criminology, 28,* 114.

LaFree, G. D. (1980). Variables affecting guilty pleas and convictions in rape cases: Toward a social theory of rape processing. *Social Forces, 58,* 833.

LaFree, G. D. (1989). *Rape and criminal justice:*

The construction of sexual assault. Belmont, CA: Wadsworth.

Langan, P., & Innes, C. (1986). *Preventing domestic violence against women.* Washington, DC: U.S. Department of Justice.

Lemon, N. (1993). Criminal cases concerning domestic violence. *Juvenile and Family Law Digest, 25,* 345–374.

Lempert, R. (1989). Humility is a virtue: On the publicization of policy-relevant research. *Law and Society Review, 23,* 145–161.

Lerman, L. G. (1986). Prosecution of wife beaters: Institutional obstacles and innovations. In M. Lystad (Ed.), *Violence in the home: Interdisciplinary perspectives.* New York: Brunner/Mazel.

Lind, E. A., & Tyler, T. R. (1988). *The social psychology of procedural justice.* New York: Plenum.

Loseke, D. R. (1989). Evaluation research and the practice of social services: A case for qualitative methodology. *Journal of Contemporary Ethnography, 18,* 202.

Lundsgaarde, H. (1977). *Murder in space city: A cultural analysis of Houston homicide patterns.* New York: Oxford University Press.

Lutzer, J. R., & Van Hasselt, V. B. (1992). Family violence. In S. M. Turner, K. S. Calhoun, & H. E. Adams (Eds.), *Clinical Behavior Therapy* (2nd ed., pp. 417–435). New York: Wiley.

Maiuro, R. D., Cahn, T. S., & Vitaliano, P. P. (1986). Assertiveness deficits and hostility in domestically violent men. *Violence and Victims, 1,* 279–290.

Margolin, G. (1988). Interpersonal and intrapersonal factors associated with marital violence. In G. T. Hotaling, D. Finkelhor, J. T. Kirkpatrick, and M. A. Straus (Eds.), *Family abuse and its consequences: New directions for research.* Newbury Park, CA: Sage.

Masters, J. C., Burish, T. G., Hollon, S. D., & Rimm, D. C. (1987). *Behavior therapy: Techniques and empirical findings* (3rd ed.). Orlando, FL: Harcourt Brace Jovanovich.

McHardy, L. W. (1993). Introduction. *Juvenile and Family Law Digest, 25,* i.

McMullin, R. E. (1986). *Handbook of cognitive therapy techniques.* New York: Norton.

Meichenbaum, D. H. (1977). *Cognitive-behavior modification.* New York: Plenum.

Meichenbaum, D. H., & Turk, D. C. (1987). *Facilitating treatment adherence: A practitioner's guidebook.* New York: Plenum.

Miethe, T. D. (1987). Stereotypical conceptions and criminal processing: The case of the victim-offender relationship. *Justice Quarterly, 4,* 571.

Miller, B. A., Downs, W. R., & Gondoli, D. M. (1988). Spousal violence among alcoholic women as compared to a random household sample of women. *Journal of Studies on Alcoholism, 50,* 533–540.

Miller, F. (1970). *Prosecution: The decision to charge a suspect with a crime.* Boston: Little, Brown.

Murphy, S. M. (1992). Orders of protection and the battered woman syndrome. *Loyola University Chicago Law Journal, 23,* 397.

Nardulli, P. (1978). *The courtroom elite.* Cambridge, MA: Ballinger.

Nardulli, P., Flemming, R., & Eisenstein, J. (1984). Unraveling the complexities of decision making in face-to-face groups: A contextual analysis of plea-bargained sentences. *American Political Science Review, 78,* 912–928.

Neidig, P. D., Friedman, D., & Collins, B. (1986). Attitudinal characteristics of males who have engaged in spouse abuse. *Journal of Family Violence, 1,* 223–233.

Novaco, R. (1976). The functions and regulation of the arousal of anger. *American Journal of Psychiatry, 133,* 1124–1128.

Ochberg, F. M. (1988). Post-traumatic therapy and victims of violence. In F. M. Ochberg (Ed.), *Post-traumatic therapy and victims of violence.* New York: Brunner/Mazel.

Okun, L. (1986). *Women abuse: Facts replacing myths.* Albany, NY: State University of New York Press.

O'Leary, K. D. (1993). Through a psychological lens: Personality traits, personality disorders, and levels of violence. In. R. J. Gelles & D. R. Loseke (Eds.), *Current controversies on family violence* (pp. 7–30). Newbury Park, CA: Sage.

O'Leary, K. D., & Arias, I. (1988). Assessing the agreement of reports of spouse abuse. In G. T. Hotaling, D. Finkelhor, J. T. Kirkpatrick, & M. A. Straus (Eds.), *Family abuse and its consequences: New directions for research*. Newbury Park, CA: Sage.

Oppelander, N. (1982). Coping or copping out: Police service delivery in domestic disputes. *Criminology, 20,* 449.

Oyler v. Boles, 368 U.S. 448 (1962).

Pagelow, M. D. (1984). *Family violence*. New York: Praeger.

Pagelow, M. D. (1992). Adult victims of domestic violence: Battered women. *Journal of Interpersonal Violence, 7,* 87.

Parnas, R. I. (1967). Police response to domestic violence. *Wisconsin Law Review, 31,* 914–960.

Parnas, R. I. (1970). The judicial response to intra-family violence. *Minnesota Law Review, 54,* 585.

Parnas, R. I. (1971). Police discretion and diversion of incidents of intra-family violence. *Law and Contemporary Problems, 36,* 539.

Pence, E., & Paymar, M. (1993). *Education groups for men who batter: The Duluth Model*. New York: Springer.

Perlin, M. (1993). What is therapeutic jurisprudence? *New York Law School Journal of Human Rights, 10,* 623–636.

Pleck, E. (1987). *Domestic tyranny: The making of social policy against family violence from colonial times to the present*. New York: Oxford University Press.

Ptacek, J. (1988). Why do men batter their wives? In K. Yllo & M. Bograd (Eds.), *Feminist perspectives on wife abuse* (pp. 133–157). Newbury Park, CA: Sage.

Rauma, D. (1984). "Going for the gold": Prosecutorial decision making in cases of wife assault. *Social Science Research, 13,* 321.

Rhodes, W. M., & Conly, C. (1981). *Analysis of federal sentencing: Final report* (Publication No. FJRP 81/004). Washington, DC: U.S. Department of Justice.

Rosenbaum, A., & O'Leary, K. D. (1981). Marital violence: Characteristics of abusive couples. *Journal of Consulting and Clinical Psychology, 49,* 63–76.

Saunders, D. G., & Azar, S. T. (1989). Treatment programs for family violence. In L. Ohlin & M. Tonry (Eds.), *Family violence: Vol. 11. Crime and justice: A review of research* (pp. 481–546). Chicago: University of Chicago Press.

Saunders, D. G., & Browne, A. (1991). Domestic homicide. In R. T. Ammerman & M. Hersen (Eds.), *Case studies in family violence* (pp. 379–402). New York: Plenum.

Schafran, L. H. (1987). Documenting gender bias in the courts: The task force approach. *Judicature, 70,* 280.

Schmidt, J., & Steury, E. (1989). Prosecutorial discretion in filing charges in domestic violence cases. *Criminology, 27,* 587–210.

Shuman, D. W. (1994). The health effects of jury service. *Law and Psychology Review, 18,* 267.

Sherman, L. W. (1992). *Policing domestic violence: Experiments and directions*. New York: Free Press.

Sherman, L. W., & Berk, R. A. (1984). The specific deterrent effects of arrest for domestic assault. *American Sociological Review, 49,* 261–272.

Shields, N., McCall, G. J., & Hanneke, C. R. (1988). Patterns of family and non-family violence: Violent husbands and violent men. *Violence and Victims, 3,* 83–98.

Simon, L. (1994). The victim-offender relationship. In T. Hirschi & M. Gottfredson (Eds.), *The generality of deviance*. New Brunswick, NJ: Transaction Press.

Sonkin, D. J., Martin, D., & Walker, L. E. (1985). *The male batterer: A treatment approach*. New York: Springer.

Sonkin, D. J., & Murphy, M. (1985). *Learning to*

live without violence: A handbook for men. San Francisco: Volcano Press.

Spector, R. G. (1993). Marital tort cases concerning domestic violence. *Juvenile and Family Law Digest, 25,* 339.

Speiker, G. (1983). What is the linkage between alcohol abuse and violence? In E. Gottheil, K. A. Druley, T. E. Skoloda, and H. M. Waxman (Eds.), *Alcohol, drug abuse, and aggression* (pp. 125–137). Springfield, IL: Charles C Thomas.

Stanko, E. A. (1985). Would you believe this woman? In N. Rafter & E. A. Stanko (Eds.), *Judge, lawyer, victim, and thief.* Boston: Northeastern University Press.

Stosny, S. (1994). *Love without hurt: Ending attachment abuse.* Unpublished manuscript.

Straus, M. A. (1983). Ordinary violence, child abuse, and wife beating: What do they have in common and why? In D. Finkelhor, R. J. Gelles, G. T. Hotaling, & M. A. Straus (Eds.), *The dark side of families: Current family violence research.* Newbury Park, CA: Sage.

Straus, M. A., & Gelles, R. J. (1986). Societal changes in family violence from 1975 to 1985 as revealed by two national surveys. *Journal of Marriage and Family, 48,* 465–478.

Sykes, G. M. & Matza, D. (1957). Techniques of neutralization: A theory of delinquency. *American Sociological Review, 22,* 667–670.

Szinovacz, M. E. (1983). Using couple data as a methodological tool: The case of marital violence. *Journal of Marriage and the Family, 45,* 633–644.

Thurman v. City of Torrington, 595 F. Supp. 1521 (D. Conn. 1984).

Tiffany, L., Avichai, Y., & Peters, G. (1975). A statistical analysis of sentencing in federal courts: Defendants convicted after trial, 1967–1968. *Journal of Legal Studies, 4,* 369.

Tolman, R. M., & Bennett, L. W. (1990). A review of quantitative research on men who batter. *Journal of Interpersonal Violence, 5,* 87.

Topliffe, E. (1992). Why civil protection orders are effective remedies for domestic violence

but mutual protection orders are not. *Indiana Law Journal, 67,* 1039.

Town of Newton v. Rumery, 480 U.S. 386 (1987).

Truninger, E. (1971). Marital violence: The legal solutions. *Hastings Law Journal, 23,* 259.

Tyler, R. R. (1990). *Why people obey the law.* New Haven, CT: Yale University Press.

Uhlman, T., & Walker, N. (1980). He takes some of my time; I take some of his: An analysis of judicial sentencing patterns in jury cases. *Law and Society Review, 14,* 23.

United States v. Cox, 342 F.2d 167 (5th Cir. 1965).

United States v. Goodwin, 457 U.S. 368 (1982).

U.S. Commission on Civil Rights. (1982). *Under the rule of thumb: Battered women and the administration of justice.* A report of the U.S. Commission on Civil Rights. Washington, DC: Author.

U.S. Department of Justice (1984). *The prevalence of guilty pleas.* Washington, DC: National Institute of Justice.

Vera Institute of Justice. (1981). *Felony arrests: Their prosecution and disposition in New York City's Courts.* New York: Author.

Waits, K. (1985). The criminal justice system's response to battering: Understanding the problem, forging the solutions. *Washington Law Review, 60,* 267.

Walker, L. E. (1979). *The battered women.* New York: Harper & Row.

Walker, L. E. (1984). *The battered woman syndrome.* New York: Springer.

Wayte v. United States, 470 U.S. 598 (1985).

Wexler, D. B. (1990). *Therapeutic jurisprudence: The law as a therapeutic agent.* Durham, NC: Carolina Academic Press.

Wexler, D. B. (1991). Health care compliance principles and the insanity acquittee conditional release process. *Criminal Law Bulletin, 27,* 18–41.

Wexler, D. B. (1992). Putting mental health into mental health law: Therapeutic jurisprudence. *Law and Human Behavior, 16,* 27–38.

Wexler, D. B. (1993a). New directions in therapeutic jurisprudence: Breaking the bounds of conventional mental health law scholarship. *New York Law School Journal of Human Rights, 10,* 759–776.

Wexler, D. B. (1993b). Therapeutic jurisprudence and the criminal courts. *William and Mary Law Review, 35,* 279–299.

Wexler, D. B., & Winick, B. J. (1991a). *Essays in therapeutic jurisprudence.* Durham, NC: Carolina Academic Press.

Wexler, D. B., & Winick, B. J. (1991b). Therapeutic jurisprudence as a new approach to mental health law policy analysis and research. *University of Miami Law Review, 45,* 979–1004.

Wexler, D. B., & Winick, B. J. (1992). Therapeutic jurisprudence and criminal justice mental health issues. *Mental and Physical Disability Law Reporter, 16,* 225–231.

Wiersema, B., & Loftin, C. (1994). *Estimates of assault by intimates from the National Crime Victimization Survey, 1987.* College Park: University of Maryland, Institute of Justice and Criminology.

Williams, K. M. (1978). *The role of the victim in the prosecution of violent offenses* (Institute for Law and Social Research, Publication No. 12). Washington, DC: U.S. Government Printing Office.

Wilson, M. I., & Daly, M. (1992). Who kills whom in spouse killings? On the exceptional sex ratio of spousal homicides in the United States. *Criminology, 189,* 206–215.

Wilt, M., & Bannon, J. (1977). *Domestic violence and the police: Studies in Detroit and Kansas City.* Washington, DC: Police Foundation.

Winick, B. J. (1991). Harnessing the power of the bet: Wagering with the government as a mechanism for social and individual change. *University of Miami Law Review, 45,* 737–816.

Worden, R. E., & Politz, A. A. (1984). Police arrests in domestic disturbances: A further look. *Law and Society Review, 18,* 105.

Yllo, K. A. (1993). Through a feminist lens: Gender, power, and violence. In R. J. Gelles & D. R. Loseke (Eds.), *Current controversies on family violence* (pp. 47–66). Newbury Park, CA: Sage.

Zahn, M. A. (1989). Homicide in the twentieth century: Trends, types, and causes. In T. R. Gurr (Ed.), *Violence in America: Vol. 1. The history of violence.* Newbury Park, CA: Sage.

Zalman, M. (1992). The courts' responses to police intervention in domestic violence. In E. S. Buzawa & C. G. Buzawa (Eds.), *Domestic violence: The criminal justice response* (pp. 79–110). Westport, CT: Auburn House.

Zimring, F. E. (1989). Toward a jurisprudence of family violence. In L. Ohlin & M. Tonry (Eds.), *Family Violence: Vol. 11. Crime and justice: An annual review of the research.* Chicago: University of Chicago Press.

Zorza, J. (1993). Civil cases concerning domestic violence. *Juvenile and Family Law Digest, 25,* 375–398.

22 ■ The Law's Response to Child Abuse and Neglect

Catherine M. Brooks
Creighton University

The response of the legal profession and the court system to child abuse and neglect has taken several paths: criminal, civil, and family court or its equivalent (sometimes called orphans court, juvenile court, or dependency court). Criminal actions have the goal of punishing those who engage in child abuse or neglect by sentencing the offender to serve time in jail, pay a fine to the court, or both. Civil actions have the goals of compensating the victim of child abuse or neglect for his or her losses and deterring acts of abuse or neglect through civil sanctions. Family court actions have the goal of protecting the child through the family court's power to order the state social service agency to remove a child from his or her home, to intervene in a family's private affairs, and to sever the legal bonds of a parent-child relationship. A child abuse or neglect case may be heard in one or more of these legal tribunals. Each of these types of child abuse and neglect cases—criminal, civil, and family—involves medical and mental health professionals who attend to the needs of children and families.

This chapter will address that complex fabric of law, with the goals of removing the facade of mysteriousness from the legal process and providing a rationale for the processes used to adjudicate the guilt of the perpetrator, the compensation of the victim, and the protection of the

child. The objectives of this chapter are to examine law, evaluate its therapeutic and anti-therapeutic effects, and offer recommendations for changes in the law.

Child Abuse and Neglect Cases in Criminal Court

Invoking the Criminal Court System

All states require that persons (such as physicians, mental health professionals) who have reason to believe that a child has been or is being abused or neglected report that suspicion to the local state social service agency or law enforcement office. Mandatory reporting has been the particular responsibility of medical professionals. Reporting laws exist because of the work of physicians seeking government protection for their young patients who had suffered harm at the hands of their parents or some other person. In 1962, C. Henry Kempe published his findings about battered children in the *Journal of the American Medical Association*, describing a pattern of trauma symptoms in young children who had been abused. These findings triggered the professional and lay movement's lobbying for legislation requiring that physicians and others report such injuries to the state authorities.

Although reporting is mandatory, some practitioners may be tempted to try working with a young patient's parents to ease the child's situation instead of calling in a state social service

I am grateful to Nancy Walker Perry, Creighton University, and to Larry L. Teply, Creighton University School of Law, for their helpful comments.

worker or law enforcement officer (Kalichman, 1993; for an example, see Kalichman, 1993, or *People v. Cavaiani*, 1988). A practitioner in that situation may see the state's presence as exacerbating the family's problems and not meeting the child's needs for emotional and physical security. When the parents are openly hostile to or more subtly uncooperative with the practitioner's efforts, the practitioner may view state intervention as backup enforcement and then report the family for its ongoing problems (Kalichman, 1993). That practitioner faces two serious risks: criminal prosecution for the failure to make a timely report and, with increasing frequency, civil liability to the young patient for the harm, because the practitioner had a legal duty to prevent such harm by invoking state authority on the child's behalf.

Five states (Kentucky, Maine, Mississippi, North Carolina, and Wyoming) do not include a specific reference to criminal penalties for failure to report; 10 states (Arkansas, Connecticut, Delaware, Maine, Massachusetts, New Jersey, Oregon, Vermont, Washington, and Wisconsin) and the District of Columbia specify penalties without labeling the reporting law violation as either a misdemeanor or a felony; the rest of the states label the violation as a misdemeanor. Illinois requires that any physician who violates the reporting law be reported to the state's medical disciplinary board. Nine states (Arkansas, Colorado, Iowa, Massachusetts, Michigan, Minnesota, Montana, New York, and Rhode Island) provide for civil liability for all damages proximately related to the failure to report. Montana and Rhode Island also extend that liability to those who prevent others from reporting.

For the medical or mental health professional who reports child abuse or child neglect, familiarity with the state's court processes may be critical to making an effective report. The report may form the basis for the state's complaint on behalf of a child; it will form the basis for the state's investigation. Thus, the report should be as detailed and legible (if written) as possible, contain direct quotes when possible, include as many differential diagnoses as were examined

and discarded, and state the findings supporting the diagnosis or suspicion of child abuse or neglect.

For many professionals, the reporting process is filled with conflicting views of their role in helping professions (Kalichman, 1993). Several scholars have investigated the impact of the reporting laws on the therapeutic relationship between the mental health professional and the adult patient or client (Anderson et al., 1992; Levine, 1992). The hypothesis may be stated as follows:

When the professional gains information in a confidential communication with an adult patient/client, the therapeutic bond which is based on trust may be injured if the patient/client thinks or feels that the professional has betrayed that confidential alliance. (Brooks, Perry, Starr, & Teply, 1994, p. 56, footnotes omitted)

Research, though, has demonstrated that after an initial injury to the relationship, the reporting process actually can be used to strengthen the relationship over time (Anderson et al., 1992).

The Criminal Court Process

Criminal court actions begin with the law enforcement investigation of a complaint made against an alleged law violator. That complaint may come from a local state social service agency or from a hotline telephone service serving a statewide area. Criminal complaints also come directly from a person reporting to a local police department or office. This discussion will primarily be concerned with only those criminal cases involving defendants who are parents or other caregivers charged with abuse or neglect of a child-victim.

After a series of court appearances on the issue of probable cause to arrest or grand jury indictment, to ensure fairness to the defendant, the defendant may be held for trial on the charges made against him or her. The parties in criminal court trials of abuse and neglect are configured just as they are in any other criminal trial. The state has the role of criminal court prosecutor; the defendant is often the parent or other caregiver but may be any person alleged to have harmed the child-victim. In the latter case, a parent present in the home may also be charged with failing to protect his or her child if evidence exists that the parent allowed harm to befall the child or failed to seek medical or other attention for the child when it was needed. Such a charge is often called "endangerment of a child."

Interestingly, the child is not considered a party to the criminal court action; the child is deemed instead to be the state's complaining witness whose interests coincide with those of the state. Those interests, though, may diverge on many issues, such as whether to prosecute, whether the child should provide testimony, and what sentence should be sought if the defendant is found guilty. The criminal court's goals are the punishment of guilty defendants, the release of innocent defendants, and the vindication of the state's interests regarding the abuse and neglect of children. The child's goals may overlap the state's goals or may diverge from them.

For example, the child may wish nothing more than to have the abuse or neglect cease. In such cases, the child may be opposed to such intrusive steps as out-of-home placement for himself or herself; removal of the perpetrator from the home—for example, to jail, to a secure medical facility, or to another home; investigation of siblings' safety in the home; or mental health treatment for himself or herself, for the perpetrator, or for other family members. Alternatively, the child may seek far more than the state criminal justice system is competent to provide, such as treatment during incarceration for the perpetrator; treatment for the nonoffending parent (or parents), siblings, or both; and treatment for self. Although the prosecutor may address this interest in making arguments to the jury regarding the defendant's alleged guilt or the defendant's sentence, the child's protection is a secondary interest in the criminal court action.

If the child is harmed in the course of the prosecution—for example, on one hand, by being required to give testimony when not psychologi-

cally ready to do so; or, on the other hand, by being denied the opportunity to give that testimony—that harm may be considered by the adults involved in the prosecution as a cost of justice being done (Berliner & Barbieri, 1984; Bross, 1987; Perry & Wrightsman, 1991). A particularly problematic issue for the child-victim may be the prosecutorial discretion to proceed with a criminal court action. The prosecutor alone decides what cases are heard, which are plea-bargained, and which are not pursued. The child may not comprehend or concur with the prosecutor's decision to allow a defendant to plead guilty to a lesser charge or to not pursue a prosecution at all. Any compromise or capitulation by the prosecutor may appear to the child to validate the perpetrator's ability to continue harming children.

Research on this specific issue would be useful in understanding the degree to which children are affected by this part of the criminal court; groundwork for such research has been laid by a scholarly investigation of prosecutorial discretion (mac Murray, 1989). Also, the complexity of the constitutionally protected rights of the criminal defendant and the absence of constitutional protection for a victim's rights may be beyond the child's ability or willingness to comprehend. Helping the child make sense of the criminal court proceeding may be an important part of the child's mental health treatment (see Schetky & Benedek, 1989). Rarely does the prosecutor or prosecution team have the time and training to make the criminal court system comprehensible to the traumatized child.

The Parties and Their Lawyers

In criminal court, the state is represented by the county or the district attorney. In some states, the prosecutor is also responsible for presenting the state's case in family court. In other states, different people are responsible for the family court role. For example, in New Jersey, state deputy attorneys general are charged with bringing court actions against those parents or guard-

ians charged with abuse or neglect of a child. The New Jersey deputy attorney general is also responsible for advocating in court for the state's interest in its social service plan for defendant parents or guardians or for proving the state's case against the parent in family court.

All prosecutors, in both criminal and family courts, are supported by law enforcement officers who have responsibility for the investigation of the charges to be brought against the defendant; the prosecutor may also have associates, law clerks, or interns who assist in the preparation of the case. The prosecutor is responsible for presenting the evidence to secure an indictment (that is, a statement of charges) against the defendant. The standard for issuing an indictment requires probable cause to believe that the defendant is the person who did the wrongs with which he or she is charged. Probable cause is the lowest possible standard against which evidence is measured. It is even lower than the civil court standard of proof by a preponderance of the evidence, which asks if something is proved to be more likely true than not true. Probable cause asks only if there is sufficient reason in fact and in law to charge the defendant with a specific law violation.

Defendants in criminal court are provided lawyers without cost if they are unable to afford to hire their own. Under the U.S. Supreme Court ruling in *Gideon v. Wainwright* (1963), all persons charged with crimes for which they may suffer loss of liberty or substantial property if they are found guilty are entitled to representation by legal counsel to be provided by the state if they are too poor to hire their own counsel. Because the various states' criminal codes provide significant punishment for the crime of child abuse or neglect, legal counsel must be provided to all indigent defendants so charged who request that assistance.

In contrast, the child-victim is not entitled to legal representation in criminal prosecutions under most state statutes, except in very limited circumstances. A child who is the subject of a child abuse or neglect legal prosecution has no right granted by the Constitution to be heard in court. It is understood in criminal jurisprudence that a victim's interests are subsumed into the interest of the public, which is represented by the prosecutor. In some instances, though, the lawyer appointed to represent the child in a concurrent civil or family court action may seek to intervene in the criminal court action to protect an interest of the child—for example, giving testimony in a protected manner—but such an intervention is not usual.

Evidentiary Issues

The Child-Victim's Testimony

In the criminal court setting, the child's testimony is crucial because the defendant has the constitutional right to be confronted by his or her accuser. Often, the child is the source of the accusation, and his or her testimony will be necessary to prove the act charged, especially in child sexual abuse cases where the central issue is the identity of the perpetrator. Of concern to all parties is the fact that the availability and clarity of the child's testimony is dependent on the child's stage of development and the level of trauma he or she has experienced. Research regarding children's testimony abounds: Loftus has examined multiple issues of memory—for example, eyewitness memory and testimony (Loftus, 1979); language and memory (Loftus, 1979); leading questions and suggestibility (Loftus & Davies, 1984). Others also have examined the issues presented by children as witnesses, both in forensic interviews and in court (Ceci & Bruck, 1993; Doris, 1991; Goodman & Bottoms, 1993; Melton, 1984; Perry & Teply, 1984–1985; Perry & Wrightsman, 1991; Walker, 1994).

Given the difficulty often faced by children offering evidence against the person accused of perpetrating wrongs against them (Claman, Harris, Bernstein, & Lovitt, 1986; Goodman & Bottoms, 1993; Schetky & Benedek, 1989; Tedesco & Schnell, 1987), special accommodations have

been provided to child witnesses in most courts (Perry, 1992). Those accommodations include testimony out of the presence of the defendant (Higgins, 1988); use of closed-circuit television (*Maryland v. Craig,* 1990); closing of the courtroom during a child-victim's testimony (*Globe Newspaper v. Superior Court,* 1982); videotaped depositions entered as evidence when the child is emotionally unavailable for testimony (for example, *Jolly v. Texas,* 1984; see also Bernstein & Claman, 1986; Colby & Colby, 1987; Gothard, 1987); and testimony of others, provided the standard exceptions to the rules against admitting hearsay into evidence are met or special exceptions to the hearsay rule are provided by statute or case law (*White v. Illinois,* 1992).

The issue of a child's emotional unavailability has been scrutinized at length by the courts. Decisions about such unavailability are made on a case-by-case, child-centered basis and on evidence that the trauma to the child in testifying justifies a release of the child from the requirement to give evidence in open court (*Coy v. Iowa,* 1988, in which such testimony was lacking; *Maryland v. Craig* 990, in which such testimony was provide

On the other hand, however, it is possible that the process of testifying can be positive and beneficial to the child. It may provide a catharsis and sense of empowerment by self-protection, provided the child is willing and able to give the needed testimony. The child may suffer significant emotional difficulty but may believe that the results of telling his or her story are well worth the emotional difficulty. Determining whether this might be the case for a particular child witness is an important issue to be addressed by the examining mental health professional (Perry & Wrightsman, 1991, citing Pynoos & Eth, 1984).

Another issue presented by the child witness' testimony is that of memory. Recalled memory, discovered memory, and other labels attached to the uncovering or discovering of information that may have been unconsciously held in the child's mind has been debated at length. This issue will be addressed later in this chapter, in the section on personal injury actions in civil court.

Testimonial Privileges

The rules of evidence, which govern the presentation of information to the court, have been fashioned to exclude unreliable data. Sometimes, though, very reliable data are excluded because of overriding social concerns about the impact of disclosing that information. For example, an overriding social concern may be the community's desire to protect the confidential nature of information communicated within certain relationships. State law recognizes privileged communications in relationships between husbands and wives, lawyers and their clients, and clergy and "penitents." Testimonial privileges between physicians and their patients are also well established in state law. More recently, state law has recognized privileged communications between mental health professionals and their patients.

The privilege that the law attaches to these communications is very specific: to invoke the privilege, the declarant must show that the communications he or she shared with the witness are protected by law because of the nature of the relationship between them, that the information communicated was given in the expectation of privacy, and that the circumstances of the communication were consistent with ensuring the confidentiality expected by the declarant. The evidentiary privilege protects information communicated confidentially in such a relationship from being repeated in court. The law thus prevents a mental health professional from testifying about the contents of a communication he or she received within the context of a protected relationship.

If the only source of the information on which to prosecute an alleged offender is the person to whom the offender entrusted the information in confidence and within the protected relationship, then the law sacrifices obtaining that information.

This sacrifice is made to satisfy society's strong interest in supporting the confidentiality of that relationship. If the court can obtain the same information from a nonprivileged source, then no real loss is experienced in the fact-finding process. It is when the court has no other source from which to obtain the information that a balance is struck in favor of the protected relationship and at the expense of the court's search for the truth. Some social concerns, however, weigh against protecting the otherwise privileged communication.

Child abuse and neglect are good examples of social concerns that outweigh an otherwise protected relationship. Since the middle of this century, the states have decided that addressing the abuse and neglect of children is more valuable than ensuring privacy in the ordinarily protected relationship between a perpetrator and his or her therapist. Thus, the states have set aside the privileges accorded professional and husband-wife relationships when children are at risk of serious harm. This decision is reflected in the reporting laws, which nullify most testimonial privileges in the face of child abuse and neglect allegations. This discussion will focus on the abrogation of the testimonial privileges attached to communications between the patient and his or her treating physician, evaluating physician, treating mental health professional, and evaluating mental health professional.

Such professionals, in relationships of normally privileged communications, who are compelled by law to report and then to give testimony about child abuse and neglect, may find themselves in particularly difficult situations. Medical or mental health evaluations undertaken for the purpose of providing evidence at court or during sentencing are easily understood by the adult subject to be part of an adversarial process. Such an arm's-length arrangement is very different from the one experienced by the patient in ongoing therapy or medical care. In the ongoing relationship, the assurance of confidentiality is the basis for the disclosures that the patient may make against his or her own legal interest. When subpoenaed for testimony, the medical or mental health professional is then caught on the horns of a dilemma: the professional must either disrupt a trusting relationship or risk being cited for contempt of court for refusing to give testimony.

Case Dispositions

There are three possible dispositions of a criminal case that reaches trial: the jury may find the defendant guilty on at least one of the counts contained in the indictment, the jury may find the defendant not guilty on all counts of the indictment, or the jury may make no determination because it lacks a sufficient number of votes for either outcome. In the latter instance, the prosecutor may decide within a specified time whether to bring the case against the defendant with a new jury.

An interesting development in the sentencing of convicted defendants is the practice of tying the duration of imprisonment to events in the victim-child's life. For example, some prosecutors have successfully argued for sentences of jail time that last until the child-victim reaches the age of majority (18 or 21). The theory underlying this practice may be that, once no longer a child, the victim may be better able to protect himself or herself from the offender. Research does not reveal published appellate opinions scrutinizing this practice; one hypothesis for this absence of appeals may be the offender's satisfaction with the jail term arrived at through the plea-bargaining process. Mental health professionals may not agree that achievement of adulthood is sufficient to accomplish all that underlies the prosecutorial expectation. The victim as a young adult may continue to be vulnerable to renewed abuses by the offender, or the child-victim may perceive that his or her own protection is the cause for jailing the offender and may mistake the true basis of the incarceration, namely punishment.

Child Abuse and Neglect Cases in Civil Court

Invoking the Civil Court System

All persons, including children, who have suffered injury because of another's intentional aggression or unreasonable carelessness have recourse to seek compensation for their losses in civil court. Although legal scholars refer to such lawsuits as tort actions, others recognize them as personal injury cases. Plaintiffs bring personal injury cases to civil court by filing a complaint alleging facts indicating the defendant's wrongdoing that has resulted in harm to the plaintiff's person or property.

Civil Court Process

Personal injury cases fall into two general categories: intentionally inflicted harms and negligently (or carelessly) inflicted harms. Intentional torts include intentionally and unlawfully touching another person without consent, which results in injury or offense (battery); creating another's perception of an imminent, intentional, unlawful touching (assault); confining another intentionally against his or her will (false imprisonment); intentionally inflicting emotional distress by an abuse of power or authority—often by language—in a way that is outrageous to the ordinary person (intentional infliction of emotional distress); and intentionally disseminating untrue information with the effect of impugning another's reputation (defamation).

Negligence cases, unlike those of intentional wrongdoing, are based on carelessness. Liability for negligence exists when a defendant causes harm to the plaintiff through conduct that is not as safe as society is entitled to expect under the circumstances. Causation is measured by its directness (from act to resulting harm) and by its nearness in space and time to the initiating event. (Lawyers ask whether the plaintiff and the kind of harm suffered were foreseeable to the careless defendant.) The basis for compensation lies in the determination that the defendant could have (and should have) foreseen the harm to the plaintiff that resulted from the defendant's act and then acted in such a way as to prevent that harm.

Compensation in both intentional and negligence suits may include an award of damages for the plaintiff's medical and other expenses, lost wages, lost earning potential, and pain and suffering. Exemplar damages, often referred to as punitive damages, may also be awarded for malicious conduct. Exemplar damages may be exacted to deter the defendant, and others similarly situated, from engaging in similar behavior in the future or to punish the defendant for the particular behavior that led to the plaintiff's injury.

A serious consideration in any case is the amount of resources the defendant has available to pay a judgment in the plaintiff's favor. Unless the defendant has the assets or insurance to satisfy a judgment, it is unlikely that a tort action will be commenced. Depending on the wrong alleged, an important source of money to satisfy the judgment is the defendant's homeowner's or professional liability insurance policy. Because most policies exclude the defendant's *intentional* wrongdoing, it is often important to prove that the child abuse was a negligent act.

Striking a child and causing serious injury appears to be an intentional tort, however, because it involves a deliberate touching to which the victim-child cannot legally consent, and it is intended to create pain or offense, resulting in injury. Additionally, it is outlawed by state statutes. Nonreflexive hitting that causes injury or outrageous demeaning epithets shouted at a child are purposeful and so qualify as intentional acts, not careless ones. Similarly, sexual abuse of a child is a nonreflexive unlawful touching that harms the child's emotional and psychological well-being, if not physical well-being as well.

Although these acts may constitute a battery, proof of battery may preclude payment by the defendant's insurer. The obstacle to recovering damages for the child-victim's intentionally inflicted harms is a significant one, and plaintiffs' lawyers have met it in a couple of ways. One route has been to argue that the child abuser is not acting deliberately, that the physical or psychological battering is an unintended consequence of the defendant's own psychological flaws, and that the sexual abuse of a child is, in fact, a response of the sexually disturbed defendant who is incapable of forming an intent or purpose. This theory is countered by the well-accepted common law premise that the rationality of one's motive in injuring another is irrelevant; intent is narrowly limited to the desire to create the contact (battery).

Another route that proved successful in one jurisdiction was to construct an argument from the language of the insurance policy to demonstrate the insurer's intent to cover more than negligently inflicted harms. For example, because a residential center had insured itself specifically against its staff's inflicting corporal punishment, it was successfully argued that the insurer had agreed to insure the residential center against intentionally wrongful acts of the staff (*Atlantic Employers Ins. Co. v. Lynch*, 1995). Hence, the insurer was required to pay for the intentionally wrongful acts of one staff member who had been found guilty of sexually abusing children at the center.

Although this approach provides funds to compensate the child, it raises serious concerns for the legal process. Specifically, by using insurance dollars to compensate any intentional wrong, the offending residential center worker and the corporate residential center entity spread the loss of those damages across the large population of premium payers. Although those premium payers may have agreed to pool resources for liabilities due to failures in risk management, they may be entirely unwilling to provide funds for those liabilities that arise from willful wrongful acts.

Damages certainly may be collected from the defendant's personal assets other than his or her insurance policies. However, by the time the civil court process is completed, such assets may be depleted by medical and mental health professionals' evaluations, expert witnesses' fees,

lawyers' fees, court costs of appealing unfavorable verdicts, and loss of employment or income due to imprisonment.

The Parties and Their Lawyers

The plaintiff in these lawsuits is the child-victim. Children, because of their minor status, are legally incapable of making certain decisions and must therefore be assisted in this process by an adult who may be called a "next friend" or "next of kin," usually the child's current caregiver. That adult person acts on the child's behalf in hiring legal counsel, filing the complaint, and—if the lawsuit is successful—safeguarding the proceeds of the damages award for the child's benefit.

A rule that establishes the last date on which a plaintiff may file a complaint in order to protect a defendant against stale claims is known as a *statute of limitations*. Usually, statutes of limitations require that lawsuits be commenced within one to three years of the event that precipitated the harm to the plaintiff. A child, however, usually has the right to bring a legal action to compensate an injury sustained during his or her childhood until the close of the statutory period of limitations after he or she has reached the age of majority.

Another modification of the statute of limitations made on behalf of children's interests allows the adult survivor of child sexual abuse to bring an action against the perpetrator once he or she "discovers" the abuse. Beginning the statute of limitations period on "discovery of the harm" is a device already available to personal injury victims. A simple example illustrates the so-called delayed discovery rule: a patient discovers a foreign substance left in his or her body during surgery, but the discovery is made too late to bring a lawsuit within the regular statutory period. An exception is allowed, but the patient-victim must bring the action within a specified time.

The problems posed by application of the discovery rule to child sexual abuse victims are varied: victims may repress the memory of all traumatic events of their childhood; they may suppress the memory of the recent abuse; their injuries may not be obvious to them; they may not recognize the causal connection between their symptomology and the originating events; or they may feel so stigmatized by the abuse that they cannot bear to bring the action until they find the personal support necessary to risk publicizing their early injuries. Suppression is understood as the "conscious intentional exclusion from consciousness of a thought or feeling" (*Merriam-Webster's Collegiate Dictionary,* 1993, p. 1185). Repression, on the other hand, is understood as "a process or mechanism of ego defense whereby wishes or impulses that are incapable of fulfillment are kept from or made inaccessible to consciousness except in disguised form [for example, a neurosis]" (*Merriam-Webster's Collegiate Dictionary,* 1993, p. 993).

Resolving the question of when the local statute of limitations terminates a plaintiff's right to bring an action for compensation is not simple in delayed discovery of child abuse. For example, in *O'Neal v. Division of Family Services* (1991), the Utah Supreme Court found that a plaintiff could not take advantage of the delayed discovery rule because the plaintiff victim had not repressed the memory of alleged childhood sexual abuse by a foster parent years earlier. Instead, the plaintiff acknowledged that he had always been conscious of the abusive behavior but psychologically unable to disclose it. In a split decision on another case, the Oklahoma Supreme Court found that the delayed discovery rule did not apply to a case in which a woman sought compensation for sexual abuse by her pastoral counselor. In that case, the plaintiff suffered from multiple personality disorder and discovered the sexual abuse from one of her personalities, a discovery that surfaced after the plaintiff learned of other offenses committed by the defendant. The Oklahoma Court held that the plaintiff was not entitled to bring her action within the statutory period of time (*Lovelace v. Keohane,* 1992).

Personal injury liability is not limited to those persons who directly inflict the harm the child-victim suffers. Professionals who fail to report child abuse and neglect despite a legislative requirement may also be liable in damages. These professionals increasingly have been named in tort actions brought by injured children. The arguments offered on behalf of the young plaintiffs highlight the duty imposed on certain professionals by most state reporting laws to notify the state social service agency or local law enforcement office when there is reason to believe that a child has suffered or is at risk of suffering abuse or neglect. Those defendants are not only responsible to the state for the failure to report (often a misdemeanor with fines up to $1000, jail time, or both), they are also liable to the child-victim for injuries that could have been prevented had the professional followed the state mandate and made the necessary report.

Another group of defendants in personal injury lawsuits are mental health professionals who evaluate alleged victims of child abuse and neglect. In a case decided in 1994, a therapist was found negligent for resolving a child abuse question without sufficient inquiry, which resulted in harm to the child-patient and to her family. The jury in that case assessed the damages in the amount of $272,231 against the mental health professional and in favor of the patient and her family (*Omaha World Herald,* 1994).

Another significant group of defendants have been the state social service agencies that are mandated to provide services to children in need of the state's protection. In one important case, *DeShaney v. Winnebago County Department of Social Services* (1989), the U.S. Supreme Court found that the Winnebago County Department of Social Services, which failed to meet young Joshua DeShaney's need for protection, was not liable to him for his harms. In *DeShaney,* all the elements of a particular kind of personal injury lawsuit were met; this federal legal action was founded on a violation of the federal code provision of 42 U.S.C.A. 1983, which governs the tortious conduct of state employees and is known colloquially as a "Section 1983 action." In

DeShaney, the Court decided that violence between two private citizens—here, Joshua's father battering him to a point of inflicting severe brain injury—could not support a federal action against a state worker who fails to act to protect the victim.

The *DeShaney* Court noted that Joshua was not in the custody of the state at the time he suffered his injuries. Had he been a state ward in foster care, he would have been due the state's protection. Several features distinguish this case: it was brought under federal law; it involved a plaintiff who was not in the custody of the state at the time the injuries were inflicted; and finally, the question of whether the child was due protection as a benefit conferred by the reporting law statute was not raised. This final point is highlighted in a footnote to the Court's opinion; why the child's lawyers failed to raise the argument of reporting law conferring a benefit upon the DeShaney child is not explained (*DeShaney v. Winnebago County Department of Social Services*, 1989, p. 194 n. 2).

Two years later, the Court considered *LaShawn et al. v. Dixon* (1991), a successful class action lawsuit brought under Section 1983 on behalf of the children who were in foster care or about to come into foster care under the supervision of the District of Columbia Department of Human Services. Other cases have been successful on behalf of individual children who were injured, abused, or neglected in their public and private foster care settings (for example, *Doe and Doe v. New York Department of Social Services* et al., 1983).

Case Dispositions

Ultimately, to prevail at trial, the plaintiff must prove by a preponderance of the evidence (that the allegation is more likely true than not true) the facts supporting the plaintiff's case.

The outcomes of a civil case for compensation include a jury or judge award that compensates the plaintiff for all actual losses including pain and suffering, for a part of those losses, or for none of them. An award may also include exemplar (or punitive) damages if the court deems such damages warranted by the facts of the plaintiff's case.

Child Abuse and Neglect Cases in Family Court

Invoking the Family Court System

The family court or its equivalent, juvenile or dependency court, is a creation of the 20th century. The family court's concern with the protection of children, however, has considerably older legal roots. This concern was inherited from England's courts of equity, which were imported into American jurisprudence during the colonial era. The English equity courts were designed to remedy instances of injustice that the law courts could not deal with effectively. Child protection was addressed by an equity court as early as the 17th century in England (Clark, 1987). Courts of equity, which are charged with ensuring fairness, are uniquely suited to issues of children's welfare. The family courts often continue to have relaxed rules of evidence and eased restrictions on procedure; increasingly, though, these courts have come under close scrutiny.

The dangers inherent in the family court's less formal decision making are serious, particularly when a parent-child relationship is being altered. For example, the search for an outcome for a particular child before the court may drive the fact-finding process to legally insupportable conclusions. For example, in *In re Interest of D.M.B.* (1992), a juvenile court made findings of fact for which the state had made no initial pleadings or amended pleadings. The defendant parent was never formally charged with the particular allegations that would have given notice of the prosecution's theory of the case and that ultimately dictated the court's findings of fact. Because of the error in the pleadings, the trial court was chastised by the state supreme court hearing the appeal. Appellate courts, confronted by case decisions not supported by the evidence adduced at trial below, have also shown more interest in imposing the constraints of the law courts on family courts.

The Parties and Their Lawyers

The local, county, or state government attorney is responsible for instituting proceedings in family court, typically with a complaint against the alleged abusing or neglectful adult family member on the child's behalf. The child is considered a party to the action under many states' statutes. The purpose of the action is to determine whether the child has been abused or neglected and is in need of protection from the risk of future harm by the alleged perpetrator. The goal of the legal action in the family court is not the punishment of the parent but rather the protection of the child.

The parent, however, may regard the action taken as punitive. Where the claim is based on an act or acts of abuse, the parent frequently makes the identity of the offender the central issue, claiming that the acts alleged in the complaint were not done by him or her. Because the question before the court is whether the evidence presented by the state is sufficient to show that the child is in need of protection, however, the inability to identify the perpetrator is not fatal for an action in family court. Instead, the parent may be charged with a failure to protect the child from the harm suffered, thus establishing the child's need for protection from further neglect. Often the second issue to be addressed in each case becomes whether the parent can provide the child with the protection needed to prevent further injury or neglect, without governmental intrusion into the family's life. The disposition that follows that finding will concern the placement of the child and services for the child and his or her family.

Some texts and legal professionals speak of prosecuting a case or parent-defendant in family court; however, *prosecution* is meant in a general

sense, not to denote a criminal court process. Indeed, no criminal finding of guilt will be made and no sentence will be imposed on the defendant, even if that defendant is found to have committed the abuse or the neglect in question, for that is not the goal of these proceedings. This difference in goals is also manifested by the difference in the standards of proof. Criminal guilt is judged on proof beyond a reasonable doubt; civil findings, such as the child's need for protection, are judged on the less stringent standard of proof by a preponderance of the evidence in some states, and on clear and convincing evidence in others. The margin between the two is wide, as the criminal proof standard is as near to certainty as the legal system comes.

When the child has been injured in the family home, the defendants are likely to be the child's parents or legal guardians. Because family court actions will not result in a finding of criminal guilt, with its attendant risk of loss of liberty or substantial property, a parent is not guaranteed representation by legal counsel. Parents may be represented if they can afford to retain a lawyer and choose to do so. However, legal counsel may not be provided to indigent parents or persons acting as parents unless state statutes provide for that representation. Most jurisdictions provide for the appointment of legal counsel at the court's discretion—when the judge believes that such appointment is necessary for fairness in the proceeding. The U.S. Supreme Court has held that legal counsel is not a constitutionally protected right in these family court actions and that judicial discretion in deciding the issue of appointment of counsel is sufficient for fairness (*Lassiter v. Durham County Department of Social Services*, 1981).

In jurisdictions where a child who is the subject of a child abuse or neglect legal action also has standing in the action, that child probably will be represented by an attorney appointed by the court. *Standing* is the right to be heard in court and is usually accorded only to the plaintiffs and the defendant in an action. The child's right of standing comes to him or her through state statutes. Because children are minors and only third-party beneficiaries of the action, they probably have no constitutionally protected right to be heard in the absence of a statutory provision.

The child's representation in these family court cases also depends on state statutes. The appointment of counsel is either discretionary (up to the family court judge) or mandatory (more likely where there is standing by statute). The appointment of counsel, though, will not depend on whether the child can afford counsel; the issue of indigence should not arise in appointing counsel to children in these protection cases. Furthermore, the court should not look to the parents or guardian to provide paid legal counsel for the child, because a conflict of interest should be presumed between the child and his or her parent or guardian once the child abuse or neglect action has been filed. Nor should counsel be paid by the parents. As the employers of legal counsel, parents may seek to direct the counsel's actions, and such a lawyer or *guardian ad litem* would be unable to zealously represent the client, the child. The lawyer would be in the untenable position of working for the parent while speaking for the child, at times advocating against the parent's interest in retaining a relationship with the child.

Many states require by statute that a defendant parent pay for the child's attorney, *guardian ad litem,* or both despite this conflict of interest. This requirement reflects the practice in divorce custody contests; opposing parents in such a contest often pay a share of their child's legal fees or costs of psychological evaluation and counseling. In child abuse or neglect cases, however, the parents are not opposed to one another but rather are opposed by the state; thus, the custody contest model underpinning the payment requirement is inapplicable. Perhaps a better practice would be to have the parents pay into a pool of funds from which all children's attorneys and *guardians ad litem* are paid and reimbursed for expenses. This pool would dilute the effect of a parent paying for a particular child's legal services.

Family court cases are often initiated by the government after negotiation with the parents has failed. The negotiation process, usually heavily weighted to the government's side, occurs between the parent or guardian and the government's social service agency. The object of the negotiation is to convince the defendant parent or guardian to accept the agency's plan. If the parent accepts the casework plan, the case will proceed on a voluntary basis without recourse to the court. The social service case plan may have many different features: the social work agency, with the parent's consent, may place the child in protective foster care and require that the parent undergo certain services. Alternatively, the agency may leave the child in the family home but supervise the family's interactions and require that the parent both receive services and provide services to the child.

The potential sanction the social service agency possesses in this negotiation is the right to remove the child under "emergency circumstances" if the parents reject a voluntary relationship with the agency. Usually within three days after such a removal, the agency will have to justify that removal to a family court judge. Justification lies in showing that there was and is probable cause to believe that an emergency did exist and continues to exist for the child in the family home. The agency must further show that if first expended reasonable efforts to prevent the child's removal to an out-of-home placement but that those efforts failed.

The agency may have no grounds or may choose not to exercise its emergency removal power. Should emergency removal be sought and the parent object to the social service agency's intervention in the family in any form, the case will proceed to court. The government's goal then becomes to prove the actual harm or risk of harm to the child in the family home, with or without an emergency removal. After such findings are made by the court, the government often requests that the court impose the social service agency's casework plan on the family and the defendant parent.

In some jurisdictions, a casework plan may or may not have an advocate in the ensuing court action once the parent rejects it. In Nebraska, for example, the local county attorney is charged with representing the interest of the people of the county, who may or may not find that interest articulated in the agency's case plan for the subject child or children. Thus, the social service agency must provide its own counsel to represent the merits of the case plan.

Although a state or county social work agency may have legal advisors and legal counsel to represent it in court actions, those legal representatives may not be present at child abuse and neglect trials in family court. The agency instead may rely on the government's attorney to present and argue for the casework plan, as he or she advocates for the underlying premise that the child is in need of governmental protection. The government's lawyer may choose to disagree with the casework plan and may propose his or her own resolution of the case to the court. He or she may also adopt the proposals of another party to the action, either from the defense or from the child's lawyer.

As with all lawsuits, child abuse and neglect actions frequently are settled before trial, and these settlements are then reduced to a "consent order." To consent, each party, through legal counsel, should understand the full implications of compliance and noncompliance with the terms of the agreement.

In the matter of consent orders and in all facets of representation, each party's lawyer should have a sound foundation of information before offering advice to the client. That foundation should include information about the extent, gravity, and duration of harm the child suffered. It should also include accurate information about the parent's capacity and willingness to change the home environment and his or her behavior to make the child safe. There is no point to agreeing to conform to the requirements of the consent order if the parent is not interested in doing so. Because noncompliance will only make the state's case for abandonment, supporting an action to sever the parent-child relationship, the noncomplying parent would be better advised to

go to trial on the merits of the charges. Impressing the parent with the gravity of the state's interest may convince the parent to comply with the dispositional orders of the court. Failing that, the court may get a clearer picture of the problems of the parent-child relationship and allow it to be severed all the earlier. Of course, of great concern in this situation are the needs of the child, and some children may not be able to tolerate such a severance.

Evidentiary Issues

"Best Interests" Issues

The usual task of the child's attorney is to present and advocate the child's expressed wishes to the court. When the attorney is concerned that those expressed wishes do not reflect the child's so-called best interests, or when the child is unable to express his or her wishes, a *guardian ad litem* may be provided to the child. The child's *guardian ad litem* is charged with presenting the child's "best interests" to the court.

The issue of best interests has been the subject of scrutiny by the courts and by legal professionals during the last several years. The "best interests of the child" is regularly touted as at least an element in all legal decisions regarding a child, including those concerning out-of-home placements, state-ordered services, alteration of relationships with parents and siblings, removal from the family's life completely, termination of parents' rights and those of all other family members, and subsequent adoptions. But judges and lawyers are hard-pressed to describe or define such best interests with any specificity. *Best* here arguably could denote the optimal outcome for the child, which could require a prohibitively great expenditure of state and family resources. Clearly, *interest* coupled with *best* has not denoted the dictionary's suggested meaning of "right, title, or legal share." No one has argued successfully that the child before the family court is entitled to the resources necessary to create an optimal outcome for him or her.

As legal professionals struggle with this difficult concept, some valuable ideas have emerged. Mnookin's (1985) work suggests that the modifier *best* be dropped and that the law focus on the child's self-interest as it does on that of the other parties. Coyne (1992) takes a different approach, one more familiar to the medical profession. In assessing the work of those charged with decision making for the child, she urges that the goal be the "least worst outcome" for the child. This viewpoint, of course, echoes the writing of Goldstein, Freud, and Solnit, who advised that legal professionals (and medical and mental health professionals) seek the least detrimental alternative for a child in any given set of circumstances. This admonition appears in their various volumes in the so-called best-interest series: *Beyond the Best Interests of the Child* (1973), *Before the Best Interests of the Child* (1979), and *In the Best Interests of the Child* (1986). Coyne's approach has significant value for two reasons: (1) it provides a real-world measure against which to develop responses to a child's needs, and (2) it can persistently remind professionals who are working with children that, although there are no "best" answers for the child-patient/client, some responses may be more satisfactory—in that they are less harmful—than others.

Federal Law Requirements on State Proceedings

Federal law requires, as a condition of federal funding, that before removing or holding a child in an out-of-home placement, the state social service agency must present evidence about its efforts to keep the family together and to prevent the child's removal. The court must decide whether the government's efforts to keep the family together were reasonable. These are known as the "reasonable efforts" findings required by the Federal Adoption Assistance and Child Welfare Act (1983), which provides for federal reimbursement of state expenses incurred in dispensing adoption and foster care services. Once a court determines that a child subject to its jurisdiction is placed or must remain outside of the home, reasonable efforts findings must be made by the court at every dispositional hearing following the adjudication of the child abuse or neglect action.

Such findings of fact prove difficult for some family courts because of basic misunderstandings regarding the federal law's reasonable efforts requirements. In fact, it is the circumstances of the child against which the issue of reasonableness must be judged. For example, certain situations are so dangerous that no efforts can create safety for a child. In such instances, a finding of no efforts serves as a finding of reasonable efforts and not as a finding of "no reasonable efforts." However, reasonable efforts for another child may involve resource expenditures that the agency may be reluctant to make, such as labor-intensive monitoring of the family at home or expensive therapeutic intervention. In the latter case, reasonable efforts may not have been expended before the child was removed or retained in an out-of-home placement, and a judge should properly find that reasonable efforts have not been made.

If the court finds that reasonable efforts were not made on a child's behalf, the judge should require that the agency make such efforts and return the child to his or her home. If a child has been removed from the home and the judge finds that reasonable efforts were made, that child may remain in an out-of-home placement pending the development of circumstances whereby a return home becomes safe—or impossible, thus freeing the child for a permanent home elsewhere.

Removal to an out-of-home placement may involve placing the child in a licensed state foster care setting, in an extended family member's home, in a residential placement such as a group home or more institutional setting, or in a psychiatric or other hospital. Federal law also requires that any placement be the least restrictive placement possible for the child, given the child's needs. The limiting factor is not the social service provider's resources but rather the child's own needs. Thus, this mandate that states spend their resources to provide for children's placement options is a strong point for argument for the child advocate.

Case Dispositions

Should the court find that the child is in need of state protection of any sort because the alleged abuse or neglect has been proved, the court may then make a dispositional order for the child's benefit. Dispositional orders frequently require mental health evaluations and the implementation of treatment recommendations derived from the assessments. These evaluations are designed to elicit the mental state of the parent perpetrator and the mental state of the child-victim. Usually the child already has been evaluated during the course of trial preparation or in the early investigation of the social service case. Such earlier evaluation may have been to assess the child's basic truthfulness, to confirm the consistency of the child's statements with known information about certain forms of abuse, and to recommend treatment. In disposing of a case, a judge may order evaluations to assess the child's family relationships, usually for the purpose of making treatment recommendations. These additional evaluations, however, may uncover other abuse or neglect allegations, beginning the process over again for another family member.

Dispositional orders require that any person identified by a preponderance of the evidence as a perpetrator of the abuse must comply with treatment recommendations such as counseling, education in parenting skills, or drug or alcohol treatment. There may well be other requirements incorporated in the dispositional order specifically designed to reunite the family, perhaps by removing stressful problems within the family. An example of such a provision may be a request to the social service agency to identify and pay for day care for youngsters in the family.

The family court's goal is to protect the child from the same perpetrator who has caused the injury that brought the child to the court's attention. This goal may require not that the child be removed from the family home and placed else-

where but that the perpetrator be removed. That removal may be accomplished in a number of ways: setting bail conditions on a corresponding criminal action to require separation between the alleged defendant and the victim-child, or issuing protection orders requiring that the alleged offender remain separate from the child.

The court must make continuing findings about the reasonable efforts expended toward family reunification. As discussed above, reasonableness is dependent on the variables presented by the family. Thus, it is sometimes inappropriate to plan to reunite a family, and reasonableness may require the termination of parental rights. This finding is particularly true when the abuse inflicted on the child has been profoundly violent, deadly, or has left the child unable or unwilling to cooperate in the reunification process. It is also true when the parent has emotionally or physically abandoned the child and has expressed over a period of time his or her desire to be free of the relationship.

Following the dispositional order, periodic court reviews of the defendant's compliance and the progress of the family toward reunification are necessary. The review process is designed to prevent the child and the family from getting "lost in the system"; adherence to the review schedule is the guarantee that this goal will be met. Court review hearings should focus on the parent's compliance with the terms of the dispositional order. The reviews also should provide the court with an opportunity to inquire into whether caseworkers have provided support for such compliance and how well the parent has understood the terms of the court order. Lack of caseworker support and genuine misunderstanding on the part of the parent may constitute valid excuses for noncompliance and should be addressed as quickly as possible.

Timely court review hearings to check compliance with the dispositional order and to identify any legitimate obstacles to that compliance are important both to the child's well-being and to safe progress from removal from to reunification with the family. Alternatively, timely reviews also allow a child to move more quickly to another permanent placement if a return home becomes impossible. State statutes provide for the termination of parental rights based on the parent's abandonment of a child. Should too much time lapse between the original dispositional order and subsequent reviews, and should it be found that the parent or parents have failed to comply with the court's orders during that gap, the consequence may be a complete loss of a meaningful parent-child relationship, actually and legally.

Expert Witness Testimony

Almost all medical and mental health issues of diagnosis and evaluation of child abuse or neglect require testimony that educates the fact finder about matters beyond his or her lay understanding. This is the proper use of expert witness testimony in child abuse and neglect trials.

Expert witness testimony is unlike lay witness testimony in that experts are allowed to give opinion testimony about causes and results of observable data, within reasonable scientific (or medical) certainty, whereas lay witnesses are not. Often the witness who is qualified, to the satisfaction of the court, as an expert will be asked for both fact and opinion testimony. Combinations of fact and opinion testimony frequently occur in a child abuse or neglect trial when a witness has observed the child or members of the family in a professional capacity. An evaluating or treating physician or mental health professional may be able to relate factual information he or she directly observed. As an expert in his or her field, that witness may also be qualified to render an opinion about the cause or likely results of what he or she observed. Such opinion testimony can be offered only if it is within the scope of the expert's field of qualifications and does not violate other rules of evidence governing testi-

mony—that the evidence be relevant, material, probative, and not unduly prejudicial.

Evidence rules are fashioned to allow only trustworthy information, as well as it can be identified, to form the basis for decision making in law. Therefore, only information that a witness has observed with his or her own senses can be considered as evidence—except in the case of the expert. The expert's main role is to make understandable to the fact finder (whether judge or jury) information that is critical to fair decision making but beyond the ordinary ken of a layperson. Such information could be the process of medical diagnosis, the interpretation and implications of medical or psychological test results, the results of scientific studies, or the consequences of events in a young child's life.

One important criticism of the relationship between legal professionals and medical and mental health professionals has been the absence of shared information about the ground rules of court procedures, that is, the rules of evidence. For example, most law offices have among their volumes the latest edition of the American Psychiatric Association's *Diagnostic and Statistical Manual of Mental Disorders* and the *Physician's Desk Reference* to pharmaceuticals as well as medical dictionaries. Because medical information is composed of many discrete groups of data, it is far more accessible to the knowledgeable reader than legal information, all of which is interrelated. This interrelatedness of legal data makes it nearly impossible to access its individual parts. A medical or mental health professional, therefore, would be well advised to consult with a legal professional on evidentiary and other legal issues.

Expert witness testimony is often the critical evidence on which a finding is made that a child needs the protection of the state. Such testimony may include medical and mental health professionals' testimony on the battered child syndrome, medical testimony about the diagnosis of sexual abuse, and psychiatric or psychological testimony on the child sexual abuse accommodation syndrome.

The Battered Child Syndrome

The battered child syndrome, first suggested by Kempe in 1962, is a diagnosis used by medical professionals to describe a pattern of trauma symptoms in a young child. The syndrome's pattern of symptoms is thought to demonstrate that a child has suffered multiple injuries at various stages of healing, caused by nonaccidental means and inflicted with mature force that is beyond the capacity of a young child. Characteristic indications of the syndrome include the following:

- Subdural hematomas, sometimes chronic and sometimes accompanied by skull fractures
- Healed and healing bone fractures, especially spiral fractures
- Other bone injuries
- Soft tissue injuries

Finally, a very important indication is that the parent's explanations for the child's injuries are inconsistent with the injuries themselves (for example, a fall is used to explain a spiral fracture, a fall downstairs to explain a hand-shaped bruise on a flat plane of the face). The battered child syndrome, in sum, is a diagnosis made by a treating or evaluating physician that a child has been injured over time in such ways that those injuries were inflicted with mature force.

Because of the parent or guardian's daily and long-term proximity to the injured child, it is assumed in the diagnosis that the parent or other caregiver is the perpetrator. If the primary caregiver has not inflicted the injuries on the child, his or her daily proximity to the child suggests a failure to protect the child, or at least failure to seek medical attention for the child. Because of the presence of the parent in the child's daily life, it is thought unlikely that such injuries would go unnoticed if they had been inflicted by another. It is the use of this syndrome for identification evidence in court that has been controversial. The diagnosis purports not only to indicate abuse but also to identify by whom—namely, someone who has repeated close access to the child over time, typically a parent or other caregiver.

The diagnosis of battered child syndrome is accepted by courts because of its apparent general acceptance in the scientific (medical) community. This acceptance as a reliable and valid diagnosis among medical professionals has led courts, without much rigorous scrutiny, to accept it as a trustworthy indicator of abuse or neglect of a child. Furthermore, because of the logic inherent in its identification of an abusing or neglectful caregiver, courts also have found that any prejudice posed by the diagnosis is outweighed by its probative, material, and relevant value.

Child Sexual Abuse Diagnosis

Expert witness testimony regarding sexual abuse presents a special issue of concern, given the secret nature of the abuse and the typical lack of forensic evidence. It is an evidentiary issue that continues to be very troubling to lawyers and judges, as well as to mental health professionals.

Although there is a vigorous legal debate about expert testimony that describes the characteristics of abusers or the abused, there is virtual unanimity of opinion that it is improper for experts to testify as to whether a particular child is telling the truth—about either the occurrence of the abuse or the identity of the alleged perpetrator. Assessing the accuracy of the child's statements is a legal issue. Questions of credibility, truthfulness, and accuracy are within the proper function of the fact finder (the judge, or the jury if there is one) alone. Whenever an expert witness seeks to offer an opinion on an individual's truthfulness, that witness is venturing into the exclusive province of the fact finder. The expert witness's assessment usurps the role of the jury (or the judge, in bench trials) as the finder of fact.

For example, an expert witness may be asked either intentionally or inadvertently by counsel for an opinion regarding the accuracy of a child's disclosure and the accuracy of the diagnosis of sexual abuse. The question goes directly to the absence of forensic data or the presence of ambiguous forensic data. The accuracy of the child's allegation and identification of the perpetrator is critical to proving the case against the alleged perpetrator. The question of accuracy, though, is an issue of credibility and goes to an ultimate conclusion of fact, which must be left to the fact finder.

A distinction can be drawn between the physical diagnosis of battered child syndrome and the psychological diagnosis of child sexual abuse regarding the nature of the evidence supporting the diagnosis. The rules of evidence are designed to be accepting of observable data (bruises that can be seen, fractures that appear on radiological studies) and wary of the spoken word (the disclosing child, the alleging adult) when the speaker cannot or is not observed by the judge or jury deciding the facts of the case.

Observations of demeanor, body language, and facial expressions are all thought necessary to the fact finder's assessment of the speaker's veracity. These observations must be made of the original speaker; it does the fact finder little good to observe the witness repeating the words of another said out of court. Such evidence is *hearsay;* statements made out of court and then offered as evidence of the truth of the matter asserted in the statement. That unwieldy definition contains two important parts: (1) the statement offered by the witness was originally made by another out of the presence of the fact finder, and (2) the witness offers the statement not only to prove that the statement was made but also to prove the truth of the content of the statement. Because the fact finder cannot ascertain the truthfulness of the original speaker, the hearsay is inadmissible as evidence of the statement's truth.

In some circumstances the trustworthiness of the context in which the statement was made allows the fact finder to accept the statement's veracity. For example, statements made to a doctor by a patient seeking treatment are considered trustworthy statements. Statements made

when the declarant is in a state of great excitement also may be considered sufficiently trustworthy. Also trustworthy are statements made by a party to a legal action when those statement go against his or her own legal interest; for example, a confession to a crime would be admissible. Such statements are exceptions to the prohibition against hearsay as evidence in court.

Some statements are considered trustworthy because they are relied on in the regular course of business; hence, business records are admissible despite their hearsay nature. Data regularly provided by a test technician to a professional for use in his or her work also may meet the necessary indicia of trustworthiness and so may be admitted as hearsay through the professional's testimony.

Child Sexual Abuse Accommodation Syndrome

Another evidentiary problem in sexual abuse cases is the prevalence of inconsistent statements by the disclosing child. This issue is addressed by the child sexual abuse accommodation syndrome, posited by Summit (1983). The potential utility of the syndrome diagnosis is for the limited purpose of explaining a child's recantation of an earlier disclosure of sexual abuse. The elements of this syndrome are a child's use of secrecy; sense of helplessness; sense of entrapment and the need to accommodate; delayed, emotionally conflicted, and unconvincing disclosure; and retraction of earlier disclosure (Summit, 1983). The syndrome explains the prevalence of children's recantations (see also Sorenson & Snow, 1991) and the circumstances under which such a recantation may be disregarded: because children are often unable to integrate the emotional, psychological, and legal consequences of the disclosure of sexual abuse, they may seek to undo the personally painful internal and external effects of the disclosure by retracting their statements.

The child sexual abuse accommodation syndrome has not been used anywhere to establish child sexual abuse and is not scientifically validated to do so. Because of the great risk of improperly legitimizing an earlier disclosure as true and accurate, the courts have been careful to limit the usefulness of the accommodation syndrome as evidence. Thus, syndrome testimony must be carefully constructed so as to only rehabilitate an earlier disclosure of child sexual abuse and nothing more. This rehabilitation of the earlier statements of disclosure is all that the syndrome diagnosis has been validated to do in social science, ensuring that a diagnosis does not have a greater usefulness in law than it does in medical or mental health practice.

Court Actions to Terminate Parental Rights

Invoking the Family Court System

The judicial termination of parental rights is a complete severing of the legal relationship between the parent and child, including all obligations of support, mutual rights to inherit, and mutual rights of contact and cohabitation. Also lost is the jurisdiction of the family court over the incidents of the nullified relationship.

The Parties and Their Lawyers

In some instances, either when circumstances are sufficiently severe or following a dispositional order and the lapse of significant time, the state may seek to terminate the rights of a defendant parent to his or her abused or neglected child. Given the severity of the outcome of such a legal action, one might expect the highest level of protection for a person's constitutional right to parent his or her child. Although an adult does have a protected right to his or her children, the state has a right to safeguard the children within its borders, often referred to as *parens patriae*. The child's need to be safe is also recognized in

termination actions. As a result of the weighing process to which the U.S. Supreme Court has subjected these competing interests, several criminal court protections are not available to the defendant parent. For example, the appointment of counsel is made at the discretion of the trial judge or by statute (*Lassiter v. Durham County Department of Social Services,* 1981), and the standard of proof to terminate a person's right to his or her children is less than that required for proof of criminal guilt (*Santosky v. Kramer,* 1982). Both of these issues will be addressed in this section.

Evidentiary Issues

The Standard of Proof

Because of the irrevocable nature of the termination action and its extraordinary intrusion into the family's privacy, safeguards have been established to protect the parent's rights in the face of extreme state action. Primary among these safeguards is the heightened standard of proof required in these cases: proof by clear and convincing evidence, more weighty than the simple preponderance of evidence, is necessary to prove a termination case. Lawyers often refer to this standard in numerical language. A preponderance is met when only 51% of the evidence indicates that the matter asserted is true. Even if the defendant shows that 49% of the evidence is in his or her favor, the standard of proof will favor a judgment for the plaintiff, the state. Clear and convincing evidence is understood to fall about midway between the preponderance standard and the standard of evidence beyond a reasonable doubt, which is placed at about 95% or higher. Thus, the "clear and convincing" standard may be said to fall at approximately 75% of the evidence.

In *Santosky v. Kramer* (1982), the U.S. Supreme Court declared that proofs supporting the termination of parental rights must be based on at least clear and convincing evidence, given

the private interest affected [the parents' loss of their

rights to their children] is commanding; the risk of error from using a preponderance standard [which asks only whether it is more likely than not that the plaintiff state has proved its case] is substantial; and the countervailing governmental interest favoring that standard [greater fiscal and administrative costs of the more rigorous proof by clear and convincing evidence and the state's interest in promoting the welfare of the children within its borders] is slight. (*Santosky v. Kramer,* 1982, p. 758)

In *Santosky,* a father and mother lost custody of three children, one after the other, for the physical abuse and medical neglect of the first two and for the risk of harm they posed to the third, a newborn. The State of New York then sought to terminate the parents' rights on the basis of their permanent neglect of their children. At that time, the New York statutes provided for a standard of proof based on a fair preponderance of the evidence. The U.S. Supreme Court found that parents in the position of losing their children because of state action were due sufficient process to make the state's action fully fair to them. Such due process included the right to a higher standard of proof, namely, proof by clear and convincing evidence. The state's strong interest in the welfare of the children within its borders was recognized in balancing that interest with the parents' constitutional right to raise their own children. The balance resulted in the clear and convincing evidence standard; the more stringent standard of proof beyond a reasonable doubt was not required by the Court.

The Grounds for Termination

In recent state court appellate decisions, it has become increasingly clear that terminations must be based not only on the best interests of the child but also on some wrongdoing on the part of the parent. In the past, the simple passage of time and a child's new attachment to a parent figure, often the state licensed foster parent, could serve as sufficient grounds for a termination action. Today, courts are wary of the "bonding" arguments used to sever original relationships in favor

of newer, state-created ones. When parents have shown good-faith compliance with dispositional orders following a family court finding of abuse or neglect, courts are more apt to deny the termination requested by the state.

The burden this situation places on the child who has formed new attachments in a replacement family cannot be overlooked, even though all parties to the arrangement understand it to be a temporary or emergency placement. Especially in situations of lengthy placement, if the courts refuse to give legal recognition to the new relationship—which has become very real for the child—the child must suffer the consequences of the state's failure to act promptly in returning child to his or her family home.

Case Dispositions

The possible legal outcomes of the termination of parental rights actions are very few. Either the state makes its case satisfactorily or it does not. The human toll, though, may be varied. Many times a parent will force the state to go through the so-called TPR (termination of parental rights) action even when it is clear that the state will be successful in its action. To avoid the guilt that may accompany voluntarily surrendering the rights to a child, the parent gives responsibility to the state for the decision to end legally the relationship that ended in reality long before.

Should the state be successful in its action, best practice would require that the state have a permanent placement available and ready for the child. There is rarely any reason to terminate the child's legal rights to the parent, including rights under a state's intestacy laws, unless there is a family willing to embrace the child in adoption or permanent foster care. A reason to do otherwise may exist if the child's psychological well-being requires the severance of the original parental relationship. In such an instance, the lawyers and the court should be advised carefully on the child's mental and emotional state by the evaluating and treating mental health professionals.

Conclusion

When a child is before the court as the victim of abuse or neglect in his or her home, that child is deprived, at least in the court's eyes, of an adequate parental advocate. Working together law, social work, medical, and mental health professionals can create an optimal environment for the child's rescue and healing. A multidisciplinary approach to meeting the child's needs educates all the professionals involved in the child's case; it also educates the community, the family members, and the child about resolving problems with respect for the others involved.

Familiarity with the three court processes involved in legal decision making is a step in that direction. More communication across disciplines will provide additional assistance to all the professionals involved in solving children's problems. Those solutions must be made on a case-by-case basis, but they cannot be made in ignorance of the larger implications each of our actions holds for children everywhere.

References

American Psychiatric Association. (1994). *Diagnostic and statistical manual of mental disorders* (4th ed.). Washington, DC: Author.

Anderson, E., Levine, M., Sharma, A., Ferretti, L., Steinberg, K., & Wallach, L. (1992). *Mandatory reporting of child abuse: The effects of compliance with the law on the therapeutic relationship.* Paper presented at the biennial meeting of the American Psychology-Law Society. San Diego, CA.

Atlantic Employers Ins. Co. v. Lynch, 280 N.J. Super. 457 (App. Div. 1995). (Confirmed in personal communication with Charles S. Lorbe, Esq., September 26, 1995).

Berliner, L., & Barbieri, M. K. (1984). The testimony of the child victim of sexual assault. *Journal of Social Issues, 40,* 125–137.

Bernstein, B. E., & Claman, L. (1986). Modern technology and the child witness. *Child Welfare, 65*(2), 155–163.

Brooks, C. M., Perry, N. W., Starr, S. D., & Teply, L. L. (1994). Child abuse and neglect reporting laws: Understanding interests, understanding policy. *Behavioral Sciences and the Law, 12,* 49–64.

Bross, D. C. (1987). Protecting child witnesses. In D. Bross & L. Freeman Michaels, (Eds.), *Foundations of child advocacy* (pp. 117–126). Longmont, CO: Bookmakers Guild.

Ceci, S. J., & Bruck, M. (1993). Suggestibility of the child witness: A historical review and synthesis. *Psychological Bulletin, 113,* 403–439.

Claman, L., Harris, J. C., Bernstein, B. E., & Lovitt, R. (1986). The adolescent as a witness in a case of incest: Assessment and outcome, *Journal of the American Academy of Child Psychiatry, 25*(4), 457–461.

Clark, H. (1987). *The law of domestic relations in the United States* (2nd ed., Vol. 2). St. Paul, MN: West.

Colby, I. C., & Colby, D. N. (1987). Videotaped interviews in child sexual abuse cases: The Texas example. *Child Welfare, 66*(1), 25–34.

Coyne, A. (1992). *On Attachment and Bonding* [Educational videotape]. National Council of Family and Juvenile Court Judges.

DeShaney v. Winnebago County Department of Social Services, 489 U.S. 198 (1989).

Doris, J. (Ed.). (1991). *The suggestibility of children's recollections.* Washington, DC: American Psychological Association.

Federal Adoption Assistance and Child Welfare Act, 42 U.S.C.A. § 471 (a) (15) (1983); as amended, 42 U.S.C.A. § 671 (a) (15) (1988).

Gideon v. Wainwright, 372 U.S. 335 (1963).

Globe Newspaper v. Superior Court, 457 U.S. 596 (1982).

Goldstein, J., Freud, A., & Solnit, A. (1973). *Beyond the best interests of the child.* New York: Free Press.

Goldstein, J., Freud, A., & Solnit, A. (1979). *Before the best interests of the child.* New York: Free Press.

Goldstein, J., Freud, A., & Solnit, A. (1986). *In the best interests of the child.* New York: Free Press.

Goodman, G. S., & Bottoms, B. (Eds.). (1993). *Child victims, child witnesses: Understanding and improving testimony.* New York: Guilford.

Goodman, G. S., Taub, E. P., Jones, D. P. H., England, P., Port, L. K., Rudy L., & Prado L. (1992). Testifying in criminal court. *Monographs of the Society for Research in Child Development, 57* (5, Serial No. 229).

Gothard, S. (1987). The admissibility of evidence in child sexual abuse cases. *Child Welfare, 66*(1), 13–24.

Higgins, R. B., (1988). Child victims as witnesses. *Law and Psychology Review, 12,* 159–166.

In re Interest of D.M.B. 481 N.W.2d 905 (Neb. 1992).

Jolly v. Texas, 681 S.W.2d 689 (Tex. App. 1984).

Kalichman, S. C. (1993). *Mandated reporting of suspected child abuse: Ethics, law, and policy.* Washington, DC: American Psychological Association.

Kempe, C. H. (1962). The battered child syndrome. *Journal of the American Medical Association, 181,* 1.

LaShawn et al. v. Dixon, 762 F. Supp. 959 (D.C. Dist. Ct. 1991).

Lassiter v. Durham County Department of Social Services, 452 U.S. 81 (1981).

Loftus, E. (1979). *Eyewitness testimony.* Cambridge, MA: Harvard University Press.

Loftus, E. (1984). Distortions in the memory of children. *Journal of Social Issues, 40,* 51–67.

Lovelace v. Keohane, 831 P.2d 624 (Okla. 1992).

mac Murray, B. K. (1989). Criminal determination for child sexual abuse: Prosecutor case-screening judgments. *Journal of Interpersonal Violence, 4*(2), 233–244.

Maryland v. Craig, 497 U.S. 836 (1990).

Melton, G. B. (1984). Child witnesses and the first amendment: A psycholegal dilemma. *Journal of Social Issues, 40,* 109–123.

Merriam-Webster's Collegiate Dictionary (10th ed.). (1993). Springfield, MA: Merriam-Webster.

Miranda v. Arizona, 384 U.S. 436 (1966).

Mnookin, R. M. (Ed.). (1985). *In the interest of children.* New York: Freeman.

Omaha World Herald (1994, January 18).

O'Neal v. Division of Family Services, 821 P.2d 1139 (Utah 1991).

People v. Cavaiani, 432 N.W.2d 409 (Mich. 1988).

Perry, N. W. (1992). When children take the stand: Permissible innovations in the U.S. courts. *Expert Evidence: The International Digest of Human Behaviour, Science, and the Law, 1,* 54–59.

Perry, N. W., & Teply, L. L. (1984–1985). Interviewing, counseling, and in-court examination of children: Practical approaches for attorneys. *Creighton Law Review, 18*(5), 1369–1426.

Perry, N. W., & Wrightsman, L. S. (1991). *The child witness: Legal issues and dilemmas.* Newbury Park, CA: Sage.

Pynoos, R. S., & Eth, S. (1984). The child as witness to homicide. *Journal of Social Issues, 40,* 87–108.

Santosky v. Kramer, 455 U.S. 745 (1982).

Schetky, D. H., & Benedek, E. P. (1989). The sexual abuse victim in the courts. *Psychiatric Clinics of North America, 12*(2), 471–481.

Sorensen, T., & Snow, B. (1991). How children tell: The process of disclosure in child sexual abuse. *Child Welfare, 70,* 3–15.

Summit, R. (1983). The child sexual abuse accommodation syndrome. *Child Abuse and Neglect, 7,* 177.

Tedesco, J. F., & Schnell, S. V. (1987). Children's reactions to sex abuse investigation and litigation. *Child Abuse and Neglect, 11*(2), 267–272.

Walker, A. G. (1994). *Handbook on questioning children: A linguistic perspective.* Washington, DC: American Bar Association Center on Children and the Law.

White v. Illinois, 502 U.S. 346 (1992).

23 Voluntary Admission and Involuntary Hospitalization of Minors

James W. Ellis
University of New Mexico

The procedures by which children may be admitted to residential facilities for treatment of mental illness or habilitation of mental retardation have been the source of much controversy. A 1979 decision by the U.S. Supreme Court (*Parham v. J. R.*) appeared to resolve the controversy, but more recent developments and new problems have revived the debate over the U.S. Constitution's Fourteenth Amendment guarantee of due process and its applicability to children. The principal focus in this debate is whether children can be institutionalized by consent of their parents alone or whether they are entitled to a hearing that is roughly comparable to the commitment hearings that adults receive before they are committed to a mental institution. Thus, the controversy implicates a series of sensitive issues, including the rights of parents, the decision-making capacity of minors (especially adolescents), and the tension between the need for mental health care by some children and the risk that other children will be stigmatized and harmed by unnecessary confinement.

This chapter will begin by surveying the nature and history of institutionalization for children with mental illness and mental retardation. This will be followed by an overview of the history of laws relating to the institutionalization of children. A detailed analysis of the U.S. Supreme Court's 1979 decision will then set the stage for a discussion of the constitutional issues involved, with particular attention to justifications for treating children differently from adults (equal protection issues) and to an analysis of the fairness of denying children a hearing on their need for confinement (due process issues). The chapter will conclude with an analysis of proposals for reforming the mental disability laws affecting children.

Treatment of Children and Adolescents with Mental Illness

Mental health problems that children and adolescents experience span a wide array of clinical conditions and differ widely in etiology, symptoms, and clinically indicated treatment and prognosis. Some of these problems are so severe that they require inpatient treatment in a residential facility, whereas the far larger number can be addressed by nonresidential approaches, such as individual or group psychotherapy. It has been estimated that there are at least 230 distinct kinds of psychological treatment used with children (Reisman & Ribordy, 1993), and there is a variety of settings in which inpatient treatment may be provided (U.S. Congress, Office of Technology Assessment, 1986).

Diagnosing children believed to have mental illness is a most inexact process. Even compared with psychiatric diagnosis and treatment of adults, intervention with children and adolescents "is more an art than a science" (Wilson, 1978, p. 93). The difficulties in diagnosing minors are partially a result of communication difficulties between adults and children or adolescents. "For example, adolescent 'turmoil' and moodiness may be mistaken for more serious symptomatology or, conversely, may obscure it" (Schwab-Stone, 1989, p. 32). These communication problems may be exacerbated by clinicians' limited understanding of mental illness in young people. "For example, the system used to classify disorders and our clinical expectations regarding the occurrence and presentation of psychopathology in this age group are based on incomplete knowledge, which further threatens diagnostic accuracy" (Schwab-Stone, 1989, p. 32). In individual cases, the reliability of a child's diagnosis may also be questionable because of the practice of "inflat[ing] or otherwise tamper[ing] with the diagnoses to meet the requirements of insurance coverage" (Mason & Gibbs, 1992, p. 452). Survey data indicate that such deliberate misdiagnoses may be widespread (Kirk & Kutchins, 1988).

Diagnostic imprecision may lead to uncertainty as to whether an individual child actually has a clinical mental disorder, as compared to the relatively ordinary process of emotional growth and development. Over the last two decades, there has been a trend toward the commitment of juveniles, particularly older teenagers, for "conduct disorder" rather than for the more traditional psychiatric diagnoses (Dalton & Forman, 1992; Jemerin & Philips, 1988).

But even when it is indisputable that the child has a mental illness, there is room for substantial disagreement among clinicians about the nature and severity of the disorder. Some therapists evaluating a child may see a mental illness so severe that it requires drastic intervention to prevent substantial deterioration of the child's condition or that it even threatens the child's health and safety, such as the potential for self-injurious behavior. Other therapists evaluating the same child may see a child with difficul-

ties that present no serious threat to the child if treatment is provided on an outpatient basis.

Diagnosis and admission decisions are particularly problematic when the child's family insists that the child be placed in a mental hospital. As the child enters adolescence, or as the child's behavior becomes more difficult, the parents may view institutionalization as the only solution for the family's problems. "The energy that previously went into tolerance [of the child's behavior] gets channeled full force into expulsion" (Perlmutter, 1986, p. 158). Institutionalizing the child or adolescent may appear to offer the prospect of restoring peace to the home and providing treatment for the individual. "Inpatient psychiatric hospitalization offers an attractive combination of treatment and control, a combination that over-stressed parents and youth services professionals may find hard to resist" (Butts & Schwartz, 1991, p. 112).

The result of these various influences in recent years has been a dramatic increase in the institutionalization of juveniles in mental facilities. There is a "growing public and professional perception that the level of utilization of psychiatric hospitalization, especially for adolescents, is inappropriate" (Hendren & Berlin, 1991, p. 6). It is equally clear that society has failed to provide adequate resources for alternatives to institutions for juveniles (Goldfine et al., 1985). But whether or not there are too many children and adolescents in mental facilities, there remain serious concerns about whether individual children require treatment in a setting that is potentially disruptive to their lives and potentially harmful to their future.

Habilitation of Children and Adolescents with Mental Retardation

Mental retardation differs from mental illness in that it primarily affects the individual's ability to learn rather than affecting the individual's emotions or thinking process. As defined by the American Association on Mental Retardation (AAMR),

[m]ental retardation refers to substantial limitations in present functioning. It is characterized by significantly subaverage intellectual functioning, existing concurrently with related limitations in two or more of the following applicable adaptive skill areas: communication, self-care, home living, social skills, community use, self-direction, health and safety, functional academics, leisure, and work. Mental retardation manifests before age 18. (Luckasson, 1992, p. 5)

What this means in practical terms is that to fall within the definition of mental retardation, a person must have an IQ of 70 to 75 or below, and this condition must have manifested itself before adulthood. The intellectual functioning component requires that the person has measured intelligence in the lowest 2.5% of the population. But for the person to be diagnosed as having mental retardation, the intellectual impairment must also cause a real disability in the person's life, including at least two of the adaptive skill areas listed by the AAMR (Ellis, 1992).

The severity of the disability experienced by individuals with mental retardation varies at least as widely as the disability caused by mental illness. Some individuals with mental retardation are so severely handicapped that they need assistance with the most simple tasks, such as feeding themselves and toileting. Some of these individuals lack mobility (because of physical disabilities that may accompany their mental disability) and may lack the ability to speak or understand speech. Individuals who have this severe a disability are a very small portion of the class of persons with mental retardation. At the other end of the spectrum, a far larger number of individuals are able, with some assistance, to learn basic academic skills and grow toward an adult life of self-support and personal independence. This latter group constitutes the vast majority of people with mental retardation—more than 90% of the total (Smith & Luckasson, 1992).

Under older systems of classification, people

with mental retardation were subdivided into four groups based on the severity of their intellectual disability: mild, moderate, severe, and profound (Ellis, 1992). These terms are no longer part of the professionals' system of diagnosis. Under the AAMR's revised system of classification, professionals identify individuals according to the intensity of the needs their disability creates. Thus, an individual can be identified as needing assistance in particular skill areas at one of four levels: intermittent, limited, extensive, or pervasive. For example, an individual's diagnosis might be "a person with mental retardation with extensive supports needed in the areas of social skills and self-direction" or "a person with mental retardation who needs limited supports in communication and social skills" (Luckasson, 1992, p. 34).

The ameliorative services provided to individuals with mental retardation have changed dramatically in recent decades. Mental retardation professionals have now developed systems of habilitation (the term preferred over *treatment*) that greatly assist people in overcoming the skill deficits that are a product of their intellectual handicap. Although it is not possible to "cure" or eliminate the intellectual disability itself, great progress has been made in teaching and training individuals with mental retardation to understand concepts and perform tasks previously thought to be beyond their capacity (Blatt, 1987; Smith & Luckasson, 1992). This is true for individuals with all degrees of severity of mental handicap.

Habilitation services for children with mental retardation are currently provided in both residential and nonresidential settings. The vast majority of children with mental retardation live with their own families; only a small minority reside in institutions (Smith & Luckasson, 1992). The trend away from institutionalization of children with mental retardation was greatly accelerated by the enactment of the Education of All Handicapped Children Act in 1975. This federal statute, which is now called the Individuals with Disabilities Education Act (IDEA, 1990), prohibited school districts from excluding children with disabilities and granted all such children the right to a free and appropriate public education. The effect of this law is to allow parents to keep at home children who previously might have been institutionalized.

As a result of the education act and the improvements in techniques of habilitation, the vast majority of children with mental retardation will never need to live in institutions. Indeed, a growing body of empirical evidence questions whether there are any individuals, whatever the level of their mental retardation, who cannot live in their home communities (Conroy & Bradley, 1985). As a result, expectations about the need for institutionalization of individuals with mental retardation are changing dramatically.

Effects of Institutionalization on Children

Residential placement in a congregate care facility is proposed for a child because it is anticipated that the child will benefit from services that the facility offers. In particular, placement may be proposed because the facility has professionals or services who can address the child's treatment or habilitation needs. But most such professionals or services could also be obtained on an outpatient basis, so other justifications for institutionalization are usually offered, explicitly or implicitly. One such justification is that the child's condition requires a more structured environment than will be experienced living at home and receiving nonresidential treatment or habilitation. It may be believed that the child's behavior will respond favorably to discipline or to other features of the management of the facility. Often this concern is expressed in terms of a desired "therapeutic milieu."

Other rationales offered for residential placement relate to the interaction between the child and family. These concerns may take several forms. One concern may be that the parents are not addressing the child's needs adequately or

that their interactions with the child may be inconsistent with the child's treatment or habilitation. Another possibility might be that the child's behavior is upsetting or disruptive to other members of the household, such as parents or siblings. A third possibility might be that the parents are unable to control the child's behavior, and the removal from the family home could assist in imposing such control.

But institutionalization may have adverse consequences for the child (Stone, 1979). For example, a child placed in a residential facility may lose contact with family and friends and may no longer be able to attend the same school. These relationships are likely to be important to the child, whether the child is identified as having mental illness or mental retardation (Strully & Strully, 1985).

Another adverse consequence of institutionalization may be the lifelong stigmatization that the child suffers as a person who had been committed to a mental facility (Edgerton, 1967; Goffman, 1963). This stigmatization, in turn, may result in discrimination against the individual. Some stigmatization is the result of societal reaction to the child's mental disability. But discrimination may also result from the official labeling as a "mentally disabled person" that is inherent in institutionalization; institutions require an "official" finding that the individual requires residential placement and that records be kept. But the effect of the label may also result from the fact that the time spent confined in the facility—especially if it is a lengthy confinement—will require explanation in later life, such as in responses to questions on job applications. The reality of stigmatization (and resulting self-stigmatization) in the lives of people who have been labeled as having a mental disability is movingly recounted in the life stories of individuals who have experienced these phenomena (Bogdan & Taylor, 1982; Zetlin & Turner, 1984).

Over and above these social consequences of residential placement, clinical consequences of institutionalization have also been documented in the clinical literature. It has long been recognized that institutionalization, particularly if it is of long duration, may have serious negative effects on the child's mental, emotional, and physical development (Bowlby, 1973; Eagle, 1994). Children who live in institutions rather than in family settings may learn more slowly and may fail to attain natural emotional and social development. Even more disturbing, judicial findings based on clinical evidence suggest that individuals with mental retardation often actually lose essential life skills that they possessed at the time of their institutional placement (*Youngberg v. Romeo*, 1982).

Children who are placed in mental institutions are frequently subjected to intrusive and even hazardous treatments, such as psychotropic medications. The treatment may also involve institutional regimentation of daily life and substantial loss of privacy that may prove to be a difficult and troubling experience for the patient (Kaysen, 1993; Warren, 1983). In addition, recurring reports indicate a troubling incidence of abuse of institutionalized children (Rindfleisch, 1988).

In a particular child's case, the clinical indications that support the proposal for residential placement may outweigh the risk of these harms, but their potential for damaging the individual makes any decision about institutionalizing a child a serious matter requiring careful consideration. It is the process through which this balance is to be struck for individual children that is at the center of the policy and legal debate about the rules governing the institutionalization of minors.

History of Laws Regarding Institutionalization of Minors

The laws that govern the institutionalization of minors are enacted at the state rather than the federal level. In most states, the laws that allow parents to place their children in mental institutions without any judicial hearing originated in the years immediately following World War II. Most of these state statutes were inspired by the

National Institute of Mental Health's *Draft Act for the Hospitalization of the Mentally Ill*, published in 1951 (Ellis, 1974). A principal feature of the *Draft Act* was to increase the ease of obtaining voluntary mental health treatment for adults. Grafted onto the provisions that authorized adults to consent to their own mental health treatment in institutions was a provision that allowed parents to place their children in such institutions. The theory and terminology of these provisions treated the children as "voluntary" patients because they were "volunteered" by their parents. The consent or acquiescence of the child was neither sought nor required under these laws.

By the 1960s, a majority of the states had adopted these "voluntary" admission laws for minors. In the years that followed this reduction of procedural protections for children, the rate of institutionalization for minors increased substantially (Ellis, 1974). Then, in the 1970s, a series of challenges were mounted against the constitutionality of laws denying to children civil commitment hearings that would be provided to adults. In a number of lower courts, these challenges were successful, and a few states changed their laws to provide commitment hearings for children. (Ellis & Carter, 1980; *In re Roger S.*, 1977). But in 1979, the U.S. Supreme Court held that the Constitution did not require that states provide children with formal hearings (*Parham v. J. R.*, 1979), and following this ruling, state reforms slowed considerably.

The *Parham* Decision

The Supreme Court's decision in 1979 arose out of constitutional challenges to the juvenile commitment statutes in Georgia and Pennsylvania. The Georgia case, *Parham v. J. R.*, involved a statute that failed to provide hearings for children said to have mental illness, and it became the lead opinion in the Supreme Court. The Pennsylvania case, *Secretary of Public Welfare v. Institutionalized Juveniles* (1979), challenged a statute that lacked procedural protections for children with mental retardation. Although at an earlier stage of the litigation the Court had warned of the potential importance of constitutional differences between the mental illness and mental retardation issues, the *Secretary of Public Welfare* decision merely echoed the justices' conclusions in the *Parham* case.

The Georgia statute at issue in *Parham* was typical of state laws that followed the model of the *Draft Act for the Hospitalization of the Mentally Ill*. The statute provided that parents could apply for, and consent to, the institutionalization of their minor children. Under the statute, if a child's parent consented to the child's placement, no hearing was required. If a child had no parents, state social workers were authorized to consent to admission.

The Lower Court Ruling

The challenge to the Georgia statute was brought in federal district court as a class action on behalf of the children institutionalized at the various Georgia residential mental health facilities. The plaintiffs claimed that the failure to provide children with the kind of hearings that adults were afforded before they could be institutionalized deprived the children of their liberty without due process of law in violation of the Fourteenth Amendment to the U.S. Constitution.

The three-judge district court that conducted the trial ruled that the Georgia statute was unconstitutional and that all children were entitled to a hearing on their need for hospitalization. The court found that the failure to provide children with independent hearings had resulted in numerous cases of inappropriate institutionalization (*J. L. v. Parham*, 1976). The state appealed this ruling to the U.S. Supreme Court.

The Supreme Court reversed the lower court and held that the Georgia procedures were constitutionally adequate, but the Court's ruling remains intensely controversial. "No modern U.S. Supreme Court civil case dealing with the rights of the mentally handicapped has been criticized as consistently or as thoroughly" (Perlin, 1994).

Because of the importance of the *Parham* decision in shaping this issue, the Supreme Court's decision will be analyzed in some detail.

The Supreme Court's Majority Opinion

In 1979, a majority of the justices of the Supreme Court of the United States concluded that the requirements of the due process clause were satisfied by Georgia's system of juvenile admissions to mental health institutions. The majority opinion, written by then–Chief Justice Warren Burger, posed the case's issue as "what process is constitutionally due a minor whose parents or guardian seek state administered institutional mental health care for the child and specifically whether an adversary proceeding is required prior to or after the commitment" (p. 587).

The majority began its analysis of this issue by holding that the child had a liberty interest in being free from unnecessary and inappropriate institutionalization. This is not the only conclusion the Court could have reached. The justices could have held that children, because of their immaturity and the rights of their parents, lack a constitutionally protected interest when their hospitalization is sought. But the Court rejected this path, holding that "a child, in common with adults, has a substantial liberty interest in not being confined unnecessarily for medical treatment" (p. 600). In reaching this conclusion, the majority "recognize[d] that commitment sometimes produces adverse social consequences for the child because of the reaction of some to the discovery that the child has received psychiatric care" (p. 600).

But recognizing a liberty interest possessed by children and the potential of harm from institutionalization was not enough for the children to win their constitutional challenge. It was also necessary for them to show that placing them in an institution required procedural protections that the Georgia statute failed to afford them. In earlier cases, the Court had set forth a formula for determining when additional "process" was "due" under the Constitution. And, in cases involving the civil commitment of adults, the Court had found that this formula required the protection of an adversarial commitment hearing (*Addington v. Texas*, 1979). So the question in *Parham* was whether children were constitutionally entitled to equivalent protections.

The Court's balancing test for determining what process is due considers four factors: (1) the nature of the individual interest involved, (2) the risk of erroneous determination if the individual was denied the procedure he or she requested, (3) the likelihood that the requested procedure would reduce the risk of erroneous deprivations of liberty, and (4) the state's interest in refusing to provide the protections requested (*Mathews v. Eldridge*, 1976; Nowak & Rotunda, 1991). The essence of the *Mathews* balancing test was weighing the individuals' interest in not losing their liberty interest against the state's interest in not paying for the procedures requested, evaluated in light of the probability that the procedures would produce fairer determinations. Having set forth the elements of the balancing test, the *Parham* majority then proceeded to evaluate each in the context of children's institutionalization and conduct the balancing.

The first element (the individual interest) is the weight or significance of the child's liberty interest in being free from unwanted and unnecessary hospitalization. Despite having described civil commitment as a "massive curtailment of liberty" in adult cases (*Humphrey v. Cady*, 1972), the *Parham* majority apparently assigned a lesser weight to the liberty interest of children. It did so by balancing the child's interest in freedom against his or her parents' interest in seeking the commitment. "[S]ince [the child's] interest is inextricably linked with the parents' interest in and obligation for the welfare and health of the child, the private interest at stake is a combination of the child's and parents' concerns" (p. 600).

The majority then proceeded to minimize the liberty interest of the child by observing that stigmatization might result from the child's "abnormal behavior" rather than from the state's application of the label of mental disability. By contrast, the parental interest was portrayed in more sympathetic terms. "Our jurisprudence historically has reflected Western civilization concepts of the family as a unit with broad parental authority over minor children" (p. 602). The majority chose to follow this historical approach both because of its lack of faith in children's judgment and its trust in the parents' judgment. "The law's concept of the family rests on the presumption that parents possess what a child lacks in maturity, experience, and capacity for judgment required for making life's difficult decisions. More important, historically it has recognized that natural bonds of affection lead parents to act in the best interests of their children" (p. 602).

The next inquiry under the *Mathews* test (the risk of error) is the likelihood that children will be erroneously committed if they are not accorded the right to a full hearing on their need for institutionalization. The *Parham* majority assessed this risk as minimal. It relied, in the first instance, on its assumption that parents would act in the best interest of their children. From this assumption, it concluded that states could grant to parents "a substantial, if not the dominant, role in the decision, absent a finding of neglect or abuse" (p. 604). But the justices recognized that there would be cases in which the parents did not act in their child's best interest. The majority expressed confidence that, in such cases, the admitting physician or staff member at the institution would be able to detect the problem. "It is unrealistic to believe that trained psychiatrists, skilled in eliciting responses, sorting medically relevant facts, and sensing motivational nuances will often be deceived about the family situation surrounding a child's emotional disturbance" (pp. 611–612).

Having concluded that the risk of error was small, the Court went on to cast doubt on whether full hearings would reduce that risk (the third criterion). It reached this conclusion by characterizing the decision to be made as essentially medical: "[N]either judges nor administrative hearing officers are better qualified than psychiatrists to render psychiatric judgments" (p. 607).

The final element of the *Mathews* test is the state's interest in avoiding giving the child the procedural protections being requested. The Court assigned substantial weight to two state interests. The first was avoiding procedural protections that might discourage parents from seeking mental health care for their children.

It is surely not idle to speculate as to how many parents who believe they are acting in good faith would forgo state-provided hospital care if such care is contingent on participation in an adversary proceeding designed to probe their motives and other private family matters in seeking the voluntary admission. (p. 605)

The other state interest the Court recognized was in avoiding spending state resources on hearings. "The State also has a genuine interest in allocating priority to the diagnosis and treatment of patients as soon as they are admitted to a hospital rather than to time-consuming procedural minuets before the admission. . . . Behavioral experts in courtrooms and hearings are of little help to patients" (pp. 605–606).

Given the foregoing analysis, the majority held that the due process clause was satisfied as long as the state provided that a medical decision maker, who has interviewed the child, determined that the child needed institutionalization.

It is not necessary that the deciding physician conduct a formal or quasi-formal hearing. A state is free to require such a hearing, but due process is not violated by use of informal, traditional medical investigative techniques. . . . [T]he decision should represent an independent judgment of what the child requires and that all sources of information that are traditionally relied on by physicians and behavioral specialists should be consulted. (pp. 607–608)

The majority also made clear that its use of the term *independent* did not indicate that the doctor must be independent of the facility to which the child's commitment was sought. Rather, it would be sufficient if the doctor had "the authority to refuse to admit any child who does not satisfy the medical standards for admission" (p. 607).

As noted earlier, some children in the *Parham* litigation had no parents involved in their commitment, either because they were orphans or because their parents had had their parental rights terminated by a court. The commitment of these children had been sought by state social workers. The issue of whether these children were entitled to a full hearing is somewhat different from that of commitments sought by parents, as there is no history of societal deference to the childraising decisions of social workers. Nevertheless, the majority opinion held that these children could be committed without hearings as well because the state statutes required that social workers act in children's best interest: "[W]e cannot assume that when the State of Georgia has custody of a child it acts so differently from a natural parent in seeking medical assistance for the child" (p. 618).

The Supreme Court's Dissenting Opinion

Justice William Brennan dissented from the majority opinion, and his dissent was joined by Justices Thurgood Marshall and John Paul Stevens. The dissenting justices were of the opinion that the Georgia statute deprived committed children of their liberty without due process.

As had the majority opinion, the dissent began with the liberty interest of the children involved, but it did not minimize the importance of that interest.

Indeed, it may well be argued that children are entitled to more protection than are adults. The consequences of an erroneous commitment decision are more tragic where children are involved. Children are, on the average, confined for longer periods than are adults. Moreover, childhood is a particularly vulnerable time of life and children erroneously institutionalized during their formative years may bear the scars for the rest of their lives. (pp. 627–628)

As it had with regard to the liberty interest, the dissent took a different view of the risk of a mistaken decision to hospitalize a child. "[T]he chances of an erroneous commitment decision are particularly great where children are involved." Justice Brennan and his colleagues then noted that the risk of error was not merely theoretical. "The National Institute of Mental Health recently found that only 36% of patients below age 20 who were confined at St. Elizabeths Hospital actually required such hospitalization," and a similar study in Georgia itself had "concluded that more than half of the State's institutionalized children were not in need of confinement if other forms of care were made available or used" (p. 629).

On the issue of the role of the child's parents, the dissenters also took a different point of view. Rather than following the line of precedents about parental authority, the dissent focused on the equally long line of cases indicating that there were limits to parental prerogatives. A generation earlier, the Court had observed that "[p]arents may be free to become martyrs themselves. But it does not follow that they are free, in identical circumstances, to make martyrs of their children" (p. 630, quoting *Prince v. Massachusetts*, 1944). Of more direct relevance to the *Parham* issue, Justice Brennan compared the case of *Planned Parenthood of Central Missouri v. Danforth* (1976). In *Danforth*, the Court had held that parents could not exercise a veto over their minor daughter's decision to seek an abortion. Justice Brennan observed that *Parham*, like *Danforth*, involved a situation in which there was a conflict of interest between parent and child.

Indeed Danforth involved only a potential dispute between parent and child, whereas here a break in family autonomy has actually resulted in the parents' decision to surrender custody of their child to a state mental institution. In my view, a child who has been ousted from his family has even greater need for an independent advocate. (p. 631)

As a result of these considerations, the dissenters concluded that both children committed by parents and children committed by social workers were entitled to a hearing.

Children incarcerated in public mental institutions are constitutionally entitled to a fair opportunity to contest the legitimacy of their confinement. They are entitled to some champion who can speak on their behalf and who stands ready to oppose a wrongful commitment. Georgia should not be permitted to deny that opportunity and that champion simply because the children's parents or guardians wish them to be confined without a hearing. The risk of erroneous commitment is simply too great unless there is some form of adversary review. And fairness demands that children abandoned by their supposed protectors to the rigors of institutional confinement be given the help of some separate voice. (pp. 638–639)

Developments since *Parham*

Despite widespread scholarly criticism of the *Parham* majority's decision (Perlin, 1981; Perry & Melton, 1983–1984; Schmidt, 1985; Schoenberger, 1981), and despite the availability of model state legislation (Mental Health Law Project, 1978; Sales & Powell, 1982), the movement to provide procedural protections for children facing institutionalization slowed considerably in the 1980s (Brakel, Parry, & Weiner, 1985).

Recent developments, however, indicate the appropriateness of reconsidering whether children should have hearings before they are institutionalized in mental health or mental retardation facilities. One important development is the growing concern that lax commitment laws are inviting the commitment of troubled children who do not have a mental disability and whose problems could and should be addressed more appropriately in other settings (Costello & Worthington, 1981).

Another widely shared concern is the explosion in the number of juvenile admissions to private psychiatric hospitals. Several studies have demonstrated that such admissions more than quadrupled during the early 1980s (Weithorn, 1988). Congressional hearings have examined the same problem (Schroeder, 1992). These studies demonstrate that private facilities have found it very profitable to treat children and adolescents whose care is paid by health insurance and that this profitability has led to serious abuses, including the commitment of children who do not need institutionalization. A variety of institutional practices, including admissions decisions, may be affected by the pervasive need to keep the facility's beds occupied by patients from whom reimbursement can be obtained (Warren, 1983). "Physicians are pressured in subtle and not so subtle ways to maintain a maximal census and thus increase profits" (Dalton & Forman, 1987, p. 13). Given the substantial potential for harm in unnecessary hospitalization, the fact that in most states these admissions receive no judicial or other independent scrutiny is a source of serious concern.

These concerns have led a number of observers to call for greater protection of children facing institutionalization (Armstrong, 1993; Schroeder, 1992; Weithorn, 1988). As one recent study concluded, "For teenagers admitted by their parents, hospitalization can be a legal twilight zone, inescapable without parental approval yet beyond legal control" (Jackson-Beeck, Schwartz, & Rutherford, 1987, p. 164).

As legislatures confront the task of deciding whether children should be given commitment hearings, they will have to weigh the same kind of considerations that went into the constitutional disputes of the 1970s.

Should Legislatures Go beyond *Parham?*

Reconsidering the Risk of Errors

In evaluating the usefulness of commitment hearings for children, it is important to consider the likelihood that a system without hearings will produce erroneous decisions. This was one of the crucial factors in the *Mathews* balancing test, and one on which the majority placed great emphasis in *Parham.* But the evaluation of any legislative proposal for reform will also require a determination of whether the current system is sufficiently protective of children's best interest and right to liberty.

The *Parham* majority concluded that the risk of error without hearings was not excessive. The justices reasoned that parents would be unlikely to seek hospitalization that was not in their child's best interest and that, if for some reason they did, mental health professionals at the institution would quickly detect this situation and deny the child's admission. This approach to the question of the prevalence of errors in a system without hearings is unsatisfactory in several ways.

The first problem is that it sets up a "straw man" in assuming that erroneous commitments could be the result only of the actions of ill-motivated parents who are unconcerned about their child's welfare. The vast majority of parents who seek the institutionalization of their child are not evilly motivated, nor are they trying to "railroad" their child into an institution. They typically are loving, concerned parents facing a situation that is beyond their ability to resolve successfully within the family home. But although their judgment that the child and family need help is likely to be correct, their judgment that the proper solution is the child's placement in an institution may well be wrong (Ellis, 1974; Perlmutter, 1986; Shapiro & Carr, 1987).

The second problem is that the majority's view rests on the assumption that the parents are supplicants asking an objective and disinterested mental health facility to determine whether their child needs institutionalization. This model may be far from accurate, particularly with regard to private, profit-seeking institutions. Such private facilities, which have been the source of the explosive growth in juvenile admissions since *Parham,* have a direct financial stake in admitting children and adolescents whose parents are able to pay (most frequently through health insurance). Indeed, some of these private facilities are active and aggressive recruiters for potential patients, and their efforts include extensive television advertising directed to parents (Armstrong, 1993; Schroeder, 1992).

If the mental health facility is actively recruiting children or adolescents as prospective patients, and if the facility stands to profit financially if the child is admitted, can the facility's officials be trusted to serve as impartial adjudicators of the minor's need for commitment (or as the *Parham* majority described the role, "neutral and detached trier[s] of fact"; p. 607)? If the child does not have access to his or her own advocate and an independent decision maker, the likelihood of an unnecessary admission rises significantly (Schmidt & Otto, 1988; Stone, 1988).

But an even more central issue is that the *Parham* majority misperceived the appropriate definition of an "error." The majority envisioned an error as a situation in which a parent decided "to abandon an emotionally normal, healthy child and thrust him into an institution" (p. 611). Without doubt, such an unlikely event would constitute an erroneous commitment; but it does not encompass the entire universe of proposed commitments that should be viewed as "errors." It is also an error to commit a child to an institution if that child has a mental disability that can be addressed successfully in a noninstitutional setting. This type of case is much more likely and much more common.

The law has for decades recognized the central importance of the "least restrictive alternative" or "least drastic means" principle in establishing limitations on coercive treatment for mental disabilities (Chambers, 1972). This doctrine has long been a part of judicial analysis of individuals' constitutional rights (*Shelton v. Tucker*, 1960) and is now codified in the mental health statutes of most states (Brakel, Parry, & Weiner, 1985).

Professional organizations concerned with mental health services for minors also have established standards that call for only limited use of institutional placement. This is a clinical version of the least-drastic-means principle. In particular, the American Academy of Child and Adolescent Psychiatry has attempted to define the circumstances in which inpatient treatment may be appropriate. These guidelines include the following requirements:

A. The psychiatric disorder must be of such severity as to cause significant impairment of daily functioning in at least two important areas of the child or adolescent's life such as school performance, social interactions, or family relationships.
B. The treatment proposed must be relevant to the problems diagnosed and adjudged likely to benefit the patient.
C. Other available less restrictive treatment resources must have been considered and determined to be not available or not appropriate to the patient's needs or have been attempted and proven unsuccessful. Examples of less restrictive treatment resources would include, but are not limited to, residential treatment, day treatment, or intensive outpatient care. (American Academy of Child and Adolescent Psychiatry, 1989, pp. 1–2).

The American Psychiatric Association has similarly endorsed the preference for less-restrictive-alternative treatment wherever possible, requiring that "no less structured means are likely to be as effective in providing" (1982, p. 972) care and treatment before a child can be committed to inpatient treatment. Mental retardation organizations have expressed similar concerns (American Association on Mental Retardation, 1981).

But the widespread legal and clinical acceptance of this principle has not meant that it is consistently implemented in the institutionalization of minors. Children are frequently proposed for institutional commitment when their mental condition could be treated on a nonresidential basis or in a residential setting smaller than an institution (such as a group home). Justice Brennan's dissent in *Parham* called attention to studies showing that most juvenile patients in institutions could be treated successfully without institutionalization. Other studies that have evaluated minors admitted to institutions also indicate that a large percentage of these children do not require hospitalization (Weithorn, 1988).

The failure to honor in practice the principle of the least restrictive alternative or least drastic means can be explained, in part, by the fact that in most states the child has no independent forum in which to test his or her need for hospitalization.

Particularly where the mental health facility stands to profit from the child's admission, whether it is clinically indicated or not, trusting its officials to decide whether a particular child needs to be hospitalized is not a system that can effectively protect children's rights. The institutionalization of a child who does have mental health problems but whose problems can be treated in his or her community is an error that can cause the child serious long-term harm.

The Role of the Parent

The majority and dissenting justices in *Parham* traced the ancestry of their arguments to contrasting lines of cases about parental autonomy and the government's ability to limit parental prerogatives. Neither line of cases provides an irrefutable tradition of authority commanding a particular result in the case of juvenile commitments. Read together, these cases teach that parents have constitutional rights to direct the upbringing of their children but that the state has the authority to override parental preferences where it discerns a need to act in the interest of children, particularly where the child's and the parents' interests may not be identical (Mnookin & Weisberg, 1989; Teitelbaum & Ellis, 1978). Thus, the Supreme Court's pre-*Parham* precedents provide some support for each side of this issue, but these cases do not by themselves resolve the question of whether children should receive a hearing.

The remaining issue is whether the *Parham* decision itself has altered the constitutional landscape—more specifically, whether the constitutional rights of parents *prevent* the legislature from granting children the right to a commitment hearing. If the parents' constitutional right to control the upbringing of their children gives them an absolute right to decide on the child's mental health care, then the state is not only *not* obligated to give the child a hearing, it is precluded from doing so.

Despite the majority's rhetoric about "Western civilization concepts of the family as a unit with broad parental authority over minor children" (p. 602), states do not violate parental rights if they choose to give children commitment hearings. The majority opinion recognizes that states may require more formal preadmission procedures than those adopted by Georgia. "A state is free to require such a hearing, but due process is not violated by use of informal, traditional medical investigative techniques" (p. 607). Thus the policy question of balancing the parents' interest in controlling medical decision making and the child's interest in liberty is left to the states.

The Child's Role in Decision Making

Another policy issue that states are free to address is what role should appropriately be afforded to juveniles in making decisions about institutionalization. In other contexts, it has been recognized that minors may have a right to make some decisions for themselves even when a decision is contrary to the wishes of their parents. This dispute has been central to both the legal and the political debates about minors' access to contraceptives (*Carey v. Population Services International*, 1977). It has also been repeatedly litigated in the context of whether a minor may obtain an abortion without the consent, or in some cases the knowledge, of her parents. The Supreme Court has held that the state may not grant parents the right to veto their minor daughter's decision to obtain an abortion (*Planned Parenthood of Central Missouri v. Danforth*, 1976). But in more recent cases, the Court has ruled that, under certain circumstances, states may require that the parents be notified of their daughter's decision so long as they are not given veto power (*H. L. v. Matheson*, 1981).

Much of this litigation over minors' claims to a right to contraceptives or to abortions centers on the decision-making ability of the minor herself. These disputes have elicited a substantial body of scholarly literature from psychologists and others on adolescents' capacity to make complex and consequential decisions (Melton, Koocher, & Saks, 1983; Scott, 1992; Weithorn, 1984). As a result, we have a relatively good understanding of the factual and theoretical issues surrounding adolescent decisions.

But it should be noted that the issue involved in institutionalization differs from the abortion or contraceptive decision in several important ways, and those differences must be factored into the public policy discussion. One central difference is that whereas abortion and contraceptive issues arise only regarding adolescents, proposals to commit a child may occur at any age. Therefore, the debate cannot presuppose a biological "floor" of an age below which the issue will not arise. Commitment may be sought for articulate adolescents who can formulate and express a preference about the issue, but it may also be sought for infants and other young children incapable of participating directly in the decision. Intuitively we know that although the law treats both as "minors," an adolescent and an infant have little in common in terms of their abilities. Thus any rules about the procedures by which commitment decisions should be made must encompass both individuals who can participate actively in the process and individuals who cannot.

However, the commitment issue differs from the abortion and contraceptive issues in another crucial respect. In the decisions about pregnancy, the child is claiming the right to make those decisions herself. This right cannot be fully recognized unless it is determined that there is reason to have confidence in her ability to make such a decision. But in the case of commitment, the claim is only that children should have an impartial decision maker and an advocate. Neither of these claims requires active and competent participation by the minor. Thus, if hearings were provided, a teenager might be directly involved in the presentation of the case, whereas a younger child would not. In each instance, the question would not be whether the child should make the decision about entering the facility but rather whether institutionalization is in the child's best interest (Mason & Gambrill, 1994). And although some may be concerned that the hearings themselves could be countertherapeutic for the minor, there is reason to believe that properly conducted proceedings can be therapeutic by assuring the juvenile that his or her position has received a fair hearing (Tyler, 1992).

Conclusion

The issue of the appropriate procedures for institutionalizing children raises complex and difficult issues. The Supreme Court's attempt to resolve these issues in 1979 has become more controversial with the passage of time. As legislatures and courts revisit the question, they will have to weigh the competing interests within the family and the substantial concern about harm to children from inappropriate placement in residential facilities.

References

Addington v. Texas, 441 U.S. 418 (1979).

American Academy of Child and Adolescent Psychiatry. (1989). *Policy statement on inpatient hospital treatment of children and adolescents.* Washington, DC: Author.

American Association on Mental Retardation (previously named American Association on Mental Deficiency). (1981). *The least restrictive alternative: Principles and practices.* Washington, DC: Author.

American Psychiatric Association. (1982). Guidelines for the psychiatric hospitalization of minors. *American Journal of Psychiatry, 139,* 971–975.

Armstrong, L. (1993). *And they call it help: The psychiatric policing of America's children.* Reading, MA: Addison-Wesley.

Blatt, B. (1987). *The conquest of mental retardation.* Austin, TX: PRO-ED.

Bogdan, R., & Taylor, S. (1982). *Inside out: Two first-person accounts of what it means to be labeled "mentally retarded."* Toronto: University of Toronto.

Bowlby, J. (1973). *Attachment and loss: Vol. 2. Separation.* London: Hogarth Press.

Brakel, S., Parry, J., & Weiner, B. (1985). *The mentally disabled and the law* (3rd ed.). Chicago: American Bar Foundation.

Butts, J., & Schwartz, I. (1991). Access to insurance and length of psychiatric stay among adolescents and young adults discharged from general hospitals. *Journal of Health and Social Policy, 3,* 91–116.

Carey v. Population Services International, 431 U.S. 678 (1977).

Chambers, D. (1972). Alternatives to civil commitment of the mentally ill: Practical guides and constitutional imperatives. *Michigan Law Review, 70,* 1108–1200.

Conroy, J., & Bradley, V. (1985). *The Pennhurst longitudinal study: A report of five years of research and analysis.* Philadelphia: Temple University, Developmental Disabilities Center.

Costello, J., & Worthington, N. (1981). Incarcerating status offenders: Attempting to circumvent the juvenile justice and delinquency prevention act. *Harvard Civil Rights–Civil Liberties Law Review, 16,* 41–81.

Dalton, R., & Forman, M. (1987). Conflict of interest associated with psychiatric hospitalization of children. *American Journal of Orthopsychiatry, 57,* 12–14.

Dalton, R., & Forman, M. (1992). *Psychiatric hospitalization of school-age children.* Washington, DC: American Psychiatric Press.

Eagle, R. (1994). The separation experience of children in long-term care: Theory, research, and implications for practice. *American Journal of Orthopsychiatry, 64,* 421–434.

Edgerton, R. (1967). *The cloak of competence: Stigma in the lives of the mentally retarded.* Berkeley: University of California.

Education for All Handicapped Children Act (1975), Pub. L. 94–142.

Ellis, J. (1974). Volunteering children: Parental commitment of minors to mental institutions. *California Law Review, 62,* 840–914.

Ellis, J. (1992). Decisions by and for people with mental retardation: Balancing considerations of autonomy and protection. *Villanova Law Review, 37,* 1779–1809.

Ellis, J., & Carter, D. (1980). Treating children under the New Mexico Mental Health and Developmental Disabilities Code. *New Mexico Law Review, 10,* 279–309.

Goffman, E. (1963). *Stigma: Notes on the management of spoiled identity.* Englewood Cliffs, NJ: Prentice Hall.

Goldfine, P., Heath, G., Hardesty, V., Berman, H., Gordon, B., & Werks, L. (1985). Alternatives to psychiatric hospitalization for children. *Psychiatric Clinics of North America, 8,* 527–535.

H. L. v. Matheson, 450 U.S. 398 (1981).

Hendren, R., & Berlin, I. (1991). A philosophy of inpatient care. In R. Hendren & I. Berlin (Eds.), *The psychiatric inpatient care of children and adolescents: A multicultural approach* (pp. 3–13). New York: Wiley.

Humphrey v. Cady, 405 U.S. 504 (1972).

Individuals with Disabilities Education Act (1990), Pub. L. 101–476.

J. L. v. Parham, 412 F. Supp. 112 (M.D. Ga. 1976).

Jackson-Beeck, M., Schwartz, I. M., & Rutherford, A. (1987). Trends and issues in juvenile confinement for psychiatric and chemical dependency treatment. *International Journal of Law and Psychiatry, 10,* 153–165.

Jemerin, J. M., & Philips, I. (1988). Changes in inpatient child psychiatry: Consequences and recommendations. *Journal of the American Academy of Child and Adolescent Psychiatry, 27,* 397–403.

Kaysen, S. (1993). *Girl, interrupted.* New York: Turtle Bay Books.

Kirk, S., & Kutchins, H. (1988). Deliberate misdiagnosis in mental health practice. *Social Service Review, 62*, 225–237.

Luckasson, R. (Ed.) (1992). *Mental retardation: Definition, classification, and systems of supports* (9th ed.). Washington, DC: American Association on Mental Retardation.

Mason, M., & Gambrill, E. (1994). *Debating children's lives: Current controversies on children and adolescents.* Newbury Park, CA: Sage.

Mason, M., & Gibbs, J. (1992). Patterns of adolescent psychiatric hospitalization: Implications for social policy. *American Journal of Orthopsychiatry, 62*, 447–457.

Mathews v. Eldridge, 424 U.S. 319 (1976).

Melton, G., Koocher, G., & Saks, M. (Eds.) (1983). *Children's competence to consent.* New York: Plenum.

Mental Health Law Project (1978). Model statute, mental health treatment for minors. *Mental Disability Law Reporter, 2*, 459–481.

Mnookin, R., & Weisberg, D. (1989). *Child, family, and state: Problems and materials on children and the law* (2nd. ed.). Boston: Little, Brown.

Nowak, J., & Rotunda, R. (1991). *Constitutional law* (4th ed.). St. Paul, MN: West.

Parham v. J. R., 442 U.S. 584 (1979).

Perlin, M. (1981). An invitation to the dance: An empirical response to Chief Justice Warren Burger's "Time-Consuming Minuets" theory in *Parham v. J. R. Bulletin of the American Academy of Psychiatry and Law, 9*, 149–164.

Perlin, M. (1994). *Law and mental disability.* Charlottesville, VA: Michie.

Perlmutter, R. (1986). Emergency psychiatry and the family: The decision to admit. *Journal of Marital and Family Therapy, 12*, 153–162.

Perry, G., & Melton, G. (1983–1984). Precedential value of social facts: *Parham* as an example. *Journal of Family Law, 22*, 633–676.

Planned Parenthood of Central Missouri v. Danforth, 428 U.S. 52 (1976).

Prince v. Massachusetts, 321 U.S. 158 (1944).

Reisman, J., & Ribordy, S. (1993). *Principles of psychotherapy with children* (2nd ed.). New York: Lexington.

Rindfleisch, N. (1988). Combating institutional abuse. In C. E. Schaefer & A. J. Swanson (Eds.), *Children in residential care* (pp. 263–283). New York: Van Nostrand Reinhold.

In re Roger S., 569 P.2d 1286 (Calif. 1977).

Sales, B., & Powell, D. (1982). *Disabled persons and the law: State legislative issues* at 409-52 (Right to Developmental Disabilities Services Act). New York: Plenum.

Schmidt, W. (1985). Considerations of social science in a reconsideration of *Parham v. J. R.* and the commitment of children to public mental institutions. *Journal of Psychiatry and Law, 13*, 339–359.

Schmidt, W. C., & Otto, R. (1988). A legal and behavioral science analysis of statutory guidelines for children's mental health and substance abuse services: The Florida case. *Journal of Psychiatry and Law, 16*, 9–65.

Schoenberger, A. (1981). "Voluntary" commitment of mentally ill or retarded children: Child abuse by the Supreme Court. *University of Dayton Law Review, 7*, 1–31.

Schroeder, P. (1992). *The profits of misery: How inpatient psychiatric treatment bilks the system and betrays our trust, Hearings Before the House Select Committee on Children, Youth, and Families*, 102d Congress, 2d Sess., April 28, 1992. (Statement of Rep. Patricia Schroeder, Chairperson)

Schwab-Stone, M. E. (1989). Diagnostic issues: DSM-III and DSM-III-R. In L. K. G. Hsu & M. Hersen (Eds.), *Recent developments in adolescent psychiatry* (pp. 31–49). New York: Wiley.

Scott, E. (1992). Judgment and reasoning in adolescent decisionmaking. *Villanova Law Review, 37*, 1607–1669.

Secretary of Public Welfare v. Institutionalized Juveniles, 442 U.S. 640 (1979).

Shapiro, E., & Carr, A. (1987). Disguised countertransference in institutions. *Psychiatry, 50*, 72–82.

Shelton v. Tucker, 364 U.S. 479 (1960).

Smith, D., & Luckasson, R. (1992). *Introduction to special education: Teaching in an age of challenge.* Boston: Allyn & Bacon.

Stone, D. (1988). The civil commitment process for juveniles: An empirical study. *University of Detroit Law Review, 65*, 679–721.

Stone, L. (1979). Residential treatment. In S. Harrison (Ed.), *Basic handbook of child psychiatry* (Vol. 3, pp. 231–262). New York: Basic Books.

Strully, J., & Strully, C. (1985). Friendship and our children. *Journal of the Association for Persons with Severe Handicaps (JASH), 10,* 224–227.

Teitelbaum, L., & Ellis, J. (1978). The liberty interest of children: Due process rights and their application. *Family Law Quarterly, 12,* 153–202.

Tyler, T. (1992). The psychological consequences of judicial procedures: Implications for civil commitment hearings. *Southern Methodist University Law Review, 46,* 433–445.

U.S. Congress, Office of Technology Assessment (1986). *Children's mental health: Problems and services.* Washington, DC: U.S. Government Printing Office.

Warren, C. (1983). The politics of trouble in an adolescent psychiatric hospital. *Urban Life, 12,* 327–348.

Weithorn, L. (1984). Children's capacities in legal contexts. In N. D. Reppucci (Ed.), *Children, mental health, and the law* (pp. 25–55). Newbury Park, CA: Sage.

Weithorn, L. (1988). Mental hospitalization of troublesome youth: An analysis of skyrocketing admission rates. *Stanford Law Review, 40,* 773–838.

Wilson, J. (1978). *The rights of adolescents in the mental health system.* Lexington, MA: Lexington Books.

Youngberg v. Romeo, 457 U.S. 307 (1982).

Zetlin, A., & Turner, J. (1984). Self-perspectives on being handicapped: Stigma and adjustment. In R. B. Edgerton (Ed.), *Lives in process: Mildly retarded adults in a large city* (pp. 93–120). Washington, DC: American Association on Mental Retardation.

24 ▮ Mental Health Issues in Juvenile Justice

Loren Warboys
Shannan Wilber
Youth Law Center

The Historical Development of the U.S. Juvenile Justice System

The U.S. juvenile justice system is almost entirely a creation of state law. The first juvenile court in the United States was established in Illinois in 1899 (Davis, 1994). Before then, any minor who committed a crime was handled in the adult criminal court. The creation of the juvenile court in the United States coincided with and was an outgrowth of the country's move from an agrarian, rural society toward a largely industrial, urban society. Its creation also reflected the values of the Enlightenment period, which emphasized the importance of social, economic, and other environmental conditions on human behavior and the belief that human behavior could be altered through proper treatment, care, and training (Teitelbaum & Harris, 1977). These changes had a profound impact on attitudes regarding the proper role of government toward families and the needs of children.

Although many institutions devoted to the care and housing of "wayward" or "delinquent" children existed in the 1800s, before the creation of juvenile court systems, it was common practice for any child over the age of 7 found guilty of a crime to suffer the same consequences as an adult, including a public trial, a permanent criminal record, and imprisonment with adult in-

mates.[1] The juvenile court movement that swept the country in the early 1900s was premised on an entirely different philosophy:

> This new court was to emphasize correctional change in the individual child. The source of each young offender's forbidden deeds was to be discovered and eliminated by treatment. Medical attention was to be given to those whose misbehavior resulted from physical ills. Psychological techniques were to be applied to the mentally disturbed. Special training would overcome behavior problems rooted in miseducation. Indeed the juvenile court was often compared to a clinic or school. (Paulsen, 1967, p. 4)

The reform era of the early 20th century resulted in a radical shift in the approach to juvenile offenders. Separate juvenile courts were developed, displacing the goal of punishment with that of rehabilitation. The jurisdiction of the new courts expanded to all children in need of state intervention, rather than just to criminal offenders. The procedure was informal, paternalistic, and nonadversarial, and courts were given broad discretion to address the child's needs. Children accused of committing criminal offenses were given few of the procedural protections available to adults in the criminal justice system (Walkover, 1984).

Because of the focus on rehabilitation and treatment, juvenile proceedings were not considered criminal in nature. Theoretically, there was no attempt to place blame or to mete out punishment. The moral responsibility or blame-

---

[1] In English common law, any child under the age of 7 was considered to be unable to possess the capacity to form the intent to commit a crime (LaFave & Scott, 1986).

worthiness of the child, therefore, was of no consequence.

In the 1960s, the juvenile courts underwent yet another reform effort. Critics asserted that the rehabilitative premise of the juvenile courts had not been actualized. Although the process was informal and discretionary, the consequences of juvenile proceedings were strikingly similar to those of the adult criminal system. Juveniles received the worst of both worlds—arbitrary decisions without procedural protections and harsh punishment. A presidential commission investigating the juvenile court concluded that "informality is often abused . . . fears have also been expressed that the formality that lawyers would bring into juvenile court would defeat the therapeutic aims of the court. But informality has no necessary connection with therapy" (President's Commission on Law Enforcement and the Administration of Justice, 1967, p. 41).

The demise of the *parens patriae* approach was acknowledged in a series of Supreme Court decisions. In *Kent v. United States* (1966), the Court held that juveniles were entitled to be represented by counsel in a full hearing before they could be transferred to criminal court to be tried as adults. *In re Gault* (1967) extended due process protections to juveniles in the adjudicatory stage of juvenile proceedings, including the rights to counsel, notice, confrontation, cross-examination, the privilege against self-incrimination, and the right to an appeal. In *In re Winship* (1970), the Court held that due process required that allegations of juvenile delinquency be proved beyond a reasonable doubt.

These decisions acknowledged that a finding of delinquency imposed a criminal stigma and that the rehabilitative goals of the juvenile justice system did not justify depriving juveniles of due process protections. The reverberations of *Gault* and its progeny were felt in every state. Due process protections were increased, delinquency court jurisdiction was limited to children alleged to have committed criminal-type offenses, and the goals of accountability and punishment were

added to the juvenile justice system's traditional rehabilitative objectives (Walkover, 1984).

The criminalization of delinquency proceedings continues today. Issues of culpability and accountability have made their way back into legal determinations at every stage of the delinquency process. Fueled by public fears and reactions to increasing rates of violent crimes by juveniles, Congress and the state legislatures have spearheaded a crackdown on juvenile offenders. The tone is distinctly punitive, and the prevailing public attitude favors increased penalties and decreased distinction between the treatment of juvenile and adult offenders.

The shifts from rehabilitation to punishment and back again have resulted in confused juvenile courts, unsure of their mission and grappling with inconsistent objectives. Should the focus of juvenile courts be to rehabilitate the child or punish minors who commit crimes? Should juveniles accused of crimes receive the same procedural protections as adults, or should the court act informally, as a parent would, in determining the best way to handle a wayward youth?[2] Virtually all states maintain the notion that the juvenile court should provide treatment and services to youthful offenders. Yet the notions of accountability, deterrence, and protection of the public have become prominent as well.

The Juvenile Justice System Today

Today, every state in the country continues to operate a juvenile court system to handle the problems of youth who commit crimes. However, because each state is free to set the parameters for that system, there are significant operational differences from state to state. Despite these differences, each state juvenile court law includes certain common elements. It is important

---

[2] This debate is most often cast in terms of treatment for the minor versus the protection of society. However, this is misleading, because those who argue for the treatment of the minor as the primary mission of the juvenile court also usually believe that this is the most effective way to ultimately achieve protection for society.

to have a basic understanding of the structure of the juvenile court system as well as some of the ways that practices vary from state to state.

The first key component addressed in every state juvenile court law is the definition of a "juvenile," which consequently determines the juvenile court's jurisdiction. The two decisive factors in making this determination are the age of the accused individual and the nature of the offense the individual is alleged to have committed.

In most states, the age of juvenile court jurisdiction is set at age 18. However, this requirement is not absolute, and a number of states use different age limits.[3] Even if a person falls within the prescribed age limit set by law, the juvenile court may not have jurisdiction over the case because the crime alleged is particularly serious or is of a certain type. Most states have laws that allow for cases involving young persons accused of serious crimes to be transferred from juvenile court to adult criminal court. In addition to handling serious crimes, adult courts in many states also automatically handle all crimes of a certain type—such as traffic offenses and fish and game violations—regardless of the age of the individual involved. The process for making this decision, the list of crimes included, and the age range of juveniles affected varies significantly from state to state.[4]

The decision to transfer jurisdiction of a minor from juvenile court to adult criminal court is extremely important and is discussed in greater detail later in this chapter. The severity of the offense alleged and an assessment of the minor's amenability to treatment and rehabilitation are generally the two most important factors in making this decision.

The basic procedural structure for juvenile court cases is the same in each state, although there are important operational differences. Typically, a juvenile court case includes the following procedural stages: (1) arrest and petition, (2) detention hearing, (3) adjudicatory hearing, and (4) dispositional hearing. Following the arrest of a juvenile, a petition is filed in juvenile court alleging that the minor has committed an offense that would be a crime if the suspect were an adult. Generally, the decision to file a petition against a minor is handled by a local juvenile probation department. The probation officer usually has significant discretion in deciding how to handle the case, ranging from the notification of the parents and release without any formal court action to the filing of a delinquency petition with a recommendation for secure detention.

The juvenile's first court appearance, in many cases, is the detention hearing. This hear-

---

[3] The jurisdiction of juvenile courts varies by both age and conduct. Juvenile court jurisdiction over delinquency (not abuse or neglect cases) ceases at age 17 in Georgia, Illinois, Louisiana, Massachusetts, and South Carolina; and at age 16 in New York, Connecticut, North Carolina, and Vermont. In Vermont, however, juveniles between 16 and 18 may petition the court to waive them back into juvenile court. Juvenile court jurisdiction does not extend to juveniles over 17 years old at all in Texas, Missouri, and Michigan. Illinois extends juvenile court jurisdiction over addicted minors to 21-year-olds (Davis, 1994).

[4] In some states, certain offenses (typically murder, kidnapping, sexual assault, and other serious crimes against the person) are excluded from the jurisdiction of the juvenile court. In Maryland, this includes crimes punishable by death or life imprisonment when committed by a child 14 years of age or older. Other states achieve the same results with mandatory waiver provisions, which typically waive juvenile court jurisdiction over serious crimes against the person, certain repeat offenders, and previously waived juveniles. In North Carolina, for example, juvenile court jurisdiction is automatically waived over a child 14 years or older who is alleged to have committed a Class A felony (Davis, 1994, pp. 2:17–2:18).

In ten jurisdictions, the juvenile and adult criminal courts have concurrent jurisdiction over juveniles of a certain age charged with committing certain offenses; in some of these states, the decision to handle the case in adult or juvenile court is a matter of prosecutorial discretion. Other states achieve essentially the same result by putting jurisdiction in the adult criminal court and granting discretion to transfer the case to juvenile court (Davis, 1994, pp. 2:23–2:24).

Additionally, every state except Nebraska, New Mexico, and New York has discretionary waiver provisions, allowing juvenile court jurisdiction to be waived by the court, the prosecutor, or the minor; these provisions range from states with no restrictions on eligibility for waiver to states with highly specific age requirements, offense requirements, or both (Davis, 1994, pp. 4:1–4:5).

ing is held to determine whether the juvenile should be securely detained pending the handling of the case. Because juveniles do not have a right to release on bail in most states (*Schall v. Martin*, 1984), the judge must determine whether detention of the minor is justified, such as to prevent the minor from committing any further offenses, to safeguard the minor, or to assure that the minor attends future court hearings.

In most cases, the next important court event is the adjudication hearing to determine whether the minor committed the offense.[5] The adjudication hearing in the juvenile court is the equivalent of the trial in an adult criminal case. The standard of proof at this hearing is the same as for adult cases—proof beyond a reasonable doubt (*In re Winship*, 1970). Assuming that the minor is found to have committed the offense, the next court appearance is the disposition hearing to determine what should be done with the juvenile. Many consider this stage to be the essence of the juvenile court process. It is at this stage that the juvenile court, with the advice of the probation department and any experts the prosecution or defense wish to call, must determine what placement or treatment services will provide the best opportunity to rehabilitate the minor and, simultaneously, protect the public.

In comparison to adult criminal court proceedings, the juvenile court process remains relatively informal. Juveniles do not have a right to jury trial in most states (*McKeiver v. Pennsylvania*, 1967); therefore, the juvenile court judge determines guilt and innocence. Most states protect the confidentiality of juvenile court proceedings, although in recent years there has been a tendency to reduce or eliminate this aspect of the juvenile court system.

---

[5] Theoretically, in between the detention hearing and the adjudicatory hearing, just as in an adult criminal court case, there may be any number of hearings on procedural issues or motions to suppress evidence. However, because the time period between arrest and adjudication in juvenile cases is generally short and the proceedings are more informal than adult cases, such procedural hearings are less common.

Interaction of the Juvenile Justice System and Mental Health Professionals

Despite the debate over the mission of the juvenile court, every state juvenile court system recognizes the importance of treatment and intervention to increase the likelihood that a juvenile will become a productive citizen. This offers mental health professionals myriad opportunities to participate in the juvenile court process (Cocozza, 1992).

Prevalence of Mental Health Issues in the Juvenile Justice System

Although delinquent behavior is often characterized as social maladjustment rather than emotional disturbance, a large number of delinquents are diagnosed as having serious emotional disturbances (Murphy, 1986). Estimates of serious emotional disorders in children and adolescents in the general population range from 2% to 7% (Brandenburg, Friedman, & Silver, 1990; National Mental Health Association, 1993). Estimates of emotional disturbances in the delinquent population range from 16% to 50% (Murphy, 1986). One federal court considering a legal challenge to a facility's failure to provide mandated special education services concluded that, nationally, 16.23% of children in correctional facilities suffered from emotional disturbance (*Green v. Johnson*, 1981). Although the figures vary significantly, it is clear that a far greater proportion of children in the juvenile justice system suffer from a serious emotional disturbance than in the general population.

Part of the difficulty in assessing the prevalence of mental health disorders is reaching definitional agreement. If mental health disorders are thought of broadly to include attention deficit disorder (ADD), attention deficit hyperactivity disorder (ADHD), substance abuse and dependence, learning disabilities, mental retardation, anxiety disorders, conduct disorders, and other diagnostic categories, then a very high proportion of children involved in the juvenile justice system present mental health issues (Cocozza, 1992). Additionally, a very high percentage of youth in the juvenile justice system have a history of child abuse, family dysfunctions, and other histories that may warrant mental health intervention.

Defining Mental Illness: A Systems Battle

There is lack of agreement in the law over the definition of juvenile mental illness. As one commentator has noted:

This lack of clarity regarding the definition of mental illness reflects both the theoretical and practical confusion about the overlap of mental illness and delinquency jurisdiction. Delinquency jurisdiction is invoked by a juvenile's actions, yet those same actions may often be seen as part of a larger constellation of mental health problems. There is no theoretical bright line indicating when the conceptualization of mental illness are more or less appropriate than the law's rubric of delinquency. (Cocozza, 1992)

Contributing to the difficulty in reaching any clear legal consensus on such definitions is that how the child's problem is defined will largely determine what service system is responsible for the child. For example, take the case of a child who has been the victim of years of physical abuse at home, who is failing at school, and who is now engaged in aggressive, acting-out behavior. From a systems perspective, this child might be handled in the child welfare system (as abused and neglected), the special education system (as seriously emotionally disturbed), the mental health system (as mentally ill), or the juvenile justice system (as a delinquent). Much of the battle over the proper definition of the child's problem is, in fact, a legal battle over what service system should take legal jurisdiction over the child. Inevitably, that battle involves many factors beyond the determination of how to provide appropriate treatment for the child. These factors

include allocating financial responsibility, making a judgment regarding the continuation of traditional parental rights, and assuring public safety and control of the child. Underlying any such decision is a strong tension in the law between protecting traditional civil rights and liberties and assuring that a child receives needed treatment.

At each stage of the juvenile court process, there are opportunities for the mental health professional to play an extremely important role. The remaining sections of this chapter will examine some of the particular stages of the juvenile court process and discuss in greater detail the opportunities for such involvement. It should not be forgotten in this discussion, however, that one of the most important questions that a mental health professional might be called on to help answer is whether a child's case should be handled by the juvenile justice system at all.

Capacity, Competency, and Culpability

Several legal issues that may be raised in a juvenile delinquency proceeding potentially involve an assessment of the juvenile's cognitive development, mental capacity, or culpability. These include (1) whether the youth validly waived his or her rights and made a voluntary confession or admission, (2) whether the youth is competent to participate in a trial and assist the attorney, (3) whether the youth is capable of distinguishing right from wrong, and (4) whether the youth should be transferred to criminal court to stand trial as an adult.

The treatment of mental health issues in juvenile delinquency proceedings varies considerably and depends largely on the juvenile court's conception of its mission. If the court views its mission as primarily to provide treatment and rehabilitation for children in need, it may consider only the minor's mental status for the purposes of making appropriate dispositional orders. If, on the other hand, the court views delinquency proceedings as criminal in nature with the potential for punitive sanctions, it is more likely to view the minor's mental status as relevant to adjudication concerns as well.

Either view may produce anomalous results. For example, in jurisdictions that do not permit a minor to assert a defense of insanity, an incompetent child with mental disorders can be forced to undergo the trauma and stigma of a trial and may be subject to punitive sanctions. On the other hand, strict compliance with due process may also place a child in jeopardy. For example, a child whose confession is found involuntary and whose case is dismissed may not receive important services that could prevent his or her escalating involvement in the juvenile justice system.

Confessions and Admissions

In *Miranda v. State of Arizona* (1966), the U.S. Supreme Court established procedural safeguards to protect the constitutional rights of an accused to be free from compelled self-incrimination during a custodial interrogation. The Court required that the accused be advised of the right to remain silent; that anything said can be used against him or her in court; and that the accused has the right to have an attorney present during the questioning, the right to have an attorney appointed if he or she cannot afford counsel, and the right to terminate the questioning at any point. Statements obtained during a custodial interrogation must be excluded from evidence unless the state establishes that the accused made a knowing, intelligent, and voluntary waiver of his or her rights.

The Supreme Court has also held that the privilege against self-incrimination and the right to counsel are among the fundamental components of due process that must be extended to juveniles in delinquency proceedings (*In re Gault*, 1967). The Court "has not yet held that *Miranda* applies with full force to exclude evi-

dence obtained in violation of its proscriptions from consideration in juvenile court proceedings (*Fare v. Michael C.*, 1979, p. 717, n.4). Nonetheless, state courts have almost uniformly held that *Miranda* is fully applicable to juvenile proceedings (*Leach v. State*, 1968; *In re William L.*, 1968). A number of states have passed juvenile statutes implementing or elaborating on *Miranda*'s requirements (*Cal. Welf. & Inst. Code* § 627.5).

Courts have also recognized that waivers by juveniles warrant closer scrutiny than do those of adults because juveniles' immaturity and vulnerability make them more susceptible to police coercion (Grisso, 1980). The Court in *In re Gault* (1967) cautioned, "[T]he greatest care must be taken to assure that [a minor's] admission was voluntary, in the sense that it was not coerced or suggested, but also that it was not the product of ignorance of rights or of adolescent fantasy, fright or despair" (p. 55). Several states require the presence of an interested adult before the juvenile's waiver of the right to remain silent is considered valid (*Commonwealth v. Markle*, 1977; *Conn. Gen. Stat. Ann.* § 46b-137(a); *Ind. Code* 31-6-7-3; *In re K.W.B.*, 1973; *N.M. Stat. Ann.* § 32A-2-14(e); Okla. Stat. Ann. tit. 10, § 1109(a)).

The admission into evidence of a minor's confession may be challenged both on the ground that it violates *Miranda*, which is based on the Fifth Amendment privilege against self-incrimination, or on the ground that it violates the due process clause of the Fourteenth Amendment. Although these theories are distinct, they are similar and often confused in the cases.

Under *Miranda*, a confession must be excluded unless the accused waives his or her rights voluntarily, knowingly, and intelligently (*Miranda v. State of Arizona*, 1966, p. 444). In *Fare v. Michael C.* (1979), the Supreme Court instructed courts to consider the totality of the circumstances to determine the voluntariness of a juvenile's waiver, including the juvenile's age, experience, education, background, intelligence, as well as the juvenile's capacity to understand the nature of the warnings, the nature of his rights, and the consequences of waiving those rights.

In *Moran v. Burbine* (1986), the Court explained that the waiver inquiry has two distinct dimensions. First, the waiver must have been

voluntary in the sense that it was the product of free and deliberate choice rather than intimidation, coercion or deception. Second, the waiver must have been made with a full awareness of both the nature of the right being abandoned and the consequences of the decision to abandon it. (p. 421)

For the waiver to have been valid, the totality of the circumstances must establish "both an uncoerced choice and the requisite level of comprehension" (p. 421). Thus, a minor must make the decision freely and must understand the decision he or she makes.

A confession that is the product of police coercion is considered involuntary, and its admission into evidence also violates the due process clause of the Fourteenth Amendment (*Brown v. Mississippi*, 1936; *Haynes v. Washington*, 1963; *Rogers v. Richmond*, 1961). Again, voluntariness is determined by the totality of the circumstances (*Payne v. Arkansas*, 1958). Thus, in an early case, the Supreme Court invalidated a confession given by a 15-year-old boy whom the police held incommunicado and questioned for five hours in the middle of the night (*Haley v. State of Ohio*, 1947). The Court stated:

The age of petitioner, the hours when he was grilled, the duration of his quizzing, the fact that he had no friend or counsel to advise him, the callous attitude of the police towards his rights combine to convince us that this was a confession wrung from a child by means which the law should not sanction. (*Haley v. State of Ohio*, 1947, pp. 600–601, n.41)

In *Colorado v. Connelly* (1986), the Supreme Court seemed to disavow at least the spirit of its earlier precedent. The Court held that, in the absence of coercive police activity, the waiver of a defendant with an active psychosis was volun-

tary and valid under both the Fifth Amendment and the Fourteenth Amendment (*Colorado v. Connelly*, 1986). The *Connelly* Court seemingly abandoned the second prong of the voluntariness test—that the waiver must be knowing and intelligent.

Although it contradicts more recent Supreme Court authority, *Connelly* apparently makes irrelevant any inquiries into a defendant's age or mental capacity to determine the validity of a waiver unless the court first finds that the police's conduct was coercive (*Derrick v. Peterson*, 1990). This approach is particularly problematic for juveniles because of the increased risk that they will waive their rights without understanding the nature of their rights or the consequences of waiver. Research has shown that the majority of juveniles under the age of 15 fail to understand at least one of the standard *Miranda* warnings, and they demonstrate significantly poorer comprehension of the nature and significance of *Miranda* rights (Grisso, 1980).

Furthermore, research has consistently shown a high correlation between delinquency and learning disabilities (Greenburg, 1991). Most youth with learning disabilities suffer from communication disorders that may further compromise their ability to understand *Miranda* rights and to communicate a valid waiver (Greenburg, 1991).

Even youth who have the cognitive capacity to understand the waiver process may be more likely than adults to make an involuntary waiver or confession. Simply by virtue of their immaturity and lack of experience, minors are more vulnerable to the various stresses associated with a custodial interrogation.

Thus, the better view is that expressed in *Fare*—the court should consider the totality of the circumstances in evaluating a juvenile's waiver, including the juvenile's age, experience, education, background, intelligence, and the capacity to understand the nature of the warnings given, the nature of Fifth Amendment rights, and the consequences of waiving those rights (*Fare v. Michael C.*, 1979). When an attorney has any question about a client's cognitive ability to make a valid waiver, the attorney should arrange for the minor to be evaluated by an experienced mental health professional. If appropriate, expert testimony should be offered to challenge admission into evidence of any confessions or admissions made by such a client.

Competency to Stand Trial

As a matter of federal constitutional law, an adult must be competent in order to stand trial for a criminal offense. The test of competency is whether the accused has sufficient present ability to consult with a lawyer with a reasonable degree of rational understanding and whether the accused has a rational as well as a factual understanding of the proceedings against him or her (*Dusky v. United States*, 1960). The purpose of the incompetency doctrine is to protect the fairness and integrity of the judicial process.

Although the Supreme Court has never addressed the issue, several states extend to an accused juvenile the right to assert incompetency in a delinquency proceeding (*Briones v. Juvenile Court of Denver*, 1975; *James H. v. Superior Court*, 1978; *Matter of Two Minor Children*, 1979; *Matter of Welfare of S.W.T.*, 1979; *State v. Kempf*, 1979; *State of Louisiana in the Interest of Pate Causey*, 1978). In some states, the right is provided by statute (*D.C. Code* 1981 § 16-2315; *Fla. R. Juv. P.*, Rule 8.095; *Me. St. T.* 15 § 3318; *Tn. St. R. Juv. P.*, Rule 29; *Tx. Family Code* § 55.04). Other jurisdictions have held as a matter of due process that a juvenile must be permitted to assert incompetency to stand trial (*Dandoy v. Superior Court*, 1980; *In the Interest of T.D.W.*, 1982; *In the Matter of W.A.F.*, 1990).

In jurisdictions that apply the competency doctrine in delinquency cases, the issue may be raised by the juvenile, the state, or the judge. When the issue of competency is raised, the court must decide whether there is sufficient evidence to justify a hearing. If there is, the court appoints a mental health professional to conduct an evaluation and make a recommendation to the court

(Woolard, Gross, Mulvey, & Reppucci, 1992). State laws typically provide that when the court determines that the minor is incompetent to stand trial, the minor is remanded to an inpatient facility for treatment to restore competency (*D.C. Code* 1981 § 16-2315(c); *Fla. R. Juv. P.*, Rule 8.095(a)(3); *Me. St. T.* 15 § 3318(1)(B); *Tn. St. R. Juv. P.*, Rule 29(a)(3)). Most of these states require that the juvenile court initiate civil commitment proceedings.[6]

Despite a general recognition of the right to assert the juvenile's incompetency to stand trial, the cases reveal confusion about the purpose of the doctrine and the circumstances under which a finding of incompetence should be made. Commentators have suggested that courts may apply the incompetency doctrine as an indirect means of gaining access to necessary treatment services (Grisso, 1992; Grisso, Miller, & Sales, 1987). For example, access to inpatient mental health services is limited by strict civil commitment standards requiring a showing of dangerousness (*Cal. Welf. & Inst. Code* § 5585.50). Prosecutors, however, have reported a willingness to stipulate to the juvenile's incompetence to stand trial when the minor needed treatment but did not meet the state's standard for involuntary commitment (Grisso, Miller, & Sales, 1987).

Statutes typically provide little or no guidance on what types of evidence courts should consider in determining whether the juvenile is competent to stand trial. Courts have considered such factors as age, intelligence, school achievement, mental illness, and prior court experience (*Matter of Welfare of S.W.T.*, 1979; *May v. State*, 1981; *State v. Kempf*, 1979; *State of Louisiana in the Interest of Pate Causey*, 1978). However, none

---

[6]The initiation of civil commitment proceedings is apparently intended to further the beneficent, rehabilitative approach to juvenile delinquency. In some states, juveniles who are incompetent to stand trial and who do not meet the standard for involuntary commitment are released (*Tn. St. R. Juv. P.*, Rule 29(a)(3)). In contrast, defendants in the adult criminal system who are found incompetent to stand trial are automatically remanded to state mental hospitals, whether or not they meet the standard for involuntary civil commitment.

of these factors is directly related to ability to assist in one's defense.

The evaluations and recommendations provided by psychiatrists and psychologists appointed to assess minors' competence are equally questionable. The typical evaluation consists of clinical interviews, mental status examinations, and psychological and educational tests. These methods are helpful in diagnosing mental disorders and describing cognitive and personality characteristics of juveniles; however, they reveal little information relevant to a minor's ability to assist in his or her own defense (Grisso, Miller, & Sales, 1987; Nicholson & Kugler, 1991).

Finally, the practice of remanding children who are incompetent to stand trial to inpatient facilities for treatment does not always make sense. A minor who is incompetent to stand trial does not necessarily suffer from a mental disorder justifying inpatient care or civil commitment. Incompetency may stem from mental retardation, learning disabilities, neurological or memory deficits, or simply lack of education and experience. These disorders do not require the type of treatment available in inpatient facilities (Grisso, Miller, & Sales, 1987).

Criminal Responsibility

A fundamental concept of our common law restricts punishment to those who are blameworthy. Traditionally, those who were unable to distinguish between right and wrong—whether by reason of youth or mental incapacity—were relieved of the moral and penal consequences of their criminal acts. Restricting punishment to those capable of forming criminal intent had its roots in concepts of fundamental fairness. It was also consistent with the common sense notion that punishment can deter a person from committing future criminal acts only if that person can distinguish between right and wrong.

The extent to which the concept of criminal responsibility is applicable in juvenile delinquency proceedings is a matter of some controversy. The courts are divided on whether a juvenile in delinquency court may interpose a defense that he or she lacked capacity to appreciate the wrongfulness of his or her conduct. This division of authority is attributable to the shifting philosophies underlying the juvenile justice system.

There was no separate juvenile court at common law. Adults and children alike were bound by the same criminal law, and their offenses were adjudicated in the same courts (Kean, 1937). At the same time, the law acknowledged that children generally are less morally blameworthy because they are less capable of understanding the wrongfulness of their acts. To address this disparity, the common law devised a series of presumptions to distinguish children who were more or less deserving of punishment.

Children under the age of 7 were conclusively presumed to lack criminal capacity and were immune from criminal prosecution; children who had reached the age of 14 were presumed capable of committing crimes. For children between the ages of 7 and 14, the common law created a rebuttable presumption of incapacity. The state had the burden of proving that a child between the ages of 7 and 14 knew the wrongfulness of his or her act (LaFave & Scott, 1986). However, with the creation of special juvenile courts in the 20th century, some courts began to reject application of the infancy defense on the ground that it would deprive children of necessary treatment (*Ex rel. Humphrey*, 1918). This ambiguity is reflected in the cases addressing the application of the infancy defense in juvenile proceedings.

Several courts have upheld the continued applicability of the infancy defense to shield nonculpable children from the consequences of a delinquency adjudication (*In re Andrew M.*, 1977; *In re Devon T.*, 1991; *In re Gladys R.*, 1970; *State v. Q. D.*, 1984; *In re William A.*, 1988). In 1970, the California Supreme Court interpreted a state penal statute to require clear proof that an accused juvenile knew the wrongfulness of his or her conduct at the time he or she allegedly committed the act (*In re Gladys R.*, 1970). Acknowledging the potentially severe consequences of sustaining a delinquency petition, the court stated, "Strong policy reasons cast doubt upon the placement of a child who is unable to appreciate the wrongfulness of his conduct in an institution where he will come into contact with many youths who are well versed in criminality" (*In re Gladys R.*, 1970, p. 680).

The Maryland Court of Appeals also upheld the application of the infancy defense in delinquency proceedings (*In re William A.*, 1988). That court asserted:

Careful review of the recent history of the juvenile court reveals that the juvenile justice system has turned from rehabilitation to principles of accountability in dealing with youthful offenders. In light of this, continued reliance on the rehabilitative ideal to undercut key protections against sanctioning the innocent in the justice process, such as the infancy defense, is intellectually and institutionally problematic. (*In re William A.*, 1988, p. 134)

Nevertheless, many other states persist in the view that the infancy defense has no place in the informal, rehabilitative scheme of juvenile court jurisdiction (*In the Interest of G. T.*, 1990; *M. S. v. State*, 1993; *State v. D. H.*, 1976; *In re Tyvonne*, 1989). The Florida Supreme Court cited the rehabilitative purposes of the juvenile court to justify its holding that the infancy defense was inapplicable (*State v. D. H.*, 1976). The court was concerned that application of the defense could frustrate the court's ability to realize its mission.

Application of the insanity defense in juvenile delinquency proceedings is subject to the same ambiguity. The defense of insanity, like that of infancy, rests on the assumption that someone who is unable to distinguish right from wrong should not be subject to criminal sanctions for his or her conduct. Following well-established Supreme Court precedent, each of the states and the federal government gives an adult accused of a crime the right to assert the defense of insanity (*Davis v. United States*, 1895).

Although the Supreme Court has never addressed the applicability of the insanity defense in juvenile proceedings, several states make the defense available to juvenile offenders (*Matter of Two Minor Children*, 1979; *People v. Superior Court for Humboldt County*, 1979; *State v. In re R.G.W.*, 1975, 1976; *State of Louisiana in the Interest of Pate Causey*, 1978; *In re Winburn*, 1966). At least one court, however, held that a juvenile has no right to interpose an insanity defense (*In re C.W.M.*, 1979). That court's rationale is reminiscent of those cases rejecting application of the infancy defense—the concept of criminal responsibility had no place in juvenile proceedings because an adjudication of delinquency would result not in the imposition of penal consequences but in rehabilitation and treatment (*In re C.W.M.*, 1979, p. 622). Accordingly, the court found that considering the juvenile's mental status at the time of disposition was adequate to ensure appropriate treatment.

Views on this subject may also be influenced by the practical consequences of permitting or rejecting interposition of the infancy or insanity defenses. In jurisdictions that apply the infancy defense, the court must dismiss the case if it is determined that the defense applies. Once the court loses jurisdiction over the minor, it has no authority to order mental health or other services that the child may need.

Some jurisdictions solve this problem at the intake level by diverting the child from the juvenile court system and referring him or her for informal supervision through the probation department. This alternative may also facilitate access to necessary services without the necessity of filing a delinquency petition.

When a delinquency petition has been filed and is denied by reason of the minor's insanity, the court typically refers the child for civil commitment proceedings or outpatient treatment (*Cal. Welf. & Inst. Code* § 702.3). Particularly when the offense was violent or otherwise egregious, there may be significant public pressure to exact punishment or retribution. This conflict is another illustration of the tension between treatment and punishment.

Waiver of Juvenile Court Jurisdiction

Under certain circumstances, minors charged with committing delinquent offenses may be prosecuted in adult criminal court rather than in juvenile court. This practice is referred to as "waiver" of juvenile court jurisdiction or "transfer" of jurisdiction from the juvenile court to the criminal court. In response to the increase in serious and violent crimes by juveniles, the trend is to increase the number of cases in which juvenile court jurisdiction is waived.

The transfer of a matter from juvenile court to criminal court is "critically important" and has significant consequences for the alleged offender (*Kent v. United States*, 1966, p. 556). Although the accused juvenile is entitled to all the due process protections reserved for adult criminal defendants, the minor is also subject to the same social stigma and range of punishment—including incarceration in adult correctional facilities in some states. The minor loses the advantages of the juvenile court system, including confidentiality, access to treatment and other services, and a limitation on the number of years of incarceration.

Every state, the District of Columbia, and the federal courts provide for waiver of juvenile court jurisdiction, but the methods of waiver vary. Some states limit juvenile court jurisdiction, either by setting an age at which jurisdiction ceases or by excluding certain offenses from juvenile court jurisdiction. For example, jurisdiction of juveniles over 16 years of age rests with the adult criminal court in Connecticut, New York, North Carolina, and Vermont (*Conn. Gen. Stat. Ann.* § 46b-120 (Supp. 1993); *N.C. Gen. Stat.* § 7A-517(1), (12), (13), (20), (21), (28), (1989); *N.Y. Fam. Ct. Act* §§ 301.2(1), 712(a) (McKinney 1983); *Vt. Stat. Ann.* tit. 33, § 5502(a)(1) (1991)).

In some states, certain enumerated offenses—usually serious crimes against the person—are always prosecuted in adult criminal court. In several jurisdictions, juvenile and adult criminal courts have concurrent jurisdiction over juveniles over a certain age who are charged with committing certain serious offenses. Often the prosecutor has discretion to determine the court in which the case will be filed.

Finally, most states permit discretionary waiver if certain criteria are met. In *Kent v. United States*, the Supreme Court approved certain criteria for discretionary waiver determinations. Many states have adopted similar formulations in their statutes. The criteria approved in *Kent* are:

1. The seriousness of the alleged offense to the community and whether the protection of the community requires waiver.
2. Whether the alleged offense was committed in an aggressive, violent, premeditated or willful manner.
3. Whether the alleged offense was against persons or against property, greater weight being given to offenses against persons especially if personal injury resulted.
4. The prosecutive merit of the complaint, i.e., whether there is evidence upon which a Grand Jury may be expected to return an indictment. . . .
5. The desirability of trial and disposition of the entire offense in one court when the juvenile's associates in the alleged offense are adults who will be charged with a crime in [adult criminal court].
6. The sophistication and maturity of the juvenile as determined by consideration of his home, environmental situation, emotional attitude and pattern of living.
7. The record and previous history of the juvenile, including previous contacts with [the juvenile justice system].
8. The prospects for adequate protection of the public and the likelihood of reasonable rehabilitation of the juvenile . . . by the use of procedures, services and facilities currently available to the juvenile court. (*Kent v. United States*, 1966, pp. 566–567)

Most state statutes do not specify the mental status of minors as a criterion to consider in the waiver determination. Some states, however, statutorily preclude a transfer of jurisdiction to criminal court when the minor suffers from mental illness or mental retardation (*Code of Ala.* § 12-15-34); *OCGA* § 15-11-39(a)(3)(c); *NDCC* § 27-20-34(b)(4)(c); *42 Pa. C.S.* § 6355(4)(B); *Va.*

Code § 16.1-269(A)(3)(c)). Although the rationale for these statutes is not explicit, one court reasoned that the minor's mental condition is relevant to the question of criminal culpability (*Anderson v. Commonwealth*, 1992). Minors with mental health problems are viewed as less culpable and more appropriately served in the juvenile justice system.

Even in the absence of statutory prescription, courts may consider the minor's mental status as part of the waiver determination. It is common, for example, for courts to appoint a mental health professional to evaluate the minor's amenability to rehabilitation. The expert's report often includes information about the minor's emotional, mental, and intellectual functioning. Not surprisingly, experts often find that the offenders suffer from mental illness, emotional disturbance, or learning disabilities. There is no consensus in the courts, however, about whether a minor's mental illness or need for mental health treatment should mitigate in favor or against retaining juvenile court jurisdiction.

In *In re Burns* (1978), in which the minor was implicated in an armed robbery and murder, an Illinois trial court denied the prosecution's motion to transfer the case to criminal court. The ruling was upheld on appeal, partly on the ground that the minor was in need of mental health treatment. The Illinois statute required the trial court to consider factors similar to those set forth in *Kent* (*Ill. Rev. Stat.* 1975, Ch. 37, par. 702-7(3)(a)). The court found that there was enough evidence for a grand jury to return an indictment on both offenses but noted that the "defendant's history was indisputably one of neglect, deprivation, emotional impoverishment and chaos" (*In re Burns*, 1978, p. 26). The court seemed to be most influenced, however, by the reports of an appointed psychologist and of an appointed psychiatrist, both of whom noted the child's serious mental health problems and her urgent need for psychiatric care.

Noting the trial court's obligation to determine whether retention in the juvenile system was in the child's best interests, the appellate court asserted that "determination of the minor's best interests could not possibly exclude consideration of the minor's mental health and the minor's need for and amenability to psychiatric treatment" (*In re Burns*, 1978, p. 28). The appellate court held that the record supported the trial court's determination; the evidence showed that retaining jurisdiction in the juvenile court could provide the minor with urgently needed psychiatric care, whereas there was no evidence that such care would be available in the adult system (*In re Burns*, 1978).

In contrast to the *Burns* opinion, the Kansas Supreme Court in *In re Ferris* (1977) upheld the trial court's transfer of jurisdiction to adult criminal court in a case in which the minor was found to suffer from acute organic brain syndrome as a result of his long-standing drug and alcohol addiction (*In re Ferris*, 1977). In *Ferris*, the minor was charged with shooting two police officers who had apprehended him for a traffic violation. Although handcuffed, the minor was able to obtain one of the officer's guns and discharge it several times.

Once again, the Kansas state statute required that the trial court consider factors similar to those approved in *Kent* (K.S.A. 1976 Supp. 38-808(b)). The minor appealed the trial court's determination on several grounds, including an argument that his mental illness required that the juvenile court retain jurisdiction. The Supreme Court held "[t]he juvenile court is not required to retain jurisdiction because of the alleged mental illness of the juvenile. A juvenile alleged to be psychotic or seriously mentally ill can raise the defense of insanity at his trial as an adult" (*In re Ferris*, 1977).

Taking yet another approach, other courts have upheld transfer determinations on the ground that the minor needed extended mental health care that was unavailable in the juvenile system. In *State v. Bickell* (1992), the Iowa Court of Appeals upheld the trial court's transfer of jurisdiction and its determination that the minor was not amenable to rehabilitation. Although the minor had no previous contact with the juvenile court, the court found that he was not amenable to rehabilitation because of "the limited rehabilitative alternatives available to the juvenile court, evidence showing [the minor's] need for professional psychological treatment, and the short period of time during which rehabilitation could occur" (*State v. Bickell*, 1992).

In a similar case, the Supreme Court of Georgia upheld the transfer of a case in which a 13-year-old was charged with murdering his 9-year-old brother (*In re J.N.B.*, 1993). The state sought waiver of juvenile court jurisdiction on the ground that the minor was not amenable to rehabilitation. The trial court relied on the testimony of experts who predicted that the minor would repeat his violent behavior unless he received intensive therapy lasting 4 to 5 years and that there was no intensive psychiatric treatment available in a secure facility in the state juvenile system for longer than 18 months. The Supreme Court found "there were reasonable grounds for the court to conclude that [the minor] could not receive appropriate treatment in a secure facility for the necessary length of time in the juvenile system" (*In re J.N.B.*, 1993, p. 203).

There is some indication, in both statutes and case law, that minors who suffer from serious mental health problems are considered less culpable and more deserving of the special solicitude of the juvenile system. However, as a practical matter, it appears that availability of appropriate mental health services dictates the waiver determination more often than not. Thus, young offenders who are amenable to treatment may be transferred to criminal court simply because the juvenile court does not have the resources to provide appropriate treatment.

Relegating impressionable minors with mental illness to the adult correctional system is both unjust and irrational (Forst & Blomquist, 1991). There is no indication that the adult system is any better equipped to provide specialized mental health treatment than the juvenile system is. Indeed, as a general rule, the state is obligated to provide more rehabilitation and programming to incarcerated youth than to adults; courts have held that, because juvenile court proceedings do not include the procedural safeguards that are available to adults, due process requires that the incarceration of juveniles be for the purpose of rehabilitation (*Gary W. v. State of Louisiana*, 1976; *Morgan v. Sproat*, 1977). The decision to waive juvenile court jurisdiction under these circumstances amounts to punishing the minor for the state's failure to implement the mission of the juvenile justice system.

Disposition and the Decision Regarding Placement and Services

The dispositional hearing is the formal stage for determining what should be done to and for the child. At the time of disposition, the child has already been determined to have committed the offense or offenses alleged in the petition and is, therefore, a delinquent youth. At disposition, the court must attempt to determine which placement and services will provide the best opportunity for rehabilitating the minor while safeguarding the public. This dual mission of the juvenile court comes into greatest conflict at this stage.

Except regarding those minors transferred to adult criminal court, virtually every state's juvenile code officially excludes "punishment" from the list of permissible sanctions that a juvenile court may consider (*Swansey v. Elrod*, 1975). An adjudication of delinquency is not considered a criminal conviction (*Cal. Welf. & Inst. Code* § 203). In fact, if a state did decide to add criminal justice punishment to the list of permissible sanctions, that state would be obligated to provide juveniles with the same constitutional safeguards that criminal defendants receive, such as jury trial and bail.

However, the preclusion of official punishment does not mean, in practice, that juveniles receive no punishment. As many observers of the juvenile justice system have noted:

> Commitment to a state "training" school often means a long period of confinement in a large, impersonal institution where the offender's contact with the community is restricted. . . . In state institutions, detention centers, and jails, children may be shut off from family and friends, subjected to filthy living conditions, denied necessary medical and psychological services, and subjected to long periods of isolation or even corporal punishment in the name of "discipline" or "institutional security." (Youth Law Center, 1981–1982, pp. 732–733)

Although the adult criminal system has moved largely to determinate sentencing, most juvenile court dispositions remain indeterminate in length. The rationale for this decision is that the juvenile court is attempting to rehabilitate the child, and it is impossible to predict precisely how long this will take. Therefore, in most states, a juvenile court disposition lasts indefinitely up to the point that the minor reaches the age of majority (usually 21) or some other age (25 in some states). As a consequence, many minors in the juvenile justice system spend more time incarcerated than do adults convicted of the same offense.

The range of dispositional options available to the juvenile court is theoretically unlimited. At one extreme, the court may allow the child to return home with a warning. At the other extreme, the child may be incarcerated in a state institution for many years. Between the two extremes, the court can place the child on probation with any number of conditions limiting the child's behavior and mandating participation in treatment and rehabilitation activities. These conditions might include mental health counseling, participation in substance abuse or victims' awareness programs, or any other activity the judge considers appropriate. The judge may also order that the child provide restitution to the victim of the crime. If the judge believes that it is inappropriate to return the child home, the court may fashion a remedy that places the child in another relative's home, a foster home, a group home, a county or state facility, a wilderness program, a private treatment center, or another residential program.

Of course, inadequate resources create a real limitation on the options of the juvenile court. Probation departments throughout the country are chronically underfunded, which substantially limits the placement options and the resources available to assess a child's needs. All too often, the availability of services, rather than a child's needs, dictates the dispositional decision. In addition, many public juvenile facilities are seriously overcrowded and provide grossly inadequate education and treatment services to minors confined to their care (Abt Associates, 1993).

A Juvenile's Right to Treatment Services: The Legal Mandate

Whether or not juveniles have a constitutional right to affirmative treatment remains an open question. The Supreme Court has never addressed the subject, and decisions from lower courts are divided on the issue (Soler et al., 1994). However, federal and state courts have determined that when a juvenile is involuntarily confined to a state or local institution, the juvenile is entitled to basic care and minimally adequate services and training so that the minor does not suffer any harm while in state custody. This elemental care includes basic education, mental health care, and medical care.

For example, in 1972, the U.S. District Court in Rhode Island held in *Inmates of Boys' Training School v. Affleck* that minors confined in juvenile detention are entitled to receive regular psychiatric or psychological counseling. The final order in *Affleck* required mental health screening within 24 hours of admission, examination by a psychiatrist within 48 hours if deemed necessary after initial interview, and ongoing access to a psychiatrist. Following *Affleck*, a number of other courts also concluded that certain mental health services must be provided to confined juveniles.

Other services that have been required by court order or consent decree include (1) individual and group therapy; (2) self-esteem programs, such as art, music, dance, and movement therapy; (3) drug and educational counseling (*Jerry M. v. District of Columbia*, 1986); (4) sufficient hiring of professional mental health staff and training for nonprofessional staff in mental health issues (*Gary H. v. Hegstrom*, 1984); (5) hiring of a full-time doctorate-level psychologist or psychiatrist (*Morgan v. Sproat*, 1977); (6) individual assessment and treatment planning that includes analysis of the child's history, educational abilities, psychiatric and psychological examinations and testing, and community evaluation (*Morales v. Turman*, 1974); (7) reasonable access to a psychiatrist for consultation and crisis intervention; (8) immediate hospital treatment following a suicide attempt unless immediately examined by a psychiatrist who waives the need for hospitalization in writing; (9) psychologist or psychiatrist involvement in a long-range treatment plan after a 20-day stay (*Martarella v. Kelley*, 1973); (10) provision for occasional neurological exams (*Benitez v. Collazo*); and (11) separate housing units providing 24-hour supervision for detainees with mental health problems (*Ahrens v. Thomas*, 1977).

The courts have also entered orders prohibiting certain control techniques or forms of aversive therapy. In *Nelson v. Heyne* (1974), the court prohibited use of tranquilizing drugs without medical prescription and required guidelines on how the drugs were to be administered to prevent dangerous side effects. Examples of similar court orders include (1) routine monitoring of the effects of psychoactive medication, (2) monthly review of the child's drug regimen by the attending physician, (3) prohibition against placing a child alone in a locked room, and (4) prohibitions on use of restraints except in situations where all other alternatives have failed and the child is endangering himself or herself or others (*Gary W. v. State of Louisiana*, 1976).

In addition to court decisions regarding the constitutional rights of confined juveniles, federal and state special education laws also provide enforceable mandates. The Individuals with Disabilities Education Act (IDEA) applies with equal force to eligible youths in state or local custody, including youths in the juvenile justice system (20 U.S.C. § 1412(6)). The IDEA applies to any youth with an educational disability, such as a serious emotional disturbance, attention deficit disorder, mental retardation, or a learning disability (20 U.S.C. § 1401(1), (15); 34 C.F.R. § 300.7). The IDEA mandates that all eligible youths receive a full assessment of their needs and a free appropriate education, including related services, such as psychological counselling (34 C.F.R. § 300.4).

In addition to court rulings on these issues, standards issued by professional groups, such as the Joint Commission on Accreditation of Healthcare Organizations and the National Commission on Correctional Health Care, also outline minimal standards of care regarding the rights of minors to mental health services (Joint Commission on Accreditation of Healthcare Organizations, 1993; National Commission on Correctional Health Care, 1992). Most professional standards regarding juvenile facilities contain similar mandates (American Correctional Association, 1991; Child Welfare League of America, 1982; National Advisory Committee for Juvenile Justice and Delinquency Prevention, 1980).

Juvenile Justice Treatment Models: Current Trends

Despite the serious limitations on the juvenile court system, there are a number of highly innovative and successful juvenile treatment programs (Lerner, 1990). Evaluations of these programs, as contrasted with traditional institutional confinement, report success measured by a number of key indicators, including reductions in recidivism rates and subsequent institutionalization (Nelson & Pearson, 1991). One of the most promising and encouraging trends is the development of cross-systems treatment approaches. These programs are premised on the belief that the involvement of a child in the juvenile justice system, rather than in the child welfare or mental health systems, is often fortuitous and that comprehensive, integrated services to troubled youths facilitates a smoother transition out of the juvenile justice system and begins to address some of the root causes of both delinquency and recidivism. Moreover, a juvenile justice system connected to the greater social services system through functional information systems and coordinated case management can begin to meet the goal of serving the whole child and his or her family. In most of these programs, the target population is youths with serious emotional problems, and the juvenile justice system is one of the agencies responsible for both identifying youths in need of services and participating in assuring the delivery of needed services.

For example, the Ventura Model in Ventura, California, is a community-based, interagency system of mental health care that targets children with mental health problems at high risk of separation from their family and possible incarceration within the juvenile justice system. Since its inception in 1984, the target population has been expanded somewhat to include youths receiving intensive public services, such as juvenile court wards. Children must have a DSM-III-R Axis I or II diagnosis plus some combination of risk indicators. The juvenile court and corrections services agencies participate in the interagency network, along with representatives from special education, social services, mental health, law enforcement, and private agencies. Within the juvenile justice subsystem, juvenile probation, detention, court, and dispositional placements are responsible for assuring that children receive screening and assessment, case management, crisis intervention, and coordinated services. Participation of private service providers is also an important component of the system (Nelson & Pearson, 1991).

A conceptually similar program operating at the statewide level is the Willie M. program in North Carolina. Named for the lawsuit *Willie M.*

v. Hunt (1983), which spurred its creation, this program targets children with serious mental health problems who have demonstrated aggressive, acting-out behavior and are at risk of institutionalization in the mental health or juvenile justice system. The program, which operates out of the state Division of Mental Health, uses a screening and assessment system to identify youths eligible for the program and then uses targeted case management to deliver largely community-based services to these children. The program has been in operation since the early 1980s and has resulted in a complete restructuring of mental health and related services for the target population; it has also had a measurable impact in reducing time and commitments to juvenile justice institutions (Dicker, 1990).

Conclusion

Unfortunately, these examples of innovative integrated services programs are still rare exceptions. Although the trend in favor of coordinated services to youths and families has made significant headway in child welfare and mental health systems, juvenile facilities, for the most part, continue to operate in isolation. As a consequence, fewer mental health, health, and educational services are available to confined youth, meaning that many children in the juvenile justice system today are simply "warehoused" for the duration of their confinement.

References

20 U.S.C. § 1401(1), (15).
20 U.S.C. § 1412(6).
34 C.F.R. § 300.4.

34 C.F.R. § 300.7.

42 Pa. C.S. § 6355(4)(B).

Abt Associates. (1993). *Conditions of confinement*. Washington, DC: Office of Juvenile Justice and Delinquency Prevention.

Ahrens v. Thomas, 434 F. Supp. 873 (W.D. Mo. 1977).

American Correctional Association. (1991). *Standards for juvenile training schools*. Laurel, MD: Author.

Anderson v. Commonwealth, 421 S.E.2d 900 (Va. 1992).

In re Andrew M., 398 N.Y.S.2d 824 (1977).

Benitez v. Collazo (Civ. No. 77-662, 77-1170)(Stipulated Agreement).

Brandenburg, N. A., Friedman, R. M., & Silver, S. E. (1990). The epidemiology of childhood psychiatric disorders: Recent prevalence findings and methodological issues. *Journal of the American Academy of Child and Adolescent Psychiatry, 29*, 76–83.

Briones v. Juvenile Court of Denver, 534 P.2d 624 (Colo. 1975).

Brown v. Mississippi, 297 U.S. 278 (1936).

In re Burns, 385 N.E.2d 22 (Ill.App. 1978).

In re C. W. M., 407 A.2d 617 (D.C. App. 1979).

Cal. Welf. & Inst. Code § 203.

Cal. Welf. & Inst. Code § 702.3.

Cal. Welf. & Inst. Code § 5585.50.

Child Welfare League of America. (1982). *Standards for residential centers for children*. New York: Author.

Cocozza, J. J. (Ed.). (1992). *Responding to the mental health needs of youth in the juvenile justice system*. Seattle, WA: National Coalition for the Mentally Ill in the Criminal Justice System.

Code of Ala. § 12-15-34.

Colorado v. Connelly, 479 U.S. 157 (1986).

Commonwealth v. Markle, 380 A.2d 346 (Pa. 1977).

Conn. Gen. Stat. Ann. § 46b-120 (Supp. 1993).

Conn. Gen. Stat. Ann. § 46b-137(a).

D.C. Code 1981 § 16-2315.

Dandoy v. Superior Court, 619 P.2d 12 (Ariz. 1980).

Davis, S. (1994). *Rights of juveniles: The juvenile justice system*. New York: Clark Boardman.

Davis v. United States, 160 U.S. 469 (1895).

Derrick v. Peterson, 924 F.2d 813 (9th Cir. 1990).

In re Devon T., 584 A.2d 1287 (Md. App. 1991).

Dicker, S. (Ed.). (1990). *Stepping stones: Successful advocacy for children*. New York: The Foundation for Child Development.

Dusky v. United States, 362 U.S. 402 (1960).

Fare v. Michael C., 442 U.S. 707 (1979).

In re Ferris, 563 P.2d 1046 (Kan. 1977).

Fla. R. Juv. P. Rule 8.095.

Forst, M., & Blomquist, M. (1991). Cracking down on juveniles: The changing ideology of youth corrections. *Notre Dame Journal of Law, Ethics, and Policy, 5*, 323–375.

Gary H. v. Hegstrom (No. 77-1039-BU)(D.Or. Dec. 17, 1984).

Gary W. v. State of Louisiana, 437 F. Supp. 1209 (E.D. La. 1976).

In re Gault, 387 U.S. 1 (1967).

In re Gladys R., 83 Cal. Rptr. 671 (1970).

Green v. Johnson, 513 F. Supp. 965 (D. Mass. 1981).

Greenburg, S. A. (1991). Learning disabled juveniles and Miranda rights: What constitutes voluntary, knowing, and intelligent waiver. *Golden Gate University Law Review, 21*, 487–524.

Grisso, T. (1980). Juveniles' capacities to waive Miranda rights: An empirical analysis. *California Law Review, 68*, 1134–1166.

Grisso, T. (1992). Five-year research update (1986–1990): Evaluations for competence to stand trial. *Behavioral Sciences and the Law, 10*, 353–369.

Grisso, T., Miller, M. O., & Sales, B. (1987). Competency to stand trial in juvenile court. *International Journal of Law and Psychiatry, 10*, 1–20.

Haley v. State of Ohio, 332 U.S. 596 (1947).

Haynes v. Washington, 373 U.S. 503 (1963).

Ex rel. Humphrey, 201 S.W. 771 (Tenn. 1918).

Ill. Rev. Stat. 1975, Ch. 37, par. 702-7(3)(a).

Inmates of Boys' Training School v. Affleck, 346 F. Supp. 1354 (1972).

In the Interest of G. T., 597 A.2d 638 (1990).

In the Interest of T.D.W. 441 N.E.2d 155 (Ill. App. 1982).

Ind. Code 31-6-7-3.

In re J. N. B., 436 S.E.2d 202 (Ga. 1993).

James H. v. Superior Court, 77 Cal.App.3d 169 (1978).

Jerry M. v. District of Columbia (C.A. No. 1519-85)(Superior Ct. of D.C., July 10, 1986)(consent decree).

Joint Commission on Accreditation of Healthcare Organizations. (1993). *Accreditation manual for mental health, chemical dependency, and mental retardation/developmental disabilities services* (Vol. 1). Oakbrook Terrace, IL: Author.

K.S.A. 1976 Supp. 38-808(b).

In re K.W.B., 500 S.W.2d 275 (Mo. Ct. App. 1973).

Kean, A.W.G. (1937). The history of the criminal liability of children. *Law Quarterly Review, 53,* 364–370.

Kent v. United States, 383 U.S. 541 (1966).

LaFave, W. R., & Scott, A. (1986). *Criminal law* (2nd ed.). St. Paul, MN: West.

Leach v. State, 428 S.W.2d 817 (Tex. Civ. App. 1968).

Lerner, S. (1990). *The good news about juvenile justice.* Bolinas, CA: Common Knowledge Press.

M. S. v. State, 625 So.2d 1187 (Ala. Cr. App. 1993).

Martarella v. Kelley, 359 F. Supp. 478 (S.D.N.Y. 1973).

Matter of Two Minor Children, 592 P.2d 166 (Nev. 1979).

Matter of W.A.F., 573 A.2d 1264 (D.C. App. 1990).

Matter of Welfare of S.W.T., 277 N.W.2d 507 (Minn. 1979).

May v. State, 398 So.2d (1981).

McKeiver v. Pennsylvania, 387 U.S. 1 (1967).

Me. St. T. 15 § 3318.

Miranda v. State of Arizona, 384 U.S. 436 (1966).

Morales v. Turman, 383 F. Supp. 53 (E.D. Tex. 1974). (rev'd on other grounds).

Moran v. Burbine, 475 U.S. 412 (1986).

Morgan v. Sproat, 432 F. Supp. 1130 (S.D. Miss. 1977).

Murphy, D. M. (1986). Prevalence of handicapping conditions among juvenile delinquents. *Remedial and Special Education, 7*(3), 7–17.

N.C. Gen. Stat. § 7A-517(1), (12), (13), (20), (21), (28) (1989).

NDCC § 27-20-34(b)(4)(c).

N.M. Stat. Ann. § 32A-2-14(e).

N.Y. Fam. Ct. Act §§ 301.2(1), 712(a) (McKinney 1983).

National Advisory Committee for Juvenile Justice and Delinquency Prevention. (1980). *Standards for the administration of juvenile justice.* Washington, DC: U.S. Government Printing Office.

National Commission on Correctional Health Care. (1992). *Standards for health services in juvenile detention and confinement facilities.* Chicago: Author.

National Mental Health Association. (1993). *All systems failure.* Alexandria, VA: Author.

Nelson v. Heyne, 491 F.2d 357 (7th Cir.), cert. denied, 417 U.S. 987 (1974).

Nelson, C. M., & Pearson, C. A. (1991). *Integrating services for children and youth with emotional and behavioral disorders.* Reston, VA: Council for Exceptional Children.

Nicholson, R., & Kugler, K. (1991). Competent and incompetent criminal defendants: A quantitative review of comparative research. *Psychological Bulletin, 109,* 355–370.

OCGA § 15-11-39(a)(3)(c).

Okla. Stat. Ann. tit. 10, § 1109(a).

Paulsen, M. G. (1967). Children's court: Gateway or last resort? *Columbia University Forum, 10,* 4.

Payne v. Arkansas, 356 U.S. 560 (1958).

People v. Superior Court for Humboldt County, 157 Cal. Rptr. 157 (Cal.App. 1979).

President's Commission on Law Enforcement and the Administration of Justice. (1967). *The challenge of crime in a free society.* Washington, DC: U.S. Government Printing Office.

Rogers v. Richmond, 365 U.S. 534 (1961).

Schall v. Martin, 467 U.S. 253 (1984).

Soler, M., Shotton, A., Bell, J., Jameson, E., Shauffer, C., & Warboys, L. (1994). *Representing the child client*. New York: Matthew Bender.

State v. Bickell, 493 N.W.2d 100 (1992).

State v. D. H., 340 So.2d 1163 (Fla. 1976).

State v. Kempf, 282 N.W.2d 704 (Iowa 1979).

State v. Q. D., 685 P.2d 557 (Wash. 1984).

State v. In re R.G.W., 342 A.2d 869 (N.J. App. 1975), aff'd, 358 A.2d 473 (N.J. 1976).

State of Louisiana in the Interest of Pate Causey, 363 So.2d 472 (La. 1978).

Swansey v. Elrod, 386 F. Supp. 1138 (N.D. Ill. 1975).

Teitelbaum, L., & Harris, L. (1977). Some historical perspectives on governmental regulation of children and parents. In L. Teitelbaum & A. R. Gough (Eds.), *Beyond control: Status offenders in the juvenile court* (pp. 1–44). Albuquerque, NM: Teitelbaum.

Thompson, E. (1991). Children in need of mental health treatment: A judge's view of revised public law and new private law proceedings. *Tulsa Law Journal, 26*, 347–404.

Tn. St. R. Juv. P. Rule 29.

Tn. St. R. Juv. P., Rule 29(a)(3).

Tx. Family Code § 55.04.

In re Tyvonne, 558 A.2d 151 (Conn. 1989).

Va. Code § 16.1-269(A)(3)(c).

Vt. Stat. Ann. tit. 33, § 5502(a)(1) (1991).

Walkover, A. (1984). The infancy defense in the new juvenile court. *UCLA Law Review, 31*, 503–562.

In re William A., 548 A.2d 130 (Md. 1988).

In re William L., 287 N.Y.S.2d 218 (1968).

Willie M. v. Hunt, 564 F. Supp. 363 (W.D. N.C. 1983).

In re Winburn, 145 N.W.2d 178 (Wis. 1966).

In re Winship, 397 U.S. 358 (1970).

Woolard, J., Gross, S., Mulvey, E., & Reppucci, N. (1992). Legal issues affecting mentally disordered youth in the juvenile justice system. In J. J. Cocozza (Ed.), *Responding to the mental health needs of youth in the juvenile justice system* (pp. 89–106). Seattle, WA: National Coalition for the Mentally Ill in the Criminal Justice System.

Youth Law Center. (1981–1982). The rights of children in the United States. *Columbia Human Rights Law Review, 13*, 675–743.

25 | Child Custody Decision Making and the Politics of Child Advocacy

Martha Albertson Fineman
Columbia University

In this chapter, I explore the development of the concepts still used to promote reforms in custody decision making, focusing on the construction and promotion of the idealized notion of "child advocacy" and its complementary assertion that mediation is superior to adjudication. It is common when discussing the current system of custody decision making to position oneself on the side of the child. In this chapter, however, I do not do so. Advocates for children typically deplore the adversary system, are critical of lawyers and judges, are disdainful of the rules of court proceedings, and generally see little value and much potential for harm to children in adjudication. I reject this attitude as a wholesale criticism. A great deal of academic and professional energy has been expended in recent years arguing for alternatives to the legal system for divorce cases, particularly in regard to the custody component. This chapter reflects more faith in the legal process.

The rhetoric of child advocacy and mediation took hold and blossomed in the medium of larger ideological struggles over the content of divorce rules. Changes were precipitated by the movement to "no-fault" divorce, which allowed the termination of a marriage at the insistence of one spouse, who did not have to specify any reasons other than that there were "irreconcilable differences." These reforms have been generated and facilitated by a sense of crisis provoked by

the perception that the family is an institution in a state of transition. Advocates of various reforms assert that the stresses of modern life, particularly the high divorce rate, change the family. Singled out for particular concern have been the children, anointed as the "victims" of the dislocations in the modern family (Felner & Farber, 1980; Mumma, 1984; Woody, 1978).

In this chapter, I will consider the factors that set the stage for the development of the concept of child advocacy as well as its early implementation. I will also examine two assumptions underlying the concept of independent child advocacy. The first assumption is that the child should be considered as separate from the parent. The second is that it is possible to define children's interests independently when these interests are conceptually separated and set apart from those of their parents.

The emphasis on child advocacy has increased the power and influence of members of the helping professions in custody decision making (Girdner, 1986). At the same time, a consensus has developed about the fairness and general desirability of "shared parenting." The implementation of independent child advocacy and the growing preference for mandatory mediation greatly increase the bargaining power of fathers in the divorce process and are of questionable benefit to children.

Furthermore, the institutionalization and professionalization of the concept of child advocacy have operated to justify regulating custody decisions at divorce in favor of increasing men's control over their children's and thus their ex-wives' lives. Proposals for reforms in this area also reflect competing perceptions of large segments of the legal and nonlegal professional communities about the functioning of families and individuals within families, the implications of divorce, and the appropriate role of the legal system in the creation and imposition of social norms (Benedek & Benedek, 1979; Fineman, 1988; Neely, 1984; Schulman & Pitt, 1982; Weitzman, 1985).

Although there is no longer serious consideration of the idea that the law should prohibit or make it difficult to divorce, the state will continue to dictate and monitor the terms of the dissolution and the structuring of postdivorce relationships.

The Rhetorical Context

Characterizing children as innocent victims in need of protection was typical of professional reformers' rhetoric at the beginning of this age of no-fault divorce. In fact, there seems to have been a strong underlying antidivorce aspect to much of this early reformist rhetoric, as well as to the proposed reforms.

The societal preference for traditional nuclear families is manifested in a variety of ways, including in rules that seek to preserve as much as possible the predivorce authority and continuing relationships between fathers and their children. To that end, although divorce is now easier to obtain and women's economic position has improved, the state's supervision of the termination process and imposition of substantive standards regulating the postdivorce mother-child unit has greatly increased (Fineman, 1988). All this is accomplished through advocacy for children.

Concern for the Child in Custody Debates

In the formal sense, the child advocate is the official legal actor charged with protecting the interests of the divorce-victimized child. Child advocates seek to position themselves beyond criticism. They claim a morally and, therefore, politically superior stance. Asserting that one's professional (or political) position is designed to advocate for children has become the rhetorical price of entry into the debate over custody policy. Of course, virtually everyone who addresses the issues that arise in divorce begins with meaningless assertions that his or her position is the one that incorporates and represents the concerns and interests of children. The child advocacy rhetoric obscures what is in large part a struggle among professional groups (that is, lawyers and mental health professionals), special interest groups (fathers' rights advocates), and legal actors over who controls the substantive standards and the process and practice of child custody decision making (judges and lawyers) (Fogelson, 1970; Herrman, McKenry, & Weber, 1979).

The fact that so many different groups use the same language of interest and advocacy to advance such radically different conclusions about ideal reforms indicates that there are profound problems with the very articulation of the concept. What, for example, are the generic child's interests to be represented? How is interest determined? By whom? Using what methods?

Mental health professionals have successfully made substantial inroads into legal decision making in this area (Girdner, 1986; Okpaku, 1976). These professionals have become accepted as experts in individual cases, as well as sources of social science information on which broad legislative standards, such as mandatory joint custody, are proposed (see Scherrer, 1976; Weil, 1982). The rhetoric of these professionals is appropriated and successfully utilized by interest groups, such as practicing mediators or fathers' rights advocates.

The control over decisions concerning the custody of children has increasingly been viewed as appropriately removed from parents and placed within the public or political sphere. This state involvement and control may occur at the macro level, as in the wholesale imposition of norms such as a presumption of joint custody, or at the micro level, as in state control over individual custody disputes by mandating the use of mediation or court-controlled experts. This shift in the perception concerning the locus of legitimate custody decision making is evident in a variety of transformations in the way the issue is discussed and understood.

Proponents of both forms justify the state involvement by asserting a need for independent advocacy for children. Increasingly, the mere presence of children at divorce, whether there is conflict over their custody or not, is viewed as mandating state involvement and control of the decision-making process to ensure that the decisions made are in the best interest of the child. Children are viewed as needing state intervention because they cannot advocate for themselves (Mumma, 1984). Because of their perceived separateness and vulnerability, children are thought to require legal protection against their parents. Thus "freed," children—or, more accurately, the idealized concept of children—present not only a problem but an opportunity for intervention by the legal system and the professional actors who cluster around it. Unencumbered by the barrier created by the presumption that mothers, unless unfit, should care for children or that parents in general protect children's best interests, the solution of child advocacy beckons seductively on a policy level. At the same time, it both symbolically and practically bestows significant influence and power on child advocates within the system.

Because, under the present conceptualization of children's position at divorce, parents cannot be trusted to act in their children's interests, advocacy ultimately becomes the state's responsibility. Coincidentally, this conceptualization fosters fierce competition among groups who

publicly assert that they seek the improvement of children's position within the legal system.

Ironically, the potent idea of an independent advocate for children in divorce actions can be traced to a series of articles that constituted a campaign by certain judges. These judges sought to provide protection for children from the adversary model (Drinan, 1962; Elkin, 1982; Hansen, 1966) and presented child advocacy as the integration of legal and social science skills (Hansen, 1964; Stone, 1982).

It is not surprising, given its legal origins, that the justification for child advocacy is set forth in the form of a "right" attached to the child. The right is based on the "recognition that children involved in a divorce are always disadvantaged parties and that the law must take affirmative steps to protect their welfare," including the appointment of a *guardian ad litem* to protect their interests (Hansen, 1964, p. 184). The first right articulated in an early Family Court "Bill of Rights for Children in Divorce Actions" established that the child is "to be treated as an interested and affected person and not as a pawn, possession or chattel of either or both parents" (Hansen, 1966, p. 184; see also *Ex parte Devine*, 1981). Note that the implication is that children have a need for and right to protection from their parents. This protection is to be implemented through a legally appointed advocate. The Family Court Bill of Rights ensures the child's right to this advocacy. The state must respond and, therefore, intervention is not only desirable but inevitable.

This legal advocacy model reflects unquestioned social science assertions that children are being used as "pawns" or are viewed as "property" by their parents. This theme was strongly presented in the influential work of Wallerstein and Kelly (1979), who stated that

[p]sychologically, an individual's rage against an ex-spouse, often expressed in litigation in which the child is the pawn, can apparently remain undiminished by the passage of time or by distance. The fight for a child may serve profound psychological needs in a parent,

including the warding off of severe depression and other forms of pathological disorganization. (p. 472)

In the "Best Interest" of the Child

Perhaps the judicial suggestion of a legally implemented child advocate position was an inevitable product of the unease generated by the widespread acceptance of no-fault divorce and by the breakdown of the best-interest-of-the-child test, the specific substantive standard used for most of this century in making custody determinations on a case-by-case basis. Determining the "best interest of the child" has theoretically involved a comparative balancing of the strengths and weaknesses of the parents. Factors such as health, wealth, education, and moral conduct have all been considered relevant by legislators and judges (Areen, 1985a). The test as fashioned is indeterminate and easily manipulated by parents, judges, and lawyers, however. Furthermore, because it is based on factual determinations that appellate courts traditionally defer to trial courts, appellate review and supervision over this trial court discretion are rare (on the breakdown of the best-interest test, see Chambers, 1984; Folberg & Graham, 1979; Mnookin, 1975). Furthermore, the best-interest test became unworkable when the old facilitation shortcuts, such as a maternal custodial preference for children of "tender years" (typically under age 7), which were used to implement it, were attacked as unacceptable standards for custody decision making.

When tests are very fact-specific, the trial judge has wide latitude in concluding which parent will act in the child's best interest. Parties are encouraged to litigate by the unpredictability of such tests. Indeterminacy increases the costs and the perception of unfairness in the system. Judges responded by developing rules of thumb to assist in making custody determinations. The preference for maternal custody embodied in the "tender years" doctrine was one such rule. In addition, the determination of fault provided a way for the traditional legal process to resolve

custody issues. Adulterers, spouse beaters, and others whom the court found at fault lost custody of their children. With such "flourishes," the best-interest test was able to resolve the vast bulk of custody cases; attorneys and parties could predict results and most cases were settled without resort to adjudication.

However, the emphasis on gender neutrality, a result of feminist agitation during the early 1960s, called into question the desirability of the presumption that children belonged with their mothers unless the mothers were unfit. Gender considerations as a way to make custody decisions began to fade from favor and were even attacked as unconstitutional in some states. This change occurred at the same time that no-fault thinking began to replace the traditional idea that, to "win" a divorce, a spouse had to show that he or she was "innocent" and his or her partner was "at fault."

As gender and fault disappeared from the process, it became apparent that the best-interest test had worked partly because these other references had served to resolve most cases. Increasingly, judges and attorneys who had to employ the best-interest-of-the-child test as thus degendered and free from fault began to view the test as unworkable (Chambers, 1984; Fineman, 1991). Unadorned, the best-interest test is so fact- and circumstance-specific that it defies any articulation of universal standards, thus encouraging litigation and promoting controversy. As a result, the search began for more predictable and progressive sources of decision making.

Understandably, courts welcomed the idea of an independent child advocate. With gendered decision making no longer permissible and no other societal norm emerging as the replacement for the preference for maternal custody, courts searched for efficient ways to make individual custody decisions.

The articulation of the substantive test has remained the best interest of the child. The best-interest test has tremendous symbolic appeal because it rhetorically focuses on the child. Continued adherence to the best-interest test has led judges, uncomfortable with the lack of specificity in the test, to resort to the "helping professions" as assessors of what constitutes a specific child's best interest.

The presence of a child advocate allows the system to continue to function unaltered. The advocate, considered a "neutral" addition to the process, is designated the task of ensuring that the child's interest is not sacrificed to the parents' anger or adversary zeal. Child advocacy presents a procedural solution that allows courts to conclude complacently that the child's interest is in fact brought to light and protected. Relying on nonjudicial decision makers to apply the best-interest standard, however, merely masks the severe problems with the substantive test. Utilization of these decision makers does not solve the problems and, in fact, allows the best-interest test to remain functional long after it should have been discarded.

The Focus of Advocacy

For advocacy purposes, the significance of the continued use of the best-interest test, post–maternal preference and postfault, is found in its theoretical separation of the child from the family. When the maternal preference was viable, the child was conceptually aligned with the mother and, absent compelling evidence, courts presumed that she acted in her child's interest (for discussions of the "tender years" doctrine, see Olsen, 1984; Zainaldin, 1979). The designation of the "innocent," not-at-fault spouse could be viewed as functioning in the same way—as a custody decision-making device. Removing these "easy" indicators meant we had to focus on the child as an independent individual with interests that might differ from those of both his or her parents. It is this development that clearly created the need for an advocate for the child as distinct from those who represent the parents or family.

The child is now viewed as a free-floating entity who is the focus of the custody proceeding. As in all assertions of rights in the United States,

with its constitutional tradition, the language used in advancing arguments for child advocacy is symbolically powerful and compelling. This is particularly true because the term *child* is highly sentimentalized in our culture.

The acceptance of children as victims is the ideological basis on which the arguments for increased state involvement have been constructed. A battery of experts presumed to act in the best interest of children is added to the process. The result is that both the questions and the solutions concerning any individual child are developed *independently of parental decisions or initiative*. The description and characterization of the problems facing the child, the important judgments to be made, and the solutions to be suggested are all in the hands of the professionals. The rationale for this delegation is that the parents, experiencing divorce, can no longer be trusted to act in the child's interest.

To child advocacy proponents, the fact that the parents are enmeshed in an adversarial contest alone is sufficient to render parents incapable of acting in their child's best interest. And if a child's future cannot be entrusted to his or her parents, a child advocate is essential. Parents are assumed to be concerned only with their own self-serving ends (for assertions to that effect, see Rosenberg, Kleinman, & Brantley, 1982).

Questions about the Child Advocacy Paradigm

Two critical problems lurk within the idea of child advocacy that should be explored. The first problem is with the creation and acceptance of the child as an independent client separable from his or her parent and in need of advocacy services at divorce. Even if the need for such advocacy were clear, however, a second problem exists concerning the process of articulating and defining the child's best interest. The very fact that the client is also a child raises questions about the feasibility of accomplishing this task of representation.

The Creation of the Child-Client

When one takes a historical look at the academic literature that underlies the notion of an advocate for children in divorce cases, one is struck by the fact that neither the arguments for nor the arguments against the institution have changed much over the past several decades. Essentially, the proponents of child advocacy assert that children need representation (Berdon, 1976), that they are victimized by divorce, and that the traditional adversarial process does not protect them and may even further victimize them. Little conceptual development has occurred beyond these assertions.

In addition, no consensus has emerged about the functions that a child advocate should perform or even who should serve as the advocate (Solender, 1976). Thus, child advocacy is an ideal that continues to be ill-defined.

We should ask two questions. The first is whether it is accurate or helpful to cast children as victims of divorce. The second question to consider is, even if children are victimized by divorce, does this necessitate the establishment of separate, independent legal advocacy? The first question should give rise to additional ones. For example, if it is true that divorcing parents are so typically self-absorbed as to use their children as "pawns," is it not appropriate that child advocates should be required in all divorces when there are children? After all, pawns are not sacrificed only in litigated cases; they are equally at risk in negotiated or uncontested cases.

Further, and most important, if a large number of parents have the tendency to sacrifice their children's well-being in this way, shouldn't we conclude that many people are unfit parents, unable to separate out their own needs and to act in their children's best interest? Could they ever be trusted to do so? Can a parent who views his or her children as "property" or treats them as "pawns" be expected to convert and be non-exploitive with the granting of a divorce decree and custody award?

Stating such alarming implications of the victim rhetoric makes it apparent that we must question the assumptions underlying the originating conclusion that parents involved in the vast majority of custody cases become temporarily incapable of acting in both their own and their children's interests. The unadorned assertions of wanton parental self-absorption and blatant sacrifice of children's interests made by critics of the judicial system are unsatisfactory, regardless of the degree of professional assurance or force with which they are made.

The second question about the ability of child advocacy to remedy victimization also raises additional considerations focused on what ideological or structural purposes such advocacy actually serves. The typical characterization of the problem places a lot of faith in professionals' and the legal system's divorce and custody decision making.

The net result of the uncritical acceptance of the child-as-victim construct is state-sponsored substitution of informal, nonlegal professional decision making for that of parents or of the courts. Clearly social workers have an enormous amount of power over the decision-making processes involved in divorce as they take control of the task of "restructuring" the family:

> [J]ust as the relationship between married spouses is a critical determination of family interaction, so, too, is the relationship between divorced spouses critical to divorced family reorganization and interaction.... The [stressful] process of coparental redefinition requires that divorced spouses separate their spousal and parental roles, terminating the former while redefining the latter. This very difficult and somewhat paradoxical process forms the nucleus of divorce family reorganization and redefinition. (Ahrons, 1981)

The significant input into the postdivorce decision-making process is no longer through parents but through professionals, inaccurately designated as "neutral" or "disinterested" and legitimated by the notion that they alone are capable of acting in the best interest of children. Furthermore, the locus for the decision making is no longer the judge but these same professionals (Podell, 1973, pp. 109–110). It is far from clear that this development is necessary to benefit children, or even desirable.

The Special Dilemma of Legal Advocacy

We have noted, then, that the terms of the substantive legal test for custody have created a climate in which we easily accept the conclusion that there is a necessity for child advocacy. A related question is how the child's best interest is to be ascertained. When the child is perceived as separate or independent—a client in need of separate counsel—there must be some way to assess what the content or goal of the representation should be. How does the child's advocate in the divorce proceeding determine what is in the child's best interest and act to defend that interest?

Advocate members of the helping professions assume that they possess the skills to make the best interest determination. Normally, however, these professionals are not advocates within the context of particular cases but are viewed as expert, neutral witnesses. Thus, professional assessments are considered evidence to assist in the determination of best interest, yet an actor is necessary to perform the advocacy role in the adversary context—to represent the child. In most instances, this advocate is a lawyer. Professionals associated with custody disputes believe that representation is the only way to protect the child(ren) of a divorce: "The most important single safeguard which could be utilized to assure the psychological best interest of the child, in a custody action, would be to provide counsel to represent him" (Watson, 1969, p. 66; see also Berdon, 1976; Genden, 1976; Girdner, 1986; Inker & Peretta, 1971; Isaacs, 1963; Podell, 1973).

The presence of an attorney as the child advocate creates problems that transcend (and complicate) the problems associated with the involvement of mental health professionals who perform custody evaluations. This is particularly true because of role confusion between these professions, coupled with uncertainty as to who and what is represented.

The Advocates

A significant component of the modern, degendered, regulatory, and highly interventionist view of divorce is the notion that the state's historic interest in protecting children establishes a legitimate avenue for the exercise of state control of parenting behavior through judgments at divorce. This judgment process depends on designating additional professional personnel for intervention into families.

If judges need to make decisions based on considerations of what is in the best interest of the child but feel unprepared to do so, they must look elsewhere for answers. For the most part, they have looked to members of the "helping professions . . . but legal specialists acting in the child's interest have also been employed" (Girdner, 1986, p. 171). It is not surprising that because the conceptual separation of the child occurs in the context of a divorce proceeding, "which is *always* a legal proceeding," child advocacy has become increasingly understood as a requirement for legal representation in divorce proceedings. The best-interest-of-the-child test, therefore, is a substantive rule that, to be appropriately implemented, must create a "client"— the child—for the legal advocate. At the same time, formalizing the idea of child advocacy allows the best-interest test to remain the substantive standard. Thus, the procedural innovation of child advocacy masks the best-interest-of-the-child test's inadequacies in a world in which social norms such as maternal custody may not be acceptable professionally or politically and, therefore, cannot be determinative legally.

Even if one accepts the idea of a need for independent child advocacy, a critical problem is connected to the perceived need for legal representation or an adversarial "champion" (Guggenheim, 1984; Shepherd, 1974). Once we establish a need, we must consider the problem of the independent child advocate's appropriate function. This creates a dilemma because the role of advocate depends on the acceptance of and belief in the child-client as a potential victim of his or her parents. If this is a true characterization, the parents cannot be trusted to provide objective or neutral information about the child and his or her interests. All information from the parents is suspect (Genden, 1976). Thus, ascertaining the child's interests involves the advocate in constructing the child's best interest—that which is to be represented or advocated in the divorce proceeding. The significant question is, How is this interest created independent of parental input?

The modern conceptualization of the child advocacy process has eliminated parents as sources of the best-interest determination, and the desire for gender neutrality has made suspect social and informal empirical observations about mothers and nurturing. We are therefore left with three potential sources of the best-interest determination. First, and easiest to dispose of, is the suggestion that the legal advocate ask the child which parent he or she prefers and then advocate whatever result the child indicates. This is roughly how an attorney should act in representing a competent adult client. However, the children's-choice approach is not considered a viable option, at least for children under the age of 14 or 15. Many children are unable or unwilling to express a preference between competing potential custodial parents. Moreover, some research indicates that it even may be harmful for older, competent children to choose between parents at divorce (Areen, 1985a).

The vast majority of legal child advocates do not adhere to such a narrow view of their responsibility. They do not conceptualize their role as being an advocate for the *child* per se but for the *child's best interest*. This is a distinction of considerable importance. In this approach, instead of merely representing the child's preference, the child's legal advocate must assess or evaluate what is in the child's best interest, independent of (though he or she may consider) the child's wishes.

The Advocate and Ascertaining Best Interest

How can the legal advocate make an evaluation of what is in a child's best interest? In practical terms, the requirement of independent advocacy means that there are two nonparental contenders for primary determiners of the best interest of the child at divorce. There is a need not only for the advocacy but also for the construction or creation of that which is urged as in the child's interest. The societal signals indicating that in most instances this would lead to a maternal preference are to be excluded by the demands of gender neutrality. Structurally, we are then presented with a choice between the two types of professionals who hover around the divorce process—the legal advocate and the helping professional.

The legal professional may make the decision, acting first as both an investigator and a collector of information and thereafter as an informed expert who has examined the evidence and reached a conclusion as to what is in the best interest of the child. This choice makes it necessary for the legal advocate to investigate, to collect information from both experts and nonexperts about the child and family, and to make a judgment about what should be the appropriate placement. Thus, the legal advocate acts in this regard as an investigator and as an expert within the legal process. The role of advocate is one with substantive dimensions.

Not only has a client been created for the legal advocate, but the characteristics of that client necessitate that one primary function of the legal advocate is to construct this client's interest in a manner that, to a large extent, is independent of the client's direction. In this instance, when the legal advocate is making an independent assessment of the quality of evidence accumulated, he or she is no better equipped than a judge to make such an assessment and would seem, for that reason alone, to be unnecessary to the process. The legal advocate's role may be more limited by the increasing value placed on the use of various mental health professionals in the divorce context. These helping professionals (psychological, psychiatric, or social work) will explicitly serve as the arbiters of the child's best interest. In this process, the legal advocate will act as nothing more than the advocate of expert helping professionals' opinions as to what is in the child's best interest. Thus, in effect, the mental health professional becomes the *substituted* client, one who speaks for the constructed child-client and is the vehicle through which the child's best interest is realized.

Increasingly, experts' conclusions in this area have centered on imposing the ideal of shared parenting after divorce (Fineman, 1991). In a gender-neutral world perceived to require the devaluation of nurturing, these experts have undertaken the task of bringing fathers back into the postdivorce picture (Abarbanel, 1979; Bowman & Ahrons, 1985; Greif, 1979). This has resulted in the creation of professional norms that would give custody to the "most generous parent," or the parent most willing to share the child with the other parent (*California Civil Code*, 1988; Child Custody Act of 1970, 1987; *Maine Rev. Statutes Annotated*, 1988; Uniform Dissolution of Marriage Act (CO), 1988). A desire for sole custody has been labeled "pathological" and is to be discouraged or punished by legal rules that mandate postdivorce cooperation and sharing (Fineman, 1991). The child advocate is thus part of a larger process whereby professional norms such as these are incorporated and made operative within the context of the legal system. The child advocate ends up representing the professional ideal.

Function of the Independent Advocate in Practical Terms

There is an important additional problem with the concept of a legal advocate as a child's *independent* advocate. It is not clear why one needs a legal advocate to interpret and assess expert and other information and reach a conclusion as to the child's best interest. Is this not what a judge would do? What does an attorney for the child add in this process? In some instances, perhaps, witnesses not called by a parent might be produced or an expert employed who was not consulted by either parent or scheduled by court personnel. One wonders how often such a positive contribution by the legal advocate occurs, however, and whether the information placed before the judge in such cases is typically dispositive or merely cumulative.

Furthermore, there are real dangers with accepting the child advocacy model. When the legal advocate represents the helping professional's opinion as to the child's best interest, the presence of an attorney designated as the child's advocate may give added and undue weight to professional advice that should be only one factor in fashioning a judge's opinion. This may result in the social worker's or psychologist's functionally being the ultimate custody decision maker.

A primary issue in the current construction of the various roles in custody decision making should be whether the legal advocate can be independent of the mental health professional. A powerful combination emerges when social worker and child's attorney agree, for whatever reason. In addition, the judge's role may be compromised. The presence of the child's legal advocate may present an easy out for the judge by providing an additional referent—another "neutral" actor who is cast as representing only the child's interest and who, for that reason, creates the illusion that his or her conclusions can be safely trusted. Furthermore, as the advocate of best interest, the legal advocate will inevitably be in the position of merely parroting the current theories of mental health professionals.

The Failures of Legal Institutions

State courts and legislatures are two legal institutions that have been instrumental in developing the idea of an independent advocacy function for children's interests at divorce. These two institutions make legal decisions in different ways and with different constraints, all of which have an impact on the institutions' respective abilities to address custody issues in a coherent manner. Courts, for example, are traditionally considered inappropriate to formulate major policy directives because they resolve disputes between individuals. The courts define and resolve custody questions in individual cases by focusing on the rights or obligations of the individual members, and the current best-interest-of-the-child test encourages such a focus.

In contrast to courts, legislatures are capable of performing as broad policymaking bodies. However, these bodies are susceptible to political pressures and the creation of simplistic, universally imposed, idealized norms. This susceptibility has been demonstrated throughout the entire spectrum of divorce reform, from marital property rules to the preference for joint custody. Legislatures have been particularly responsive to the equality rhetoric of fathers' rights groups in reference to divorce. Equality as a model for decision making has symbolic as well as political appeal. In the case of child advocacy, many state legislatures now require separate representation for children when custody is contested, and a few have proposed that such advocacy be provided whenever a divorce involves children, even if there is no contest over custody.

Complicating the problems inherent in view-ing legislatures or courts as rational policymaking and decision-making institutions is the fact that doctrinal family law during the past several decades has rejected the idea that the family has rights associated with it as a unit or as an entity. The thrust of law concerning the family currently reflects an adherence to the notion that the family is nothing more than a collection of individuals, each with specific and potentially conflicting rights. Therefore, the real unit of modern concern for family law and policy and the legal institutions that implement them is the individual. Laws focus on single issues isolated from other circumstances to "help" specific family members. In fact, family law has begun to reflect an assumption that the family may be harmful to an individual's (economic, emotional, and physical) health.

To minimize the evils inherent in divorce, the law focuses on and identifies the rights of the individuals. When the individual is a child, the situation mandates the use of state authority to intervene in a "protective" manner (Counts & Sacks, 1985; Herrman et al., 1979; Mumma, 1984). Children as one set of individuals with rights and interests separate from and potentially conflicting with those of their parents need an "advocate," and the state is the logical supplier of persons to fill that role.

Political and Policy Implications of Child Advocacy

As stated earlier, the crux of the problem is that the substantive standard of best interest of the child is so amorphous, undirected, incomprehensible, and indeterminate as to be meaningless without a substantial extrajudicial implementation team. The only response to a degendered, no-fault divorce system—short of scrapping the best-interest-of-the-child test—is to create alternative decision makers and refer all substantive decisions to them. There are problems with this response, no matter which professional is the source of the best-interest determination. However, as discussed earlier, the problems for a legal advocate are extreme.

The legal advocate functions to give the illusion of neutrality to the decision-making process. The illusion allows the system to limp along without serious reassessment of the political and practical roles played by mental health professionals and others who seek to define the best interests of children through processes and standards that enhance the position and power of their own professions. Custody decision making and the rules that govern it involve more than just making individual decisions regarding placement of children. Submerged in the rules and processes are political and ideological conflicts between "mothers" (or nurturing and caretaking values) and "fathers" (or independence and financial security values); between the legal profession (or advocacy and adversariness as values) and the helping professions (or treatment and therapy as values); between the moralists (who would impede or discourage divorce and punish those who seek to divorce; see Kleinfeld, 1970) and the secularists (who would seek to implement rules ensuring that individuals did not lose too much if they decided to end their marriage; see Fineman, 1983; Neely, 1984). The illusion and pretense of objectivity and neutrality, of which the legal advocate is but one part, serve the interests of those empowered by the status quo and the bias in professional opinion making.

This increased state regulation of the postdivorce family has occurred against the backdrop of significant social and legal developments that characterized the establishment of and the response to the women's movement in the United States. During the 1970s, there were successful attempts in most states to make laws gender neutral (Fineman, 1983, 1991). Such changes were particularly significant in family law, in which gendered rules had been the norm. Feminists concerned with law reform considered the push for degendered rules a symbolic imperative even when they recognized that such reforms might actually result in removing an arguable advantage for women, as in the case of maternal preference rules for deciding custody cases (Fineman & Opie, 1987; Zainaldin, 1979).

By rejecting the dominant ideology that defined a woman's role as that of mother and wife and by arguing for a more equitable redistribution of parental responsibilities, feminists hoped to break down the barriers that excluded them from the market and to make parenthood more of a joint effort than it had been traditionally. However, the studies indicate that this has not in fact occurred to any great degree (Fuchs, 1986). Mothers still perform not only the vast bulk of child care but also the majority of housework. In addition, women in far greater proportions than men seem to plan their careers to accommodate child care responsibilities, illustrating that a combination of mothering and professional career is desirable for them (Chambers, 1984; Fuchs, 1986; "Project," 1982).

In addition, the women's movement's push for equality in the family and workplace generated various backlashes. For example, amid rhetoric that labeled delinquent fathers as "deadbeats," state and federal governments passed economic reforms concerning property divisions at divorce and enacted stringent state and federal provisions for collecting past-due child support. These reforms spurred the formation of fathers' rights groups (Polikoff, 1982; Raschick, 1985; Shiffman, 1985). These groups appropriated and successfully employed the feminist rhetoric of equality and gender neutrality to force reforms in family law, such as mandatory joint custody, that were not particularly beneficial to women and children.

The feminist rhetoric of gender neutrality was particularly susceptible to being employed against women and children by fathers' rights groups as they attacked the notion of motherhood as distinct from parenthood (Everett, 1984). The fathers' rights groups also argued for the child's "right" to access to both parents and the right of the noncustodial father to be equally involved in postdivorce decisions concerning the child (Everett, 1984). Much of the rhetoric of these groups concerns the importance of fathers in the postdivorce family (Chambers, 1984; Lamb & Sagi, 1983).

Various professionals involved in the divorce process, who viewed the traditional rules as imbalanced in favor of women, fueled the success of fathers' rights groups. These professionals built on the images of excluded (but worthy and caring) fathers to fashion a professional standard of "shared parenting" after divorce. This new norm was to be implemented via the mediation skills of these same professionals. The shared parenting discourse entails an uncritical acceptance of the empirical notion that the contributions of women and men to parenting are exchangeable (Abarbanel, 1979; see Fineman & Opie, 1987).

It is interesting to note how much more successfully the equality model has been adopted and implemented in the context of family law than with respect to more general laws (Fineman, 1995). As equality and the concurrent concept of gender neutrality have been incorporated into divorce decision making, the old, tested gendered rules that permitted predictable, inexpensive decisions to be made without protracted litigation have been set aside. One problem confronting the newly, formally degendered family law system is the need to create new gender-neutral factors or processes to handle the cases. The need for an authoritative articulation of alternative standards has set the stage for political and ideological battles.

One consequence of the power and persuasiveness of the attack on gendered decision making that should be of particular concern to those who identify with the plight of children at divorce is the devaluation of nurturing as a basis for decision making. Changes in divorce practice have had more profound impacts than merely making the legislatures' or judges' tasks more

difficult. The obsession with gender neutrality has affected the articulation of what substantively constitutes the best interest of the child and of what safeguards are considered necessary to achieve it.

In fact, it seems that the force of the gender-neutral logic has extended beyond attacking explicitly gendered rules to attacking those that operate merely to produce results that tend to favor one gender over the other. For example, rules that focus on the performance of nurturing or caretaking tasks as the basis for preferencing parents have been attacked, not because they are explicitly gender biased but because in operation they will favor women who traditionally perform such tasks. Nurturing as a decisional measure, even though it is not inherently gendered and is potentially a choice for both men and women, is thus devalued. David Chambers (1984) provides a good example of the effect of such neutrality when he writes:

[I]t is not at all clear, even in the context of a traditional marriage, that the primary caretaker *should* be considered to have "earned" the child any more than the other parent. The other parent, usually today the father, has typically supported the family by working in the labor force. His earnings paid for the food the mother cooked and the clothes she washed. If the primary caretaker "deserves" the child because of her contributions as childraiser, then the other parent "deserves" to keep all stock and other assets held in his name, because they were acquired from his labors. (p. 477)

An expanded and uncritically accepted version of neutrality favors fathers. Labeling tasks gendered removes the things women tend to stereotypically do for children, which are grouped under the term *nurture*. Neutrality in the context of an active and operating gendered system of lived social roles is antimaternal and is hardly gender neutral in its impact.

What is even more problematic, however, is that often the search is not only for language but for *factors* that are gender neutral. This unfortunate and misguided position can be seen in the position of Judith Areen, an influential family law casebook author, who, in the teachers' manual that accompanies the second edition of her *Cases and Materials on Family Law* (1985b), concluded that the nurturing parent or primary caretaker determination should not be adopted:

On balance, I find the primary caretaker approach . . . objectionable because it does not look first to the needs of the children, and because it is at the same time unnecessarily hostile to men because more gender neutral reforms (i.e. economic reforms) could be adopted to offset inequities in bargaining power. . . . I believe a more appropriate way to offset financial disadvantage is by direct modification of statutes governing child support, alimony and division of property, not by a presumption that is not gender neutral in impact. (p. 124)

Areen thus dismisses caretaking, elevates the concern for fathers, and naively minimizes the harmful economic consequences of a divorce system that refuses to acknowledge material disadvantages associated with custodial parenting by assuming that both spouses are equal in opportunities and circumstances.

It is interesting to note that this devaluing of the nurturing role undermines the rhetoric of the transformative prospects inherent in changing custody policy. That is, moving away from gender bias while simultaneously devaluing nurturing considerably diminishes the likelihood that men will assume more responsibility for child care.

Even if the ultimate goal is gender neutrality, imposing rules that embody such a view within the context of family law issues is disingenuous because the effect is to the detriment of those who have constructed their lives around "genderized" roles. In this regard, one risks significant emotional as well as economic costs under reformed divorce laws. For example, shifting custody policy means the threat of potential loss of children for many mothers at divorce. To most, this risk is too great to contemplate. As a result, many

mothers exchange a bargained-down property settlement to avoid a custody contest because many mothers, in contrast to fathers, consider custody a "nonnegotiable" issue (Fineman, 1991).

Furthermore, the choice of a gender-neutral position over one that focuses more specifically on child nurturing, such as the primary caretaker rule, makes no empirical sense. Gendered contributions are not equal. There are qualitative differences between the contributions of primary caretakers (typically mothers) and primary earners (typically fathers) to their children's upbringing; the income contributions fathers make for their families cannot be classified as "sacrifices." In the process of generating family income, fathers are simultaneously establishing themselves in their professions, a benefit they retain throughout their careers. Although this undeniably affords advantages to the entire family during marriage, the sharing of the benefit generally diminishes significantly after divorce, as evidenced by data relative to fathers' postdivorce child support payment patterns (Weitzman, 1985).

By contrast, mothers' sacrifices in providing daily care to children yield no collateral advantages, except in terms of the attachment that forms between mother and child. Children consume the services mothers provide to them, with the years spent in childrearing representing a depletable amount of the mother's nonrenewable resources. Similarly, the time a woman spends away from career development probably disadvantages her throughout her work life.

In addition, this expanded concept of neutrality operates to set the stage for increased state control over custody decisions. Experts, those from the legal as well as the helping professions, are considered necessary to construct and implement new degendered standards and procedures under the best-interest test. The rationale for this increased intervention is, of course, the presence of children. Children are used politically as the imprimatur for the development of processes and rules that conceptually alienate children from their parents and place their futures in the control of state-designated experts.

The Ideal Child Advocate

In spite of these problems, advocates could perform two valuable functions in custody decision making. First, in individual cases, an advocate sensitive to process concerns could bring legal values, such as due process and a preference for public decision making, back into a process that has become so informal and nonlegal as often to operate according to the whims of politically unaccountable professionals or to be driven by professional fads and biases.

Second, on a general societal level, an advocate could perform a public function by lobbying for the replacement of the best-interest-of-the-child test with a more substantive rule—one more susceptible to the protection of traditional legal decision making and more responsive to actual caretaking responsibilities. The most sensible rule is one that rewards past care and concern for children and minimizes the role and power of the helping professionals in custody decision making.

The primary caretaker rule has been criticized as merely being the old maternal preference in gender-neutral terms because it would operate within our current social situation to award custody more often to mothers than to fathers. That this is offered as a criticism shows how far we have strayed from real concern for children to a desire to adhere to simplistic notions of equality between spouses at divorce. The primary caretaker rule *is* gender neutral on its face, and men can change their behavior if they want to have an opportunity to get custody. The rule values nurturing and caretaking and rewards it. This is appropriate.

In addition, one advantage of the primary caretaker rule is that the evidence on which it relies can be gleaned in open court according to our notions of due process and publicly accountable decision making. The primary caretaker rule provides that children need day-to-day care and that the parent who has performed this primary care during marriage should get custody (*Garska v. McCoy*, 1981; Neely, 1984). It avoids the need for speculative assessments about psychological consequences of attributes and refocuses responsibility for the decision on the parents and, if they cannot agree, on the judge who must make the factual finding as to who has cared for the child. Therefore, the rule takes decision making away from the helping professionals.

Conclusion

Voices of doubt have always been raised in the legal community about the effectiveness of the current system, given its reliance on predictions about the future well-being of children based on scanty evidence of questionable validity. There is a special role for a legal advocate who can best serve children's interests by not viewing himself or herself as only a part of a best-interest team. The legal advocate should not be aligned with any other professional but should remain skeptical and critical of them all. The helping professional experts would be presumed to be useful only to weed out or identify those parents who are *clearly* unfit to care for their children. Provided that the tests and methods of such professionals are reliable, they can tell us who falls below a legally defined bright line. Their opinions as to the superior parent—the one who most resembles their professional ideal, which in current practice would be the best-interest recommendation—should be viewed as just an opinion. At most, it would be entitled to no more respect than any other opinion. Optimally, it would be excluded as irrelevant in most custody determinations.

The legal advocate's function, in those few cases when necessary, would ensure that the helping professional's opinion was not overvalued in contrast with information more relevant to the determination of who had acted as the primary caretaker—that supplied by teachers, neighbors, and others who have more extensive exposure to the individual child. The legal advocate would act as a check on this private, informal decision-making process. In this way, professional biases (such as the current ones favoring shared parenting or creating a custody preference for the most generous parent) would be recognized as ideological and be subjected to vigorous and critical probing. This would truly be in the child's best interest.

When an expert testifies, the legal advocate would explore his or her education and experience. Supervision and a critical assessment of the fact-gathering process of the mental health professional would be essential functions for the legal advocate in fulfilling his or her responsibility to the child. The goal would be to expose, and thus examine, the process of reaching a nonlegal professional opinion.

What has been lost under current practice are legal procedural values—due process, adherence to clear standards, and the right to cross-examination—in addition to the undervaluing of nurturing and caretaking. The current referral to extrajudicial personnel may make lawyers and judges feel more secure because we can believe that some other profession is appropriately taking care of the custody business; but that illusion may not work in the best interest of the children.

References

Abarbanel, A. (1979). Shared parenting after separation and divorce: A study of joint custody. *American Journal of Orthopsychiatry, 49*, 320–329.

Ahrons, C. R. (1981). The continuing coparental relationship between divorced spouses. *American Journal of Orthopsychiatry, 51*, 415–428.

Areen, J. (1985a). *Cases and materials on family law* (2nd ed.). Mineola, NY: Foundation Press.

Areen, J. (1985b). *Cases and materials on family law: Teachers' manual.* Mineola, NY: Foundation Press.

Benedek, E. P., & Benedek, R. S. (1979). Joint custody: Solution or illusion? *American Journal of Psychiatry, 136*, 1540–1544.

Berdon, R. I. (1976). A child's right to counsel in a contested custody proceeding resulting from a termination of the marriage. *Connecticut Bar Journal, 50*, 150–167.

Bowman, M. E., & Ahrons, C. R. (1985). Impact of legal custody status on fathers' parenting postdivorce. *Journal of Marriage and the Family, 47*, 481–488.

California Civil Code, § 4600(b)(1) (West Suppl. 1988).

Chambers, D. (1984). Rethinking the substantive rules for custody disputes in divorce. *Michigan Law Review, 83*, 518–520.

Child Custody Act of 1970, MI Compiled Laws Annotated, § 722.23(j) (West Suppl. 1987).

Counts, R. M., & Sacks, A. (1985). The need for crisis intervention during marital separation. *Social Work, 30*, 146–150.

Drinan, R. F. (1962). The rights of children in modern American family law. *Journal of Family Law, 2*, 101–109.

Elkin, M. (1982). The missing links in divorce law: A redefinition of process and practice. *Journal of Divorce, 6*, 37–63.

Everett, W. J. (1984). Shared parenthood in divorce: The parental covenant and custody law. *Journal of Law and Religion, 2*, 85–99.

Ex parte Devine, 398 So.2d 686 (Ala. 1981).

Felner, R. D., & Farber, S. S. (1980). Social policy for child custody: A multidisciplinary framework. *American Journal of Orthopsychiatry, 50*, 341–347.

Fineman, M. A. (1991). *The illusion of equality: The rhetoric and reality of divorce reform.* Chicago: University of Chicago Press.

Fineman, M. A. (1995). *The neutered mother, the sexual family, and other twentieth century tragedies.* New York: Routledge.

Fineman, M. L. (1983). Implementing equality: Ideology, contradiction, and social change. *Wisconsin Law Review, 1983,* 789–886.

Fineman, M. L. (1988). Dominant discourse, professional language, and legal change in child custody decisionmaking. *Harvard Law Review, 101,* 727–774.

Fineman, M. L., & Opie, A. (1987). The uses of social science data in legal policymaking: Custody determinations at divorce. *Wisconsin Law Review, 1987,* 107–158.

Fogelson, F. B. (1970). How social workers perceive lawyers. *Social Casework, 51,* 95–101.

Folberg, H. J., & Graham, M. (1979). Joint custody of children following divorce. *U.C.D. Law Review, 12,* 523–581.

Fuchs, V. R. (1986). Sex differences in economic well-being. *Science, 232,* 459–464.

Garska v. McCoy, 278 S.E.2d 357 (W. Va. 1981).

Genden, J. K. (1976). Separate legal representation for children: Protecting the rights and interests of minors in judicial proceedings. *Harvard Civil Rights–Civil Liberties Law Review, 11,* 565–595.

Girdner, L. K. (1986). Child custody determination: Ideological dimensions of a social problem. In E. Seidman & J. Rappaport (Eds.), *Redefining social problems* (pp. 165–183). New York: Plenum.

Greif, J. B. (1979). Fathers, children, and joint custody. *American Journal of Orthopsychiatry, 49,* 318–319.

Guggenheim, M. (1984). The right to be represented but not heard: Reflections on legal representation for children. *New York University Law Review, 59,* 76–155.

Hansen, R. W. (1964). *Guardians ad litem* in divorce and custody cases: Protection of the child's interests. *Journal of Family Law, 4,* 181–184.

Hansen, R. W. (1966). The role and rights of children in divorce actions. *Journal of Family Law, 6,* 1–14.

Herrman, M. S., McKenry, P. C., & Weber, R. E. (1979). Attorneys' perceptions of their role in divorce. *Journal of Divorce, 2,* 313–322.

Inker, M. L., & Peretta, C. A. (1971). A child's right to counsel in custody cases. *Family Law Quarterly, 5,* 108–120.

Isaacs, J. L. (1963). The role of the lawyer in representing minors in the new family court. *Buffalo Law Review, 12,* 501–521.

Kleinfeld, A. J. (1970). The balance of power among infants, their parents, and the state. *Family Law Quarterly, 4,* 320–350.

Lamb, M. E., & Sagi, A. (Eds.). (1983). *Fatherhood and family policy.* Hillsdale, NJ: Erlbaum.

Maine Rev. Statutes Annotated, Title 19, § 752.5H (Suppl. 1988).

McKenry, P. C. (1979). Mediation eases the split. *Practice Digest, 2,* 8–10.

Mnookin, R. H. (1975). Child-custody adjudication: Judicial functions in the face of indeterminacy. *Law and Contemporary Problems, 39,* 226–293.

Mumma, E. W. (1984). Mediating disputes. *Public Welfare, 42,* 22–30.

Neely, R. (1984). The primary caretaker parent rule: Child custody and the dynamics of greed. *Yale Law and Policy Review, 3,* 168–186.

Okpaku, S. R. (1976). Psychology: Impediment or aid in child custody cases? *Rutgers Law Review, 29,* 1117–1153.

Olsen, F. (1984). The politics of family law. *Law and Inequality, 2,* 1–19.

Podell, R. J. (1973). The "why" behind appointing guardians ad litem for children in divorce proceedings. *Marquette Law Review, 57,* 103–110.

Polikoff, N. D. (1982). Why are mothers losing: A brief analysis of criteria used in child custody determinations. *Women's Rights Law Reporter, 7,* 235–243.

Project: Law firms and lawyers with children: An empirical analysis of family/work conflict. (1982). *Stanford Law Review, 34,* 1263–1307.

Pruhs, A., Paulsen, M. L., & Tysseling, W. R. (1984). Divorce mediation: The politics of integrating clinicians. *Social Casework, 65,* 532–540.

Raschick, M. (1985). *Wisconsin non-custodial parents' groups.* Unpublished manuscript.

Rosenberg, E., Kleinman, J., & Brantley, T. I. (1982). Custody evaluations: Helping the family reorganize. *Social Casework, 63,* 203–208.

Scherrer, J. L. (1976). How social workers help lawyers. *Social Work, 21,* 279–283.

Schulman, J., & Pitt, V. (1982). Second thoughts on joint child custody: Analysis of legislation and its implications for women and children. *Golden Gate University Law Review, 12,* 539–577.

Shepherd, R. E., Jr. (1974). Solomon's sword: Adjudication of child custody questions. *University of Richmond Law Review, 8,* 151–200.

Shiffman, M. (1985, August). *The men's movement: An exploratory empirical investigation.* Paper presented at the 80th annual meeting of the American Sociological Association, Washington, DC.

Solender, E. K. (1976). The guardian ad litem: A valuable representative or an illusory safeguard? *Texas Tech Law Review, 7,* 619–643.

Stone, O. M. (1982). *The child's voice in the court of law.* Toronto: Butterworths.

Uniform Dissolution of Marriage Act, CO Rev. Statutes, § 14-10-124(1.5)(f) (Suppl. 1988).

Wallerstein, J. S., & Kelly, J. B. (1979). Children and divorce: A review. *Social Work, 24,* 468–475.

Watson, A. S. (1969). The children of Armageddon: Problems of custody following divorce. *Syracuse Law Review, 21,* 55–86.

Weil, M. (1982). Research on issues in collaboration between social workers and lawyers. *Social Service Review, 56,* 393–405.

Weitzman, L. J. (1985). *The divorce revolution: The unexpected social and economic consequences for women and children in America.* New York: Free Press.

Woody, J. D. (1978). Preventive intervention for children of divorce. *Social Casework, 59,* 537–544.

Zainaldin, J. S. (1979). The emergence of a modern American family law: Child custody, adoption, and the courts, 1796–1851. *Northwestern University Law Review, 73,* 1038–1089.

Name Index

Subject Index